INDEX TO
TENNESSEE CONFEDERATE PENSION APPLICATIONS.

Revised Edition

By
TENNESSEE STATE LIBRARY

Revised Edition
Transcribed and Edited by
SAMUEL SISTLER

JANAWAY PUBLISHING, INC.
Santa Maria, California

Index to Tennessee Confederate Pension Applications. Revised Edition.

Originally published in 1964 by Tennessee State Library.
Updated and revised in 1995 by Samuel Sistler.
Revised edition published in 1995.

Copyright © 1995, Byron Sistler & Associates

ALL RIGHTS RESERVED. Written permission must be secured
from the author or publisher to use or reproduce any part of
this book, in any form or by any means, including
electronic reproduction, except for brief
quotations in critical reviews
or articles.

Reprinted by:

Janaway Publishing, Inc.
732 Kelsey Ct.
Santa Maria, California 93454
(805) 925-1038
www.JanawayGenealogy.com

2014

ISBN: 978-1-59641-327-6

Made in the United States of America

DIRECTIONS

Entries are arranged alphabetically by surname. All three pension files for Soldiers, Widows, and Colored Men's applications are intermingled in this index. Entry types can be distinguished by the prefix S (Soldiers), W (Widows), or C (Colored) preceding each application number. Entries are arranged as follows:

SOLDIERS AND COLORED MEN'S ENTRIES:

1. **Surname** of applicant
2. **First Name** of applicant
3. **Application Number(s)**:
    S + number indicates Soldier's Application
    C + number indicates "Colored Man's" Application
4. **County Abbreviation** (See Key to County Symbols, on reverse of this page)
5. **Unit** served in (official Confederate War Dept. regiment designation)
6. **Comments** (any further locating information not included above)

e.g.: PATTERSON, John W., S11437, BR, 1st (Carter's) Cav.
    means John W. Patterson applied for a Soldier's Pension while living in Bradley County. He served with Carter's Cavalry and his application was numbered 11437.

WIDOWS ENTRIES:

1. **Surname** of applicant
2. **First Name** of applicant
3. **Application Number(s)**:
    W + number indicates Widow's Application
4. **County Abbreviation** (See Key to County Symbols)
5. **Surname** of Soldier
6. **First Name** of Soldier
7. **Comments**

e.g.: HILBERT, Nancy F., W4280, WA, Hilbert, Samuel D.
    means Nancy F. Hilbert applied for a Widow's Pension while living in Washington County. She applied on the service of her husband Samuel D. Hilbert and her application was numbered 4280.

KEY TO COUNTY SYMBOLS

A	Anderson	HA	Hancock	MOO	Moore
B	Bedford	HR	Hardeman	MG	Morgan
BE	Benton	HD	Hardin	O	Obion
BL	Bledsoe	HM	Hamblen	OV	Overton
BO	Blount	HW	Hawkins	P	Perry
BR	Bradley	HY	Haywood	PI	Pickett
C	Campbell	HE	Henderson	PO	Polk
CA	Cannon	HN	Henry	PU	Putnam
CR	Carroll	HI	Hickman	R	Rhea
CT	Carter	HO	Houston	RO	Roane
CE	Cheatham	HU	Humphreys	RB	Robertson
CH	Chester	J	Jackson	RU	Rutherford
CL	Claiborne	JA	James*	S	Scott
CY	Clay	JE	Jefferson	SE	Sevier
CO	Cocke	JO	Johnson	SQ	Sequatchie
CF	Coffee	K	Knox	SH	Shelby
CC	Crockett	L	Lauderdale	SM	Smith
CU	Cumberland	LA	Lawrence	ST	Stewart
D	Davidson	LE	Lewis	SU	Sullivan
DE	Decatur	LK	Lake	SN	Sumner
DK	DeKalb	LI	Lincoln	T	Tipton
DI	Dickson	LO	Loudon	TR	Trousdale
DY	Dyer	M	Macon	U	Unicoi
F	Fayette	MA	Madison	UN	Union
FE	Fentress	MR	Marion	V	Van Buren
FR	Franklin	MS	Marshall	W	Warren
G	Gibson	MU	Maury	WA	Washington
GI	Giles	MC	McMinn	WY	Wayne
GR	Grainger	MN	McNairy	WE	Weakley
GE	Greene	ME	Meigs	WH	White
GU	Grundy	MO	Monroe	WI	Williamson
H	Hamilton	MT	Montgomery	WL	Wilson

* James Co. does not appear on modern maps. This county was formed from part of Hamilton Co. in 1870, and was reunited with Hamilton in 1919.

PREFACE

In 1964 the Confederate Pension Applications were indexed by the Tennessee State Library and Archives. This index was published in a book that has long been out of print. Since its publication, many errors have come to light. Papers were found out of place on the microfilm, individuals were listed under misread surnames, and there were applicants missing entirely. Chuck Sherrill, Director of Public Services at the State Library, approached us about correcting and reprinting the book, as the information in these applications is of great value to genealogical and military researchers.

This project turned into considerably more work than I expected, but as I got further into the process of making corrections, I realized just how badly this new book is needed. I consulted the microfilm and original applications when necessary to confirm information. With the help of the computer, a tool unavailable to the staff who originally prepared the index, it was possible to catch a great number of errors.

In this revision, there are about 300 additional applicants not in the original volume, and considerably more changes to existing entries. Cross-references are included for equivalent entries and widows previously listed only under their remarried names are now also listed by their soldiers' surnames. It was very much worth the effort; this is a much more complete volume than the original.

I would like to thank the staff of the Tennessee State Library and Archives for their help and cooperation with this project; especially Julia Rather who saved me much time checking original Soldiers' applications. I also would like to thank Chuck Sherrill & Edna Wiefering for the use of their book *Tennessee's Confederate Widows and Their Families*. This book is an indexed numerical listing of the Widows' applications and was invaluable for checking information rapidly without having to consult the microfilm.

Sam Sistler
Nashville, Tennessee
December 1994

INTRODUCTION

In 1891 the State of Tennessee enacted legislation which established a Board of Pension Examiners. The membership consisted of the State Comptroller, the Attorney General, and three ex-Confederate soldiers recommended by the Tennessee Division of Confederate Veterans and appointed by the Governor. These men had the authority to decide (a) if a Confederate veteran applying for pension was incapable of "making a support," and (b) if his service was honorable. The burden of proof rested with the veteran, who was obligated to prove disability and/or indigency and separation from the service under honorable conditions.

Both Federal and Confederate veterans who were residents of Tennessee for at least one year before making application were eligible for pension, provided they met the qualifications set forth by the Pension Act. However, the Federal Government's earlier and more liberal pensions to their veterans prompted men who had served both sides at one time or another (a surprising number did change sides in mid-stream) to apply to that government rather than to the Tennessee Board. There was a common agreement among states granting pensions to Confederate veterans that the applicant should apply to the pension board OF THE STATE IN WHICH HE RESIDED WHEN MAKING APPLICATION, although this was often not the state in whose forces he served.

Most pension applications and their supporting papers contain information of much interest to soldiers' descendants, to genealogists, and to other researchers. They are more informative than official service records because they give more detailed information about a soldier's military, personal, and family history. The application lists the veteran's place of enlistment, unit, period of service, battles participated in, and whether he was wounded or captured. Made out in questionnaire form, it also asked such information as place of birth, number of children, and value of personal and real property owned by the veteran.

Pensions for soldiers' widows were first issued in 1905. Their applications show place of birth for both widow and husband, and in many instances the names and ages of children. As proof of marriage was required for admission to the pension rolls, a copy of the marriage certificate is often found in widow applications. Supporting papers consist of correspondence between the applicant and the Pension Board, letters or sworn affidavits from old comrades and neighbors attesting to the veteran's character and the nature of his military service, and abstracts of the soldier's service record furnished by the Federal War Department.

The Board kept three separate rolls, one for soldiers, one for widows, and one for so-called "colored" soldiers. These are filed in the Archives in the same grouping. There are 16693 soldiers' pension applications, 11188 widows' pension applications, and 285 colored soldiers' applications. Some of these (as noted in the Appendix) are missing.

Note that this revised index is arranged differently than its predecessor. All three pension files are intermingled in this volume. Entry types can be distinguished by the prefix S (Soldiers), W (Widows), or C (Colored) preceding each application number. A soldier's entry includes his name followed by his application number(s), the county of residence at the time of the application, and the unit in which the soldier served. A widow's entry includes her name followed by her application number(s), county of residence at the time of application, and the name of her Confederate soldier husband. County names are abbreviated and can be identified by the Key to County Symbols, reverse of Directions page.

The following explanations clarify the terms used within this book:

(1) Most of the Confederate veterans pensioned under Tennessee law served in units with a Tennessee designation, e.g., 1st Tennessee Cavalry, 7th Tennessee Infantry. For this reason, state designations are included only in instances where the veteran served in the forces of a state OTHER THAN Tennessee.

(2) In cases where a veteran served in more than one unit, the one in which he spent the majority of his military career is listed in the index.

(3) All units listed were of regimental size unless otherwise specified.

(4) Many units known in the field by one regimental number were officially recognized by the Confederate War Department under another number. For example, the 1st East Tennessee Rifles was officially designated the 37th Tennessee Infantry Regiment, and the 2nd (Barteau's) Tennessee Cavalry was officially listed as the 22nd (Barteau's) Tennessee Cavalry. In order to avoid confusion, the official designation is used in this book.

(5) The term "Undetermined" is used in cases where the data given is insufficient to determine the unit in which the veteran served.

(6) "Unassigned" denotes instances in which the veteran was not assigned to a field company but was detailed or assigned to a job which was necessary to the war effort. The Colored Men's entries frequently show such positions. Some of these occupations were tailor, mechanic (carpenter), teamster, blacksmith, and miner.

    A photocopy of a pension application may be obtained from the Tennessee State Library and Archives, Research Services, 403 7th Ave N, Nashville, TN 37243-0312 ph: (615) 741-2764. Visitors to the Archives Section can make their own copies from the microfilm.

    There are a few entries in this book marked "On Misc. microfilm reel." They were found just before publication of this revision. Contact the State Library for information regarding these applicants.

Index to Tennessee Confederate Pension Applications

AARON, T. N. S6739, DE, 52nd Inf
ABBOTT, Annie Laura, W7355, W9196, D, Abbott, Henry Harrison
ABBOTT, Henry H. S14557, D, Burrough's Co. Lt. Art.
ABBOTT, Laura S. W9504, LI, Abbott, Napoleon Bonaparte
ABBOTT, Marth Catherine, W4952, FR, Abbott, George Washington
ABBOTT, Mary, W10388, Abbott, Lenard B.
ABBOTT, N. B. S9543, LI, 1st (Turney's) Inf.
ABBOTT, Sarah Margaret, W9532, LI, Abbott, Thomas Benjamin
ABBOTT, Sterling S. S8343, RO, Thomas Legion, N.C.
ABBOTT, Thomas B. S2619, LI, 28th Inf.
ABERNATHY, Alfred E. S9293, GI, 32nd Inf.
ABERNATHY, Anna Dyer, W11015, GI, Abernathy, M. Thomas
ABERNATHY, C. G. S4620, LA, 35th Ala. Inf.
ABERNATHY, Emma Day, W9044, H, Abernathy, Y. L.
ABERNATHY, Henry G. S15402, GI, 6th (Wheeler's) Cav.
ABERNATHY, J. C. S6548, WE, 27th Inf.
ABERNATHY, J. E. S10437, LA, 27th Ala. Inf.
ABERNATHY, J. L. S14091, GI, 3rd (Clack's) Inf.
ABERNATHY, J. M. S2770, HE, 21st Cav.
ABERNATHY, J. Press, S16148, S16041, GI, 3rd (Clack's) Inf.
ABERNATHY, John W. S14606, GI, 53rd Inf.
ABERNATHY, L. E. S11825, GI, 60th Inf.
ABERNATHY, Lucy Alice, W8475, CC, Abernathy, Richard Tucker
ABERNATHY, M. T. S16184, GI, 3rd (Clack's) Inf.
ABERNATHY, Mary, W8970, GU, Abernathy, Thomas Coke
ABERNATHY, Richard T. S505, HY, 53rd Inf
ABERNATHY, Ruff, C14, GI, 3rd Tenn. Inf.
ABERNATHY, Sarah Elizabeth, W8514, GI, Abernathy, Andrew Jackson
ABERNATHY, Susie Caldania, W4885, SH, Abernathy, Jessie Franklin
ABERNATHY, Thomas C. S1574, GU, 21st (Wilson's) Cav.
ABERNATHY, Y. L. S16107, H, 1st (Carter's) Cav.
ABESTON, Julyett Amanda, W3555, CY, Abeston, Lipscomb Petett
ABNER, James W. S8663, ST, 7th Inf.

ABSHERE, Ezekiel, S2819, HW, 43rd Inf.
ABSHIRE, Susan, W4596, HW, Abshire, Ezekiel
ABSTON, Julyett Amanda, W663, CY, Abston, Lipscomb Pedit
ACHEY, J. H. S13201, MT, 14th Inf.
ACHORD, Anna Amanda, W1311, HR, Achord, William Anderson
ACKLEN, Joseph M. S4310, FR, 17th Inf.
ACKLEN, Lucy Jane, W1671, FR, Acklen, Joseph Milton
ACKLEN, Sarena W. W5047, FR, Acklen, Gustin
ACKLIN, T. F. S14699, LA, 48th (Nixon's) Cav.
ACOCK, W. M. S14524, K, 62nd Inf.
ACREE, J. H. S11264, MT, 14th Inf.
ACREE, Louisa, W9847, MA, Acree, John Smith
ACUFF, Albert, S880, GR, 26th Inf.
ACUFF, Betsy Emeline, W3326, GR, Acuff, John
ACUFF, Eva Craton, W3907, B, Acuff, John W.
ACUFF, Mary Tennessee, W7838, BL, Acuff, James Hamable
ACUFF, R. W. S3997, HY, 27th Tex. Cav.
ACUFF, Stokely, S261, UN, 26th Inf.
ADA, John, S15759, GI, 11th (Holman's) Cav.
ADAIR, Eliza Catherine, W2640, G, Adair, William Nelson
ADAIR, Jeff, S182, T, 2nd Miss. Inf.
ADAIR, P. S11806, WH, Unassigned (Blacksmith)
ADAMS, Alabama America, W3057, HN, Adams, Jasper
ADAMS, Albert Madison, S12852, MU, 14th (Neely's) Cav.
ADAMS, Alexander, S10874, BE, 7th Ky. Mtd. Inf.
ADAMS, America, W1817, MOO, Adams, Pinkney
ADAMS, Ann E. W1305, GI, Adams, Robert
ADAMS, Anna Malone, W11122, T, Adams, John Wesley
ADAMS, Annie Lewis, W8409, HY, Adams, James Britton
ADAMS, Annie Senter, W10488, G, Adams, J. J. R.
ADAMS, B. S. S13607, HO, Phillips' Co. Lt. Art.
ADAMS, Carrie Jenkins, W7565, D, Adams, William H.

Index to Tennessee Confederate Pension Applications

ADAMS, Charles, S13336, CF, 28th Cav.
ADAMS, Chesley T. S9921, G, 52nd Inf.
ADAMS, Cleo, W9583, DK, Adams, Pleasant C.
ADAMS, Cynthia Artealue, W7796, Adams, James Peter
ADAMS, Dollie, W5045, MS, Adams, R. A.
ADAMS, Eliza, W6219, MS, Adams, John Milton
ADAMS, Eliza Jane, W1810, TR, Adams, S. D.
ADAMS, Elizabeth, W3307, H, Adams, Charles
ADAMS, Eunice, W2395, MT, Adams, William
ADAMS, F. N. S13119, RB, 50th Inf.
ADAMS, Henry, S4726, WE, 5th Inf.
ADAMS, Houston, S163, MT, 49th Inf.
ADAMS, J. B. S15445, HY, 14th (Neely's) Cav.
ADAMS, J. C. S15549, G, 3rd Mo. Cav.
ADAMS, J. H. S6692, RU, 45th Inf.
ADAMS, J. H. S7588, MS, 48th Inf.
ADAMS, J. I. J. S4073, DI, 11th Inf.
ADAMS, J. R. S9539, 21st Cav.
ADAMS, J. W. S11022, L, 9th Inf.
ADAMS, James K. S10198, WE, Cox's Bn. Cav.
ADAMS, James Madison, S12855, O, 15th Cav.
ADAMS, John, S13644, CF, 37th Inf.
ADAMS, John Calvin, S965, S673, ST, 50th Inf.
ADAMS, John M. S4947, MS, 50th Ala. Inf.
ADAMS, Joseph J. S2504, HN, 5th Inf.
ADAMS, Josephine, W10664, CF, Adams, Charles
ADAMS, Laura, W10047, DI, Adams, W. T.
ADAMS, Laura Isabel, W9948, MC, Adams, Henry Clay
ADAMS, Lee, S10413, K, 63rd Inf.
ADAMS, Lizzie Coleman, W2861, SH, Adams, Walter Warren
ADAMS, Margaret, W2844, K, Adams, Thomas Fletcher
ADAMS, Margaret Jane, W8751, W6440, ST, Adams, John C.
ADAMS, Martha, W515, DI, Adams, Montgomery
ADAMS, Martha Elnora, W4810, T, Adams, William Hunley
ADAMS, Martin V. S10755, S15879, WA, 10th (De Moss') Cav.
ADAMS, Mary, W6459, K, Adams, Lee Andrew
ADAMS, Mary Ann, W6275, MT, Adams, Houston
ADAMS, Mary Elizabeth, W4299, SH, Adams, Thomas Patton
ADAMS, Mary Jennette, W3915, Adams, Joseph J.
ADAMS, Mary Lizabeth, W2474, T, Adams, G. M.
ADAMS, Mary Lucinda, W9135, W8182, WA, Adams, Martin Van Buren
ADAMS, N. M. S9027, M, 19th Inf.
ADAMS, N. W. S3698, MC, 5th Cav.
ADAMS, Nancy, W11024, CU, Adams, R. Thomas
ADAMS, R. A. S8689, MS, 17th Inf.
ADAMS, R. M. S7261, HR, 14th Cav.
ADAMS, S. D. S8170, M, 24th Inf.
ADAMS, Sarah, W6630, PO, Adams, Newton Washington
ADAMS, Sarah Letticia, W8307, MS, Adams, J. D.
ADAMS, Sarah R. W4328, RU, Adams, Jesse H.
ADAMS, Susan, W8245, G, Adams, John Craig
ADAMS, Unity Ann, W194, WE, Adams, William Andrew
ADAMS, W. H. S15535, D, 3rd Ky. Cav.
ADAMS, W. J. S11631, S12154, LA, 50th Inf.
ADAMS, W. T. S4183, DI, 11th Inf.
ADAMS, W. W. S6343, SH, 21st Miss. Inf.
ADAMS, William, S2497, BR, 3rd (Lillard's) Mtd. Inf.
ADAMS, William C. S1774, WE, McCutcheon's? Co. Inf.
ADAMS, William Judson, S12237, K, 29th Ala. Inf.
ADAMS, William L. S693, LO, 3rd Inf.
ADAMSON, F. W. M. S4411, G, 19th & 20th Cons. Cav.
ADCOCK, Bolin, S6727, DY, 15th Cav.
ADCOCK, Bowlin, S10022, DY, 15th (Stewart's) Cav.
ADCOCK, David, S1308, DK, 23rd Inf.
ADCOCK, David Joseph, S9810, MN, Moreland's Regt. AL Cav.
ADCOCK, Demerias, W3329, DK, Adcock, Joseph
ADCOCK, Frances, W1056, DK, Adcock, Thomas
ADCOCK, Harriet Emoline, W6381, DK, Adcock, James Welconi
ADCOCK, J. W. S3575, DI, 11th Inf.
ADCOCK, Louisa, W3860, WH, Adcock, John
ADCOCK, M. E. S6304, DK, 16th Inf.
ADCOCK, Martin V. S6242, DI, 11th Inf.
ADCOCK, Sarah, W6885, DI, Adcock, Thomas Benton
ADCOCK, Susan E. W4971, DI, Adcock, Martin T.

ADCOCK, Thomas, S1305, DK, Undetermined
ADCOCK, t. B. S6814, DI, 11th Inf.
ADDY, J. S. S3910, SN, 46th Inf.
ADEN, Sarah Ann, W6910, SH, Aden, Riley Baughman
ADKINS, E. P. S10799, MU, 19th (Biffle's) Cav.
ADKINS, Ed, S8107, B, 53rd Inf.
ADKINS, J. C. S5180, WE, 38th Va. Inf.
ADKINS, Narcissa Frances, W2518, MU, Adkins, William Sidney
ADKISSON, George Lafayette, S13282, MU, 6th (Wheeler's) Cav.
ADKISSON, Matilda Agnes, W8980, MU, Adkisson, Abner
ADKISSON, Samuel, S10819, DE, 52nd Inf.
ADKISSON, W. F. S9902, MU, 48th (Voorhies') Inf.
AGEE, Frances, W8062, CU, Agee, I. N.
AGEE, G. M. S15440, K, 51st Va. Inf.
AGEE, Isaac N. S6313, BL, 43rd Inf.
AGEE, James M. S710, HW, 42nd Inf.
AGEE, James M. S1472, HW, 42nd Va. Inf.
AGNEW, J. M. S13579, MU, 53rd Inf.
AGNEW, James K. P. S8906, BE, 11th Cav.
AGNEW, Selina Adline, W7996, BE, Agnew, James K. Polk
AIKEN, Amanda J. W6089, BR, Aiken, Jasper N.
AIKEN, J. C. S11767, WA, Lynch's Co. Lt. Art.
AIKEN, John G. S5067, LO, Undetermined.
AIKEN, Mary Elizabeth, W8929, WA, Aiken, James
AIKEN, Mary Lou, W8605, WA, Aiken, John Chapman
AIKIN, James, S2687, WA, Winston's Co. Lt. Art.
AIKMAN, John S. S2972, ME, 5th Cav.
AIKMAN, John S. S3664, ME, 5th (McKenzie's) Cav.
AILOR, Nicholas, S12647, MR, 2nd (Ashby's) Cav.
AIRHEART, Sarah Jane, W9117, MO, Airheart, Isham
AKENS, I. N. S10963, BE, 20th (Russell's) Cav.
AKERS, A. J. S6597, HW, 10th Ky. Cav.
AKERS, B. F. S10436, BE, 3rd Inf.

AKERS, Harriet Nelson Colli, W10490, K, Akers, Edwin Archer
AKERS, Mary Frances, W5379, BE, Akers, Benjamin F.

AKERS, Sarah Elizabeth, W5450, HW, Akers, Andrew Jackson
AKIN, Emma, W8152, SH, Akin, William Morgan
AKIN, J. F. S15183, DE, 52nd Inf.
AKIN, Lena Oden, W9354, WI, Akin, J. H.
AKIN, Robert E. S14281, SH, 51st Inf.
AKIN, Thomas, S10686, H, 3rd Inf.
AKIN, Virginia, W8695, MU, Akin, John W.
AKIN, William Morgan, S6264, SH, 13th Inf.
AKINS, Andrew J. S11389, SU, 61st Inf.
AKINS, Isaac, S1413, SU, 60th Inf.
AKINS, John, C221, D, 9th Cav.
ALBERTINO, Daniel, S481, GE, 5th N.C. Inf.
ALBERTINO, Daniel, S2182, GE, 5th N.C. Inf.
ALBERTINO, Mary Elizabeth, W4289, GE, Albertino, Daniel
ALBIN, James Shannon, S10875, K, 33rd Va. Inf.
ALBRIGHT, J. A. S7354, DI, 10th Cav.
ALCORN, Richard, S1069, PU, 17th Inf.
ALDERSON, Emma Susan, W6258, MG, Alderson, Thomas John
ALDERSON, Isaac, S15376, MA, 43rd Inf.
ALDERSON, Mary Ann A. W1452, MA, Alderson, Thomas Ballard
ALDERSON, Sarah, W4679, MU, Alderson, Thomas Edward
ALDERSON, T. J. S6807, MG, 2nd Va. Cav.
ALDERSON, Thomas E. S6086, MU, 9th Bn. (Gantt's) Cav.
ALDRICH, Louisiana Aramenta, W10349, RU, Aldrich, Thomas Joyce
ALDRIDGE, Amanda E. W10779, MC, Aldridge, Richard Moteville
ALDRIDGE, James W. S8900, MO, 1st N.C. Cav.
ALDRIDGE, R. M. S9913, MO, Detailed Conscripts
ALEN, G. P. S6374, CF, Ramsey's Battery, Art.
ALEWINE, Daniel, S4311, JE, 9th S.C. Inf.
ALEWINE, Mary Ann, W2505, JE, Alewine, Daniel
ALEXANDER, Adelene, W967, D, Alexander, N. B.
ALEXANDER, Amanda M. W3245, SM, Alexander, Albert M.

ALEXANDER, Andrew Jackson, S13453, MU, 48th Inf.
ALEXANDER, Celia Ann, W240, D, Alexander, John F.

ALEXANDER, D. F. S13630, HN, 5th Inf.
ALEXANDER, E. C. S15248, MU, 1st Heavy Art.
ALEXANDER, E. F. S5962, MS, 17th Inf.
ALEXANDER, Ebin P. S10911, MU, 19th (Biffle's) Cav.
ALEXANDER, Edwin F. S12361, MA, 51st Inf.
ALEXANDER, Elizabeth, W6430, HE, Alexander, John W.
ALEXANDER, Elizabeth A. W1564, WI, Alexander, James Rankin
ALEXANDER, Emma, W2384, MS, Alexander, E. F.
ALEXANDER, Estelle, W, Some papers with #11183 on film
ALEXANDER, G. D. S11503, WL, 4th (McLemore's) Cav.
ALEXANDER, G. L. S8198, S1464, HY, 9th Inf.
ALEXANDER, G. W. S13325, WL, 7th Inf.
ALEXANDER, G. W. S14921, G, 19th (Biffle's) Cav.
ALEXANDER, Gideon, S15359, RU, 8th (Smith's) Cav.
ALEXANDER, Gideon Blackburn, S11366, WL, 22nd (Barteau's) Cav.
ALEXANDER, Harriet Joanna, W6653, MA, Alexander, Thomas H.
ALEXANDER, J. A. S11067, RU, 2nd Inf.
ALEXANDER, J. B. S3890, MA, 51st Inf.
ALEXANDER, J. D. S2381, HN, 3rd Ark. Inf.
ALEXANDER, J. E. K. S9086, CA, 8th (Dibrell's) Cav.
ALEXANDER, J. H. S8398, RU, 45th Inf.
ALEXANDER, J. W. S5812, HE, 27th Inf.
ALEXANDER, J. Wallace, S674, WI, 4th (McLemore's) Cav.
ALEXANDER, James Benton, S12231, T, 18th Tex. Inf.
ALEXANDER, James F. S8282, HN, 51st Inf.
ALEXANDER, James W. S7843, RU, 45th Inf.
ALEXANDER, Jennie Hendley, W9536, MU, Alexander, John Newton
ALEXANDER, John E. S12789, F, 35th Ala. Inf.
ALEXANDER, John W. S15950, RU, 2nd (Robison's) Inf.

ALEXANDER, Josephine, W10902, HY, Alexander, George Lucas
ALEXANDER, Julia A. W8561, MA, Alexander, Edwin Franklin

ALEXANDER, M. C. S4659, B, 45th Inf.
ALEXANDER, Margaret Williams, W9189, WI, Alexander, Thomas Benton
ALEXANDER, Martha, W7774, RU, Alexander, J. A.
ALEXANDER, Martha, W10190, HU, Alexander, Robert Perry
ALEXANDER, Martha Cleopatra, W1862, WI, Alexander, Jesse Wallace
ALEXANDER, Martha Delia, W2737, MU, Alexander, Joseph Washington
ALEXANDER, Martha Foster, W7110, WL, Alexander, Gideon Blackburn
ALEXANDER, Mary Dean, W3371, SH, Alexander, Thomas William
ALEXANDER, Mary Elizabeth, W4321, LO, Alexander, Robert Hinton
ALEXANDER, Mary Jane, W5083, W8904, M, Alexander, William Patterson
ALEXANDER, Mattie Ann, W2982, F, Alexander, William Julius
ALEXANDER, Maudiville, W3713, HN, Alexander, William Perry
ALEXANDER, Melville B. S244, HN, 5th Inf.
ALEXANDER, Parilee, W591, WL, Alexander, Samuel Madison
ALEXANDER, Parilee, W8263, WL, Alexander, G. D.
ALEXANDER, R. H. S3599, G, 47th Inf.
ALEXANDER, Robert, S16488, HD, 9th Cav.
ALEXANDER, S. D. W3389, SH, Alexander, I. E.
ALEXANDER, S. M. S14985, FR, 41st Inf.
ALEXANDER, Sallie Idella, W5222, WE, Alexander, Melvin Bruce
ALEXANDER, Sannie B. W2527, RU, Alexander, James M.
ALEXANDER, Sarah Jane, W11083, MU, Alexander, Eben P.
ALEXANDER, T. E. S. S8828, SH, 154th Sr. Regt. Inf.
ALEXANDER, T. H. S8247, MA, 51st Inf.
ALEXANDER, Thomas Benton, S14223, WI, Sparkman's Co. Lt. Art.
ALEXANDER, Valeria A. W9767, MA, Alexander, James W.
ALEXANDER, W. D. S7304, L, 154th Sr. Regt. Inf.
ALEXANDER, W. H. S6422, RU, 25th Inf.
ALEXANDER, W. M. S7567, RO, 60th N.C. Inf.

Index to Tennessee Confederate Pension Applications

ALEXANDER, W. M. S15022, H, 8th (Smith's) Cav.
ALEXANDER, W. P. S14148, CO, 25th N.C. Inf.
ALEXANDER, William J. S6740, F, 13th Inf.
ALEXANDER, William T. S15796, H, 30th Ala. Inf.
ALFORD, Alex W. S11766, H, 2nd (Ashby's) Cav.
ALFORD, Amanda, W9256, ME, Alford, William A.
ALFORD, Cora, W2358, HD, Alford, William L.
ALFORD, E. A. S11996, DY, 21st Va. Cav.
ALFORD, J. R. S5763, HR, 18th Inf.
ALFORD, James, S409, RU, 4th TX Inf./45th TN Inf.
ALFORD, James Madden, S1991, LA, 9th Cav.
ALFORD, John, S10993, SU, 26th Inf.
ALFORD, Martha, W6452, DY, Alford, Elkoney Andrew
ALFORD, R. N. S12443, LA, 9th Cav.
ALFORD, Sallie, W2135, MU, Alford, Monroe
ALFORD, Sarah E. W4013, H, Alford, Alexander
ALFORD, T. J. S9005, RU, 45th Inf.
ALFORD, William A. S10395, S15979, ME, 3rd (Lillard's) Inf.
ALGEE, Martha Elizabeth, W6225, G, Algee, William H.
ALISON, Robert B. S3426, SU, 19th Inf.
ALISON, W. A. S2865, CH, 52nd Inf.
ALISON, William P. S14692, SN, 3rd (Forrest's) Cav.
ALLBRIGHT, Sophronia, W7549, DI, Allbright, John
ALLDAY, Ella Herman, W10238, WI, Allday, Benjamin Franklin
ALLEN, A. S9773, O, 12th Ky. Cav.
ALLEN, A. J. S11872, MA, 1st (Field's) Inf.
ALLEN, A. J. S12170, G, 12th Inf.
ALLEN, A. S. S14932, D, 44th Inf.
ALLEN, Allie, W2906, WE, Allen, Z. W.
ALLEN, Amanda Elizabeth, W4485, G, Allen, Christopher Daniel
ALLEN, B. F. S4984, D, 18th Inf.
ALLEN, Benjamin Franklin, S16628, K, 29th N.C. Inf.
ALLEN, C. D. S205, G, 15th Cav.
ALLEN, C. G. S14731, WI, 11th (Holman's) Cav.
ALLEN, Cain, W10985, D, Allen, James

ALLEN, Carrie C. W6592, D, Allen, Andrew Jackson
ALLEN, Catherine, W394, HA, Allen, Green
ALLEN, Chelton, S13983, TR, 22nd (Barteau's) Cav.
ALLEN, Cornelia Jane, W3805, O, Allen, George W.
ALLEN, Cornell Tipton, S5885, 5th Inf.
ALLEN, D. A. S15566, O, 1st N.C. Inf.
ALLEN, Darthula Jane, W1868, HM, Allen, John Edward Layton
ALLEN, Drew C. S3239, FR, 44th Ala. Inf.
ALLEN, Edd, S7254, MS, 5th (McKenzie's) Cav.
ALLEN, Elender, W5143, WA, Allen, Thomas O.
ALLEN, Elijah, S3561, J, 4th (Murray's) Cav.
ALLEN, Eliza A. W3912, SH, Allen, James H.
ALLEN, Eliza L. W3947, FR, Allen, J. H.
ALLEN, Elizabeth V. W3491, H, Allen, I. David
ALLEN, Emma Bell, W9261, O, Allen, Benjamin Totten
ALLEN, Fannie L. W474, D, Allen, Gran T.
ALLEN, Frances Catherine, W7473, J, Allen, Dave
ALLEN, Frances Elizabeth, W4642, P, Allen, Joseph Henry
ALLEN, George Whitfield, S7966, O, 14th Inf.
ALLEN, Granville T. S2211, D, 45th Inf.
ALLEN, Hattie Lou, W2922, D, Allen, John Bell
ALLEN, Henrietta Anna, W2359, D, Allen, James Calhum
ALLEN, Hulda, W6789, DE, Allen, W. M.
ALLEN, J. D. S5335, H, 9th Ga. Cav.
ALLEN, J. H. S3170, FR, 37th Inf.
ALLEN, J. H. S4774, SH, 38th Inf.
ALLEN, J. J. S14812, MS, 4th (McLemore's) Cav.
ALLEN, J. W. S9029, SH, 38th Inf.
ALLEN, J. W. S13858, HN, 5th Inf.
ALLEN, J. Wesley, S13629, J, 25th Inf.
ALLEN, James, S3968, CO, 5th (McKenzie's) Cav.
ALLEN, James B. S934, CL, Undetermined
ALLEN, James H. S4143, WL, 4th (McLemore's) Cav.
ALLEN, James O. S8482, D, 1st (Wheeler's) Cav.
ALLEN, James W. S7234, WI, Baxter's Co. Lt. Art.
ALLEN, John, S7020, BR, 2nd Cav.

-5

ALLEN, John B. S2106, BR, 2nd Cav.
ALLEN, John J. S6071, CO, 62nd Inf.
ALLEN, John Simpson, S9939, 8th (Smith's) Cav.
ALLEN, John T. S6568, CO, 62nd Inf.
ALLEN, Joseph Carol, S6868, WI, 32nd Inf.
ALLEN, Josie E. W3758, O, Allen, John W.
ALLEN, M. R. S7506, MS, 32nd Inf.
ALLEN, Malvina Frances, W8416, WL, Allen, William Riley
ALLEN, Martha, W6634, MS, Allen, Ed.
ALLEN, Martha, W9154, PU, Allen, Jesse P.
ALLEN, Martha A. W30, HR, Allen, Thompson
ALLEN, Martha Elender, W1135, SM, Allen, Charles
ALLEN, Martha Jane, W9750, RU, Allen, William Albert
ALLEN, Mary A. W7840, MA, Allen, Andrew Jackson
ALLEN, Mary C. W2285, SU, Allen, W. E.
ALLEN, Mary E. W10727, MT, Allen, Kemer C.
ALLEN, Mary Norman, W7674, D, Allen, Alphonso S.
ALLEN, Mary Stovall, W10155, O, Allen, Daniel Alvis
ALLEN, Mary Susan, W8151, BR, Allen, John B.
ALLEN, Matilda, W534, ST, Allen, Henry
ALLEN, Matilda, W5867, CO, Allen, James
ALLEN, Melvina Victoria, W5686, Allen, Cornell Tipton
ALLEN, Nancy, W147, MS, Allen, John
ALLEN, Nancy F. W8646, HN, Allen, James Watson
ALLEN, Robert, S2595, GR, 9th Bn. (Day's) Cav.
ALLEN, Roxana V. W7750, SH, Allen, Thomas
ALLEN, Sally C. W11164, D, Allen, Robert B.
ALLEN, Sarah Alice, W5117, MT, Allen, William Carney
ALLEN, Sarah C. W5693, TR, Allen, Robert Baker
ALLEN, Sarah E. W336, H, Allen, Thomas A.
ALLEN, Susan, W498, MS, Allen, John F.
ALLEN, Susan, W2222, D, Allen, Benjamin F.
ALLEN, Susie Morgan, W2394, SH, Allen, Sam Houston
ALLEN, T. H. S4307, B, 37th Inf.
ALLEN, Thomas, S10279, SH, 15th Cav.
ALLEN, Thomas B. S4512, H, 3rd Inf.
ALLEN, Thomas O. S10193, WA, 29th N.C. Inf.
ALLEN, Tip, S6452, G, 18th Cav.
ALLEN, Vesta, W1515, GR, Allen, Robert

ALLEN, W. A. S3509, WL, 8th (Smith's) Cav.
ALLEN, W. D. S2810, WL, Allison's Squadron Cav.
ALLEN, W. E. S9997, SU, 16th Inf.
ALLEN, W. G. S7110, R, 5th Cav.
ALLEN, W. J. S12362, WE, 31st Inf.
ALLEN, W. J. F. S15113, SH, 47th Inf.
ALLEN, W. N. S13261, D, 10th (DeMoss') Cav.
ALLEN, W. R. S14630, SM, 22nd (Barteau's) Cav.
ALLEN, William, S356, RU, 1st Inf.
ALLEN, William, S5132, J, 2nd Ky. Cav.
ALLEN, William, S11323, WL, Allison's Squadron, Cav.
ALLEN, William C. S2214, CO, 62nd Inf.
ALLEN, Young Washington, S5540, G, 47th Inf.
ALLEY, A. K. S9842, BR, 35th Inf.
ALLEY, Amanda, W941, W, Alley, L.
ALLEY, Amanda Rockanna M. W1413, HO, Alley, David
ALLEY, Andrew D. S2940, A, 6th N.C. Cav.
ALLEY, Ann P. W3043, WY, Alley, Fredrick Leroy
ALLEY, Elizabeth, W7617, G, Alley, Wm. Riley
ALLEY, Louisa C. W9178, G, Alley, Melas Glen
ALLEY, Melissa H. W10117, D, Alley, Samuel James
ALLEY, Milas G. S7628, G, 19th (Biffle's) Cav.
ALLEY, William R. S13905, G, 3rd (Clack's) Inf.
ALLGOOD, John, S9403, MO, 3rd (Lillard's) Mtd. Inf.
ALLISON, Alexander, S12479, K, 7th Inf.
ALLISON, Benjamin Franklin, S1784, HW, 63rd Inf.
ALLISON, Bettsy A. W171, B, Allison, Kemtro T.
ALLISON, Caroline, W696, SM, Allison, Joseph
ALLISON, Catherine Elizabeth, W5823, WA, Allison, Robert
ALLISON, Herbert, S1071, CO, 62nd Inf.
ALLISON, Hester, W8611, W, Allison, Wm.
ALLISON, Ida Harris, W6948, K, Allison, Alex.
ALLISON, Kisiah J. W670, HU, Allison, Robert W.
ALLISON, L. F. S4826, LE, 1st Cav.
ALLISON, Lytle T. S1870, CF, 24th Inf.
ALLISON, Mary E. W623, B, Allison, Thomas B.
ALLISON, Nancy Jane, W4550, HW, Allison, Benjamin Franklin

Index to Tennessee Confederate Pension Applications

ALLISON, R. A. S935, D, 5th Ark. Inf.
ALLISON, Sadie Vaughn, W10839, D, Allison, John
ALLISON, Sam, C170, HY, 7th Cav.
ALLISON, W. C. S12746, HU, 1st (Feild's) Inf.
ALLISON, William, S8075, W, 35th Inf.
ALLISON, William D. S1361, RO, 16th Inf.
ALLMAN, Velie, W5204, O, Allman, Louis Collins
ALLMON, D. A. S5666, SU, Burrough's Co. Lt. Art.
ALLMON, L. C. S8745, O, 29th Inf.
ALLOWAY, John H. S14085, MC, 19th Inf.
ALLRED, B. W. S3309, H, 25th Inf.
ALLRED, C. M. S9247, MA, 14th N.C. Inf.
ALLRED, Etta T. W6984, MA, Allred, Clemmons M.
ALLRED, John, S9613, GI, 13th Ark. Vols.
ALLRED, Lou Frank, W5718, H, Allred, Blockston W.
ALLRED, William, S266, OV, 25th Inf.
ALLRED, William J. S594, OV, 59th Inf.
ALMAN, Josephine B. W1572, HO, Alman, Perry A.
ALMANY, Francis M. S1387, MR, 63rd Inf.
ALMANY, James M. S10251, SU, 63rd Inf.
ALMANY, Kate, W5934, MR, Almany, F. M.
ALRED, John W. S5635, OV, 25th Inf.
ALRED, Malinda, W3970, CF, Alred, Samuel A.
ALSOP, Mary L. W1948, GI, Alsop, John
ALSPAUGH, Josiah C. S9325, DI, 11th Inf.
ALSPAUGH, Mary Zeinob, W7114, DI, Alspaugh, Josiah Clifton
ALSTON, J. B. S15729, D, 4th (McLemore's) Cav.
ALSTON, J. J. S14444, DY, 20th Inf.
ALSTON, Joan Currie, W6027, L, Alston, Solomon G.
ALSTON, Laura E. W5246, MA, Alston, Arther L.
ALSTON, Mary Connie, W10072, DY, Alston, Joe John
ALSTON, Nannie V. W3646, MA, Alston, John R.
ALSTON, Samuel J. S14535, D, 4th (McLemore's) Cav.
ALSTON, Samuel J. S15170, D, 4th (McLemore's) Cav.
ALSUP, Hannah, W5860, RU, Alsup, Thomas Edwin

ALSUP, Jacob, S16631, WL, 12th Cav.
ALSUP, James, S1514, RU, 16th Inf.
ALSUP, John, S7577, GI, 32nd Inf.
ALSUP, Martha Elizabeth, W9347, MU, Alsup, John V.
ALSUP, S. T. S5551, WL, 45th Inf.
ALSUP, Virginia W. W1133, WL, Alsup, Samuel Thompson
ALTMAN, W. J. S15556, G, 30th Ark. Inf.
ALVIS, Wylie B. S8860, HW, Winston's Co. Lt. Art.
AMBERS, Jane, W3345, CO, Ambers, Farle
AMES, Nancy Katherine, W10905, CC, Ames, Jesse Burton
AMIS, H. B. S7676, HW, 12th Bn. (Day's) Cav.
AMIS, Joseph Thomas, S12943, MA, 21st (Wilson's) Cav.
AMIS, S. S. S10129, HE, 13th Inf.
AMIS, Tolbert F. S15564, MA, 21st (Wilson's) Cav.
AMMONS, B. F. S4742, MN, 1st Heavy Art.
AMMONS, Christian Caroline, W2971, HR, Ammons, Robert F.
AMMONS, J. A. S6718, K, 2nd N.C. Cav.
AMMONS, James H. S6486, MN, 14th (Neely's) Cav.
AMMONS, R. F. S285, HR, Undetermined
AMMONS, Sallie Agnes, W10264, MN, Ammons, Benjamin Franklin
AMMONS, Sarah Frances, W9827, MN, Ammons, James A.
AMMONS, W. H. S7016, H, 12th Ga. Cav.
AMONETT, Casander, W4707, PI, Amonett, Newton
AMONETT, M. V. S1686, PI, Shaw's Bn. Cav.
AMONETTE, A. J. S15117, LA, 1st Bn. (Colm's) Inf.
AMONS, Sallie A. W8181, MN, Amons, B. F.
AMOS, J. P. S11925, LI, 49th Ala. Inf.
AMOS, Mary E. W6538, LI, Amos, John P.
AMY, Pete, C143, K, Unassigned (Supply Wagon)
ANDERSON, A. J. S9802, MO, 59th Inf.
ANDERSON, A. M. S8489, MT, 14th Inf.
ANDERSON, Andrew J. S7629, CF, 24th Inf.
ANDERSON, Ann L. W4461, B, Anderson, Green B.
ANDERSON, Aurelia A. W3010, K, Anderson, Joseph J.
ANDERSON, B. F. S4775, FR, 1st (Turney's) Inf.

ANDERSON, B. P. S15289, PU, 8th Cav.
ANDERSON, Bettie, W3393, HR, Anderson, Miles E.
ANDERSON, C. S. S14075, HM, Griffin's Co. VA Lt. Art.
ANDERSON, Cader B. S14656, D, 7th Inf.
ANDERSON, D. J. S975, S15791, RB, 25th Inf.
ANDERSON, David L. S8931, LI, 1st (Turney's) Inf.
ANDERSON, E. H. S8789, F, 14th Cav.
ANDERSON, Eliza Ellen, W5296, CF, Anderson, Andrew Jackson
ANDERSON, Elizabeth, W2191, FR, Anderson, Benjamin F.
ANDERSON, Elizabeth, W3373, W1340, DK, Anderson, James Madison
ANDERSON, Elizabeth C. W3647, OV, Anderson, Wm. Joseph
ANDERSON, Elizabeth Calline, W2054, BE, Anderson, Marcus Lafayette
ANDERSON, Ella, W10639, SU, Anderson, Wm. Spurgeon
ANDERSON, Ella L. W7296, D, Anderson, Robert Meredith
ANDERSON, Ella Otey,   See Ella Otey Mason
ANDERSON, Ellen M. W3292, K, Anderson, Curren M.
ANDERSON, Etta, W4112, MU, Anderson, Philander P.
ANDERSON, Frances, W10540, G, Anderson, Wm. Persley
ANDERSON, Frances Elizabeth, W1340, W3373, DK, Anderson, James Madison
ANDERSON, Francis, S3271, MO, 4th Cav.
ANDERSON, Frank, S857, MO, 4th Inf.
ANDERSON, Frank, S11775, D, 8th (Smith's) Cav.
ANDERSON, Frank Ogleby, S16250, MT, 14th Inf.
ANDERSON, G. W. S4942, OV, 8th (Dibrell's) Cav.
ANDERSON, George, C216, HI, 9th Cav.
ANDERSON, Grace Ann, W2344, HI, Anderson, Erastus C.
ANDERSON, H. H. S13236, WE, 10th Cav.
ANDERSON, Henry, S14816, O, 40th N.C. Inf.
ANDERSON, Hixie J. W8259, D, Anderson, Orren B.
ANDERSON, Ike, C96, ST, 1st Ky. Cav.
ANDERSON, J. A. S16347, 10th Cav.

ANDERSON, J. M. S3660, SH, Forrest's Old Regt.
ANDERSON, J. R. S3674, SH, 9th Inf.
ANDERSON, J. T. S7883, HI, 48th Inf.
ANDERSON, James, S5662, F, 4th Miss. Inf.
ANDERSON, James A. S9159, SN, 8th (Dibrell's) Cav.
ANDERSON, James E. S2175, J, 8th Cav.
ANDERSON, James E. S4413, SN, 7th Cav.
ANDERSON, Jessie L. W6051, K, Anderson, Daria D.
ANDERSON, John A. S14839, 10th (DeMoss') Cav.
ANDERSON, John B. S8395, CL, 27th Bn. Va. Cav.
ANDERSON, John D. S7718, HE, 18th (Newsom's) Cav.
ANDERSON, Judia, W5474, PU, Anderson, James Edward
ANDERSON, Laura L. W9884, FR, Anderson, Edward Davidson
ANDERSON, Laura Lucretia, W3703, FR, Anderson, Edward Davidson
ANDERSON, Lavina, W1049, HI, Anderson, John Thomas
ANDERSON, Louisa Emily, W5217, OV, Anderson, George Washington
ANDERSON, M. D. S9006, DY, 15th (Stewart's) Cav.
ANDERSON, M. L. S9478, DK, 8th (Dibrell's) Cav.
ANDERSON, Martha, W148, J, Anderson, Andrew Jackson
ANDERSON, Mary A. W8539, HI, Anderson, W. S.
ANDERSON, Mary E. W2862, BR, Anderson, Jefferson C.
ANDERSON, Mary Susan, W7190, HM, Anderson, Asa
ANDERSON, Mattie, W7272, DK, Anderson, Sidney
ANDERSON, N. H. S11929, CF, 28th Cav.
ANDERSON, Nancy, W4968, J, Anderson, Miles Wesley
ANDERSON, Nannie, W782, CF, Anderson, W. M.
ANDERSON, O. V. S13491, CF, Huggin's Co. Lt. Art.
ANDERSON, P. P. S9437, WI, 9th Bn. (Gantt's) Cav.
ANDERSON, Parthena, W3625, HI, Anderson, E. Campbell

ANDERSON, R. F. S11069, HU, 9th Bn. (Gantt's) Cav.
ANDERSON, R. M. S15236, D, 44th Va. Cav.
ANDERSON, Richard, S15914, HI, 6th (Wheeler's) Cav.
ANDERSON, Robert R. S13223, SU, 60th Inf.
ANDERSON, Sallie, W7468, FR, Anderson, William C.
ANDERSON, Sallie E. W2519, D, Anderson, Benjamin Franklin
ANDERSON, Sarah Adaline, W1380, P, Anderson, Robert Drake
ANDERSON, Sarah Emiline, W2865, WH, Anderson, Joel Polk
ANDERSON, Sarah Jane, W4824, CF, Anderson, Marion
ANDERSON, Sidney, S12892, DK, 16th Inf.
ANDERSON, Sophronia, W2402, WH, Anderson, William
ANDERSON, T. B. S8726, SN, 28th Inf.
ANDERSON, T. D. W. S15172, D, 1st (Turney's) Inf.
ANDERSON, Virginia, W4415, MT, Anderson, Alfred Minor
ANDERSON, W. C. S8183, FR, 44th Inf.
ANDERSON, W. J. S370, PU, 8th Cav.
ANDERSON, W. J. S13440, HR, 14th Cav.
ANDERSON, W. J. Polk, S14960, MU, 48th (Voorhies') Inf.
ANDERSON, W. T. S12688, MA, 6th Inf.
ANDERSON, William A. S7511, SN, Stark's Bn. Art.
ANDERSON, William M. S7005, LI, Huggin's Co. Lt. Art.
ANDERSON, Winnie Catharine, W5308, SU, Anderson, Robert R.
ANDERTON, J. W. S7269, MOO, 37th Inf.
ANDERTON, James W. S7277, MOO, 37th Inf.
ANDERTON, Mary, W2485, MOO, Anderton, John Washington
ANDERTON, Nancy Evaline, W1166, MOO, Anderton, Thomas E.
ANDES, J. W. S12245, MR, 4th (McLemore's) Cav.
ANDES, Nancy Louisa, W9708, MR, Andes, John Wesley
ANDES, Sarahannia, W626, WA, Andes, Peter B.
ANDES, William L. S9504, MO, 4th (McLemore's) Cav.
ANDREWS, A. G. S13815, MA, 27th Inf.
ANDREWS, B. T. S2158, DI, 1st Heavy Art.

ANDREWS, Henry C. S10662, MOO, 7th Ala. Cav.
ANDREWS, J. K. P. S13058, S15703, MU, 17th Inf.
ANDREWS, John J. S12508, D, 20th Inf.
ANDREWS, M. L. S15345, D, 4th (McLemore's) Cav.
ANDREWS, Martha Jane, W4592, SE, Andrews, George Ashford
ANDREWS, Mary Ann, W924, DI, Andrews, B. F.
ANDREWS, Mary Dixon, W9231, D, Andrews, William M.
ANDREWS, Mary Elizabeth, W4758, D, Andrews, John Jefferson
ANDREWS, Mary Jane, W1441, MU, Andrews, William Carroll
ANDREWS, Mary Kenedy, W9182, WI, Andrews, Thomas Edward
ANDREWS, Nannie Elizabeth, W2484, O, Andrews, Michael Patric
ANDREWS, P. H. S8450, O, 9th Cav.
ANDREWS, Patrick Henry, S10442, HR, Forrest's Old Regt. Cav.
ANDREWS, R. W. S12466, H, 6th Inf.
ANDREWS, Sarah Elizabeth, W8606, D, Andrews, Elbert Gray
ANDREWS, Sarah Wilson, W9716, D, Andrews, Mark L.
ANDREWS, W. H. S8831, TR, 9th (Ward's) Cav.
ANDREWS, W. M. S11318, D, 20th Inf.
ANDREWS, William H. S5082, CO, 5th Tex. Inf.
ANGEL, A. G. S942, S1363, CT, 4th Va. Hvy. Art., Also with 34th Va. Inf.
ANGEL, Eliza, W7759, HM, Angel, William G.
ANGEL, James M. S13371, K, 36th Va. Inf.
ANGEL, Nancy Caroline, W6289, CF, Angel, Richard
ANGEL, Richard, S6087, CF, 37th Inf.
ANGEL, W. G. S13228, CO, 29th N.C. Inf.
ANGEL, William, S5238, BL, 8th Inf.
ANGELL, George W. S8434, CF, 24th Inf.
ANGELL, Martha A. W6008, CF, Angell, George W.
ANGLE, L. W. S16524, SN, 3rd Ky. Mtd. Inf.
ANGLEA, Fredonia, W10745, SN, Anglea, John Wesley
ANGLIN, Daniel, S13568, WI, 20th Inf.
ANGLIN, F. M. S11558, SH, 24th Inf.

ANGLIN, J. M. S14543, WI, 9th Bn. (Gantt's) Cav.
ANGLIN, Newton J. S272, WI, 24th Inf.
ANTHONY, Amanda, W8971, B, Anthony, James F.
ANTHONY, Birdie Daniel, W9112, CF, Anthony, R. S.
ANTHONY, Emma C. W7600, GI, Anthony, W. W.
ANTHONY, Ephraim M. S4902, B, 17th Inf.
ANTHONY, Fannie, W6820, G, Anthony, John Frank
ANTHONY, J. F. S14955, B, 28th Inf.
ANTHONY, Jake, S14359, LI, 41st Inf.
ANTHONY, King Fletcher, S9619, SH, 17th Inf.
ANTHONY, Mariah, W1022, B, Anthony, Anderson
ANTHONY, P. S. S7921, B, 17th Inf.
ANTHONY, Peter S. S6027, B, 17th Inf.
ANTHONY, R. S. S11402, MOO, 1st (Turney's) Inf.
ANTHONY, Sarah Caroline, W1254, B, Anthony, Daniel
ANTHONY, Sarah Jane, W4228, B, Anthony, Peter S.
ANTHONY, W. W. S12121, GI, 4th Ala. Cav.
APPERSON, C. S7969, BR, 7th Va. Inf., On misc. microfilm reel
APPERSON, Susan A. W6306, BR, Apperson, Cincinnati
APPLE, L. D. S8188, SM, 28th Inf.
APPLE, M. V. S14466, DY, 53rd N.C. Inf.
APPLE, Needoam, S2984, PU, 28th Inf.
APPLE, Sarah Ann, W6344, SM, Apple, A. J.
APPLEBERRY, Edwin, S15306, F, 1st Confederate Cav.
APPLETON, W. P. S4399, GI, 1st (Feild's) Inf.
APPLEWHITE, A. M. S1845, SH, 18th Miss. Cav.
APPLING, J. F. S8560, SH, 18th Miss. Cav.
APPLING, W. A. S9559, SH, 17th Miss. Inf.
ARBUCKLE, Mary J. W1042, D, Arbuckle, C. T. L.
ARBUCKLE, S. B. S13034, SH, Henderson's Scouts (MS)
ARCHER, Joseph, S1420, WA, 29th Inf.
ARCHER, William R. S16206, MS, 41st Inf.
ARGO, Lizzie, W7880, W, Argo, Eiza Jones
ARGO, Lucinda, W325, Argo, Ervin H.
ARGO, Willis, S16510, GU, Warren County Home Guards
ARMES, I. T. R. S11149, CY, 28th Inf.

ARMISTEAD, Cleo [Ferrill], W10383, WL, Armistead, John Mack, [Later married Ferrill]
ARMISTEAD, Elizabeth Baker, W4297, SH, Armistead, Fountaine
ARMISTEAD, John Mack, S253, SM, 8th (Smith's) Cav.
ARMISTEAD, Marcella Eugenia, W8468, W9787, SH, Armistead, Robert Alexander
ARMOR, Elizabeth Augusta, W2648, H, Armor, Robert Cowden
ARMS, A. C. S12728, CY, 8th Inf.
ARMS, Belle, W9835, PU, Arms, Newton M.
ARMS, Celina Olive, W10193, CY, Arms, Alvin Cullom
ARMS, Newton M. S15585, CY, 13th (Dibrell's) Cav.
ARMS, Rebecca, W6696, CY, Arms, Henry Martin
ARMSTRONG, A. C. S3282, MN, 9th Inf.
ARMSTRONG, Attie, W4541, H, Armstrong, M. V.
ARMSTRONG, Catharine, W859, RU, Armstrong, John James
ARMSTRONG, Elizabeth Josephine, W8671, MS, Armstrong, J. B. G.
ARMSTRONG, H. S15528, HD, 30th Ala. Inf.
ARMSTRONG, Joseph Benton, S13424, MS, 17th Inf.
ARMSTRONG, Lizzie, W3280, SH, Armstrong, John
ARMSTRONG, Louisa Charlott, W5449, SH, Armstrong, William James
ARMSTRONG, Lucy, W1696, MT, Armstrong, George W.
ARMSTRONG, M. V. S7096, ME, 5th (McKenzie's) Cav.
ARMSTRONG, Martha J. W6297, H, Armstrong, John William
ARMSTRONG, Martha M. W1232, HW, Armstrong, James G.
ARMSTRONG, Mattie Matilda, W9674, G, Armstrong, Ezekiel Jessie
ARMSTRONG, N. N. S209, RB, 30th Inf.
ARMSTRONG, Samuel M. S11948, WE, 12th Ky. Cav.
ARMSTRONG, W. R. S5133, PO, 29th Inf.
ARMSTRONG, William, S4088, MS, 17th Inf.
ARMSTRONG, William B. S1287, PO, 29th Inf.

Index to Tennessee Confederate Pension Applications

ARNETT, Eliza Catherine, W8479, HW, Arnett, Augustus Gallehoe
ARNETT, Elizabeth, W5593, MS, Arnett, John J.
ARNETT, J. H. S6893, LI, 19th (Biffle's) Cav.
ARNETT, J. H. S13045, LI, 8th (Dibrell's) Cav.
ARNETT, Martha A. W8311, RU, Arnett, Henry
ARNETT, Mary Delia, W5573, DY, Arnett, Joseph W.
ARNETT, T. J. S15097, WY, 9th Bn. Cav.
ARNETT, W. R. S15521, HR, 1st (Turney's) Inf.
ARNEY, John J. S5105, MU, 29th Va. Inf.
ARNEY, Sallie, W5372, PI, Arney, William Ervin
ARNO, John L. S1712, CF, 16th Miss. Inf.
ARNOLD, A. S7201, B, 18th Inf.
ARNOLD, A. H. S11223, G, 1st Ark. Cav.
ARNOLD, Almedia Fredora, W6421, H, Arnold, Francis Fieldon
ARNOLD, Almira J. W10445, DY, Arnold, John G.
ARNOLD, Antionette, W10618, SH, Arnold, Charles Demps
ARNOLD, B. F. S16249, HI, 24th Inf.
ARNOLD, Baker, S10646, HW, 29th Inf.
ARNOLD, Docia, W4377, BE, Arnold, Wm. Pinkney
ARNOLD, E. C. S8086, HI, 48th Inf.
ARNOLD, Eliza, W10302, JO, Arnold, James, see if same as Eliza J.
ARNOLD, Eliza C. W4263, O, Arnold, John Beakley
ARNOLD, Eliza J. W7816, JO, Arnold, James, see if same as Eliza
ARNOLD, Ellie, W6155, G, Arnold, A. H.
ARNOLD, Emma, W10600, RU, Arnold, Marion Francis
ARNOLD, F. M. S14877, RU, 18th Inf.
ARNOLD, G. S5496, DY, 1st Cav.
ARNOLD, Gideon, S7698, HI, 42nd Inf.
ARNOLD, J. Thomas, S9055, HI, 8th (Dibrell's) Cav.
ARNOLD, James, S585, HW, 29th Inf.
ARNOLD, James, S12232, JO, 30th Va.
ARNOLD, Jarett, S9989, JO, 37th N.C. Art.
ARNOLD, Joel T. S13305, HI, 10th Cav.
ARNOLD, John W. S8825, WE, 51st Inf.
ARNOLD, Mary, W295, RU, Arnold, Henry
ARNOLD, Mary Jane, W3066, B, Arnold, Avelius
ARNOLD, Molie, W4511, WH, Arnold, Seth

ARNOLD, Nancy, W851, HW, Arnold, William
ARNOLD, Nathan R. S16418, HW, Hawkins' Co. Home Guards
ARNOLD, Polk, C5, B, Forrest's Escort, Cav.
ARNOLD, R. A. S1645, G, 12th Inf.
ARNOLD, Robert, S12937, JO, 8th Va. Inf.
ARNOLD, Samuel Graham, S6942, MA, 154th Sr. Regt. Inf.
ARNOLD, Sarah Catherine, W9614, RU, Arnold, William Thomas
ARNOLD, Sarah Jane, W7357, G, Arnold, Reese Alby
ARNOLD, Thomas, S312, RU, 23rd Inf.
ARNOLD, William, S7465, K, 8th (Smith's) Cav.
ARNOLD, William Thomas, S4290, RU, 45th Inf.
ARNOTT, A. G. S6503, HW, 5th (McKenzie's) Cav.
ARNOTT, H. M. S6639, HW, 60th Inf.
ARNWINE, Reese Jackson, W8653, W6814, MC, Arnwine, Thomas L.
ARNWINE, Thomas L. S14113, MC, 3rd (Lillard's) Mtd. Inf.
ARRANT, Jacob, S13046, MO, 37th N.C. Inf.
ARRANT, Mary Ann, W7365, MO, Arrant, Jacob
ARRANTS, Catherine, W671, SU, Arrants, Nathan M.
ARRINGTON, Elizabeth C. W1578, W, Arrington, William
ARRINGTON, Henry C. S15902, SH, 28th Inf.
ARRINGTON, Sallie A. W3161, MA, Arrington, John Alonzo
ARROWSMITH, Florence Harris, W8717, GI, Arrowsmith, Field
ARTHER, Felix, S6072, MC, 29th Inf.
ARTHER, Milton A. S11876, GI, Phillip's Co. Lt. Art.
ARTHUR, James M. S4370, GI, 19th (Biffle's) Cav.
ARTHUR, Lou C. W11065, MS, Arthur, Benjamin C.
ARTHUR, Sallie A. W2857, GI, Arthur, James Monroe
ASBELL, Dan, S6098, HD, 12th Miss. Cav.
ASBERRY, Spencer, S833, CL, Undetermined
ASBILL, J. M. S3481, MN, 34th Inf.
ASH, Daniel, S1012, BR, 69th N.C. Inf.
ASH, Jane, W1720, SM, Ash, William
ASHBURN, D. D. S13152, SU, Unassigned: NC Conscripts

Index to Tennessee Confederate Pension Applications

ASHBY, Asbury, S7845, LI, Huggin's Co. Lt. Art.
ASHBY, E. W. S12433, LI, 5th Ky. Inf.
ASHBY, John L. S2025, MOO, 9th Ky. Inf.
ASHBY, Mattie, W10215, LI, Ashby, Asbury
ASHBY, Rebecca E. W5599, LI, Ashby, E. W.
ASHBY, T. N. S13889, LI, Huggin's Battery Lt. Art.
ASHCRAFT, H. C. S5773, CH, 2nd Bn. Cav.
ASHCRAFT, Lettie, W10585, DY, Ashcraft, John White
ASHCROFT, John W. S14665, DY, 6th Cav.
ASHFORD, E. W. S8609, CA, 18th Inf.
ASHFORD, Margaret Montgomery, W9930, H, Ashford, Robert James
ASHFORD, W. W. S12807, GI, 32nd Inf.
ASHLEY, Eleanor Jane, W653, CF, Ashley, Simeon
ASHLEY, Elizabeth Ann, W2088, CF, Ashley, William
ASHLEY, George W. S14447, G, 20th Inf.
ASHLEY, J. M. S802, P, Undetermined
ASHLEY, Louisa Evaline, W5306, H, Ashley, William Cinton
ASHLEY, Nannie Missouri, W8521, G, Ashley, Benjamin Franklin
ASHLEY, Serena Iavena, W6304, G, Ashley, Robert Martin
ASHWORTH, Mainda E. W5415, MU, Ashworth, Sam Wilson
ASHWORTH, Perlina B. W9018, WI, Ashworth, Joseph Sephus
ASHWORTH, S. W. S2476, MU, 34th Inf.
ASKEW, Eula Utley, W10068, MA, Askew, Joseph David
ASKEW, G. A. S3284, CO, 2nd N.C. Inf.
ASKEW, G. H. S12363, HY, 38th N.C. Inf.
ASKEW, J. D. S15882, MA, 6th Inf.
ASKEW, J. F. S14891, CO, 53rd N.C. Inf.
ASKEW, John, S16580, BE, Unassigned
ASKEW, W. F. S15413, D, Allison's Squadron, Cav.
ASKEW, W. T. S5449, SN, 44th Inf.
ASKEW, William, S12638, G, 6th Inf.
ASKINS, Mary Elizabeth, W3243, HI, Askins, Joseph
ASLIN, J. A. S13966, G, 12th Ky. Cav.

ASTON, Sarah Ann, W2214, WA, Aston, Washington Jackson
ASTON, W. H. S5343, WA, 61st Inf.
ATCHISON, B. F. S6641, SN, 30th Inf.

ATCHLEY, Elizabeth Frances, W1870, H, Atchley, James M.
ATCHLEY, George W. S2493, ME, 3rd (Lillard's) Mtd Inf.
ATCHLEY, James M. S2252, R, 26th Inf.
ATCHLEY, Joshua, S1102, ME, 5th Cav.
ATCHLEY, M. L. S6305, ME, 3rd (Lillard's) Mtd. Inf.
ATCHLEY, Mary A. W988, ME, Atchley, Josh
ATCHLEY, Robert, S9207, R, 5th Cav.
ATCHLEY, Sarah j. W460, ME, Atchley, Noah R.
ATKERSON, B. R. S5667, MU, Maury Lt. Art.
ATKERSON, John W. S4877, HN, 46th Inf.
ATKERSON, Martha Roean, W790, MU, Atkerson, Benjamin Reeves
ATKINS, Annie, W9615, K, Atkins, Kennerly Carson
ATKINS, Augustine T. S9343, T, 11th (Holman's) Cav.
ATKINS, Easter, W6879, MO, Atkins, James M.
ATKINS, Henry, S12265, K, 12th Bn. Cav.
ATKINS, J. E. S12434, O, 7th Cav.
ATKINS, J. M. S8425, MO, 37th Inf.
ATKINS, James Jesse, S12146, HN, 21st (Wilson's) Cav.
ATKINS, James M. S5041, BO, 2nd (Ashby's) Cav.
ATKINS, John B. S5239, HN, 46th Inf.
ATKINS, John S. S2690, MN, 4th Inf.
ATKINS, Johnnie, W4153, MN, Atkins, John S.
ATKINS, Joseph T. S59, WE, 46th Inf.
ATKINS, K. C. S14619, K, 63rd Va. Inf.
ATKINS, L. C. S14079, RB, 3rd Ky. Cav.
ATKINS, Lavinia Ruth, W9495, DY, Atkins, James A.
ATKINS, Mattie D. W887, SH, Atkins, William Henry
ATKINS, Nancy Graves, W4038, O, Atkins, James Elias
ATKINS, Obedience Cardwell, W711, HN, Atkins, Richard Lee
ATKINS, R. L. S3677, HN, 20th (Russell's) Cav.
ATKINS, S. L. S14500, CF, 55th Va. Inf.
ATKINS, Sue, W364, HN, Atkins, Wm. Edward
ATKINS, W. G. S9746, HD, 4th Inf.
ATKINSON, Ben F. S11480, GR, 60th Inf.
ATKINSON, Cordelia Marcella, W9469, GR, Atkinson, Ben F.
ATKINSON, F. M. S8101, D, Forrest's Escort, Cav.

Index to Tennessee Confederate Pension Applications

ATKINSON, Frances Marion, W3440, D, Atkinson, Joe Webb
ATKINSON, James S. S12332, GR, 60th Inf.
ATKINSON, S. W. S685, CY, Hamilton's Bn. Cav.
ATKINSON, Sallie, W3784, MT, Atkinson, Qunitus Cincinnatus
ATKINSON, William Thomas, S13492, SH, 8th Ga. Cav.
ATKISON, Avarillo E. W4246, HN, Atkison, S. P.
ATKISON, Ellen Olivia, W4199, SH, Atkison, Martin VanBuren
ATKISSON, Thomas J. S12690, MU, 48th (Voorhies') Inf.
ATNIP, John, S11759, DK, 16th Inf.
ATTKISSON, James Martin, S12689, MU, 19th (Biffle's) Cav.
ATTKISSON, T. J. S7326, MU, 48th Inf.
AUBREY, John J. S8223, RU, 45th Inf.
AULT, C. W. S3576, R, 1st (Carter's) Cav.
AUSBROOKS, Pleasant H. S1600, SN, 25th Inf.
AUSBROOKS, W. C. sr. S5157, SN, 44th Inf.
AUST, Mary E. W10384, WL, Aust, W. H.
AUSTELL, A. L. B. S6567, FR, 28th Cav.
AUSTIN, Amanda, W3648, HW, Austin, John
AUSTIN, Ann Elizabeth, W2916, WE, Austin, Moses Vincent
AUSTIN, C. V. S14841, DI, 11th Inf.
AUSTIN, Ed, S2618, WH, 25th Inf.
AUSTIN, George W. S3482, HE, 2nd Ark. Inf.
AUSTIN, H. G. S9951, DI, Napier's Bn. Cav.
AUSTIN, J. J. S14219, DE, 19th (Biffle's) Cav.
AUSTIN, J. T. S3898, SN, 7th Bn (Bennett's) Cav.
AUSTIN, Jacob, S6441, MN, 14th N.C. Inf.
AUSTIN, James, S6592, WA, 29th Inf.
AUSTIN, John, S1952, WH, 16th Inf.
AUSTIN, John, S2511, HW, 4th Va. Inf.
AUSTIN, Johnathan, S13172, SQ, 35th Inf.
AUSTIN, Louiza, W1809, L, Austin, John R.
AUSTIN, Lucinda Jane, W5039, HM, Austin, William
AUSTIN, Mary Ann, W428, DI, Austin, George Wyatt
AUSTIN, Mary Lucy, W8796, DE, Austin, John J.
AUSTIN, Nathaniel Glenn, S1806, WH, 28th Inf.
AUSTIN, Robert, S2498, WH, 8th (Dibrell's) Cav.
AUSTIN, Robin, S5181, WH, 8th (Dibrell's) Cav.
AUSTIN, Sarah Edna, W8493, DI, Austin, Charles Van Buren
AUSTIN, Susan, W9859, HY, Austin, Albert Morris
AUSTIN, Thomas, S11466, WH, 28th Inf.
AUSTIN, William H. S10724, WH, 25th Inf.
AUTEN, Edmond G. S1136, MN, Col. Jeff Forest Regt.
AUTEN, Livona, W7814, MN, Auten, Edmond Green
AUTREY, William H. S95, PU, 16th Inf.
AUTRY, S. J. S1692, BE, 52nd Inf.
AVANS, F. M. S2280, ME, 62nd Inf.
AVANT, Alfred Scott, C275, RU, Regiment not given
AVANT, Belle, See Belle Findley
AVANTS, James T. S13461, O, 2nd Miss. Cav.
AVARITT, R. H. S9733, RU, 18th Inf.
AVENT, Maggie Ogden, W3764, RU, Avent, Benjamin
AVERILL, E. W. S2290, D, 3rd Ala. Inf.
AVERITT, Albert, C45, RU, 18th Inf.
AVERITT, E. W. S5095, TR, 2nd Inf.
AVERITT, W. R. S1142, RU, 11th Cav.
AVERY, Margaret, W6841, WE, Avery, Granvil Piller
AWALT, J. F. S7782, FR, 17th Inf.
AYDELATT, M. P. S12774, O, 48th (Voorhies') Inf.
AYDELOTT, William C. S15789, MU, 6th (Wheeler's) Cav.
AYERS, Delilah Jane, W9870, W, Ayers, John Lenny
AYERS, Powell, S2612, GI, 44th Inf.
AYERS, Sarah L. W1377, B, Ayers, Calvin W.
AYLOR, Mattie, W10679, WE, Aylor, Joseph Smith
AYMETT, Ada A. W8672, GI, Aymett, F. D.
AYMETT, Edward Fields, S15932, GI, 6th (Wheeler's) Cav.
AYMETT, Hance Hamilton, S2160, GI, 53rd Inf.
AYRES, F. S. S4560, M, 9th Bn. (Bennett's) Cav.
AYRES, J. P. S9893, HU, 6th (Wheeler's) Cav.
AYRES, James, S3399, GI, 23rd Inf.
AYRES, Millie J. W8028, GI, Ayres, Powell
AYRES, Nancy Cathrine, W7227, HU, Ayres, John Poke
AYRES, Olivia B. W6388, HU, Ayres, Thomas E.
AYRES, Thomas J. S13708, RB, 6th (Wheeler's) Cav.

BABB, Henry, S3535, G, 47th N.C. Inf.
BABB, Stephen Oliver, S12444, HR, 22nd Inf.
BABER, C. C. S13696, CE, 9th Bn. (Bennett's) Cav.
BACHELOR, C. S. S10381, HE, 6th Inf.
BACHMAN, L. H. S1391, SU, 1st Cav.
BACON, Jane, W441, RO, Bacon, John Harrison
BACON, John, S15154, WA, 60th Inf.
BACON, John H. S463, RO, 2nd Cav.
BADGETT, B. F. S15515, K, 63rd Inf.
BAGARLY, J. W. S2426, CE, 30th Inf.
BAGGETT, Anna Caroline, W2681, MT, Baggett, Hezekiah
BAGGETT, Elias, S6447, MT, 49th Inf.
BAGGETT, Joe, S11626, MT, 49th Inf.
BAGLEY, C. B. S16343, LI, 41st Inf.
BAGLEY, James M. S9563, LI, 41st Inf.
BAGLEY, Margaret Susan, W3807, LI, Bagley, James M.
BAILEY, A. B. S297, HW, 29th Inf.
BAILEY, A. J. S605, K, 54th Va. Inf.
BAILEY, Alpha, S13380, HR, 14th Cav.
BAILEY, Annie C. W8333, HW, Bailey, Henry
BAILEY, B. S. S11636, CF, 13th Cav.
BAILEY, Charlotte E. W2967, T, Bailey, Jeremiah
BAILEY, E. L. S15844, U, 2nd N.C. Home Guards
BAILEY, Eliza, W8365, W6207, HW, Bailey, Jessie
BAILEY, Ellen Louisa, W1796, D, Bailey, James William
BAILEY, F. M. S9510, HW, 31st Inf.
BAILEY, Frank M. S2176, J, 28th Inf.
BAILEY, G. W. S5835, RU, 23rd Inf.
BAILEY, G. W. S6741, MU, 1st Mo. Inf.
BAILEY, J. A. S2424, CA, 18th Inf.
BAILEY, J. A. S5590, SH, 9th Miss. Inf.
BAILEY, J. C. S10894, CL, 25th Va. Cav.
BAILEY, J. M. S3629, G, 12th Inf.
BAILEY, J. W. S1872, D, 4th Cav.
BAILEY, Jacob, S2941, WA, 61st Inf.
BAILEY, James A. S13278, K, 1st Va. Cav.
BAILEY, James A. S14970, D, 1st (Feild's) Inf.
BAILEY, James H. S3675, BO, 3rd East Tenn. Cav.
BAILEY, Jennie, W7044, W, Bailey, James A.
BAILEY, Jessee, S9887, HW, 29th Inf.
BAILEY, John, S4008, HD, 4th Ala. Cav.
BAILEY, Joseph, S5510, HW, 31st Inf.
BAILEY, Jubel, S8227, G, 12th Inf.

BAILEY, L. J. S3190, CO, 1st Inf.
BAILEY, Manerva L. W6991, J, Bailey, Francis Marion
BAILEY, Margaret E. W742, JE, Bailey, Joseph
BAILEY, Martha W. W7714, D, Bailey, James A.
BAILEY, Mary Catherine, W9023, LI, Bailey, Cullen
BAILEY, Mary E. W296, WA, Bailey, Jacob
BAILEY, Mary E. W932, HW, Bailey, W. N.
BAILEY, Mary Jane, W4534, H, Bailey, Vardell
BAILEY, Mary Rebecca, W1545, MU, Bailey, George Washington
BAILEY, Mary W. W6578, SH, Bailey, Joshua G.
BAILEY, Missouri J. W3880, CH, Bailey, Samuel Truman
BAILEY, Nancy L. W4201, MOO, Bailey, Owen Jefferson
BAILEY, Nathaniel, S13705, GE, 61st Inf.
BAILEY, Robert, S11598, W, 18th Inf.
BAILEY, Sophrona C. W1092, G, Bailey, Thomas B.
BAILEY, Thomas B. S6154, O, 3rd Inf.
BAILEY, Vista Street, W10885, U, Bailey, Elbert Lenore
BAILEY, Vod, S1289, H, 40th Inf.
BAILEY, W. A. S14307, B, Forrest's Escort, Cav.
BAILEY, Zac. T. S11784, MT, 14th Inf.
BAILIFF, Eliza Jane, W8761, DK, Bailiff, J. M.
BAILIFF, Elizabeth M. W261, DK, Bailiff, Joab
BAILIFF, James M. S5336, DK, Undetermined
BAIN, Frederick Washington, S7331, GI, 48th Inf.
BAIN, Jasper, S4541, W, 4th (Murray's) Cav.
BAIN, John, S5357, DK, 50th Inf.
BAIN, Martha A. W1214, DK, Bain, John
BAIN, Mary, W4940, W2940, WH, Bain, William, 2940 found with 4940 on film
BAIN, Palestine, W9996, W, Bain, Alfred Monroe
BAINE, William, S2236, WH, 1st Bn. (Colm's) Inf.
BAINS, Mary Ann, W2860, WA, Bains, Nathan
BAINS, Mattie, W8357, SU, Bains, Samuel
BAINS, Samuel, S8636, SU, 60th Inf.
BAIRD, C. L. S6742, S9564, WL, 45th Inf.
BAIRD, Eliza E. W7253, WL, Baird, William Alex
BAIRD, F. M. S6403, SH, 11th Miss. Cav.

Index to Tennessee Confederate Pension Applications

BAIRD, Fannie M. W1131, MA, Baird, R. Harrison
BAIRD, James P. S11426, SU, 11th Va. Inf.
BAIRD, L. M. S11620, CF, 45th Inf.
BAIRD, Maggie A. W8613, RU, Baird, Newton Harrison
BAIRD, Marie, W8100, BR, Baird, William Thomas
BAIRD, Martha Cathern, W7118, CF, Baird, Lemuel Moore
BAIRD, N. H. S13055, RU, 38th Inf.
BAIRD, Samuel H. S7431, WL, 16th S.C. Inf.
BAIRD, Winnifred, W2146, D, Baird, Martin L.
BAKER, Alfred, S6104, BO, 6th Ga. Cav.
BAKER, Amanda Few, W8674, HU, Baker, James Wilkens
BAKER, Amanda P. W6422, GI, Baker, John Frazier
BAKER, C. L. S3175, SU, 59th Inf.
BAKER, Calaway, S1546, K, 4th Inf.
BAKER, Cassie E. W4711, SH, Baker, Vardra Edward
BAKER, Catherine, W10937, SN, Baker, W. P.
BAKER, Charity Barton, W4505, WE, Baker, Wm. Henry
BAKER, D. M. S15738, MN, 1st Regt. NC Jr. Reserves
BAKER, Eliza P. W8378, SH, Baker, William Henry
BAKER, Eliza S. W4158, HI, Baker, James P.
BAKER, Elizabeth A. W6237, G, Baker, L. C. sr.
BAKER, Elizabeth Jane, W1858, BE, Baker, John P.
BAKER, Ely, S9102, L, 8th (Smith's) Cav.
BAKER, Emily, W6414, WH, Baker, Robert F.
BAKER, Emily Jane, W1811, DI, Baker, George Washington
BAKER, G. V. S4058, HI, 2nd Ky. Cav.
BAKER, H. C. S11529, D, 9th (Ward's) Cav.
BAKER, H. O. S5362, T, 9th Miss. Inf.
BAKER, Hannah, W10247, PU, Baker, William L.
BAKER, Isaac, S4366, WA, Lynch's Battery, Lt. Art.
BAKER, J. B. S15694, DY, 22nd (Barteau's) Cav.
BAKER, J. F. S8887, F, 38th Inf.
BAKER, J. H. S7030, DY, 42nd Inf.
BAKER, J. W. S11755, C, 13th Inf.
BAKER, Jennie Margaret, W4000, D, Baker, Beverly
BAKER, Jim, C239, F, Unassigned (Laborer)
BAKER, John, S2146, HU, 1st (Maney's) Inf.
BAKER, John Jonas, S16575, L, 47th North Miss. Inf.
BAKER, John M. S8861, FR, 4th (McLemore's) Cav.
BAKER, John R. S7597, HA, 43rd Inf.
BAKER, Julia Maria, W7608, FR, Baker, John Martin
BAKER, L. C. sr. S12010, G, 12th Ky. Cav.
BAKER, Laura J. W2827, HA, Baker, Andrew L.
BAKER, Leander K. S9103, CC, 7th (Duckworth's) Cav.
BAKER, Leon B. S7604, K, 2nd (Ashby's) Cav.
BAKER, Louisa, W113, WH, Baker, Samuel M.
BAKER, Marinda Gaines, W2556, Baker, Thomas H.
BAKER, Marticia M. W272, HI, Baker, Fielding H.
BAKER, Mary E. W1102, CU, Baker, Samuel
BAKER, Mary E. W2437, D, Baker, A. L.
BAKER, Matilda, W4165, CO, Baker, Wm. Andrew Russell
BAKER, Nancy Elizabeth, W2565, DI, Baker, Wyley Johnson
BAKER, Nancy Ellen, W8612, D, Baker, Thos. Richmund
BAKER, Nannie C. W8766, HD, Baker, Wm. James
BAKER, Nathaniel J. S14924, K, Unassigned (Railroad Wk.)
BAKER, Paralee, W1490, CC, Baker, Alfred Thomas
BAKER, R. D. S731, WH, 16th Inf.
BAKER, R. F. S14836, WH, 8th (Dibrell's) Cav.
BAKER, Rabeca Euphamia, W3175, DI, Baker, Chambers B.
BAKER, Robert Howell, S16111, WL, Pettus' Escort
BAKER, Sarah, W4113, MA, Baker, Henry Thomas
BAKER, Sarah Jane, W6654, HI, Baker, George Venable
BAKER, Sarah Jane, W10717, SH, Baker, Moses
BAKER, T. D. S6364, D, Undetermined
BAKER, Thomas, S7787, DI, 10th Cav.
BAKER, W. E. S15681, FR, 4th (McLemore's) Cav.
BAKER, W. H. S615, HI, 11th Inf.

Index to Tennessee Confederate Pension Applications

BAKER, W. L. S2920, WH, 1st Bn. (Colm's) Inf.
BAKER, W. P. S7928, SN, 30th Inf.
BAKER, Wiley J. S5240, DI, 11th Inf.
BAKER, William D. S1619, PU, 28th Inf.
BAKER, William E. S15243, FR, 4th (McLemore's) Cav.
BALCH, Adeline S. W4840, CO, Balch, Philip Hinkle
BALDING, M. D. L. S13091, JE, 60th N.C. Inf.
BALDRIDGE, Edmund T. S8874, G, 14th Cav.
BALDRIDGE, J. P. S11779, CC, 9th Inf.
BALDRIDGE, J. S. S9472, CC, 27th Inf.
BALDWIN, Chesley, S4754, D, 19th Inf.
BALDWIN, Ellen, W6280, D, Baldwin, Chesley
BALDWIN, John M. S11799, MR, 60th Ga. Inf.
BALDWIN, N. M. S2545, CL, Undetermined
BALDWIN, T. G. S14358, SH, 29th Ga. Bn. Cav.
BALDY, Rosa Virginia, W5563, HR, Baldy, William H.
BALDY, W. H. S12485, HR, 1st Miss. Cav.
BALES, Jesse, S7598, HM, 1st (Carter's) Cav.
BALL, Elizabeth Jane, W4813, SU, Ball, John Wesley
BALL, G. W. S5820, SU, 31st Inf.
BALL, J. L. S12677, GI, 53rd Inf.
BALL, James H. S10854, WI, 26th Ala. Inf.
BALL, John M. S5193, JE, 60th N.C. Inf.
BALL, John W. S12375, GI, 6th (Wheeler's) Cav.
BALL, M. E. S6092, GE, 31st Inf.
BALL, Martha A. W1315, MA, Ball, William Lawson
BALL, Milton E. S2783, GE, 31st Inf.
BALL, T. T. S2704, MC, 5th (McKenzie's) Cav.
BALL, W. J. S3948, WA, 51st Va. Inf.
BALL, Wesley, S12426, HW, Hewald's Battery Art.
BALLANFANT, J. L. S895, MU, Forrest's Cav.
BALLARD, Benjamin F. S6550, HN, 7th Cav.
BALLARD, George H. S10443, WA, 29th N.C. Inf.
BALLARD, James H. S2933, K, 3rd Conf. Engineer Troops
BALLARD, Louis J. S11084, SH, 29th Miss. Inf.
BALLARD, Peter J. S96, SM, 8th Cav.
BALLARD, Rutha Frances, W402, WH, Ballard, James Catlip
BALLARD, Susan Talitha, W5653, SH, Ballard, George Alexander
BALLARD, Thomas A. S4509, CC, 9th Inf.
BALLENTINE, Benjamin Wesly, S1204, MT, 14th Inf.
BALLEW, George, S2804, LO, 1st S.C. Inf.
BALLEW, Sallie Wright, W5726, SH, Ballew, Benjamin Franklin
BALLZONEY, John, S6992, F, 20th Miss. Inf.
BALTHROP, Elizabeth Frances, W4535, RB, Balthrop, Wm. Henry
BALTHROP, John H. S12072, MT, 49th Inf.
BANCOM, J. J. S12722, O, 9th Inf.
BANCUM, Melvina Jane, W10509, HN, Bancum, John Lilly
BANDY, A. G. S1410, HW, 49th Inf.
BANDY, E. A. S3650, HN, 18th Inf.
BANDY, Emily Ann, W7909, PO, Bandy, James Thomas
BANDY, H. Q. S1924, HW, 18th N.C. State Troops
BANDY, J. H. S10896, WE, 51st Inf.
BANDY, Margaret, W2465, CU, Bandy, T. E.
BANDY, Thomas J. S14668, PO, 43rd Inf.
BANDY, Virginia, W2533, D, Bandy, Wm. Pierce
BANGUS, Robert Benjamin, S7884, O, 3rd (Clack's) Inf.
BANISTER, David M. S8120, D, 17th Ala. Inf.
BANISTER, Sarah, W8498, D, Banister, D. M.
BANKS, Charlie Simpkins, S15743, D, 30th Ala. Inf.
BANKS, E. O. S12397, SH, 3rd (Forrest's) Cav.
BANKS, Emma Frances, W3504, G, Banks, Wm. Ambrose
BANKS, Florence T. W9319, D, Banks, Charles
BANKS, John W. S11790, HI, 48th (Voorhies') Inf.
BANKS, Martha Elizabeth, W10366, RU, Banks, Solomon
BANKS, Porter, C50, D, 2nd Inf.
BANKS, S. G. S4662, CF, 17th (Newman's) Cav.
BANKS, Thomas J. S15896, LE, 48th (Voorhies') Inf.
BANKS, Weatley D. S6223, DK, 35th Inf.
BANKS, William, S11144, CA, 18th Inf.
BANKSMITH, Sophie, W4531, SH, Banksmith, Ansel
BANKSTON, John H. S13341, H, 1st Inf.
BANKSTON, Sarah Jane, W5855, H, Bankston, John Henry
BANKSTON, Wilson L. S14220, LI, 44th Ala. Inf.

Index to Tennessee Confederate Pension Applications

BANTHER, Patton, S16432, H, Folder only contains affadavits
BANTON, Charles M. S12273, LI, 8th Inf.
BARANGER, Mary Ann, W3188, G, Baranger, George
BARB, Eliza Jane, W1957, HW, Barb, John
BARBEE, Margaret Elizabeth, W6595, SH, Barbee, James Pleasant
BARBEE, Maria E. W1325, H, Barbee, George Washington
BARBEE, Mary Elizabeth, W4155, Barbee, Jefferson Monroe, Applied from Logan Co. Ky.
BARBEE, R. M. S4948, WL, Allison's Squadron, Cav.
BARBEE, Sarah Elizabeth, W8037, WL, Barbee, R. M.
BARBEE, Sarah Louis, W3848, SH, Barbee, J. O.
BARBER, Harriet Lavinia, W10052, SN, Barber, William Allen
BARBER, I. W. S7437, P, 10th Cav.
BARBER, J. G. S2437, SN, 7th Inf.
BARBER, John L. S7630, D, Carter's Scouts, Cav.
BARBER, Manerva, W9993, SN, Barber, Joseph G.
BARBER, Martha A. W4890, D, Barber, John L.
BARBER, Martha Mosley, W2931, GI, Barber, Robt. J.
BARBER, R. J. S2134, GI, 3rd Inf.
BARBER, W. A. S5774, SN, 30th Inf.
BARE, George Lilburn, S15372, SU, Kain's Co. Lt. Art.
BARE, Samuel, S6453, HW, 13th Va. Art.
BAREFIELD, William, S6605, WA, 34th N.C. Inf.
BARFIELD, M. T. S1775, HN, 67th N.C. Inf.
BARFIELD, T. P. S8865, D, 9th Bn. Ga. Art.
BARFIELD, W. H. S14379, HN, 20th Cav.
BARGER, Mary E. W1132, SU, Barger, Nicholas
BARGER, Sophronia Eudora, W8883, WE, Barger, W. G.
BARHAM, Annie Dickson, W9505, MT, Barham, John Henry
BARHAM, C. E. W255, CH, Barham, L. P.
BARHAM, Ida, W10593, HN, Barham, Newton J.
BARHAM, J. W. S4251, GE, 61st Inf.
BARHAM, L. P. S4300, CH, 21st (Wilson's) Cav.
BARHAM, N. S. S9969, SH, 18th Miss. Cav.
BARHAM, Sophie Ann, W9675, HI, Barham, Hartwell Freeman
BARKER, Annie E. W9740, LK, Barker, James Allen
BARKER, Eloysa, W4606, DY, Barker, Raleigh White
BARKER, Francis M. S11661, K, Burrough's Co. Art.
BARKER, Henry W. S13041, K, Thomas' Legion, N.C.
BARKER, J. A. S16149, LK, 55th Inf.
BARKER, James, S10677, SQ, 35th Inf.
BARKER, John K. S1355, 32nd Inf.
BARKER, Nancy, W2166, SQ, Barker, Abner
BARKLEY, G. W. S5206, MN, 7th Miss. Cav., Also spelled Bartlett & Bartley in app.
BARKLEY, James M. S12001, WA, 63rd Inf.
BARKLEY, John T. S12406, O, 2nd Cav.
BARKSDALE, Cornelia, W10973, G, Barksdale, Wm. Warren
BARKSDALE, Dicie J. W3346, O, Barksdale, James R.
BARKSDALE, Eliza B. W2161, SM, Barksdale, Wm. H.
BARKSDALE, G. T. S7964, G, 20th (Russell's)
BARKSDALE, Henderson, C102, G, 12th Inf.
BARKSDALE, John F. S8448, MA, 12th Inf.
BARKSDALE, W. W. S15620, G, 4th Bn. S.C. Reserves
BARLER, J. S. S12530, GI, 48th (Nixon's) Inf.
BARLEW, Ella F. W7138, MR, Barlew, Zebedee
BARLEW, Libby, W7321, GU, Barlew, Wm.
BARLEW, William, S11703, GU, 4th (McLemore's) Cav.
BARLEW, Z. S1861, MR, 5th Cav.
BARLEW, Zebadee, S532, MR, 6th (Wheeler's) Cav.
BARLEY, Joseph W. S6299, H, 3rd (Forrest's) Cav.
BARLOW, John J. S1822, CE, 2nd Cav.
BARLOW, Joseph, S10002, HM, 23rd Va. Bn. Inf.
BARLOW, Robert D. S10453, WE, 12th Ky. Cav.
BARLOW, W. A. S3860, O, 5th Ark. Inf.
BARNARD, Elvis, S6612, SN, Undetermined
BARNARD, P. B. S4516, GR, 5th Cav.
BARNARD, Robert, S14912, CL, 37th Inf.

-17

BARNARD, Wiley M. S9287, HW, 19th Inf.
BARNES, A. A. S5241, HN, 5th Inf.
BARNES, A. J. S4294, BR, Winston's Co. Lt. Art.
BARNES, A. J. S7350, GU, 35th Inf.
BARNES, Andrew Jackson, S14241, RB, 14th Inf.
BARNES, C. A. S9932, MT, 14th Ky. Cav.
BARNES, Charles, S814, BE, 5th Inf.
BARNES, Dennis, S7415, FR, 17th Inf.
BARNES, Elijah, S16117, S16038, SU, 59th Inf.
BARNES, George, S16586, HO, 14th Inf.
BARNES, H. C. S9140, MA, 6th Inf.
BARNES, Isaac, S12880, W, 35th Inf.
BARNES, J. T. S4633, SU, 19th Inf.
BARNES, James A. S803, P, Undetermined
BARNES, James A. S1500, DE, 6th Inf.
BARNES, James W. S10922, D, 55th Inf.
BARNES, Jehu, S3856, W, 1st Ga. Inf.
BARNES, Jehu, S4998, WH, 1st Ga. Inf.
BARNES, Joel Lucas, S9513, GI, 3rd (Brown's) Inf.
BARNES, John B. S11193, D, 20th Inf.
BARNES, John H. S10713, MR, Barry's Co. Lt. Art.
BARNES, John W. S16220, O, 4th (Starne's) Cav.
BARNES, John Warren, S10308, D, 1st (Field's) Inf.
BARNES, Jonetta, W4568, D, Barnes, Wm. Dickey
BARNES, L. T. S7758, S10293, PU, 8th (Dibrell's) Cav.
BARNES, Lizzie [Henry], W11084, MA, Barnes, Edwin, [Later married Henry]
BARNES, M. S12874, W, 35th Inf.
BARNES, Margaret, W5504, OV, Barnes, Jesse Adison
BARNES, Mary A. W7719, SU, Barnes, James
BARNES, Mary J. W411, SU, Barnes, Wm. E.
BARNES, Mary L. W7330, RB, Barnes, Andrew Jackson
BARNES, Mary M. W5963, SU, Barnes, John T.
BARNES, Mary R. W7767, MR, Barnes, John H.
BARNES, Mattie J. W6415, MA, Barnes, Henry Clay
BARNES, R. S. S8228, G, 20th Cav.
BARNES, Rebecca M. W8977, SU, Barnes, Elijah C.
BARNES, Sallie Jane, W2600, D, Barnes, James Marion
BARNES, Sarah J. W5978, SU, Barnes, George R.
BARNES, W. J. S6602, MR, 44th Inf.
BARNES, W. R. S4963, HD, 12th Miss. Inf.
BARNES, William C. S12713, GU, 35th Inf.
BARNES, William T. S5612, MA, 38th Inf.
BARNETT, Bettie, W6124, ST, Barnett, Jessie J.
BARNETT, E. H. S4534, HW, 12th Bn. Cav.
BARNETT, F. G. S11063, MA, 19th (Biffle's) Cav.
BARNETT, Isaac W. S2155, R, 19th Inf.
BARNETT, J. J. S9406, ST, 14th Inf.
BARNETT, J. W. S969, MA, 6th Inf.
BARNETT, J. W. S15296, LI, 1st Va. Art.
BARNETT, Ransom, S10790, P, 10th Cav.
BARNETT, S. M. S13774, P, 5th Inf.
BARNETT, Sarah Ann, W8308, W9655, P, Barnett, Wm. Ransom
BARNETT, Susan Collier, W8906, W5392, MU, Barnett, James
BARNETT, Thomas A. S4397, BR, 4th Ga. Cav.
BARNETT, Tinnie D. [Mincy], W10757, CC, Barnett, Wm. Jarrett, [Later married Mincy]
BARNETT, W. C. S9973, BR, 62nd Inf.
BARNETT, W. Ranson, S9466, BE, 10th Cav.
BARNETT, William R. S3200, HD, 30th Inf.
BARNETT, William R. S14544, K, 5th Cav.
BARNHILL, Elizabeth, W6873, WI, Barnhill, Vachel I.
BARNHILL, J. M. S15954, HD, 12th Confederate Cav.
BARNHILL, J. M. S16163, HD, 1st Confederate Cav.
BARNHILL, M. E. S11453, WL, 7th Inf.
BARNHILL, Marguerette Allice, W10109, HD, Barnhill, James Monroe
BARNHILL, V. J. S5242, WI, Baxter's Co. Lt. Art.
BARNS, Lavinia Ann, W326, Barns, Wm. Calvin
BARNWELL, Florence O. W3252, FR, Barnwell, Bower Williamson
BARR, John H. S13873, HI, 11th Inf.
BARR, Joseph, S9952, SU, 59th Inf.
BARR, Sarah Russel, W4964, SH, Barr, Wm. M.

Index to Tennessee Confederate Pension Applications

BARR, Susan, W6137, SU, Barr, Jacob Alexander
BARR, Susan, W6338, SU, Barr, Joseph
BARR, T. W. S10517, WL, 28th Inf.
BARRETT, Alexander, S1911, CA, 2nd Cav.
BARRETT, Callie Lou, W5624, D, Barrett, Jeremiah
BARRETT, Ellen, W6683, HW, Barrett, Ezekiel Haynes
BARRETT, Evaline, W16, SM, Barrett, Isaac Joshua
BARRETT, H. F. S4017, WL, 4th (McLemore's) Cav.
BARRETT, James A. S13544, SM, 24th Inf.
BARRETT, John C. S10826, HW, Unassigned (Miner)
BARRETT, John L. S6520, HW, 12th Bn. (Day's) Cav.
BARRETT, Laura A. W1795, O, Barrett, Lasrus S.
BARRETT, Miles, S4166, S478, MS, 8th Inf.
BARRETT, Sallie M. W7317, HW, Barrett, John L.
BARRETT, Sarah Florence, W7462, BR, Barrett, Wm. Franklin Lee
BARRETT, Susan J. W896, HW, Barrett, Thos. T.
BARRETT, W. F. S12775, BR, 43rd Inf.
BARRETT, William N. S3165, MN, 26th Miss. Inf.
BARRETT, William R. S11072, BR, 43rd Inf.
BARRON, Grace, W8452, SH, Barron, Samuel Lee
BARRON, H. Thomas, S12691, MS, 32nd Inf.
BARRON, Hiram T. S8235, MS, 32nd Inf.
BARRON, John M. S10970, WA, 19th Inf.
BARRON, L. J. S13166, MO, 54th Ga. Inf.
BARRON, S. L. S6487, F, 38th Inf.
BARRON, Salina, W5861, G, Barron, W. J.
BARRON, Susan M. W5807, F, Barron, Wm. I.
BARRON, William J. S1916, G, 51st Inf.
BARRON, William P. S10464, K, 60th Inf.
BARROW, Alice Vickie, W7424, M, Barrow, Henry Clay
BARROW, H. C. S10396, M, 24th Inf.
BARROW, W. J. S9269, F, 13th Inf.
BARROW, William Henry, S15997, WL, 18th Inf.
BARRY, Carrie Franklin, W1877, SN, Barry, John N.
BARRY, Daniel, S10863, D, 19th (Biffle's) Cav.
BARRY, Emma Jane, W7500, D, Barry, Daniel

BARRY, J. L. S15509, WL, 8th (Smith's) Cav.
BARRY, R. W. S6691, SN, 30th Inf.
BARRY, Thomas V. S15820, RB, 30th Inf.
BARTELS, Annie, W9535, SH, Bartels, Harrison
BARTLETT, G. W. See G. W. Barkley
BARTLETT, I. A. S10159, CL, 1st (Carter's) Cav.
BARTLETT, James, S6315, FR, 2nd Miss. Inf.
BARTLETT, Martha Eliz. Turner, W8730, MS, Bartlett, Andrew Jackson
BARTLETT, Mary Ann, W5868, RB, Bartlett, James Thomas
BARTLETT, R. J. S10532, JE, 61st Inf.
BARTLETT, Rebecca L. W7987, HM, Bartlett, Robt. Jesse
BARTLEY, G. W. See G. W. Barkley
BARTON, Charlotte, W3649, WL, Barton, J. C.
BARTON, Delila Ann, W3941, R, Barton, Thomas Jefferson
BARTON, Dora, W7890, D, Barton, Daniel Johnson
BARTON, J. E. S10552, T, 3rd Ky. Cav.
BARTON, Laura Clementine, W2654, CF, Barton, Starns Wiggins
BARTON, Lottie, W7445, WL, Barton, James Conway
BARTON, Margaret, W446, PI, Barton, Benjamin Straton
BARTON, S. T. S15004, SH, 15th Cav.
BARTON, Sammie Taylor, W6938, T, Barton, James Edmunds
BARTON, Sarah Jane, W6987, Barton, John Andrew
BARTON, T. J. S4025, R, 1st (Carter's) Cav.
BARTON, William, S2942, K, 2nd (Ashby's) Cav.
BASHAM, J. P. S16461, D, 7th Inf.
BASHEARS, Alexander, S2390, C, 22nd (Barteau's) Cav.
BASHERS, W. P. S4371, LA, 19th (Biffle's) Cav.
BASKERVILLE, J. A. S4653, TR, 2nd (Smith's) Cav.
BASKERVILLE, Pattie Pursley, W10867, TR, Baskerville, John Alexander
BASKET, John, S323, MC, 19th Inf.
BASKETTE, Mary C. W7056, MC, Baskette, William Henry
BASKETTE, William H. S6613, MC, 18th Ark. Inf.
BASKIN, W. C. S8108, WL, 45th Inf.

BASKINS, B. F. S5243, WL, 45th Inf.
BASKINS, B. F. S14597, RU, 45th Inf.
BASS, Elizabeth Frances, W9270, WL, Bass, Wm. Ensley
BASS, F. M. S13527, GI, 6th (Wheeler's) Cav.
BASS, Fredonia, W10576, L, Bass, Patrick H.
BASS, J. C. S10118, CT, 3rd S.C. Inf.
BASS, J. M. S12662, GI, 32nd Inf.
BASS, James Riley, S16528, D, 4th (McLemore's) Cav.
BASS, Jennie S. W1647, RU, Bass, H. P.
BASS, Jethro, S14892, ST, 14th Inf.
BASS, John B. S15341, GI, 3rd (Clack's) Inf.
BASS, John T. S4216, WL, 4th (McLemore's) Cav.
BASS, John W. S3814, W, 5th Inf.
BASS, Mahala, W593, FR, Bass, Henry Coleman
BASS, Martha J. W5006, GI, Bass, Francis Marion
BASS, Mary, W2893, WL, Bass, Edward P.
BASS, Melissa, W3650, WL, Bass, W. S.
BASS, Rachel, W2923, W, Bass, John W.
BASS, T. P. S15639, GI, Morton's Battery Lt. Art.
BASS, W. E. S2564, WL, 4th (McLemore's) Cav.
BASS, W. J. S14914, SH, 3rd Ark. Cav.
BASS, William B. S2725, GI, 53rd Inf.
BASSETT, James E. S12239, K, 64th N.C. Inf.
BASSHAM, J. A. S7605, GI, 48th (Nixon's) Inf.
BASSHAM, J. L. S8447, LA, 20th Cav.
BATE, H. H. S5898, SN, 2nd (Robison's) Inf.
BATE, James H. S16119, SN, 2nd Inf.
BATE, Nancy D. W5157, SN, Bate, Humphrey Howell
BATE, Nellie Boone, W10075, D, Bate, Henry Clay
BATEMAN, Albert, S14222, SU, 5th Bn. Va. Reserves
BATEMAN, Artie, W10536, BE, Bateman, John Jerry
BATES, B. B. S9448, HI, 9th Bn. (Gantt's) Cav.

BATES, Cornelia Clagett, W9041, HI, Bates, Jasper Alonzo
BATES, Frances C. W4977, LE, Bates, John
BATES, G. M. S6723, PO, 3rd Inf.
BATES, Henry, C188, MO, Regiment not given
BATES, Josie, W7346, HI, Bates, R. B.
BATES, Lewis, S10815, HI, 42nd Inf.

BATES, Lucinda Alice, W9506, H, Bates, Miller McAfee
BATES, Martha Jane, W8469, HI, Bates, Zebulun Bail
BATES, Mary A. W3651, BR, Bates, Sterling V.
BATES, Noah, S10839, A, 39th N.C. Inf.
BATES, Noah, S14459, MG, 39th N.C. Inf.
BATES, P. R. S4903, PO, 59th Inf.
BATES, R. B. S8480, JA, 34th Ga. Inf.
BATES, R. B. S10051, HI, 9th Bn. (Gantt's) Cav.
BATES, Robert, S1364, SU, 19th Inf.
BATES, W. T. S1245, WE, 31st Inf.
BATES, Z. B. S15869.5, HI, 24th Inf.
BATEY, B. B. S13619, RU, 1st (Feild's) Inf.
BATEY, Ben, S16351, RU, 21st Cav.
BATEY, George, S13081, MS, 45th Inf.
BATEY, H. J. S9903, CF, 18th Inf.
BATEY, Mary Caroline, W4105, RU, Batey, Wm. Overton
BATSON, Madison F. S9412, H, Carter's Scouts, Cav.
BATTLE, A. S15551, SH, 9th Inf.
BATTLE, Martha E. W4114, WI, Battle, John
BATTLE, Sarah Jane, W2396, WI, Battle, Isaac J.
BATTOE, Annie Elizabeth, W6254, SH, Battoe, Wm. Tandy
BATTOE, William Tandy, S12364, SH, 4th Ky. Inf.
BATTS, John W. S3852, DK, Allison's Squadron, Cav.
BATTS, L. S9493, LE, 8th Ky. Cav.
BATTY, J. S. S8982, RU, 18th Inf.
BAUCOM, William, S4210, DE, 52nd Inf.
BAUGH, E. L. S9473, D, 1st (Feild's) Inf.
BAUGH, Emma J. W7655, D, Baugh, Elijah L.
BAUGH, John M. S4184, RU, 11th Cav.
BAUGH, Louisa Lnra. [Fudge], W10782, SH, Baugh, Wm. Frederick, [Later married Fudge]
BAUGH, Lucy Raleigh, W10637, GI, Baugh, John Lemons
BAUGH, Willis, C, RU, Regiment not given, Application is missing.
BAUGHN, William, S10548, MU, 1st (Feild's) Inf.
BAXTER, Andrew J. S3577, SH, 1st Hvy. Art.
BAXTER, Hugh B. S9743, CC, 2nd Inf.
BAXTER, James M. S16656, D, 5th Cav.
BAXTER, Joe H. S8647, MOO, 23rd Battalion, Inf.

Index to Tennessee Confederate Pension Applications

BAXTER, John F. S5174, MA, 44th Inf.
BAXTER, John L. S14212, H, 1st (Turney's) Inf.
BAXTER, Lutita, W6039, CC, Baxter, H. B.
BAXTER, Martha Ann, W1367, WI, Baxter, Joseph S.
BAXTER, Mary Elizabeth, W6151, RU, Baxter, Richard
BAXTER, Mourning Cathren, W4455, O, Baxter, John Franklin
BAXTER, Virginia Tate, W4789, D, Baxter, Montgomery
BAXTER, W. M. S12480, HI, 11th Inf.
BAXTER, W. S. S15339, F, 14th (Neely's) Cav.
BAY, Nancy, W6775, WL, Bay, Thomas
BAY, Thomas, S6514, WL, 9th (Bennett's) Cav.
BAYCE, Mary Louisa, W9214, LE, Bayce, George Washington
BAYETTE, J. A. S63, MS, 17th Inf.
BAYLESS, Asa, S15680, HM, 5th (McKenzie's) Cav.
BAYLESS, B. J. S8286, MC, 2nd Cav.
BAYLESS, Cassie B. W8143, HM, Bayless, Asa
BAYLESS, Deborah Lucinda, W11055, WA, Bayless, Luke S.
BAYLESS, Elizabeth C. W314, WA, Bayless, Elkanah W.
BAYLESS, Elizabeth Robinson, W1973, WA, Bayless, John Washington
BAYLESS, John Washington, S8203, WA, 60th Inf.
BAYLESS, Julia A. W6793, WA, Bayless, Robert R.
BAYLESS, Mary A. W3891, WA, Bayless, Albert G.
BAYLESS, R. R. S11911, WA, 60th Inf.
BAYLESS, Samuel G. S8989, MS, 12th Bn. Cav.
BAYLESS, Sarah J. W2635, GI, Bayless, Samuel G.
BAYLESS, Texana, W7393, MC, Bayless, Benjamin J.
BAYLESS, William M. S1520, WA, Undetermined

BAYLOR, Martha Edmonia, W5904, HO, Baylor, R. N.
BAYNHAM, Alexander, S16597, MT, 50th Inf.
BAYNHAM, Eliza Jane, W10747, MT, Baynham, Alexander
BAZELL, G. W. S8310, RU, 24th Inf.
BAZELL, William D. S5477, WI, 24th Inf.

BEACH, John, S1538, H, 17th Va. Inf.
BEADLE, Joshua S. S13502, D, 1st (Feild's) Inf.
BEAIRD, G. W. S5134, CC, 9th Inf.
BEAL, Charles Curtis, S16687, MA, 18th (Newsom's) Cav.
BEAL, George, S36, D, 8th Inf.
BEAL, Hattie A. W6250, D, Beal, George
BEAL, Mary Ann, W7659, MA, Beal, Charles Curtis
BEAL, Sallie G. W7255, F, Beal, Thomas Sidney
BEAL, T. S. S13298, F, 13th Inf.
BEAL, W. H. S7052, F, 14th (Neely's) Cav.
BEAL, W. M. S13845, 16th Bn. (Neal's) Cav.
BEAL, Z. B. J. S10496, BE, 54th Inf.
BEALL, John B. S7311, D, 19th Ga. Inf.
BEAM, J. A. S12884, WH, 28th Inf.
BEAN, Benjamin L. S10587, HW, 12th Cav.
BEAN, Eliza, W1885, MOO, Bean, Ezekiel Marion
BEAN, J. S. S12630, O, 1st Ga. Inf.
BEAN, John C. S14331, RB, 30th Inf.
BEAN, John L. S2067, J, 28th Inf.
BEAN, Malvina, W4214, HW, Bean, Benjamin L.
BEAN, Mary Eilzabeth, W6182, O, Bean, Joseph Simmon
BEAN, Mary Jane, W907, CF, Bean, Conner H.
BEAN, Nora, W5928, MA, Bean, Richard L.
BEAN, Sallie Ann, W6583, RB, Bean, John Charles
BEAN, Sarah Elizabeth, W6878, MA, Bean, John Lausden
BEARD, Ada J. W8945, HO, Beard, Wm. E.
BEARD, Annie, W1304, CC, Beard, George W.
BEARD, Arthur Hopkins, S15449, SH, 4th Ala. Cav.
BEARD, Charles Edmond, S12776, SH, 21st Va. Cav.
BEARD, D. C. W9279, SH, Beard, Arthur H.
BEARD, Delia, W6169, SU, Beard, G. W.
BEARD, Eugenia Montague, W10817, K, Beard, Richd. A.
BEARD, Eva, W2555, OV, Beard, Moses
BEARD, Frank, S10617, HI, 9th Bn. Cav.
BEARD, George W. S2985, SU, 59th Inf.
BEARD, Henry, S9231, G, 27th (O'Neal's) Ala. Cav.
BEARD, Hugh L. S6709, RO, 7th Inf.
BEARD, Ida S. W9586, LI, Beard, Wm. Davis
BEARD, James H. S8808, P, 43rd Inf.

-21

Index to Tennessee Confederate Pension Applications

BEARD, James Henry, S7762, R, 1st (Carter's) Cav.
BEARD, Jane, W5084, HI, Beard, Frank
BEARD, Mary, W9088, GI, Beard, Will
BEARD, Mary Elizabeth, W3193, SU, Beard, James Taylor
BEARD, N. P. W3785, SU, Beard, Wm. E.
BEARD, Pocahontas, W6907, W7233, R, Beard, James Henry
BEARD, Richard, S15821, RU, 9th Confederate Inf.
BEARD, Richard, S16164, RU, 5th Confederate Cav.
BEARD, Samuell, S11256, HN, 46th Inf.
BEARD, Step. S3299, WI, 9th Bn. Cav.
BEARD, W. D. S7552, MS, 53rd Inf.
BEARD, W. E. S9375, SU, 60th Inf.
BEARD, William, S5783, WI, 9th Bn. Cav.
BEARDEN, Mary, W2880, GI, Bearden, Rufus McLin
BEARDEN, R. K. S7934, MN, 6th Ga. Cav.
BEARDEN, R. M. S6220, GI, 44th Inf.
BEARDEN, William C. S4006, MS, 3rd Inf.
BEARDEN, William Morgan, S13219, D, 1st Va. Cav.
BEASLEY, A. S5003, WE, 51st & 52nd Cons. Inf.
BEASLEY, A. B. S12167, BE, 5th Inf.
BEASLEY, Abigail Corlister, W8242, W9995, SH, Beasley, James Dean
BEASLEY, Archer, S8642, MS, 41st Inf.
BEASLEY, B. H. S6151, RU, 3rd S.C. Inf.
BEASLEY, Bettie, W1359, W1639, CC, Beasley, John M. (James M.?)
BEASLEY, Charles D. S9709, S7499, T, 19th Ala. Inf.
BEASLEY, David H. S9689, GI, 41st Inf.
BEASLEY, E. H. S1851, SM, 4th Cav.
BEASLEY, H. H. S2083, PU, 8th Cav.
BEASLEY, H. H. S8768, SM, 8th Inf.
BEASLEY, H. W. S13144, D, 44th Inf.
BEASLEY, Hester Anne, W6646, HU, Beasley, Jacob Browning
BEASLEY, Isaac J. S2636, SM, 24th Inf.
BEASLEY, J. C. S15503, HU, 10th (DeMoss') Cav.
BEASLEY, J. D. S14689, SH, 12th Cav.
BEASLEY, James M. S5919, CC, 1st (Feild's) Inf.
BEASLEY, Jane, W1201, SM, Beasley, Jesse
BEASLEY, Jesse, S2190, SM, 17th Inf.

BEASLEY, John, S10313, WE, 55th (Brown's) Inf.
BEASLEY, John P. S10931, SM, 7th Inf.
BEASLEY, Josiah H. S557, S955, M, 28th Inf.
BEASLEY, Lula D. W10493, WE, Beasley, John
BEASLEY, Mary Ann, W6807, MS, Beasley, David Hobbs
BEASLEY, Merriman L. S7411, BO, 22nd S.C. Inf.
BEASLEY, Robert, S1657, T, 4th Ala. Bn.
BEASLEY, William, S3105, T, 34th Ga. Inf.
BEATEY, George, See George Baty
BEATTY, A. N. S3069, LE, 24th Inf.
BEATTY, H. K. S4780, LE, 9th Inf.
BEATY, W. G. S14368, MA, 33rd Inf.
BEAUMONT, Ben, C109, ST, 10th Cav.
BEAVER, A. J. S9742, WH, 38th Inf.
BEAVER, Alfred C. S12500, H, 65th Ga. Inf.
BEAVER, D. L. S397, MC, 9th Inf.
BEAVER, David L. S1968, MC, 29th Inf.
BEAVER, H. O. S5244, H, 5th Cav.
BEAVER, John L. S11668, LI, 1st Inf.
BEAVER, R. L. S14383, CC, 21st (Wilson's) Cav.
BEAVER, W. H. S1206, HW, 58th N.C. Inf.
BEAVER, W. M. S9644, SU, 58th N.C. Inf.
BEAVER, William A. S11828, FR, 3rd (Clack's) Inf.
BEAVERS, A. J. S6432, WH, 38th Inf.
BEAVERS, Ann Eliza, W1285, GI, Beavers, Wm. Henry
BEAVERS, Hozie Alexander, S7351, MC, 65th Inf.
BEAVERS, James H. S14266, 22nd Inf.
BEAVERS, Josie C. W4884, LI, Beavers, W. S.
BEAVERS, M. M. S15388, PO, 36th Ga. Inf.
BEAVERS, W. H. S5175, GI, 23rd Inf.
BEAZLEY, E. C. W365, RU, Beazley, John E.
BECK, J. Z. S7529, SN, 8th (Dibrell's) Cav.
BECK, John T. S6540, DI, Baxter's Co. Lt. Art.
BECK, Mattie Houston, W10291, MC, Beck, Wm. Henry
BECK, Nancy Jane, W1741, CH, Beck, Jefferson Wilson
BECKHAM, W. T. S14700, LA, 19th (Biffle's) Cav.
BECKHAM, William N. S12521, GI, 6th (Wheeler's) Cav.
BECTON, B. M. S12491, RU, 47th Inf.
BECTON, Harriet Ann, W6311, G, Becton, L. F.

BECTON, Sara, W9202, H, Becton, Benjamin May
BEDDINGFIELD, James A. S16449, LI, 6th (Wheeler's) Cav.
BEDDINGFIELD, W. J. S1483, LI, 32nd Inf.
BEDWELL, Nancy Elena, W890, BR, Bedwell, Hiram Francis
BEECH, Beulah L. W11051, WI, Beech, Richard Thomas
BEECH, C. B. S8044, DY, 47th Inf.
BEECH, Hurmon Henry, S2350, LI, 8th Inf.
BEECH, James T. S2762, LI, 28th Inf.
BEECH, Nicie America, W7002, DY, Beech, Cincinnati
BEECH, Paul B. S8156, WI, 20th Inf.
BEECH, R. T. S15212, S16329, WI, 20th Inf.
BEECHAM, Arminty, W2811, HU, Beecham, Jesse Edward
BEECHAM, Loma F. W664, HU, Beecham, Alex
BEEDLE, Ann Leda, W8772, D, Beedle, Joshua Smith
BEELER, Adalid, W1402, JE, Beeler, Joseph Cleveland
BEELER, Joseph C. S4167, JE, 59th Inf.
BEELER, Lucinda Ellender, W5881, GR, Beeler, Jacob
BEENE, L. J. S15516, MR, 4th Inf.
BEESLY, William, S7900, D, 1st (Feild's) Inf.
BEGBIE, Sarah Frances, W2984, WI, Begbie, Charles Alexander
BEGLEY, James, S13288, HA, 16th Bn. (Neal's) Cav.
BEIDLEMAN, Elizabeth, W7219, SU, Beidleman, Henry C.
BEIDLEMAN, H. C. S11157, SU, 63rd Inf.
BELCHER, A. S. S6672, MO, 62nd Inf.
BELCHER, F. P. S4134, WL, 9th (Ward's) Cav.
BELCHER, J. M. S4308, WL, 23rd Inf.
BELCHER, Mary Jane, W4454, TR, Belcher, J. M.
BELEW, William, S16408, LA, 32nd Inf.
BELL, A. D. S688, HN, 20th Cav.
BELL, A. E. S13911, SN, 9th (Ward's) Cav.
BELL, Ann Elizabeth, W6855, T, Bell, Marmaduke
BELL, Calvin C. S15688, H, 53rd Inf.
BELL, Camille Bright, W10864, MA, Bell, Tracy Wayne
BELL, Carrie, W9596, WY, Bell, Wm. Levy
BELL, Charley, C68, DI, 11th Inf., Alias Charley Harris

BELL, E. P. S16299, RU, 45th Inf.
BELL, Ella Williams, W9699, D, Bell, Leonidas Dean
BELL, Frances, W1421, SN, Bell, Q. S.
BELL, Hollin, W10693, MT, Bell, Sam
BELL, J. B. S9721, GI, 9th (Ward's) Cav.
BELL, J. M. S10126, FR, 44th Inf.
BELL, J. W. S13666, DY, 4th Ky. Inf.
BELL, Jane Smith, W5089, CC, Bell, J. H.
BELL, John Franklin, S12404, G, 44th Inf.
BELL, John W. S7017, WY, 6th (Wheeler's) Cav.
BELL, Katherine Reeves, W9352, GI, Bell, Wm. Edward
BELL, Margaret R. W2284, D, Bell, John Martin
BELL, Martha Jane, W3124, FR, Bell, J. M.
BELL, Mary E. W7762, HN, Bell, John W.
BELL, Mary Jane, W6281, CC, Bell, Wm.
BELL, N. E. S7823, 21st (Wilson's) Cav.
BELL, NAncy jane, W1579, Bell, Robert J. Adison
BELL, P. S14046, O, 10th (DeMoss') Cav.
BELL, Paralee, W872, G, Bell, Andy
BELL, Quint S. S7591, SN, 22nd (Barteau's) Cav.
BELL, R. L. S15233, D, 18th Inf.
BELL, Robert F. S892, MS, 17th Inf.
BELL, S. H. S13020, WA, 63rd Inf.
BELL, Sallie A. W4764, H, Bell, Martin Van Buren
BELL, Susan Jane, W4879, CA, Bell, Wm. Carson
BELL, W. H. S13167, HY, 51st Inf.
BELL, W. J. S15029, D, 8th (Smith's) Cav.
BELL, W. T. S11284, RU, 4th Inf.
BELL, Washington F. S43, CH, 17th Cav.
BELL, William A. S16238, W, 16th Inf.
BELL, William C. S10553, C, 1st/3rd Mo. Cav. (Cons.)
BELL, William Carroll, C139, RB, 30th Inf.
BELL, William H. H. S1430, B, 1st Cav.
BELLAMY, Andrew B. S3245, CL, Undetermined
BELLAMY, Ophelia Jane, W6571, MT, Bellamy, Richd. Watson
BELLAMY, R. W. S7410, MT, 14th Inf.
BELLAMY, T. J. S15285, K, 4th Ga. Inf.
BELLAR, Jonathan, S6979, SM, 8th (Dibrell's) Cav.
BELLAR, Virginia E. W1023, SM, Bellar, James

Index to Tennessee Confederate Pension Applications

BELLENFANT, Mahala Jones, W3379, B, Bellenfant, Absalom Scales
BELMAR, Sarah J. W6725, SH, Belmar, Jefferson O.
BELOTE, Celia T. W7712, MT, Belote, Isaac N.
BELOTE, Isaac N. S9288, MT, 14th Inf.
BELOTE, Wesley F. S313, HR, 14th Miss. Inf.
BELSHA, Martha Catherine, W5578, WY, Belsha, James Calvin
BELT, Sarah W. W852, BO, Belt, John Wallace
BELTON, Rea, S1421, WA, 45th N.C. Inf.
BELYEW, Frances, W7077, BE, Belyew, John
BELYEW, John, S11505, BE, 55th Inf.
BEMEY, J. H. S9087, BE, Undetermined
BENDALL, Annie Lee, W6394, SH, Bendall, Wm. Edward
BENDERMAN, O. S10027, MU, 6th (Wheeler's) Cav.
BENDERMAN, Sophronia E. W8531, MU, Benderman, Tom
BENHAM, John M. S5112, WY, 19th (Biffle's) Cav.
BENHAM, Miriam, W7431, WY, Benham, John Vincent
BENNETT, A. H. S6255, MN, 31st Inf.
BENNETT, Ambrose, S2831, LI, 1st (Turney's) Inf.
BENNETT, Ann Henry, W6942, GI, Bennett, Wm. Oliver
BENNETT, D. C. S4887, B, 23rd Bn. Inf.
BENNETT, F. M. S7073, BE, 15th Cav.
BENNETT, Fannie P. W3999, D, Bennett, Jacob C.
BENNETT, J. N. S13682, F, 38th Inf.
BENNETT, J. W. S7885, WL, 7th Inf.
BENNETT, John B. S13128, WE, 12th Ky. Cav.
BENNETT, L. B. S2052, OV, 8th Cav.
BENNETT, L. B. S3932, OV, 8th (Dibrell's) Cav.
BENNETT, Laura Ann, W3115, BL, Bennett, John Parsley
BENNETT, Louella Anna Cheairs, W7653, F, Bennett, John Newton
BENNETT, Louisa, W4673, OV, Bennett, L. B.
BENNETT, Martha, W9118, OV, Bennett, Alfred
BENNETT, Martha Jane, W8614, O, Bennett, John William
BENNETT, Martha Virginia, W4718, WL, Bennett, Wm. Jordan
BENNETT, Nancy, W5293, MN, Bennett, Andrew Houston
BENNETT, Nancy, W8934, W, Bennett, Wm. Riley
BENNETT, Nancy Ann, W6851, LA, Bennett, Francis Marion
BENNETT, Powhattan P. S10397, MA, 10th Ark. Inf.
BENNETT, Sallie, W7422, WI, Bennett, T. J.
BENNETT, Samuel H. S12294, S15584, MR, 4th & 8th (Smith's) Cav.
BENNETT, Sarah A. W5036, HN, Bennett, Thomas Jefferson
BENNETT, T. J. S12866, HN, 20th (Russell's) Cav.
BENNETT, Thomas J. S14149, WI, 11th Miss. Inf.
BENNETT, W. M. S13862, D, 24th Inf.
BENNETT, William J. S12625, SN, 9th (Ward's) Cav.
BENNETT, William Oliver, S12648, GI, 6th (Wheeler's) Cav.
BENSON, Arguile, S6380, G, 23rd Inf.
BENSON, G. W. S7686, RU, 23rd Inf.
BENSON, John B. S9655, FR, 41st Inf.
BENSON, John Henry, S11265, D, Huggin's Co. Lt. Art.
BENSON, S. W. S15311, SH, 17th Miss. Inf.
BENSON, Sallie Fine, W7243, D, Benson, John H.
BENTAL, Theodoria Elizabeth, W7373, MA, Bental, Alexander
BENTHAL, Alex, S9409, MA, 52nd Inf.
BENTON, Margaret, W2976, H, Benton, L. P. S.
BERCHEEN, Eliza Jane, W548, MU, Bercheen, Josiah
BERDON, Gustavus, S13299, MA, 22nd Miss. Inf.
BERKELY, James W. S10955, GR, 22nd Va. Bn. Inf.
BERKLEY, Annie T. W10735, SU, Berkley, Charles Radford
BERKLEY, Mary A. W4234, GR, Berkley, J. W.
BERKSHIRE, Bettie, W5484, SH, Berkshire, Wm. Henry
BERNARD, Elizabeth E. W1914, D, Bernard, John
BERNARD, Patience, W4146, HW, Bernard, Riley Kendrick
BERRETT, John, S10821, HW, 31st Inf.

BERRY, A. C. S11943, MO, Thomas' Legion, N.C.
BERRY, C. C. S5857, MO, Thomas' Legion, N.C.
BERRY, George, S4120, GE, 1st Mo. Inf.
BERRY, George H. S15624, D, 3rd Va. Reserves
BERRY, I. S. S5478, MU, 44th Inf.
BERRY, J. A. S9843, SU, 60th Inf.
BERRY, J. B. S13092, MN, 6th Miss. Cav.
BERRY, J. H. S5704, SU, 60th Inf.
BERRY, J. L. S8664, G, 47th Inf.
BERRY, James, S7190, MO, 31st Inf.
BERRY, Martha, W867, BE, Berry, Isaac Galloway
BERRY, Martha, W9229, WL, Berry, Toab
BERRY, Martha C. W7741, WL, Berry, H. N.
BERRY, Martha Jane, W2804, K, Berry, Thomas
BERRY, Martha Jane, W3221, G, Berry, James L.
BERRY, Nancy, W897, WA, Berry, Wm. A.
BERRY, Nancy, W9230, WL, Berry, George Doak
BERRY, Sallie H. See Blair, Sallie H.
BERRY, Sarah Annie, W1475, CF, Berry, Ulys. Newland Moffit
BERRY, Sarah Ellen, W1175, MU, Berry, Isaac Short
BERRY, Thomas, S3640, SE, 3rd Inf.
BERRY, U. N. M. S402, HU, 47th Inf.
BERRY, W. H. S11013, D, 2nd Ky. Cav.
BERRY, W. P. S14993, SH, 1st Miss. Cav.
BERRY, William A. S3350, MO, 59th Inf.
BERRYHILL, J. S. S7777, FR, 28th Cav.
BERRYHILL, L. T. S5613, LI, 23rd Inf.
BERRYHILL, Mary Elizabeth, W5716, FR, Berryhill, J. S.
BERRYHILL, Sarah, W5738, LI, Berryhill, L. T.
BERRYMAN, Anderson, S9496, LI, 38th Inf.
BERTRAND, Louisa Arterburn, W4085, SN, Bertrand, Robert Boyers
BESS, Mary A. W6205, D, Bess, Charles H.
BESS, Mollie Hill, W10911, D, Bess, James Riley
BESS, Tempy, W9691, W, Bess, John
BESS, Wiley, S15207, W, 16th Inf.
BESSENT, John C. S7692, G, 9th (Bennett's) Cav.
BEST, James, S5968, BO, 31st Inf.
BEST, Samuel, S4976, CO, 25th N.C. Inf.

BETHSHEARS, Manerva M. W5629, WI, Bethshears, W. H.
BETHSHEARS, W. H. S6119, WI, Baxter's Co. Lt. Art.
BETHUNE, James, S6852, L, 41st Inf.
BETTERSON, Zephana, W2223, K, Betterson, John Nathan
BETTERSWORTH, Eugene, S653, D, 2nd Inf.
BETTIS, Alice, W3844, L, Bettis, Martin VanBuren
BETTIS, Bradley, S12895, HM, 1st (Carter's) Cav.
BETTIS, M. V. S10269, L, 15th Cav.
BETTIS, Priscilla Catharine, W5900, HM, Bettis, Bradley
BETTS, C. C. S13174, WE, 12th Inf.
BETTS, Evander M. S12486, MA, 51st Inf.
BETTS, J. J. S900, MA, 19th Cav.
BETTS, Jessie, W8343, WE, Betts, C. C.
BETTS, Mary Ellen, W10179, MA, Betts, Evonder M.
BETTS, Pervilla, W490, CC, Betts, John Jefferson
BETTS, Sallie S. W4138, D, Betts, Wm. James
BETTY, Jennie V. W2116, D, Betty, Horatio C.
BETTY, Mary Ann, W8486, MA, Betty, Wesley Taylor
BETTY, Olivia, W4786, D, Betty, James Keelen
BETTY, W. T. S14370, MA, 6th Inf.
BETTY, William F. M. S2009, WL, 28th Inf.
BEVELS, E. G. S9007, LI, 44th Inf.
BEVELS, G. M. S739, LI, 32nd Inf.
BEVELS, Louisa Elizabeth, W6522, LI, Bevels, Elisha Green
BEVELS, Mary Ellen, W6382, LI, Bevels, George M.
BEVIL, Mary Ratcliff, W9592, SH, Bevil, Alex.
BEVILL, A. H. S15580, HU, 19th (Biffle's) Cav.
BEVILLE, M. L. S7730, MA, 3rd (Forrest's) Cav.
BIBB, E. S10023, HI, 11th Inf.
BIBB, Kate T. W6723, PU, Bibb, Lockart
BIBB, Nancy W. W5198, L, Bibb, S. H.
BIBB, Stephen H. S11023, L, 1st Cav.
BIBB, William, C136, RU, 12th Ala. Inf.
BIBEE, M. J. S13812, MA, 2nd Miss. Cav.
BIBEE, Mary Russell, W10720, MA, Bibee, Marion Jasper
BICE, Amos N. S6471, H, Barry's Co. Lt. Art.
BICE, J. G. S260, PO, 4th Cav.

BICE, Mary, W477, H, Bice, John Garner
BICE, O. M. D. W4822, H, Bice, Wm. W.
BICE, W. W. S5245, H, 9th Ga. Inf.
BICKLEY, Mary Jane, W5632, D, Bickley, Wm. Lewis
BICKNELL, Amelia, W4317, SH, Bicknell, Byron J.
BICKNELL, Byron J. S12649, SH, 1st Miss. Cav.
BICKNELL, D. K. S2784, CF, 37th Inf.
BIFFLE, J. K. S16234, MU, 19th (Biffle's) Cav.
BIGBIE, Frances Elizabeth, W9754, HD, Bigbie, Wm. S.
BIGGER, Elizabeth F. W403, B, Bigger, Joseph T.
BIGGER, R. B. S14269, RB, 42nd Inf.
BIGGERS, Fannie, W7271, H, Biggers, Lorenzo J.
BIGGERS, Lorenzo J. S12467, H, Pemberton's Co. Ga. Home Guards
BIGGERSTAFF, Helen G. W, Some papers with #11183 on film
BIGGS, Augusta E. W4441, K, Biggs, James Alexander
BIGGS, Hester A. W262, SN, Biggs, Sanford
BIGGS, J. E. S1846, RB, 2nd (Morgan's) Ky. Cav.
BIGGS, James A. S10497, K, 31st Inf.
BIGGS, Jane Wilkins, W7986, RB, Biggs, J. E.
BIGGS, Jesse, S15237, S8853, SH, 8th Ky. Cav.
BIGGS, Robert J. S3142, SH, 14th (Neely's) Cav.
BIGGS, Sophie Jones, W9207, SH, Biggs, Jesse
BIGGS, Zack, S15554, G, 55th Inf.
BIGHAM, Barbary A. W7694, HU, Bigham, E. S.
BIGHAM, Elbert Sanford, S2670, HU, 14th Inf.
BIGHAM, T. P. S3483, HM, 62nd N.C. Inf.
BIGLEY, Annie Lowe, W4520, D, Bigley, Thomas Jefferson
BIGLEY, Thomas J. S7099, D, 20th Inf.
BILBREY, C. C. S7262, OV, 25th Inf.
BILBREY, F. G. S10049, OV, 8th (Dibrell's) Cav.
BILBREY, F. M. S12046, OV, 8th (Dibrell's) Cav.
BILBREY, I. J. S13109, S14120, OV, 25th Inf.
BILBREY, Jefferson, S777, OV, 8th Cav.
BILBREY, Joseph, S9527, OV, 5th Cav.
BILBREY, Malinda G. W4722, OV, Bilbrey, Isaac jr.
BILBREY, Margaret Elizabeth, W9986, OV, Bilbrey, M. V.
BILBREY, Martha J. W8517, PU, Bilbrey, Seane D.
BILBREY, Martin V. S5479, OV, 8th Inf.
BILBREY, S. D. S7641, PU, 14th Ark. Inf.
BILBREY, Sallie, W10753, OV, Bilbrey, Felix Grundy
BILBREY, Sarah Jane, W7601, OV, Bilbrey, Joseph
BILBREY, William C. S589, OV, 25th Inf.
BILBREY, William H. S15867, OV, 13th (Gore's) Cav.
BILBREY, Winey, W4659, PI, Bilbrey, Jefferson
BILDERBACK, Lucy Jane, W6689, SH, Bilderback, Wm. Stuart
BILES, D. C. S7553, GI, 6th (Wheelers') Cav.
BILES, Kitty L. W5964, WH, Biles, Thomas B.
BILES, Lydia Palinia, W5374, GI, Biles, DeWitt Clinton
BILES, T. B. S13640, WH, 16th Inf.
BILLINGS, Drucilla, W10835, WL, Billings, George W.
BILLINGS, George W. S15930, S16439, WL, 38th Inf.
BILLINGS, J. M. S9201, GI, 8th Inf.
BILLINGS, James W. S12097, DK, 8th (Dibrell's) Cav.
BILLINGSBY, James A. S3434, RO, 43rd Inf.
BILLINGSLEY, B. F. S639, LO, 62nd Inf.
BILLINGSLEY, Mary J. W7934, HN, Billingsley, R. D.
BILLINGSLEY, R. D. S11947, HN, 21st (Wilson's) Cav.
BILLINGSLY, Leander T. S10718, BL, 2nd (Ashby's) Cav.
BILLINGSLY, Lucy, W9486, BL, Billingsly, Leander Travis
BILLS, L. P. S7677, B, 17th Inf.
BILLS, Maud, W11008, LA, Bills, Wm. Goshum
BILLS, Nancy C. E. W306, MS, Bills, Wm. Jackson
BING, L. G. S1992, DK, 16th Inf.
BINGHAM, Julia Frances, W3518, DE, Bingham, Leonidus E.
BINGHAM, L. E. S424, DE, 27th Inf.
BINGHAM, Lowdie Jane, W3918, RU, Bingham, Robt. Tuckson
BINGHAM, Mattie, W7857, WL, Bingham, Thos. Jefferson

BINGHAM, R. J. S7666, B, 4th (McLemore's) Cav.
BINGHAM, S. F. S16311, WL, 4th (McLemore's) Cav.
BINKLEY, H. C. S14601, D, 4th (McLemore's) Cav.
BINKLEY, M. B. S14092, D, 8th (Dibrell's) Cav.
BINKLEY, Minerva Emma, W4050, RB, Binkley, James Monroe
BINKLEY, W. H. S5207, DI, 11th Inf.
BIRAM, S. A. S10370, CL, 43rd Inf.
BIRCH, G. W. S1630, W, 1st Cav.
BIRCH, Whitey, S5541, SE, 36th Ga. Inf.
BIRCH, garrett, S13137, SE, 36th Ga. Inf.
BIRCHETT, Ada R. W6453, MN, Birchett, James M.
BIRCHETT, J. M. S13775, MU, 7th Ala. Cav.
BIRD, Ellen, W7630, LA, Bird, Valentine Ausburn
BIRD, James N. S8479, HN, 46th Inf.
BIRD, Martha, W2690, BR, Bird, James
BIRD, Martha Whitlow, W6960, HD, Bird, Wm. Jasper
BIRD, Mary William, W6771, HN, Bird, James N.
BIRD, T. P. S8051, HE, 55th Inf.
BIRD, V. A. S10331, LA, 4th Ala. Cav.
BIRD, W. J. S6099, HD, 4th Ala. Cav.
BIRDSONG, Henry L. S7332, GI, 32nd Inf.
BIRDWELL, Benjamin F. S1084, J, 28th Inf.
BIRDWELL, E. T. S13347, MR, 4th Inf.
BIRDWELL, J. M. S9294, RB, 28th Inf.
BIRDWELL, Jacob Logan, S2935, GE, 3rd (Lillard's) Mtd. Inf.
BIRDWELL, John J. S746, RB, 28th Inf.
BIRDWELL, Mariah M. W6113, RB, Birdwell, John
BIRDWELL, Mary, W10529, MR, Birdwell, Thos. Edward
BIRDWELL, William, S10471, J, 28th Inf.
BIRMINGHAM, S. T. S12435, SH, 18th Miss. Cav.
BISHOP, Amanda J. W1288, WA, Bishop, Ed H.
BISHOP, Benjamin T. S10237, SH, 6th Ky. Inf.
BISHOP, David, S12922, HR, 14th Inf.
BISHOP, Edward H. S2047, WA, 63rd Inf.
BISHOP, F. F. S8326, LA, 12th Cav.
BISHOP, Harriet, W10575, D, Bishop, Andrew
BISHOP, James L. S15972, LI, 19th (Biffle's) Cav.

BISHOP, John C. S826, PO, 2nd (Walker's) Inf.
BISHOP, Louisa, W8878, HR, Bishop, David
BISHOP, Lucinda, W3376, MO, Bishop, Washington
BISHOP, Manerva, W10469, Bishop, David A.
BISHOP, Mary Elizabeth, W3183, MC, Bishop, James Monroe
BISHOP, Nancy Jane, W2520, LA, Bishop, Frederick F.
BISHOP, Nancy P. W8919, ST, Bishop, John Franklin
BISHOP, S. I. S11618, CH, 21st Cav.
BISHOP, Sarah Isabelle, W863, MC, Bishop, Robt.
BISHOP, Sarah Jane, W8544, W11077, PO, Bishop, John O.
BISHOP, Sylvester, S6561, BR, 59th Inf.
BISSELL, William, S3638, HU, 20th Inf.
BISZELL, William H. S595, HY, 6th Inf.
BITER, Lucy J. W1318, MT, Biter, Wm. A.
BITTICK, Harriet A. W8118, O, Bittick, J. H.
BITTICK, J. H. S10651, O, 9th Inf.
BITTLE, Mollie E. W4830, K, Bittle, Robt. F.
BITTLE, Robert F. S10388, SU, 50th Va. Inf.
BIVENS, DeWitt Clinton, S15816, LA, 53rd Inf.
BIVENS, Dicy, W2829, BE, Bivens, Wm. E.
BIVENS, E. C. S10041, MO, 59th Inf.
BIVENS, J. W. S16216, L, 31st Inf.
BIVINS, Donie Emaline, W11082, D, Bivins, John Anderson
BIZZELL, Sarah Elizabeth, W4252, HR, Bizzell, Thos. Henry
BIZZELL, T. H. S9446, HR, 14th (Neely's) Cav.
BIZZLE, J. R. S12923, HR, 14th Cav.
BLACK, A. S13569, D, 8th (Dibrell's) Cav.
BLACK, Alexander, S3351, K, 16th Ga. Inf.
BLACK, Barbry Ann, W786, WH, Black, Isaac
BLACK, Beny Katherine, W7651, WE, Black, Wm. Anderson
BLACK, D. L. S5948, HO, Maury's Battery, Lt. Art.
BLACK, Elizabeth Ann, W4130, MT, Black, Alfred
BLACK, Ella Henderson, W5433, RU, Black, Jas. Morton
BLACK, Emma, W5654, MA, Black, George Baley
BLACK, George W. S5390, WH, 28th Inf.
BLACK, J. B. S12757, G, 14th (Neely's) Cav.
BLACK, J. H. S4173, CY, 8th Inf.
BLACK, J. M. S7475, T, 51st Inf.

Index to Tennessee Confederate Pension Applications

BLACK, J. S. S15171, CO, 72nd N.C. Inf.
BLACK, J. W. S5886, CF, 23rd Inf.
BLACK, James Franklin, S1726, 27th Inf.
BLACK, James M. S7932, RU, 45th Inf.
BLACK, John C. S8561, T, 33rd N.C. Inf.
BLACK, Lou Ann, W2601, CY, Black, John Hudspeth
BLACK, Margaret Hale, W8843, MU, Black, David S.
BLACK, Martha J. W7011, D, Black, Alexander
BLACK, Mary Ann, W797, B, Black, James Lawrence
BLACK, Mary Ella, W9935, SH, Black, Perry Mitchell
BLACK, Nannie C. W89, RU, Black, James F.
BLACK, Nannie Virginia, W7182, SH, Black, Napoleon B.
BLACK, Sallie I. W7390, SH, Black, W. F.
BLACK, Sarah Elizabeth, W4699, SM, Black, David Cothron
BLACK, Sarah V. W9874, T, Black, James McFinin
BLACK, Thomas, S6042, GE, 26th Inf.
BLACK, Thomas Giles, S1303, MA, 6th Inf.
BLACK, Virginia Margaret, W5984, MA, Black, Thomas Gideon
BLACK, W. A. S10182, WE, 21st (Wilson's) Cav.
BLACK, W. A. S16144, RU, 20th & 21st (Consolidated) Cav.
BLACK, Wiley L. S5118, MT, 50th Inf.
BLACK, William, S15084, G, 1st Ark. Inf.
BLACK, William F. S13430, SH, 7th (Duckworth's) Cav.
BLACKBURN, A. J. S5246, DE, 9th Cav.
BLACKBURN, C. D. S16541, RB, 14th Inf.
BLACKBURN, E. J. S4571, SN, 7th Inf.
BLACKBURN, Emma, W4739, DI, Blackburn, John R.
BLACKBURN, Florence, W9819, SH, Blackburn, Charles Buck
BLACKBURN, G. H. S12970, A, 33rd Inf.
BLACKBURN, H. B. S12324, G, 12th Inf.
BLACKBURN, Hugh M. S2296, HW, 63rd Inf.
BLACKBURN, J. H. S4838, CF, 44th Inf.
BLACKBURN, J. R. S6574, DI, 49th Inf.
BLACKBURN, James Lafayette, S599, BR, 2nd Cav.
BLACKBURN, Lila T. W8313, D, Blackburn, John W.
BLACKBURN, Mary Eilzabeth, W1230, SN, Blackburn, James B.
BLACKBURN, Sarah, W4207, CF, Blackburn, John H.
BLACKBURN, Sarah Jane, W1679, SN, Blackburn, Elisha J.
BLACKBURN, Sarah Paralee, W8207, B, Blackburn, George Washington
BLACKBURN, Susan D. W8250, DI, Blackburn, Wm. Henry
BLACKBURN, W. H. S7829, DI, 11th Inf.
BLACKBURN, William Spinks, S15532, SH, 18th Bn. Miss. Cav.
BLACKMAN, M. T. W3582, MA, Blackman, B. T.
BLACKMON, James Robert, S16608, MA, 21st (Wilson's) Cav.
BLACKMORE, Matilda A. W6509, SN, Blackmore, Andrew L.
BLACKSHIRE, Martha J. W567, MN, Blackshire, Jacob
BLACKWELL, A. H. S4895, TR, 8th Inf.
BLACKWELL, Abe, C187, F, Regiment not given
BLACKWELL, Alfred, S7800, ME, 26th Inf.
BLACKWELL, Charles F. S11718, S10042, LI, 41st Inf.
BLACKWELL, J. M. S16304, MS, 41st Inf.
BLACKWELL, John, S2671, W, 35th Cav.
BLACKWELL, John Y. S157, TR, 8th Inf.
BLACKWELL, Leathy Jane, W2360, TR, Blackwell, John Y.
BLACKWELL, Lillie, W7870, L, Blackwell, Thos. John
BLACKWELL, Margaret Eiline, W4503, W, Blackwell, John
BLACKWELL, Permelia C. W6431, SH, Blackwell, Wesley Coke
BLACKWELL, R. H. S14819, MU, 9th Bn. Cav.
BLACKWELL, Robert L. S5937, WL, 2nd Cav.
BLACKWELL, Sophronia, W3102, SH, Blackwell, B. M.
BLACKWELL, T. J. S13968, L, 31st Miss. Inf.
BLACKWOOD, Newton J. S6055, HN, 46th Inf.
BLAIR, Andrew C. S841, SM, 7th Inf.
BLAIR, Cornelia, W1393, GR, Blair, Jacob
BLAIR, Cornelia E. W4086, W, Blair, John B.
BLAIR, Harriet E. W9547, CT, Blair, James B.
BLAIR, J. B. S15683, CT, 6th N.C. Cav.
BLAIR, J. C. S12902, SM, 28th Inf.
BLAIR, J. H. S8999, MU, 11th Cav.
BLAIR, J. J. S13659, D, 22nd (Barteau's) Cav.
BLAIR, J. L. W. S4730, FR, 1st (Feild's) Inf.

Index to Tennessee Confederate Pension Applications

BLAIR, James, S1531, WL, 7th Inf.
BLAIR, James D. S15305, MU, 22nd (Barteau's) Cav.
BLAIR, John B. S3478, W, 35th Inf.
BLAIR, Margaret, W5282, SM, Blair, A. C.
BLAIR, Martha Jane, W4759, FR, Blair, Calvin Taylor
BLAIR, Sallie H. [Berry], W5421, WA, Blair, Samuel Cunningham, [Later married Berry]
BLAIR, Samuel C. S1613, S1856, WA, 5th Cav.
BLAKE, Sue M. W7948, MA, Blake, Wm. A.
BLAKE, Theda Crowder, W9604, SH, Blake, Larkin Lafayette
BLAKELY, E. C. S10321, BE, 1st Va. Engineer Corps
BLAKEMORE, Ada, W7645, SN, Blakemore, Henry A.
BLAKEMORE, Florence, W1629, WE, Blakemore, John W.
BLAKEMORE, H. A. S14131, SN, 8th Inf.
BLAKEMORE, J. H. S14277, G, 20th (Russell's) Cav.
BLAKENEY, O. T. S1429, HD, 1st Mo. Cav.
BLALOCK, Eliza S. W540, PU, Blalock, John
BLALOCK, John, S3699, PU, 8th (Dibrell's) Cav.
BLALOCK, Ollie Gertrude, W10557, HR, Blalock, Frederick Stanton
BLANCHARD, T. S9942, BE, 5th Inf.
BLAND, Julia Demaris, W8982, CH, Bland, James Robert
BLAND, Silas, S10518, D, 44th Inf.
BLAND, W. H. S6337, SU, 36th Va. Inf.
BLANKENSHIP, Cate, W57, MO, Blankenship, John T.
BLANKENSHIP, G. J. S16054, BL, 25th Inf.
BLANKENSHIP, G. W. S14726, HO, 2nd Ky. Cav.
BLANKENSHIP, J. F. S15685, WE, Davies' Bn. Ark. Cav.
BLANKENSHIP, J. J. S4733, SN, 4th (McLemore's) Cav.
BLANKENSHIP, John, S9419, U, 4th Ga. Cav.
BLANKENSHIP, Margaret Palina, W1484, PO, Blankenship, Albert Berton
BLANKENSHIP, Sarah jane, W10776, HO, Blankenship, G. W.
BLANKENSHIP, Victoria Allice, W9404, WE, Blankenship, John Frasher
BLANKINSHIP, W. W. S6294, ME, 26th Inf.
BLANKS, H. W. S7863, W, 16th Inf.

BLANKS, John S. B. S16217, W, 16th Inf.
BLANKS, Winnie A. W4172, CA, Blanks, Wm.
BLANTON, Annie Elizabeth, W8660, FR, Blanton, Robert Newton
BLANTON, David M. S8742, CF, 1st (Turney's) Inf.
BLANTON, Eudora Lizzie, W4498, MT, Blanton, Wm. Carroll
BLANTON, Febia Perline, W571, MN, Blanton, Powhatan
BLANTON, J. C. S5848, D, 23rd Inf.
BLANTON, Robert Newton, S6176, FR, 4th (McLemore's) Cav.
BLANTON, Virginia Frances, W10674, O, Blanton, Wm. Carpenter
BLANTON, W. C. S5574, MT, 14th Inf.
BLANTON, W. N. S3468, HD, 26th Miss. Inf.
BLASINGAME, William P. S12751, MN, 1st Bn. Mo. Lt. Art.
BLAYDES, Elizabeth Boyd, W10570, SH, Blaydes, James Elliott
BLAYDES, J. J. S14099, CC, 12th (Green's) Cav.
BLAYLOCK, Elisha D. S40, WE, 5th Ky. Inf.
BLAYLOCK, F. S. S11092, HR, 7th (Duckworth's) Cav.
BLAYLOCK, Florence C. [Felts], W10568, HR, Blaylock, Edward P. [Later married Felts]
BLEDSOE, A. S. S7468, H, 17th Inf.
BLEDSOE, Alexander Green, S616, SN, 7th Inf.
BLEDSOE, G. W. S12436, MA, 19th & 20th Consolidated Cav.
BLEDSOE, Lee, W7541, H, Bledsoe, Anthony Street
BLEDSOE, Lou, W9575, LI, Bledsoe, Lewis Jefferson
BLEDSOE, Mary Elizabeth, W1032, FR, Bledsoe, James
BLEDSOE, Nancy Elizabeth, W1830, DI, Bledsoe, Thomas
BLEDSOE, Thomas N. S12587, MOO, 41st Inf.
BLEDSOE, W. I. S13949, G, 47th Inf.
BLEDSOE, Wm. Anthony, C127, MA, 6th Inf.
BLESSING, J. P. S2080, B, 41st Inf.
BLEVINS, A. C. S2313, R, 26th Inf.
BLEVINS, Amanda C. W5356, ME, Blevins, Batholmew King
BLEVINS, Calvin, S3086, SU, 26th Inf.
BLEVINS, Christenah, W580, SU, Blevins, Wm. L.

BLEVINS, Cynthia E. W3133, D, Blevins, Wm. S.
BLEVINS, D. M. S12336, ME, 3rd (Lillard's) Mtd. Inf.
BLEVINS, Fannie, W4244, ME, Blevins, David Mossengale
BLEVINS, H. H. S3553, SU, 26th Inf.
BLEVINS, Hiram, S12761, SU, 26th Inf.
BLEVINS, Isaac, S3612, WA, 61st N.C. Inf.
BLEVINS, J. D. S9241, MC, 5th Cav.
BLEVINS, J. P. S11145, ME, 3rd (Lillard's) Inf.
BLEVINS, John W. S15565, SU, Detailed Conscripts
BLEVINS, Maggie, W7156, SU, Blevins, Hiram
BLEVINS, Mary Catherine, W10846, SU, Blevins, John Wesley
BLEVINS, Mary Corda,   See Mary Corda Watson
BLEVINS, Rebecca Jane, W960, SU, Blevins, Henry Hufman
BLEVINS, S. L. S2906, R, 1st (Carter's) Cav.
BLEVINS, Taritha Jane, W2620, K, Blevins, John J.
BLEVINS, Virginia Cathrine, W2980, R, Blevins, Alfred Carter
BLEVINS, W. B. S3643, ME, 5th Cav.
BLEVINS, W. F. S7111, R, 5th Cav.
BLEVINS, William S. S103, D, 35th Ala. Inf.
BLEWITT, Mary, W1237, D, Blewitt, Daniel
BLICK, Lula Ann, W8625, MA, Blick, Wm. Jefferson
BLICK, William Jefferson, S9505, MA, 9th Va. Inf.
BLIGH, Thomas, S7255, MS, 53rd Inf.
BLIZZARD, James G. S4674, HW, 48th Va. Inf.
BLOCK, Mary Margarette, W1593, W, Block, Charles Guy
BLOCKER, Amanda, W10689, HI, Blocker, Thomas P.
BLOCKER, J. A. S10811, SH, 1st S.C. Cav.
BLOCKER, Mary Ellen, W5082, SH, Blocker, James Alfred
BLOCKER, Thomas P. S15963, HI, 6th (Wheeler's) Cav.
BLOODWORTH, Elizabeth, W500, RB, Bloodworth, Alex
BLOODWORTH, William, S1353, WL, 18th Inf.
BLOUNT, James E. S7987, HD, 1st Cav.
BLUE, Daritha, W1190, CA, Blue, Neptoline Jackson

BLUE, Elizabeth, W5895, SN, Blue, John Franklin
BLUE, John F. S10753, SN, 2nd (Robison's) Inf.
BLUE, W. N. S9301, LA, 23rd Inf.
BLUME, Mattie F. W8391, D, Blume, F. M.
BLUNKALL, Amanda C. W83, D, Blunkall, Patrick H.
BLUNT, I. J. S6018, WH, 4th Maryland Battery
BLYTHE, Josh, S2975, WL, 2nd (Smith's) Cav.
BOARD, Stephen, S15255, O, 7th Tex. Inf.
BOATMAN, John, S14454, HM, 61st Inf.
BOATMAN, T. M. S5223, MN, 51st Inf.
BOATMAN, Thomas M. S134, MN, 51st Inf.
BOATMON, John, S2344, PU, 8th Cav.
BOAZ, Leatham, W8458, LI, Boaz, Thomas A.
BOAZ, Lucy S. W6599, LI, Boaz, W. M.
BOAZ, W. N. S12915, LI, 44th Inf.
BOAZ, W. R. S2570, O, 7th Cav.
BOBBITT, Carter, C148, MA, 14th Cav.
BOBBITT, Sallie Olivia, W4589, W8101, F, Bobbitt, Thomas Falkner
BOBBITT, Sarah Ann, W6312, MA, Bobbitt, John Richard
BOBBITT, W. D. S13851, G, 19th & 20th Consolidated Cav.
BOBBITT, W. J. S15931, CE, 49th Inf.
BOBO, K. J. S5068, MOO, 1st (Turney's) Inf.
BOBO, Susan, W5451, MOO, Bobo, Kindred Jackson
BOBO, William L. S2384, MOO, 14th Inf.
BODEN, G. B. S13414, HN, 46th Inf.
BODEN, Hudnall A. S10350, HN, 10th (DeMoss') Cav.
BODEN, Josephine, W791, WE, Boden, Andrew V.
BODEN, Laura, W8139, HN, Boden, H. A.
BODKINS, W. R. S6614, WE, Thrall's Battery, Ark. Art.
BOENCH, Leonora, W6663, WL, Boench, Walter Bernard
BOENCH, W. B. S13175, WL, 9th (Ward's) Cav.
BOGAR, F. A. S3135, LA, 9th Bn. Cav.
BOGART, Frances Eveline, W6572, LO, Bogart, Henry Madison
BOGART, H. M. S856, LO, 62nd Inf.
BOGART, Samuel, S6324, MO, 37th Inf.
BOGGS, C. B. S4107, HD, 7th Ala. Inf.
BOGGS, Caldwell, S11645, SH, 23rd Ark. Inf.
BOGGS, Joseph R. S2039, LI, 47th Inf.
BOGGS, Mary Jane, W5949, SH, Boggs, Caldwell

Index to Tennessee Confederate Pension Applications

BOGGS, Pleasant L. S7458, LI, 34th Inf.
BOGLE, Elizabeth Cox, W10321, LO, Bogle, John C. M.
BOGLE, Erastus Harris, S5415, WA, 45th Va. Inf.
BOGLE, J. Y. S7074, CA, 23rd Inf.
BOGLE, Sallie Stout, W10298, SU, Bogle, Erastus H.
BOGLE, Sarah Ann, W1435, G, Bogle, Samuel Franklin
BOHANNAN, Phillman, S13350, MC, 62nd Inf.
BOHANNON, Margaret Jane, W8195, PU, Bohannon, Thomas
BOHANON, Charles, S16271, FR, 6th Cav.
BOHANON, Thomas, S7774, PU, 16th Inf.
BOILES, Naomi E. W755, GR, Boiles, Jasper
BOISSEAU, W. H. S13322, RB, 50th Inf.
BOKER, J. F. S3815, GI, 1st Cav.
BOLDING, Samuel H. S1840, HR, 43rd Inf.
BOLES, Annie, W8374, W8445, WH, Boles, George R.
BOLES, Elizabeth, W7952, JE, Boles, J. A.
BOLES, G. R. S2792, J, 8th (Dibrell's) Cav.
BOLES, Hiram B. S5871, MC, 29th Inf.
BOLES, Mary Jane, W469, BR, Boles, John
BOLES, Melvina, W2224, GE, Boles, Robert
BOLES, Perlina M. W4869, OV, Boles, Robert
BOLES, Robert, S8638, GE, 64th N.C. Inf.
BOLES, Sarah Annie, W8445, W8374, WH, Boles, George Randolph
BOLIN, Adaline, W9326, G, Bolin, William
BOLIN, E. M. S15054, FR, 34th Inf.
BOLIN, Elizabeth A. W376, LI, Bolin, Pinkney J.
BOLIN, H. C. S2161, MOO, 1st (Turney's) Inf.
BOLIN, M. B. S3365, W, 35th Inf.
BOLIN, Mary Ann, W5770, DE, Bolin, William
BOLIN, P. J. S3840, LI, 32nd Inf.
BOLING, E. A. S5511, SU, 26th Inf.
BOLING, Elizabeth A. W6114, SU, Boling, William G.
BOLING, George W. S12073, CC, 9th Inf.
BOLING, Mary, W3226, SU, Boling, Daniel J.
BOLLES, Robert jr. S410, OV, 8th Inf.
BOLLI, Mary, W2172, K, Bolli, Emanuel
BOLLING, Jane, W1096, SU, Bolling, Larking B.
BOLLING, Willie J. W5496, SH, Bolling, Warner Thomas
BOLTON, E. B. H. S10319, WL, 7th Inf.
BOLTON, Hattie John, W3861, WI, Bolton, John Goodloe

BOLTON, John Dean, S13746, SM, 7th Inf.
BOLTON, Julia E. W8287, D, Bolton, Wm. H.
BOLTON, Louisa, W6613, SM, Bolton, John D.
BOLTON, Nancy A. W5351, WA, Bolton, John M.
BOLTON, Samuella S. W10225, GU, Bolton, Virgil V.
BOLTON, Sarah Elizabeth, W10380, WA, Bolton, Samuel Pearce
BOLTON, William R. S2599, MU, 9th Bn. Cav.
BOMAR, Martha Virginia, W2466, K, Bomar, G. H.
BOMAR, Sally F. W75, B, Bomar, James Brooks
BOMAR, W. S. S14434, HN, 20th (Russell's) Cav.
BOND, Adella M. W8077, SH, Bond, Russell Perry
BOND, Bettie Harrison, W4536, O, Bond, R. T.
BOND, Charles A. S12790, WI, 4th (McLemore's) Cav.
BOND, David L. S13352, D, 4th Cav.
BOND, Eaton D. S6619, MA, 14th Cav.
BOND, Elbert G. S11049, WA, 59th Inf.
BOND, Ellen M. W2506, SH, Bond, Nicholas P.
BOND, Fannie, W8328, PO, Bond, Marion Pink
BOND, J. H. S14235, D, 7th Inf.
BOND, James H. S10525, SU, 59th Inf.
BOND, Jemima E. W2211, H, Bond, Bartlett W.
BOND, Jennie V. W10825, HY, Bond, John Roscoe
BOND, John B. W. S4262, W, 35th Inf.
BOND, John C. S15572, RU, 8th (Smith's) Cav.
BOND, John R. S16409, HY, 21st (Wilson's) Cav.
BOND, Lavinia A. W6270, SH, Bond, Peter Napoleon
BOND, M. P. S14572, PO, 11th Miss. Inf.
BOND, Martha E. W6542, G, Bond, Winfrey Earl
BOND, Mary Cason, W7956, D, Bond, James Houston
BOND, Mary Willard, W11027, SU, Bond, Elbert Gipson
BOND, Nannie, W7474, SH, Bond, James Pearson
BOND, Peter N. S10608, SH, 4th Inf.
BOND, R. P. S15511, SH, 5th Miss. Cav.
BOND, Rachel, W11129, LO, Bond, James Houston
BOND, Rachel, W11129, LO, Bond, Jas. Houston

BOND, Sallie Ann, W9011, WE, Bond, George Alexander
BOND, Solomon, S14343, RU, 45th Inf.
BOND, Susan Virginia, W8850, RU, Bond, Joseph Green
BOND, Winfrey E. S4806, MA, 47th Inf.
BONDS, A. L. S11637, BE, 14th Inf.
BONDS, Samuel W. S1931, GI, 32nd Inf.
BONDS, Susan K. W3480, BE, Bonds, Alfred L.
BONDURANT, B. T. S16355, WE, 19th & 20th (Consolidated) Cav.
BONDURANT, Mary Lou, W9070, WE, Bondurant, Benjamin Thomas
BONDURANT, R. K. S5920, GU, 2nd Va. Cav.
BONE, J. P. S8799, SH, 3rd (Forrest's) Cav.
BONE, Linnie Kyle, W6726, SH, Bone, James Preston
BONE, Peter B. S11498, HU, 53rd Inf.
BONE, William J. S12522, SH, 56th Ga. Inf.
BONER, Ann Ross, W1599, D, Boner, Christopher Stump
BONNER, Andrew J. S1504, D, 8th Inf.
BONNER, Ann Eliza, W9945, W, Bonner, Andrew Jackson
BONNER, Miles, S9723, W, 11th (Holman's) Cav.
BOOHER, Annaliza, W7325, SU, Booher, George
BOOHER, B. P. S16084, SU, 61st Inf.
BOOHER, Eli, S3938, SU, 63rd Inf.
BOOHER, George, S4452, SU, 63rd Inf.
BOOHER, Laura, W1712, SU, Booher, E.
BOOHER, Laura, W7881, WA, Booher, Carson
BOOHER, N. C. S11348, SU, 61st Inf.
BOOHER, Peter W. S8276, SU, 61st Inf.
BOOHER, Sarah J. W2259, SU, Booher, W. B.
BOOHER, Sarah Jane, W4853, SU, Booher, Peter Wesley
BOOHER, Taritha J. W2260, SU, Booher, Jonathan T.
BOOHER, Virginia, W2682, SU, Booher, Adam C.
BOOKER, Amanda, W7954, HI, Booker, James A.
BOOKER, David S. S7171, HW, 31st Inf.
BOOKER, J. P. S6177, HI, 1st (Feild's) Inf.
BOOKER, J. T. S164, SM, 28th Inf.
BOOKER, James A. S3484, S3077, HI, 42nd Inf.
BOOKER, John A. M. S5829, CL, 59th Inf.
BOOKER, M. Ellen, W90, SM, Booker, Samuel D.
BOOKER, R. J. S8037, HI, 42nd Inf.
BOOKER, Sarah, W8184, SM, Booker, J. T.
BOON, James E. S273, WE, 12th Inf.
BOON, John P. S14884, CT, 6th N.C. Inf.
BOON, W. B. S12455, WL, 45th Inf.
BOONE, Margaret Ann, W6764, SH, Boone, Levy Jesse
BOONE, Martha Matilda, W2390, HO, Boone, Etheldred
BOONE, Mary Jane, W4265, MOO, Boone, David Crockett
BOONE, Thomas E. S14196, MC, 59th Inf.
BOOTH, Alexander, S1365, WA, Undetermined
BOOTH, F. M. S4026, F, 154th Sr. Regt. Inf.
BOOTH, W. C. S6961, H, Lookout Art.
BOOTHE, Lettie J. W2132, H, Boothe, William C.
BOOTHE, Mary Emmelene, W1472, F, Boothe, Francis Marion
BOOTHE, Rachel T. W1224, CT, Boothe, Alexander
BORDEN, L. M. W282, BR, Borden, Thomas J.
BOREN, J. W. S5849, MA, 16th Cav.
BOREN, M. D. S2672, W, 35th Inf.
BOREN, Paralee Williams, W4043, W, Boren, Michael Dean
BOREN, Sue Neal, W9752, MA, Boren, Wm. Aaron
BORING, J. W. S6778, SU, 59th Inf.
BORING, Martha Jane, W2385, SU, Boring, James Wesley
BORING, Peter H. S11408, WA, 3rd (Lillard's) Mtd. Inf.
BORROW, George W. S14828, ST, 50th Inf.
BOSHERS, Jason W. S15594, MU, 48th (Voorhies') Inf.
BOSTIC, Sarah Ann, W9776, FR, Bostic, Berry Rice
BOSTICK, B. R. S15833, FR, 3rd Ky. Cav.
BOSTICK, Pullin, W3319, FR, Bostick, Forest Green
BOSTON, James Calvin, S10700, HR, 34th Miss. Inf.
BOSTON, William A. S11829, S10199, LA, Allison's Squadron, Cav.
BOSWELL, Annie E. W1780, HR, Boswell, D. M.
BOSWELL, J. S. S2571, OV, 25th Inf.
BOSWELL, Laura Ann, W2780, HE, Boswell, John
BOSWELL, Lutetia Tide, W2814, HE, Boswell, Sanders

BOTT, J. T. S6728, SU, 37th Va. Inf.
BOTT, W. L. S9703, H, 9th Va. Inf.
BOTTOMS, Marandy, W2094, W, Bottoms, James Armstead
BOULDIN, Ann, W5739, V, Bouldin, Nathan
BOULDIN, Eilzabeth, W10220, W, Bouldin, Moses
BOULTON, Joan White, W7669, W8585, SM, Boulton, Isaac G.
BOULTON, Joe Anne, W8585, W7669, SM, Boulton, Isaac G.
BOULTON, Rachel Ellen, W7366, O, Boulton, Edward B. H.
BOUNDS, Mary, W11162, WH, Bounds, Thomas B.
BOUNDS, Talitha, W7813, W, Bounds, Wm. C.
BOUNDS, W. C. S1555, W, 2nd Miss. Inf.
BOUNDS, William C. S738, W, 2nd Inf.
BOURNE, Irene Florence, W10480, MT, Bourne, Joseph Wimberly
BOURNE, Susie Ellen, W10327, MT, Bourne, Wm. Henry
BOUTON, James E. S13950, SU, White's Co. Sullivan Co. Reserves
BOUTON, Martha, W2167, SU, Bouton, James V.
BOUTON, Mary Ann "Mag", W8471, SU, Bouton, J. E.
BOWDEN, D. J. S15454, WE, 20th Cav.
BOWDEN, J. G. S7852, MS, 17th Inf.
BOWDEN, James, S9748, LI, 32nd Inf.
BOWDEN, John W. S7583, 5th Inf.
BOWDEN, Lucretia Henry, W1850, HN, Bowden, Wm. Jordan
BOWDEN, S. B. S15087, S12737, HD, 5th N.C. Inf., Also applied from McNairy County
BOWDEN, Thomas P. S7655, T, 51st Inf.
BOWE, J. C. S10620, CT, 34th Bn. Va. Cav.
BOWE, Leona, W8058, HU, Bowe, Peter Brown
BOWEN, Cilla, W10255, HU, Bowen, Wm. Reece
BOWEN, Enoch S. S7097, HW, 16th Bn. Cav.
BOWEN, J. F. S7173, G, 15th (Stewart's) Cav.
BOWEN, James A. S5194, B, 45th Inf.
BOWEN, M. Alexina, W7579, D, Bowen, Arthur Campbell
BOWEN, Mark, S9056, DY, 20th (Russell's) Cav.
BOWEN, Mary Frances, W1968, DY, Bowen, Mark
BOWEN, Rachel L. W3449, H, Bowen, Marion

BOWENS, Mary L. W5935, RB, Bowens, Bailey Thompson
BOWERS, A. B. S3398, SU, 21st Va. Inf.
BOWERS, Adam, S7901, D, 18th Inf.
BOWERS, Alexander McGee, S4465, MO, 3rd (Clack's) Inf.
BOWERS, Allen L. S10003, SU, 13th Cav.
BOWERS, Annie Belle, W5596, G, Bowers, Orrin Harris
BOWERS, Annie Henry, W4065, D, Bowers, Wm. Franklin
BOWERS, Ansel S. S13953, MC, 50th Inf.
BOWERS, Anthony, S11823, H, 39th N.C. Inf.
BOWERS, Belle, W3732, G, Bowers, Orrin H.
BOWERS, Bettie D. W10532, HN, Bowers, George W.
BOWERS, Caldonia, W8448, LI, Bowers, James Nathaniel
BOWERS, Cordelia H. W4665, MT, Bowers, John C.
BOWERS, E. S. S10749, WL, Howell's Battery, Art.
BOWERS, Eliza, W4308, HN, Bowers, John
BOWERS, Elmira Mildred, W697, MO, Bowers, Alexander
BOWERS, Ephraim, S6318, W, 35th Inf.
BOWERS, Fredonia, W1836, D, Bowers, Adam
BOWERS, George W. S3109, FR, 1st Inf.
BOWERS, George W. S8590, MO, 1st N.C. Cav.
BOWERS, Geraldus C. W6584, SH, Bowers, John T.
BOWERS, H. C. S7592, T, 12th Cav.
BOWERS, Isaac N. S8777, CT, 59th Inf.
BOWERS, J. H. S10964, FR, 1st (Turney's) Inf.
BOWERS, J. N. S12250, LI, 62nd Ala. Inf.
BOWERS, J. T. S13042, SH, 28th Miss. Cav.
BOWERS, James A. S3519, MO, 3rd (Clack's) Inf.
BOWERS, John, S3485, HN, 5th Inf.
BOWERS, John C. S8045, MT, 49th Inf.
BOWERS, Liddie J. W1928, SU, Bowers, Abraham
BOWERS, Martha Jane, W1223, FR, Bowers, George Washington
BOWERS, Mary (Polly), W6893, H, Bowers, Anthony
BOWERS, Mary A. W4683, FR, Bowers, John Henry
BOWERS, Mary E. W7298, W, Bowers, Ephraim

BOWERS, Mary Jane, W627, MO, Bowers, Allen Harvey Mathews
BOWERS, Minnie Everline, W6341, T, Bowers, Henry Clay
BOWERS, S. W. S2848, MO, 1st N.C. Inf.
BOWERS, Susan, W898, K, Bowers, Wm. G.
BOWERS, Thomas, S5061, GR, Undetermined
BOWERS, William H. S5512, MS, 8th Inf.
BOWERY, C. R. S8241, SU, 59th Inf.
BOWERY, Elizabeth C. W3652, SU, Bowery, Wm.
BOWERY, Louisiana Elizabeth, W7826, WA, Bowery, James H.
BOWERY, Samuel, S13102, SU, 19th Inf.
BOWINGTON, John, S606, PU, 2nd Inf.
BOWINGTON, Margaret, W4510, PU, Bowington, John
BOWLDER, John M. S912, MR, 60th Ga. Inf.
BOWLES, A. J. S8093, MT, 21st Va. Inf.
BOWLES, Daniel, S7031, R, 16th Bn. (Neal's) Cav.
BOWLING, A. A. S11800, SN, 14th Inf.
BOWLING, Allen, S11120, T, 8th Ala. Inf.
BOWLING, J. W. S5433, FR, 41st Inf.
BOWLING, Larkin, S6019, SU, 3rd (Lillard's) Mtd. Inf.
BOWLING, Sarah Jane, W4958, FR, Bowling, George Washington
BOWLING, William, S1104, S, 24th Inf.
BOWLING, William W. S16581, F, 44th Miss. Inf.
BOWMAN, Benjamin T. S10791, H, 18th Inf.
BOWMAN, C. C. S1328, CT, 60th Inf.
BOWMAN, Daniel, S5724, H, 4th Ala. Bn.
BOWMAN, Elzira Carolyn, W6959, K, Bowman, William B.
BOWMAN, Eusibius, S989, S1912, CY, 4th Cav.
BOWMAN, G. W. S6515, GE, Regt. of Ark. Inf.
BOWMAN, J. P. S2139, SM, 23rd Inf.
BOWMAN, Jacob, S2749, BR, 33rd Inf.
BOWMAN, Jacob S. S4943, JE, 61st Inf.
BOWMAN, Josephine, W4161, W8631, RU, Bowman, James Carmichael
BOWMAN, Martha A. W7647, SM, Bowman, James K. P.
BOWMAN, Mary E. W5772, WA, Bowman, R. C.
BOWMAN, R. C. S14137, WA, 60th Inf.
BOWMAN, Robert M. S3251, D, 23rd Inf.
BOWMAN, Susan J. W7726, GE, Bowman, G. W.

BOWMAN, William B. S2943, K, 61st Mtd. Inf.
BOWMAR, H. D. S15436, SH, 3rd Ky. Mtd. Inf.
BOWREY, Barsheba, W516, SU, Bowrey, John
BOWREY, James H. S2514, WA, 19th Inf.
BOWREY, William, S5766, SU, 1st Cav.
BOY, Adam A. S10494, HW, 4th Inf.
BOY, Eleanor Jane, W6736, SU, Boy, Wm. Adams
BOY, J. W. S14769, SU, 1st (Carter's) Cav.
BOY, P. J. S11785, SU, 63rd Inf.
BOYD, B. B. S530, GU, 8th Cav.
BOYD, B. K. S11337, F, 38th Inf.
BOYD, Barbara A. W4397, MO, Boyd, Jeremiah
BOYD, C. J. S11542, F, Forrest's Old Regt. Cav.
BOYD, Charles W. S8157, WI, 44th Inf.
BOYD, E. B. S3857, LE, 23rd Inf.
BOYD, Elizabeth, W507, HW, Boyd, Joseph B.
BOYD, Emily G. W4501, HR, Boyd, Robt. Alexander
BOYD, F. S. S2738, DE, Jackson's Lt. Art.
BOYD, George, C281, MC, Regiment not given
BOYD, J. D. S2832, CH, 2nd N.C. Inf.
BOYD, J. H. S11582, JA, 43rd Inf.
BOYD, J. W. S4076, WY, 9th Cav.
BOYD, James A. S1208, PU, 16th Inf.
BOYD, James T. S12407, G, 7th Cav.
BOYD, John S. S1933, HW, 64th Va. Cav.
BOYD, Joseph, S2115, HW, 63rd Inf.
BOYD, Lillie Lincoln, W9405, F, Boyd, Calvin Jones
BOYD, Lydia Caroline, W6703, GI, Boyd, Wm. Miles
BOYD, Martha B. W5109, HW, Boyd, Wm. Brownlow
BOYD, Mary Emeline, W4481, D, Boyd, Benjamin Bradford
BOYD, Mary Tamah, W9576, SH, Boyd, C. M.
BOYD, Mattie Shook, W7631, D, Boyd, Thomas Aaron
BOYD, Nancy Mayfield, W1427, MS, Boyd, Benjamin Franklin
BOYD, Naomi, W4369, BR, Boyd, Robt.
BOYD, Parmelia Catherine, W1958, D, Boyd, Francis Marion
BOYD, R. A. S13535, HR, Forrest's Old Regt. Cav.
BOYD, Robert, S12228, O, 46th Inf.
BOYD, Robert F. S7179, WI, 4th Cav.
BOYD, Sarah A. W7028, F, Boyd, B. K.
BOYD, W. A. S16159, GI, 35th Ala. Inf.

Index to Tennessee Confederate Pension Applications

BOYD, W. B. S10932, HW, 29th Inf.
BOYD, W. C. S11333, D, 51st Inf.
BOYD, William M. S11605, GI, 11th Cav.
BOYD, Wm. Susan Bradshaw, W2236, MU, Boyd, Leonidas Augustus
BOYDSTEN, J. K. P. S12472, SH, 1st Con. Cav.
BOYDSTON, J. M. S5363, H, 4th Ga. Cav.
BOYDSTUN, Emma Elizabeth, W4864, L, Boydstun, A. Wood
BOYKEN, Sarah Ann, W752, SM, Boyken, Hesikirer R.
BOYKIN, C. M. S13159, MA, 6th Inf.
BOYKIN, James M. S11979, CC, 6th Inf.
BOYKIN, Louise Batey, W10231, MO, Boykin, Wm. Orsborn
BOYLES, Mary Margaret, W1976, LI, Boyles, George Ball
BOYSE, Sarah Frances, W4353, FR, Boyse, Wm. Frank
BOYSE, W. M. S11804, FR, 32nd Inf.
BOZARTH, Jesse D. S11922, DK, 16th Inf.
BOZARTH, Sarah, W7104, DK, Bozarth, Jesse D.
BOZE, Clarissa, W7989, SM, Boze, Wm. C.
BOZE, Fannie, W613, SM, Boze, Wm.
BOZE, W. C. S14734, SM, 7th Inf.
BOZEMAN, Elizabeth Jane, W3365, K, Bozeman, Crawford Ward
BRAAKS, Rolin, S5881, GR, 26th Inf.
BRACH, J. M. S2285, HO, 14th Inf.
BRACK, Mary Louisa, W7117, HO, Brack, James Monroe
BRACKEN, A. L. S8289, H, 4th Cav.
BRACKEN, Laura A. W6223, H, Bracken, Archie L.
BRACKETT, Cora Lee, W9516, MC, Brackett, Wm. Adkins
BRACKETT, William Adkins, S10810, MC, 16th Cav.
BRACKETT, William M. S14842, PO, 5th Ga. Inf.
BRACKIN, Calie, W8124, MA, Brackin, Thomas
BRACKIN, Thomas, S15808, K, 29th N.C. Inf.
BRACKING, T. G. S15915, D, Baxter's Confederate Cav.
BRADBERRY, E. S734, LO, 31st Va. Inf.
BRADEN, H. J. S7878, DY, 2nd (Ashby's) Cav.
BRADEN, Martha Marie, W2174, SH, Braden, Wm. H.
BRADFORD, A. S9558, HI, 9th Bn. Cav.

BRADFORD, Alford M. S3527, HE, 6th Inf.
BRADFORD, Bettie, W9312, SM, Bradford, Thomas Crutchfield
BRADFORD, Charles, S10796, PU, 25th Inf.
BRADFORD, Edmund B. S351, MC, 31st Inf.
BRADFORD, J. C. S10239, CH, 18th (Newsom's) Cav.
BRADFORD, J. G. S6853, L, 15th Inf.
BRADFORD, James F. S5480, MC, 5th (McKenzie's) Cav.
BRADFORD, John, S15993, D, 28th Inf.
BRADFORD, Malittie Magdalene, W10177, WI, Bradford, Alexander
BRADFORD, Martha Jane, W5505, HY, Bradford, Hiram Scott
BRADFORD, Mary Ann, W7046, PU, Bradford, Charles
BRADFORD, Mary Elizabeth, W9625, CH, Bradford, James Claiborn
BRADFORD, Susan Jane, W951, HE, Bradford, James
BRADFORD, T. J. S4074, WH, 16th Inf.
BRADFORD, Thomas Crutchfield, S13726, SM, 9th (Ward's) Cav.
BRADLEY, A. J. S14126, S15427, SM, 7th Inf.
BRADLEY, A. W. S5404, SN, 30th Inf.
BRADLEY, Andrew S9940, H, 1st Ga. Inf.
BRADLEY, Andrew, S12794, H, 36th Ga. Inf.
BRADLEY, Andrew A. S9871, SH, Wood's Regt. Miss. Cav.
BRADLEY, B. B. S3449, SH, 1st Hvy. Art.
BRADLEY, B. C. S16256, RB, 42nd Inf.
BRADLEY, Dora, W9682, SN, Bradley, J. W.
BRADLEY, Ella Dowlen, W10400, RB, Bradley, Baily Peyton
BRADLEY, Ellen E. W5062, SH, Bradley, Andrew Alexander
BRADLEY, Eugenia, W9283, WL, Bradley, Thomas E.
BRADLEY, George, S7611, RB, 30th Inf.
BRADLEY, J. A. S4296, MS, Undetermined
BRADLEY, J. B. S13283, CC, 7th (Duckworth's) Cav.
BRADLEY, J. C. S7256, HW, 31st Inf.
BRADLEY, J. D. S7723, HN, 5th Inf.
BRADLEY, J. W. S10971, SN, 30th Inf.
BRADLEY, Lizzie Goff, W3155, WI, Bradley, Thos. H.
BRADLEY, Marene G. W7453, HW, Bradley, Jesse C.

BRADLEY, Margaret [Kittrell], W10682, SM, Bradley, George Washington, [Later married Kittrell]
BRADLEY, Martha Emiline, W4489, H, Bradley, Lute Clifford
BRADLEY, Mary C. W899, L, Bradley, Henry Carroll
BRADLEY, Mary E. W1910, D, Bradley, Samuel Green
BRADLEY, Mary Webster, W3524, SN, Bradley, Wm. Thomson
BRADLEY, Nannie E. W2629, SN, Bradley, Vincent
BRADLEY, R. H. C104, MA, 29th Miss. Inf.
BRADLEY, Sarah Francis, W1607, M, Bradley, John Davis
BRADLEY, Stephen, S4658, K, Thomas' Legion, N.C.
BRADLEY, T. E. S12738, SN, 23rd Inf.
BRADLEY, T. E. S15899, WL, 8th Inf.
BRADLEY, Thomas Edward, S15701, WL, 8th Inf.
BRADLEY, Thomas H. S9542, WI, 4th Cav.
BRADLEY, W. H. S2448, SM, 23rd Inf.
BRADLEY, W. T. S1727, SN, 7th Inf.
BRADLEY, William W. S13935, K, 22nd N.C. Inf.
BRADOW, Henry H. S11967, SH, 12th Inf.
BRADSFORD, See Bransford
BRADSHAW, A. J. S6911, HN, 154th Sr. Regt. Inf.
BRADSHAW, Anthony A. S807, FR, 4th Inf.
BRADSHAW, Catharine, W2557, HW, Bradshaw, Joseph B.
BRADSHAW, I. R. S2605, HD, 34th Miss. Inf.
BRADSHAW, J. S14154, O, 1st Cav.
BRADSHAW, John W. S13888, WL, 45th Inf.
BRADSHAW, Margaret L. W5605, HD, Bradshaw, I. R.
BRADSHAW, Mary Pinion, W10497, H, Bradshaw, John
BRADSHAW, Mattie E. W8710, WL, Bradshaw, Thomas W.
BRADSHAW, Rosa, W3228, HN, Bradshaw, Andrew J.
BRADSHER, Margaret Elizabeth, W9877, F, Bradsher, Stephen Garrett
BRADSHER, S. G. S8458, F, 7th Cav.
BRADY, Alvarez, W4001, GR, Brady, Gilford L.
BRADY, Ann, W3311, OV, Brady, Francis Marion
BRADY, Annie C. W2576, MA, Brady, Charles T.
BRADY, Edward, S2268, WH, 28th Inf.
BRADY, Ellen, W4129, CU, Brady, S. H.
BRADY, John, S15287, MU, 19th (Biffle's) Cav.
BRADY, M. V. S6239, WH, 1st (Carter's) Cav.
BRADY, O. B. S3248, CY, 4th (Murray's) Cav.
BRADY, Patrick, S2197, WH, 28th & 84th (Consolidated) Inf.
BRADY, Rosa, W10953, MU, Brady, John
BRADY, Samuel, S13399, W, 1st (Carter's) Cav.
BRAGDEN, Joseph, S8862, 16th Cav.
BRAGDON, Emily, W6395, Bragdon, Joseph
BRAIN, John C. S1058, K, Confederate States Navy
BRAKE, Thomas, S2165, ST, 14th Inf.
BRAKEFIELD, Mary, W1365, FR, Brakefield, Barton
BRALEY, Robert C. S13104, GI, 11th (Holman's) Cav.
BRALEY, Sarah Elizabeth, W7556, GI, Braley, J. C.
BRALY, Gentile, S8534, GU, 13th Miss. Inf.
BRALY, J. S. S228, MN, 23rd Inf.
BRALY, James C. S6344, GI, 11th Miss. Cav.
BRAME, Geraldine A. W6702, D, Brame, John Lemuel
BRAMHAM, Isaac N. S11546, O, 33rd Inf.
BRAMLETT, H. M. S15881, PO, 11th Ga. Cav.
BRANCH, Alice Cummins, W8487, D, Branch, Walter Preston
BRANCH, Eugenia, W10670, SN, Branch, John
BRANCH, Hugh, S13688, CC, 7th (Duckworth's) Cav.
BRANCH, J. M. F. S10404, SH, 51st Inf.
BRANCH, John, S13317, SN, 1st Fla. Reserves
BRANCH, Leah, W327, MOO, Branch, D. G.
BRANCH, Letitia, W963, CC, Branch, Kinon
BRANCH, M. V. S403, BE, 17th Miss. Inf.
BRANCH, Martin Vanburon, S949, BE, 17th Miss. Inf.
BRANCH, Priscilla E. W1779, MU, Branch, R. E. J.
BRANCH, Tena Davis, W9605, CC, Branch, Hu.
BRANCH, William T. S4265, LA, 23rd Inf.
BRANDON, Alfred G. S13141, CA, 8th (Smith's) Cav.
BRANDON, Ann Elizabeth, W6596, CA, Brandon, Alford George

Index to Tennessee Confederate Pension Applications

BRANDON, Charles L. S5078, SN, 7th Inf.
BRANDON, D. W. S14438, L, 10th Ala. Inf.
BRANDON, Edmund Tennyson, S13069, CA, 23rd Inf.
BRANDON, Elizabeth, W2245, CA, Brandon, Joseph A.
BRANDON, J. B. S6962, ME, 63rd Inf.
BRANDON, Joe A. S4029, CA, 4th Cav.
BRANDON, Mamie M. W4264, W7089, L, Brandon, Jessie Scott
BRANDON, Martha Jane, W120, CA, Brandon, Arch.
BRANDON, Mary Marie, W7089, W4264, L, Brandon, Jesse Scott
BRANDON, Nannie E. W6606, D, Brandon, James Polk
BRANDON, P. A. S10187, H, 12th Ala. Inf.
BRANDON, Robert B. S13677, RU, 8th Mo. Cav.
BRANDON, Sarah Jane, W84, R, Brandon, Gideon Thompson
BRANHAM, George, S10640, SN, 9th Cav.
BRANHAM, John W. S14502, SN, 9th (Ward's) Cav.
BRANHAM, Julius, S10280, BR, 36th Inf.
BRANN, Emaline E. W1356, WE, Brann, Thomas Jefferson
BRANNOCK, J. P. S10977, HE, 2nd Mo. Cav.
BRANNON, Arena, W3808, GU, Brannon, George Washington
BRANNON, Bettie, W5172, MO, Brannon, James
BRANNON, David, S11158, SU, 10th Ga. Cav.
BRANNON, G. A. S8024, BO, 2nd (Ashby's) Cav.
BRANNON, James, S2791, MO, 39th N.C. Inf.
BRANNON, Nancy Ann, W7711, BO, Brannon, G. A.
BRANNON, Richard, S13570, SH, 11th Ala. Inf.
BRANNUM, J. C. S10797, ME, 59th Inf.
BRANSFORD, A. T. S1473, M, 30th Inf.
BRANSFORD, Araminta Dormer, W2188, SM, Bransford, Samuel Moody
BRANSFORD, Emma, W10698, O, Bransford, Thomas Leroy
BRANSON, J. R. S5358, H, 41st Inf.
BRANSON, J. S. S13516, G, 12th Ky. Cav.
BRANSON, Lena Roberts, W6785, D, Branson, Wm.
BRANSON, Sarah E. W11071, G, Branson, John Steele

BRANSON, T. W. S11591, G, 20th (Russell's) Cav.
BRANSON, Tabitha Caroline, W5570, G, Branson, Thomas Wilson
BRANSON, William, S12138, D, 2nd (Ashby's) Cav.
BRANTLEY, Margaret A. W4204, HY, Brantley, George L.
BRANTLEY, Mary Frances, W7092, WE, Brantley, Wm. Carrol
BRANTLEY, Robert E. S14455, CF, 17th Inf.
BRANTLEY, S. N. S12358, L, 7th (Duckworth's) Cav.
BRANTLEY, William C. S12303, WE, 6th (Wheeler's) Cav.
BRANUM, William Riley, S6476, R, 37th Inf.
BRASFIELD, J. J. S7442, CC, 9th Ark. Cav.
BRASHEAR, Annie L. W5287, RU, Brashear, John
BRASHEARS, Julia Ann, W1518, GI, Brashears, James
BRASHER, Charles, S217, CH, 31st Inf.
BRASHER, Frances Louizer, W6790, MN, Brasher, Henry Collins
BRASHER, H. C. S2856, MN, 18th Ala. Inf.
BRASHER, Margaret C. W2391, MA, Brasher, Charles R. App. between 216 & 217 on Soldiers film
BRASHER, Sam D. S1599, DE, 27th Inf.
BRASSELL, Henry T. S10368, SN, 7th (Bennett's) Cav.
BRASSFIELD, Joshua E. S13168, CC, 9th Ark. Inf.
BRASSFIELD, Sophronia A. W3653, G, Brassfield, John J.
BRASSWELL, A. D. S11401, SN, 7th Ky. Cav.
BRASSWELL, Isabel, W6526, D, Brasswell, Dallas
BRASWELL, H. K. S12991, SM, 8th (Smith's) Cav.
BRASWELL, Paradine, W7172, D, Braswell, Alonzo Franklin
BRATCHER, Thomas J. S218, DK, Unknown
BRATTON, John F. S6854, L, 1st Cav.
BRATTON, Mary W. W2904, D, Bratton, Sam Houston
BRATTON, Narcissa, W1341, HI, Bratton, Robert Franklin
BRAUGHTON, Ben, S3545, LI, 8th Inf.
BRAUGHTON, Jane, W3849, B, Braughton, James

Index to Tennessee Confederate Pension Applications

BRAWNER, Betsy Ann, W195, WE, Brawner, John
BRAWNER, J. H. S11488, WE, 52nd Inf.
BRAY, Eliza Adline, W8431, CH, Bray, James Franklin
BRAY, F. M. S8617, CH, 51st Inf.
BRAY, I. M. S9778, CH, 16th Cav.
BRAY, J. F. S10536, CH, 6th Inf.
BRAY, John R. S7741, CH, 21st (Wilson's) Cav.
BRAY, M. W. S5737, HR, 22nd Inf.
BRAY, Margaret Adaline, W4223, CH, Bray, Wm. Hamlin
BRAY, Rebecca Malinda, W4136, GI, Bray, John Butler
BRAY, W. . S8359, PU, 25th Inf.
BRAZEL, James, S4312, HU, 11th Inf.
BRAZELTON, Maggie C. W6359, D, Brazelton, Wm.
BRAZELTON, Margaret E. W1093, FR, Brazelton, Abram
BRAZELTON, William G. S5135, FR, 1st (Turney's) Inf.
BRAZIER, T. N. S2297, MOO, 44th Inf.
BREADY, Nannie H. W4660, G, Bready, Isaac Newton
BREEDEN, Cecile, W2617, HO, Breeden, John Oliver
BREEDEN, Isham, S5710, HO, 50th Inf.
BREEDEN, J. G. C. S489, MO, Undetermined
BREEDEN, John L. S8066, HO, 49th Inf.
BREEDEN, John O. S769, HO, 49th Inf.
BREEDEN, L. O. S1291, HO, 14th Inf.
BREEDEN, Mary, W7689, HO, Breeden, John L.
BREEDEN, Nancy C. W2699, MO, Breeden, John
BREEDEN, Pomp, S6993, HU, 50th Inf.
BREEDEN, Rebecca E. W4410, HO, Breeden, Linsey Oliver
BREEDEN, Rufus S. S5391, LO, 62nd Inf.
BREEDEN, Samuel Young, S9620, HR, 7th Cav.
BREEDING, Margaret, W751, CL, Breeding, Pryar Lilburn
BREEDING, Samuel, S5539, CL, 63rd Inf.
BREEDLOVE, Christopher Columbus, S16589, W, Unassigned
BREEDLOVE, Lutitia, W3041, HN, Breedlove, Robt. Jos. Montgomy.
BREEDLOVE, Nancy Elizabeth, W3751, Breedlove, Smith C.
BREEDLOVE, Robert H. S10684, HN, 10th Cav.
BREEN, Daniel, S1493, HR, 1st Lt. Art.
BRENDLE, H. P. S10170, PO, Thomas' Legion, N.C.
BRENT, Albert H. S11382, D, 6th (Wheeler's) Cav.
BRENTS, Victoria T. W4556, MS, Brents, Wilson Payne
BRENTS, W. P. S8844, LI, 41st Inf.
BRESLER, Abe, S15015, LI, Trigg's Battery, Ark. Lt. Art.
BREVARD, Sallie Malone, W9956, W8630, O, Brevard, Alfred Lee
BREWER, Ada B. W5936, Brewer, Henry Clay
BREWER, Anderson, S4414, GR, 29th Inf.
BREWER, Carthen, W4522, HA, Brewer, Jackson Theodore
BREWER, David, S14299, LK, 22nd Inf.
BREWER, Elizabeth, W4474, LA, Brewer, C. C.
BREWER, G. A. S3858, LE, 6th (Wheeler's) Cav.
BREWER, George W. S2907, R, 60th Ga. Inf.
BREWER, H. C. S14406, 12th Ky. Cav.
BREWER, Harmon, S9311, SH, 16th Inf.
BREWER, James A. S454, HA, 29th Inf.
BREWER, James R. S10876, W, 35th Inf.
BREWER, John J. S4135, WY, 10th Inf.
BREWER, John T. S7735, RU, 18th Inf.
BREWER, John W. S74, RU, 4th Cav.
BREWER, Katherine C. W5633, UN, Brewer, Richard
BREWER, Lauvina J. W2418, UN, Brewer, Anderson
BREWER, Lina, W5411, HR, Brewer, Albert Andrew
BREWER, Lucy, W6860, SH, Brewer, Lorenzo Dow
BREWER, Margrett E. W9838, RU, Brewer, Joel
BREWER, Paralee, W2225, RU, Brewer, John Thomas
BREWER, Parrie, W2435, CA, Brewer, James Russel
BREWER, R. F. S3070, WY, 23rd Inf.
BREWER, Richard, S4835, UN, 2nd (Ashby's) Cav.
BREWER, Sam, S15194, S12259, MR, 34th Inf.
BREWER, W. H. S5813, SN, 30th Inf.
BREWER, W. J. S11756, LA, 10th Miss. Cav.
BREWER, W. S. S9679, BE, 20th (Russell's) Cav.

Index to Tennessee Confederate Pension Applications

BREWER, William J. S3420, GI, 44th Inf.
BREWINGTON, Joseph, S2105, CY, 13th Cav.
BREWSTER, Josiah, S9695, BO, 65th Ga. Inf.
BRICKHOUSE, John Beasley, S4801, D, 10th Ala. Inf.
BRICKHOUSE, Mary Elizabeth, W3654, MT, Brickhouse, John Beasley
BRIDGEFORTH, Minnie E. W9652, HI, Bridgeforth, Benjamin
BRIDGER, Redmon, S7317, CC, 29th Miss. Inf.
BRIDGES, B. H. S4684, MN, 32nd Inf.
BRIDGES, C. B. S6446, WE, 12th Ky. Cav.
BRIDGES, D. A. S13114, WL, 4th (McLemore's) Cav.
BRIDGES, D. F. S2805, MN, 13th Miss. Inf.
BRIDGES, D. W. S9506, MC, 1st Ga. Cav.
BRIDGES, E. C. L. S13560, GI, 3rd (Clack's) Inf.
BRIDGES, Emaline, W2137, BE, Bridges, Hosia B.
BRIDGES, G. T. S12018, P, 19th (Biffle's) Cav.
BRIDGES, John, S9366, D, 8th (Smith's) Cav.
BRIDGES, John W. S7194, WE, 38th Inf.
BRIDGES, Martha Ann, W4499, MN, Bridges, Berry Hicks
BRIDGES, Plasie, W1875, CO, Bridges, Henderson
BRIDGES, Rachel Elizabeth, W10335, G, Bridges, George Terry
BRIDGES, Sarah E. W6567, MN, Bridges, D. F.
BRIDGES, Sarah Elizabeth, W3281, MC, Bridges, David Watson
BRIDGES, Si Anderson, S9071, WE, 12th Ky. Cav.
BRIDGES, Virginia M. W7979, SH, Bridges, Wm. G.
BRIDGES, William Bolivar, S11211, WE, 38th Inf.
BRIDGES, William Gale, S15517, SH, 3rd Confederate Infantry
BRIDGFORTH, William, S15349, GI, 32nd Inf.
BRIDGMAN, M. S. S13460, SU, 63rd Va. Inf.
BRIGANCE, Martha A. W654, DE, Brigance, John D.
BRIGANCE, William M. S625, SN, 1st (Turney's) Inf.
BRIGG, Henry M. S15375, GI, Tenn. Hvy. Art.
BRIGGS, A. Wesley, S7446, CT, 29th N.C. Inf.
BRIGGS, Annie Victoria, W7401, GI, Briggs, John Gideon
BRIGGS, Dora, W9831, MU, Briggs, James F.

BRIGGS, Isabella A. W7205, MA, Briggs, Robert Allen
BRIGGS, Jesse F. S578, B, 9th Cav.
BRIGGS, John G. S7507, GII, 53rd Inf.
BRIGGS, Joseph R. S10912, GI, 11th (Gordon's) Cav.
BRIGGS, Lizzie, W10280, GI, Briggs, J. R.
BRIGGS, R. A. S15202, MA, 4th Ala. Cav.
BRIGGS, R. S. S3388, SU, 29th N.C. Inf.
BRIGGS, W. J. S197, WA, 37th Va. Inf.
BRIGGS, William H. S14077, RB, 9th (Bennett's) Cav.
BRIGHAM, A. C. S6606, ST, 1st Hvy. Art.
BRIGHAM, J. H. S14474, ST, 33rd Inf.
BRIGHAM, Lucy A. W4334, ST, Brigham, A. C.
BRIGHT, Emma, W10054, WL, Bright, Ben Porter
BRIGHT, Mahala, W3519, DE, Bright, George Whitfield
BRIGHTWELL, Thomas H. S15225, SH, 18th Va. Inf.
BRIGMAN, N. K. S13633, CO, 1st N.C. Cav.
BRILEY, J. N. S11319, D, 9th Cav.
BRILEY, J. N. S14796, MA, 9th Cav.
BRIM, W. B. S6724, CE, 49th Inf.
BRINKLEY, J. A. S15489, 12th Ky. Cav.
BRINKLEY, J. C. S11801, HW, 18th N.C. Inf.
BRINKLEY, J. E. S15522, SH, 154th Sr. Regt. Inf.
BRINKLEY, L. H. S5004, RU, 45th Inf.
BRINKLEY, Mollie Greenway, W9406, F, Brinkley, Thomas William
BRINKLEY, Sallie Lacy, W10651, Brinkley, John Alexander
BRINKLEY, T. W. S13304, F, 12th Cav.
BRINKLEY, Walter J. S5872, WE, 46th N.C. Inf.
BRINKLY, John, S5680, RU, 45th Inf.
BRISCOE, Sarah E. W5941, K, Briscoe, James W.
BRISTER, Lufty R. W7770, SH, Brister, W. T.
BRISTER, W. T. S13974, SH, 3rd (Clack's) Inf.
BRITTAIN, Elizabeth Ferrell, W6080, FR, Brittain, Wm. Washington
BRITTAIN, Elizabeth Jane, W9811, RU, Brittain, Peyton S.
BRITTAIN, Frances Matilda, W6794, RU, Brittain, Columbus Lafayette
BRITTAIN, Joseph F. S11606, MS, 11th Cav.
BRITTON, Ellen T. W5165, GI, Britton, James M.

BRITTON, J. H. S14886, GE, 31st Inf.
BRITTON, James M. S8204, GI, 53rd Inf.
BRITTON, Joseph, S114, HW, 19th Inf.
BRITTON, Millie Temperance, W3085, MA, Britton, James Patrick
BRITTON, Thomas C. S15692, WI, 11th Cav.
BRIXEY, Helon Martha, W1179, CF, Brixey, Jonathan Wooten
BRIXEY, Samuel H. S3762, B, 24th Inf.
BRIXEY, William T. S6524, CF, 16th Inf.
BRIZENDINE, Marion J. S13093, S16255, SN, 9th (Ward's) Cav.
BRIZENDINE, Thomas J. S1719, WE, 5th Inf.
BRIZENDINE, W. M. S11376, WE, 7th Cav.
BROACH, Lucy S. W7661, Broach, Sidney Abner
BROADAWAY, J. E. S15848, S10287, LI, 8th Inf.
BROCH, F. M. S13216, PO, 43rd Inf.
BROCK, Ama, W628, CL, Brock, Moses
BROCK, David, S7599, BR, 3rd Inf.
BROCK, John W. S383, PO, 19th Inf.
BROCK, Judie Catherine, W2510, WE, Brock, John Merrill
BROCK, Mary Ann, W6391, H, Brock, Richard Emerson
BROCK, Sarah C. W1351, PO, Brock, John W.
BROCK, T. G. S14171, HE, 31st Inf.
BROCKWELL, W. S. S4332, O, 47th Inf.
BROGDEN, J. W. S9687, WE, 5th Inf.
BROGDEN, Sarah Ann Elizabeth, W2119, HN, Brogden, F. M.
BROGDON, Francis Marion, S3661, HN, 7th Cav.
BROMLEY, Elizabeth, W846, G, Bromley, James Harvey
BROMLEY, James H. S1962, G, 19th Bn. (Gantt's) Cav.
BROMLEY, S. C. S3153, WY, 9th Cav.
BROMLEY, W. D. S6710, F, 3rd (Forrest's) Cav.
BROMLEY, W. F. S4416, MT, 14th Inf.
BROMLEYE, J. M. S11048, MT, 14th Inf.
BRONSON, Elizabeth, W8049, H, Bronson, John Rufus
BROOK, Leonard H. S819, SM, 28th Inf.
BROOKS, Albert M. S2421, GI, 9th Ala. Inf.
BROOKS, Allen, S10163, CL, 1st (Carter's) Cav.
BROOKS, Allen, S11583, CO, 26th Inf.
BROOKS, C. B. S8019, GR, 3rd (Lillard's) Mtd. Inf.
BROOKS, C. C. S48, RU, 1st Inf.
BROOKS, C. G. S13616, TR, 8th (Smith's) Cav.
BROOKS, Elizabeth, W3545, RO, Brooks, Thomas R.
BROOKS, Ellen Byrum, W10821, LE, Brooks, Thomas Brantley
BROOKS, Elvira, W9786, MO, Brooks, Adolphus
BROOKS, J. C. S4303, MN, 154th Sr. Regt. Inf.
BROOKS, J. C. S10715, CL, 29th Inf.
BROOKS, Jackson P. S1485, SM, 28th Inf.
BROOKS, James L. S4415, A, 16th N.C. Inf.
BROOKS, James M. S14376, B, 20th Inf.
BROOKS, James P. S2623, WE, 33rd Inf.
BROOKS, James P. S13928, WE, 19th & 20th (Consolidated) Cav.
BROOKS, John W. S3221, CL, 29th Inf.
BROOKS, L. S. S5785, CO, 60th Inf.
BROOKS, Malinda Elvira, W9303, MO, Brooks, Adolphus
BROOKS, Margaret, W4080, H, Brooks, Wm. Houston
BROOKS, Martha, W8030, SM, Brooks, John P.
BROOKS, Mary J. W8084, MN, Brooks, Joseph C.
BROOKS, Octavia, W8879, HR, Brooks, Tudar Frith
BROOKS, R. A. S3528, CL, 29th Inf.
BROOKS, Rissa L. W1693, SM, Brooks, Leonidas H.
BROOKS, Roland, S718, GR, 26th Inf.?, On misc. microfilm reel
BROOKS, Sarah Magnolia, W7032, GI, Brooks, John Milton
BROOKS, Susan Anne, W9265, SM, Brooks, Charles Green
BROOKS, Thomas F. S499, S1246, K, 16th N.C. Inf.
BROOKS, W. A. S14747, DY, 26th N.C. Inf.
BROOKS, W. H. S15968, TR, 23rd Inf.
BROOKS, W. J. S15307, MA, 13th Inf.
BROOKS, William H. S8687, H, 16th Inf.
BROOKSHER, Elizabeth, W2551, D, Brooksher, Joseph
BROOKSHER, Joseph, S233, D, 45th Inf.
BROOKSHIRE, E. C. sr. S11081, SH, 3rd Inf.
BROOM, John P. S14395, HI, 9th Bn. (Gantt's) Cav.
BROOME, Martha, W7171, MT, Broome, W. F.
BROTHERS, Benjamin, S4258, CF, 4th (McLemore's) Cav.

Index to Tennessee Confederate Pension Applications

BROTHERS, Martha, W1483, RU, Brothers, Thomas
BROUGHTON, Thomas, S6118, BE, 5th Inf.
BROUGHTON, Thomas T. S10994, 5th Inf.
BROWDER, Nancy, W1511, BR, Browder, Samuel David
BROWDER, S. D. S893, BR, 5th Cav.
BROWDER, Sallie Elizabeth, W6774, RO, Browder, John Franklin
BROWER, W. A. S7312, HE, 27th Inf.
BROWES, Sarah Jane, W2419, HE, Browes, Wesley A.
BROWN, A. C. S8751, OV, 28th Inf.
BROWN, A. E. S10096, WE, 21st (Wilson's) Cav.
BROWN, A. F. S7181, H, Border's Tex. Cav.
BROWN, A. J. S16090, HI, 48th (Voorhies') Inf.
BROWN, Abbie, W4175, CU, Brown, Jackson Van Buren
BROWN, Abner, S11576, K, 50th Inf.
BROWN, Adaline, W104, OV, Brown, Samuel
BROWN, Adeline Nannie, W10090, HN, Brown, Nathaniel jr.
BROWN, Alfred, C233, BR, Regiment not given
BROWN, Alfred, S5575, CT, 21st Va. Cav.
BROWN, Alfred, S10571, JE, 51st Va. Inf.
BROWN, Alfred H. S9813, SH, 13th Inf.
BROWN, Allen Foot, S9040, WA, Lynch's Co. Lt. Art.
BROWN, Amanda, W172, OV, Brown, S. L.
BROWN, Amanda Dora Bayless, W5061, WA, Brown, Robert Columbus
BROWN, Amanda J. W3219, WA, Brown, Allen F.
BROWN, Anderson, C209, MA, Unassigned (Horse Shoer)
BROWN, Ann, W8442, LO, Brown, George Washington
BROWN, Arizona Alice, W10118, RU, Brown, Daniel Swept
BROWN, B. S3588, HO, 50th Inf.
BROWN, B. F. S1754, U, 63rd Inf.
BROWN, B. F. S3475, DI, Baxter's Co. Lt. Art.
BROWN, Barbara Elizabeth, W7149, U, Brown, Alfred P.
BROWN, Beulah Benton, W9366, L, Brown, Alexander Y. Some papers with 11183
BROWN, C. G. S13415, RB, 28th Inf.
BROWN, Caleb, S298, MR, 23rd Ga. Inf.
BROWN, Cansada, W8984, PU, Brown, A. C.
BROWN, Charles, S4104, WE, 31st Inf.

BROWN, Charles H. S6647, SN, 9th (Ward's) Cav.
BROWN, Commodore P. S5750, HW, 43rd Inf.
BROWN, D. S. S15652, RU, 2nd Inf.
BROWN, Dolly D. W3273, H, Brown, John H.
BROWN, E. D. S8496, MC, 19th Inf.
BROWN, E. F. S2277, MOO, 1st (Turney's) Inf.
BROWN, E. L. S16572, MT, 1st Inf.
BROWN, Ecloey, W4139, HI, Brown, James A.
BROWN, Eliza E. W5377, JE, Brown, Alfred
BROWN, Eliza Wilson, W3360, MT, Brown, Jerry
BROWN, Elizabeth, W925, PU, Brown, H. A.
BROWN, Elizabeth E. W2095, H, Brown, James E.
BROWN, Elizabeth Frances, W4783, MOO, Brown, James W.
BROWN, Elvira, W4974, RU, Brown, John Clark
BROWN, Elyanie, W9717, H, Brown, James B.
BROWN, Emaline, W6783, CT, Brown, Alfred
BROWN, Emily Alice, W11114, HD, Brown, James Knoch Polk
BROWN, Emma, W11144, SH, Brown, Milton A.
BROWN, Enoch, S3582, S331, CY, 7th Inf.
BROWN, Finettie, W4188, MOO, Brown, Elbert Franklin
BROWN, Frank M. S11247, A, 6th Ga. Cav.
BROWN, G. B. S7937, D, 9th Bn. Cav.
BROWN, G. T. S6400, DE, 16th Inf.
BROWN, G. T. S15005, D, Monsarrat's Battery
BROWN, G. W. S3300, PU, 8th Inf.
BROWN, G. W. S5569, LO, 2nd (Ashby's) Cav.
BROWN, G. W. S6743, MU, 9th Bn. Cav.
BROWN, G. W. S12088, OV, 25th Inf.
BROWN, G. W. S16629, CF, 3rd Ga. Cav.
BROWN, G. W. G. S3816, CL, 63rd Inf.
BROWN, George W. S11134, H, Barry's Co. Lt. Art.
BROWN, H. R. S13120, O, 22nd (Barteau's) Cav.
BROWN, Henry K. S14251, CO, 14th N.C. Bn.
BROWN, Hiram, S5195, SN, 30th Inf.
BROWN, I. N. S7469, WL, 9th (Bennett's) Cav.
BROWN, Irene Harris, W8765, RO, Brown, William L.
BROWN, Isaac, S6623, R, 19th Inf.
BROWN, J. A. S1010, HW, 63rd Inf.
BROWN, J. C. S4330, FR, 25th Inf.
BROWN, J. E. S12445, DI, 48th Inf.
BROWN, J. H. S7910, H, 4th Cav.

Index to Tennessee Confederate Pension Applications

BROWN, J. H. L. S16188, J, 28th Inf.
BROWN, J. J. S12116, DI, 11th Inf.
BROWN, J. M. S4144, HE, 21st (Wilson's) Cav.
BROWN, J. P. S5232, SN, 20th Inf.
BROWN, J. P. S12207, WH, 1st Bn. (Colm's) Inf.
BROWN, J. S. S11730, H, 1st (Carter's) Cav.
BROWN, J. T. S5392, MA, Rice's Battery, Lt. Art.
BROWN, J. V. S430, PI, 16th Inf.
BROWN, J. W. S9145, SN, 20th Inf.
BROWN, Jabez, S10766, O, 9th Inf.
BROWN, Jacob, S3831, U, 63rd Inf.
BROWN, Jacob A. S12870, SU, 36th Inf.
BROWN, James A. S11109, HI, 11th Inf.
BROWN, James D. S4685, SN, 4th (McLemore's) Cav.
BROWN, James E. S1703, FR, 17th Inf.
BROWN, James G. S12456, H, 17th Ga. Inf.
BROWN, James M. S10218, MA, 16th Cav.
BROWN, James P. S10579, SN, 20th Inf.
BROWN, James R. S1566, MOO, 8th Inf.
BROWN, James T. S14424, SH, 2nd Ga. Cav.
BROWN, James W. S7811, MOO, 23rd Inf.
BROWN, Jannie, W10581, GU, Brown, R. L.
BROWN, Jesse F. S9440, K, 54th Va. Inf.
BROWN, Jessie Elizabeth, W10958, WL, Brown, Wm. Andrew
BROWN, John, S352, W, Tenn. Confederate Regt.
BROWN, John, S1755, JO, 28th N.C. Inf.
BROWN, John, S7200, FR, 44th Inf.
BROWN, John A. S5687, K, 31st Inf.
BROWN, John D. S235, S1125, CO, 16th N.C. Inf.
BROWN, John H. S13915, D, Forrest's Old Regt. Cav.
BROWN, John L. C186, H, 20th Inf.
BROWN, John M. S15144, DY, 19th (Biffle's) Cav.
BROWN, John P. S9662, CY, 8th (Dibrell's) Cav.
BROWN, John S. S7836, GE, 60th Mtd. Inf.
BROWN, Joseph C. S1209, HM, 1st Regt. Sharpshooters
BROWN, Joseph Franklin, S4698, RU, 8th Bn. Ga. Inf.
BROWN, Joseph M. S2505, RO, 5th Cav.
BROWN, Joseph R. S4890, HM, 31st Inf.
BROWN, Julia A. W9091, O, Brown, Joe R.
BROWN, Kittie, W1585, SN, Brown, Wm. H.
BROWN, L. B. S5625, CU, 28th Inf.
BROWN, L. V. S6396, FR, 4th Ga. Cav.
BROWN, Lewis, S2237, HD, 9th Inf.
BROWN, Lila, W7642, FR, Brown, John
BROWN, Lou Ezree, W7049, D, Brown, George Tully
BROWN, Louis B. S15912, D, 44th Inf.
BROWN, Lucinda, W4268, GE, Brown, Peter
BROWN, Lucretia, W114, U, Brown, Benjamin Franklin
BROWN, Lucy, W8954, WL, Brown, R. M.
BROWN, Lucy E. W5338, WL, Brown, Ross M.
BROWN, Lucy Malissa, W9969, B, Brown, Frederick
BROWN, Malcy Jane, W5252, G, Brown, Milton
BROWN, Margaret Frances, W7265, WL, Brown, Samuel Leonidas
BROWN, Margaret Jane, W10067, MA, Brown, Robert Bruce
BROWN, Margaret V. W8189, D, Brown, Floyd Bazelle
BROWN, Martha Elizabeth, W11131, SH, Brown, Jessie Newton
BROWN, Martha J. W2267, D, Brown, Sterling C.
BROWN, Mary, W6011, SH, Brown, Andrew Coler
BROWN, Mary A. W4239, HM, Brown, Richard Wesley
BROWN, Mary A. W10158, G, Brown, Peterway
BROWN, Mary Amanda, W3474, SE, Brown, Elijah
BROWN, Mary Ann, W740, GI, Brown, Wm. Alexander
BROWN, Mary Frances, W7413, MA, Brown, John Irvin
BROWN, Mary Frances, W8438, R, Brown, Isaac
BROWN, Mary Frances, W10417, HN, Brown, Wm.
BROWN, Mary J. W1792, R, Brown, W. F. Polk
BROWN, Mary Jane, W1457, B, Brown, Robert Marion
BROWN, Mary Octavia, W5183, SH, Brown, Thomas Benton
BROWN, Matilda M. W297, RO, Brown, Thomas
BROWN, Medora Bunch, W11161, MU, Brown, Wm. Hugh, Papers found mixed with 11157 on film

Index to Tennessee Confederate Pension Applications

BROWN, Missouri, W10450, HN, Brown, Charles C.
BROWN, N. L. S14643, 20th (Russell's) Cav.
BROWN, Nancy A. W163, HU, Brown, Perry L.
BROWN, Narcissus H. W7120, SH, Brown, Wiley D.
BROWN, Parlee, W1677, W, Brown, Abner
BROWN, R. B. S6571, CH, 27th Inf.
BROWN, R. F. S10750, TR, 2nd (Robison's) Inf.
BROWN, R. F. S13268, CC, 6th Inf.
BROWN, R. L. S1171, S459, GU, 16th Inf.
BROWN, R. L. S13591, DK, 14th Inf.
BROWN, R. M. S4245, WL, 6th (Wheeler's) Cav.
BROWN, R. M. S4550, B, 45th Inf.
BROWN, R. S. S12617, S15534, H, 17th Inf.
BROWN, Rachel Adney, W2938, O, Brown, Osborn Ross
BROWN, Rebecca Ann, W3134, Brown, John
BROWN, Richard, S1989, CF, 4th (McLemore's) Cav.
BROWN, Richard W. S9691, HM, 61st Inf.
BROWN, Robert, S5725, HR, 9th Inf.
BROWN, Robert, S6059, MU, 24th Inf.
BROWN, Robert C. S3053, WA, 60th Inf.
BROWN, Rosa Caroline, W9564, G, Brown, John Thomas
BROWN, Russell, S1794, HU, 11th Inf.
BROWN, S. A. S1458, MA, 38th Inf.
BROWN, S. C. S2515, CF, 17th Inf.
BROWN, S. C. S15085, MU, 1st (Feild's) Inf.
BROWN, S. C. S15558, DI, 22nd (Barteau's) Cav.
BROWN, S. W. S9608, PU, 8th Cav.
BROWN, Sallie A. W9664, SN, Brown, H.
BROWN, Sam, S2317, CY, 20th Inf.
BROWN, Samuel, S8972, HU, 11th Inf.
BROWN, Samuel M. S4836, B, 44th Inf.
BROWN, Sarah Delaney, W1594, JE, Brown, Benjamin H.
BROWN, Sarah Dorcas, W6638, K, Brown, Jesse F.
BROWN, Sarah M. W9385, HR, Brown, Robert
BROWN, Starling Tucker, S1513, MU, 48th Inf.
BROWN, Stephen W. S14503, LI, 33rd Ala. Cav.
BROWN, Susan Fannie, W8474, HI, Brown, Delon Lemuel
BROWN, Susan Frances, W8880, GI, Brown, James Cardial
BROWN, T. B. S9922, SH, 16th Miss. Cav.

BROWN, T. J. S12113, WI, 11th (Holman's) Cav.
BROWN, T. W. S3745, T, 37th Inf.
BROWN, Thomas, S8739, F, 60th Inf.
BROWN, Thomas, S11320, PO, 1st Cav.
BROWN, Thomas C. S758, S1022, J, 4th (Murray's) Cav.
BROWN, Thomas sr. S1422, SU, 1st N.C. Cav.
BROWN, Vina, W9252, DK, Brown, Wm. Henderson
BROWN, W. G. S2238, MN, 21st Cav.
BROWN, W. H. S14089, SH, 154th Sr. Regt. Inf.
BROWN, W. L. S7680, RO, 18th Ga. Inf.
BROWN, W. M. S6367, RU, 23rd Inf.
BROWN, W. N. S12194, WE, 21st (Wilson's) Cav.
BROWN, W. R. S15494, MOO, 23rd Inf.
BROWN, Wade W. S9015, J, 4th (Murray's) Cav.
BROWN, William, S5073, HR, 14th Cav.
BROWN, William, S7953, MOO, 4th Inf.
BROWN, William, S14180, WA, 60th Inf.
BROWN, William A. S617, HW, 63rd Inf.
BROWN, William A. S14457, WL, 8th (Smith's) Cav.
BROWN, William C. S2973, CT, Barry's Co. Lt. Art.
BROWN, William C. S6653, WL, Carter's Bn. Mtd. Scouts, Cav.
BROWN, William C. S8527, WA, Winston's Battery, Art.
BROWN, William F. S11750, MA, 18th (Newsom's) Cav.
BROWN, William G. S5393, OV, 8th (Smith's) Cav.
BROWN, William H. S314, RU, 23rd Inf.
BROWN, William M. S13307, CO, 14th N.C. Bn.
BROWN, William S. S2457, LA, 9th Ky. Inf.
BROWN, Zach T. S16228, D, 8th (Smith's) Cav.
BROWNING, Abraham, S10444, UN, 2nd (Ashby's) Cav.
BROWNING, David A. S7976, WE, 16th Cav.
BROWNING, F. M. S647, RB, 30th Inf.
BROWNING, G. W. S15967, HO, Maney's Battery, Art.
BROWNING, Mary A. W2849, UN, Browning, Abraham
BROWNING, R. M. S392, HM, 7th Inf.

-43

BROWNING, Susan, W9382, HO, Browning, George
BROWNING, William Henry, S1026, WE, 15th Inf.
BROWNING, William W. S2774, GU, 47th Ala. Inf.
BROWNLEE, A. M. S13890, SH, 18th Miss. Cav.
BROWNLEE, Mary Jane, W7052, SH, Brownlee, R. A.
BROWNLEE, R. A. S15010, SH, 18th Miss. Cav.
BROWNLOW, Emily J. W1277, GI, Brownlow, John L.
BROYLES, Andrew Coffee, S14571, K, Unassigned (Nitre Bureau)
BROYLES, Charity C. W5485, SU, Broyles, Lewis A.
BROYLES, E. A. S9616, K, 5th Cav.
BROYLES, Elizabeth Jane, W847, WA, Broyles, Marion Wilhoit
BROYLES, Frances L. W395, WA, Broyles, Larance V.
BROYLES, H. S. S14659, K, 58th N.C. Inf.
BROYLES, Harvey, S581, GE, 63rd Inf.
BROYLES, I. N. S7540, R, 1st (Carter's) Cav.
BROYLES, J. S. S2276, UN, 5th Cav.
BROYLES, James M. S2944, WA, 61st Inf.
BROYLES, Jesse, S8277, GE, 61st Inf.
BROYLES, Louis S. S8680, SU, 26th Va. Inf.
BROYLES, Margaret A. W4392, K, Broyles, Edwin A.
BROYLES, Margaret Adelia, W6472, U, Broyles, John S.
BROYLES, Martha E. W2683, SU, Broyles, James
BROYLES, Mary, W5362, WA, Broyles, Harvey
BROYLES, Mary A. W2286, WH, Broyles, John Summerfield
BROYLES, Mary Jane, W1651, WA, Broyles, Isaac Newton
BROYLES, Mattie Ann, W8657, GE, Broyles, Wm. Gibson
BROYLES, O. G. S3301, WH, 1st Cav.
BROYLES, Salina, W4491, GE, Broyles, Simeon
BROYLES, Simeon, S9194, WA, 61st Inf.
BROYLES, T. . S2945, GE, 61st Inf.
BROYLES, W. G. S2546, GE, 29th Inf.
BROYLES, W. N. S10975, SU, 5th (McKenzie's) Cav.

BRUCE, A. M. S14162, CL, 2nd Cav.
BRUCE, D. H. S13400, GR, 51st Va. Inf.
BRUCE, Finis, S15996, SN, 30th Inf.
BRUCE, J. A. S10432, MOO, 44th Inf.
BRUCE, J. H. S9826, WI, 11th (Holman's) Cav.
BRUCE, J. I. S13189, HR, 9th Inf.
BRUCE, James M. S1191, SN, 18th Inf.
BRUCE, John, S2917, WL, 45th Inf.
BRUCE, Levi N. S12597, HM, 7th Cav.
BRUCE, Lucretia, W7782, CL, Bruce, A. M.
BRUCE, Margaret V. W263, D, Bruce, James Madison
BRUCE, Mary Bell, W11147, HW, Bruce, Levi N.
BRUCE, O. P. S5416, LI, 3rd Inf.
BRUCE, Sarah Jane, W1225, WL, Bruce, John J.
BRUCE, Virginia A. W10715, MS, Bruce, James Hardaman
BRUCKNER, Mary Jane, W4916, SH, Bruckner, J. T.
BRUMAGER, J. W. S15179, BE, 1st Confederate Cav.
BRUMBELOW, Mary Louisa, W10567, HR, Brumbelow, James H.
BRUMBY, E. R. S15211, H, 7th Ga. Cav.
BRUMIT, Albert H. S2382, MC, 19th Inf.
BRUMLEY, A. E. S12102, T, 15th (Stewart's) Cav.
BRUMLEY, Dave, S13309, G, 16th Ala. Inf.
BRUMLEY, Matt, S12122, SH, 15th (Stewart's) Cav.
BRUMMETT, Corinne Belle, W11030, UN, Brummett, John B.
BRUMMITT, J. H. S9148, WE, 44th N.C. Inf.
BRUMMITT, Mattie, W9470, WE, Brummitt, John Henry
BRUMMITT, Sarah Elizabeth, W2350, WE, Brumitt, David A.
BRUNK, Lessie, W10319, K, Brunk, Michael Edward
BRUNSON, Jeff, S1954, T, 21st Inf.
BRUNSON, John R. S3595, MU, 15th Cav.
BRUNSON, R. J. S16170, GI, 32nd Inf.
BRUSEN, Margaret R. W630, SH, Brusen, George Jefferson
BRUSHINGHAM, Mary, W2917, SU, Brushingham, Cornelius
BRUTON, W. H. S14958, SH, 6th Inf.
BRYAN, C. J. S1649, SH, 4th Inf.
BRYAN, Caroline M. W4744, SU, Bryan, Robert C.

BRYAN, Elizabeth, W8769, CF, Bryan, John C.
BRYAN, Elizabeth Ridley, W4612, WL, Bryan, James Nelson
BRYAN, Evaline Frances, W7465, CF, Bryan, James Lafayette
BRYAN, Henry W. S4161, SU, 20th Bn. Va. Art.
BRYAN, J. A. S10146, CF, 28th Inf.
BRYAN, J. L. S2558, CF, 28th Inf.
BRYAN, Jake, S1486, MT, 11th Inf.
BRYAN, Jennie Ducker, W9683, MA, Bryan, Finis Ewing
BRYAN, Jesse W. S4785, FR, 1st Ala. Cav.
BRYAN, John C. S11810, CF, 4th (McLemore's) Cav.
BRYAN, Joseph D. S13378, WA, 1st N.C. Cav.
BRYAN, M. W. S165, MT, 11th Inf.
BRYAN, Margaret Emma, W10987, H, Bryan, Wm. Duncan
BRYAN, N. A. S9492, O, 39th Ga. Inf.
BRYAN, R. C. S12233, SU, 48th Va. Inf.
BRYAN, R. I. S12971, MA, 6th Inf.
BRYAN, Thomas, S2060, CF, 4th Cav.
BRYANT, A. S1634, PU, 17th Inf.
BRYANT, Aleathia Melvina, W918, Bryant, Albert Danson
BRYANT, Amos, S9992, JO, 45th Va. Inf.
BRYANT, Autinette, W8230, D, Bryant, Phillip Henry
BRYANT, Brummitt, S3623, CO, 26th Inf.
BRYANT, Charles Henry, S8845, L, 15th Inf.
BRYANT, Charlotte, W3789, SQ, Bryant, John W.
BRYANT, Cynthia Rena, W8213, L, Bryant, Charles H.
BRYANT, D. F. S4226, MS, 17th Inf.
BRYANT, D. J. S1003, HI, 42nd Inf.
BRYANT, Eliza, W9739, MS, Bryant, Wm. A.
BRYANT, Elizabeth, W4697, CT, Bryant, Peter
BRYANT, Ellen, W7309, MU, Bryant, Wm. Demoss
BRYANT, Emma L. W8380, MU, Bryant, Isaiah B.
BRYANT, Frances Cordelia, W9060, MU, Bryant, Lucius Rhodes
BRYANT, Henry, C169, ME, Unassigned (Recruit Off.)
BRYANT, I. Barney, S14722, MU, 6th (Wheeler's) Cav.
BRYANT, J. F. S15676, RU, 1st (Carter's) Cav.
BRYANT, J. W. S11564, D, 7th Inf.
BRYANT, James E. S12811, G, 22nd Inf.

BRYANT, James L. S7452, MS, Forrest's Escort, Cav.
BRYANT, John, S5578, MC, 3rd Ga. Cav.
BRYANT, John C. S12618, B, Forrest's Escort, Cav.
BRYANT, John D. S11557, LI, 44th Inf.
BRYANT, John T. S7833, HU, 10th (DeMoss') Cav.
BRYANT, John W. S10898, GU, 35th Inf.
BRYANT, Julia, W10980, JO, Bryant, Amos
BRYANT, Mariah Louise, W6199, Bryant, Richard H.
BRYANT, Martha E. W10133, G, Bryant, James E.
BRYANT, Martin, S2198, MOO, 44th Inf.
BRYANT, Mary, W3881, M, Bryant, William R.
BRYANT, Mary Caroline, W6057, PU, Bryant, A.
BRYANT, Mary Jane, W1770, LI, Bryant, W. J.
BRYANT, Minervia, W5546, MT, Bryant, W. H.
BRYANT, Mozella Adams, W11073, RU, Bryant, John Frank
BRYANT, Nancy Ann, W5438, PO, Bryant, Wm. Franklin
BRYANT, Nancy Clementine, W3110, MS, Bryant, James L.
BRYANT, Nancy E. W964, HI, Bryant, David Jackson
BRYANT, P. H. S8773, HU, 10th Cav.
BRYANT, Peter, S3278, CT, 18th Inf.
BRYANT, Phoebe, W707, LI, Bryant, W. E.
BRYANT, R. A. S9788, 55th Inf.
BRYANT, R. H. S1181, Undetermined
BRYANT, S. E. S16112, HU, 10th Cav.
BRYANT, Smith M. S16235, PU, 17th Inf.
BRYANT, Thomas H. S8469, MU, 3rd (Brown's) Inf.
BRYANT, Thomas R. S4493, D, 11th Inf.
BRYANT, W. H. S12729, MT, 14th Inf.
BRYANT, W. L. S14933, SH, 4th Bn. Ark. Inf.
BRYANT, W. R. S6815, SH, 3rd (Lillard's) Mtd. Inf.
BRYANT, William, S1264, CO, 5th Cav.
BRYANT, William, S1603, DK, 23rd Inf.
BRYANT, William D. S9963, HI, 9th Bn. (Gantt's) Cav.
BRYANT, William E. S2857, LI, 44th Inf.
BRYANT, William G. S1428, WL, 20th Inf.
BRYANT, William J. S8669, LI, 44th Inf.
BRYANT, William Lane, S9915, CA, 23rd Inf.

Index to Tennessee Confederate Pension Applications

BRYANT, William R. S371, M, 28th Inf.
BRYON, Thomas M. S663, O, 47th Inf.
BRYSON, E. D. S10256, CA, 22nd (Barteau's) Cav.
BRYSON, John H. S1095, R, 1st Cav.
BRYSON, William Holmes, S13466, CA, 18th Inf.
BUCHANAN, C. M. S14569, LI, 8th Inf.
BUCHANAN, Claudius, S16462, D, 20th Inf.
BUCHANAN, Dora Duncan, W4643, D, Buchanan, Samuel Jones
BUCHANAN, E. B. S11931, WI, 4th Inf.
BUCHANAN, F. M. S14339, LK, Ham's Miss. Cav.
BUCHANAN, G. Y. S14751, BO, 58th N.C. Inf.
BUCHANAN, Henry, C114, RU, 12th Inf.
BUCHANAN, Henry, S10376, DY, 20th (Russell's) Cav.
BUCHANAN, J. P. S267, HO, 14th Inf.
BUCHANAN, J. P. S13731, LI, 41st Inf.
BUCHANAN, James A. S6876, LK, 9th Inf.
BUCHANAN, John A. S13742, L, 2nd Miss. Cav.
BUCHANAN, John M. S11609, HR, 37th Va. Inf.
BUCHANAN, John P. S16481, RU, 4th Ala. Cav.
BUCHANAN, Kate McClelland, W5342, LI, Buchanan, Felix G.
BUCHANAN, L. W. S2057, LA, 35th Ala. Inf.
BUCHANAN, Louisa, W7419, O, Buchanan, James A.
BUCHANAN, Margaret, W404, O, Buchanan, John H.
BUCHANAN, Mary Eliza, W8780, LI, Buchanan, John D.
BUCHANAN, Mattie F. W69, WI, Buchanan, John P.
BUCHANAN, Mattie S. W4941, MS, Buchanan, Wm. A.
BUCHANAN, Moses R. S11229, D, 21st (Carter's) Cav.
BUCHANAN, Roxie, W9850, B, Buchanan, Wm. Fletcher
BUCHANAN, Sallie E. W3200, D, Buchanan, George R.
BUCHANAN, Sallie Jane, W10081, O, Buchanan, James M.
BUCHANAN, Samuel Jones, S8881, D, 20th Inf.
BUCHANAN, Sarah Caroline, W7865, LI, Buchanan, Charles McKinney
BUCHANAN, Sarah Richard, W4149, HR, Buchanan, John Matthew
BUCHANAN, Susie, W7170, HO, Buchanan, John Poleman
BUCHANAN, Thelia Spragins, W6134, SH, Buchanan, Joseph Williams
BUCHANAN, Thomas E. S10560, G, 19th & 20th (Consolidated) Inf.
BUCHANAN, W. G. S10130, CT, 29th Inf.
BUCK, Elias J. S9361, SN, 9th (Bennett's) Cav.
BUCK, J. A. S740, OV, 28th Inf.
BUCK, Jesse H. S11454, PU, 8th Cav.
BUCK, Martha E. W2397, SN, Buck, M. A.
BUCK, Nancy Ann, W9418, PU, Buck, Isaac Newton
BUCKALOO, George Washington, S7691, DY, 1st (Turney's) Inf.
BUCKALOO, Mary A. W6590, DY, Buckaloo, George W.
BUCKINGHAM, Jennie Alsbrooks, W10392, ST, Buckingham, Peter Terry
BUCKLES, C. R. S7174, SU, 61st Mtd. Inf.
BUCKLES, John M. S5591, SU, 63rd Inf.
BUCKLES, Robert, S5627, SU, Unassigned (Nitre & Mining Bureau)
BUCKLES, Sally N. W2457, SU, Buckles, Cam
BUCKLEY, John H. S102, SH, 51st Inf.
BUCKLEY, John sr. S6725, WE, 46th Inf.
BUCKLEY, Mary Lutisha, W1526, CH, Buckley, Nathaniel Terry
BUCKLEY, Thomas A. S3427, K, 1st (Carter's) Cav.
BUCKNER, E. D. S9044, MU, 9th Cav.
BUCKNER, J. S. S15111, D, 27th Miss. Inf.
BUCKNER, Jacob B. S13135, OV, 25th Inf.
BUCKNER, John A. S7082, L, 30th Va. Inf.
BUCKNER, Lit, W8991, OV, Buckner, Jacob
BUCKNER, Martha Jane, W7650, CF, Buckner, Garrett D.
BUCKNER, Nannie, W10263, FR, Buckner, William W.
BUCKNER, Sarah Ann, W1583, FR, Buckner, Richmon T.
BUCKNER, Stacey Emily, W7322, MU, Buckner, Elisha Dodson
BUCKNER, Susan, W6922, G, Buckner, Greene Sophrona
BUCKNER, William Henry, S8947, L, 64th N.C. Inf.
BUCKWELL, Margaret Bell, W17, K, Buckwell, George
BUCY, John H. S12446, HN, 33rd Inf.

Index to Tennessee Confederate Pension Applications

BUDDE, John, S11042, DE, 27th Inf.
BUDDE, Martha E. W9496, DE, Budde, John
BUFFALOE, J. W. S1770, HY, Phillip's Co. Lt. Art.
BUFFALOE, Turner, S12067, HY, 9th Inf.
BUFFET, Augustus G. S13588, K, 37th Inf.
BUFFETT, Sarah Lamar, W9251, K, Buffett, A. G.
BUFFORD, Martha Jane, W8775, W6862, ST, Bufford, John Harvey
BUFORD, E. G. S15242, D, 3rd (Clack's) Inf.
BUFORD, Emma Sidney, W3277, MA, Buford, Whittaker John
BUFORD, Florence, W3859, D, Buford, John T.
BUFORD, John C. S1907, DI, 3rd Ala. Inf.
BUFORD, Spencer, S5434, CC, 9th Inf.
BUFORD, William, C18, WI, 9th Inf.
BUGG, Annie E. W7340, GI, Bugg, Henry Martin
BUGG, Martha Ann Margaret, W2885, D, Bugg, James Green
BUGG, Mary Cox, W486, D, Bugg, Samuel
BUGG, R. W. S11701, TR, 2nd (Robison's) Inf.
BUGG, Robert M. S8752, GI, 23rd Tex. Cav.
BULL, Joseph, S3920, 60th Inf., Applied from Coles Co. IL
BULLARD, Benjamin, S13050, W, 23rd Inf.
BULLEN, Ben, S12451, RO, 63rd Inf.
BULLEN, Nancy ann, W9457, GE, Bullen, Samuel Dudley
BULLEN, Samuel D. S3479, GE, 12th Cav.
BULLEN, Vina J. W2261, GR, Bullen, Wm.
BULLEN, W. S. S6051, W, 16th Inf.
BULLEN, William, S4949, S3217, GR, 37th Inf.
BULLINER, H. C. S10423, CH, 52nd Inf.
BULLINGTON, D. A. S15429, 19th & 20th (Consolidated) Cav.
BULLINGTON, J. P. S482, GE, 13th S.C. Inf.
BULLINGTON, James, S13448, CO, 6th S.C. Cav.
BULLINGTON, John, S7500, D, 16th Inf.
BULLINGTON, R. E. S16518, SH, 18th Miss. Cav.
BULLINGTON, Sarah Mariah, W6, D, Bullington, Wm.
BULLOCK, A. H. S2314, WA, 63rd Inf.
BULLOCK, Frances Dowell, W10040, PU, Bullock, Frank M.
BULLOCK, Isabella, W919, WI, Bullock, John H.
BULLOCK, Mary Ella, W5494, MU, Bullock, Robt. Sloane

BUMARGNER, A. L. S7493, CO, 29th N.C. Inf.
BUMGARNER, Charity, W7273, CO, Bumgarner, Anthony L.
BUMPASS, Milton, S15473, CC, Forrest's Escort, Cav.
BUMPASS, Sarah E. W2282, W8868, D, Bumpass, James A.
BUMPASS, W. P. S10859, HN, 20th (Russell's) Cav.
BUMPASS, William J. S3436, MA, 6th Inf.
BUNCH, B. M. S3850, GI, 32nd Inf.
BUNCH, Benjamin F. S8399, H, 1st Cav.
BUNCH, David, S7530, GR, 1st (Carter's) Cav.
BUNCH, F. M. S12501, GI, 3rd (Clack's) Inf.
BUNCH, G. B. S3379, D, 48th Inf.
BUNCH, Martin, S11441, GR, 29th Inf.
BUNCH, Mary E. W564, P, Bunch, George Dabney
BUNCH, Mary Jane, W18, GI, Bunch, Enoch Houston
BUNCH, Mary Jones, W4497, D, Bunch, George Burton
BUNCH, Rebecca, W10930, GR, Bunch, David
BUNCH, Robert, S13497, HW, 25th N.C. Inf.
BUNDREN, Angeline, W5095, JE, Bundren, J. B.
BUNDREN, J. B. S10775, JE, 26th Inf.
BUNDY, Penelipy, W1398, TR, Bundy, William
BUNN, J. H. S11900, CC, 1st Hvy. Art.
BUNN, James H. S15782, L, 2nd Bn. Ark. Hvy. Art.
BUNN, William, S4665, SU, 48th Va. Inf.
BUNTIN, Emma, W2558, MA, Buntin, Asa
BUNTING, Pauline, W5616, SH, Bunting, Edward Morgan
BUNTLEY, Andrew J. S2723, LI, 1st (Turney's) Inf.
BUNTON, Mariah Elizabeth, W5041, WE, Bunton, Isaac
BURCH, Clementine, W5311, CL, Burch, Wiley Patton
BURCH, G. W. S3603, CA, 3rd Hvy. Art.
BURCH, H. A. S6584, HU, 11th Bn. (Holman's) Cav.
BURCH, J. M. S4881, R, 35th Inf.
BURCH, James A. S1092, BL, 2nd Cav.
BURCH, Julia H. W264, HI, Burch, James Monroe
BURCH, Mary J. W5310, SH, Burch, James Edward
BURCHAM, John D. S9566, SH, 37th Va. Cav.

-47

BURCHARD, Zianna, W3790, HI, Burchard, Abraham Volentine
BURCHELL, John G. S1349, GR, 37th Inf.
BURCHETT, George B. S4634, CL, 1st (Carter's) Cav.
BURCHETT, John, S11952, S13759, WA, 33rd Va. Inf.
BURCHETT, Larkin F. S13233, CL, 1st (Carter's) Cav.
BURCHETT, Mary Adalaid, W3167, CL, Burchett, James F.
BURCHETT, Melvina, W3485, CY, Burchett, John
BURCHETT, W. C. S2223, OV, 25th Inf.
BURCHFIELD, James A. S2016, HW, 17th Bn. Cav.
BURCHFIELD, Joseph, S2946, CL, 2nd (Ashby's) Cav.
BURCHFIELD, N. S5417, PO, 5th (DeWitt's) Cav.
BURCHFIELD, Phebe A. W828, CL, Burchfield, James
BURCHFIELD, Willis, S1186, R, 43rd Inf.
BURDETT, Eliza Hume, W10633, LO, Burdett, George Madre
BURDETT, L. J. S13517, WI, 13th Ala. Inf.
BURDETT, S. M. S15903, WI, 13th Ala. Inf.
BURDETT, Sarah Stewart, W11107, D, Burdett, S. M.
BURDETTE, R. C. S14711, WE, 20th (Russell's) Cav.
BUREN, Julia C. W7204, HW, Buren, Henry S.
BURGE, Westley, S929, GI, 53rd Inf.
BURGESS, J. M. S7135, PU, 8th Cav.
BURGESS, J. M. S11638, TR, 17th Inf.
BURGESS, Joseph, S11218, J, 17th Inf.
BURGESS, Margaret King, W3551, GI, Burgess, J. C. J.
BURGESS, Nancy, W9730, J, Burgess, Joseph
BURGESS, Rebecca Ann, W6660, PU, Burgess, James Marion
BURGETT, John, S16596, MS, 51st Ga. Inf.
BURGUR, John, S11170, MO, 59th Inf.
BURK, John, S4267, WA, 5th Cav.
BURK, Josephine, W35, WL, Burk, Josiah Newton
BURK, M. A. S1089, SN, 7th Inf.
BURK, Mary E. W246, WI, Burk, John A.
BURK, Richard, S10221, CL, 1st (Carter's) Cav.
BURK, Sarah Ann Elizabeth, W2912, WI, Burk, Wm. Caster

BURK, Sarah Elizabeth, W5405, CL, Burk, Richard
BURK, Thomas H. S8344, WI, 24th Inf.
BURK, William H. S15913, D, 8th (Dibrell's) Cav.
BURK, William M. S12626, Morton's Co. Lt. Art.
BURKE, Hannah, W4484, RB, Burke, Mike
BURKE, J. L. S4795, WL, 4th (McLemore's) Cav.
BURKE, Martha Ann, W2482, D, Burke, Nathan C.
BURKE, Martha J. W3931, WI, Burke, Thomas H.
BURKE, Martin, S8, D, Major Stuart Horse Art. Va.
BURKE, Mary Elizabeth, W6210, WL, Burke, James Lewis
BURKE, Michael, S8949, RB, 8th Ky. Inf.
BURKE, Nancy Glovina, W9933, WE, Burke, William Jasper
BURKE, S. V. S6844, CC, 20th Inf.
BURKE, V. R. S6786, 15th Inf.
BURKE, W. J. S16219, WE, 12th Ky. Cav.
BURKE, Walter, S135, O, 22nd Inf.
BURKETT, Alvin, S10488, HE, 5th Inf.
BURKETT, Sarah, W1656, G, Burkett, Wm. Henry
BURKHART, Louisa Jane, W7818, H, Burkhart, Wm. Carroll
BURKHART, W. C. S7783, H, 35th Inf.
BURKHARTZ, Mary Jane, W2981, D, Burkhartz, Joseph
BURKHEAD, E. H. S7197, CH, 21st Cav.
BURKHEAD, Nannie, W7793, CH, Burkhead, Eli Harrison
BURKS, C. L. S5196, FR, 17th Inf.
BURKS, D. M. S5036, CF, 44th Inf.
BURKS, Eliza F. W8399, OV, Burks, Robt. Lee
BURKS, R. L. S14614, OV, 4th (McLemore's) Cav.
BURKS, S. B. S14316, HD, 34th Inf.
BURLISON, D. A. S14254, HY, 48th (Nixon's) Inf.
BURLISON, Elizabeth P. W8271, HY, Burlison, D. A.
BURLISON, Mary Elizabeth, W8930, HY, Burlison, David Anderson
BURLISON, William, S5435, MO, 3rd Inf.
BURNETT, A. G. S11575, D, 11th (Gordon's) Cav.

BURNETT, Cordelia A. W5284, K, Burnett, Wm.
BURNETT, Decatur, S6372, SU, 63rd Inf.
BURNETT, Eliza, W1652, SU, Burnett, Cyrus
BURNETT, Emma C. W6045, O, Burnett, Newland S.
BURNETT, George W. S12256, K, Burrough's Co. Lt. Art.
BURNETT, J. K. P. S14176, UN, 1st (Carter's) Cav.
BURNETT, James H. S15493, D, 20th Inf.
BURNETT, James M. S6130, 22nd Inf.
BURNETT, John, S2624, UN, 1st Cav.
BURNETT, John A. S5599, SU, 50th Va. Inf.
BURNETT, Justina, W10274, D, Burnett, James Richardson
BURNETT, L. B. S10730, MR, 7th Ala. Inf.
BURNETT, Lou J. W4023, SU, Burnett, Franklin Marion
BURNETT, M. B. S15715, SU, Burrough's Co. Lt. Art.
BURNETT, N. S. S10192, O, 52nd Inf.
BURNETT, Relda Jane, W2924, UN, Burnett, Martin
BURNETT, Sarah Jane, W8574, SU, Burnett, M. B.
BURNETT, Simon, S6205, SU, 63rd Inf.
BURNETT, T. J. S6259, D, 1st Cav.
BURNETT, W. B. S14977, HR, Polk's Battery, Lt. Art.
BURNETT, William, S5844, UN, 2nd (Ashby's) Cav.
BURNETTE, Louisa Angel. Carter, W9295, UN, Burnette, James Knox Polk
BURNEY, J. D. S12658, DI, 49th Inf.
BURNEY, W. L. S10867, RB, 30th Inf.
BURNLEY, Melvina, W5985, SN, Burnley, W. D.
BURNLEY, William Daniel, S7184, SN, 7th Ky. Cav.
BURNS, A. P. S10200, MN, 21st Inf.
BURNS, Becky E. A. W1420, LA, Burns, James W.
BURNS, Brunnette, W6647, SN, Burns, Wm. Harrison
BURNS, Dave, C123, WY, 8th Cav.
BURNS, Eliza Ann, W2071, HE, Burns, Wm. M.
BURNS, Elizabeth, W6619, SN, Burns, James
BURNS, H. C. S5767, 22nd Inf.
BURNS, J. B. S7078, WY, 19th (Biffle's) Cav.
BURNS, J. W. S1247, D, 23rd Inf.

BURNS, James M. S10647, HI, 48th Ala. Inf.
BURNS, M. V. S8331, ME, 16th Cav.
BURNS, Mary Frances, W6378, HI, Burns, James M.
BURNS, Nancy, W4147, H, Burns, George Henderson
BURNS, Pattie E. W3089, LE, Burns, Jacob Biffle
BURNS, Thomas Yeatman, S558, SM, 30th Inf.
BURNS, W. H. S11777, GU, Sterling's Co. Lt. Art.
BURNS, William, S10767, PO, 39th Ga. Inf.
BURNS, William R. S6145, MO, 62nd Inf.
BURRELL, Frances C. W3534, D, Burrell, Henry
BURRESS, Jesse, S15557, O, 31st Inf.
BURREY, Prudie F. W8150, SN, Burrey, W. L.
BURRIS, Dollie C. W6092, MO, Burris, James M.
BURRIS, James M. S12836, MO, 1st N.C. Cav.
BURRIS, John M. S5841, J, 8th Inf.
BURRIS, Thomas D. S145, J, 8th (Dibrell's) Cav.
BURRIS, margaret, W633, MC, Burris, John Tipton
BURROUGHS, A. H. S14114, SU, 11th Va. Inf.
BURROUGHS, John S. S2177, J, 8th Cav.
BURROUGHS, Zach, S3801, GE, 44th Inf.
BURROW, A. G. S2811, SH, 3rd Forrest's Cav.
BURROW, A. H. S14397, MN, 21st Inf.
BURROW, Eliza, W6926, MN, Burrow, Harrison Andrew
BURROW, Finis J. S3313, SH, 4th Inf.
BURROW, J. A. S16636, M, 24th Inf.
BURROW, Mary Adeline, W6835, SH, Burrow, Finis Jefferson
BURROW, N. C. S13105, Undetermined
BURROW, Newton L. S8201, CC, 22nd Inf.
BURROWS, Mary Katherine, W1264, RU, Burrows, T. W.
BURROWS, Matilda a. W2641, K, Burrows, Benjamin F.
BURRUM, Charles R. S28, MOO, 37th Inf.
BURRUS, Joseph S. S2782, M, 8th (Smith's) Cav.
BURRUS, Margaret Louverne, W3394, HR, Burrus, Joseph Marion
BURRUS, Mattie E. W2853, D, Burrus, Lucien B.
BURT, Annie, W6576, CF, Burt, John Gaston
BURT, Charles F. S2559, MOO, 17th Inf.
BURT, J. G. S11733, CF, 7th Inf.

Index to Tennessee Confederate Pension Applications

BURT, J. Green, S8109, GI, 8th Inf.
BURT, J. L. S3907, B, 3rd Ark. Battery
BURT, John, S4168, CF, 1st (Turney's) Inf.
BURT, Millie E. W6769, GI, Burt, J. Green
BURT, Vesty Mary, W2280, SH, Burt, Andrew Dosey
BURT, W. W. S6902, FR, 4th Inf.
BURTON, Amelia A. W1050, F, Burton, Henry Lyne
BURTON, D. W. S2745, B, 18th Inf.
BURTON, Eliza Ann. W11135, K, Burton, Henry
BURTON, Ermine, W2026, O, Burton, James Monroe
BURTON, Jackson, S680, SM, 28th Inf.
BURTON, James A. S950, RU, 10th Inf.
BURTON, Lucy W. W7702, F, Burton, James W.
BURTON, R. A. S15387, HY, 5th Inf.
BURTON, Sarah E. W1642, HU, Burton, Willis Jasper
BURTON, Susan Jane, W9991, WL, Burton, George M.
BURTON, Tom, S1436, RU, 45th Inf.
BUSBEE, Jacob L. S2372, LI, 22nd Ala. Inf.
BUSBY, David, S4227, HR, 6th Miss. Cav.
BUSBY, Philip R. S12871, D, 29th Miss. Inf.
BUSBY, W. H. S1137, HO, 50th Inf.
BUSH, Green, S4075, SM, 4th Cav.
BUSH, I. F. S8842, D, Undetermined
BUSH, L. D. S3233, CA, 18th Inf.
BUSH, Mattie jane, W3065, SM, Bush, Green
BUSH, R. Y. S13406, MT, Hvy. Art.
BUSH, William, S11395, WY, 19th (Biffle's) Cav.
BUSHONG, Mary Catherine, W1506, SU, Bushong, David
BUSHONG, Mary Ellen, W2918, SU, Bushong, David Erwin
BUSICK, Eliza, W5212, HW, Busick, James B.
BUSICK, J. B. S13447, HW, 45th N.C. Inf.
BUSSELL, C. C. S6912, DE, 52nd Inf.
BUSSELL, C. C. H. S14575, K, 5th (McKenzie's) Cav.
BUSSELL, Charlotte Cathrine, W5910, HW, Bussell, John L.
BUSSELL, Ella E. W3539, HI, Bussell, Absalom T.
BUSSELL, John L. S808, HW, 60th Inf.
BUTCHER, Jackson, S5882, CL, 21st N.C. State Troops

BUTCHER, Nancy, W7506, CL, Butcher, Jackson
BUTLER, A. S. S8371, CH, 34th Inf.
BUTLER, Ada Glass, W9821, L, Butler, W. P. H.
BUTLER, Anna Montgomery, W3564, GI, Butler, John Denny
BUTLER, B. R. S9536, G, 20th Cav.
BUTLER, Bailey, S14582, S1582, CY, 8th Inf.
BUTLER, D. D. S8171, SM, 44th Inf., Also see entry for Demarcus D. Butler
BUTLER, Delia Taylor, W9249, GI, Butler, Samuel Warren
BUTLER, Demarcus D. S633, SM, 44th Inf., Also see entry for D. D. Butler
BUTLER, Elizabeth, W541, OV, Butler, Lecaroy Bonapart
BUTLER, Elizabeth, W665, PU, Butler, Wm. Little
BUTLER, G. C. S8143, CH, 14th (Neely's) Cav.
BUTLER, George W. S75, RU, 8th Ga. Inf.
BUTLER, Henry C. S16520, CY, 2nd Ky. Cav.
BUTLER, J. B. S470, MR, 8th Ga. Inf.
BUTLER, J. B. S14044, HU, 11th Inf.
BUTLER, J. H. S12218, SH, 2nd Miss. Inf.
BUTLER, J. P. S3953, SU, 63rd Inf.
BUTLER, J. W. S9548, CH, 31st Inf.
BUTLER, James A. S4314, MA, 51st Inf.
BUTLER, James K. S766, M, undetermined
BUTLER, Jerome, S765, M, 44th Inf.
BUTLER, John, S3009, DI, 1st La. Cav.
BUTLER, John David Calvin, S16620, GI, 44th Inf.
BUTLER, Joseph N. S7169, SU, 12th Bn. Cav.
BUTLER, L. B. S4185, OV, 4th (Murray's) Cav.
BUTLER, L. J. S8372, CH, 16th Inf.
BUTLER, Louisa Elvira, W7364, CT, Butler, James N.
BUTLER, M. D. F. S4796, RO, Thomas' Legion, N.C.
BUTLER, M. J. S2409, DY, 15th Inf.
BUTLER, Martha Ann, W3854, GI, Butler, George Henderson
BUTLER, Mary Creek, W9698, MR, Butler, Thomas J.
BUTLER, Minnie Bell, W10402, DY, Butler, James
BUTLER, Mittie Edward, W7683, GI, Butler, Wm. Thomas
BUTLER, P. H. S11341, G, 51st Inf.
BUTLER, Sebrena, W5765, DI, Butler, John

Index to Tennessee Confederate Pension Applications

BUTLER, Susan Ellen, W6398, WA, Butler, Joel S.
BUTLER, T. H. S10304, MC, 5th (McKenzie's) Cav.
BUTLER, W. G. S4770, GE, 63rd Va. Inf.
BUTLER, W. R. S1583, SH, 7th Cav.
BUTLER, W. S. S14056, MS, 41st Inf.
BUTLER, W. Solomon, S7278, W, 16th Inf.
BUTLER, Wade H. S831, J, 28th Inf.
BUTLER, William E. S10458, MA, Lynch's Co. Lt. Art.
BUTNER, Marian V. W6132, CF, Butner, Thomas Malone
BUTNER, Thomas M. S7185, CF, 44th Inf.
BUTRAM, Elizabeth, W884, G, Butram, Simeon
BUTRAM, Lucinda B. W6043, WH, Butram, John
BUTT, Carrie Baskin, W7915, SH, Butt, Benj. Watkins Leigh
BUTTER, Martha Alzird, W5159, G, Butter, Philop Harrison
BUTTERY, J. M. S2758, WI, Baxter's Co. Lt. Art.
BUTTLER, Thomas J. S15768, MR, 17th Inf.
BUTTON, Charles H. S13898, D, Forrest's Regt. Cav.
BUTTRAM, Cynthia P. W1403, R, Buttram, James Calloway
BUTTREY, Eliza Jane, W2609, DI, Buttrey, Wm. George Demarks
BUTTREY, Tennessee, W7477, WI, Buttrey, James Monroe
BUTTRY, J. F. S4964, WI, Baxter's Battery Lt. Art.
BUTTS, Elmira O. W9250, MU, Butts, M. M.
BUTTS, Melmon Marion, S12261, U, Maury's Lt. Art.
BUTTS, T. W. S12169, L, 35th Inf.
BYARS, D. W. S3352, W, 16th Inf.
BYARS, H. D. S13859, HN, 9th Inf.
BYARS, Senith, W3428, DK, Byars, Perry G.
BYARS, Thomas, S10908, D, 8th (Smith's) Cav.
BYARS, Z. P. S14361, HN, 4th Inf.
BYBEE, L. S. S711, OV, 44th Inf.
BYBEE, N. C. S712, J, 8th Cav.
BYBEE, P. J. W4543, J, Bybee, N. C.
BYBEE, Sarah Elizabeth, W2628, J, Bybee, L. S.
BYERLY, Kittie A. W298, BL, Byerly, John W.
BYERS, David, S10438, JO, 53rd N.C. Inf.
BYERS, Eleanor Barbara, W2718, MT, Byers, George Newton

BYERS, Loudelia, W4316, OV, Byers, Wm. Harrison
BYERS, Louise, W2361, MU, Byers, Isaac Newton
BYERS, W. H. S7687, OV, 25th Inf.
BYERS, Watson C. S10033, PU, 3rd Tex. Cav.
BYINGTON, J. B. S2183, HW, 64th Va. Inf.
BYINGTON, Mary Emiline, W4576, HW, Byington, Isaac
BYNUM, E. J. S12919, W, 8th (Smith's) Cav.
BYNUM, J. T. S13757, LK, 12th Inf.
BYNUM, John H. S9664, WE, 10th Cav.
BYNUM, Leonora Anna, W4002, SH, Bynum, Britton Slith
BYNUM, Sarah Roxie, W7998, W, Bynum, E. Z.
BYNUM, W. G. S10141, O, 4th Inf.
BYRAM, A. C. S3666, SN, 30th Inf.
BYRD, D. T. S5663, TR, 9th (Bennett's) Cav.
BYRD, F. M. S16300, WI, 35th Ala. Inf.
BYRD, J. J. S5233, P, 54th Ala. Inf.
BYRD, James, S2319, BR, 62nd Inf.
BYRD, Jane, W6963, TR, Byrd, Dabney Thomas
BYRD, John M. S12762, WI, Undetermined
BYRD, Martha Loveina, W6093, O, Byrd, G. W.
BYRD, Nannie F. W11042, SU, Byrd, Ezekiel Kunsey
BYRD, Robert F. S13095, T, 12th Inf.
BYRD, Sarah Ophilia, W5975, T, Byrd, Robert F.
BYRD, W. M. S3991, SH, 16th Inf.
BYRD, W. P. S5664, LA, 48th (Nixon's) Inf.
BYRD, William, S4315, HD, Eldridge's Battery, Art.
BYRD, William B. S11464, WI, 40th Inf.
BYRD, William J. S9367, WH, 16th N.C. Inf.
BYRN, Bettie, W4055, SN, Byrn, James D.
BYRN, Sarah E. W588, RU, Byrn, James Harvey
BYRNE, G. D. S12248, PU, 17th Inf.
BYRNE, J. P. S15490, D, 17th Inf.
BYRNS, J. W. S13049, SN, 22nd (Barteau's) Cav.
BYROM, Catherine, W7234, MOO, Byrom, James Wilson
BYROM, George W. S10043, FR, 34th Inf.
BYROM, James W. S1899, FR, 1st (Turney's) Inf.
BYROM, Jennie, W6023, FR, Byrom, Joe

Index to Tennessee Confederate Pension Applications

BYROM, Jo, S2327, B, 1st (Turney's) Inf. See also entry for Joe Byron
BYROM, Tranquilla, W2534, CF, Byrom, Asbury M.
BYRON, Joe, S668, B, 1st (Turney's) Inf. See also entry for Jo Byrom
BYRUM, Catherine, W1523, GU, Byrum, Jesse
BYRUM, J. T. S8099, MA, 51st Inf.
BYRUM, James M. S3569, MOO, 37th Inf.
BYRUM, Lydia G. W7542, CA, Byrum, John Thomas
BYRUM, S. Alexander, S13481, H, 43rd Inf.
BYRUM, Wade, S9791, HY, 14th Inf.
CABLE, C. B. S6458, SU, 1st Ky. Inf.
CABLE, G. W. S9251, JO, 37th N.C. Inf.
CABLE, Martha E. W4430, SU, Cable, C. B.
CABLE, Mary Jane, W6148, K, Cable, L. H.
CABLE, W. D. S10305, LO, 14th Inf.
CABLER, James F. S4999, RU, 45th Inf.
CADE, G. W. S15971, RO, 10th Cav.
CADE, J. W. S15982, ME, 26th Inf.
CAGE, Lucy Blackwell, W10514, MT, Cage, James Edward
CAGE, Sallie Douglas, W4452, D, Cage, Jessee
CAGLE, Charles, S14355, HD, 1st Conf. Inf.
CAGLE, Easter Caroline, W10020, HD, Cagle, Charlie
CAGLE, Henry C. S6935, DY, 27th Inf.
CAGLE, Isaac, S7578, SU, 63rd Inf.
CAGLE, J. H. S11304, BE, 1st Cav.
CAGLE, Martha A. W2659, MO, Cagle, Marton
CAGLE, N. C. S14375, CH, 3rd Ga. Cav.
CAGLE, Robert V. S13199, LA, White's Ala. Art.
CAGLE, Sarah, W6370, SU, Cagle, Isaac
CAGLE, Sarah, W8414, LE, Cagle, Charles
CAGLE, Susan Catherine, W9960, MO, Cagle, Elijah
CAIN, A. M. S3908, CE, 18th Inf.
CAIN, Cornelia Ann, W7656, D, Cain, Thomas Marton
CAIN, G. L. S14669, G, 7th Ky. Inf.
CAIN, J. B. S4035, CE, 42nd Inf.
CAIN, John, S2298, WA, 60th Inf.
CAIN, Reuben, S1539, D, 3rd Inf.
CAIN, Tennessee, W6163, D, Cain, Reuben J.
CAIN, Thomas Jefferson, S15393, HO, 14th Cav.
CAIN, Victoria, W1826, D, Cain, Andrew Newton
CAIN, William Jesse, S16493, D, 2nd Inf.
CALAHAN, J. K. S10641, MS, 32nd Inf.

CALAWAY, Giles M. S9966, CT, 26th N.C. Inf.
CALAWAY, Hiram, S9208, CT, 26th N.C. Inf.
CALBERT, Ella Foster, W11064, LA, Calbert, Robert William
CALDWELL, A. W. S11259, O, 27th Inf.
CALDWELL, Albert Andrew, S9856, B, 1st (Carter's) Cav.
CALDWELL, Ann Roberts, W8393, WI, Caldwell, Joseph A.
CALDWELL, Claudie, W5188, B, Caldwell, Edward
CALDWELL, Hardy, S11230, SN, 20th Inf.
CALDWELL, James Ephram, S14177, O, 20h Cav.
CALDWELL, James P. S8637, MU, 3rd Inf.
CALDWELL, James W. S7846, Morton's Co. Lt. Art.
CALDWELL, Joe E. S3487, S8690, O, 33rd Inf.
CALDWELL, John, C83, D, 1st Cav.
CALDWELL, Joseph A. S4068, WI, Thomas' Legion, N.C.
CALDWELL, Kate Livingston, W4056, HM, Caldwell, Edward
CALDWELL, Malinda Jane, W2151, Caldwell, James Wallace
CALDWELL, Marie Elizabeth, W9809, DY, Caldwell, James Ephrim
CALDWELL, Martha E. W5679, SH, Caldwell, Henry L.
CALDWELL, Mary, W6016, MN, Caldwell, Carroll
CALDWELL, Mary Ann, W4345, O, Caldwell, Alexander W.
CALDWELL, Mary Caroline, W801, H, Caldwell, Isaac Anderson
CALDWELL, Mary Jane, W3830, O, Caldwell, James Madison
CALDWELL, NAncy, W1163, SN, Caldwell, Hardy
CALDWELL, Nancy Jane, W7618, DI, Caldwell, Oscar Dunreth
CALDWELL, Nancy Roena, W2072, FR, Caldwell, Wm. Alexander
CALDWELL, O. D. S4344, DI, 49th Inf.
CALDWELL, R. R. S15178, D, 12th Cav.
CALDWELL, S. A. S9656, PO, 59th Inf.
CALDWELL, S. J. S12421, D, 64th Ga. Inf.
CALDWELL, Sallie M. W7725, MU, Caldwell, John W.
CALDWELL, Susie, W8190, JE, Caldwell, John M.

Index to Tennessee Confederate Pension Applications

CALDWELL, William Ashley, S11985, MU, 3rd (Clack's) Inf.
CALDWELL, William D. S10871, MC, 59th Inf.
CALE, John, S12620, J, 17th Inf.
CALE, Mat, C181, G, Capt. Ross's Cav.
CALFEE, Isaac, S4246, CO, 31st Inf.
CALHOUN, A. F. S6169, SH, 33rd Inf.
CALHOUN, Anna r. W6533, SH, Calhoun, Andrew F.
CALHOUN, C. B. S14778, HN, 46th Inf.
CALHOUN, Clara J. W4980, SH, Calhoun, Wm. Semms
CALHOUN, Dicey M. W2866, O, Calhoun, George Washington
CALHOUN, J. S1140, RB, 14th Inf.
CALHOUN, James, S10804, CT, 58th N.C. Inf.
CALHOUN, John W. S15161, O, 22nd (Barteau's) Cav.
CALHOUN, Missouri G. W6371, RB, Calhoun, John C.
CALHOUN, S. H. S4535, S5079, SH, 9th Inf.
CALHOUN, Samuel L. S2179, WL, 7th Inf.
CALL, D. S12415, HN, 46th Inf.
CALL, Henry C. S626, MR, 4th (McLemore's) Cav.
CALL, James H. S8562, CF, 44th Inf.
CALLAHAM, A. H. S5247, W, 24th Inf.
CALLAHAN, D. K. S14820, MA, 8th Va. Cav.
CALLAHAN, Jennie, W10069, W, Callahan, Acholiese Herndon
CALLAHAN, Lydia M. W8138, U, Callahan, Levi
CALLAHAN, Margaret L. W8359, U, Callahan, Levi
CALLAHAN, Mary Ella, W7922, MA, Callahan, David Kelley
CALLAHAN, William, S6302, U, 64th Inf.
CALLICOTT, J. W. S13117, HN, 46th Inf.
CALLOWAY, J. W. S1138, CO, 16th N.C. Inf.
CALLOWAY, William R. S11141, HN, 5th Inf.
CALLUP, Mary Elizabeth, W8303, W8876, WA, Callup, Wm. Henry
CALTON, Winfield, S9096, HW, 48th Va. Inf.
CALVARD, Wiley M. S9106, BL, 8th (Dibrell's) Cav.
CALVERT, Joseph W. S11125, LA, 54th Inf.
CALVERT, L. N. S990, S1598, MU, 3rd (Clack's) Inf.
CALVERT, Nancy Emma, W8240, W9657, LA, Calvert, Joseph Warren

CALVERT, Narcissa E. W1537, MU, Calvert, Louis Nelson
CALVERT, Robert W. S11126, LA, 54th Inf., One of his papers with previous #11125
CALVERT, T. J. S11093, GI, 1st Cav.
CALWELL, Hardy, sr. S48.5, SN, 1st Cav.
CAMBRON, Martha H. W6739, LI, Cambron, Elijah J.
CAMBRON, W. J. S3730, LI, 5th Ala. Bn. Inf.
CAMERON, Allen McD. S1380, HY, 6th Inf.
CAMERON, E. M. S15034, HY, 6th Inf.
CAMERON, James A. S13211, SH, Rice's Battery, Lt. Art.
CAMERON, Margaret, W1630, CO, Cameron, Thomas
CAMERON, Maria O. W4829, SH, Cameron, James Alexander
CAMERON, Thomas, S1955, CO, 31st Inf.
CAMERON, William L. S7922, K, "Young Guards of Memphis" & C.S.A. Navy
CAMERON, Z. J. S13620, WH, 1st Bn. (Colm's) Inf.
CAMP, A. A. S4316, FR, 32nd Inf.
CAMP, B. F. S14946, K, 2nd S.C. Cav.
CAMP, Elizabeth C. W5979, D, Camp, Miles Newton
CAMP, G. C. S15176, BE, 5th Inf.
CAMP, George A. S10371, D, 2nd (Robison's) Inf.
CAMP, Rebecca, W1442, CF, Camp, Anderson A.
CAMPBELL, A. J. S3613, K, 34th Inf.
CAMPBELL, Alexander, S10803, H, 37th N.C. Inf.
CAMPBELL, Amanda c. W10061, WE, Campbell, Mark Patterson
CAMPBELL, Amos A. S6952, H, 20th N.C. Inf.
CAMPBELL, Ann E. W4796, D, Campbell, W. J.
CAMPBELL, Annie Dixon, W4793, MA, Campbell, Alexander Wm.
CAMPBELL, Benjamin D. S4108, FR, 7th Ark. Inf.
CAMPBELL, Callie H. W11134, SH, Campbell, Wm. Joseph
CAMPBELL, Caroline V. W5480, SH, Campbell, Joseph Borum
CAMPBELL, Carrie, W5689, D, Campbell, James
CAMPBELL, Claiborne, S14145, B, 17th Inf.

-53

Index to Tennessee Confederate Pension Applications

CAMPBELL, Cornelia, W2839, HR, Campbell, Garner Duncan
CAMPBELL, Elizabeth, W2528, LI, Campbell, William G.
CAMPBELL, Elizabeth, W5536, GE, Campbell, James
CAMPBELL, Elizabeth Claiborne, W629, CA, Campbell, W. B. L.
CAMPBELL, Ella Vanleeor, W9861, G, Campbell, James Samuel
CAMPBELL, Ezekiel D. S851, WI, 48th Inf.
CAMPBELL, G. C. S15813, D, 7th Inf.
CAMPBELL, G. D. S6529, HR, 9th Inf.
CAMPBELL, G. R. S11630, CF, 16th Inf.
CAMPBELL, G. W. S7531, CF, 1st (Turney's) Inf.
CAMPBELL, George W. S10583, MU, 11th (Holman's) Cav.
CAMPBELL, Green B. S7501, D, 41st Inf.
CAMPBELL, Helen, W164, D, Campbell, Thomas Taylor
CAMPBELL, Henry, S8817, CA, 4th Cav.
CAMPBELL, I. D. S2099, PI, 8th Cav.
CAMPBELL, J. B. S11000, SH, 51st Inf.
CAMPBELL, J. D. S5248, W, 4th Cav.
CAMPBELL, J. M. S7146, LE, 1st Cav.
CAMPBELL, J. P. S15780, GI, 53rd Inf.
CAMPBELL, J. W. C. S1392, WA, 21st Va. Inf.
CAMPBELL, James, S13572, D, 1st Inf.
CAMPBELL, James, S15888, D, 13th (Gore's) Cav.
CAMPBELL, James M. S3310, SU, 63rd Inf.
CAMPBELL, James N. S8519, FR, 37th Inf.
CAMPBELL, Joe, S16667, K, 1st Inf.
CAMPBELL, John, S14683, LK, 16th Inf.
CAMPBELL, John E. S1648, LE, 10th Cav.
CAMPBELL, Joseph B. S3777, WA, 60th Mtd. Inf.
CAMPBELL, Lucy Ann, W337, B, Campbell, James Harvey
CAMPBELL, Malacia, S9611, R, 1st (Carter's) Cav.
CAMPBELL, Mary C. W7959, HY, Campbell, Wm. Riley
CAMPBELL, Mary E. W1573, SU, Campbell, Thos. J.
CAMPBELL, Mary Lynch, W2511, K, Campbell, A.
CAMPBELL, Mildred, W7287, WE, Campbell, Thomas
CAMPBELL, Robert, S8901, CA, 8th (Smith's) Cav.
CAMPBELL, Sallie, W10517, CT, Campbell, Wm.
CAMPBELL, Samuel, S853, WE, Undetermined
CAMPBELL, Sarah E. W4763, Campbell, Wm.
CAMPBELL, Tabitha Ann, W8347, WI, Campbell, Ezekiel D.
CAMPBELL, Thomas, S1642, MA, 19th Cav.
CAMPBELL, Thomas, S10933, WE, 15th Inf.
CAMPBELL, Thomas I. S5963, RO, 59th Inf.
CAMPBELL, Thomas J. S1276, SU, 1st Inf.
CAMPBELL, Thomas M. S7778, D, 38th Inf.
CAMPBELL, W. S10034, 15th Inf.
CAMPBELL, W. A. S16128, GI, 3rd (Clack's) Inf.
CAMPBELL, W. B. L. S1270, CF, 16th Inf.
CAMPBELL, W. C. S4676, RU, 16th Inf.
CAMPBELL, William, S66, WH, 3rd Inf. & 62nd Inf.
CAMPBELL, William, S11550, WA, 63rd Inf.
CAMPBELL, William, S13096, CT, Marshall's Co. Art.
CAMPBELL, William F. S16583, SU, 72nd Va. Inf.
CAMPBELL, William R. S384, HY, 8th Ark. Inf.
CAMPBELL, William T. S9690, MA, 7th Cav.
CAMPER, Andrew J. S4863, HM, 60th Inf.
CAMPER, David, S8750, WA, Jeffres' Battery Lt. Art.
CAMPER, Ollie Elizabeth, W5912, SH, Camper, Andrew Jackson
CAMPER, Samuel P. S2797, SU, 48th Va. Inf.
CAMPFIELD, S. J. S11933, LA, 48th (Nixon's) Inf.
CAMPSAY, J. B. S7502, MU, 24th Inf.
CAMPTON, Ella W. W5398, HY, Campton, Wm. Henry
CANADA, James C. S2884, LK, 3rd (Lillard's) Mtd. Inf.
CANADA, Ophelia A. W1734, G, Canada, James Patrick
CANADAS, James P. S7520, G, 12th Cav.
CANADY, James W. S2691, WI, 9th Cav.
CANDLE, Jesse B. S16076, O, 27th Inf.
CANEER, Joseph A. S6787, S5377, MS, 8th Inf.
CANEER, W. L. S14024, MS, 8th Inf.
CANIPE, J. W. S2766, SH, 56th Inf.
CANIPE, Mary Watts, W3643, SH, Canipe, John Wm.
CANNON, A. H. S14514, K, Brown's Co. Home Guards

CANNON, Benjamin J. S1993, OV, 8th (Dibrell's) Cav.
CANNON, Bessie Rembert, W9917, SH, Cannon, Henry E.
CANNON, Charles, C217, SH, 154th Sr. Regt. Inf.
CANNON, Emaline, W5043, OV, Cannon, W. J.
CANNON, G. B. S3847, SN, 22nd (Barteau's) Cav.
CANNON, H. P. S11849, G, 9th Ga. Inf.
CANNON, James, S7584, OV, 8th (Dibrell's) Cav.
CANNON, Jennie McEwen, W10684, WI, Cannon, Newton
CANNON, Josephine Taylor, W5574, K, Cannon, W. A.
CANNON, L. A. W4669, SN, Cannon, G. B.
CANNON, L. W. W1202, MO, Cannon, John O.
CANNON, M. V. S15464, J, Shaw's Bn. Cav.
CANNON, Mary C. W5406, G, Cannon, Henry P.
CANNON, Nancy, W3902, F, Cannon, Stephen
CANNON, W. A. S14037, K, 59th Inf.
CANNON, W. J. S1853, OV, 25th Inf.
CANNON, William H. S8419, D, 49th Inf.
CANNON, William N. S3680, T, 1st Cav.
CANSLER, Hugh Lawson, C122, K, 43rd Inf.
CANTER, James H. S2152, WA, 63rd Va. Inf.
CANTRELL, A. P. S13239, DK, 23rd Inf.
CANTRELL, Aaron, S6994, DK, 1st Bn. (Colm's) Inf.
CANTRELL, Alexander, S3718, SE, 1st N.C. Cav.
CANTRELL, C. C. S11941, WH, 21st (Carter's) Cav.
CANTRELL, Cleve A. S16522, W, 16th Inf.
CANTRELL, D. W. S5042, W, 16th Inf.
CANTRELL, Elizabeth, W2761, W, Cantrell, Peter
CANTRELL, Florence Hart, W5273, SN, Cantrell, John M.
CANTRELL, George W. S2088, O, 49th Inf.
CANTRELL, Hiram P. S533, S6995, DK, 23rd Inf.
CANTRELL, Hosel H. S2224, DK, 39th Ga. Inf.
CANTRELL, Isaac, S6673, DK, 16th Inf.
CANTRELL, J. C. S13504, H, 4th Ga. Inf.
CANTRELL, J. H. S767, RB, 18th Inf.
CANTRELL, J. J. S3712, WE, 7th Cav.
CANTRELL, Jane L. W2295, SE, Cantrell, Phydilla P.
CANTRELL, John, S2178, DK, 16th Inf.

CANTRELL, Joseph, S1592, DK, 8th Ga. Bn. Inf.
CANTRELL, Julia Ann, W8020, DK, Cantrell, Joseph
CANTRELL, L. R. S10798, W, 11th Ga. Cav.
CANTRELL, Lawson, S4845, DK, 16th Inf.
CANTRELL, Martha Ann, W6866, HD, Cantrell, James K. Polk
CANTRELL, Martha J. W1641, DK, Cantrell, Wm. Carrell
CANTRELL, Martha Jane, W3332, WL, Cantrell, Wm. Carrol
CANTRELL, Mary Ellen, W5869, W, Cantrell, Lewis K.
CANTRELL, Mary J. W4546, DK, Cantrell, C. A.
CANTRELL, Mary Jane, W5870, MU, Cantrell, Tillman Dodson
CANTRELL, Mary Jane, W10742, DK, Cantrell, P. F.
CANTRELL, Nancy Ellen, W658, WE, Cantrell, W. H.
CANTRELL, P. F. S16509, W, 22nd Bn. Inf.
CANTRELL, Perry G. S1635, DK, 16th Inf.
CANTRELL, Sarah, W9163, DK, Cantrell, Aaron
CANTRELL, Stephen O. S7593, SE, 7th Inf.
CANTRELL, Sue, W1783, W, Cantrell, Samuel
CANTRELL, T. D. S9737, MU, 9th Ky. Cav.
CANTRELL, Watson, S6168, DK, 16th Inf.
CANTRELL, William Carroll, S9688, CA, 16th Inf.
CAPELL, James Thomas, S13545, DY, 31st Inf.
CAPERTON, Thomas E. S14416, WI, 11th (Holman's) Cav.
CAPLENOR, Lina, W9570, WL, Caplenor, W. C.
CAPLENOR, Mary Isabel, W9569, WL, Caplenor, John Wilson
CAPP, Margaret, W5543, GE, Capp, John
CAPPS, Bettie, W2287, D, Capps, B. F.
CAPPS, E. F. S9449, D, 6th (Wheeler's) Cav.
CAPPS, J. R. S1266, 31st Miss. Inf.
CAPPS, John A. S2273, UN, 1st Cav.
CAPPS, Ollie Abaline, W3586, D, Capps, Ephraim Foster
CARATHERS, David, S11249, WA, 29th Inf.
CARBARY, John, S5208, SU, 60th Inf.
CARBARY, Sarah E. W5058, SU, Carbary, John
CARDEN, C. C. S3681, SU, 19th Inf.
CARDEN, Elbert, S910, SU, 63rd Inf.

CARDEN, Mattie S. W8125, H, Carden, W. C.
CARDEN, Polly, W634, MC, Carden, Wm. Jones
CARDEN, R. C. S8029, CF, 16th Inf.
CARDEN, Samuel R. S9699, JE, 2nd (Ashby's) Cav.
CARDEN, W. C. S15164, H, Ga. Cadets
CARDIN, G. W. S3758, MO, 3rd Inf.
CARDIN, Larkin, S2184, GI, 3rd Inf.
CARDIN, Mary, W451, MO, Cardin, G. W.
CARDING, J. B. S6178, DI, 49th Inf.
CARDWELL, J. T. S5418, CF, 1st (Feild's) Inf.
CARDWELL, James, S11239, W, 11th (Holman's) Cav.
CARDWELL, James A. S483, SM, 1st Inf.
CARDWELL, James R. S4217, GR, 26th Inf.
CARDWELL, John B. S12619, SM, 9th (Ward's) Cav.
CARDWELL, Joseph L. S14179, WL, 24th Inf.
CARDWELL, L. P. S2458, S1678, DY, 18th (Newsom's) Cav.
CARDWELL, Lucy F. W429, SM, Cardwell, James A.
CARDWELL, Malissie, W4278, GR, Cardwell, James R.
CARDWELL, Margie Eugenia, W2249, SM, Cardwell, Samuel Sullivan
CARDWELL, T. D. S2434, DY, 18th (Newsom's) Cav.
CARDWELL, Theresa Elvira, W3855, FR, Cardwell, Joseph Taylor
CARDWELL, Virginia, W1733, WE, Cardwell, John Westley
CAREY, B. B. S11287, D, 30th Inf.
CAREY, Ellen Rhea, W10463, SH, Carey, Hunsdon
CAREY, Laura Dickerson, W8874, D, Carey, Benjamin Brister
CARGILE, Eliza, W7851, CF, Cargile, Henry K.
CARGILE, Henry K. S6943, CF, 24th Miss. Inf.
CARLEN, Mary, W2051, HR, Carlen, H. W.
CARLETON, Peggie Elliott, W11078, FR, Carleton, John H.
CARLIN, William B. S2299, PU, 4th Cav.
CARLISLE, Bettie, W806, D, Carlisle, Samuel H.
CARLISLE, Ellis, S5436, S7063, J, 8th Cav.
CARLISLE, Newton, S8144, J, 8th (Dibrell's) Cav.
CARLTON, A. M. S12143, HY, 7th Cav.
CARLTON, Adam, S4466, SU, 19th Inf.
CARLTON, D. C. S1560, B, 24th Inf.

CARLTON, Elias H. S14294, FR, 4th Inf.
CARLTON, Martha Angeline, W2120, RU, Carlton, Daniel Carral
CARLTON, Thomas H. S5830, RU, 12th Inf.
CARLTON, William H. H. S12537, WE, 12th Inf.
CARMACK, C. C. S16037, SU, 10th Ky. Cav.
CARMACK, Evan, S2888, CL, 1st (Carter's) Cav.
CARMACK, G. W. S5942, WA, 8th (Smith's) Cav.
CARMACK, G. W. S13784, O, 9th Inf.
CARMACK, J. D. S13733, OV, Shaw's Bn. Cav.
CARMACK, Jesse W. S6882, OV, 8th Inf.
CARMACK, Jim C. S13732, OV, Shaw's Bn. Cav.
CARMACK, Lucy M. W8107, OV, Carmack, Jesse W.
CARMACK, Martha Jane, W6863, O, Carmack, G. W.
CARMACK, Nannie Elizabeth, W2771, FR, Carmack, Samuel Wm.
CARMACK, Robert R. S6345, WA, 12th Bn. (Day's) Cav.
CARMACK, T. B. S7719, HW, 63rd Inf.
CARMACK, W. H. S14753, LA, 37th Va. Inf.
CARMAN, Edward R. S15619, D, 2nd (Robison's) Inf.
CARMAN, Emma, W8897, TR, Carman, Thomas
CARMAN, John, S10642, SN, 9th Cav.
CARMAN, T. G. S10481, TR, 8th Inf.
CARMAN, W. B. S10104, M, 7th Bn. Cav.
CARMIACAEL, J. H. S8769, SH, 42nd Miss. Inf.
CARMICHAEL, Edna Davis, W10969, HM, Davis, Thos.
CARMICHAEL, Jacob G. S9104, MC, 2nd (Ashby's) Cav.
CARMICHAEL, Martha P. W4024, WI, Carmichael, James H.
CARMICHAEL, Mary Selina, W7573, D, Carmichael, George Washington
CARMICHAEL, Priscilla, W6880, SH, Carmichael, John H.
CARNAHAN, J. C. S15834, RU, 8th (Smith's) Cav.
CARNAHAN, James M. S14247, CA, 8th (Smith's) Cav.
CARNAHAN, Mary Frances, W8241, RU, Carnahan, James Calvin

CARNATHAN, M. J. W6136, D, Carnathan, Wiley J.
CARNELL, J. N. S7564, L, 16th (Logwood's) Cav.
CARNES, Anna Lord, W9010, K, Carnes, John Minton
CARNES, John W. S10725, SQ, 14th Va. Cav.
CARNEY, Alfred, S1356, H, 19th Inf.
CARNEY, Daniel J. S4927, D, 28th Inf.
CARNEY, Joshua, S8387, TR, 9th Cav.
CARNEY, Lavina, W4897, CE, Carney, Wm. M.
CARNEY, Leacy, W5551, TR, Carney, Joshua
CARNEY, Martha Ann, W2750, D, Carney, Elijia Wilson
CARNEY, Mary Jane, W299, D, Carney, Joseph E.
CARNEY, N. B. S5980, MN, 50th Inf.
CARNEY, Rebecca Jane, W10732, BE, Carney, Norfleet Bryan
CARNEY, Romalus S. S324, S1608, HY, 154th Sr. Regt. Inf.
CARNEY, Sidney E. W229, WL, Carney, Daniel Johnson
CAROTHERS, H. R. S14076, HI, 42nd Inf.
CAROTHERS, Josephine, W5740, WL, Carothers, Thomas J.
CAROTHERS, Mary Porter, W7015, WI, Carothers, R. B.
CAROWAY, Albert S. S2583, WL, 38th Inf.
CARPENTER, Emma Anderson, W5524, SH, Carpenter, A. S.
CARPENTER, George W. S4591, CL, 63rd Inf.
CARPENTER, J. P. S15622, SH, 2nd Ark. Mtd. Rifles
CARPENTER, John W. S3150, LI, 44th Inf.
CARPENTER, Joshua, S6887, T, 2nd Ark.
CARPENTER, Malissa, W5529, CL, Carpenter, G. W.
CARPENTER, Nice Bell, W7919, MS, Carpenter, Thomas Benjamin
CARPENTER, Tom B. S1956, MU, 3rd Ky. Inf.
CARPENTER, William H. S14953, HA, 63rd Inf.
CARR, Benjamin, S15458, OV, 25th Inf.
CARR, E. W. S471, J, 4th Cav.
CARR, Elijah W. S909, J, 4th & 25th Inf.
CARR, Elizabeth Arthula, W4087, TR, Carr, Daniel Anderson
CARR, Elizabeth F. W19, PU, Carr, Elijah Watson
CARR, Elkana, S5249, CT, 634d Inf.
CARR, F. M. S11008, OV, 25th Inf.
CARR, Hannah Frances, W4135, RB, Carr, John
CARR, J. J. S3094, WY, 27th Ala. Inf.
CARR, J. T. S2336, OV, 28th Inf.
CARR, James, S9235, SU, 59th Inf.
CARR, James, S12255, TR, 24th Inf.
CARR, Josh H. S10899, SH, 29th Miss. Inf.
CARR, Martha, W6890, OV, Carr, Francis Marion
CARR, Mary Eliza, W2305, PU, Carr, Zebedee
CARR, Mary Matilda, W10996, WE, Carr, Thomas Jefferson
CARR, Nancy Emily, W1259, OV, Carr, John Tipton
CARR, Pattie Ann, W1015, TR, Carr, John Doak
CARR, Sarah J. W521, WL, Carr, John O.
CARR, Susan, W7290, WA, Carr, James
CARR, Tennessee C. W5767, DI, Carr, T. J.
CARR, Thomas J. S2496, DI, Baxter's Co. Lt. Art.
CARR, William, S1984, SU, 61st Mtd. Inf.
CARR, William, S2068, WH, 1st Bn. (Colm's) Inf.
CARR, Zebedee, S9420, PU, 8th (Dibrell's) Cav.
CARRALL, Nettie, W4684, HU, Carrall, James E.
CARRAWAY, E. W. S11873, HY, 13th Inf.
CARRAWAY, Sarah B. W8092, F, Carraway, E. W.
CARRELL, Absalom P. S11532, MN, 13th Ga. Inf.
CARRICK, Thomas F. S9803, GU, 21st (Wilson's) Cav.
CARRIER, C. N. S13847, SU, Unassigned (Chopped Wood)
CARRIER, E. A. S4854, SU, 63rd Inf. See also Eldridge Carrier
CARRIER, Elbert, S6607, SU, Tenn. Reserves
CARRIER, Eldridge, S5640, SU, 63rd Inf. See also E. A. Carrier
CARRIER, Elizabeth E. W7450, SU, Carrier, Eldridge
CARRIER, J. A. S5377, S6787, MS, 8th Inf.
CARRIER, J. C. S14998, SU, Unassigned (Iron Worker)
CARRIER, J. P. S2969, SU, 61st Inf.
CARRIER, James R. S4382, SU, 21st Va. Cav.
CARRIER, John M. S2947, K, 4th (McLemore's) Cav.
CARRIER, Leroy, S2948, SU, 63rd Inf.

CARRIER, Martha Jane, W9127, SU, Carrier, James Parrot
CARRIER, Nancy J. W2907, SU, Carrier, Leroy
CARRIER, Sarah, W6607, SU, Carrier, James R.
CARRIER, W. D. S14995, SU, Chumbley's Home Guards
CARRIER, W. H. S8594, WA, Finney's Nitre and Mining Bureau
CARRIER, W. W. S998, SU, 63rd Inf.
CARRIGAN, H. M. S15405, D, 6th (Wheeler's) Cav.
CARRIGAN, Kate, W5445, D, Carrigan, W. H.
CARRIGAN, W. H. S393, D, 8th Inf.
CARRIGER, Britton F. S124, LI, 8th Inf.
CARRIGER, James A. S16015, HM, 59th Mtd. Inf.
CARRIGER, Polly Burrow, W9407, MOO, Carriger, Britton F.
CARROLL, Ben, S15235, MU, 3rd Confederate Cav.
CARROLL, C. H. S10483, O, 22nd (Barteau's) Cav.
CARROLL, Charles, S2750, MN, 25th Inf.
CARROLL, Clementine Hodge, W7804, CF, Carroll, Henry
CARROLL, E. C. S10785, O, 9th Inf.
CARROLL, Eliza Jane, W4222, L, Carroll, James Alexander
CARROLL, George Ann, W2186, HE, Carroll, Joseph
CARROLL, George W. S8283, MC, 2nd Cav.
CARROLL, Henry, S5364, CF, 23rd Bn. Inf.
CARROLL, J. C. S4752, CH, 10th Cav.
CARROLL, J. S. S7156, CH, 21st Tex. Cav.
CARROLL, James Jackson, S968, HI, 11th Inf.
CARROLL, John, S2345, LE, 48th Inf.
CARROLL, John H. S7155, CH, 51st Inf.
CARROLL, Josephine, W10872, SH, Carroll, Addison R.
CARROLL, Levi, S4367, RB, 43rd Inf.
CARROLL, Louisa Jane, W6094, CH, Carroll, John H.
CARROLL, Lucinda Susan, W1631, FR, Carroll, John W.
CARROLL, Mandy, W7760, MN, Carroll, Charles
CARROLL, Marcus C. S3451, RO, 4th (McLemore's) Cav.
CARROLL, Margie, W2834, HW, Carroll, James Madison

CARROLL, Martha, W1160, CL, Carroll, Wm. T.
CARROLL, Martha A. W452, CH, Carroll, Thomas Benton
CARROLL, Martha Amanda, W8008, DI, Carroll, James Jackson
CARROLL, Martha R. W3635, G, Carroll, W. T.
CARROLL, Mary Catherine, W1667, LE, Carroll, John
CARROLL, Mary J. W1085, FR, Carroll, Zachariah N.
CARROLL, Mattie, W8673, SH, Carroll, John William
CARROLL, Mattison, S683, C, 19th Inf.
CARROLL, Octavia, W5960, HD, Carroll, Samuel Addison
CARROLL, Patrick, S8477, MU, 21st Ala. Inf.
CARROLL, Sabelia Frances, W3039, CH, Carroll, James Stirling
CARROLL, W. C. S10692, O, 13th Ark. Hvy Art.
CARROLL, W. T. S2718, CL, 1st Cav.
CARROLL, William T. S8254, G, 20th Cav.
CARROLL, Z. N. S4834, FR, 44th Inf.
CARROWAY, A. G. S13960, SH, 1st Bn. (Cox's) Inf.
CARRUTH, Elizabeth Victoria, W8655, H, Carruth, Wm. H.
CARRUTHERS, Barbara Elizabeth, W3205, SH, Carruthers, Nathan S.
CARRUTHERS, Linnie Lou, W10252, SH, Carruthers, Thomas Neely
CARSON, Benjamin F. S7406, D, 1st (Feild's) Inf.
CARSON, Benjamin F. S14674, WA, 61st Inf.
CARSON, D. W. S11926, D, 30th Inf.
CARSON, J. M. S2606, LE, 24th Inf.
CARSON, James L. S1511, TR, 30th Inf.
CARSON, John L. S791, S4186, CY, 28th Inf.
CARSON, Joseph, S897, HW, Undetermined
CARSON, Julia Ann, W8460, WA, Carson, John Ross
CARSON, Margaret Jane, W10416, SU, Carson, James Campbell
CARSON, Mary Jane, W4582, CY, Carson, John L.
CARSON, Mollie E. W7257, WA, Carson, Benjamin F.
CARSON, Sallie S. W1802, WI, Carson, Benjamin Franklin
CARSON, W. O. S15151, SH, 13th Miss. Cav.

Index to Tennessee Confederate Pension Applications

CARSON, W. S. S6293, CH, 6th Inf.
CARTER, Alfred B. S2446, SH, 6th Va. Cav.
CARTER, Almarinda, W6282, WH, Carter, Wm. H.
CARTER, B. H. S10540, HM, 37th Inf.
CARTER, Bettie, W6285, Carter, John
CARTER, Bettie, W7713, SN, Carter, W. N.
CARTER, Bob, C101, F, Regiment not given
CARTER, Borous, S13375, F, 13th Inf.
CARTER, Chesley C. S11484, MO, 59th Inf.
CARTER, Coly Elizabeth, W1345, HM, Carter, Enoch Henry
CARTER, Cynthia, W1782, GI, Carter, James Thompson
CARTER, D. G. S5471, RU, 1st (Feild's) Inf.
CARTER, Frances Lucinda, W6672, WA, Carter, P. J.
CARTER, Fred T. S2771, CL, 25th Va. Cav.
CARTER, H. C. S3125, MN, 16th Ala. Inf.
CARTER, H. M. S2929, S3488, B, 41st Inf.
CARTER, Isaac, S11642, SH, 27th Ala. Cav.
CARTER, J. A. S10203, D, 4th (McLemore's) Cav.
CARTER, J. L. S6194, WY, 23rd Inf.
CARTER, J. T. S3489, CF, 4th (McLemore's) Cav.
CARTER, J. W. S3455, SN, 20th Inf.
CARTER, James, S540, J, 28th Inf.
CARTER, James W. S13133, O, 22nd (Barteau's) Cav.
CARTER, John, S7790, RU, 45th Inf.
CARTER, John, S9953, 22nd Inf.
CARTER, John Edward, S9149, HY, 24th Inf.
CARTER, John Hughes, S11250, D, Wheeler's Scouts, Cav.
CARTER, Joseph, S4278, SN, 9th (Ward's) Cav.
CARTER, Martha, W2671, MA, Carter, Marcus DeLafayette
CARTER, Martha Ellen, W10856, WA, Carter, James Henry
CARTER, Martha Jane, W2158, O, Carter, Edward Polk
CARTER, Mary, W10066, SH, Carter, Thomas Jefferson
CARTER, Mary A. W3955, HW, Carter, Robert W.
CARTER, Mary E. W2262, MN, Carter, Henry C.
CARTER, Mary E. W8130, GI, Carter, W. E.
CARTER, Mary Elizabeth, W5727, B, Carter, Henry Marion
CARTER, Mary Jane, W9778, O, Carter, Ezekiel Columbus
CARTER, Narcissa, W7274, CF, Carter, S. A.
CARTER, Parilee, W3304, J, Carter, Thackston
CARTER, Philip J. S11029, WA, 42nd Va. Inf.
CARTER, R. L. S13198, SH, 24th Inf.
CARTER, R. S. S700, J, Undetermined
CARTER, R. S. S976, S1288, J, 17th Inf.
CARTER, Rebecca Ellen, W9591, OV, Carter, Zibe
CARTER, S. A. S4253, PU, 1st Bn. Inf.
CARTER, S. A. S7817, B, 4th (McLemore's) Cav.
CARTER, Sallie A. W7527, G, Carter, Thomas B.
CARTER, Thaxton, S729, J, 25th Inf.
CARTER, Thomas, S1497, 25th Inf.
CARTER, Thomas J. S15757, SH, 2nd Regt. Miss. Partisan Rangers
CARTER, Thomas T. S10572, GI, 3rd (Clack's) Inf.
CARTER, Tom B. S837, MA, Undetermined
CARTER, Virginia Anne, W2016, K, Carter, John Davis
CARTER, W. N. S11430, SN, 7th Cav.
CARTER, W. W. S764, CO, 2nd Cav.
CARTER, William, S9354, RU, 45th Inf.
CARTER, William B. S669, M, 44th Inf.
CARTER, William B. S11917, LI, 8th Inf.
CARTER, William Egbert, S10693, GI, 20th Cav.
CARTER, William H. S1570, 22nd Inf.
CARTER, William H. S11043, WH, 60th N.C. Inf.
CARTER, William Riley, S14300, T, 2nd Miss. Inf.
CARTER, Z. B. S7049, CY, 8th (Dibrell's) Cav.
CARTER, Z. P. S14280, HW, 7th Bn. Ky. Cav.
CARTHEL, Elizabeth Ivie, W9840, G, Carthel, John T.
CARTMELL, Emaline J. W2142, WL, Cartmell, H. M.
CARTMELL, James Martin, S6651, MA, 6th Inf.
CARTMELL, Julia Ann, W1512, SH, Cartmell, Robert D.
CARTWELL, J. H. S444, MA, 6th Inf.
CARTWRIGHT, Mary H. W5124, SU, Cartwright, S. G.
CARTWRIGHT, W. T. S7993, LI, 23rd Bn. Inf.
CARTY, Henry K. S816, LI, 8th Inf.

CARUTH, Isaac A. S6684, WL, 9th (Ward's) Cav.
CARUTHERS, Amanda Lewis, W8727, W7256, HR, Caruthers, Wm. A.
CARUTHERS, B. F. S2356, PU, 28th Inf.
CARUTHERS, John, C241, WL, 48th Inf.
CARUTHERS, William Adolphus, S13169, HR, Polk's Battery, Lt. Art.
CARVAN, J. J. S7834, CH, 14th (Ward's) Bn. Miss. Lt. Art.
CARVAN, Sarah E. W3399, CH, Carvan, Jordan Jones
CARVER, A. J. S8121, WL, 45th Inf.
CARVER, Pleasant P. S11770, FR, Huggin's Co. Lt. Art.
CARVER, Sarah Elizabeth, W4431, RB, Carver, John Alven
CARY, David, S8222, HE, 16th Cav.
CASE, John L. S1013, K, 29th N.C. Inf.
CASE, Sarah Ann, W4942, K, Case, John L.
CASEY, Dennis, S1344, CO, 1st S.C. Art.
CASEY, Elizabeth, See Elizabeth Scott
CASEY, Frances Rebecca, W9646, SH, Casey, Wm. Pryor
CASEY, Isaac N. S6346, SH, 13th Inf.
CASEY, J. C. S14745, CC, 7th Cav.
CASEY, John Daniel Randall, S8984, HR, 14th Cav.
CASEY, Martha Jane, W11061, HR, Casey, J. D. R.
CASEY, William, S15662, CT, 59th Inf.
CASH, Catherine, W91, CF, Cash, James
CASH, Charity, W4607, LE, Cash, W. M.
CASH, James W. S13667, WH, 8th (Dibrell's) Cav.
CASH, John, S3946, SU, Sullivan Co. Reserves, Local Defense
CASH, Lizzie E. W2067, OV, Cash, James M.
CASH, Mary, W10451, WH, Cash, Wm. Simpson
CASH, Mary Alice, W8963, HI, Cash, Thomas Woodson
CASH, Sarah Elizabeth, W8288, SH, Cash, Green Benjamin
CASH, Shadrick, S3039, A, 29th N.C. Inf.
CASH, Thomas W. S13302, HI, 3rd Inf.
CASH, William, S10477, JO, 11th (Holman's) Cav.
CASH, William M. S8417, LE, 10th Cav.
CASH, William Simpson, S1508, WH, 25th Inf.
CASHION, Arch, S6704, LI, 1st (Turney's) Inf.

CASHION, Elizabeth, W6103, LI, Cashion, Arch.
CASHION, Elizabeth Monday, W6707, LI, Cashion, Wm. Henry
CASHION, Franklin, S1225, CO, 56th N.C. Inf.
CASHION, James, S3063, MOO, 8th Inf.
CASHION, Newton G. S4222, K, 8th (Smith's) Cav.
CASHION, Sarah Louisa, W121, K, Cashion, Newton Gillespie
CASHION, W. H. S2406, LI, 1st (Turney's) Inf.
CASHION, William A. S2243, MOO, 1st (Turney's) Inf.
CASHON, Ava W. W5321, O, Cashon, R. W.
CASKEY, Missouri E. W3948, MU, Caskey, Wm. S.
CASKEY, R. H. S15050, MU, 6th (Wheeler's) Cav.
CASKEY, Sarah Ann, W4047, GI, Caskey, Samuel Willerson
CASON, D. D. S13182, MS, 11th (Holman's) Cav.
CASON, Frazier, C173, CH, 31st Inf.
CASON, W. C. S13116, MA, 18th (Newsom's) Cav.
CASS, James Moses, S16606, WH, Edmundson's Bn. Cav.
CASSELL, John M. S9751, HM, 51st Va. Inf.
CASSON, S. E. S12873, H, 34th Va. Bn. Cav.
CASTEEL, Joseph, S9875, MC, 16th Cav.
CASTEEL, Ruth, W5179, MC, Casteel, Joseph
CASTEEL, Surbina J. W300, SU, Casteel, J. G.
CASTELLOW, J. M. S15263, RB, 6th (Wheeler's) Cav.
CASTELLOW, James W. S11231, HY, 7th Cav.
CASTELMAN, Charles C. S9072, D, 30th Inf.
CASTELMAN, G. S6342, MS, 7th Inf.
CASTELMAN, George W. S12079, CC, 20th Inf.
CASTELMAN, Jacob M. S2253, W, 16th Inf.
CASTELMAN, James D. S1390, D, 20th Inf.
CASTELMAN, John Fielder, S1812, CC, 20th Inf.
CASTILE, J. M. S4462, BE, 55th Inf.
CASTILE, P. A. S15292, ST, 9th Inf.
CASTLEBERRY, Frances Jane, W1499, FR, Castleberry, James Marion
CASTLEBERRY, Rebecca Almida, W1500, FR, Castleberry, Timothy
CASTLEBERRY, T. M. S2357, FR, 32nd Inf.
CASTLEMAN, Lavinia E. W3759, D, Castleman, Gad

Index to Tennessee Confederate Pension Applications

CASTLEMAN, Mary Leila, W9153, D, Castleman, Charles Newton
CASTLEMAN, Nancy Cathron, W8859, W1136, RU, Castleman, James Hardin
CATE, A. W. S9085, MC, Unassigned (Worked in pork factory)
CATE, Elisha P. S3362, JE, Marshall's Co. Lt. Art.
CATE, Eliza F. W10006, W8302, G, Cate, Atlas Jones
CATE, Ephraim B. S8052, CO, Marshall's Co. Lt. Art.
CATE, Grunbury, S12365, H, Undetermined
CATE, James Polk, S14356, HN, 21st (Wilson's) Cav.
CATE, Martha A. W283, HN, Cate, James Franklin
CATE, R. E. S8347, MC, 43rd Inf.
CATE, Rebeker A. W3704, HN, Cate, Wm. D.
CATE, Silas, S14108, HN, 20th (Russell's) Cav.
CATE, Tennessee, W2630, H, Cate, Henry
CATE, William, S14393, HN, 20th (Russell's) Cav.
CATES, C. T. S6361, MOO, 37th Inf.
CATES, Dixon, S5344, L, 18th Inf.
CATES, Eliza F. W8302, W10006, G, Cates, Atlas
CATES, Elzira Jane, W27, B, Cates, Wm. Carroll
CATES, Isaah, S4417, HU, Undetermined
CATES, J. W. S16365, O, 20th Inf.
CATES, Jesse Calvin, S15326, G, 20th (Russell's) Cav.
CATES, John, S945, RO, 26th Inf.
CATES, N. C. S274, B, 41st Inf.
CATES, Sarah James, W1029, B, Cates, Charles Timothy
CATHCART, Sarah Adelaide, W3802, GI, Cathcart, Wm. Hugh
CATHCART, William H. S3314, GI, 1st Cav., Filed under Cothcutt
CATHEY, E. N. S5359, DI, 11th Inf.
CATHEY, Fanny M. W7768, MU, Cathey, Jethro B.
CATHEY, Harriet, W117, RU, Cathey, James Newton
CATHEY, J. S. S7445, L, 18th Miss. Cav.
CATHEY, M. M. S916, HO, 14th Inf.
CATHEY, M. V. S7837, MS, Courtney's Bn. Ala. Art.
CATHEY, Mary Jane, W8872, DI, Cathey, Elias Newton
CATHEY, Rovania Jane, W8771, MS, Cathey, Thos. J.
CATHEY, Sallie A. W10374, ST, Cathey, Henry L.
CATHEY, T. J. S12588, MS, 11th (Holman's) Cav.
CATLETT, Tom, C189, MO, Regiment not given
CATO, Helen E. W301, SM, Cato, Wm. H.
CATON, George T. S10965, HN, 7th (Duckworth's) Cav.
CATON, Sarah Ann, W3051, WE, Caton, James
CATRON, John, S15313, F, 3rd (Forrest's) Cav.
CATRON, W. P. S4457, SU, 48th Va. Inf.
CAUDEL, William A. S10934, WE, 22nd (Barteau's) Cav.
CAUGHRON, Elizabeth, W1252, MO, Caughron, Wm.
CAULK, S. S13372, SH, West's Battery, Ark. Art.
CAUSBY, G. W. S13021, LI, 8th Inf.
CAUSEY, Elizabeth, W5285, ST, Causey, Hubert Asberry
CAUSEY, H. A. S12606, ST, 14th Inf.
CAUSEY, Mary Jane, W10093, LI, Causey, George Washington
CAUTHORN, Emily Margaret, W9773, H, Cauthorn, Wm. A.
CAVANAUGH, John, S7242, O, 9th Inf.
CAVANDAR, Hugh, S16588, MT, 22nd (Barteau's) Cav.
CAVANDER, Zilpha Ann, W11079, MT, Cavander, Hugh
CAVANER, George W. S10864, MS, 20th (Nixon's) Cav.
CAVANON, N. C. S2449, GI, 53rd Inf.
CAVE, R. Lin, S14472, D, 13th Va. Inf.
CAVENDER, Margaret, W1560, DI, Cavender, George Bryant
CAVENER, Amanda Early, W7332, GE, Cavener, George C.
CAVENER, G. C. S6020, GE, 29th Inf.
CAVIN, Eli, S5513, HW, 31st Inf.
CAVIN, Eliza, W4621, HW, Cavin, Eli
CAVIN, Enoch, S7670, HW, 29th Inf.
CAVIN, William, S6030, SU, 31st Inf.
CAVITT, William S. S11802, WE, 31st Inf.
CAWOOD, Malinda, W445, HW, Cawood, David J.
CAWTHEN, Frances, W6612, Cawthen, John W.

-61

CAWTHORN, A. W. S6988, WL, Carter's Scouts
CAWTHORN, Bettie, W8103, RU, Cawthorn, John T.
CAWTHORN, Frank M. S12791, S14872, SH, 55th Inf.
CAWTHORN, Sallie Ann, W8899, RU, Cawthorn, Augustus Wilson
CAWTHORNE, Sally A. W8576, RU, Cawthorne, A. W.
CECIL, Eliza C. W3336, WA, Cecil, Giles S.
CECIL, Luzelle [Hardy], W10617, MU, Cecil, John W. [Later married Hardy]
CERTAIN, William, S2431, DK, 1st Bn. (Colm's) Inf.
CHADWELL, George, S9156, WI, 20th Inf.
CHADWELL, James P. S10533, RU, 6th (Wheeler's) Cav.
CHALK, James W. S6603, DE, 27th Inf.
CHAMBERLAIN, B. F. S13689, LA, 9th Bn. (Gantt's) Cav.
CHAMBERLAIN, C. C. S5005, SU, 19th Inf.
CHAMBERLAIN, D. P. S13690, LA, 9th Bn. (Gantt's) Cav.
CHAMBERLAIN, F. F. S16245, WL, 7th Inf.
CHAMBERLAIN, John W. S15456, SH, 9th Ark. Inf.
CHAMBERLAIN, Laura, W7721, M, Chamberlain, W. F.
CHAMBERLAIN, Martha, W3742, SH, Chamberlain, Benjamin
CHAMBERLAIN, Mollie B. W2329, MU, Chamberlain, James Layfayett
CHAMBERLAIN, Ruth, W10650, WL, Chamberlain, Foster F.
CHAMBERLAIN, Sarah Elizabeth, W4619, LA, Chamberlain, Benjamin Franklin
CHAMBERS, Andrew H. S14214, GI, 31st Inf.
CHAMBERS, Caroline, W1057, MT, Chambers, Eli Jackson
CHAMBERS, Eli Jackson, S5250, MT, 1st Inf.
CHAMBERS, Elizabeth Ann, W4212, W8814, SH, Chambers, John Dupee
CHAMBERS, F. M. S11032, S, 22nd Inf.
CHAMBERS, H. C. S9334, MN, 18th (Newsom's) Cav.
CHAMBERS, H. D. S15432, O, 12th Ky. Cav.
CHAMBERS, J. C. S14311, HI, Stewart's Bn. Ala. Cav.
CHAMBERS, J. H. S14982, SM, 9th (Ward's) Cav.

CHAMBERS, James Wilson, S6855, L, 15th Cav.
CHAMBERS, Maria Barry, W2129, SM, Chambers, Wm. Wert
CHAMBERS, Mary Ann, W9115, GI, Chambers, Andrew Hopkins
CHAMBERS, Mary Ella, W9308, G, Chambers, Robert Thomas
CHAMBERS, Mary J. W3402, LA, Chambers, John May
CHAMBERS, Robert T. S7476, G, 31st Inf.
CHAMBERS, Sadie, W10892, O, Chambers, John Burette
CHAMBERS, Sarah P. W3418, HY, Chambers, Josias A.
CHAMBERS, William, S12502, GI, 3rd (Clack's) Inf.
CHAMLEE, Thomas A. S9192, MC, 31st Inf.
CHAMPION, J. H. S11190, CA, 22nd (Barteau's) Cav.
CHAMPION, Martha Jane, W5690, FR, Champion, Benjamin Franklin
CHAMPION, Matilda B. W3867, H, Champion, Wm. Coke
CHANCE, Elizabeth, W2919, SU, Chance, Thomas Franklin
CHANDLER, A. L. S5345, WL, 45th Inf.
CHANDLER, Allen, S7383, HA, 48th West Va. Inf.
CHANDLER, Annie M. W9237, HY, Chandler, Daniel Smith
CHANDLER, Elizabeth, W1008, Chandler, Archibald B.
CHANDLER, Irena Catherine, W9914, WL, Chandler, A. L.
CHANDLER, J. D. S12954, CY, 8th Inf.
CHANDLER, John D. S4121, CY, 8th (Dibrell's) Cav.
CHANDLER, John P. S1709, M, 4th (McLemore's) Cav.
CHANDLER, Mary Frances, W7361, G, Chandler, John James
CHANDLER, Melissa Atlantic, W6513, HI, Chandler, Wm. Kimmine
CHANDLER, W. T. S15406, D, 8th Ky. Cav.
CHANDLER, William K. S10763, HI, 48th (Voorhies') Inf.
CHANDOIN, Nancy, W6153, D, Chandoin, Wm. M.
CHANEY, D. M. S9711, D, 15th Cav.
CHANEY, M. L. S10484, HI, 6th (Wheeler's) Cav.

Index to Tennessee Confederate Pension Applications

CHANEY, Malinda Jane, W3743, HW, Chaney, Nathaniel Jefferson
CHANEY, Martha R. [Hassell], W10361, MU, Chaney, A. J. [Later married Hassell]
CHANEY, Mary Lucy, W4852, LU, Chaney, David Sampson
CHANNELL, Johnson, S11431, SH, 56th Ala. Inf.
CHAPIN, L. W. S9330, OV, 8th (Dibrell's) Cav.
CHAPIN, Mattie J. W3246, OV, Chapin, Loyd W.
CHAPIN, Sibba Daugherty, W5218, PU, Chapin, Wm. Paul
CHAPMAN, Barbara, W8183, WH, Chapman, Isaac
CHAPMAN, C. C. S8563, CF, 44th Inf.
CHAPMAN, C. S. S2998, B, 32nd Inf.
CHAPMAN, E. W. M. S15347, DY, 1st Regt. Ga. Regulars
CHAPMAN, Elizabeth W. W2002, G, Chapman, W. O.
CHAPMAN, Isaac, S3208, DK, 44th Inf.
CHAPMAN, James, S1396, SU, 29th Inf.
CHAPMAN, James, S6368, MU, 6th (Wheeler's) Cav.
CHAPMAN, John Wert, S16619, MU, Capt. Wm. Sander's Co. 17th Cav.
CHAPMAN, Mary Amanda, W9709, GI, Chapman, Francis Marion
CHAPMAN, Mary Catharine, W1269, CF, Chapman, Christopher Columbus
CHAPMAN, Nancy A. W8156, MS, Chapman, Bennett F.
CHAPMAN, Nancy Ellen, W8055, MS, Chapman, Carroll Swanson
CHAPMAN, Sallie Fairfax, W2121, HY, Chapman, Benjamin Washington
CHAPMAN, Susanna McMillion, W10023, GI, Chapman, Wm. Edmond
CHAPMAN, Toney, C15, D, 4th Cav.
CHAPMAN, William, S5559, SU, Unassigned
CHAPMAN, William Edmond, S15837, GI, 11th Bn. (Gordon's) Cav.
CHAPPEL, Levi, S16127, F, 52nd Inf.
CHAPPEL, Martin J. S8348, S4069, HI, 42nd Cav.
CHAPPEL, N. P. S16420, WY, 48th Inf.
CHAPPELL, Amanda Louise, W6017, HI, Chappell, M. J.
CHAPPELL, Angeline N. W1161, SN, Chappell, Wm. Martin

CHAPPELL, Nancy Jane, W4462, HU, Chappell, Hosea W.
CHARLES, H. L. S9646, HW, 31st Inf.
CHARLES, John O. S8735, CF, 24th Inf.
CHARLES, L. H. S11556, HM, 29th Inf.
CHARLES, Lou E. W9355, WA, Charles, Wiley W.
CHARLES, Matilda S. W3006, HW, Charles, John B.
CHARLTON, Bettie, W9967, D, Charlton, James D.
CHARLTON, Elizabeth Jane, W7950, JE, Charlton, Joseph Edward
CHARLTON, J. E. S8243, JE, 5th Cav.
CHARLTON, Mosura Frances, W1067, ST, Charlton, J. W.
CHARTER, C. J. S12251, MU, 9th Bn. Cav.
CHARTER, Levinia Victoria, W4970, D, Charter, Cave Johnson
CHASE, C. M. S14902, WA, 61st Inf.
CHASE, Elizabeth,   See Elizabeth Lady
CHASE, Harvey L. S1393, WA, 19th Inf.
CHASE, Isaac P. S1394, SU, 19th Inf.
CHASE, Isabella T. W5871, D, Chase, Irvine Keith
CHASE, J. C. S9490, WA, 60th Inf.
CHASE, John N. S10740, SU, 19th Inf.
CHASE, Mary, W173, SU, Chase, Richard Finlay
CHASE, Matilda, W6732, WA, Chase, John N.
CHASE, Nelson D. S10935, WA, 60th Inf.
CHASE, Sarah E. W9096, GE, Chase, Joseph C.
CHASE, William M. S1395, WA, 60th Inf.
CHASTAIN, John, S2584, CU, 2nd Ga. Inf.
CHASTEEN, B. B. S4950, FR, 1st (Turney's) Inf.
CHASTEEN, Sarah Jane, W4025, FR, Chasteen, Benjamin Berry
CHATMAN, Mary Jane, W544, HN, Chatman, Marion Edwary
CHATMAN, Samuel, S14150, BO, Unassigned (Wagon Shop)
CHAUDOIN, William M. S12047, D, 8th Ark. Inf.
CHEATHAM, Josephine A. W9359, O, Cheatham, Joseph Rye
CHEATHAM, Lou Z. W5804, GI, Cheatham, Fletcher H.
CHEATHAM, Mary N. W9984, DK, Cheatham, Tillman F.
CHEATHAM, Sallie Ann, W10148, MS, Cheatham, Wm. Thomas

Index to Tennessee Confederate Pension Applications

CHEATWOOD, Evie Mai, W11156, D, Cheatwood, Wm. Marion
CHEEK, Annie J. W5274, MS, Cheek, James A.
CHEEK, Bettie, W8063, SH, Cheek, John L.
CHEEK, Luther B. S13574, SM, Allison's Squadron, Cav.
CHENAULT, Colby, S14720, SN, 9th (Ward's) Cav.
CHENEY, Hampton J. S14094, D, 2nd (Robison's) Inf.
CHENEY, Martha Florence, W10614, H, Cheney, Robert Dee
CHERRY, Andrew Lemuel, S14779, MT, 14th Inf.
CHERRY, Annie, W8920, D, Cherry, Henry Sowell, On microfilm after Soldiers #13358
CHERRY, Henry Belle, W1217, HN, Cherry, Calvin Washington
CHERRY, Henry S. S9296, D, 9th Bn. Cav.
CHERRY, James B. S11743, CY, Hamilton's Bn. Cav.
CHERRY, John T. S3254, CC, 47th Inf.
CHERRY, Robert, S16513, BE, 5th Tenn. Recruits
CHERRY, Sterling M. S13359, D, 4th Inf.
CHERRY, W. H. S16310, WI, 4th (McLemore's) Cav.
CHESHIRE, C. M. S6381, B, 17th Inf.
CHESHIRE, Mary Ann, W20, B, Cheshire, Weldon Polk
CHESHIRE, Susan L. W5701, CF, Cheshire, C. Madison
CHESHIRE, Weldon T. S2219, B, 23rd Inf.
CHESNEY, James P. S2300, UN, 22nd (Barteau's) Cav.
CHESNEY, Phebe E. W2180, UN, Chesney, James Polk
CHESSOR, Jesse A. S11285, HI, 42nd Inf.
CHESTER, John M. S7710, WI, 20th Inf.
CHESTER, Joseph, S2199, WI, 49th Inf.
CHESTER, Sallie T. W5755, G, Chester, S. J.
CHESTER, William, S11515, ST, 49th Inf.
CHICK, Missouri, W2992, F, Chick, Fred
CHICK, Sarah E. W940, CF, Chick, W. D.
CHICK, W. D. S2453, CF, 3rd (Forrest's) Cav.
CHILCUTT, William F. S4654, S1128, HN, 5th Inf.
CHILDERS, Starling, S7895, WE, 46th Inf.
CHILDRESS, A. B. S11495, G, 19th & 20th Cav.
CHILDRESS, Andrew Jackson, S9926, MR, 43rd Inf.
CHILDRESS, Ella Graham, W6271, SU, Childress, John Bird
CHILDRESS, Lucy E. W5921, JE, Childress, Wm. M.
CHILDRESS, Mary Lyon, W8985, D, Childress, John Whitsett
CHILDRESS, Sarah A. W3262, SU, Childress, Thomas Houston
CHILDRESS, T. M. S3796, DI, Cobb's Legion of Cav. GA
CHILDRESS, W. C. S12002, SH, 34th Miss. Inf.
CHILDRESS, William, S13832, JE, Burrough's Co. Lt. Art.
CHILDREY, B. B. S9738, MU, 3rd (Clack's) Inf.
CHILDREY, Mattie, W3949, MU, Childrey, Robert Benjamin
CHILDREY, N. T. S1292, MU, 3rd Inf.
CHILDREY, Warren Madison, S8484, DY, 9th Cav.
CHILDS, H. T. S10028, LI, 1st (Turney's) Inf.
CHILES, Elizabeth Tihitia, W7173, A, Chiles, Wm. McCagah
CHILES, J. T. S16082, O, 22nd (Barteau's) Cav.
CHILES, Mary W. W491, GI, Chiles, Willis Paul
CHILES, William M. S4839, A, Thomas' Legion, N.C.
CHILTON, A. L. S1722, CY, 28th Inf.
CHILTON, J. A. S4030, CF, 2nd Cav.
CHILTON, Joshua L. S4840, PI, 8th Inf.
CHILTON, L. B. S6625, MT, 1st Ky. Cav.
CHILTON, Virginia Benton, W1088, CY, Chilton, Andrew Lafayette
CHILTON, W. H. S3985, OV, 8th Inf.
CHILTON, W. H. S14352, MS, 53rd Inf.
CHINOWITH, Mary E. W5789, WA, Chinowith, Wm.
CHINOWITH, William, S4721, WA, 60th Inf.
CHISAM, Mary L. W807, WH, Chisam, Wm.
CHISM, Florence, W9225, WH, Chism, James W.
CHISOM, J. W. S5182, W, 38th Inf.
CHISOM, William, S1460, WH, 38th Inf.
CHISUM, M. C. W2176, MA, Chisum, James S.
CHITWOOD, Edmond, S15792, SH, 15th Cav.
CHITWOOD, Martha Ann, W8488, DY, Chitwood, Shedrick Alvonza

CHOAT, John, S4445, HU, 11th Inf.
CHOAT, John D. S10731, MR, 8th (Smith's) Cav.
CHOAT, T. J. S11680, RB, 14th Inf.
CHOATE, M. L. F. W3552, RB, Choate, T. J.
CHOATE, Mary Duke, W4801, DI, Choate, James Marion
CHOATE, N. A. S14371, MU, 6th (Wheeler's) Cav.
CHOATE, Rufus, S9105, HU, 1st (Feild's) Inf.
CHOATE, S. E. S13980, HU, 11th Inf.
CHRISMAN, Mary Almyra Frances, W7515, WI, Chrisman, John Fredrick Hay
CHRISMAN, Sabra Delphia, W7147, WI, Chrisman, Silas Wilburn
CHRISTENBERRY, Annie, W8106, WE, Christenberry, Jasper
CHRISTENBERRY, J. J. S8965, 1st Ark. Inf.
CHRISTENBERRY, T. D. S9047, MA, 12th Ky. Cav.
CHRISTENBERRY, W. S. S49, G, 15th Inf.
CHRISTIAN, A. F. S16400, OV, 13th (Gore's) Cav.
CHRISTIAN, Allen, S9083, WE, 19th Inf.
CHRISTIAN, Allen, S11862, HW, 19th Inf.
CHRISTIAN, Benson P. S5251, OV, 8th Inf.
CHRISTIAN, Elizabeth, W4551, J, Christian, B. P.
CHRISTIAN, J. W. S14599, LE, 48th (Voorhies') Inf.
CHRISTIAN, John L. S14889, H, 42nd Inf.
CHRISTIAN, L. Jack, S5158, HU, 42nd Inf.
CHRISTIAN, Mary Elizabeth, W5544, W, Christian, O. B.
CHRISTIAN, Mattie, W11119, OV, Christian, Arkley Fiske
CHRISTIAN, Moffit A. S6329, OV, 25th Inf.
CHRISTIAN, Nancy Jane, W1414, HW, Christian, George Maxwell
CHRISTIAN, O. B. S11240, W, 11th (Holman's) Cav.
CHRISTIAN, Robert N. S12509, SH, 34th Miss. Inf.
CHRISTIAN, W. R. S8061, G, 12th Inf.
CHRISTIE, Jasper N. S2631, WA, 63rd Inf.
CHRISTIE, Thomas J. S6860, WY, 6th (Wheeler's) Cav.
CHRISTMAN, Albert, S1146, D, 2nd Inf.
CHRISTMAN, Martha, W3421, HN, Christman, James M.
CHRISTMAN, W. D. S16014, WI, 4th (McLemore's) Cav.

CHRISTOPHER, S. P. S15883, S16190, PU, 63rd Ga. Inf.
CHRISTOPHER, William, S8907, SE, 31st Inf.
CHRISTY, Jasper Newton, S5425, WA, 63rd Inf.
CHRISTY, William K. S11899, WA, 63rd Inf.
CHRONISTER, Sarah A. W4865, LA, Chronister, James H.
CHUMBLEY, James N. S10741, MU, 11th (Holman's) Cav.
CHUMLEY, David A. S1850, RU, 1st Bn. Hvy. Art.
CHUMLEY, Fanny Leviny, W1478, RU, Chumley, David Acon
CHUNN, W. N. S12986, G, 6th Inf.
CHURCH, A. B. S16262, MU, 19th (Biffle's) Cav.
CHURCH, Amanda Mell, W10200, FR, Church, Thomas Grant
CHURCH, Elizabeth Jane, W6718, JO, Church, H. M.
CHURCH, Emory N. S8814, O, 1st Inf.
CHURCH, Eva, W10338, H, Church, F. G.
CHURCH, F. G. S16175, H, 22nd Bn. Ga. Hvy. Art.
CHURCH, George, S12520, HW, 2nd (Ashby's) Cav.
CHURCH, H. M. S7924, JO, 26th N.C. Vols.
CHURCH, Henry, C19, WI, 48th Inf.
CHURCH, Henry, S1143, WI, 48th Inf.
CHURCH, Hiram, S9844, HA, 2nd (Ashby's) Cav.
CHURCH, Hugh M. S4504, JO, 26th N.C. Inf.
CHURCH, Jacob C. S2464, FR, 18th (Newsom's) Cav.
CHURCH, John R. S9923, HI, 9th Bn. (Gantt's) Cav.
CHURCH, Laura E. W4003, HA, Church, Hiram
CHURCH, Margaret A. W5486, FR, Church, John Fletcher
CHURCH, Mary A. W5254, HI, Church, John R.
CHURCH, Mary M. W3698, FR, Church, Henderson
CHURCH, Robert Burr, S16263, MU, 48th (Voorhies') Inf.
CHURCH, Sarah S. W8634, WI, Church, Joshua Pinkney
CHURCH, Susan, W6476, HA, Church, George
CHURCHILL, John, C212, HR, Undetermined

-65

Index to Tennessee Confederate Pension Applications

CHURCHMAN, DeWitt C. S1628, S3366, G, 22nd Inf.
CHURCHMAN, Margaret Ann, W1797, Churchman, D. W. C.
CHURCHWELL, J. B. S16460, LE, 9th Cav.
CHURCHWELL, J. E. S16257, LE, 19th (Biffle's) Cav.
CIERLEY, W. H. S3458, S4345, HD, 19th & 21st (Consolidated) Cav.
CIERLY, Catherine C. W7523, HD, Cierly, Wm. Henry
CISCO, S. S848, J, 28th Inf.
CLAIBORN, C. L. S16529, DY, 1st N.C. Jr. Reserves
CLAIBORNE, Eugenia Frances, W2991, DY, Claiborne, Robert F.
CLAIBORNE, J. A. S11009, SH, 7th (Duckworth's) Cav.
CLAIBORNE, Robert F. S6803, DY, 30th N.C. Inf.
CLAIBORNE, Susan A. W10819, DY, Claiborne, Charles F.
CLAMAN, Pleasant, S7988, SU, 13th Bn. Va. Art.
CLAMPETT, George W. S325, BR, 8th Ga. Inf.
CLAMPETT, Martha J. W3655, H, Clampett, George W.
CLANUCH, J. E. S1035, LI, 44th Inf.
CLARE, Mary Hadley, W1878, D, Clare, Wm.
CLARK, A. B. S5498, SU, 44th Va. Inf.
CLARK, A. J. S7313, SN, Hamilton's Bn. Cav.
CLARK, Amelia Frances, W5837, F, Clark, T. J.
CLARK, Angenline, W3926, DY, Clark, Benton J.
CLARK, Bettie, W4396, F, Clark, David
CLARK, C. S4279, HO, 14th Inf.
CLARK, C. H. S3771, V, 16th Inf.
CLARK, Cal, S6944, F, 12th Cav.
CLARK, Charles, S11487, SN, 9th (Ward's) Cav.
CLARK, D. C. S8311, MC, 1st Cav.
CLARK, E. S11760, MOO, Forrest's Escort, Cav.
CLARK, E. R. W3772, SU, Clark, Arthur B.
CLARK, Edward F. S484, SN, 44th Inf.
CLARK, Eleanor Jane, W4856, SU, Clark, Job H.
CLARK, Elizabeth Allison, W1939, D, Clark, John Columbus
CLARK, Elizabeth Ann, W5775, CF, Clark, James Carter
CLARK, Francis S. S8539, LI, 41st Inf.

CLARK, G. R. S14209, K, 1st Va. Cav.
CLARK, H. K. S11075, MC, 43rd Inf.
CLARK, H. T. S9340, GI, 3rd Ala. Cav.
CLARK, H. W. S14452, RU, 18th Inf.
CLARK, Harriet, W7348, D, Clark, Solomon C.
CLARK, Harry, S1492, WI, Baxter's Co. Art.
CLARK, Henry, S13328, SN, 17th Inf.
CLARK, Hester, See Hester Marberry
CLARK, J. A. S12150, LI, 44th Inf.
CLARK, J. P. S13594, 4th Ark. Inf.
CLARK, James A. S6744, RU, 45th Inf.
CLARK, James C. S4603, CF, 8th Inf.
CLARK, James H. S14713, HD, 27th Inf.
CLARK, James J. S1005, D, 11th Inf.
CLARK, James P. S2269, WH, 8th (Dibrell's) Cav.
CLARK, Jane, W12, DI, Clark, George W.
CLARK, Job H. S10597, SU, 5th Bn. (McClellan's) Cav
CLARK, John A. S13653, CC, 14th Cav.
CLARK, John E. S11078, G, 12th Cav.
CLARK, John M. S14170, ME, 10th Cav.
CLARK, Joseph, S2140, M, 23rd Inf.
CLARK, Joshaway, S2986, O, Undetermined
CLARK, Josiah, S8623, HO, Undetermined
CLARK, L. B. S12304, WL, 28th Inf.
CLARK, L. H. S15771, GI, White's Ala. Art.
CLARK, Laura A. W11006, F, Clark, Calvin
CLARK, Laura F. W10378, D, Clark, S. H.
CLARK, Lita Pauline, W9244, SH, Clark, John C.
CLARK, Lou, W5911, G, Clark, Malcomb
CLARK, M. S7853, G, 22nd Inf. See also Malcom Clark
CLARK, M. M. K. W2781, WI, Clark, Harvy
CLARK, Malcom, S10405, G, 22nd Inf. See also M. Clark
CLARK, Margaret, W3229, H, Clark, Carroll
CLARK, Martha H. W8322, LI, Clark, Francis M.
CLARK, Martha Louise, W3809, SN, Clark, Charles
CLARK, Mary, W2572, HD, Clark, Robt. L.
CLARK, Mary Elizabeth, W9929, K, Clark, George Rogers
CLARK, Mary I. W1, D, Clark, James J.
CLARK, Mary Jane, W2876, HO, Clark, Coleman
CLARK, Melia Roxanna, W9374.5, LE, Clark, Robert Dodson
CLARK, N. S15203, HO, 7th Bn. Ark. Cav.
CLARK, Nancy A. W315, MC, Clark, John

Index to Tennessee Confederate Pension Applications

CLARK, Nancy J. W8682, FR, Clark, Joseph M.
CLARK, Parmelia Jane, W9277, W9074, FR, Clark, Robert
CLARK, Permelia R. W4800, HI, Clark, Robert D.
CLARK, R. D. S11159, HI, 24th Inf.
CLARK, Richard, S3685, SN, 20th Inf.
CLARK, Sabria Caroline, W7690, W9266, R, Clark, Wm. Raleigh
CLARK, Sarah, W6479, MU, Clark, Henry T.
CLARK, Sarah Caroline, W7162, MC, Clark, David Cobb
CLARK, Sarah J. W1785, LA, Clark, Benjamin F.
CLARK, Solomon C. S4057, D, McClung's Art.
CLARK, T. J. S12589, B, 55th Inf.
CLARK, Thomas C. S15288, MU, 32nd Inf.
CLARK, W. A. S9467, HI, 42nd Inf.
CLARK, W. T. S4807, CO, 16th N.C. Inf.
CLARK, William, S13269, K, 2nd (Ashby's) Cav.
CLARKE, Stephen, S3075, U, 51st Va. Inf.
CLARKE, Virginia Stokes, W6156, H, Clarke, Isaac Lewis
CLARY, James A. S9255, WL, 8th Cav.
CLAUD, Philip, S12503, HI, 9th Cav.
CLAUDE, Etta, W10481, GI, Claude, L. B.
CLAUDE, L. B. S15625, GI, 6th (Wheeler's) Cav.
CLAWSON, Sarah Malinda, W5818, CL, Clawson, Thomas Johnson
CLAWSON, Thomas J. S13575, CL, 64th Va. Inf.
CLAXTON, M. D. S2301, GI, 3rd Tenn. Vols.
CLAXTON, William, S7399, LI, 10th Ky. Cav.
CLAXTON, William H. S7470, G, 2nd Mo. Cav.
CLAY, D. D. S112, D, 1st Inf.
CLAY, Eliza J. W351, WA, Clay, George Lemuel
CLAY, Fanny, W7131, D, Clay, David Dickerson
CLAY, John R. S6068, S2866, SU, 59th Inf.
CLAY, Rebecca M. W7722, WY, Clay, W. S.
CLAY, W. S. S15658, WY, 45th Inf.
CLAYBORN, Antonette, W1547, HI, Clayborn, Henry Franklin
CLAYMAN, Emeline, W1113, SU, Clayman, George
CLAYMAN, George W. S3951, SU, 63rd Inf.
CLAYTON, A. C. S15838, MS, 5th Inf.

CLAYTON, Fannie J. W4463, D, Clayton, Wiley McDonald
CLAYTON, Francis M. S14565, MN, 13th Inf.
CLAYTON, Hadassah C. W4709, RU, Clayton, James
CLAYTON, James, S11185, RU, 23rd Inf.
CLAYTON, John T. S16042, S11444, SH, 12th Cav.
CLAYTON, Leona, W10641, BE, Clayton, Solomon Smith
CLAYTON, S. S. S15278, BE, 20th Inf.
CLAYTON, Sam, C234, D, 46th Inf.
CLAYTON, William J. S11171, K, 3rd (Lillard's) Mtd. Inf.
CLEAGE, Hattie Ewing, W2212, K, Cleage, Samuel
CLEARY, Mary Jane, W6830, MN, Cleary, Wm. J.
CLEEK, A. J. S11989, CC, 15th Cav.
CLEEK, E. A. S14306, O, 44th Inf.
CLEEK, Sarah Virginia, W10250, SU, Cleek, James David
CLEM, John Henry, S1932, GI, 50th Ala. Inf.
CLEMENS, Alexander C. S600, SM, 28th Inf.
CLEMENT, H. C. S3341, O, 31st Inf.
CLEMENT, James C. S8404, WE, 31st Inf.
CLEMENT, Mollie, W3810, O, Clement, Henry Clay
CLEMENTS, C. H. S4919, WE, 38th Va. Inf.
CLEMENTS, Francis M. S16185, D, 21st Cav.
CLEMENTS, W. R. S15576, HN, 20th (Russell's) Cav.
CLEMMONS, Frances B. W3612, WL, Clemmons, Randall Thompson
CLEMMONS, J. W. S9757, WL, 7th Inf.
CLEMMONS, James L. S8460, WL, 45th Inf.
CLEMMONS, Mary, W7399, W10174, WL, Clemmons, John W.
CLEMMONS, Mollie, W10174, W7399, WL, Clemmons, J. W.
CLEMMONS, Myra, W9015, WL, Clemmons, Elham Alexander
CLEMMONS, Nannie Bomer, W6826, WL, Clemmons, James Lee
CLEMMONS, Samuel B. S12639, WL, 4th (McLemore's) Cav.
CLEMONS, Henry, S9447, BO, 37th Inf.
CLEMONS, Isaac, S14295, D, 11th Inf.
CLEMONS, R. P. S9499, B, 44th Inf.
CLENDENEN, Eliza, W3942, W, Clendenen, Charles Washington
CLENDENEN, J. N. S1048, W, 16th Inf.

CLENDENIN, Mattie Lou, W10418, HN, Clendenin, John Wilson
CLENDENIN, W. F. S11127, HN, 20th (Russell's) Cav.
CLENDENING, Annie Elizabeth, W3214, D, Clendening, Wm. Alexander
CLENDENING, J. C. S9660, SN, 5th Inf.
CLENDENING, J. S. S6064, SN, 9th Cav.
CLENDENING, William A. S6662, D, 7th Inf.
CLENDENNING, Isori, W9530, SN, Clendenning, James Curren
CLENDENON, J. P. S12034, L, 19th (Biffle's) Cav.
CLENNY, Harriet F. W2757, D, Clenny, Henry
CLENNY, Henry, S6883, D, 7th Inf.
CLEVELAND, A. M. S2932, GR, 1st (Carter's) Cav.
CLEVELAND, Elizabeth H. W9479, D, Cleveland, Barnette Franklin
CLEVELAND, Maurice Adams, C200, GI, Undetermined
CLEVELAND, W. N. S11517, M, 2nd Ark. Inf.
CLICK, Samuel, S4046, HW, 27th Va. Inf.
CLIFFORD, Elizabeth Caroline, W1646, WL, Clifford, John
CLIFT, Mary Elizabeth, W8329, MS, Clift, Albert Gipson
CLIFT, Mary Jane, W4979, SH, Clift, James Knox Polk
CLIFT, Mattie M. W11014, O, Clift, Harrison Davis
CLIFT, William P. S8595, S16381, MS, 3rd Inf.
CLIFTON, Burrel A. S1309, DI, 11th Inf.
CLIFTON, Cyntha Adaline, W7226, DI, Clifton, Burel A.
CLIFTON, Isaac A. S1318, FR, 1st Inf.
CLIFTON, J. A. S1105, FR, 1st Inf.
CLIFTON, J. K. S7112, DI, 11th Inf.
CLIFTON, J. M. S1317, LA, 9th Inf.
CLIFTON, Sarah Elizabeth, W3979, LA, Clifton, Doctor Wisdom
CLIFTON, Tennessee Ann, W8394, DI, Clifton, James Kirby
CLIMER, Margaret, W1700, DI, Climer, Charles Elbert
CLIMER, Susan Adeline, W4573, D, Climer, James Marion
CLINARD, Archibald Wilson, S3041, D, Forrest's Old Regiment, Cav.
CLINARD, Julia, W3540, RB, Clinard, Jefferson
CLINARD, Martha Caroline, W1321, ST, Clinard, Robert Henry

CLINE, George H. S6397, DI, 8th N.C. Inf.
CLINE, George W. S11377, S16434, SU, 16th Va. Cav.
CLINE, Louisa E. W747, SN, Cline, John Wm.
CLINE, P. L. S12478, JE, 61st Inf.
CLINTON, A. M. S9834, CE, 38th Inf.
CLINTON, George W. S8114, H, 1st Inf.
CLINTON, John Franklin, S11342, CY, 8th (Dibrell's) Cav.
CLINTON, Mildred, W6763, HY, Clinton, Alexander Murrey
CLINTON, Walter E. S834, J, 16th Inf.
CLINTON, louisiana, W8995, HR, Clinton, Samuel Hardeman
CLOAR, Ann McCalister, W9573, W7602, O, Cloar, James Anderson
CLOAR, Green, S8882, O, 33rd Inf.
CLOAR, J. A. S7292, O, 33rd Inf.
CLOAR, J. E. S15480, O, 22nd (Barteau's) Cav.
CLOAR, John, S8697, O, 33rd Inf.
CLONTS, M. L. S12382, MC, 1st Ga. Cav.
CLOPTON, Nancy E. W7326, WL, Clopton, Wm. Wartus
CLOSE, Nancy, W726, BL, Close, Henry Love
CLOUCH, J. B. S12048, MR, 63rd Inf.
CLOUCH, Martha M. W4996, MR, Clouch, John Barron
CLOUD, A. M. S11632, HA, 25th Va. Cav.
CLOUD, J. F. S5560, SH, 17th Inf.
CLOUD, Mary, W4322, K, Cloud, Thomas
CLOUD, Thomas, S1758, S2007, K, 26th Inf.
CLOUD, William H. S13954, SU, 29th Va. Inf.
CLOURS, Elizabeth, W60, GE, Clours, George Washington
CLOUSE, James P. S9195, H, 3rd (Forrest's) Cav.
CLOUSE, Minerva, W5537, H, Clouse, James P.
CLOUSE, William C. S78, MR, 6th Ala. Inf.
CLOWERS, John C. S10485, GE, 29th Inf.
CLOWERS, Martha, W7127, GE, Clowers, John C.
CLOYD, J. S. S230, WH, 25th Inf.
CLOYD, James, S5217, WH, 25th Inf.
CLUCK, Benjamin S. S4860, WL, 45th Inf.
CLYCE, J. F. S12151, SU, 61st Inf.
CLYCE, Sarah Jane, W6194, SU, Clyce, James Ferdinand
CLYMOR, Narcissa Jane, W9934, O, Clymor, Joe Henry
COADY, Ransom L. S550, DE, 23rd Inf.
COAKLEY, Z. D. S9567, GE, 16th N.C. Inf.
COAL, W. A. S346, HD, 26th Miss. Inf.

Index to Tennessee Confederate Pension Applications

COATS, A. J. S10168, HI, 48th Inf.
COATS, E. G. S3081, HI, 48th Inf.
COATS, Henry H. S8312, B, 41st Miss. Inf.
COATS, J. H. S15824, S14488, HN, 18th Inf.
COATS, Mary F. W4698, HI, Coats, Elijah Griffin
COATS, Solomon, S12181, T, 4th Inf.
COATS, Wilson, W. S9823, T, 7th (Duckworth's) Cav.
COBB, G. A. G. S2596, GI, 11th Bn. (Holman's) Cav.
COBB, J. P. S10851, WI, 2nd Ark. Inf.
COBB, James F. S7209, MC, 1st (Carter's) Cav.
COBB, Jefferson S. S14218, CC, 26th Ala. Inf.
COBB, Joseph, S10406, MC, 1st (Carter's) Cav.
COBB, Kate, W5680, HW, Cobb, Thomas W.
COBB, M. R. S10372, O, 1st (Turney's) Inf.
COBB, Missouri Ann, W10808, WI, Cobb, James Pulaski
COBB, W. J. S7961, H, 19th Inf.
COBB, William P. S2456, WH, Thomas' Legion, N.C.
COBBLE, Emma, W10309, FR, Cobble, Eph. A.
COBBLE, Frederick W. S6135, GE, 61st Inf.
COBBLE, John L. S1282, OV, 8th Cav.
COBBLE, Malinda jane, W4870, OV, Cobble, John
COBELL, W. C. S7798, G, 7th Ky. Cav.
COBLE, D. H. S15755, FR, 44th N.C. Inf.
COBLE, Millie Caroline, W9017, P, Coble, Wm. Riley
COBLE, W. H. S12323, P, 10th (DeMoss') Cav.
COBURN, Henry G. S5252, CC, 15th Cav.
COCHRAN, Christopher C. S6246, MS, 17th Inf.
COCHRAN, Dulin, S4463, MS, 41st Inf.
COCHRAN, Emma L. W5555, SH, Cochran, A. O.
COCHRAN, G. W. S12885, H, 3rd Cav.
COCHRAN, Harder P. S16473, WI, 2nd Ala. Cav.
COCHRAN, Louisa J. W386, LI, Cochran, Benjamin Fleachran
COCHRAN, Mary Ann, W5582, MS, Cochran, Wm. Essex
COCHRAN, Nancy L. W419, MS, Cochran, Hugh
COCHRAN, Quincy Williams, W8545, MU, Cochran, Jas. Thos. Lafayette
COCHRAN, Robert L. S8611, MO, 63rd Inf.
COCHRAN, S. W. S12763, HN, 46th Inf.
COCHRAN, Sallie B. W6697, HI, Cochran, Sam
COCHRAN, Sam, S10678, HI, 9th Bn. Cav.
COCHRAN, William E. S7257, MS, 6th (Wheeler's) Cav.
COCHRAN, William M. S16547, SH, 7th Ky. Mtd. Inf.
COCK, Anna F. W3216, W, Cock, Wm. Henry
COCKE, Adelaide Sledge, W10830, SH, Cocke, John L.
COCKE, J. W. S7769, K, 60th N.C. Inf.
COCKE, Samuella, W6313, SN, Cocke, Thomas Webb
COCKRAN, Jacson J. S1114, MO, 52nd Inf.
COCKRELL, E. G. S16639, SN, 12th Cav.
COCKRELL, Josie P. W11094, LA, Cockrell, Ed J.
COCKRILL, Mary Matilda, W6203, MU, Cockrill, Newton Granville
COCKRILL, N. G. S9739, MU, 6th (Wheeler's) Cav.
COCKRILL, William Goodloe, S15550, T, 7th Cav.
CODAY, John L. S5253, O, 27th Inf.
CODY, A. J. S7366, T, 39th N.C. Inf.
CODY, J. L. S997, SH, 16th Ala. Inf.
CODY, Lucy Ella, W7634, W8599, T, Cody, James Franklin, Also applied from Shelby County
CODY, T. J. S8293, SH, Forrest's Old Regt. Cav.
COE, Jane, W1297, WL, Coe, Jesse F.
COE, William, S1698, PI, Hamilton's Bn. Cav.
COFFEE, A. A. S6227, H, 52nd Ga. Inf.
COFFEE, A. S. S8070, W, 1st Ark. Cav.
COFFEE, Amanda, W10694, BO, Coffee, Cleveland Monroe
COFFEE, Aricie C. W6339, OV, Coffee, John
COFFEE, James A. S6373, MA, 10th Ga. Inf.
COFFEE, Martha, W1906, OV, Coffee, Richard N.
COFFEE, R. D. S14759, SM, 24th Inf.
COFFEE, Sarah, W699, HA, Coffee, Ira
COFFEY, Alberta H. W9222, HR, Coffey, Thomas David
COFFEY, Ira, S534, GR, 26th Inf.
COFFEY, John, S9188, GR, 12th Bn. (Day's) Cav.
COFFEY, John B. S14721, MC, 58th N.C. Inf.
COFFEY, Martha Ann, W3398, GI, Coffey, Samuel Madison

COFFEY, Mary Ann Elafare, W4680, CH, Coffey, James Alexander
COFFEY, S. M. S5136, GI, 6th (Wheeler's) Cav.
COFFEY, T. D. S15890, HR, 9th Inf.
COFFIN, Clarkson, S5419, CO, 13th Bn. Va. Reserves
COFFMAN, C. H. S1734, DE, 50th Ala. Inf.
COFFMAN, Catherine S. W6444, SU, Coffman, David
COFFMAN, David, S9196, SU, 1st (Carter's) Cav.
COFFMAN, Ida Small, W10634, GI, Coffman, James S.
COFFMAN, J. F. S1066, GI, 50th Ala. Inf.
COFFMAN, Jacob, S2853, UN, 1st (Carter's) Cav.
COFFMAN, Jacob, S12030, OV, 22nd Inf.
COFFMAN, James S. S7484, GI, 1st Bn. Ala. Vols.
COFFMAN, Robert E. S16020, GI, 10th Ala. Cav.
COFFMAN, Telitha Cuni, W1218, HR, Coffman, William
COFFMAN, W. H. S16363, SU, 1st (Carter's) Cav.
COGDELL, James B. S4675, CO, 60th N.C. Inf.
COGDILL, L. B. S4301, SE, 1st Ga. Inf.
COGDILL, Louise Elizabeth, W10888, BR, Cogdill, Nelson Crowder
COGDILL, Nancy J. W6999, CO, Cogdill, Wm. R.
COGDILL, W. R. S14248, CO, 2nd Bn. N.C.
COGGIN, J. J. S129, D, 18th Inf.
COGGIN, John C. S7699, D, 18th Inf.
COGGIN, Mattie Pauline, W7066, D, Coggin, James Jordan
COGGINS, Joseph A. S11879, MS, 14th Cav.
COGGINS, SArah Jane, W6032, MS, Coggins, Joseph Atlas
COGSWELL, Mary A. W4812, WA, Cogswell, W. B.
COHEN, Morris, S3428, K, 1st Tex. Cav.
COKELY, James, S5916, WH, 8th Cav.
COKER, James C. S3262, FR, 32nd Inf.
COKER, John T. S11647, T, 43rd Miss. Inf.
COKER, Mary, W7992, FR, Coker, Colin
COKER, Mary Elizabeth, W5368, T, Coker, John Thadis
COLBERT, James C. S3717, LI, 8th Inf.
COLBY, Annie Powel, W6276, SH, Colby, Eli Elliott
COLDWELL, Rilla Ayers, W7638, BO, Coldwell, Albert Andrew
COLE, A. J. S7367, MS, 11th Cav.
COLE, B. T. S9236, LI, 32nd Inf.
COLE, Benjamin G. S8836, HW, 37th Va. Inf.
COLE, Elizabeth, W1485, WH, Cole, Walter Wilkins
COLE, Elizabeth T. W6307, P, Cole, James Washington
COLE, Emily, W10367, WE, Cole, John
COLE, F. S1080, SU, 37th Inf.
COLE, Henry, S2949, UN, 63rd Inf.
COLE, J. B. S9491, LI, 32nd Inf.
COLE, J. H. S16451, HN, Undetermined
COLE, J. M. S510, MA, 6th Inf.
COLE, J. W. S9710, WY, 27th Ark. Inf.
COLE, James, S3353, MR, 29th Inf.
COLE, James C. S10573, D, 49th Inf.
COLE, James M. S9057, G, 12th Ky. Cav.
COLE, John F. S13578, G, 47th Inf.
COLE, Jud. Mary Henrietta, W9662, L, Cole, Wm. Henry
COLE, Lafayette, S3778, D, 11th Inf.
COLE, Lean, W1334, HA, Cole, James
COLE, Lewis, S2653, BE, 55th Inf.
COLE, Louisa Elizabeth, W4306, GI, Cole, Louis Houston
COLE, Louisa F. W2653, G, Cole, Stephen S.
COLE, Martha Jane, W7503, JE, Cole, Edward Richard
COLE, Mary Belle, W3882, G, Cole, Richard Swinney
COLE, Minnie, W9424, WL, Cole, Henry Clay
COLE, Nancy C. W430, RB, Cole, Rozzy
COLE, Nannie Lavinia, W2112, D, Cole, Perry M.
COLE, Polley (Mary E.), W2675, BE, Cole, Mark
COLE, Rebecca A. W2408, MS, Cole, Andrew J.
COLE, Sallie E. W3385, MA, Cole, Wm. R.
COLE, Sarah A. W1653, BE, Cole, James R.
COLE, Sue Ann, W9719, MA, Cole, Wm. George
COLE, Susanna, W4773, HW, Cole, Ben G.
COLE, T. J. S15321, RB, 30th Inf.
COLE, W. F. S3014, GI, 1st (Feild's) Inf.
COLE, W. H. S7554, HR, 1st Ala. Tenn. & Miss. Inf.
COLE, W. H. S14905, L, 2nd Ky. Cav.
COLE, Walter, S222, WH, 16th Inf.
COLE, William K. S1889, MC, 3rd Cav.
COLE, William R. S7050, MA, 9th Ga. Inf.

COLEMAN, Adline, W1923, WE, Coleman, Lewis
COLEMAN, Amy L. [Hollins], W10983, SN, Coleman, Theopilus Neal, [Later married Hollins]
COLEMAN, Arabella McClure, W8594, SH, Coleman, Nicholas
COLEMAN, C. O. S6877, WE, 7th Ky. Mtd. Inf.
COLEMAN, Calvin K. S8993, CL, 27th Va. Inf.
COLEMAN, Carr, S12101, HN, 7th Ky. Inf.
COLEMAN, David B. C100, GI, 6th Ala. Inf.
COLEMAN, Elizabeth, W9007, RU, Coleman, John Calvin
COLEMAN, G. J. S10558, 5th Inf.
COLEMAN, Isaac M. S7243, RU, 45th Inf.
COLEMAN, Isabella, W6432, RU, Coleman, John F.
COLEMAN, J. F. S7355, G, Truehardt's Battery, Ala. Art.
COLEMAN, Jacob, C2, GI, 11th Ala. Inf.
COLEMAN, John B. S7879, WE, 45th Inf.
COLEMAN, L. R. S13868, SH, 7th (Duckworth's) Cav.
COLEMAN, Lucinda Jones, W2854, D, Coleman, John William
COLEMAN, Mary, W7048, SH, Coleman, James P.
COLEMAN, Mary, W7676, RB, Coleman, Robert Lafayette
COLEMAN, Mary E. W1361, RU, Coleman, James R.
COLEMAN, Mattie Bowden, W9305, W6844, HN, Coleman, Carr
COLEMAN, Polk, S13881, WH, 8th (Dibrell's) Cav.
COLEMAN, R. L. S6629, RB, 17th S.C. Inf.
COLEMAN, Rebecca, W760, CL, Coleman, George Washington
COLEMAN, Robert B. S6219, RU, 45th Inf.
COLEMAN, Sallie, W3656, RU, Coleman, Isaac
COLEMAN, Sarah Elizabeth, W5190, G, Coleman, Wm. P.
COLEMAN, Sarah Elizabeth, W5402, HU, Coleman, John Calhoun
COLEMAN, Sarah Margaret, W1271, FR, Coleman, Charles Alexander
COLEMAN, T. J. S10694, O, 4th (Consolidated) Inf.
COLEMAN, Thomas P. S6437, D, 11th Cav.
COLEMAN, W. J. S6894, HD, 3rd Ga. Inf.
COLEMAN, W. R. S8651, R, Walker's Bn. Thomas' Legion, N.C.

COLES, G. M. S3631, SN, 4th (McLemore's) Cav.
COLES, Henry C. S19, WL, 4th Cav.
COLES, Kate, W4288, SH, Coles, Robt. Jonathan
COLES, Robert F. S4538, WL, 18th Inf.
COLEY, Mary, W9238, HN, Coley, Richard Archer
COLEY, W. F. S11714, RO, 5th (McKenzie's) Cav.
COLLAKE, C. V. S9421, MO, 62nd Mtd. Inf.
COLLAY, John, S372, BE, 10th Inf.
COLLET, James L. S3139, S4360, MO, 3rd Inf.
COLLEY, W. G. S3899, SN, 22nd (Barteu's) Cav.
COLLIER, B. P. S13796, WL, 4th (McLemore's) Cav.
COLLIER, C. C. S16174, S15504, J, 25th Inf.
COLLIER, D. W. S3391, SH, Forrest's Old Cav.
COLLIER, Eula Steed, W11018, MU, Collier, John Albert
COLLIER, George M. S16193, D, 45th Inf.
COLLIER, Hugh Lawson, S12747, S16129, MU, 6th (Wheeler's) Cav.
COLLIER, J. M. S7368, DI, 3rd Cav.
COLLIER, Julia Rebecca Lee, W10543, SH, Collier, Charles Henry
COLLIER, Lutitia, W9119, WE, Collier, Alonzo H.
COLLIER, Marcus M. S16693, GE, Napier's Bn. Cav.
COLLIER, Mary Delana, W9992, WL, Collier, B. P.
COLLIER, Sam, C211, C257, MA, 6th Inf.
COLLIER, Susana Brewer, W5600, D, Collier, John Matthew
COLLIER, W. M. S13697, MT, 14th Inf.
COLLINS, A. W. S12523, FR, 5th Ala. Cav.
COLLINS, Adaline D. W220, K, Collins, Arthur C.
COLLINS, Annie Cox, W10096, G, Collins, John Jarrett
COLLINS, C. E. S13924, A, Thomas' Legion, N.C.
COLLINS, Calvin C. S6737, WA, 60th Inf.
COLLINS, Delcena, W316, GE, Collins, Isaac Tipton
COLLINS, Elizabeth Frances, W5266, D, Collins, Carson Wm.
COLLINS, Fannie D. W10056, WL, Collins, Wm. A.

Index to Tennessee Confederate Pension Applications

COLLINS, Fredonia, W6075, HU, Collins, Henry M.
COLLINS, Green, S3107, CL, 12th Cav.
COLLINS, Griffin, S10883, GR, 26th Inf.
COLLINS, H. S2262, HU, 11th Inf.
COLLINS, H. H. S11528, JE, 64th N.C. Inf.
COLLINS, Helen, W9887, CA, Collins, Jere B.
COLLINS, Henry M. S5576, HU, 11th Inf.
COLLINS, Hugh M. S14663, HN, 5th Inf.
COLLINS, J. T. S12714, MS, 53rd Inf.
COLLINS, J. W. S13583, S11816, MS, 2nd Miss. Inf.
COLLINS, Jack J. S4020, O, 8th Inf.
COLLINS, James, S6244, WA, 29th Inf.
COLLINS, James W. S245, O, 17th Inf.
COLLINS, Jellina, W2678, GR, Collins, Noble
COLLINS, John B. S11295, D, 22nd (Barteau's) Cav.
COLLINS, John C. S9924, BR, 43rd Inf.
COLLINS, John Clark, S13425, MA, 43rd Inf.
COLLINS, John James, S13423, G, 6th Inf.
COLLINS, Josie, W8264, MS, Collins, Leroy B.
COLLINS, L. B. S7838, MS, 17th Inf.
COLLINS, Loucinda Frances, W10162, MS, Collins, Henry L.
COLLINS, M. L. S14288, MA, 57th Ga. Inf.
COLLINS, Malissa, W648, K, Collins, Thos. D.
COLLINS, Mary Adaline, W10475, SN, Collins, Monroe Joshua
COLLINS, Mary Elizabeth, W3871, D, Collins, Richd. Wm.
COLLINS, Mary Jane, W4956, H, Collins, N. J.
COLLINS, Milam, S5254, HA, 50th Va. Inf.
COLLINS, Nealie Jane, W8764, MA, Collins, J. E.
COLLINS, Polly, W3072, HA, Collins, Milam
COLLINS, R. E. S11833, D, 6th (Wheeler's) Cav.
COLLINS, R. T. S6804, LI, 6th (Wheeler's) Cav.
COLLINS, Sarah Catherine, W3657, GI, Collins, Wm. R.
COLLINS, Sophronia, W8324, W8762, MA, Collins, Wm. Lafayette
COLLINS, T. H. S14907, SH, 15th Miss. Inf.
COLLINS, Thomas W. S3023, D, 20th Inf.
COLLINS, Thurman, S8959, HA, 50th Va. Inf.
COLLINS, V. D. S6338, SU, 61st Mtd. Inf.
COLLINS, W. E. S511, WA, 2nd Ky. Cav.
COLLINS, W. L. S13546, MA, Undetermined
COLLINS, William A. S2707, SU, 63rd Inf.
COLLINS, William M. S1951, R, 5th (McKenzie's) Cav.
COLLINSWORTH, Bettie Rains, W8797, G, Collinsworth, Andrew Jackson
COLLIS, Mary Elizabeth, W2573, SH, Collis, Clean
COLLOM, Hiram, S11653, MC, 3rd Inf.
COLLOM, R. N. S11194, WA, 63rd Inf.
COLLUM, Fannie Malinda, W9548, H, Collum, John Basil
COLMAN, John C. S13793, HU, 50th Inf.
COLN, George J. S12347, MN, Moreland's Regt. Ala. Cav.
COLN, Thomas Theodore, S3878, MN, 6th Miss. Cav.
COLQUIT, William, S7494, WL, 4th (McLemore's) Cav.
COLQUITT, Ludie F. W6664, WL, Colquitt, Wm.
COLQUITT, William T. S5255, MU, 1st Inf.
COLSTON, E. C. S618, MR, 1st Ky. Cav.
COLSTON, Elizabeth, W5672, MR, Colston, Ephrum
COLSTON, Jackson, S299, MR, 6th Ala. Inf.
COLVARD, Euphremia L. W10146, BL, Colvard, W. M.
COLVERT, George H. S3279, DK, 1st Bn. (Colm's) Inf.
COLVERT, John E. ("Dock"), S12764, MU, 1st Bn. (Colm's) Inf.
COLVILLE, Young, S8960, R, 16th Bn. Cav.
COLWELL, Edward, S436, RU, 2nd Inf.
COLWELL, J. G. S4557, MU, 45th Inf.
COLWELL, Mary A. W138, WI, Colwell, John G.
COMBET, Virginia Moses, W4804, SH, Combet, Joseph
COMBS, Daniel C. S13051, H, 5th Ky. Inf.
COMBS, Elma Victory, W1051, MN, Combs, Charles Augustus
COMBS, Eveline, W6686, T, Combs, David C.
COMBS, James H. S9376, BE, 5th Inf.
COMBS, John V. S10561, SU, 61st Inf.
COMBS, Louisa M. W7861, SU, Combs, John V.
COMBS, Mack, S7377, MR, 34th Inf.
COMBS, Martha A. E. W398, D, Combs, David
COMBS, Nancy, W2624, SU, Combs, Wm. B.
COMBS, Oliver Calwell, S15527, DY, 21st Miss. Inf.
COMBS, R. F. S15418, CL, 45th Inf.
COMBS, Sarah, W3760, CT, Combs, Wm.

COMBS, W. B. S10995, SU, 26th Inf.
COMER, Eliza Jane, W1137, HN, Comer, Edward A.
COMER, W. H. S6031, S13106, SH, 2nd Miss. Cav.
COMPTON, A. B. S16150, CH, Salisbury Prison Guard Bn. (NC Defense)
COMPTON, Callie, W1739, D, Compton, Richard
COMPTON, Eli, S8167, 5th Inf.
COMPTON, H. C. W1069, D, Compton, W. B.
COMPTON, Mary G. W7968, Compton, Eli
COMPTON, Richard, S8950, D, 9th Bn. Cav.
COMPTON, Wealthy W. W1619, R, Compton, Wm. Anderson
COMSTOCK, Alvizary A. W2475, HE, Comstock, Charles Marvin
COMSTOCK, Charles Marvin, S9598, HE, 32nd Inf.
CONASTER, Martha Englantine, W4450, PI, Conaster, James K.
CONAWAY, A. L. S8741, LI, 41st Inf.
CONAWAY, Rane M. S379, LI, 41st Inf.
CONDER, Martin L. S8809, DE, 3rd Vol. Inf.
CONDITT, Mary, W3460, SM, Conditt, Wm. H.
CONDRA, Delilah, W1848, MR, Condra, Howell
CONDRA, Esther, W2661, MR, Condra, Wm.
CONDRA, William, S1896, MR, 4th (McLemore's) Cav.
CONE, G. W. S11735, L, 14th Inf.
CONE, John R. S2561, MN, 21st (Wilson's) Cav.
CONE, Mary C. W10391, L, Cone, G. M.
CONE, W. W. S8122, L, 47th Inf.
CONKIN, Moses, S7036, SU, 60th Inf.
CONKLIN, Alfred, S9986, L, 15th (Stewart's) Cav.
CONKLIN, Bettie Bowen, W4179, SH, Conklin, James Franklin
CONLEY, Easter, W2310, PI, Conley, James
CONLEY, Eliza Ann, W3705, BE, Conley, Wm.
CONLEY, James, S241, D, 10th Inf.
CONLEY, L. P. S10249, WH, 25th Inf.
CONLEY, M. H. S5836, HI, 17th Inf.
CONLEY, Matilda M. W2046, HI, Conley, Milton H.
CONLEY, Nancy, W245, GE, Conley, Franklin
CONLEY, Sarah Elizabeth, W7563, DY, Conley, Thomas G.
CONLEY, T. G. S6580, DY, 50th Inf.
CONN, George Adams, C198, B, Unassigned

CONN, J. A. S10402, FR, 32nd Inf.
CONN, James, S12142, K, 59th Inf.
CONN, Jesse, S3939, O, 14th Cav.
CONNALLY, Thadeus B. S14398, MA, 4th Ala. Cav.
CONNELL, J. M. S37, RB, 11th Inf.
CONNELL, Mattie J. W3302, G, Connell, John W.
CONNELLY, James, S866, D, 10th Inf.
CONNELLY, John, S2010, K, 10th Inf.
CONNER, George T. S9629, JE, 2nd N.C. Cav.
CONNER, John C. S15525, WE, 12th Ky. Cav.
CONNER, Joseph F. S13456, MA, 51st Inf.
CONNER, Laura Adelaide, W7302, H, Conner, Wm. Franklin
CONNER, Margaret A. W4524, JE, Conner, George T.
CONNER, P. N. S13720, L, 9th Inf.
CONNER, Robert, S14262, SE, Unassigned (Enrolling Officer)
CONNER, W. B. S500, H, 55th Inf.
CONNOR, C. C. sr. S16313, L, 11th Cav.
CONNOR, Hutoka, W8914, WE, Connor, Samuel Martin
CONNOR, J. C. S15437, GI, 5th Miss. Cav.
CONNOR, Thomas, S153, D, 10th Inf.
CONRY, Mary Cox, W6805, H, Conry, Peter
CONWAY, Lawrance F. S3404, SH, 1st Art.
CONWAY, Timothy, S11315, SH, 2nd Bn. Ala. Lt. Art.
CONYERS, T. F. S5450, CC, 15th Cav.
COOK, A. Jenkins, S4910, B, 55th Inf.
COOK, A. S. S4089, G, 9th Cav.
COOK, Alta, W11168, D, Cook, Benjamin F.
COOK, B. F. S12452, D, 1st Cav.
COOK, Bettie, W7576, WE, Cook, John W.
COOK, Delilah, W3744, HO, Cook, Carroll A.
COOK, E. K. S15541, WL, 4th (McLemore's) Cav.
COOK, E. M. S14680, WH, 43rd Ga. Inf.
COOK, Eliza, W132, SU, Cook, David
COOK, Eliza G. W3, WI, Cook, Edmund Collingsworth
COOK, Elizabeth, W5401, CT, Cook, W. A. D.
COOK, Elizabeth Taylor, W2425, DI, Cook, Wm. Richard
COOK, Ellen, W1574, RB, Cook, Jacob
COOK, G. J. S6745, MN, 21st (Wilson's) Cav.
COOK, George E. S2925, GI, 32nd Inf.
COOK, I. W. S8951, G, Sparkman's Lt. Art.
COOK, J. A. S9417, F, 24th N.C. Inf.

COOK, J. A. W. S7064, MO, 3rd (Lillard's) Mtd. Inf.
COOK, J. D. S705, F, 47th Inf.
COOK, J. E. S8596, RB, 9th Ky. Inf.
COOK, J. F. S8038, G, 22nd Inf.
COOK, J. G. S16314, D, 8th Cav.
COOK, J. N. S8172, WE, 12th Ky. Cav.
COOK, J. T. S13215, G, 19th (Biffle's) Cav.
COOK, James F. S3044, MS, 4th (McLemore's) Cav.
COOK, James M. S4871, D, 1st (Feild's) Inf.
COOK, John, S14001, OV, 25th Inf.
COOK, John F. S7989, G, 14th Inf.
COOK, John F. S8136, MO, 13th Tex. Inf.
COOK, John H. S12286, SU, 46th N.C. Militia
COOK, John W. S5893, WE, 31st Inf.
COOK, Julia Ann, W8415, OV, Cook, John
COOK, Lemuel, S14093, D, 49th Ala. Inf.
COOK, Lucinda Mayo, W9395, HY, Cook, Hartwell
COOK, Martha Eliza, W1640, G, Cook, Wm. M.
COOK, Mary Elizabeth, W7045, HR, Cook, Robert Alexander
COOK, Mary Fannie, W1416, G, Cook, Anthony Shem
COOK, Mary Jane, W891, MS, Cook, James David
COOK, R. A. S1792, HR, 13th Inf.
COOK, S. L. S3865, CF, 39th Ga. Inf.
COOK, Sue L. W508, GI, Cook, George Edmund
COOK, Susan, W10175, WL, Cook, E. K.
COOK, Tempey, W1716, O, Cook, W. B.
COOK, Thaddeus C. S2120, GI, 32nd Inf.
COOK, Thomas, S6828, MS, 4th (McLemore's) Cav.
COOK, Thomas F. S4418, UN, 1st Cav.
COOK, W. A. S4904, SH, 29th Ark. Inf.
COOK, W. A. D. S4211, CT, 64th Va. Inf.
COOK, W. N. S750, T, 47th Inf.
COOK, W. P. S13534, MU, Sparkman's Co. Lt. Art.
COOK, William, S8005, G, 14th Cav.
COOK, William L. S6408, WE, 22nd N.C. Inf.
COOKE, Ann Rebecca, W4825, F, Cooke, Joseph Atlas
COOKE, Hartwell, S14259, HY, 9th Inf.
COOKE, Matilda H. W3974, MC, Cooke, John Brazelton
COOKE, Robert A. S2852, RU, 45th Inf.
COOKE, Susan P. W3526, RU, Cooke, Robert A.

COOKLEY, Louisa, W7428, WH, Cookley, James
COOKSEY, E. N. S9606, MT, 50th Inf.
COOKSEY, W. M. S11696, SM, 44th Inf.
COOKSTON, Isaac, S1612, MC, 5th Cav.
COOKSTON, Mary, W4502, H, Cookston, Isaac
COOLEY, John F. S4145, WH, 15th Cav.
COOLEY, John M. S12229, LO, 16th Bn. Cav.
COOLEY, L. B. S16542, S15866, G, 10th Cav.
COOLEY, Missouri Tennessee, W2007, W2521, SN, Cooley, Albert Gallalin
COOLEY, Phillip M. S4433, SQ, 3rd Cav.
COOLEY, T. J. S275, HD, 2nd Miss. Inf.
COOP, James H. S12590, S15174, B, 18th Inf.
COOPER, Ada Frances [Ramsey], W10966, Cooper, Robert Allen, [Later married Ramsey]
COOPER, Ada Hill, W4670, HN, Cooper, James Porter
COOPER, Alfred T. S6677, LE, 19th (Biffle's) Cav.
COOPER, Alice Greenlee, W9304, JE, Cooper, Thomas J.
COOPER, Barshaba, W5972, HM, Cooper, William J.
COOPER, Bettie, W5358, H, Cooper, Joseph
COOPER, Daniel Brooks, S15350, CH, 51st Inf.
COOPER, Delila Clementine, W892, CA, Cooper, Isaac
COOPER, F. M. S3811, ME, 3rd Inf.
COOPER, F. P. S8224, MA, 19th Cav.
COOPER, G. G. S12235, DY, 51st Inf.
COOPER, G. M. S5378, PU, 8th Cav.
COOPER, G. W. S12401, MA, 6th Inf.
COOPER, George M. S11834, R, 69th N.C. Inf.
COOPER, George W. S10626, D, 18th Inf.
COOPER, George W. S16306, J, 12th Cav.
COOPER, H. L. S3547, HM, 60th Inf.
COOPER, Isaac, S902, GI, 1st Cav.
COOPER, J. A. S9818, CA, 8th (Smith's) Cav.
COOPER, J. G. S14589, JA, 60th Ga. Inf.
COOPER, J. P. S9892, SU, 59th Inf.
COOPER, J. W. S4617, FR, 1st (Turney's) Inf.
COOPER, Jacob G. S9451, S15066, 27th Inf.
COOPER, James L. S8564, DY, 20th (Russell's) Cav.
COOPER, James M. S8641, D, 1st (Turney's) Inf.
COOPER, James Porter, S4786, HN, 5th Inf.
COOPER, Jane Catharine, W4826, K, Cooper, Wm. Jacob
COOPER, John A. S5324, H, 35th Inf.

Index to Tennessee Confederate Pension Applications

COOPER, John L. S7343, C, 2nd Cav.
COOPER, Jonathan N. B. S11362, GR, 59th Mtd. Inf.
COOPER, Jones Walker, S16691, G, 1st Ark. Cav.
COOPER, Joseph, S3131, ME, 17th Ky. Cav.
COOPER, L. B. S1197, LE, 3rd Inf.
COOPER, Maggie Ellen, W10512, FR, Cooper, Thomas M.
COOPER, Margaret Elizabeth, W6620, CA, Cooper, Joseph A.
COOPER, Martha, W4704, PU, Cooper, Nathan C.
COOPER, Martha Ann, W1961, PU, Cooper, G. M.
COOPER, Martin, S5000, SN, 55th Inf.
COOPER, Mary Elizabeth, W8752, SH, Cooper, Wm. Manuel
COOPER, Nancy Lasly, W10569, HR, Cooper, Solomon Edwin
COOPER, Nathan, S2542, PU, 8th (Dibrell's) Cav.
COOPER, O. M. S8016, SM, 8th (Dibrell's) Cav.
COOPER, P. P. S2107, CY, 28th Inf.
COOPER, Rebecca Jane, W5620, FR, Cooper, J. W.
COOPER, Robert T. S10870, FR, 17th Inf.
COOPER, S. Caroline L. W5641, W5909, PU, Cooper, Wm. K.
COOPER, S. G. S12145, G, 20th (Russell's) Cav.
COOPER, Sallie Virginia, W5681, G, Cooper, Sinai Graves
COOPER, Sarah E. W6157, GR, Cooper, Harpeth L.
COOPER, Susan E. W5182, D, Cooper, James Monroe
COOPER, Susan Levina, W9120, SU, Cooper, James P.
COOPER, T. J. S4235, JE, 60th Inf.
COOPER, Thomas M. S3333, FR, 4th Cav.
COOPER, W. H. S6980, CF, 4th Inf.
COOPER, W. K. S5325, PU, 8th Cav.
COOPER, W. T. S11327, BE, William's Co. Cav.
COOPER, William M. S16689, SH, 1st Bn. Ark. Inf.
COOPER, William T. S12242, J, 17th Inf.
COPASS, M. S. S1366, SU, 60th Inf.
COPE, A. J. S15340, WH, 16th Inf.
COPE, Arrany, W8908, WH, Cope, Harrison H.

COPE, D. J. S15197, DY, 20th (Russell's) Cav.
COPE, Elizabeth, W8265, G, Cope, Daniel J.
COPE, J. M. S115, WH, 16th Inf.
COPE, Jane, W2479, WH, Cope, Jesse
COPE, Minerva Jane, W568, OV, Cope, Joseph Marion
COPE, Nancy Jane, W3605, WH, Cope, James Madison
COPELAND, A. J. S11445, OV, 25th Inf.
COPELAND, B. A. S13955, S16002, WH, 28th & 84th Consolidated Inf.
COPELAND, Bitha Ann, W6433, OV, Copeland, S. Leander
COPELAND, Eliza, W7900, OV, Copeland, Andrew Jackson
COPELAND, F. M. S404, OV, 25th Inf.
COPELAND, James E. S4400, PU, 28th Inf.
COPELAND, Mary L. W4277, OV, Copeland, James Calvin
COPELAND, Mary Lewis, W10237, G, Copeland, Wm. Edward
COPELAND, Melvina, W224, OV, Copeland, Mathew
COPELAND, S. L. S185.5, D, 8th Inf.
COPELAND, Sarah A. W3658, CU, Copeland, S. A.
COPELAND, Soloman Addison, S7158, CU, 25th Inf.
COPELAND, W. M. S6268, CY, 8th Inf.
COPENHAVER, Henry, S9762, RO, 63rd Va. Inf.
COPLAND, A. J. S1044, OV, 19th (Biffle's) Cav.
COPLAND, Rhoda, W346, MOO, Copland, Nickles
COPP, John, S2495, WA, 63rd Inf.
COPP, Kissie Elizabeth, W6870, WA, Copp, Wm. David
COPP, M. S12994, WA, 63rd Inf.
COPPENGER, Alice, W7743, MO, Coppenger, E. E.
CORBETT, Mary E. W1643, JE, Corbett, Wm. J.
CORBETT, William J. S4827, JE, 12th Bn. Cav.
CORBIN, Sarah A. W3500, CL, Corbin, Alvis C.
CORBITT, H. B. S14788, HN, 5th Inf.
CORBITT, Joseph M. S8895, D, 11th Inf.
CORBITT, Ruth Josephine, W2667, BE, Corbitt, Jacob Smith
CORBITT, W. D. S14611, O, 10th Cav.

CORDELL, Susan Emelin, W2311, H, Cordell, Wiley
CORDER, Benjamin Green, S7080, LI, 44th Inf.
CORDER, Hannah Elizabeth, W557, LI, Corder, John Andrew
CORDER, J. A. S2632, LI, 17th S.C. Vols.
CORDER, Robert A. S10574, WI, 8th (Smith's) Cav.
CORE, Louise Gillespie, W3088, WI, Core, Jessee Gillis
CORKRAN, P. H. S4136, RB, 2nd Inf.
CORLETT, Sarah Eilzabeth, W3843, W4983, MS, Corlett, Alphonso Work
CORLEW, Mary, W227, DI, Corlew, John Randolph
CORLEY, John B. S8685, D, 8th Inf.
CORLEY, Mary Ann, W7673, MA, Corley, Nat C.
CORLEY, Nannie Rosamond, W6342, D, Corley, John Burford
CORLEY, Nathan, S873, DK, 24th Inf.
CORLEY, Nathaniel C. S8123, G, 47th Inf.
CORLEY, Seth M. S7555, SM, 23rd Inf.
CORN, Cullie, W9890, CF, Corn, Wm. Jefferson
CORN, Jesse B. S5360, FR, 17th Inf.
CORN, T. J. S4401, FR, 32nd Inf.
CORNANT, Amanda A. W3888, LI, Cornant, James H.
CORNELISON, Jesse, S4169, CF, 1st (Turney's) Inf.
CORNELIUS, John E. S16274, MN, 11th Cav.
CORNELIUS, Nannie E. W10775, MN, Cornelius, Ira E.
CORNET, John, S8928, CT, 58th N.C. Inf.
CORNETT, James A. S15655, SU, 37th Va. Inf.
CORNETT, John, S16032, CT, 58th N.C. Inf.
CORNWELL, F. C. S9463, TR, 9th (Bennett's) Cav. See also Fuscha Cornwell
CORNWELL, Fuscha, S13190, SM, 9th (Ward's) Cav. See also F. C. Cornwell
CORNWELL, James W. S5379, GE, 29th Inf.
CORNWELL, John S. S4162, WL, 24th Inf.
CORPIER, Sarah J. W4943, GI, Corpier, W. A.
CORPIER, W. A. S2726, S4951, LI, 32nd Inf.
CORRELL, George W. S14273, U, 1st Bn. (Colm's) Inf.
CORTNER, Bettie S. W9128, D, Cortner, Matthew
CORTNER, Daniel, S16013, B, 23rd Inf.
CORUM, Adline, W6058, DY, Corum, Abigo
CORUM, D. C. S3536, O, 23rd Inf.

CORUM, Georgia Ann, W10531, JO, Corum, Robert Galen
CORUM, H. C. S7438, SN, 28th Inf.
CORUM, Martha Jane, W1614, D, Corum, Ila Douglas
CORUM, Mary jane, W5173, O, Corum, Don Carliss
CORUM, Rachel Frances, W5324, SN, Corum, Henry Clinton
CORUM, Robert G. S10044, JO, 20th Inf.
CORUM, S. R. S2585, SM, 25th Inf.
COSBY, E. H. S4402, GI, 3rd (Clack's) Inf.
COSBY, Ella Bush, W9894, H, Cosby, Williamson Marion
COSBY, John, S8914, RU, 7th Inf.
COSBY, Missouri Jane, W4367, GI, Cosby, Epharnam H.
COSSENBERRY, Ephriam N. S501, WY, 1st Mo. Inf.
COSSON, Cassie Almyra, W7164, HM, Cosson, S. E.
COSTNER, Joseph W. S10956, CO, 49th N.C. Inf.
COSTNER, Thomas, S3133, BO, 38th N.C. Inf.
COTHAM, Ida, W10904, HI, Cotham, Wm. S.
COTHAM, W. S. S15411, HI, 24th Inf.
COTHCUTT, William H. See Cathcart, William H.
COTHRAN, Bettie, W7214, T, Cothran, Eldridge G.
COTHRAN, Gilford, S16633, WE, 1st (Feild's) Inf.
COTHRAN, Mary Ellen, W5880, SM, Cothran, Wm. Harris
COTHRAN, R. W. S2212, HI, 48th (Voorhies') Inf.
COTHREN, F. D. S1886, WE, 23rd Inf.
COTHREN, Martha J. W1155, DY, Cothren, Franklin D.
COTHREN, Mary Ann, W8894, CH, Cothren, Robert
COTNAM, J. M. S14328, MR, 3rd Confederate Cav.
COTTEN, R. J. S5380, SH, 4th Inf.
COTTEN, William A. S1477, W, 16th Inf.
COTTER, Barbara A. W2486, SU, Cotter, George W.
COTTER, George W. S286, SU, 59th Inf.
COTTON, Alonzo, C283, D, Undetermined
COTTON, Amanda, W7194, K, Cotton, James
COTTON, Ida, W5458, DY, Cotton, Tom

Index to Tennessee Confederate Pension Applications

COTTON, James, S11177, K, 3rd GA Bn. Sharpshooters
COTTON, James R. S9549, SH, 9th Miss. Inf.
COTTON, John N. S13801, SH, 23rd Ark. Inf.
COTTON, John P. S10636, WH, 23rd Inf.
COTTON, Mary Ann, W2714, W, Cotton, Wm. Alexander
COTTON, Mary V. W2990, SH, Cotton, James Richard
COTTON, R. F. S15247, WI, 4th (McLemore's) Cav.
COTTON, Sarah J. W2011, HI, Cotton, Jessie V.
COTTRELL, George Washington, S1891, LA, 27th Ala. Inf.
COTTRELL, J. T. S7854, WA, 5th (McKenzie's) Cav.
COTTRELL, J. W. S7855, WA, 5th (McKenzie's) Cav.
COTTRELL, Lydia M. W2738, LA, Cottrell, George W.
COTTRELL, Richard, S6050, MO, 62nd Inf.
COUCH, D. I. S8468, H, 4th Cav.
COUCH, Frances Josephine, W8080, WI, Couch, Joseph E.
COUCH, J. D. S14168, D, 4th Cav.
COUCH, John, S5995, ME, 26th Inf.
COUCH, Joseph E. S8746, WI, 4th (McLemore's) Cav.
COUCH, Mary Ellen, W6171, D, Couch, Edgar William
COUCH, Nancy Ann, W9941, H, Couch, George Washington
COUCH, Nancy P. W109, W, Couch, Joseph W.
COUDER, Elizabeth, W1329, LI, Couder, John Jefferson
COUGHLIN, Thomas, S15665, D, 10th Bn. Ga. Inf.
COULESTON, S. S7477, MN, 32nd Inf.
COULTER, A. J. S14461, H, 16th Bn. Cav.
COULTER, Sarah Jane, W2189, BO, Coulter, Robert Riley
COUNCIL, Joseph C. S10358, HE, 27th Inf.
COUNCIL, Sarah Elizabeth, W4202, O, Council, Thomas Dudley
COUNCIL, Sarah Warner, W3659, DI, Council, Willis
COUNCIL, T. D. S10314, O, 42nd Inf.
COUNTESS, E. H. S5873, SU, 13th Bn. Art.
COUNTISS, Robert, S15324, FR, 28th Cav.
COURSEY, Joseph, S5050, CA, 24th Inf.

COURTNEY, Catherine Anne, W5617, HW, Courtney, John Riley
COURTNEY, Stephen, S3339, GE, 61st Inf.
COURTNEY, W. W. S13899, WI, 32nd Inf.
COUSER, T. L. S6021, FR, 37th Inf.
COUSINS, Fannie Ellen, W3068, L, Cousins, Nathaniel Milton
COUSINS, Mary Ann, W3875, W1205, CC, Cousins, Robert Thomas
COUSINS, Nathan Milton, S2543, L, 27th Inf.
COVEY, L. E. S11599, O, 1st (Feild's) Inf.
COVEY, W. R. S9276, MU, 1st (Feild's) Inf.
COVINGTON, Della McCord, W8891, RU, Covington, John J.
COVINGTON, E. A. S3154, B, 23rd Inf.
COVINGTON, E. H. S12650, HN, 14th Inf.
COVINGTON, E. J. S6504, MT, 6th N.C. Inf.
COVINGTON, India C. W8667, CA, Covington, John A.
COVINGTON, J. A. S14694, WE, 20th (Russell's) Cav.
COVINGTON, J. F. S4648, SN, 13th Inf.
COVINGTON, Matilda, W6523, SN, Covington, J. F.
COVINGTON, Ruth Franklin, W377, RU, Covington, Wm. Franklin
COVINGTON, T. L. S11235, D, 20th Inf.
COVINGTON, Tennessee, W6063, D, Covington, Robert W.
COWAN, Eliza J. W8291, FR, Cowan, John R.
COWAN, Florence E. W2932, DI, Cowan, John Max
COWAN, Hattie McGavock, W9539, WI, Cowan, George Limerick
COWAN, James B. S11290, CF, 3rd (Forrest's) Cav.
COWAN, Lucy C. W2845, CF, Cowan, James Benjamin
COWAN, Maggie B. W7425, D, Cowan, James C.
COWAN, Mahlon S. S15659, SU, 37th Va. Inf.
COWAN, Mary Louise Murta, W11159, SH, Cowan, John Stephen Randall, Papers found mixed with 11157 on film
COWAN, Samantha Catherine, W6024, FR, Cowan, Wm. Michael
COWAN, Sarah Bell, W2317, HY, Cowan, Robert Cameran
COWARD, James W. S9630, MA, 1st S.C. Cav.
COWARD, Matilda, W6915, K, Coward, Thomas

COWARD, Thomas, S14548, K, 3rd (Lillard's) Mtd. Inf.
COWARDIN, Ella R. W7615, WE, Cowardin, Henry C.
COWARDIN, H. C. S7963, WE, 2nd (Robison's) Inf.
COWART, Jennie A. W5642, H, Cowart, Thomas
COWDEN, Lizzie, W5780, MS, Cowden, Wm. Morris
COWELL, Martha Ellen, W248, BE, Cowell, Berry
COWEN, George W. S823, SM, 28th Inf.
COWEN, Martha A. W5810, PU, Cowen, George W.
COWEN, W. M. S7479, LK, 1st (Turney's) Inf.
COWLES, R. S. S14648, WI, 45th Inf.
COWSER, Sallie A. W1390, FR, Cowser, Thomas L.
COWSETT, Isaac K. S4677, WI, 3rd Inf.
COX, Asa, S5579, HN, 7th Cav.
COX, Clarisa A. W8388, JE, Cox, Wm. K.
COX, David, S13365, CU, 45th Inf.
COX, Elvira V. W3714, SU, Cox, A. J.
COX, Endora, W2972, MA, Cox, Wm. Hamlin
COX, F. M. S12924, HR, 14th (Neely's) Cav.
COX, Fannie Lou, W11023, SU, Cox, Jesse Hyder
COX, G. S. S385, O, 33rd Inf.
COX, George W. S11051, T, 12th Cav.
COX, Hardie, S9910, CU, 16th Bn. (Neal's) Cav.
COX, Henry, S5943, LA, 48th (Nixon's) Inf.
COX, J. A. S15756, MR, 2nd Ga. Bn. Inf.
COX, J. D. S15213, O, Forrest's Scouts, Cav.
COX, J. H. S7814, SU, 4th Ky. Cav.
COX, J. M. S8268, SM, 24th Inf.
COX, J. M. S9444, SU, 4th Ky. Cav.
COX, J. P. S9484, O, 5th Inf.
COX, J. R. S11033, ST, 1st Ky. Cav.
COX, J. R. S11744, SU, 29th Inf.
COX, Jacob, S10592, MU, 2nd (Ashby's) Cav.
COX, James, S8932, ME, 5th Cav.
COX, James H. S2328, HW, 12th Cav.
COX, James Madison, S3324, R, 1st (Carter's) Cav.
COX, Joel, S10705, MU, 10th (DeMoss') Cav.
COX, John, S11371, S12056, WL, 4th (McLemore's) Cav.
COX, John B. S5256, HM, 61st Inf.
COX, John B. S11866, K, 3rd S.C. Cav.

COX, John N. S16428, MN, 18th (Newsom's) Cav.
COX, Lawson J. S16610, HN, 20th (Russell's) Cav.
COX, Leroy, S2597, JE, 1st Cav.
COX, Louisa C. W9694, HI, Cox, John M.
COX, Louise, W2538, K, Cox, John Bartlett
COX, Louisie Columbia, W4839, O, Cox, John Marion
COX, Martha L. W2762, SU, Cox, Henry W.
COX, Martin V. S1785, HW, 16th Bn. Cav.
COX, Mary Ann, W8627, CU, Cox, David
COX, Mary Docia, W10196, WA, Cox, Wm. Taylor
COX, Mary E. W1368, WI, Cox, J. T.
COX, Mary L. W7308, SM, Cox, James Madison
COX, Nancy, W5233, RU, Cox, Thomas D.
COX, Nathan M. S2132, PU, 4th Cav.
COX, Noah, S11731, SU, 60th Inf.
COX, Rachel Emeline, W6241, SU, Cox, Samuel R.
COX, Ritta M. W731, HR, Cox, Wilson W.
COX, Robin, S2549, WL, 4th (McLemore's) Cav.
COX, S. R. S8940, SU, 60th Inf.
COX, Susan Jane, W1541, MU, Cox, William James
COX, Susannah Elizabeth, W2450, PU, Cox, Henry Clifton
COX, Tabitha Louisa, W599, CC, Cox, Robert Henry
COX, Taylor, S10877, WA, 1st (Carter's) Cav.
COX, Terrasena, W10356, ST, Cox, Joseph Robert
COX, Thomas D. S2263, RU, 44th Inf.
COX, Virginia Emeline, W2805, SU, Cox, James G.
COX, W. F. S12925, HR, 14th (Neely's) Cav., Also see other W. F. Cox
COX, W. F. S16093, HR, 14th Cav., Also see other W. F. Cox
COX, W. H. S8883, WE, 27th Inf.
COX, W. H. S11251, MA, 19th (Biffle's) Cav.
COX, W. J. S1957, MU, 3rd Inf.
COX, W. K. S15351, JE, 60th Inf.
COX, William L. S10475, GI, 9th Ala. Inf.
COX, lucie Jane, W8882, HR, Cox, Wm. Franklin
COZART, B. F. S8452, LE, 24th Inf.
COZART, Gilbert, S6488, DY, 32nd Tex. Cav.
COZART, James, S1922, HE, 27th Inf.

Index to Tennessee Confederate Pension Applications

COZART, James W. S5257, CL, 1st Cav.
COZORT, Nancy, W3850, CL, Cozort, James W.
CRABB, J. F. S5739, SN, 2nd Inf.
CRABB, Mary E. W1144, GI, Crabb, Freeland
CRABB, William, S2077, SN, 2nd Cav.
CRABTREE, Aurilla, W7731, CF, Crabtree, J. C.
CRABTREE, Emily, W412, OV, Crabtree, John Wesley
CRABTREE, Ewell, S12408, RO, 5th Cav.
CRABTREE, F. F. S8033, LI, 32nd Inf.
CRABTREE, George W. S14132, LI, 8th Inf.
CRABTREE, J. C. S3490, MN, 1st N.C. Inf.
CRABTREE, J. C. S3706, CF, 25th Ark. Inf.
CRABTREE, J. H. S5394, LI, 32nd Inf.
CRABTREE, J. H. S8837, J, 5th Cav.
CRABTREE, James, S7105, RB, 14th Inf.
CRABTREE, Mary J. W1431, GI, Crabtree, Wm. Nathaniel
CRABTREE, Nancy, W8472, RO, Crabtree, Ewell
CRABTREE, Nancy S. W1362, MS, Crabtree, Wm. Meridick
CRABTREE, Roena Emmaline, W7143, LI, Crabtree, John Henry
CRABTREE, Sarah, W2498, RO, Crabtree, Wm.
CRABTREE, W. I, S12110, GU, 44th Inf.
CRABTREE, W. N. S5740, GI, 44th Inf.
CRADDOCK, Catherine E. W1306, CC, Craddock, Wm. Millard
CRADDOCK, N. L. S9568, RU, 24th Inf.
CRAFTON, C. A. S9724, DY, 23rd Va. Inf.
CRAFTON, G. H. S15631, O, 11th (Holman's) Cav.
CRAFTON, Sallie M. W9369, D, Crafton, Daniel Shelburn
CRAFTON, Soloman, S12678, WI, 42nd Inf.
CRAFTON, William S. S13217, D, 11th (Holman's) Cav.
CRAIG, B. C. S2908, R, 31st Inf.
CRAIG, Elizabeth P. W572, WE, Craig, Columbus F.
CRAIG, Felicia Elizabeth, W6004, MU, Craig, Samuel Monroe
CRAIG, George W. S6028, B, 41st Inf.
CRAIG, J. E. S3921, DI, 10th Cav.
CRAIG, J. J. S14802, SH, 19th (Biffle's) Cav.
CRAIG, James Lafayette, S13344, HM, 61st Inf.
CRAIG, Jane, W1033, R, Craig, Barton C.
CRAIG, Margaret A. W2537, MU, Craig, Robert Elihu
CRAIG, Margaret Ruth, W8927, LA, Craig, Rufus Franklin
CRAIG, Martha F. W122, LA, Craig, James Archibald
CRAIG, Martha Jane, W328, MS, Craig, Burrell B.
CRAIG, Millie Mildred, W366, D, Craig, Larkin Brooks
CRAIG, N. S. S12944, MU, 48th (Voorhies') Inf.
CRAIG, Nancy Ann, W2788, D, Craig, Wm. S.
CRAIG, Nancy Elizabeth, W7636, W4180, P, Craig, Eleazor Hardman
CRAIG, Newton H. S15905, SH, 12th Cav.
CRAIG, P. H. S14408, WY, 20th (Nixon's) Cav.
CRAIG, R. F. S9848, LA, 3rd (Clack's) Inf.
CRAIG, Robert M. S1585, DY, 17th Inf.
CRAIG, S. E. S16548, WY, 48th (Nixon's) Inf.
CRAIG, S. S. S7147, MU, 3rd Inf.
CRAIG, S. S. S7378, MU, 48th Inf.
CRAIG, W. D. S5716, DY, 48th Inf.
CRAIG, Woodford, S14639, D, 22nd (Barteu's) Cav.
CRAIGHEAD, W. J. S2626, SM, 44th Inf.
CRAIN, E. W. S16303, S16593, L, 14th Mo. Inf.
CRAIN, Mary Frances, W5211, WY, Crain, Henry Stratton
CRANE, Martin V. S5006, SU, 5th Ga. Battery
CRANE, Viney, W7681, K, Crane, Wm.
CRANE, William, S4613, CL, 64th Inf.
CRASS, F. H. S13256, RU, 1st (Feild's) Inf.
CRAVANS, P. C. S2026, OV, 25th Inf.
CRAVEN, Ewell L. S13136, G, 21st (Wilson's) Cav.
CRAVEN, J. W. S15155, O, 7th Cav.
CRAVER, D. F. S12340, O, 42nd N.C. Inf.
CRAWFORD, Alex N. S31, MS, 32nd Inf.
CRAWFORD, Ann, W4044, SU, Crawford, James
CRAWFORD, C. Y. S4419, K, 4th Va. Inf.
CRAWFORD, David H. S3290, MR, 10th S.C. Inf.
CRAWFORD, E. D. S3400, H, 19th Inf.
CRAWFORD, Ephraim, S464, HW, 29th Inf.
CRAWFORD, Ezekiel N. S7574, LI, 1st (Turney's) Inf.
CRAWFORD, Fannie A. W4039, SU, Crawford, Samuel H.

CRAWFORD, Fannie J. W5354, F, Crawford, John Kerr
CRAWFORD, G. W. S5637, WH, 6th Ky. Cav.
CRAWFORD, J. R. S6438, R, 26th Inf.
CRAWFORD, J. R. S9079, FR, 41st Inf.
CRAWFORD, J. R. S9647, S9593, SU, 60th Inf.
CRAWFORD, Jackson, S4375, SU, 29th Inf.
CRAWFORD, Jemima Frances, W4040, Crawford, James S. A. Applied from Henrico Co. Va.
CRAWFORD, Julia F. W3929, H, Crawford, Wm. Harvey
CRAWFORD, Margaret Elizabeth, W3594, HU, Crawford, John R.
CRAWFORD, Martha E. W761, SU, Crawford, Ephraim
CRAWFORD, Mary C. W3406, R, Crawford, James R.
CRAWFORD, Mary M. W6810, K, Crawford, Robert R.
CRAWFORD, Matilda Caroline, W9755, HR, Crawford, Robert Raford
CRAWFORD, Nathan E. S9533, GE, 60th Inf.
CRAWFORD, R. N. S7709, HR, 32nd Ark. Inf.
CRAWFORD, R. R. S14764, HR, Polk's Battery, Lt. Art.
CRAWFORD, Samuel, S9116, HW, 1st Bn. (Colm's) Inf.
CRAWFORD, Samuel H. S5395, SU, 63rd Inf.
CRAWFORD, Sarah Hester, W3377, K, Crawford, Thomas Ellis
CRAWFORD, Thomas C. S8055, MU, 14th Inf.
CRAWFORD, Thomas N. S11694, HR, 7th Cav.
CRAWFORD, W. E. S12366, F, 13th Inf.
CRAWFORD, William P. S4333, S1196, C, 19th Inf.
CREAMER, C. B. S14101, HY, 11th Ala. Cav.
CREASEY, J. R. S12812, HW, 12th Bn. (Day's) Cav.
CREASMAN, William L. S13833, WA, 66th N.C. Troops
CREASY, J. M. S4567, DE, 52nd Inf.
CREASY, J. M. S14072, M, 24th Inf.
CREASY, Joseph, S7990, SN, 1st Cav.
CREASY, William H. S1660, HW, 12th Cav.
CREECH, Barbara, W3100, HW, Creech, Elijah H.
CRENSHAW, F. M. S13831, SH, 51st Inf.
CRENSHAW, Hardin, S7053, D, 20th Inf.
CRENSHAW, J. M. S12086, TR, 2nd (Robison's) Inf.

CRENSHAW, James C. S10884, D, 55th Inf.
CRENSHAW, Sinai T. W305, TR, Crenshaw, Thomas Jefferson
CRESAP, N. A. S15835, G, 47th Inf.
CRESAP, Nancy Jane, W8917, HD, Cresap, Virgil Augustus
CRESON, Denis H. S1669, RU, 45th Inf.
CRESS, A. J. S7062, LO, 3rd Engineer Troops
CRESS, Mary E. W6510, LO, Cress, Andrew J.
CRESSELL, Martha Elizabeth, W6912, SU, Cressell, Thomas C.
CRESSELL, Sarah E. W8131, WA, Cressell, James
CRESSELL, Thomas C. S4146, SU, 60th Inf.
CRESSELL, W. B. S10216, SU, Huwall's Battery, Art.
CRESSWELL, Sarah Elizabeth, W1262, G, Cresswell, Wm. Campbell
CRETSINGER, N. P. S3005, SU, Marshall's Co. Art.
CRETSINGER, Susannah, W1990, SU, Cretsinger, Wm. B.
CREWDSON, Sallie A. W2662, SH, Crewdson, Gus H.
CREWS, Alford H. S12031, 22nd Inf.
CREWS, C. C. S14999, SH, 4th Inf.
CREWS, Emily, W5040, GR, Crews, J. W.
CREWS, J. H. S13834, WE, 46th Inf.
CREWS, John W. S5258, 20th Cav.
CREWS, John W. S10426, GR, 37th Inf.
CREWS, R. B. S9030, WE, 27th Inf.
CREWS, Sarah F. W2392, Crews, John W.
CREWS, Treecy [Hall], W10706, Crews, David Anderson, [Later married Hall]
CREWSE, Louisa Ann, W6393, PO, Crewse, Henry Knox Polk
CRICHLOW, Anna Louise, W1443, D, Crichlow, Samuel P.
CRIDER, Preston Columbus, S8102, G, 19th & 20th Consolidated Cav.
CRIDER, Rebecca C. W4026, G, Crider, F. H.
CRIGGER, J. H. S12607, MS, 9th Va. Inf.
CRIGGER, James Preston, S8190, MS, 28th Va. Inf.
CRIGGER, Mary Jane, W9745, MS, Crigger, John Henry
CRIGGER, Nancy, W5783, DY, Crigger, James Madison
CRIM, Henry C. S3104, D, 11th Inf.
CRIM, Mary Frances, W85, D, Crim, Henry Clay
CRIPPS, John, S8184, SM, 28th Inf.

Index to Tennessee Confederate Pension Applications

CRISMAN, J. F. H. S14505, D, 22nd (Nixon's) Cav.
CRISP, D. J. S13842, F, 14th S.C. Inf.
CRISP, R. A. S12457, CT, 22nd N.C. Inf.
CRISSON, Louisa Elizabeth, W7610, A, Crisson, Mack Wilson
CRISSWELL, Sophronia, W7202, D, Crisswell, James Henry
CRISWELL, J. H. S8004, D, 7th Inf.
CRISWELL, Jennette Frances, W3549, D, Criswell, Robert Terry
CRISWELL, John T. S4174, WL, 7th Inf.
CRISWELL, Robert T. S9665, D, 7th Inf.
CRISWELL, S. D. S1178, WI, Undetermined
CRISWELL, T. A. S10816, G, 24th Inf.
CRITTENDEN, J. S13918, HR, 9th Ala. Cav.
CRITTENDON, Florence A. W2637, SH, Crittendon, Emmet W.
CROCKER, Elizabeth Watson, W479, D, Crocker, Benjamin F.
CROCKER, James M. S7974, G, 9th Mo. Cav.
CROCKER, Miriam, W2386, GE, Crocker, James M.
CROCKER, Sarah, W1146, D, Crocker, Benjamin
CROCKER, Sinthy, W4350, HD, Crocker, Wiley S.
CROCKER, Wiley S. S2705, HD, 2nd Ala. Cav.
CROCKETT, A. W. S11034, S15408, O, 9th Inf.
CROCKETT, Eliza, W7242, K, Crockett, O. P.
CROCKETT, Fountain P. S42, RU, Owen's Battery, Ark.
CROCKETT, James H. S6276, WI, 25th Va. Cav.
CROCKETT, Mary M. W4527, WI, Crockett, James Hunter
CROCKETT, Nancy Morandia, W10205, HU, Crockett, Wm. Henry
CROCKETT, Rachel Lou, W8851, RU, Crockett, Granville Hinton
CROCKETT, W. C. S15766, S16236, RU, 5th Ala. Cav.
CROFFORD, J. A. S15240, SH, 3rd (Forrest's) Cav.
CROFFORD, Kate Hill, W8254, SH, Crofford, John Alexander
CROFT, George W. S7143, MO, 43rd Inf.
CROFT, T. A. S7344, MO, 3rd Inf.
CROFTS, Lillie, W10796, MC, Crofts, W. M.
CROFTS, William, S14929, MO, 3rd Inf.
CROLEY, S. N. S11908, LI, 44th Inf.

CROMER, J. H. S6663, RU, 24th Inf.
CRON, Anne Elizabeth, W9373, SN, Cron, Joseph Ellison
CRON, J. E. S16358, SN, 9th (Ward's) Cav.
CRONK, Sallie D. W1357, HN, Cronk, Richard Henry
CROOK, C. B. S13129, PU, 28th Inf.
CROOK, Edna, W284, Crook, David W.
CROOK, Elliott H. S2466, HE, 13th Inf.
CROOK, G. M. S8753, F, Ballentine's Regt. Tex. Cav.
CROOK, Mary Jane, W6104, L, Crook, George Madison
CROOK, Nancy Adline, W4797, HE, Crook, Elliott Harrison
CROOK, P. F. S7690, K, 26th Inf.
CROOK, S. Rebecca, W6293, WL, Crook, David Lee
CROOK, Z. V. S10222, LA, 48th Inf.
CROOM, Susan [Williams], W10889, SU, Croom, John Wilson, [Later married Williams]
CROPPER, Hiram, S878, WL, 4th Cav.
CROSBY, Bridget Agnes, W10769, SH, Crosby, John C.
CROSBY, Frances E. W5015, GR, Crosby, George W.
CROSLEY, Sudie, W9695, SH, Crosley, Abraham Hughes
CROSS, Abbie Josephine, W1476, W1326, HI, Cross, Harry Newton
CROSS, Becky, W6252, W8251, GI, Cross, Stephen Shelton
CROSS, Catherine, W5315, WA, Cross, J. L.
CROSS, David, S4699, SU, 63rd Inf.
CROSS, David M. S3592, SU, 60th Inf.
CROSS, Elizabeth, W4346, HR, Cross, Napoleon Bonaparte
CROSS, Esterh E. W317, SU, Cross, Jesse P.
CROSS, H. N. S1677, S921, HI, 24th Inf.
CROSS, J. N. S13234, D, 19th (Biffle's) Cav.
CROSS, Jackson L. S2673, WA, 60th Inf.
CROSS, Jennie C. W6165, MU, Cross, S. H.
CROSS, Joe B. S12765, A, 2nd (Ashby's) Cav.
CROSS, John, S4109, SU, 60th Mtd. Inf.
CROSS, John B. S2950, HO, 14th Inf.
CROSS, John F. S13783, SU, 29th Inf.
CROSS, Lucy Ann, W1114, HO, Cross, John B.
CROSS, Margaret J. W753, HN, Cross, Samuel Stacker
CROSS, Martha, W3383, SU, Cross, W. A.
CROSS, Mary A. W672, SU, Cross, Elkana

-81

CROSS, Mary Florence, W6577, SU, Cross, John
CROSS, Mary M. W6072, O, Cross, Moses
CROSS, Mary Margaret, W10648, O, Cross, Moses Henry
CROSS, Newt, S15465, D, 19th (Biffle's) Cav.
CROSS, R. B. S9845, SU, 60th Inf.
CROSS, S. L. S14930, SU, 60th Inf.
CROSS, S. R. S13315, F, 19th Inf.
CROSS, S. S. S4031, GI, 3rd Inf.
CROSS, Sallie E. W673, SU, Cross, Jacob G.
CROSS, Shelton Henry, S10758, MU, 3rd Inf.
CROSS, W. W. S16436, SU, 59th Inf.
CROSS, William, S2562, GI, 14th Cav.
CROSS, William, S7412, SU, 59th Inf.
CROSS, William A. S6213, SU, 29th Inf.
CROSS, William S. S5996, SU, White's Co. Sullivan County Reserves
CROSSETT, Frances Jane, W764, F, Crossett, James Greer
CROSSLIN, A. M. S7919, CF, 44th Inf.
CROSSNOE, W. W. S12000, CC, 19th (Biffle's) Cav.
CROSSWELL, John R. S698, HN, 5th Inf.
CROSSWELL, Tom, W666, HU, Crosswell, James T.
CROSTWAIT, A. L. S15264, D, Carter's Scouts
CROTZER, Artemise, W2356, D, Crotzer, Leaner Washington
CROTZER, James H. S5542, MT, 14th Inf.
CROUCH, Abigail M. W8064, WA, Crouch, Joseph H.
CROUCH, D. C. S1987, HN, 19th & 20th Cav.
CROUCH, Elizabeth, W318, GU, Crouch, Estern Mosely
CROUCH, Franklin Jackson, S13354, SN, 55th Inf.
CROUCH, George P. S11757, WA, 62nd Inf.
CROUCH, John L. S11277, WA, 60th Inf.
CROUCH, Joseph H. S167, WA, 29th Inf.
CROUCH, Josie Anderson, W7670, D, Crouch, Peter W.
CROUCH, Lilah, W5584, WA, Crouch, George Preston
CROUCH, Malissa Thomas, W10007, B, Crouch, Zachary Taylor
CROUCH, Mitt, W3765, SH, Crouch, J. W.
CROUCH, Naomi Emiline, W2082, CF, Crouch, Wm. H.
CROUCH, Peter W. S316, HI, 7th Ky. Cav.
CROUCH, Robert C. S16430, HM, 19th Inf.
CROUCH, W. R. S12327, HN, 5th Inf.

CROUCH, William H. S2017, CF, 4th Ky. Cav.
CROUSHORN, William H. S1857, CL, 63rd Inf.
CROW, Finn, S12786, H, 35th Inf.
CROW, J. W. S9753, MN, 31st Ala. Inf.
CROW, Rebecca, W2663, H, Crow, Isaac L.
CROW, Rebecca, W5014, H, Crow, F. M.
CROW, Sarah L. W2941, H, Crow, Christopher C.
CROW, Zachariah, S1448, WA, 63rd Inf.
CROWDEN, Jane, W3111, BO, Crowden, Joe T.
CROWDER, Elizabeth McCarmally, W6901, MU, Crowder, Wm. Jackson
CROWDER, J. C. S11387, HY, Undetermined
CROWDER, Joseph T. S5668, S1540, BO, 62nd Inf.
CROWDER, R. B. S3787, DY, 3rd Cav.
CROWDER, W. J. S8973, MU, 9th Bn. Cav.
CROWDER, Willie B. W9565, HY, Crowder, John Archer
CROWE, A. S2860, MN, Undetermined
CROWEL, W. H. S14492, FR, 48th (Voorhies') Inf.
CROWELL, George Washington, S12715, HU, 24th Bn. Inf.
CROWELL, J. D. S13785, WA, 13th Bn. Va. Art.
CROWELL, John S. S7943, G, 11th Inf.
CROWELL, Mary Rosanna, W4633, WA, Crowell, James Daly
CROWLEY, W. G. S4952, DK, 23rd Inf.
CROWNOVER, W. B. S822, HE, 27th Inf.
CROXDALE, Jehiel, S5170, HM, Unassigned
CRUDUPS, Henry Davis, C8, WL, 7th Inf.
CRUMLEY, D. J. S11030, SU, 36th Inf.
CRUMLEY, Eliza, W3733, BR, Crumley, J. C.
CRUMLEY, Elizabeth, W961, SU, Crumley, Phillip H.
CRUMLEY, Elizabeth, W4102, SU, Crumley, Daniel J.
CRUMLEY, Elizabeth, W7580, PO, Crumley, David N.
CRUMLEY, J. C. S980, BR, 24th Ga. Inf.
CRUMLEY, Mary Louisiana, W4650, WA, Crumley, David James
CRUMLEY, Mary S. W1713, SU, Crumley, Wm. L.
CRUMLEY, S. M. S1025, S1367, WA, 37th Va. Inf.
CRUMLEY, Sallie C. W3422, WA, Crumley, John H.

Index to Tennessee Confederate Pension Applications

CRUMLY, Lucinda Cathrine, W10506, SU, Crumly, Cass Polk
CRUMP, Andrew J. S16437, D, 2nd (Robison's) Inf.
CRUMP, G. K. S8521, D, 3rd Inf.
CRUMP, J. M. S14039, SH, 17th Miss. Inf.
CRUMP, Lula W. W9307, LA, Crump, John Osborn
CRUMP, Marcus V. S14019, HY, 22nd (Barteau's) Cav.
CRUMP, Mary, W1364, D, Crump, George Kinnaird
CRUMP, Missouri Baggett, W9756, SH, Crump, John Moorman
CRUMP, Sarah Braden, W7159, HU, Crump, Fendall
CRUNK, A. J. S4781, D, 2nd (Robison's) Inf.
CRUNK, George N. S9358, WI, 4th (McLemore's) Cav.
CRUNK, John E. S6306, WI, 4th (McLemore's) Cav.
CRUNK, Mary E. W239, WI, Crunk, John E.
CRUSE, Henry A. S10732, 22nd Inf.
CRUSSELL, Elizabeth J. W7, WI, Crussell, Thomas M.
CRUSSELL, William, S3775, SU, 19th Inf.
CRUTCHER, Alice W. W6655, WI, Crutcher, Thomas S.
CRUTCHER, D. B. S10179, WI, 11th Cav.
CRUTCHER, Eliza Bell, W4629, WI, Crutcher, Wm. Henry
CRUTCHER, Hester A. W2568, DI, Crutcher, J. P.
CRUTCHER, Jack, C26, WI, 20th Inf.
CRUTCHER, M. M. S13758, MS, 1st (Feild's) Inf.
CRUTCHER, Mary C. W1185, WL, Crutcher, Price Perkins
CRUTCHER, Rowena Margery, W6616, SH, Crutcher, Wm. Henry
CRUTCHER, Sallie McHenry, W9104, D, Crutcher, Lawson Mantiply
CRUTCHER, Sarah Josephine, W8362, D, Crutcher, Wm. A.
CRUTCHER, Thomas S. S9507, WI, 55th Inf.
CRUTCHER, William A. S495, WI, 20th Inf
CRUTCHFIELD, Amos, S3895, CL, 63rd Inf.
CRUTCHFIELD, Cynthia Elizabeth, W4927, MR, Crutchfield, J. W.
CRUTCHFIELD, E. J. S4494, RU, 45th Inf.
CRUTCHFIELD, J. B. S6669, RU, 2nd Ga. Cav.
CRUTCHFIELD, J. S. S10555, 9th Inf.
CRUTCHFIELD, J. W. S9209, MR, 7th Ala. Cav.
CRUTCHFIELD, John H. S146, D, 7th Ky. Inf.
CRUTCHFIELD, Martha Virginia, W9138, WE, Crutchfield, John Seymore
CRUTCHFIELD, Sallie, W9184, CL, Crutchfield, Amos
CRUTCHFIELD, W. H. S16342, L, 4th Inf.
CUFF, John M. S13291, BE, 55th Inf.
CUFF, Malissie, W2138, BE, Cuff, David S.
CUFF, Sarah, W1242, BE, Cuff, Francis Asbury
CULBERSON, Mary Lizette, W8888, SH, Culberson, John Hugh
CULBERTSON, J. H. S14852, SH, 3rd S.C. Inf.
CULBREATH, J. M. S9441, F, 51st Inf.
CULBREATH, John Macklin, S11688, T, 7th Cav.
CULBREATH, John R. S1728, SN, 7th Bn. Cav.
CULBREATH, Mary Jane, W4876, SN, Culbreath, John R.
CULBREATH, Sarah J. W6738, T, Culbreath, Jordan Clark
CULLEY, James W. S6656, CF, 17th Inf.
CULLEY, W. L. S4988, B, 17th Inf.
CULLIP, Joseph, S7799, HM, 23rd Inf.
CULLIPHER, G. W. S1115, CC, 12th Cav.
CULLIPHER, J. G. S8294, G, 19th & 20th Cav.
CULLIPHER, Mary Margaret, W7126, CC, Cullipher, John Green
CULLIPHER, Nancy, W4814, CC, Cullipher, George Washington
CULLOM, Candis Love, W8815, SH, Cullom, Edward
CULLOM, Ed, S3746, D, 4th Inf.
CULLOM, Mary Adel. Elliston, W236, D, Cullom, Benjamin Lovell
CULLOM, Sam, C58, OV, 8th Inf.
CULLOM, Sam W. C232, RB, Undetermined, Application is missing.
CULLUM, E. F. S4170, HU, 5th Inf.
CULLUM, E. G. S8158, DI, 18th Inf.
CULLUP, Elizabeth Crockett, W8876, W8303, SU, Cullup, Wm. Henry
CULLY, J. M. S5964, MS, 17th Inf.
CULPEPPER, C. T. S12137, HN, 20th Inf.
CULPEPPER, Eliza Ann, W4088, HN, Culpepper, James Warren
CULPEPPER, Gideon Alston, S8733, SH, 48th Inf.
CULPEPPER, Sarah J. W8946, HN, Culpepper, C. T.
CULPS, Robert L. S417, GI, 9th Ala. Inf.

CULTON, Harriett McConnell, W9710, BR, Culton, James Mattock
CULTON, James M. S9321, BR, 43rd Inf.
CULVER, J. J. S11481, H, 31st Ala. Inf.
CUMBEY, Nancy, W285, WH, Cumbey, James
CUMBY, Fannie, W2680, PU, Cumby, James Henry
CUMMINGS, Berthany, W8861, W5444, W, Cummings, Wm. Tilford
CUMMINGS, Florence Adaline, W7343, G, Cummings, Pleasant Jasper
CUMMINGS, G. M. S3371, PU, 55th Inf.
CUMMINGS, J. D. S12608, V, 35th Inf.
CUMMINGS, Josie, W4880, CA, Cummings, Warren
CUMMINGS, MArtha L. W2089, WH, Cummings, Gabriel M.
CUMMINGS, Margaret Jane, W9057, O, Cummings, David
CUMMINGS, Mary Elizabeth, W5924, H, Cummings, John
CUMMINGS, Mollie, W9981, O, Cummings, Virgil Baxter
CUMMINGS, P. J. S12437, G, 33rd Inf.
CUMMINGS, Surilda, W6233, WL, Cummings, John Wm.
CUMMINGS, Thomas David, S16266, S14885, O, 48th (Nixon's) Inf.
CUMMINGS, W. S12949, CA, 8th (Smith's) Cav.
CUMMINGS, William T. S12707, W, 22nd (Barteau's) Cav.
CUMMINS, Dixie L. W4160, HI, Cummins, John W.
CUMMINS, Fannie, W1771, LI, Cummins, John Jackson
CUMMINS, J. J. S147, LI, 8th Inf.
CUMMINS, J. W. S12041, WL, 45th Inf.
CUMMINS, John H. S16386, LI, 55th Inf.
CUMMINS, Mollie, W10870, LI, Cummins, John H.
CUNDIFF, J. C. S10936, MS, 4th (McLemore's) Cav.
CUNNINGHAM, A. E. W2610, WA, Cunningham, John R.
CUNNINGHAM, Bettie J. W5602, BE, Cunningham, Richard Maury
CUNNINGHAM, Calvin, S7923, SN, 7th Inf.
CUNNINGHAM, Charles, S4377, LI, 32nd Inf.
CUNNINGHAM, D. P. S246, O, 32nd Inf.
CUNNINGHAM, Ediom, S9322, GR, 37th Inf.
CUNNINGHAM, Eliza J. W165, WI, Cunningham, John F.
CUNNINGHAM, Ellen Elizabeth, W9851, HU, Cunningham, James Henderson
CUNNINGHAM, Eve Ann, W4564, R, Cunningham, Franklin L.
CUNNINGHAM, George W. S1871, B, 4th Inf.
CUNNINGHAM, Henrietta, W8278, O, Cunningham, Demarcus Perry
CUNNINGHAM, Henry, S1017, SH, 15th Inf.
CUNNINGHAM, Henry Marlin, S596, SQ, 3rd (Lillard's) Mtd. Inf.
CUNNINGHAM, Henry P. S104, WI, 20th Inf.
CUNNINGHAM, J. D. S16374, O, 9th Inf.
CUNNINGHAM, James, S2897, G, 38th Inf.
CUNNINGHAM, James A. S16471, B, 44th Inf.
CUNNINGHAM, Joseph, S3511, CF, 4th Mo. Inf.
CUNNINGHAM, Lane, S11639, PU, 28th Inf.
CUNNINGHAM, Lenora Stalcup, W10320, TR, Cunningham, Frank
CUNNINGHAM, Lucy B. W7548, SN, Cunningham, Calvin
CUNNINGHAM, Maggie, W9378, B, Cunningham, James A.
CUNNINGHAM, Mary, W8964, LI, Cunningham, Wm. Anthony
CUNNINGHAM, Mary, W10134, B, Cunningham, James Knox Polk
CUNNINGHAM, Mischner, S16492, D, 4th Cav.
CUNNINGHAM, Nathaniel H. S1888, MO, 37th Inf.
CUNNINGHAM, Osborne, C87, WI, 1st Cav.
CUNNINGHAM, R. M. S10878, MT, 8th (Smith's) Cav.
CUNNINGHAM, Sallie, W4418, MOO, Cunningham, George Washington
CUNNINGHAM, Sarah Jane, W2096, W, Cunningham, Hugh A.
CUNNINGHAM, Susan F. W8701, WI, Cunningham, Henry P.
CUNNINGHAM, T. J. S8180, CF, 4th (Murray's) Cav.
CUNNINGHAM, T. N. L. S3078, R, 19th Inf.
CUNNINGHAM, Thomas, S735, HI, 24th Inf.
CUNNINGHAM, Tim L. S10195, SN, 2nd Inf.
CUNNINGHAM, W. A. S12591, LI, 1st (Turney's) Inf.
CUNNINGHAM, W. C. S2329, MOO, 4th Inf.
CUNNINGHAM, W. P. S9708, CC, 31st Inf.
CUNNINGHAM, William E. S551, D, 41st Inf.

CUNNINGHAM, William M. S16221, O, 9th Inf.
CUNYNGHAM, Bettie, W7461, R, Cunyngham, Thomas Newton Lack
CUPP, J. G. S9849, WE, 12th Inf.
CUPP, J. O. S2974, HW, 63rd Inf.
CUPP, Maticia Jane, W7057, GE, Cupp, James Orville
CUPPET, Malvina C. W2803, WL, Cuppet, George W.
CUPPLES, Elie, S7373, HD, 52nd Inf.
CUPPLES, Thomas J. S6861, HD, 21st (Wilson's) Cav.
CURD, Mary, W9636, WL, Curd, John N.
CURL, Ada Vaughan, W10221, P, Curl, John Burton
CURL, J. B. S15891, P, 19th (Biffle's) Cav.
CURL, Mary Sidney, W1788, W, Curl, John Henry
CURL, William, S9663, P, 11th Ark. Inf.
CURLE, David S. S4587, B, 23rd Inf.
CURLE, Fannie, W9853, B, Curle, David S.
CURLEE, C. D. S5361, RU, 4th Cav.
CURLEY, Bridget, W2567, W8719, D, Curley, James
CURLIN, E. C. S9898, O, 14th (Neely's) Cav.
CURLIN, Missouri Belle, W6943, O, Curlin, Edmond Cooper
CURNEY, Deborah Ann, W6650, MN, Curney, Joseph Henry
CURRENT, Jesse, S12099, FR, 5th Ky. Cav.
CURREY, J. B. S8615, HN, 20th (Nixon's) Cav.
CURREY, Millie Ann, W3049, P, Currey, John Wesley
CURRIE, Araminta H. W6375, HY, Currie, Wm. Thomas
CURRIE, Joseph M. S10519, SH, 7th Cav.
CURRIE, Malvina P. W5954, HY, Currie, Newton
CURRIE, Mary Isabella, W6224, SH, Currie, Joseph Mitchell
CURRIE, Susan, W6748, W9390, HY, Currie, Neil Archibald
CURRIN, Addie, See Addie Maroney
CURRIN, George w. S158, WI, 24th Inf.
CURRIN, Julia Ann, W1278, D, Currin, George Washington
CURRY, J. H. S6551, MN, 8th (Dibrell's) Cav.
CURRY, J. S. S9872, HN, 7th Inf.
CURRY, Larceny, W10601, HN, Curry, Jermon Baker
CURRY, M. V. S8428, GI, 50th Ala. Vols.

CURRY, Mary Jane, W6690, GI, Curry, Martin VanBuren
CURRY, S. H. S3207, WE, 7th Cav.
CURSEY, J. E. S16353, G, 12th Cav.
CURTHBERTSON, hn, S7168, HN, 46th Inf.
CURTIS, Adaline, W1089, MO, Curtis, David Berton
CURTIS, Addie, W8193, SU, Curtis, J. E.
CURTIS, Armsted C. S12504, WA, 29th Inf.
CURTIS, Eliza, W7167, DI, Curtis, James Alford
CURTIS, Elizabeth, W231, DK, Curtis, Wm.
CURTIS, Emma Lou, W7283, MN, Curtis, Jesse H.
CURTIS, J. E. S10169, SU, 4th Va. Inf.
CURTIS, James A. S2779, DI, 50th Inf.
CURTIS, Jesse W. S542, HD, 4th Ala. Inf.
CURTIS, John, S2084, WA, 1st Cav.
CURTIS, John W. S13470, B, 8th (Dibrell's) Cav.
CURTIS, Louiza, W7249, OV, Curtis, Thomas Sanford
CURTIS, M. C. W835, MN, Curtis, Wm. Woodson
CURTIS, R. J. S10719, GI, 6th (Wheeler's) Cav.
CURTIS, Selma Florentine, W8557, JO, Curtis, Finley Patterson
CURTIS, Symantha Ann, W9101, GI, Curtis, Robert John
CURTIS, Thomas S. S8957, OV, 25th Inf.
CURTIS, William, S15868, BO, 37th Inf.
CURTIS, Wilson H. S8237, B, 41st Inf.
CURTON, Eliza Jane, W1636, K, Curton, Pleasant Smith
CUSTER, J. S. S11954, CF, 44th Inf.
CUTRELL, Martha Ann, W8600, D, Cutrell, Ephraim Frankland
CUTRELL, Pattie S. W8981, W8102, RB, Cutrell, Joseph F.
CUTTEN, Sophrania, W4749, H, Cutten, Peter E.
CYPHERS, Arminta, W6408, MR, Cyphers, Jacob
CYPHERS, Jacob, S14818, MR, 154th Sr. Regt. Inf.
DABBS, Annie R. W577, D, Dabbs, James Polk
DABBS, Eliza J. W4695, LA, Dabbs, Richard I.
DABBS, Mary Elizabeth, W10227, LE, Dabbs, Stephen V.
DABBS, Stephen V. S455, WY, 9th Cav.
DABNEY, Mack, C90, MU, 3th Inf.
DABNEY, Mack, S8520, S6779, MS, 3rd Inf.

DABNEY, Mary Frances, W3543, G, Dabney, George Washington
DABNEY, S. D. S8700, GI, 11th Cav.
DABNEY, Susan S. W2136, MU, Dabney, Lewis
DABNEY, Tennie, W7426, GI, Dabney, Samuel Day
DACUS, James A. S12909, MC, 38th Ga. Inf.
DAFFRON, Arvazine, W7823, MR, Daffron, Captain
DAFFRON, Captain, S6489, MR, 35th Inf.
DAGGETT, J. P. S11191, SU, 59th Inf.
DAIL, Martha C. W9923, C, Dail, Wm. N.
DAIL, William N. S5768, UN, 2nd Cav.
DAILEY, Wilmoth, W8355, MT, Dailey, Charles Henry
DAILY, G. W. S12518, CY, Shaw's Bn. Cav.
DAILY, Henry Ellis, S13250, HR, 49th Ala. Inf.
DAILY, J. A. S6919, HU, 20th Inf.
DAILY, Sarah DePriest, W10089, HU, Daily, John Andrew
DAILY, W. M. S5924, DE, 20th Inf.
DAILY, W. R. S16359, HU, 42nd Inf.
DAILY, William R. S13059, P, 42nd Inf.
DAINGERFIELD, Amanda, W10675, MT, Daingerfield, Wm. L.
DAINWOOD, George G. S15965, MU, 24th Inf.
DAINWOOD, S. W. S15802, MU, 3rd Consol. Inf.
DAKE, Elizabeth L. W110, ME, Dake, Phillip M.
DALBY, Lucinda, W5980, WE, Dalby, James Weathers
DALE, A. L. S9041, CY, 28th Inf.
DALE, C. E. S15169, CY, 28th Cav.
DALE, J. F. S9667, CY, 8th (Dibrell's) Cav.
DALE, Jake M. S14276, MO, 39th N.C. Inf.
DALE, Margaret McLean, W10152, MU, Dale, Wm. Jason
DALE, Martha Lousetta, W10428, OV, Dale, A. L.
DALE, Mary K. W8566, D, Dale, A. C.
DALE, Sarah Jane, W4447, PO, Dale, Wm. Decatur
DALE, Susie Toombs, W8261, MU, Dale, James Thomas
DALE, William D. S11321, PO, 19th N.C. Cav.
DALTON, Amos, S6260, CL, 51st Va. Inf.
DALTON, Catherine, W9892, G, Dalton, Daniel Harrison
DALTON, Colby, S6347, GR, 26th Inf.
DALTON, Elizabeth, W2775, GR, Dalton, Wm. Nelson
DALTON, Elizabeth, W3025, K, Dalton, James Thomas
DALTON, Harram, S10318, GR, 59th Inf.
DALTON, Isham, S3688, HW, 29th Inf.
DALTON, Israel Thomas, S11070, T, 27th Inf.
DALTON, J. C. S13747, TR, 9th (Ward's) Cav.
DALTON, J. T. S14194, PU, 25th Inf.
DALTON, Jane, W1773, GR, Dalton, John W.
DALTON, L. A. S15664, S14224, S5876, H, 17th Inf.
DALTON, Margaret, W7266, HW, Dalton, Isham
DALTON, N. P. S10778, GR, 12th Bn. (Day's) Cav.
DALTON, Reuben, S506, GR, 37th Inf.
DALTON, T. B. S11073, 49th Inf., Applied from Todd Co. KY
DALTON, W. N. S7279, GR, 26th Inf.
DALY, C. H. S10035, MT, 4th (McLemore's) Cav.
DAMERON, Mary Elizabeth, W5268, MA, Dameron, Wm. Franklin
DAMRON, G. D. S7413, CF, 34th Inf.
DANCE, George, C46, MOO, 8th Inf.
DANCEY, Fredonia Avent, W3501, SH, Dancey, Wm. Stodard
DANCY, Emily B. W4186, SH, Dancy, Frank B.
DANCY, Frank B. S10017, SH, 154th Sr. Regt. Inf.
DANIEL, A. L. S5741, K, 11th Inf.
DANIEL, Bettie, W2815, DY, Daniel, George W.
DANIEL, Bird, S2064, T, 28th Inf.
DANIEL, C. S. S14541, MT, 2nd Ky. Cav.
DANIEL, Elizabeth, W7863, PU, Daniel, Emory
DANIEL, Emory, S1185, WH, 28th Inf.
DANIEL, F. N. S11106, MT, 2nd Ky. Cav.
DANIEL, G. W. S7447, DY, 4th Inf.
DANIEL, H. J. S6331, HU, 23rd Inf.
DANIEL, Ickabod B. S9021, CF, 45th Inf.
DANIEL, J. W. S2247, OV, 8th Cav.
DANIEL, James E. S7568, HN, 5th Inf.
DANIEL, John W. S8220, GI, 11th Cav.
DANIEL, Leonard, S4435, GU, 16th Inf.
DANIEL, Louvica Ann, W1917, T, Daniel, E. B.
DANIEL, Lucy Ann, W8395, WI, Daniel, Thomas Anderson
DANIEL, Lucy Jones, W7854, MT, Daniel, Cole Spence Daniel

Index to Tennessee Confederate Pension Applications

DANIEL, Martha Victoria, W6109, HR, Daniel, Chester Columbus
DANIEL, Mary C. W76, HN, Daniel, Charles Parrish
DANIEL, Nancy A. W3404, HU, Daniel, Hiram J.
DANIEL, Robert, S15735, MA, 2nd Ky. Cav.
DANIEL, Rufus A. S12505, CC, Freeman's Battery, N.C. Troops
DANIEL, Sarah Frances, W10111, HR, Daniel, Martin Rolinton
DANIEL, T. A. S11577, WI, 24th Inf.
DANIEL, T. J. S13627, OV, 3rd (Lillard's) Mtd. Inf.
DANIEL, W. B. S16133, LI, 1st (Turney's) Inf.
DANIEL, W. G. S13866, K, 4th S.C. Inf.
DANIEL, W. H. S8650, HN, 5th Inf.
DANIEL, William, S630, PU, 8th Cav.
DANIELS, C. C. S5083, HR, 9th Miss. Inf.
DANIELS, Mary, W2139, PU, Daniels, Wm. Noah
DANIELS, William, S15403, WY, 16th Inf.
DANLEY, John, S9745, MT, 3rd Cav.
DANSBEE, Lizzie Gray, W2789, D, Dansbee, Robert Charter
DARBY, B. F. S13351, MN, 19th Ark. Inf.
DARBY, J. Goodwyn, S14164, K, 2nd S.C. Cav.
DARDEN, A. J. S10160, HE, 27th Inf.
DARDEN, Adeline, W8314, RB, Darden, Charles Byrus
DARDEN, Charles B. S14956, RB, 11th Inf.
DARDEN, Josephine E. W6806, SH, Darden, Morgan Monroe
DARDEN, Nancy T. W4221, SH, Darden, Abraham J.
DARDEN, Sarah O. W2954, RB, Darden, Thomas Berry
DAREN, Joe C. S3644, MOO, 9th Ky. Inf.
DARMOND, Henry, S10900, WA, 4th La. Inf.
DARNELL, J. H. S8094, LI, 8th Inf.
DARNELL, Joseph, S10309, GI, 8th Inf.
DARNELL, L. J. S3143, HO, 14th Inf.
DARNELL, Logan, S9212, CF, 34th Inf.
DARNELL, Nancy Jane, W1219, O, Darnell, Thomas Lacy
DARNELL, P. H. S15744, CF, 34th Inf.
DARNELL, Samuel H. S65, O, 14th Inf.
DARR, J. H. S1905, BR, 43rd Inf.
DARR, Maggie Elizabeth, W7017, H, Darr, Samuel Curtis
DARR, Nannie F. W2226, BR, Darr, James H.
DARR, Ressie, W3514, BR, Darr, Mathews

DARR, S. C. S8400, H, 5th Ark. Inf.
DARSEY, W. H. S14082, WI, 32nd Ga. Inf.
DARWAIN, P. B. S8067, FR, 44th Inf.
DARWIN, J. W. S16134, TR, 25th Inf.
DARWIN, Louisa Jane, W2728, FR, Darwin, Peyton B.
DAUGHERTY, Benjamin Rush, S16559, SH, Capt. Dickerson's Co., No further unit info.
DAUGHERTY, H. C. S15874, L, 4th La. Inf.
DAUGHERTY, James Madison, S15864, WL, 45th Inf.
DAUGHERTY, Leah Adams, W8661, HM, Daugherty, Issac
DAUGHERTY, Nancy Jane, W1680, MO, Daugherty, Thomas A.
DAUGHERTY, Robert, S11363, MT, Undetermined
DAUGHERTY, Sallie T. W6441, CT, Daugherty, John Canedy
DAUGHERTY, T. J. S5038, ST, 1st Hvy. Art.
DAUGHERTY, William L. S4636, MU, 24th Inf.
DAUGHTRY, Ellen C. W54, SN, Daughtry, W. T.
DAUGHTRY, R. G. S7600, SE, 9th (Ward's) Cav.
DAUGHTRY, William Thomas, S3202, SN, 30th Inf.
DAVANT, Elizabeth Baker, W7232, SH, Davant, Frank Flicking
DAVANT, F. F. S14909, SH, 2nd S.C. Cav.
DAVAULT, Eliza Jane, W8069, SU, Davault, Michael Weaver
DAVENPORT, Charles W. S4735, HR, 34th Miss. Inf.
DAVENPORT, H. F. S5645, HN, 33rd Inf.
DAVENPORT, J. D. S1577, T, 3rd Inf.
DAVENPORT, J. R. S11460, CL, 13th Va. Inf.
DAVENPORT, J. W. S12162, HO, 50th Inf.
DAVENPORT, James, S6079, C, 60th Inf.
DAVENPORT, John, S3581, J, 28th Inf.
DAVENPORT, John S. S13243, CA, Unassigned (Salt Peter Works)
DAVENPORT, Lizzie, W9533, CA, Davenport, Abraham H.
DAVENPORT, Mollie A. W1046, GI, Davenport, Henry Spencer
DAVENPORT, Syrena Elizabeth, W6981, H, Davenport, Luke Levander
DAVENPORT, Walter R. S12471, W, 3rd Cav.

DAVENPORT, Zuba Tubbs, W6423, LA, Davenport, Thomas Daniel
DAVES, James W. S14324, SH, 22nd Miss. Inf.
DAVES, John H. S14325, SH, 31st Miss. Inf.
DAVIDSON, A. L. S14528, G, 31st Inf.
DAVIDSON, Andrew, S2666, SU, 19th Inf.
DAVIDSON, Elias, S631, J, 17th Inf.
DAVIDSON, Eliza Ann, W3027, SU, Davidson, Andrew
DAVIDSON, Elizabeth, W5359, CH, Davidson, Wm. A.
DAVIDSON, Ella M. W4899, B, Davidson, Hugh Albert
DAVIDSON, G. N. S10149, G, 19th & 20th Cav.
DAVIDSON, J. C. S7872, G, Caruther's Battery, Hvy. Art.
DAVIDSON, John F. S2739, HW, 12th (Day's) Cav.
DAVIDSON, John M. S16160, MU, 48th Inf.
DAVIDSON, Nettie, W367, D, Davidson, Benjamin W.
DAVIDSON, Robert, S5365, HA, 12th Cav.
DAVIDSON, Rufus E. S726, CF, 23rd Inf.
DAVIDSON, Sarah Elizabeth, W4490, MT, Davidson, John Wesley
DAVIDSON, Simie E. W5719, LI, Davidson, George W.
DAVIDSON, Thalia, See Thalia Stain
DAVIDSON, Thomas C. S9410, HN, 1st Ky. Battery
DAVIDSON, W. A. S7417, CH, 52nd Inf., App. between 7390 & 7391 on film
DAVIS, A. A. S5711, MOO, 17th Inf.
DAVIS, A. J. S15400, MS, 17th Inf.
DAVIS, Absalom, S15343, WH, 28th (Consol.) Inf.
DAVIS, Albert C. S3929, FR, 4th Ala. Cav.
DAVIS, Allen, S10377, MU, 19th (Biffle's) Cav.
DAVIS, Almira, W6680, PU, Davis, C. Jackson
DAVIS, Amanda Elizabeth, W7981, JO, Davis, Shade Lee
DAVIS, Ann, W8111, L, Davis, James A.
DAVIS, Ann, W8153, WH, Davis, George W.
DAVIS, Anna Washington, W5070, H, Davis, Wm. Galius
DAVIS, Arabela, W1024, HO, Davis, Robert Abna
DAVIS, Archie, C208, T, 2nd Cav.
DAVIS, Arminda, W9813, OV, Davis, Samuel
DAVIS, Arthur, S14984, L, 15th Cav.
DAVIS, B. S8774, SH, 154th Sr. Regt. Inf.

DAVIS, B. F. S12926, S10701, HR, 14th (Neely's) Cav.
DAVIS, Ben, C39, SH, Forrest's Headquarters
DAVIS, Bettie, W4420, PO, Davis, Robert
DAVIS, Bettie, W6015, W, Davis, James Thomas
DAVIS, Bettie A. W8615, D, Davis, George Washington
DAVIS, Blake, S8250, O, 3rd Inf.
DAVIS, C. J. S8829, PU, 13th Cav.
DAVIS, C. M. S7216, HE, 43rd N.C. Inf.
DAVIS, Caldona, W4198, FR, Davis, Albert Chadrac
DAVIS, Charles W. S11102, K, 64th N.C. Inf.
DAVIS, Christine, W5064, HD, Davis, James D.
DAVIS, Clabourn F. S1838, B, 1st Tenn. Vols.
DAVIS, D. C. S8327, JO, 1st N.C. Cav.
DAVIS, David, S9312, R, 7th Va. Inf.
DAVIS, Dona, W7746, LA, Davis, Arthur B.
DAVIS, Donnie, W11072, SH, Davis, Jas. P.
DAVIS, E. J. S16482, MU, 9th Cav.
DAVIS, Elias M. S1119, DK, 1st Bn. (Colm's) Inf.
DAVIS, Elijah, S10888, JO, 52nd N.C. Inf.
DAVIS, Elizabeth, W8404, B, Davis, George Washington
DAVIS, Elizabeth Marion, W1238, J, Davis, Alexander C.
DAVIS, Ella, W8342, SH, Davis, Hugh
DAVIS, Emily B. W8685, MU, Davis, John Calvin
DAVIS, F. M. S23, MS, 32nd Inf.
DAVIS, F. T. S1263, BR, 5th Ky. Inf.
DAVIS, Fannie Elizabeth, W818, SH, Davis, John D.
DAVIS, Francis M. S148, SN, 20th Inf.
DAVIS, G. W. S9384, B, 44th Inf.
DAVIS, George W. S12359, WH, 8th (Dibrell's) Cav.
DAVIS, George Washington, S13348, SH, 22nd Inf.
DAVIS, H. H. S9792, 49th N.C. Inf.
DAVIS, H. M. S5259, CF, 41st Inf.
DAVIS, H. M. S12978, H, 2nd Ga. Cav.
DAVIS, Harriet, W2080, CH, Davis, Noah
DAVIS, Harvey L. S14133, H, 6th N.C. Cav.
DAVIS, Henry Bryson, S10466, D, 3rd (Clack's) Inf.
DAVIS, Henry Jackson, S16392, MS, 4th Inf.
DAVIS, Ida, W9958, RU, Davis, Oscar M.
DAVIS, J. B. S9385, B, 11th (Holman's) Cav.
DAVIS, J. C. S8995, CL, 12th Bn. Cav.

Index to Tennessee Confederate Pension Applications

DAVIS, J. D. S7495, HD, 48th Miss. Inf.
DAVIS, J. E. S8413, CH, 19th Cav.
DAVIS, J. J. S7847, CA, 23rd Inf.
DAVIS, J. L. S725, CY, 8th Inf.
DAVIS, J. M. S7280, SQ, Undetermined
DAVIS, J. R. S15067, O, 9th Inf.
DAVIS, J. T. S15851, MU, 6th (Wheeler's) Cav.
DAVIS, J. W. S14018, HW, 63rd Va. Inf.
DAVIS, Jacob H. S6968, PU, 8th (Dibrell's) Cav.
DAVIS, James M. S6065, BL, 8th Cav.
DAVIS, James P. S5858, F, 14th Cav.
DAVIS, James T. S3405, WI, 44th Inf.
DAVIS, James W. S2346, G, 47th Inf.
DAVIS, John, S6066, SQ, 4th Cav.
DAVIS, John, S6195, JO, 37th N.C. Inf.
DAVIS, John, S11473, W, 35th Inf.
DAVIS, John H. S2302, LI, 16th Inf.
DAVIS, John H. S7886, MU, 20th Inf.
DAVIS, John Henry, S8533, WL, 4th Cav.
DAVIS, John N. S7840, ME, 5th (McKenzie's) Cav., On misc. microfilm reel
DAVIS, John Q. A. S806, WL, Undetermined
DAVIS, John R. S11150, WY, 19th (Biffle's) Cav.
DAVIS, John W. S168, CY, 8th Inf.
DAVIS, Katie, W6808, K, Davis, Charles W.
DAVIS, L. F. S2682, DE, 31st Inf.
DAVIS, Lavinia H. W1748, SH, Davis, George Wesley
DAVIS, Loutitie, W4070, MT, Davis, A. L.
DAVIS, Lucindia, W1177, SN, Davis, F. M.
DAVIS, Lydia Ann, W2467, PU, Davis, Henry Polk
DAVIS, Maggie, W9105, MS, Davis, Wm. Green
DAVIS, Margaret, W6314, SQ, Davis, John
DAVIS, Margaret Eliza, W1983, MA, Davis, James Mason
DAVIS, Martha Ann, W2034, MU, Davis, Newton Anderson
DAVIS, Martha Ann, W3074, HE, Davis, Lawson Asberry
DAVIS, Martha Elizabeth, W6295, MU, Davis, Wm. Hamlin
DAVIS, Mary, W1623, ME, Davis, John N.
DAVIS, Mary, W3660, MO, Davis, Nathan J.
DAVIS, Mary, W9557, W9409, WA, Davis, James H.
DAVIS, Mary Ann, W3459, HM, Davis, Wm. Johnson
DAVIS, Mary Ann, W4960, MC, Davis, Harrison
DAVIS, Mary B. W8844, W6573, MU, Davis, John Hamilton
DAVIS, Mary Elizabeth, W1632, WE, Davis, John
DAVIS, Mary H. W4706, CA, Davis, Jonathan Jones
DAVIS, Mary J. W8266, ME, Davis, T. A.
DAVIS, Mary Jane, W6268, SM, Davis, Rufus Baker
DAVIS, Mary Jane, W10121, D, Davis, Isaac Luckett
DAVIS, Mary Kercheval, W2552, DI, Davis, Josiah Knox
DAVIS, Matilda E. W1536, MA, Davis, Louis Franklin
DAVIS, Mattie Harriet, W10901, L, Davis, Arthur
DAVIS, Melvin D. S15904, D, 23rd Inf.
DAVIS, Minerva E. W11058, MC, Davis, Nathan
DAVIS, Moses Aaron, S6981, MS, 17th Inf.
DAVIS, N. C. S9666, MA, 19th (Biffle's) Cav.
DAVIS, N. J. S3132, MO, 59th Inf.
DAVIS, Nancy Ann, W9130, MU, Davis, Robert Evans
DAVIS, Nancy Elizabeth, W765, BL, Davis, Wm. Scott
DAVIS, Nancy Elizabeth, W4674, SN, Davis, John Wilson
DAVIS, Nancy Elizabeth, W7238, WI, Davis, Thomas Alexander
DAVIS, Nancy Jane, W1838, MT, Davis, James B.
DAVIS, Nathan, S6585, PO, 64th N.C. Inf.
DAVIS, Nattie Jane, W10976, MS, Davis, Henry Jackson
DAVIS, Noah, S619, CH, 27th Inf.
DAVIS, Palina, W5821, CY, Davis, Jesse L.
DAVIS, Parrasetta, W273, WH, Davis, N. C.
DAVIS, R. E. S6845, MS, 19th (Biffle's) Cav.
DAVIS, R. P. S2407, FR, 41st Inf.
DAVIS, R. R. S7407, O, 1st (Turney's) Inf.
DAVIS, R. T. S15500, WL, 7th Inf.
DAVIS, Rachel Adilay, W3125, R, Davis, David
DAVIS, Rachel J. W7552, D, Davis, Richard Thomas
DAVIS, Richard E. S5053, WI, 18th Va. Inf.
DAVIS, Robert, S5108, MC, 3rd (Lillard's) Mtd. Inf.

DAVIS, Robert H. S13486, WI, 4th (McLemore's) Cav.
DAVIS, Robert W. S2378, O, 9th Inf.
DAVIS, Rufus B. S11913, SM, 23rd Inf.
DAVIS, Sadie, W10194, CY, Davis, James K. Polk
DAVIS, Sallie Thornton, W10515, D, Davis, Wm. Thornton
DAVIS, Samuel, S7844, OV, 25th Inf.
DAVIS, Sarah, W8647, LI, Davis, W. L.
DAVIS, Sarah E. W5375, JO, Davis, John
DAVIS, Sarah Elizabeth, W4472, JE, Davis, Thadeus D.
DAVIS, Sarah Elizabeth, W4816, H, Davis, Thomas P.
DAVIS, Sarah Elizabeth, W5091, W, Davis, John
DAVIS, Scott D. S16003, MS, 4th (McLemore's) Cav.
DAVIS, Shade L. S9918, JO, Allison's Squadron, Cav.
DAVIS, Sophronia Candace, W9110, U, Davis, Wm. Tilson
DAVIS, Susan Thalitha, W6186, GE, Davis, Thomas A.
DAVIS, Susie, W9656, G, Davis, Henry Hartwood
DAVIS, T. A. S6780, WI, 1st Ala. Cav.
DAVIS, T. A. S6953, ME, 5th (McKenzie's) Cav.
DAVIS, T. A. S7281, SU, 31st Inf.
DAVIS, T. C. S5764, GI, 53rd Inf.
DAVIS, T. F. S9008, LA, 32nd Inf.
DAVIS, T. J. S2696, W, 16th Inf.
DAVIS, T. P. S5786, H, 14th Ga. Inf.
DAVIS, T. V. S16552, CY, 8th Inf.
DAVIS, T. W. P. S10512, BO, 1st N.C. Cav.
DAVIS, Tennessee O. W1097, MS, Davis, Moses A.
DAVIS, Thaddeus D. S6249, JE, 61st Inf.
DAVIS, Thomas, S3549, D, 17th Inf.
DAVIS, Thomas, S11746, HM, 61st Inf.
DAVIS, Virginia Isadora, W4696, LA, Davis, James W.
DAVIS, W. A. S2530, WL, 2nd (Robison's) Inf.
DAVIS, W. B. S9508, CO, 49th N.C. Inf.
DAVIS, W. G. S1830, OV, 4th (Murray's) Cav.
DAVIS, W. H. S14385, MU, 19th (Biffle's) Cav. See also William Hamblin Davis
DAVIS, W. H. S15419, SH, 38th N.C. Inf.
DAVIS, W. O. S12867, ME, 5th (McKenzie's) Cav.
DAVIS, W. S. S9277, CY, 28th Inf.
DAVIS, W. S. S10834, GE, 31st Inf.
DAVIS, W. T. S1210, U, 26th Inf.
DAVIS, William, S9850, SQ, 34th Ga. Inf.
DAVIS, William A. S13314, MS, 17th Inf.
DAVIS, William G. S10029, MS, 11th (Holman's) Cav.
DAVIS, William G. S10923, D, 18th Inf.
DAVIS, William Hamblin, S9878, MU, 19th (Biffle's) Cav. See also W. H. Davis
DAVIS, William Scott, S1388, BL, 4th Cav.
DAWKINS, Martha Ann, W4439, SH, Dawkins, Benjamin Ferrell
DAWN, Rachel Ann, W2694, K, Dawn, Wm. Hardwick
DAWNING, Adrian M. S9240, MS, 8th Inf.
DAWS, Bell, W7004, GI, Daws, Isaac
DAWS, Isaac, S9107, GI, 11th (Gordon's) Cav.
DAWS, William, S4688, S741, J, 25th Inf.
DAWSON, Henry J. S1424, SM, 7th Inf.
DAWSON, I. H. S9983, DY, 15th Cav.
DAWSON, J. J. S7642, SH, 1st Mo. Inf.
DAWSON, John Gaston, S9123, MU, 9th Bn. (Gantt's) Cav.
DAWSON, John N. S6165, MR, 1st Ga. Cav.
DAWSON, MAttie C. W4448, DY, Dawson, Isaac Henderson
DAWSON, Mary, W6593, MA, Dawson, Wm. Franklin
DAWSON, Mary Christine, W7827, MT, Dawson, Wm. Henry
DAWSON, Mary Jane, W6770, K, Dawson, Elijah Pedigo
DAWSON, Mary Southern, W10168, MU, Dawson, Reuben Kemper
DAWSON, Nancy, W2847, SH, Dawson, John Jefferson
DAWSON, W. S8896, MT, 13th Ky. Cav.
DAWSON, W. F. S9621, G, 31st Inf.
DAWSON, W. H. S10541, S15129, MU, 48th (Voorhies') Inf.
DAWSON, W. P. S15320, CC, 50th Inf.
DAWSON, W. T. S15573, G, 1st S.C. Inf.
DAY, Alice, W417, HA, Day, Jesse
DAY, Eliza Jane, W1026, MA, Day, Wm. Peater
DAY, I. B. S8449, MA, 6th Inf.
DAY, James M. S9783, MA, 51st Inf.
DAY, John R. S11641, D, 13th Bn. Va. Art.
DAY, Martha Matilda, W9555, MA, Day, James Meek
DAY, Mary C. W1208, H, Day, Samuel Houston
DAY, Mary Clay, W5030, HM, Day, John E.

Index to Tennessee Confederate Pension Applications

DAY, W. P. S1533, HR, 33rd Inf.
DEADERICK, A. V. S16414, U, 37th Inf.
DEADERICK, Carter Luster, W2529, WA, Deaderick, Alfred Shelby
DEADERICK, E. L. S14733, WA, 1st (Carter's) Cav.
DEADERICK, Inslee, S13358, K, 2nd Cav.
DEADERICK, Maggie, W8176, K, Deaderick, Oakley
DEADERICK, Oakley, S11427, K, 2nd Cav.
DEAKINS, A. L. S7293, SQ, 35th Inf.
DEAKINS, J. D. S8381, MR, 35th Inf.
DEAKINS, Josephine, W1882, MR, Deakins, S. B.
DEAKINS, M. E. S10901, SQ, 35th Inf.
DEAKINS, Martha, W6416, SQ, Deakins, Mose E.
DEAKINS, Mary D. W2324, H, Deakins, Frank
DEAKINS, Nancy, W9924, W, Deakins, George Stewart
DEAL, Andrew, S4358, MOO, 50th Ala. Inf.
DEAL, Eliza Ann, W4424, LI, Deal, John Small
DEAL, John S. S4359, MOO, 41st Inf.
DEAL, Maggie, W7882, MC, Deal, J. L.
DEAL, Syntha, W6505, MOO, Deal, Andrew
DEAMORE, W. J. S234, MA, 16th Cav.
DEAN, Catherine, W2726, SH, Dean, James Samuel
DEAN, Clare, W8423, H, Dean, John Robert
DEAN, Dave, S16369, O, 2nd Cav.
DEAN, E. A. S11452, HI, 11th Inf.
DEAN, Florence Stuart, W9213, SH, Dean, Robert James
DEAN, J. A. S10706, FR, 23rd Inf.
DEAN, James, S922, P, 20th Inf.
DEAN, John R. S3973, H, 17th Inf.
DEAN, M. L. S12291, HI, 10th Cav.
DEAN, M. M. S9256, CF, 8th Inf.
DEAN, Mannie Lou, See Mannie Lou Kirby
DEAN, Mariah Virginia, W5781, K, Dean, Thomas Jefferson
DEAN, Mary Jane, W11076, HI, Dean, Marcus Lafayette
DEAN, Samuel A. S15853, SH, 9th Miss. Inf.
DEAN, Sue Anderson, W6930, HI, Dean, Ephraim Aurelina
DEAREN, Nancy Caroline, W347, B, Dearen, Hopkins Lee
DEARMON, Levi L. S3630, D, 28th Inf.
DEASON, H. H. S10110, WI, 32nd Inf.
DEASON, Mary, W9540, WE, Deason, Wm. E.
DEASON, W. E. S12758, WE, 31st Inf.

DEASON, W. R. S12468, DI, 49th Inf.
DEATHERAGE, Allen, S1045, OV, Undetermined
DEATHERAGE, Artymiss Stewart, W4566, HU, Deatherage, Henry Clay
DEATHERAGE, W. M. S13604, RO, 26th Inf.
DEATHERIDGE, Artie Missie, W9381, MA, Deatheridge, Henry C.
DEATON, V. F. S9998, SU, 11th Va. Inf.
DEBARDELEBEN, Daniel, S8712, HM, 8th Ala. Cav.
DEBOND, John W. S1673, BL, 60th Mtd. Inf.
DEBOW, A. B. S13876, TR, Raum's Co. Miss. Cav.
DEBRUCE, Mary Jane, W3121, BE, DeBruce, John H.
DEBUSH, Campbell, S6869, CL, 29th Inf.
DEBUSH, Martha, W704, GE, Debush, Shadrick
DEBUSK, Eliza, W3811, CL, Debusk, Campbell
DECK, Alvin C. S6795, OV, 25th Inf.
DECK, America, W7152, OV, Deck, Alvin C.
DECK, J. V. S2450, S13408, HO, 24th Bn. Sharpshooters
DECK, John V. S7043, FE, 25th Inf.
DECKER, W. M. S7542, FR, 33rd Ala. Inf.
DECKER, W. R. S8062, MC, 31st Inf.
DECKERD, Nancy Mariah, W3987, PU, Deckerd, John C.
DECKHERD, John, S742, J, 4th Bn. Cav.
DECOSTA, Julia Adeline, W10381, H, DeCosta, A. C.
DEDMAN, Elizabeth, W8804, DK, Dedman, Patterson
DEEK, William C. S8219, B, 41st Inf.
DEEN, Siann Malinda, W2202, O, Deen, Josiah
DEEP, J. G. B. S8869, O, 3rd Inf.
DEERING, isabelle Jane, W3745, B, Deering, Fountain Farris
DEES, Steve, S5679, WE, 154th Sr. Regt. Inf.
DEETS, B. G. S5159, HN, 5th Inf.
DEFORE, Anna Yother, W, Some papers with #11183 on film
DEFRESE, Robert H. S13257, SU, 13th Bn. Va. Reserves
DEGRAFFENREID, Nathan, C16, F, 154th Sr. Regt. Inf.
DEJOURNETT, Charles P. S10627, MA, 57th N.C. Inf.
DEJOURNETTE, Sarah, W10157, MC, DeJournette, James Rufus
DELANEY, B. F. S3871, 21st (Wilson's) Cav.

Index to Tennessee Confederate Pension Applications

DELANEY, H. H. S15379, SU, 8th (Smith's) Cav.
DELASHMIT, G. W. S7620, T, 12th (Greene's) Cav.
DELBRIDGE, E. W. S3861, RU, 2nd (Walker's) Inf.
DELBRIDGE, Mattie F. W4727, RU, Delbridge, Edward W.
DELES, William G. S15073, SH, Donaldsville Art. La.
DELK, David, S2600, CY, 8th Inf.
DELK, W. D. S9827, HI, 9th Bn. (Gantt's) Cav.
DELLINGER, Margaret Susana, W4583, WE, Dellinger, Jacob Riley
DELOACH, Catherin Emma, W3903, MA, Deloach, John
DELOACH, Eliza Turner, W3950, CC, Deloach, Wm. Turner
DELONAS, William, S5787, DI, 19th Inf.
DELONES, Rebecca Ann, W5348, DI, Delones, Wm.
DELONG, Emiley, W1569, DK, Delong, David C.
DELOP, George W. S13975, MO, 1st (Carter's) Cav.
DELOZIER, Ann B. W8400, RU, Delozier, James Alexander
DELOZIER, J. A. S7301, RU, 63rd Inf.
DELOZIER, T. L. S3602, K, 3rd Inf.
DELPH, Philip, S2924, DY, 22nd Inf.
DEMENT, Charles, S5931, RU, 45th Inf.
DEMENT, Thomas J. S10392, H, 6th Va. Cav.
DEMENT, Zoe Louise, W6084, D, Dement, Thomas Jefferson
DEMING, C. W. S7938, HR, 22nd Inf.
DEMING, Henry A. S10272, G, 26th Cav.
DEMING, M. M. S8145, CH, 18th (Newsom's) Cav.
DEMING, W. J. S3678, WE, 22nd Inf
DEMONBREUN, Sarah Ann, W5492, WI, Demonbreun, John Forsythe
DEMONBREUN, Timothy, S1141, RB, Baxter's Co. Lt. Art.
DEMOSS, L. W. S5119, 12th Ky. Cav.
DEMOSS, S. C. S7249, D, 10th (DeMoss') Cav.
DEMOSS, W. F. S9599, D, 5th Mo. Cav.
DEMPSEY, A. W. S13683, F, 1st Ark. Inf.
DEMPSEY, Ann E. W44, SN, Dempsey, John Washington
DEMPSEY, John A. S5867, SU, 48th Va. Inf.
DEMPSEY, John W. S1269, D, 30th Inf.

DEMPSEY, Martha Ann, W3991, SU, Dempsey, John A.
DENHAM, A. E. S16048, RU, 6th (Wheeler's) Cav.
DENHAM, Andrew E. S14491, DY, 6th (Wheeler's) Cav.
DENHAM, R. H. S1604, GE, 1st (Carter's) Cav.
DENHAM, Sarah A. W6555, DY, Denham, A. E.
DENISON, John V. S12481, D, 20th Inf.
DENNEY, David, S1211, SM, 55th Inf.
DENNIGAN, Pat, S13641, SH, 15th Inf.
DENNING, Bettie, W10647, RB, Denning, John Will
DENNING, John William, S15529, RB, 22nd Cav.
DENNING, Mary Frances, W10677, WE, Denning, Thomas Jefferson
DENNIS, D. H. S2374, ME, 29th Inf.
DENNIS, G. C. S8231, SU, Stark's Bn. Va. Inf.
DENNIS, G. W. S2027, OV, 8th Cav.
DENNIS, John, S8803, R, 43rd Inf.
DENNIS, Lamanda Melseny, W916, CO, Dennis, Carey
DENNIS, Pauline Frances, W8572, CA, Dennis, Henry
DENNIS, Sarah C. W9764, OV, Dennis, Geo. Wash. Lafayette
DENNIS, T. J. S6250, PI, 8th (Dibrell's) Cav.
DENNISON, Henry, S14467, HM, 12th Bn. (Day's) Cav.
DENNISON, Louisa R. W5797, D, Dennison, John V.
DENNISON, William, S276, HM, 43rd Inf.
DENNY, Aggie, W6801, SM, Denny, Wyatte Benjamin
DENNY, E. H. S5396, PO, 6th Ga. Legion
DENNY, George S. S2425, WA, Unassigned
DENNY, James A. S14701, SH, Semmes Bn. La. Lt. Art.
DENNY, Jemia S. W2998, SU, Denny, John L.
DENNY, L. H. S13373, SU, 61st Inf.
DENNY, Lydie E. W7903, WA, Denny, George S.
DENNY, Rachel, W549, RU, Denny, Benjamin Rush
DENNY, W. B. S13819, SM, 24th Inf.
DENSFORD, Caroline, W5876, T, Densford, James O.
DENSFORD, J. O. S5969, T, 12th (Green's) Cav.

DENSON, Stanton A. S2443, FR, 1st (Turney's) Inf.
DENT, Martha A. W1867, WE, Dent, Elly Rolandus
DENTON, Emanuel, S13755, JO, 6th N.C. Inf.
DENTON, Frances, W6709, CO, Denton, Wm. Anderson
DENTON, Frank Desha, S14830, SH, 8th Ark. Inf.
DENTON, Fronie C. W10448, JO, Denton, Emanuel
DENTON, Isaac, S8622, S12868, DK, 5th Inf.
DENTON, Isaac A. S6746, SE, 2nd Cav.
DENTON, J. H. S15426, WI, 3rd (Clack's) Inf. See also James H. Denton
DENTON, James H. S10590, WI, 3rd (Clack's) Inf. See also J. H. Denton
DENTON, James R. S13916, H, 26th Inf.
DENTON, John Berryman, S5366, WL, 28th Inf.
DENTON, John H. S14957, RO, 16th Inf.
DENTON, Nannie, W9126, WI, Denton, James H.
DENTON, O. D. S7864, S2697, W, 35th Inf.
DENTON, S. J. S12721, RU, 8th (Dibrell's) Cav.
DENTON, Samantha, W286, P, Denton, Elihah
DENTON, Samantha Jane, W8234, W, Denton, Isaac
DENTON, W. A. S5797, CO, 26th Inf.
DEPRIEST, John R. S12460, G, 42nd Inf.
DERLIN, Bettie Brister, W5998, SH, Derlin, James Calvin
DEROSSETT, John, S2536, WH, 28th Inf.
DEROSSETTE, John, S6256, WH, 28th Inf.
DERRICK, Susannah Margaret, W5707, LA, Derrick, Joshua Adam
DERRYBERRY, A. J. S9227, HR, 14th Cav.
DERRYBERRY, Eugenia Frances, W9349, MU, Derryberry, Wm. Alexander
DERRYBERRY, J. H. S9638, MS, 24th Inf.
DERRYBERRY, Mary Elizabeth, W8051, MA, Derryberry, Andrew Jesse
DERRYBERRY, Mary Frances, W9873, D, Derryberry, Christopher Columbus
DERRYBERRY, Nancy, W7739, MN, Derryberry, Columbus
DERRYBERRY, Sarah C. W4495, MA, Derryberry, J. W. C.
DESAUSSURE, C. A. S16511, SH, Beaufort (S.C.) Vol. Art.

DESHA, Edith Louise, W10903, H, DeSha, Hamilton
DESHA, Hamilton, S16088, S13684, H, Edmondson's Bn. Ga. Cav.
DESHA, Hampton, S16089, S13685, H, Edmondson's Bn. Ga. Cav.
DESHAZO, J. W. S15220, CC, 6th Miss. Cav.
DESHAZO, Larkin Columbus, S13769, CC, 8th Miss. Cav.
DESHELES, William G. S11852, MT, 8th Inf.
DEVASHER, A. L. S13428, SN, 1st Ky. Cav.
DEVAULT, John A. S14002, GE, 64th N.C. Inf.
DEVAULT, Martin V. S13140, WA, 29th Inf.
DEVAULT, Mary, W812, GR, Devault, Pryor H.
DEVAULT, Prior H. S835, GR, Undetermined
DEVIN, David W. S11621, MS, 17th Inf.
DEVINE, Charles, S8137, H, 2nd Ark. Inf.
DEVINEY, James L. S14189, L, 3rd Mo. Cav.
DEVINEY, John, S14506, HI, 10th Cav.
DEVINNEY, Almyra Forsythe, W6059, L, DeVinney, J. L.
DEVORE, W. E. S14315, SH, 25th Ala. Cav.
DEVOTI, Anthony, S4923, GE, 64th N.C. Inf.
DEW, Leathey Ann, W123, WH, Dew, John Moran
DEW, Nancy Louisa, W9067, W9020, G, Dew, Thomas Jefferson
DEW, Thomas J. S16275, G, 6th Inf.
DEWALD, Nancy E. W5388, WA, Dewald, James Miller
DEWBERRY, Annie Hart, W7379, L, Dewberry, James Whitfield
DEWBERRY, James W. S1799, L, 37th Ga. Inf.
DEWBERRY, T. M. S11279, CH, 27th Inf.
DEWITT, James T. S2065, GE, 62nd Inf.
DIAL, J. J. S2547, BR, 35th Ga. Inf.
DIAL, Martha C. W7487, H, Dial, Jonathan Jackson
DIAMOND, Robert, S870, SC, 22nd N.C. Inf.
DIARMOND, See DARMOND
DIBRELL, Flora, W5063, WH, Dibrell, Joseph Anthony
DIBRELL, J. A. S13536, WH, 8th (Dibrell's) Cav.
DIBRELL, Jennie, W10502, WH, Dibrell, W. L.
DIBRELL, W. L. S14758, WH, 8th (Dibrell's) Cav.
DICE, Henry, S8384, CE, 4th (McLemore's) Cav.
DICE, John S. S7294, TR, 8th Inf.
DICK, Jackson, S3774, R, 18t.ı Inf.

DICK, Mary L. W7107, K, Dick, Jackson
DICKENS, Hiram L. S10317, S16233, O, 12th Ky. Inf.
DICKENS, John Clay, S11094, RB, 22nd (Barteau's) Cav.
DICKENSON, James, S479, GE, 29th Inf.
DICKENSON, John C. S8266, S8039, D, 37th Va. Inf.
DICKERSON, A. E. S876, BE, 27th Inf.
DICKERSON, B. Susan, W10884, SH, Dickerson, Wm. Thomas
DICKERSON, Edwin, S2512, DI, 23rd N.C. Inf.
DICKERSON, Eliza F. W2106, WE, Dickerson, John Adams
DICKERSON, Emeline, W9906, CF, Dickerson, James
DICKERSON, Isaiah, S2126, RO, 26th Inf.
DICKERSON, Marendie V. W10571, MN, Dickerson, Andrew J.
DICKERSON, Martha Emeline, W5884, H, Dickerson, A. C.
DICKERSON, Susan Martha, W8068, SH, Dickerson, Wm. T.
DICKERSON, W. D. S11865, SM, 28th Inf.
DICKERSON, Winnie, W8507, DI, Dickerson, Ed
DICKEY, D. C. S7656, BE, 5th Inf.
DICKEY, G. Q. S14016, DY, 12th Inf.
DICKEY, James M. S10045, DY, 12th Inf.
DICKEY, John M. S15227, LI, 44th Inf.
DICKEY, John P. S8280, OV, 2nd (Ashby's) Cav.
DICKEY, N. S10655, O, 84th Inf.
DICKEY, William T. S10273, MOO, "Buckner Guards" Ky. Cav.
DICKINS, William B. S16191, CF, 44th Inf.
DICKINSON, Gertrude E. W9899, WA, Dickinson, Wm. A.
DICKINSON, James E. S14988, MA, 7th Cav.
DICKINSON, Mary Evelyn, W9686, RU, Dickinson, Thomas William
DICKINSON, Robert T. S4928, WI, 6th (Wheeler's) Cav.
DICKINSON, Susan Elizabeth, W937, G, Dickinson, J. H.
DICKINSON, W. a. S15126, WA, 22nd (Barteau's) Cav.
DICKISON, Martha, W1436, WA, Dickison, David
DICKS, Emma I. W3492, H, Dicks, Joseph
DICKSON, A. F. S859, DY, 12th Inf.
DICKSON, Bettie White, W7386, G, Dickson, Enoch
DICKSON, Charles H. S607, DE, 31st Inf.
DICKSON, Enoch, S13813, G, 21st Cav.
DICKSON, Jacob Tipton, S6093, P, 10th (DeMoss') Cav.
DICKSON, James G. S10459, HD, 12th Cav.
DICKSON, Joshua M. S16413, MN, 21st Inf.
DICKSON, Julia Paralee, W8034, P, Dickson, James B.
DICKSON, Martha Euphrasier, W10301, MT, Dickson, John McCauley
DICKSON, Mary E. W10025, Dickson, David M. Applied from Wayne Co. Michigan
DICKSON, Nellie mayes, W2325, SH, Dickson, Barton
DICKSON, Nicie Ann, W10549, MN, Dickson, Joshua
DICKSON, Pimena Durind, W7102, DI, Dickson, Wm. Henry
DICKSON, Rachel Jane, W10710, W8267, T, Dickson, James Fentress
DICKSON, Richard W. S10393, H, 35th Ala. Inf.
DICKSON, Robert A. S11748, R, Unassigned (Blacksmith)
DICKSON, Sallie, W10850, SH, Dickson, John Robb
DICKSON, W. H. S7211, DI, 11th Inf.
DIEMER, S. L. S15660, MS, Huggin's Co. Lt. Art.
DIGGONS, George A. S1681, D, 10th Inf.
DIGGONS, Mattie Gertrude, W8853, D, Diggons, George Alfred
DIGGS, Elizabeth, W1586, BE, Diggs, Wm.
DIGGS, James, S15598, SH, 3rd Miss. Cav.
DIGGS, John W. S7675, G, 31st Inf.
DIGGS, Robert Pleasant, S15531, D, 5th Inf.
DILDINE, Emeline Frances, W5237, WE, Dildine, James Dier
DILDINE, J. D. S7113, WE, 41st Inf.
DILDINE, NAncy J. W4767, WE, Dildine, Andrew J.
DILL, Felix G. S490, WL, 7th & 18th Inf.
DILL, H. M. S3817, WL, 18th Inf.
DILL, J. C. S14598, H, 62nd Inf.
DILL, W. C. S9423, WL, 22nd (Barteau's) Cav.
DILLAHAY, James T. S2854, SM, 24th Inf.
DILLAHINTY, Millie Frances, W3699, Dillahinty, Wm. Alonzo
DILLAHUNTY, Mary Tenny, W4843, D, Dillahunty, Lewis

Index to Tennessee Confederate Pension Applications

DILLARD, E. G. S4053, WL, 44th Inf.
DILLARD, F. M. S15672, B, 23rd Inf.
DILLARD, Huldah, W9527, D, Dillard, John
DILLARD, J. A. S8146, BR, 4th Ga. Cav.
DILLARD, Jerusha D. W1453, B, Dillard, Isaac Vanburin
DILLARD, John, S5502, DI, Baxter's Co. Lt. Art.
DILLARD, Martha Jane, W777, WL, Dillard, Ephraim G.
DILLARD, Mary J. W3798, SM, Dillard, P. G.
DILLARD, Nancy Caroline, W831, WL, Dillard, Wm. Henry Harrison
DILLARD, Oney, W55, SM, Dillard, Osborne
DILLARD, Osborn, S1164, SM, 28th Inf.
DILLARD, P. G. S9000, O, 7th Inf.
DILLARD, Sally J. W1568, WL, Dillard, A. A.
DILLEHAY, Frances, W8407, SM, Dillehay, John Harvie
DILLEHAY, Lucy, W1474, SM, Dillehay, James T.
DILLEHAY, Mary E. W8731, MU, Dillehay, Wm. Gilliam
DILLEHAY, Mattie, W7928, D, Dillehay, Wm. C.
DILLEHAY, R. J. S4812, M, 24th Inf.
DILLEHAY, W. C. S11244, D, 6th (Wheeler's) Cav.
DILLEHAY, W. G. S13047, MU, 53rd Inf.
DILLEN, Martha, W578, OV, Dillen, David
DILLEN, S. B. S3238, OV, 8th Inf.
DILLIARD, T. J. W. S15587, S8191, SH, 38th Inf., Also applied from Fayette County
DILLINGER, Jacob Riley, S9954, WE, 34th N.C. Inf.
DILLINGHAM, H. Bent, S7631, MOO, 17th Inf.
DILLINGHAM, Sam, S13240, MOO, 8th (Smith's) Cav.
DILLON, Cora Jane, W2664, SM, Dillon, James W.
DILLON, D. T. S2044, OV, 8th Inf.
DILLON, Ellen R. W5811, K, Dillon, Harvey
DILLON, George W. S2368, RU, 18th Inf.
DILLON, Henry J. S8804, PI, 25th Inf.
DILLON, J. L. S2877, RU, 8th (Smith's) Cav.
DILLON, James W. S1768, SM, 8th Inf.
DILLON, Jim, C89, D, 47th Inf.
DILLON, MArtha paralee, W9434, OV, Dillon, Wm. Thomas
DILLON, Martha Ann, W2539, RU, Dillon, George W.

DILLON, Mary Jane, W447, CA, Dillon, Joseph Marion
DILLON, Mary Jane, W3831, RU, Dillon, Johnny Lester
DILLON, Nannie Matilda, W7084, PI, Dillon, H. J.
DILLON, Sarah L. W9855, SM, Dillon, Thomas S.
DILLON, Thomas S. S14484, D, 9th (Ward's) Cav.
DILLOW, C. C. S9728, SU, Lynch's Battery, Art.
DINKLE, Annie E. W2631, WA, Dinkle, Calvin Newton
DINSMORE, Oliver, S13910, HW, Unassigned (Salt Mines)
DINSMORE, Preston, S2841, CL, 61st Inf.
DINWIDDIE, Malissa Frances, W2700, MT, Dinwiddie, Wm. H.
DINWIDDLE, M. B. S13891, HN, 5th Inf.
DIRICKSON, John M. S8805, D, 23rd Inf.
DISHNER, Margaret Albany, W7144, SU, Dishner, Andrew Jackson
DISHNER, William, S10157, SU, 63rd Va. Inf.
DISMUKES, Abraham, C67, MA, Unassigned (Shoeman)
DISMUKES, G. W. S13273, SN, 21st Ala. Inf.
DISMUKES, Ida, W8500, D, Dismukes, Wm. Henry
DISMUKES, Maggie L. W2494, MA, Dismukes, W. A.
DISMUKES, Minerva Hays, W6401, MA, Dismukes, Thomas Carter
DISMUKES, W. H. S10211, D, 41st Inf.
DITMORE, H. M. S8612, MO, 1st Cav.
DITTS, B. J. S14849, CC, 12th Cav.
DIXON, Daniel H. S12945, CU, 4th (Murray's) Cav.
DIXON, Edom, S4953, MO, 11th Inf.
DIXON, Ellie, W3661, W3508, DE, Dixon, Wallace
DIXON, J. M. S14399, MN, 21st Inf.
DIXON, James T. S7805, GI, 41st Inf.
DIXON, John A. S2410, D, Baxter's Co. Lt. Art.
DIXON, John H. S4745, MC, 16th N.C. Inf.
DIXON, Lutitia Ellison, W3508, W3661, DE, Dixon, Wallace
DIXON, Margaret C. W3312, GR, Dixon, Pleasant
DIXON, Martha, W3791, SU, Dixon, Wm.
DIXON, Martha Elizabeth, W10106, SU, Dixon, John

Index to Tennessee Confederate Pension Applications

DIXON, Mary Elizabeth, W10550, ST, Dixon, Ephram F.
DIXON, Mattie, W9480, MS, Dixon, Wm. Henry
DIXON, Moses L. S13989, HW, 2nd Va. Cav.
DIXON, Pleasant, S4649, GR, 18th N.C. Inf.
DIXON, Simeon A. S10792, BR, Thomas' Legion, N.C.
DIXON, William, S4564, SU, 1st Cav.
DOAK, Buena Vista, W7845, WL, Doak, John F.
DOAK, Elizabeth Henrietta, W4842, CA, Doak, Thomas Jefferson
DOAK, Ella, W9271, WL, Doak, Andrew H.
DOAK, Margaret J. W7846, W4765, WL, Doak, Wm. Harrison
DOAK, Sue J. W4802, K, Doak, Joe A.
DOAN, W. A. S2798, WH, 25th Inf.
DOBBINS, Emma Ann, W9365, HN, Dobbins, James Leaper
DOBBINS, James P. S8588, LA, 14th Cav.
DOBBINS, Mary White Fleming, W8935, MU, Dobbins, Albert Newton
DOBBINS, Mollie M. W1507, GI, Dobbins, James P.
DOBBINS, Sarah N. W1738, HD, Dobbins, Wm. Jessee
DOBBINS, Susie Ida, W5758, SN, Dobbins, Albert Carson
DOBBINS, T. E. S11160, LI, 32nd Inf.
DOBBS, Acijane, W6308, W9087, MC, Dobbs, James Pryar
DOBBS, Axie Jane, W9087, W6308, MC, Dobbs, James Pryor
DOBBS, J. P. S10315, MC, 3rd (Lillard's) Mtd. Inf.
DOBBS, Joseph, S15940, WY, 48th (Voorhies') Inf.
DOBBS, R. I. S2349, LE, 48th Inf.
DOBBS, Samantha E. W338, SN, Dobbs, James Chesley
DOBSON, J. E. S5894, T, 14th (Neely's) Cav.
DOBSON, Robert, S15230, GE, 16th Bn. (Neall's) Cav.
DOBYNS, Nellie Marie, W5914, SH, Dobyns, Henry Clay
DODD, A. J. S7957, MC, 4th Cav.
DODD, Albert M. S4946, CA, 8th (Smith's) Cav.
DODD, Artia Missie, W9121, H, Dodd, Henry Clay
DODD, B. P. S9009, DY, 1st Bn. (McNairy's) Cav.
DODD, David D. S1043, CA, 18th Inf.
DODD, Florence G. W29, D, Dodd, Thomas J.
DODD, Gabriella Augusta, W2250, MC, Dodd, Andrew Jackson
DODD, Hamie, W8747, RU, Dodd, Alfred
DODD, Henry Clay, S6103, H, 23rd Inf.
DODD, J. M. S5218, G, 19th & 20th Cav.
DODD, James M. S3196, O, 32nd Inf.
DODD, James W. S2909, H, 31st Inf.
DODD, Joel, S15241, MS, 8th Inf.
DODD, Joel Jackson, S6330, MS, 32nd Inf.
DODD, Kizzie Turner, W2559, MS, Dodd, Joel Jackson
DODD, Sarah Jane, W352, R, Dodd, Wm. Henderson
DODD, Serena C. W5862, GE, Dodd, Nathan
DODD, Sophia, W3832, BR, Dodd, Wm. Washington
DODDS, J. C. S3616, CH, 16th (Wilson's) Cav.
DODDS, Mary Elizabeth, W396, CH, Dodds, James Crook
DODDS, R. L. S12708, HN, 5th Inf.
DODGENS, Margaret, W4191, SE, Dodgens, Joseph Henry
DODSON, Agnes C. W1434, WI, Dodson, Bird E.
DODSON, Clarinda I. W6953, FR, Dodson, Woodard Crockett
DODSON, Crocket, S2676, WH, 25th Inf.
DODSON, D. B. S11763, CC, 47th Inf.
DODSON, E. M. S6040, HM, 1st Ga. Inf.
DODSON, Emily Elizabeth, W2025, WI, Dodson, John W.
DODSON, Esther Leonard, W5581, CC, Dodson, David B.
DODSON, J. E. S16450, DI, 4th Cav.
DODSON, James A. S10433, MU, 6th (Wheeler's) Cav.
DODSON, Kate, W9882, W, Dodson, James
DODSON, Lanetta, W9400, MU, Dodson, Raleigh T.
DODSON, Maggie A. W6315, WL, Dodson, George Thomas
DODSON, Martha, W7833, MG, Dodson, Henry
DODSON, Mary Ann, W6565, G, Dodson, Wm. Henry
DODSON, Noah, S345, V, 1st Inf.
DODSON, Sarah Jane, W9980, MU, Dodson, John C.

DODSON, Vonie Hight, W10110, MU, Dodson, Paul Weisman
DOE, E. S. S16454, RB, 14th Ky. Cav.
DOGAN, J. W. S14139, F, 13th Inf.
DOGGETT, A. P. S16122, MS, 20th (Nixon's) Cav.
DOGGETT, Jasper, S4640, MS, 48th (Voorhies') Inf.
DOGGETT, Jemima A. W4794, MS, Doggett, Jasper
DOGGETT, MArtha Amarica, W3567, MS, Doggett, Newton
DOGGETT, P. M. S4486, MS, 53rd Inf.
DOLAND, Alfred, See Alfred Dowland
DOLBY, D. H. S13817, O, 9th Inf.
DOLBY, Woodson Night, S373, B, 44th Inf.
DOLEN, Henry, S1651, CE, 30th Inf.
DOLEN, John, S3491, T, 9th Inf.
DOLES, Hannah Ellis, W8491, SH, Doles, Wm. G.
DOLL, Bettie Hunter, W2439, K, Doll, Richard McSherry
DOLLAR, J. P. S5260, LI, 8th Inf.
DONAHEW, A. V. S11448, UN, 5th Bn. Cav.
DONAHOE, R. F. S10214, K, 3rd Inf.
DONALDSON, John R. S9160, CY, 28th Inf.
DONALDSON, Pauline, W, Some papers with #11183 on film
DONALDSON, Permelia Catherine, W1657, CY, Donaldson, John Richmond
DONALDSON, R. S. S14564, FR, 38th Inf.
DONALDSON, William E. S10557, MR, 1st (Turney's) Inf.
DONALDSON, William R. S4471, D, 45th Inf.
DONEHEW, Berry L. S8905, UN, 2nd (Ashby's) Cav.
DONEHUE, Mary E. W7910, K, Donehue, Barry L.
DONELSON, R. S. S9673, SH, 13th Inf.
DONNEL, Nancey Emaline, W4279, RU, Donnel, Newton
DONNELL, David Crockett, S5069, WL, 45th Inf.
DONNELL, Francis M. S5109, S12692, WL, 4th (McLemore's) Cav.
DONNELL, George Ewing, S9914, 4th (McLemore's) Cav.
DONNELL, J. P. S16440, WL, 4th Cav.
DONNELL, J. W. S10793, O, 33rd Inf.
DONNELL, Martha Eliza, W802, WL, Donnell, Silas Morrison

DONNELL, Mary, W5742, WL, Donnell, David C.
DONNELL, Mollie, W9228, WL, Donnell, Alonzo E.
DONNELL, Nancy Emaline, W9008, W9558, W6892, RU, Donnell, Newton
DONNELL, Tennie, W9220, WL, Donnell, R. T.
DONNELL, Wm. M. C51, B, Comm. Dept.
DONOHO, A. G. sr. S13877, TR, 2nd (Robison's) Inf.
DONOHO, Amanda, W3069, M, Donoho, John Wiseman
DONOHO, J. S. S9474, WL, 2nd Inf.
DOOLEY, Mary Ann, W1886, MU, Dooley, Martin Pemberton
DOOLIN, M. E. S15605, D, 6th Ky. Cav.
DOOLIN, Mary Mal, W10223, D, Doolin, Milford Elliott
DORAN, T. J. S6393, S13932, WE, 33rd Inf.
DORRIS, Elizabeth, W461, RB, Dorris, James Dawson
DORRIS, Henry Jane, W1363, SN, Dorris, Isiah Thornsbury
DORRIS, Isaac N. S3969, SN, 30th Inf.
DORRIS, Isah T. S2123, SN, 7th Inf.
DORRIS, J. D. S947, RB, 14th Inf.
DORRIS, James D. S16563, SN, 14th Inf.
DORRIS, Louisa Agnes, W2888, SN, Dorris, James Richard
DORRIS, Sarah Frances, W2010, M, Dorris, Wm. Asa
DORRIS, Susan Ellen, W10874, H, Dorris, Wm. Willis
DORRIS, W. A. S7702, RB, 14th Inf.
DORRIS, W. J. S13853, RB, 9th (Bennett's) Cav.
DORRIS, W. W. S12409, GU, 20th Cav.
DORSEY, John R. S8616, H, 4th Ga. Inf.
DORTCH, Charles, C152, MT, 2nd Ky. Cav.
DORTIN, Joeanna Elizabeth, W5125, HI, Dortin, Henderson Jackson
DOSS, H. A. S11805, MA, 14th (Neely's) Cav.
DOSS, James Monroe, S4578, DY, 33rd Inf.
DOSS, Mary J. W3411, DY, Doss, James Monroe
DOSS, Sarah Elizabeth, W2366, GI, Doss, Wm. Blount
DOSS, Sarah Frances, W9139, MA, Doss, Henry Ayres
DOSS, Thomas J. S3453, GI, 32nd Inf.
DOSS, W. Y. S9073, M, 20th Inf.

DOSS, William Blount, S1518, S522, GI, 3rd Inf.
DOSS, Zubie, W6427, SH, Doss, James Hurd
DOSSON, J. F. S4604, R, 19th Inf.
DOSTER, E. C. S10087, WE, Jeff Davis' Legion, Miss. Cav.
DOSTER, Mary Elizabeth, W7973, WE, Doster, Ellison Caraway
DOSTER, W. Z. A. S14003, GI, 16th Ga. Inf.
DOTSON, David N. S418, GR, 37th Inf.
DOTSON, Eliza, W2012, HW, Dotson, John Wesley
DOTSON, H. C. S796, M, 9th (Bennett's) Cav.
DOTSON, J. P. S8401, FR, 32nd Inf.
DOTSON, Joel C. S3201, GR, 3rd (Lillard's) Mtd. Inf.
DOTSON, John, S11968, LI, 41st Inf.
DOTSON, John A. S13262, G, 18th (Newsom's) Cav.
DOTSON, John W. S8800, DI, 3rd (Forrest's) Cav.
DOTSON, Martha, W4808, FR, Dotson, John Payne
DOTSON, Mary, W302, GR, Dotson, Charles
DOTSON, Mary Ann, W4803, WA, Dotson, Berry Wilson
DOTSON, Nancy Catherine, W7397, HU, Dotson, John W.
DOTSON, Sarah L. W756, M, Dotson, Hiram C.
DOTSON, W. B. S2903, GR, 12th Inf.
DOTY, F. M. See F. M. Doughty
DOTY, J. M. S13229, HN, 20th (Nixon's) Cav.
DOTY, John A. S7195, DI, 49th Inf.
DOTY, Susan, W4051, MA, Doty, Robert I.
DOUGHERTY, A. M. S15024, JO, Waugh's Home Gaurds, Mo.
DOUGHERTY, D. M. S9305, GI, 3rd (Clack's) Inf.
DOUGHERTY, E. H. S13097, BO, 6th N.C. Cav.
DOUGHERTY, Hattie Haynes, W9429, D, Dougherty, J. R.
DOUGHERTY, J. R. S13384, RU, 2nd Cav.
DOUGHERTY, M. B. S7757, RO, 63rd Inf.
DOUGHERTY, Mary White, W9626, JO, Dougherty, T. L.
DOUGHTON, W. C. S9248, HI, 11th Inf.
DOUGHTRY, Jesse, S14119, RU, 2nd (Robison's) Inf.
DOUGHTY, Francis M. S7958, ST, 2nd Ky. Cav.
DOUGHTY, J. F. S13052, HN, 46th Inf.

DOUGHTY, Syntha, W6784, ST, Doughty, T. J.
DOUGHTY, T. J. S8229, ST, 3rd Ky. Inf.
DOUGLAS, Electra Louise, W9860, RU, Douglas, Edwin Henry
DOUGLAS, Fannie, W4805, SH, Douglas, Joseph Benjamin
DOUGLAS, J. J. S11715, RU, 23rd Inf.
DOUGLAS, J. W. S7939, HN, 22nd Miss. Inf.
DOUGLAS, Maggie M. W2549, DI, Douglas, David
DOUGLASS, Alexander, S1351, CT, Undetermined
DOUGLASS, Alfred H. S9702, D, 9th Cav.
DOUGLASS, Charles S. S15678, SN, 30th Inf.
DOUGLASS, Cornelia, W1668, SH, Douglass, Howard Franklin
DOUGLASS, Edwin C. S1326, F, 154th Sr. Regt. Inf.
DOUGLASS, Harriet B. W4238, BE, Douglass, Wesley Austin
DOUGLASS, Henrietta, W5262, O, Douglass, John H.
DOUGLASS, J. H. S13734, O, 33rd Inf.
DOUGLASS, J. P. S15363, FR, 16th Cav.
DOUGLASS, J. P. S15893, W, 16th Inf.
DOUGLASS, J. W. S13300, HN, 22nd Miss. Inf.
DOUGLASS, Joseph A. S7327, O, 33rd Inf.
DOUGLASS, Levi, C99, HY, Regt. not given
DOUGLASS, Lizzie, W1070, D, Douglass, Charles Adam
DOUGLASS, Mari Etta, W9844, MU, Douglass, Hugh B.
DOUGLASS, Mary Frances, W9374, D, Douglass, Thomas Jefferson
DOUGLASS, R. S13728, SN, 9th (Bennett's) Cav.
DOUGLASS, Sallie Ann, W8598, SH, Douglass, Ila Elmo
DOUGLASS, W. A. S4920, HN, 1st Inf.
DOUGLASS, Zudie Kirkpatrick, W10760, D, Douglass, Edward
DOUTHIT, James H. S9391, MR, Barry's Co. Lt. Art.
DOVE, George R. S5552, SU, 4th Inf.
DOVE, James W. S4420, W, 25th Inf.
DOVE, Nancy Jane, W5569, CC, Dove, Hiram
DOVE, Rosie, W6325, SU, Dove, George Ringold
DOVE, Susie, W6005, W, Dove, James W.
DOVER, David, S456, LA, 22nd Ala. Inf.
DOVER, William, S300, G, 12th & 47th Consolidated Inf.

Index to Tennessee Confederate Pension Applications

DOWDY, Angeline, W9185, HN, Dowdy, Henry
DOWDY, Eliza, W5275, WY, Dowdy, Joe
DOWDY, G. W. S14934, HR, 3rd (Forrest's) Cav.
DOWDY, Henry, S11215, HN, 46th Inf.
DOWDY, L. H. S210, RB, 24th Inf.
DOWDY, M. J. S8124, G, 51st Inf.
DOWDY, P. L. S11600, P, 19th (Biffle's) Cav.
DOWDY, Rachel, W1806, G, Dowdy, M. J.
DOWDY, Sallie Elizabeth, W9086, HR, Dowdy, George
DOWELL, Alice Deborah, W3235, MU, Dowell, James B. F.
DOWELL, Mary Elizabeth, W9310, SM, Dowell, Horace P.
DOWELL, Sarah Ann, W4798, PU, Dowell, George Rufus
DOWELL, Virginia, W5309, RB, Dowell, Wm. Tandy
DOWELL, William T. S6179, RB, 18th Va. Inf.
DOWLAND, Alfred, S1321, 5th N.C. Inf.
DOWLEN, Henry, S6073, CE, 30th Inf.
DOWLEN, Sarah E. W7779, CE, Dowlen, Henry
DOWNEY, Rebecca E. W1011, GE, Downey, John A.
DOWNING, Ella E. W3237, MS, Downing, Adrian M.
DOWNING, F. M. S1803, LI, 8th Inf.
DOWNING, John G. S10298, LA, 41st Inf.
DOWNING, Mary J. W7772, Downing, W. A.
DOWNS, A. S9197, ST, 50th Inf.
DOWNS, Ann F. W9507, ST, Downs, Alphard
DOWTIN, S. C. S10207, 55th Inf.
DOYAL, A. S5726, F, 24th N.C. Inf.
DOYAL, H. P. S14807, DY, 4th Inf.
DOYAL, J. H. S6420, H, 53rd Ga. Inf.
DOYAL, J. W. S14573, LE, 1st (Jackson's) Hvy. Art.
DOYAL, James William, S10233, HD, 1st Confederate Cav.
DOYAL, John, S15275, MR, 4th Cav.
DOYAL, John C. S8499, H, 2nd Cav.
DOYAL, John R. S11001, HR, 14th Inf.
DOYAL, S. J. S10341, MU, 11th Cav.
DOYLE, Cleopatra Ann, W7849, H, Doyle, John C.
DOYLE, Margaret White, W7181, SH, Doyle, James
DOYLE, Minervia Selden, W8196, SH, Doyle, W. J.
DOYLE, Sarah Adeline, W3105, D, Doyle, Samuel Jackson
DOZIER, Henry, S14947, G, 47th Inf.
DOZIER, Henry C. S7733, DY, 12th Inf.
DOZIER, Mary Ann, W542, MS, Dozier, Joseph Thomas
DRAKE, Andrew J. S10526, SU, 6th Inf.
DRAKE, D. A. S8983, SU, 59th Inf.
DRAKE, D. C. S4327, B, 17th Inf.
DRAKE, Drew James, W2742, HY, Drake, Richer Baxter
DRAKE, Edwin L. S9851, FR, 2nd (Robison's) Inf.
DRAKE, G. W. C93, D, 16th Inf.
DRAKE, G. W. S3648, SU, 19th Inf.
DRAKE, J. G. S11232, HY, 6th Inf.
DRAKE, J. P. S2413, HY, 14th Cav.
DRAKE, James, S7754, CF, 4th (McLemore's) Cav.
DRAKE, James A. S5007, R, 29th Inf.
DRAKE, Lucy, W8854, W, Drake, Uriah York
DRAKE, Lucy Varner, W8490, CC, Drake, W. L.
DRAKE, Martha Jane, W1229, WA, Drake, John Morrell
DRAKE, Reuben Miller, S1018, L, 8th Inf.
DRAKE, Richard, S15424, SH, 2nd Miss. Inf.
DRAKE, W. H. S14737, WL, 7th Inf.
DRAKE, William B. S14190, L, Davies' Va. Art.
DRAKE, Willis, S7032, R, 62nd Inf.
DRANE, James H. S16346, G, 12th Inf.
DRAPER, A. J. S16252, G, 15th Cav.
DRAPER, Frances Rachel, W10812, SH, Draper, Andrew Jackson
DRAPER, Mary Jane, W2748, W8965, WL, Draper, Wm.
DRAPER, Stephen P. S12808, G, 12th Cav.
DRAUGHON, Anna Northern, W10323, SH, Draughon, James Harris
DRAUGHON, J. B. S94, D, 30th Inf.
DRENNAN, Jane, W8921, WL, Drennan, Thomas Jefferson
DRENNAN, John N. S7033, RU, Carter's Scouts
DRENNEN, Elvina Ann, W876, WL, Drennen, John G.
DRINNEN, Mary Jane, W2362, K, Drinnen, Thomas
DRINNEN, Thomas, S3047, SE, 43rd Inf.
DRINNEN, William H. S2502, SE, 43rd Inf.

Index to Tennessee Confederate Pension Applications

DRISKELL, Nancy Ann, W6610, MN, Driskell, Joel Jefferson
DRISKILL, O. B. S8443, K, 12th Cav.
DRIVER, C. M. S5997, D, 2nd Ky. Cav.
DRIVER, J. M. S8683, S, 6th Wheeler's Cav.
DRIVER, Jeptha, S7217, DK, Allison's Squadron, Cav.
DRIVER, Malisa Jane, W616, DK, Driver, Giles
DRIVER, Mary Emily, W926, HU, Driver, John Macklan
DRIVER, Sidney J. W7780, MOO, Driver, T. N.
DRIVER, Simon P. S15219, L, 7th Cav.
DRIVER, Thomas N. S2036, MOO, 45th Inf.
DRIVER, W. O. S3567, D, 1st (Feild's) Inf.
DRIVER, Wiley, S2194, MS, 17th Inf.
DROKE, Christena, W4091, SU, Droke, G. W.
DROKE, Sarah Anne, W4877, SU, Droke, Andrew Jackson
DROKE, W. C. S7643, SU, 59th Inf.
DRUMMOND, J. H. S4361, 55th Inf.
DRUMMOND, John H. S6328, K, 2nd (Ashby's) Cav.
DRUMMONDS, Laura Frances, W2157, T, Drummonds, Robert M.
DRUMMONDS, R. M. S1810, SH, 51st Inf.
DRUMMONDS, Rutha L. W1394, Drummonds, John H.
DRUMRIGHT, W. b. S11723, MR, 1st (Feild's) Inf.
DRUMRIGHT, William Robert, S15028, T, 56th Va. Inf.
DRURY, A. B. S7121, WL, 25th Inf.
DRYDEN, E. R. S8933, RU, 17th Inf.
DRYDEN, Maria E. W3590, RU, Dryden, Ephraim R.
DUBLIN, Polly Ann New, W10095, LK, Dublin, Wm. Thomas
DUBOSE, Elizabeth Egleston, W3626, FR, DuBose, Rob Marion
DUBREE, J. M. S6634, CY, 8th (Dibrell's) Cav.
DUCK, Daniel W. S4616, GE, 64th N.C. Inf.
DUCK, Robert M. S6170, GE, 5th Bn. N.C. State Troops
DUCKWORTH, D. F. S14318, H, 5th (McKenzie's) Cav.
DUCKWORTH, Harriet Emmeline, W5942, HY, Duckworth, Wm. Lafayette
DUCKWORTH, Irena, W5446, ME, Duckworth, Wm. Jasper
DUCKWORTH, W. J. S1559, ME, 3rd Cav.
DUCKWORTH, William, S3054, ME, 5th (McKenzie's) Cav.

DUDLEY, Catherine, W2338, H, Dudley, Christopher Columbus
DUDLEY, Christopher C. S5837, H, 4th Inf.
DUDLEY, E. J. S11186, HI, 49th Inf.
DUDLEY, Nannie M. W10965, HM, Dudley, Thomas T.
DUDLEY, Rufus, S3512, WE, 12th Ky. Cav.
DUE, N. E. S16139, MU, Vaughn's Scouts
DUER, C. L. S11672, SN, 30th Inf.
DUFF, Hugh T. S4788, LI, 59th Inf.
DUFF, J. M. S12974, HM, 64th Va. Inf.
DUFFER, Margaret A. W7414, SN, Duffer, Wm. T.
DUFFER, Millie, W9915, SN, Duffer, Robert
DUFFER, Robert A. S2836, SN, 7th Cav.
DUFFER, W. T. S10100, TR, 9th (Ward's) Cav.
DUFFEY, Patrick, S1456, HN, 1st Inf.
DUFFORD, Amanda, W6475, O, Dufford, Eugene
DUGGAN, Jane Steed, W8221, W4104, B, Duggan, Benjamin Fredrick
DUGGAN, W. S. S8125, L, 1st Cav.
DUGGER, J. A. S16336, ME, 8th Ga. Bn. Cav.
DUGGER, Mattie Ann, W10218, LA, Dugger, Robert Reece
DUGGER, R. R. S11288, MS, 3rd Inf.
DUGGER, Sallie Thomas, W6857, MA, Dugger, Adrian Dorian
DUGGER, T. M. S6577, GI, 11th Bn. (Holman's) Cav.
DUIGNAN, Ann, W5343, JE, Duignan, Michael
DUKE, Alfred, C190, SH, 3rd (Forrest's) Cav.
DUKE, Felix T. S7226, HD, Undetermined
DUKE, H. L. S8652, SH, 1st Miss. Cav.
DUKE, J. W. S15135, O, 17th Miss. Inf.
DUKE, James K. S8100, WE, 31st Inf.
DUKE, James M. S8889, SH, 5th Ala. Inf.
DUKE, James M. S10663, HY, 5th Bn. N.C. Lt. Art.
DUKE, Jessie Moss, W3839, D, Duke, John Timberlake
DUKE, John, S5316, WL, 7th Inf.
DUKE, L. T. S14824, WA, 15th Va. Inf.
DUKE, Martha Isabla, W4282, WE, Duke, James Knox
DUKE, Newton J. S1093, DE, Marshall's Co. Art.
DUKE, Nora L. W9095, O, Duke, James W.
DUKE, Pattie J. W6334, HY, Duke, James M.
DUKE, Polly Ann, W2512, WL, Duke, James Alfred

DUKE, Sarah Lane, W8478, WL, Duke, John Thomas
DUKE, Susan Y. W1263, G, Duke, James A.
DUKE, W. H. H. S332, SM, 7th Inf.
DUKES, Henry, S1747, HW, Undetermined
DULANEY, Ephraim, S14525, WA, 60th Inf.
DULIN, Fouzie S. S5883, HR, 48th N.C. Inf.
DULWORTH, James, S11811, CY, 8th Inf.
DULWORTH, Polly Ann, W4229, CY, Dulworth, James
DUNAHOO, Sophronia Idella, W2673, DY, Dunahoo, Alexander
DUNAVANT, John D. S8393, DY, 6th (Wheeler's) Cav.
DUNAVANT, John W. S6954, L, 1st Cav.
DUNAVANT, Susan Ellen, W10802, L, Dunavant, Oscar Reid
DUNAWAY, J. W. S6423, D, 45th Inf.
DUNAWAY, L. C. S14213, HI, 42nd Inf.
DUNAWAY, Samuel W. S9362, HI, 42nd Inf.
DUNCAN, A. M. S4305, HR, 42nd Inf.
DUNCAN, A. N. M. S15450, CF, 4th (McLemore's) Cav.
DUNCAN, Anna Eliza, W9292, HD, Duncan, Joseph Kelly
DUNCAN, Annie, W9367, CC, Duncan, Wm. Daniel
DUNCAN, Annie M. W10657, DY, Duncan, Wm. D. L.
DUNCAN, Belle, W7785, K, Duncan, James M.
DUNCAN, C. A. S1407, HR, 10th Ark. Inf.
DUNCAN, C. P. S14873, D, 1st Ky. Inf.
DUNCAN, Daniel, S6705, CF, 44th Inf.
DUNCAN, Elizabeth, W5103, MS, Duncan, Newton C.
DUNCAN, Elizabeth, W7786, K, Duncan, J. H.
DUNCAN, Elizabeth M. W1754, O, Duncan, Edward Madison
DUNCAN, Ethanzia A. W2522, HN, Duncan, Andrew V.
DUNCAN, George R. S7202, WA, 63rd Inf.
DUNCAN, H. C. S14631, R, 5th Cav.
DUNCAN, Ida S. W9408, H, Duncan, Daniel Lewis
DUNCAN, J. C. S11055, MS, 17th Inf.
DUNCAN, J. G. S6733, WA, 60th Inf.
DUNCAN, J. G. S6917, MS, 17th Inf.
DUNCAN, J. M. S5975, K, 2nd Regt. Engineer Troops
DUNCAN, J. M. S6539, HW, 7th Ky. Cav.
DUNCAN, J. P. S11485, FR, 17th Inf.
DUNCAN, James, C271, HD, 1st Inf.

DUNCAN, James D. S15803, SN, 9th (Ward's) Cav.
DUNCAN, James K. P. S14652, MN, 45th Inf.
DUNCAN, Jennie C. W7116, FR, Duncan, James Polk
DUNCAN, John E. S7594, H, 3rd (Lillard's) Mtd. Inf.
DUNCAN, Joseph, S12174, HD, 19th (Biffle's) Cav.
DUNCAN, Julia A. W3662, RB, Duncan, S. Jourdan
DUNCAN, L. S. S812, CF, 4th Inf.
DUNCAN, Louisa B. W387, WL, Duncan, James Harvey
DUNCAN, Maggie, W7734, CF, Duncan, L. S.
DUNCAN, Martha Elizabeth, W1883, H, Duncan, John E.
DUNCAN, Mary, W8214, SU, Duncan, Benjamin
DUNCAN, Mary Ann, W2330, MS, Duncan, James Wesley
DUNCAN, Mary Elizabeth, W2777, K, Duncan, Robert G.
DUNCAN, Mary M. W462, GU, Duncan, John Franklin
DUNCAN, Newton C. S6536, MS, 17th Inf.
DUNCAN, P. S12766, HI, 10th Cav.
DUNCAN, S. J. S9906, RB, 3rd Ky. Cav.
DUNCAN, Sallie, W3210, SH, Duncan, Elihu Duncan
DUNCAN, Sallie Louise, W8849, HR, Duncan, Calvin Anderson
DUNCAN, Sarah Love, W99, CF, Duncan, Wm. Anderson
DUNCAN, Signore H. W7341, HN, Duncan, Christopher Pritchel
DUNCAN, Thomas, S5628, GE, 23rd S.C. Inf.
DUNCAN, William A. S11780, WE, 9th Cav.
DUNCAN, Z. D. S3473, CF, 34th Inf.
DUNGAN, William A. S13212, MA, 6th Inf.
DUNHAM, Drucilla, W274, WH, Dunham, David Lafayette
DUNHAM, Nancy, W1215, DK, Dunham, Wm. Ray
DUNING, Harriet Elizabeth, W3147, HR, Duning, Charles Wesley
DUNKIN, Martha C. W3348, WH, Dunkin, John Thomas
DUNLAP, Antionette A. W4545, SH, Dunlap, David R.
DUNLAP, D. R. S7759, SH, 13th Inf.
DUNLAP, I. P. S6484, WE, 5th Inf.

DUNLAP, John C. S14539, SH, 4th Ga. Cav.
DUNLAP, Mary Eliza, W10070, WE, Dunlap, Silas Wright
DUNLAP, Mary Melcinia, W4635, WE, Dunlap, Isaac P.
DUNLAP, Robert W. S11252, WE, 51st Inf.
DUNLAP, S. W. S11817, WE, 21st (Wilson's) Cav.
DUNLAP, Sarah Frances, W10524, LK, Dunlap, Finis Ewing
DUNLAP, Susan, W8222, G, Dunlap, Wm. Newton Lafayette
DUNLAP, W. A. S11819, WE, 21st (Wilson's) Cav.
DUNLOP, J. R. S7037, G, 40th Ala. Inf.
DUNN, Allen S. H. S16562, SN, 14th Inf.
DUNN, Allie A. W7022, MC, Dunn, Napoleon B.
DUNN, Anna Elizabeth, W2835, SH, Dunn, John Frost
DUNN, Elizabeth, W8816, W440, RU, Dunn, John Allen
DUNN, J. F. S10398, RB, 2nd Ky. Cav.
DUNN, J. J. S6576, WE, 37th Inf.
DUNN, J. L. S11690, DY, 45th Inf.
DUNN, James, C121, TR, 7th Cav.
DUNN, Julia Ann, W2447, RB, Dunn, S. S.
DUNN, L. C. S4771, PO, 3rd Inf.
DUNN, Louisa E. W10, RU, Dunn, T. F.
DUNN, Martha J. W3333, H, Dunn, W. W.
DUNN, Mary Eilzabeth, W787, SH, Dunn, Bernard
DUNN, Mary Jane, W10909, D, Dunn, Blackman Hayes
DUNN, Newton C. S9080, WL, 23rd Inf.
DUNN, Rachel C. W2867, WL, Dunn, Newton Cannon
DUNN, Sallie, W3042, PO, Dunn, Thomas
DUNN, Sally Anderson, W2507, WE, Dunn, James Jackson
DUNN, William, S4828, HU, 26th Inf.
DUNNAGAN, William L. S12730, WE, 49th Inf.
DUNNAGON, A. C. S1958, HU, 42nd Inf.
DUNNAVANT, Samuel M. S7443, GI, 53rd Inf.
DUNNIVANT, Thomas, S2586, GI, 32nd Inf.
DUNSTON, J. H. S9399, DY, Cummings' Regt. Ga. Inf.
DUPREE, George F. S15840, F, 3rd (Forrest's) Cav.
DUPREE, P. H. S1131, GI, 9th Cav., On misc. microfilm reel

DUPREE, Sallie E. W8417, F, Dupree, George F.
DURBIN, Ara Alice, W9193, SH, Durbin, G. W.
DURBIN, G. W. S846, MN, 9th Ala. Reg.
DUREN, M. J. S13208, S12551, MN, Phillip's Co. Lt. Art.
DURHAM, B. C. S14310, L, 1st Miss. Inf.
DURHAM, B. C. sr. S15577, L, 1st Miss. Inf.
DURHAM, Columbia A. W5413, RO, Durham, James
DURHAM, F. G. S650, SN, 20th Inf.
DURHAM, Fannie E. W3258, SM, Durham, James A.
DURHAM, Favious, S3334, B, 2nd (Robison's) Inf.
DURHAM, H. H. S4872, FR, 17th Inf.
DURHAM, Harriet, W6662, RB, Durham, John C.
DURHAM, Henry, S8446, LI, Moreland's Regt. Ala. Cav.
DURHAM, J. C. S5788, RB, 1st Cav.
DURHAM, J. H. S12731, SN, 20th Inf.
DURHAM, J. O. S15919, MA, 31st Inf.
DURHAM, J. S. S357, RO, 26th Inf.
DURHAM, James A. S1375, SM, 28th Inf.
DURHAM, John, S14184, MR, 4th Ga. Cav.
DURHAM, John A. S12209, J, 5th Cav.
DURHAM, Leoni Alis, W8732, SN, Durham, Frances Gooseberry
DURHAM, Martha H. W61, D, Durham, Thomas Matthew
DURHAM, R. H. S3583, HU, Undetermined
DURHAM, Sam, S4558, MT, Baxter's Co. Lt. Art.
DURHAM, Sarah E. W2237, B, Durham, Fabious
DURHAM, Susannah Durham, W1432, MT, Durham, Sam
DURHAM, W. M. S13878, SN, 9th (Ward's) Cav.
DURHAM, William E. S12293, SN, 9th (Ward's) Cav.
DURHAM, William M. S5491, SN, 20th Inf.
DURM, John, S6963, MR, 4th Ga. Cav.
DURRENT, Mary Elizabeth, W5189, HR, Durrent, David Edgar
DURRETT, Lee, W8918, LA, Durrett, Solomon
DURRETT, Lennza Jernigan, W9720, D, Durrett, Wm. T.
DURRETT, Solomon, S255, LA, 54th Inf.
DURRETT, W. R. S13658, MA, McD. Carrington's Co. Va. Lt. Art.

Index to Tennessee Confederate Pension Applications

DURRETT, William T. S4446, D, 14th Inf.
DURRUM, J. P. S11578, SH, 2nd Mo. Cav.
DURRUM, Maria L. W8363, SH, Durrum, James P.
DUTTON, Wiley, S183, S1233, O, 24th Inf.
DUVALL, T. M. S11853, JO, 26th N.C. Inf.
DYAL, A. J. S970, DE, 32nd Inf.
DYCHE, James L. S655, SU, 1st Cav.
DYCUS, Andrew, S9960, MU, 9th Bn. (Gantt's) Cav.
DYCUS, J. M. S4565, HE, 3rd (Clack's) Inf.
DYCUS, J. T. S6982, ST, 14th Inf.
DYCUS, James Q. A. S11509, P, 3rd (Clack's) Inf.
DYE, Mary Rebecca, W3962, B, Dye, Osborne
DYE, O. S6816, B, 16th Inf.
DYER, Amanda, W5033, BO, Dyer, John
DYER, America, W8645, PU, Dyer, Logan Robinson
DYER, Angus Washington, S5600, HW, 61st Inf.
DYER, Benjamin A. S1542, BO, 19th Inf.
DYER, Bettie Ross, W5037, W9546, MA, Dyer, John W.
DYER, Elizabeth, W10074, PU, Dyer, James P.
DYER, Ephriam, S13610, W, Thomas' Legion, N.C.
DYER, J. H. S5895, HO, 49th Inf.
DYER, James, S3384, O, 9th Bn. (Gantt's) Cav.
DYER, James P. S13874, PU, 17th Inf.
DYER, John Alexander, S3166, WA, 60th Inf.
DYER, John W. S399, GI, 3rd Inf.
DYER, Logan R. S12960, J, 28th Inf.
DYER, Louis, S1283, HW, 61st Inf.
DYER, Martha Ann Frances, W1997, RU, Dyer, Isiah W.
DYER, Sarah, W3715, UN, Dyer, John A.
DYER, W. R. S8925, UN, 2nd (Ashby's) Cav.
DYER, W. W. S14746, PU, 28th Inf.
DYER, William L. S2092, PU, 8th (Dibrell's) Cav.
DYER, Zachary Taylor, S9946, GI, 3rd (Clack's) Inf.
DYKES, D. D. S10439, HY, 4th Ala. Cav.
DYKES, E. M. W7313, HY, Dykes, Daniel
DYKES, Harriet, W4806, HW, Dykes, John Robison
DYKES, Isham B. S966, HW, 31st Inf.
DYKES, J. R. S6032, HW, 31st Inf.
DYKES, John N. S9884, RU, 31st Inf.
DYKES, Margaret Elizabeth, W5819, RU, Dykes, John Netherlands

DYKES, Mollie Walker, W8993, GU, Dykes, Robert Tyler
DYKES, Robert T. sr. S14702, GU, 35th Inf.
DYKES, Sarah Elizabeth, W2043, HW, Dykes, Isham Bailess
DYSART, James Milton, S6273, MS, 4th (McLemore's) Cav.
DYSART, Mary Frances, W2296, MS, Dysart, James M.
DYSART, Thomas J. S8095, B, 4th (McLemore's) Cav.
DYSON, Minerva Dunn, W2432, D, Dyson, Thomas Edward
DYSON, W. A. S13343, D, 3rd N.C. Inf.
EADS, A. K. S12064, SU, 8th (Smith's) Cav.
EADS, D. C. S10966, SU, Unassigned (Mining Nitre)
EADS, Martha H. W2508, CL, Eads, Stephen N.
EADS, William W. S8034, B, 16th Bn. (Neal's) Cav.
EAGAN, James M. S13218, WL, 45th Inf.
EAGAN, Mary, W1286, GI, Eagan, Richard Baugh
EAGIN, R. B. S5984, GI, 44th Inf.
EAKENS, Andrew Jackson, S4086, R, 62nd Inf.
EAKER, Alfred, S7720, UN, 16th N.C. Inf.
EAKER, D. W. S11521, MN, 3rd (Forrest's) Cav.
EAKER, Mary, W5034, UN, Eaker, Alfred
EAKES, G. W. S6608, WL, 20th Inf.
EAKIN, James N. S1011, FR, 1st Inf.
EAKIN, Milbrey Ewing, W5031, B, Eakin, Spencer
EAKS, W. M. S3380, LI, 41st Inf.
EALEM, J. W. S2435, MN, 22nd (Barteau's) Cav.
EANES, Annis P. W1927, SU, Eanes, Thomas B.
EANES, Elizabeth M. W5604, SH, Eanes, Wm. Woods
EANES, Emma P. W3812, SU, Eanes, Robert P.
EANES, Joe C. S12901, WH, 4th (McLemore's) Cav.
EARHEART, John L. S3134, WL, 20th Inf.
EARL, Peter T. S6681, HW, 63rd Inf.
EARLE, Turner, C73, F, 3rd Cav.
EARLE, William T. S1352, W, Undetermined
EARLES, James, S4348, W, 44th Inf.
EARLES, Minerva D. W4379, W, Earles, J. N.
EARLES, P. G. S11942, D, 44th Inf.
EARLES, Sophia, W9471, W, Earles, Wm. T.

-103

EARLEY, Laura, W2878, SH, Earley, Jessie Thomas
EARLEY, W. C. S14649, SH, McGehee's Ark. Cav.
EARLEY, William B. S1293, WI, 4th Cav.
EARLS, Nathaniel, S2822, CL, 37th Inf.
EARLS, William, S2823, CL, 37th Inf.
EARLY, Medoria O. W1220, RU, Early, Jesse
EARNEST, Eva Taylor, W3138, WA, Earnest, Felix Wells
EARNEST, M. M. S9219, BR, 60th Ga. Inf.
EARP, Leonora Kellogg, W5453, SH, Earp, Wm. Malcolm
EARWOOD, Andrew Jackson, S9344, T, 2nd Miss. State Cav.
EASLEY, A. J. S6180, SH, 13th Ark. Inf.
EASLEY, E. W. S8432, HI, 24th Inf.
EASLEY, Edom, C237, HI, 10th Cav.
EASLEY, Elizabeth, W2684, DI, Easley, John Wesley
EASLEY, Gillie Ann, W5843, SH, Easley, Andrew Jackson
EASLEY, Jane, W3067, HI, Easley, Thomas Stewart
EASLEY, John W. S9081, DI, 1st (Feild's) Inf.
EASLEY, Margarett Elizabeth, W4173, HI, Easley, Edward Wade
EASLEY, Mary Harris, W10511, DY, Easley, Martin Van Buren
EASLEY, Mary J. W8074, T, Easley, James D.
EASLEY, Mary M. W5768, HI, Easley, S. B.
EASLEY, Rebecca Jane, W4027, CH, Easley, Campbell Smith
EASLEY, S. B. S11207, HI, 12th Cav.
EASLEY, W. M. C10, HI, 24th Inf.
EASON, Bettie Bowen, W11138, SH, Eason, Edmund Epps
EASON, Clayton A. S2383, GI, 1st (Feild's) Inf.
EASON, Elizabeth J. W3773, GE, Eason, George Jefferson
EASON, Emeline Kizzie, W9342, DE, Eason, Robert W.
EASON, George J. S568, GE, 15th Ala. Inf.
EASON, Joella, W3663, Eason, Wm. H.
EASON, Mary Catherine, W1272, GI, Eason, Clayton Alfred
EASON, R. W. S11791, DE, 52nd Inf.
EASON, William H. S5454, 22nd Inf.
EAST, George Washington, C13, D, 4th Tex. Cav.
EAST, J. D. S12391, K, 10th Va. Inf.
EAST, J. R. S7865, C, 22nd Va. Cav.

EAST, Joseph, S347, HD, Undetermined
EAST, Lelia Lee, W5276, K, East, James Dickerson
EAST, Mary E. W7812, SU, East, Wm. Martin
EAST, Thomas J. S6913, MT, 32nd Inf.
EAST, W. M. S4882, SU, 21st Va. Cav.
EASTERLEY, Mary Elizabeth, W6434, BR, Easterley, John E. C.
EASTERLY, J. E. C. S10116, BR, 7th Bn. Cav.
EASTES, Thomas J. S14871, SM, 22nd (Barteau's) Cav.
EASTLACK, J. T. S12965, HR, 3rd (Forrest's) Cav.
EASTLAND, Ellen Lucrecia, W8691, HI, Eastland, Wm. Cyrus
EASTRIDGE, Barnabas, S15548, JE, 58th N.C. Inf.
EASTWOOD, F. A. S14476, O, 33rd Inf.
EATHERLEY, William, S15184, CE, 18th Inf.
EATHERLY, Emily E. W7168, W4951, WL, Eatherly, J. J.
EATHERLY, Hattie Ellen, W8860, CE, Eatherly, Benjamin Hamilton
EATHERLY, Mary E. W5051, WL, Eatherly, Winfield Scott
EATHERLY, Wm. C285, D, Regiment not given
EATON, Andrew J. S4772, D, Shaw's Bn. Cav.
EATON, Catherine Ward, W232, DK, Eaton, Wm. Jasper
EATON, Martha Jane, W10542, D, Eaton, Thomas Lewis
EATON, Thomas L. S9108, J, Allison's Squadron, Cav.
EAVES, Ben, S4128, MC, 43rd Inf.
EAVES, J. F. S5859, H, 8th Bn. Ga. Inf.
EAVES, John J. S211, BE, 33rd Inf.
EAVES, Mattie, W3980, H, Eaves, John F.
ECHOLS, J. B. S12813, SN, 9th (Bennett's) Cav.
ECHOLS, J. W. S10656, GU, 25th Bn. Ala. Cav.
ECHOLS, Louisa Elizabeth, W8001, GU, Echols, James V.
ECHOLS, William T. S2090, DK, 2nd Inf.
ECKEL, James R. S2740, OV, 25th Inf.
ECKFORD, William W. S14301, T, 4th Inf.
ECKLES, B. E. S14333, SH, 38th Inf.
EDDINS, Columbia Elizabeth, W7275, SH, Eddins, Wm. Louis
EDDINS, Margaret Ann, W5495, WL, Eddins, George Washington

Index to Tennessee Confederate Pension Applications

EDDINS, Mary Lila, W9272, WL, Eddins, Thomas H.
EDDINS, W. L. S13289, SH, 34th Miss. Inf.
EDDINS, Wash, S8349, CH, 33rd Inf.
EDENS, F. M. S12345, MOO, 1st (Turney's) Inf.
EDENS, Mary E. W4760, FR, Edens, Sam W.
EDENS, Sallie George Stone, W10927, MOO, Edens, F. M.
EDENS, Talitha Coats, W6189, FR, Edens, Wm.
EDENTON, Florence Tharp, W10449, MA, Edenton, Wm. Henry
EDENTON, Kate Ayres, W10635, MA, Edenton, James Caswell
EDGAR, Martha Ann, W9757, HN, Edgar, R. T.
EDGAR, Mary Elizabeth, W9678, W2208, HN, Edgar, Lewis Calvin
EDGAR, R. T. S14367, HN, 46th Inf.
EDGE, Harriet, W2367, DK, Edge, Wm.
EDGEMAN, Elija, S2919, MOO, 45th Inf.
EDGEMAN, Keziah, W3339, ME, Edgeman, Kimbal
EDGEMAN, Sarah Rutheny, W4574, MC, Edgeman, Simeon Grishom
EDGEMON, James, S8205, ME, 5th Cav.
EDGEMON, S. G. S10111, MC, 19th Inf.
EDGMON, Nancy Rebecca, W9610, BR, Edgmon, James E.
EDINGTAND, Mary Jane, W1256, MO, Edingtand, Abraham A.
EDINGTON, Harrison, S11949, JE, Lynch's Co. Lt. Art.
EDLIN, Bobbie, W5140, MT, Edlin, John Bell
EDLIN, G. C. S10265, MT, 2nd Ky. Cav.
EDLIN, John B. S4378, MT, 49th Inf.
EDMONDS, C. A. S11370, HY, 49th Ala. Inf.
EDMONDS, Drucilla Price, W4372, RU, Edmonds, Joseph Sterling
EDMONDS, H. L. S4317, WI, Undetermined
EDMONDS, Hettie A. W7083, SU, Edmonds, Wm. F.
EDMONDS, J. S. S12961, RU, 24th Inf.
EDMONDSON, Anderson K. S13225, LI, 1st (Turney's) Inf.
EDMONDSON, F. R. S11151, UN, 37th Inf.
EDMONDSON, James B. S13, WI, 1st Inf.
EDMONDSON, James M. S6983, MS, 11th Cav.
EDMONDSON, Josephine Neale, W9687, RU, Edmondson, Thomas Pinkney
EDMONDSON, Robert H. S7021, MT, 14th Inf.

EDMONDSON, Samuel, S16686, D, 2nd (Morgan's) Ky. Cav.
EDMONDSON, Sarah Boid, W8763, SN, Edmondson, David C.
EDMONSON, Mary E. W1444, SH, Edmonson, Wm. Bryant
EDMONSON, Mary Elizabeth, W8088, D, Edmonson, Samuel S.
EDMONSTON, Sallie E. W3150, WE, Edmonston, Wm. Monroe
EDMUNDSON, Henry, S13571, D, 1st Bn. (McNairy's) Cav.
EDMUNDSON, Janie Hamrick, W10556, SH, Edmundson, Wm. Lane
EDMUNDSON, May Farrow, W10485, SH, Edmundson, Edward A.
EDMUNDSON, Tennie Elizabeth, W10427, G, Edmundson, John Bergan
EDNEY, Marvel N. B. S8147, CT, 16th Miss. Inf.
EDWARDS, A. M. S3942, RU, 1st (Feild's) Inf.
EDWARDS, Alice, W6442, T, Edwards, Wm. Battle
EDWARDS, Arthor O. S11110, LI, 37th Inf.
EDWARDS, B. B. S634, T, 13th Ala. Inf.
EDWARDS, Dugenia, W3864, MS, Edwards, Gray Hillman
EDWARDS, Eula Ann, W11099, D, Edwards, Weldon James
EDWARDS, G. H. S7557, MS, 53rd Inf.
EDWARDS, George W. S5758, JE, 3rd Bn. N.C. Lt. Art.
EDWARDS, Hattie Tillett, W6511, D, Edwards, Thomas
EDWARDS, Henry H. S6945, RU, 4th (McLemore's) Cav.
EDWARDS, J. S14504, RB, 50th Inf.
EDWARDS, J. D. S16557, MS, 3rd (Forrest's) Cav.
EDWARDS, J. W. S10498, HU, 1st (Feild's) Inf.
EDWARDS, Jesse B. S7218, WI, Baxter's Co. Lt. Art.
EDWARDS, John J. S8576, U, 29th N.C. Inf.
EDWARDS, Josephus Monroe, S11152, O, 6th Tex. Cav.
EDWARDS, Kate, W4567, GE, Edwards, Samuel M.
EDWARDS, Louise, W3086, RU, Edwards, Thomas S.
EDWARDS, Martha E. W979, RU, Edwards, Leander Herriford

-105

EDWARDS, Mary E. W149, D, Edwards, Thomas
EDWARDS, Mary Elizabeth, W7218, O, Edwards, Josephus Monroe
EDWARDS, Mary Fannie, W3288, RB, Edwards, John F.
EDWARDS, Mary Neal, W1554, GI, Edwards, Washington McMahon
EDWARDS, Mary Rebecca, W7157, MU, Edwards, Wm. Henry
EDWARDS, Minerva Ann, W7259, RB, Edwards, Wiley
EDWARDS, Nancy C. W4981, WY, Edwards, R. A.
EDWARDS, Nannie Duncan, W2925, D, Edwards, Charles Henry
EDWARDS, R. A. S8934, P, 9th Bn. Cav.
EDWARDS, R. E. S13973, G, 20th (Russell's) Cav.
EDWARDS, S. H. S8046, MA, 21st (Wilson's) Cav.
EDWARDS, S. T. S10802, DY, 20th Inf.
EDWARDS, Sarah E. W6195, MA, Edwards, S. W.
EDWARDS, Sarah Elizabeth, W3535, RU, Edwards, Wm. Houston
EDWARDS, Sarah Frances, W7805, MT, Edwards, Zadock Daniel
EDWARDS, Silas W. S9485, MA, 12th Ky. Cav.
EDWARDS, Susie Aldrich, W10341, RU, Edwards, Robert Wilson
EDWARDS, Thomas, S6535, RU, 6th Ark. Inf.
EDWARDS, Thomas, S14529, D, 17th Inf.
EDWARDS, Thomas Jefferson, S15876, S15985, HN, 20th (Russell's) Cav.
EDWARDS, W. J. S7839, MS, 8th (Smith's) Cav.
EDWARDS, W. J. S16669, HO, 8th (Smith's) Cav.
EDWARDS, W. T. S41, D, 3rd Inf.
EDWARDS, W. W. S2812, LI, 1st (Turney's) Inf.
EDWARDS, Wiley, S14302, RB, 11th Inf.
EDWARDS, William H. S293, MU, 9th Cav.
EDWARDS, Z. D. S16677, MT, 5th Inf.
EELBECK, Frank C. S9941, WI, 20th Inf.
EFFLER, William, S1744, U, 60th Inf.
EGAN, John J. S1152, HY, 38th Inf.
EGAN, Perlefna Lin, W2421, D, Egan, John
EIDSON, J. R. S6016, SN, 7th Inf.
EIDSON, Josiah R. S9526, SN, 7th Inf.
EIDSON, Missouria A. W763, SN, Eidson, John C.
EIDSON, Thomas H. S586, HW, 63rd Inf.
EIFFERT, H. A. S14342, BR, 2nd Mo. Cav.
EIFFERT, Susan Theresa, W8455, BR, Eiffert, H. A.
ELAM, Alice Hurley, W6714, T, Elam, John Calhoun
ELAM, Andrew Hart, S10972, T, 12th (Green's) Cav.
ELAM, Daniel W. S308, SN, 7th Inf.
ELAM, Dora, W5899, W, Elam, Marion Randolph
ELAM, John, S8313, CF, 11th Cav.
ELAM, John T. S11270, MA, 12th Inf.
ELAM, John T. S14771, O, 18th Va. Inf.
ELAM, Martha E. W182, SN, Elam, D. W.
ELAM, Mary, W2871, CA, Elam, John
ELAM, Nancy Jane, W1584, MU, Elam, Robert Snowden
ELAM, Sallie N. W3792, D, Elam, Thomas A.
ELAM, Sallie T. W8351, O, Elam, John
ELAM, W. T. S12869, SH, 2nd Ky. Cav.
ELAM, W. W. S543, OV, 8th Inf.
ELAM, William R. S1265, RB, 18th Inf.
ELDER, A. M. S1714, PI, 6th Ky. Cav.
ELDER, G. W. S11020, S14191, GI, 53rd Inf.
ELDER, Hal, C273, G, Regiment not given
ELDER, Sarah Bell Bright, W3600, SH, Elder, Charles Alexander
ELDERS, Bob, S16390, BR, Davenport's Labor Brigade
ELDRIDGE, Bettie, W9454, G, Eldridge, Wm. Spencer
ELDRIDGE, Frances, W4622, CU, Eldridge, John
ELDRIDGE, J. M. S1341, OV, 8th Cav. See also James M. Eldridge
ELDRIDGE, J. W. S13725, OV, 16th Bn. (Neal's) Cav.
ELDRIDGE, James M. S1050, OV, 8th Cav. See also J. M. Eldridge
ELDRIDGE, John, S6317, SE, 8th (Dibrell's) Cav.
ELDRIDGE, Martin, S11880, OV, 8th (Dibrell's) Cav.
ELDRIDGE, W. S. S201, G, 55th Inf.
ELEAZOR, S. G. S9476, DI, 49th Inf.
ELEY, J. H. S16361, D, 44th Inf.
ELIZER, T. D. S9837, SN, 44th Inf.
ELKIN, Mary Jane, W3298, RU, Elkin, James Davis

ELKINS, Alice, W8401, HE, Elkins, James Napoleon
ELKINS, Eliza Parlee, W5952, HI, Elkins, David Franklin
ELKINS, J. L. S16515, DY, 33rd Inf.
ELKINS, J. N. S15817, HE, 12th Ky. Cav.
ELKINS, James Davidson, S366, S2023, G, 23rd Inf.
ELKINS, John Wesley, S3671, G, 13th Inf.
ELKINS, Mary Jane, W5808, CC, Elkins, John Wesley
ELKINS, Mary Jane, W10286, HI, Elkins, Samuel
ELKINS, Spicie, W6110, RU, Elkins, Woodson
ELKINS, T. D. S13721, CA, 22nd (Barteau's) Cav.
ELLER, Darthual, W4513, D, Eller, John Harrison
ELLER, David W. S10653, GU, 1st N.C. Cav.
ELLER, G. H. S15000, H, 24th Ga. Inf.
ELLER, James, S5121, S2485, WH, 25th Inf.
ELLER, Jane, W62, WH, Eller, James
ELLETT, J. F. S11010, HR, 5th Ala. Inf.
ELLINGTON, F. W. S13060, CC, 10th Ark. Inf.
ELLINGTON, Ida Lee, W9356, CC, Ellington, F. W.
ELLINGTON, Ida Maie, W9081, CC, Ellington, James Edward
ELLIOTT, Altha S. W3613, K, Elliott, H. C.
ELLIOTT, Elizabeth, W3363, CE, Elliott, John Mathews
ELLIOTT, Emma, W4618, CC, Elliott, Wm. Jonathan
ELLIOTT, F. M. S7880, B, 23rd Inf.
ELLIOTT, F. P. S15013, D, 1st Inf.
ELLIOTT, Hiram C. S4672, K, 11th N.C. Inf.
ELLIOTT, Isabella Petrikin, W655, K, Elliott, Wm. Powell
ELLIOTT, Jerome P. S301, G, 9th Cav.
ELLIOTT, Joseph J. S14166, D, 2nd Cav.
ELLIOTT, Margaret Cyntha, W1901, DK, Elliott, Milton M.
ELLIOTT, Mattie Fountain, W7086, D, Elliott, Joseph Jackson
ELLIOTT, S. F. S11812, SN, 2nd (Robison's) Inf.
ELLIOTT, Samuel, S4802, C, 3rd (Lillard's) Mtd. Inf.
ELLIOTT, T. A. S3662, SH, 8th Ala. Inf.
ELLIOTT, W. V. S12006, SU, 48th Va. Inf.
ELLIOTT, W. W. R. S8747, HR, 154th Sr. Regt. Inf.

ELLIOTT, William S. S4100, SN, 7th Inf.
ELLIS, A. B. S15217, SH, 13th Inf.
ELLIS, A. C. S13976, ST, 5th Inf.
ELLIS, Benjamin F. S4546, B, 41st Inf.
ELLIS, C. J. S15854, D, 30th Inf.
ELLIS, Cordelia V. W5239, GR, Ellis, Pryor F.
ELLIS, Ellen Ann, W8738, ST, Ellis, Alexander Carroll
ELLIS, F. M. S12107, CH, 21st (Wilson's) Cav.
ELLIS, Fannie I. W4928, WI, Ellis, Christopher Columbus
ELLIS, George, S13990, BE, 1st Heavy Art.
ELLIS, Gertrude V. W4137, WE, Ellis, Henry
ELLIS, Hattie Lou, W8540, LI, Ellis, Wiley Benton
ELLIS, J. G. S13612, RB, 1st Miss. Inf.
ELLIS, J. H. S2535, D, 69th Inf.
ELLIS, J. J. S12640, D, 20th Inf.
ELLIS, J. J. S15088, MN, 4th N.C. State Troops
ELLIS, J. M. S5879, LI, 11th Ga. Inf.
ELLIS, James E. S1438, O, 2nd Va. Hvy. Art.
ELLIS, James I. S11494, HD, 16th Cav.
ELLIS, Jasper, S3263, LI, 4th (McLemore's) Cav.
ELLIS, John, S3445, SE, 31st Inf.
ELLIS, John W. S2951, LI, 3rd Ga. Inf.
ELLIS, Katie, W6998, CO, Ellis, James
ELLIS, Laura Reid, W1188, SH, Ellis, Van Rensader
ELLIS, Lou Etta, W9482, SH, Ellis, Wm. Wallace
ELLIS, Maggie E. W10786, D, Ellis, Charles James
ELLIS, Martha, W2093, K, Ellis, John
ELLIS, Mollie J. W9802, F, Ellis, Wm. Augustus
ELLIS, Nancy, W348, J, Ellis, Lewis B.
ELLIS, P. S. S1664, SH, 13th Inf.
ELLIS, Partheny, W7251, CH, Ellis, Francis Marion
ELLIS, R. J. S14963, MT, Napier's Bn. Cav.
ELLIS, S. M. S14032, H, 1st Cav.
ELLIS, Theophilus, S12846, MO, 39th N.C. Inf.
ELLIS, Thomas S. S1715, SN, 30th Inf.
ELLIS, Thomas W. S1683, S1605, MR, 3rd Inf.
ELLIS, W. A. S4656, H, 6th (Wheeler's) Cav.
ELLIS, W. T. S12972, HW, 12th Bn. (Day's) Cav.
ELLIS, W. W. S559, SH, 13th Inf.
ELLIS, Wiley B. S15976, LI, 4th (McLemore's) Cav.

ELLIS, William F. S15049, RO, 16th (Neal's) Bn. Cav.
ELLISON, Benjamin, S5536, SE, 39th Inf.
ELLISON, D. A. S5130, LI, 12th Ala. Inf.
ELLISON, Lindsey, S15301, JO, 27th N.C. Inf.
ELLISON, Manerva, W1129, ME, Ellison, Elisha
ELLISON, Peter, S6682, R, 5th (McKenzie's) Cav.
ELLISON, Sophia Sawyer, W7195, D, Ellison, Samuel H.
ELLISON, W. F. S1636, S1578, O, 32nd Inf.
ELLSBERRY, Benjamin, S12499, WE, 22nd Inf.
ELMORE, A. M. S7314, HY, 7th Cav.
ELMORE, Alfred, S13310, CU, 28th Inf.
ELMORE, Edna J. W2819, HY, Elmore, Armstead Marshall
ELMORE, John E. S4003, HE, 55th Inf.
ELMORE, Mary Jane, W6411, RU, Elmore, P. H.
ELMORE, P. H. S4755, RU, 24th Inf.
ELMORE, Paralee, W6568, BE, Elmore, John E.
ELMORE, W. F. S7565, L, 8th N.C. Inf.
ELROD, Andrew Jackson, S1302, PU, 28th Inf.
ELROD, Delilah C. W5526, WA, Elrod, Wiley C.
ELROD, Elizabeth, W8453, TR, Elrod, John
ELROD, Giles, S1953, WH, 1st Bn. (Colm's) Inf.
ELROD, John, S2200, SM, 28th Inf.
ELROD, Martha Frances, W10948, DI, Elrod, Jacob J.
ELROD, Sabra Jane, W5010, PU, Elrod, Andrew Jackson
ELROD, Senith, W1000, WH, Elrod, Giles
ELROD, W. C. S6274, WA, 37th Va. Inf.
ELSOM, Nannie C. W5024, WA, Elsom, Richard S.
ELSWICK, Giles L. S5902, SU, 63rd Va. Inf.
ELY, John A. S9927, H, 4th Ky. Cav.
ELY, Ruth Prigmore, W5760, H, Ely, John Alexander
ELY, Sarah Elizabeth, W9290, D, Ely, J. H.
ELZEY, Mary Tennessee, W5313, T, Elzey, Andrew Jackson
EMBREY, Jesse W. S2459, MOO, 8th Cav.
EMBREY, M. D. S4829, FR, 4th (McLemore's) Cav.
EMBRY, Alexina, See Alexina Hogan
EMBRY, Lucias Jones, S11644, MU, 48th Inf.
EMERSON, A. L. S15581, MU, 12th Ky. Cav.

EMERSON, A. R. S6181, HR, 14th Cav.
EMERSON, Horatio T. S8629, D, 53rd Inf.
EMERSON, J. L. S7182, MS, 41st Inf.
EMERSON, Mary Crisp, W8817, SH, Emerson, Owan Calhoun
EMERSON, Nancy E. W4907, HN, Emerson, David B.
EMERSON, W. M. S14677, MS, 17th Inf.
EMERT, Rebecca, W161, SU, Emert, James W.
EMERY, F. M. S8481, W, 4th Cav.
EMMERSON, Nancy Jane, W1708, MS, Emmerson, J. L.
EMMERT, Ben W. S2119, SU, 26th Inf.
EMMERT, David W. S169, SU, 53rd Inf.
EMMERT, Fannie, W4944, SU, Emmert, D. W.
EMMERT, George, S3832, HY, 63rd Inf.
EMMERT, John W. S4459, SU, 63rd Inf.
EMMERT, Mary, W2979, HY, Emmert, George
EMMETT, Annie, W6883, SU, Emmett, John W.
EMMONS, Rebecca, W4283, MN, Emmons, H. M.
EMORY, Isaac Carroll, S5641, W, 35th Inf.
EMORY, Sarah Ann, W1722, A, Emory, James
ENDSLEY, Alexander M. S7139, MS, 4th Cav.
ENDSLEY, Julia C. W250, LI, Endsley, John Payne
ENDSLEY, Nancy Louisa, W1853, MS, Endsley, Alexander M.
ENGLAND, C. D. S6570, WH, 1st Ark. Cav.
ENGLAND, D. S. S8078, WH, 8th (Dibrell's) Cav.
ENGLAND, Elvira Jane, W10130, CF, England, T. J.
ENGLAND, Joseph S. S7606, RB, 14th Inf.
ENGLAND, T. J. S11135, W, 19th Ala. Inf.
ENGLISH, J. M. S6387, MC, 21st (Wilson's) Cav.
ENGLISH, Lizzie, W9907, MU, English, Thomas Young
ENLOE, John T. S4014, A, 69th N.C. Inf.
ENNIS, Nancy Jane, W10579, HU, Ennis, Wm. R.
ENOCHS, Elizabeth Ann, W6967, B, Enochs, M. A. L.
ENOCHS, George W. S14592, LI, Forrest's Escort
ENOCHS, M. A. L. S14507, B, 1st (Turney's) Inf.
ENOCHS, Sarah [McKnight], W11172, DY, Enochs, Robert H. [Later married McKnight]

Index to Tennessee Confederate Pension Applications

ENSER, J. K. S8148, SU, Unassigned (Nitre Mining)
ENSMINGER, J. T. S3294, R, 19th Inf.
ENSOR, Mary W. W3353, SU, Ensor, J. K.
EPPERSON, Bettie Jane, W4416, MA, Epperson, Thomas Newsom
EPPERSON, E. E. S5910, C, 51st Va. Inf.
EPPERSON, Florence A. W4613, C, Epperson, E. E.
EPPERSON, James T. S4905, RU, 17th Inf.
EPPERSON, James sr. S7163, BR, 2nd (Ashby's) Cav.
EPPERSON, Margaret Jane, W7481, RU, Epperson, James K. Polk
EPPERSON, Sallie C. W6665, MS, Epperson, James Thomas
EPPES, Mary Elizabeth, W5412, SH, Eppes, Wm.
EPPS, Anderson B. S9284, WI, 4th (McLemore's) Cav.
EPPS, Armstrong P. S11390, WI, 4th (McLemore's) Cav.
EPPS, Florence, W9632, LI, Epps, John Norris
EPPS, George, S5261, DI, 11th Inf.
EPPS, John Norris, S353, LI, 8th Inf.
EPPS, Lawrence, S8704, RU, 8th Inf.
EPPS, Mary Iserbeller, W3981, DI, Epps, George
EPPS, Peter, S1716, HW, 61st Inf.
EPPS, Sarah, W70, HM, Epps, Peter
EPPS, W. H. S5063, RU, 45th Inf.
ERVEN, James, S13028, GI, 59th Inf.
ERVIN, A. W. S6747, MO, 3rd (Lillard's) Mtd. Inf.
ERVIN, Andy J. S1273, RO, 1st Inf.
ERVIN, J. C. S12053, K, 3rd S.C. Inf.
ERVIN, Joe J. S2834, HR, 7th Cav.
ERVIN, John C. S2999, GE, 16th N.C. Inf.
ERVIN, Panthy Troy, W4827, HW, Ervin, John C.
ERVIN, Theophilus, S13818, HR, 35th Ark. Inf.
ERVIN, W. H. S13735, CH, 24th Inf.
ERVIN, W. M.   See William Ervin
ERVIN, William, S16094, S7516, S15719, DK, 23rd Inf.
ERWIN, A. W. S2987, MO, 3rd Inf.
ERWIN, Andrew J. S1389, H, 1st Cav.
ERWIN, Elizabeth Gray, W7680, MU, Erwin, Robert H.
ERWIN, Ella, W4254, H, Erwin, Andrew Jackson

ERWIN, George Washington, S12592, MU, 6th (Wheeler's) Cav.
ERWIN, H. L. S13760, FR, 41st Inf.
ERWIN, J. C. S14983, BR, 6th Ga. Cav.
ERWIN, J. J. T. S13441, MU, 6th (Wheeler's) Cav.
ERWIN, John, S7188, ME, 1st East Tenn. Cav.
ERWIN, John A. S1294, BR, 29th Inf.
ERWIN, Joseph Buchanan, S11960, MU, 9th Bn. (Gantt's) Cav.
ERWIN, Julia Frances, W6349, MU, Erwin, Wm. Turner
ERWIN, Lou F. W4945, MU, Erwin, J. R.
ERWIN, Louiza, W174, MN, Erwin, J. D.
ERWIN, Margaret, W4623, MC, Erwin, John A.
ERWIN, Minerva J. W3932, SU, Erwin, John
ERWIN, Nancy Rebecca, W8046, HR, Erwin, Joseph John
ERWIN, Rebecca Jane, W5655, WH, Erwin, Wm. Lawson
ERWIN, Robert Hardin, S12545, MU, 6th (Wheeler's) Cav.
ERWIN, Sallie A. W434, HI, Erwin, Wm. B.
ERWIN, Sam W. S15191, MU, 9th Bn. Cav.
ERWIN, Samuel, S212, SH, 51st Inf.
ERWIN, T. F. S7235, MOO, 37th Inf.
ERWIN, Virginia Caroline, W3151, HI, Erwin, Wm. Thomas
ERWIN, W. B. S1295, MC, 32nd Inf.
ERWIN, William A. S2225, TR, 22nd (Barteau's) Cav.
ERWIN, William P. S4714, HN, 154th Sr. Regt. Inf.
ERWIN, William T. S13963, MU, 6th (Wheeler's) Cav.
ESCUE, A. S849, SN, 44th Inf.
ESCUE, Lucinda M. W453, SN, Escue, Wm. A.
ESCUE, Susan, W10382, WL, Escue, George Granderson
ESKEW, John C. S15618, WL, 45th Inf.
ESKRIDGE, S. A. W4, HU, Eskridge, Thomas V.
ESKRIDGE, Thomas V. S2509, HU, 45th Inf.
ESLICK, Eliza E. W303, LI, Eslick, Thomas Austin
ESLICK, John, S2829, LI, 8th Inf.
ESLICK, Levi, S11969, LI, 3rd (Clack's) Inf.
ESLICK, Maldo Wallace, W9014, CF, Eslick, Levy
ESLICK, Newton G. S6635, GI, 6th (Wheeler's) Cav.

Index to Tennessee Confederate Pension Applications

ESPEY, Nancy Melinda, W3146, RU, Espey, Samuel Erastus
ESPEY, William H. S1183, O, 13th Inf.
ESPY, Albert M. S9174, H, 22nd Ala. Inf.
ESSARY, Elbert S. S3641, S2898, CL, 22nd Va. Cav.
ESSARY, Martha J. W4290, CL, Essary, Elbert S.
ESSARY, Mary Ann, W7532, CL, Essary, W. E.
ESSARY, W. E. S9999, CL, 22nd Va. Cav.
ESSEX, T. H. S3731, SN, 20th Inf.
ESTEP, Rachel A. W1681, PO, Estep, Abner
ESTES, Augusta, W10303, SH, Estes, James Millon
ESTES, Eliza Jane, W3851, MU, Estes, Ferdanan Russell
ESTES, Emily T. W1784, MS, Estes, John T.
ESTES, G. G. S15063, DI, 11th (Holman's) Cav.
ESTES, H. H. S7333, MS, 4th (McLemore's) Cav.
ESTES, Indiana, W3083, WL, Estes, Wm.
ESTES, J. A. S11592, OV, 45th Inf.
ESTES, J. G. S3823, DI, 11th Cav.
ESTES, J. W. S12531, DY, Undetermined
ESTES, Marcellor E. W1221, FR, Estes, Elbert
ESTES, Martha Elizabeth, W1162, MU, Estes, Wm. Asbury
ESTES, Minnie Bacon, W10408, DY, Estes, Joel Henry
ESTES, Nannie J. W6112, RB, Estes, Henry Harrison
ESTES, Sara Anderson, W6077, K, Estes, Christopher Tompkins
ESTES, William, S4921, WL, 45th Inf.
ESTILL, Winn, W1186, FR, Estill, Samuel
ETHERAGE, William E. S6996, DK, 28th Inf.
ETHERIDGE, Eliza J. W942, D, Etheridge, George W.
ETHERIDGE, William T. S9904, HU, 11th Inf.
ETHRIDGE, Collie, W4061, D, Ethridge, Wm. G.
ETHRIDGE, Elizabeth, W2318, MU, Ethridge, Jesse
ETHRIDGE, J. H. S2274, SH, 9th Inf.
ETHRIDGE, J. S. S13082, FR, 1st (Turney's) Inf.
ETHRIDGE, John, S874, DK, 28th Inf.
ETHRIDGE, Sarah M. W5384, DI, Ethridge, John
ETTER, Ada Gertrude, W9497, W, Etter, James K. Polk

ETTER, George H. S6800, W, 16th Inf.
ETTER, John M. S2303, HW, 63rd Inf.
ETTER, Leonidas L. S2011, HW, 63rd Inf.
ETTER, Roysdon R. S16035, W, 16th Inf.
EUBANK, Asa Jackson, S9468, GI, 53rd Inf.
EUBANK, J. T. S9045, GI, 53rd Inf.
EUBANK, John R. S9512, GI, 32nd Inf.
EUBANK, John W. S9814, T, 12th Cav.
EUBANK, Josie, W9537, DI, Eubank, Richard Daley
EUBANK, Mary E. W368, HR, Eubank, James Thomas
EUBANKS, Theodosia, W8439, T, Eubanks, John Wesley
EUDALEY, Lucelia Caroline, W4532, WI, Eudaley, Moses
EUSEY, Mary J. W4748, CF, Eusey, Wm. L.
EVANS, A. W. S5197, WA, Wooding's Art. Va.
EVANS, Amanda Melvina, W2124, CY, Evans, Francis Marion
EVANS, Elliott, S3082, HW, 29th Va. Inf.
EVANS, Elmina, W5863, CO, Evans, Jessee
EVANS, Elura E. W9857, CO, Evans, Thomas J.
EVANS, Francis M. S4553, CY, 38th Inf.
EVANS, Henry Clay, S3467, SH, 2nd (Walker's) Inf.
EVANS, Isaac, S8691, GI, 53rd Inf.
EVANS, J. B. S6228, SM, 16th Inf.
EVANS, J. Frank, S16012, S16404, MU, 9th Bn. Cav.
EVANS, J. M. S8456, CC, 12th Inf.
EVANS, JEsse, S8018, CO, 25th N.C. Inf.
EVANS, James Frank, S16246, MU, 9th Bn. (Gantt's) Cav.
EVANS, James Wilkerson, S389, HW, 12th Cav.
EVANS, Jesse E. S1200, WY, 2nd Inf.
EVANS, John J. S7453, CE, 3rd Miss. Cav.
EVANS, Josephine, W4987, CE, Evans, John J.
EVANS, Julia Ann, W6644, LI, Evans, Green Berry
EVANS, Larkin H. S5556, MO, 3rd Inf.
EVANS, Lean Frances, W1109, CY, Evans, Pearce
EVANS, Margaret E. W609, PU, Evans, Thomas Jefferson
EVANS, Mary A. W2039, RU, Evans, W. C.
EVANS, Matilda, W2712, CC, Evans, James Madison
EVANS, Mollie, W4335, MT, Evans, Ross
EVANS, NAncy Jane, W3198, F, Evans, Simpson
EVANS, Robert L. S5183, GI, 53rd Inf.

Index to Tennessee Confederate Pension Applications

EVANS, Ross, S569, MT, 49th Inf.
EVANS, Samuel F. S1836, GI, 53rd Inf.
EVANS, Sarah, W8477, CE, Evans, Wm. Milton
EVANS, Simpson, S10219, F, Ark. Cav.
EVANS, Susan, W2108, SM, Evans, J. B.
EVANS, Susan Brown, W8990, W10703, WE, Evans, Wm. L.
EVANS, T. W. S16478, SM, 4th Cav.
EVANS, Thomas F. S14510, CC, 7th Cav.
EVANS, Thomas J. S7770, CL, 63rd Inf.
EVANS, Thomas J. S12482, CC, Forrest's Old Regt. Cav.
EVANS, Thomas James, S13426, CO, 1st (Carter's) Cav.
EVANS, W. H. S13454, L, 5th S.C. Cav.
EVANS, Wallace W. S113, B, 20th Inf.
EVANS, William C. S2136, RU, 45th Inf.
EVANS, William M. S13537, CE, 26th Inf.
EVERETT, J. J. S13395, CE, 49th Inf.
EVERETT, John H. S9326, SU, 1st N.C. State Troops
EVERETT, Nancy C. W3813, BO, Everett, John Newton
EVERETT, Signer, S4803, C, 3rd Inf.
EVERHART, James Henderson, S238, HW, 31st Inf.
EVETT, Nathan, S1756, K, 23rd Ga. Inf.
EVETT, Sarah M. W2288, K, Evett, Nathan
EVETTS, J. W. S5907, TR, 9th (Ward's) Cav.
EVINS, Ella Lowrance, W8774, D, Evins, James Thomas
EVINS, Mary Elizabeth, W4034, B, Evins, Wesley Smith
EVITTS, M. V. S13648, D, 44th Inf.
EWELL, Adeline L. W8025, MA, Ewell, Joe D.
EWELL, J. D. S10508, MA, 51st Inf.
EWELL, Mary Elizabeth, W10619, G, Ewell, Thomas Wiley
EWELL, Thomas W. S386, MA, 18th (Newsom's) Cav.
EWIN, Mattie J. W3565, HU, Ewin, Wm. Goodwin
EWING, A. J. S11863, MS, 17th Inf.
EWING, Alberta, W2069, MS, Ewing, Argule
EWING, Fannie Lewis, W6170, WY, Ewing, Martin Luther
EWING, J. H. S11082, HN, 46th Inf.
EWING, James A. S16039, MS, 17th Inf.
EWING, Johnanna C. W1138, W936, D, Ewing, Wm. Randle
EWING, Kate B. W10741, WI, Ewing, Zewingle W.

EWING, Luther C. S7688, MS, 41st Inf.
EWING, Martin L. S3255, WY, 1st Ark. Cav.
EWING, Mary C. W5647, MS, Ewing, Luther C.
EWING, Mary J. W3716, ME, Ewing, Jacob M.
EWING, Nancy L. W1662, MS, Ewing, George Wyth
EWING, Susan C. W6666, MS, Ewing, Andrew J.
EWTON, C. J. S287, W, 5th Inf.
EWTON, F. P. S10902, SQ, 28th Cav.
EXUM, G. W. S13761, HU, 20th Inf.
EXUM, Harriet Josephine, W6839, HU, Exum, George Wm.
EXUM, Mary Jane, W1034, T, Exum, Wm. C.
EXUM, Sarah Moore, W10232, MA, Exum, Martin Van Buren
EZELL, Alice J. W10030, D, Ezell, James B.
EZELL, Allen, S6829, LA, 32nd Inf.
EZELL, Annie Haislip, W4778, SH, Ezell, Wm. Henry
EZELL, Elon H. S16506, GI, 20th Cav.
EZELL, H. F. S15273, MS, 11th (Holman's) Cav.
EZELL, J. B. S12831, CC, 11th (Holman's) Cav.
EZELL, John, S5262, FR, 51st Ala. Cav.
EZELL, John H. S2706, GI, 1st (Feild's) Inf.
EZELL, Lafayette, S4392, K, 20th Inf.
EZELL, Mary E. W1140, GI, Ezell, M. P.
EZELL, Mary F. W1762, ST, Ezell, Thomas
EZELL, Rebecca Jane, W9511, HN, Ezell, J. B.
EZELL, Sallie, W9083, CC, Ezell, Joseph Burkett
EZELL, W. H. S1167, WE, 4th Cav.
EZZELL, M. S12743, WE, 52nd Inf.
EZZELL, Mary Jane, W4648, WE, Ezzell, Mace
FAGAN, Emaline, W3347, JE, Fagan, Thompson Jefferson
FAGAN, Thomas, S5989, SU, 19th Inf.
FAGANS, George W. S5633, WU, 59th Inf.
FAIDLEY, Joseph G. S7727, D, 32nd Tex. Cav.
FAIL, William Thomas, S13411, MA, 33rd Ala. Inf.
FAIN, Amie Catherine, W4236, D, Fain, Richard Walker
FAIN, Carrie V. W2719, SU, Fain, John
FAIN, G. P. S6642, HW, 60th Inf.
FAIN, S. L. S11180, MS, Carter's Scouts, Cav.
FAIN, Sallie Elizabeth, W5520, HW, Fain, George Paul
FAIN, T. L. S7244, MT, 11th Inf.

FAIN, William A. S11877, JE, 1st (Carter's) Cav.
FAIR, Samuel H. S1915, CT, Marshall's Co. Lt. Art.
FAIRCHILD, J. B. S11738, MG, 2nd (Ashby's) Cav.
FAIRES, W. A. S13637, SH, 38th Miss. Cav.
FAIRFAX, Annie Eliza, W3028, SU, Fairfax, Raymond
FAISON, Delia, W6909, SH, Faison, James
FALLS, Delilah, W7582, ME, Falls, W. A.
FALLS, Narcissa L. W2894, BR, Falls, Thomas
FALLS, Thomas, S1757, R, 5th Cav.
FALLS, W. O. S2634, MC, 5th Cav.
FALWELL, Hallie Louise, W720, SH, Falwell, Henry Calvin
FALWELL, Tennessee Jane, W584, WE, Falwell, James Taylor
FAMBOUGH, Mussa, W6350, MT, Fambough, Robert
FAMBROUGH, N. B. S4101, MT, 18th Inf.
FAMBROUGH, Robert, S10257, CE, 18th Inf.
FANCETTE, Susan Virginia, W8895, SH, Fancette, Chesley John
FANNING, Alfred, S4789, DE, 18th (Newsom's) Cav.
FANNING, Benjamn F. S6553, LI, 44th Inf.
FARABEE, B. F. S10665, SH, 13th Inf.
FARE, H. C. S465, PO, 1st Ga. Inf.
FARIES, Emily, W5522, PU, Faries, Thomas
FARIES, Thomas, S5563, PU, 8th (Dibrell's) Cav.
FARIS, C. A. D. S15526, H, 11th (Holman's) Cav.
FARIS, J. W. S8159, RU, 11th Cav.
FARIS, R. W. S15016, MR, 24th Inf.
FARLESS, James M. S14717, W, 4th (McLemore's) Cav.
FARLEY, Celia, W2708, PU, Farley, John
FARLEY, Clayton, S14935, MU, Thomas' Legion, N.C.
FARLEY, Cora, W10951, SM, Farley, Wm. M.
FARLEY, David, S6825, PU, 8th (Dibrell's) Cav.
FARLEY, F. H. S5008, GE, 7th Va. Inf.
FARLEY, G. M. S14978, F, 12th Va. Inf.
FARLEY, James, S8197, PU, 8th (Dibrell's) Cav.
FARLEY, John, S2100, PU, 8th (Dibrell's) Cav.
FARLEY, Julia F. W3308, F, Farley, Wm.
FARLEY, L. S3824, DY, 33rd Inf.

FARLEY, Louvada Jane, W5005, BO, Farley, Wm. Van Buren
FARLEY, Maggie Kay Kendell, W8277, SH, Farley, James Deverick
FARLEY, Nannie, W10565, PU, Farley, James
FARLEY, P. H. S9016, G, 20th Va. Inf.
FARLEY, Rubin, S16551, WH, 13th (Gore's) Cav.
FARLEY, T. A. S2337, OV, 58th Va. Inf.
FARLEY, Thomas P. S13670, HD, 12th Va. Inf.
FARLEY, W. V. B. S2411, K, 25th N.C. Inf.
FARLEY, William, S3557, SM, 55th (McKoin's) Inf.
FARLEY, William N. S12461, D, 10th Cav.
FARLISS, James, S6022, W, 35th Inf.
FARMER, A. S5593, MR, 6th Ala. Inf.
FARMER, A. F. S13445, WI, 1st (Feild's) Inf.
FARMER, B. F. S14781, BE, 55th Inf.
FARMER, Berry, S6398, CL, 3rd Bn. S.C. Art.
FARMER, Daniel, S1461, MR, 6th Ala. Inf.
FARMER, Elizabeth, W9205, HN, Farmer, John
FARMER, J. C. S7384, RU, 45th Inf.
FARMER, J. H. S11768, GR, 1st (Carter's) Cav.
FARMER, J. W, S6439, SH, 7th Ark. Inf.
FARMER, James, S8582, K, 63rd Inf.
FARMER, John, S12016, HN, 5th Inf.
FARMER, John B. S3016, WE, 7th Cav.
FARMER, John F. S14157, RO, McClung's Battery, Art.
FARMER, Lucinda M. W1464, MR, Farmer, Daniel
FARMER, Margaret I. W3362, MC, Farmer, Thomas F.
FARMER, Martha E. W8114, BE, Farmer, John C.
FARMER, Mary A. W502, PO, Farmer, Isaac
FARMER, Mary A. W6490, MR, Farmer, A.
FARMER, Mary Elizabeth, W9253, WE, Farmer, Wm. Henry
FARMER, Nancy L. W1355, B, Farmer, Benjamin F.
FARMER, Phoebe, W10967, A, Farmer, Berry
FARMER, S. J. S15988, SH, 7th Ga. Cav.
FARMER, Sarah Amanda, W1268, PO, Farmer, John
FARMER, W. H. S959, CL, Undetermined
FARMER, W. J. S10924, JA, 3rd (Lillard's) Mtd. Inf.
FARR, John R. S1901, RU, 18th Inf.
FARRAR, See also Farrow
FARRAR, J. T. S16145, LI, 1st (Turney's) Inf.
FARRELL, H. W. S10330, CF, 44th Inf.

Index to Tennessee Confederate Pension Applications

FARRELL, Michael, S4596, D, 2nd Inf.
FARRINGTON, Joe, C9, LK, 5th N.C. Cav.
FARRIS, Andrew Jackson, S12659, DY, Forrest's Old Regt. Cav.
FARRIS, C. C. S1809, HM, 63rd Inf.
FARRIS, Frances, W2246, SH, Farris, Oliver B.
FARRIS, H. F. S13584, H, 26th Inf.
FARRIS, J. K. S8345, CF, 41st Inf.
FARRIS, J. P. S11161, SU, 42nd Va. Inf.
FARRIS, John, S5009, PU, 8th (Dibrell's) Cav.
FARRIS, John C. S13349, WY, 4th Ala. Inf.
FARRIS, Laura, W972, FR, Farris, Reuben
FARRIS, Martha Jane, W8464, FR, Farris, Thomas C.
FARRIS, Martha L. W7708, MR, Farris, R. W.
FARRIS, Mary Elizabeth, W10100, RU, Farris, John W.
FARRIS, Mary H. W3971, MU, Farris, Wm. H.
FARRIS, Mary Hubbard, W8000, H, Farris, Charles Ambrose
FARRIS, Mary Jane, W5420, PU, Farris, John
FARRIS, Mary Rosalie, W5487, SH, Farris, Miles H.
FARRIS, Miles H. S13729, SH, Unassigned (Machinist & Pistol Factory)
FARRIS, S. J. H. S7959, FR, 41st Inf.
FARRIS, Sallie E. W4849, SU, Farris, Johnson Petty
FARRIS, T. J. S10147, HR, 3rd (Forrest's) Cav.
FARRIS, W. G. S5864, HD, 16th Cav.
FARROW, See also Farrar
FARROW, Gillie Adaline, W2277, CH, Farrow, Samuel Wilks
FARROW, I. J. S11955, S16165, CF, 44th Inf.
FARTHING, Carrie C. W6974, JO, Farthing, David Jesse
FATHERA, John R. S787, RU, 8th (Smith's) Cav.
FAUCETTE, C. J. S15650, SH, Ashby's Scouts, Cav.
FAUGHT, Samuel, S6157, T, 14th (Neely's) Cav.
FAULK, J. D. S15978, SH, 12th Cav.
FAULKNER, John P. S8103, FR, 44th Inf.
FAULKNER, Mary Elizabeth, W3919, T, Faulkner, Thomas Lesley
FAULKNER, T. L. S9341, T, 12th Cav.
FAUSLER, George W. S582, HW, 12th Cav.
FAY, Rebecca Mary, W9544, B, Fay, Robert E.
FAZZI, John, S15228, SH, 3rd (Forrest's) Cav.
FEAGINS, Anna, W4766, HW, Feagins, J. H.
FEAGINS, J. H. S6033, SU, 31st Inf.

FEAGINS, William, S4223, HW, 31st Inf.
FEATHER, G. W. S11994, HW, 26th Inf.
FEATHERS, A. M. S9622, HM, 63rd Inf.
FEATHERS, Elkana, S6009, SU, 63rd Inf.
FEATHERS, J. H. S1440, SU, 26th Inf.
FEATHERS, Nannie Salena, W1977, H, Feathers, Alvin Marion
FEATHERS, Rachel L. W3591, SU, Feathers, Eli
FEATHERS, William B. S8545, SU, Burrough's Co. Art.
FEATHERSTON, Eliza Jane, W5300, D, Featherston, John
FEATHERSTON, J. R. S15064, LI, 41st Inf.
FEATHERSTON, John, S5887, MS, 19th (Biffle's) Cav.
FEATHERSTON, Mary J. W800, RU, Featherston, Oliver P.
FEATHERSTON, Sallie Ann, W6758, DY, Featherston, Willis Vaughn
FEATHERSTON, W. G. S10012, RU, 1st (Feild's) Inf.
FEEZELL, J. R. S10005, BO, 39th N.C. Inf.
FEEZELL, Sophronia Jane, W10499, BO, Feezell, James Robinson
FELAND, W. B. S15552, D, 6th Ky. Cav.
FELKER, Louisa, W2194, BR, Felker, Wm. Marion
FELLERS, Catharine, W3927, WA, Fellers, D. M.
FELLERS, D. M. S4403, WA, 61st Inf.
FELLERS, D. M. S9569, GE, 61st Inf.
FELPS, C. W. S2304, MOO, 1st (Turney's) Inf.
FELPS, G. W. S8149, B, Forrest's Escort, Cav.
FELPS, Sarah Eveline, W4399, B, Felps, George Washington
FELTON, John, S15244, WH, 8th (Dibrell's) Cav.
FELTS, A. S11470, HR, 55th Inf.
FELTS, Addie T. W5416, D, Felts, Joseph W.
FELTS, D. B. S8389, CC, 12th Cav.
FELTS, Dullie Parilee, W8017, HR, Felts, Alexander Green
FELTS, Florence C. See Florence C. Blaylock
FELTS, Frances Bragg, W10538, SH, Felts, James Medicus
FELTS, J. W. S3797, CC, 9th Inf.
FELTS, J. W. S11782, D, 22nd Inf.
FELTS, Kate E. W9027, RB, Felts, Rufus Mallory
FELTS, Mollie Frances, W11000, D, Felts, Thomas L.

FELTS, Phebe, W8122, H, Felts, T. B.
FELTS, Rufus M. S8585, RB, 49th Inf.
FELTS, S. R. S14703, HY, 14th (Neely's) Cav.
FELTS, Sarah Elizabeth, W7632, CC, Felts, David Benjamin
FELTS, Thomas L. S15855, D, 22nd (Nixon's) Cav.
FELTY, G. L. S11914, MO, 21st Va. Cav.
FELTY, Michael, S5209, SU, 63rd Va. Inf.
FELTZ, J. C. S6152, D, 20th Inf.
FENLEY, R. S8522, MN, 11th Miss. Cav.
FENTRESS, A. J. S8096, D, 18th Inf.
FENTRESS, Bettie Bradley, W4152, WI, Fentress, Francis
FERGASON, Iva Jane, W5704, MR, Fergason, Wm. Thomas
FERGASON, W. T. S8528, LI, 4th Ala. Cav.
FERGERSON, Emma Lee, W, Some papers with #11183 on film
FERGUS, J. T. S12422, RU, 45th Inf.
FERGUSON, A. M. S4187, SU, 34th Va. Cav.
FERGUSON, A. M>, S5868, WA, 37th Va. Inf.
FERGUSON, B. F. S5326, PU, 8th Cav.
FERGUSON, C. D. S2326, D, 24th Inf.
FERGUSON, Elizabeth, W5734, BL, Ferguson, James Schoolfield
FERGUSON, George S. S6080, HU, 11th Inf.
FERGUSON, H. J. S9830, G, 55th Inf.
FERGUSON, H. L. N. S8926, R, 16th Bn. Cav.
FERGUSON, H. T. S14904, CL, 50th Va. Inf.
FERGUSON, Henry T. S14230, CL, 50th Va. Inf.
FERGUSON, Jacabina Rosaline, W4352, Ferguson, Thomas Lemuel
FERGUSON, Jackson, S11111, MA, 42nd Inf.
FERGUSON, James S. S9919, BL, 43rd Inf.
FERGUSON, John T. S380, R, 16th Cav.
FERGUSON, Joseph, S15885, HI, 9th Bn. (Gantt's) Cav.
FERGUSON, Mary Drusilla, W10848, W3793, D, Ferguson, Ferdinand
FERGUSON, Phoebe, W8253, D, Ferguson, Nimrod
FERGUSON, Samuel J. S12815, MT, 14th Inf.
FERGUSON, Sarah M. W7970, G, Ferguson, John G.
FERGUSON, Susan Long, W11037, MN, Ferguson, James
FERGUSON, Thursey E. W8070, R, Ferguson, Perry Newton
FERGUSON, W. H. S3343, ME, 2nd (Ashby's) Cav.

FERRELL, B. B. S6348, WL, 7th Inf.
FERRELL, Darthula, W5937, CF, Ferrell, James A.
FERRELL, David Peterson, S9494, DY, 15th Inf.
FERRELL, Dulsena, W10201, OV, Ferrell, A. J.
FERRELL, E. N. S3600, CA, 8th (Smith's) Cav.
FERRELL, Elizabeth, W2035, K, Ferrell, James P.
FERRELL, James A. S50, CF, 1st Inf.
FERRELL, Martha McDowell, W1091, WI, Ferrell, Oscar C.
FERRELL, Sarah Isabelle, W4045, CA, Ferrell, Enoch N.
FERRELL, Thomas H. S5998, DY, 13th Inf.
FERRELL, W. E. S1994, CA, 35th Inf.
FERRIL, A. J. S1046, OV, 25th Inf.
FERRILL, Cleo, See Cleo Armistead
FERRILL, John Burton, S12139, HR, Forrest's Old Regt. Cav.
FERRILL, Nancy S. W105, HR, Ferrill, Thomas
FERRIS, Benjamin Franklin, S14268, D, 23rd Inf.
FERRISS, Henrietta N. W2087, D, Ferriss, Josiah
FERRISS, J. S. S10018, D, 20th Inf.
FERRISS, S. L. S7763, G, 20th (Russell's) Cav.
FERRISS, Susan Elmora, W6524, G, Ferriss, Samuel Lee
FERRITER, James, S3068, SU, 26th Inf.
FESMIRE, William, S15686, 21st (Wilson's) Cav.
FESSMIRE, Ellen, W2056, HE, Fessmire, John Wesley
FEW, Cyntha Jane, W3700, HU, Few, Wm.
FEWELL, G. P. S7994, HY, 15th Cav.
FIELD, R. E. S6969, MS, 4th Cav.
FIELDBURG, Charles P. S5054, SU, Unassigned (Torpedo Bureau)
FIELDER, Annette, W7073, MT, Fielder, James Washington
FIELDER, J. W. S11867, CE, 42nd Inf.
FIELDER, John, S4929, L, 4th Ala. Inf.
FIELDER, R. J. S12453, O, 15th Cav.
FIELDER, Sallie, W9925, O, Fielder, R. J.
FIELDS, A. S12341, O, 1st Mo. Inf.
FIELDS, Abner, S2889, CL, 29th Inf.
FIELDS, Cordelia, W7874, HW, Fields, Joseph P.
FIELDS, D. H. S3144, HD, 26th Miss. Inf.
FIELDS, Fannie Rebecca, W8795, G, Fields, John Henry

Index to Tennessee Confederate Pension Applications

FIELDS, George H. S9955, MN, 26th Miss. Inf.
FIELDS, Hands A. S6865, G, 12th (Green's) Cav.
FIELDS, J. W. S6115, WI, 4th (McLemore's) Cav.
FIELDS, James D. S2215, SM, 7th Inf.
FIELDS, James F. S1875, GE, 60th Inf.
FIELDS, John, S4458, H, 4th Cav.
FIELDS, Joseph Preston, S1761, HW, 16th Cav.
FIELDS, Maria Price, W6585, O, Fields, John Samuel
FIELDS, Martha E. W5380, HD, Fields, Daniel H.
FIELDS, Martha Jane, W4603, D, Fields, Dennis M.
FIELDS, Martherry, W6986, O, Fields, Abslom
FIELDS, Martin, S14966, LK, 41st Inf.
FIELDS, Mary, W3515, MS, Fields, Robert E.
FIELDS, Mary L. W836, D, Fields, James M.
FIELDS, Mollie, W9845, LK, Fields, Martin
FIELDS, Sue Sugg, W7604, RU, Fields, Wm. R.
FIELDS, W. R. S9749, RU, 4th (McLemore's) Cav.
FIELDS, W. T. S14216, DY, 12th Inf.
FIGUERS, Thomas N. S16616, MU, 32nd Inf.
FIKES, Harriett F. W9058, SN, Fikes, Wm. H.
FINCH, Carline Granville, W5442, O, Finch, George Washington
FINCH, George M. S7054, CF, 44th Inf.
FINCH, John F. S262, CF, 1st Inf.
FINCH, Sarah Melissa, W2676, FR, Finch, Hilliand
FINCH, Senie, W9459, CF, Finch, John F.
FINCH, W. H. S11870, D, 4th (McLemore's) Cav.
FINCH, William F. S13012, SH, 14th Bn. Miss. Lt. Art.
FINCH, William H. S1904, CF, 44th Inf.
FINCHEM, Martin, S11673, JE, 1st Bn. (Colm's) Inf.
FINCHUM, John, S12814, CO, 1st (Carter's) Cav.
FINCHUM, Katie, W2038, FR, Finchum, John F.
FINCHUM, Mary E. W6025, FR, Finchum, Polk
FINCHUM, Polk, S4896, FR, 16th Cav.
FINCHUM, W. M. S16095, FR, 1st (Turney's) Inf.
FINDLEY, Belle [Avant], W11102, K, Findley, Thomas Jefferson, [Later married Avant]
FINDLEY, W. V. S9821, SH, 8th Ga. Bn. Inf.

FINE, Elijah, S14051, LO, 1st (Carter's) Cav.
FINE, John A. S10407, MO, 3rd (Lillard's) Mtd. Inf.
FINE, Miranda, W6122, CT, Fine, Wm. R.
FINE, Mollie L. W7794, LO, Fine, Elijah
FINE, Sarah, W5381, WA, Fine, Jacob
FINE, Stephen V. S3459, SE, 16th Cav.
FINE, William Vinson, S10942, CO, 60th Inf.
FINELY, W. F. S6964, MS, 41st Inf.
FINEY, P. P. S3928, FR, 24th Inf.
FINGER, J. H. S3880, MN, Crews' Bn. Inf.
FINLEY, Albert, S295, G, 5th Ark. Inf.
FINLEY, Bettie Lou, W9467, MS, Finley, Newton Marshal
FINLEY, Daniel, S5455, CF, 4th Inf.
FINLEY, James S. S8199, LA, 32nd Inf.
FINLEY, Ophelia Akin, W4166, MU, Finley, Samuel Keny
FINN, William R. S14627, SN, 22nd Bn. Inf.
FINNEY, A. J. S12050, MOO, 35th Inf.
FINNEY, H. L. T. S4095, FR, 32nd Inf.
FINNEY, J. W. S12051, FR, 5th Inf.
FINNEY, John, S10194, S1860, A, 61st Inf.
FINNEY, L. L. S5137, FR, 44th Inf.
FINNEY, R. W. S4238, DY, 45th Inf.
FINNEY, W. R. S5727, FR, 32nd Inf.
FINNY, John T. S5705, FR, 24th Inf.
FIRTH, Margaret Ann, W9164, SH, Firth, Wm. Silas
FIRTH, Thomas Julian, S12837, SH, 8th (Smith's) Cav.
FISER, Ann Booker, W6149, G, Fiser, Robert Hicks
FISH, W. M. S15109, CO, 14th Bn. N.C. Cav.
FISHBURN, Martha A. W4672, BO, Fishburn, Peter I.
FISHBURN, P. J. S4487, BO, 24th Va. Inf.
FISHER, A. J. S10150, H, 3rd Inf.
FISHER, A. L. S6521, DE, 52nd Inf.
FISHER, Alfred, S11710, WH, 8th (Dibrell's) Cav.
FISHER, Amanda, W8425, W3774, WH, Fisher, George
FISHER, E. C. W23, WH, Fisher, Madison Lee
FISHER, Elizabeth, W5318, DK, Fisher, John
FISHER, Emma (Pettigrew), W10912, DE, Fisher, Thomas J.
FISHER, Enoch, S7400, SM, 28th Inf.
FISHER, George W. S3117, B, 55th Inf.
FISHER, Henderson, S1300, R, 1st Cav.
FISHER, Hettie C. D. W1595, DE, Fisher, Wm. Hickory

FISHER, I. F. S11664, H, 16th Bn. Cav.
FISHER, J. H. S9615, DE, 52nd Inf.
FISHER, J. H. S15074, SH, 4th Inf.
FISHER, J. S. S15147, DY, 2nd Mo. Inf.
FISHER, Jacob, S5367, RU, 55th Inf.
FISHER, James C. S9528, GE, 21st Va. Mtd. Inf.
FISHER, John, S4666, DK, 16th Inf.
FISHER, John P. S4989, DK, 16th Inf.
FISHER, L. B. S2291, DK, 16th Inf.
FISHER, Lou C. W1532, WL, Fisher, John W.
FISHER, Margaret McEwen, W2530, WI, Fisher, Wm. Stratton
FISHER, Mary Elizabeth, W4167, GE, Fisher, James Campbell
FISHER, Mary Elizabeth, W8232, MS, Fisher, Frank
FISHER, Missouri, W8170, DE, Fisher, J. H.
FISHER, Mournin, W184, DK, Fisher, Wm.
FISHER, P. A. S9455, G, 12th Inf.
FISHER, Rachel C. W10326, G, Fisher, Ples A.
FISHER, Sallie, W3442, WH, Fisher, Alfred
FISHER, Samuel H. S3395, S15575, FR, 36th Ga. Inf.
FISHER, Sarah Jane, W8666, SM, Fisher, Enoch
FISHER, Thomas B. S13764, HO, 11th (Holman's) Cav.
FISHER, W. F. S10835, M, 24th Inf.
FISK, Milton, S2166, WH, 1st Bn. (Colm's) Inf.
FITCH, John, S2910, S5728, ME, 62nd Inf.
FITE, Alice, W8542, LE, Fite, Peter Francis
FITE, E. C. S14026, SN, Sterling's Co. Hvy. Art.
FITE, Emma, W6160, WL, Fite, J. L.
FITE, Susie Comer, W8510, SN, Fite, Edwin Campbell
FITE, W. F. S10290, LE, 3rd Inf.
FITTS, John W. S6277, HD, 29th Ala. Inf.
FITTS, Tennessee, W4174, HD, Fitts, John Wilson
FITZGERALD, Abe, S8138, MU, Maury's Co. Lt. Art.
FITZGERALD, Charity Lewis, W9817, MU, Fitzgerald, Buford Hanks
FITZGERALD, Daniel E. S6542, G, 1st (Feild's) Inf.
FITZGERALD, John Martin, C74, MU, 48th Inf.
FITZGERALD, Lucinda, W3048, MU, Fitzgerald, Wm. D.
FITZGERALD, M. C. S13671, G, 14th La. Inf.
FITZGERALD, Margaret Jane, W1197, MU, Fitzgerald, Cornelous P. Wilson

FITZGERALD, Mary Elizabeth, W10959, MU, Fitzgerald, Rufus P.
FITZGERALD, Nancy Angeline, W5281, MU, Fitzgerald, Carroll Green
FITZGERALD, Nannie E. W4700, G, Fitzgerald, Daniel E.
FITZGERALD, Nannie H. W3717, SH, Fitzgerald, Rufus
FITZGERALD, O. G. S14803, SH, 3rd (Forrest's) Cav.
FITZGERALD, R. P. S16207, MU, Maury's Co. Lt. Art.
FITZGERALD, Richard, S1398, SU, 1st Cav.
FITZGERALD, Roena E. W780, Fitzgerald, B. A.
FITZGERALD, Sarah J. W5946, G, Fitzgerald, M. C.
FITZGERALD, Woodson, S795, H, 36th Inf.
FITZHUGH, Cora E. W10058, WI, Fitzhugh, J. A.
FITZHUGH, James W. S277, HY, 7th Cav.
FITZPATRICK, Catherine, W4691, D, Fitzpatrick, Michael W.
FITZPATRICK, John, S10337, GI, 3rd (Clack's) Inf.
FITZPATRICK, Samuel, S5263, SM, 8th Cav.
FITZPATRICK, T. W. S10373, K, 29th Inf.
FIZER, Fannie, W6494, FR, Fizer, Simon Washington
FIZER, J. T. S12752, HO, 24th Bn. Inf.
FIZER, S. W. S3492, RB, Erwin's Bn. Miss. Inf.
FLANAGIN, J. W. S4965, HD, 16th Cav.
FLANARY, Margaret Johnson, W8729, UN, Flanary, Isaac
FLANERY, Jane, W4196, HU, Flanery, Isaac
FLANIGAN, Epsie Lee, W10057, SH, Flanigan, John D.
FLANIGAN, Isaac W. S7124, HW, 3rd Conf. Engineer Troops
FLANIGAN, John D. S8935, SH, 51st Inf.
FLANIKEN, Ellen E. W3988, SH, Flaniken, Isaac W.
FLANNAGAN, Paul, S170, SH, 2nd Inf.
FLANTT, John D. S12157, GI, 3rd (Clack's) Inf.
FLATT, Annie Lee, W7571, RB, Flatt, David
FLATT, Clara Jane, W603, DY, Flatt, Wm. T.
FLATT, George W. S576, J, Undetermined
FLATT, H. M. S14443, G, Forrest's Ala. Cav.
FLEEMAN, James M. S2736, M, 2nd Cav.
FLEENOR, Abraham, S7127, SU, 3rd Bn. Art.

FLEENOR, I. B. S12068, SU, Unassigned (Blacksmith)
FLEENOR, J. H. S6657, HM, 48th Va. Inf.
FLEENOR, Susan, W4892, SU, Fleenor, Abram
FLEMING, B. W. S13511, S10748, O, 22nd (Barteau's) Cav.
FLEMING, Bettie T. W1296, MU, Fleming, Robert Josiah
FLEMING, Elijah Coleman, S16030, MU, 6th (Wheeler's) Cav.
FLEMING, Elizabeth, W5258, SU, Fleming, James B.
FLEMING, Elizabeth, W9166, MU, Fleming, Ranson Green
FLEMING, Ella D. W9498, SH, Fleming, Samuel Thomas
FLEMING, G. D. S10188, RU, 23rd Inf.
FLEMING, J. W. S1842, HR, 14th Cav.
FLEMING, James B. S2835, SU, Campbell's Scouts, Miss. Cav.
FLEMING, John H. S1902, MC, 24th Ala. Inf.
FLEMING, John W. S5693, LI, 8th Inf.
FLEMING, Martha C. W4857, OV, Fleming, Wm. H.
FLEMING, Martha D. W7806, RU, Fleming, G. D.
FLEMING, Mary H. W3059, SN, Fleming, Berry N.
FLEMING, Sam T. S16280, SH, 34th Miss. Inf.
FLEMING, Sarah Martha, W7018, H, Fleming, Wm. W.
FLEMING, Thomas F. S14255, MU, 48th (Voorhies') Inf.
FLEMING, W. H. S9996, OV, 25th Inf.
FLEMING, W. J. P. S15589, MC, 60th N.C. Inf.
FLEMING, William, S3285, CO, 2nd N.C. Inf.
FLEMING, William W. S13329, H, 43rd Inf.
FLETCHER, Athusa, W388, RU, Fletcher, John S.
FLETCHER, Catherine, W667, CY, Fletcher, Melton A.
FLETCHER, Elizabeth, W10328, G, Fletcher, Wm. Allison
FLETCHER, Franklin, S13542, CL, 7th Inf.
FLETCHER, Jacob M. S2085, MG, 64th Va. Inf.
FLETCHER, James K. S1397, S1449, WA, 29th Inf.
FLETCHER, James L. S2579, HW, 64th Va. Inf.
FLETCHER, Joseph T. S4122, MT, 14th Inf.
FLETCHER, Mary J. W8201, CL, Fletcher, B. M.
FLETCHER, Mary J. A. W207, CF, Fletcher, James K. P.
FLINN, Candace Ann, W1013, H, Flinn, Wm. Griffith
FLINN, William Griffin, S1701, H, 26th Inf. & 39th Mtd. Inf.
FLINT, Younger T. S13130, LI, 5th Miss. Cav.
FLIPPEN, James D. S15206, D, 44th Inf.
FLIPPEN, Martha Tennessee, W6891, D, Flippen, Armistead Brooks
FLIPPEN, Samuel A. S9631, SM, 4th Cav.
FLIPPIN, Armistead B. S8606, D, 3rd Ark. Cav.
FLIPPIN, George C. S11717, SM, 55th Inf.
FLIPPIN, Hiram Laurence, S10913, WI, 8th (Smith's) Cav.
FLIPPIN, Joseph, S8173, D, 3rd (Lillard's) Mtd. Inf.
FLIPPIN, Lou,   See Lou Patton
FLIPPIN, Virginia Adaline, W1481, GI, Flippin, Thomas Jefferson
FLIPPIN, W. H. S6897, SM, 8th (Smith's) Cav.
FLIPPO, Susan Ann Jane, W1561, MOO, Flippo, Jefferson
FLORA, Elizabeth H. W7705, HW, Flora, W. D.
FLORA, Mary Ann, W7923, R, Flora, Theo
FLORA, N. A. S8941, HW, 60th Inf.
FLORA, Theodore, S9894, R, 35th Inf.
FLORA, W. D. S1699, HW, 63rd Inf.
FLORENCE, Cynthia J. W5016, BE, Florence, J. B.
FLORENCE, J. W. S6477, BE, 55th Inf.
FLORIDA, Louvinia, W10033, RU, Florida, Patrick Bethel
FLOWERS, Eliza Frances, W10537, G, Flowers, Martin Ervin
FLOWERS, Frances Virginia, W9255, T, Flowers, James Henry
FLOWERS, I. H. S13581, G, 12th Inf.
FLOWERS, J. H. jr. S16239, T, 7th Cav.
FLOWERS, J. T. S15569, G, 12th Inf.
FLOWERS, J. W. S11794, D, 11th Inf.
FLOWERS, M. E. S10562, G, 20th (Russell's) Cav.
FLOWERS, Manerva Frances, W2387, G, Flowers, Michael Marion
FLOWERS, Marion J. S12693, PI, 13th Ark. Inf.
FLOWERS, Mary Elizabeth, W9472, G, Flowers, Isaac Henry
FLOWERS, Sarah A. W868, D, Flowers, General Green
FLOWERS, W. M. S7681, WL, 45th Inf.
FLOWERS, William A. S14458, DY, 4th Inf.

FLOYD, Fannie E. W5567, MS, Floyd, Josiah W. E.
FLOYD, J. T. S2607, LE, 48th Inf.
FLOYD, J. W. E. S13308, MS, 23rd Inf.
FLOYD, John D. S14961, B, 17th Inf.
FLOYD, John T. S16135, SH, 26th Miss. Inf.
FLOYD, Katherine, W8042, BE, Floyd, Thomas W.
FLOYD, Marion, S14009, B, 13th Ark. Inf.
FLOYD, Mary E. W4954, WH, Floyd, Robert Dowell
FLOYD, Mary Elizabeth, W9768, W9336, SH, Floyd, Wm. Smith
FLOYD, R. D. S11432, WH, 7th Inf.
FLOYD, R. E. B. S6206, B, Forrest's Escort, Cav.
FLOYD, Sallie E. See Sallie E. Motlow
FLOYD, Sarah Ellen, W5277, BE, Floyd, Sterling Brewer
FLOYD, Sterling B. S7081, BE, 5th Inf.
FLOYD, T. W. S10843, BE, 20th (Nixon's) Cav.
FLOYD, W. J. S6856, RU, 24th Inf.
FLOYD, W. T. S12679, WH, 7th Inf.
FLOYD, William, S13628, K, 16th Bn. (Neal's) Cav.
FLOYD, William S. S4188, G, 47th Inf.
FLY, Edline, W2398, WI, Fly, George W.
FLY, G. W. S8692, MU, 1st Cav.
FLY, J. C. S1212, G, 38th Inf.
FLY, J. M. S14843, HI, 24th Inf.
FLY, James W. S11409, WI, 41st Inf.
FLY, Mary Elizabeth, W5643, MU, Fly, George Washington
FLY, Melissa Ann, W7955, G, Fly, James Calvin
FLY, Sarah Ashburn, W3135, G, Fly, John Lon
FLYNN, Agnes, W6406, DK, Flynn, James W.
FLYNN, George W. S451, J, 4th (Murray's) Cav.
FLYNT, Paralee, W4762, LI, Flynt, Y. T.
FOELDEN, Martha, W185, GR, Foelden, Wm. R.
FOGG, H. U. S3315, GI, 32nd Inf.
FOGG, J. Fred, S2587, GI, 32nd Inf.
FOGG, Nancy Jane, W6927, GI, Fogg, Horace Upshaw
FOGG, Sallie A. W4291, GI, Fogg, J. Ted
FOGG, William H. sr. S5706, GI, 53rd Inf.
FOLAND, Julia, W635, RO, Foland, George Harvey
FOLSOM, Benjamin F. S1541, CT, 60th Inf.

FONTAINE, Charles D. S15157, SH, Coits' Bn. Miss. Art.
FONVILLE, John F. S14070, MA, 6th Ala. Inf.
FONVILLE, William G. S4440, DE, 3rd & 13th N.C. Inf.
FOOSHEE, Sarah F. W8148, WH, Fooshee, Joseph Michael
FOOTE, James Theodore, S6349, SH, Ballentine's Regt. Cav.
FOOTE, Mary Alice, W5587, F, Foote, Wm. Henry
FOOTE, W. H. S13631, F, 35th Ala. Inf.
FORBES, Jennie Melvine, W10767, SH, Forbes, Allen J.
FORBES, S. F. S15561, WL, 7th Inf.
FORBESS, J. M. S5010, T, 51st Inf.
FORBESS, Thomas J. S11807, T, 51st Inf.
FORD, Andrew Jackson, S5096, PU, Undetermined
FORD, Ann E. W3432, SU, Ford, John W.
FORD, Benjamin F. S4105, SU, 19th Inf.
FORD, Charley, S1368, SU, 29th Inf.
FORD, Della, W9458, BE, Ford, M. C. W.
FORD, Elizabeth, W4482, SM, Ford, Squire
FORD, Henry K. S4291, SU, 19th Inf.
FORD, James H. S7006, WA, 63rd Inf.
FORD, James M. S3219, ME, 5th Cav.
FORD, John B. S4820, HW, 29th Inf.
FORD, Loyd, S4705, HW, 12th Bn. (Day's) Cav.
FORD, M. N. S15555, SM, 28th Inf.
FORD, Mary Ellen, W6187, SU, Ford, Benjamin Franklin
FORD, Mary Jane, W5566, PU, Ford, Green Berry
FORD, N. C. S5011, H, 21st Va. Inf.
FORD, Powel, S3605, L, 15th Cav.
FORD, Sarah Bolling, W6829, WL, Ford, Addison Burette
FORD, Squire, S7455, J, 4th Cav.
FORD, W. T. S. S9042, RU, 16th Inf.
FORD, William, S4059, WA, 29th Inf.
FORD, William Henry, S14290, HY, 9th Inf.
FORE, L. P. S3682, SH, 18th Va. Inf.
FORE, Margaret Eveline, W5950, BR, Fore, H. C.
FORE, Martha E. W5579, SH, Fore, Leonidas P.
FOREHAND, John L. S4047, HI, Baxter's Co. Lt. Art.
FOREHAND, T. D. S4782, CE, 1st Bn. (McNairy's) Cav.

Index to Tennessee Confederate Pension Applications

FOREMAN, A. J. S2952, GE, 5th (McKenzie's) Cav.
FORESTER, E. S12875, HN, 48th Inf.
FORESTER, Isaac V. S16161, LI, 8th Inf.
FORESTER, Mary, W420, HI, Forester, Silas M.
FORESTER, Sarah, W3367, HU, Forester, Richard
FORHAND, William, S2069, D, 44th Inf.
FORKUM, Asberry, S730, J, 28th Inf.
FORLEY, J. J. S4441, SQ, 23rd Inf.
FORMWALT, Ida O. W11096, LI, Formwalt, John A.
FORREST, Cordelia Ann, W8220, K, Forrest, Orren Perry
FORREST, Jacob T. S3354, K, 37th Va. Inf.
FORREST, Margaret M. W166, HU, Forrest, John T.
FORREST, Martha Jane, W5385, MC, Forrest, Wm. H.
FORREST, Thornton, C48, C151, SH, Gen. Forrest's Steward
FORREST, W. H. S11119, MC, 31st Inf.
FORREST, William Montgomery, S9866, SH, White's Co. MacDonald's Bn. Cav.
FORRESTER, Eliza Ann, W6871, SH, Forrester, John F.
FORRESTER, Louvenie, W582, HI, Forrester, Josiah
FORRESTER, Maggie Ann, W6708, LI, Forrester, N. S.
FORRESTER, N. S. S3316, LI, 8th Inf.
FORSHEE, George, S5789, MO, 3rd (Lillard's) Mtd. Inf.
FORSHEE, Lottie Emaline, W4343, WY, Forshee, Elijah
FORSIE, Mary, W10290, D, Forsie, Wade W.
FORSYTH, J. W. S2117, LA, 44th Inf.
FORSYTH, Julia, W7924, GI, Forsyth, R. Harry
FORSYTH, W. A. S3531, MN, 16th Inf.
FORSYTHE, Clementine, W3238, GI, Forsythe, Jessie Walker
FORSYTHE, Elizabeth, W6326, T, Forsythe, Joseph
FORSYTHE, Jerry M. S12566, DI, 49th Inf.
FORSYTHE, Jesse W. S5148, GI, 44th Inf.
FORSYTHE, Julia, W3581, GI, Forsythe, Robert Harrison
FORTENBERRY, Margaret I. W4790, K, Fortenberry, E. C.
FORTENBURY, E. C. S9852, K, 2nd (Ashby's) Cav.
FORTNER, D. R. S1162, BO, 31st Inf.

FORTNER, M. V. S14287, O, 20th Inf.
FORTNER, Nancy J. W2875, DI, Fortner, John Estes
FORTNER, Theresa Jamima, W5434, HI, Fortner, Charles D.
FORTNER, Wiley, S4990, PO, Lookout Battery, Art.
FORTNER, William, S6888, HU, 10th (DeMoss') Cav.
FORTUNE, George T. S9297, MA, 6th Inf.
FORTUNE, John W. S11068, H, 21st Ga. Inf.
FORTUNE, Mary J. W927, MT, Fortune, S. T.
FORTUNE, Nancy, W7598, HR, Fortune, John T.
FOSS, Bettie M. W8133, SH, Foss, H. R.
FOSS, H. R. S15431, SH, 4th Ala. Inf.
FOSTER, Albert, S15472, FR, 41st Inf.
FOSTER, Alfred, S2167, WA, 60th Inf.
FOSTER, B. F. S12458, MS, 9th Cav.
FOSTER, Fred, S7830, MS, 8th Inf.
FOSTER, George A. S8953, WI, 19th Va. Inf.
FOSTER, George W. S5327, MS, 8th Inf.
FOSTER, Hannah Mildred, W813, HD, Foster, Robert Wm.
FOSTER, Hulda Gilliam, W8902, D, Foster, Travis Brooks
FOSTER, I. T. S15958, GR, 5th Bn. Va. Reserves
FOSTER, J. G. S7198, MC, 29th Inf.
FOSTER, J. J. S10666, D, 63rd Inf.
FOSTER, J. W. S12423, 12th Ky. Cav.
FOSTER, James, S1030, WE, 27th Inf.
FOSTER, James D. S4517, H, 33rd Ala. Inf.
FOSTER, James L. S8332, MOO, 23rd Bn. Inf.
FOSTER, James M. S4093, WE, 27th Inf.
FOSTER, Joe, C277, HI, 9th Cav.
FOSTER, John A. S12427, MS, 3rd Inf.
FOSTER, John T. S4539, MN, 14th Cav.
FOSTER, K. B. S11944, T, 10th Ark. Inf.
FOSTER, L. A. S10288, 5th Inf.
FOSTER, Martha C. W155, LI, Foster, Wm. Hopwood
FOSTER, Martha N. W9728, LA, Foster, Daniel M.
FOSTER, Mary, W7210, MN, Foster, John Thomas
FOSTER, Mary Eliza, W7695, MS, Foster, Benjamin Franklin
FOSTER, Mary F. W6945, MS, Foster, Fred
FOSTER, Mary Frances, W5640, WI, Foster, George Andrew

Index to Tennessee Confederate Pension Applications

FOSTER, Mary Frances, W6443, DY, Foster, Wm. Thomas
FOSTER, Mary J. W6255, SH, Foster, Edward
FOSTER, Mary Jane, W3512, MC, Foster, John Goss
FOSTER, Mattie Lee, W10815, MC, Foster, Pryor Lee
FOSTER, Nancy A. W1347, HE, Foster, Henry W.
FOSTER, Nannie Elizabeth, W9444, LI, Foster, George Washington
FOSTER, Oliver H. S10294, SN, 7th Inf.
FOSTER, Peter, S7755, B, 41st Inf.
FOSTER, R. A. S9345, GI, 48th (Voorhies') Inf.
FOSTER, Rowland T. S6369, SM, Allison's Squadron, Cav.
FOSTER, S. B. S14059, GU, 18th Inf.
FOSTER, Susan, W9428, RU, Foster, Ike
FOSTER, T. B. S11289, D, 30th Inf.
FOSTER, T. J. S11893, F, 1st (Turney's) Inf.
FOSTER, Tabitah Rachel, W3334, MU, Foster, Joseph Molloy
FOSTER, Tennessee Josephine, W9436, W, Foster, James Porter
FOSTER, Thomas A. S12183, SH, 12th Ala. Inf.
FOSTER, W. H. S2701, LI, 41st Inf.
FOTSOM, Sarah Elizabeth, W2319, CT, Fotsom, Henderson M.
FOUNTAINE, W. D. S8784, K, 13th Ga. Inf.
FOUNTAINE, Willis (Will), C184, LK, 6th Miss. Inf.
FOUST, David B. S9879, SU, 34th Va. Cav.
FOUST, Emma, W1273, R, Foust, George W.
FOUST, H. D. S5328, DK, 45th Inf.
FOUST, Mary Matilda, W233, HN, Foust, Elija
FOUST, Sarah Elizabeth, W6351, G, Foust, Wm.
FOUST, Susan E. W10559, SU, Foust, David B.
FOUST, Susanna Maryline, W307, R, Foust, N. B.
FOUST, William, S14338, G, 15th Cav.
FOUST, William A. S12631, HN, 5th Inf.
FOUTCH, America Frances, W7581, DK, Foutch, Francis Lafayette
FOUTCH, Elijah, S7693, D, 7th Inf.
FOUTCH, F. L. S387, DK, 7th Inf.
FOUTCH, J. C. S11225, W, 24th Inf.
FOUTCH, J. W. S2049, DK, Allison's Squadron, Cav.
FOUTCH, Julie Emaline, W6087, W, Foutch, John Calvin

FOUTCH, Martha Jane, W7095, D, Foutch, Elijah
FOUTCH, Sarah Jane, W5625, DK, Foutch, J. W.
FOWLER, B. F. S5957, D, 2nd (Walker's) Inf.
FOWLER, Bettie, W2836, DK, Fowler, Daniel
FOWLER, H. T. S4790, SN, 22nd (Barteau's) Cav.
FOWLER, J. G. S2572, LI, 22nd Cav.
FOWLER, Lucy Caroline, W492, HN, Fowler, James Elisha
FOWLER, Nancy Ann, W2487, HD, Fowler, John S.
FOWLER, Patience, W4518, SN, Fowler, Henry Thomas
FOWLER, R. H. S6236, ST, 50th Inf.
FOWLER, S. W. S16010, T, 6th Ala. Inf.
FOWLER, William M. S5624, MS, 41st Inf.
FOWLKES, John A. S10696, HI, 10th Cav.
FOWLKES, Mary Caroline, W4106, SH, Fowlkes, J. L.
FOWLKES, Rebecca Jane, W5417, HI, Fowlkes, John Alston
FOX, Benjamin B. S2149, J, 28th Inf.
FOX, Cornelius R. S16053, H, 36th Ga. Inf.
FOX, E. B. S117, WI, 20th Inf.
FOX, Ezekiel, S10069, JE, 26th Inf.
FOX, Harriet A. W449, RU, Fox, John M.
FOX, J. H. S333, 7th Cav.
FOX, James M. C. S159, WI, 49th Inf.
FOX, John M. S4830, CO, 62nd Inf.
FOX, Joseph A. S116, MU, 20th Inf.
FOX, Martha Jane, W11174, PU, Fox, John B.
FOX, Mary Ann, W8662, RU, Fox, Samuel
FOX, Mollie Smith, W10945, LI, Fox, Joseph P.
FOX, N. H. W. S12694, J, 28th Inf.
FOX, Sallie F. W10304, J, Fox, James F.
FOX, Skelton, S15110, WA, 58th N.C. Inf.
FOX, Stephen, S5742, K, 26th Inf.
FOX, Susan E. W2535, RU, Fox, John E.
FOXALL, John J. S5198, MU, 48th (Voorhies') Inf.
FRAKER, W. M. S12492, H, 39th Ga. Inf.
FRALEY, John G. S14931, SH, 17th Inf.
FRALIX, James Milton, S9514, GI, 37th Inf.
FRALIX, Martha Jane, W7334, GI, Fralix, James Milton
FRAME, Henrietta D. W759, B, Frame, J. W.
FRANCE, J. M. S8270, OV, 8th Cav.
FRANCE, Jasper Henry, S1569, PU, 8th Cav.
FRANCE, John B. S10986, OV, 8th (Dibrell's) Cav.

Index to Tennessee Confederate Pension Applications

FRANCES, J. D. S4855, CA, 14th Cav.
FRANCIS, C. C. S12695, CA, 22nd (Barteau's) Cav.
FRANCIS, Edward, C213, FR, Hospital Steward
FRANCIS, M. C. S8288, CA, 4th Cav.
FRANCIS, M. H. S924, S518, CA, 2nd Inf.
FRANCIS, Mary L. W4347, CA, Francis, Matthew Howel
FRANCIS, Thomas W. S11646, LO, 63rd Inf.
FRANCISCO, C. F. S14394, HM, 64th Va. Mtd. Inf.
FRANCISCO, Terrissa Fuller, W8910, HM, Francisco, Cornelius Fugate
FRANCISCO, William F. S16625, HW, 37th Va. Inf.
FRANK, A. B. S6706, GI, 1st Ark. Inf.
FRANKLE, A. S15980, B, 22nd La. Inf.
FRANKLE, Lizzie Yancey, W9062, B, Frankle, Abraham
FRANKLIN, Ambrose N. S13183, S9182, GI, 8th Inf., Also applied from Marshall County
FRANKLIN, B. J. S2911, R, 1st (Carter's) Cav.
FRANKLIN, Bettie, W2399, SN, Franklin, A. R.
FRANKLIN, Bettie P. W2458, SN, Franklin, James
FRANKLIN, David A. S15181, LI, 1st (Turney's) Inf.
FRANKLIN, Eliza, W3129, D, Franklin, Smith C.
FRANKLIN, J. P. S4889, WH, 9th Tex. Inf.
FRANKLIN, James, S4318, WY, 8th Inf.
FRANKLIN, Jese H. S5514, HR, 17th Miss. Inf.
FRANKLIN, John T. S8508, FE, 8th Cav.
FRANKLIN, L. M. S628, SM, 28th Inf.
FRANKLIN, Martha Ann, W5422, WY, Franklin, James
FRANKLIN, Martha Rebecca, W10731, H, Franklin, James S.
FRANKLIN, Mary, W5510, SH, Franklin, Thomas
FRANKLIN, Mary Ann,   See Mary Ann Smith
FRANKLIN, Mary Jane, W7420, WH, Franklin, John P.
FRANKLIN, Mary Lavinia, W2238, HR, Franklin, Jesse Hardin
FRANKLIN, Mollie, W5564, MA, Franklin, James Weeden
FRANKLIN, Peter H. S6644, GE, 13th Bn. N.C. Lt. Art.
FRANKLIN, Salena E. W1400, H, Franklin, Benjinett J.

FRANKLIN, Smith C. S9310, D, 9th (Bennett's) Cav.
FRANKLIN, Susan Frances, W2943, D, Franklin, Robert H.
FRANKLIN, W. C. S8063, TR, 13th Inf.
FRANKS, Amanda E. W3224, WH, Franks, Peter Buren
FRANKS, Ann Dill, W10083, D, Franks, Samuel Baldwin
FRANKS, S. H. S10201, WH, 8th Cav.
FRANKS, W. H. S11477, MN, 3rd Inf.
FRASER, Carrie F. W5423, F, Fraser, E. I.
FRASER, E. I. S12417, F, 7th Cav.
FRASER, William L. S10223, SH, 1st Cav.
FRASHER, P. S12712, DI, 7th Ky. Inf.
FRASHER, Sarah E. W7990, DI, Frasher, Pleasant
FRASHER, W. P. A. S6171, DI, Baxter's Co. Lt. Art.
FRAYSER, Mary Isab. Neighbors, W1915, SH, Frayser, Wm. Henry
FRAZIER, Andrew Jackson, S12355, HD, 20th (unit incomplete)
FRAZIER, Ann Eliza, W506, GE, Frazier, Thomas Jefferson
FRAZIER, Austin, S5420, CO, 60th Inf.
FRAZIER, George Winchester, S7985, L, 7th Inf.
FRAZIER, H. E. S8485, HN, 20th Cav.
FRAZIER, Isaac, S6685, CF, 24th Inf.
FRAZIER, J. B. S12376, K, 18th Inf.
FRAZIER, J. B. (Mrs.), W11180, Frazier, J. B. Contents of file missing
FRAZIER, J. H. S9888, O, 14th N.C. Inf.
FRAZIER, J. L. S11271, BE, 5th Inf.
FRAZIER, Janie Elizabeth, W7404, D, Frazier, Wm. Bowling
FRAZIER, John, S8269, G, Undetermined
FRAZIER, John B. S7657, CF, 4th Inf.
FRAZIER, Judith, W8456, CF, Frazier, Isaac
FRAZIER, Louisa E. W1293, R, Frazier, Beriah
FRAZIER, Lucrecia A. W939, MT, Frazier, Wm.
FRAZIER, Martha, W1981, SU, Frazier, Thomas C.
FRAZIER, Mary, W2239, Frazier, Wm. Franklin
FRAZIER, Nancy, W7803, DY, Frazier, John
FRAZIER, Nannie Jane, W7029, HD, Frazier, Andrew Jackson
FRAZIER, Nicholis P. S4605, BL, 19th Inf.
FRAZIER, P. B. S9600, D, 1st Mo. Cav.

FRAZIER, Sarah J. W7902, R, Frazier, Nicholas Polk
FRAZIER, T. M. S10073, W, 35th Inf.
FRAZIER, Thomas C. S9456, SU, 19th Inf.
FRAZIER, W. G. S12028, HI, 11th Inf.
FRAZIER, W. G. S15462, HI, 10th Cav.
FRAZIER, William B. S12252, D, 20th Inf.
FRAZOR, J. M. S4734, SN, 6th Ark. Inf.
FRAZOR, Margaret Jane, W5799, SN, Frazor, Wm. Andrew
FRAZOR, W. A. S4641, SN, 44th Inf.
FRAZURE, Thomas, S6182, SE, 60th Inf.
FRAZZIER, A. M. S11704, BE, 55th Inf.
FREANO, J. R. S14594, CC, 7th Cav.
FREE, Joe, S6159, RU, 8th Bn. Ga. Inf.
FREEDLE, J. H. S10814, TR, 9th (Ward's) Cav.
FREEDLE, O. H. S14378, SN, 2nd Inf.
FREELAND, J. P. S5769, K, 60th Inf.
FREELS, W. M. S13121, HY, 9th Inf.
FREEMAN, A. C. S3707, LI, 8th Inf.
FREEMAN, Almedia C. W6347, W9045, HE, Freeman, Wm. Henry
FREEMAN, Andrew Jackson, S7970, O, 10th Ala. Cav.
FREEMAN, Annie, W7644, HR, Freeman, W. L.
FREEMAN, Armina, W389, BL, Freeman, James M.
FREEMAN, C. B. S14650, SH, Unassigned (Courier in Forrest's Cav.)
FREEMAN, C. H. S9545, WE, 22nd Inf.
FREEMAN, Christian, S14695, GR, 1st (Carter's) Cav.
FREEMAN, D. H. S6183, H, 2nd S. C. Rifles
FREEMAN, G. H. S7295, G, 29th Inf
FREEMAN, H. F. S7767, F, 3rd (Lillard's) Mtd. Inf.
FREEMAN, J. C. S9907, MA, 7th Inf.
FREEMAN, J. R. S7801, MS, 41st Inf.
FREEMAN, James M. S4610, BL, 43rd Inf.
FREEMAN, James N. S105, 55th Inf.
FREEMAN, Jap, S15995, LA, 42nd Inf.
FREEMAN, Jap, S16447, LA, 48th Inf.
FREEMAN, Joseph, S14547, CT, 29th N.C. Inf.
FREEMAN, Julia C. W7850, H, Freeman, Hutcherson
FREEMAN, M. E. S8426, MO, 55th Inf.
FREEMAN, M. W. S14272, D, 18th Inf.
FREEMAN, Martha Ann Elizabeth, W1004, MS, Freeman, James Frank
FREEMAN, Martha B. W7560, G, Freeman, George Hamilton

FREEMAN, Martha Jane, W3935, LE, Freeman, Samuel D.
FREEMAN, Mary F. W1887, WL, Freeman, Wm. F.
FREEMAN, Nora Manley, W9807, DY, Freeman, Clinton Blackwell
FREEMAN, R. J. S15709, MA, 27th Ala. Inf., Alias J. M. Walker - 14962
FREEMAN, Rosamond, W6316, GR, Freeman, John
FREEMAN, Sallie, W6827, D, Freeman, James Calvin
FREEMAN, Samuel, S6107, CT, 58th N.C. Inf.
FREEMAN, Samuel D. S7788, LE, 16th Ark. Cav.
FREEMAN, Susan, W3270, Freeman, James Newton
FREEMAN, W. J. S10342, CH, 21st (Wilson's) Cav.
FREEMAN, W. M. S8267, O, 4th Inf.
FREEMAN, William, S13573, MA, (Calvert's) Bn. Ark. Lt. Art.
FREEMAN, William J. S4328, B, 8th Inf.
FREEZE, Mary Anne, W9799, CF, Freeze, Solomon H.
FREEZE, S. H. S3754, W, 4th Inf.
FRENCH, G. A. sr. S16537, BE, 5th Inf.
FRENCH, G. H. S15068, HO, 11th Inf.
FRENCH, George D. S15103, HM, 7th Bn. Va. Cav.
FRENCH, John A. S4254, T, 7th Inf.
FRENCH, Joseph S. S9956, HM, 51st Va. Inf.
FRENCH, Larkin, S13723, P, 51st Inf.
FRENCH, Lennis Bolton, W6712, HM, French, Joseph St. Clair
FRENCH, Louise M. W9724, MA, French, Robert Henry
FRENCH, Sophia Hass, W7980, HM, French, George D.
FRENCH, William, S992, GE, 61st Inf.
FRERICHS, Sarah J. W6750, MO, Frerichs, John H.
FRERICKS, John H. S256, MO, Undetermined
FRESHOUR, J. V. S4334, MN, 56th Ala. Inf.
FRESHOUR, John, S5405, GE, 64th N.C. Inf.
FREY, C. J. S10855, SN, 30th Inf.
FREY, Martha, W2109, RB, Frey, James Eldridge
FRICKS, Elizabeth C. W6575, H, Fricks, Napolian B.
FRIDDLE, Alfred, S6196, B, 37th Inf.
FRIDDLE, Jessee, S5368, B, 41st Inf.

Index to Tennessee Confederate Pension Applications

FRIDDLE, Nancy Caroline, W4400, B, Friddle, Jesse
FRIEND, August, S12005, D, 1st (Feild's) Inf.
FRIEND, Frances N. W10129, GU, Friend, H. R.
FRIEND, H. R. S14952, GU, 4th La. Cav.
FRIERSON, James L. S7558, DI, Cabell's Bn. Ga. Art.
FRIERSON, Lizzie Anne, W10459, RU, Frierson, Robert Moore
FRIERSON, Lucy Serena, W10292, MU, Frierson, Albert Davidson
FRIERSON, Mary Little, W9287, B, Frierson, Robert Poyner, App. follows 9288 on film
FRINK, Sarah Jane, W6617, MN, Frink, Martin N.
FRISBEE, J. A. S8758, PO, 3rd Inf.
FRITCH, John, S1945, D, 1st (Feild's) Inf.
FRIZZELL, Emma H. W953, FR, Frizzell, Nathan
FRIZZELL, L. P. S315, RU, 44th Inf.
FROST, Eliza J. W5230, SU, Frost, George Washington
FROST, Fanna, W2868, CF, Frost, Wm. D.
FROST, G. W. S7227, SU, 47th Bn. Va. Cav.
FROST, Joe, S5935, MU, 17th Ala. Inf.
FROST, N. A. W602, HO, Frost, Wm. Carroll
FROST, Stephen, S8653, UN, 4th Bn. Cav.
FROST, Terrissa Ann, W4873, MU, Frost, Joe
FROST, White, S2305, CU, 28th Inf.
FRY, Anderson, S4335, T, 21st N.C. Inf.
FRY, Elizabeth E. W2668, H, Fry, Hugh Lawson
FRY, Harvey, S4888, MC, 59th Inf.
FRY, Isaac M. S9774, CE, 1st (Turney's) Inf.
FRY, J. M. S13258, MS, 3rd (Clack's) Inf.
FRY, Joe W. S9706, CH, 52nd Inf.
FRY, John P. S6218, SU, Undetermined
FRY, Mary A. W6047, H, Fry, George Thompson
FRY, Mary Emmaline, W914, BR, Fry, Thomas Claiborne
FRY, Nancy Ann, W7853, WL, Fry, Wm. Jasper
FRY, Nancy Ann Caroline, W509, GI, Fry, Lewis
FRY, Sue E. W4871, GE, Fry, Robert C. G.
FRY, T. J. S14010, MA, 18th (Newsom's) Cav.
FRY, Telite, W636, H, Fry, Hardin Grunlesly
FRY, W. J. S7418, WL, 4th Inf.
FRYAR, Martha E. W100, D, Fryar, James F.
FRYER, Amanda Geneva, W8570, RB, Fryer, W. M.

FRYER, W. M. S14231, RB, 8th Ky. Cav.
FUDGE, Louisa Leonora, See Louisa Leonora Baugh
FULGHAM, Clementine Minerva, W6196, Fulgham, Jesse Mercer
FULGHAM, Jesse M. S11918, 12th Ga. Bn. Art.
FULGHUM, Alice Buntin, W5831, D, Fulghum, Sylanus
FULGHUM, J. E. S15105, G, 47th Inf.
FULGHUM, Nannie, W6721, G, Fulghum, J. E.
FULGHUM, W. R. S4181, DY, 47th Inf.
FULGRUM, Sylvanus, S5729, SN, 30th Inf.
FULK, Maggie J. W1763, RU, Fulk, John Washington
FULKERSON, Thomas G. S12057, CL, 63rd Inf.
FULKERSON, Virginia Gill, W7059, MT, Fulkerson, Charles F.
FULKERSON, W. W. S7296, WL, 25th Inf.
FULKS, James M. S10351, B, 4th (McLemore's) Cav.
FULKS, Rebecca J. W7096, B, Fulks, J. M.
FULLER, Amanda, W6154, D, Fuller, Joseph H.
FULLER, Elizabeth, W3092, MU, Fuller, John
FULLER, G. C. S12035, O, 48th (Nixon's) Inf.
FULLER, H. R. S15455, RO, 16th Bn. Cav.
FULLER, Joseph H. S5592, D, 13th Inf.
FULLER, Lee, C86, F, 5th Ala. Cav.
FULLER, Martha, W7507, RO, Fuller, O. B.
FULLER, O. B. S9031, RO, 43rd Inf.
FULLER, Thomas, S14964, SM, 22nd (Barteu's) Cav.
FULLERTON, Henry Thomas, S13538, O, 13th Inf., Also applied from Gibson County
FULLERTON, M. A. S7487, O, 21st (Wilson's) Cav.
FULLERTON, Robert J. S5084, MA, 10th Cav.
FUNK, John P. S13029, RU, 43rd Inf.
FUNK, Medora Woodward, W10726, RU, Funk, John Pennywitt
FUNK, Samuel, S12187, SH, 43rd Inf.
FUQUA, Elizabeth America, W1645, RU, Fuqua, Joel
FUQUA, J. E. S12260, WL, 30th Inf.
FUQUA, J. J. S10403, HU, 11th Inf.
FUQUA, James C. S374, M, 24th Inf.
FUQUA, Margaret F. W3928, HU, Fuqua, Jesse J.
FUQUA, Sarah Jane, W850, TR, Fuqua, James Caster
FUQUA, William J. S12267, 19th & 20th Cav.

FURCHES, Mary Lou, W6263, WA, Furches, Samuel Wesley
FURCHES, S. W. S1502, WA, 13th Inf.
FURGUS, Amanda Virginia, W8953, RU, Furgus, John Tylor
FURRY, H. C. S5790, CL, 29th Inf.
FURRY, Rosa, W8583, W10857, CL, Furry, Henry Clay
FURRY, William J. S5503, K, Crews' Battery, Va. Art.
FUSELL, W. N. S9754, MA, 52nd Inf.
FUSSELL, J. J. S10817, 18th (Newsom's) Cav.
FUSSELL, Joe H. S14809, MU, 6th (Wheeler's) Cav.
FUSSELL, Josephine, W4362, G, Fussell, Wm. N.
FUSSELL, Margaret Roberts, W6161, MU, Fussell, Joseph Henry
FUSSELL, Sarah E. W463, MA, Fussell, Jason W.
FUSTON, J. M. S5798, D, 16th Inf.
FUSTON, J. S. S4542, W, 4th (Murray's) Cav.
FUTHEY, A. B. S2226, HN, 20th Cav.
FUTRELL, Andrew Jackson, S6108, HD, 20th Miss. Inf.
FUTRELL, J. G. S15001, MA, 6th Inf.
FUTRELL, Martha A. W6648, G, Futrell, James Green
GACHET, Charles, S11702, SH, 3rd Ala. Inf.
GADD, Matilda, W2023, R, Gadd, John Dallas
GADDIS, Arch W. S16006, MO, 62nd Ga. Inf.
GADSBY, A. E. W5953, CC, Gadsby, John Edward
GAFFNEY, Mary Kate, W8595, H, Gaffney, James Mathew
GAFFORD, Isaac, S7954, ST, 49th Inf.
GAFFORD, Nancy Dianna, W5414, CD, Gafford, Wm. Jefferson
GAINES, Elizabeth Ann, W3142, H, Gaines, John Henry
GAINES, George W. S15860, OV, 25th Inf.
GAINES, J. H. S6686, H, 38th Ga. Inf.
GAINES, Marcellus R. S10949, 20th (Russell's) Cav.
GAINES, Martha, W4357, GR, Gaines, Thomas Elvin
GAINES, R. K. S2953, GR, 59th Inf.
GAINES, Thomas E. S8535, GR, 13th Cav.
GAITHER, Amelia Elizabeth, W5720, CA, Gaither, Wm. Pinkney
GAITHER, B. S4032, CA, 4th Cav.
GAITHER, John H. S3868, CF, 18th Inf.

GAITHER, Laura T. W8014, CF, Gaither, John H.
GAITHER, R. L. S15444, B, 41st Inf.
GAITHER, Thomas Asariah, S9157, CA, 8th (Smith's) Cav.
GAITHER, W. P. S8639, CA, 8th (Smith's) Cav.
GAITHER, William M. S8244, F, 13th Inf.
GALAWAY, Doctor, S13122, SE, 6th N.C. Inf.
GALAWAY, James, S1527, CA, 35th Inf.
GALBRAITH, J. L. S14727, HM, 29th Inf.
GALBRAITH, J. N. S5451, CH, 55th Inf.
GALBREATH, G. W. S12084, BE, 55th Inf.
GALBREATH, John R. S15957, D, 20th (Russell's) Cav.
GALESPIE, Carline, W225, LA, Galespie, Wm.
GALIGAN, Patrick, S1118, D, 18th Inf.
GALLAHAN, Rachel J. W4637, CL, Gallahan, W. H.
GALLAHAN, W. H. S4038, CL, 27th Va. Cav.
GALLAHER, A. H. S13434, LO, 2nd (Ashby's) Cav.
GALLAHER, Frances Louisa, W7145, LO, Gallaher, Albert Hugh
GALLAHER, Harriet Adelia, W7614, K, Gallaher, Thomas Jefferson
GALLAHER, Hugh, S1423, K, 48th Va. Inf.
GALLAHER, Martha E. W5721, RO, Gallaher, David Houston
GALLAHER, Pleasant P. S2654, H, 5th Cav.
GALLAHER, Sarah, W4895, K, Gallaher, George H.
GALLAHER, Thomas J. S14863, K, 26th Inf.
GALLAWAY, James S. S5896, WH, 8th (Dibrell's) Cav.
GALLOWAY, A. S3923, CE, 18th Inf.
GALLOWAY, Eliza H. W6090, WA, Galloway, Samuel
GALLOWAY, Elizabeth Rebecca, W8520, MU, Galloway, Wm. Thomas
GALLOWAY, G. W. S6643, SU, 59th Inf.
GALLOWAY, John B. S4468, MU, 9th Bn. Cav.
GALLOWAY, Lucinda, W4249, RU, Galloway, James
GALLOWAY, Mary J. W9711, WA, Galloway, Nathan
GALLOWAY, Robert A. S8871, MU, 3rd Inf.
GALLOWAY, Samuel, S7408, WA, 60th Inf.
GALLOWAY, Susan C. W7318, SU, Galloway, George W.
GALLOWAY, Susan H. W2806, F, Galloway, Narffet Wiston

Index to Tennessee Confederate Pension Applications

GALLOWAY, Thomas J. S12876, WA, Unassigned (Commissary Dept.)
GALOWAY, A. C. S12936, CE, 18th Inf.
GAMBELL, Susan, W1210, DY, Gambell, James Jefferson
GAMBILL, Fannie Ellen, W4584, MS, Gambill, Wm. Stewart
GAMBILL, John Tilford, S8633, D, 28th Inf.
GAMBILL, Lou, W10259, WL, Gambill, W. J.
GAMBILL, Martha Louise, W6460, WL, Gambill, Wm. James
GAMBILL, William S. S9522, MS, 41st Inf.
GAMBLIN, G. W. S13943, BR, 37th Inf.
GAMBLIN, Mary L. W6670, BR, Gamblin, George Washington
GAMBLIN, Rodie Jane, W10097, HN, Gamblin, John S.
GAMMON, Bettie, W10394, O, Gammon, Wm. Carroll
GAMMON, George A. S13778, K, 63rd Inf.
GAMMON, H. C. S10727, D, 30th Inf.
GAMMON, J. R. S7607, D, 9th (Bennett's) Cav.
GAMMON, John M. S3049, TR, 30th Inf.
GAMMON, Louis A. S6390, GE, 42nd Inf.
GAMMON, Margaret Hale, W5903, K, Gammon, George Alexander
GAMMON, Mary A. W1198, SM, Gammon, John Monroe
GAMMON, W. B. S15731, SH, 1st (Carter's) Cav.
GAMMON, W. C. S8917, O, 4th Inf.
GANAWAY, Sarah Adline, W1076, B, Ganaway, John
GANDY, Sophia Alice, W952, CA, Gandy, Wm.
GANDY, William A. S4085, CA, 4th Cav.
GANN, George W. S15507, WL, 8th (Smith's) Cav.
GANN, Jim C. S7831, SM, 8th (Smith's) Cav.
GANN, Lenora Jane, W4314, SM, Gann, James Campbell
GANN, Martha A. W3269, SM, Gann, Thomas
GANN, Nancy M. W995, SM, Gann, Wm.
GANN, Nathan, S2808, CA, Allison's Squadron, Cav.
GANN, Thomas, S2837, SM, 4th Cav.
GANN, William H. S4453, CA, Allison's Squadron, Cav.
GANNAWAY, E. N. S6136, R, 16th Bn. (Neal's) Cav.
GANNAWAY, Mary A. W1454, H, Gannaway, Thomas Cotlett

GANNON, Amanda, W2809, DY, Gannon, Wm. Carroll
GANNON, Harvey, S5337, RB, 4th Cav.
GANNON, W. H. S15828, W, 8th (Smith's) Cav.
GANSNER, Nick, S9386, ST, 50th Inf.
GANT, Christian Elizabeth, W353, SN, Gant, Wm. T.
GANT, Daniel P. S10105, HD, 1st Cav.
GANT, L. James, S12301, WA, 61st Inf.
GANT, Malinda Frances, W2145, SN, Gant, Wm. Henry
GANT, W. H. S5012, SN, 1st Cav.
GANTT, W. J. S13825, MA, 15th Miss. Inf.
GARBER, Sol, S9828, HW, 25th Va. Cav.
GARDENHIRE, James A. W4905, D, Gardenhire, James Alexis
GARDNER, Alfred, S8693, MU, 1st Cav.
GARDNER, Cannie, W5815, Gardner, Jacob Henry
GARDNER, Charles N. S16459, RB, 11th Inf.
GARDNER, David Alexander, S3168, T, 4th Inf.
GARDNER, E. M. S15871, D, 6th Miss. Cav.
GARDNER, Ellen Lipscomb, W10771, D, Gardner, James I.
GARDNER, George W. F. S13554, DY, 11th Inf.
GARDNER, James H. S14478, K, 21st Va. Cav.
GARDNER, John A. S852, SN, 10th Inf.
GARDNER, Joseph E. S15596, JE, 12th Va. Cav.
GARDNER, Luzianna Jackson, W11069, MA, Gardner, Nathan Andrew
GARDNER, Martha Cate, W10787, K, Gardner, Joe E.
GARDNER, Minerva Jane, W1987, T, Gardner, David Alexander
GARDNER, Nancy Elender, W4678, MO, Gardner, James Bryant
GARDNER, S. B. S15823, MU, 6th (Wheeler's) Cav.
GARDNER, Sarah E. W5042, BO, Gardner, Elishey M.
GARDNER, Sarah E. W10185, SU, Gardner, Soloman
GARDNER, Stephen G. S15533, W, 4th (Murray's) Cav.
GARNER, Alice, W7454, FR, Garner, Wm. Wallace
GARNER, E. H. S15906, MU, 9th Bn. Cav.

-125

Index to Tennessee Confederate Pension Applications

GARNER, George, C29, C246, FR, 1st Inf., 246 is missing.
GARNER, I. C. S2058, H, 1st (Turney's) Inf.
GARNER, J. D. S15286, G, 10th (DeMoss') Cav.
GARNER, J. M. S4430, A, 18th Tex. Inf.
GARNER, J. T. S14693, SH, 4th Ala. Inf.
GARNER, L. G. S12524, D, 4th (McLemore's) Cav., On misc. microfilm reel
GARNER, Malissa Carrie, W2657, D, Garner, Wiley Washington
GARNER, Mary, W2753, MU, Garner, Samuel L.
GARNER, Mary Ann, W9955, MU, Garner, Elijah Hanks
GARNER, Mary Pryor, W480, FR, Garner, Irvin Clark
GARNER, S. L. S5406, MU, 9th Bn. Cav.
GARNER, W. B. S2794, SH, 21st Inf.
GARNER, W. W. S5074, FR, 1st (Turney's) Inf.
GARNES, R. C. S2751, W, 35th Inf.
GARREN, John W. S7137, MO, 2nd Cav.
GARRETT, Bettie Brandon, W8936, MS, Garrett, Thomas Eason
GARRETT, D. B. S12532, GI, 3rd (Clack's) Inf.
GARRETT, Electy C. W1682, CC, Garrett, Wm.
GARRETT, F. E. S16264, WE, 19th & 20th (Consolidated) Cav.
GARRETT, G. F. S15037, MU, 48th (Voorhies') Inf.
GARRETT, George W. C244, SH, Regiment not given
GARRETT, George W. S16444, SH, 3rd Engineer Corps
GARRETT, Harriet L. W1181, O, Garrett, Pat
GARRETT, J. C. S4388, OV, 8th (Smith's) Cav.
GARRETT, J. G. S16438, RU, 11th Cav.
GARRETT, J. H. S13068, SH, 18th (Newsom's) Cav.
GARRETT, J. M. S14675, RU, 11th Cav.
GARRETT, J. W. S2248, OV, 28th Inf.
GARRETT, J. W. S11410, SN, 44th Inf.
GARRETT, J. W. S11705, BE, 16th Va. Cav.
GARRETT, James B. S3694, SN, 7th Inf.
GARRETT, John L. S12578, H, Freeman's Mo. Cav.
GARRETT, Mary B. W10398, SH, Garrett, Wm. E.
GARRETT, Mary Elizabeth, W2201, SH, Garrett, Wm. Hardison
GARRETT, Mary Elizabeth, W10764, D, Garrett, Wm. David
GARRETT, Mary J. W1673, B, Garrett, James S.
GARRETT, Mary Jane, W2040, D, Garrett, Samuel James
GARRETT, Mary Lasater, W10099, WE, Garrett, F. Ellen
GARRETT, Nancy Adaline, W251, WL, Garrett, William
GARRETT, Nannie Lee, W11090, WI, Garrett, Daniel B.
GARRETT, Nannie Smith, W5147, SH, Garrett, James H.
GARRETT, Noah, C, GR, Regiment not given, Application is missing.
GARRETT, Pollie, W9665, OV, Garrett, Joshua Winchester
GARRETT, R. C. S11162, B, Forrest's Escort, Cav.
GARRETT, Rebecca Alexander, W10246, G, Garrett, Jerome Kemp
GARRETT, S. L. P. S4346, MS, 3rd Inf.
GARRETT, Sue Ella, W6061, O, Garrett, Jessee
GARRETT, T. W. S14653, RU, 24th Inf.
GARRETT, Thomas E. S15677, MS, 15th Ky. Cav.
GARRETT, Virginia Crider, W9194, WE, Garrett, Noah Jackson
GARRETT, William, S4189, WL, 6th (Wheeler's) Cav.
GARRETT, William H. S9990, SH, 154th Sr. Regt. Inf.
GARRETT, William N. S5877, HD, 1st N.C. Inf.
GARRETT, William Thomas, S12680, MS, 11th (Gordon's) Cav.
GARRIGUS, J. M. S9306, WE, 9th Bn. (Gantt's) Cav.
GARRISON, Helen, W4784, W9961, F, Garrison, John Thomas
GARRISON, J. T. S10250, F, 7th Cav.
GARRISON, John L. S662, J, 28th Inf.
GARRISON, Mattie Elizabeth, W3868, K, Garrison, Wm. Winder
GARRISON, William E. S2399, GI, 32nd Inf.
GARRISON, Wilson P. S461, DK, 44th Inf.
GARTON, Edmon T. S12204, WI, 49th Inf.
GARTON, Moses, S2553, DI, 11th Inf.
GARTON, Salonia Omega, W7098, DI, Garton, Martin
GARVIN, S. V. S4583, MN, 16th Ala. Inf.
GARVIN, T. J. S5826, D, 23rd Inf.
GARY, F. M. S10914, DI, 1st (Feild's) Inf.

Index to Tennessee Confederate Pension Applications

GARY, Nancy Ann, W7091, DI, Gary, F. M.
GASKILL, Maud, W9566, MU, Gaskill, Thomas C.
GASKILL, Thomas Christopher, S14754, MU, 3rd Mo. Cav.
GASKINS, Thomas Green, S11889, WE, 15th Inf.
GASS, A. J. S9307, FR, 34th Ga. Inf.
GASTON, D. M. S14530, G, 27th Inf.
GATE, Mary Ellis, W1209, D, Gate, Wm. Dudley
GATELY, John H. S15599, 52nd Inf.
GATES, Frances T. W1865, K, Gates, John
GATES, Georgia A. W1071, MA, Gates, John W.
GATES, Mamie Long, W10018, SH, Gates, Wm. Beverly
GATES, Spencer C. S1880, MS, 17th Inf.
GATES, Thomas M. S11200, MA, 6th Inf.
GATES, William Ward, S12003, MA, 19th & 20th (Consolidated) Cav.
GATEWOOD, Emma F. W6405, DI, Gatewood, John F.
GATEWOOD, Wesly, C131, SH, 7th Miss. Inf.
GATHER, Elizabeth Ann, W1691, MU, Gather, James
GATHINGS, Frances Isabel, W3982, HE, Gathings, Milton Carmell
GATHINGS, Sarah Ann, W4963, HE, Gathings, Joseph John
GATLIN, Albert G. S12927, S11011, HR, 14th Cav.
GATLIN, Benjamin, S2775, D, 11th Cav.
GATLIN, Jacob, S11338, BR, 62nd Inf.
GATLIN, Lucy, W1184, WI, Gatlin, Benjamin Franklin
GATLIN, Mary E. W7969, BR, Gatlin, Jacob
GATLIN, Sarah A. W275, GI, Gatlin, Isaac Thomas
GATLING, J. J. S4873, DE, 18th (Newsom's) Cav.
GATTIS, Amanda H. W175, CH, Gattis, George Carson
GATTIS, Elizabeth, W6506, MOO, Gattis, Isaac Van Buren
GATTIS, I. V. S5949, MOO, 8th Inf.
GATTIS, Mary J. W709, FR, Gattis, Willis Moore
GATTISH, T. M. S13163, HD, 21st (Wilson's) Cav.
GATTON, Nancy E. W1103, WL, Gatton, Joseph W.

GAULDIN, M. D. S9426, DY, 12th Inf.
GAULT, Mary Walter, W6317, WI, Gault, John M.
GAUSE, Adam Mary, W10342, HY, Gause, Fredrick Becoat
GAUT, Bettie Latimore, W9009, MO, Gaut, Rufus
GAYLER, James, S10266, C, 5th Bn. Ala. Cav.
GAYLOR, John L. S12317, WE, 12th Inf.
GEAGLEY, Hannah M. W6980, LO, Geagley, Henry
GEAN, Cheatham Catherine, W10869, WY, Gean, Wm. Henderson
GEAN, W. H. S9725, WY, 9th Bn. (Gantt's) Cav.
GEE, J. D. S10448, D, 6th (Wheeler's) Cav.
GEE, J. M. S6360, WI, 45th Inf.
GEE, James, S5317, RU, 1st (Feild's) Inf.
GEE, M. M. S9812, D, 6th (Wheeler's) Cav.
GEE, Mary Addie, W5454, D, Gee, Marcellus Madison
GEE, Qunitus R. S10036, D, 2nd Inf.
GEE, Sallie, W118, MA, Gee, George Washington
GEE, Sally Ann, W2349, WI, Gee, James Lucas
GEE, Susan A. W3176, WI, Gee, James Whitfield
GEE, T. A. S7738, RU, 8th (Dibrell's) Cav.
GEER, W. I. S2306, WH, 28th Inf.
GENNOE, Calvin, S8734, H, 43rd Inf.
GENNOE, Carrie, W9635, R, Gennoe, Hezekiah
GENNOE, Hezekiah, S14915, R, 43rd Inf.
GENTRY, Ann Catherine, W5322, D, Gentry, M. S.
GENTRY, Dorcus, W973, MC, Gentry, Gilbert
GENTRY, Frank, S6004, MO, 62nd Inf.
GENTRY, J. W. S11961, S10171, H, 8th Ga. Bn. Cav.
GENTRY, James, C154, MS, 17th Inf.
GENTRY, M. B. S706, PU, 25th Inf.
GENTRY, Mary Eliz. Rector, W8955, PU, Gentry, Isaac Easley
GENTRY, Mary Jane, W3122, WE, Gentry, Wm. Licurgus
GENTRY, Milam S. S10505, D, 5th S.C. Inf.
GENTRY, W. P. S11573, HI, 9th Bn. (Gantt's) Cav.
GENTRY, William T. S4151, CF, 4th (McLemore's) Cav.
GEORGE, A. Jack, S9124, LE, 10th (DeMoss') Cav.
GEORGE, A. Sinclair, S5235, HN, 14th Inf.

GEORGE, Alice, W5209, LE, George, Andrew J.
GEORGE, F. S14430, HI, 48th (Voorhies') Inf.
GEORGE, H. P. S16344, LI, 8th Inf.
GEORGE, Mary Ann, W1012, ME, George, John C.
GEORGE, Mollie H. W6724, SH, George, Thomas Fletcher
GEORGE, Permelia Burnham, W11167, WE, Burnham, John W.
GEORGE, Susan McLaughlin, W10138, LI, George, Henderson P.
GEORGE, T. F. S15052, SH, 32nd Inf.
GEORGE, W. H. S14480, S12753, S4851, WL, Allison's Squadron, Cav., Also #3030
GHALAN, Celia Frances, W5148, O, Ghalan, Wm.
GHORMLEY, W. G. S12135, MO, 3rd (Lillard's) Mtd. Inf.
GHORMLEY, W. H. S8706, H, 2nd Cav.
GIBBONS, C. C. S9700, DY, 18th Cav.
GIBBONS, Cynthia A. W9727, CC, Gibbons, H. F.
GIBBONS, H. F. S12684, CC, 20th (Nixon's) Cav.
GIBBONS, N. H. S202, HU, 42nd Inf.
GIBBONS, R. R. S14027, HU, 42nd Inf.
GIBBONS, Sarah Frances, W3061, HU, Gibbons, George Yarbrough
GIBBS, Ella Virginia, W5848, WE, Gibbs, Jesse Allen
GIBBS, Fred, S73, SM, 7th Inf.
GIBBS, T. H. S13967, ST, 14th Inf.
GIBBS, Tennessee, W1270, SM, Gibbs, Richard C.
GIBBS, Thomas S. S7282, WI, 1st (Carter's) Cav.
GIBSON, Allen, S3601, G, 13th Inf.
GIBSON, Ann Elizabeth, W5717, SU, Gibson, Andrew Jackson
GIBSON, B. F. S4611, WE, 5th Inf.
GIBSON, Elias P. S13126, MC, Winston's Co. Lt. Art.
GIBSON, Elizabeth, W7075, PU, Gibson, Joseph
GIBSON, F. P. S5421, HW, 22nd Va. Cav.
GIBSON, Frank T. S6335, FR, 17th Inf.
GIBSON, G. W. S14041, S14122, S15617, GI, 3rd (Clack's) Inf.
GIBSON, Hannah E. W2254, HR, Gibson, Stephen Hardy
GIBSON, Hettie, W5214, FR, Gibson, Wm. Carrell

GIBSON, J. H. S6034, MU, 28th Consolidated Inf.
GIBSON, J. L. S10710, BR, 39th N.C. Inf.
GIBSON, J. L. S11471, HR, 7th Miss. Cav.
GIBSON, J. T. S12185, HR, 14th (Neely's) Cav.
GIBSON, J. W. S12377, BE, 29th Tex. Cav.
GIBSON, Jerry, S11456, H, 57th N.C. Inf.
GIBSON, John, C274, HI, Regiment not given
GIBSON, Leaner, W7041, HA, Gibson, Richard
GIBSON, Lou, W10027, H, Gibson, Jeremiah
GIBSON, Lucy A. W6894, D, Gibson, Thomas
GIBSON, Lucy Ann, W2715, SH, Gibson, Henry Clay
GIBSON, Margaret E. W4590, CL, Gibson, Zachariah
GIBSON, Martha L. W5488, WE, Gibson, Benjamin Franklin
GIBSON, Mary D. W1603, MN, Gibson, Samuel R.
GIBSON, Mary E. W5844, Gibson, Albert
GIBSON, Mary F. W4735, MA, Gibson, Jesse T.
GIBSON, Partheia, W150, MN, Gibson, Lemuel J. A.
GIBSON, R. M. S7270, DI, 10th (DeMoss') Cav.
GIBSON, Richard, S14382, HA, 50th Va. Inf.
GIBSON, Rosa Lee, W9798, MO, Gibson, Joseph L.
GIBSON, S. R. S4528, MN, 1st Ala. Miss. & Tenn.
GIBSON, Sallie, W6920, HA, Gibson, John B.
GIBSON, T. F. S13992, MC, Unassigned (Iron Worker)
GIBSON, Thomas J. S10779, ME, 5th Cav.
GIBSON, Wesley, S7694, GI, 25th N.C. Inf.
GIBSON, William C. S1417, FR, 17th Inf.
GIBSON, William R. S11273, WE, 31st Inf.
GIDCOME, Thomas, S4389, MU, 6th (Wheeler's) Cav.
GIESLER, Nancy Ann, W3162, SU, Giesler, Henry
GIESLER, W. R. S8365, SU, 59th Inf.
GILBERT, A. J. S5581, CL, 63rd Inf.
GILBERT, Amanda J. W484, HW, Gilbert, Greene B.
GILBERT, Carrie W. W2203, Gilbert, James Monroe
GILBERT, George C. S9413, JO, 29th Inf.
GILBERT, Hester Anna, W5785, C, Gilbert, Jabas Onsby
GILBERT, India Phillip, W4624, GI, Gilbert, Edward

Index to Tennessee Confederate Pension Applications

GARY, Nancy Ann, W7091, DI, Gary, F. M.
GASKILL, Maud, W9566, MU, Gaskill, Thomas C.
GASKILL, Thomas Christopher, S14754, MU, 3rd Mo. Cav.
GASKINS, Thomas Green, S11889, WE, 15th Inf.
GASS, A. J. S9307, FR, 34th Ga. Inf.
GASTON, D. M. S14530, G, 27th Inf.
GATE, Mary Ellis, W1209, D, Gate, Wm. Dudley
GATELY, John H. S15599, 52nd Inf.
GATES, Frances T. W1865, K, Gates, John
GATES, Georgia A. W1071, MA, Gates, John W.
GATES, Mamie Long, W10018, SH, Gates, Wm. Beverly
GATES, Spencer C. S1880, MS, 17th Inf.
GATES, Thomas M. S11200, MA, 6th Inf.
GATES, William Ward, S12003, MA, 19th & 20th (Consolidated) Cav.
GATEWOOD, Emma F. W6405, DI, Gatewood, John F.
GATEWOOD, Wesly, C131, SH, 7th Miss. Inf.
GATHER, Elizabeth Ann, W1691, MU, Gather, James
GATHINGS, Frances Isabel, W3982, HE, Gathings, Milton Carmell
GATHINGS, Sarah Ann, W4963, HE, Gathings, Joseph John
GATLIN, Albert G. S12927, S11011, HR, 14th Cav.
GATLIN, Benjamin, S2775, D, 11th Cav.
GATLIN, Jacob, S11338, BR, 62nd Inf.
GATLIN, Lucy, W1184, WI, Gatlin, Benjamin Franklin
GATLIN, Mary E. W7969, BR, Gatlin, Jacob
GATLIN, Sarah A. W275, GI, Gatlin, Isaac Thomas
GATLING, J. J. S4873, DE, 18th (Newsom's) Cav.
GATTIS, Amanda H. W175, CH, Gattis, George Carson
GATTIS, Elizabeth, W6506, MOO, Gattis, Isaac Van Buren
GATTIS, I. V. S5949, MOO, 8th Inf.
GATTIS, Mary J. W709, FR, Gattis, Willis Moore
GATTISH, T. M. S13163, HD, 21st (Wilson's) Cav.
GATTON, Nancy E. W1103, WL, Gatton, Joseph W.

GAULDIN, M. D. S9426, DY, 12th Inf.
GAULT, Mary Walter, W6317, WI, Gault, John M.
GAUSE, Adam Mary, W10342, HY, Gause, Fredrick Becoat
GAUT, Bettie Latimore, W9009, MO, Gaut, Rufus
GAYLER, James, S10266, C, 5th Bn. Ala. Cav.
GAYLOR, John L. S12317, WE, 12th Inf.
GEAGLEY, Hannah M. W6980, LO, Geagley, Henry
GEAN, Cheatham Catherine, W10869, WY, Gean, Wm. Henderson
GEAN, W. H. S9725, WY, 9th Bn. (Gantt's) Cav.
GEE, J. D. S10448, D, 6th (Wheeler's) Cav.
GEE, J. M. S6360, WI, 45th Inf.
GEE, James, S5317, RU, 1st (Feild's) Inf.
GEE, M. M. S9812, D, 6th (Wheeler's) Cav.
GEE, Mary Addie, W5454, D, Gee, Marcellus Madison
GEE, Qunitus R. S10036, D, 2nd Inf.
GEE, Sallie, W118, MA, Gee, George Washington
GEE, Sally Ann, W2349, WI, Gee, James Lucas
GEE, Susan A. W3176, WI, Gee, James Whitfield
GEE, T. A. S7738, RU, 8th (Dibrell's) Cav.
GEER, W. I. S2306, WH, 28th Inf.
GENNOE, Calvin, S8734, H, 43rd Inf.
GENNOE, Carrie, W9635, R, Gennoe, Hezekiah
GENNOE, Hezekiah, S14915, R, 43rd Inf.
GENTRY, Ann Catherine, W5322, D, Gentry, M. S.
GENTRY, Dorcus, W973, MC, Gentry, Gilbert
GENTRY, Frank, S6004, MO, 62nd Inf.
GENTRY, J. W. S11961, S10171, H, 8th Ga. Bn. Cav.
GENTRY, James, C154, MS, 17th Inf.
GENTRY, M. B. S706, PU, 25th Inf.
GENTRY, Mary Eliz. Rector, W8955, PU, Gentry, Isaac Easley
GENTRY, Mary Jane, W3122, WE, Gentry, Wm. Licurgus
GENTRY, Milam S. S10505, D, 5th S.C. Inf.
GENTRY, W. P. S11573, HI, 9th Bn. (Gantt's) Cav.
GENTRY, William T. S4151, CF, 4th (McLemore's) Cav.
GEORGE, A. Jack, S9124, LE, 10th (DeMoss') Cav.
GEORGE, A. Sinclair, S5235, HN, 14th Inf.

GEORGE, Alice, W5209, LE, George, Andrew J.
GEORGE, F. S14430, HI, 48th (Voorhies') Inf.
GEORGE, H. P. S16344, LI, 8th Inf.
GEORGE, Mary Ann, W1012, ME, George, John C.
GEORGE, Mollie H. W6724, SH, George, Thomas Fletcher
GEORGE, Permelia Burnham, W11167, WE, Burnham, John W.
GEORGE, Susan McLaughlin, W10138, LI, George, Henderson P.
GEORGE, T. F. S15052, SH, 32nd Inf.
GEORGE, W. H. S14480, S12753, S4851, WL, Allison's Squadron, Cav., Also #3030
GHALAN, Celia Frances, W5148, O, Ghalan, Wm.
GHORMLEY, W. G. S12135, MO, 3rd (Lillard's) Mtd. Inf.
GHORMLEY, W. H. S8706, H, 2nd Cav.
GIBBONS, C. C. S9700, DY, 18th Cav.
GIBBONS, Cynthia A. W9727, CC, Gibbons, H. F.
GIBBONS, H. F. S12684, CC, 20th (Nixon's) Cav.
GIBBONS, N. H. S202, HU, 42nd Inf.
GIBBONS, R. R. S14027, HU, 42nd Inf.
GIBBONS, Sarah Frances, W3061, HU, Gibbons, George Yarbrough
GIBBS, Ella Virginia, W5848, WE, Gibbs, Jesse Allen
GIBBS, Fred, S73, SM, 7th Inf.
GIBBS, T. H. S13967, ST, 14th Inf.
GIBBS, Tennessee, W1270, SM, Gibbs, Richard C.
GIBBS, Thomas S. S7282, WI, 1st (Carter's) Cav.
GIBSON, Allen, S3601, G, 13th Inf.
GIBSON, Ann Elizabeth, W5717, SU, Gibson, Andrew Jackson
GIBSON, B. F. S4611, WE, 5th Inf.
GIBSON, Elias P. S13126, MC, Winston's Co. Lt. Art.
GIBSON, Elizabeth, W7075, PU, Gibson, Joseph
GIBSON, F. P. S5421, HW, 22nd Va. Cav.
GIBSON, Frank T. S6335, FR, 17th Inf.
GIBSON, G. W. S14041, S14122, S15617, GI, 3rd (Clack's) Inf.
GIBSON, Hannah E. W2254, HR, Gibson, Stephen Hardy
GIBSON, Hettie, W5214, FR, Gibson, Wm. Carrell
GIBSON, J. H. S6034, MU, 28th Consolidated Inf.
GIBSON, J. L. S10710, BR, 39th N.C. Inf.
GIBSON, J. L. S11471, HR, 7th Miss. Cav.
GIBSON, J. T. S12185, HR, 14th (Neely's) Cav.
GIBSON, J. W. S12377, BE, 29th Tex. Cav.
GIBSON, Jerry, S11456, H, 57th N.C. Inf.
GIBSON, John, C274, HI, Regiment not given
GIBSON, Leaner, W7041, HA, Gibson, Richard
GIBSON, Lou, W10027, H, Gibson, Jeremiah
GIBSON, Lucy A. W6894, D, Gibson, Thomas
GIBSON, Lucy Ann, W2715, SH, Gibson, Henry Clay
GIBSON, Margaret E. W4590, CL, Gibson, Zachariah
GIBSON, Martha L. W5488, WE, Gibson, Benjamin Franklin
GIBSON, Mary D. W1603, MN, Gibson, Samuel R.
GIBSON, Mary E. W5844, Gibson, Albert
GIBSON, Mary F. W4735, MA, Gibson, Jesse T.
GIBSON, Partheia, W150, MN, Gibson, Lemuel J. A.
GIBSON, R. M. S7270, DI, 10th (DeMoss') Cav.
GIBSON, Richard, S14382, HA, 50th Va. Inf.
GIBSON, Rosa Lee, W9798, MO, Gibson, Joseph L.
GIBSON, S. R. S4528, MN, 1st Ala. Miss. & Tenn.
GIBSON, Sallie, W6920, HA, Gibson, John B.
GIBSON, T. F. S13992, MC, Unassigned (Iron Worker)
GIBSON, Thomas J. S10779, ME, 5th Cav.
GIBSON, Wesley, S7694, GI, 25th N.C. Inf.
GIBSON, William C. S1417, FR, 17th Inf.
GIBSON, William R. S11273, WE, 31st Inf.
GIDCOME, Thomas, S4389, MU, 6th (Wheeler's) Cav.
GIESLER, Nancy Ann, W3162, SU, Giesler, Henry
GIESLER, W. R. S8365, SU, 59th Inf.
GILBERT, A. J. S5581, CL, 63rd Inf.
GILBERT, Amanda J. W484, HW, Gilbert, Greene B.
GILBERT, Carrie W. W2203, Gilbert, James Monroe
GILBERT, George C. S9413, JO, 29th Inf.
GILBERT, Hester Anna, W5785, C, Gilbert, Jabas Onsby
GILBERT, India Phillip, W4624, GI, Gilbert, Edward

Index to Tennessee Confederate Pension Applications

GILBERT, J. H. S5085, CO, 42nd Inf.
GILBERT, J. R. S1127, LO, 26th Inf.
GILBERT, Jabez O. S3203, C, 2nd Va. Cav.
GILBERT, John E. S10467, GI, 50th Ala. Inf.
GILBERT, Margaret Jane, W7235, LA, Gilbert, Wesley H.
GILBERT, R. M. S9179, WE, 7th (Duckworth's) Cav.
GILBERT, Sallie Finney, W6661, H, Gilbert, Stephen M.
GILBERT, Sarah Elizabeth, W1408, FR, Gilbert, Jesse Gilford
GILBERT, Tranguila R. W1150, MU, Gilbert, J. C.
GILBERT, W. W. S9392, MC, 1st N.C. Cav.
GILBERT, Wesley H. S1304, LA, 48th Inf.
GILBERT, William C. S358, DK, 1st Inf.
GILBERT, William M. S368, HA, 63rd Inf.
GILBREATH, J. A. S15484, MO, 62nd Inf.
GILBREATH, L. C. S3672, SE, 16th S.C. Inf.
GILBREATH, Thaney, W6267, SE, Gilbreath, L. C.
GILCHRIST, John M. S15090, S15369, MC, 21st (Wilson's) Cav.
GILES, C. Y. S10259, MA, 20th Inf.
GILES, D. N. S4442, SU, 59th Mtd. Inf.
GILES, Delia, W6018, RO, Giles, Lydney Lafayette
GILES, Dollie, W2190, MO, Giles, Reuben
GILES, J. F. S10822, HI, 4th (McLemore's) Cav.
GILES, J. M. S2418, RO, 54th N.C. Inf.
GILES, James Calvin, S5730, R, 43rd Inf.
GILES, John W. S13237, LA, 41st Ga. Inf.
GILES, Lula, W10377, WL, Giles, Paschal
GILES, Margaret Elln, W5786, CT, Giles, Wm. Harrison
GILES, Mary S. W10561, D, Giles, John F.
GILES, Nathaniel C. S10489, MA, 18th (Newsom's) Cav.
GILES, Olive, W6318, RO, Giles, James M.
GILES, Perin, S1310, CO, Undetermined
GILES, Ruffus, S10950, MO, 59th Inf.
GILES, Sarah Helan, W6888, MA, Giles, N. C.
GILES, Sarah Jane, W1077, WI, Giles, Thomas Perrin
GILES, Sidney L. S1479, A, 35th N.C. Inf.
GILES, W. H. S3156, CT, 26th Inf.
GILHAM, C. W. S10234, SH, 12th Cav.
GILL, A. B. S5527, WL, 24th Inf.
GILL, B. F. S9282, G, 154th Sr. Regt. Inf.
GILL, C. H. S11904, MT, 50th Inf.

GILL, Elizabeth P. W36, GR, Gill, Wm. T.
GILL, Ellen Arminta, W5973, T, Gill, Charlie Henry
GILL, J. D. S13013, DI, 48th (Nixon's) Inf.
GILL, John Young, S11301, D, 44th Inf.
GILL, Louisa Clinton, W10022, DI, Gill, John Wm.
GILL, Mary E. W2895, D, Gill, John Y.
GILL, Rebecca, W4226, HD, Gill, Wm. B.
GILL, W. T. S11014, MS, 4th (McLemore's) Cav.
GILLENWATER, James J. S11391, K, 6th Ga. Cav.
GILLESPIE, Addie Newman, W5142, LI, Gillespie, John Field
GILLESPIE, Catherine Pickett, W10950, T, Gillespie, Green Berry
GILLESPIE, Dora, W10554, FR, Gillespie, Richard Johnson
GILLESPIE, Eliza Watkins, W4754, SN, Gillespie, J. C.
GILLESPIE, Green Berry, S16584, T, 1st Ga. Cav.
GILLESPIE, James, S7128, SM, 7th Inf.
GILLESPIE, James, S8290, K, 8th Cav.
GILLESPIE, James S. S11522, MT, 24th Inf.
GILLESPIE, Jessie C. S11822, SN, 7th Inf.
GILLESPIE, M. H. S7812, K, 11th Cav.
GILLESPIE, Margaret, W4990, SM, Gillespie, James
GILLESPIE, Nancy J. W7415, K, Gillespie, M. H.
GILLESPIE, Sallie Hannah, W6283, LI, Gillespie, George Carmack
GILLESPY, Nancy Adaline, W537, BO, Gillespy, Samuel T.
GILLEY, Elizabeth, W6284, CF, Gilley, J. H.
GILLEY, James Harvey, S9570, CA, 8th (Smith's) Cav.
GILLEY, Martha Ann Eliz. W1723, CA, Gilley, John W.
GILLIAM, Amanda Jane, W7292, HE, Gilliam, James Harvey
GILLIAM, David M. S. S7589, SN, 20th Inf.
GILLIAM, J. H. S14496, HE, 51st Inf.
GILLIAM, J. M. S3537, HY, 12th Cav.
GILLIAM, Jessup, S4846, FR, 24th Inf.
GILLIAM, Josephine, W8949, GU, Gilliam, Wm.
GILLIAM, Lucy Ann, W4141, HY, Gilliam, Alonzo P.

GILLIAM, Lucy S. W1717, SN, Gilliam, David M. S.
GILLIAM, Marcus Austin, S9744, M, 9th (Ward's) Cav.
GILLIAM, Millie A. W7545, SN, Gilliam, W. B.
GILLIAM, N. C. S4137, MU, 6th (Wheeler's) Cav.
GILLIAM, Nancy Ellen, W3856, D, Gilliam, Wm. H.
GILLIAM, Nancy J. W933, MU, Gilliam, James M.
GILLIAM, Nancy Jane, W4168, WE, Gilliam, Willis Nelson
GILLIAM, Robert, C185, SH, Undetermined
GILLIAM, Sam, S15612, GU, 28th Cav.
GILLIAM, Samuel N. S7995, MR, 4th Inf.
GILLIAM, Thomas Jefferson, S12904, MU, 48th (Voorhies') Inf.
GILLIAM, W. B. S3695, SN, 20th Inf.
GILLIAM, William, S13490, GU, 4th Inf.
GILLIAM, Willis N. S9, WE, 31st Inf.
GILLIAND, Frank, S11317, S14673, OV, 8th (Dibrell's) Cav.
GILLIAND, James A. S8414, G, 30th Inf.
GILLILAND, Sallie L. W7451, G, Gilliland, James A.
GILLMORE, S. G. S5688, G, 11th Bn. (Gordon's) Cav.
GILLOCK, James W. S9766, DI, 6th Ky. Mtd. Inf.
GILLOCK, Susan Matilda, W9161, DI, Gillock, James Worton
GILLOOLEY, Frank, S3295, SH, Unassigned
GILLUM, J. H. S14870, CA, 8th (Smith's) Cav.
GILLUM, Martha Alice, W9461, CA, Gillum, J. Henry
GILLUM, Martha V. W2462, ST, Gillum, John R.
GILLUM, William D. S5264, MS, 41st Inf.
GILMAN, Cornelius P. S9173, DY, 10th Bn. Va. Art.
GILMAN, Mary Elizabeth, W2850, D, Gilman, Joseph Warren
GILMAN, Sophia H. W8085, DY, Gilman, Cornelius Pleasant
GILMORE, Annie HIx, W9046, B, Gilmore, Grandison
GILMORE, M. S. S9313, B, 18th Inf.
GILMORE, Mattie H. W4921, SH, Gilmore, Nathaniel Alston
GILMORE, Nannie J. W9549, RU, Gilmore, M. S.
GILMORE, Permelia E. W3718, LA, Gilmore, James M.
GILMORE, W. H. S7856, G, 23rd Inf.
GILMORE, William C. S5070, WL, 45th Inf.
GILPIN, B. F. S1564, T, 21st Cav.
GILPIN, John W. S1565, T, 21st Cav.
GILROY, Barney, S26, SH, 6th Inf.
GIPSON, Amanda, W4208, HA, Gipson, Jarvis
GIPSON, Emily, W815, J, Gipson, Lycurgus M.
GIPSON, Jarvis, S9141, HW, 50th Va. Inf.
GIPSON, John B. S2633, HA, 64th Va. Inf.
GIPSON, Joseph, S797, J, 4th Cav.
GIRTMAN, Nick, S13981, SU, 26th Inf.
GIST, Mary Jane, W124, WH, Gist, Vance Carrick
GIST, Nancy, W1944, CU, Gist, John
GIVAN, J. D. S7907, DK, 23rd Inf.
GIVENS, F. M. S14723, O, 19th (Biffle's) Cav.
GIVENS, George W. S8969, MA, 14th Cav.
GIVENS, R. S. S3373, S5528, HN, 20th Inf.
GIVENS, Sarah E. W3294, MA, Givens, George W.
GIVENS, Sarah F. W8648, DK, Givens, Thomas
GIVENS, Thomas, S15920, DK, 23rd Inf.
GIVIN, Alice Madera, W6435, Givin, John Elias
GLADDEN, A. C. S5697, T, 12th Cav.
GLADDEN, Bettie, W10479, P, Gladden, Felix Madison
GLADISH, W. J. S15384, H, 26th La. Inf.
GLADNEY, J. A. S13709, MA, 14th (Neely's) Cav.
GLASCO, Sandy C. S7318, GI, 1st Cav.
GLASGOW, Cynthia Elizabeth, W7933, O, Glasgow, John Mason
GLASGOW, John M. S10563, O, 20th (Russell's) Cav.
GLASGOW, John W. S7, D, 2nd Inf.
GLASGOW, L. A. S118, D, 14th Inf.
GLASGOW, Mary Blanchard, W788, SH, Glasgow, John W.
GLASS, Alexander, S748, CU, 22nd N.C. Inf.
GLASS, J. C. S11881, S13007, O, 7th (Duckworth's) Cav.
GLASS, J. K. S9298, T, 1st Hvy. Art.
GLASS, John E. S13599, MA, 51st Inf.
GLASS, John M. S16384, WE, 20th (Hollis') Cav.
GLASS, Piety Ann, W8339, LA, Glass, Thomas Jefferson
GLASS, Sue A. W5512, MA, Glass, John E.
GLASS, T. J. S9393, LA, 20th Cav.

GLASSCOCK, Easter, W5104, OV, Glasscock, John J.
GLASSCOCK, J. J. S4393, OV, 4th (Murray's) Cav.
GLAZE, Martha Ophelia, W10312, GI, Glaze, Andrew Louis
GLAZE, Tennessee Mildred, W58, GI, Glaze, Monroe Jepthy
GLEAVES, Deliah Baker, W2937, D, Gleaves, Wm. Carrel
GLEAVES, George W. S13937, D, 1st (Feild's) Inf.
GLEAVES, James T. S16186, D, 9th Ky. Cav.
GLEAVES, Josephine, W9294, HD, Gleaves, Felix
GLEAVES, Mollie Payne, W10010, D, Gleaves, Jackson M.
GLEAVES, W. C. S6609, D, 30th Inf.
GLEAVES, W. M. S11953, D, 18th Inf.
GLEEN, Alexander, S3807, WH, 16th Inf.
GLENN, Benjamin, S2588, UN, 30th Bn. Va. Sharpshooters
GLENN, C. C. L. S186, MS, 17th Inf.
GLENN, D. W. S7544, RU, 11th (Holman's) Cav.
GLENN, Elizabeth, W2147, WL, Glenn, Sanderson
GLENN, G. W. S3241, LI, 32nd Inf.
GLENN, George C. S7971, MS, 41st Inf.
GLENN, J. T. S13787, MS, 11th Cav.
GLENN, J. W. S15070, S8848, CC, 16th Ala. Inf.
GLENN, James M. S2486, MS, 18th (Newsom's) Cav.
GLENN, L. C. S3524, MS, 17th Inf.
GLENN, Lucy Ann, W287, MS, Glenn, Lorenzo Clark
GLENN, Lucy Randolph, W11004, W10002, WL, Glenn, Daniel Webster
GLENN, Margaret E. W1596, MS, Glenn, James Henry
GLENN, Martha E. W2758, MS, Glenn, C. C. L.
GLENN, Newton C. S5013, L, 7th Cav.
GLENN, Patrick, S9716, HU, 11th Inf.
GLENN, Sanderson, S2417, WL, 45th Inf.
GLENN, Sarah Ann, W8802, MS, Glenn, Robert N.
GLENN, Sarah Catherine, W3922, LI, Glenn, George Whitfield
GLENN, T. S. S10720, SN, 2nd (Robison's) Inf.
GLENN, Thomas M. S8490, MU, 1st Cav.

GLENN, Virginia Exim, W5208, WI, Glenn, R. C.
GLIDEWELL, Timothy, S5850, HR, 14th (Neely's) Cav.
GLIDEWELL, William Lafayette, S10476, DY, 26th Miss. Inf.
GLIMP, John A. S11724, S1385, L, 1st Cav.
GLOSSUP, James H. S7644, GI, 37th Inf.
GLOVER, B. F. S12280, K, Home Guards
GLOVER, Fannie, W7338, O, Glover, Joshua Perry
GLOVER, Francis M. S15270, CT, 59th Mtd. Inf.
GLOVER, George Clinton, S13811, RB, 30th Inf.
GLOVER, Henry C. S5791, SU, 4th Cav.
GLOVER, I. L. S4715, SN, 44th Inf.
GLOVER, J. F. S7784, HD, Williams' Regt. Art.
GLOVER, John, S2844, SU, 4th Cav.
GLOVER, John W. S12243, GI, 1st Inf.
GLOVER, Julia Belle, W10500, HD, Glover, John F.
GLOVER, Katherine, W7513, SU, Glover, Henry Clay
GLOVER, Mary A. W7558, CT, Glover, Francis M.
GLOVER, Mary Ellen, W4736, SU, Glover, Samuel
GLOVER, Nancy, W5877, SM, Glover, Newton H.
GLOVER, Newton H. S10925, SM, 28th Inf.
GLOVER, Sallie E. W9702, D, Glover, Ira Levy
GLOVER, Samuel, S12203, SU, 61st Inf.
GLOVER, Sarah, W6226, SU, Glover, John
GLOVER, Susie, W10611, G, Glover, James Raleigh
GLOVER, W. A. S12598, S6748, HN, 46th Inf
GLOVER, William, S4748, SU, 20th Inf.
GLYMP, John H. See John Glimp
GLYMP, Marthy Madora, W848, RU, Glymp, John Henry
GOAD, C. E. S13638, SM, 28th Inf.
GOAD, J. C. S6649, MU, Maury's Lt. Art.
GOAD, Joshua, S5437, SM, 24th Inf.
GOAD, Margaret Ann, W4097, D, Goad, Willis Washington
GOAD, Mary Ann, W1019, MU, Goad, James Reison
GOAD, Mary C. W9676, WE, Goad, James Edward
GOAD, Virginia, W92, SM, Goad, Jefferson
GOAD, W. H. S10267, LA, 54th Inf.

Index to Tennessee Confederate Pension Applications

GOANS, A. T. S2936, A, 22nd (Barteau's) Cav.
GOANS, Arin W. S12546, A, 2nd (Ashby's) Cav.
GOANS, F. W. S3493, K, 8th (Smith's) Cav.
GOBBLE, C. B. S5605, WA, 22nd Va. Cav.
GOBER, Elizabeth, W9320, H, Gober, Dempsey Conner
GOBER, Silas, C140, F, 3rd Cav.
GOBLE, Simon P. S5014, L, 7th Ala. Cav.
GODSEY, Clementine, W5559, SU, Godsey, Jackson
GODSEY, D. G. S2164, T, 5th Cav.
GODSEY, Hamilton, S1696, SU, 63rd Inf.
GODSEY, Jackson, S10362, SU, 63rd Inf.
GODSEY, John H. S14808, HR, 7th Miss. Cav.
GODSEY, Margaret E. W4908, F, Godsey, Daniel G.
GODSEY, Mary Catharine, W4631, SU, Godsey, Alexander Hamilton
GODWIN, Calvin T. S450, HD, 52nd Inf.
GODWIN, Ida, W2032, JE, Godwin, John W.
GODWIN, Mary D. W2415, DI, Godwin, George M. Between 450 and 451 on Soldiers' Film
GODWIN, Susan, W4017, GR, Godwin, John P.
GOENS, John C. S13295, L, 5th Ala. Bn. Inf.
GOFORTH, Dan B. S5717, PO, 29th Inf.
GOFORTH, Fannie, W3242, BO, Goforth, George W.
GOFORTH, G. W. S6272, MC, 3rd (Lillard's) Mtd. Inf.
GOFORTH, George W. S6319, BO, 31st Inf.
GOFORTH, James H. S6404, MO, 3rd Inf.
GOFORTH, Mary Elizabeth, W6776, PO, Goforth, John G.
GOFORTH, N. B. S2902, MC, 31st Inf.
GOFORTH, Nancy Carline, W4020, PO, Goforth, Daniel Boon
GOFORTH, Rebecca Adaline, W1488, MC, Goforth, Napoleon Bonapart
GOIN, John, S4518, CL, 37th Inf.
GOIN, Rhoda Elizabeth, W7958, L, Goin, John Callioner
GOINS, Alfred, S10394, HD, 4th Ala. Cav.
GOINS, Elizabeth, W8435, HA, Goins, Sam
GOINS, G. W. S8686, GR, 26th Inf.
GOINS, John, S10879, S13379, BR, Thomas' Legion, N.C.
GOINS, Liddie J. W4066, GR, Goins, George W.
GOINS, Manda Jane, W6247, BR, Goins, John
GOINS, Samuel, S6598, HA, 29th Inf.
GOINS, Thankful Talitha, W4300, HI, Goins, Jordan R.
GOLD, J. E. S15921, SM, 24th Inf.
GOLD, Laurie Alice, W7860, WA, Gold, Sylvanus Hill
GOLD, S. H. S11044, S5044, WA, 1st N.C. Cav.
GOLDBAUM, Rosina, W6812, SH, Goldbaum, Morris
GOLDEN, J. J. S14519, LI, 8th Ala. Cav.
GOLDEN, James, S3048, MOO, 17th Inf.
GOLDEN, Loula, W10733, L, Golden, Richard G.
GOLDEN, Sarah A. W6266, LI, Golden, John J.
GOLDMAN, Joe, S2259, GI, 3rd Inf.
GOLDMAN, Mary Emely, W4469, GI, Goldman, Joe
GOOCH, Allice E. W5260, RB, Gooch, J. W. M.
GOOCH, Ann E. W4768, MN, Gooch, Jesse
GOOCH, B. L. S14462, K, 10th Ky. Cav.
GOOCH, Cordelia White, W6867, MA, Gooch, James C.
GOOCH, Gillie P. W6754, K, Gooch, Bartlett L.
GOOCH, J. T. S10827, RU, 7th Bn. Ala. Cav.
GOOCH, James, C240, C259, D, 4th (McLemore's) Cav.
GOOCH, Jesse, S4585, MN, 1st Ala. Miss. & Tenn. Inf.
GOOCH, John Y. S9198, GI, 32nd Inf.
GOOCH, M. A. S4158, WH, 28th (Consolidated) Inf.
GOOCH, Margaret R. W8109, D, Gooch, Nathaniel
GOOCH, Martha Jane, W2050, HY, Gooch, John Claiborne
GOOCH, Mary E. W4115, WI, Gooch, Allen G.
GOOCH, R. B. S12552, LA, 16th Ala. Inf.
GOOCH, S. K. S9614, GI, 1st (Feild's) Inf.
GOOCH, Willim R. S4856, 5th Inf.
GOOD, A. C. S12627, RU, 8th (Smith's) Cav.
GOOD, Angelina, W3340, CA, Good, Wm. Henry
GOOD, Italy, W, Some papers with #11183 on film
GOOD, Lafayette, S9010, HA, 64th Va. Inf.
GOOD, Martin S. S10545, SU, 61st Inf.
GOOD, T. H. C. S3708, MN, 27th Inf.
GOOD, William H. S496, H, 43rd Inf.
GOODEN, A. J. S5499, LO, 63rd Inf.
GOODIN, B. A. S3826, HN, 5th Inf.
GOODLETT, Eliza Jane, W7497, SH, Goodlett, Robert Spartan

Index to Tennessee Confederate Pension Applications

GOODLETT, Robert S. S6711, SH, 4th Ark. Inf.
GOODLIN, Mary, W9186, K, Goodlin, Napoleon Alexander
GOODLOE, Eugenia Crocker, W4593, D, Goodloe, Bennett Rucker
GOODLOE, J. C. S15704, RU, 4th Ala. Cav.
GOODLOE, Mary E. W10071, MU, Goodloe, John P.
GOODLOE, W. H. S15498, D, 11th Ala. Cav.
GOODMAN, A. C. S2954, GE, 46th N.C. Inf.
GOODMAN, D. L. S14724, P, 19th (Biffle's) Cav.
GOODMAN, G. W. S1399, WA, 60th Inf.
GOODMAN, J. L. S13353, BE, 23rd Inf.
GOODMAN, John, S16222, S15887, O, 3rd Cav.
GOODMAN, John A. S6314, SU, 26th Inf.
GOODMAN, Mary, W5299, GE, Goodman, Aaron Columbus
GOODMAN, Terrell R. S1219, LA, 53rd Inf.
GOODMAN, l. M. W1314, K, Goodman, Solomon P.
GOODNER, Mattie, W10322, DK, Goodner, Thomas Wesley
GOODRICH, D. H. S15328, HU, 2nd Mo. State Guards
GOODRICH, G. W. S5149, R, 1st (Feild's) Inf.
GOODRICH, J. P. S4901, DI, 49th Inf.
GOODRICH, John T. S15056, LI, 10th & 11th (Consolidated) Cav.
GOODRICH, M. B. S8764, D, 8th (Smith's) Cav.
GOODRICH, Martha Ann, W877, MA, Goodrich, George P.
GOODRICH, Mary Landers, W7908, LI, Goodrich, John T.
GOODRICH, R. C. S6412, SH, 1st Miss. Inf.
GOODRICH, Sallie C. W9234, HU, Goodrich, D. H.
GOODRICH, Tennessee White, W3886, H, Goodrich, George Washington
GOODRUM, Harrison, S1323, 53rd Inf.
GOODRUM, James L. S1753, B, 23rd Inf.
GOODRUM, Matilda Ann, W5708, D, Goodrum, James L.
GOODSON, C. S3264, W, 25th Inf.
GOODSON, Cyrus R. S485, HW, 37th Va. Inf.
GOODSON, Lucinda, W2090, RB, Goodson, Thomas R.
GOODSON, S. S12487, H, 5th La. Inf.
GOODSON, Thomas R. S1130, GE, 25th Inf.
GOODSON, Thomas R. S1691, W, 25th Inf.

GOODWIN, Edward P. S6339, HD, 52nd Inf.
GOODWIN, J. A. S11482, D, 18th Inf.
GOODWIN, Jane, W2024, D, Goodwin, Robert
GOODWIN, Margaret, W7040, D, Goodwin, Wm. Thomas
GOODWIN, Texas Frost, W2735, DY, Goodwin, C. W. Applied from Limestone Co. Ala.
GOODWIN, W. A. S10714, MA, 21st (Wilson's) Cav.
GOODWIN, William, S13903, S13391, WH, 25th Inf.
GOODWIN, William T. S10119, D, 6th (Wheeler's) Cav.
GOODWYN, John Hudson, S13602, WE, 1st S.C. Inf.
GOOKIN, Charles, S523, WA, 4th Ala. Inf.
GOOLSBY, W. F. S9371, PU, 19th Va. Inf.
GOOLSBY, William Edward, S5346, K, 21st N.C. Inf.
GOOSTREE, T. J. S4911, SN, 30th Inf.
GORDON, Andrew R. S12838, MS, 11th (Holman's) Cav.
GORDON, Charley E. S860, S11411, WY, 48th (Nixon's) Inf.
GORDON, David Leonidas, S16494, GI, 9th Cav.
GORDON, Fannie A. W3494, MU, Gordon, John C.
GORDON, James Payne, S13024, MU, 2nd (Robison's) Inf.
GORDON, Jesse B. S317, B, 2nd Inf.
GORDON, John C. S15563, SH, Nelson's Ala. Lt. Art.
GORDON, Joshua, S5219, BR, 5th Cav.
GORDON, Lucy Jane, W6466, MU, Gordon, James Payne
GORDON, M. B. L. S2793, GI, 11th Cav.
GORDON, Mary Camp, W10065, MU, Gordon, Richard Cross
GORDON, Mary L. W3425, H, Gordon, Cicero Newton
GORDON, Matilda Margruda, W9363, MU, Gordon, Wm. Bradshaw
GORDON, Nancy, W10519, MU, Gordon, Nathan
GORDON, Nathan, C53, MU, 11th Cav.
GORDON, Queen Victory, W6352, BR, Gordon, Joshua
GORDON, Sarah, W45, B, Gordon, John Polk
GORDON, Vandy E. W46, B, Gordon, Jessie Bird

GORE, Elisha, S5925, FR, 9th Ky. Inf.
GORE, F. M. S2024, OV, 4th Cav.
GORE, Henry, C132, D, 8th Cav.
GORE, Isaac, S12910, OV, 25th Inf.
GORE, J. G. S2365, MOO, 34th Inf.
GORE, J. T. S1006, OV, 28th Inf.
GORE, Martha, W10186, OV, Gore, Isaac
GORE, Pattie J. W10055, DY, Gore, Wm. John
GORE, Sarah Ann Margaret, W2468, HN, Gore, J. D.
GORE, Sarah M. W8803, MOO, Gore, Hezekiah
GORHAM, R. T. S16321, S16382, ST, 1st & 2nd Ky. Cav.
GORMAN, E. W. S3617, SH, 13th Inf.
GORRELL, E. S2506, CO, 16th Bn. (Neal's) Cav.
GORRELL, William N. S7087, CO, 5th (McKenzie's) Cav.
GORSUCH, Walter, S12525, SH, 11th Ala. Cav.
GOSLIN, Lafayette A. S342, MU, 33rd N.C. State Troops
GOSNALD, Nannie F. W4218, GE, Gosnald, James Elbert
GOSNELL, Amanda Josephine, W8959, GI, Gosnell, George Washington
GOSNOLD, J. E. S2101, GE, 29th Inf.
GOSS, Henderson, S4808, T, 51st Inf.
GOSS, John, S12205, T, 7th Cav.
GOSSAGE, T. J. S9335, D, 17th Inf.
GOSSETT, Amanda C. W2985, HN, Gossett, Wm. Richard
GOSSETT, D. A. S10889, BE, 5th Inf.
GOSSETT, Elizabeth Virginia, W7828, BE, Gossett, David Alexander
GOSSETT, Jack, S9908, SN, 30th Inf.
GOSSETT, Louisa, W2368, BE, Gossett, Abr. Miles Colwell
GOTHARD, Henry, S2220, BR, 16th Bn. (Neal's) Cav.
GOUDLING, B. L. S15460, H, 1st Ga. Inf.
GOUGE, Sarah, W3287, CT, Gouge, Edmond, Applied from Mitchell Co. N.C.
GOULDING, Sarah V. W5184, SU, Goulding, Theodore P.
GOULDMAN, John M. S5039, GI, 55th Va. Inf.
GOURLEY, Lisa, W1384, ME, Gourley, John
GOURLEY, Mary L. W1637, SN, Gourley, James Robert
GOURLY, Eveline, W608, SN, Gourly, James F.
GOW, Clairsa, W8368, J, Gow, John A.
GOWAN, Richard W. S10564, K, 42nd N.C. Troops

GOWEN, William Franklin, S9109, SH, 13th Inf.
GRABLE, D. F. S13531, B, 17th Inf.
GRACE, Susan A. W8090, LI, Grace, Thomas
GRACEY, Altie, W3737, PU, Gracey, Crockett Dibrell
GRACEY, W. B. S12973, MU, 6th (Wheeler's) Cav.
GRACY, A. E. W5000, HI, Gracy, James S.
GRACY, Andrew R. S9905, HI, 9th Bn. (Gantt's) Cav.
GRACY, Henrietta C. W4649, HI, Gracy, Andrew Bud
GRACY, Susan, W900, L, Gracy, Wm. Lattemore
GRADY, A. W. S749, SH, 12th Cav.
GRADY, J. N. S14864, SH, 3rd (Lillard's) Mtd. Inf.
GRADY, John, S9829, R, 59th Inf.
GRADY, Sarah, W8643, G, Grady, Joseph Turner
GRAGG, Iola S. W6298, SH, Gragg, Wm. Henry
GRAGG, W. H. S14000, SH, 12th Cav.
GRAGSON, G. W. S3437, DK, 7th Inf.
GRAHAM, Albert K. S6490, SH, 7th Cav.
GRAHAM, C. C. S12040, CU, 40th Ala. Inf.
GRAHAM, Carrie Almire, W6719, H, Graham, John Alexander
GRAHAM, David, S12553, SU, 21st Va. Cav.
GRAHAM, Eliakim G. S2053, GE, 16th Bn. (Neal's) Cav.
GRAHAM, Elmira Jane, W2560, F, Graham, Walter Scott
GRAHAM, Frances Stegall, W9964, WI, Graham, Wm. Henry
GRAHAM, H. C. S11438, ST, 50th Inf.
GRAHAM, Henrietta Josephine, W5119, CU, Graham, Christopher Columbus
GRAHAM, Isham F. S10460, MN, 41st Ala. Inf.
GRAHAM, J. S. S14725, WY, 19th (Biffle's) Cav.
GRAHAM, James D. S2400, DY, 31st Inf.
GRAHAM, Jonathan T. S1674, HW, 37th Va. Inf.
GRAHAM, Mack. S14940, R, 6th N.C. Inf.
GRAHAM, Martha Organ, W6473, MN, Graham, Isom Franklin
GRAHAM, Mary Love, W1300, MA, Graham, James Douglass
GRAHAM, R. S6448, ME, 2nd (Ashby's) Cav.
GRAHAM, R. M. S12469, HR, 63rd Inf.

Index to Tennessee Confederate Pension Applications

GRAHAM, R. M. S16396, D, 1st E. Tenn. Cav.
GRAHAM, Robert M. S3720, CA, 18th Inf.
GRAHAM, Sarah Catharine, W5200, HR, Graham, Robert Matthew
GRAHAM, Susie C. W8447, MR, Graham, Thomas Newell
GRAHAM, W. A. S1883, PU, 16th Cav.
GRAHAM, W. M. S4547, MN, 31st Inf.
GRAHAM, W. M. S13018, LI, 34th Inf.
GRAHAM, W. R. S3515, A, Undetermined
GRAHAM, William, S4510, CU, 40th Ala. Inf.
GRAHAM, William, S11543, MR, 55th Ala. Inf.
GRAHAM, William H. S10310, RU, 45th Inf.
GRAIG, James Polk, S3227, HR, 11th Inf.
GRAINGER, Gervis D. S2730, SN, 6th Ky. Inf.
GRAINGER, John T. S6749, HN, 7th Cav.
GRAINGER, Ora Walton, W3755, SN, Grainger, G. D.
GRAMMAR, Milford, S4912, MOO, 17th (Newman's) Inf.
GRAMMER, Benjamin F. S10338, L, 36th Ark. Inf.
GRAMMER, George A. S3115, LI, Swett's Miss. Battery
GRAMMER, John, S2163, MOO, 9th Ky. Inf.
GRAMMER, Mary Ann, W6798, MOO, Grammer, John
GRAMMER, Mary E. W4181, MA, Grammer, George Albert
GRAMMER, Sophia, W9321, FR, Grammer, James M.
GRANGER, John Giles, S10506, HR, 6th Inf.
GRANT, Dave, S15805, SU, 2nd Cav.
GRANT, Frances, W9681, JO, Grant, Hugh Tolliver
GRANT, James Z. S13713, MT, 49th Inf.
GRANT, John B. S16417, FR, 17th Inf.
GRANT, Joseph C. S4491, FR, 17th Inf.
GRANT, Mary, W8149, JO, Grant, Park S.
GRANT, Susan Ann, W10399, MG, Grant, Thomas V.
GRANT, T. H. S4268, FR, 17th Inf.
GRANT, T. J, S6418, H, 17th Inf.
GRANT, Thomas, S14616, MG, 25th N.C. Inf.
GRANT, W. J. S5338, MT, 49th Inf.
GRANT, William, S14035, CC, 9th Inf.
GRANT, William (Sandy), S13176, SM, 9th (Ward's) Cav.
GRANT, William Thomas, S11725, T, 5th S.C. Inf.
GRANTHAM, James H. S8305, MN, 18th Cav.
GRANTHAM, Louis, S13795, D, 24th Inf.

GRAVES, See also Groves
GRAVES, Alfred, S34, MR, 26th Inf.
GRAVES, B. H. S1242, D, 24th Inf.
GRAVES, C. C. S5015, LI, 28th N.C. Inf.
GRAVES, G. J. S745, SN, 20th Inf.
GRAVES, Hannah Emeline, W2351, HU, Graves, Thomas Jefferson
GRAVES, Henry E. S13374, D, 20th Inf.
GRAVES, J. B. S11909, BR, 43rd Inf.
GRAVES, J. E. S13471, D, 9th (Ward's) Cav.
GRAVES, Jason P. S12599, HM, 61st Inf.
GRAVES, John L. S15221, MO, 7th Bn. N.C. Cav.
GRAVES, Julia E. W9296, D, Graves, Henry E.
GRAVES, Mark, S9686, 12th Inf.
GRAVES, Mary F. W8300, D, Graves, S. W.
GRAVES, Mary Jane, W3005, D, Graves, Lorenzo John
GRAVES, Melvina, W10315, GI, Graves, Nathaniel Basil
GRAVES, N. T. B. S3568, GI, 32nd Inf.
GRAVES, Nancy Jane, W7531, HR, Graves, John G.
GRAVES, S. S11403, WL, 7th Inf.
GRAVES, Sallie Frances, W4893, HY, Graves, James Edwards
GRAY, A. J. S15753, D, 45th Inf.
GRAY, Albert, C224, HI, 24th Inf.
GRAY, Alice, W6658, SH, Gray, Wm. Stewart
GRAY, B. B. S7212, G, 19th & 20th (Consolidated) Cav.
GRAY, B. E. S8374, D, 17th Miss. Inf.
GRAY, B. F. S10747, O, 9th Ala. Inf.
GRAY, D. S1372, MN, 26th Miss. Inf.
GRAY, Darthula, W2263, SU, Gray, J. F.
GRAY, Dock, C218, HI, Undetermined
GRAY, E. H. S11349, SU, 63rd Inf.
GRAY, Edmon, S318, 23rd Inf.
GRAY, Elizabeth, W2459, SU, Gray, J. S.
GRAY, Elizabeth, W4042, CO, Gray, Tillman
GRAY, Elizabeth Catharine, W10385, WA, Gray, Nelson Anderson
GRAY, Elizabeth M. W493, LI, Gray, Joseph W. N.
GRAY, Fielding W. S4495, H, Berry's Co. Lookout Art.
GRAY, Frances Josephine, W9791, H, Gray, Wm.
GRAY, G. W. S2767, CL, Ramsey's Battery, Art.
GRAY, H. P. S15539, G, 41st Ala. Inf.
GRAY, Harrison, S6224, CO, 62nd Inf.

-135

GRAY, Henry Anderson, S583, H, 19th Inf.
GRAY, Hosea M. S13835, B, 17th Va. Cav.
GRAY, J. F. S6846, SU, 25th Va. Cav.
GRAY, J. H. S9509, T, 4th Inf.
GRAY, J. W. S4102, SN, 7th Inf.
GRAY, James, S5407, WL, 45th Inf.
GRAY, James, S10166, SU, 60th Inf.
GRAY, James H. S16623, WA, 22nd Va. Cav.
GRAY, James P. S15595, SH, 51st Inf.
GRAY, James T. S11355, LI, 44th Inf.
GRAY, Jesse, S14351, HW, 60th Inf.
GRAY, John, S1333, S14249, WA, 60th Inf.
GRAY, John, S8597, T, 23rd Miss. Inf.
GRAY, John S. S9377, SU, 60th Inf.
GRAY, John Saml. Alexander, S12519, MU, 9th Bn. (Gantt's) Cav.
GRAY, John W. S3242, T, 45th Inf.
GRAY, John Wesley, S6857, N, 3rd (Forrest's) Cav.
GRAY, Joseph, S10856, WA, 2nd Ark. Mtd. Rifles, Cav.
GRAY, Joseph A. S13555, SU, 2nd (Ashby's) Cav.
GRAY, Joseph R. S8025, SU, 1st (Carter's) Cav.
GRAY, Josephine, W7574, WA, Gray, Joshua
GRAY, Joshua, S1925, WA, 60th Inf.
GRAY, Lida W. W9985, CA, Gray, Wiley W.
GRAY, Louisa Clarina, W9758, O, Gray, Joseph Henry
GRAY, Lucy Ann, W2078, SN, Gray, James Wesley
GRAY, Lucy Ellen, W8223, K, Gray, Francis Marion
GRAY, Margaret, W1818, D, Gray, James
GRAY, Marget, W3141, HD, Gray, Luther
GRAY, Mariah Elizabeth, W8720, SU, Gray, E. H.
GRAY, Martha A. W329, GR, Gray, Pleasant J.
GRAY, Mary, W4182, MT, Gray, John Joseph
GRAY, Mary A. W4723, SN, Gray, James Franklin
GRAY, Mattie Elizabeth, W4028, D, Gray, Frank F.
GRAY, Nelson A. S11584, WA, 29th Inf.
GRAY, Pinkney C. S12108, MU, 19th (Biffle's) Cav.
GRAY, Rebecca C. W8466, ST, Gray, Andrew Jackson
GRAY, Sallie Catherine, W6527, SU, Gray, Moses
GRAY, Sallie Glenn, W6639, SU, Gray, Joseph Alexander

GRAY, Sarah Almedia, W8584, MU, Gray, John Saml. Alexander
GRAY, Sarah C. W7799, SU, Gray, Moses
GRAY, Sophronia J. W2041, W8837, LI, Gray, James P.
GRAY, Susan Ann, W7342, O, Gray, Benjamin Franklin
GRAY, Thomas, S1813, HD, 3rd Bn. Cav.
GRAY, Tilman, S7903, CO, 5th Cav.
GRAY, Vertie, W11116, WA, Gray, James H.
GRAY, W. A. S2955, CL, 2nd (Ashby's) Cav.
GRAY, W. A. S14081, SN, 9th (Ward's) Cav.
GRAY, W. B. S8337, HI, 6th (Wheeler's) Cav.
GRAY, W. M. S1781, MA, Crews' Bn. Inf.
GRAY, W. R. S8079, H, 60th Ga. Inf.
GRAY, W. W. S16196, CA, 4th (Smith's) Cav.
GRAY, William M. S4476, SN, 7th Inf.
GRAY, Willis, S15057, CO, 31st Inf.
GRAYSON, Ava R. W5634, G, Grayson, John Anderson
GRAYSON, Jane Davis, W9607, DY, Grayson, Lemuel Franklin
GRAYSON, Josie Louisa, W8915, MR, Grayson, Anderson Cheek
GRAYSON, Lemuel F. S12058, DY, 42nd Inf.
GRAYSON, Patrick Henry, S9777, MR, 3rd Cav.
GREAVES, Annie Maria, W3814, L, Greaves, Edwin Bennett
GREAVES, E. B. S999, L, 3rd (Forrest's) Cav.
GREAVES, Josephine R. W6778, L, Greaves, R. J.
GREAVES, Reuben J. S8355, L, 7th Cav.
GREAVES, W. F. S16057, HY, 6th Inf.
GREDIG, Abram, S13241, K, Kain's Battery, Lt. Art.
GREDIG, Frances Marion, W7925, K, Gredig, Abraham
GREEN, A. J. S10185, F, 13th Inf.
GREEN, A. W. S11923, LA, 9th Cav.
GREEN, Adeline, W3230, SU, Green, James N.
GREEN, Albert, S6116, HI, Baxter's Co. Lt. Art.
GREEN, Anna M. W1879, SN, Green, Elmore Harris
GREEN, B. H. S1554, D, 9th Bn. Cav.
GREEN, Baley, S1729, SM, 28th Inf.
GREEN, Bashie, See Bashie Harkleroad
GREEN, Catherine, W5612, TR, Green, A. C.
GREEN, Cynthia Munroe, W10073, MT, Green, W. H.
GREEN, D. C. S11886, WE, 33rd Inf.
GREEN, D. W. S11720, CL, 16th N.C. Inf.

GREEN, Dave, S16100, D, 22nd (Barteau's) Cav.
GREEN, Elias H. S13788, W, 16th Inf.
GREEN, Elizabeth, W4737, CO, Green, James A.
GREEN, Elizabeth, W5167, LA, Green, John L.
GREEN, Emily, W573, MU, Green, George A.
GREEN, Emmaline Cathrine, W617, B, Green, Jasin
GREEN, Frances Catharine, W2377, B, Green, Wm. Orville
GREEN, Gardner, S119, WH, 16th Inf.
GREEN, George W. S3344, CO, 62nd Inf.
GREEN, H. J. S5481, SQ, 4th Inf.
GREEN, Harriet C. W2004, HM, Green, John
GREEN, Henry P. S15647, RO, 26th Inf.
GREEN, Henry R. S4687, H, 23rd Inf.
GREEN, Isaac, S4381, D, 44th Inf.
GREEN, J. A. S54, MS, 53rd Inf.
GREEN, J. A. S14490, CC, 12th Ala. Cav.
GREEN, J. A. Y. S6858, L, 7th Cav.
GREEN, J. C. S15166, MS, 53rd Inf.
GREEN, J. H. S13098, 21st (Wilson's) Cav.
GREEN, J. L. S8491, MO, 39th N.C. Inf.
GREEN, J. M. S4992, SE, 62nd N.C. Inf.
GREEN, J. R. S14651, HY, 35th Inf.
GREEN, James A. S1182, CO, 62nd N.C. Inf.
GREEN, James H. S13276, SE, 60th N.C. Inf.
GREEN, James N. S3891, SU, 61st Inf.
GREEN, Jessee H. S11643, LA, 19th Cav.
GREEN, Jessie W. S1490, DK, 23rd Inf.
GREEN, John, C261, HM, Undetermined
GREEN, John, S1450, HW, 4th Cav.
GREEN, John, S4982, K, 1st N.C. Cav.
GREEN, John S. S12134, CC, 9th Inf.
GREEN, John W. S8324, MA, 14th Cav.
GREEN, Julia Anne, W8005, DY, Green, John Wells
GREEN, Katherine Somerville, W7489, HY, Green, Thomas Wallace
GREEN, Lewis L. S2683, WH, 8th Cav.
GREEN, Lucy J. W4253, K, Green, John
GREEN, Luraine E. W5652, DY, Green, H. H.
GREEN, Margaret Eugenia, W10673, CC, Green, Robert A.
GREEN, Martin V. S364, K, 63rd Inf.
GREEN, Mary A. E. W2763, MU, Green, Wm. E. B.
GREEN, Mary E. W288, MS, Green, Newton A.
GREEN, Mary E. W7732, HI, Green, Albert
GREEN, Missouri Ann, W5682, CL, Green, Daniel W.

GREEN, Mollie A. W10495, LA, Green, Ace Washington
GREEN, Nancy C. W8369, Green, Moses F.
GREEN, Qunitos A. S6470, MC, 2nd N.C. Cav.
GREEN, R. D. S5694, MS, 17th Inf.
GREEN, R. F. S296, HI, 24th Inf.
GREEN, Riley, S12955, WH, 2nd Ga. Scouts
GREEN, Robert Andrew Jacks. S7779, CC, 48th (Nixon's) Inf.
GREEN, Robert F. S8724, HI, 24th Inf.
GREEN, Rosa L. W9508, CC, Green, I. A.
GREEN, Sallie (Sarah) E. W3250, CF, Green, W. M.
GREEN, Samuel, S15442, RB, 11th Inf.
GREEN, Sarah E. W9343, Green, T. L.
GREEN, Sarah W. W151, CF, Green, Washington Irving
GREEN, T. J. S8806, HR, Forrest's Old Regt. Cav.
GREEN, Thomas L. S14485, 20th (Russell's) Cav.
GREEN, Thomas P. S1759, SQ, 5th Inf.
GREEN, Thomas Wallace, S12131, HY, 12th Ky. Cav.
GREEN, Ursula Dudley, W8537, HY, Green, John Rufus
GREEN, W. C. S16366, WL, 2nd Ky. Cav.
GREEN, W. F. S12163, G, 1st Miss. Cav.
GREEN, W. H. S2956, K, 60th Inf.
GREEN, W. H. S7058, HO, 10th Cav.
GREEN, W. M. S5318, CF, 44th Inf.
GREEN, W. W. S8846, SH, 18th (Newsom's) Cav.
GREEN, W. W. S16104, D, 19th Inf.
GREEN, William Allen, S917, WE, 3rd Inf.
GREEN, William C. S927, GR, 26th Inf.
GREEN, William M. S8080, HO, 2nd Ky. Cav.
GREENE, Elzina, W1170, MN, Greene, D. B.
GREENE, Irvin P. S16397, B, 4th Inf.
GREENE, Nannie E. W2099, SH, Greene, Wm. Worth
GREENE, William, S2799, SU, Kain's Co. Lt. Art.
GREENER, Martha C. W3719, K, Greener, Addison Wesley
GREENHILL, Florindy Ann, W7660, MT, Greenhill, Henry Winfield
GREENHILL, H. W. S11002, MT, 2nd Ky. Cav.
GREENHILL, R. C. S14590, ST, 2nd Ky. Cav.
GREENHILL, Sallie Fredonia, W10680, ST, Greenhill, Richd. Courtney

GREENLEE, Ann Eliza, W651, BR, Greenlee, Benjamin Franklin
GREENLEE, Mary Rebecca, W7911, H, Greenlee, James Augustus
GREENLEE, Sarah, W7304, WA, Greenlee, W. W.
GREENLEE, William W. S11334, CT, 31st Inf.
GREENLOE, Rutha A. W5889, CF, Greenloe, H. L.
GREENWAY, Bettie, W6799, D, Greenway, James
GREENWAY, James, S8211, D, 48th Ala. Inf.
GREENWAY, Lydia Diana, W5497, SU, Greenway, Wm. C.
GREENWAY, W. G. S6750, WA, 61st Inf.
GREENWAY, William C. S2018, SU, 63rd Inf.
GREENY, D. B. S3243, MN, 31st Inf.
GREER, A. D. S5237, D, 4th Cav.
GREER, A. J. S12241, D, 1st Cav.
GREER, Agnes Elizabeth, W405, WL, Greer, Charles Marion
GREER, Alamba L. W9627, HI, Greer, L. C.
GREER, Alex, S15315, JO, 6th N.C. Cav.
GREER, B. K. S8852, D, 1st Cav.
GREER, Calvin, S7471, WL, 4th (McLemore's) Cav.
GREER, Celestia Price, W4466, T, Greer, Lemuel Bert
GREER, Elizabeth, W4666, RB, Greer, Daniel Webster
GREER, G. B. S5487, BE, 55th Inf.
GREER, George E. S13526, SU, 8th (Smith's) Cav.
GREER, J. J. H. S14165, MA, 17th Miss. Inf.
GREER, J. P. S2957, CL, 2nd Cav.
GREER, James H. S5533, HI, 24th Inf.
GREER, Joe Silas, S10957, D, 20th Inf.
GREER, John, S2976, CL, 29th Inf.
GREER, John J. S11601, LI, 44th Inf.
GREER, Jones, C61, MS, Forrest's Escort, Cav.
GREER, Josephine, W3963, CL, Greer, John P.
GREER, L. C. S10052, HI, 9th Bn. (Gantt's) Cav.
GREER, Lavisa, W9215, P, Greer, Joseph A.
GREER, Mahala, W4380, GR, Greer, John M.
GREER, Martha Ann, W6995, RB, Greer, Oliver Cormel
GREER, Mary, W1104, DK, Greer, Mat
GREER, Mazie J. W4712, BE, Greer, Wm. Washington
GREER, Nancy, W7570, JO, Greer, Alexander

GREER, O. C. S703, RB, 3rd Ky. Cav., On misc. microfilm reel
GREER, Parlee T. W837, D, Greer, Abram Davidson
GREER, R. S. S15124, D, 1st Mo. Inf.
GREER, Rhoda N. W252, LI, Greer, Joseph Henry
GREER, Robert, S3525, CL, 2nd Ky. Cav.
GREER, Thomas, S6693, HA, 29th Inf.
GREER, Thomas V. S14186, LI, 44th Inf.
GREER, W. J. S10618, HI, 9th Cav.
GREER, W. M. S5092, WL, 4th (McLemore's) Cav.
GREER, W. W. S3716, BE, 55th Inf.
GREER, William H. S10434, LA, 6th (Wheeler's) Cav.
GREGG, Amanda Jane, W6720, GE, Gregg, J. H.
GREGG, Ellen, W4934, T, Gregg, Wm. H.
GREGG, Emma, W3390, MC, Gregg, Albert Barnes
GREGG, J. H. S14850, GE, 16th Bn. Cav.
GREGG, Joseph H. S8790, MS, 1st Inf.
GREGG, Margaret C. W4911, MS, Gregg, J. H.
GREGG, Samuel, S5543, MC, 59th Inf.
GREGG, T. H. S12410, SH, 9th Miss. Inf.
GREGG, William H. S5553, T, 7th Miss. Cav.
GREGGS, Manervia Caroline, W454, T, Greggs, John Lewis
GREGORY, Dorcas, W712, ME, Gregory, James F. H.
GREGORY, E. B. S2616, SM, 15th Cav.
GREGORY, E. B. S3228, SM, 9th (Ward's) Cav.
GREGORY, E. N. S5265, MC, 5th Cav.
GREGORY, Ellen Stephenson, W10572, D, Gregory, Alfred
GREGORY, Emily Jane, W1445, SM, Gregory, E. B.
GREGORY, Fannie Clay, W6364, L, Gregory, Bascom Green
GREGORY, Frances Annie, W6971, MC, Gregory, James Lafayette
GREGORY, George W. S8661, B, 1st Cav.
GREGORY, Herriett Ellen, W6631, RB, Gregory, John
GREGORY, J. S. S8139, RU, 18th Inf.
GREGORY, James, S5266, H, 68th Inf.
GREGORY, James B. S3252, P, 1st Hvy. Art.
GREGORY, John, S1741, RB, 6th Ky. Inf.
GREGORY, John, S16498, CC, 14th (Neely's) Cav.

GREGORY, John T. S14193, B, 41st Inf.
GREGORY, Joseph, S6350, RU, 18th Inf.
GREGORY, Julia Ann, W9878, SH, Gregory, John Edward
GREGORY, Loula, W3116, MA, Gregory, Beverly James
GREGORY, Mary A. W1336, FR, Gregory, Thomas D.
GREGORY, Ned, C3, FR, 1st (Turney's) Inf.
GREGORY, Sarah Cooper, W6139, B, Gregory, George W.
GREGORY, T. F. S13870, DY, 9th Bn. (Gantt's) Cav.
GREGORY, W. J. S9205, TR, 24th Inf.
GREGORY, William A. S519, SN, 24th Inf.
GREGSON, Francis M. S247, HN, 46th Inf.
GREYSON, Nancy Frances, W5917, HN, Greyson, Francis Marion
GRIAMS, Joshua, S9394, CL, 25th Va. Cav.
GRIBBLE, Ezekiel, S9899, BO, 39th N.C. Inf.
GRIBBLE, G. W. S4529, CA, 8th (Smith's) Cav.
GRIBBLE, J. M. (Dock), S16243, W, 38th Inf.
GRIBBLE, Julia Miller, W9579, W, Gribble, J. M.
GRIBBLE, Mrth. Levada Melvina, W5974, BO, Gribble, Ezekiel
GRIBBLE, S. C. S4284, FR, 16th Inf.
GRIDER, John H. S4632, B, 17th Inf.
GRIDER, William, S1976, PU, 16th Inf.
GRIFFIN, Barbara Powell, W10658, O, Griffin, Wm. H.
GRIFFIN, Butler, C150, SH, 26th Ga. Inf.
GRIFFIN, J. B. S12723, T, 2nd Ala. Cav.
GRIFFIN, J. H. S8497, WL, 7th Inf.
GRIFFIN, James P. S1268, WE, 33rd N.C. Inf.
GRIFFIN, John L. S6442, HU, 48th (Voorhies') Inf.
GRIFFIN, L. B. S6160, CO, 60th Inf.
GRIFFIN, Louisa, W9269, WL, Griffin, J. H.
GRIFFIN, Maria Rosser, W10792, SH, Griffin, Durrell Fears
GRIFFIN, Martha Elizabeth, W2685, H, Griffin, Samuel Columbus
GRIFFIN, Mary, W5393, D, Griffin, Hugh
GRIFFIN, Mary Ann, W6497, MA, Griffin, W. T.
GRIFFIN, Mollie T. W4552, DY, Griffin, W. J.
GRIFFIN, P. S. S5075, DI, 48th Inf.
GRIFFIN, Rufus, S4924, K, 31st Inf.
GRIFFIN, Samuel J. S354, WH, 5th Cav.
GRIFFIN, Sarah Malissa, W10665, GI, Griffin, J. Anthony
GRIFFIN, Thiophus W. S16604, RU, 1st (Carter's) Cav.
GRIFFIN, W. J. S2522, DY, 55th Inf.
GRIFFIN, W. T. S512, MA, 27th Inf.
GRIFFIN, W. W. S8360, S12305, D, 7th Inf.
GRIFFIN, William A. S6280, MU, Maury's Co. Lt. Art.
GRIFFIN, William T. S871, S1213, HE, 27th Inf.
GRIFFIS, H. D. S12043, LI, 41st Inf.
GRIFFIS, James D. S1837, MS, 53rd Inf.
GRIFFIS, Josephine, W10586, GI, Griffis, Hugh Dailey
GRIFFIS, Julia Fox, W9447, MS, Griffis, Thomas W.
GRIFFIS, Nancy Caline, W9297, MS, Griffis, Wm. Wesley
GRIFFIS, Nannie H. W8371, MU, Griffis, Andrew Jackson
GRIFFITH, Annie Morgan, W9177, MA, Griffith, Joseph Dickson
GRIFFITH, Isaac, S3406, BR, 5th Cav.
GRIFFITH, J. D. S16318, MA, 15th Cav.
GRIFFITH, James O. S206, BR, 62nd Inf.
GRIFFITH, John E. S1516, PO, 37th Inf.
GRIFFITH, Mary L. W2028, PO, Griffith, John Ervin
GRIFFITH, Solomon, S8056, BR, 62nd Inf.
GRIGG, Mary Elizabeth, W3664, D, Grigg, Edmund Tompkins
GRIGG, Rhodie, W8767, RU, Grigg, Andrew Pride
GRIGG, T. H. S5681, M, 22nd (Barteau's) Cav.
GRIGGS, Eliza Ann, W1370, D, Griggs, Medrith Gentry
GRIGGS, George H. S8509, HE, 27th Inf.
GRIGGS, Louisa Emeline, W4692, HE, Griggs, George H.
GRIGGS, M. C. W1843, MA, Griggs, John Henry
GRIGGS, Mahala Caroline, W2411, L, Griggs, Robert
GRIGGS, Martha, W934, L, Griggs, Wm.
GRIGGS, N. J. S11739, GI, 12th Miss. Cav.
GRIGGS, Peter B. S3224, GI, 12th Cav.
GRIGGS, Robert, S2292, L, 1st Cav.
GRIGGS, Robert Berry, S16632, G, Unassigned (Recruiting Service)
GRIGGS, Turner S. S3120, HE, 51st Inf.

Index to Tennessee Confederate Pension Applications

GRIGSBY, Elizabeth, W3481, HW, Grigsby, Jesse
GRIGSBY, J. P. S15086, DY, 12th Inf.
GRIGSBY, Jane, W2933, DI, Grigsby, Thomas Kinley
GRIGSBY, Jesse, S1024, HW, 31st Inf.
GRIGSBY, John C. S16553, GI, 11th Cav.
GRIGSBY, Samuel, S840, HW, 60th Inf.
GRIGSBY, Teletha B. W47, ME, Grigsby, Washington Lafayette
GRIGSBY, Thomas A. C30, SH, 15th Cav.
GRILLS, R. S. S2977, K, 8th (Smith's) Cav.
GRILLS, Thomas W. S3045, WA, 11th Va. Inf.
GRIMES, Addie M. W4654, G, Grimes, Dock Green
GRIMES, B. F. S5630, CH, Moreland's Regt. Ala. Cav.
GRIMES, D. G. S4724, LA, 27th Ark. Inf.
GRIMES, Dan W. C231, Application is missing.
GRIMES, Daniel W. C228, RB, 11th Inf.
GRIMES, Elizabeth H. W10122, SH, Grimes, George F.
GRIMES, Elizabeth Hannah, W6777, T, Grimes, George Franklin
GRIMES, Elizabeth Mahonie, W7665, CE, Grimes, Thomas Jefferson
GRIMES, Isaac, S14867, SU, Sullivan's Co. Home Guards
GRIMES, J. B. S8328, MT, 50th Inf.
GRIMES, J. P. S14661, LA, 9th Bn. Cav.
GRIMES, J. P. S16568, DI, 11th Inf.
GRIMES, J. S. S1499, HU, 44th Inf.
GRIMES, Margaret E. W4388, WY, Grimes, John Calvin
GRIMES, Mary E. W7775, SU, Grimes, Isaac W.
GRIMES, Mike, S13676, DY, 29th Inf.
GRIMES, Parmelia J. W3341, CH, Grimes, Benjamin J.
GRIMES, Richard, S2627, LI, 41st Inf.
GRIMES, S. H. S11045, LA, 9th Bn. (Gantt's) Cav.
GRIMES, T. J. S10106, CE, 11th Inf.
GRIMES, T. L. S9216, HI, 9th Bn. Cav.
GRIMES, Tabitah Frances, W6332, HU, Grimes, John Samuel
GRIMES, Thomas L. S15875, S12249, D, 10th (DeMoss') Cav.
GRIMM, A. S10996, SN, 13th Cav.
GRIMSLEY, Fannie G. W1399, OV, Grimsley, George K.
GRIMSLEY, G. K. S2028, OV, 8th Cav.
GRINDER, James M. S1725, LE, Undetermined
GRINDER, Polly Ann, W659, WY, Grinder, R. M.
GRINDER, R. m. S4077, WY, 9th Cav.
GRINDER, W. M. S2020, LE, 9th Cav.
GRINDER, W. M. S12621, LE, 19th (Biffle's) Cav.
GRINDLES, Sarah Ann, W4500, H, Grindles, Wm.
GRINER, W. P. S11808, HI, 2nd (Ashby's) Cav.
GRISHAM, Eliza, W3497, SM, Grisham, T. D.
GRISHAM, James, S923, ME, 19th Inf.
GRISHAM, John A. S13151, D, 44th Inf.
GRISHAM, Susan P. W9168, MA, Grisham, Wm. Henderson
GRISHAM, T. D. S1852, SM, 4th Cav.
GRISHAM, William, S2679, ME, 43rd Inf. See also William G. Grisham
GRISHAM, William G. S560, ME, 43rd Inf. See also William Grisham
GRISSOM, Ann, W1054, V, Grissom, James C.
GRISSOM, J. C. S1239, V, 38th Inf.
GRISSOM, Permelia, W6227, V, Grissom, Esau
GRISSOM, R. A. S14047, WE, C. S. Navy
GRISSOM, S. B. S9571, V, 8th (Dibrell's) Cav.
GRISSOM, Savannah, W10370, WE, Grissom, Robert A.
GRISSOM, T. W. S10575, HE, 55th (Brown's) Inf.
GRIZZARD, Eva E. W10814, D, Grizzard, M. T.
GRIZZARD, Lou, W5180, MT, Grizzard, Wm.
GRIZZARD, M. T. S11286, D, 2nd (Robison's) Inf.
GRIZZARD, W. H. S11959, ST, 2nd Cav.
GRIZZEL, G. W. S2656, CA, 8th (Smith's) Cav.
GRIZZEL, J. H. S13252, UN, 2nd Ky. Cav.
GRIZZEL, Martha, W5196, UN, Grizzel, John H.
GRIZZORD, W. B. S14140, Greer's Regt. Partisan Rangers
GROCE, Nety Caroline, W10079, PI, Groce, Granville Jackson
GROCE, Thomas, S15777, LI, 41st Inf.
GROOMES, C. R. S5851, G, 31st Inf.
GROOMES, Cartha Ann, W4381, G, Groomes, C. B.
GROSECLOSE, Levi, S10744, SU, 45th Va. Inf.
GROSS, Adam H. S12993, D, 1st Art.
GROSS, Callie Brewer, W8372, D, Gross, A. H.
GROSS, Eliza, W2215, SU, Gross, Jacob C.

Index to Tennessee Confederate Pension Applications

GROSS, Ella, W10840, SH, Gross, Charles Conrad
GROSS, J. A. S16023, S16690, GU, 35th Inf., #16690 Never fully acted on by board.
GROSS, J. C. S5958, SU, 59th Inf.
GROSS, W. M. S12077, BE, Undetermined
GROSSCLOSE, Solomon, S3061, GR, 4th Va. Inf.
GROVE, J. R. S9346, W, 11th (Holman's) Cav.
GROVE, Mary E. W7423, W, Grove, Joseph R.
GROVE, Mary Emma, W3556, HY, Grove, Richard Rowan
GROVE, R. D. S14520, SH, 7th Cav.
GROVES, See also Graves
GROVES, G. W. S5594, V, 10th Inf.
GROVES, John, S5638, RB, 30th Inf.
GROVES, John, S13710, HR, 14th (Neely's) Cav.
GROVES, Lou, W5790, SH, Groves, Robert Douglass
GROVES, Lydia L. W5766, LI, Groves, Caleb C.
GROVES, Melvina, W1459, FR, Groves, Richmond A.
GROVES, R. A. S2180, FR, 41st Inf.
GROVES, Sarah Ann, W1395, SU, Groves, Samuel
GRUBB, A. J. S13420, ME, 5th (McKenzie's) Cav.
GRUBB, B. A. S6729, WE, 33rd Inf.
GRUBB, Samuel H. S646, HW, 63rd Inf.
GRUBBS, Fanny, W7499, GI, Grubbs, Sylvanus Hensley
GRUBBS, Hensley, S10593, GI, 6th (Wheeler's) Cav.
GRUBBS, Mahala, W211, RB, Grubbs, Peterson
GRUBBS, Sarah V. W3211, SU, Grubbs, Robert Lewis
GRUBBS, Thomas, S14052, HN, 7th (Duckworth's) Cav.
GRUBBS, W. A. S431, RB, 30th Inf.
GRYMES, William Jasper, S5561, MT, 49th Inf.
GUDGER, Mary Rebecca, W6213, MC, Gudger, Marcus Farmer
GUESS, J. C. S13361, WA, 48th Va. Inf.
GUESS, N. C. S9895, SU, 48th Va. Inf.
GUEST, Celia Jane, W858, RU, Guest, John Dervin
GUEST, J. T. S14846, FR, 28th Inf.
GUEST, John D. S3881, RU, 2nd (Robison's) Inf.
GUFFEE, A. S9560, WI, 5th Cav.

GUFFEE, A. W. S3095, ME, 5th Mtd. Inf.
GUFFEE, Elizabeth Harris, W1009, WE, Guffee, John Henry
GUFFEE, H. S. S8206, LO, 5th Cav.
GUFFEE, J. H. S6530, WE, 16th Inf.
GUFFIN, Butler, C150, SH, 26th Ga. Inf.
GUILD, George B. S14344, D, 8th (Smith's) Cav.
GUILLIAMS, L. G. S14062, CH, 48th Inf.
GUIN, Pat M. S1606, WA, 60th Inf.
GUINN, Eliza M. W6556, FR, Guinn, G. D.
GUINN, Elizabeth J. W959, WA, Guinn, M. S.
GUINN, G. D. S10158, FR, 4th Inf.
GUINN, Jesse H. S14115, ME, 3rd (Lillard's) Mtd. Inf.
GUINN, Louise Franklin, W3756, WI, Guinn, George W.
GUINN, Margaret Mariah, W9499, GE, Guinn, P. M.
GUINN, William, S1552, HM, 29th Inf.
GUINTON, N. G. S3265, MN, 26th Miss. Inf.
GUITON, Margaret, W7001, MN, Guiton, Nathaniel
GULLET, G. W. S10274, PU, 25th Inf.
GULLEY, James V. S6172, S4250, LI, 8th Inf.
GULLEY, L. F. S2988, HW, 61st Inf.
GULLEY, Martha A. W6687, HW, Gulley, Samuel Osborne
GULLICK, Nancy C. W2242, LA, Gullick, Willis C.
GULLY, Samuel O. S13355, HW, 12th Bn. Cav.
GUNN, A. J. S11046, DI, 1st (Feild's) Inf.
GUNN, E. W. S9572, RB, 11th Inf.
GUNN, J. A. S11566, MT, 1st Ky. Inf.
GUNN, James G. S1789, CF, 37th Inf.
GUNN, Lyman C. S14167, D, 4th Inf.
GUNN, Nancy A. W3090, CF, Gunn, James Gray
GUNN, Nancy A. W9069, W9006, FR, Gunn, John B.
GUNN, Sallie Boyd, W5639, D, Gunn, Lyman C.
GUNSON, W. D. S15948, ST, 50th Inf.
GUNTER, Dorthula, W5060, MG, Gunter, Pleasant Calvin
GUNTER, Hiram W. S15936, LI, 32nd Inf.
GUNTER, J. H. S2427, LI, 32nd Inf.
GUNTER, Laura Ann, W8483, L, Gunter, Napoleon Bonaparte
GUNTER, Lou, W8838, LI, Gunter, H. W.
GUNTER, Mary S. W9490, LI, Gunter, Wm. Henry

-141

GUNTER, Napoleon B. S1165, G, 23rd Inf.
GUNTER, P. C. H. S2093, MG, 25th Inf.
GUNTER, Samantha Waldrop, W10183, MC, Gunter, Jasper S.
GUNTER, William H. S10428, LI, 32nd Inf.
GUPTON, Calvin, S933, CE, 42nd Inf.
GUPTON, E. J. S13064, MT, 42nd Inf.
GUPTON, Joseph P. S12946, MS, 12th N.C. Inf.
GUPTON, Margaret [Craig], W10412, MS, Gupton, Joseph P. [Later married Craig]
GURLEY, Nancy Mary Ann, W3592, HE, Gurley, John Autry
GUTHREY, D. M. S5267, H, 3rd Confederate Cav.
GUTHRIE, Ann Eliza, W9449, D, Guthrie, J. C.
GUTHRIE, Esther Jane, W5728, HN, Guthrie, Wm. Francis
GUTHRIE, H. C. S16327, D, 30th Inf.
GUTHRIE, Henry C. S12538, MS, 20th Inf.
GUTHRIE, J. C. S9125, D, 20th Inf.
GUTHRIE, J. M. S9424, SN, 9th (Bennett's) Cav.
GUTHRIE, Nannie Eilza, W6245, D, Guthrie, Wm. Wolf
GUTHRIE, Nathan L. S14705, D, 7th Inf.
GUTHRIE, W. F. S13662, HN, 7th (Duckworth's) Cav.
GUTHRIE, W. W. S12450, D, 20th Inf.
GUY, Margaret Florence, W10577, O, Guy, George Albert
GUY, Susan Maclin, W3972, SH, Guy, Wm. Wallace
GWIN, Frances Josephine, W6749, SH, Gwin, Robert Greer
GWIN, J. E. S16587, HU, 24th Inf.
GWIN, Mary Ann Eliza, W1533, SN, Gwin, Jesse
GWIN, Medorah Alice, W1889, Gwin, John Elias
GWIN, Nancy, W1658, HU, Gwin, James Montica
GWIN, Sarah Elizabeth, W10283, Gwin, Robert Donnell
GWYN, H. C. S13170, F, 13th Inf.
GWYN, R. R. S9411, F, 2nd Partisan Rangers, Miss.
HABIN, J. M. S2978, SE, 29th N.C. Inf.
HABIN, John, S5936, HM, 37th Inf.
HACKER, I. N. S8830, K, 5th Cav.
HACKER, Matilda I. W5826, MC, Hacker, Samuel M.

HACKER, S. M. S817, MC, Undetermined
HACKER, Susan C. W1147, HM, Hacker, Julius C.
HACKERSMITH, John Wesley, S1815, FR, 31st Ala. Inf.
HACKETT, Mary E. W935, SM, Hackett, E. H.
HACKETT, Peter, S5751, SM, 23rd Inf.
HACKNEY, Gildie Jane, W8205, HR, Hackney, Wm. Perry
HACKNEY, James H. S13205, SH, 59th Va. Inf.
HACKNEY, Martha Rebecca, W6586, MU, Hackney, Joseph James
HACKNEY, Sarah Elizabeth, W5149, SH, Hackney, Jesse Edwards
HACKNEY, Sarah Louisa, W5988, JO, Hackney, John Wesley
HACKNEY, William P. S7315, HE, 41st N.C. Volunteers
HACKWORTH, Elijah A. S13651, K, 11th Va. Inf.
HACKWORTH, Fannie S. W6319, K, Hackworth, Elijah Alonzo
HACKWORTH, Levi, S9445, SQ, 35th Inf.
HACKWORTH, William H. S11832, S15416, MR, 4th (McLemore's) Cav.
HADDOCK, I. N. S4078, WY, 9th Cav.
HADDON, Thomas W. S3235, K, 6th N.C. Cav.
HADLEY, Etta Pope, W9159, D, Hadley, Ferdinan Columbus
HADLEY, Mary Jane, W5017, T, Hadley, Wm. Manley
HADLEY, William M. S10549, T, 18th Miss. Inf.
HAGAN, Anderson, S3983, D, 4th (McLemore's) Cav.
HAGAN, Bettie Hobson, W2128, D, Hagan, Leonardos Polk
HAGAN, William H. S127, LA, 9th Cav.
HAGAR, Elizabeth, W2164, D, Hagar, James Riley
HAGER, Cornelia A. W8698, D, Hager, George Fount
HAGER, Margaret, W4831, D, Hager, James Madison
HAGER, Mary Jane, W2343, WL, Hager, Rubin Benjamin
HAGER, Reuben B. S156, WL, 7th Inf.
HAGERTY, Richard, S1434, HY, 5th Inf.
HAGERTY, Sarah Caroline, W5751, WY, Hagerty, Thomas
HAGERTY, Thomas, S3649, WY, 13th Ark. Inf.

Index to Tennessee Confederate Pension Applications

HAGGARD, Emily, W1633, CF, Haggard, Henderson
HAGGARD, J. T. S5815, H, 17th (Newman's) Inf.
HAGGARD, James R. S3090, B, 17th Inf.
HAGGARD, John A. S11533, CH, 55th Inf.
HAGGARD, Mary, W1078, B, Haggard, James R.
HAGGARD, Mary Thedora, W839, B, Haggard, Wm. McGinnis
HAGGARD, Nancy Elizabeth, W6228, CH, Haggard, John Anderson, Follows 6229 on film
HAGGARD, S. H. S5199, CF, 4th (McLemore's) Cav.
HAGGARTY, Sarah, W5312, HY, Haggarty, Richard
HAGLER, Bettie Pollard, W3665, HO, Hagler, B. F.
HAGLER, W. L. S12632, HN, 5th Inf.
HAGOOD, E. T. S5712, DI, 14th Inf.
HAILE, Alma, W9895, CY, Haile, Thomas Harrison
HAILE, J. T. S10196, LA, 32nd Inf.
HAILE, James A. S12877, S15863, J, 28th Inf.
HAILE, Mary Angeline, W4363, LA, Haile, J. T.
HAILE, Merlin D. S9357, J, 8th Inf.
HAILE, Strickney R. W8518, J, Haile, James A.
HAILE, T. H. S16017, CY, 28th Inf.
HAILEY, Albert, C56, D, 44th Inf.
HAILEY, Amanda, W4923, O, Hailey, John Anderson
HAILEY, J. A. S3206, O, 27th Inf.
HAILEY, J. C. S12367, WI, 6th (Wheeler's) Cav.
HAILEY, J. C. S12493, G, 16th Cav.
HAILEY, John Gee, S13472, D, 1st (Feild's) Inf.
HAILEY, Josephine, W7406, WI, Hailey, John C.
HAILEY, Kate E. W5455, D, Hailey, John Gee
HAILEY, Mary Adline, W1769, Hailey, Samuel Harvey
HAILEY, Nora Adell, W4312, G, Hailey, Jasper Collumbus
HAILEY, R. T. S3742, WI, 6th (Wheeler's) Cav.
HAILEY, V. H. S8302, CA, 11th Cav.
HAINEY, Levi, S5426, WH, 1st (Feild's) Inf.
HAIRSTON, John, C183, LI, Regiment not given
HALBERT, James Crawford, S14181, LI, 41st Inf.

HALBERT, Sarah E. W10045, LI, Halbert, Pleasant Washington
HALBERT, Susie J. W10470, WL, Halbert, Wm. Hays
HALE, See also Hall
HALE, Edna R. W6320, D, Hale, George W.
HALE, Eliza, W6600, WA, Hale, Jessee W.
HALE, Elizabeth C. W319, RU, Hale, Joseph Pomphey
HALE, Ferrie, W11005, SN, Hale, Hugh Barnett
HALE, H. B. S13897, SN, 9th (Ward's) Cav.
HALE, Ira G. S5369, SU, 60th Inf.
HALE, J. H. S2278, WH, 25th Inf.
HALE, J. H. S3062, ME, 16th Cav.
HALE, J. H. S5911, R, 16th Cav.
HALE, J. P. S4573, RU, 45th Inf.
HALE, J. W. S9715, CF, 45th Inf.
HALE, Jesse W. S13242, WA, 60th Inf.
HALE, John W. S4574, CF, 45th Inf.
HALE, John W. S12092, SN, 4th Cav.
HALE, Joseph L. S1330, S1253, WA, 60th Inf.
HALE, Margaret, W2996, R, Hale, John H.
HALE, Margaret E. W5044, MOO, Hale, George W.
HALE, Martha, W1437, J, Hale, Thomas
HALE, Myra Duffy, W9396, SM, Hale, J. B.
HALE, Reuben Grissim, C6, WL, Qtrmaster Dept. 4th Inf.
HALE, T. P. S8396, CF, 18th Inf.
HALE, Talmage H. W8039, TR, Hale, Wm. J.
HALE, Thomas, S4147, WA, 60th Inf.
HALE, W. F. S7881, HD, 5th (McKenzie's) Cav.
HALE, W. H. S5427, SM, 6th (Wheeler's) Cav.
HALE, W. H. S6281, HE, Lyle's Ark. Cav.
HALE, W. J. S13879, TR, 2nd (Robison's) Inf.
HALEY, A. H. S5614, SM, 4th (McLemore's) Cav.
HALEY, Albert S. S12098, SM, 8th (Smith's) Cav.
HALEY, Cornelia Cecelia, W5155, H, Haley, Joel Thomas
HALEY, Eliza J. W3387, SM, Haley, J. S.
HALEY, Elizabeth, W8642, K, Haley, Wellington M.
HALEY, G. W. S5370, W, 11th Cav.
HALEY, H. D. S15141, SH, 18th Miss. Cav.
HALEY, J. A. S8008, CF, 44th Inf.
HALEY, J. C. S10890, S6005, CF, 44th Inf.
HALEY, J. H. S16607, HR, 4th (Murray's) Cav.
HALEY, J. T. S5040, WE, 51st & 52nd (Consolidated) Inf.

Index to Tennessee Confederate Pension Applications

HALEY, John C. S9936, H, 2nd (Ashby's) Cav.
HALEY, Mary, W6030, CA, Haley, George W.
HALEY, Mary Bazell, W9465, WI, Haley, Richard Thomas
HALEY, Mary E. W3720, G, Haley, Wm. P.
HALEY, Mollie E. W3669, D, Haley, Wm. Richard
HALEY, Nan P. W3374, M, Haley, Wm.
HALEY, Perneacy C. W3495, MU, Haley, John F.
HALEY, Robert T. S12473, SH, Wood's Regt. Cav.
HALEY, S. F. S14676, CC, 12th Inf.
HALEY, Sarah Evangeline, W1415, WE, Haley, Wm. F.
HALEY, T. J. S13462, G, 15th (Stewart's) Cav.
HALEY, Thomas, S15783, SM, 4th (McLemore's) Cav.
HALEY, W. C. S16208, B, Douglass' Bn. Cav.
HALEY, W. F. S4954, WE, 51st Inf.
HALEY, William B. S4593, CA, 23rd Inf.
HALFORD, L. W. S7824, G, 47th Inf.
HALFORD, Mary, W4189, MA, Halford, Licurgus Winchester
HALL, See also Hale
HALL, A. J. S5016, SH, 1st (Feild's) Inf.
HALL, Agnes, W9280, M, Hall, Hilliard
HALL, Alex H. S9378, SU, 60th Inf.
HALL, Alexander M. S5944, HN, 5th Inf.
HALL, Almon Calvis, S10326, T, 12th (Green's) Cav.
HALL, Almon G. S12893, MU, 6th (Wheeler's) Cav.
HALL, Andrew J. S7792, RB, 30th Inf.
HALL, Ann Eliza, W4599, WE, Hall, Williamson
HALL, B. F. S1638, WI, 45th Inf.
HALL, B. F. S6146, DI, 11th Inf.
HALL, B. F. S12858, CY, 8th (Dibrell's) Cav.
HALL, Caroline, W3595, FR, Hall, George R.
HALL, Dora Conner, W11100, WA, Hall, Samuel
HALL, E. B. S9883, SU, 3rd (Lillard's) Mtd. Inf.
HALL, E. H. S10006, D, 6th (Wheeler's) Cav.
HALL, E. J. S9422, CE, 18th Inf.
HALL, Emma, W4746, D, Hall, Everrett
HALL, Emma Elizabeth, W8916, WL, Hall, Dock J.
HALL, Emmaline, W3833, WI, Hall, James Henderson
HALL, G. R. S2227, FR, 41st Inf.
HALL, George W. S7793, RB, 30th Inf.

HALL, H. D. S11392, MR, 11th Inf.
HALL, Harriet S. W4738, SU, Hall, David Nathaniel
HALL, Hattie, W9288, B, Hall, John Virgil
HALL, Hilliard, S15304, M, 19th S.C. Inf.
HALL, J. A. S2159, DI, 1st Hvy. Art.
HALL, J. A. S7088, GE, 1st (Carter's) Cav.
HALL, J. F. S14197, FR, 41st Inf.
HALL, J. H. S9088, HU, 1st (Feild's) Inf.
HALL, J. P. S14741, H, 1st Ga. Cav.
HALL, J. S. S2858, CL, 48th Va. Inf.
HALL, J. W. S2216, CO, 5th (McKenzie's) Cav.
HALL, Jacob, S422, WL, 45th Inf.
HALL, James, S8716, J, 7th Ark. Inf.
HALL, James D. S3187, CL, 48th Va. Inf.
HALL, James H. S2711, WI, Baxter's Co. Lt. Art.
HALL, James L. S2076, FR, 1st (Turney's) Inf.
HALL, Jesse J. A. S2482, RO, 22nd Ga. Inf.
HALL, John G. S87, RB, 8th Inf.
HALL, John M. S5941, PO, 3rd (Lillard's) Mtd. Inf.
HALL, John T. S5482, PU, 8th (Dibrell's) Cav.
HALL, Leona, W10439, HN, Hall, Thomas Jefferson
HALL, Lucinda, W3157, WA, Hall, Ebenezer B.
HALL, Lusanna Mitchell, W1967, HW, Hall, John Bradford
HALL, Lydia, W5568, MS, Hall, W. W.
HALL, M. A. S10919, SH, 23rd Miss. Inf.
HALL, Martha, W7090, SM, Hall, Pleas Athanel
HALL, Martha Adeline, W11007, SH, Hall, Wm. Jasper
HALL, Martha Frances, W729, WL, Hall, Littleton C.
HALL, Martha J. W133, RU, Hall, Jacob
HALL, Martha Louise, W10981, MA, Hall, Wm. H.
HALL, Mary Ann, W9232, MT, Hall, E. J.
HALL, Mary Jane, W2686, DI, Hall, Benjamin Franklin
HALL, Mary Jane, W7547, T, Hall, James I.
HALL, Mary Lee, W4507, MS, Hall, Pleasase Creace
HALL, Matilda, W1618, CO, Hall, John Wesley
HALL, Mattie E. W5603, T, Hall, Joseph R.
HALL, Nancy, W6286, CO, Hall, Wm.
HALL, Nancy Jane, W1275, WI, Hall, Benjamin Franklin
HALL, Nannie, W6699, MR, Hall, Henry David
HALL, Nannie C. W2540, SH, Hall, Andrew James

Index to Tennessee Confederate Pension Applications

HALL, Nannie L. W789, TR, Hall, Benjamin Perkins
HALL, Nannie Prewitt, W5613, FR, Hall, George Newton
HALL, P. A. S13810, SM, 24th Inf.
HALL, P. C. S8453, MS, 53rd Inf.
HALL, Paulina Ann, W4256, W4197, PU, Hall, John T.
HALL, Pauline L. W4976, SH, Hall, R. R.
HALL, Polly M. W8162, FR, Hall, James L.
HALL, R. R. R. S10735, SH, 2nd Ky. Cav.
HALL, Robert G. S570, SH, 13th Inf.
HALL, S. D. S13107, SU, 60th Inf.
HALL, S. H. S16538, BE, 5th Inf.
HALL, Samuel, S9126, FR, 33rd Ala. Inf.
HALL, Samuel, S11534, WA, 60th Inf.
HALL, Samuel S. S5775, SU, 60th Inf.
HALL, Sarah E. W1433, DI, Hall, Joe A.
HALL, Susan Burnettee, W9300, WH, Hall, Benjamin Franklin
HALL, Susan Catherine, W10629, G, Hall, James Madison
HALL, Susan Margrett, W4341, MA, Hall, Andrew Jackson
HALL, Susan P. W5925, RB, Hall, Andrew J.
HALL, T. J. S6997, HU, 1st (Feild's) Inf.
HALL, Thomas, S9804, BL, 8th (Dibrell's) Cav.
HALL, Thomas, S10546, D, 20th Inf.
HALL, Thomas Alexander, S14973, SH, Wood's Cav. Miss.
HALL, Treecy,   See Treecy Crews
HALL, W. D. S5529, HN, 5th Inf.
HALL, W. W. S1848, WI, 49th Inf.
HALL, William, S5422, CO, 35th N.C. Inf.
HALLEY, Bettie, W8385, GI, Halley, W. G.
HALLEY, John W. S13649, SH, 4th Inf.
HALLIBURTON, Charles, S446, SH, 11th Inf.
HALLIBURTON, D. F. S15520, G, 12th Inf.
HALLIBURTON, David, S4756, MT, 49th Inf.
HALLIBURTON, James A. S15590, ST, 50th Inf.
HALLIBURTON, Margaret Ann, W4336, MT, Halliburton, David
HALLIBURTON, Mary Frances Eliz. W6292, G, Halliburton, Wm. B.
HALLIBURTON, Missouri H. W8805, ST, Halliburton, James A.
HALLIBURTON, Virginia Ann, W2433, MT, Halliburton, Turner
HALLOM, Martha Ann, W2097, CH, Hallom, Noah Phillip

HALLON, James, S11535, GI, 1st (Turney's) Inf.
HALLUM, M. S16108, O, 20th (Russell's) Cav.
HALLUM, Malissa Ann, W9521, WE, Hallum, Robert P.
HALLUM, Martha Parlee, W10299, D, Hallum, George Washington
HALLY, Margaret Liza, W4215, MN, Hally, Grant Hamilton
HALTON, Martha Taylor, W2934, MA, Halton, Elisha Starks
HAM, Annie, W5132, SH, Ham, Mortimer Randolph
HAM, Bradley K. S16197, CA, 21st Cav.
HAM, Emma Briscoe, W2843, SH, Ham, George W.
HAM, I. W. S2483, CE, 20th Inf.
HAM, J. R. S7271, G, 45th Inf.
HAM, James R. S15329, SH, 18th Miss. Cav.
HAM, Jesse D. S2484, CE, 50th Inf.
HAM, Mary, W7790, G, Ham, J. R.
HAM, Mortimer Randolph, S13962, SH, 15th Miss. Inf.
HAM, Sophronia Jane, W9077, GI, Ham, Thomas L.
HAM, Thomas L. S15075, GI, 11th Ala. Cav.
HAMBLEN, Parmalier, W196, GE, Hamblen, Harrable
HAMBREE, Nerva, W1546, K, Hambree, Jasper
HAMBRICK, A. J. S571, MT, 49th Inf.
HAMBRIGHT, Aaron W. S9929, LO, 1st Ga. Inf.
HAMBY, George, S12605, LI, 41st Inf.
HAMBY, J. A. S8532, PI, 28th Inf.
HAMBY, John H. S4505, JO, 52nd N.C. Inf.
HAMBY, Kate, W8753, CU, Hamby, Albert N.
HAMBY, M. D. L. S2499, LI, 8th Inf.
HAMBY, Mattie, W10376, PI, Hamby, Julius A.
HAMBY, Nancy Frances, W7221, CU, Hamby, Wm. Anderson
HAMBY, William A. S12074, CU, 28th Inf.
HAMEL, John N. S4123, SU, 61st Inf.
HAMIL, Millie Frances, W5018, CC, Hamil, John Alexander
HAMILTON, Annie Eliza, W8560, DY, Hamilton, Ephraim Edward
HAMILTON, Cornelia, W10704, SH, Hamilton, Frank B.
HAMILTON, D. D. S7038, D, 7th Inf.
HAMILTON, D. G. S7931, SU, 12th Bn. Cav.
HAMILTON, David N. S14151, O, 15th Inf.
HAMILTON, E. S8306, MA, 14th Cav.

Index to Tennessee Confederate Pension Applications

HAMILTON, Elizabeth Jane, W4878, G, Hamilton, Wm. Wilkins Nelson
HAMILTON, F. B. S6460, MA, 6th Inf.
HAMILTON, G. W. S10284, WA, 60th Inf.
HAMILTON, Isaach H. S12567, WA, Unassigned (Nitre Bureau)
HAMILTON, Isaiah, S10507, SH, 1st Miss. Inf.
HAMILTON, J. G. S14515, WL, 4th (McLemore's) Cav.
HAMILTON, J. P. S16279, LI, 4th Ala. Cav.
HAMILTON, James, S5381, HE, 6th Cav.
HAMILTON, Jennie, W10464, FR, Hamilton, J. P.
HAMILTON, John L. S7106, SN, 2nd Inf.
HAMILTON, Josie Penelope, W5011, D, Hamilton, Joseph Porter
HAMILTON, Julia Ann, W7010, WL, Hamilton, James Gourley
HAMILTON, Maggie, W10754, CY, Hamilton, Wm. C.
HAMILTON, Margaret Amanda, W7795, D, Hamilton, D. D.
HAMILTON, Mary A. W10016, O, Hamilton, Wm. F.
HAMILTON, N. A. S8110, FR, 44th Inf.
HAMILTON, T. J. S9048, RO, 63rd Inf.
HAMILTON, W. G. S9993, SH, 47th Inf.
HAMILTON, W. H. S3947, D, 18th Inf.
HAMILTON, W. H. S12240, RU, Carter's Scouts
HAMILTON, W. R. S3885, MC, 1st Ga. State Troops
HAMIT, G. W. S982, WA, 60th Inf.
HAMLET, Charlotte, W48, J, Hamlet, Joseph
HAMLET, David M. S4175, J, 8th Inf.
HAMLET, John A. S11854, ST, 14th Inf.
HAMLET, Solomon, S9127, GI, 4th Ala. Cav.
HAMLETT, Amanda Jane, W7755, SH, Hamlett, W. J.
HAMLETT, D. W. S16043, A, 21st (Wilson's) Cav.
HAMLETT, J. M. S9110, MA, 51st Inf.
HAMLETT, W. J. S7191, SH, 26th Cav.
HAMLIN, Joseph William, S11797, 7th Inf.
HAMLIN, Julia Pride Kemp, W7675, Hamlin, Joe Wm.
HAMLIN, William Thomas, S10060, GI, 3rd (Clack's) Inf.
HAMM, Cyntha A. W7765, MN, Hamm, James M.
HAMM, Nicie Jane, W10273, MN, Hamm, Archibald Benton

HAMM, William C. S443, O, 9th Ala. Inf.
HAMMER, Elizabeth, W4638, SU, Hammer, James Cyrus
HAMMER, Kate E. W3913, SU, Hammer, John P.
HAMMERLY, Ada F. W7026, MA, Hammerly, Richard Henry
HAMMERLY, R. H. S10675, MA, 12th Ky. Cav.
HAMMERS, John T. S16668, SH, 4th Miss. Cav.
HAMMETT, E. R. S4018, WA, 60th Inf.
HAMMETT, Hannah, W5093, WA, Hammett, Ezekiel Reece
HAMMOCK, James, S7044, OV, 25th Inf.
HAMMOCK, John, S986, J, 8th Cav.
HAMMOCK, L. H. S11148, OV, 8th (Dibrell's) Cav.
HAMMOCK, Nannie Pink, W10293, SU, Hammock, N. J. T.
HAMMOCK, Polley, W1822, CL, Hammock, Sterling
HAMMOCK, Sterling, S207, GR, 26th Inf.
HAMMOCK, William, S2185, GR, 1st Cav.
HAMMON, Louisa Rowe, W4440, WL, Hammon, David Francis
HAMMON, Samuel, S3793, DI, 11th Inf.
HAMMOND, Amos, S6155, HA, 64th Va. Inf.
HAMMOND, Cas T. S9327, HM, 3rd (Lillard's) Mtd. Inf.
HAMMOND, Cynthia C. W7599, K, Hammond, Caswell Thomas
HAMMOND, D. F. S10263, WL, 3rd Confederate Cav.
HAMMOND, H. L. S12424, G, 47th Inf.
HAMMOND, Susan, W2896, MR, Hammond, John A.
HAMMOND, W. H. S7601, HM, 31st Inf.
HAMMONDS, Joseph Carroll, S15395, DY, 47th Inf.
HAMMONDS, Maria C. W8316, LA, Hammonds, G. W.
HAMMONS, John A. S2239, HR, 14th Cav.
HAMMONTREE, J. J. S2402, FR, 34th Inf.
HAMNER, Annie Shepherd, W4404, T, Hamner, Lorenzo Dew
HAMNER, Lorenzo Dow, S13284, T, C. S. Navy
HAMPSON, Ida E. W8513, SH, Hampson, Wm. Andrew
HAMPTON, B. F. S288, HD, 5th Ky. Vols.
HAMPTON, Carey D. S12080, WY, 20th Inf.

Index to Tennessee Confederate Pension Applications

HAMPTON, David M. S1763, MA, 51st Inf.
HAMPTON, James C. S1639, GE, 64th Inf.
HAMPTON, Laura Ann, W5548, MA, Hampton, David M.
HAMPTON, Malisia Colline, W2897, ST, Hampton, James
HAMPTON, Mary Catherine, W6140, WH, Hampton, Wm. Overton
HAMPTON, Noah J. S6839, D, 18th Inf.
HAMPTON, Parthenia, W2493, D, Hampton, Noah Jaspy
HAMPTON, Thomas J. S1419, WA, 63rd Inf.
HAMREN, J. J. S1940, WA, 3rd Cav.
HAMRICK, Mary E. W7662, W5353, F, Hamrick, Wm.
HANCOCK, A. H. S12696, HN, 5th Inf.
HANCOCK, Ada N. W3286, OV, Hancock, Amos W.
HANCOCK, Elizabeth Parilee, W7323, HN, Hancock, Azariah Harrison
HANCOCK, Eva C. W3964, HD, Hancock, Samuel S.
HANCOCK, G. D. S14100, HN, 1st Bn. (McNairy's) Cav.
HANCOCK, J. G. S6131, HN, 5th Inf.
HANCOCK, Nora, W7228, H, Hancock, Henry Crawford
HANCOCK, R. B. S85, PO, 10th N.C. Inf.
HANCOCK, R. P. S12017, 20th (Russell's) Cav.
HANCOCK, R. T. S9017, CA, 8th (Smith's) Cav.
HANCOCK, Richard R. S1711, CA, 22nd (Barteau's) Cav.
HANCOCK, W. W. S9573, HE, 1st Cav.
HANCOCK, Zemri, S1695, WE, 10th Bn. Hvy. Art.
HANDCOCK, Nancy Caroline, W6562, WE, Handcock, Zemri
HANDLEY, John R. S11278, D, 17th Inf.
HANDLIN, Dora, W10995, HU, Handlin, John Nathaniel
HANDLIN, John N. S16360, HU, 11th Inf.
HANDLY, Lizzie Caldwell, W5746, D, Handly, Claiborne Russ
HANDY, George, S14291, SH, 10th Miss. Inf.
HANES, Ella, W4587, D, Hanes, David Mosby
HANES, Ella, W10044, HI, Hanes, Peter Cornelius
HANEY, Sallie, W9155, PU, Haney, Elijah
HANKAL, James M. B. S2708, WA, 29th Inf.

HANKINS, Alfred, S3001, WL, 4th (McLemore's) Cav.
HANKINS, J. T. S12282, W, 2nd Cav.
HANKINS, Mildred H. W993, WL, Hankins, Wm. T.
HANKINS, Satira H. W1020, HR, Hankins, Wm. D.
HANKINS, W. J. S11406, HO, 14th Inf.
HANKS, Calvin J. S15423, SH, 1st Bn. Ark. Cav.
HANLEY, Frances, W1855, TR, Hanley, Thomas Jefferson
HANLEY, N. B. S4897, TR, 8th Inf.
HANN, J. C. S10515, HI, 26th Inf.
HANNA, George, C252, HI, 3rd (Forrest's) Cav.
HANNA, H. B. S6751, MU, 9th Inf.
HANNA, J. F. S11433, GI, 32nd Inf.
HANNA, J. S. S4572, MN, 26th Miss. Inf.
HANNA, Mary Louise, W8262, MU, Hanna, Hugh Brom
HANNA, Nancy M. W2707, GI, Hanna, Thomas
HANNA, W. C. S15832, T, 12th Cav.
HANNAH, A. L. S14744, RO, 25th N.C. Inf.
HANNAH, B. F. S2528, CE, 11th Inf.
HANNAH, Bettie, W10242, CE, Hannah, George Woodard
HANNAH, E. M. S3052, WA, 29th Inf.
HANNAH, Harriet Susan, W6105, SN, Hannah, James Alison
HANNAH, James A. S5120, CO, 62nd N.C. Inf.
HANNAH, Jerry, C254, MU, Regiment not given
HANNAH, John G. S58, FR, 41st Inf.
HANNAH, Nancy Rachel, W4190, FR, Hannah, John G.
HANNAH, S. A. S6426, FR, 45th Inf.
HANNER, Mary Parrish, W10666, WI, Hanner, John Wesley
HANNIET, Nancy, W1736, WA, Hanniet, George Washington
HANSARD, Joseph K. S15453, S15512, CL, 29th Inf.
HANSEL, James, S6124, K, 61st Inf.
HAQUEWOOD, B. A. S6545, DY, 51st Inf.
HARALSON, Mary Frances, W9747, WL, Haralson, Joseph Stanfield
HARBER, Mary Magdaline, W5534, G, Harber, James Washington
HARBERT, Tennessee Hutchison, W10584, G, Harbert, Thomas C.
HARBIN, Margaret, W3876, HM, Harbin, John

-147

HARBIN, Nannie M. W2649, H, Harbin, Wm. John
HARBIN, Sarah E. W6246, SH, Harbin, Samuel M.
HARBIN, Sarah Emeline, W6387, SE, Harbin, Jasper McDaniel
HARBISON, D. F. S2689, MU, 48th Inf.
HARBISON, Elizabeth George, W3112, HI, Harbison, M. M.
HARBISON, M. M. S984, HI, 48th Inf.
HARBISON, William M. S10915, MU, 19th (Biffle's) Cav.
HARBOUR, S. T. S449, HD, 1st Cav.
HARBSOOK, Mary Luvinia, W3101, K, Harbsook, George Lundamood
HARDAWAY, Sarah E. W191, D, Hardaway, Wm. W.
HARDCASTEL, Joseph P. S3079, W, 35th Inf.
HARDCASTLE, Charity E. W3666, DE, Hardcastle, John
HARDCASTLE, John, S4813, DE, 18th (Newsom's) Cav.
HARDEE, Lemuel, S9991, MA, 14th (Neely's) Cav.
HARDEMAN, B. J. S7309, O, 16th Cav.
HARDEMAN, Drucilla Ann, W8524, GI, Hardeman, Jasper Marion
HARDEMAN, J. M. S12306, GI, 21st (Wilson's) Cav.
HARDEN, Susan, W1998, BE, Harden, Isaac Henry
HARDER, Sarah A. W2409, P, Harder, Wm. Henry
HARDER, William Henry, S1745, P, 23rd Inf.
HARDIMAN, J. T. S15430, LA, 53rd Inf.
HARDIN, Cornelius, S4355, RO, 3rd N.C. Inf.
HARDIN, Hose, S15165, CO, 62nd Inf.
HARDIN, J. H. S8112, LI, 44th Inf.
HARDIN, J. N. S3110, WY, 9th Cav.
HARDIN, James O. S14353, MU, Orleans Lt. Horse Cav. La.
HARDIN, Jennie F. W10430, HD, Hardin, A. G. (Pony)
HARDIN, Margaret Jane, W3330, MN, Hardin, Bartlett
HARDIN, Marget A. W5878, LI, Hardin, James H.
HARDIN, Martha Ann, W4530, G, Hardin, A. R.
HARDIN, Peter, S6211, GU, 17th Inf.
HARDIN, Phena Ann, W186, LI, Hardin, Lovel C.

HARDIN, Sarah E. W10591, LE, Hardin, George W.
HARDIN, Thomas J. S16302, WY, 1st Confederate Cav.
HARDIN, W. D. S4935, MN, 32nd Miss. Inf.
HARDIN, Watt, S16169, HD, 1st Confederate Cav.
HARDING, Isadore, W7847, R, Harding, Sol
HARDING, James, C25, D, 9th Cav.
HARDING, Solomon, S4757, R, Lookout Art.
HARDISON, H. A. S14441, RU, 6th (Wheeler's) Cav.
HARDISON, Hampton Jeremiah, S12554, MU, 20th (Nixon's) Cav.
HARDISON, J. J. S16373, G, Forrest's Cav.
HARDISON, M. T. S13407, SH, 9th Ky. Inf.
HARDISON, Martin V. S6847, MU, 24th Inf.
HARDISON, Mattie, W10613, MU, Hardison, Hampton Jeremiah
HARDISON, R. C. S14036, WL, 6th (Wheeler's) Cav.
HARDISON, W. D. S15966, S14372, MU, 24th Inf.
HARDY, Frances Ann, W618, GI, Hardy, Alfred
HARDY, Luzelle,   See Luzelle Cecil
HARDY, Samuel, S9515, OV, 8th Cav.
HARGETT, John Alfred, S13634, O, 12th Inf.
HARGIS, John W. S10316, GU, 44th Inf.
HARGIS, Mary Eliz. Travis, W9281, GU, Hargis, Abraham Dallas
HARGROVE, Benjamin, S12859, MU, 48th (Nixon's) Inf.
HARGROVE, D. J. S12778, K, 3rd N.C. Inf.
HARGROVE, David E. S15495, GI, 10th Ala. Cav.
HARGROVE, Flora Jane, W3396, SH, Hargrove, John Calhoun
HARGROVE, J. A. S4286, GI, 3rd Cav.
HARGROVE, J. C. S7933, SH, 14th Miss. Inf.
HARGROVE, Lucinda, W7030, WE, Hargrove, Benjamin
HARGROVE, Sarah Ellen, W7067, K, Hargrove, David James
HARKINS, Caldonia Elisabeth, W2352, LI, Harkins, Thomas Marion
HARKLEROAD, Bashie [Green], W11120, SU, Harkleroad, Jacob Isaac, [Later married Green]
HARKLEROAD, George W. S10657, SU, 26th Inf.
HARKLEROAD, J. I. S7908, SU, Nitre & Mining

Index to Tennessee Confederate Pension Applications

HARKLEROAD, W. D. S12033, SU, 26th Inf.
HARKREADER, H. R. S10215, WL, 7th Inf.
HARLAN, Cullen Mack, S11975, HR, 23rd Miss. Inf.
HARLAN, Josephine, W4681, MU, Harlan, Henry C.
HARLAN, R. E. S7955, G, 12th Cav.
HARLAN, Thomas, S219, WL, 24th Inf.
HARLESS, Martha Jane, W7320, SU, Harless, Wm. A.
HARLESS, W. A. S5500, SU, 22nd Va. Cav.
HARLEY, H. E. S4454, D, 25th Inf.
HARLEY, Polly M. W4457, D, Harley, Hiram Ellison
HARLOW, Lucy C. W10955, MU, Harlow, Marion L.
HARLOW, Marion L. S12032, MU, 32nd Inf.
HARMAN, E. C. S14419, CT, 58th N.C. Inf.
HARMAN, G. W. S9574, PO, 29th Inf.
HARMAN, J. P. S11499, HN, 5th Inf.
HARMAN, Margaret J. W8692, MU, Harman, James Alexander
HARMAN, Mary Elizabeth, W10426, D, Harman, Charles Wesley
HARMAN, Sarah Jane, W3437, MC, Harman, Leonard J.
HARMAN, W. A. S11831, SU, 11th Bn. N.C. Inf.
HARMON, B. H. S13768, CC, 47th Inf.
HARMON, Benjamin A. S8990, HM, 64th N.C. Inf.
HARMON, D. J. S8918, HM, 60th Inf.
HARMON, Henry, S6207, GE, 64th N.C. Inf.
HARMON, J. H. S9628, O, 52nd Inf.
HARMON, Jacob F. S6010, HM, 64th N.C. Inf.
HARMON, James W. S14414, LA, 35th Ala. Inf.
HARMON, Jarusha Grady, W1833, CF, Harmon, Thomas Jefferson
HARMON, Kittie C. W3317, MU, Harmon, Frederick
HARMON, Leonard J. S3700, R, 26th Inf.
HARMON, Martha A. W4755, HM, Harmon, Daniel Jackson
HARMON, Mary Ann, W9703, SU, Harmon, Wiley Almon
HARMON, Rebecca C. W3667, MC, Harmon, George W.
HARMON, Sarah J. W3806, MC, Harmon, Leonard J.
HARMON, Tom, S7419, S10610, MU, 24th Inf.

HARMOND, James T. S3066, GI, 1st (Turney's) Inf.
HARNEY, Martha J. W8406, MO, Harney, Newton Lafayett
HARPER, A. N. S16476, D, 20th Cav.
HARPER, Hugh W. S3962, GE, 31st Inf.
HARPER, J. A. S16389, 7th Ky. Cav.
HARPER, J. B. S1002, D, 55th Inf.
HARPER, J. M. S9278, SM, 24th Inf.
HARPER, James A. S5654, WE, 7th Ky. Inf.
HARPER, Kittie, W8686, SM, Harper, Wm. Alexander, Same app. number as Emma Davis Long
HARPER, Louisa, W5390, O, Harper, John P.
HARPER, Martha Frances, W928, SN, Harper, Wm. T.
HARPER, Mary Elizabeth, W6802, SH, Harper, John A.
HARPER, Mary Frances, W8788, SM, Harper, Joseph H.
HARPER, Ora D. W1058, G, Harper, Samuel W.
HARPER, Rebecca Harrison, W11043, D, Harper, John Bell
HARPER, S. W. S2201, S2970, G, 12th Inf.
HARPER, T. M. S8375, GI, 32nd Inf.
HARPER, Thomas D. A. S1205, CO, 3rd Inf.
HARPER, William I. S16421, LI, 1st S.C. Inf.
HARPOLE, Ann, W1847, CF, Harpole, Martin VanBuren
HARPOLE, John T. S12333, G, 8th Ky. Cav.
HARPOLE, M. V. S5932, CF, 4th Inf.
HARR, Adam, S1451, SU, 63rd Inf.
HARR, E. D. S5912, SU, 63rd Inf.
HARR, Jacob D. S6674, SU, 59th Inf.
HARR, James, S3302, SU, 60th Inf.
HARR, James L. S7176, SU, 59th Inf.
HARR, John J. S9379, SU, 60th Inf.
HARR, Joseph D. S9648, SU, 61st Inf.
HARR, Lydia C. W7895, SU, Harr, Simon Wesley
HARR, Mary Elizabeth, W4935, SU, Harr, John Joseph
HARR, Mary R. W413, SU, Harr, Wm. M.
HARR, Mattie, W10189, SU, Harr, E. D.
HARR, S. J. E. S7144, SU, 59th Inf.
HARR, Sallie A. W7505, SU, Harr, Jacob D.
HARR, Simon W. S7245, SU, 59th Inf.
HARR, William D. S6712, SU, 59th Inf.
HARREL, John T. S4153, RU, 23rd Inf.
HARRELL, A. J. S76, RU, 2nd Inf.
HARRELL, Calvin S. S9755, GR, 12th Cav.

HARRELL, Emma Landon, W11128, T, Harrell, John Frank
HARRELL, Fanney, W9977, DY, Harrell, James Crogan
HARRELL, G. B. S11307, CF, 17th Inf.
HARRELL, H. M. S4394, RU, 2nd (Walker's) Inf.
HARRELL, J. B. S9672, SH, 9th Inf.
HARRELL, J. H. S10759, WA, 12th Bn. (Day's) Cav.
HARRELL, Maggie, W10483, CF, Harrell, Gilbert B.
HARRELL, Martha, W3443, GR, Harrell, Calvin Scot
HARRELL, N. H. S2958, CL, 12th Bn. (Day's) Cav.
HARRELL, Rebecca Angeline, W1740, MU, Harrell, John Washington
HARRELL, Robert H. S7075, GR, 51st Va. Inf.
HARRELL, Robert N. S4024, S4791, SH, 9th Inf.
HARRELL, Sarah Elizabeth, W8095, SH, Harrell, Robert A.
HARRELL, T. A. S4575, HW, 12th Bn. (Day's) Cav.
HARRIGAN, Thomas, S11181, SU, 2nd Ala. Cav.
HARRINGTON, Elizabeth, W5295, WE, Harrington, George Washington
HARRINGTON, Emma, W2278, D, Harrington, Alfus Truman
HARRINGTON, G. W. S7780, WE, 26th N.C. Inf.
HARRINGTON, J. D. S7569, CE, 18th Inf.
HARRINGTON, J. D. S9680, HI, 24th Inf.
HARRINGTON, J. M. S13339, SH, 1st Ark. Inf.
HARRINGTON, Jennie L. W6528, CE, Harrington, John D.
HARRINGTON, Lottie, W4929, SH, Harrington, John M.
HARRINGTON, Tennessee, W2531, HI, Harrington, James D.
HARRINGTON, W. B. S11316, U, 21st Va. Cav.
HARRINGTON, W. H. S9220, WL, 45th Inf.
HARRINGTON, W. W. S14090, LK, 24th Inf.
HARRIS, A. D. S12392, WA, 60th Inf.
HARRIS, A. J. S11015, SH, 19th Miss. Inf.
HARRIS, A. L. S9654, LA, 48th (Nixon's) Inf.
HARRIS, Almeadia, W1043, D, Harris, Lafayette
HARRIS, America, W421, J, Harris, Bryant

HARRIS, Anne E. W8702, GI, Harris, Charles N.
HARRIS, Benjamin, S13805, CY, 1st (Carter's) Cav.
HARRIS, CHarles Edwin, S15938, S16624, HR, 3rd (Forrest's) Cav.
HARRIS, Catherine Jane, W5161, CF, Harris, Rawly Cunningham
HARRIS, Charles N. S13230, GI, 12th Miss. Cav.
HARRIS, Charley, C68, DI, 11th Inf., Alias Charley Bell
HARRIS, David Porter, S3869, CA, 18th Inf.
HARRIS, Dora, W9911, HU, Harris, O. Wit
HARRIS, Eliza Ann, W8806, MA, Harris, John Wesley
HARRIS, Eliza H. W4909, SH, Harris, Henry Macon
HARRIS, Elizabeth Jane, W2898, MN, Harris, David Thomas
HARRIS, Emeline [Pressley], W10348, OV, Harris, Franklin, [Later married Pressley]
HARRIS, Emily C. W2451, MA, Harris, John W.
HARRIS, Fannie A. W3668, H, Harris, Wm.
HARRIS, Fannie Davis, W3892, SH, Harris, Fergus Sloan
HARRIS, Florence Frazer, W6013, MA, Harris, Howell DeWitt
HARRIS, Flovilla Hoyle, W2376, FR, Harris, Robert
HARRIS, Frank, S14252, CL, 37th Va. Inf.
HARRIS, Fredonia Ann, W8638, LE, Harris, John Franklin
HARRIS, G. L, S11809, MN, 18th (Newsom's) Cav.
HARRIS, G. W. S14682, 55th Inf.
HARRIS, George W. S15829, 55th Inf.
HARRIS, Grandison, S125, S1631, RU, 18th Inf.
HARRIS, H. M. S4270, SH, 17th Miss. Inf.
HARRIS, H. R. C. W2646, HY, Harris, J. W.
HARRIS, HAttie Gibson, W10306, CT, Harris, Nathaniel Edwin
HARRIS, I. T. S6817, MA, 4th Inf.
HARRIS, I. T. S9740, MU, 3rd (Clack's) Inf.
HARRIS, J. F. S14542, LE, 1st Bn. (McNairy's) Cav.
HARRIS, J. M. S12642, S15466, BO, Thomas' Legion, N.C.
HARRIS, J. N. S10611, RU, 4th Cav.

HARRIS, J. N. S11489, CC, 47th Inf.
HARRIS, J. R. S423, WL, 18th Inf.
HARRIS, J. R. S12835, ST, 48th (Nixon's) Inf.
HARRIS, J. T. S10021, SH, 2nd Miss. Cav.
HARRIS, J. T. S12438, O, 12th Cav.
HARRIS, J. W. S3763, CH, 21st (Wilson's) Cav.
HARRIS, J. W. S16105, MU, 19th Ala. Inf.
HARRIS, Jacob T. S11530, D, 45th Inf.
HARRIS, James A. S4837, O, 15th Cav.
HARRIS, James M. S13730, LI, 2nd Ga. State Troops
HARRIS, James R. S10580, D, 6th Inf.
HARRIS, James U. S15775, S15872, 55th Inf.
HARRIS, James U. S16033, 22nd Inf.
HARRIS, James W. S7503, HY, 12th (Green's) Cav.
HARRIS, Jane, W7005, CL, Harris, Frank
HARRIS, John A. S8569, SM, 4th Cav.
HARRIS, John D. S5428, B, 41st Inf.
HARRIS, John W. S12, RU, 18th & 4th Cav.
HARRIS, Julia C. W7736, RU, Harris, Charles N.
HARRIS, Julia D. W6483, SH, Harris, John Vincent
HARRIS, Laura E. W2921, MT, Harris, Aquilla
HARRIS, Lillie Sophronia, W4565, SH, Harris, Andrew Jackson
HARRIS, Louisa, W3544, SN, Harris, John Dudley
HARRIS, Louise C. W10982, W10766, BO, Harris, James Madison
HARRIS, Lucretia, W558, CE, Harris, Byness Franklin
HARRIS, Lucy Ann, W5210, H, Harris, Tazwell Polk
HARRIS, M. L. S15712, SU, 48th Va. Inf.
HARRIS, Maggie Green, W6078, RU, Harris, John C.
HARRIS, Margaret G. W6335, CC, Harris, Rollen G.
HARRIS, Margaret R. W7297, O, Harris, John C.
HARRIS, Mary, W7707, D, Harris, J. R.
HARRIS, Mary Eliza, W10405, GI, Harris, Wm. Searcy
HARRIS, Mary H. W3532, MA, Harris, Wm. Irbin
HARRIS, Mary Hillman, W9677, WE, Harris, Louis Allen
HARRIS, Mattie Emerson, W4967, CC, Harris, James Nathaniel

HARRIS, Mildred, W8913, MS, Harris, David L.
HARRIS, Mollie Anne, W5987, SH, Harris, Alonzo
HARRIS, Nancy Hill, W620, MA, Harris, George Washington
HARRIS, Nannie C. W7737, B, Harris, Wm. J.
HARRIS, Nannie Halbert, W8497, LI, Harris, James Mathew
HARRIS, Nannie Rebecca, W7007, CH, Harris, Jessie Winborn
HARRIS, Newton C. S2891, D, Huggin's Co. Lt. Art.
HARRIS, Orris, S11305, HR, 7th Cav.
HARRIS, Paralee, W10762, MN, Harris, W. H.
HARRIS, R. C. S7305, CF, 1st Inf.
HARRIS, R. J. S12950, WI, 19th (Biffle's) Cav.
HARRIS, Rebecca L. W4569, CA, Harris, David P.
HARRIS, Richard A. S8826, RU, 24th Inf.
HARRIS, Robert, S666, MR, 9th Ga. Inf.
HARRIS, Ruth, W9123, CC, Harris, Leven Hill
HARRIS, S. L. S713, ME, 2nd Cav.
HARRIS, Sallie Mitchell, W4875, SH, Harris, John L.
HARRIS, Samuel, S3469, R, 63rd Inf.
HARRIS, Sarah A. W354, MU, Harris, Edward
HARRIS, Sarah F. W414, MT, Harris, John Richard
HARRIS, Stacie Jane, W6420, LI, Harris, Newton Franklin
HARRIS, Susan Elizabeth, W2150, OV, Harris, James Carroll
HARRIS, T. D. S7334, CH, 33rd Inf.
HARRIS, T. G. S3296, SN, 20th Inf.
HARRIS, T. J. S9308, DI, 11th Inf.
HARRIS, Tennessee R. W3897, D, Harris, W. W. S.
HARRIS, Tennie F. W1798, R, Harris, Samuel L.
HARRIS, Thomas A. S1576, HW, 50th Inf.
HARRIS, Thomas G. S531, SN, 20th Inf.
HARRIS, Tina, W10766, W10982, BO, Harris, James M.
HARRIS, Victoria, W1176, M, Harris, Winton Bates
HARRIS, W. C. S11128, MS, 6th (Wheeler's) Cav.
HARRIS, W. F. S14422, MA, 31st Inf.
HARRIS, W. H. S13642, MN, 21st (Wilson's) Cav.

HARRIS, W. H. H. S8991, CU, 1st (Carter's) Cav.
HARRIS, W. R. S8126, J, 8th (Dibrell's) Cav.
HARRIS, W. T. S15807, O, 15th Cav.
HARRIS, Wash. C163, GI, Undetermined
HARRIS, Wesley, S5762, HN, 5th Inf.
HARRIS, William, S11786, BE, 49th Inf.
HARRIS, William D. S15508, WL, 45th Inf.
HARRIS, William F. S13056, HN, 5th Inf.
HARRIS, William H. S3930, H, 1st (Carter's) Cav.
HARRIS, William H. S14417, G, 7th Inf.
HARRIS, William P. S7459, MU, 8th (Smith's) Cav.
HARRISON, A. J. S14043, HD, 53rd Inf.
HARRISON, B. F. S10869, JE, 31st Inf.
HARRISON, B. P. S10131, SH, 20th Inf.
HARRISON, Benjamin F. S8908, GE, 31st Inf.
HARRISON, C. T. S7658, MA, 12th Miss. Cav.
HARRISON, Charles, S2500, WA, 60th Inf.
HARRISON, D. P. S2122, WI, 20th Inf.
HARRISON, D. Z. S12795, G, 32nd Inf.
HARRISON, Ella Pleasant, W7369, MU, Harrison, Wm. B.
HARRISON, Fanny E. W1284, WI, Harrison, W. H.
HARRISON, Gertrude, W4881, MU, Harrison, Wyatt Cary
HARRISON, Harriet Elmira, W783, HD, Harrison, Thomas Robert
HARRISON, J. M. S6640, WA, 62nd N.C. Inf.
HARRISON, J. M. S11336, WI, 20th Inf.
HARRISON, James M. S16231, D, Forrest's Escort, Cav.
HARRISON, Jessie Miles, W11074, W, Harrison, John Samuel
HARRISON, John, S3256, SM, 38th Inf.
HARRISON, John, S6970, HW, 64th Va. Inf.
HARRISON, John M. S13986, SM, 45th Inf.
HARRISON, Lavena, W2729, WA, Harrison, Joseph Mitchell
HARRISON, Lempy J. W5502, DK, Harrison, John
HARRISON, Margaret, W9620, WI, Harrison, Daniel P.
HARRISON, Martha Louisa, W1704, GE, Harrison, Washington
HARRISON, Martin V. S12036, T, 4th Inf.
HARRISON, Mary Elizabeth, W559, SN, Harrison, James Wm.
HARRISON, Mary Jane, W7985, WI, Harrison, James Mitchell
HARRISON, Mary Lou, W5256, MA, Harrison, Columbus T.
HARRISON, Mary Lou, W10594, SH, Harrison, Wm. David
HARRISON, Mattie C. W5700, D, Harrison, James P.
HARRISON, Mattie Jane, W2962, MA, Harrison, Wm. Henry
HARRISON, N. F. S6295, SH, 13th Inf.
HARRISON, Parilee V. W4924, F, Harrison, Rufus Knight
HARRISON, R. K. S1829, F, 13th Inf.
HARRISON, Salina Bendon, W784, OV, Harrison, John Randolph
HARRISON, Sallie Hogan, W10333, O, Harrison, Daniel Zeno
HARRISON, Sarah A. W3076, JE, Harrison, B. F.
HARRISON, Susan Catherine, W2597, G, Harrison, James
HARRISON, T. L. S8335, WI, 4th Cav.
HARRISON, Thomas T. S8770, D, 1st Inf.
HARRISON, W. E. S6971, GE, 64th Va. Inf.
HARRISON, W. G. S5665, MS, 32nd Inf.
HARRISON, W. H. S7887, MA, 6th Inf.
HARRISON, Washington, S5642, GE, 61st Inf.
HARRISON, William B. S15322, MU, Unassigned (Chief Surgeon)
HARRISON, Wilmoth [Phillips], W10897, WE, Harrison, Adison L. [Later married Phillips]
HARSTON, Jarrod, S279, HY, 6th Inf.
HART, C. V. S12007, MA, 6th Inf.
HART, Elizabeth Mary, W3596, G, Hart, John
HART, Emma Buntin, W3475, MA, Hart, James Neely
HART, H. L. S15937, O, 12th S.C. Inf.
HART, J. M. S7027, WE, 15th Tex. Cav. (Dismounted)
HART, James, S3538, SH, 21st Inf.
HART, James H. S491, CC, 51st Inf.
HART, John, S8510, MC, 43rd Inf.
HART, Martha Locke, W6447, SH, Hart, Ben
HART, Nancy Artimazia, W8644, MA, Hart, Wm. Joseph
HART, R. D. S8759, MA, 6th Inf.
HART, S. S6753, HN, 46th Inf.
HART, Sadie Amanda, W6064, MA, Hart, Calvin Vancourt
HARTLEY, Alice C. W7123, SH, Hartley, James Douglass
HARTLEY, Washington, S7794, WI, 24th Inf.

HARTLINE, Henry Sims, S3037, MO, 19th Ala. Inf.
HARTMAN, George W. S14919, D, 15th Ky. Cav.
HARTMAN, J. C. S12428, MN, 18th N.C. Inf.
HARTMAN, James Henry, S15859, L, 22nd (Nixon's) Cav.
HARTMAN, Margaret, W7192, MN, Hartman, James C.
HARTMAN, Sallie Mitchel, W8855, DY, Hartman, J. H.
HARTMAN, William, S8818, D, 20th Inf.
HARTNESS, John A. S7306, SU, 60th Inf.
HARTSELL, Joseph, S14109, RO, 64th N.C. Inf.
HARTSFIELD, W. S. S11079, G, 47th Inf.
HARTSFIELD, William Sidney, S14253, G, 47th Inf.
HARTSOOK, George L. S5408, S4966, BO, 27th Va. Cav.
HARVEY, Abner, S3192, CL, 37th Inf.
HARVEY, Drury A. S15078, WA, Brumit's Co. Tenn. Home Guards
HARVEY, F. S. S8251, DY, 15th Cav.
HARVEY, George W. S4190, LI, 41st Inf.
HARVEY, John W. S991, CO, 50th Inf.
HARVEY, Mary Frances, W7495, MT, Harvey, Oney S.
HARVEY, O. S. S7159, MT, 11th Inf.
HARVEY, Sarah Elizabeth, W2677, CL, Harvey, Thomas
HARVEY, Thomas, S2921, GR, 12th Cav.
HARWARD, Harriett, W864, OV, Harward, Bry
HARWELL, Allen C. S8265, SH, 9th Cav.
HARWELL, Florence Pierce, W3936, D, Harwell, Frank Eugene
HARWELL, H. M. S16497, GI, Unassigned (Ala. Nitre & Mining Corps)
HARWELL, J. N. S8160, SH, 3rd (Forrest's) Cav.
HARWELL, L. C. S11335, CC, 47th Inf.
HARWELL, L. C. S11607, L, 42nd Inf.
HARWELL, L. S. S4039, HY, 9th Ala. Inf.
HARWELL, Mary Frances, W5090, GI, Harwell, Richard Sevier
HARWELL, Richard L. S3472, GI, 1st (Feild's) Inf.
HARWELL, T. J. S10499, MN, 21st (Wilson's) Cav.
HARWELL, Tempie Lou, W8724, W5610, MS, Harwell, Richard Mason
HARWELL, Wilkes, S14178, GI, 11th Ala. Cav.

HARWOOD, Alzie, W4029, R, Harwood, B. F.
HARWOOD, B. F. S7093, BL, 26th Inf.
HARWOOD, Frances Louisa, W2369, DY, Harwood, James Harvey
HARWOOD, Hattie Mead, W10768, SH, Harwood, Wm. Hugh
HARWOOD, J. E. S3092, WA, 63rd Va. Inf.
HARWOOD, Joseph S. S5776, ME, 3rd Inf.
HARWOOD, Mary Eugenia, W6068, D, Harwood, Richard Drury
HASH, J. B. S1439, SU, 50th Inf.
HASHAW, William R. S2565, GI, 17th Inf.
HASKINS, Creek, S14349, DY, 19th & 20th Consolidated Cav.
HASKINS, Jasper N. S7065, HR, 2nd Miss. Inf.
HASKINS, John Gaston, S981, MT, 49th Inf.
HASLAM, Polk, S9244, D, 1st Inf.
HASLETT, W. P. S13561, MOO, 23rd Inf.
HASLEY, H. S7403, S11754, DI, 10th (DeMoss') Cav.
HASSELL, E. T. S9202, HO, 50th Inf.
HASSELL, Elisha M. S10987, WI, 11th Cav.
HASSELL, Martha Ruth, See Martha R. Chaney
HASSELL, Mary Jane, W9943, D, Hassell, E. T.
HASSELL, Nancy Salina, W2856, HI, Hassell, Zebulon
HASSELL, Nannie W. W4918, G, Hassell, George Ellis
HASSELL, W. B. S14182, DI, 10th Cav.
HASTIN, H. F. S9011, U, 56th N.C. Inf.
HASTIN, J. G. C84, MO, 42nd Ga. Cav., Application is missing.
HASTING, James, S11608, HN, 5th Inf.
HASTING, Mirah, W545, V, Hasting, James
HASTING, Nettie, W8173, HN, Hasting, E. J.
HASTINGS, Alex, C141, B, 17th Inf.
HASTINGS, E. J. S14345, HN, 5th Inf.
HASTINGS, Francis Marion, S4280, HN, 46th Inf.
HASTINGS, John M. S3750, B, 17th Inf.
HASTINGS, Joseph H. S1214, B, 17th Inf.
HASTINGS, Lawrence Green, S5483, HN, 46th Inf.
HASTINGS, Sarah Malinda, W6265, HN, Hastings, Lawrence Green
HASTINGS, T. M. S3757, HN, 46th Inf.
HASTON, Joanna, W8390, WH, Haston, Samuel Shockley
HASTON, John T. S3539, V, 1st Cav.
HASTON, Samuel S. S10824, V, 16th Inf.
HASTY, J. T. S16441, WL, 16th Inf.

Index to Tennessee Confederate Pension Applications

HASTY, Martha, W6328, D, Hasty, James Pleasant
HASTY, W. M. S11404, HU, 17th Inf.
HATCH, Willie ADams, W9538, H, Hatch, Lemuel Durant
HATCHER, Alex, S3303, B, 23rd Inf.
HATCHER, Amelia Edna, W6740, SH, Hatcher, Samuel Archibald
HATCHER, Elizabeth C. W1710, SU, Hatcher, Henry
HATCHER, George R. S10240, BR, 4th Ga. Cav.
HATCHER, Lillie, W5969, B, Hatcher, Alex
HATCHER, Lucrecia Frances, W885, WE, Hatcher, D. M. W.
HATCHER, Mary Jane, W9056, WI, Hatcher, Spootwood Henry
HATCHER, Sarah Elizabeth, W5085, H, Hatcher, George Radford
HATCHER, W. R. S2029, OV, 28th Inf.
HATCHER, William B. S3311, SU, 3rd Inf.
HATCHES, Eutatia, W2782, SU, Hatches, Wm. B.
HATCHET, Nathan C. S13187, B, 2nd (Robison's) Inf.
HATCHETT, Ann, W9696, FR, Hatchett, Isham W.
HATCHETT, George W. S3740, B, 2nd (Robison's) Inf.
HATCHETT, J. H. S8127, MS, 33rd Inf.
HATCHETT, Jennie, W8632, B, Hatchett, Thomas
HATCHETT, Margaret, W10406, B, Hatchett, Nathan C.
HATCHETT, Thomas, S12234, B, 2nd Inf.
HATFIELD, Annie, W4585, LO, Hatfield, George Gibson
HATFIELD, Charles L. S2147, FR, 12th Inf.
HATFIELD, F. M. S6320, HA, 29th Inf.
HATFIELD, George Gibson, S1257, LO, 5th Cav.
HATFIELD, Julia, W1732, SQ, Hatfield, Wm. Emery
HATFIELD, Malvina, W619, H, Hatfield, Franklin Miller
HATFIELD, Mary, W1299, SQ, Hatfield, Wm. H.
HATFIELD, Nancy Jane, W7937, FR, Hatfield, Charles Leander
HATFIELD, Pricy, W2014, SQ, Hatfield, David C.
HATFIELD, William, S11677, GU, 1st Confederate Cav.
HATFIELD, William E. S3229, SQ, 2nd (Ashby's) Cav.
HATFIELD, William G. S5933, WH, 5th Cav.
HATFIELD, William P. S16640, H, 16th Ga. Inf.
HATHCOCK, John T. S7674, T, 31st Inf.
HATHCOCK, L. H. S415, RU, 44th Inf.
HATHWAY, J. A. S4182, DY, 12th Inf.
HATHWAY, Missouri Parlee, W4817, DY, Hathway, James Adison
HATLEY, H. C. S798, WL, 8th (Smith's) Cav.
HATLEY, N. G. S2095, DI, 1st Hvy. Art.
HATLEY, P. H. S3805, BE, 12th Ga. Cav.
HATLEY, William E. S4022, HD, 9th Ky. Inf.
HATTON, Sophia K. W1075, WI, Hatton, Robert
HAUGHTON, A. G. S14615, MA, Kyser's Scouts
HAUGHTON, Annie Gill, W6561, MA, Haughton, Alzemon G.
HAUKAL, M. K. S2062, WA, 29th Inf.
HAVELEY, C. B. S9482, HM, 63rd Inf.
HAVELEY, Jacob M. S7203, K, 3rd Conf. Engineer Troops, 3rd Confederate Engineer Troops
HAVELY, James, S8854, K, 19th Inf.
HAVELY, Jerome H. S15435, HM, 25th Bn. Va. Cav.
HAVELY, Malinda, W943, K, Havely, Jacob M.
HAVNER, Jacob, S1116, HE, 52nd Inf.
HAVNOR, Ardena, W7788, HE, Havnor, Jacob
HAVRON, James P. S5086, MR, 4th (McLemore's) Cav.
HAVRON, Rebecca Y. W3123, H, Havron, Hodges H.
HAWK, H. D. S15924, SU, 19th Inf.
HAWK, James, S5554, SU, 60th Inf.
HAWK, James M. S13345, SU, 19th Inf.
HAWK, S. F. S10074, SH, 18th Miss. Inf.
HAWK, Sarah M. W9456, SU, Hawk, James Meredith
HAWK, Tim, S13312, MO, 16th Bn. Mtd. Inf.
HAWKES, Alelia Alice, W4769, SH, Hawkes, Archer Everett
HAWKES, Archer Everett, S12276, SH, 3rd Va. Cav.
HAWKES, Martha Ann, W6115, RU, Hawkes, John Archey
HAWKINS, Bettie J. W1279, D, Hawkins, Thomas Solomon

HAWKINS, E. E. S14412, CC, 12th Inf.
HAWKINS, Evaline, W2100, J, Hawkins, James I.
HAWKINS, Florence, W7245, CA, Hawkins, J. I.
HAWKINS, H. L. S16659, R, Unassigned
HAWKINS, James, S5582, J, 28th Inf.
HAWKINS, James M. S7015, MS, 53rd Inf.
HAWKINS, Joe D. S2637, CA, 11th Cav.
HAWKINS, Joe I. S14618, W, 11th (Holman's) Cav.
HAWKINS, Julia Amanda, W4309, WE, Hawkins, Moses Henry
HAWKINS, Lauretta, W5531, WL, Hawkins, Henry
HAWKINS, Livinia, W280, D, Hawkins, E. T.
HAWKINS, Louisa A. W6409, MS, Hawkins, James Marion
HAWKINS, Mary Ellen, W10589, SH, Hawkins, Wm. Robert
HAWKINS, Mary Frances, W1613, FR, Hawkins, Henry J.
HAWKINS, Phillip, S15586, GU, 1st (Turney's) Inf.
HAWKINS, Sallie Merrit, W8616, FR, Hawkins, Phillip
HAWKINS, William B. S7335, CA, 23rd Inf.
HAWKS, John, S2244, ME, 43rd Inf.
HAWKS, John Taylor, S14626, D, 9th (Ward's) Cav.
HAWKS, P. H. S15277, SH, 6th Inf.
HAWKS, Sarah jane, W9660, CF, Hawks, James T.
HAWLEY, A. M. S11934, BE, 59th Inf.
HAWLEY, David A. J. S4469, SU, 1st (Carter's) Cav.
HAWLEY, James A. S2460, BE, 19th Inf.
HAWLEY, Nancy W. W5065, BE, Hawley, A. M.
HAWLEY, Susan, W7597, BE, Hawley, James A.
HAWTHORN, James E. S8212, MA, 51st Inf.
HAWTHORNE, E. D. C105, L, 7th Cav.
HAWTHORNE, Isabella Allen, W5943, D, Hawthorne, Eli Pitchford
HAY, H. B. S10095, WI, 48th (Voorhies') Inf.
HAY, John T. S11178, CC, 16th Ga. Inf.
HAY, Mary, W9330, CC, Hay, John Thomas
HAY, Mary B. W8950, RU, Hay, Baylom
HAYES, Alexander A. S11519, G, 8th (Smith's) Cav.
HAYES, Alice Maples, W10780, WI, Hayes, John P.
HAYES, Almira, W2926, D, Hayes, Newton M.
HAYES, Angeline, W5822, GR, Hayes, Henderson E.
HAYES, Barnet, S684, GR, 26th Inf.
HAYES, C. J. S7488, BO, 3rd (Lillard's) Mtd. Inf.
HAYES, C. L. S6620, MT, 11th Inf.
HAYES, Caesar, C34, SH, 154th Sr. Regt. Inf.
HAYES, E. T. S2524, MC, 3rd (Lillard's) Mtd. Inf.
HAYES, Elizabeth, W607, WA, Hayes, Jacob
HAYES, Elizabeth Ann, W5525, CL, Hayes, Green Berry
HAYES, Freeling, S15845, D, Shaw's Bn. Cav.
HAYES, G. B. S5268, CL, 12th Cav.
HAYES, H. E. S7153, GR, 2nd (Ashby's) Cav.
HAYES, H. H. S9480, MC, 3rd Cav.
HAYES, Harmon M. S4615, HA, 5th (McKenzie's) Cav.
HAYES, Henry Lafayette, S12549, W, 16th Inf.
HAYES, Ibby S. W5247, W3701, G, Hayes, Alexander A.
HAYES, J. P. S16406, WI, 3rd (Forrest's) Cav.
HAYES, J. S. S14407, SH, 56th Ala. Cav.
HAYES, James, S6818, CL, 26th Inf.
HAYES, John S. S2959, K, 3rd Inf.
HAYES, John T. S12281, WH, 23rd Inf.
HAYES, L. W. S14110, LA, 43rd Ga. Inf.
HAYES, Lizzie Martin, W7619, D, Hayes, Charles Morgan
HAYES, Lydia, W3178, GR, Hayes, Robertson
HAYES, Mary E. W8115, WA, Hayes, P. P.
HAYES, Mollie, W7907, T, Hayes, James W.
HAYES, Nancy Eilzabeth, W8370, LA, Hayes, Lewis Wesley
HAYES, Nancy Jane, W7388, W, Hayes, Henry Layfatte
HAYES, R. P. S6801, WH, Undetermined
HAYES, Rachel O. W5545, BO, Hayes, C. J.
HAYES, Ruthy M. W4936, GR, Hayes, Barnett
HAYES, W. H. S7140, GI, 53rd Inf.
HAYES, W. J. S11907, K, 16th N.C. Inf.
HAYLEY, William A. S11446, MA, 51st Inf.
HAYNES, A. H. S15281, RU, 55th Inf.
HAYNES, Emma, W8117, WA, Haynes, John
HAYNES, Emma L. W2731, CA, Haynes, Wm. Jefferson
HAYNES, George W. S10142, DE, 52nd Inf.
HAYNES, Georgia Ann Victoria, W9339, SH, Haynes, John Jones
HAYNES, H. C. S16205, SN, 2nd Inf.
HAYNES, Henry H. S3298, B, 18th Inf.

HAYNES, J. N. S6972, CC, 12th Ky. Cav.
HAYNES, J. N. S8544, G, Undetermined
HAYNES, J. P. S15290, CO, 62nd N.C. Inf.
HAYNES, J. W. A. S8707, RU, 11th Cav.
HAYNES, Jacob, S7632, U, 1st (Carter's) Cav.
HAYNES, James, S14330, MN, Phillip's Legion, Cav.
HAYNES, James A. S13123, HN, 10th (DeMoss') Cav.
HAYNES, Jennie Louise, W7099, SH, Haynes, Alonzo Augustus
HAYNES, John, S14577, U, 12th Cav.
HAYNES, John A. S9154, WI, 24th Inf.
HAYNES, John J. S11112, SH, 9th Miss. Cav.
HAYNES, Lela Forrest, W9904, CC, Haynes, Wm. A.
HAYNES, Louisa, W10573, DY, Haynes, Wm. W.
HAYNES, M. E. S681, DE, 52nd Inf.
HAYNES, Marinda Ellen, W9055, SN, Haynes, Henry Clay
HAYNES, Melvina, W8071, W9494, HO, Haynes, David James
HAYNES, Roxanna, W8789, CA, Haynes, Newton Alexander
HAYNES, Samuel P. S2628, HW, 63rd Inf.
HAYNES, Sarah Elizabeth, W968, RU, Haynes, John Wm.
HAYNES, Sophia M. W9741, RU, Haynes, Wm. Rufus
HAYNES, Susan Elizabeth, W8736, HN, Haynes, Wm. Dillahunty
HAYNES, Susana Rebecca, W7206, WI, Haynes, John A.
HAYNES, W. A. S6069, HO, 50th Inf.
HAYNES, W. A. S16240, CC, 3rd (Forrest's) Cav.
HAYNES, W. D. S15367, HN, 15th Cav.
HAYNES, W. R. S16064, RU, 45th Inf.
HAYNES, Washington, C64, HN, 5th Inf.
HAYNIE, Amanda Crews, W5126, D, Haynie, Jessie E.
HAYNIE, Blanche, W11140, LO, Haynie, James Jackson
HAYNIE, Elizabeth Townes, W3152, SH, Haynie, Thomas James
HAYNIE, Jesse E. S334, SM, 23rd Inf.
HAYNIE, John L. S12298, T, 12th Cav.
HAYNIE, Martin B. S335, SM, 9th Cav.
HAYS, Almeda, W7175, W10410, LA, Hays, Jones
HAYS, Bettie, W330, ST, Hays, James Washington
HAYS, E. W. S5515, HN, 46th Inf.
HAYS, Elizabeth J. W1919, GE, Hays, John
HAYS, Ellen Douglass, W1303, D, Hays, Stokley Hannon
HAYS, G. B. S9683, BR, 2nd (Ashby's) Cav.
HAYS, James W. S9763, T, 51st Inf.
HAYS, John C. S8341, DK, 8th (Smith's) Cav.
HAYS, Jones, S7454, LA, 19th (Biffle's) Cav.
HAYS, Josephine G. W1747, SH, Hays, Robert Butler
HAYS, Josey, W10751, K, Hays, James L.
HAYS, Luke, C279, CC, Regiment not given
HAYS, Mary D. W2183, BR, Hays, G. B.
HAYS, Mary Eliza, W7971, CC, Hays, Wm. Lawson
HAYS, N. B. S10478, K, 3rd Confederate Engineer Troops
HAYS, Nancy Ann, W4575, WL, Hays, James Bryant
HAYS, P. R. S12933, HN, 46th Inf.
HAYS, Unity Jane, W3989, BR, Hays, Wm. Grant
HAYS, W. A. S16330, DI, 11th Inf.
HAYS, W. H. S15355, DK, 24th Inf.
HAYS, W. P. S763, WL, 45th Inf.
HAYS, William, S8035, RU, 23rd Inf.
HAYS, William L. S9784, CC, 19th Ala. Inf.
HAYSE, Peter P. S14878, WA, Waugh's Regt. Home Guards
HAYWOOD, John, S336, T, 7th Cav.
HAYWORTH, Martha, W8807, JO, Hayworth, Nathan J.
HAYZE, Lydia, W1061, HA, Hayze, Robertson
HAZELWOOD, W. E. S14469, F, 3rd (Forrest's) Cav.
HAZLERIGG, A. J. S3813, WE, 22nd (Barteau's) Cav.
HAZLERIGG, W. H. S4027, O, 4th Inf.
HAZLEWOOD, G. F. S11146, LA, 53rd Inf.
HAZLEWOOD, John, S12096, GI, 11th Ala. Cav.
HAZLEWOOD, John R. S1572, WE, 7th Inf.
HAZLEWOOD, Mattie, W8282, HR, Hazlewood, Wm. E.
HAZLEWOOD, W. D. S9283, F, 5th Ala. Cav.
HAZLEWOOD, W. T. S6483, HR, 3rd (Forrest's) Cav.
HAZZLERIGG, William Henry, S213, O, 33rd Inf.

HEACKER, W. J. S13836, GR, 2nd (Ashby's) Cav.
HEAD, Amanda R. W2774, G, Head, E. Alex.
HEAD, E. A. S4738, G, 9th Bn. (Gantt's) Cav.
HEAD, J. W. S16079, O, 22nd (Barteau's) Cav.
HEAD, John W. S3021, WA, 25th N.C. Inf.
HEAD, M.E. S16199, S16267, SN, 2nd (Robison's) Inf.
HEAD, Martha Jane, W7592, W9451, PU, Head, Thomas A.
HEAD, Mattie Jane, W9451, W7592, PU, Head, Thomas Anthony
HEAD, Thomas A. S1721, V, 16th Inf.
HEAD, W. H. S1966, V, 16th Inf.
HEADDEN, S. A. S390, DY, 12th Inf.
HEADRICK, James M. S13386, H, 23rd Ga. Inf.
HEAFER, Fannie Totten, W4602, D, Heafer, Simeon Newton
HEARD, Sarah Jane, See Sarah Jane Simpson
HEARN, Adelia, W9522, WL, Hearn, Orrin D.
HEARN, I. G. S9415, CH, 18th (Newsom's) Cav.
HEARN, Jo Ann, W4187, G, Hearn, Wm. Grattus
HEARN, Thomas N. S4054, WL, 7th Inf.
HEARN, W. T. S7472, CH, 34th N.C. Troops
HEARNE, Elizabeth E. W8525, MA, Hearne, Rufus Davidson
HEART, James H. S1551, MA, 51st Inf.
HEARTLY, Washington, S1277, WI, 24th Inf.
HEATH, A. J. S12600, SN, 9th (Ward's) Cav.
HEATH, Dave, S4584, RU, 24th Inf.
HEATH, George W. S7028, LI, 17th Inf.
HEATHCOCK, James B. S8291, WI, 20th Inf.
HEATHCOCK, Sallie, W422, WI, Heathcock, Larkin
HEATHMAN, E. D. S9550, CE, 49th Inf.
HEATHMAN, Lutitia Jeniva, W2045, CE, Heathman, Erascus Darvin
HEATON, S. J. S8161, RU, 9th (Ward's) Cav.
HECK, A. S. S2470, HW, 31st Inf.
HECK, J. W. S6225, HW, 63rd Inf.
HECK, Mary, W2783, HW, Heck, Adam Steward
HEDGCOCK, Joseph, S3992, 11th Inf.
HEDGECOCK, Rachel, W10919, Hedgecock, Joseph
HEDGECOUTH, J. C. S7432, MS, 2nd (Ashby's) Cav.
HEDGEPATH, C. R. S14388, CE, 45th Inf.
HEDGEPATH, Neal, S16328, D, 45th Inf.

HEDRICK, A. B. S2886, CO, 16th Bn. (Neal's) Cav.
HEEL, Laura H. W2611, HU, Heel, James Calvin
HEFFERON, Thomas, S16474, S16375, SH, 9th Miss. Inf.
HEFLIN, D. J. S3789, LI, 7th Cav.
HEFLIN, Henry, S3461, WL, 1st Hvy. Art.
HEFLIN, Hester Jane, W10447, O, Heflin, James K. Polk
HEFLIN, James K. P. S15975, O, 2nd (Woodward's) Ky. Cav.
HEGGIE, L. A. S16600, MT, 2nd Ky. Cav.
HEIFNER, J. R. S8557, BR, 29th Inf.
HEIFNER, Malinda, W6815, BR, Heifner, Jessie Richard
HEIGHT, Harry, S6436, D, 3rd Tex. Cav.
HEIGHT, Pocahontas, W4251, D, Height, Harry
HEINS, Dorathea, W6765, K, Heins, Gaudens
HEINS, Gandens, S7448, K, 32nd Ala. Inf.
HEINS, Jacob, S7489, K, 1st (Feild's) Inf.
HEINS, Lena Matilds, W3271, K, Heins, Jacob
HEISTAND, D. C. S13944, SH, 4th Inf.
HELM, Lou, W4620, G, Helm, Miles S.
HELM, Nancy S. W4938, JE, Helm, Gideon B.
HELM, Thomas J. S13906, O, 46th Inf.
HELMECK, Nancy, W167, GI, Helmeck, Hiram
HELMICK, Andrew J. S9117, GI, 53rd Inf.
HELMS, Eli, S5809, S2840, H, Unassigned (Forman of a cattle drive)
HELMS, M. S. S2360, G, 55th (Brown's) Inf.
HELMS, Sarah Ellen, W5127, SH, Helms, John Thomas
HELMS, T. H. S7079, O, 46th Inf.
HELTON, Calloway, S1748, HW, 60th Inf.
HELTON, Cynthia M. W435, HM, Helton, D. D.
HELTON, Daniel, S10909, HM, 61st Inf.
HELTON, F. M. S15939, W, 35th Inf.
HELTON, Harriet, W2602, K, Helton, J. M.
HELTON, J. H. S16512, WA, 24th Va. Inf.
HELTON, J. T. S13002, HM, 12th Inf.
HELTON, J. W. S7602, JE, 1st (Carter's) Cav.
HELTON, James M. S15089, K, 2nd Mo. Cav.
HELTON, John N. S4983, JE, 58th N.C. Inf.
HELTON, Martha Virginia, W8856, RU, Helton, Anderson P.
HELTON, Mary Ann, W24, WH, Helton, James
HELTON, Samuel P. S1779, B, 4th Inf.
HEMBREE, Elizabeth, W6287, WH, Hembree, Martin Vanburen
HEMBREE, Jasper M. S1926, K, 61st Inf.

-157

HEMBREE, M. V. S3288, WH, 16th Inf.
HEMPHILL, J. A. S7645, A, 55th Inf.
HEMPHILL, Mary C. W7115, HE, Hemphill, J. A.
HENDERSON, A. A. S7940, BR, 43rd Inf.
HENDERSON, A. C. S1008, BO, 2nd Cav.
HENDERSON, A. M. S8440, FR, 13th Tex. Inf.
HENDERSON, A. Martha, W10000, LA, Henderson, James
HENDERSON, Benjamin, S5484, CO, Thomas' Legion, N.C.
HENDERSON, Charles P. S15496, LA, Phillips' Legion, Ga. Vols.
HENDERSON, Cordelia Caroline, W5100, W4076, WA, Henderson, Oliver Perry
HENDERSON, D. H. S10782, G, 22nd (Barteau's) Cav.
HENDERSON, Delpha R. W320, HN, Henderson, James Washington
HENDERSON, Emma D. W21, K, Henderson, John James
HENDERSON, G. L. S10588, HW, 12th Cav.
HENDERSON, H. G. S15513, K, 27th Va. Cav.
HENDERSON, H. H. S9281, DI, 11th Inf.
HENDERSON, Henry, C88, WH, Regiment not given
HENDERSON, J. P. S5184, MC, 19th Inf.
HENDERSON, Jacob, S3345, CO, 16th N.C. Inf.
HENDERSON, James, S10983, GI, 9th Ga. Bn. Art.
HENDERSON, James F. S1827, MU, 3rd Inf.
HENDERSON, James K. S3407, SE, 58th N.C. Inf.
HENDERSON, James T. S13473, WH, 1st (Feild's) Inf.
HENDERSON, Jennie, W8386, CH, Henderson, M. A.
HENDERSON, John H. S11385, JO, 6th N.C. Inf.
HENDERSON, John Jackson, S4482, O, 46th Inf.
HENDERSON, Julia Ann, W6973, HW, Henderson, Wm. Winton
HENDERSON, M. A. S2375, CH, 31st Inf.
HENDERSON, Martha, W9124, GI, Henderson, John
HENDERSON, Mary, W7672, K, Henderson, John
HENDERSON, Mary Elizabeth, W3536, MO, Henderson, Wm. Franklin
HENDERSON, Mary O. W6412, SH, Henderson, Samuel Augustus
HENDERSON, Mattie, W8033, MA, Henderson, Wm. Taylor
HENDERSON, Mattie, W10646, SH, Henderson, Anderson Bedford
HENDERSON, Melvina A. W8144, WA, Henderson, A. P.
HENDERSON, Mollie Young, W6730, CF, Henderson, Reese Keyser
HENDERSON, Nora, W4946, WH, Henderson, James T.
HENDERSON, O. P. S302, WA, Hampton's Legion, S.C. Inf.
HENDERSON, Reese K. S13326, RU, 2nd Inf.
HENDERSON, Robert Franklin, S13131, MA, 21st (Wilson's) Cav.
HENDERSON, S. A. S13509, SH, 17th Miss. Inf.
HENDERSON, Susan A. W1233, MU, Henderson, Wm. A.
HENDERSON, W. S. S8621, CH, 6th (Gould's) Bn. Tex. Cav.
HENDERSON, W. T. S12061, MA, 14th (Neely's) Cav.
HENDERSON, William F. S8850, O, 33rd Inf.
HENDERSON, William W. S11434, HW, 2nd Cav.
HENDLEY, H. L. S15250, MU, 9th Bn. Cav.
HENDON, America Ellen, W8889, MG, Hendon, John Thompson
HENDRICK, Ann B. W2696, RU, Hendrick, John L.
HENDRICK, Isabella, W2029, D, Hendrick, James
HENDRICK, John L. S8662, RU, 10th Confederate Cav.
HENDRICK, Lamentina Endora, W1567, Hendrick, Sanford
HENDRICKS, E. L. S45, MS, 5th Inf.
HENDRICKS, Elam L. S620, G, 3rd (Forrest's) Cav.
HENDRICKS, George M. S8913, DY, 12th Inf.
HENDRICKS, M. R. S8486, DY, 12th Inf.
HENDRICKS, Mary Isabell, W9523, DY, Hendricks, Wm. Lafayette
HENDRICKS, N. J. S15668, DY, 4th Ala. Inf.
HENDRICKS, Rachel Sophronia, W4169, G, Hendricks, Elam Loton
HENDRICKS, Sallie Emeline, W3007, DY, Hendricks, Morten R.
HENDRICKS, Sarah Jane, W197, HN, Hendricks, Robert

HENDRICKS, W. D. S7617, HN, 5th Inf.
HENDRICKSON, India V. W7543, CT, Hendrickson, E. D.
HENDRIX, Calvin M. S394, DK, 23rd Inf.
HENDRIX, G. L. S11813, MN, 31st Inf.
HENDRIX, H. H. S2403, FR, 4th Inf.
HENDRIX, James, S4612, FR, 17th Inf.
HENDRIX, Luther, S2127, K, 26th Inf.
HENDRIX, Malinda, W9217, CF, Hendrix, C. M.
HENDRIX, Martha C. W3937, MS, Hendrix, Elijah L.
HENDRIX, Mary C. W7745, W3560, FR, Hendrix, Henry H.
HENDRIX, Neely J. W2179, HI, Hendrix, Smith G.
HENDRIX, R. J. S15934, MN, 51st Inf.
HENDRIX, Sarah Caroline, W10946, MN, Hendrix, Richard Ivy
HENDRIX, W. B. S11280, MN, 6th Inf.
HENDRIX, W. B. S12860, MN, 21st (Wilson's) Cav.
HENDRIX, W. T. S5171, FR, 1st (Turney's) Inf.
HENDRIXON, E. D. S4191, CT, 28th Va. Inf.
HENDRIXON, Mary Ann, W242, DK, Hendrixon, Pleasant A.
HENGLEY, Lewis H. S4700, WL, 45th Inf.
HENKEL, Chris, S9789, SH, 10th Miss. Inf.
HENKEL, Ellen, W3557, SH, Henkel, Christopher
HENLEY, Charles F. S12222, MO, 26th Inf.
HENLEY, Edmonia E. W9957, WA, Henley, Landon H.
HENLEY, Frances, W869, WA, Henley, Isaac
HENLEY, G. P. S983, HR, 24th Miss. Inf.
HENLEY, J. C. S15981, GU, 28th Cav.
HENLEY, John H. S15697, GU, 28th Inf.
HENLEY, John M. S10537, SU, Unassigned (Slaughter House)
HENLEY, John Samuel, S6421, HI, 3rd (Clack's) Inf.
HENLEY, L. H. S16018, WA, 61st Inf.
HENLEY, Lura Estella, W10977, GU, Henley, James Campbell
HENLEY, Margaret A. W5595, WA, Henley, John S.
HENLEY, Martha Jane, W8327, HI, Henley, John S.
HENLEY, P. B. S9333, SN, 23rd Va. Inf.
HENLEY, Sarah Ann, W4496, SN, Henley, Peter Branch
HENLEY, Sarah Elizabeth, W8462, BO,

Henley, Charles Fairfax
HENLEY, T. G. S1668, L, 7th (Duckworth's) Cav.
HENLEY, Tennessee, W10788, GU, Henley, John H.
HENNESSEE, Cora, W9600, W, Hennessee, Hamilton Mortimer
HENNESSEE, H. M. S13623, CA, 16th Inf.
HENNESSEE, John, S6914, W, 35th Inf.
HENNESSEE, Lucinda, W6817, WH, Hennessee, H. A.
HENNESSEE, P. A. S12779, WH, 25th Inf.
HENNESSEE, Symantha Elizabeth, W9950, CU, Hennessee, Scott Patrick
HENNING, James A. S5055, T, 9th Inf.
HENNING, James H. S9185, SH, 4th Va. Inf.
HENNING, Judith Elvira, W1988, T, Henning, James Allen
HENRY, Apsley W. W6376, SH, Henry, David Wescot
HENRY, Caroline, W6346, D, Henry, Overton
HENRY, Cassie, W106, R, Henry, Cyrus W.
HENRY, Eliza Smith, W553, K, Henry, Wm. Jasper
HENRY, Elizabeth, W6846, PU, Henry, Wm. J.
HENRY, F. B. S10760, DI, 24th Inf.
HENRY, G. S1097, WH, 25th Inf.
HENRY, Harriet A. W5665, D, Henry, Owen
HENRY, J. M. S13998, TR, 55th Inf.
HENRY, Jane, W9891, L, Henry, Wm.
HENRY, Jasper, S15014, PU, 84th Inf.
HENRY, Joel L. S7316, R, 1st Cav.
HENRY, John, S3408, O, 48th Inf.
HENRY, Lizzie,   See Lizzie Barnes
HENRY, M. N. S10449, JE, 5th (McKenzie's) Cav.
HENRY, M. S. S5492, SN, 2nd Cav.
HENRY, Martha M. W3458, CO, Henry, Cicero Alexander
HENRY, Mary A. W722, D, Henry, William
HENRY, Mary Finni, W1986, MA, Henry, Wm. Franklin
HENRY, Mary Fitzpatrick, W10638, SN, Henry, John Franklin
HENRY, Mary J. W7752, R, Henry, J. L.
HENRY, Mattie E. W2412, L, Henry, Amzie Bradshaw
HENRY, Ophelia, W11130, H, Henry, Wm. Frank
HENRY, Overton, S13814, D, 9th Ky. Inf.
HENRY, Owen, S9575, D, 24th Inf.

HENRY, Rachel, W6197, PU, Henry, George W.
HENRY, S. R. S9257, SH, 19th Inf.
HENRY, Sallie Ellen, W3020, D, Henry, Fountain J.
HENRY, W. H. S1222, BO, 4th Cav.
HENRY, W. J. S13849, WH, 28th Inf.
HENRY, West (Wess), C78, TR, 2nd & 21st Cav.
HENRY, William, S12881, SH, 5th Ark. Inf.
HENRY, William R. S11935, R, 1st (Carter's) Cav.
HENSHAW, Thomas B. S8536, O, 33rd Inf.
HENSLEE, Mary Ann, W5562, MO, Henslee, Fielden Hampton
HENSLEY, A. S10568, U, 64th N.C. Inf.
HENSLEY, Fielden H. S2674, MO, 25th N.C. Inf.
HENSLEY, Isaac, S1172, SM, 1st Inf.
HENSLEY, John, S12748, HW, 64th Va. Inf.
HENSLEY, John A. S6872, U, 58th N.C. Inf.
HENSLEY, Louisa Jane, W4492, HR, Hensley, George Washington
HENSLEY, M. S2981, MOO, 17th Inf.
HENSLEY, Margaret Eveline, W9136, WH, Hensley, Eli Lasson
HENSLEY, Orville, S6989, B, 2nd (Robison's) Inf.
HENSLEY, R. W. S16453, HR, 3rd Miss. Inf.
HENSLEY, Richard, S1873, WH, 16th Inf.
HENSLEY, Sallie, W6200, U, Hensley, George W.
HENSLEY, Susan Ann, W5658, WH, Hensley, Richard
HENSLEY, Susan Organ, W1888, W, Hensley, Carral Jackson
HENSLEY, T. J. S3924, WA, 61st Inf.
HENSLEY, Telitha T. W5115, HW, Hensley, John L.
HENSLEY, Vicie, W1839, HI, Hensley, James Bartlet
HENSON, Ella C. W3670, GU, Henson, James Thadeus
HENSON, Ethelindia Jane, W4307, MN, Henson, George Henry
HENSON, G. H, S3523, MN, 20th Miss. Inf.
HENSON, G. S. S12189, MA, 18th (Newsom's) Cav.
HENSON, Gurtrude, W7286, WA, Henson, Pinkney
HENSON, Mary Ann, W3139, BL, Henson, Wm.
HENSON, Pinkney, S2330, WA, 60th Inf.
HERALD, Frank M. S13679, MC, 1st (Carter's) Cav.
HERBERT, J. G. S15941, WI, 11th (Holman's) Cav.
HERBERT, J. H. S9001, D, 4th Tex. Inf.
HERBERT, Lillie McEwen, W10826, WI, Herbert, John Green
HERBERT, Mollie, W9550, W8198, SH, Herbert, George H.
HERBERT, Olivia, W6081, D, Herbert, David Cummins
HERBERT, Sallie, W9426, WI, Herbert, George W. Snead
HERBERT, William T. S487, MA, 31st Inf.
HERBISON, R. B. S6048, DI, 49th Inf.
HERBISON, W. J. S4050, HI, 20th Inf.
HERD, Sarah Evaline, W125, WH, Herd, James Vance
HERD, William A. S16499, GI, Undetermined
HEREFORD, Ella Robinson, W10979, GI, Hereford, Robert Strong
HEREFORD, Robert S. S16312, LI, 4th Ala. Cav.
HERMON, John H. S10702, MT, 4th La. Battery, Lt. Art.
HERNDON, B. J. S14354, D, 42nd Ga. Inf.
HERNDON, Catharine (Kate), W3505, HW, Herndon, George W.
HERNDON, James P. S16091, D, Phillips' Co. Lt. Art.
HERNDON, Mary George, W9971, DY, Herndon, James
HERNDON, Nancy Jane, W9909, BE, Herndon, Wm. Carroll
HERNDON, Thomas, S12979, MT, 14th Inf.
HERNDON, W. W. S1377, CC, 52nd Inf.
HERNDON, William C. S4798, DE, Undetermined
HERON, Elizdann, W6468, HW, Heron, Hiram
HERON, Hiram, S1841, HA, 16th Cav.
HERRIN, Mary jane, W7529, LA, Herrin, James L.
HERRIN, Thomas B. S10132, BE, 20th Cav.
HERRING, A. A. S4913, MT, 14th Inf.
HERRING, Francis A. S535, SM, 23rd Inf.
HERRING, J. T. S9359, SN, 9th (Ward's) Cav.
HERRING, Lema, W9286, HY, Herring, John West
HERRING, Mary Jane, W2370, SN, Herring, Davie Grant

Index to Tennessee Confederate Pension Applications

HERRING, Matilda A. W93, SM, Herring, Francis Asbury
HERRING, Mollie Isabella, W5773, SN, Herring, John Taylor
HERRING, Nannie E. W5370, SH, Herring, Silas Leonidas
HERRING, Naomi Jane, W3568, SH, Herring, Robert Franklin
HERRING, R. G. S10926, M, 9th (Ward's) Cav.
HERROD, Margarette, W1962, RU, Herrod, David Andrew
HERRON, Elizabeth, W5443, SH, Herron, Wm.
HERRON, Hattie Everline, W9556, MA, Herron, Harrison
HERRON, J. W. S9540, HE, 19th Cav.
HERRON, John S. S5037, WL, 45th Inf.
HERRON, Juletta, W2490, L, Herron, John S.
HERRON, Mary Jane, W5856, RU, Herron, Benjamin Franklin
HERRON, William S. S5743, WA, 16th Va. Cav.
HESS, N. I. S14445, CC, 12th Inf.
HESS, Sidnie N. W7593, CC, Hess, N. I.
HESSEE, Elizabeth L. W4947, K, Hessee, Edward
HESSEY, Annie R. W3836, D, Hessey, Flavus F.
HESSEY, F. F. S4192, D, 30th Inf.
HESSEY, James M. S11669, D, 20th Inf.
HESSEY, W. N. S12724, FR, 20th Inf.
HESSON, Amorintha, W7305, M, Hesson, Wm.
HESSON, Peter A. S16349, SM, 22nd (Barteau's) Cav.
HESSON, William A. S10114, S9534, SM, 30th Inf.
HESTAND, Mary E. W2859, CY, Hestand, E. D.
HESTER, J. H. S14825, WE, 12th Ky. Cav.
HESTER, Jeddiah Gideon, S15615, S16200, MO, 42nd Ga. Inf.
HESTER, Jennie, W2379, ST, Hester, Obediah F.
HESTER, Mary Elizabeth, W9700, WE, Hester, John Henry
HESTER, Mary Lou, W6365, HN, Hester, Wm. Franklin
HESTER, O. F. S5113, ST, 14th Inf.
HESTER, R. m. S11302, SN, 14th Bn. Ala. Cav.
HESTER, Sarah Alice, W126, B, Hester, James W.
HESTER, W. B. S4628, RB, 9th (Bennett's) Cav.

HESTLAND, E. D. S2096, CY, 4th Bn. (Branner's) Cav.
HEVERIN, Mary Cox, W2440, D, Heverin, Hugh
HEWELL, J. D. S12075, MT, 50th Inf.
HEWGLEY, G. H. S8238, WL, 38th Inf.
HEWGLEY, Martha Siloan, W1353, MU, Hewgley, Alfred Washington
HEWGLEY, Mattie, W8503, D, Hewgley, Augustus
HEWITT, A. J. S8552, SM, 28th Inf.
HEWITT, Egbert B. S15579, GI, 19th (Biffle's) Cav.
HEWITT, Louisa, W7809, CE, Hewitt, Wm.
HEWITT, M. D. S1082, SM, 28th Inf.
HEWITT, Mary E. W94, SM, Hewitt, Milton D.
HEWITT, Sarah Elizabeth, W683, MS, Hewitt, Richard James
HEWITT, William, S348, CE, 14th Inf.
HIATT, Marion E. S13482, CL, 64th Va. Inf.
HIBBETT, A. J. S15467, SN, Allison's Squadron, Cav.
HICE, Cynthia Jane, W4991, MOO, Hice, W. B.
HICE, William B. S4163, MOO, 37th Inf.
HICKAM, Jane Elizabeth, W5020, SE, Hickam, Robert Berton
HICKERSON, Clay, C79, CF, 24th Inf.
HICKERSON, J. H. S4028, CF, 3rd Inf.
HICKERSON, J. M. S10254, HU, 49th Inf.
HICKERSON, Jennie, W5477, CF, Hickerson, J. H.
HICKERSON, Martha Ann, W5263, HU, Hickerson, James Marshall
HICKERSON, Samuel, S4005, P, 9th Cav.
HICKEY, George, S736, WH, 25th Inf.
HICKEY, J. B. S12863, WH, 8th (Dibrell's) Cav.
HICKEY, James P. S520, RO, 26th Inf.
HICKEY, John C. S3770, K, 1st Art.
HICKEY, John M. S561, MU, 6th Mo. Inf.
HICKEY, Mary, W5938, WH, Hickey, John B.
HICKEY, W. N. S1626, K, 31st Inf.
HICKLE, Drury A. S10567, U, 1st (Carter's) Cav.
HICKLE, Mary J. W5892, UN, Hickle, D. A.
HICKMAN, Andrew Jackson, S2451, LA, 53rd Inf.
HICKMAN, Callie, W5334, GI, Hickman, E. T.
HICKMAN, E. T. S9273, GI, 53rd Inf.
HICKMAN, Eliza J. W2734, GI, Hickman, Riley
HICKMAN, J. R. S3421, GI, 39th Inf.

-161

HICKMAN, John, S1821, WH, 1st Va. Inf.
HICKMAN, John P. S16253, D, 7th Bn. Cav.
HICKMAN, Mahala, W6095, GI, Hickman, James Riley
HICKMAN, Martha Caroline, W2303, LA, Hickman, Andrew Jackson
HICKMAN, R. B. S2845, SE, 60th N.C. Inf.
HICKMAN, Samuel C. S1415, ME, 5th Cav.
HICKMAN, Sarah Elizabeth, W3569, ME, Hickman, Samuel Calvin
HICKS, A. G. S16403, SH, 12th Ky. Cav.
HICKS, A. J. S349, BE, 27th Inf.
HICKS, Alice L. W9587, WA, Hicks, Nathaniel F.
HICKS, B. N. S16325, S16379, DK, 16th Inf.
HICKS, Barbara A. W6996, SU, Hicks, Samuel R.
HICKS, Calvin, S14511, WA, 1st (Carter's) Cav.
HICKS, Catharine, W3266, SU, Hicks, Ruben N.
HICKS, E. M. S9928, H, 4th (McLemore's) Cav.
HICKS, Elizabeth, W6192, H, Hicks, Elijah M.
HICKS, George W. S3312, SU, 63rd Inf.
HICKS, H. J. S6506, SU, 6th (Wheeler's) Cav.
HICKS, J. C. S15682, H, 35th Ga. Inf.
HICKS, J. D. S15656, CE, 26th Inf.
HICKS, J. H. S9076, SU, 8th (Smith's) Cav.
HICKS, J. N. S14468, CC, 3rd (Forrest's) Cav.
HICKS, J. P. S3585, SU, 63rd Inf.
HICKS, James M. S5056, S1610, SN, 30th Inf.
HICKS, Jane E. W1620, HN, Hicks, James
HICKS, Joanne G. W7942, WA, Hicks, Joseph S.
HICKS, Joe S. S2414, SU, 19th Inf.
HICKS, John, S3882, SU, 60th Inf.
HICKS, John, S15252, F, 21st Ala. Inf.
HICKS, Josephine, W6242, SU, Hicks, W. C.
HICKS, Mary, W2426, MO, Hicks, Abraham
HICKS, Mary, W3803, SU, Hicks, John
HICKS, Mary Emma, W9781, SH, Hicks, Robert Goodwin
HICKS, Mary Jane, W1094, CT, Hicks, Jacob
HICKS, Mary Leeper, W10420, HN, Hicks, Nathaniel Smith
HICKS, Mary Lucia, W7887, H, Hicks, James C.
HICKS, Mary Pasteur, W10144, SE, Hicks, Abraham Jackson
HICKS, Mathias, S3280, CT, 18th Inf.
HICKS, Matilda, W2084, HW, Hicks, James
HICKS, Matilda E. W2801, WA, Hicks, Russell Sanders

HICKS, Matthew, S5827, MO, Undetermined
HICKS, Nancy J. W2047, MC, Hicks, James N.
HICKS, Nathan, S752, OV, 8th Cav.
HICKS, Nathaniel, S10120, SU, 19th Inf.
HICKS, R. K. S12697, RB, 2nd Ky. Cav.
HICKS, R. S. S2658, WA, 45th Va. Inf.
HICKS, Ruth, W3639, SU, Hicks, George W.
HICKS, S. R. S7230, SU, 1st (Carter's) Cav.
HICKS, Sofrona Jane, W3143, SN, Hicks, James Marion
HICKS, Stephe J. S3456, BR, 7th Inf.
HICKS, Susan Frances, W946, G, Hicks, John M.
HICKS, Susanna, W1789, SU, Hicks, Wm.
HICKS, Thomas Harrison, S12129, HY, 6th Inf.
HICKS, W. C. S7231, SU, 6th (Wheeler's) Cav.
HICKS, W. R. S7164, S16192, BE, 46th Inf.
HICKS, W. S. S7177, WE, 47th Inf.
HICKS, William, S2662, SU, 60th Inf.
HICKS, William, S10252, BO, 31st Inf.
HICKS, William A. S3902, P, Napier's Bn. Cav.
HICKS, William K. S11113, BE, 7th Cav.
HICKS, Wilson Chapson, S10813, MC, 59th Inf.
HICKS, Zilpha J. W7448, CC, Hicks, James Nelson
HIESTAND, Miriam Finley, W384, SH, Hiestand, Thomas J.
HIGDON, J. H. S15482, BO, 16th N.C. Inf.
HIGDON, Michael C. S5080, PO, 2nd Bn. Cav.
HIGGARSON, John T. S11224, MA, 20th Inf.
HIGGASON, Richard P. S9347, MA, 44th Inf.
HIGGASON, Thomas H. S1194, SN, 18th Inf.
HIGGERSON, L. D. S562, SN, 44th Inf.
HIGGINBOTHAM, Aaron, S15298, W, 16th Inf.
HIGGINBOTHAM, J. H. S8303, MOO, 41st Inf.
HIGGINS, Bettie, W5352, WY, Higgins, Taylor Chamberlain
HIGGINS, J. P. S8610, CA, 18th Inf.
HIGGINS, Joel C. S7750, MN, Crew's Bn. Inf.
HIGGINS, Nancy Ann, W9910, DK, Higgins, John P.
HIGGINS, William F. S8717, CA, 18th Inf.
HIGGS, J. A. J. S9980, 31st Inf.
HIGGS, J. K. S13099, SH, 21st (Wilson's) Cav.
HIGGS, Mary Affire, W4434, F, Higgs, John Wiley Roland
HIGGS, T. J. S15626, WE, 31st Inf.
HIGH, Ben R. S2452, SM, 8th Inf.
HIGH, C. D. S10482, TR, 23rd Inf.

Index to Tennessee Confederate Pension Applications

HIGH, Edmond Durant, S10421, SH, Cobb's Legion, Ga. Vols.
HIGH, Sallie, W5552, TR, High, C. D.
HIGH, Solomon S. S7715, D, 28th Inf.
HIGHSMITH, C. S9822, RB, 30th Inf.
HIGHSMITH, William D. S8833, RB, 30th Inf.
HIGHT, Carrie Margaret, W6780, D, Hight, Oliver Hazzard
HIGHT, Edna Elizabeth, W9970, B, Hight, Wm. Garrett
HIGHT, Wm. G. S15689, B, Nixon's Cav.
HIGHTOWER, Bythenia Eleanora, W1695, MS, Hightower, James Harvey
HIGHTOWER, Leander, S5744, A, 63rd Inf.
HIGHTOWER, Louisa Hume, W4194, D, Hightower, Richard Robertson
HIGHTOWER, Margaret E. R. W4125, SH, Hightower, Wm.
HIGHTOWER, Mattie Moore, W10555, H, Hightower, T. H.
HIGHTOWER, T. H. S14304, BR, Lynch's Co. Lt. Art.
HILBERT, Nancy F. W4280, WA, Hilbert, Samuel D.
HILBERT, Samuel D. S2639, WA, 60th Inf.
HILBERT, Sarah E. W198, WA, Hilbert, John H.
HILDERBRAND, S. J. S15865, SH, 3rd (Forrest's) Cav.
HILDRETH, John, S15193, MU, 3rd (Clack's) Inf.
HILL, A. P. S4096, LI, 8th Inf.
HILL, Alfred H. S6808, GR, 31st Inf.
HILL, Angerona Rosetta, W3520, MA, Hill, Leonidas John
HILL, Arthur L. S2138, CY, 43rd Inf.
HILL, Ava, W10923, SH, Hill, L. B.
HILL, Bailey, S10569, CF, 32nd Inf.
HILL, C. H. S6552, MN, 19th Inf.
HILL, Clary Ann Elizabeth, W8203, HN, Hill, Nelson Cameron
HILL, Clementine, W235, CF, Hill, Sam
HILL, Cornelia, W8040, MS, Hill, Ike H.
HILL, Eliza Calista, W3487, SH, Hill, John C.
HILL, Eugenia, W8163, W, Hill, Wm. Isaiah
HILL, F. P. S9161, HY, 9th Inf.
HILL, Flora L. W7486, HN, Hill, Wm. Abram
HILL, Frances Elizabeth, W647, MN, Hill, Charles Henry
HILL, Henry W. S9729, B, 17th Inf.
HILL, I. B. S12853, W, 5th Inf.
HILL, I. H. S14095, MS, 53rd Inf.

HILL, J. A. S9517, DY, 24th Inf.
HILL, J. B. S1271, B, 1st Inf.
HILL, J. G. S16301, LK, 7th Cav.
HILL, J. L. S14437, D, 1st Ga. Inf.
HILL, J. W. S12609, CF, 45th Inf.
HILL, James Alexander, S14755, D, 24th Inf.
HILL, James Charlton, S12568, T, 7th (Duckworth's) Cav.
HILL, James Milton, S154, WI, 1st Inf.
HILL, James R. S9961, CO, 62nd N.C. Inf.
HILL, James W. S1849, RU, 8th Tex. Rangers
HILL, James W. S3145, MU, 4th Inf.
HILL, Jane Isabella, W6096, DY, Hill, Hugh Andrew
HILL, John C. S11670, SH, Unassigned (Commissary Agent)
HILL, John R. S4995, H, 20th Inf.
HILL, Joseph A. S2079, D, 1st Cav.
HILL, Margaret Ann, W6480, G, Hill, James Terry Cahal
HILL, Margaret Evelyn, W10992, CO, Hill, J. R.
HILL, Margaret Moore, W10051, T, Hill, Jonathan Sloan
HILL, Martha, W10087, HN, Hill, Joseph T.
HILL, Mary, W1086, D, Hill, Frank
HILL, Mary, W3845, LO, Hill, Oliver Perry
HILL, Mary Ann, W2499, CL, Hill, Jacob Manning
HILL, Mary Ann Emily, W1280, D, Hill, Frank Marion
HILL, Mary Emma, W9318, OV, Hill, George Washington
HILL, Mary Josephine, W1863, HY, Hill, Fountain Pitts
HILL, N. C. S4259, HN, 8th S.C. Inf.
HILL, N. K. S1457, MS, 8th Inf.
HILL, O. P. S160, LO, 2nd (Ashby's) Cav.
HILL, Preston Y. S15960, S16000, WL, 7th Inf.
HILL, Riley H. S7725, MN, 62nd Inf.
HILL, Robert G. S12610, SN, 24th Inf.
HILL, S. E. W4614, HR, Hill, John W.
HILL, Samuel J. S13493, G, 12th Cav.
HILL, Sarah Elizabeth, W5314, G, Hill, Samuel Joseph
HILL, Sarah Elizabeth, W10287, D, Hill, John B.
HILL, Sarah Frances, W7791, H, Hill, Wm. H.
HILL, Sophia Reddick, W4081, SN, Hill, Robert Gwynn
HILL, Susan, W556, MU, Hill, J. W.
HILL, Thomas, S3292, D, McClung's Co. Lt. Art.

HILL, W. A. S12980, HN, 19th Miss. Inf.
HILL, W. H. S10172, H, 1st Ga. Inf.
HILL, W. I. S10465, W, 11th (Holman's) Cav.
HILL, W. T. S5934, H, 24th Ga. Inf.
HILL, William J. S677, LI, 41st Inf.
HILL, William J. S11087, CL, 60th Inf.
HILLARD, F. R. S11553, K, Martin's Co. Post Guard, Va.
HILLIARD, A. D. S5057, 55th Inf.
HILLIARD, Fannie Lester, W9047, F, Hilliard, W. C.
HILLIARD, John A. S5971, B, 56th Ala. Inf.
HILLIARD, John A. S10262, F, 16th (Logwood's) Cav.
HILLIARD, Laura, W7575, W9034, MU, Hilliard, Alvis Thomas
HILLIARD, Maacha A. W424, T, Hilliard, James A.
HILLIARD, Virginia C. W5176, WE, Hilliard, Wm. Harrison
HILLIARD, W. H. S15410, S15621, JO, 37th N.C. Inf.
HILLIS, Amanda Ellen, W10896, WE, Hillis, Sebern J.
HILLIS, Lawson H. S7356, V, 38th Inf.
HILLIS, M. Jane, W7875, W, Hillis, Isaah
HILLIS, P. C. W2331, WE, Hillis, J. J.
HILLIS, Robert O. S16391, W, 16th Inf.
HILLIS, Woodson P. S14187, V, 22nd Inf.
HILLS, J. B. S3392, SH, 4th Inf.
HILTON, Calloway, S411, HW, 63rd Inf.
HILTON, James, S3839, K, 19th Inf.
HILTON, John M. S16501, SU, 19th Inf.
HIMEBAUGH, Virginia Higgins, W3951, LI, Himebaugh, Peter
HIMES, James H. S8081, CF, 17th Inf.
HIMES, Martha Ann, W5832, B, Himes, Wm. Calvin
HINDMAN, Elihu L. S9407, GI, 19th (Biffle's) Cav.
HINDS, Fannie H. W6547, SH, Hinds, Joseph L.
HINDS, Martha Ann, W2701, FR, Hinds, Robert C.
HINDS, Mary Flanagan, W4835, SH, Hinds, Wm. Newton
HINDS, R. C. S6094, FR, 41st Inf.
HINE, Augusta E. W4092, SU, Hine, Thomas Levi
HINES, Elmira, W7368, SN, Hines, Thomas L.
HINES, Isaac J. S84, SM, 28th Inf.
HINES, James K. P. S9249, MU, 9th Bn. Cav.
HINES, John, S4155, LK, 12th Ky. Cav.

HINES, L. S. W974, FR, Hines, Porter
HINES, Louarky Jane, W2727, CF, Hines, Wm. James
HINES, Mary Jane, W550, SH, Hines, Turner Wm.
HINES, Thomas L. S4519, SN, 23rd Inf.
HINES, Thomas L. S10632, TR, 23rd Inf.
HINES, William C. S7022, B, 41st Inf.
HINES, William E. S5397, TR, 20th Inf.
HINES, William G. S8471, O, 47th Inf.
HINKEL, J. T. S12622, RB, 9th (Ward's) Cav.
HINKLE, Emma A. W7319, RB, Hinkle, Joseph A.
HINKLE, H. H. S13547, RB, 9th (Ward's) Cav.
HINKLE, Jesse Isaac, S5224, RB, 14th Cav.
HINKLE, Josiah A. S12295, 30th Inf.
HINSLEY, W. M. S901, SN, 7th Inf.
HINSLEY, William, S2601, SN, 7th Inf.
HINSON, Amanda M. W9690, D, Hinson, James Hartwell
HINSON, E. L. S6936, P, 10th (DeMoss') Cav.
HINSON, Eli H. S8936, WE, 46th Inf.
HINSON, Emeline L. W6356, D, Hinson, Warren J.
HINSON, G. W. S6245, LE, 48th (Voorhies') Inf.
HINSON, J. H. sr. S16268, S12767, P, 10th (DeMoss') Cav.
HINSON, James H. S15187, S9722, MS, 20th Inf., 1st Application is missing.
HINSON, Jane P. W2691, G, Hinson, W. H.
HINSON, John M. S13952, LK, 7th Ky. Mtd. Inf.
HINSON, Mollie Jackson, W10160, HU, Hinson, E. Larkin
HINSON, R. C. S8511, ST, 50th Inf.
HINSON, Sarah Pochantas, W9952, P, Hinson, James Harvey
HINSON, W. H. S7857, G, 12th Inf.
HINSON, W. J, S101, D, 17th Inf.
HINTON, Samuel G. S9500, SH, McGehee's Regt. Ark. Cav.
HIPSHER, Delpha, W6787, GR, Hipsher, Wm. L.
HIPSHER, George, S416, GR, Undetermined
HIPSHER, George W. S1357, GR, 12th Cav.
HIPSHER, Nancy M. W838, GR, Hipsher, George Washington
HISE, H. H. S3157, WA, Undetermined
HITCH, S. K. S1814, BO, 63rd Inf.
HITCHCOCK, John, S1240, V, 35th Inf.
HITER, Sallie, W3766, CC, Hiter, Wm. Young

HITT, Margaret Maria, W8786, HD, Hitt, Joseph Robinson
HIX, Isaac, S3003, J, 25th Inf.
HIX, James B. S12555, B, 17th Inf.
HIX, John, S1285, MO, Undetermined
HIX, Martha Melvina, W1604, BO, Hix, Sam Marion
HIX, Rose Ann, W2061, WH, Hix, Isaac
HIXSON, Dona, W10438, H, Hixson, Wilson
HIXSON, John, S6046, H, 1st (Carter's) Cav.
HIXSON, Roda Jane, W10606, H, Hixson, Billie
HIXSON, Wilson, S6047, H, 1st (Carter's) Cav.
HIZER, Jasper, S5270, HR, 14th Cav.
HOARD, Cornelia, W11032, HW, Hoard, George
HOARD, John, S2715, HW, 60th Inf.
HOATH, Robert D. S7585, WE, 25th Ark. Inf.
HOBBS, Amanda, W594, DI, Hobbs, Wilham Marion
HOBBS, Fannie Lou, W9481, GI, Hobbs, Richard Compton
HOBBS, Ferdinand, S1007, WE, 11th N.C. Inf.
HOBBS, Harriet E. W8177, LI, Hobbs, Thomas B.
HOBBS, J. L. S12947, MU, 48th (Voorhies') Inf.
HOBBS, J. N. S9916, D, 48th (Voorhies') Inf.
HOBBS, J. T. S12083, TR, 4th (McLemore's) Cav.
HOBBS, James, S15977, GU, 5th Inf.
HOBBS, John Westley, S1168, FR, 1st Inf.
HOBBS, Mattie, W9421, WL, Hobbs, John H.
HOBBS, Priscilla E. W2881, HU, Hobbs, James K.
HOBBS, R. C. S8863, GI, 4th (McLemore's) Cav.
HOBBS, Sarah Dikes, W8790, W, Hobbs, James
HOBBS, Susan H. W8174, SH, Hobbs, J. H.
HOBBS, W. W. S4385, HU, 10th (DeMoss') Cav.
HOBBY, F. M. S12287, MS, 17th Inf.
HOBBY, William Carroll, S3971, MS, 11th Cav.
HOCKERSMITH, Catherine, W2227, FR, Hockersmith, John Wesley
HOCKERSPITH, George D. S9320, RB, 30th Inf.
HOCKERSPITH, Hubert Holman, S2613, RB, 30th Inf.
HODGE, Annie M. W2228, HW, Hodge, John Preston

HODGE, Barbara, W8382, DY, Hodge, Henry Clay
HODGE, Bettie, W6448, W9361, W8249, WI, Hodge, James J.
HODGE, E. D. S3900, HM, 61st Inf.
HODGE, Elizabeth Jane, W8249, W6448, W9361, WI, Hodge, James Joseph
HODGE, H. C. S10352, DY, 15th (Stewart's) Cav.
HODGE, J. H. S5122, WA, Marshall's Co. Art.
HODGE, J. M. S2847, MU, 6th (Wheeler's) Cav.
HODGE, J. M. S7283, SU, 60th Inf.
HODGE, James, S8207, GR, 7th Cav.
HODGE, James C. S2589, MN, 31st Inf.
HODGE, James J. S8006, WI, 45th Inf.
HODGE, John Preston, S8174, HW, 59th Mtd. Inf.
HODGE, Julia A. W7534, SU, Hodge, Robert Chester
HODGE, Malinda, W3916, R, Hodge, A. B.
HODGE, Mary Emma Sarena, W7825, H, Hodge, Robert Jackson
HODGE, Mary Frances, W4858, WI, Hodge, James Robert
HODGE, Mattie M. W2949, WA, Hodge, John T.
HODGE, R. C. S7760, SU, 59th Inf.
HODGES, Amanda, W3300, GE, Hodges, Thomas C.
HODGES, Ann, W7960, SU, Hodges, John Chrst. Columbus
HODGES, Anson, S9846, SU, 1st (Carter's) Cav.
HODGES, C. A. S8150, SU, Unassigned (Nitre Mining)
HODGES, Caloway, S4520, K, 29th Inf.
HODGES, E. P. S11980, WE, 38th Va. Inf.
HODGES, H. T. S7170, WE, 15th Cav.
HODGES, Harriet F. W156, SN, Hodges, Daniel Smith
HODGES, J. C. C. S9901, SU, Unassigned (Nitre Mining)
HODGES, J. D. S13791, SH, 41st Miss. Inf.
HODGES, J. M. S7129, SU, 29th Inf.
HODGES, J. W. S13320, SH, 14th Cav.
HODGES, Jennie Edna, W8986, SU, Hodges, Anson
HODGES, Joannah, W2863, W6133, CH, Hodges, Newton Jasper
HODGES, Lillian Parish, W11166, SH, Parish, Isaac W.

HODGES, Lou Rayner, W9775, SH, Hodges, Wm. Robert
HODGES, Louisa, W524, SU, Hodges, James G.
HODGES, Mary, W9340, HM, Hodges, Wm.
HODGES, Mary Angaline, W2810, HM, Hodges, James Calloway
HODGES, Mary Ann, W5001, K, Hodges, Calloway
HODGES, R. A. S13277, SN, 44th Inf.
HODGES, S. A. P. W355, H, Hodges, John Pettus
HODGES, Susan A. W10046, SN, Hodges, Richard A.
HODGES, T. C. S1776, GE, Hamilton's Bn. Cav.
HODGES, Virginia Ann, W1971, F, Hodges, John Wesley
HODGES, W. B. S8030, GR, 26th Inf.
HODGES, W. H. S1863, GI, 3rd Inf.
HODGES, William, S14965, HM, 37th Inf.
HODGES, ohn, S2625, UN, 2nd Cav.
HOFFMAN, Mary Jane, W2999, BO, Hoffman, John George
HOFFNER, G. V. S9295, WI, 11th Cav.
HOGAN, Alexina [Embry], W10204, D, Hogan, Alexander, [Later married Embry]
HOGAN, Elizabeth, W6425, MU, Hogan, Thomas Moitland
HOGAN, George W. S12212, D, 55th Inf.
HOGAN, James L. S16517, CY, South Cumberland Bn. (U.S.A.)
HOGAN, James Polk, S15471, SH, 7th Cav.
HOGAN, Linda, W9462, SH, Hogan, James Polk
HOGAN, Linda Collins, W8252, SH, Hogan, James Polk
HOGAN, Malinda, W9462, SH, Hogan, James Polk
HOGAN, Sarah E. W684, ST, Hogan, John Randle
HOGAN, William, S10520, MN, 20th (Russell's) Cav.
HOGE, Sarah Tommie, W4134, FR, Hoge, Samuel Copeland
HOGINS, W. M. S11208, DI, 49th Inf.
HOGUE, Martha A. W7435, SH, Hogue, W. G.
HOGUE, W. G. S11901, SH, 12th Ky. Cav.
HOLBROOK, F. M. S2008, O, 4th Inf.
HOLCOMB, Letha Ann, W10476, HY, Holcomb, Nevill
HOLCOMB, Mary D. W5162, D, Holcomb, John R.
HOLCOMB, Nevill, S14413, HY, 4th Ala. Inf.
HOLCOMB, P. M. S14765, MU, McGehee's Regt. Ark. Cav.
HOLCOMB, S. C. S6472, HN, 12th Ky. Cav.
HOLDEN, Abraham, S3999, SE, 26th N.C. State Troops
HOLDEN, D. M. S8714, H, 45th Inf.
HOLDEN, J. M. S5319, B, 45th Inf.
HOLDEN, S. S15038, L, Coleman's Regt. Mo. Cav.
HOLDEN, Sallie A. W7282, SQ, Holden, John M.
HOLDER, B. F. S8558, FR, 4th (McLemore's) Cav.
HOLDER, Crockett, S5713, FR, 41st Inf.
HOLDER, D. W. S12393, JO, 58th N.C. Inf.
HOLDER, Dennis, S7284, MOO, 23rd Inf.
HOLDER, Elijah T. S1170, BO, 58th N.C. Inf.
HOLDER, Frances Wilson, W4292, MS, Holder, Wesley
HOLDER, Henry, S4044, GI, Undetermined
HOLDER, J. A. S7462, RU, 24th Inf.
HOLDER, J. F. S7982, WE, 12th Cav.
HOLDER, J. H. S8670, RB, 17th Inf.
HOLDER, J. M. S4891, FR, 17th Inf.
HOLDER, J. S. S11121, WH, 1st (Carter's) Cav.
HOLDER, J. W. S16585, D, 17th Inf.
HOLDER, John F. S3836, FR, 17th Inf.
HOLDER, Mack sr. S7272, CO, 60th Inf.
HOLDER, Mary, W9329, WH, Holder, John Simpson
HOLDER, Mary Frances, W2632, FR, Holder, Benjamin Franklin
HOLDER, Mary Frances, W10360, G, Holder, Josiah
HOLDER, Mary Rose, W1925, SN, Holder, T. J.
HOLDER, Rebeccah, W2448, BO, Holder, Thomas
HOLDER, Wesley, S5269, MS, 23rd Bn. Inf.
HOLDER, William, S9779, W, 5th Inf.
HOLDER, William A. S8213, 21st N.C. Inf.
HOLE, Nettie, W11092, K, Hole, W. J.
HOLE, W. J. S16573, K, Unassigned (Guarded Prisoners)
HOLEMAN, Larkin A. S8232, HW, 25th La. Inf.
HOLIFIELD, J. N. S1764, MA, 12th Ky. Inf.
HOLLADAY, Mary Ellen, W5407, MG, Holladay, Robert Alexander
HOLLADAY, S. W. S11787, BE, 55th Inf.
HOLLAND, A. A. S9350, ME, 43rd Inf.
HOLLAND, A. C. S5472, DE, 51st Inf.

Index to Tennessee Confederate Pension Applications

HOLLAND, A. H. S13776, M, 30th Inf.
HOLLAND, Amanda A. W2913, R, Holland, Adolphus Alexander
HOLLAND, Benjamin F. S8778, H, 37th Inf.
HOLLAND, Erophely S. W3313, GI, Holland, Robert F.
HOLLAND, Frank A. S16424, B, 17th Inf.
HOLLAND, Harriet Elizabeth, W10656, MA, Holland, Wm.
HOLLAND, J. L. S2387, HD, 27th Ala. Inf.
HOLLAND, J. R. S3571, M, 24th Inf.
HOLLAND, J. W. S9911, WL, 28th Inf.
HOLLAND, James J. S16507, WI, 20th Inf.
HOLLAND, James P. S8546, MS, 8th Inf.
HOLLAND, Jesse A. S6461, LI, 3rd Inf.
HOLLAND, John, S4650, RB, 8th (Smith's) Cav.
HOLLAND, Madora C. W4269, WL, Holland, J. W.
HOLLAND, Margaret Davidson, W6009, LI, Holland, Robert T.
HOLLAND, Martha Ann, W10491, BE, Holland, James Madison
HOLLAND, Mary Jane, W10799, WI, Holland, John James
HOLLAND, Mary S. W1035, MU, Holland, Wm.
HOLLAND, N. B. S1927, BE, 55th Inf.
HOLLAND, P. S10891, BE, 55th Inf.
HOLLAND, R. F. S11172, GI, 32nd Inf.
HOLLAND, R. T. S5799, LI, 17th Inf.
HOLLAND, Roxana, W3257, BE, Holland, P.
HOLLAND, W. S. S13751, D, 11th Inf.
HOLLAND, William, S2830, CL, 37th Inf.
HOLLAND, William M. S10378, FR, 44th Inf.
HOLLANDER, Marguerite, W4747, SH, Hollander, Ben
HOLLANDSWORTH, James G. S6112, DY, 8th (Smith's) Cav.
HOLLANDSWORTH, William, S9203, WH, 8th Cav.
HOLLEMAN, Henry H. S686, SM, 28th Inf.
HOLLEMAN, James G. S13826, J, 28th Inf.
HOLLEMAN, Matilda, W7957, J, Holleman, James G.
HOLLERAM, James, S3818, SH, 21st Inf.
HOLLEY, G. H. S3355, MN, 10th Miss. Inf.
HOLLEY, Isaac P. S11372, GI, 32nd Inf.
HOLLEY, J. S4484, DI, 14th Inf.
HOLLEY, John, S11085, HD, 28th Ala. Inf.
HOLLIDAY, Eliza, W418, SM, Holliday, Wm. F.
HOLLIFIELD, A. S. S11972, SH, 6th Ga. Cav.
HOLLINGSHEAD, Julia Ann, W6488, L, Hollingshead, Wm. E.
HOLLINGSWORTH, G. H. S9957, BE, R. W. Ayer's Guard Co.
HOLLINGSWORTH, Nancy, W1956, WY, Hollingsworth, Wm.
HOLLINS, Amy L. See Amy L. Coleman
HOLLINS, J. L. S1818, HD, 3rd Miss. Inf.
HOLLINSWORTH, Mary Jane, W7964, O, Hollinsworth, James Galen
HOLLIS, Elizabeth, W954, CE, Hollis, Jonathan
HOLLIS, Isaac W. S4799, CH, 13th Inf.
HOLLIS, J. P. S11331, MT, 7th Ky. Cav.
HOLLIS, Julia C. C. W5565, H, Hollis, George E.
HOLLIS, Martha, W10141, CA, Hollis, W. J.
HOLLIS, Martha S. W1165, RB, Hollis, Wm. H.
HOLLIS, Mary H. W1344, CA, Hollis, James Bell
HOLLIS, Mary James, W7311, GI, Hollis, Wilbowby Alexander
HOLLIS, R. G. S2768, W, 8th (Smith's) Cav.
HOLLIS, W. J. S3911, W, 18th Inf.
HOLLIS, William, S1466, S1027, SN, 30th Inf.
HOLLODAY, Cornelia A. W8043, BE, Holloday, Stephen Washington
HOLLOMAN, E. S5777, BE, 5th Inf.
HOLLOMAN, S. S. S14900, WL, Hamilton's Bn. Cav.
HOLLON, J. M. S4619, GI, 32nd Inf.
HOLLOW, Emeline, W10852, SU, Hollow, Wm. B.
HOLLOW, W. B. S6445, JO, 37th N.C. Inf.
HOLLOWAY, A. J. S6862, OV, 8th (Dibrell's) Cav.
HOLLOWAY, Anna, W10931, O, Holloway, Wm. Wallace
HOLLOWAY, B. F. S44, R, 1st Cav.
HOLLOWAY, Elizabeth, W888, T, Holloway, Daniel Reed
HOLLOWAY, Emma Pass, W2320, R, Holloway, B. F.
HOLLOWAY, J. F. S7178, CH, 51st Inf.
HOLLOWAY, J. H. S6359, MO, 3rd (Lillard's) Mtd. Inf.
HOLLOWAY, John, S13681, HD, 24th N.C. Inf.
HOLLOWAY, Josie, W9019, SU, Holloway, W. J.
HOLLOWAY, Judy, W3721, J, Holloway, George Washington

HOLLOWAY, L. H. W. S15352, WL, 45th Inf.
HOLLOWAY, Leopatra, W1911, R, Holloway, Samuel Houston
HOLLOWAY, Margaret J. W4203, MO, Holloway, James H.
HOLLOWAY, Miranda Hartful, W10807, RB, Holloway, Wm. Samuel
HOLLOWAY, Nancy Stanley, W816, D, Holloway, James John
HOLLOWAY, S. H. jr. S1662, CU, 8th (Dibrell's) Cav.
HOLLOWAY, Sarah Milbern, W1039, O, Holloway, James K. Polk
HOLLOWAY, W. S. S16370, RB, 2nd Ky. Cav.
HOLLOWAY, William T. S1491, RO, 16th Cav.
HOLLY, Eliza Green, W4580, GI, Holly, John Pink
HOLLY, Sarah Marthey, W226, MS, Holly, Wm. M.
HOLLY, William G. S14558, GI, 32nd Inf.
HOLMAN, Elizabeth Carlin, W8711, D, Holman, Robert Augusta
HOLMAN, James S. S2045, PU, 28th Inf.
HOLMAN, Jennie Thomas, W1951, SH, Holman, Wm. Pitts
HOLMAN, Martha [Purkey], W10707, HW, Holman, Larkin A. [Later married Purkey]
HOLMAN, Mattie, W5394, MU, Holman, Wm. Fletcher
HOLMAN, R. S. S12669, RB, 49th Inf.
HOLMAN, T. C. S13206, H, 41st Ga. Inf.
HOLMES, Alexander, S8181, WA, 63rd Inf.
HOLMES, Amanda Mildina, W6445, W8703, SN, Holmes, Calvin B.
HOLMES, C. C. S5649, L, 22nd Ala. Inf.
HOLMES, Calvin B. S7873, SN, 20th Inf.
HOLMES, Emily, W7496, HU, Holmes, James M.
HOLMES, G. P. S9668, CF, 4th (McLemore's) Cav.
HOLMES, Henry F. S16102, H, 12th Bn. Ga. Lt. Art.
HOLMES, J. J. S13636, H, 4th (McLemore's) Cav.
HOLMES, J. M. S289, 12th Inf.
HOLMES, J. M. S15115, HU, 10th Cav.
HOLMES, J. R. S15708, RO, 5th (McKenzie's) Cav.
HOLMES, James A. S445, HO, 14th Inf.
HOLMES, John R. S2097, MU, 1st (Feild's) Inf.

HOLMES, Julia Ann, W6772, SN, Holmes, Robert Yancey
HOLMES, Mary, W10173, GU, Holmes, B. F.
HOLMES, Mary Frances, W3761, RU, Holmes, Charles Ready
HOLMES, Mattie Jane, W10098, G, Holmes, Marion C.
HOLMES, Ophelia Josephine, W1800, D, Holmes, Joseph Anthony
HOLMES, Pandora, W9327, HO, Holmes, James A.
HOLMES, R. C. S16319, HO, 50th Inf.
HOLMES, R. Y. S13065, SN, 20th Inf.
HOLMES, Sarah Catherine, W4728, CF, Holmes, G. P.
HOLMES, Thomas L. S4297, 1st Mo. Inf.
HOLMES, Toffield D. S16061, MR, Quantrell's Guerillas
HOLMES, W. F. S3211, G, 12th Inf.
HOLMES, W. S. S5874, W, 4th (McLemore's) Cav.
HOLMES, William, S278, RB, 30th Inf.
HOLMES, William F. S4766, RU, 4th (McLemore's) Cav.
HOLMES, William S. S14996, CF, 4th (McLemore's) Cav.
HOLMS, Marion, S4455, J, 8th (Smith's) Cav.
HOLT, A. Y. W95, SN, Holt, Novel L.
HOLT, Andrew M. S7858, GI, 32nd Inf.
HOLT, Caleb, S1892, H, 5th Cav.
HOLT, Charles M. S507, GE, 54th Inf.
HOLT, E. G. W. S4861, RB, 50th Inf.
HOLT, Eliza M. W5435, HM, Holt, Thomas R.
HOLT, Elzira Ann, W3044, GI, Holt, Elijah Wilson
HOLT, H. C. S11352, SH, 9th Bn. (Gantt's) Cav.
HOLT, H. H. S13035, FR, 37th Inf.
HOLT, Isabel, W2577, GE, Holt, Sparrel
HOLT, J. C. S548, S1154, DY, 16th Cav.
HOLT, James Monroe, S10015, D, 44th Inf.
HOLT, James R. S6240, GI, 21st Miss. Inf.
HOLT, John, S14057, GE, 29th Inf.
HOLT, John P. S1543, WI, Undetermined
HOLT, Lizora Jane, W8742, GI, Holt, Wyatt Lafayette
HOLT, Lucinda, W3450, GI, Holt, J. R.
HOLT, Mary Ann, W4900, SU, Holt, James H.
HOLT, Mary Cathrine, W5360, DY, Holt, W. M.
HOLT, Mary Elizabeth, W3846, SH, Holt, Robert James

Index to Tennessee Confederate Pension Applications

HOLT, Melissa Jane, W4594, GE, Holt, Charles Mabry
HOLT, N. D. S2724, CF, 37th Inf.
HOLT, Nicholas Perkins, S14160, D, 17th Inf.
HOLT, R. W. S15635, GI, 5th Inf.
HOLT, Spurrel, S508, GE, 54th Va. Inf.
HOLT, Stephen Henry, S16657, D, 3rd (Forrest's) Cav.
HOLT, Thomas Huston, S9084, GI, 3rd (Clack's) Inf.
HOLT, Thomas R. S12601, HM, 61st Inf.
HOLT, W. M. S8338, B, 17th Inf.
HOLT, Wes M. S11678, DY, 1st Ky. Inf.
HOLTON, Allen, S1522, SU, 34th Inf.
HOLTON, N. P. S1562, CH, 27th Inf.
HOLTON, Susan F. W531, RU, Holton, John R.
HOLYFIELD, E. C. S14123, MN, 21st (Wilson's) Cav.
HOLYFIELD, Mary Ann, W485, CH, Holyfield, John H.
HONEYCUT, John W. S3543, HD, 9th Ala. Cav.
HONEYCUTT, James A. S10927, SN, 8th Ky. Inf.
HONNOLL, Mary Elizabeth, W5787, SH, Honnoll, James Wiseman
HOOBERRY, Martha C. W4284, D, Hooberry, John W.
HOOD, Annie E. W8129, SH, Hood, Vinson A.
HOOD, Bettie, W10355, G, Hood, John Warmeth
HOOD, Daniel, S15042, GI, 1st Ala. Cav.
HOOD, James C. S11963, RU, 8th (Smith's) Cav.
HOOD, James Dorrel, S12745, MU, Sparkman's Co. Lt. Art.
HOOD, Newton Alexander, S11025, HY, Undetermined
HOOD, Susan, W481, R, Hood, Rufus
HOOD, Thomas L. S16665, RO, 5th (McKenzie's) Cav.
HOOD, Z. a. S13356, LA, 41st Ga. Inf.
HOOFMAN, S. W. S3466, WE, 15th Inf.
HOOKER, Martha Ann, W6727, MN, Hooker, Thomas Benton
HOOKER, T. B. S13458, MN, 27th Ala. Inf.
HOOKER, William R. S3663, DY, 62nd Inf.
HOOKS, A. D. S15724, T, 51st Inf.
HOOKS, J. B. S8021, SH, 5th Miss. Cav.
HOOKS, Thomas, S3024, A, Kain's Co. Lt. Art.
HOOPER, A. S2128, CE, 11th Inf.
HOOPER, A. B. S12049, HU, 10th Cav.

HOOPER, Ann JAne, W2234, MT, Hooper, James Obediah Raglin
HOOPER, C. S. S12981, CE, 11th (Holman's) Cav.
HOOPER, Elizabeth, W7421, D, Hooper, Joseph Harrison
HOOPER, Emily, W1110, P, Hooper, Benjamin
HOOPER, Fannie L. W9483, DI, Hooper, Jessie Owen
HOOPER, Frances A. W583, SN, Hooper, Daniel S.
HOOPER, Gabriella Ellenor, W1406, MT, Hooper, Marcellus Jordan
HOOPER, J. H. S12230, HN, 13th N.C. Inf.
HOOPER, J. H. S15266, D, McClung's Co. Lt. Art.
HOOPER, J. O. S8162, DI, 50th Inf.
HOOPER, J. O. S11353, MA, 7th Mo. Cav.
HOOPER, James, S3954, HI, 24th Inf.
HOOPER, John, S7213, PO, 29th Inf.
HOOPER, John L. S7490, O, 50th Inf.
HOOPER, M. J. S3083, MT, 49th Inf.
HOOPER, Margaret Ann, W2920, RU, Hooper, George Washington
HOOPER, Martha Hunnora, W6402, MA, Hooper, John O.
HOOPER, Mary Ann, W7344, CE, Hooper, Claborn Stuart
HOOPER, Mary P. W1669, H, Hooper, Warren Franklin
HOOPER, Myra Cantrell, W4103, SN, Hooper, Andrew Jackson
HOOPER, Nancy W. W4777, DI, Hooper, A.
HOOPER, S. W. A. S4936, DK, Shaw's Bn. Cav.
HOOPER, Sarah Jane, W2851, DI, Hooper, Simpson Homes
HOOPER, T. J. S2422, DI, Baxter's Co. Lt. Art.
HOOPER, T. M. S16151, DK, 16th Inf.
HOOPER, W. H. S7369, S8163, HI, 11th Inf.
HOOPER, William, S10024, HI, 11th Inf.
HOOSER, William M. S4503, WH, 17th Inf.
HOOTEN, Jesse, S1061, J, 8th Cav.
HOOTEN, Martha, W157, MU, Hooten, John R.
HOOVER, B. R. S7151, CF, 4th Cav.
HOOVER, E. Bell, W2101, RU, Hoover, Rueben Lawson
HOOVER, F. D. W8114.5, W8398, RU, Hoover, J. P. J.
HOOVER, J. S. S9561, HI, 9th Bn. Cav.
HOOVER, James M. S3035, W, 2nd Inf.

Index to Tennessee Confederate Pension Applications

HOOVER, Mary Kay, W10035, B, Hoover, Rufus Archibald
HOOVER, Mary L. W6251, HI, Hoover, Joseph S.
HOOVER, Mattie Emeline, W8624, RU, Hoover, Wm. Murphree
HOOVER, Millie, W8873, CA, Hoover, Thomas J.
HOOVER, Samuel sr. S3546, HI, 2nd Bn. (Biffle's) Cav.
HOPE, Francis Manning, S4818, RU, 18th Inf.
HOPE, Hugh L. S2050, RU, 45th Inf.
HOPE, James King, S9302, B, 5th Inf.
HOPE, Kate, W5253, RU, Hope, F. M.
HOPE, Martha J. W1479, GE, Hope, Adam
HOPE, Rachel Jane, W7337, K, Hope, John W.
HOPE, S. W. S15861, D, 6th (Wheeler's) Cav.
HOPKINS, Lavena Dill, W5163, RU, Hopkins, Wilburn Harris
HOPKINS, Martha Susan, W1319, MR, Hopkins, Baird Scott
HOPKINS, Mollie, W3799, MN, Hopkins, T. B.
HOPKINS, Sam J. S14470, CC, 7th (Duckworth's) Cav.
HOPKINS, Thomas B. S4336, MN, 19th Cav.
HOPPER, Elizabeth Jane, W1859, LI, Hopper, George W.
HOPPER, George W. S5999, LI, 32nd Inf.
HOPPER, Jesse, S2960, CL, 63rd Inf.
HOPPERS, F. J. S14155, JO, 61st N.C. Inf.
HORD, Annie Gray, W7781, D, Hord, Benjamin McCulloch
HORD, B. M. S15370, D, 1st Ark. Cav.
HORD, Frederick R. C62, HW, 2nd Cav.
HORN, Belle, W9420, WL, Horn, James Marion
HORN, C. D. S9552, ST, 14th Inf.
HORN, Eliza, W525, D, Horn, Joseph
HORN, Ella Barbee, W9156, ST, Horn, Cornelius Dave
HORN, H. L. S13253, SM, 28th Inf.
HORN, Henry H. S11108, D, 50th Inf.
HORN, James T. S11241, D, 10th Inf.
HORN, Joel E. S11496, D, 9th Cav.
HORN, Julia Ann, W4318, JO, Horn, Lewis Henderson
HORN, Lewis H. S7362, JO, 18th N.C. Inf.
HORN, Louise [Kirkpatrick], W7370, D, Horn, Joel Lee, [Later married Kirkpatrick]
HORN, Lucy Ann, W2591, H, Horn, John
HORN, Malinda P. W674, CH, Horn, John Wilson
HORN, Mary A. W8165, PU, Horn, Sherrod
HORN, Mindy, W6934, D, Horn, Henry
HORN, Palestine E. S7560, LA, 53rd Inf.
HORN, Paulina, W7412, D, Horn, James Thomas
HORN, Sherard, S8503, CU, 28th Inf.
HORN, W. D. S14066, BE, 10th Cav.
HORNBEAK, Rash, C260, HI, Undetermined
HORNBERGER, G. E. S8909, RB, 50th Inf.
HORNBERGER, Louisa B. W7237, RB, Hornberger, Wm. Wiley
HORNBERGER, W. W. S12550, RB, 11th Inf.
HORNBERGER, Wiley, S4247, RB, 11th Inf.
HORNBUCKLE, J. W. S12488, SN, 49th Inf.
HORNBURGER, C. E. S1682, RB, 50th Inf.
HORNE, A. C. S2892, MU, 3rd (Clack's) Inf.
HORNE, Henrietta C. W7997, D, Horne, David Edward
HORNE, Letitia, W11163, SH, Horne, Jack
HORNE, Matilda, W2298, K, Horne, Wm.
HORNE, Palestine, S4000, LA, 53rd Inf.
HORNER, J. S8603, P, 42nd Inf.
HORNER, L. K. S3618, G, 20th Inf.
HORNER, Melvinia, W9351, W8997, OV, Horner, Marion Spencer
HORNER, Minnie Iola, W6236, D, Horner, Jessee Pleasant
HORNER, N. S. sr. S8577, P, 42nd Inf.
HORNER, O. M. W8997, W9351, OV, Horner, S. M.
HORNER, S. M. S13409, OV, 8th (Dibrell's) Cav. See also J. H. Pollard #8997
HORNER, Thomas, S2640, P, 9th Inf.
HORNSBY, Ruth Anna, W5711, CH, Hornsby, Wm. Sibestean
HORSFORD, Mandy, W6741, MS, Horsford, Wm.
HORTON, Frances, W8292, HE, Horton, Jesse S.
HORTON, G. R. S12886, MN, 9th Ga. Art.
HORTON, H. J. S425, HW, 12th Cav.
HORTON, J. D. S6162, HE, 13th Inf.
HORTON, J. H. S12732, HD, 19th (Biffle's) Cav.
HORTON, Lucy Henderson, W10547, W9760, WI, Horton, Henry Claiborne
HORTON, Martha Ann, W6019, H, Horton, Samuel Virgil
HORTON, Martha Jane, W4185, RU, Horton, Robert N.
HORTON, Mary A. W8089, WY, Horton, George Riley

170-

HORTON, Mary Dee, W4370, CC, Horton, W. H.
HORTON, Mary Elizabeth, W2732, Horton, Edwin Ruthorn
HORTON, T. T. S14427, HA, 10th Ky. Cav.
HORTON, W. A. S15663, H, 43rd Inf.
HORTON, W. H. S9428, JO, 58th N.C. Inf.
HORTON, W. P. S11544, CT, 22nd Va. Cav.
HOSKINS, Frances M. W9113, WI, Hoskins, Charles Henry
HOSS, Ellen Eliza, W5430, SU, Hoss, Samuel E.
HOSS, J. M. S3393, U, 45th Inf.
HOSTON, See Haston
HOUCHINS, John C. S5544, S3283, HW, 50th Va. Inf., 3283 follows 5544: out of order on film
HOUSE, Emelia E. W8593, D, House, Thomas Bryant
HOUSE, Harwell, S11461, S5329, H, 4th (McLemore's) Cav.
HOUSE, J. F. S3409, WI, 4th (McLemore's) Cav.
HOUSE, J. W. S11467, G, 21st Cav.
HOUSE, Joshua T. S16692, 4th Ky. Inf., Applied from Boulder County, CO.
HOUSE, Martha W. W3441, D, House, Wm. Henry
HOUSE, Mary E. W3349, H, House, Hartwell
HOUSE, W. D. S1117, WE, 11th Inf.
HOUSE, William J. S12526, WL, 1st Cav.
HOUSE, Winbourn, S88, D, 23rd Inf.
HOUSEAL, Augusta Addy, W6858, SH, Houseal, J. T.
HOUSER, George W. S4097, SU, Home Guards
HOUSER, J. H. S7100, SU, 48th Va. Inf.
HOUSER, John T. S3625, K, 15th N.C. Cav.
HOUSEWRIGHT, Henry, S1591, HW, 1st Cav.
HOUSTON, Abbigail, W2743, HY, Houston, James Lafayette
HOUSTON, Eliza Jane, W1548, R, Houston, John McCarney
HOUSTON, Emma Louisa, W6803, SH, Houston, Horace Myers
HOUSTON, J. L. S7570, HY, 18th Cav.
HOUSTON, J. M. S3494, R, 16th Bn. Cav.
HOUSTON, J. W. S10121, SU, Unassigned (Nitre Mining)
HOUSTON, Levi, S7859, S2813, MN, 11th Miss. Cav.
HOUSTON, Mary Hicks, W8808, MA, Houston, Wm. Washington

HOUSTON, Sarah Eliza, W10539, GI, Houston, Frederick Newton
HOVIS, Emily, W6507, HD, Hovis, Winfield Taylor
HOVIS, W. T. S8523, MN, 2nd Miss. Cav.
HOWARD, Ada G. W10616, MU, Howard, Bithal
HOWARD, C. P. S10327, R, Ralston's Bn. Ga. Cav.
HOWARD, Emily A. W980, WE, Howard, James R.
HOWARD, Esther B. W2255, K, Howard, Asa O.
HOWARD, Frances E. W10080, H, Howard, Thomas J.
HOWARD, G. N. S7214, GI, 32nd Inf.
HOWARD, G. W. S5714, WL, 45th Inf.
HOWARD, Isabella, W4577, MA, Howard, Joseph Thomas
HOWARD, J. D. S12297, MU, 48th Inf.
HOWARD, J. W. S13248, HN, 5th Inf.
HOWARD, James A. S5852, MA, 51st Inf.
HOWARD, James C. S10584, BO, 2nd (Ashby's) Cav.
HOWARD, James D. S10742, MR, 18th Ala. Cav.
HOWARD, James T. S1201, ME, 5th Cav.
HOWARD, Martha Evelyn, W5403, W, Howard, James Wm.
HOWARD, Mary Ann, W2460, MR, Howard, A. L.
HOWARD, Mary Elizabeth, W2915, GI, Howard, George Newton
HOWARD, Mary Ellen, W5459, ME, Howard, James Turner
HOWARD, Mattie P. W4657, MU, Howard, J. D.
HOWARD, Penelope, W308, R, Howard, R. T.
HOWARD, S. W. S7456, GI, 32nd Inf.
HOWARD, Sarah Lucinda, W8779, CF, Howard, John Gilliland
HOWARD, Stephen M. S3689, D, 9th Inf.
HOWARD, Thaden Milton, S6125, SH, 1st Miss. Inf.
HOWARD, Thomas H. S7433, SU, 60th Inf.
HOWARD, Thomas J. S4193, H, 16th Cav.
HOWARD, W. J. S9137, MU, 48th (Nixon's) Inf.
HOWARD, W. J. F. S4091, SN, 2nd Ky. Cav.
HOWELL, C. S8405, FR, 49th Ala. Inf.
HOWELL, D. C. S6407, HR, 14th (Neely's) Cav.

Index to Tennessee Confederate Pension Applications

HOWELL, D. P. S8512, S4643, HD, 18th (Newsom's) Cav.
HOWELL, Elizabeth C. W1052, FR, Howell, Joseph M.
HOWELL, F. M. S14728, LK, 38th Inf.
HOWELL, J. C. J. S1595, WI, 48th Inf.
HOWELL, J. H. S4513, MN, 14th Inf.
HOWELL, James M. S14655, HU, 42nd Inf.
HOWELL, Jerre, S2890, SE, 16th N.C. Inf.
HOWELL, Jessie C. S13089, MU, 53rd Inf.
HOWELL, John H. S13292, MU, 53rd Inf.
HOWELL, John W. S11536, G, 22nd (Barteau's) Cav.
HOWELL, Julia Franklin, W, Some papers with #11183 on film
HOWELL, Lee J. S15632, MN, 18th (Newsom's) Cav.
HOWELL, Lucinda J. W3466, O, Howell, George Washington
HOWELL, Margaret A. W957, K, Howell, John Haven
HOWELL, Martha Jane, W5732, WI, Howell, Y. C. Y.
HOWELL, Martha L. W7284, MN, Howell, David P.
HOWELL, Mary Ann, W826, FR, Howell, J. F.
HOWELL, Nancy A. W8019, HR, Howell, Richard C.
HOWELL, Nancy J. W1312, HR, Howell, David Crawford
HOWELL, Newton Cannon, S4421, K, 31st Inf.
HOWELL, R. C. S2608, HR, 9th Inf. See also Richard C. Howell
HOWELL, Richard C. S4514, HR, 9th Inf. See also R. C. Howell
HOWELL, Ruthie N. W6327, CO, Howell, Jere
HOWELL, S. D. S6615, U, 58th N.C. Inf.
HOWELL, S. J. S3925, G, 8th Inf.
HOWELL, Sarah Melinda, W3541, JE, Howell, Isaac Barton
HOWELL, Sophia Head, W10409, H, Howell, John Edward
HOWELL, Steven, S5516, P, 19th (Biffle's) Cav.
HOWELL, William, S6752, P, 19th (Biffle's) Cav.
HOWELL, Willis Cazy, S11153, CC, 12th Cav.
HOWES, George H. S7603, D, 9th Ala. Inf.
HOWK, Jesse, S10527, SU, 1st (Carter's) Cav.
HOWLAND, Ephraim, S13254, RU, 23rd Inf.
HOWLAND, L. B. S5382, CF, 2nd Inf.
HOWLAND, R. L. S12856, CF, 2nd (Robison's) Inf.
HOWLETT, Bettie, W3561, MU, Howlett, James Stokley
HOWLETT, Isaac J. S14645, D, 48th (Voorhies') Inf.
HOWREN, James J. S3410, WA, 3rd Cav.
HOWS, Margaret A. W2965, D, Hows, Racy Jerome
HOWS, Nannie Lovell, W9129, D, Hows, Stephen Harrison
HOWS, S. H. S16338, D, 5th Cav.
HOWSE, J. S. S12368, HY, 14th Cav.
HOWSE, L. C. S12334, HR, 14th (Neely's) Cav.
HOWSE, Lycurgus H. S9815, RU, 1st (Feild's) Inf.
HOWSER, Margaret, W455, H, Howser, John M.
HUBBARD, Ella, W3407, WI, Hubbard, Josiah Rucks
HUBBARD, Henry C. S9968, SM, 28th Inf.
HUBBARD, J. H. S2846, D, 1st (Turney's) Inf.
HUBBARD, John Milton, S12178, SH, 7th (Duckworth's) Cav.
HUBBARD, Mary, W9344, SH, Hubbard, John Milton
HUBBARD, R. M. S6998, L, 3rd (Clack's) Inf.
HUBBLE, Thomas Ganaway, S6237, JE, 1st Va. Cav.
HUBBS, Ellen, W2030, D, Hubbs, James Monroe
HUBBS, G. W. S1978, U, 2nd (Ashby's) Cav.
HUBBS, Martha Elizabeth, W1501, O, Hubbs, John T.
HUCKABY, Sarah Ann, W1611, HW, Huckaby, James
HUCKS, Andy, S1452, K, 29th Inf.
HUDDLESTON, A. C. S2012, PU, 8th Cav.
HUDDLESTON, D. D. S7485, PU, 8th (Dibrell's) Cav.
HUDDLESTON, Eunice, W3706, PU, Huddleston, D. D.
HUDDLESTON, J. R. S1995, FR, 6th Miss. Cav.
HUDDLESTON, John P. S7977, PU, 25th Inf.
HUDDLESTON, Joseph A. S3732, FR, 6th Miss. Cav..
HUDDLESTON, Mary E. W8260, WL, Huddleston, Wm. L.
HUDDLESTON, Mary Elizabeth, W7140, RO, Huddleston, Wm. Washington

HUDDLESTON, Mary Lou, W2264, HI, Huddleston, Wm. Howell
HUDDLESTON, Samuel, S14893, L, 23rd N.C. Inf.
HUDDLESTON, Sarah Caroline, W10049, PU, Huddleston, John P.
HUDDLESTON, T. J. S3933, B, 7th Ala. Cav.
HUDDLESTON, William Washington, S6889, S2157, RO, 2nd (Ashby's) Cav.
HUDDLETON, Pleasant M. S13419, HR, 18th (Newsom's) Cav.
HUDGENS, Agnes, W9500, DI, Hudgens, F. M.
HUDGENS, America Caroline, W7982, WH, Hudgens, James Pleasant
HUDGENS, B. W. S3281, CE, 15th Inf.
HUDGENS, Joe, S7941, PU, 8th Cav.
HUDGENS, Joseph, S541, HM, Undetermined
HUDGENS, T. H. S13075, CE, 49th Inf.
HUDGGINS, Sarah, W9151, SN, Hudggins, Wm.
HUDGINS, Ann, W1001, WH, Hudgins, James
HUDGINS, Ellinor Nancy, W7314, D, Hudgins, Richard Christopher
HUDGINS, James P. S10037, WH, 8th (Dibrell's) Cav.
HUDGINS, Mary Jane, W11046, WI, Hudgins, Wm. J.
HUDGINS, Sarah, W796, SN, Hudgins, Wm.
HUDGINS, W. J. S10943, HU, 42nd Inf.
HUDGINS, W. J. S13070, WI, 23rd Bn. Inf.
HUDSON, Bettie, W9098, D, Hudson, George James
HUDSON, C. C. S16179, BE, 5th Inf.
HUDSON, Carroll Tipton, S12928, HR, 14th (Neely's) Cav.
HUDSON, Charles W. S13396, MA, 16th Cav.
HUDSON, Edward, S232, DK, 26th Inf.
HUDSON, Effie, W10943, MA, Hudson, Chas. Whitfield
HUDSON, Elijah D. S13978, 1st Va. Reserves
HUDSON, F. G. S11706, BE, 55th Inf.
HUDSON, F. L. S13053, G, 19th & 20th (Consolidated) Cav.
HUDSON, G. J. S7401, D, 45th Inf.
HUDSON, Henry H. S15922, T, 22nd Ala. Inf.
HUDSON, J. C. S1019, RU, 24th Inf.
HUDSON, James, S12780, OV, Hamilton's Bn. Cav.
HUDSON, James E. S778, HR, 9th Inf.
HUDSON, Jo G. S9808, BE, 5th Inf.
HUDSON, John B. S171, O, 33rd Inf.
HUDSON, John C. S466, RU, 24th Inf.

HUDSON, Julia, W10724, OV, Hudson, James A.
HUDSON, Julina Elizabeth, W2403, WH, Hudson, Wm. C.
HUDSON, Lucy Alice, W9804, LI, Hudson, Wm. B.
HUDSON, O. C. S10906, BE, 5th Inf.
HUDSON, P. W. S9408, BE, 55th Inf.
HUDSON, Sallie Elizabeth, W9989, Hudson, Elijah David
HUDSON, Sarah, W873, DI, Hudson, Robert Anderson
HUDSON, Susan A. W3267, BE, Hudson, P. W.
HUDSON, Tabitha Charity, W5255, G, Hudson, Ferdinand Leonidas
HUDSON, Thomas D. S6946, CH, 21st (Wilson's) Cav.
HUDSON, Vitura Virginia, W1016, G, Hudson, John H.
HUDSON, W. L. S12929, HR, 14th Cav.
HUDSON, William Perry, S9881, MU, 1st (Feild's) Inf.
HUDSPETH, Dicy Ann, W8325, HI, Hudspeth, David Crockett
HUDSPETH, J. A. S7370, DI, 4th Inf.
HUEY, Andrew Jackson, S3701, MS, 7th Ark. Inf.
HUEY, Eliza Jane, W1999, W1410, MU, Huey, James Hillman
HUFF, David, S1512, PO, 3rd Inf.
HUFF, Isaac M. S7352, ME, 3rd Confederate Cav.
HUFF, J. E. S9523, RU, 31st Miss. Inf.
HUFF, John, S12054, ME, 26th Inf.
HUFF, Mary A. W3671, ME, Huff, Isaac M.
HUFF, Mary Elizabeth, W2170, J, Huff, Pendleton
HUFF, P. S2548, J, 8th Inf.
HUFF, Susan Clearrinda, W7184, ME, Huff, John
HUFFAKER, Mary A. W10268, SE, Huffaker, Abner Henry
HUFFER, P. A. S5347, OV, 13th Cav.
HUFFER, T. H. S1346, OV, 8th Inf.
HUFFMAN, Ellen, W6036, WL, Huffman, Robert D.
HUFFMAN, Ephraim, S6923, MU, 45th Va. Inf.
HUFFMAN, John W. S1969, D, 2nd Inf.
HUFFMAN, Martha, W4519, MU, Huffman, Ephraim
HUFFMAN, Mary, W7263, SU, Huffman, Wm.

Index to Tennessee Confederate Pension Applications

HUFFMAN, Nancy Elizabeth, W9036, B, Huffman, John P.
HUFFMAN, R. D. S9912, WL, 44th Inf.
HUFFMASTER, A. D. S16479, HW, 43rd Inf.
HUFFMEISTER, Josephill M. S6161, K, 60th Inf.
HUFMAN, William D. S4011, SU, 48th Va. Inf.
HUGGINS, Elizabeth, W2077, MN, Huggins, James Monroe
HUGGINS, Elmina, W8373, DI, Huggins, J. M.
HUGGINS, John, S2086, MN, 13th Inf.
HUGGINS, S. C. S7310, MS, 53rd Inf.
HUGGINS, Sarah, W9039, SN, Huggins, Wm.
HUGGINS, Sarah M. W5303, MS, Huggins, Solomon C.
HUGHES, See also Hughs
HUGHES, A. L. S8369, SH, 2nd Miss. Inf.
HUGHES, Aaron, S6117, W, 16th Inf.
HUGHES, Archelaus M. S16354, MU, 9th Cav.
HUGHES, Columbia, W8596, D, Hughes, James C.
HUGHES, David, S3955, U, 29th N.C. Inf.
HUGHES, Evelene, W11045, SM, Hughes, George Washington
HUGHES, F. E. S11035, 48th Inf.
HUGHES, Francis M. S14158, F, 4th Inf.
HUGHES, George R. S13563, WI, 4th (McLemore's) Cav.
HUGHES, Georgia Allen, W5009, MA, Hughes, James Emmett
HUGHES, Harriett E. W10932, M, Hughes, George Lafayette
HUGHES, Hutson, S1843, H, 43rd Inf.
HUGHES, J. B. S7978, CU, 12th Bn. Cav.
HUGHES, J. C. S10679, MR, 7th Ky. Cav.
HUGHES, J. D. S9089, PU, 22nd (Barteau's) Cav.
HUGHES, J. W. V. S11526, S7813, SH, 15th (Stewart's) Cav.
HUGHES, James B. S4176, TR, 4th (McLemore's) Cav.
HUGHES, James B. S15055, D, 4th (McLemore's) Cav.
HUGHES, James E. S10538, MA, 6th Inf.
HUGHES, James Hilry, S13991, CC, 7th (Duckworth's) Cav.
HUGHES, James R. S7716, O, 1st (Feild's) Inf.
HUGHES, Jemima Gentry, W5251, D, Hughes, Arch.
HUGHES, Jennie Langston, W5958, WI, Hughes, George Richard

HUGHES, Jesse B. S16582, L, 19th (Biffle's) Cav.
HUGHES, John C. S14797, W, 16th Inf.
HUGHES, Joseph, S544, SN, 24th Inf.
HUGHES, Kate, W2790, WL, Hughes, Robert H.
HUGHES, Laura Tennessee, W5623, RU, Hughes, Richard Bartin
HUGHES, Martha Ann, W523, D, Hughes, Wm. T.
HUGHES, Martha Cordelia, W3097, WY, Hughes, James Edmond
HUGHES, Martha Jane, W1683, HI, Hughes, James A.
HUGHES, Mary, W2951, W, Hughes, Aaron
HUGHES, Mary Irene, W1555, WI, Hughes, John M.
HUGHES, Mildred A. W3516, SM, Hughes, James B.
HUGHES, N. P. S15158, D, 9th (Ward's) Cav.
HUGHES, Nannie Frances, W9197, W, Hughes, John Calhoon
HUGHES, Sallie E. W3775, WI, Hughes, James Kemp
HUGHES, Susan, W5660, MT, Hughes, Theo Michael
HUGHES, T. M. S13362, MT, Georgia Volunteers
HUGHES, W. C. S1238, OV, 25th Inf.
HUGHES, William B. S15849, MU, 5th Ala. Cav.
HUGHES, William Dallas, S12562, MU, 5th Ala. Cav.
HUGHES, William P. S6221, SH, 6th Inf.
HUGHES, Winnie Almeda, W1945, LA, Hughes, Jesse Patterson
HUGHES, Witt Eva, W7250, SH, Hughes, Barney
HUGHEY, George L. S13875, GI, 9th Ala. Cav.
HUGHEY, William H. S16533, SH, 1st Miss. Inf.
HUGHLETT, James, S4033, SN, 30th Inf.
HUGHLETT, Susan, W1876, SN, Hughlett, James
HUGHS, See also Hughes
HUGHS, A. J. S1059, BO, 3rd Inf.
HUGHS, Hiram B. S524, GE, 48th Va. Inf.
HUGHS, J. P. S8677, RB, 2nd Cav.
HUGHS, Perella, W6964, OV, Hughs, Wm. C.
HUGINS, F. M. S11368, DI, 11th Inf.
HUHN, Mary B. W6373, SH, Huhn, John Daniel
HULIN, Mary A. W2592, HD, Hulin, Rubin

HULIN, Matthew, S1971, K, Kain's Co. Lt. Art.
HULL, J. C. S9797, SU, 59th Inf.
HULL, Levinah, W3435, SU, Hull, John C.
HULL, William Rogers, S9553, SU, 63rd Inf.
HULME, Sarah James, W6191, GI, Hulme, J. W.
HULME, William F. S699, LI, 1st Inf.
HULME, William Henry, S16637, SH, Unassigned
HULSE, Sarah F. W2240, WA, Hulse, Wm. P.
HULSEY, Martha, W3309, D, Hulsey, James Calvin
HUMBER, Benjamin W. S11026, MT, 49th Inf.
HUMBLE, N. P. S2580, 35th Inf.
HUMES, Mary Catherine, W7866, K, Humes, Thomas Wm.
HUMES, Thomas W. S13716, K, 1st Miss. Inf.
HUMMEL, J. M. S753, CY, 8th Cav.
HUMMEL, W. H. S1347, OV, 28th Inf.
HUMPHREY, B. B. S6754, WH, 50th Inf.
HUMPHREY, James E. S16569, GI, 4th S.C. Inf.
HUMPHREY, Noah, S15707, K, Home Guards, Ga.
HUMPHREY, Sallie Annie, W5539, D, Humphrey, James Rayfus
HUMPHREYS, D. J. S13596, WA, 5th Cav.
HUMPHREYS, James B. S1584, WA, 63rd Inf.
HUMPHREYS, Mary E. W64, WA, Humphreys, Olliver Miller
HUMPHREYS, William H. S6738, WA, 63rd Inf.
HUMPHRIES, H. J. S1437, H, 43rd Inf.
HUNIGAN, O. H. S6719, SU, 54th Va. Inf.
HUNNICUT, D. R. S6006, D, 15th Cav.
HUNNICUTT, Albert, S10649, B, 30th Bn. Ga. Cav.
HUNNICUTT, Harriet L. W101, SN, Hunnicutt, Thomas F.
HUNNIGAN, Mary Susan, W7612, SU, Hunnigan, Oliver H.
HUNT, A. J. S15818, T, 12th (Green's) Cav.
HUNT, Artelia Priscilla, W6121, RU, Hunt, Elisha Bell
HUNT, Benjamin Minor, S11027, MT, 58th Va. Inf.
HUNT, Catherine, W37, WA, Hunt, George
HUNT, Clyde M. W10718, MT, Hunt, Benjamin Marvin
HUNT, David, S4892, FR, 41st Inf.
HUNT, David N. S6809, RO, 59th Inf.
HUNT, Dilphie, W10652, LA, Hunt, Daniel
HUNT, E. K. S14943, WA, 19th Inf.
HUNT, Elizabeth, W7449, MO, Hunt, Thomas Jefferson
HUNT, Ella, W9782, HR, Hunt, Charles M.
HUNT, Harry B. S5875, MT, 49th Inf.
HUNT, J. F. S4171, T, 7th Cav.
HUNT, J. M. S754, DY, Undetermined
HUNT, J. W. S79, GE, 50th Inf.
HUNT, Jane Callen, W4067, O, Hunt, T. J.
HUNT, Jennie, W3672, RU, Hunt, Sim
HUNT, John O. S12192, D, 9th (Ward's) Cav.
HUNT, Joseph, S13438, D, 3rd Ky. Inf.
HUNT, Joseph E. S12698, D, 20th Inf.
HUNT, Lucius L. S11981, SH, 26th Inf.
HUNT, Mariah J. W637, GE, Hunt, Washington S.
HUNT, Martha Vandelia, W304, D, Hunt, Cyrus Washington
HUNT, Mary, W6791, MO, Hunt, Zachary Taylor
HUNT, Mary P. W8, WL, Hunt, George W.
HUNT, Robert H. S16603, G, 20th (Russell's) Cav.
HUNT, Sarah Frances, W6755, T, Hunt, John Hilliard
HUNT, Sarah J. W96, WL, Hunt, James H.
HUNT, Sarah Mariah, W10249, W5532, SU, Hunt, Adam Miller
HUNT, Sasannah M. W638, GE, Hunt, Wm.
HUNT, Simeon, S948, RU, 45th Inf.
HUNT, Susan Ellen, W9580, D, Hunt, W. C.
HUNT, Susan M. W5363, SH, Hunt, Wm.
HUNT, T. J. S14899, MO, 3rd (Lillard's) Mtd. Inf.
HUNT, U. H. S5271, WA, 60th Inf.
HUNT, Z. T. S12379, MO, 59th Inf.
HUNTER, B. R. S18, WL, 17th Inf.
HUNTER, Booker, C92, WI, Undetermined
HUNTER, David W. S16618, MS, Undetermined
HUNTER, Donie Cannon, W11160, LI, Hunter, Wm. M. Papers found mixed with 11157 on film
HUNTER, Eliza Jane, W8669, W1337, SM, Hunter, John B.
HUNTER, Elizabeth A. W2587, K, Hunter, Peter L.
HUNTER, George W. S5429, SN, 30th Inf.
HUNTER, H. D. S4776, RB, 3rd Ky. Inf.
HUNTER, Henry C. S7276, D, 2nd (Robinson's) Inf.

HUNTER, ISadora E. W969, WL, Hunter, Burchett R.
HUNTER, J. A. S13706, H, 39th Ga. Inf.
HUNTER, J. D. S4694, MN, 22nd Cav.
HUNTER, J. P. S15545, JE, 3rd Mtd. Art.
HUNTER, James, S6000, H, 10th Ga. Inf.
HUNTER, James Alexander, S16120, H, Edmondson's Bn. Ga. Cav.
HUNTER, James W. S9224, WH, Unassigned
HUNTER, Jonathan, S3690, CO, N.C. Regt.
HUNTER, Mary Catherine, W5948, B, Hunter, James Bradshaw
HUNTER, Mary E. W7917, MN, Hunter, James D.
HUNTER, Mary Virginia, W7072, D, Hunter, Wm. Allen
HUNTER, Nancy Jane, W10988, W5307, CE, Hunter, Thomas William
HUNTER, Nannie E. W3054, MS, Hunter, W. A.
HUNTER, P. E. S4644, R, 5th (McKenzie's) Cav.
HUNTER, Samuel, S4967, S5843, SM, 28th Inf.
HUNTER, Sophronia, W9334, H, Hunter, James Albert
HUNTER, Susie Vance, W7962, SH, Hunter, Willis Osborne
HUNTER, Thomas, S1441, H, 2nd (Walker's) Inf.
HUNTER, Thomas W. S12816, CE, 42nd Inf.
HUNTER, W. S1690, SN, 30th Inf.
HUNTER, W. W. S7618, J, 4th Cav.
HUNTER, William A. S9659, D, 22nd (Barteau's) Cav.
HUNTER, William H. H. S14901, DY, 24th Inf.
HUNTER, William M. S2030, OV, 25th Inf.
HUNTER, William M. S16166, LI, 25th Inf.
HURD, Nancy Jane, W2400, DY, Hurd, John Carroll
HURLEY, George W. S14029, MN, 20th (Russell's) Cav.
HURLEY, T. J. S14030, MN, 20th (Russell's) Cav.
HURSH, Henly, S1680, CL, 1st (Carter's) Cav.
HURST, A. J. S4914, MN, 3rd Confederate Engineer Troops
HURST, Amanda Melvina, W532, CL, Hurst, Chrisley B.
HURST, C. B. S813, CL, Undetermined
HURST, Catherine, W581, CL, Hurst, Nathan
HURST, Eldridge, S2685, UN, 49th Inf.
HURST, John, S12593, HM, 63rd Inf.

HURST, Mary, W4018, CL, Hurst, Andrew
HURST, Mary B. W1251, SU, Hurst, Daniel
HURST, Mary J. W7658, HR, Hurst, A. J.
HURST, Nancy Jane, W3315, CH, Hurst, Wm. Haywood
HURST, Nathan, S2657, CL, 12th Bn. Cav.
HURST, P. L. S4814, CL, 1st Cav.
HURST, Polly Anne, W8659, UN, Hurst, Napoleon
HURST, Roadman, S2373, CL, 61st Inf.
HURST, Roland, S10671, HM, 5th (McKenzie's) Cav.
HURST, W. H. S1920, CH, 3rd Inf.
HURST, W. H. S2688, CL, 63rd Inf.
HURT, Ada, W7893, Hurt, Wm.
HURT, Eliza Caroline, W610, CH, Hurt, Joel F.
HURT, Florida, W9427, D, Hurt, Milton
HURT, Indiana, W10127, WE, Hurt, Wm. M.
HURT, John, S11518, D, 30th Inf.
HURT, John A. S1028, O, 47th Inf.
HURT, Lizzie N. W10345, MA, Hurt, John D.
HURT, Martha B. W5120, D, Hurt, John
HURT, Mary Ann, W2175, HU, Hurt, Wm. Riley
HURT, Mary Louisa, W2658, D, Hurt, Josiah
HURT, Sophia (Monil), W893, G, Hurt, Anthony Bennezette
HURT, Thomas Benjamin, S11367, HR, 21st (Wilson's) Cav.
HURT, W. R. S405, HU, 37th Inf.
HURT, W. R. S1083, HU, 24th Bn. Inf.
HURT, William, S7894, 22nd Inf.
HURT, William W. S6694, D, 30th Inf.
HUSKIN, John, S14058, MO, Thomas' Legion, N.C.
HUSKINS, Marguerite Lucille, W7333, SC, Huskins, Wm. Graham
HUSKITH, Letitia F. W803, WE, Huskith, James Little
HUSSEY, Ella Moss, W4327, D, Hussey, Wm. B.
HUTCHENS, Caroline, W7624, HW, Hutchens, Wm. A.
HUTCHENS, Lawson H. S1947, WH, 50th Inf.
HUTCHENS, Sarah Jane, W5029, WH, Hutchens, Lasson Lafayette
HUTCHENS, T. Jeff. S3619, K, 12th Cav.
HUTCHENS, W. A. S12832, HW, 12th Bn. (Day's) Cav.
HUTCHERSON, Bettie, W3866, HI, Hutcherson, James
HUTCHERSON, E. S9252, G, 42nd Inf.

Index to Tennessee Confederate Pension Applications

HUTCHERSON, George, S14481, WL, Allison's Squadron, Cav.
HUTCHERSON, James C. S5981, T, Forrest's Old Regt. Cav.
HUTCHERSON, Z. R. S5409, W, 4th Ky. Inf.
HUTCHESON, Elizabeth Maclin, W11133, L, Hutcheson, Guilford Jones
HUTCHESON, G. J. S16180, L, 1st Hvy. Art.
HUTCHESON, J. C. S10581, HI, 24th Inf.
HUTCHESON, James L. S6557, BL, 43rd Inf.
HUTCHESON, Miles, S13995, MU, 1st (Feild's) Inf.
HUTCHESON, Thomas, S5150, RU, 23rd Inf.
HUTCHINSON, Andrew, S1996, ST, 50th Inf.
HUTCHINSON, Auston P. S4483, RO, 54th Va. Inf.
HUTCHINSON, Mary Elizabeth, W5982, SH, Hutchinson, Wm. Dodson
HUTCHINSON, William H. S3216, B, 1st (Turney's) Inf.
HUTCHISON, G. W. S16352, RU, 45th Inf.
HUTCHISON, John, S7083, G, 55th Inf.
HUTCHISON, Mariah Elizabeth, W5916, T, Hutchison, Minor Ellis
HUTCHISON, Miner Ellis, S4670, T, 12th (Green's) Cav.
HUTCHISON, Nancy, W7609, HI, Hutchison, James Calvin
HUTCHISON, Sarah Jane, W3368, CH, Hutchison, George Washington
HUTCHKISS, J. J. S854, LO, 62nd Inf.
HUTCHUSON, M. D. S309, ST, 50th Inf.
HUTSON, John, S16531, D, 29th Ga. Inf.
HUTTON, A. A. S343, HM, 4th Va. Inf.
HUTTON, A. P. S7761, BR, 63rd Va. Inf.
HUTTON, J. O. S7746, BR, 63rd Va. Inf.
HUTTON, J. W. S4079, WY, 9th Cav.
HUTTON, Laura, W10526, H, Hutton, Cornelius Marion
HUTTON, Mary Janes, W4823, BR, Hutton, James O.
HUTTON, Susan Jane, W4761, BR, Hutton, A. D.
HUX, Catherine, W2042, CO, Hux, John Nelson
HUX, Isaac Alexander, S11187, HM, 29th Inf.
HUX, John N. S5423, S3289, CO, 26th Inf.
HYATT, Emily J. W9227, MC, Hyatt, Nathan N.
HYATT, Mary Louise, W10749, HA, Hyatt, Maroni E.
HYATT, N. N. S11761, MC, Thomas' Legion, N.C.
HYDE, Fannie Scott, W10941, D, Hyde, Henry Clay
HYDE, Josiah W. S10202, BL, 11th Ga. Cav
HYDE, Margaret Adeline, W7374, SQ, Hyde, Josiah Washington
HYDER, J. N. S9012, PU, 8th (Dibrell's) Cav.
HYDER, Jasper, S2573, CU, 16th Bn. (Neal's) Cav.
HYDER, Martha, W4151, CU, Hyder, Jasper
HYEMANN, Elizabeth Pauline, W7060, H, Hyemann, Solomon
HYETT, John, S2051, WA, 29th Inf.
HYLES, L. D. S5583, G, 6th (Wheeler's) Cav.
HYLTON, Mary E. W998, WA, Hylton, Solomon
HYNES, Litel, S770, GE, 29th Va. Inf.
ICEHOUT, S. A. S5517, CT, 3rd N.C. Reserves
ICEHOWER, Nalie, W10508, WA, Icehower, Solomon
ICEHOWER, S. A. S7219, CT, 8th Bn. N.C. Junior Reserves, Inf.
ING, J. B. S3411, G, 31st Inf.
ING, Robert B. S3401, G, 20th Cav.
INGE, Richard, S3268, T, 12th Cav.
INGLE, Alonzo, S12768, GE, 31st Inf.
INGLE, Eliza Jane, W9391, Ingle, James Alexander
INGLE, Elizabeth J. W1608, ME, Ingle, Jacob
INGLE, Elizabeth Jane, W8547, WA, Ingle, Alonzo
INGLE, Ellis, S11479, GE, 2nd (Ashby's) Cav.
INGLE, G. Q. S11478, S5718, MN, 8th Miss. Cav.
INGLE, J. A. S9475, 53rd N.C. Inf.
INGLE, Jacob, S1498, ME, 1st Cav.
INGLE, James, S10703, K, 20th Inf.
INGLE, Virginia Alice, W6451, B, Ingle, James P.
INGLE, W. H. S8605, LI, 8th Inf.
INGLES, M. S5647, SU, 19th Inf.
INGLES, William C. S10253, SE, 4th Cav.
INGRAM, Bessie Lowe, W10119, WL, Ingram, J. C.
INGRAM, I. L. S12602, MO, 22nd (Barteau's) Cav.
INGRAM, J. C. S14637, WL, 7th Inf.
INGRAM, John, S11655, CH, 31st Inf.
INGRAM, Margaret Jane, W6212, CH, Ingram, John
INGRAM, Mary C. W6939, MO, Ingram, Isac L.
INGRAM, N. T. S16322, SH, 1st Ark. Inf.

INGRAM, Pines R. S1867, FR, 1st Inf.
INGRAM, Sue L. W10171, MA, Ingram, Hazael Hewitt
INGRAM, W. W. S13191, GI, 11th (Holman's) Cav.
INGRUM, Nancy Jane, W9749, MU, Ingrum, Jonas M.
INGUL, Ephraim, S7069, HR, 16th N.C. Inf.
INKLEBARGER, Adeline, W4866, UN, Inklebarger, John T.
INKLEBARGER, Chesley J. S4651, K, 2nd (Ashby's) Cav.
INKLEBURGER, John T. S11449, CL, 5th Bn. Cav.
INMAN, Adline, W10855, P, Inman, Ezekiel
INMAN, Clavin E. S4507, P, 23rd Inf.
INMAN, Eliza, W8188, O, Inman, T. R.
INMAN, Ezekiel, C43, P, 5th Cav., Application is missing.
INMAN, J. H. S8851, MU, 5th Miss. Inf.
INMAN, James L. S1658, GI, 5th Inf.
INMAN, Margaret, W4437, P, Inman, Joseph S.
INMAN, Mary A. W2102, O, Inman, C. W.
INMAN, Mary C. W3547, MU, Inman, John Harrison
INMAN, S. E. S15603, P, 19th (Biffle's) Cav.
INMAN, Susan, W6026, P, Inman, Calvin E.
INMAN, Thomas R. S13512, O, 27th Inf.
INMAN, William B. S3136, HM, 62nd N.C. Inf.
INSCOE, Sallie A. W7101, WA, Inscoe, W. H.
INSCOE, William H. S14976, WA, 44th N.C. Inf.
INSCORE, James, S525, GE, 30th N.C. Inf.
IRBY, Tempie, W2837, HR, Irby, Lundy Robert
IRELAND, Addie Kelly, W10008, D, Ireland, Rufus Morgan
IRELAND, R. M. S14228, D, 9th (Bennett's) Cav.
IRICK, Lawrence, S7480, K, 2nd (Ashby's) Cav.
IRICK, Susan, W6012, K, Irick, Lawrence
IRVIN, Alice, W6143, WI, Irvin, Wm. D.
IRVIN, Amelia A. W244, WI, Irvin, J. C.
IRVIN, Emma Jane, W10357, G, Irvin, Robert Steel
IRVIN, Emmarilla, W4227, WH, Irvin, A. T. D.
IRVIN, G. W. S1581, WA, 60th Inf.
IRVIN, R. S. S11691, L, 7th Cav.
IRVIN, W. L. S6734, WH, 25th Inf.
IRVIN, William D. S1278, WI, 32nd Inf.
IRVINE, Crawford W. S6312, MU, 1st (Feild's) Inf.
IRVING, Jane, W1591, GU, Irving, Wm. Clark

IRWIN, A. T. D. S5903, WH, 16th Inf.
IRWIN, Cornelia Broyles, W8675, HD, Irwin, James Wm.
IRWIN, Ellen, W49, D, Irwin, Thomas
IRWIN, Hettie, W6446, G, Irwin, Larkin Huston
IRWIN, J. B. S11066, HR, 3rd Miss. Cav.
IRWIN, Lenora L. W4451, HR, Irwin, J. B.
IRWIN, Mary Hellen, W8864, MU, Irwin, King
IRWIN, Mattie Roth, W9561, MU, Irwin, Samuel Whifield
IRWIN, W. D. S2055, WL, 4th (McLemore's) Cav.
IRWIN, W. W. S4492, HI, 48th Inf.
IRWIN, William Daniel, S149, SM, 4th Cav., Follows #150 on film
ISBELL, David J. S10521, HU, 32nd Inf.
ISBELL, Elizabeth A. W3414, MO, Isbell, Wash.
ISBELL, G. W. S1573, SH, 29th Miss. Inf.
ISBELL, H. B. S15297, MU, 32nd Inf.
ISBELL, John G. S6870, O, 50th Inf.
ISBELL, Pendleton, S4404, SN, 6th Inf.
ISBELL, Pendleton M. S3713, MO, 3rd Inf.
ISBELL, W. H. S14906, SH, 29th Miss. Inf.
ISBELL, William, S6947, SN, 59th Inf.
ISBILL, Louisa Jane, W5676, LO, Isbill, Marcus Lafayette
ISBILL, M. S. S11303, LO, 3rd (Lillard's) Mtd. Inf.
ISBILL, Washington, S2141, MO, 37th Inf.
ISHAM, Rebecca Emaline, W3983, B, Isham, Wm. Hosea
ISHAM, William Hosia, S7341, B, 17th Inf.
ISLEY, Samuel, S7040, MS, 53rd Inf.
ISOM, G. F. S8684, LI, 8th Inf.
ISOM, Joseph B. S4893, B, 17th Inf.
ISOM, Mollie Ellen, W2660, B, Isom, Joseph Bird
IVEY, B. F. S4831, FR, 42nd Inf.
IVEY, H. J. S6658, D, 8th (Smith's) Cav.
IVEY, J. H. S3096, FR, 4th Inf.
IVEY, Mary Elender, W1824, DE, Ivey, John Jasper
IVEY, R. L. S7765, SH, Forrest's Old Regt. Cav.
IVEY, Sarah Ann, W4068, WI, Ivey, Wm. Lewis
IVEY, William B. S7682, MO, 42nd Inf.
IVIE, Roxanna, W7371, D, Ivie, Henry J.
IVIE, Wiley Sutton, C52, B, Quartermasters
IVY, A. J. S15334, MA, 7th Cav.
IVY, James K. S7633, DE, 18th Cav.
IVY, Montgomery, S10332, HU, 4th (Russell's) Ala. Cav.

Index to Tennessee Confederate Pension Applications

JACK, Lida Mitchell, W9746, HM, Jack, Samuel Walter
JACKSON, Aggie Elizabeth, W4142, DE, Jackson, James Holden
JACKSON, Alexander, S755, G, 8th Cav.
JACKSON, Amanda, W7403, HN, Jackson, R. J.
JACKSON, Amy Ann, W3887, K, Jackson, Andrew
JACKSON, C. S2474, HD, 4th Ala. Cav.
JACKSON, Caroline, W1059, WL, Jackson, I. G.
JACKSON, Charles Edward, S13483, SH, 7th (Duckworth's) Cav.
JACKSON, Cynthia S. W2187, GE, Jackson, Wm. E. V.
JACKSON, D. W. S5778, RB, 30th Inf.
JACKSON, Dora, W8434, RB, Jackson, Daniel Washington
JACKSON, Elias H. S8329, MO, 52nd Ga. Inf.
JACKSON, Elizabeth, W2289, CF, Jackson, D. C.
JACKSON, Elizabeth T. W208, RU, Jackson, Wm. H.
JACKSON, Emma, W8857, W8721, DY, Jackson, John Adkins
JACKSON, F. M. S3304, CC, 33rd Inf.
JACKSON, F. M. S15578, WE, 12th Ky. Cav.
JACKSON, Frances Emma, W8590, SH, Jackson, Charles Edward
JACKSON, G. W. S6391, WA, 22nd N.C. Inf.
JACKSON, G. W. S10359, SH, 7th (Duckworth's) Cav.
JACKSON, George W. S4589, B, 70th N.C. Inf.
JACKSON, H. A. S8397, MT, 14th Inf.
JACKSON, Hannah Liza, W187, WA, Jackson, David
JACKSON, Henry, C149, SH, Undetermined
JACKSON, J. C. S11393, HR, 52nd Inf.
JACKSON, J. E. S6755, DY, 42nd Ala. Inf.
JACKSON, J. M. S2338, OV, 28th Inf.
JACKSON, J. N. S282, HW, 12th Cav.
JACKSON, J. V. S16114, DI, 2nd (Woodward's) Ky. Cav.
JACKSON, J. W. S521, S1319, PU, 28th Inf.
JACKSON, J. W. S9170, O, 21st (Wilson's) Cav.
JACKSON, James A. S10916, SN, 20th Inf.
JACKSON, James H. S2930, HE, 31st Inf.
JACKSON, James H. S7059, ME, 19th Inf.
JACKSON, James S. S14768, RU, 11th Inf.
JACKSON, Jeff, S5430, W, 9th Bn. (Gannt's) Cav.
JACKSON, Jesse H. S1383, G, 12th Inf.
JACKSON, John A. S2142, WY, 20th Cav.
JACKSON, John A. S6898, HN, 20th (Russell's) Cav.
JACKSON, John B. S14069, D, Undetermined
JACKSON, John E. S6382, MO, Orr's Brigade, 2nd S.C. Rifles
JACKSON, John H. S15609, MO, 24th Ga. Inf.
JACKSON, John L. S7820, RU, 24th Inf.
JACKSON, John Murrow, S2124, L, 3rd Inf.
JACKSON, L. B. S1879, WA, 60th Inf.
JACKSON, L. M, S1382, WA, 60th Inf.
JACKSON, Laura Adeline, W7835, SH, Jackson, Joseph Columbus
JACKSON, Levi, S12164, HA, 37th Va. Inf.
JACKSON, Levinia Josephine, W3738, DI, Jackson, Gillins P.
JACKSON, Lizzie, W2816, B, Jackson, W. H.
JACKSON, Louisa R. W6461, HN, Jackson, Thomas H.
JACKSON, M. R. S231, D, 24th Inf.
JACKSON, Margaret E. W9666, OV, Jackson, Henry
JACKSON, Martha, W6811, WA, Jackson, Laib McCoy
JACKSON, Martha Ann, W4562, WY, Jackson, John Alexander
JACKSON, Martha Drucilla, W9331, W9246, CC, Jackson, Wm. Henry
JACKSON, Martha M. W6731, SU, Jackson, John
JACKSON, Mary A. W2165, SH, Jackson, Thomas Shepherd
JACKSON, Mary A. W9541, HN, Jackson, John A.
JACKSON, Mary A. P. W158, RB, Jackson, Sanford G. M.
JACKSON, Mary J. W5153, B, Jackson, George W.
JACKSON, Mollie Davis, W9218, D, Jackson, David G.
JACKSON, N. M. W4653, HR, Jackson, Jessy C.
JACKSON, Nathan R. S3551, SU, 60th Inf.
JACKSON, Penelope, W5994, HD, Jackson, Elisha W.
JACKSON, R. J. S11585, HN, 5th Inf.
JACKSON, R. W. S12059, HN, 5th Inf.
JACKSON, Rachel Anna, W8739, RU, Jackson, Francis Marion
JACKSON, Rebecca, W3956, MO, Jackson, J. E.

JACKSON, Rebecca James, W2978, SH, Jackson, George W.
JACKSON, Richard W. S9387, MT, 14th Inf.
JACKSON, Robert M. S6700, H, 2nd Bn. Ala. Cav.
JACKSON, S. H. S5160, MR, 4th Cav.
JACKSON, Sallie D. W3746, D, Jackson, Wm. Henry
JACKSON, Sarah Jane, W754, SM, Jackson, Wm.
JACKSON, Susan, W808, HN, Jackson, Daniel Wilson
JACKSON, Susan, W10838, SU, Jackson, Nathan Bradford
JACKSON, Susan Elizabeth, W2532, RU, Jackson, John L.
JACKSON, T. A. S11983, HN, 20th (Russell's) Cav.
JACKSON, T. A. S13030, DI, 49th Inf.
JACKSON, Texas Clementine, W5864, R, Jackson, James H.
JACKSON, Theodora Fagundus, W4010, SN, Jackson, Bailie Peyton
JACKSON, Thomas, S2719, CL, 1st Cav.
JACKSON, Thomas Neely, S3993, MA, 22nd Inf.
JACKSON, Virginia Ann, W8781, LI, Jackson, John Matthew
JACKSON, W. C. S12665, SN, 9th (Bennett's) Cav.
JACKSON, W. H. S9576, CC, 19th Cav.
JACKSON, W. a. S13977, SH, 18th Miss. Cav.
JACKSON, Wiley H. S10997, SH, 2nd Mo. Cav.
JACKSON, William, S1997, F, 10th Inf., On misc. microfilm reel
JACKSON, William, S15200, CE, 18th Inf.
JACKSON, William, S16072, GE, 60th Mtd. Inf.
JACKSON, William H. S14561, D, Cobb's Legion, Ga. Vols. Cav.
JACKSON, William Thomas, S3825, WE, 7th Ky. Inf.
JACKSON, alfred, S4537, SN, 9th (Bennett's) Cav.
JACO, John W. S303, W, 5th Inf.
JACO, O. D. S14326, W, 35th Inf.
JACOBS, Alice S. W6681, CF, Jacobs, Wesley B.
JACOBS, Edward Wesley, S867, HR, 14th Cav.
JACOBS, J. W. S4857, RU, 2nd (Robison's) Inf.
JACOBS, John W. S8985, HR, 14th Cav.

JACOBS, Mary O. W7276, G, Jacobs, Wm. Green
JACOBS, Mattie, W10906, RU, Jacobs, John Wesley
JACOBS, Robert M. S1470, MU, 1st Inf.
JACOBS, Sarah Frances, W7590, HR, Jacobs, Edward Wesley
JACOBS, Stokely, S12539, RU, 17th Inf.
JACOBS, Thomas Benton, S14045, RU, 4th (McLemore's) Cav.
JACOBS, Thomas Harvey, S4582, D, 48th (Voorhies') Inf.
JACOBS, W. G. S14707, G, 12th Inf.
JACOWAY, Isabelle, W5940, MR, Jacoway, Samuel Wesley
JACOWAY, S. W. S9546, MR, 49th Ala. Inf.
JAMES, Bell, W9206, GI, James, Wm. Newton
JAMES, Bobbie Cobb, W4376, MT, James, Barclay Army
JAMES, Dallis W. S3578, SE, 16th N.C. Inf.
JAMES, Dorcas, W7761, BO, James, E. L.
JAMES, Elenora Hampton, W3196, MA, James, Wm. Pinkney
JAMES, Elijah, S14105, BO, 1st (Carter's) Cav.
JAMES, Elizabeth, W6477, G, James, Wm. Jasper
JAMES, J. A. S16650, O, 19th & 20th (Consolidated) Cav.
JAMES, Joe B. S15422, FR, 4th Ala. Cav.
JAMES, Mary Amanda, W10804, O, James, J. A.
JAMES, Mattie Annie, W8704, W8304, WL, James, Rufus Quinten
JAMES, R. P. S2663, SH, 19th Inf.
JAMES, R. Q. S13957, WL, 8th (Smith's) Cav.
JAMES, Sallie I. W77, MS, James, Wm. C.
JAMES, Susanna R. W2074, WE, James, Thomas H.
JAMES, W. F. S7925, RU, 45th Inf.
JAMES, W. J. S13043, G, 17th Inf.
JAMES, W. T. S11814, GI, 6th (Wheeler's) Cav.
JAMES, W. W. S15946, S16387, HU, 12th (Green's) Cav.
JAMISON, Ida, W10880, SH, Jamison, Henry
JAMISON, J. W. S7385, RU, 45th Inf.
JAMISON, Robert Garner, S15323, T, 12th Cav.
JAMISON, Sam, S972, T, 22nd Inf.
JAMISON, T. E. S14020, WI, 48th (Voorhies') Inf.
JANUARY, Minerva, W5905, L, January, Wm. Houston

Index to Tennessee Confederate Pension Applications

JANUARY, W. H. S12148, L, 20th (Russell's) Cav.
JAPLIN, Thomas Moses, S6599, D, 1st Bn. Cav. (Coleman's) Scouts
JAQUERS, Margaret Jane, W456, J, Jaquers, John Lofton
JAQUES, John L. S361, J, 28th Inf.
JAQUESS, G. B. S5631, T, 16th Inf.
JAQUESS, J. G. S526, J, 28th Inf.
JAQUESS, Mary A. W7031, J, Jaquess, Joseph G.
JARED, C. B. S12029, PU, 8th (Dibrell's) Cav.
JARED, Elizabeth Frances, W7188, PU, Jared, Wm. James
JARED, Mariah, W3978, PU, Jared, Charles Branchford
JARED, W. C. S13231, PU, 7th Inf.
JARED, W. J. S11383, SM, 28th Inf.
JARMAN, Mary Frances, W7470, B, Jarman, Lafayette Bilbro
JARMON, L. B. S13540, B, 8th (Smith's) Cav.
JARNAGIN, Pleasant D. S7806, JE, 26th Inf.
JARNAGIN, Rebecca Jane, W9084, CA, Jarnagin, A. J.
JARNAGIN, Virginia Rouhs, W10805, H, Jarnagin, Gustavous Henry
JARNIGAN, A. S4521, HA, 50th Inf.
JARNIGAN, David, C31, K, 16th Cav.
JARNIGAN, Nancy, W595, GR, Jarnigan, Aaron
JARNIGAN, S. C. S13626, HM, 1st (Carter's) Cav.
JARNIGAN, Sarah Jane, W9053, HM, Jarnigan, Spencer Clark
JARRATT, A. W. S7521, MT, 45th Inf.
JARRATT, Susie Anna, W10313, D, Jarratt, Wm. Daniel
JARRATT, William D. S6805, D, 3rd (Clack's) Inf.
JARRELL, J. S. S4727, MA, 18th Inf.
JARRELL, James C. S1192, CF, 24th Inf.
JARRELL, Kate, W4675, CF, Jarrell, J. C.
JARRELL, L. J. S10244, G, 14th Cav.
JARRELL, Nancy Basket, W8818, B, Jarrell, Benjamin Franklin
JARRELL, R. R. S11236, D, 4th (McLemore's) Cav.
JARRETT, H. B. S14366, SH, 44th Miss. Inf.
JARRETT, R. R. S7532, GI, 53rd Inf.
JARRETT, Sarah Ann, W6848, DI, Jarrett, T. G.
JARRETT, Sarah E. W3208, SE, Jarrett, Edward S.

JARRETT, T. G. S12160, DI, 45th Inf.
JARVIS, James W. S7374, CO, 56th N.C. Inf.
JARVIS, Sylvester, S2245, WH, 8th Cav.
JEAN, Catharine, W1005, LI, Jean, James
JEAN, David, S7609, MS, 44th Inf.
JEAN, Rosanna, W4131, CF, Jean, Wiley
JEANS, Wiley, S3317, MOO, Huggin's Co. Lt. Art.
JEFFREES, Cora Lee, W10587, WE, Jeffrees, James A.
JEFFREES, Laura J. W2321, SH, Jeffrees, Richard J.
JEFFREY, John, S8681, MU, 23rd Ala. Inf.
JEFFREYS, Maria A. W2235, WH, Jeffreys, Robert Jordan
JEFFRIES, Frances Ann, W8011, B, Jeffries, James D.
JEFFRIES, J. D. S15025, B, 23rd Inf.
JEFRIES, Nancy Callie, W9688, W, Jefries, Isham Duane
JENKINS, A. A. S9111, HI, 9th Bn. (Gantt's) Cav.
JENKINS, Beulah Clement, W2022, D, Jenkins, James Franklin
JENKINS, Charles W. S15952, D, 30th Inf.
JENKINS, Charlotte J. W7703, WI, Jenkins, S. G.
JENKINS, Daniel Calvin, S11122, WE, 154th Sr. Regt. Inf.
JENKINS, Ephraim, S8819, H, 23rd Ga. Inf.
JENKINS, F. T. S1637, T, 1st Va. Cav.
JENKINS, Florence V. W8361, SU, Jenkins, Wm. H.
JENKINS, J. A. S1414, WE, 52nd Inf.
JENKINS, J. H. S11707, BE, 5th Inf.
JENKINS, Joe P. S9046, HN, 154th sr. Regt. Inf.
JENKINS, John Franklin, S8012, SH, 9th (Ark.) Cav.
JENKINS, John S. S136, HD, 4th Inf.
JENKINS, John S. S527, J, 28th Inf.
JENKINS, Martha Alice, W10136, G, Jenkins, John Sandford
JENKINS, Mary Elizabeth, W9440, HI, Jenkins, Amos Anderson
JENKINS, N. M. S8671, LI, 44th Inf.
JENKINS, Nannie, W5144, HM, Jenkins, Alfred
JENKINS, R. R. S13153, RB, 8th Ky. Cav.
JENKINS, Sallie Anjalette, W5601, SH, Jenkins, James Lafayette
JENKINS, Sallie R. W4486, W4022, CF, Jenkins, Wm. H. 4022 is missing

-181

JENKINS, Sarah James, W5516, F, Jenkins, Isaac
JENKINS, W. F. S10418, MOO, 20th Inf.
JENKINS, William C. S4447, CF, 17th Inf.
JENKINS, William H. S7904, CF, 24th Inf.
JENNETT, Henry P. S15474, D, 10th (DeMoss') Cav.
JENNINGS, A. W. S13083, WL, 8th (Smith's) Cav.
JENNINGS, Alice, See Alice White
JENNINGS, Charles E. S15175, U, 19th Va. Inf.
JENNINGS, Enos, S16388, WL, 7th Inf.
JENNINGS, G. M. S5114, WL, 7th Inf.
JENNINGS, Harriet Amanda, W339, WL, Jennings, Erastus Smith
JENNINGS, J. B. S12744, CC, 12th Cav.
JENNINGS, J. H. S11740, WE, 52nd Inf.
JENNINGS, J. M. S13762, DI, 14th Inf.
JENNINGS, J. W. S14920, SH, 11th Miss. Inf.
JENNINGS, James E. S9138, CL, 1st (Carter's) Cav.
JENNINGS, John H. S8607, H, 19th Ala. Inf.
JENNINGS, Joseph, C116, HM, 12th Cav.
JENNINGS, Lindsey R. S10805, JO, 33rd Inf.
JENNINGS, Martha E. W8134, JO, Jennings, T. R.
JENNINGS, Rebecca, W4319, JO, Jennings, Wiley
JENNINGS, Samuel, S8648, CL, Burrough's Co. Art.
JENNINGS, Sarah Emmerline, W5267, HI, Jennings, John P.
JENNINGS, Uriah, S4800, CA, 8th (Smith's) Cav.
JENNINGS, W. S. S15700, WI, 3rd Inf.
JENNINGS, William N. S2228, D, 1st Cav.
JENNOE, David, S898, R, 43rd Inf.
JERNIGAN, A. A. sr. S12579, HR, 18th (Newsom's) Cav.
JERNIGAN, A. Green, S15167, RB, 30th Inf.
JERNIGAN, Andrew Jesse, S16167, CA, 23rd Inf.
JERNIGAN, Cynthia Elizabeth, W3965, G, Jernigan, Marshall Henry
JERNIGAN, G. W. S8589, B, 44th Inf.
JERNIGAN, George W. S5655, MN, 18th (Newsom's) Cav.
JERNIGAN, I. W. S3496, CF, 44th Inf.
JERNIGAN, Isaac, S3495, FR, 22nd Bn. Inf.
JERNIGAN, L. W. S4708, FR, 23rd Inf.
JERNIGAN, Lucy, W1381, FR, Jernigan, Isaac
JERNIGAN, M. H. S4695, HR, 14th Cav.

JERNIGAN, Mary Jane, W5800, FR, Jernigan, Lewis J.
JERNIGAN, S. M. S15249, FR, 17th Inf.
JERNIGAN, Susan, W7654, CF, Jernigan, George W.
JERRETT, Ely, S12168, U, 58th N.C. Inf.
JERRIGAN, A. J. S12769, CA, 23rd Inf.
JESTER, A. J. S4083, CH, 18th Cav.
JESTER, Elizabeth Marinio, W1760, CH, Jester, Andrew Jackson
JETER, Levena Elizabeth, W10031, WY, Jeter, Neal
JETT, C. M. S10509, JE, 31st Inf.
JETT, Eliza, W4896, WH, Jett, Archibald O.
JETT, Elizabeth, W3923, WH, Jett, Thomas J.
JETT, Parmelia, W3279, JE, Jett, C. M.
JETT, R. W. S7192, RB, 14th Inf.
JETT, Thomas B. S3994, MS, 24th Inf.
JETTON, A. J. S4239, CA, 22nd (Barteau's) Cav.
JETTON, C. F. S10528, CA, 18th Inf.
JETTON, Carrie W. W7189, RU, Jetton, James Thompson
JETTON, J. T. S13303, CA, 18th Inf.
JETTON, Robert Henderson, S15614, L, 12th Cav.
JEWELL, J. H. S719, R, 26th Inf.
JEWELL, James M. S5669, R, 26th Inf.
JEWELL, Mary Ann, W1446, CC, Jewell, Henry Hutton
JEWELL, Tennie, W8283, R, Jewell, John Henninger
JEWELL, W. A. S13524, R, 3rd (Clack's) Inf.
JOBE, B. A. S14804, HN, 8th (Smith's) Cav.
JOBE, J. T. S14566, WE, 46th Inf.
JOBE, Judith A. W2500, HN, Jobe, Luke A.
JOBE, Paralee, W10887, HN, Jobe, Wm. Madison
JOBE, Sophronia C. W442, HD, Jobe, Francis Marion
JOBE, W. M. S10681, HN, 7th Inf.
JOHN, A. K. S5800, MC, 31st Inf.
JOHN, Z. T. S6999, C, 31st Inf.
JOHNS, A. J. S11657, LA, 3rd Inf.
JOHNS, E. F. S6322, CL, 17th Va. Inf.
JOHNS, E. P. S828, D, 18th Inf.
JOHNS, Eliza Ophelia, W10622, SM, Johns, Wm. R.
JOHNS, John B. S6735, RU, 18th Inf.
JOHNS, Mary McCullough, W5597, RU, Johns, Beverly H.

Index to Tennessee Confederate Pension Applications

JOHNS, Mollie, W11019, MC, Johns, Alfred King
JOHNS, W. R. S15949, SM, Nixon's Regt. Cav.
JOHNSON, A. D. S12159, LI, 41st Inf.
JOHNSON, A. J. S11050, GI, 53rd Inf.
JOHNSON, A. M>, S9885, WL, 8th (Dibrell's) Cav.
JOHNSON, A. S. S14225, HD, 55th Inf.
JOHNSON, Ada, W8044, D, Johnson, Albert Sidney
JOHNSON, Adline, W10669, MU, Johnson, Henry
JOHNSON, Amilia, W1755, DI, Johnson, John Pinkerton
JOHNSON, B. C. S4925, LO, 25th N.C. Inf.
JOHNSON, B. D. S10007, WI, 24th Inf.
JOHNSON, B. H. S7130, MN, Moreland's Ala. Cav.
JOHNSON, B. H. (Mrs.), W11178, Johnson, B. H. Contents of file missing
JOHNSON, B. J. G. S4177, SU, 19th Inf.
JOHNSON, B. N. S4422, A, Burrough's Co. Lt. Art.
JOHNSON, B. R. S15787, D, 30th Inf.
JOHNSON, Bettie, W945, CC, Johnson, C. R.
JOHNSON, Bettie, W5241, D, Johnson, Charles S.
JOHNSON, Bettie A. W2085, WI, Johnson, Wm. L.
JOHNSON, Bob, S10743, SH, 12th (Green's) Cav.
JOHNSON, Caroline, W705, WL, Johnson, Timothy Alexander
JOHNSON, Carrie Lurton, W7136, MT, Johnson, Thomas Dickson
JOHNSON, Charles Green, S12090, WI, 11th (Holman's) Cav.
JOHNSON, Charles S. S8009, D, 20th Inf.
JOHNSON, Claiborne G. S11243, D, 20th Inf.
JOHNSON, Cornelia Ann, W5193, WY, Johnson, Fredric Volentine
JOHNSON, D. S. S6184, O, 9th Bn. Cav.
JOHNSON, David W. S9736, MA, 14th Cav.
JOHNSON, Dee, W5560, B, Johnson, John Faris
JOHNSON, Delia Elizabeth, W8607, MT, Johnson, Thomas Addison
JOHNSON, Demaris M. W10667, O, Johnson, Abner
JOHNSON, Diza A. W9762, SN, Johnson, John C.
JOHNSON, E. P. S12462, MC, 31st Inf.
JOHNSON, E. R. S11999, LA, 9th Cav.
JOHNSON, E. T. S6937, WE, 4th Inf.
JOHNSON, Elias, S14671, SU, 6th N.C. Cav.
JOHNSON, Elijah, S11885, SE, 31st Inf.
JOHNSON, Eliza A. W10455, HD, Johnson, Leonard
JOHNSON, Eliza B. W2322, SU, Johnson, Benjamin J. G.
JOHNSON, Eliza Jane, W860, HD, Johnson, Lorenzo Dow
JOHNSON, Eliza Jane, W10413, A, Johnson, George Washington
JOHNSON, Elizabeth Ann, W6340, GR, Johnson, James R.
JOHNSON, Elizabeth White, W5192, MA, Johnson, Robert Fenner
JOHNSON, Ella, W10350, PU, Johnson, Sam L.
JOHNSON, Ella S. W9559, D, Johnson, Virgil Foster
JOHNSON, F. A. S12540, CH, 1st Cav.
JOHNSON, F. M. S7608, B, 41st Inf.
JOHNSON, Fannie Willis, W3673, D, Johnson, John Albert
JOHNSON, Felix G. S3050, O, 9th Ark. Inf.
JOHNSON, Frances Artemisa, W7135, MU, Johnson, Obey
JOHNSON, G. D. S9368, CL, 64th Va. Inf.
JOHNSON, G. H. S15852, SH, Forrest's Old. Regt.
JOHNSON, G. P. S3876, G, 38th Inf.
JOHNSON, G. W. S10217, A, 2nd (Ashby's) Cav.
JOHNSON, G. W. S14210, K, 63rd Inf.
JOHNSON, George Floyd, C201, K, Undetermined
JOHNSON, George Washington, S7731, MA, 6th Inf.
JOHNSON, Geraldus, S2896, D, 1st Cav.
JOHNSON, Gus, S11100, ST, 4th Ky. Inf.
JOHNSON, H. C. S5017, HD, 9th Ala. Inf.
JOHNSON, Hanner, W5989, HA, Johnson, James
JOHNSON, Harriet Thomas, W8035, F, Johnson, Bob
JOHNSON, Hattie B. W2339, WA, Johnson, M. H.
JOHNSON, Henry, S16483, S16401, MU, 1st Cav.
JOHNSON, Henry Clay, S11586, MA, 19th Inf.
JOHNSON, Isaiah W. S12556, SH, 2nd Tex. Inf.
JOHNSON, Isom Andrew, S13576, MU, 19th (Biffle's) Cav.
JOHNSON, J. A. S14868, D, 45th Inf.

-183

Index to Tennessee Confederate Pension Applications

JOHNSON, J. B. S15446, LI, Unassigned (Wagon Maker, Q.M. Corps)
JOHNSON, J. B. S16181, DI, 50th Inf.
JOHNSON, J. G. S15053, H, 2nd Ga. Cav.
JOHNSON, J. I. S15133, LA, 45th Ga. Inf.
JOHNSON, J. K. S3589, WI, 2nd (Walker's) Inf.
JOHNSON, J. M. S5595, V, 35th Inf.
JOHNSON, J. M. S11500, HR, 10th Tex. Cav.
JOHNSON, J. M. S16415, RU, 11th (Holman's) Cav.
JOHNSON, J. O. S8361, WH, 22nd (Murray's) Bn. Inf.
JOHNSON, J. T. S15986, DI, Harvey's Scouts
JOHNSON, James, S3006, HA, 50th Va. Inf.
JOHNSON, James, S11656, MC, 3rd Inf.
JOHNSON, James E. S13948, DY, 12th Cav.
JOHNSON, James H. S3266, WL, 4th Cav.
JOHNSON, James M. S3934, WL, 45th Inf.
JOHNSON, James M. S4007, GU, 17th Inf.
JOHNSON, James R. S6695, GR, 19th Inf.
JOHNSON, Jane, W1934, MA, Johnson, W. T.
JOHNSON, Jennie, W4052, LE, Johnson, Leonidas Alexander
JOHNSON, Joel H. S14501, BR, 43rd Inf.
JOHNSON, John, S1155, K, Undetermined
JOHNSON, John, S2358, DK, 5th Inf.
JOHNSON, John A. S11439, WI, 45th Inf.
JOHNSON, John C. S513, P, 44th Inf.
JOHNSON, John C. S3305, GI, 11th Cav.
JOHNSON, John C. S12557, HD, 48th (Nixon's) Inf.
JOHNSON, John F. S4645, B, 41st Inf.
JOHNSON, John N. S15308, H, 1st Bn. Ky. Cav.
JOHNSON, Joseph, S6546, SU, 22nd Va. Cav.
JOHNSON, Josiah, S8350, MC, 31st Inf.
JOHNSON, L. A. S4432, LE, 6th (Wheeler's) Cav.
JOHNSON, L. T. S14640, P, 11th (Holman's) Cav.
JOHNSON, Larkin, S437, BR, 36th Inf.
JOHNSON, Laura Sirls, W10442, D, Johnson, Tim
JOHNSON, Levi, S3007, HA, 50th Va. Inf.
JOHNSON, Lewis L. S768, WI, 44th Inf.
JOHNSON, Lillie Charlotte, W8553, SH, Johnson, Isaiah
JOHNSON, Lucinda Ann, W4645, LA, Johnson, E. R.
JOHNSON, Lucy Ann, W8905, RB, Johnson, Turner Lawrence

JOHNSON, M. H. S1400, WA, 9th Ala. Inf. See also Marshall H. Johnson
JOHNSON, M. J. S10151, MU, King's Battery, Ga. Lt. Art.
JOHNSON, M. M. S10343, SQ, 35th Inf.
JOHNSON, Margrett Jane, W10978, WH, Johnson, Wesley
JOHNSON, Mariah Elizabeth, W9779, MC, Johnson, R. H.
JOHNSON, Marshall H. S388, WA, 9th Ala. Inf. See also M. H. Johnson
JOHNSON, Martha, W7295, A, Johnson, Benglor Neal
JOHNSON, Martha Ann Tate, W10716, G, Johnson, Pleasant Green
JOHNSON, Martha Jane, W378, HI, Johnson, James Augusta
JOHNSON, Mary Eliza, W3403, SH, Johnson, Young Haywood
JOHNSON, Mary Elizabeth, W4832, MU, Johnson, Sidney
JOHNSON, Mary Elizabeth, W6904, Johnson, Eli Travis
JOHNSON, Mary Elizabeth, W7476, DK, Johnson, Wm. Allen
JOHNSON, Mary Irene, W9810, MT, Johnson, Mastain Clark
JOHNSON, Mary Jane, W168, GI, Johnson, John Clinton
JOHNSON, Mary Jane, W6842, DY, Johnson, Claudius Galian
JOHNSON, Mary Jane, W8907, WL, Johnson, Thomas Harrison
JOHNSON, Mary L. W8168, LA, Johnson, John Iverson
JOHNSON, Mary L. W9642, SQ, Johnson, Malcom M.
JOHNSON, Mary Lockhart, W8870, LI, Johnson, Wm. Alexander
JOHNSON, Mary M. W2891, BO, Johnson, James Richard
JOHNSON, Mary Maud, W4089, D, Johnson, John McFerrin
JOHNSON, Matilda J. W1735, GE, Johnson, Benjamin G.
JOHNSON, Mattie, W9692, WL, Johnson, James
JOHNSON, Mattie E. W8530, CH, Johnson, Felix A.
JOHNSON, Mollie A. W3857, D, Johnson, John Thomas

Index to Tennessee Confederate Pension Applications

JOHNSON, Mollie I. W7043, MT, Johnson, M. C.
JOHNSON, N. B. S2334, K, 63rd Inf.
JOHNSON, Nannie, W8756, LI, Johnson, Agnug (Dick)
JOHNSON, Nannie J. W8320, GU, Johnson, James Miles
JOHNSON, Nannie N. W3852, O, Johnson, Jerry F.
JOHNSON, Noah, S12934, OV, 8th (Dibrell's) Cav.
JOHNSON, Noble, S12804, A, Thomas' Legion, N.C.
JOHNSON, Obadiah, S11447, MU, 11th Mo. Inf.
JOHNSON, Parlee, W1157, DK, Johnson, Isaac
JOHNSON, Peter, C191, HI, Undetermined
JOHNSON, R. E. S11728, K, Thomas' Legion, N.C.
JOHNSON, R. L. S16456, WL, 1st (Feild's) Inf.
JOHNSON, R. Y. S11036, MT, 49th Inf.
JOHNSON, Richard, C40, SH, 14th Miss. Inf.
JOHNSON, S. A. S14420, WL, 10th (Smith's) Bn. Cav.
JOHNSON, S. C. S6163, HE, 10th Cav.
JOHNSON, S. W. S6375, PU, 25th Inf.
JOHNSON, Sallie, W2404, OV, Johnson, T. H.
JOHNSON, Sallie I. W8160, GR, Johnson, W. T.
JOHNSON, Sallie John, W6651, MU, Johnson, Barclay Martin
JOHNSON, Sam L. S15538, PU, 8th Cav.
JOHNSON, Samuel, S13593, WH, 8th (Dibrell's) Cav.
JOHNSON, Samuel G. S12809, S13477, CF, 8th (Smith's) Cav.
JOHNSON, Sarah, W9939, G, Johnson, Needham Brantly
JOHNSON, Sarah A. W234, D, Johnson, Lylton Harrison
JOHNSON, Sarah E. W3815, CL, Johnson, G. W.
JOHNSON, Sarah Jo, W9131, MU, Johnson, Barclay M.
JOHNSON, Sarah John, W8224, MU, Johnson, Barclay Martin
JOHNSON, Sarah Lou, W8281, H, Johnson, Elias Pressnel
JOHNSON, Serena Frances, W1600, MO, Johnson, Thomas Jefferson
JOHNSON, Sidney, S13782, MU, 10th Cav.
JOHNSON, Sofina, W9931, MA, Johnson, Ruben
JOHNSON, Susan Catherine, W8436, R, Johnson, Asa
JOHNSON, Susan Elizabeth, W6106, MU, Johnson, John Adkins
JOHNSON, Susie F. W2744, WI, Johnson, Louis L.
JOHNSON, T. D. S15267, MT, 14th Inf.
JOHNSON, T. H. S13886, S15348, WL, 7th Inf.
JOHNSON, T. H. S15415, H, 4th Ga. Cav.
JOHNSON, T. L. S15956, RB, 24th Inf.
JOHNSON, T. P. S3828, SN, 2nd Inf.
JOHNSON, Tabitha, W9581, WL, Johnson, John
JOHNSON, Tabitha, W9701, OV, Johnson, Wm.
JOHNSON, Tennessee C. W660, MN, Johnson, Wm. Turner
JOHNSON, Tennie, W10683, GI, Johnson, W. H.
JOHNSON, Thomas M. S7621, L, 6th Inf.
JOHNSON, Tom, C75, WI, 50th Inf.
JOHNSON, Virginia M. W2306, WI, Johnson, B. D.
JOHNSON, W. A. S4898, DK, 23rd Inf.
JOHNSON, W. B. S1537, HN, Kizer's Regt. Cav.
JOHNSON, W. D. S86, G, 31st Inf.
JOHNSON, W. H. S2827, LA, 50th Inf.
JOHNSON, W. H. S6132, HR, 14th (Neely's) Cav.
JOHNSON, W. M. S3764, CA, 35th Inf.
JOHNSON, W. S. S16567, G, 12th Inf..
JOHNSON, W. T. S951, WI, 1st Cav.
JOHNSON, W. T. S10270, F, 54th Inf.
JOHNSON, W. T. S12483, B, 24th Inf.
JOHNSON, William, C27, WI, Undetermined
JOHNSON, William, S3051, GE, 61st Inf.
JOHNSON, William, S11936, OV, 9th Ky. Inf.
JOHNSON, William H. S15873, SH, 1st Miss. Bn. Sharpshooters
JOHNSON, William P. S4506, WA, 61st Inf.
JOHNSON, William T. S9139, JO, 31st Inf.
JOHNSON, William T. S14799, GR, 2nd (Ashby's) Cav.
JOHNSON, Willis R. S2419, DI, 44th Inf.
JOHNSON, Y. H. S6491, D, 48th Inf.
JOHNSTON, Ellen, W6515, GE, Johnston, John Thomas
JOHNSTON, Emeline M. J. W6141, MU, Johnston, Milton Jones

Index to Tennessee Confederate Pension Applications

JOHNSTON, Fontain Bascum, S16131, B, 28th Inf.
JOHNSTON, J. W. S2741, DE, 27th Inf.
JOHNSTON, James A. S15983, MO, 59th Inf.
JOHNSTON, James T. S16601, DI, 11th Inf.
JOHNSTON, John H. S10197, MO, 2nd (Ashbys) Cav.
JOHNSTON, John L. S7122, MA, 6th Inf.
JOHNSTON, Mary F. W9785, MA, Johnston, John L.
JOHNSTON, Miles Eldridge, S13539, WL, 25th Bn. Ala. Cav.
JOHNSTON, Nannie Jackson, W9721, G, Johnston, Ward Richmond
JOHNSTON, Susan Adella, W10653, LI, Johnston, Thomas Larkin
JOICE, Cynthia S. W1266, WY, Joice, John
JOINER, W. S. S11965, F, 17th Miss. Inf.
JOINS, Spencer, S6938, DK, 1st Bn. (Colm's) Inf.
JOLLY, Isaac, S4678, R, 5th (McKenzie's) Cav.
JOLLY, J. W. S2401, BR, 5th (McKenzie's) Cav.
JOLLY, James W. S11262, H, 66th Ga. Inf.
JOLLY, Jennie, W1920, BR, Jolly, James W.
JOLLY, Mary Jane, W3179, CF, Jolly, W. M.
JOLLY, Sally, W10288, H, Jolly, James W.
JOLLY, William, S1706, LA, 11th Ala. Inf.
JONES, A. B. S10245, FR, 18th Inf.
JONES, A. J. S5926, SU, 59th Inf.
JONES, Adeline Josephine, W7395, G, Jones, Wm. Parks
JONES, Alexander Mitchell, S5272, G, 9th Bn. Cav.
JONES, Aley, W3674, H, Jones, James W.
JONES, Alfred W. S7671, TR, 9th (Ward's) Cav.
JONES, Alice T. W7724, SH, Jones, James C.
JONES, Amanda, W6069, HN, Jones, Marshall Pitts
JONES, Amanda Jane, W1379, D, Jones, James Elias
JONES, Amos B. S15112, WE, 6th Inf.
JONES, Andrew, S5801, D, 20th Inf.
JONES, Ann Elizabeth, W6566, MA, Jones, David Henry
JONES, Annie, W9766, D, Jones, Richard Thomas M.
JONES, Annie Batt, W2900, CC, Jones, George W. D.
JONES, Annie Huddleston, W10153, SM, Jones, John H.

JONES, Arthur Baker, S6806, SH, 13th Inf.
JONES, B. B. S8292, FR, 23rd Bn. Inf.
JONES, B. F. S9372, 12th (Green's) Cav.
JONES, B. F. M. S2125, CU, 28th Inf.
JONES, B. J. C106, K, 3rd Inf.
JONES, B. T. S779, CC, 6th Inf.
JONES, Bettie, W6129, HY, Jones, Willy B.
JONES, Burl B. S7634, DE, 18th (Newsom's) Cav.
JONES, Burrel, S15226, BE, 5th Inf.
JONES, C. C. S4498, HD, 41st Miss. Inf.
JONES, C. J. W4705, HA, Jones, Calvin Jasper
JONES, C. W. S6884, SU, Marshall's Co. Art.
JONES, Calvin J. S503, HA, 63rd Inf.
JONES, Catherine Elizabeth, W9936, SM, Jones, Wm. Thomas
JONES, Celestia Reed, W1428, GI, Jones, Thomas Madison N.
JONES, Charles B. S14583, MU, 9th Cav.
JONES, Clementine E. W830, SH, Jones, Arthur Baker
JONES, Cordelia, W10750, DI, Jones, James Yell
JONES, D. C. S8810, G, 4th Cav.
JONES, D. H. S12155, MA, Polk's Battery, Lt. Art.
JONES, D. M. S8961, G, 23rd Inf.
JONES, D. S. S3209, MU, 24th Inf.
JONES, Daniel, S5210, MO, 43rd Inf.
JONES, David B. S15452, MU, 6th (Wheeler's) Cav.
JONES, Della, W10795, DY, Jones, John Alfred
JONES, E. B. S9964, O, Forrest's Old Regt. Cav.
JONES, E. J. S6197, MT, 13th Ky. Cav.
JONES, Eli, S2354, W, 11th Cav.
JONES, Eli M. S140, HN, 5th Inf.
JONES, Elia Ann, W9257, CF, Jones, Wm. Henry
JONES, Elisha, S8415, MT, 13th Ky. Cav.
JONES, Eliza Gideon, W9024, SN, Jones, Henry Paris
JONES, Eliza Jennie, W10803, SH, Jones, Marshall Burns
JONES, Elizabeth, W2764, SU, Jones, W. F.
JONES, Elizabeth, W7682, MN, Jones, Jonathan
JONES, Elizabeth, W10963, HU, Wallace, James Tyler, See also Elizabeth Wallace
JONES, Elizabeth Adaline, W2229, O, Jones, James Joseph

JONES, Elizabeth Ann, W1871, WY, Jones, Wm. Riley
JONES, Elizabeth Collins, W8556, SH, Jones, George Washington
JONES, Elizabeth M. W10548, D, Jones, Wm. P.
JONES, Elizabeth Morley, W2908, SU, Jones, Peter M.
JONES, Ellen Jane, W2185, G, Jones, D. M.
JONES, Emily Biles, W3767, GI, Jones, Willis Henry
JONES, Emma, W9518, H, Jones, James
JONES, Emma H. W8098, MU, Jones, John L.
JONES, Emma P. W2889, MA, Jones, Thomas P.
JONES, Esther A. W7888, MS, Jones, James J.
JONES, Eunolia, See Eunolia Lowery
JONES, Eva Sowell, W10784, MU, Jones, Benjamin Harrison
JONES, George W. S4194, GI, 35th Ala. Inf.
JONES, Griffith Rogan, S4545, HW, 64th Va. Inf.
JONES, Harriet, W8326, W, Jones, Hesekiah Lee
JONES, Hattie G. W8578, RU, Jones, Gershom Hunt
JONES, Helen, W6952, MA, Jones, Willis
JONES, Henry, S1568, CO, 35th N.C. Inf.
JONES, Henry, S11138, SU, 63rd Inf.
JONES, I. S9681, BE, Nixon's Regt. Cav.
JONES, Ida Lacy, W10962, SH, Jones, Louis Henderson
JONES, Isaac, S12489, GR, 45th Va. Inf.
JONES, Isaac Newton, S6675, CE, McClung's Co. Lt. Art.
JONES, Isham, S14739, MT, 50th Inf.
JONES, J. S10255, SH, 2nd Ala. Cav.
JONES, J. C. S4292, SU, 26th Inf.
JONES, J. C. S6965, SU, 59th Inf.
JONES, J. D. S6449, RU, Allison's Squadron, Cav.
JONES, J. E. S10984, M, 24th Inf.
JONES, J. F. S16448, MA, 21st (Wilson's) Cav.
JONES, J. G. S9947, CF, 28th Cav.
JONES, J. J. S4883, SU, 1st (Carter's) Cav.
JONES, J. J. S9816, HR, 1st N.C. Inf.
JONES, J. L. S11139, SU, 63rd Inf.
JONES, J. M. S2590, TR, 24th Inf.
JONES, J. R. S12316, HR, 22nd Inf.
JONES, J. S. S9279, CH, 26th N.C. Inf.
JONES, J. S. S9303, MA, 22nd Inf.
JONES, J. T. S7514, MU, 9th Cav.
JONES, J. T. S8500, RB, 11th Inf.
JONES, J. W. S7379, HO, 50th Inf.
JONES, J. W. S15229, B, 20th Cav.
JONES, J. Y. S16083, S10075, DI, 23rd Inf.
JONES, James, S11527, W, 16th Inf.
JONES, James C. S2325, WA, 34th Va. Cav.
JONES, James I. S11772, F, 154th Sr. Regt. Inf.
JONES, James J. S16491, S16331, O, 7th (Duckworth's) Cav.
JONES, James M. S3185, D, 20th Inf.
JONES, James M. S7659, G, 12th Ky. Cav.
JONES, James W. S2881, MR, 4th (Murray's) Cav.
JONES, James W. S5945, BO, 2nd S.C. Inf.
JONES, Jennette, W1125, SU, Jones, Wm.
JONES, Jennie M. W1534, D, Jones, John W.
JONES, Jerre M. S3949, DY, Undetermined
JONES, Jim, S14314, MA, 1st (Carter's) Cav.
JONES, Joe, S14941, HR, 1st (Carter's) Cav.
JONES, John, S1334, D, 18th Inf.
JONES, John, S5211, S2686, WL, 7th Inf.
JONES, John, S8325, RU, 2nd Inf.
JONES, John, S11173, HW, 64th Va. Inf.
JONES, John B. S2702, DK, 154th Sr. Regt. Inf.
JONES, John B. S9612, HR, 12th Miss. Inf.
JONES, John H. S11283, MA, 51st Inf.
JONES, John H. S15870, SM, 28th Inf.
JONES, John J. S14756, RO, 61st Inf.
JONES, John L. S15841, MN, Moreland's Ala. Cav.
JONES, John T. S5626, MO, 59th Inf.
JONES, John W. S12633, HN, 7th (Duckworth's) Cav.
JONES, John Wesley, S1959, M, 24th Inf.
JONES, Joseph M. S4655, CF, 1st Bn. (McNairy's) Cav.
JONES, Joshua F. S9118, G, 12th (Green's) Cav.
JONES, Josiah, S1743, HE, 3rd (Forrest's) Cav.
JONES, Josiah A. S1176, DE, 16th Inf.
JONES, Julia A. W2541, MS, Jones, B. F.
JONES, Julia Ann, W9443, WI, Jones, John Wilson
JONES, Julia S. W8135, BE, Jones, Isham
JONES, Julius A. S8513, MA, 1st Confederate Cav.
JONES, L. D. S10967, S6076, JE, 59th Inf.
JONES, L. W. S2574, HE, 21st Cav.
JONES, Leonidas, S441, J, Undetermined
JONES, Leroy, C120, T, 4th Inf.
JONES, Lettie S. W6201, U, Jones, Wilson
JONES, Lewis H. S15728, SH, 4th Miss. Cav.

Index to Tennessee Confederate Pension Applications

JONES, Lila Anne, W6321, SM, Jones, Judithan Monroe
JONES, Lizzie, W3862, DY, Jones, Jerry M.
JONES, Lora, W3627, MO, Jones, Thomas C.
JONES, Louisa, W369, RB, Jones, James Long
JONES, Louisa, W3130, SU, Jones, T. W.
JONES, Loving Dean, W9830, RB, Jones, James Samuel
JONES, Lucinda, W7375, CH, Jones, Landrim Woodard
JONES, Lucy Evelyn, W3877, HR, Jones, Thomas Jefferson
JONES, Lucy Malinda, W1832, WH, Jones, Harmon Lafayette
JONES, Lula Euthea, W9492, SH, Jones, Peter Brown
JONES, Lydia Caroline, W8877, RU, Jones, John Linsey
JONES, M. H. S5398, HE, 55th Inf.
JONES, M. H. S8736, RU, 8th (Smith's) Cav.
JONES, M. V. S12817, BR, 5th Cav.
JONES, Madonna, W3597, SH, Jones, Joe
JONES, Maggie, W10316, G, Jones, Benjamin Morton
JONES, Margaret, W349, SU, Jones, Wm.
JONES, Margaret, W10785, MA, Jones, Jacob Franklin
JONES, Marian Lisebeth, W1538, M, Jones, Wm. Burl
JONES, Marion C. S497, GE, 64th N.C. Inf.
JONES, Marshall B. S11263, SH, 12th Cav.
JONES, Martha, W1544, D, Jones, Alexander
JONES, Martha, W9865, H, Jones, Wm. Thomas
JONES, Martha A. W139, HN, Jones, Harison S.
JONES, Martha A. W8185, CF, Jones, Thomas E.
JONES, Martha Alice, W6145, CF, Jones, Jesse Gardin
JONES, Martha Ann, W2219, CF, Jones, T. H.
JONES, Martha J. W9805, HN, Jones, John W.
JONES, Martha Susannah, W2371, HU, Jones, George Marion
JONES, Mary, W499, L, Jones, Isaac Carol
JONES, Mary, W1786, SM, Jones, Simeon
JONES, Mary Adeline, W399, W, Jones, Noah
JONES, Mary Adeline, W4926, CU, Jones, B. F. M.
JONES, Mary Ann, W31, CF, Jones, Nathan
JONES, Mary Ann, W5854, MA, Jones, David Adisson
JONES, Mary C. W6073, MS, Jones, Wm. Thomas

JONES, Mary Caroline, W7288, W8871, LI, Jones, Wm. Harrison
JONES, Mary Clemintine, W9075, LI, Jones, Wm. Carroll
JONES, Mary E. W3438, G, Jones, James M.
JONES, Mary Elizabeth, W2401, H, Jones, Elias P.
JONES, Mary Elizabeth, W4555, HD, Jones, Perry Clark
JONES, Mary Elizabeth, W7240, HR, Jones, James Riley
JONES, Mary Ellen, W10086, SH, Jones, Marshall Branch
JONES, Mary Emeline, W2268, MU, Jones, James T.
JONES, Mary Emma, W6688, Jones, Robert Clinton
JONES, Mary H. W212, BE, Jones, P. M.
JONES, Mary J. W7977, RO, Jones, John J.
JONES, Mary Josephine, W2553, HU, Jones, Samuel Green
JONES, Mary Josephine, W10478, GI, Jones, Wm. Riley
JONES, Mary L. W9455, D, Jones, J. H.
JONES, Mary Lou, W10415, MU, Jones, Sam Willis
JONES, Mary Louise, W8204, SE, Jones, Eli Hutsel
JONES, Mary M. W2652, LI, Jones, John L.
JONES, Mary Pate, W8172, K, Jones, Reps
JONES, Mary Virginia, W5052, W3865, WA, Jones, Wm. Walter
JONES, Matilda, W5339, HW, Jones, G. R.
JONES, Mattie Gober, W9905, SH, Jones, Daniel Curd
JONES, Mattie P. W6360, RU, Jones, John
JONES, Maxie Harris, W8687, MS, Jones, Alfred
JONES, Monroe, C41, SH, Miss. Art.
JONES, N. G. S9151, SH, 51st Inf.
JONES, Nancy, W464, RU, Jones, Sam W.
JONES, Nancy E. W3990, SU, Jones, B. D.
JONES, Nannie G. W10777, FR, Jones, W. L.
JONES, Nannie L. [Smith], W10702, SH, Jones, Francis James, [Later married Smith]
JONES, Nannie Nicholson, W7648, MU, Jones, Robb
JONES, Nathaniel, S8299, WL, 55th Inf.
JONES, Noah, S2614, W, 5th Inf.
JONES, Nora Elizabeth, W10527, FR, Jones, Henry Leslie
JONES, O. W. S5537, SH, 38th Inf.

Index to Tennessee Confederate Pension Applications

JONES, Parthina Watkins, W1966, D, Jones, Him Leandor
JONES, Penelope Beatrice, W6020, DY, Jones, Samuel Jarrett
JONES, Peter B. S11798, T, 19th (Biffle's) Cav.
JONES, Peter M. S5950, WA, Unassigned (Made nails for horse shoes)
JONES, Polly, W10644, SN, Jones, Joseph Addison
JONES, Polly Ann, W65, J, Jones, Lon
JONES, R. A. S5927, ME, 5th (McKenzie's) Cav.
JONES, R. C. S12459, 46th Inf.
JONES, R. D. S4132, CL, 1st Cav.
JONES, R. T. M. S9800, D, 14th Ky. Cav.
JONES, R. W. S12494, SQ, 6th Ky. Cav.
JONES, Rachel, W3055, BO, Jones, John W.
JONES, Rachel D. W778, WL, Jones, Christopher Columbus
JONES, Raymond, S5802, SN, 2nd (Robison's) Inf.
JONES, Rebecca, W5931, MU, Jones, Dan H.
JONES, Rebecca C. W218, CC, Jones, Benjamin Thomas
JONES, Rebecca J. W6823, MO, Jones, R. A.
JONES, Richard, S2333, K, 12th Cav.
JONES, Richard C. S3182, RU, 2nd Inf.
JONES, Robert L. S6282, SH, 51st Inf.
JONES, Robert W. S7945, SH, 11th Va. Inf.
JONES, Ruth Ann, W861, W, Jones, Eli
JONES, Ruthie Jane, W9983, HR, Jones, J. A.
JONES, S. T. S8875, CH, 27th Inf.
JONES, Sackie Frances, W9054, MU, Jones, Silas
JONES, Sallie, W2195, WL, Jones, Raymond
JONES, Sallie E. W3823, SN, Jones, Thomas Allen
JONES, Samuel, S1647, RU, 18th Inf.
JONES, Sarah Amelia, W6877, LO, Jones, Eli Cleveland
JONES, Sarah Elizabeth, W6333, CL, Jones, Richard Daniel
JONES, Sarah Elvina, W639, MC, Jones, P. W.
JONES, Sarah L. W4285, SU, Jones, John W.
JONES, Sarah Margaret, W6495, SU, Jones, J. C.
JONES, Sebern E. S2191, FR, 17th Inf.
JONES, Selina, W397, HE, Jones, Josiah
JONES, Silas M. S15137, MU, 19th (Biffle's) Cav.
JONES, Sophia E. W6022, D, Jones, Thomas Jefferson

JONES, Stephen, S1418, K, 50th Va. Inf.
JONES, T. A. S5273, SN, 6th Ky. Inf.
JONES, T. H. S3669, CF, 17th Inf.
JONES, T. J. S10472, TR, 30th Inf.
JONES, T. J. S12801, B, 8th Inf.
JONES, T. S. S15536, CC, 45th Inf.
JONES, T. W. S7319, V, 50th Inf.
JONES, T. W. S10976, SU, 12th Bn. (Day's) Cav.
JONES, Tempy, W2110, SM, Jones, Wm. J.
JONES, Tennessee Hatton, W1963, MT, Jones, Wm. Henry
JONES, Thomas, S4985, C, 29th Inf.
JONES, Thomas, S15933, TR, 30th Inf.
JONES, Thomas E. S8430, CF, 24th Inf.
JONES, Thomas F. S4337, HI, 10th Cav.
JONES, Thomas H. S14236, MU, 24th Inf.
JONES, Thomas J. S1831, HR, 16th Cav.
JONES, Thomas Jefferson, S5606, HN, 154th Sr. Regt. Inf.
JONES, Thomas W. S7114, DK, 35th Inf.
JONES, Tiney, W6273, G, Jones, Daniel C.
JONES, Virginia Ann, W3675, GI, Jones, George W.
JONES, W. F. S14362, G, 12th (Green's) Cav.
JONES, W. H. S5985, GI, 3rd (Clack's) Inf.
JONES, W. H. S12660, LI, 41st Inf.
JONES, W. H. H. S2603, O, 11th Inf.
JONES, W. M. S9265, 15th Consol. Cav.
JONES, W. M. S10606, G, 3rd N.C. Inf.
JONES, W. P. S9577, G, 48th Inf.
JONES, W. R. S2307, WY, 45th Inf.
JONES, W. R. S13663, WE, 46th Inf.
JONES, W. S. S9271, RU, 45th Inf.
JONES, W. T. S1676, FE, 11th Ga. Cav.
JONES, W. T. S4874, SE, 7th Inf.
JONES, William, S977, CY, 28th Inf.
JONES, William, S3978, SU, 63rd Inf.
JONES, William, S12569, T, 6th Ga. Cav.
JONES, William B. S5274, O, 33rd Inf.
JONES, William D. S7635, LI, 41st Inf.
JONES, William F. S10658, SU, Jackson's Home Guards
JONES, William Francis, S14275, DY, 1st Va. Reserves
JONES, William H. S155, SH, 12th Cav.
JONES, William H. H. S2560, O, 11th Inf.
JONES, William Henry, S13777, MC, Moreland's Ala. Cav.
JONES, William L. S9835, MS, 32nd Inf.
JONES, William L. S16576, FR, 28th Inf.
JONES, William M. S4055, CY, 8th Cav.

Index to Tennessee Confederate Pension Applications

JONES, William T. S6984, MS, 17th Inf.
JONES, Willis, C278, CC, Regiment not given
JONES, Willis, S13263, MA, 26th N.C. Inf.
JONES, Y. B. S5784, HO, 38th Va. Inf.
JONES, Zack, C117, HI, 24th Inf.
JORDAN, Annias, S11860, Unassigned (Teamster)
JORDAN, Annie Hendrix, W10248, MS, Jordan, Clement Lee
JORDAN, Annie Ruth, W9293, B, Jordan, Tandy Johnson Monroe
JORDAN, Arch C. S4568, WE, 20th (Russell's) Cav.
JORDAN, B. B. S6863, MN, Undetermined
JORDAN, Berry, S5670, BE, 5th Inf.
JORDAN, C. L. S6336, RU, 4th (McLemore's) Cav.
JORDAN, Christiana, W1203, SU, Jordan, Thomas J.
JORDAN, Dora, W4646, MS, Jordan, Wm. Carroll
JORDAN, Edward H. S15781, SH, 19th (Biffle's) Cav.
JORDAN, Fannie Everline, W6404, D, Jordan, Edward Jackson
JORDAN, J. H. S11902, 22nd Inf.
JORDAN, J. Monroe, S172, B, 1st Inf.
JORDAN, J. Morris (Rev.), S11257, LI, 20th Inf.
JORDAN, James H. S3118, LE, 35th Ga. Inf.
JORDAN, John A. S7807, RU, 24th Inf.
JORDAN, John T. S7841, T, 7th Miss. Cav.
JORDAN, Jonathan M. S15003, SH, 2nd S.C. Cav.
JORDAN, Lamera H. W3293, WE, Jordan, A. C.
JORDAN, Laura James, W2655, WI, Jordan, Robert Archer
JORDAN, Lizzie Vandergriff, W10894, H, Jordan, James
JORDAN, Margaret Isabella, W7153, G, Jordan, Arch.
JORDAN, Mary P. W6587, LI, Jordan, John Morris
JORDAN, Nannie Virginia, W5678, BR, Jordan, Gideon Luther
JORDAN, P. C. S7167, MG, 49th Inf.
JORDAN, R. C. S6533, HR, 21st S.C. Inf.
JORDAN, Rhoda, W596, BE, Jordan, Wm. Wright
JORDAN, Ruben, S8151, CH, 44th N.C. Troops
JORDAN, Sarah Miller, W4548, T, Jordan, John Thomas
JORDAN, Susan Jane, W1601, B, Jordan, Wm. Archer
JORDAN, Thomas H. S15592, HE, 19th (Biffle's) Cav.
JORDEN, Jackson, S10704, GR, 12th Bn. (Day's) Cav.
JORDON, Benjamin F. S14172, WH, Welcher's Bn. Cav.
JORDON, Mary A. W8227, MA, Jordon, N. E.
JORDON, W. C. S6578, GI, 3rd Bn. Ky. Cav.
JOSLIN, Daniel W. S3396, SE, 17th Miss. Inf.
JOSLIN, Robert C. S7936, CE, 3rd Tex. Cav.
JOSLIN, W. B. S12770, DI, Fisher's Co. Art.
JOURDAN, Needom C. S7742, HE, 18th (Newsom's) Cav.
JOURNEY, Esther Jane, W7817, MU, Journey, Emmanuel Thomas
JOURNEY, Mary E. W406, O, Journey, James C.
JOWERS, A. R. S882, HE, 27th Inf.
JOY, A. A. S635, O, 4th Cav.
JOY, Robert, S1717, S1550, T, 45th Inf.
JOYCE, Bettie, W8440, B, Joyce, Thomas James
JOYCE, G. W. S15274, MS, 11th (Holman's) Cav.
JOYCE, James A. S14687, D, 17th Inf.
JOYCE, Samuel Alexander, S13023, D, 17th Inf.
JOYNER, Arch, S6198, HE, 13th Inf.
JOYNER, Claudia Wilson, W1119, Joyner, Newsom Lafayette
JOYNER, E. M. S8115, 55th Inf.
JOYNER, Fannie, W2786, O, Joyner, Wm. Thomas
JOYNER, George S. S15732, O, 14th (Neely's) Cav.
JOYNER, Joe, S5759, HE, 13th Inf.
JOYNER, Margaret Ellen, W10143, O, Joyner, George S.
JOYNER, Martha Jane, W10167, Joyner, Edmon Marshal
JOYNER, N. L. S7497, 55th Inf.
JOYNER, Nancy Emiline, W2420, HE, Joyner, Arch.
JOYNER, Sue, W7613, TR, Joyner, Thomas
JOYNER, Thomas H. S9090, TR, 9th (Bennett's) Cav.
JUDD, A. J. S6875, PU, 8th (Dibrell's) Cav.
JUDD, Amos W. S16096, H, Dyke's Co. Fla. Lt. Art.
JUDD, Celiann, W10920, PU, Judd, George W.

Index to Tennessee Confederate Pension Applications

JUDD, G. W. S7728, PU, 8th (Dibrell's) Cav.
JUDD, Ida Eakin, W9475, H, Judd, Amos Wilson
JUDKINS, B. R. S8553, LA, 16th Inf.
JUDKINS, Elizabeth Hannah, W3606, D, Judkins, Thomas David
JUDKINS, W. L. S10726, DK, 16th Inf.
JULIAN, Bettie J. W219, H, Julian, Wm. I.
JULIAN, John A. S11554, MS, 20th (Russell's) Cav.
JULIN, W. P. S3102, CH, 21st Ark. Inf.
JUSTICE, Alfred, S9535, GE, 61st Inf.
JUSTICE, Bettie Melinda, W11041, SM, Justice, Frances E.
JUSTICE, Elizabeth Abigal, W652, B, Justice, Henry Allen
JUSTICE, F. E. S6185, SM, 24th Ga. Inf.
JUSTICE, J. C. S1100, S936, HR, 14th Cav.
JUSTICE, Nancy Jane, W5349, GE, Justice, James
JUSTICE, Thomas L. S4207, DI, Harding Artillery
JUSTICE, W. W. S13387, CT, 25th N.C. Inf.
JUSTUS, Nannie, W10960, CO, Justus, Reuben Allen
JUSTUS, Reuben Allen, S13003, S1094, CO, 61st Inf.
KAGLE, Isaac, S7055, SU, 1st Cav.
KANESTER, A. L. S645, PO, 29th Inf.
KANIPE, Henry, S12044, HM, 49th N.C. Inf.
KANIPE, Louise, W7023, HM, Kanipe, Henry
KANNON, Martha E. W5224, MU, Kannon, Edward W.
KARR, John M. S13143, D, 32nd Inf.
KARR, R. W. S7386, SN, 6th Ky. Inf.
KARR, Sarah, W675, SN, Karr, Aaron
KASIRE, David, S1960, MC, 43rd Inf.
KATES, Isaiah, S3800, HU, 42nd Inf.
KEA, W. W. S2408, WY, 9th Cav.
KEALHOFER, Alice Starr, W5687, SH, Kealhofer, Charles Wm.
KEARNEY, J. R. S10176, SH, 21st Inf.
KEARNEY, Nancy Cordelia, W7261, Kearney, Wm. Henry
KEATHEY, Willis, S2131, J, 8th (Dibrell's) Cav.
KEATHLEY, William, S2420, WH, 8th (Dibrell's) Cav.
KEATON, Calvin S. S2680, K, 53rd N.C. Inf.
KEATON, G. C. S6133, CA, 1st (Turney's) Inf.
KEATON, J. W. S6538, RU, Allison's Squadron, Cav.

KEATON, Mary A. W8635, DK, Keaton, James W.
KEATON, Polly, W5213, CA, Keaton, Gabriel C.
KEATON, William S. S7967, SU, 58th Va. Inf.
KECK, John M. S8672, B, 17th Inf.
KEE, B. T. S1085, S1663, CH, 52nd Inf.
KEE, Elizabeth, W8726, BE, Kee, Thomas J.
KEE, G. B. S5115, CH, 21st (Wilson's) Cav.
KEE, John J. S11699, BE, 14th Cav.
KEE, T. J. S10576, BE, 49th Inf.
KEE, Vick T. W10986, BE, Kee, Wm. Riley
KEE, W. R. S16276, BE, 5th Inf.
KEEF, Amanda, W2427, H, Keef, Wm. Daley
KEEF, Ross, S3733, CA, 7th Inf.
KEEF, W. D. S6478, H, 37th Inf.
KEEL, Caroline, W3531, ST, Keel, Wm. Henry
KEEL, Delitha, W9611, W3958, CF, Keel, Green Richard
KEELE, Eliza A. W1790, CA, Keele, Thomas Melton
KEELE, George M. S2013, GI, 4th Cav.
KEELE, John William, S11711, SM, 17th Inf.
KEELE, Marion, S14373, RB, 44th Inf.
KEELE, T. M. S3702, CA, 8th (Smith's) Cav.
KEELING, George Calvin, S6560, P, 23rd Inf.
KEELING, John Francis, S9756, S15733, DY, 23rd Inf.
KEEN, Emily J. W713, SN, Keen, Alexander M.
KEEN, Mary B. W4409, M, Keen, Wm.
KEEN, William, S4622, M, 20th Inf.
KEENER, Hannah R. W4150, MO, Keener, John F.
KEERL, William S. S14279, U, 2nd Va. Inf.
KEESLING, Matilda Caroline, W5452, SU, Keesling, Melville Greever
KEETON, Hettie, W10311, DE, Keeton, Marcus D. Lafayette
KEETON, Sarah E. W2890, K, Keeton, Calvin S.
KEEVER, Mary E. W8086, U, Keever, Daniel Nelson
KEHOE, Malinda, W4989, SH, Kehoe, Joe
KEILEN, James, S1459, SU, 13th (Gore's) Cav.
KEISTER, Sarah Angeline, W10691, K, Keister, Henley Crocket
KEITH, C. L. S10046, RU, 1st Ky. Cav.
KEITH, Isaac, S9150, WE, Home Guards, N.C.
KEITH, John, S838, J, 25th Inf.
KEITH, John L. S2821, FR, 1st (Turney's) Inf.
KEITH, Levi, S14654, O, 48th Ala. Inf.

KEITH, Lou E. W10375, FR, Keith, Pleasant Brown
KEITH, Mary Constance, W2650, H, Keith, John Bailey
KEITH, Mary Elijah, W6125, FR, Keith, Wm. McGehee
KEITH, Rebecca, W698, J, Keith, Francis Marion
KEITH, Roswell, S4597, CA, 7th Inf.
KEITH, Susan Frances, W2993, RU, Keith, Charley Ledbetter
KEITH, Virginia E. W9797, MA, Keith, John Yancey
KEITH, W. H. S4689, FR, 4th (McLemore's) Cav.
KEITH, W. L. S10961, FR, 41st Inf.
KEIZER, G. M. V. S5689, MU, 6th (Wheeler's) Cav.
KELL, Henry T. S3195, SQ, 35th Inf.
KELL, Rebecca Lugana, W407, W, Kell, James Elliott
KELLAR, Joseph H. S16201, HR, 18th (Newsom's) Cav.
KELLER, Abe J. S16132, HR, 18th Cav.
KELLER, George B. S8077, LI, 8th Inf.
KELLER, George W. S8501, HR, 6th Inf.
KELLER, Isaac, S6462, H, 36th Ga. Inf.
KELLER, John H. S8737, K, Walker's Bn. Thomas' Legion, N.C.
KELLER, Lucinda, W471, B, Keller, Francis Marion
KELLER, Mary E. W4354, HR, Keller, James B.
KELLER, Matilda Elizabeth, W7203, K, Keller, Wm. Swan
KELLER, Nannie, W6854, MA, Keller, George Washington
KELLER, William S. S11736, K, 1st Cav.
KELLEY, A. S4832, SH, 12th (Green's) Cav.
KELLEY, Addie, W9431, WA, Kelley, Wm. J.
KELLEY, Albert, S7896, SN, 30th Inf.
KELLEY, Albert Andrew, S5690, T, 12th (Green's) Cav.
KELLEY, Amanda, W1422, CL, Kelley, John Wesley
KELLEY, America, W2380, MOO, Kelley, Thomas
KELLEY, America Josephine, W8323, MU, Kelley, George W.
KELLEY, C. C. S6512, DE, 16th Cav.
KELLEY, Charles O. S2763, K, 2nd Va. Cav.
KELLEY, Cordelia A. W2476, H, Kelley, Calven

KELLEY, Elisha, S7986, LE, 9th Cav.
KELLEY, Eliza A. W2697, R, Kelley, Wm. A.
KELLEY, Ellen Bruner, W10059, U, Kelley, Wm. R.
KELLEY, J. B. S9785, CE, 42nd Inf.
KELLEY, J. H. S6463, RO, 43rd Inf.
KELLEY, James, S667, D, 1st (Turney's) Inf.
KELLEY, James Thomas, S4878, WI, 9th Bn. Cav.
KELLEY, John, S9578, BO, 31st Inf.
KELLEY, John M. S6307, FR, 17th Inf.
KELLEY, Joseph, S2825, HI, 9th Cav.
KELLEY, Maggie, W10169, DE, Kelley, Christopher Columbus
KELLEY, Martha Ann, W2107, SH, Kelley, Wm. Johnethen
KELLEY, Mary W. W5134, D, Kelley, Terrance
KELLEY, N. S. S3412, MU, 2nd Bn. Cav.
KELLEY, S. H. S3446, K, 42nd Inf.
KELLEY, Sarah Elizabeth, W2013, SH, Kelley, James McHenry
KELLEY, Sarah Frances, W809, WL, Kelley, Wm. J.
KELLEY, Susan V. W2621, K, Kelley, Charles O.
KELLEY, Thomas J. S106, F, 3rd Ark. Cav.
KELLEY, Virginia E. W8896, RU, Kelley, Robert C.
KELLEY, W. H. S1819, R, 19th Inf.
KELLEY, W. H. S11006, K, 42nd Inf.
KELLEY, W. J. S2692, WA, 19th Inf.
KELLEY, Wiley, S5779, MU, 34th Inf.
KELLEY, William H. S855, HW, 6th Inf.
KELLOW, Alice Mathis, W8998, MT, Kellow, John
KELLOW, John, S15571, MT, 4th Ky. Cav.
KELLOW, N. J. S13124, WI, 20th Inf.
KELLOW, W. T. S5545, DY, 47th Inf.
KELLY, Amelia J. W8178, GU, Kelly, John
KELLY, Campbell, S2513, UN, 2nd (Ashby's) Cav.
KELLY, Caroline, W1949, UN, Kelly, Samuel Nathan
KELLY, E. S11788, DE, 52nd Inf.
KELLY, J. S. S9518, WI, 2nd Bn. Cav.
KELLY, J. W. S14666, SU, 45th Va. Inf.
KELLY, Juda A. W9801, SU, Kelly, J. W.
KELLY, Lucelle Elder, W3601, SH, Kelly, Wm. Owen
KELLY, M. F. S682, HI, 10th Ala. Inf.
KELLY, Marica Heseltine, W8901, FR, Kelly, Thomas

Index to Tennessee Confederate Pension Applications

KELLY, Martha A. W2015, GU, Kelly, Charles R.
KELLY, Mary, W10562, WI, Kelly, James Thomas
KELLY, Mary Susan, W10761, MC, Kelly, Wm. Gogden
KELLY, Nancy E. W4192, SH, Kelly, Samuel M.
KELLY, Rebecca Jones, W714, K, Kelly, Alexander
KELLY, Susie Frances, W10516, T, Kelly, Albert Andrew
KELLY, Terrence, S3956, D, 16th Ala. Inf.
KELLY, W. J. S7579, GI, 32nd Inf.
KELSEY, Eunice H. W3256, D, Kelsey, Wm. T.
KELSEY, Jasper, S9839, GI, 23rd Inf.
KELSEY, William T. S11091, DI, 1st (Feild's) Inf.
KELSO, Elizabeth Strong, W7051, LI, Kelso, James Cowan
KELSO, Margaret, W6256, HR, Kelso, J. F.
KELSO, Mary Virginia, W4272, LI, Kelso, Alfred Donald
KELTNER, Thomas W. S12045, H, 19th Ga. Inf.
KELTNER, William Franklin, S13525, MU, 48th (Nixon's) Inf.
KELTON, J. T. S7504, RU, 23rd Inf.
KEMP, Allie Laurie, W9820, SH, Kemp, Franklin Smith
KEMP, Amanda, W8091, SM, Kemp, John M.
KEMP, J. M. S10928, SM, 24th Inf.
KEMP, James A. S1521, SM, 44th Inf.
KEMP, John, S187, SM, 55th Inf.
KEMP, Logan H. S760, SM, 44th Inf.
KEMP, Nancy C. W965, DE, Kemp, John
KEMP, Sallie Frances, W8257, G, Kemp, John Calvin
KEMP, Sallie Susan, W3676, SM, Kemp, James
KEMP, Thomas M. S15786, BR, 1st Ky. Inf.
KEMP, W. L. jr. S9432, SM, 9th (Ward's) Cav.
KEMPER, Delia Elizabeth, W38, D, Kemper, Wm. A.
KENDALL, Frank, S2254, SN, 8th Inf.
KENDALL, Martha, W7564, SN, Kendall, Frank
KENDALL, W. D. S10598, HN, 5th Inf.
KENDALL, William F. S11593, WE, 5th Inf.
KENDRICK, Frank B. S7220, D, 1st (Feild's) Inf.
KENDRICK, Margaret Victoria, W7891, D, Kendrick, Frank Bateman

KENDRICK, Rufus Franklin, S9032, RO, 16th Bn. (Neal's) Cav.
KENNADY, Daniel, S3734, R, 1st Cav.
KENNEDY, A. E. S15641, SH, 3rd Ark. Cav.
KENNEDY, Alice Leslie, W7993, LA, Kennedy, John Booker
KENNEDY, D. T. S13401, FR, 1st (Turney's) Inf.
KENNEDY, Ebby C. W4750, WI, Kennedy, James W.
KENNEDY, George W. S9562, CF, 16th Inf.
KENNEDY, H. S. S9820, D, 18th Inf.
KENNEDY, John, S4937, RB, 7th Inf.
KENNEDY, John B. S11560, LA, 3rd (Clack's) Inf.
KENNEDY, John M. S16074, K, 2nd (Ashby's) Cav.
KENNEDY, Joseph, S8504, GI, 3rd Volunteers
KENNEDY, Joseph S. S9049, HE, 7th Ala. Cav.
KENNEDY, Josie M. W9735, SH, Kennedy, Frank B.
KENNEDY, Julia Ann, W3722, CA, Kennedy, Wm. Clark
KENNEDY, Louella, W10952, LI, Kennedy, Dan Turner, Some papers are mixed with 11157 on film
KENNEDY, Manuel, C161, SH, 15th Miss. Cav.
KENNEDY, Martha, W7733, DE, Kennedy, S. H.
KENNEDY, Mary E. W5105, Kennedy, D. A.
KENNEDY, Mary Jane, W5121, WE, Kennedy, Robert Finley
KENNEDY, Obe, S12930, HR, 21st (Wilson's) Cav.
KENNEDY, Olly B. W3148, WI, Kennedy, W. H.
KENNEDY, Rachel C. W3776, ME, Kennedy, W. G.
KENNEDY, S. H. S5469, DE, 21st (Wilson's) Cav.
KENNEDY, Sarah Angeline, W1167, GI, Kennedy, Wm. Henry
KENNEDY, Simeon, S3703, OV, 10th Va. Cav.
KENNEDY, Susanna, W503, DE, Kennedy, Wm. G.
KENNEDY, W. C. S2717, CA, 2nd Cav.
KENNEDY, Zora Ellis, W7941, D, Kennedy, Henry S.
KENNEKLY, James, C253, HN, 46th Inf.
KENNERLY, John A. S6261, WA, 19th Inf.
KENNERLY, John P. S15713, CF, 32nd Inf.

KENNON, Adelia O. W8006, F, Kennon, Thomas W.
KENNON, T. W. S13179, F, 17th Miss. Inf.
KENT, D. C. S6126, HN, 4th Ala. Cav.
KENT, George H. S15593, D, 3rd (Forrest's) Cav.
KENT, Jennie, W2817, HN, Kent, David Christopher
KENYON, Edward Clayton, S4124, M, 63rd Inf.
KENYON, Tempy Louisa, W5448, M, Kenyon, Edward Clayton
KEOUGH, Martha A. W3265, SH, Keough, Peter
KEOUGH, Peter, S4702, SH, 10th Ga. Inf.
KERKIS, Sarah A. W3354, L, Kerkis, J. T.
KERLEY, Jack, S13582, MT, 1st Ky. Inf.
KERN, Frances Almira, W5691, HO, Kern, Joseph Travis
KERN, J. T. S4569, HO, 50th Inf.
KERNELL, T. J. S3819, ST, 14th Inf.
KERNEY, W. H. S6789, 6th Inf.
KERNS, Burton, S9948, H, 33rd Ga. Inf.
KERR, A. D. S12725, SH, 9th Inf.
KERR, Alfred, S2867, GI, 1st Cav.
KERR, J. L. S16029, D, 6th Tex. Cav.
KERR, James C. S9390, BO, 5th (McKenzie's) Cav.
KERR, Mary Frances, W1524, GI, Kerr, Addison Mitchell
KERR, Mary Larissa, W8623, MU, Kerr, Marshall Newton
KERR, Mildred Mollisse, W10088, LO, Kerr, Wm. H.
KERR, Minerva A. W3386, MU, Kerr, Robert S.
KERR, Ophelia Jane, W9671, D, Kerr, James Lawson
KERR, Phoebe Sharp, W10041, W6484, HY, Kerr, Wm. Fletcher
KERR, Robert s. S7420, MU, 6th (Wheeler's) Cav.
KERR, Sarah M. W8951, RU, Kerr, Sam
KERR, W. H. S12190, LO, 2nd (Ashby's) Cav.
KERSEY, F. M. S5340, GI, 53rd Inf.
KERSEY, T. J. S12195, O, 33rd Inf.
KERSEZ, Andrew Jackson, S4746, MS, 48th (Voorhies') Inf.
KERSH, Adella Williams, W9140, SH, Kersh, Wyatt Curtis
KERTERSON, William, S9726, GE, 61st Inf.
KESMODEL, Maria Louise, W6990, SH, Kesmodel, Charles
KESTERSON, W. A. S15258, GE, 61st Inf.

KETCHEN, James, S12253, K, Kain's Co. Lt. Art.
KETCHUM, I. H. S4449, DY, 7th Miss. Cav.
KETCHUM, Thomas J. S608, MS, 41st Inf.
KEVER, Daniel Nelson, S3128, U, 55th N.C. Inf.
KEWIN, James, S8262, HR, Confederate States Gunboat, Ark.
KEY, Carrie Belle, W11080, DK, Key, James Marcus
KEY, Catherine F. W7555, O, Key, Leroy Cage
KEY, George, S5001, SN, 44th Inf.
KEY, George M. S14221, SM, 7th Inf.
KEY, Hepsibath Louise, W1112, LI, Key, Campbell G.
KEY, James M. S12699, SM, 23rd Inf.
KEY, John Taylor, S10513, D, 61st Miss. Inf.
KEY, Leroy Cage, S12011, O, 7th (Duckworth's) Cav.
KEY, Lucius Eugene, S13377, H, 13th Ga. Inf.
KEY, Margaret Ann, W1580, MA, Key, Richard
KEY, Mary Emma Leona, W10159, MA, Key, Napolion B.
KEY, Nancy H. W2491, D, Key, Thomas Jefferson
KEY, Sally, W3050, D, Key, John Taylor
KEY, Valvie Olivia, W8987, SM, Key, George Milton
KEY, W. H. S7848, HN, 46th Inf.
KEYS, Caroline, W727, SU, Keys, Benjamin
KEYS, George W. S1272, WA, 12th Ala. Inf.
KEYS, William S. S1248, WA, 60th Inf.
KIBBLE, B. B. S220, BR, 3rd Inf.
KIBERT, Callis, W5712, CL, Kibert, James
KIBERT, G. W. S11064, CL, 29th Inf.
KIBERT, James A. S11689, CL, 29th Inf.
KIDD, J. J. S12371, W, 28th Cav.
KIDD, Joe P. S16288, LA, 9th Cav.
KIDD, K. L. S10430, HR, 19th Miss. Inf.
KIDWELL, Alexander, S3113, GI, 7th (Duckworth's) Cav.
KIDWELL, Maria Jane, W2598, JE, Kidwell, Joshua J.
KIDWELL, Samuel H. S1454, HM, 1st Cav.
KIEROFF, S. E. S14644, CC, 27th Inf.
KIKER, Alice, W2736, D, Kiker, E. W.
KILBY, J. P. S9443, D, 4th Va. Cav.
KILGORE, G. W. C. S9373, HN, 33rd Inf.
KILGORE, Marion M. S16611, GU, 28th Cav.
KILGORE, Matilda, W249, GE, Kilgore, Wm. Anderson

Index to Tennessee Confederate Pension Applications

KILGORE, Susan S. W3636, HA, Kilgore, James
KILLEBREW, A. J. S9758, HN, 20th (Russell's) Cav.
KILLEBREW, Charlotta Elizabeth, W706, WE, Killebrew, James Franklin
KILLEBREW, Martha Ann, W1615, WE, Killebrew, T. L.
KILLEBREW, Mary Emiline, W1396, WE, Killebrew, J. M.
KILLEBREW, T. L. S8791, WE, 33rd Inf.
KILLEN, James Thomas, S13036, G, 20th (Russell's) Cav.
KILLGONE, G. W. C. S6916, WE, 33rd Inf.
KILLGORE, Susie Mary, W7329, WE, Killgore, Geo. Wash. Easy
KILLIAM, Lennie L. W5951, W9386, W, Killiam, Jerry D.
KILLIAN, J. H. S15671, GU, 40th Inf.
KILLIAN, Jeremiah, S11970, W, 3rd (Forrest's) Cav.
KILLIAN, Martha, W10574, GU, Killian, John Houston
KILLINGER, Frances Elizabeth, W11026, JE, Killinger, Ezia Terrell
KILLINGSWORTH, J. T. S2665, MS, 17th Inf.
KILLINGSWORTH, Nancy, W7883, MS, Killingsworth, J. T.
KILLOUGH, W. D. S10619, RU, 45th Inf.
KILLPATRICK, James A. S1854, WY, 48th Inf.
KILPATRICK, Delana, W3202, L, Kilpatrick, Nias B.
KILPATRICK, Elizabeth C. W6667, MC, Kilpatrick, Elisha
KILPATRICK, Frances Susan, W7416, SH, Kilpatrick, John Wilson
KILPATRICK, Maud Ann, W908, WY, Kilpatrick, James A.
KILPATRICK, W. A. S14987, T, 4th Miss. Cav.
KILZER, Annis Hawkins, W1916, G, Kilzer, John W.
KIMBALL, Mary Ann, W6831, SH, Kimball, Wm. W.
KIMBRO, David A. S13994, B, 41st Inf.
KIMBRO, Emma Frances, W1776, D, Kimbro, John
KIMBRO, J. W. S16171, GI, 20th Cav.
KIMBRO, John, S1659, D, 1st Ky. Inf.
KIMBRO, John W. S10689, N, 33rd Inf.
KIMBRO, Lizzie, W676, B, Kimbro, Newton J.
KIMBRO, Nancy Elizabeth, W10197, HN, Kimbro, John W.

KIMBROUGH, Fannie Serena, W1257, L, Kimbrough, Nathaniel Madin
KIMBROUGH, H. F. S15291, GI, 19th (Biffle's) Cav.
KIMBROUGH, Mary Ann, W4661, MC, Kimbrough, Robert Franklin
KIMBROUGH, R. M. S10862, RO, 16th Inf.
KIMBROUGH, Sarah Bryant, W3275, L, Kimbrough, Duke Love
KIMSEY, H. M. S6631, CF, 17th Inf.
KINAHELOE, Mary Jane, W1597, WA, Kinaheloe, Eldridge F.
KINCAID, D. W. S6830, GI, 3rd Inf.
KINCAID, John L. S4894, MU, 32nd Inf.
KINDALL, Benjamin, S39, 5th Inf.
KINDLEY, James, C253, HN, 46th Inf.
KINDRICK, J. A. S11095, MN, 20th (Russell's) Cav.
KINDRICK, T. B. S11096, MN, 19th Cav.
KING, Abraham Benjamin, S994, SM, 28th Inf.
KING, Addie, W6229, RU, King, Wm.
KING, Alice C. W5326, MS, King, Boling Woodson
KING, Amanda M. W9043, WL, King, John Henry
KING, Anderson, S4751, WI, Baxter's Co. Lt. Art.
KING, Andrew Jackson, S1811, CC, 14th Cav.
KING, Angeline, W7054, W9704, WE, King, Robert Burton
KING, Ann P. W3777, HN, King, Jesse P.
KING, Anne Maria, W5849, HY, King, Joseph
KING, Charles N. S12903, SH, 3rd Mo. Inf.
KING, Charlotte Lorena, W7588, GI, King, Frank Richardson
KING, D. A. S7905, MA, 51st Inf.
KING, E. C. S13600, DY, 8th Inf.
KING, E. H. S4125, SU, 61st Inf.
KING, E. J. S10076, MS, 8th Inf.
KING, E. R. S10892, SU, 19th Inf.
KING, Elizabeth Burk, W9348, MU, King, Meredith David
KING, Ellen Elizabeth, W11022, SU, King, John Thomas
KING, F. R. S3, LI, 18th Ga. Inf.
KING, Fannie Elizabeth, W792, RB, King, Theodore H.
KING, Fannie Saphire, W1274, PU, King, Joseph Calloway
KING, G. W. S319, ST, 50th Inf.
KING, George, S6479, MR, 33rd Ala. Inf.

KING, Griselda Frances, W9856, HU, King, Decatur Russell
KING, H. J. S7866, W, 16th Inf.
KING, Hannah L. W7376, BR, King, Harvey
KING, Harvey, S14327, M, Ledford's Regt. Ga.
KING, J. A. S11242, SU, Unassigned (Mining Nitre)
KING, J. B. S16173, MC, 16th Inf.
KING, J. C. S4696, MN, 1st Ala. Miss. & Tenn. Inf.
KING, J. Dudley, S1684, HU, 50th Inf.
KING, J. H. S502, GE, 5th Tenn. Cav.
KING, J. M. S3915, DY, 47th Inf.
KING, J. Polk, S12700, HW, 31st Inf.
KING, J. R. D. S7123, CF, 16th Inf.
KING, Jane, W183, WI, King, Anthony
KING, Jo C. S2461, PU, 8th Inf.
KING, John B. S1824, CF, 44th Inf.
KING, John B. S7371, HW, 61st Inf.
KING, John H. S11993, W, 5th Ark. Inf.
KING, John H. S15125, RU, 11th (Holman's) Cav.
KING, Johnson W. S7706, LI, 4th N.C. Inf.
KING, Joseph, S4707, SN, 9th (Bennett's) Cav.
KING, Katherine Rutledge, W5897, HM, King, Oliver C.
KING, L. M. S4758, R, 5th (McKenzie's) Cav.
KING, Lee, W9599, MA, King, Napolion Barfield
KING, Lucinda Marthy, W7062, DY, King, James Michel
KING, M. O. W1955, MC, King, James C.
KING, Malinda Amanda Emily, W9534, D, King, Marion Deculd
KING, Margaret Ann, W4694, GE, King, John Harvey
KING, Margaret Ann, W10486, G, King, Edwin Thomas
KING, Margaret J. W289, King, Jackson
KING, Mary, W649, ST, King, Robert T.
KING, Mary A. W2126, MN, King, John
KING, Mary Ann, W4014, ST, King, George W.
KING, Mary Catherine, W5066, WI, King, James Vinson
KING, Mary Elizabeth, W7936, DK, King, Wm. Robert, Follows 7937 on film
KING, Mary P. W8053, SU, King, Edward Rutledge
KING, Mary Turner, W7087, RU, King, Thomas Moore
KING, Nancie Emeline, W4301, SU, King, Eldridge Hard

KING, Nancy Catherine, W5606, SH, King, Wm. Calvin
KING, Parmelia, W431, WI, King, Wm. E.
KING, Pearlie, W11142, SM, King, Abraham Benjamin
KING, Robert H. S4530, CA, 8th (Smith's) Cav.
KING, S. M. S5518, HE, 21st (Wilson's) Cav.
KING, Sarah Cecelia, W4116, MA, King, D. Hamner
KING, Sarah Jane, W1374, B, King, John E.
KING, Sarah Lacenia, W2162, CC, King, Andrew Jackson
KING, Sarah M. W5561, HI, King, Luke
KING, Susanna, W2265, LI, King, John W.
KING, T. H. S3072, RB, 30th Inf.
KING, T. M. sr. S12580, RU, 1st (Feild's) Inf.
KING, Thomas C. S12152, SU, 37th Va. Inf.
KING, Thomas S. S15987, D, 9th (Ward's) Cav.
KING, Tilman A. S13748, GI, 9th Ala. Inf.
KING, W. A. S9747, CC, 12th Inf.
KING, W. B. S5928, SN, 6th Ark. Inf.
KING, W. C. S12288, SH, 4th Inf.
KING, W. R. S4601, DK, 24th Inf.
KING, W. S. S14588, HM, 21st N.C. Inf.
KING, William, S8864, LO, 24th Va. Inf.
KING, William P. S2759, 55th Inf.
KINGSALVER, Malinda J. W748, GR, Kingsalver, John
KINGSLEY, Nannie J. W5576, GE, Kingsley, Roswell E.
KINGSTON, A. J. S13452, WE, 31st Inf.
KINISLEY, James R. S7882, JE, 31st Inf.
KINKSTON, William, S2316, B, 4th (McLemore's) Cav.
KINKTON, Malinda, W781, B, Kinkton, Wm. Henry
KINNAIRD, Alexander, S675, PU, 8th Inf.
KINNAIRD, Virginia, W762, PU, Kinnaird, Alexander
KINNARD, Newton Cannon, S13736, WI, 20th Inf.
KINNARD, Sallie, W4007, PU, Kinnard, Ezekiel Ray
KINNARD, Taylor, C227, HY, 54th Inf.
KINNERY, Mary Lavania, W10032, WE, Kinnery, James Louis
KINNIE, Nancy Tabitha, W6972, SH, Kinnie, George Alexander
KINNIER, E. R. S4899, PU, 22nd Inf.
KINNON, Taylor, C203, HY, 24th Inf.
KINSER, Barsheby, W528, MC, Kinser, Isaac
KINSER, Isaac, S326, MC, 59th Inf.

KINSER, J. A. S4477, BR, 4th Ga. Cav.
KINSER, Jacob, S5033, MO, 62nd Inf.
KINSER, Louvenia, W5838, MO, Kinser, Jacob
KINSER, M. L. S3032, A, 1st Ark. Inf.
KINSER, T. J. S10628, LO, 2nd Cav.
KINSLER, Isaac W. S12749, HA, 7th Ky. Bn. Cav.
KINSLER, Millie K. W6436, HA, Kinsler, Isaac W.
KINSLEY, Deborah, W9737, CO, Kinsley, J. R.
KINSLEY, S. E. G. S4759, UN, 31st Inf.
KINZALOW, Elizabeth, W1982, H, Kinzalow, Wm. L.
KINZER, George A. S10978, MU, 1st Cav.
KINZER, Josie, W1969, D, Kinzer, John W.
KINZER, Lou J. W2944, MU, Kinzer, Wm. H.
KINZER, Mary Eliza, W6693, MU, Kinzer, George Asberry
KINZER, Roe A. W4741, MU, Kinzer, Wm. Francis Marion
KIRBY, Adeline, W1231, K, Kirby, Levi
KIRBY, Ann O. W4772, MA, Kirby, Curtis Confield
KIRBY, C. C. S8966, MA, 42nd Miss. Inf.
KIRBY, David H. S12594, SM, 9th (Ward's) Cav.
KIRBY, F. M. S4040, SN, 30th Inf.
KIRBY, J. C. J. S3943, W, 16th Inf.
KIRBY, Joseph Jackson, S13993, SH, 1st Ark. Cav.
KIRBY, Laban, S1098, V, 8th Cav.
KIRBY, Laben, S14865, WH, 8th (Dibrell's) Cav.
KIRBY, Levi, S1109, K, 63rd Inf.
KIRBY, Levi, S1507, K, 26th Inf.
KIRBY, M. R. S15238, K, 72nd N.C. Inf. Reserves
KIRBY, Malinda J. W7753, W, Kirby, J. C. J.
KIRBY, Mannie Lou [Dean], W5171, HN, Kirby, Richard Pickney, [Later married Dean]
KIRBY, N. M. S6756, SM, 8th Inf.
KIRBY, Richmond P. S141, HN, 5th Inf.
KIRBY, William E. S3178, WE, 46th Inf.
KIRK, Betty, W10748, K, Kirk, Wm. Reed
KIRK, Clarrinda Cammel, W5556, MU, Kirk, George Orney
KIRK, Elizabeth, W2977, MN, Kirk, W. J. N.
KIRK, Harriet L. W3227, SN, Kirk, Wm. T.
KIRK, J. L. S12975, HM, 37th Inf.
KIRK, James B. S3863, GU, 44th Inf.
KIRK, Sam, C125, RU, Hospital Service

KIRK, W. T. S5225, SN, 9th Cav.
KIRKES, Temperance A. W9987, H, Kirkes, James Washington
KIRKHAM, Jane, W3644, SN, Kirkham, Euel
KIRKHAM, Thomas, S5161, SN, Undetermined
KIRKHAM, William J. S11835, GR, 59th Inf.
KIRKLAND, Callie Brush, W10294, HN, Kirkland, Wm. Frank
KIRKLAND, Franky, W10300, MO, Kirkland, James
KIRKLAND, J. C. S4598, C, Thomas' Legion, N.C.
KIRKLAND, J. C. S9395, MO, 3rd (Clack's) Inf.
KIRKLAND, John, S3751, PO, 3rd Inf.
KIRKLAND, Levi, S2709, O, 50th Inf.
KIRKLAND, Lucy Ann, W7050, HN, Kirkland, Thomas B.
KIRKLAND, Mariah Jane, W3570, HR, Kirkland, Richard Henry
KIRKLAND, Mary Sophrona, W5947, MO, Kirkland, John Henderson
KIRKLAND, Nancy J. W71, HR, Kirkland, Joseph B.
KIRKLAND, R. H. S10691, F, 12th Cav.
KIRKLAND, Sarah Luisia, W5225, MO, Kirkland, James Calvin
KIRKLAND, T. B. S2229, HN, 154th Sr. Regt. Inf.
KIRKLAND, Tina, W4811, A, Kirkland, Charles Johnson
KIRKPATRICK, A. M. S14464, MR, 3rd Confederate Cav.
KIRKPATRICK, Annie Wilson, W3573, D, Kirkpatrick, Samuel Bradford
KIRKPATRICK, J. T. S11423, H, 1st Ga. Inf.
KIRKPATRICK, James A. S10510, WA, 2nd (Ashby's) Cav.
KIRKPATRICK, Louise, See Louise Horn
KIRKPATRICK, Melvina, W1692, OV, Kirkpatrick, Fisk
KIRKPATRICK, Rowena I. W3093, WA, Kirkpatrick, James Albert
KIRKPATRICK, Sumner, S13779, D, 2nd Bn. Inf. State Guards, Ga.
KIRKPATRICK, Thomas Curry, S16209, L, 9th Cav. & 18th Inf.
KIRKSEY, Missouri Julia, W6028, H, Kirksey, George W.
KISTLER, D. S. S11836, HM, 71st N.C. Inf.
KISTLER, Mary A. W8093, HM, Kistler, David Sidney

Index to Tennessee Confederate Pension Applications

KITCHENS, M. F. W. W78, LA, Kitchens, B. D.
KITCHENS, Martha Ann, W5959, K, Kitchens, Zephinia L. Butler
KITE, DAniel, S9112, HW, 31st Inf.
KITE, Hiley, W3762, GE, Kite, Henderson
KITE, John jr. S2814, HW, 31st Inf.
KITE, Peter, S239, GE, 31st Inf.
KITE, W. A. S1401, WA, 31st Inf.
KITTLEBRAND, S. D. S13487, D, 25th S.C. Inf.
KITTRELL, Agnes Dobbins, W6598, MU, Kittrell, J. Hunter
KITTRELL, Bill, C266, MU, Undetermined, Application is missing.
KITTRELL, Callie Stewart, W7129, CA, Kittrell, George W.
KITTRELL, George W. S15299, CA, 7th Inf.
KITTRELL, Margaret, See Margaret Bradley
KITTRELL, Mary Ann, W5389, WL, Kittrell, Isaac Edmond
KITTRELL, Mollie May, W10612, MU, Kittrell, Hinton Greene
KITTRELL, William, S587, WH, 38th Inf.
KITTRELL, William Edward, S13410, SM, 28th Inf.
KITTS, C. N. S2087, UN, 2nd Cav.
KITTS, John, S2341, UN, 1st (Carter's) Cav.
KITTS, John, S2843, GR, 26th Inf.
KITTS, Mary Emeline, W1675, UN, Kitts, Carack Nelson
KITTS, Vina, W7427, GR, Kitts, John
KITTS, William, S4240, UN, 1st Cav.
KITZMILLER, Annis, W5518, SU, Kitzmiller, Henry
KITZMILLER, Henry, S3374, SU, 3rd Mtd. Art.
KIZER, J. B. S9425, SN, 9th (Bennett's) Cav.
KIZER, John, S375, WA, 5th Cav.
KIZER, Joseph A. S13624, CO, 16th Bn. (Neal's) Cav.
KIZER, Mollie, W7709, W, Kizer, John
KIZER, Nicolas, S8873, HE, 27th Inf.
KIZER, William C. S9657, G, 21st (Wilson's) Cav.
KLICK, Margaret Ann, W592, F, Klick, Hayne Irby
KLINKINBEARD, John L. S8666, WA, 2nd Va. Cav.
KLUTTS, Christiann Elizabeth, W9946, WE, Klutts, Samuel Carrol
KLUTTS, Cordelia A. W3878, HN, Klutts, Tobias Franklin

KLUTTS, Emma Elizabeth, W10432, HN, Klutts, Tobe Franklin
KLUTTS, Tobias Franklin, S3683, WE, Wilson's Regt. Cav.
KNEE, J. C. L. S5696, SE, Orr's Regt. S.C.
KNEEDSON, Margaret Talitha, W290, MS, Kneedson, Ole
KNIGHT, Aaron, S9038, D, 4th (McLemore's) Cav.
KNIGHT, Amanda F. See Amanda F. Pettus
KNIGHT, Andrew J. S4590, FR, 17th Inf.
KNIGHT, Archy, S10717, JE, 31st Inf.
KNIGHT, B. F. S13900, FR, 17th Inf.
KNIGHT, David James, S10301, MR, 56th Ga. Inf.
KNIGHT, David M. S7739, GE, 39th N.C. Inf.
KNIGHT, E. H. S15344, SM, 7th Inf.
KNIGHT, Eliza Fain, W7931, J, Knight, Elijah Haynie
KNIGHT, Eliza Tennessee, W8502, FR, Knight, Benjamin Franklin
KNIGHT, Fannie Hill, W9800, SM, Knight, John A.
KNIGHT, Henry C. S8897, HU, 10th Cav.
KNIGHT, John, S8738, RU, 4th Cav.
KNIGHT, John A. S8233, M, 9th (Bennett's) Cav.
KNIGHT, John H. S4138, HU, 4th Inf.
KNIGHT, Lewis (Louis), C124, FR, 17th Inf.
KNIGHT, Maggie [Stubblefld.], W11060, JE, Knight, Archy, [Later married Stubblefield]
KNIGHT, R. C. S426, R, 26th Inf.
KNIGHT, Rebecca [Smith], W10595, D, Knight, Wm. Leonard, [Later married Smith]
KNIGHT, Sallie Davis, W6529, HU, Knight, Henry Clay
KNIGHT, Thomas J. S5043, GE, 22nd N.C. Inf.
KNIGHT, W. L. S7396, CE, 2nd Inf.
KNIGHT, W. T. S4955, MN, 22nd Cav.
KNIX, Charlotte, W1540, MT, Knix, Ike
KNOTT, J. C. S5348, K, 52nd N.C. Inf.
KNOTT, Martha, W3244, HR, Knott, Wm. L.
KNOWLES, Stacey Ann, W611, WH, Knowles, Cason S.
KNOX, Arch, S9651, CU, 8th (Dibrell's) Cav.
KNOX, Benjamin F. S5615, WL, 22nd (Barteau's) Cav.
KNOX, David C. S12510, CU, 1st (Carter's) Cav.
KNOX, F. M. S11188, F, 17th Miss. Inf.
KNOX, H. H. S8175, BR, 43rd Inf.

Index to Tennessee Confederate Pension Applications

KNOX, Henry, S1331, HW, 3rd Inf.
KNOX, J. F. S13505, B, 4th (McLemore's) Cav.
KNOX, J. R. S839, D, 4th Cav.
KNOX, Josiah Henry, S12217, SH, 36th Ala. Inf.
KNOX, Laura Adelaide, W10844, SH, Knox, Micajah Halbert
KNOX, Mary Elizabeth, W8535, RU, Knox, Wm. Francis
KNOX, Mary Ruth, W10729, D, Knox, James Franklin
KNOX, Nancy B. W3869, RU, Knox, Benjamin F.
KNOX, R. L. S15099, SH, 17th Miss. Inf.
KNOX, S. R. S137, HD, 4th Inf.
KNOX, Sophia McClune, W11063, SH, Knox, Robert Lee
KNOX, Susan M. W804, RO, Knox, Samuel
KNOX, W. F. S12739, RU, 23rd Inf.
KOELING, John Francis, S2655, G, 23rd Inf.
KOEN, Ann Boggan, W5470, SH, Koen, Robert Benjamin
KOEN, Robert Benjamin, S13646, SH, 38th Inf.
KOFFMAN, Laura Christina, W10149, G, Koffman, Isaiah Jefferson
KOGER, J. D. S15071, CF, 8th (Smith's) Cav.
KOLWYCK, J. W. S4743, HE, 1st Art.
KOON, Robert, S6433, GI, 60th Ga. Inf.
KOONCE, J. F. S12378, SH, 14th (Neely's) Cav.
KOONCE, James Madison, S9579, DY, 31st Inf.
KOONCE, Mary D. W9059, LI, Koonce, Needham Perry
KOONCE, N. P. S3244, LI, 8th Inf.
KROPFF, Owen, S5929, CO, 42nd Va. Inf.
KROUSE, Elizabeth, W6947, SH, Krouse, Jacob
KROUSE, Jacob, S3691, 2nd Mo. Cav.
KUHN, Dorothea, W1727, D, Kuhn, David Jarsh
KUHN, J. R. S4405, SU, 59th Inf.
KUHN, Lucinda, W6641, SU, Kuhn, J. R.
KURD, Isaiah, S7404, SU, 63rd Inf.
KUTCH, W. H. S2989, WY, 9th Cav.
KUYKENDALL, George W. S11219, GE, 56th N.C. Inf.
KUYKENDALL, H. M. S1259, MA, 23rd Miss. Inf.
KUYKENDALL, W. T. S2551, PU, 16th N.C. Inf.
KYKER, A. J. S9175, WA, 1st Hvy. Art.
KYLE, Delia Carter, W9148, K, Kyle, Wm. Sterling

KYLE, Jane Elizabeth, W9706, SH, Kyle, Wm. D.
KYLE, Joseph, S6573, HW, 2nd (Ashby's) Cav.
KYLE, Martha, W2381, K, Kyle, James Gideon
KYLE, Mary Kate, W9672, D, Kyle, Robert
KYLE, S. B. S15268, F, 15th Cav.
KYLE, Sarah, W3461, LA, Kyle, James T.
LACEWELL, M. L. S10133, O, 21st Cav.
LACKEY, Mary Elizabeth, W7569, SH, Lackey, Wm. Bunting
LACKEY, Obediah, S3542, HW, 3rd (Clack's) Inf.
LACKEY, Robert P. S2566, LI, 44th Inf.
LACY, Daniel S. S16019, LA, 18th (Newsom's) Cav.
LACY, Fanny, W5185, O, Lacy, Richard Johnson
LACY, George, C223, MA, 14th Cav., Application is missing.
LACY, George, S15094, MA, 14th (Neely's) Cav.
LACY, Sarah Elizabeth, W10626, MA, Lacy, George
LADD, Balis, S13066, MR, 33rd Ala. Inf.
LADD, Margaret Elizabeth, W1684, MU, Ladd, Wm. Henry
LADD, Mary Jane, W9621, WE, Ladd, John Thomas
LADD, Nelly, W5135, WI, Ladd, Thomas J.
LADD, Virginia Reed, W8862, FR, Ladd, Bates
LADD, W. H. S8694, MU, 1st Cav.
LADY, Elizabeth [Chase], W10743, WA, Lady, James R. [Later Married Chase]
LADY, Mary E. W10583, WA, Lady, W. D.
LADY, Nancy, W1245, SU, Lady, Henry H.
LADY, W. D. S14708, WA, 34th Bn. Va. Cav.
LAFERTY, Sarah Ann, W749, O, Laferty, Daniel M.
LAFFERTY, D. M. S3222, O, 30th Inf.
LAFFERTY, Mira, W1152, WY, Lafferty, Oze
LAIL, William, S5884, SU, 6th N.C. Inf.
LAIN, Almeda Abigail, W1460, WL, Lain, Richard R.
LAIN, J. R. S1805, WL, 7th Inf.
LAINE, Mary Frances, W7530, WL, Laine, John Randolph
LAINE, Sallie, W9769, WL, Laine, Thornton H.
LAIRD, John T. H. S16046, SH, 2nd Miss. Cav.
LAKIN, John, S7946, RO, 37th Inf.
LAKINS, W. M. S536, GR, 26th Inf.
LAMAR, Isadore Brooks, W8476, MU, Lamar, Thomas Wilson

LAMAR, J. W. S5138, GI, 3rd Inf.
LAMAR, Larkin Samuel, S11174, MU, 3rd (Clack's) Inf.
LAMAR, Nancy Elizabeth, W6220, GI, Lamar, John Wesley
LAMAR, T. C. S8370, SH, 1st Miss. Cav.
LAMASTUS, William Henry, S381, DI, 10th Cav.
LAMB, B. F. S5564, WI, 45th Inf.
LAMB, Benjamin F. S4260, HA, 5th Cav.
LAMB, Elizabeth, W4304, HN, Lamb, Thomas B.
LAMB, G. H. S6405, WI, Undetermined
LAMB, J. P. S12196, WE, 5th Inf.
LAMB, James, S13837, HN, 46th Inf.
LAMB, Jefferson, S9162, CL, 5th (McKenzie's) Cav.
LAMB, Mary Jane, W3077, GE, Lamb, Wm. Riley
LAMB, P. J. S4556, K, 5th (McKenzie's) Cav.
LAMB, Susan, W7524, HA, Lamb, Benjamin F.
LAMB, Thomas W. S1446, HN, 5th Inf.
LAMB, W. R. S412, GE, 29th Inf.
LAMB, W. R. S6973, RU, 2nd (Robison's) Inf.
LAMB, William, S4736, GE, 64th N.C. Inf.
LAMBERT, Emily, W10609, G, Lambert, Wm. H.
LAMBERT, H. C. S4224, LI, 8th Inf.
LAMBERT, Harvey H. S6948, CF, 1st (Turney') Inf.
LAMBERT, J. R. S11616, UN, 29th Va. Inf.
LAMBERT, James, S2806, CL, 64th Va. Inf.
LAMBERT, James F. S4362, M, 6th (Wheeler's) Cav.
LAMBERT, Joel, S2533, LI, 27th Ala. Inf.
LAMBERT, Lillie, W4311, CL, Lambert, James
LAMBERT, Martha C. W8344, D, Lambert, Joel
LAMBERT, Narcissa Elizabeth, W2688, SH, Lambert, Walton Eldridge
LAMBERT, W. E. S5700, SH, 1st Miss. Inf.
LAMBERT, W. J. S12114, CC, 26th N.C. Inf.
LAMBERT, Wiliam Henry, S13982, G, 21st (Wilson's) Cav.
LAMBETH, Charles Monroe, S11418, HR, Forrest's Old Regt. Cav.
LAMBRIGHT, Anna H. W2879, K, Lambright, George William
LAMONS, Martha Jane, W4132, SM, Lamons, Gideon B.
LAMPLEY, A. J. S11745, DI, Baxter's Co. Lt. Art.

LANARD, Mary, W4443, SH, Lanard, John
LANCASTER, Dora Eliza, W9195, DY, Lancaster, John Adams
LANCASTER, Henry, S14844, F, 7th Miss. Cav.
LANCASTER, James, S7942, ST, 50th Inf.
LANCASTER, John H. S16260, D, 48th (Nixon's) Inf.
LANCASTER, Josie Alice, W3747, MU, Lancaster, John Sebron
LANCASTER, Martha Tennessee, W833, DE, Lancaster, Benjamin Marion
LANCASTER, Mary Lane, W8652, ST, Lancaster, James
LANCASTER, Richard, S601, ST, 14th Inf.
LANCASTER, S. M. S5970, 11th Inf., Applied from Calloway Co. KY
LANCASTER, Sallie, W8863, MS, Lancaster, Wm. James
LANCASTER, T. C. S4172, HU, 11th Inf.
LANCASTER, W. J. S11019, MU, 48th (Nixon's) Inf.
LANCE, J. J. S8573, W, 11th Cav.
LANCE, J. N. S8572, W, 11th Cav.
LANCE, Nancy, W975, CA, Lance, James H.
LAND, Allison, S8964, MO, 31st Inf.
LAND, Birdie J. W5668, K, Land, James J.
LAND, Elizabeth Evalina, W1581, SH, Land, Wm. Leonard
LAND, H. M. S5577, MA, 38th Va. Inf.
LAND, Ida, W11132, SH, Land, Johnson Monroe
LAND, J. C. S5275, S12844, SH, 51st Inf.
LAND, J. T. S10486, SH, 13th Inf.
LAND, James Jeffrson, S6668, GE, 63rd Inf.
LAND, W. L. S5276, SH, 12th Cav.
LANDERS, Allen, S3438, GI, 7th Ala. Inf.
LANDERS, F. S. S15499, B, 23rd Inf.
LANDERS, Luke, S2712, MO, 3rd (Lillard's) Mtd. Inf.
LANDIS, Janet, W9622, D, Landis, Wm. Harrison
LANDMAN, Robert S. S14847, SH, 4th Ala. Cav.
LANDRUM, Ann, W11089, G, Landrum, John Monroe
LANDRUM, Annie E. W9644, W8269, SU, Landrum, Patrick Henry
LANDRUM, Nan, W5850, HM, Landrum, W. N.
LANDRUM, W. N. S3465, HM, 10th Ala. Inf.
LANE, Abbie Crowder, W5409, MU, Lane, Pink

Index to Tennessee Confederate Pension Applications

LANE, Abraham, S438, GE, 61st Inf.
LANE, Adeline, W1774, MC, Lane, Charles Patrick
LANE, Almira Gill, W7518, G, Lane, Thomas Franklin
LANE, Alvina Estelle, W3424, SH, Lane, Richard Candour
LANE, Elias, S1869, DK, 23rd Inf.
LANE, Emma C. W390, W, Lane, Hardin Smith
LANE, Granville, S2091, DK, 23rd Inf.
LANE, H. M. S2479, HO, 14th Inf.
LANE, Indiana, W1884, WL, Lane, John Armstead
LANE, J. M. S14042, H, Phillips' Legion, Ga.
LANE, James N. S198, D, 4th (McLemore's) Cav.
LANE, John, S7743, CF, 4th (McLemore's) Cav.
LANE, John, S13647, ST, 16th Ala. Inf.
LANE, John W. S10456, SH, 7th Inf.
LANE, Louisa Ellen, W6742, D, Lane, John King
LANE, Margaret C. W5683, RU, Lane, Owen
LANE, Owen, S5609, RU, 45th Inf.
LANE, P. S10493, MU, 9th Bn. (Gantt's) Cav.
LANE, R. C. S8322, SH, 9th Inf.
LANE, Samuel P. S5546, HW, 64th Va. Inf.
LANE, Sarah Frances, W9982, WL, Lane, Mathias A.
LANE, Thomas, S4368, DI, 11th Inf.
LANE, Thomas F. S11769, G, 1st Ga. Inf.
LANE, W. T. S12701, MC, 19th Inf.
LANE, Walker, S16486, MR, Caruther's Battery, Hvy. Art.
LANE, William Franklin, S8591, SU, 26th Inf.
LANE, William J. S7522, SU, 1st (Carter's) Cav.
LANERD, John, S588, SH, 2nd Inf.
LANEY, Susan Frances, W9974, WL, Laney, Wm. Noah
LANFORD, William W. S3883, A, 1st S.C. Inf.
LANG, Harriet M. W2353, SU, Lang, John Patterson
LANGDON, J. J. S12796, F, 13th Inf.
LANGDON, Jennie, W9793, F, Langdon, J. J.
LANGFORD, Alice G. W1661, RB, Langford, Augustus Mabrie
LANGFORD, David, S3497, PO, 59th Inf.
LANGFORD, George H. S5341, OV, 28th Inf.
LANGFORD, Matthew, S1733, OV, 8th Cav.
LANGFORD, Noah C. S2014, JE, 2nd Cav.
LANGFORD, Sophia Boyles, W1522, RB, Langford, Nathaniel Talmadge

LANGFORD, Wiley B. S11871, MA, 21st (Wilson's) Cav.
LANGHROM, Samuel Marion, S13922, WA, 26th Inf.
LANGLEY, Henry J. S3325, D, 49th Ala. Inf.
LANGLEY, James, S6074, SU, 34th Va. Cav.
LANGLEY, James M. S8356, L, 1st Conf. Cav.
LANGLEY, Mahaly A. W1525, HU, Langley, Thomas Lankford
LANGLEY, Malvina E. W8622, L, Langley, James Matthew
LANGLEY, Mary Ann, W7889, O, Langley, T. H.
LANGLEY, T. H. S12021, O, 3rd (Clack's) Inf.
LANGLEY, T. L. S6903, HU, 42nd Inf.
LANGLEY, W. A. S13478, L, 14th (Neely's) Cav.
LANGSTON, Jonathan, S2385, FR, 44th Inf.
LANGSTON, Thomas J. S10836, FR, 1st Bn. Ala. Partisan Rangers
LANIER, John, S5965, RU, 7th Inf.
LANIER, John S. S492, L, 1st & 27th Consolidated Inf.
LANIER, Lavonia Wilson, W2117, WL, Lanier, Wm. Osborne
LANIER, Lewis, S10659, SU, 42nd N.C. Inf.
LANIER, R. N. S10633, MS, 20th Inf.
LANIER, Richard F. S12771, WE, 1st Bn. (McNairy's) Cav.
LANIER, S. H. S8013, HR, 9th Inf.
LANIER, W. S. S11507, GI, 11th Inf.
LANIUS, Arabella Vanhooser, W10518, WL, Lanius, Richard Price
LANIUS, Richard P. S13306, WL, Huggin's Battery, Art.
LANKFORD, D. H. S7273, DI, Baxter's Co. Lt. Art.
LANKFORD, Josie, W5012, MS, Lankford, Wm. S.
LANKFORD, Kiziah, W2163, DI, Lankford, Dillard H.
LANKFORD, M. V. B. S12352, H, 1st S.C. Art.
LANKFORD, Marvel Cathrine, W1249, HN, Lankford, Daniel Mason
LANKFORD, P. L. S15850, SH, 3rd (Forrest's) Cav.
LANKFORD, T. P. S5504, DI, Baxter's Co. Lt. Art.
LANKFORD, W. S. S13249, HN, 5th Inf.
LANNOM, J. D. S5176, WL, 45th Inf.
LANNOM, Mary E. W3255, WL, Lannom, Thomas E.

-201

LANNOM, Robert T. S6474, RU, 1st (Carter's) Cav.
LANNOM, T. M. S6664, WL, 11th Cav.
LANNOM, Thomas E. S6654, RU, Carter's Bn. Mtd. Scouts, Cav.
LANNOM, W. M. S8140, WL, 45th Inf.
LANNON, John Thomas, S13987, D, 45th Inf.
LANOM, Mary Ann, W1107, WL, Lanom, J. R. Wilson
LANSDEN, Louisa, W1746, OV, Lansden, John M.
LANSDOWNE, Matilda Jane, W3357, MU, Lansdowne, Lavick
LARD, R. G. S14440, Davenport's Bn. Miss. Cav.
LARGEN, H. M. S3937, LI, 8th Inf.
LARGENT, Annie B. W3723, F, Largent, J. C.
LARGENT, J. C. S5853, S8771, F, 154th Sr. Regt. Inf.
LARGENT, Serena Idell, W6786, HO, Largent, John
LARKIN, Ophelia, W6677, FR, Larkin, Thomas Jefferson
LARKINS, B. B. S13661, HU, 49th Inf.
LARKINS, Elizabeth Frances, W920, DI, Larkins, J. H.
LARKINS, J. H. S4739, DI, 11th Inf.
LARKINS, J. J. S15477, S15705, DI, 11th Cav.
LARKINS, John Thomas, S13457, LK, 6th (Wheeler's) Cav.
LARKINS, Louisa Palestine, W8446, DI, Larkins, Samuel Putnam
LARKINS, S. P. S6283, DI, 49th Inf.
LARKINS, William Y. S621, HW, 12th Cav.
LARMER, E. S. S15333, HM, 26th Va. Cav.
LARMER, Rebecca Anna, W9282, R, Larmer, Evans Spencer
LARUE, John W. S5900, MS, 17th Inf.
LARWILL, Joseph H. S8382, CH, 9th Cav.
LASATER, J. W. S14550, O, 33rd Inf.
LASATER, T. H. S11648, WL, 12th Ky. Cav.
LASETER, Mary Louise, W6579, D, Laseter, John Hambrick
LASETER, Tilitha C. W7134, WL, Laseter, Thomas Harrison
LASKY, Mary Jane, W1869, HM, Lasky, Obediah
LASLEY, J. T. S11039, O, 22nd (Barteau's) Cav.
LASLEY, W. H. S1086, D, 48th Ala. Inf.
LASSATER, P. C. S10529, RU, 18th Inf.
LASSITER, L. C. S11824, D, 55th Inf.

LASSITER, Mary Frances, W8529, CA, Lassiter, Peyton Campbell
LASSITER, W. F. S10450, D, 13th Cav.
LASTER, E. S720, O, 2nd Inf.
LASTER, Lucinda, W1844, DE, Laster, George Washington
LASTER, Mary War Narr, W715, O, Laster, Elias
LASTER, Tom, S16293, CC, 47th Inf.
LATEN, Margaret Ann, W6588, LI, Laten, Joshua Simpson
LATHAM, M. A. S11440, CH, 21st Cav.
LATHAM, Neal, S9199, CH, 21st (Wilson's) Cav.
LATHAM, Olivia Jones, W2513, MU, Latham, John Jefferson
LATHIM, Claiborne W. S1039, GR, 20th Inf.
LATIMER, H. A. S931, WE, 12th Miss. Inf.
LATIMER, James H. S14380, D, 49th Ga. Inf.
LATIMER, Josephine, W8519, BE, Latimer, James Thomas
LATIMER, Lizzie Walker, W6214, O, Latimer, Thomas Jefferson
LATIMER, T. J. S13513, O, 9th Inf.
LATIMER, William Mitchell, S6874, CA, 18th Inf.
LATTA, Elizabeth A. W3768, MU, Latta, Wm. W.
LATTA, Mary S. W370, D, Latta, Wm. A.
LATTA, Sims, S16124, S15900, MU, 6th (Wheeler's) Cav.
LATTA, Thomas, S16259, MU, 1st Inf.
LATTA, W. D. S12905, MN, 27th Inf.
LATTIMER, R. A. S3950, HU, 1st (Feild's) Inf.
LATTY, James L. S5899, HU, 10th Cav.
LAUD, Sarah Ann, W7897, SH, Laud, John Tyler
LAUDERBACK, L. S15391, HW, 2nd (Ashby's) Cav.
LAUDERDALE, Ann Rebecca, W8346, DY, Lauderdale, Josiah Mallory
LAUDERDALE, E. C. S1672, HD, 53rd Inf.
LAUDERDALE, J. G. S13969, SH, 3rd (Clack's) Inf. See also John G. Lauderdale
LAUDERDALE, J. M. S5177, GR, 2nd (Robison's) Inf.
LAUDERDALE, John G. S5064, SH, 3rd (Clack's) Inf. See also J. G. Lauderdale
LAUDERDALE, Josephine, W8912, LI, Lauderdale, Wm. Thomas

Index to Tennessee Confederate Pension Applications

LAUDERDALE, Quennie Tipton, W5187, DY, Lauderdale, John Wood
LAURENT, Edward, S15717, D, 1st (Carter's) Cav.
LAUTHNER, John A. S6627, HW, 61st Inf.
LAUTHNER, Mary Ann, W4676, HW, Lauthner, John Anderson
LAVENDER, Mary Tennessee, W1338, D, Lavender, Richard Blythe
LAVENDER, W. R. S2114, WH, 2nd Ga. Cav.
LAW, A. H. S1935, SM, 24th Inf.
LAW, Anna, W1079, SM, Law, Hugh L.
LAW, Mary Frances, W7568, SM, Law, Adison Henry
LAW, Sarah E. W10452, SM, Law, Jesse
LAWLER, Aaron, S4228, G, 27th Inf.
LAWLESS, James K. S9237, HM, 3rd Inf.
LAWLESS, R. J. S11771, H, 55th Ala. Inf.
LAWRENCE, Amanda, W7754, O, Lawrence, B. F.
LAWRENCE, Anna, W1860, O, Lawrence, Wm. Henry Harrison
LAWRENCE, B. F. S9869, O, 11th (Gordon's) Cav.
LAWRENCE, C. C. S11897, LA, 12th Bn. Ala. Cav.
LAWRENCE, Cynthia L. W7003, SN, Lawrence, T. J.
LAWRENCE, Eliza, W3602, P, Lawrence, Miles L.
LAWRENCE, Ella A. Richardson, W3908, K, Lawrence, Wm. Wallace
LAWRENCE, Frances Martin, W9179, SH, Lawrence, Wm. E.
LAWRENCE, J. B. S6949, DI, 11th Inf.
LAWRENCE, J. W. S7094, CF, 4th (McLemore's) Cav.
LAWRENCE, Lewis H. S14260, H, 33rd N.C. Inf.
LAWRENCE, Mary, W4163, GTR, Lawrence, James
LAWRENCE, Miles L. S8406, P, 10th Cav.
LAWRENCE, Nannie Lou [Whites.], W10564, B, Lawrence, James Polk, [Later married Whiteside]
LAWRENCE, Otilia Josephine, W2752, D, Lawrence, Augustus Henry
LAWRENCE, R. C. S5087, WL, 18th Inf.
LAWRENCE, Robert F. S12563, SN, 4th Inf.
LAWRENCE, Sallie Reed, W9552, MA, Lawrence, Swomie Burrows

LAWRENCE, Sophronia A. W1625, CF, Lawrence, John W.
LAWRENCE, T. K. S7496, HN, 5th Inf.
LAWRENCE, Thomas J. S5139, SN, 30th Inf.
LAWRENCE, W. H. H. S16694, O, 11th Inf.
LAWS, John, S8673, CL, 25th Va. Cav.
LAWS, Kitora Arington, W1719, MA, Laws, John
LAWS, Martha E. W2593, H, Laws, Guilford C.
LAWSON, Bettie, W576, HW, Lawson, Orvile B.
LAWSON, Calaway, S6229, HW, 60th Inf.
LAWSON, D. C. S7387, MR, 5th Cav.
LAWSON, David, S10534, MR, 5th (McKenzie's) Cav.
LAWSON, Eliz. Jane (Pierce), W9099, MC, Lawson, Eli Davis, Follows 9100 on film
LAWSON, Elizabeth, W3284, V, Lawson, Wm.
LAWSON, Howell, S2882, FR, 1st Ga. Inf.
LAWSON, Isibel, W3952, FR, Lawson, Levi
LAWSON, J. B. S8785, K, 1st Cav.
LAWSON, John, S7636, HI, 1st (Carter's) Cav.
LAWSON, John F. S2386, HI, 9th Tenn. Bn. Cav.
LAWSON, Levi, S2388, FR, 34th Inf.
LAWSON, Mary T. W6500, CF, Lawson, Howell
LAWSON, N. F. S11986, MG, 1st (Carter's) Cav.
LAWSON, Nola,   See Nola Womack
LAWSON, R. C. S9388, H, 5th Cav.
LAWSON, R. T. S5200, BR, 36th Inf.
LAWSON, Sarah, W6637, MR, Lawson, David C.
LAWSON, Sarah E. W7215, J, Lawson, Woody
LAWSON, Sarah Jane, W11165, BR, Lawson, Arthur
LAWSON, Susan Ann, W8972, PU, Lawson, Terry
LAWSON, W. L. S2361, HW, 50th Va. Inf.
LAWSON, William M. S6186, R, 5th (McKenzie's) Cav.
LAWSON, William Marshal, S829, S1661, PO, 62nd Inf.
LAX, Mary E. W2299, HR, Lax, Robert M.
LAXON, Emily G. W39, GU, Laxon, Jesse Ferril
LAXSON, J. F. S4376, FR, 4th Inf.
LAY, David, S10445, UN, 5th Bn. N.C. Cav.
LAYCOCK, Mirna Elzira, W1577, PU, Laycock, Thomas
LAYCOCK, Thomas, S1296, PU, 16th Inf.

LAYNE, Betty, W11093, SH, Layne, Edward D.
LAYNE, Elizabeth Vermilia, W9900, L, Layne, Wm. Marin
LAYNE, Mary Ann, W188, CF, Layne, James M.
LAZENBY, J. H. S3651, GI, 32nd Inf.
LAZENBY, James, S10650, D, 9th Cav.
LEA, A. C. S10053, WL, 38th Inf.
LEA, John H. S11016, OV, 8th (Dibrell's) Cav.
LEA, Laura, W7947, OV, Lea, J. H.
LEA, Martha J. W834, OV, Lea, Clem Hickman
LEABOW, S. L. S10189, CL, 61st Inf.
LEACH, Louvisa Peoples, W11176, WA, Peoples, P. I. C.
LEACH, Mary J. W6491, WA, Leach, W. T.
LEACH, W. S. S11850, SH, 12th Miss. Inf.
LEACH, W. T. S1332, WA, Undetermined
LEAHEY, Licena Caroline, W10645, H, Leahey, Jeremiah
LEAKE, Kate Emma, W6782, D, Leake, Berry Brown, Applied from Fulton Co. Ga.
LEATH, Eliza Jane, W9187, D, Leath, W. J.
LEATH, James K. S5939, HR, 18th Miss. Cav.
LEATH, Jennie, W6896, F, Leath, Polk
LEATH, Polk, S12171, F, 18th Miss. Cav.
LEATH, W. J. S3741, RU, 12th Inf.
LEATHERS, Fielding Dixon, S1314, S1004, HI, 48th Inf.
LEATHERS, W. L. S11154, RU, 21st (Carter's) Cav.
LEATHERWOOD, John A. S15762, MN, 7th Miss. Cav.
LEATHERWOOD, Pheby Jane, W10789, MN, Leatherwood, John A.
LEATHERWOOD, Thomas, S8064, BO, 26th Inf.
LEAVELL, Millrey Ewing, W7926, SH, Leavell, Napoleon Lewis
LEBOW, G. T. S14146, BO, 1st (Carter's) Cav.
LEDBETTER, E. W. S10408, OV, 8th (Dibrell's) Cav.
LEDBETTER, H. C. sr. S4302, O, 48th Inf.
LEDBETTER, H. H. S138, S1406, HD, 48th Miss. Inf.
LEDBETTER, J. W. S12709, MN, Phillips' Co. Lt. Art.
LEDBETTER, Martha Ann, W1027, DY, Ledbetter, Andrew
LEDBETTER, Martha Ann, W4393, MN, Ledbetter, Henry Harrison
LEDBETTER, P. H. S2320, OV, 16th Inf.
LEDBETTER, Ralph, C54, D, 1st Inf.

LEDBETTER, Syntha Jane, W7797, MN, Ledbetter, James Warren
LEDFORD, Caroline, W9097, MC, Ledford, James M.
LEDFORD, James L. S1510, MC, 16th Inf.
LEDFORD, Lucius S. S13455, BR, 62nd N.C. Inf.
LEDFORD, M. M. W817, MN, Ledford, Marion Henderson
LEDFORD, Mary E. W11170, MC, Ledford, James
LEDFORD, Minerva, W1199, PO, Ledford, James K.
LEDFORD, T. L. S13285, BO, 52nd Ga. Inf.
LEDFORD, W. P. S14013, LI, 31st Inf.
LEDSINGER, Mary Louise, W9848, DY, Ledsinger, Thomas Fowlkes
LEE, A. Y. S676, K, 26th Inf.
LEE, Alexander, S5018, J, Hamilton's Bn. Cav.
LEE, Alice, W10999, D, Lee, Harry Rene
LEE, Alsa J. S7189, MU, 11th Cav.
LEE, B. G. S12319, CL, 29th Inf.
LEE, Belle, W6380, SH, Lee, Martin
LEE, Beulah Dickey, W, Some papers with #11183 on film
LEE, Clark, C107, H, Regiment not given
LEE, Claudia, W2869, SH, Lee, Wm. Edward
LEE, Edward F. S15644, MU, 38th Inf.
LEE, Eliza Jane, W7350, TR, Lee, John F.
LEE, F. M. S2772, HD, 2nd Miss. Inf.
LEE, H. C. S4760, HN, 46th Inf.
LEE, Harriet Louise, W2791, TR, Lee, James Monroe
LEE, Harry R. S16254, D, 34th Miss. Inf.
LEE, Henry B. S7363, MU, 53rd Inf.
LEE, Isaac N. S6616, RB, 2nd Cav.
LEE, J. F. S12561, HN, 46th Inf.
LEE, J. H. S2471, CH, 52nd Inf.
LEE, James C. S1979, K, 63rd Inf.
LEE, James M. S3441, RU, 45th Inf.
LEE, John, S11778, G, Thomas' Legion, N.C.
LEE, John, S16577, SN, 20th Inf.
LEE, John C. S6939, SH, 8th S.C. Inf.
LEE, John F. S4456, TR, 23rd Inf.
LEE, John H. S9144, MN, 52nd Inf.
LEE, John M. S7786, OV, 25th Inf.
LEE, John P. S5151, HN, 48th (Nixon's) Inf.
LEE, Joshua S. S649, SN, 55th Inf.
LEE, Louis H. S4852, HW, 29th Inf.
LEE, M. B. S16469, SN, 8th Cav.
LEE, M. J. W700, MN, Lee, Thomas S.
LEE, Marcia, W9815, D, Lee, James Sonford

Index to Tennessee Confederate Pension Applications

LEE, Margaret Edmondson, W921, RU, Lee, James M.
LEE, Margaret Jane, W6516, MO, Lee, Wm.
LEE, Mariah, W3904, SN, Lee, Joshua S.
LEE, Martha, W8564, SH, Lee, David W.
LEE, Martha Ann, W7111, HN, Lee, Henry C.
LEE, Martha Susan, W4183, MU, Lee, Henry B.
LEE, Mary Martilie, W8716, J, Lee, Rubin Cashioner
LEE, Matilda F. W3254, SN, Lee, Stephen
LEE, Polly Louny, W6066, OV, Lee, John Madison
LEE, Preston, S5019, OV, 6th Ark. Inf.
LEE, Rachel A. W8597, WL, Lee, James Benjamin
LEE, Rachel R. W4515, D, Lee, John F.
LEE, Robert, S1188, H, 37th Inf.
LEE, Sallie, W9410, WL, Lee, A. C.
LEE, Sarah Emmaline, W4057, B, Lee, Thomas Jefferson
LEE, Virginia F. W4757, D, Lee, Zebulon Lee
LEE, W. J. S12651, K, 63rd Inf.
LEE, W. W. S14685, HN, 20th Cav.
LEE, William, S6974, WA, McClung's Co. Lt. Art.
LEE, William J. S8082, MU, 48th Inf.
LEE, Z. P. S1544, DK, 23rd Inf.
LEECH, James M. S8208, SH, 19th Miss. Inf.
LEEDY, Joseph, S9245, HA, 64th Va. Mtd. Inf.
LEEPER, F. L. S14869, FR, 8th (Wade's) Confederate Cav.
LEEPER, Hallie M. Coffee, W10861, W, Leeper, Frack L.
LEEPER, Hannibal, S9396, K, 29th Inf.
LEEPER, Katharine Walters, W4030, HW, Leeper, Frank
LEETH, Nancy Elleanor, W1905, HD, Leeth, Joseph Damron
LEFTWICH, Elizabeth, W3350, LI, Leftwich, Littlebury
LEFTWICH, Henry C. S8880, SU, 2nd Cav.
LEGG, George W. S3926, SN, 30th Inf.
LEGG, Isaac W. S1980, RO, 63rd Inf.
LEGG, Mary E. W50, ME, Legg, Meredith Webb
LEGG, Mary Elizabeth, W3314, K, Legg, James Alexander
LEGG, William E. S2893, SN, 7th Cav.
LEGGETT, Artimissa, W730, MT, Leggett, Matthew
LEGGETT, Frances D. W9818, D, Leggett, John L.

LEGGETT, Marthy Jane, W612, SN, Leggett, Isaac Daniel
LEGGETT, Mary Jane, W6869, HR, Leggett, Wm. Marcus
LEGGETT, William M. S203, HR, 154th Sr. Regt. Inf.
LEHEW, C. F. S4823, WL, 18th Inf.
LEIGH, J. W. S9554, H, 8th Ga. Inf.
LEIGON, T. W. S13872, CH, 20th (Nixon's) Cav.
LEIPER, James A. S15815, W, 11th (Holman's) Cav.
LEIPER, Priscilla Macon, W10935, SH, Leiper, Wm. D.
LEIRD, Ann Eliza, W9524, L, Leird, James
LEITH, Josephine Watkins, W7230, K, Leith, Wm. Henry
LELAND, Charles, S15035, SH, 4th Inf.
LEMARR, D. F. S11894, CL, 48th Va. Inf.
LEMASTER, Nettie, W6601, SH, Lemaster, Peter Adison
LEMAX, F. R. S4229, HU, 10th (DeMoss') Cav.
LEMAY, J. C. S4319, CF, 18th Inf.
LEMOND, J. W. S3381, CC, 6th Inf.
LEMONS, Abraham, S9380, SU, 44th Ga. Inf.
LEMONS, Calvin D. S4866, HN, 46th Inf.
LEMONS, W. V. S8644, K, 1st Cav.
LENAHAN, Ida Morrison, W6174, D, Lenahan, Joseph
LENARD, William, S1575, WA, 60th Inf.
LENEASE, Susan Frances, W9175, SH, Lenease, David Washington
LENEHAN, Annie E. W8640, D, Lenehan, Dan
LENNING, Drew V. W10034, RU, Lenning, James H.
LENOIR, Nannie L. W10365, RU, Lenoir, Lycurgus B.
LENOIR, W. T. S15582, MO, 43rd Inf.
LENTZ, G. W. S14448, MU, 6th (Wheeler's) Cav.
LENTZ, Martha E. W7533, B, Lentz, John Jackson
LENTZ, Nancy Jane, W8819, W8444, MS, Lentz, Benjamin Franklin
LEONARD, Andrew, S3979, SU, 63rd Va. Inf.
LEONARD, C. Burk, S1336, WA, 63rd Inf.
LEONARD, Debby, W4412, HW, Leonard, John
LEONARD, Frank S. S597, WA, 60th Inf.
LEONARD, J. C. S10634, MS, 32nd Inf.
LEONARD, J. M. S15961, GI, 32nd Inf.
LEONARD, Jacob, S7018, SU, 59th Inf.
LEONARD, Jeff, S2487, LI, 44th Inf.

LEONARD, John, S609, HW, 60th Inf.
LEONARD, John, S10786, SU, 60th Inf.
LEONARD, Martain, S5020, K, 63rd Va. Inf.
LEONARD, Martha, W6864, MS, Leonard, Jesse Calvin
LEONARD, Nancy, W2230, SU, Leonard, Andrew
LEONARD, Nancy Messick, W6795, SU, Leonard, Peter H.
LEONARD, Susan J. W5344, SU, Leonard, Rufus S.
LESLEY, Elizabeth Ann, W2057, LI, Lesley, Wm. Crawford
LESLEY, Margaret E. W1017, WA, Lesley, Wm. Alexander
LESLEY, W. A. S4968, WA, 60th Inf.
LESLEY, William C. S7926, LI, 17th Bn. (Newman's) Cav.
LESLIE, Emma Rains, W9141, SU, Leslie, Hamilton Wade
LESLIE, Hamilton W. S7478, RO, 45th Va. Inf.
LESLIE, Nancy Elizabeth, W6040, MO, Leslie, James W.
LESTER, Cassie E. W1401, WL, Lester, James W.
LESTER, Eliza J. W2488, DK, Lester, Thomas J.
LESTER, J. W. S7007, RU, 7th Inf.
LESTER, James H. S16599, MG, 16th Va. Cav.
LESTER, John, S14845, K, 37th Va. Inf.
LESTER, Richard, C4, GI, 3rd Inf.
LESTER, Robert, C126, D, 8th Inf.
LESTER, Sallie Williamson, W5816, WL, Lester, James R.
LESTER, William J. S17, WL, 4th Cav.
LETSINGER, Catharine Ann, W1685, MU, Letsinger, Wm. James
LEVAN, Calma Libonia, W5158, GU, Levan, Samuel Celsie
LEVERTON, Ben T. S4320, GU, 17th Inf.
LEVI, Jasper N. S3786, H, 2nd Cav.
LEVI, Nancy, W7920, R, Levi, Jasper Newton
LEVY, Paul T. S12982, SH, 1st Miss. Lt. Art.
LEWELLEN, F. G. S4070, HR, 23rd Miss. Inf.
LEWELLING, Mary Frances, W2692, DY, Lewelling, James Newton
LEWELLYN, Mary A. W1941, DY, Lewellyn, John Edward
LEWELLYN, Sarah Elizabeth, W4093, K, Lewellyn, Charles Howard
LEWIS, A. N. S12197, H, 4th (McLemore's) Cav.

LEWIS, Abraham, S10241, CL, 1st Cav.
LEWIS, Amos, S7380, MR, 4th Cav.
LEWIS, Bettie, W9789, HO, Lewis, Robert T.
LEWIS, C. R. S11751, L, Phillips' Battery, Art.
LEWIS, Caroline Tennie, W7554, W8002, ST, Lewis, James Madison
LEWIS, Cornelia Virginia, W5756, ST, Lewis, J. G.
LEWIS, David, S1000, SN, 16th Inf.
LEWIS, Edward, S4281, LK, 15th Inf.
LEWIS, Elija W. S5277, HE, 27th Inf.
LEWIS, Elijah, S908, CO, 26th Inf.
LEWIS, Emily A. W1002, WH, Lewis, Jacob A.
LEWIS, Fredonia, W1115, HE, Lewis, Elijah Willis
LEWIS, G. M. S13334, SH, 6th Inf.
LEWIS, G. R. S11346, ST, 49th Inf.
LEWIS, G. W. S15195, HI, 12th (Green's) Cav.
LEWIS, George Washington, S6113, SH, 4th Inf.
LEWIS, Gorla, W7595, ST, Lewis, George Rufus
LEWIS, Henry H. S15897, SH, 14th (Neely's) Cav.
LEWIS, Irwin, S1402, WA, Undetermined
LEWIS, Isaac, S8467, WA, 26th N.C. Inf.
LEWIS, J. A. S10019, WE, 11th Inf.
LEWIS, J. G. S5632, S263, ST, 50th Inf.
LEWIS, J. G. S8786, DI, Baxter's Co. Art.
LEWIS, J. K. P. S5959, P, 7th Ky. Inf.
LEWIS, J. M. S3516, T, 3rd Mo. Inf.
LEWIS, James, S9798, FR, 3rd Inf.
LEWIS, James, S10246, MC, 5th Cav.
LEWIS, James W. S10306, LE, 48th (Voorhies') Inf.
LEWIS, Jane, W574, ME, Lewis, John
LEWIS, Jane, W2588, G, Lewis, John R.
LEWIS, Jasper, S3647, WH, 50th Inf.
LEWIS, John, S1373, HE, 46th Ga. Inf.
LEWIS, John F. S6284, D, 22nd (Barteau's) Cav.
LEWIS, John H. S2620, MOO, 17th Inf.
LEWIS, John T. S8578, P, 42nd Inf.
LEWIS, Joseph W. S15312, JO, 21st Va. Cav.
LEWIS, Lou, W4656, LK, Lewis, E. J.
LEWIS, Louise J. W3203, MOO, Lewis, Cainouth Marion
LEWIS, Lucy C. W5122, DI, Lewis, James G.
LEWIS, M. S9465, MC, 5th (McKenzie's) Cav.
LEWIS, M. G. S11957, D, 8th Cav.
LEWIS, M. J. W2674, WA, Lewis, Isaac
LEWIS, Margaret Ann, W4069, H, Lewis, Archibald Newton

Index to Tennessee Confederate Pension Applications

LEWIS, Martha Ann, W5684, HR, Lewis, Nathaniel B.
LEWIS, Mary C. W604, FR, Lewis, Wm. Martin
LEWIS, Mary T. W1276, WI, Lewis, Leander M.
LEWIS, Mattison Alexander, S4669, S223, MR, 4th (McLemore's) Cav.
LEWIS, Minnie P. W9942, G, Lewis, Meredith P.
LEWIS, N. B. S8958, F, 49th Ala. Inf.
LEWIS, Nancy Paxton, W2300, CO, Lewis, R. H.
LEWIS, Narcissa Howry, W2405, HI, Lewis, John Calvin
LEWIS, Nathaniel M. S16622, S16634, RU, 11th (Gordon's) Cav.
LEWIS, Peter E. S1839, WE, 1st Cav.
LEWIS, R. H. S1076, CO, 26th and 5th Inf.
LEWIS, Salina, W3677, WA, Lewis, Irvine
LEWIS, Samuel J. S11297, MS, 1st (Feild's) Inf.
LEWIS, Sarah, W2204, MC, Lewis, M.
LEWIS, Sarah Ann, W5141, WI, Lewis, Thomas Harden
LEWIS, Sarah E. W140, SN, Lewis, Wm. A.
LEWIS, Syntha Jane, W1714, MOO, Lewis, John Henry
LEWIS, T. J. S6416, WH, 50th Inf.
LEWIS, T. J. S10682, SN, 44th Inf.
LEWIS, Tennie, W7554, W8002, ST, Lewis, James Madison
LEWIS, Thomas H. S11017, WI, 20th Inf.
LEWIS, William I. S3042, WH, 1st Bn. (Colm's) Inf.
LEWTER, J. H. S3389, LI, 55th Inf.
LEWTER, Nancy, W7209, GI, Lewter, J. H.
LIGGETT, Frances Fox, W7935, MU, Liggett, Wm. Cissero
LIGGETT, H. N. S8856, MS, 4th Cav.
LIGGETT, H. T. S3552, 4th Cav.
LIGGETT, R. M. C160, RO, 2nd Cav.
LIGGETT, W. H. S9580, MS, 53rd Inf.
LIGHT, Amanda, W10161, HW, Light, George
LIGHT, Bayless, S6251, HW, 29th Inf.
LIGHT, George, S3848, HW, 31st Inf.
LIGHT, Hannah, W2209, HW, Light, Jonathan
LIGHT, Nathan, S643, SU, 29th Inf.
LIGHT, Samuel, S467, HW, 29th Inf.
LIGHT, Samuel, S13330, H, 4th Ga. Cav.
LIGON, Anna Rebecca, W2342, D, Ligon, Osborne Lockett
LIGON, Augustus B. S5856, SN, 23rd Inf.
LIGON, Henry, C179, O, 14th Inf.

LIGON, Mary Jane, W8541, CH, Ligon, Timothy Walton
LIGON, Mattie, W7685, G, Ligon, John
LIGON, T. W. See T. W. Leigon
LILLARD, Charles J. S9266, SH, 9th Inf.
LILLARD, J. S. V. S6757, ME, 3rd (Lillard's) Mtd. Inf.
LILLARD, Jennie M. W2252, ME, Lillard, James S. V.
LILLARD, Letitia Penelope, W6279, K, Lillard, Calvin
LILLARD, Robert, S5601, PO, 3rd Inf.
LILLARD, Sarah, W134, ME, Lillard, James E.
LILLARD, W. G. S15021, D, 4th (McLemore's) Cav.
LILLEY, Andrew J. S6940, SU, 59th Inf.
LILLEY, G. G. S12666, H, 4th Ala. Cav.
LIMBAUGH, Sarah Grant, W976, FR, Limbaugh, Peter
LIMBAUGH, Susan, W977, FR, Limbaugh, Mike
LIMING, William Holland, S14439, SH
LINCH, John T. S5110, RU, 2nd (Robison's) Inf.
LINCH, Parlee I. W6097, RU, Linch, John T.
LINCOLN, John M. S268, WA, 19th Inf.
LINCOLN, John M. S7402, D, 16th Bn. Cav.
LINDAMOOD, George M. S1988, WA, 63rd Inf.
LINDAMOOD, M. W. S11628, SU, 4th Cav.
LINDER, Gabriel, S100, D, 1st Inf.
LINDER, George W. S2861, CU, 4th Cav.
LINDER, Katherine Ellen, W11085, SH, Linder, John McDonald
LINDER, Mary Lovetta, W5956, CU, Linder, George Washington
LINDER, Perlina Emeline, W6486, OV, Linder, Wm.
LINDER, William, S344, OV, Undetermined
LINDSAY, Thomas F. S845, GI, 3rd Inf.
LINDSEY, Alonzo, S16590, D, 3rd (Clack's) Inf.
LINDSEY, Demeris, W766, WL, Lindsey, Wm.
LINDSEY, Eliza Elizabeth, W6845, GU, Lindsey, Wm. David
LINDSEY, Eliza S. W2858, SH, Lindsey, Moses
LINDSEY, J. H. S13479, HN, 22nd Miss. Inf.
LINDSEY, James E. S4321, B, Legion's Ga. Inf.
LINDSEY, N. S. S486, CH, 27th Inf.
LINDSEY, W. W. S9210, MN, 27th Inf.
LINEBAUGH, Joel, S12411, FR, 17th Inf.

LINEBAUGH, Lizzie, W1440, FR, Linebaugh, Rufus
LINEBAUGH, Sarah A. W8820, FR, Linebaugh, Joel
LINEBERGER, John D. S2369, LI, 37th N.C. Inf.
LINEBERRY, P. J. S11781, P, 19th (Biffle's) Cav.
LINEBERRY, Rebecca Susan, W6117, P, Lineberry, Peter Jasper
LINEHAM, Dan, S14684, D, 1st (Turney's) Inf.
LINER, A. J. S9253, H, 43rd Inf.
LINER, J. B. S12995, S12089, MC, 43rd Inf.
LINER, Lucy Vail, W865, MC, Liner, James Smith
LINGERFEET, Elijah, S5278, MO, 3rd Inf.
LINGERFELT, Martha C. W4930, MC, Lingerfelt, Jacob
LINGERFELT, Rebecca, W321, PO, Lingerfelt, Alfred
LINK, Clarinda, W3973, SN, Link, Thomas Wesley
LINK, Elida Elizabeth, W6379, JE, Link, John Henry
LINK, R. H. S7320, SN, 30th Inf.
LINK, Thomas W. S72, SN, 2nd Cav.
LINKHAUER, Addie, W8067, SH, Linkhauer, John A.
LINKINHOKER, C. B. S10295, LA, 57th Inf.
LINKINHOKER, Mollie, W9103, LA, Linkinhoker, Cary Breckinridge
LINSLEY, E. L. S14657, WL, 4th (McLemore's) Cav.
LINTNER, John, S13896, RU, 20th Inf.
LINTON, Cora P.   See Cora P. Roach
LINTON, J. E. S671, S1700, DY, 15th Cav.
LINTZ, Sarah Eleanor, W11145, U, Lintz, Wm. Jackson
LINVILLE, Worley, S1403, WA, 60th Inf.
LINZEY, Julia C. W8094, DI, Linzey, Wm. Henry Harrison
LINZEY, W. H. H. S2879, DI, 11th Inf.
LIPE, W. P. S658, HW, 63rd Inf.
LIPFORD, W. A. S11175, JO, 8th Va. Inf.
LIPPS, H. R. S7646, SU, 3rd (Clack's) Inf.
LIPPS, Jacob W. S14207, GR, 10th Ky. Mtd. Inf.
LIPSCOMB, John, S16651, FR, 41st Inf.
LIPSCOMB, Joseph Allison, S16543, SH, 30th Va. Inf.
LIPSCOMB, Laura, W10809, FR, Lipscomb, John

LIPSCOMB, Lina E. W4756, FR, Lipscomb, John Thomas
LIPSCOMB, T. E. S15371, CC, 52nd Inf.
LIPSCOMB, Theodore Erwin, S13385, MU, 9th Bn. Cav.
LIPSCOMB, Thomas, C63, O, 9th Bn. Cav.
LIPSCOMB, W. H. S15123, MU, 9th Bn. Cav.
LISENBEY, Della M. W5387, D, Lisenbey, Wm. H.
LITTLE, A. J. S9632, G, Hudson's Battery, Miss. Lt. Art.
LITTLE, A. P. S8116, WA, Unassigned (Mining)
LITTLE, Annie Rebecca, W4743, WI, Little, Joseph L.
LITTLE, Catherine, W1222, SU, Little, George W.
LITTLE, David H. S4106, O, 1st Miss. Inf.
LITTLE, G. W. S2684, SU, 63rd Inf.
LITTLE, G. W. S9186, HU, 60th Inf.
LITTLE, J. L. S12805, WI, 44th Inf.
LITTLE, J. W. S6927, RU, 41st Inf.
LITTLE, M. M. S16292, P, 9th Miss. Cav.
LITTLE, Malinda E. W205, D, Little, David
LITTLE, Martha, W9100, WE, Little, John Richard
LITTLE, Mary Elizabeth, W9828, WI, Little, Wm. D.
LITTLE, Mary Jane, W3036, G, Little, Austin Joseph
LITTLE, Mary R. W8728, K, Little, Wm. Gray
LITTLE, Nancy Elizabeth, W5106, OV, Little, H. G.
LITTLE, Nannie Victoria, W7097, RU, Little, John Westley
LITTLE, Thomas H. S460, P, 32nd Inf.
LITTLE, Tom C. S16140, LI, Forrest's Escort, Cav.
LITTLE, W. J. S6895, HU, 32nd Inf.
LITTLEFIELD, Mary Polk, W992, D, Littlefield, Wm.
LITTLEFORD, J. H. S4255, SU, 1st Va. Cav.
LITTLEFORD, Willis L. S9097, SU, 8th (Smith's) Cav.
LITTLEJOHN, John W. S15637, MU, 15th S.C. Inf.
LITTLEJOHN, Lousetta A. W3527, HN, Littlejohn, James Thomas
LITTLEJOHN, Mary J. W7892, MU, Littlejohn, John W.
LITTLEJOHN, S. S. S9487, MN, 19th & 20th Consolidated Cav.

Index to Tennessee Confederate Pension Applications

LITTLEJOHN, W. J. S7051, MN, 18th Cav.
LITTLETON, George W. S10277, DY, 16th Ga. Inf.
LITTLETON, I. F. S16480, S15613, HN, 7th (Duckworth's) Cav.
LITTLETON, Manervie, W8983, G, Littleton, Wm. Sparks
LITTLETON, Mary Louise, W8295, SN, Littleton, James
LITTLETON, Robert S. S12439, O, 3rd Inf.
LITTLETON, William S. S1654, S9389, G, 4th Ala. Inf. 9th Cav.
LITTON, Martha Ann, W2877, HI, Litton, Wm. Carrol
LITTRELL, Charles, S2397, LI, 1st Inf.
LITTRELL, Charley, C168, HR, 14th Cav.
LITTRELL, William, S7548, CL, 3rd Confederate Engineer Troops
LIVELY, E. M. S10828, H, 3rd Cav.
LIVELY, James R. S15127, H, 37th Ga. Inf.
LIVESAY, Lafayette, S8630, HA, 64th Va. Cav.
LIVING, J. D. S15574, MA, 27th S.C. Inf.
LIVINGSTON, Amanda L. W565, DE, Livingston, Nicholas Foister
LIVINGSTON, G. W. S14257, GR, 62nd N.C. Inf.
LIVINGSTON, L. W. S5707, C, 62nd N.C. Inf.
LIVINGSTON, Louisa, W8678, SN, Livingston, Robert Newman
LIVINGSTON, R. N. S3657, SN, 24th Inf.
LIZENBERY, William, S1616, WA, 63rd Inf.
LLOYD, A. C. S3665, HW, 31st N.C. Inf.
LLOYD, A. J. S5650, L, 28th N.C. Inf.
LLOYD, Anna Elizabeth, W4542, SH, Lloyd, Atlas J.
LLOYD, Ellen, W8191, WA, Lloyd, James H. Follows 8189 on film
LLOYD, Kate, W10386, B, Lloyd, James Knox Polk
LLOYD, Lucy J. W4732, JE, Lloyd, Robert Barton
LLOYD, W. A. S14817, L, 4th Inf.
LOCK, Benjamin, S4164, WH, 16th Inf.
LOCK, James M. S13566, PO, 3rd (Lillard's) Mtd. Inf.
LOCK, Joseph, S9002, J, 4th (Murray's) Cav.
LOCK, Margaret Atline, W821, MO, Lock, Robert Harison
LOCKE, Alfred, C147, R, 1st Cav.
LOCKE, Anna, W10353, LA, Locke, John S.
LOCKE, Augustus S. S9519, J, 28th Inf.
LOCKE, John S. S13860, C, 6th Ky. Inf.
LOCKE, Letha J. W8579, J, Locke, Joe
LOCKE, Sarah Elizabeth, W8931, WI, Locke, Berry
LOCKE, Sidney, S11483, GI, 32nd Inf.
LOCKETT, Mary Ann, W391, D, Lockett, Eli Franklin
LOCKEY, B. S14084, FR, 45th Inf.
LOCKEY, J. F. S7357, B, 23rd Inf.
LOCKEY, William B. S10550, SH, 1st S.C. Cav.
LOCKHART, J. S. S10136, GU, 16th Inf.
LOCKHART, J. W. S15542, G, 19th (Biffle's) Cav.
LOCKHART, Lucy, W7706, GU, Lockhart, J. S.
LOCKHART, Lydia E. W7306, F, Lockhart, Thomas J.
LOCKHART, Margaret, W6902, SH, Lockhart, Thomas Jefferson
LOCKHART, T. J. S12405, F, Forrest's Old Regt. Cav.
LOCKHART, Tennessee, W7217, GU, Lockhart, James M.
LOCKHART, Thomas J. S10409, SH, 17th Miss. Inf.
LOCKHART, W. T. S14004, SH, 14th Miss. Inf.
LOCKHART, Willie Tucker, W8166, SH, Lockhart, Wm. Thomas
LOCKMAN, Elizabeth, W7452, MN, Lockman, John Richardson
LOCKMAN, I. N. S16495, H, Ga. Lt. Art.
LOCKMAN, J. R. S4531, MN, 18th (Newsom's) Cav.
LOCKMAN, Lula L. W10228, H, Lockman, Isaac N.
LOCKRIDGE, G. B. S13724, WI, 3rd (Clack's) Inf.
LOCKRIDGE, Jennie, W5882, WI, Lockridge, Gideon B.
LOCKRIDGE, Jennie Davis, W5136, MU, Lockridge, John Williamson
LOCKRIDGE, John Williamson, S12570, MU, 3rd (Clack's) Inf.
LODEN, James, S10107, CU, 16th Cav.
LODEN, William, S11118, D, 19th (Biffle's) Cav.
LOFLAND, Charles, S920, SH, 49th Inf.
LOFTICE, Warren, S2602, GR, 59th Inf.
LOFTIN, Benjamin F. S99, D, 32nd Inf.
LOFTIN, E. C. S359, D, 28th Inf.
LOFTIN, Ellen Smith, W9157, MU, Loftin, E. E.
LOFTIN, James Joseph, S12495, MU, 9th Cav.
LOFTIN, John A. S5616, RU, 11th Cav.

-209

Index to Tennessee Confederate Pension Applications

LOFTIN, T. J. S3533, DY, 16th (Wilson's) Cav.
LOFTIN, W. H. S12652, MS, 24th Inf.
LOFTIN, W. R. S5473, O, 1st Cav.
LOFTIS, Calidonia F. W8315, HI, Loftis, James G.
LOFTIS, Ella, W1701, J, Loftis, Henry H.
LOFTIS, Francis, S11622, OV, 25th Inf.
LOFTIS, Louisa Tennessee, W8032, OV, Loftis, Frances
LOGAN, Elizabeth C. W4997, LI, Logan, George Cass
LOGAN, Fannie Victory, W6847, G, Logan, T. P.
LOGAN, James N. S5534, FR, 17th Inf.
LOGAN, James W. S10299, S13196, PI, 5th Ky. Inf.
LOGAN, Joab D. S8624, H, 23rd Ga. Inf.
LOGAN, L. P. S15134, GI, 7th Inf.
LOGAN, Mary L. W3177, H, Logan, Joab Drury
LOGUE, J. B. S7236, MU, 9th Bn. (Gantt's) Cav.
LOKEY, Mary Frances, W3966, SH, Lokey, Wiley Hoet
LOMAX, J. W. S11347, HU, 10th (DeMoss') Cav.
LOMAX, Margaret, W7751, DE, Lomax, James W.
LOMAX, Susannah Janes, W2929, HY, Lomax, John Franklin
LONAS, William B. S16475, K, 12th Bn. (Day's) Cav.
LONDON, C. C. S6127, LA, 3rd Inf.
LONDON, Caroline, W1539, H, London, Martin VanBuren
LONDON, Enoch C. S13145, MS, 17th Inf.
LONDON, Sallie, W10210, MS, London, Enoch C.
LONES, Jasper, S4536, K, Burrough's Co. Art.
LONES, Mary, W4062, K, Lones, Jasper
LONG, A. C. S9299, BO, Thomas' Legion, N.C.
LONG, A. T. S2202, GI, 53rd Inf.
LONG, Alfred, S4809, DI, 11th Inf.
LONG, Alice, W7953, FR, Long, Samuel
LONG, Benton W. S6758, MS, 4th (McLemore's) Cav.
LONG, Bettie M. W1794, MA, Long, Wm. Harrison
LONG, Branch T. S6624, HW, 31st Inf.
LONG, Cordelia, W1697, PU, Long, James Mitchell
LONG, Daniel W. S9623, GR, 59th Inf.
LONG, Dolly, W8127, FR, Long, Henry
LONG, E. L. S4331, HM, 59th Inf.
LONG, Emma Davis, W8686, MU, Long, Richard Thomas, Same app. number as Kittie Harper
LONG, G. T. S6790, BO, 37th Inf.
LONG, Isaac, S12887, HM, 37th Inf.
LONG, Isaac D. S809, HW, 31st Inf.
LONG, Isham, S868, BR, 29th Inf.
LONG, J. C. S1379, G, 12th Inf.
LONG, J. H. S3161, HM, 37th Inf.
LONG, J. M. S12447, SH, 2nd N.C. Jr. Inf.
LONG, J. N. S12344, D, 15th (Stewart's) Cav.
LONG, James, S2769, CH, 16th Cav.
LONG, James H. S8242, HE, 6th Confederate Cav.
LONG, James P. S13707, FR, 24th Inf.
LONG, John, S6035, HW, 31st Inf.
LONG, John, S8954, LO, 2nd (Walker's) Inf.
LONG, John, S12175, GR, 2nd (Ashby's) Cav.
LONG, John R. S4977, BR, 62nd Inf.
LONG, Lou Gray, W9947, SH, Long, Julius Marion
LONG, Lucy Hamilton, W6305, SH, Long, Henry Clay
LONG, Mary Adline, W2517, DI, Long, Alfred
LONG, Mary Catherine, W7488, HM, Long, Joseph H.
LONG, Mary Frances, W4293, MS, Long, Burton W.
LONG, Matilda Caroline, W855, GI, Long, Augustus Tillman
LONG, Nannie, W5614, G, Long, J. C.
LONG, Nathan P. S8128, L, 16th Cav.
LONG, R. T. S7481, MU, 4th (McLemore's) Cav.
LONG, R. W. S6413, LI, 41st Inf.
LONG, Robert L. S14969, GR, 59th Inf.
LONG, Samuel, S11758, FR, 24th Inf.
LONG, Sarah A. W8389, GR, Long, John
LONG, Sarah Elizabeth, W4458, BO, Long, A. C.
LONG, Sarah Elizabeth, W4850, HU, Long, James Howe
LONG, Susan C. W5638, HM, Long, Levi
LONG, Susanna E. W989, GR, Long, John
LONG, Thomas J. S6736, FR, 32nd Inf.
LONG, W. C. S1340, OV, 28th Inf.
LONG, W. H. S11633, HM, 59th Inf.
LONG, William, S9920, SQ, 31st Inf.
LONG, William, S11163, HM, 37th Inf.
LONGMIRE, J. S. S12308, SH, 7th Miss. Cav.

Index to Tennessee Confederate Pension Applications

LONGMIRE, Lorena Dawson, W8526, SH, Longmire, James Sylvester
LONGMIRE, Martha Ann, W9871, MA, Longmire, Wm. Martin
LOONEY, Elizabeth Caroline, W2831, Looney, James Fergus
LOONEY, J. B. S14545, FR, Hunter Bn. Ala. Cav.
LOONEY, J. C. S13621, FR, 17th Inf.
LOONEY, James F. S7860, 27th Inf.
LOONEY, John D. S9018, HN, 25th Inf.
LOONEY, Samuel, S10242, HW, 12th Bn. Cav.
LOONEY, Tennessee Hays, W2855, HN, Looney, Jonathan Davis
LOONEY, William, S11416, HW, 59th Inf.
LOOP, Harvey, S13270, HM, Unassigned (Government Shop)
LOOP, Louisa, W5174, CL, Loop, William
LOOP, William, S2800, CL, 29th Inf.
LOOPER, W. H. S10988, OV, Shaw's Bn. Cav.
LORANCE, Mattie A. W3571, SH, Lorance, John I.
LORANCE, Rebecca J. W6437, CA, Lorance, W. W.
LORANCE, W. W. S4841, CA, 18th Inf.
LORE, Margaret Elizabeth, W8293, MU, Lore, Joel
LOTT, Sallie, W8366, CH, Lott, Wm. Henderson
LOTT, William H. S10612, CH, 52nd Inf.
LOUDENBER, Minnie Ingersol, W7389, H, Loudenber, Frank W.
LOUDON, Irena A. W309, MS, Loudon, Amos
LOUDON, Priscilla A. W310, MS, Loudon, Thomas Honis
LOUIS, Stephen N. S12670, FR, 41st Inf.
LOVE, Henry, S4623, M, Undetermined
LOVE, Jacob D. S1229, U, 63rd Inf.
LOVE, James A. S7008, SU, 19th Inf.
LOVE, James M. S9003, MO, 31st Inf.
LOVE, James R. S1256, U, 37th Inf.
LOVE, Joel, S6257, MU, 19th (Biffle's) Cav.
LOVE, John, S7336, MU, 9th Bn. Cav.
LOVE, John R. S1230, U, 39th N.C. Inf.
LOVE, Joseph, S14607, MU, 48th Inf.
LOVE, L. G. S15943, DK, 16th Inf.
LOVE, Louisa J. W3498, K, Love, Wm. Alva
LOVE, Margaret Clementine, W4296, DY, Love, John Wesley
LOVE, Margaret E. W6710, MU, Love, Joel
LOVE, Margaret R. W2514, WA, Love, Thomas Elias
LOVE, Martha Jane, W7965, SU, Love, Winston
LOVE, Mary Jane, W5317, MU, Love, John A.
LOVE, Mary Mallisia, W5186, SE, Love, Preston Blount
LOVE, Mary Susan, W677, G, Love, Stephen Jordan
LOVE, Mexie, W9823, SH, Love, Volney Arnol
LOVE, Noah J. S14487, JO, 33rd N.C. Inf.
LOVE, P. B. S3642, SE, 31st Inf.
LOVE, Phebe, W4770, U, Love, Jacob D.
LOVE, Sallie Wilkes, W8681, MU, Love, Joseph
LOVE, Sarah J. W4745, U, Love, John R.
LOVE, Sarah L. W7546, H, Love, Wiley B.
LOVE, Susan, W1745, M, Love, Henry
LOVE, Thomas, S1884, WA, 4th Va. Inf.
LOVE, Thomas, S15362, JO, 37th N.C. Inf.
LOVE, Thomas R. S14121, SN, 9th (Bennett's) Cav.
LOVE, Walter C. S8667, MR, 31st Inf.
LOVE, Winton, S3790, SU, 19th Inf.
LOVELACE, D. W. S3684, K, 1st Inf.
LOVELACE, George W. S1596, GU, 1st Inf.
LOVELACE, Nancy Ann, W4625, CC, Lovelace, Simeon
LOVELACE, Victoria, W10494, SH, Lovelace, Peter Collins
LOVELESS, Ella McLaurine, W2416, GI, Loveless, DeWitt Franklin
LOVELL, C. B. S12541, D, 50th Inf.
LOVELL, Mary Elizabeth, W3730, SN, Lovell, Robert Elmore
LOVELL, R. E. S4195, SN, 13th Inf.
LOVETT, H. H. S2912, CC, 11th Bn. (Holman's) Cav.
LOVETT, Melissa, W7716, CC, Lovett, H. H.
LOVETTE, Martha Ann, W438, HI, Lovette, Newton Carroll
LOVING, A. W. S8351, G, 12th Cav.
LOVING, H. W. S10186, SH, 7th Cav.
LOVING, John C. S1975, DK, 65th Ga. Inf.
LOVING, Sarah Jane, W1587, G, Loving, Alexander Wilson
LOVING, W. R. S16141, LI, 14th Tex. Cav.
LOVITT, Nancy, W322, G, Lovitt, George Washington
LOVVORN, W. A. S16556, RU, 45th Inf.
LOW, John, S8902, A, Kain's Co. Lt. Art.
LOWDERMILK, Marriott, W10719, HN, Lowdermilk, Stephen Jasper
LOWDY, George W. S4159, S8698, SU, 59th Inf.

LOWDY, Mary E. W7429, SU, Lowdy, George Washington
LOWE, A. T. S5172, GR, 2nd (Ashby's) Cav.
LOWE, Angie L. W6924, GR, Lowe, John M.
LOWE, Calvin C. S4133, RU, 23rd Inf.
LOWE, Elizabet J. W2442, MT, Lowe, J. S.
LOWE, J. M. S10088, GR, 59th Inf.
LOWE, J. Y. S15006, RU, 8th (Smith's) Cav.
LOWE, John A. S5279, SH, 49th N.C. Inf.
LOWE, Mary Frances, W3391, G, Lowe, Nathan Jasper
LOWE, N. J. S8166, G, 28th Cav.
LOWE, Neri, sr. S8792, WL, 3rd Ky. Cav.
LOWE, Sarah Ellen, W5747, RU, Lowe, Thomas Newton
LOWE, Sarah Winston, W6520, SH, Lowe, James Nicholas
LOWE, Susan Payne, W901, D, Lowe, Wm. K. Bowling
LOWE, Thomas B. S1243, WH, 8th Cav.
LOWE, W. C. S4436, SH, Undetermined
LOWERY, Eunolia [Jones], W11117, Lowery, J. Lambon, [Later married Jones]
LOWERY, Fletcher, S71, BR, 5th Cav.
LOWERY, G. B. S3356, WL, 6th Ga. Cav.
LOWERY, James R. S16044, WY, Undetermined
LOWERY, Mary, W9862, BE, Lowery, Tobe
LOWERY, Simpson, S3002, WH, 25th Inf.
LOWERY, W. H. S12987, DI, 5th Inf.
LOWERY, William, S16, D, 2nd Inf.
LOWEY, Thomas, S14559, WA, Thomas' Legion, N.C.
LOWREY, John Wesley, S1816, WH, 16th Inf.
LOWRY, Bettie, W5621, SH, Lowry, Van P.
LOWRY, Eliza, W2770, H, Lowry, Benjamin C.
LOWRY, F. C. S14581, W, 35th Inf.
LOWRY, George W. S15923, HM, 62nd Inf.
LOWRY, J. J. S12671, S13226, HN, 5th Inf.
LOWRY, J. L. S12685, HN, 20th (Russell's) Cav.
LOWRY, J. T. S14832, WL, 6th Ga. Cav.
LOWRY, Mary E. W8349, WL, Lowry, John T.
LOWRY, Sarah A. W8076, W, Lowry, Fessington C.
LOWRY, Susana A. W4608, HO, Lowry, Wm.
LOWRY, T. W. S8472, HN, 46th Inf.
LOWRY, W. H. S10968, MO, 26th Inf.
LOWRY, William, S3877, HO, 50th Inf.
LOWRY, William, S11971, WH, 16th Inf.
LOWSON, Frank, S7206, MR, 1st (Carter's) Cav.

LOWY, A. G. S4842, GI, 6th (Wheeler's) Cav.
LOWY, G. B. S5140, WL, 6th Ga. Cav.
LOYD, B. F. S5990, BL, 5th (McKenzie's) Cav.
LOYD, Caroline Jane, W7566, BL, Loyd, Benjamin Franklin
LOYD, Charlotte, W2152, GI, Loyd, Alexander Green
LOYD, Frances A. W2698, R, Loyd, W. C.
LOYD, George, S8884, U, 58th N.C. Inf.
LOYD, J. H. S13930, WA, Ellington's Battery, N.C. Inf.
LOYD, J. K. S8319, B, 17th Inf.
LOYD, Joshua Thompson, S7329, HW, 12th Bn.
LOYD, Lou, W7871, HW, Loyd, John T.
LOYD, Mary, W10816, HN, Loyd, Wm. David
LOYD, Phebe Elizabeth, W5713, GE, Loyd, George Nichols
LOYD, Victoria C. W3026, MS, Loyd, W. G.
LOYD, W. G. S11539, MS, 2nd La. Inf.
LOYD, William A. S15847, HN, 47th N.C. Inf.
LUCADO, Margaret, W6781, T, Lucado, Edward P.
LUCAS, Eliza, W5424, HW, Lucas, George W.
LUCAS, George W. S12429, HW, Hewalld's Battery
LUCAS, J. T. S5438, HU, 42nd Inf.
LUCAS, John W. S8357, L, 15th Cav.
LUCAS, L. R. S10849, H, 5th Tex. Inf.
LUCAS, Sallie Isabel, W6558, MR, Lucas, L. R.
LUCK, Andrew Jackson, S1611, WL, 4th Cav.
LUCK, Julia, W7198, HO, Luck, L. B.
LUCK, L. B. S8890, HO, 14th Inf.
LUCKETT, Annie S. W7407, HU, Luckett, W. K.
LUCKETT, Will K. S7948, HU, 9th Bn. Cav.
LUCKEY, Frances, W8332, MA, Luckey, Thomas
LUCKEY, Martha M. W6923, D, Luckey, Wm. Harris
LUCKEY, William H. S9146, D, Allison's Squadron, Cav.
LUCY, William H. S3375, GI, 3rd (Clack's) Inf.
LUMLEY, J. G. S12957, MN, 23rd Miss. State Troops
LUMPKIN, Catherine M. W9738, T, Lumpkin, David
LUMPKIN, Martha A. W3637, HR, Lumpkin, Wilson M.
LUNA, Allen P. S13044, LA, 23rd Inf.
LUNA, J. M. S4098, LI, 8th Inf.
LUNA, James M. S2520, LI, 8th Inf.
LUNA, John S. S7193, MS, 53rd Inf.

LUNA, Maggie, W8330, MS, Luna, John B.
LUNA, Nancy Jane, W10331, LA, Luna, Allen P.
LUNA, Sarah J. W1192, MS, Luna, Wm. C. A.
LUNDY, A. T. S12496, JO, 4th Va. Inf.
LUNDY, Leonora Texana, W9335, HO, Lundy, John Green
LUNN, J. N. S9652, MS, 4th (McLemore's) Cav.
LUNN, John A. S6297, DI, 17th Inf.
LUNN, Mary A. W199, WI, Lunn, John Aldon
LUNN, Nicholas G. S8435, MU, 17th Inf.
LUNN, Robina N. W8845, MU, Lunn, Eli jr.
LUNN, Sarah Frances, W8683, MU, Lunn, Felix
LUNN, W. S. S15106, WI, 10th Inf.
LUNSFORD, James, S5485, HU, 11th Inf.
LUNSFORD, william, S3692, CO, 16th N.C. Inf.
LUSK, Elizabeth, W7268, GU, Lusk, F. L.
LUSK, J. A. S3442, CF, 1st (Turney's) Inf.
LUSK, John H. S10829, MC, 1st (Carter's) Cav.
LUSK, Lucinda M. W5169, L, Lusk, Richard N.
LUSK, Margaret Tennessee, W8932, MU, Lusk, Samuel Scott
LUSK, Mary Vincent, W6083, CF, Lusk, Edmund
LUSK, Rhoda, W3259, CF, Lusk, John
LUSK, Sarah Candace, W9473, BR, Lusk, John Harrison
LUSK, W. H. S15892, GU, Unassinged
LUTHER, J. M. S5330, WE, 28th N.C. Inf.
LUTHER, Martin D. S1740, MC, 25th N.C. Inf.
LUTHER, Mary A. W4241, SE, Luther, W. A.
LUTHER, William A. S8919, K, 11th N.C. Troops
LUTON, J. T. S11058, D, 19th Inf.
LUTTRELL, Calvin, S5488, GE, 31st Inf.
LUTTRELL, Eldes, W4413, HR, Luttrell, John Washington
LUTTRELL, Elizabeth, W2618, MN, Luttrell, R. J.
LUTTRELL, Elizabeth, W6041, FR, Luttrell, James
LUTTRELL, J. J. S3040, LA, 41st Miss. Inf.
LUTTRELL, Louis M. S1972, K, 1st (Carter's) Cav.
LUTTRELL, Martha J. W1111, GE, Luttrell, Calvin
LUTTRELL, Thornton, S3008, LI, 44th Inf.
LUTTRELL, W. P. S13324, CH, 11th Miss. Cav.
LYLE, Ceina Ann, W1995, HI, Lyle, W. W.

LYLE, George M. S1369, WA, 23rd Va. Inf.
LYLE, Henry T. S14334, MT, 2nd Ky. Cav.
LYLE, J. D. S4867, MC, Winston's Co. Lt. Art.
LYLE, J. Y. S15481, H, 24th Ala. Inf.
LYLE, Joe, S14341, MT, 49th Inf.
LYLE, John M. S7091, JE, 31st Inf.
LYLE, Sarah Butter, W4121, WA, Lyle, Cyrus W.
LYLE, Sarah Jane, W8007, H, Lyle, Jefferson Y.
LYLE, W. P. S4930, PO, 62nd Inf.
LYLES, John, S12244, LO, 62nd Inf.
LYLES, Martha Ann, W10387, SH, Lyles, W. W.
LYNAM, Alice E. W6908, DK, Lynam, Marcus A.
LYNAM, M. A. S11450, DK, C. S. Navy
LYNCH, David, S11792, FR, 41st Inf.
LYNCH, David J. S283, SM, 7th Inf.
LYNCH, J. D. S11510, FR, 17th Inf.
LYNCH, Sarah Jane, W9872, D, Lynch, Wm. Berry
LYNCH, W. M. S1833, WY, 20th Inf.
LYNN, Andrew, S11343, CY, 8th (Dibrell's) Cav.
LYNN, Buck, S5816, OV, 13th Cav.
LYNN, Carrie Matilda, W9643, SH, Lynn, Wm. Everett
LYNN, Celina, W3136, OV, Lynn, David
LYNN, Cornelia Ann, W5478, SH, Lynn, Charles
LYNN, David, S440, CY, Undetermined
LYNN, Filena, W8286, J, Lynn, Wm. M.
LYNN, J. D. S10206, HR, 15th (Stewart's) Cav.
LYNN, Lany, W4955, HI, Lynn, J. D.
LYNN, M. H. S11882, MC, 9th Tex. Art.
LYNN, William, S9053, HI, 42nd Inf.
LYNN, William, S9935, OV, 8th (Dibrell's) Cav.
LYON, A. Augustine, S12193, D, 48th Miss. Inf.
LYON, Alexander, S13232, RU, 8th (Smith's) Cav.
LYON, Almita E. W2130, CC, Lyon, J. R.
LYON, E. C. S10333, WE, 31st Inf.
LYON, Emeline, W8760, CA, Lyon, Nathan James Smoot
LYON, John S. S6646, SU, 59th Inf.
LYON, Lucy, W7517, WE, Lyon, Edward Coleman
LYON, Margaret, W4726, SU, Lyon, John S.
LYON, Mary Lucy, W9588, WE, Lyon, Edward Coleman
LYON, Richard H. S3106, D, 3rd Inf.

Index to Tennessee Confederate Pension Applications

LYON, Ruthy, W10460, RU, Lyon, Alexandria
LYON, W. B. S6214, SU, 59th Mtd. Inf.
LYONS, A. S. S15725, HW, 12th Bn. Cav.
LYONS, Albertine, W3199, K, Lyons, Edward Farrell
LYONS, E. H. S8927, HW, 12th Bn. Cav.
LYONS, Livie M. W1950, HW, Lyons, Clinton G.
LYONS, Richard, S1557, R, 19th Inf.
LYTLE, Frank, S9262, MU, 16th Inf.
LYTLE, Kate B. W7831, RU, Lytle, Evander
MABE, David, S1998, WH, 28th Inf.
MABE, Hezakiah, S1487, HA, 63rd Inf.
MABE, William sr. S190, HA, 63rd Inf.
MABERRY, John P. S836, J, 16th Inf.
MABERRY, Malvina Jn. Huffines, W1648, J, Maberry, Silas
MABRY, Adenia Mason, W5092, H, Mabry, Thomas Milligan
MABRY, Parmelia C. R. W79, HN, Mabry, Thomas Asbury
MABRY, Pattie, W8783, FR, Mabry, Moses Jamilan
MABRY, R. F. S12004, O, 45th Inf.
MABRY, R. M. S6985, WL, 45th Inf.
MACINNA, John P. S6153, CT, 58th Inf.
MACKBEE, Robert Theadore, S12840, SH, 14th Inf.
MACKEY, Lillie A. W4795, HI, Mackey, W. J.
MACKEY, W. J. S11905, HI, 22nd (Barteau's) Cav.
MACLIN, Helen E. W1996, GI, Maclin, Michael M.
MACLIN, James, C192, L, 7th Cav.
MACLIN, Nancy J. W4209, SH, Maclin, James Nathaniel
MACLIN, Robert Landen, S3450, GI, 6th (Wheeler's) Cav.
MACON, Frances Elizabeth, W1281, RU, Macon, Henry Harrison
MADDEN, J. M. S1267, BE, 5th Inf.
MADDEN, J. W. S5349, H, 23rd Ga. Inf.
MADDEN, Sarah Wilmouth, W10050, HN, Madden, John Morgan
MADDEN, T. W. S3342, D, 8th Inf.
MADDIN, James Monroe, S9727, D, 6th (Wheeler's) Cav.
MADDOX, Frank, S13605, F, Hanover's Va. Art.
MADDOX, Mattie, W8360, LI, Maddox, J. J.
MADDOX, N. G. S5818, LI, 8th Inf.
MADDUX, A. V. S11007, RU, 45th Inf.
MADDUX, Mary Jane, W6368, RB, Maddux, Alfred V.
MADDUX, Nancy R. W7789, LI, Maddux, N. G.
MADDUX, Taylor L. S15716, J, 25th Inf.
MADENA, T. H. S12968, FR, 3rd Miss. Cav.
MADEWELL, Emma, W8937, W8577, W, Madewell, Wm.
MADEWELL, James, S14389, V, Unassigned (Shoe Maker)
MADISON, Eliza Lee, W11095, SH, Madison, James Marion
MADISON, John R. S4196, MS, 17th Inf.
MADOUX, Andrew J. S12337, PO, 59th Inf.
MAGEE, E. A. S13830, P, 19th (Biffle's) Cav.
MAGEE, Joseph, S16685, MA, 24th Ala. Inf.
MAGEE, Lear, W7432, DY, Magee, Thomas
MAGEE, Margaret, W8397, MA, Magee, Joseph
MAGEE, Thomas, S804, DY, 9th Cav.
MAGNESS, L. J. S6569, DK, 23rd Inf.
MAGNESS, Sallie A. W875, D, Magness, Richard Marion
MAHAFFEY, J. H. S4931, DK, 23rd Inf.
MAHONEY, Asenath J. W3174, GI, Mahoney, Thomas
MAHONEY, John, S14936, D, 21st Ala. Inf.
MAHONEY, Mary M. W409, T, Mahoney, John
MAHONEY, Rose Elizabeth, W10773, H, Mahoney, John Thomas
MAHONEY, William, S3257, RO, 3rd Engineer Troops
MAHONEY, Willie Ann, W10373, D, Mahoney, Wm. Benjamin
MAIDEN, W. F. S11997, BE, 48th Va. Inf.
MAIDEN, William H. S14053, K, 48th Va. Inf.
MAIN, Alice Eulalia, W9832, K, Main, Henry Kinnamon
MAINARD, Ailsie Jane, W1556, MA, Mainard, Alfred Alpins
MAINARD, Elizabeth, W4425, CY, Mainard, Lewis C.
MAINES, James H. S14633, CT, 30th Va. Inf.
MAINORD, L. C. S4395, OV, 25th Inf.
MAINORD, S. D. sr. S2249, OV, 25th Inf.
MAJOR, Annie, W9273, WL, Major, A. M.
MAJOR, Sarah Elizabeth, W1212, WL, Major, Thomas Merrit
MAJORS, Alsie Jane, W6916, HR, Majors, Benjamin Franklin
MAJORS, B. F. S4532, HR, 45th Inf.
MAJORS, J. W. S2432, FR, 1st (Turney's) Inf.
MAJORS, John, S4287, RO, 43rd Inf.

Index to Tennessee Confederate Pension Applications

MAJORS, John M. S5519, HD, 43rd Miss. Inf.
MAJORS, Mary Marinda, W3967, FR, Majors, Robert Murphy
MAJORS, Sarah, W605, GR, Majors, James P.
MAJORS, William, S4036, FR, 1st (Turney's) Inf.
MALLARD, Eldridge T. S12906, B, 45th Inf.
MALLARD, Susan Evyline, W5669, B, Mallard, Eldridge Thornton
MALLICOAT, J. D. S9119, GR, 37th Inf.
MALLICOAT, Rachel M. W5364, GR, Mallicoat, John Daniel
MALLORY, Jennie Greer, W4127, SH, Mallory, George Jones
MALLORY, Josiah, S7221, WI, 1st (Feild's) Inf.
MALLORY, Leacy Amelia, W5618, MT, Mallory, Thomas Ebb
MALLORY, Martha Kyle, W2986, SH, Mallory, Theophilus S.
MALONE, B. F. S5320, S2693, LI, 53rd Inf.
MALONE, C. P. S11059, HR, 26th Miss. Inf.
MALONE, Caswell, S8968, T, 13th Inf.
MALONE, David, S6866, SU, 63rd Inf.
MALONE, David E. S12857, GI, 53rd Inf.
MALONE, Elendor, W5833, LI, Malone, Jesse E.
MALONE, Eva S. W678, SU, Malone, James K.
MALONE, F. M. S14898, SU, Sullivan's Co. Home Guards
MALONE, Frances Elizabeth, W8745, DK, Malone, Jim
MALONE, G. W. S5860, CT, 59th Inf.
MALONE, George B. S15616, SH, 3rd (Forrest's) Cav.
MALONE, J. B. S11883, SN, 2nd (Robison's) Inf.
MALONE, J. H. S6105, WE, 5th Inf.
MALONE, James, S3529, SU, 61st Inf.
MALONE, John M. S4230, HY, 63rd Inf.
MALONE, John W. S10951, S5410, SN, 22nd (Barteau's) Cav.
MALONE, Katie, W8589, SN, Malone, James Bryson
MALONE, Lula Susan, W9875, MA, Malone, Charles Pinkney
MALONE, M. A. S3103, LI, 1st S.C. Inf.
MALONE, Margaret J. W4107, MN, Malone, Wm. B.
MALONE, Martha, W6111, LI, Malone, John Edward
MALONE, Mary C. W6539, SU, Malone, David

MALONE, Mary Elizabeth, W9301, SU, Malone, Wm. C.
MALONE, Mary Jane, W7447, LI, Malone, Marion A.
MALONE, Mitissa, W2148, D, Malone, Willis D.
MALONE, Polk, S10115, L, 12th Ky. Cav.
MALONE, Rebecca W. W10604, SH, Malone, Robert Carroll
MALONE, Sallie, W9176, SU, Malone, Francis Marion
MALONE, Sarah Ann, W9528, SU, Malone, George Jefferson
MALONE, Sarah E. W601, LI, Malone, Benjamin F.
MALONE, T. B. S1786, HD, 51st Inf.
MALONE, W. B. S9363, MN, 13th Inf.
MALONE, W. C. S12275, SU, State Reserves
MALSH, Patrick, S827, 15th Inf.
MALUGEN, Nancy Carolyn, W5594, LE, Malugen, Henry Jackson
MALUGIN, Jane Woolard, W8348, HI, Malugin, Robert B.
MALUGIN, Mary S. W8459, HI, Malugin, George W.
MANER, A. B. S8754, MT, 2nd (Ashby's) Cav.
MANES, John, S1878, SE, 48th Inf.
MANES, Rissie, W2983, SE, Manes, John
MANES, William, S3340, GE, 61st Inf.
MANESS, July Saphronia, W2960, DE, Maness, James
MANESS, Martha Jane, W3231, L, Maness, Thomas Jefferson
MANESS, Mary, W3369, CH, Maness, Moab
MANESS, T. J. S973, L, 52nd Inf.
MANESS, W. J. S10613, MN, 52nd Inf.
MANESS, W. M. S7968, CH, 21st Cav.
MANESS, Yancey, S1160, HW, 50th Va. Inf.
MANEY, James, C164, RU, 1st (Feild's) Inf.
MANEY, Thomas H. S14021, D, 1st (Feild's) Inf.
MANGRAM, Wesley, S2516, CE, 20th Inf.
MANGREM, Lou, W5395, MU, Mangrem, James
MANGRUM, J. C. S12198, WI, Baxter's Co. Lt. Art.
MANGRUM, Sallie Elizabeth, W4266, CE, Mangrum, Wesley
MANGUM, W. T. S10787, CF, 17th Inf.
MANIER, Allen Howes, S2396, D, 17th Inf.
MANIER, Frank Luzette, S1773, D, 20th Inf.

MANIER, Lucy, W6467, CF, Manier, A. Webb
MANING, Mike, S6410, HN, 5th Inf.
MANIRE, A. W. S6630, CF, 24th Inf.
MANIS, F. A. S4087, RO, 2nd Cav.
MANIS, George S. S11047, MO, 2nd (Ashby's) Cav.
MANIS, James Harvey, S12126, MC, 2nd (Ashby's) Cav.
MANIS, Lousinda, W1729, MO, Manis, John
MANISE, D. C. S5141, RU, 24th Inf.
MANKIN, Lucy T. W9751, RU, Mankin, Welcom
MANKIN, Sallie J. W9031, RU, Mankin, R. P.
MANLEY, Andrew R. S8275, WI, 10th Cav.
MANLEY, B. F. S11776, O, 11th Inf.
MANLEY, Benjamin, S7145, HU, 11th Inf.
MANLEY, Clementine E. W4063, Manley, Newton Eldridge
MANLEY, Esther Adelia, W1935, F, Manley, Franklin Carr
MANLEY, H. H. S2753, GU, 44th Inf.
MANLEY, Mary E. W4647, GU, Manley, H. H.
MANLEY, Mary Ella, W5355, SH, Manley, William Lightner, Applied from Desoto Co. Miss.
MANLEY, Tennessee Adeline, W7536, O, Manley, Benjamin Franklin
MANLY, C. A. S11773, MA, 3rd (Forrest's) Cav.
MANN, Dissie, W465, Mann, T. J.
MANN, Henry C. S15524, JE, 1st (Carter's) Cav.
MANN, Henry W. S16269, MU, 17th Inf.
MANN, James W. S5456, 22nd Inf.
MANN, Julia Elizabeth, W7191, G, Mann, Wm. Walker
MANN, Mary Frances, W522, Mann, Wm. Alvis
MANN, Mary J. W1182, HW, Mann, Daniel A.
MANN, R. E. S2734, WL, 28th Inf.
MANN, William W. S4906, G, 37th Inf.
MANNING, A. F. S13654, MR, 8th Ga. Inf.
MANNING, Amos Smith, S10687, H, 34th Ga. Inf.
MANNING, Martty, W955, HN, Manning, Mike
MANNIS, John, S3046, MC, 3rd (Lillard's) Mtd. Inf.
MANSON, E. P. S14396, MT, 14th Inf.
MANTLO, R. W. S11405, D, 30th Inf.
MANTLO, W. J. S80, RB, 30th Inf.
MANTOOTH, Dicie Ann, W10563, MC, Mantooth, Doctor H.
MANTZ, P. G. S7722, SU, 23rd Va. Inf.
MANUS, Bartley, S2195, WH, 25th Inf.
MAPLES, Cage R. S14063, WA, 5th (McKenzie's) Cav.
MARABLE, James R. S10773, SH, 11th (Holman's) Cav.
MARANE, Christopher Columbus, S13004, HI, 11th Inf.
MARBERRY, Hester [Clark], W10624, HU, Marberry, John Monroe, [Later married Clark]
MARBERRY, Louise, W2483, HO, Marberry, Franklin
MARBERRY, Nancy, W10234, HN, Marberry, A. E.
MARBERY, Jerraldine, W950, ST, Marbery, George
MARBURY, Jarupa S. W3575, CF, Marbury, Moses P.
MARBURY, P. H. S14267, HY, 9th Inf.
MARCH, Sallie E. W3786, D, March, Wm. Finch
MARCHBANKS, Linnie A. W3017, D, Marchbanks, Columbus
MARCUS, Margarette Jane, W7666, WE, Marcus, Wm. Brown
MARGRAVES, Sallie Ann, W9362, HW, Margraves, George Washington
MARGROVE, W. P. S12055, K, Lynch's Co. Lt. Art.
MARION, Mathew, S8168, SU, 60th Inf.
MARKHAM, Annie Hayes, W5110, GI, Markham, James D.
MARKHAM, Elizabeth F. W1803, BE, Markham, James M.
MARKHAM, George Somervill, S4978, S4423, T, 7th (Duckworth's) Cav.
MARKHAM, John, S8040, K, 27th Va. Cav.
MARKS, Bell, W11106, GI, Marks, Jas. Thos.
MARKS, James T. S14006, GI, 1st (Wheeler's) Cav.
MARKS, Lizzie, W4217, GI, Marks, Lewis Harwell
MARKS, Martha Ann, W1375, LA, Marks, John Henry
MARKS, Samuel, S8152, S5281, MA, 17th Miss. Inf.
MARKS, Thomas C. S2591, GI, 6th (Wheeler's) Cav.
MARKUM, Barney O. S3841, HW, 14th Va. Inf.
MARKUM, M. C. S4740, CA, 8th (Smith's) Cav.

Index to Tennessee Confederate Pension Applications

MARKUM, Sarah Ann, W5096, HW, Markum, Barnett O.
MARLER, Mary Elizabeth, W10592, LI, Marler, David Alexander
MARLER, Mattie, W9770, WL, Marler, Richard
MARLER, Susan, W8312, R, Marler, Francis Marion
MARLIN, A. J. S5617, HE, 51st Inf.
MARLIN, Anna Elisa, W2561, MS, Marlin, J. W.
MARLIN, Estes A. W3464, HE, Marlin, A. J.
MARLIN, J. W. S9581, MS, 45th Inf.
MARLIN, Joe, S6678, RU, 45th Inf.
MARLIN, Joseph B. S8182, WI, 32nd Inf.
MARLIN, Nannie E. W8712, CF, Marlin, Wm. B.
MARLIN, Sallie, W10012, WI, Marlin, W. B.
MARLIN, W. B. S12081, WI, 32nd Inf.
MARLIN, W. B. S12156, RU, 2nd (Robison's) Inf.
MARLOW, J. A. S5282, LI, 8th Inf.
MARLOW, James A. S7009, GI, 8th Inf.
MARLOW, Nancy, W1984, WH, Marlow, Wm. C.
MARLOW, Sarah, W970, PU, Marlow, James
MARLOW, William C. S398, WH, 28th Inf.
MARONEY, Addie [Currin], W11148, SH, Maroney, James, [Later married Currin]
MARONEY, James, S10852, HR, Forrest's Old Regt. Cav.
MARONEY, Laura Jane, W8294, W9392, WL, Maroney, Lewis
MARONEY, Lewis, S10067, MA, 22nd Inf.
MARR, A. M. S6265, SH, 55th Inf.
MARR, B. F. S14497, K, 6th Ky. Mtd. Inf.
MARR, Joseph, S4349, BR, 3rd Inf.
MARR, Mary M. W870, LI, Marr, Richard
MARR, Richard, S7010, LI, 41st Inf.
MARR, W. M. S2070, D, 10th Inf.
MARR, W. W. S11950, MO, 2nd (Ashby's) Cav.
MARRS, G. W. S6873, P, 53rd Inf.
MARRS, Lucinda, W3191, P, Marrs, George Washington
MARRS, Sallie M. W8621, LI, Marrs, Marcus
MARSH, Amanda Huey, W7783, H, Marsh, Charles Wesley
MARSH, C. W. S12878, H, Lee's Battery, Va.
MARSH, D. M. S33, DI, 1st Bn. Hvy. Art.
MARSH, D. M. S14309, MA, 12th Ark. Inf.
MARSH, Dan G. S14621, MA, 70th N.C. Inf.

MARSH, Drewey Milton, S5608, MT, 1st Art.
MARSH, E. J. S590, HU, Hawkins' Scouts
MARSH, James M. S10382, SU, 21st Va. Cav.
MARSH, Mary Anna, W6621, SH, Marsh, Frank Corbett
MARSH, Mollie Evylin, W9033, MA, Marsh, D. M.
MARSH, Virginia Caroline, W5513, SU, Marsh, James Madison
MARSHALL, A. G. S1944, G, 22nd Inf.
MARSHALL, Annie F. W9618, T, Marshall, Thomas Hardeman
MARSHALL, David, S9601, 22nd Inf.
MARSHALL, Drury F. S5634, MT, 14th Inf.
MARSHALL, Eva Francies, W2452, G, Marshall, Alvis G.
MARSHALL, F. W. S5088, M, 2nd (Walker's) Inf.
MARSHALL, H. H. S4009, SN, 18th Inf.
MARSHALL, J. K. S16218, WI, 20th Inf.
MARSHALL, J. M. S8333, HN, 46th Inf.
MARSHALL, J. W. S14518, WL, 30th Inf.
MARSHALL, James B. S9511, MS, Burkner's Guards, Ky.
MARSHALL, John J. S11475, MA, 51st Inf.
MARSHALL, Lavinia Lee, W1391, K, Marshall, Wm. E.
MARSHALL, Leonidas Polk, S14005, T, 12th Cav.
MARSHALL, Lottie A. W9833, T, Marshall, Wm. H.
MARSHALL, Martha W. W4742, GE, Marshall, John C.
MARSHALL, Mary Jane, W5748, MT, Marshall, Drue Francis
MARSHALL, Molly Frances, W6221, D, Marshall, Henry Harrison
MARSHALL, Thomas H. S3596, HN, 27th Inf.
MARSHALL, Thomas H. S11685, T, 51st Inf.
MARSHALL, W. A. S2610, 22nd Inf.
MARSHALL, W. A. S15269, CF, 1st (Turney's) Inf.
MARSHALL, W. H. S14587, SH, 4th Tex. Inf.
MARSHALL, W. S. S6611, RU, 24th Inf.
MARSHALL, William E. S3357, K, 12th Cav.
MARSHALL, William H. S2703, SN, 18th Inf.
MARSHALL, Willie Mai, W7377, CF, Marshall, Wm. Alexander
MARTIN, Alexander, S12020, T, 6th (Wheeler's) Cav.
MARTIN, Amanda Eliza, W3240, MU, Martin, Wm. Carroll

MARTIN, Amy Iola, W10233, PO, Martin, Layfayatt
MARTIN, Andrew, S13617, T, 25th Ala. Inf.
MARTIN, B. C. S5283, W, 35th Inf.
MARTIN, B. P. S13368, WL, 1st Cav.
MARTIN, Benjamin H. S15962, RO, 39th Ga. Inf.
MARTIN, Benjamin Thomas, S12581, MU, 48th (Nixon's) Inf.
MARTIN, C. M. S6427, CF, 4th (McLemore's) Cav.
MARTIN, C. M. S9328, GU, 4th (McLemore's) Cav.
MARTIN, Catherine, W1880, BE, Martin, Wm.
MARTIN, D. W. S10161, SH, 9th Inf.
MARTIN, Dicy, W3469, MT, Martin, Morgan
MARTIN, Dinmer, S5284, B, 35th Inf.
MARTIN, Dora, W3467, T, Martin, Sidney Baxter
MARTIN, E. H. S3726, H, 60th Ga. Inf.
MARTIN, E. O. S13807, SH, 154th Sr. Regt. Inf.
MARTIN, E. P. S14555, ST, 10th Cav.
MARTIN, Ellen B. W4949, W, Martin, Dimmon
MARTIN, Emma, W10970, GI, Martin, John Jas.
MARTIN, Emma N. W5663, SH, Martin, John C.
MARTIN, Etta Barnes, W9332, RB, Martin, John Milton
MARTIN, Fannie E. W7510, W8078, SH, Martin, Wm. Luther
MARTIN, Fannie Margaret, W10150, SH, Martin, Bollin James
MARTIN, Frances Elizabeth, W8078, W7510, SH, Martin, Wm. Luther
MARTIN, Frances R. W4435, Martin, Milton Scoot
MARTIN, G. W. S847, S13933, RB, 30th Inf.
MARTIN, G. W. S9793, SN, 9th (Bennett's) Cav.
MARTIN, G. W. S10736, HY, 9th Inf.
MARTIN, George H. S11359, SH, 14th (Neely's) Cav.
MARTIN, George H. S16068, SH, Hudson's Miss. Lt. Art.
MARTIN, George W. S2859, FR, 44th Inf.
MARTIN, H. A. S9853, D, 18th (Newsom's) Cav.
MARTIN, H. C. S3884, RU, 8th (Smith's) Cav.
MARTIN, Hannah Elizabeth, W7629, HU, Martin, John W.

MARTIN, Harriet, W5467, MR, Martin, John A.
MARTIN, Hiram, S15506, S13595, PU, 25th Inf.
MARTIN, I. B. S10030, LI, 9th Ky. Mtd. Inf.
MARTIN, I. F. S12967, DI, 10th Cav.
MARTIN, Irene, W10728, ST, Martin, Edward P.
MARTIN, J. D. S3709, DK, 7th Inf.
MARTIN, J. D. S8514, DI, 10th Cav.
MARTIN, J. G. S3659, GI, 32nd Inf.
MARTIN, J. J. S11697, DK, 16th Inf.
MARTIN, J. M. S9582, W, 28th Cav.
MARTIN, J. S. S14704, HY, 12th Cav.
MARTIN, J. T. S7215, DI, 11th Inf.
MARTIN, J. W. S2615, WI, Baxter's Co. Lt. Art.
MARTIN, James B. S8529, MR, 4th Inf.
MARTIN, James C. S2150, WH, 1st Bn. Inf.
MARTIN, James H. S3963, WL, 7th Va. Inf.
MARTIN, James H. S13110, HI, 10th Cav.
MARTIN, James I. S12628, V, 16th Inf.
MARTIN, Jane, W7225, CF, Martin, Cornelius McGuire
MARTIN, Jane D. W776, WI, Martin, Benjamin Franklin
MARTIN, Jerry H. S10685, ST, 50th Inf.
MARTIN, John, S2873, MR, 43rd Inf.
MARTIN, John C. S4579, SH, 12th (Green's) Cav.
MARTIN, John C. S15723, HE, 19th (Biffle's) Cav.
MARTIN, John J. S15223, GI, 20th Cav.
MARTIN, John M. S15784, RB, 30th Inf.
MARTIN, L. G. S12879, H, 5th (McKenzie's) Cav.
MARTIN, L. M. S10446, PO, 64th N.C. Inf.
MARTIN, Lettie Larcenia, W9132, MU, Martin, Wm. M. Graves
MARTIN, Louisa J. W621, MS, Martin, Overton C.
MARTIN, M. C. W189, DI, Martin, John Shelby
MARTIN, Maggie Susan, W5961, RU, Martin, Henry Clay
MARTIN, Margaret A. E. W1542, WL, Martin, John H.
MARTIN, Martha Ann, W3574, DK, Martin, John
MARTIN, Mary A. W206, CF, Martin, Isaac Thomas
MARTIN, Mary Ann, W1861, SN, Martin, James Glascow

Index to Tennessee Confederate Pension Applications

MARTIN, Mary Catherine, W7522, HN, Martin, Calvin Gaines
MARTIN, Mary E. W688, DK, Martin, John D.
MARTIN, Mary E. W4210, HN, Martin, James Polk
MARTIN, Mary Emma, W11013, W, Martin, Joseph Franklin
MARTIN, Mary Jane, W2705, ME, Martin, John C.
MARTIN, Mary Louise, W10597, HY, Martin, Isaiah Benjamin
MARTIN, Mary Rebecca, W7193, ST, Martin, Samuel
MARTIN, Mattie, W9487, HI, Martin, James Hillard
MARTIN, Mattie J. W8755, LI, Martin, Ben F.
MARTIN, Mattie Jane, W11098, RO, Martin, Benjamin Harley
MARTIN, Milton Scott, S11887, Greer's Regt. Partisan Rangers, Cav.
MARTIN, Missouri, W10461, WL, Martin, Joe J.
MARTIN, N. H. S10092, 22nd Inf.
MARTIN, N. R. S3293, FR, 17th Inf.
MARTIN, Nancy, W3325, HE, Martin, Wm. F.
MARTIN, Nannie Elizabeth, W5181, CC, Martin, John Roe
MARTIN, Overton C. S1881, B, 4th Cav.
MARTIN, P. P. S5686, RB, 1st Inf.
MARTIN, P. T. S15761, WI, 17th Inf.
MARTIN, Perneley T. W4429, J, Martin, Thomas L.
MARTIN, Ransom Gwyn, S16066, W, 16th Inf.
MARTIN, Robert, S6351, WE, 21st Va. Inf.
MARTIN, Rose Ellen, W10871, RB, Martin, George Patrick
MARTIN, S. R. S14774, CY, 25th Inf.
MARTIN, Sally Lucy, W2524, SH, Martin, Wiley Pnkny. Mangrum
MARTIN, Sam, S11129, MT, 6th Ky. Inf.
MARTIN, Sampson, S5213, W, 16th Inf.
MARTIN, Sarah Elizabeth, W9563, DK, Martin, Josiah Franklin
MARTIN, Sarah G. W866, MC, Martin, Washington Franklin
MARTIN, Sarah Jane, W2882, MA, Martin, Wm. Dawson
MARTIN, Sue Brittain, W10654, WL, Martin, Andrew Bennett
MARTIN, Sue Mary, W2269, D, Martin, Henry Alexander
MARTIN, Susana, W732, T, Martin, John Wallace
MARTIN, T. S10385, CE, 2nd Ala. Inf.
MARTIN, Tennessee A. W1187, DI, Martin, Cave Johnson
MARTIN, Thomas L. S1249, J, 1st Inf.
MARTIN, Thomas T. S7736, MU, 11th (Holman's) Cav.
MARTIN, Thurse A. W6021, WH, Martin, Julius C.
MARTIN, Virginia Ann, W3840, H, Martin, James Monroe
MARTIN, W. P. M. S7861, SH, 34th Miss. Inf.
MARTIN, William, S14718, MO, 63rd N.C. Inf.
MARTIN, William Thomas, S10511, DY, 9th Inf.
MARTIN, William W. S842, SM, 4th Cav.
MARTINDALE, D. W. S473, L, 13th N.C. Inf.
MARTINDALE, Susan Jane, W2966, T, Martindale, Daniel Webster
MARTINDALE, W. M. S6252, MN, 32nd Miss. Inf.
MASENGALE, Joseph, S877, GU, 16th Inf.
MASENGIL, R. N. S11258, PO, 2nd Ga. Cav.
MASEY, L. R. S8300, W, 11th Cav.
MASH, A. D. S7911, CF, 24th Inf.
MASH, America Elizabeth, W6166, B, Mash, Wm.
MASH, William, S14706, B, 2nd Inf.
MASHBORN, Aaron, S3430, SE, 62nd Inf.
MASHBURN, Anderson, S11052, SE, 62nd Inf.
MASHBURN, Eliza Jane, W2091, HR, Mashburn, James Edward
MASHBURN, Marilla, W3395, U, Mashburn, Calaway
MASHBURN, Nancy C. W7021, SE, Mashburn, A.
MASON, Bennet, S2366, DI, 11th Inf.
MASON, D. D. S9529, RB, 3rd Ky. Cav.
MASON, D. J. S5226, WL, 7th Bn. Cav.
MASON, E. C. S10712, D, 3rd Ky. Cav.
MASON, E. R. S15338, T, 22nd (Barteau's) Cav.
MASON, Ella Otey [Anderson], W10314, G, Mason, Thomas Walton, [Later married Anderson]
MASON, F. Y. S12634, F, 7th (Duckworth's) Cav.
MASON, G. S661, RB, 30th Inf.
MASON, Harrison, S8026, RO, 58th N.C. Inf.
MASON, Isabell Coleman, W10849, SH, Mason, Jackson Lafayette

MASON, J. E. S10937, RU, 24th S.C. Inf.
MASON, J. F. S5461, DK, Marshall's Co. Lt. Art.
MASON, Jackson L. S13503, SH, 17th Miss. Inf.
MASON, James E. S9163, MA, 20th Inf.
MASON, James J. S12223, RU, Carter's Scouts, Cav.
MASON, John, S1184, CO, 62nd N.C. Inf.
MASON, John, S1215, GR, 19th Inf.
MASON, John, S13005, CA, 16th Inf.
MASON, John L. S6123, BO, 29th N.C. Inf.
MASON, L. H. S2043, CC, 20th Inf.
MASON, Larkin, S2143, MO, 3rd Inf.
MASON, Lucinda P. W7639, D, Mason, Elbert C.
MASON, Martha J. W5168, WL, Mason, David Thomas
MASON, Mary Candyce, W4339, RB, Mason, Gustavus Henry
MASON, Mary E. W3197, D, Mason, Bennett
MASON, P. D. S8214, G, 38th Inf.
MASON, Pernelia Angilina, W8733, RU, Mason, Wm. McGun
MASON, Peter, S6701, MO, 56th Va. Inf.
MASON, Plunk, C182, HI, Unassigned, Wagon Train
MASON, R. M. S11492, MR, 3rd Confederate Cav.
MASON, Susan E. W8120, T, Mason, Jesse W.
MASON, Texie, W7356, MO, Mason, Larkin
MASON, W. B. S16021, FR, 48th (Nixon's) Inf.
MASON, William D. S11245, CO, 62nd N.C. Inf.
MASONER, Amanda, W575, ME, Masoner, John T.
MASONER, John T. S4690, ME, 5th (McKenzie's) Cav.
MASSENGALE, James M. S9457, MR, 4th Ga. Cav.
MASSENGILL, A. P. S9780, CH, 21st (Wilson's) Cav.
MASSENGILL, I. J. S2433, CH, 52nd Inf.
MASSENGILL, Jasper, S5792, CH, 51st Inf.
MASSENGILL, John D. S15358, SU, 8th (Smith's) Cav.
MASSENGILL, Louie V. W7800, O, Massengill, Wm. Zachariah
MASSENGILL, Martha A. W7784, PO, Massengill, R. N.
MASSENGILL, Mary Ann, W10701, CH, Massengill, Sidney Monroe

MASSENGILL, Mary E. W2272, SU, Massengill, George Dallus
MASSENGILL, Mattie E. W7437, CH, Massengill, Isaac Jasper
MASSENGILL, Nancy E. W311, R, Massengill, James M.
MASSENGILL, S. D. S2575, CH, 21st Cav.
MASSENGILL, S. M. S6516, CH, 21st (Wilson's) Cav.
MASSENGILL, Sarah, W11097, MN, Massengill, Allen P.
MASSEY, B. L. S4609, WL, 11th Mo. Inf.
MASSEY, Catherine Elizabeth, W929, W1447, WL, Massey, John Wm.
MASSEY, Fannie, W5456, MS, Massey, Wm. G.
MASSEY, George W. S3889, SU, 63rd Va. Inf.
MASSEY, J. H. S1033, CO, 62nd Inf.
MASSEY, James F. S6199, MOO, 8th Inf.
MASSEY, John, S9880, D, 9th (Ward's) Cav.
MASSEY, John W. S4592, WL, 31st Miss. Inf.
MASSEY, Lucinda E. W4426, WL, Massey, Benjamin Lewis
MASSEY, Margaret, W9219, WL, Massey, Arch.
MASSEY, Margaret J. W4508, MOO, Massey, George Washington
MASSEY, Martha M. W392, D, Massey, James
MASSEY, Mattie, W8809, B, Massey, Constant Smith
MASSEY, Narsis Alcy, W10615, HN, Massey, Wm. Henry Harrison
MASSEY, Sarah Williams, W3614, WL, Massey, Wm. Y.
MASSEY, W. G. S2246, G, 4th Cav.
MASSEY, William A. S14593, SU, 37th Va. Inf.
MASSEY, William G. S81, MS, 1st Inf.
MASSON, Harrison, S13780, MC, 43rd Inf.
MASTERS, Joyce Lou, W9489, CY, Masters, Thomas Carrol
MASTERS, Lucy A. W4108, OV, Masters, Samuel Thomas
MASTERS, M. A. S3073, OV, 8th Cav.
MASTERS, T. C. S12533, J, Shaw's Bn. Cav.
MASTIN, Richard, S14423, HM, 30th Va. Inf.
MATHENY, Almira, W915, PI, Matheny, James L.
MATHENY, James L. S15381, WE, 5th Inf.
MATHENY, James M. S11890, WE, 15th Inf.
MATHERLY, D. F. S12225, SN, 7th Inf.
MATHERLY, Mary Elizabeth, W7921, SN, Matherly, Daniel Francis

MATHERLY, S. H. S13388, WL, 45th Inf.
MATHES, E. A. S14243, RU, 8th (Smith's) Cav.
MATHES, J. Harvey, S3548, SH, 37th Inf.
MATHES, J. R. S16289, WL, 18th Inf.
MATHES, W. G. S15079, RU, 8th (Smith's) Cav.
MATHEWS, Linsey, S2962, MO, 26th Inf.
MATHEWS, R. S. S9263, CC, 6th Inf.
MATHEWS, William, S11841, D, 2nd Ky. Cav.
MATHIS, Ann, W3168, ST, Mathis, Wm. E.
MATHIS, C. S9734, CT, 1st N.C. Bn.
MATHIS, Dal, C159, HY, Undetermined
MATHIS, David, S9206, HA, 63rd Inf.
MATHIS, J. B. S1350, WI, 1st Ala. Inf.
MATHIS, John A. S4618, SN, 2nd Ky. Inf.
MATHIS, Lorina A. W8353, CT, Mathis, J. Calvin
MATHIS, Martha Alice, W10339, W8159, P, Mathis, Jesse Manuel
MATHIS, Mollie, W9606, RU, Mathis, E. A.
MATHIS, Nellie E. W8158, DI, Mathis, W. J.
MATHIS, R. W. S7023, LK, 7th (Duckworth's) Cav.
MATHIS, W. H. S6383, S14563, LE, 3rd (Clack's) Inf.
MATHIS, W. H. S11378, WE, 12th Ky. Cav.
MATHIS, W. J. S11184, D, 11th Inf.
MATHIS, W. J. S11462, O, 12th Inf.
MATLEY, Sarah M. W6152, F, Matley, James J.
MATLOCH, Philip N. S14729, O, Carter's Scouts, Cav.
MATLOCK, A. H. S9874, PO, 5th (McKenzie's) Cav.
MATLOCK, Ann Rebecca, W3583, PO, Matlock, Abraham Harris
MATLOCK, Mary Ann, W1265, MN, Matlock, Moses M.
MATLOCK, Mary I. W7544, O, Matlock, Phillip N.
MATLOCK, Prudilla, W14, D, Matlock, James P.
MATLOCK, Rhoda Ann, W538, DI, Matlock, Lewis
MATLOCK, W. H. S8772, PU, 25th Inf.
MATLOCK, William, S406, HU, 54th Inf.
MATTHEWS, Alice Bailey, W10332, D, Matthews, George I.
MATTHEWS, Amanda, W8956, OV, Matthews, Richard D.
MATTHEWS, Amanda J. W3493, D, Matthews, Henry Clay
MATTHEWS, B. F. S269, HU, 24th Inf.
MATTHEWS, Cloie M. W10921, MC, Matthews, J. C.
MATTHEWS, Cynthia C. W6303, K, Matthews, Glover Harrison
MATTHEWS, Emily J. W7254, D, Matthews, Daniel H.
MATTHEWS, Euphemia, W6759, F, Matthews, James Still
MATTHEWS, G. H. S10285, K, 27th Va. Cav.
MATTHEWS, J. A. S11435, HN, 9th Bn. Cav.
MATTHEWS, J. A. S15177, MU, 9th Bn. Cav.
MATTHEWS, J. C. S7711, MC, 8th (Dibrell's) Cav.
MATTHEWS, J. F. S14061, G, 6th Inf.
MATTHEWS, J. H. S9464, MA, 38th Inf.
MATTHEWS, J. S. S2108, OV, 25th Inf.
MATTHEWS, J. S. S8287, F, 13th Inf.
MATTHEWS, J. T. S5817, D, 20th Inf.
MATTHEWS, James H. S9043, HU, 10th Cav.
MATTHEWS, James W. S2129, CU, 1st Cav.
MATTHEWS, John T. S4243, DI, 11th Inf.
MATTHEWS, John V. S14144, SH, Cocke's Regt. Ark. Inf.
MATTHEWS, Martha, W7252, MC, Matthews, Linzy
MATTHEWS, Mary Catherine, W1261, WA, Matthews, Felix Henry
MATTHEWS, Matthew, S13854, S14449, SM, 22nd (Barteau's) Cav.
MATTHEWS, Nancy Jane, W7528, OV, Matthews, John Sims
MATTHEWS, Nannie L. W7521, CC, Matthews, Robert
MATTHEWS, R. D. S2646, OV, 8th Inf.
MATTHEWS, S. E. S15510, GI, 3rd (Clack's) Inf.
MATTHEWS, S. J. S1693, LA, 9th Ala. Inf.
MATTHEWS, Samuel, S9364, G, 19th & 20th Consolidated Cav.
MATTHEWS, Sarah Elizabeth, W2693, G, Matthews, Wm. Edward
MATTHEWS, Susanna J. W2469, O, Matthews, Wm. Taylor
MATTHEWS, Virginia Finch, W1946, LA, Matthews, Ben Franklin
MATTHEWS, W. H. S10837, D, 20th Inf.
MATTHEWS, Wilhelmina, W5330, SH, Matthews, Wm. L.
MATTHEWSON, George, C37, HN, Ga. Troops
MATTHIAS, W. J. S9949, D, 2nd (Robison's) Inf.

MATTOX, Nancy S. C. W2243, SU, Mattox, John J.
MAUDLIN, W. A. S12839, MA, 42nd Ga. Inf.
MAUK, Amanda Melvina, W3914, WA, Mauk, Alfred Embree
MAULDIN, Virginia Washington, W6900, HR, Mauldin, Wm. Dread
MAULEY, Sarah Frances, W3324, MA, Mauley, Caleb Allen
MAUPIN, Annie B. W8123, SH, Maupin, James H.
MAUPIN, Henry, S9164, C, 2nd (Ashby's) Cav.
MAUPIN, J. A. S14835, O, 22nd (Barteau's) Cav.
MAUPIN, James H. S11848, WE, 22nd Inf.
MAUPIN, James J. S12571, WA, Unassigned (Nitre Bureau)
MAUPIN, Nan Rebecca, W8306, O, Maupin, J. A.
MAUPIN, R. T. S15018, O, 33rd Inf.
MAUPIN, W. C. S12463, WA, Lynch's Lt. Art.
MAURY, Branch, C128, F, 17th Miss. Inf.
MAURY, F. C. S11671, D, 42nd Inf.
MAURY, Matt F. S13469, WI, Baxter's Co. Lt. Art.
MAUZY, Ida A. W10015, SH, Mauzy, John W. Plunkett
MAXEY, A. B. S10122, DI, 14th Inf.
MAXEY, H. L. S6826, K, Ramsey's Battery, Art.
MAXEY, Joseph P. S799, M, 44th Inf.
MAXEY, Luvisa L. W4889, M, Maxey, Joseph P.
MAXEY, Martha E. W996, FR, Maxey, Wm. H.
MAXWELL, Albert, S6394, H, 43rd Inf.
MAXWELL, Carline, W5439, H, Maxwell, Albert
MAXWELL, Elisha D. S636, T, Hvy. Art.
MAXWELL, Elizabeth, W689, PO, Maxwell, James
MAXWELL, Isabella, W11081, HA, Maxwell, Jas. H.
MAXWELL, J. C. S4728, SN, 30th Inf.
MAXWELL, J. H. S13037, HW, 25th N.C. Inf.
MAXWELL, J. L. S15793, MU, 3rd (Clack's) Inf.
MAXWELL, Jhn W. S8515, HN, 5th Inf.
MAXWELL, Nancy Matilda, W685, PU, Maxwell, David Mock
MAXWELL, R. H. S16578, WI, Forrest's Scouts, Cav.
MAXWELL, R. P. S382, O, Undetermined
MAXWELL, Robert A. S16258, DK, 24th Inf.
MAXWELL, Sallie B. W11075, D, Maxwell, R. H.
MAXWELL, William F. S8002, RU, 45th Inf.
MAY, Ben, S6121, LI, 4th (McLemore's) Cav.
MAY, Benjamin F. S3169, D, 44th Inf.
MAY, Callie Dona, W9432, LA, May, Albert Harrison
MAY, Charles W. S15836, GI, 6th (Wheeler's) Cav.
MAY, J. C. S9200, S16527, HN, 44th Inf.
MAY, J. F. S15280, GI, 19th (Biffle's) Cav.
MAY, J. W. S1306, MN, 4th Cav.
MAY, J. W. S11472, HR, 7th Miss. Cav.
MAY, James L. S4218, SH, 14th Ala. Inf.
MAY, Jane, W5404, LI, May, Ben
MAY, Jesse, S3043, HU, Napier's Bn. Cav.
MAY, Louisa Jane, W8336, HU, May, Henry
MAY, Mary Jane, W2422, D, May, Benjamin Franklin
MAY, Sallie E. W2826, GI, May, Daniel Wm.
MAY, Sarah, W5839, HR, May, Wm. C.
MAY, W. C. S3919, HR, 1st Cav.
MAY, W. H. S5656, SN, 9th (Bennett's) Cav.
MAYBERRY, Elizabeth Jane, W5851, LA, Mayberry, Robert Newton
MAYBERRY, Elizabeth M. W5475, WI, Mayberry, Henry George W.
MAYBERRY, Jim, C204, HI, 24th Inf.
MAYBERRY, Lucinda, W554, WI, Mayberry, Edward
MAYBERRY, Margaret S. W7787, J, Mayberry, John P.
MAYBERY, Catherine, W216, WH, Maybery, Wm. Thomas
MAYES, Burrel C. S8743, RB, 30th Inf.
MAYES, Harrison, C44, MU, 1st Cav.
MAYES, Henry S. S14813, MU, 6th (Wheeler's) Cav.
MAYES, J. F. S6617, SN, 30th Inf.
MAYES, J. M. S8631, SC, 35th Inf.
MAYES, Mary Eveline, W7667, GI, Mayes, Richard Franklin
MAYES, Nancy Jane, W7583, D, Mayes, Burwell Chester
MAYFIELD, Bernice Henderson, W3528, MA, Mayfield, George Washington
MAYFIELD, Della, W9774, MU, Mayfield, Wm.
MAYFIELD, Isaac, S5081, CF, 32nd Inf.
MAYFIELD, J. R. S11540, HR, 22nd Inf.
MAYFIELD, Jasper A. S12042, SC, 38th Inf.

Index to Tennessee Confederate Pension Applications

MAYFIELD, John Henderson, S2441, WI, 9th (Ward's) Cav.
MAYFIELD, John W. S7533, RU, 18th Inf.
MAYFIELD, Mary E. W7710, RU, Mayfield, John W.
MAYFIELD, T. B. S2647, CY, 4th Cav.
MAYFIELD, W. E. S14757, S480, DI, 49th Inf.
MAYHAM, Billy, S4815, O, 33rd Inf.
MAYHEW, Mary Kendrick, W10295, SH, Mayhew, George Washington
MAYNARD, Britana, W8567, V, Maynard, Kendrick M.
MAYNARD, Henrietta, W8310, MT, Maynard, Alfred
MAYNARD, K. M. S12402, V, 1st Confederate Cav.
MAYNARD, Mary Jane, W8947, L, Maynard, Paschal Thaddeus
MAYNOR, Elizabeth, W1964, M, Maynor, Vincent
MAYO, Agnes Frances, W5128, K, Mayo, Roderick Payne
MAYO, Albert, S7388, SH, 4th Inf.
MAYO, Freelove Albatine, W5840, WE, Mayo, George D.
MAYO, G. D. S8974, WE, 20th Cav.
MAYO, Margaret Ellen, W6671, T, Mayo, Henry Jordan
MAYO, Mary Joanna, W3078, SH, Mayo, Albert
MAYO, O. B. S2742, DE, Undetermined
MAYO, William H. S7796, G, 43rd N.C. Inf.
MAYS, A. H. S8225, MA, 19th Cav.
MAYS, Bettie, W3506, D, Mays, Silas Linton
MAYS, D. D. S12527, F, 14th (Neely's) Cav.
MAYS, E. S16261, DE, 14th (McCarver's) Ark. Inf.
MAYS, Francis A. S3886, WI, Sparkman's Co. Lt. Art.
MAYS, James, S1808, SC, 16th Inf.
MAYS, Mahala Margaret, W1116, MA, Mays, Marlin Thadeus
MAYS, Sallie, W5425, MA, Mays, A. H.
MAYS, Samuel L. S150, HU, 10th Cav., On misc. microfilm reel
MAYS, Stewart, S4479, WI, 10th Cav.
MAYS, William F. S14620, 12th Inf.
MAYSE, Matilda G. W457, HM, Mayse, Joseph C.
MCABEE, Lucinda, W3255, MA, McAbee, Pinkney J.
MCABEE, P. J. S5288, MA, 16th N.C. Inf.
MCABEE, Susan, W3679, GE, McAbee, T. L.
MCABEE, T. L. S2681, GE, 16th S.C. Inf.
MCABEE, W. B. S7421, RU, 39th Ga. Inf.
MCADAMS, E. M. S7920, MS, 17th Inf.
MCADAMS, Elizabeth S. W1301, MS, McAdams, E. M.
MCADAMS, G. J. S7165, D, 20th Inf.
MCADAMS, James B. S7534, SN, 20th Inf.
MCADAMS, Martha J. W4886, H, McAdams, Wm. J.
MCADAMS, Sarah Elizabeth, W9278, SN, McAdams, James Boles
MCADOO, J. C. S15736, S14553, RU, 4th (McLemore's) Cav.
MCADOO, Mollie Byrn, W3975, WL, McAdoo, James Clark
MCADOO, Sallie, W2031, McAdoo, Wm. Josephus
MCADOO, Sarah F. W680, G, McAdoo, Adolphis Evins
MCADOO, Sophronia C. W631, McAdoo, Robert E.
MCADOO, Sue Brown, W11044, McAdoo, J. C.
MCADOO, W. J. S7748, 12th Inf.
MCAFEE, Amanda, W9291, W7434, W9350, MU, McAfee, Thomas Rowe
MCAFEE, Eliza A. W1749, LI, McAfee, James Monroe
MCAFEE, Martha Elizabeth, W7460, H, McAfee, Thomas Wesley
MCAFEE, T. R. S11547, P, 16th Ga. Inf.
MCAFEE, Thomas W. S14483, H, 63rd Ga. Inf.
MCAFFNEY, Jennie Loyd, W4651, K, McAffney, John A.
MCAFFREY, John A. S1730, K, 1st Ga. Regulars
MCALISTER, R. M. S9855, HI, 11th (Holman's) Bn. Cav.
MCALISTER, Thomas M. S12897, HM, Unassigned (Sapers and Miners)
MCALPIN, Nancy A. W2792, MN, McAlpin, Benjamin Franklin
MCALPINE, C. H. S15583, MU, Unassigned
MCANALLY, John W. S4642, B, 17th Inf.
MCANLEY, Martha Maria, W7844, SH, McAnley, Gus H.
MCANLEY, R. R. S11520, HO, 50th Inf.
MCARTHUR, Matilda, W8141, WI, McArthur, P. P.
MCARTHUR, Mattie Lucy, W9441, WI, McArthur, John Littleton

Index to Tennessee Confederate Pension Applications

MCATEER, H. D. S3376, MS, 17th Inf.
MCAULEY, A. M, S5719, HO, 50th Inf.
MCAULEY, G. H. S11003, HO, 14th Inf.
MCBEE, G. B. S10457, PO, 11th Ga. Mtd. Inf.
MCBEE, G. D. S12572, MA, 60th Inf.
MCBEE, Isaac, S2961, CL, 12th Bn. (Day's) Cav.
MCBEE, J. M. S7389, MG, 1st Cav.
MCBEE, John, S2764, CL, 2nd (Ashby's) Cav.
MCBEE, John W. S2488, GR, 22nd (Barteau's) Cav.
MCBEE, Margaret J. W8167, PO, McBee, G. B.
MCBEE, Mary Christine, W7064, RO, McBee, John Montgomery
MCBRAYER, Elizabeth J. W5694, MO, McBrayer, Wm. E.
MCBRAYER, W. E. S13938, MO, 52nd Ga. Inf.
MCBRIDE, Albert, S2876, RB, 25th Inf.
MCBRIDE, B. F. S12668, MU, 6th (Wheeler's) Cav.
MCBRIDE, F. E. P. S13398, D, 23rd Inf.
MCBRIDE, Jane, W7019, W, McBride, Mathew
MCBRIDE, John Osier, S14286, O, 35th Inf.
MCBRIDE, Matthew, S5289, W, 16th Inf.
MCBRIDE, Sarah, W2159, CF, McBride, Albert
MCBRIDE, W. B. S8547, WH, 25th Inf.
MCBRIDE, W. B. S16412, MO, 4th Mo. Cav.
MCBRIDE, W. C. S4996, W, 16th Inf.
MCBRIDE, William P. S1545, V, 5th Inf.
MCBROOM, Flem, S6187, PU, 17th Inf.
MCBROOM, Nancy E. W2542, G, McBroom, John Wm.
MCBRYDE, Martha Leonard, W10503, D, McBryde, Samuel H.
MCCABE, James A. S242, D, Forrest's Old Regt. Cav.
MCCABE, Maggie, W169, D, McCabe, James Alexander
MCCABE, Margaret, W1907, MT, McCabe, Thomas
MCCABE, Thomas, S3735, MT, 10th Inf.
MCCAGE, Aaron R. S14312, G, 10th Cav.
MCCAGE, S. L. S14313, G, 53rd Inf.
MCCAIN, Mary E.   See Mary E. Mitchell
MCCAIN, R. S. S5021, HN, 46th Inf.
MCCAIN, William S. S7869, 46th Inf.
MCCALEB, Thomas P. S10058, HI, 11th Inf.
MCCALL, H. L. S8271, SM, 24th Inf.
MCCALL, James, S747, S1218, J, Hamilton's Bn. Cav.
MCCALL, Lillie Dance, W7258, G, McCall, Wm. Martin

MCCALL, T. C. S14641, HN, 8th Fla. Inf.
MCCALL, T. W. S14208, SH, 18th Miss. Cav.
MCCALL, Vina, W4255, ME, McCall, Wm.
MCCALL, William, S8780, ME, 26th Inf.
MCCALL, William M. S14203, G, 7th Inf.
MCCALL, William S. S248, HN, 12th Ky. Cav.
MCCALLA, J. G. S13816, SH, 12th (Green's) Cav.
MCCALLA, Martha L. W1965, SH, McCalla, Thomas G.
MCCALLUM, Lourinda Hardin, W3008, K, McCallum, James Rogers
MCCALLUM, Mary Amanda, W8305, P, McCallum, James K. Polk
MCCALLUM, Medora Rose, W2449, GI, McCallum, James Joseph
MCCALLUM, Sallie M. W8079, SH, McCallum, John F.
MCCAMPBELL, A. J. S11602, MR, 42nd Inf.
MCCAMPBELL, C. B. S14117, BO, Lynch's Battery, Art.
MCCAMPBELL, James, S8411, BO, 4th Ga. Inf.
MCCAMPBELL, Mary Elizabeth, W7411, BO, McCampbell, James
MCCAMY, Annie Ruth, W6519, GE, McCamy, Calvin D.
MCCAMY, C. D. S5439, GE, 29th Inf.
MCCANDLESS, Martha, W4891, SH, McCandless, Wm. Henry
MCCANDLESS, Rebecca, W5396, MU, McCandless, Thomas Brown
MCCANLESS, J. B. S5889, JE, 3rd (Clack's) Inf.
MCCANLESS, Lavinia W. W312, JE, McCanless, Samuel H.
MCCANLESS, Nancy A. W2955, GI, McCanless, Thomas Samuel
MCCANLESS, Samuel Houston, S391, JE, 3rd Inf.
MCCANLEY, Virginia Elizabeth, W7033, HU, McCanley, Richmond
MCCANN, Frances Lemyra, W1068, HR, McCann, James
MCCANN, James, S6023, HR, 22nd Inf.
MCCANN, Jemima Jane, W425, P, McCann, Edward
MCCANSE, William P. S4261, LI, 8th Inf.
MCCARLEY, George W. S6928, D, 18th Inf.
MCCARLEY, Sallie Phillips, W3894, D, McCarley, George W.
MCCARRELL, William, S883, LO, 43rd Inf.

MCCARTER, E. C, S5738, SH, 9th Inf.
MCCARTER, G. W. S3004, M, 4th Bn. Cav.
MCCARTER, Rhoda, W5656, SE, McCarter, George Birdett
MCCARTER, S. A. S10062, HR, 14th Inf.
MCCARTER, Wm. C171, BO, 62nd Inf.
MCCARTNEY, Threet H. S13532, WL, 45th Inf.
MCCARTY, Eliza, W10916, MG, McCarty, James Carmichael
MCCARTY, George W. S2059, DK, 28th Inf.
MCCARTY, J. C. S204, GR, 59th Inf.
MCCARTY, J. C. S11548, MG, 60th Inf.
MCCARTY, John, S6485, BR, 5th (McKenzie's) Cav.
MCCARTY, Malissa Elen, W2695, BR, McCarty, John
MCCARTY, Margaret W. W2231, BR, McCarty, Thomas Cowan
MCCARTY, Mary, W2605, DK, McCarty, George Washington
MCCARTY, Samuel, S8217, BR, 62nd Inf.
MCCARVER, L. A. S12635, D, 25th Inf.
MCCARVER, Mary, W10843, GU, McCarver, Elias
MCCARVER, W. H. S16077, D, 25th Inf.
MCCASKILL, Cynthia, W5776, HR, McCaskill, John E.
MCCASKILL, Faith Elizabeth, W265, HR, McCaskill, James Armstrong
MCCASKILL, John E. S12702, HR, 4th Inf.
MCCASKILL, W. H. S14866, F, 12th Cav.
MCCASLIN, B. T. S12313, DI, Fisher's Co. Art.
MCCASLIN, Martha Elizabeth, W9048, HI, McCaslin, Benjamin Tidwell
MCCASLIN, S. J. S7535, G, 12th Ky. Cav.
MCCAUL, Mary Elizabeth, W2131, SH, McCaul, Robert Franklin
MCCAUL, Robert F. S10721, GI, 11th (Holman's) Cav.
MCCAULEY, John C. S11837, HU, 11th Inf.
MCCAULEY, Louisa Eugenia, W8029, HU, McCauley, John C.
MCCAULEY, Richmond, S320, HU, 11th Inf.
MCCAULEY, W. H. S14603, DI, 11th Inf.
MCCLAIN, Daniel W. S7756, WE, 16th (Logwood's) Cav.
MCCLAIN, Frances Elizabeth, W4162, MN, McClain, McD.
MCCLAIN, G. W. S11721, O, 5th Inf.
MCCLAIN, George Alexander, S13843, LI, 31st Inf.

MCCLAIN, Harry H. S13274, D, 7th Inf.
MCCLAIN, J. R. S4322, HO, 4th Ky. Inf.
MCCLAIN, James P. S3319, HE, 18th Inf.
MCCLAIN, L. D. S7359, D, 4th Ga. Inf.
MCCLAIN, Martha, W1589, HE, McClain, James P.
MCCLAIN, Martin, S13577, LE, 3rd (Clack's) Inf.
MCCLAIN, McDonald, S10989, MN, 6th (Wheeler's) Cav.
MCCLAIN, Sue L. W6819, WL, McClain, John B.
MCCLAIN, William A. S8309, WE, 36th Ala. Inf.
MCCLAMRACK, G. W. S15741, MS, 4th Inf.
MCCLAMROCH, Mary Catherine, W7946, W9433, D, McClamroch, George Washington
MCCLANAHAN, Arthusa Jane, W8770, HI, McClanahan, Wm. M.
MCCLANAHAN, Ellen Davy, W10964, DE, McClanahan, Pinckney M.
MCCLANAHAN, Frances, W3872, LE, McClanahan, R. L.
MCCLANAHAN, H. D. S10473, D, 10th (DeMoss') Cav.
MCCLANAHAN, John A. S1928, D, 12th Ky. Cav.
MCCLANAHAN, M. B. S751, WI, 11th Inf.
MCCLANAHAN, W. W. S15196, HI, 9th Cav.
MCCLARAN, Annie, W9240, RU, McClaran, Thomas J.
MCCLARD, Leah Elvada, W5507, TR, McClard, T. J.
MCCLARD, T. J. S9811, TR, 8th Inf.
MCCLAREN, Bob, C180, SH, 13th Cav.
MCCLARTY, John W. S15984, S15152, SH, 3rd (Forrest's) Cav.
MCCLATCHEY, Julia Eliza, W7459, H, McClatchey, Wm. Perrin
MCCLATCHEY, W. P. S15451, H, Caper's Ga. Cadets
MCCLAUAHAN, J. M. S11508, HI, 9th Bn. (Gantt's) Cav.
MCCLEAREN, A. C. S14646, LE, 24th Inf.
MCCLEAREN, John F. S2874, HD, 22nd (Barteau's) Cav.
MCCLEAREN, Sarah A. W6049, HI, McClearen, John Addams
MCCLEAREN, Susan Ann, W9578, LE, McClearen, Wm. Addison
MCCLELLAN, A. S131, SU, 4th Cav.

MCCLELLAN, Margaret, W7514, LI, McClellan, Wm. Wilson
MCCLELLAN, W. C. S15076, SM, Buck Hart's Independent Co.
MCCLELLAN, William W. S9775, LI, 1st (Turney's) Inf.
MCCLELLAND, John R. S15314, MS, 53rd Inf.
MCCLELLAND, Mary M. W2606, SU, McClelland, Samuel A.
MCCLELLAND, R. A. S4478, BR, Undetermined
MCCLELLAND, Samuel A. S5746, SU, 13th Bn. Va. Reserves
MCCLELLON, I. L. S5058, HW, 3rd Inf.
MCCLELLON, S. P. S889, M, 28th Inf.
MCCLENDON, James C. S13389, D, 20th Inf.
MCCLENDON, Mary, W930, ME, McClendon, Dennis
MCCLENDON, Tabitha Graves, W10860, D, McClendon, James Clark
MCCLENNY, John W. S2489, LI, 44th Inf.
MCCLEUR, James, S6247, GU, 1st (Turney's) Inf.
MCCLINTOCK, Joe, S6267, MS, 24th S.C. Inf.
MCCLINTOCK, Kate M. W9624, MA, McClintock, David Fletcher
MCCLISTER, J. H. S16154, HM, 2nd (Ashby's) Cav.
MCCLISTER, Maggie Ford, W9880, HM, McClister, James Henry
MCCLUNEY, A. G. S9972, T, 2nd Ala. Cav.
MCCLUNEY, Catherine Elizabeth, W4071, T, McCluney, Wm. Watus
MCCLUNEY, Mary Jane, W3171, T, McCluney, Adam Garrison
MCCLUNY, S. G. S13403, T, 2nd Ala. Cav.
MCCLURE, Beckey D. W7442, FR, McClure, John Wesley
MCCLURE, Emma Clara, W5108, WA, McClure, Ewing Graham
MCCLURE, F. M. S13850, HN, 12th Ky. Cav.
MCCLURE, Henry M. S1009, MS, 53rd Inf.
MCCLURE, John Wesley, S2581, HW, 1st (Turney's) Inf.
MCCLURE, Mollie Ann, W6262, O, McClure, Samuel Houston
MCCLURE, Sallie, W7179, GU, McClure, James
MCCLURE, W. F. S11617, HU, 1st Inf.
MCCLURKAN, Nancy Frances, W624, DI, McClurkan, Samuel Brison
MCCOLGAN, J. T. S14632, SN, 14th Ky. Cav.

MCCOLLUM, A. N. S15679, SH, Palmetto, Lt. Art.
MCCOLLUM, B. C. S8722, G, 22nd Inf.
MCCOLLUM, Callie, W9560, CH, McCollum, Edwin Layfayette
MCCOLLUM, E. A. S11611, MS, 53rd Inf.
MCCOLLUM, E. L. S10353, CH, 21st (Wilson's) Cav.
MCCOLLUM, Elizabeth Sally, W8284, LE, McCollum, James Egbert
MCCOLLUM, J. E. S2609, LE, 42nd Inf.
MCCOLLUM, J. E. S7098, LE, 42nd Inf.
MCCOLLUM, Martha E. W6931, G, McCollum, Benjamin C.
MCCOLLUM, Martha J. W6746, MS, McCollum, Ephraim A.
MCCOLLUM, Thomas Jefferson, S7622, G, 20th Inf.
MCCOLPIN, Elisha Henderson, S12911, MA, 15th Cav.
MCCONICO, John M. S4956, GI, 45th Inf.
MCCONICO, Kate T. W7244, GI, McConico, John M.
MCCONKEY, A. B. S15318, D, 3rd (Lillard's) Mtd. Inf.
MCCONKEY, Mary Sue, W5288, MO, McConkey, John
MCCONNEL, Mary V. W3509, MS, McConnel, A. S.
MCCONNELL, Ella Goff, W5730, SH, McConnell, Benjamin Franklin
MCCONNELL, Hugh, S6924, SH, 21st Inf.
MCCONNELL, Isaac, S2979, GR, 16th Bn. (Neal's) Cav.
MCCONNELL, J. C. S8705, DY, Jones' Battery, Hvy. Art.
MCCONNELL, J. W. S13259, MS, 11th (Holman's) Cav.
MCCONNELL, John W. S14436, D, 16th Inf.
MCCONNELL, Mary A. W7594, MU, McConnell, W. E.
MCCONNELL, Mary J. W8132, MS, McConnell, Jackson W.
MCCONNELL, Pamela Jane, W8658, MS, McConnell, Wm. Jasper
MCCONNELL, Sam H. S10205, GR, 16th Bn. Cav.
MCCONNELL, Thomas J. S14549, HW, 7th Bn. Cav.
MCCONNELL, Tinnie, W10115, D, McConnell, Samuel P.

Index to Tennessee Confederate Pension Applications

MCCONNELL, W. E. S13260, MS, 11th (Holman's) Cav.
MCCONNELL, William W. S11436, HN, 7th Cav.
MCCOOL, J. Vince, S11541, CE, 2nd (Robison's) Inf.
MCCOOL, Martha J. W5798, MS, McCool, Arch E.
MCCORD, Ellen A. W2619, LI, McCord, F. O.
MCCORD, F. O. S1113, LI, 9th Ky. Inf.
MCCORD, James A. S10097, WI, 32nd Inf.
MCCORD, John H. B. S12784, G, 51st Inf.
MCCORD, Lillie, W9515, MS, McCord, Henry G.
MCCORD, M. M. S15653, S15846, HU, 10th Cav.
MCCORD, Margaret Ann, W3968, GI, McCord, Luther Wood
MCCORD, Martha, W8782, HU, McCord, Marion McDonald
MCCORD, Mary Tennessee, W5741, WI, McCord, James A.
MCCORD, Sidney Jane, W476, DI, McCord, Calvin McDonald
MCCORKLE, A. J. S15081, DY, 20th (Russell's) Cav.
MCCORKLE, F. A. S7612, DY, 20th (Russell's) Cav.
MCCORKLE, Francis H. S2537, MC, 5th (McKenzie's) Cav.
MCCORKLE, Mary Emeline, W2910, HE, McCorkle, Frankle Biye
MCCORKLE, Mollie E. W4394, ME, McCorkle, Frank H.
MCCORKLE, William A. S11603, HW, 2nd Cav.
MCCORMACK, Dollie R. W6142, SN, McCormack, James Wm.
MCCORMACK, I. L. S9602, OV, 25th Inf.
MCCORMACK, Julia Ann, W2502, OV, McCormack, Wade H.
MCCORMACK, Lucy Jane, W4525, W, McCormack, George E.
MCCORMACK, R. T. S4276, H, 2nd Bn. Cav.
MCCORMACK, R. T. S5290, H, 1st (Carter's) Cav.
MCCORMICK, F. M. S884, DK, 35th Inf.
MCCORMICK, Mary M. W853, SM, McCormick, Tilmon H.
MCCORMICK, Palestine Christian, S8943, MU, 23rd Inf.
MCCORMICK, R. D. S12841, MU, 19th (Biffle's) Cav.
MCCORMICK, Susan, W771, DK, McCormick, F. M.
MCCOURY, M. C. S5972, U, 16th N.C. Inf.
MCCOY, Alexander, S13752, BR, 27th Ala. Inf.
MCCOY, Charles W. S6379, SE, 6th Ala. Inf.
MCCOY, F. M. S5917, FR, 41st Inf.
MCCOY, John J. S1060, HI, 48th Inf.
MCCOY, John L. S13552, V, 8th (Dibrell's) Cav.
MCCOY, M. A. W546, HI, McCoy, Robert
MCCOY, Martha L. W1563, RU, McCoy, Andrew H.
MCCOY, Mary A. W982, FR, McCoy, David F.
MCCOY, Mary Frances, W10801, HE, McCoy, Sam Elum
MCCOY, Samuel E. S12754, HE, 7th Ala. Cav.
MCCOY, Samuel H. S659, GI, 3rd Inf.
MCCOY, W. L. S1597, HM, 5th Cav.
MCCRACKEN, David, S1503, HW, 37th Va. Inf.
MCCRACKEN, J. A. S3476, ST, 1st (Carter's) Cav.
MCCRACKEN, J. B. S9584, LI, 37th Inf.
MCCRACKEN, Madison, S12573, JO, 21st Va. Cav.
MCCRACKEN, Martha, W7139, McCracken, Wm. Leonidas
MCCRACKEN, Mary Cicily, W8290, W51, W8708, GI, McCracken, John Calvin
MCCRACKEN, W. L. S9267, 12th Ky. Cav.
MCCRACKIN, Emily Jane, W6837, LA, McCrackin, Elbert
MCCRACKIN, John H. S13313, HW, 61st Inf.
MCCRADY, Sarah, W3405, FR, McCrady, John
MCCRARY, A. A. S8258, RU, 18th Inf.
MCCRARY, George B. S9635, HM, 3rd Inf.
MCCRARY, George W. S1751, K, 5th Cav.
MCCRARY, J. B. S9171, HM, 63rd Inf.
MCCRARY, James A. S1280, SM, 28th Inf.
MCCRARY, Joe, S16241, HU, 11th Inf.
MCCRARY, John M. S5059, SU, 61st Inf.
MCCRARY, Malinda, W1317, RU, McCrary, Joseph Hamilton
MCCRARY, Mary E. W3169, WL, McCrary, John
MCCRARY, Samuel W. S7704, HM, 63rd Inf.
MCCRARY, Sarah Savilla, W7995, HM, McCrary, James Bluford
MCCRARY, William M. S12996, D, 9th Bn. Ga. Art.

MCCRAVEY, J. B. S14551, HM, 26th Va. Cav.
MCCRAVY, Sarah J. W7081, D, McCravy, Wm. Marion
MCCREARY, John, S5399, WL, 7th Inf.
MCCREARY, Martha, W5688, SM, McCreary, James A.
MCCREIGHT, W. Y. S5493, T, 51st Inf.
MCCRORY, Eveline, W2778, D, McCrory, James
MCCRORY, H. D. S62, MS, 17th Inf.
MCCRORY, J. L. S7512, MS, 14th Cav.
MCCRORY, Margaret, W7637, MS, McCrory, James L.
MCCRORY, Nannie Jane, W2308, WI, McCrohan, Wm.
MCCRUTCHEN, Fannie, W10922, DE, McCrutchen, Robert C.
MCCRUTCHEN, Robert C. S16635, DE, 53rd Inf.
MCCULLEY, A. T. S13165, BL, 37th Inf.
MCCULLEY, Elmira V. W6091, WA, McCulley, Robert F.
MCCULLEY, John A. S12534, CH, 1st Cav.
MCCULLEY, Mary Hix, W1234, F, McCulley, W. C.
MCCULLEY, Samuel, S11501, SU, 60th Inf.
MCCULLOCH, Alexander, S15044, HN, 20th Cav.
MCCULLOCH, Andrew, S13008, WL, Carter's Scouts, Cav.
MCCULLOCH, Delea, W10240, D, McCulloch, James L.
MCCULLOCH, G. E. N. S10089, WE, 15th (Stewart's) Cav.
MCCULLOCH, Minerva Jane, W10276, DY, McCulloch, Gabriel Edwd. Nelson
MCCULLOCK, R. E. S14411, MT, 14th Inf.
MCCULLOCK, Rachel C. W5685, WL, McCullock, J. G.
MCCULLOCK, Sam, S6188, LI, 5th Ky. Inf.
MCCULLOUGH, C. R. S11623, MS, 10th & 11th Cav.
MCCULLOUGH, Eudora Jane, W10011, HN, McCullough, Alex
MCCULLOUGH, Fannie, W6014, LI, McCullough, Samuel
MCCULLOUGH, James R. S5458, CA, 23rd Inf.
MCCULLOUGH, John, S10946, G, 15th (Stewart's) Cav.
MCCULLOUGH, Martha, W10077, G, McCullough, John W.

MCCULLOUGH, Mary A. W8087, RU, McCullough, Allen P.
MCCULLOUGH, Ned, C137, RU, 17th Inf.
MCCULLOUGH, Sinai Ann, W5500, T, McCullough, Wm. Dawson
MCCULLOUGH, W. L. S16654, DY, 12th Ky. Cav.
MCCULLY, Beckie A. W3297, F, McCully, I. S.
MCCURDY, Harriet, W6274, MS, McCurdy, Wm. A.
MCCURDY, William A. S7815, MS, 4th (McLemore's) Cav.
MCCUTCHAN, Mary Elizabeth, W5371, G, McCutchan, Joe D.
MCCUTCHEN, Fannie, W4600, HN, McCutchen, Robert D.
MCCUTCHEN, James Thomas, S11164, MA, 4th Arizona Brigade
MCCUTCHEN, Linnie Valentine, W4818, MA, McCutchen, David McAlpine
MCDADE, Sarah Ann, W10369, WE, McDade, Nathan Gilbert
MCDANIEL, Addie, W6384, RO, McDaniel, James Nathaniel
MCDANIEL, Adrian, S12236, LI, 4th Cav.
MCDANIEL, Caswell W. S7660, ME, 2nd (Ashby's) Cav.
MCDANIEL, E. M. S1640, T, 10th Miss. Inf.
MCDANIEL, Fannie Edith, W7873, LI, McDaniel, Wm. Thomas
MCDANIEL, G. E. S13363, G, 14th Cav.
MCDANIEL, Hessie, W9201, MA, McDaniel, John C.
MCDANIEL, J. A. S15214, SH, 5th Confederate Inf.
MCDANIEL, J. C. S10268, MA, 14th Cav.
MCDANIEL, J. W. S14748, G, 22nd (Barteau's) Cav.
MCDANIEL, J. Y. S2727, S2287, S6660, LI, 8th Inf.
MCDANIEL, James N. S12603, RO, 16th Bn. (Neal's) Cav.
MCDANIEL, Margaret, W1627, BL, McDaniel, John
MCDANIEL, Margaret A. W1207, RO, McDaniel, Wm. Toliver
MCDANIEL, Martha Ann, W1386, MO, McDaniel, Roten Calvin
MCDANIEL, Nancy Prarilla, W3510, PU, McDaniel, Thomas Franklin

MCDANIEL, Peter, S376, LK, 154th Sr. Regt. Inf.
MCDANIEL, Pheraby Drucilla, W560, SH, McDaniel, James Jackson
MCDANIEL, Sarah P. W2434, G, McDaniel, R. E.
MCDANIEL, Tabitha Adom, W5283, HN, McDaniel, Peter
MCDANIEL, W. J. S5794, MO, 62nd Inf.
MCDANIEL, W. T. S8177, LI, Huggin's Co. Lt. Art.
MCDANIEL, William T. S2826, RO, 3rd Inf.
MCDAVID, Samuel, S6929, DY, 13th Inf.
MCDEARMAN, W. J. S10774, G, 12th Inf.
MCDEARMON, Mary E. W8827, WE, McDearmon, Clem Clark
MCDERMONT, James W. S12703, D, McClung's Co. Lt. Art.
MCDERMOTT, Fannie, W7848, D, McDermott, James Washington
MCDERMOTT, Margaret Park, W2068, K, McDermott, Samuel Augustus
MCDONALD, Alexander W. S13698, MU, 6th (Wheeler's) Cav.
MCDONALD, Andrew, S16364, PU, Hamilton's Bn. Cav.
MCDONALD, Daniel, S960, P, 10th Cav.
MCDONALD, G. W. S8215, MA, 12th Inf.
MCDONALD, Isabella, W107, RU, McDonald, George W.
MCDONALD, J. A. S6920, B, 24th Inf.
MCDONALD, J. A. S13864, BR, 43rd Inf.
MCDONALD, J. K. S9741, MU, 6th (Wheeler's) Cav.
MCDONALD, Jesse, S2675, FR, 17th Inf.
MCDONALD, Joseph A. S7422, MU, 2nd (Robison's) Inf.
MCDONALD, Josephine, W7578, G, McDonald, Thomas Benton
MCDONALD, Kate Adair, W6514, SH, McDonald, George Alexander
MCDONALD, Luvina C. W3234, WE, McDonald, R. J.
MCDONALD, Martha, W11173, CC, McDonald, Francis
MCDONALD, Martha Jane, W5696, SH, McDonald, James Avant
MCDONALD, Mary E. W1028, CY, McDonald, James M.
MCDONALD, Nancy A. W1156, HO, McDonald, John W.
MCDONALD, R. J. S4994, WE, 33rd Inf.

MCDONALD, S. S. S14321, SM, 28th Inf.
MCDONALD, Sarah A. W3408, MO, McDonald, W. A.
MCDONALD, Sarah D. W6635, MU, McDonald, Alexander Wilson
MCDONALD, Sarah Permelia, W1799, HI, McDonald, Wm. Collin
MCDONALD, W. R. S3055, HD, 4th Inf.
MCDONALD, Wesley, S11604
MCDONALD, Wiley A. S3798, MO, 25th S.C. Inf.
MCDONALD, William George, S1655, WL, 9th (Ward's) Cav.
MCDONOUGH, J. S. S11345, K, 63rd Inf.
MCDONOUGH, Mary Lenoir, W5968, K, McDonough, James Sevier
MCDOUGAL, A. G. S6797, MN, 6th Tex. Cav.
MCDOUGAL, Elizabeth S. W2336, D, McDougal, Wm. Campbell
MCDOUGAL, Lou, W7567, HD, McDougal, Alex A. G.
MCDOUGAL, P. R. S10212, LA, 47th Ala. Inf.
MCDOUGALD, Tennessee Hamilton, W3609, G, McDougald, Clinton
MCDOWELL, Andrew, C230, PU, 5th Bn. Cav., Application is missing.
MCDOWELL, B. G. S13464, SU, 39th N.C. Inf.
MCDOWELL, C. P. S10958, F, 62nd N.C. Inf.
MCDOWELL, M. L. S13884, FR, 2nd (Robison's) Inf.
MCDOWELL, Mattie, W8839, MOO, McDowell, Sam
MCDOWELL, Nettie, W3295, WH, McDowell, Thomas
MCDOWELL, Sallie, W7720, F, McDowell, C. P.
MCDOWELL, Samuel, S13770, MOO, 22nd (Barteau's) Cav.
MCDOWELL, Thomas, S944, DK, 1st Inf.
MCDUFFIE, Sallie, W3184, LO, McDuffie, Robert Newton
MCEACHIN, Julia Frances, W6733, SH, McEachin, Daniel L.
MCELROY, A. J. S8849, LI, 1st Inf.
MCELROY, Frances E. W5521, LI, McElroy, Thomas B.
MCELROY, John, S4352, MT, 10th Inf.
MCELROY, Louise E. W10523, McElroy, Henry D.
MCELROY, R. A. S14971, ST, 50th Inf.
MCELROY, Rufus C. S9400, LI, 4th (McLemore's) Cav.

MCELROY, T. B. S2370, LI, 44th Inf.
MCELVAY, Mary L. W5002, MT, McElvay, John
MCELWEE, W. E. S15530, RO, 26th Inf.
MCELYEA, Brunette, W6898, DI, McElyea, Thomas Benton
MCELYEA, Thomas B. S92, DI, 1st (Feild's) Inf.
MCEWEN, A. A. S10354, B, Forrest's Escort, Cav.
MCEWEN, George W. C95, D, 1st Inf.
MCEWEN, Laura Hughes, W7065, WI, McEwen, J. F.
MCEWIN, James F. S13520, WI, 1st (Feild's) Inf.
MCFADDEN, Alcy Ann, W10329, F, McFadden, Wm. Steele
MCFADDEN, John W. S13138, WI, 45th Inf.
MCFADDEN, Julia A. W6429, SH, McFadden, Peter Culp
MCFADDEN, Mary Buford, W10845, WI, McFadden, John Wesley
MCFADDEN, Samuel N. S14990, G, 45th Inf.
MCFALL, Emma Florida, W5021, MU, McFall, Wm. Hamlet
MCFALL, George W. S11104, WA, 63rd Inf.
MCFALL, J. R. S537, HD, 1st Cav.
MCFALL, William H. S3470, MU, 9th Bn. (Gantt's) Cav.
MCFARLAND, Dal, C159, HY, Undetermined
MCFARLAND, Elizabeth Ann, W5286, McFarland, Robert Jahu
MCFARLAND, John W. S14752, WL, 28th Inf.
MCFARLAND, Kate, W6911, WL, McFarland, J. W.
MCFARLAND, Laura F. W9998, W5003, HN, McFarland, Wm. Henry
MCFARLAND, Margaret M. W1566, HM, McFarland, Sherman Rice
MCFARLAND, Pauline, W3589, WL, McFarland, John Porter
MCFARLAND, Robert J. S8748, 7th Cav.
MCFARLAND, Sallie, W10636, G, McFarland, A. Sylvester
MCFARLAND, W. L. S9022, CT, Lynch's Co. Lt. Art.
MCFARLAND, William H. S6254, HN, 7th Cav.
MCFAUL, Robert Henry, S5845, K, 31st Inf.
MCFERRIN, Litton Burt, S16198, CA, 18th Inf.
MCFERRIN, Thomas M. S10063, LI, 41st Inf.
MCGAHEY, G. W. S13711, HI, 20th Inf.

MCGANN, Charles H. S3772, SH, 14th Inf.
MCGANN, James L. S14204, WI, 22nd (Barteau's) Cav.
MCGAR, L. R. S9891, D, 19th (Biffle's) Cav.
MCGAR, Nancy Jane, W6485, D, McGar, L. R.
MCGARRITY, Mattie Addison, W10135, SH, McGarrity, James
MCGARRY, Margaret E. W962, SU, McGarry, John W.
MCGARVEY, Emma, W3748, G, McGarvey, John Williams
MCGAUGH, B. F. S257, MS, 3rd Inf.
MCGAUGH, Fannie A. W1709, MS, McGaugh, George W.
MCGAUGHY, Martha A. W3473, H, McGaughy, Henry Clay
MCGEE, C. J. S11384, SU, 48th Va. Inf.
MCGEE, Elizabeth J. W2936, SU, McGee, Charles James
MCGEE, G. W. S11747, RB, 7th Ky. Cav.
MCGEE, John A. S16523, W, 5th Inf.
MCGEE, M. C. S9958, GI, 53rd Inf.
MCGEE, Margaret Ann, W1036, MN, McGee, Andrew J.
MCGEE, Nannie, W8968, HR, McGee, Henry Lafayette
MCGEE, W. A. S4744, MN, 14th Ga. Inf.
MCGEE, William, S4682, B, 41st Inf.
MCGHEE, Samuel, S7375, H, 43rd Inf.
MCGHEE, Virginia W. W9590, H, McGhee, Sam
MCGHEE, W. F. S12833, MT, 3rd Ky. Cav.
MCGILL, Albert M. S6667, CA, 8th (Smith's) Cav.
MCGILL, T. J. S13794, WE, 20th Cav.
MCGIMPSEY, J. L. S13267, FR, 8th N.C. Home Guards
MCGIMPSEY, Maldonia V. W7679, HM, McGimpsey, Junius Lenvir
MCGINNIS, Carrie Ellen, W5297, SH, McGinnis, John Mathis
MCGINNIS, Mary, W6968, DK, McGinnis, Richard
MCGINNIS, R. W. S5772, DK, 16th Inf.
MCGLAMERY, Jacob, S13022, JE, 34th N.C. Inf.
MCGLASSON, Martha A. W9567, PU, McGlasson, Oliver P.
MCGLASSON, Maryanne D. W7436, PU, McGlasson, Jasper Green
MCGLASSON, Oliver P. S15487, J, 8th (Dibrell's) Cav.

Index to Tennessee Confederate Pension Applications

MCGOLDRICK, Thomas, S10419, GR, 37th Inf.
MCGOUIRK, George W. S9585, GU, 1st Ga. Bn.
MCGOUIRK, Martha E. W6766, GU, McGouirk, George Washington
MCGOWAN, Alicent Taylor, W6438, SH, McGowan, Samuel Petty
MCGOWAN, C. E. S7638, RU, 7th Cav.
MCGOWAN, Elizabeth, W10258, D, McGowan, W. T.
MCGREGOR, Ada Byron, W9236, T, McGregor, Ransford Rob Roy
MCGREGOR, Albert F. S11700, MS, 17th Inf.
MCGREGOR, Andrew, S11189, WL, 4th (McLemore's) Cav.
MCGREGOR, Cora, W10810, W, McGregor, Marshall
MCGREGOR, Marshall, S11561, W, 35th Inf.
MCGREGOR, Mary A. W4874, MS, McGregor, Albert
MCGREGOR, Mary Eliza, W6804, SH, McGregor, Amos Flowers
MCGREGOR, Mary Wallace, W8992, W, McGregor, James Robert
MCGREGOR, Rob Roy, S7321, T, 7th Cav.
MCGREW, Louisa Ruth, W7927, GI, McGrew, Neil
MCGREW, Neil, S14450, GI, 6th (Wheeler's) Cav.
MCGRIFF, Ellen, W3462, H, McGriff, Jefferson
MCGRINER, Mary Margerit, W7696, HI, McGriner, Wm. Pleasant
MCGUIN, N. C. S9128, K, 13th N.C. Inf.
MCGUINE, Horace, S2003, DK, 16th Inf.
MCGUIRE, Elizabeth, W4261, SU, McGuire, Robert Walker
MCGUIRE, Jeremiah, S11179, MO, 59th Inf.
MCGUIRE, Mary, W656, CF, McGuire, James
MCGUIRE, R. R. S5720, GI, 1st Inf.
MCGUIRE, William A. S6650, WI, 32nd Inf.
MCHANEY, Anna Eliza, W7222, HE, McHaney, Cornelius Felix
MCHANEY, C. F. S15327, HE, 21st (Wilson's) Cav.
MCHENRY, David, S9937, RU, 11th Cav.
MCHENRY, William, S2001, MT, 1st Ala. Inf.
MCHUGHES, Simpson, S13404, MN, 18th (Newsom's) Cav.
MCINTIRE, Evaline, W566, WL, McIntire, James C.
MCINTIRE, John, S16550, WL, 7th Inf.

MCINTOSH, John L. S6077, HI, 20th Inf.
MCINTOSH, M. H. S14509, D, 1st Ark. Mtd. Rifles
MCINTOSH, Mary Isabella, W9328, HO, McIntosh, Samuel Benjamin
MCINTOSH, Verona. W7299, D, McIntosh, Martin Harvey
MCINTYRE, John, S5651, L, 5th N.C. Cav.
MCINTYRE, W. T. S16612, WL, 4th (McLemore's) Cav.
MCKAIG, Elizabeth, W7684, H, McKaig, Francis
MCKAMEY, Mary Catharine, W2008, SU, McKamey, Robert
MCKAMY, Alice, W8231, BR, McKamy, J. W.
MCKAMY, Jasper N. S5671, BR, 43rd Inf.
MCKAMY, Julia Eliza, W5626, BR, McKamy, Wm. Hannah
MCKAMY, Robert, S1946, SU, 60th Inf.
MCKAMY, S. M. S1941, WA, 59th Inf.
MCKAUGHAN, James P. S1281, J, 4th Bn. Cav.
MCKAUGHAN, William M. S1001, J, 28th Inf.
MCKAY, A. B. S10830, JE, 60th N.C. Inf.
MCKAY, Alexander Washington, S14245, LI, 19th (Biffle's) Cav.
MCKAY, B. M. S2332, GE, 3rd Inf.
MCKAY, Campbellim, W2651, GE, McKay, Martin
MCKAY, Elizabeth Catharine, W1752, WA, McKay, George Edward
MCKAY, Harriet Wood, W8734, D, McKay, Wm. Lewis
MCKAY, J. S13220, WI, 5th Mo. Inf.
MCKAY, Robert H. S14289, WI, 20th Inf.
MCKAY, W. L. S724, D, 18th Inf.
MCKEE, Andrew J. S13369, MU, 11th Cav.
MCKEE, Elizabeth C. W7930, WI, McKee, Andrew Jackson
MCKEE, Lenora R. W5774, SH, McKee, Wm. Henry
MCKEE, Lula, W8215, D, McKee, George Washington
MCKEE, W. H. S12093, S12535, SH, 21st (Wilson's) Cav.
MCKEE, William, S5234, HR, 9th Inf.
MCKEEHAN, Mary C. W3351, K, McKeehan, Alexander
MCKEEHAN, William W. S4252, K, 1st (Carter's) Cav.
MCKEELY, Jane, W785, G, McKeely, Americus Pond

MCKELDIN, Mary Sehorn, W2612, MC, McKeldin, Wm. Brazelton
MCKENNON, Alma Isabella, W5890, RU, McKennon, Leroy
MCKENNON, James A. S9896, K, 37th Va. Inf.
MCKENNON, Leroy, S14028, RU, 9th Bn. (Gantt's) Cav.
MCKENNON, Mary Frances, W1283, MU, McKennon, Thomas James
MCKENNON, T. J. S6890, MU, 9th Bn. Cav.
MCKENRY, A. P. S13694, SU, 14th Va. Cav.
MCKENRY, Mary E. W4774, SU, McKenry, A. P.
MCKENZIE, Anna M. W2205, MN, McKenzie, George B.
MCKENZIE, Elias G. S11858, ME, 5th (McKenzie's) Cav.
MCKENZIE, G. B. S6517, MN, 19th Cav.
MCKENZIE, George M. S7141, ME, 5th Cav.
MCKENZIE, H. M. S6209, ME, 16th Bn. (Neal's) Cav.
MCKENZIE, Laura, W8798, McKenzie, John David
MCKENZIE, M. M. S7545, MN, 19th Cav.
MCKENZIE, Mary R. W8110, SH, McKenzie, John W.
MCKENZIE, Penelope A. W3291, ME, McKenzie, Elias Green
MCKENZIE, Sarah Fine, W7100, H, McKenzie, Wm. Morrison
MCKENZIE, W. M. S6955, MC, 5th (McKenzie's) Cav.
MCKENZIE, William Allen, S1532, K, 33rd Inf.
MCKEOWN, Sarah C. W3824, ME, McKeown, Wm. M.
MCKEOWN, William, S2321, ME, 5th Cav.
MCKEZIE, W. A. S5747, K, 33rd Inf.
MCKIBBEN, Henrietta C. W8038, D, McKibben, Benjamin Alexander
MCKINLEY, Mary Polk, W2613, D, McKinley, Wm. Robert
MCKINLEY, Sarah Frances, W7246, PU, McKinley, James D.
MCKINLEY, Sarah james, W7640, D, McKinley, Wm. G.
MCKINLEY, W. J. S2554, SN, 7th Inf.
MCKINLY, James D. S6061, PU, 17th Inf.
MCKINNEY, Christopher C. S4139, MS, 8th Inf.
MCKINNEY, E. H. S4792, K, 21st N.C. Inf.
MCKINNEY, Eliza, W1211, K, McKinney, Samuel

MCKINNEY, Fannie Lea, W3870, K, McKinney, John Lintun
MCKINNEY, J. A. S16643, LI, 1st Inf.
MCKINNEY, J. F. S10695, SH, 154th Sr. Regt. Inf.
MCKINNEY, James, S863, OV, 8th Inf.
MCKINNEY, John V. S14293, H, 1st (Turney's) Inf.
MCKINNEY, Lucy, W6997, FR, McKinney, Russell
MCKINNEY, Lusindey M. W2997, M, McKinney, George W.
MCKINNEY, MArtha J. W66, GI, McKinney, Galon A.
MCKINNEY, Margaret J. W7723, D, McKinney, George C.
MCKINNEY, Martha J. W990, LI, McKinney, James A.
MCKINNEY, Mary A. W3680, OV, McKinney, James
MCKINNEY, Mary Jane, W10305, HE, McKinney, Wm. Akin
MCKINNEY, Mike, S5185, SH, 7th Miss. Cav.
MCKINNEY, Nancy, W5523, CT, McKinney, John P.
MCKINNEY, Russell, S1607, FR, 41st Inf.
MCKINNEY, S. J. W4779, LI, McKinney, Joe C.
MCKINNIE, Ella H. W9180, D, McKinnie, Virgins
MCKINNIE, M. J. S11298, HR, 7th (Duckworth's) Cav.
MCKINNIE, P. H. S15026, SH, 7th Cav.
MCKINNIE, Sarah Frances, W5571, MA, McKinnie, John Arthur
MCKINSEY, John, S2389, FR, 1st (Turney's) Inf.
MCKINSTRY, Pinkie E. W8218, F, McKinstry, John Wilson
MCKISSACK, O. W. S304, MU, Forrest's Escort, Cav.
MCKISSACK, Sarah Bunch, W10862, MU, McKissack, Alonzo
MCKNETT, Luta, W5447, SH, McKnett, Henry Harrison
MCKNIGHT, A. B. S15497, CA, Allison's Squadron, Cav.
MCKNIGHT, Amanda Eliza, W10005, P, McKnight, James Hewie
MCKNIGHT, Andrew M. S7997, RU, 4th Cav.
MCKNIGHT, Delia Louise, W8280, G, McKnight, Wm. Hall

MCKNIGHT, F. A. S12176, RU, 8th (Smith's) Cav.
MCKNIGHT, J. M. S6147, G, 35th Tex. Cav.
MCKNIGHT, J. R. S6581, RU, 18th Inf.
MCKNIGHT, James, S7390, JE, 1st Bn. (Colm's) Inf.
MCKNIGHT, James H. S14025, P, 14th Cav.
MCKNIGHT, James N. S6696, RU, 62nd Inf.
MCKNIGHT, Joe, S12969, MS, 41st Inf.
MCKNIGHT, John N. S6831, RU, 2nd (Smith's) Cav.
MCKNIGHT, M. B. S5603, MA, 51st Inf.
MCKNIGHT, Martha A. W1461, RU, McKnight, James N.
MCKNIGHT, Mary Elizabeth, W7929, RU, McKnight, James Robert
MCKNIGHT, R. M. S9091, RU, 8th (Smith's) Cav.
MCKNIGHT, Rachel L. W8427, JE, McKnight, James M.
MCKNIGHT, Sarah, See Sarah Enochs
MCKNIGHT, Sarah Frances Adlade, W1521, LI, McKnight, Charles Lucius
MCKNIGHT, Sarah Martha, W819, FR, McKnight, John H.
MCKNIGHT, Unity T. E. W4819, G, McKnight, J. M.
MCKOIN, John G. S13691, SN, 30th Inf.
MCLAIN, Mary Caroline, W1857, MR, McLain, Moudica Robert
MCLAIN, W. A. S1910, WE, 36th Ala. Inf.
MCLAMORE, Marthie, W5651, G, McLamore, Egbert
MCLANE, Elizabeth, W5078, FE, McLane, John L.
MCLANE, John L. S8858, OV, 29th N.C. Inf.
MCLAREN, Cynthia Carry, W6605, HR, McLaren, Anthony Augustus
MCLARRIN, William J. S879, R, 19th Inf.
MCLAUGHLIN, Cora Lorean, W9242, SH, McLaughlin, John Robert
MCLAUGHLIN, J. R. S10873, SH, 9th Inf.
MCLAUGHLIN, M. B. S6049, LI, 41st Inf.
MCLAUGHLIN, Nancy T. W8136, D, McLaughlin, W. T.
MCLAUGHLIN, Sallie Kilcrean, W482, LI, McLaughlin, Elijah C.
MCLAURINE, J. W. S13111, GI, 53rd Inf.
MCLAURINE, Pattie, W9239, GI, McLaurine, R. J.
MCLAURINE, R. J. S9315, GI, 6th (Wheeler's) Cav.

MCLEAN, Dora I. W4730, LA, McLean, J. L.
MCLEAN, E. J. S2990, WY, 9th Cav.
MCLEAN, J. L. S2063, LA, 3rd Inf.
MCLEAN, Lucinda Ann, W5814, WY, McLean, E. J.
MCLEAN, Martha Burnside, W6033, D, McLean, Richard Ogilvie
MCLEAN, Nancy Lucinda, W6198, WY, McLean, Wm. Williams
MCLEAN, R. O. S9670, D, 8th (Smith's) Cav.
MCLEAN, T. L, S4522, K, 59th Inf.
MCLEAN, U. R. S6024, HD, 9th Cav.
MCLEAN, W. L. S13598, SH, 12th Bn. Ark. Sharpshooters
MCLEAN, William, S11595, LA, 48th (Nixon's) Inf.
MCLEMORE, Delphy C. W2802, MN, McLemore, Wm.
MCLEMORE, Egbert, S1656, G, 20th Cav.
MCLEMORE, Margaret C. W3423, G, McLemore, James Knox Polk
MCLENDON, Susan Ellen, W8075, SH, McLendon, Green S.
MCLEOD, A. H. S15300, G, 14th Miss. Inf.
MCLEOD, Fannie, W3681, FR, McLeod, C. H.
MCLEOD, J. P. S11428, HY, 7th Cav.
MCLEOD, John A. S7917, G, 1st Ky. Inf.
MCLERAN, A. A. S12070, HR, 26th Miss. Inf.
MCLIN, R. L. S2490, MS, 6th (Wheeler's) Cav.
MCLISTER, John C. S15295, T, 12th Cav.
MCLUSKEY, Nancy A. W41, LI, McLuskey, Wm.
MCMACKIN, M. J. S16591, HU, 10th Cav.
MCMAHAN, A. A. S9981, D, 24th Inf.
MCMAHAN, Arthur, S9537, F, 9th La. Inf.
MCMAHAN, Emeline, W1105, DK, McMahan, Wm.
MCMAHAN, G. W. S13926, SE, Thomas' Legion, N.C.
MCMAHAN, James, S940, LA, 35th Inf.
MCMAHAN, James F. S8098, WY, 5th Ark. Inf.
MCMAHAN, Martha J. W4859, LA, McMahan, James
MCMAHON, Daniel B. S9838, CF, 28th Cav.
MCMAHON, Eliza Ann, W9111, WY, McMahon, James Franklin
MCMAHON, Lemuel L. S9586, WI, 24th Inf.
MCMAHON, Mary Jane, W5883, W8676, B, McMahon, Abraham
MCMAHON, Mary Jane, W8146, CF, McMahon, Daniel B.

Index to Tennessee Confederate Pension Applications

MCMAHON, Thomas G. S9289, GI, 3rd (Clack's) Inf.
MCMAHON, William W. S672, L, Undetermined
MCMANUS, G. A. S14636, D, 19th (Biffle's) Cav.
MCMANUS, John P. S6011, CF, 37th Inf.
MCMASTER, T. J. S12654, MA, Forrest's Escort, Cav.
MCMASTER, W. G. S10190, MA, 14th Cav.
MCMASTERS, John, S14763, GI, 48th (Nixon's) Inf.
MCMEEN, Margaret E. W2196, MU, McMeen, Joseph B.
MCMEENS, J. O. S9028, MU, 1st (Feild's) Inf.
MCMENNANY, W. E. S15310, WE, 45th Inf.
MCMICHAEL, J. F. S3704, D, 5th Inf.
MCMICHAEL, J. S. S8105, CF, 4th (McLemore's) Cav.
MCMICHAEL, Mary L. W2070, CF, McMichael, James Searcy
MCMILLAN, James C. S15361, M, 8th (Dibrell's) Cav.
MCMILLAN, Jasper, S1707, CE, 4th (McLemore's) Cav.
MCMILLAN, William, C210, K, 77th Va. Cav.
MCMILLEN, Alvis, S15319, GR, 1st (Carter's) Cav.
MCMILLIN, Edna Rebecca, W32, LI, McMillin, Robert
MCMILLIN, Elizabeth Lucretia, W323, WL, McMillin, Thomas
MCMILLIN, Samuel D. S6459, SU, 51st Va. Inf.
MCMILLIN, W. B. S2667, S5383, LI, 44th Inf.
MCMILLION, A. H. S780, GI, 3rd Inf.
MCMILLION, Josephine C. W7586, GI, McMillion, Gustavus Henry
MCMINN, Adaline, W983, MU, McMinn, Oliver P.
MCMINN, John W. S16034, G, 20th Cav.
MCMINNS, C. W. S3186, HD, 16th Ala. Inf.
MCMURRAY, C. C. S15331, H, 15th N.C. Inf.
MCMURRAY, Eliza N. W266, ME, McMurray, Wm. Elsy
MCMURRAY, Emma Alexander, W8235, H, McMurray, Francis Goudling
MCMURRAY, Francis G. S13139, H, 23rd Ala. Inf.
MCMURRAY, J. D. S15687, MU, 48th (Voorhies') Inf.
MCMURRAY, Laura, W7078, H, McMurray, Christopher Columbus
MCMURTRY, J. H. S11915, SN, 9th (Ward's) Cav.
MCMURTRY, James B. S6428, SM, 9th (Bennett's) Cav.
MCMURTRY, Mattie O. Uttey, W9001, SN, McMurtry, Jacob H.
MCNABB, Charles Andrew, S8996, RU, 4th Cav.
MCNABB, Elizabeth, W4572, SH, McNabb, Ezekiel Baptist
MCNABB, Ida B. W6833, RU, McNabb, Charles Andrew
MCNABB, J. F. S4225, DK, 4th Cav.
MCNABB, John, S15667, BR, Thomas' Legion, N.C. Troops
MCNABB, Nancy Ellen, W1041, D, McNabb, Richard Toliver
MCNABB, Richard, S905, LO, 3rd Inf.
MCNABB, Sarah Elizabeth, W11062, WL, McNabb, John Farrow
MCNATT, Mary James, W3707, CH, McNatt, Richd. Muse Davidson
MCNATT, P. B. S2828, CH, 21st Cav.
MCNATT, R. M. D. S7024, CH, 21st (Wilson's) Cav.
MCNEAL, Elizabeth J. W5585, DI, McNeal, John Rilley
MCNEAL, Margaret, W3098, C, McNeal, John
MCNEAL, Sam Simpson, C146, SH, 7th Inf.
MCNEAL, Young, S1593, WI, 20th Inf.
MCNEECE, W. T. S16142, LA, 48th (Nixon's) Inf.
MCNEELEY, Emily Jane, W9858, W4640, GI, McNeeley, Wm. Jabez
MCNEELEY, J. S12270, HU, 26th Ark. Inf.
MCNEELEY, Sam, C21, SH, 14th Cav.
MCNEELEY, William C. S11928, SH, 23rd Ark. Inf.
MCNEELY, Rachel Ann, W7858, G, McNeely, James Yatts
MCNEELY, Rush, C172, MA, 27th Inf.
MCNEES, E. L. S5097, WA, 12th Bn. Cav.
MCNEESE, Joseph, S8938, GI, 3rd Inf.
MCNEIL, Ausburn, C115, F, Unassigned, Teamster
MCNEIL, Eliza, W2689, CL, McNeil, A. J.
MCNEIL, Elizabeth Brown, W10139, D, McNeil, Andrew Jackson
MCNEIL, John R. S1202, DI, 48th Inf.

Index to Tennessee Confederate Pension Applications

MCNEIL, Theodosia Brown, W10477, SH, McNeil, Thomas Archibald
MCNEILL, A. J. S2221, D, 14th Inf.
MCNEILL, D. T. C. S7586, HN, 20th (Russell's) Cav.
MCNEILL, J. A. S11076, L, 14th (Neely's) Cav.
MCNEILL, J. B. S1556, SN, 2nd Inf.
MCNEILL, Lucy E. W1320, HN, McNeill, T. C.
MCNEILL, Mary, W8994, BE, McNeill, James David
MCNEILL, Sue, W6088, McNeill, Nathan W.
MCNEILLY, J. T. S8461, BO, 7th N.C. Troops
MCNICHOLS, J. T. S12733, MT, 14th Inf.
MCNICKOLS, Ann, W379, DI, McNickols, Thomas
MCNIEL, J. A. S10535, CL, 61st Inf.
MCNULTY, Elizabeth B. W10125, H, McNulty, Peter Cuttino
MCNUTT, Elizabeth, W4701, MC, McNutt, James
MCNUTT, Fannie V. W7963, K, McNutt, George Anderson
MCNUTT, George Anderson, S8444, K, Kain's Co. Lt. Art.
MCPEAK, Clarissa G. W5872, SH, McPeak, Elihu
MCPEAK, G. B. S7107, RU, 13th Ark. Inf.
MCPEAK, Granville, S517, WL, 45th Inf.
MCPEAK, Lucy Ann, W4733, RU, McPeak, Gervis B.
MCPEAK, Martha, W9689, RU, McPeak, Luther
MCPEAK, Martha F. W9258, RU, McPeak, Anderson
MCPEAKE, Angelina, W3144, WL, McPeake, Robert Knox
MCPEETERS, C. L. S16485, HM, 16th N.C. Inf.
MCPETTERS, Julia, W9966, HM, McPetters, Charles Lafayette
MCPHERSON, Amanda Jane, W1243, R, McPherson, James H.
MCPHERSON, Catherine J. W4262, R, McPherson, John Marshall
MCPHERSON, J. M. S10479, R, 1st (Carter's) Cav.
MCPHERSON, Joel Lewis, S10077, R, 11th Tex. Cav.
MCPHERSON, Nancy Jane, W1159, K, McPherson, Richard Franklin
MCPHERSON, W. W. S13927, SH, 2nd Miss. Inf.

MCQUEAN, D. N. S472, F, 4th N.C. State Troops
MCQUEEN, Martha E. W2354, F, McQueen, Wm.
MCQUIGG, Martha Ann, W9640, MU, McQuigg, Abner Turner
MCQUIRTER, Patience, W9667, SN, McQuirter, Thomas Samuel
MCRAE, Alexander C. S8314, BE, 55th Inf.
MCRAE, Annie, W3615, W10833, SH, McRae, Wm. Hinson
MCRAE, J. H. S8464, HW, 5th N.C. Inf.
MCRAE, Lenora Ann, W1244, BE, McRae, Alexander Collins
MCRAE, Mary Susie, W7763, SH, McRae, James F.
MCREE, Carroll, S2550, GI, 44th Inf.
MCREE, Lizzie, W6150, F, McRee, Richard A.
MCREE, R. A. S12082, F, 1st Cav.
MCREE, W. F. S15553, G, 47th Inf.
MCREYNOLDS, Robert, S4627, K, Undetermined
MCRIMMON, Harrison, S15657, MN, 18th Inf.
MCSWAIN, Betty, W6119, HN, McSwain, John A.
MCSWAIN, Sarah Virginia, W3640, HN, McSwain, Thomas Smith
MCTHENEY, B. D. S6600, OV, 31st Va. Inf.
MCVEY, Leroy Pope, S5212, SH, 9th Miss. Inf.
MCWATERS, J. P. (Mrs.), W11179, McWaters, J. P. Contents of file missing
MCWATTERS, J. P. S7983, MA, 17th S.C. Inf.
MCWHERTER, Nancy Henry, W2345, WE, McWherter, Robert
MCWHIRTER, A. G. S11266, D, Huggin's Co. Lt. Art.
MCWHIRTER, F. L. S6707, WE, 33rd Inf.
MCWHIRTER, Robert, S25, WE, 33rd Inf.
MCWHIRTER, Sallie [Stevens], W10659, RU, McWhirter, Sam A. [Later married Stevens]
MCWHIRTER, W. L. S3122, HI, 27th Inf.
MCWHORTER, Samuel, S3320, LI, 44th Inf.
MCWHORTER, W. M. S14642, LI, 44th Inf.
MCWILLIAMS, J. L. S5847, CH, 52nd Inf.
MCWILLIAMS, Joanna, W7074, T, McWilliams, Pressly Baldrich
MCWILLIAMS, Presley B. S5104, T, 1st S.C. Art.
MEACHAM, Pina Jane, W2111, WI, Meacham, Milton Skiles
MEAD, Mattie, W10956, G, Mead, Edgar A.

MEADE, Henry Nathaniel, S16641, SU, 1st Va. Inf.
MEADOR, B. F. S6713, R, 52nd Ga. Inf.
MEADOR, J. H. A. S10800, HI, 9th Bn. (Gantt's) Cav.
MEADOR, John A. S3198, DI, 24th Inf.
MEADOR, Mallie, W10336, M, Meador, J. P.
MEADOR, Martha Sue, W10091, TR, Meador, Ira
MEADOR, Pleasant G. S9418, M, 24th Inf.
MEADOWS, Elizabeth Hannah, W5019, B, Meadows, Wm. Henry
MEADOWS, Harriet, W1378, H, Meadows, James Washington
MEADOWS, Ida C. W10347, WA, Meadows, Emanuel
MEADOWS, James, S8087, CH, 21st (Wilson's) Cav.
MEADOWS, John, S9270, HE, 27th Inf.
MEADOWS, John D. S1519, SU, 4th N.C. Inf.
MEADOWS, Maria Watts, W8559, DY, Meadows, James Gus
MEADOWS, Sarah M. W7728, SU, Meadows, John D.
MEARS, Susan, W7484, CA, Mears, Wm.
MEARS, William, S2168, CA, 18th Inf.
MEBANE, Lou, W5845, Mebane, Wm. E.
MEBANE, W. E. S12318, 55th Inf.
MEDARIS, Hiram, S4409, MC, 16th Bn. (Neal's) Cav.
MEDARIS, Sarah M. W7169, MC, Medaris, Hiram
MEDLEY, Green, S69, CF, 16th Inf.
MEDLEY, John, S264, CF, 5th Inf.
MEDLEY, Laura Ann, W254, W, Medley, Wm. Marion
MEDLIN, Amanda A. W6322, HE, Medlin, J. R.
MEDLIN, Dillie Ann, W9360, CC, Medlin, Moses
MEDLIN, Jacob C. S8575, 15th Cav.
MEDLIN, James R. S10440, HE, 27th Inf.
MEDLIN, M. W. S16429, CC, 7th Cav.
MEDLIN, S. H. S3986, 5th Inf.
MEDLIN, W. R. S12497, D, 20th Inf.
MEDLIN, William T. S7131, HY, 7th Cav.
MEDLOCK, Louizie, W4184, MN, Medlock, D. D.
MEE, Thomas, S14054, HW, 61st Inf.
MEEK, Alice E. W1527, GR, Meek, W. H.
MEEK, Eliza Ann, W3062, HD, Meek, Robert White
MEEK, Eliza J. W3355, RO, Meek, James H.
MEEK, James, S14532, JE, 4th Ky. Cav.
MEEK, Lucy Malissia, W3337, HW, Meek, Robert Joseph
MEEK, M. H. S15597, BO, 11th Inf.
MEEK, Mary Ann, W3217, K, Meek, Wm.
MEEK, William, S9233, K, 31st Inf.
MEEKS, B. S8779, WI, 1st Ala. Inf.
MEEKS, Catherine Veoger, W9079, GU, Meeks, Elijah
MEEKS, Elijah, S13934, GU, 28th Cav.
MEEKS, J. L. S15100, MN, 3rd (Forrest's) Cav.
MEEKS, Melinda, W5419, GU, Meeks, Thomas Jefferson
MEEKS, Sarah Meritte, W2393, G, Meeks, Noah M.
MEEKS, Susie, W10752, SH, Meeks, Wm. Nathan
MEEKS, W. N. S8634, L, 32nd Inf.
MEHAFFEY, Susan W. W1438, K, Mehaffey, John Knox
MEHIGAN, Cornelius, S11567, MT, 14th Inf.
MEHIGAN, Elizabeth Irene, W8367, MT, Mehigan, Cornelius
MELLON, John, S11874, MT, 49th Inf.
MELTON, A. H. S9809, BE, 55th Inf.
MELTON, C. B. S8765, BR, 1st N.C. Inf.
MELTON, David M. S6406, BE, 55th Inf.
MELTON, Emma L. W3413, SH, Melton, James Francis
MELTON, Evaline, W10811, BE, Melton, Asa Herndson
MELTON, G. W. S8249, BR, 27th Ala. Vols.
MELTON, J. T. S4372, SH, 9th Inf.
MELTON, James, S2428, LI, 32nd Inf.
MELTON, James F. S11195, SH, 9th Ala. Inf.
MELTON, John, S12470, R, 5th Cav.
MELTON, John H. S5505, HN, 5th Inf.
MELTON, Levi Benton, S10667, T, 2nd Miss. Inf.
MELTON, Mary, W1940, BE, Melton, P. M.
MELTON, P. J. W2820, BR, Melton, G. W.
MELTON, Silas, S5888, GE, 61st Inf.
MELTON, Tennessee, W4571, G, Melton, Marcus Montrose
MELTON, W. M. S3513, R, 3rd Inf.
MELTON, William, S2429, CH, 13th Inf.
MENATUE, D. G. S3272, GI, 53rd Inf.
MENATUE, George W. S3273, GI, 53rd Inf.
MENDENHALL, Emiline Victory, W5426, UN, Mendenhall, Obediah Ruffin Smith
MENDENHALL, O. S. R. S2186, UN, 37th N.C. Inf.

Index to Tennessee Confederate Pension Applications

MENEES, Henry B. S7696, D, 2nd (Robison's) Inf.
MENEFEE, William Oscar, S14882, T, 12th Cav.
MENIFEE, Mattie M. W10535, MS, Menifee, Willis G.
MERCER, Ella Madora, W6905, SH, Mercer, Wm. Abner
MERCER, Manerva Jane, W4205, W7643, J, Mercer, Thomas J. jr.
MERCER, Mary E. W2638, D, Mercer, Isaac N.
MERCER, Susan, W5242, MC, Mercer, John Samuel
MERCER, Thomas, S13264, HW, 31st Inf.
MERCER, Thomas E. S16554, MA, 33rd Inf.
MERCER, W. A. S9193, MA, 33rd Inf.
MEREDITH, Ed, S1571, WH, 8th Cav.
MEREDITH, Mary Minerva, W5164, WY, Meredith, Andrew Medows
MEREDITH, Mary S. W6218, K, Meredith, David Crockett
MEREDITH, Mildred A. W6897, G, Meredith, James Samuel
MEREDITH, William H. S1081, WH, 25th Inf.
MERIDITH, David Crockett, S14202, K, Unassigned (Wagon Guard)
MERIDITH, E. C. W26, WH, Meridith, Edward
MERIWEATHER, Margaret Barker, W10004, MT, Meriweather, James McClure
MERIWETHER, M. D. S12351, MA, 6th Inf.
MERRILL, Montie T. W650, D, Merrill, Richard
MERRILL, Virginia E. W6656, WI, Merrill, John O.
MERRIMAN, Irvin, S10048, CA, 18th Inf.
MERRIMAN, James H. S13484, WY, 54th Inf.
MERRITT, B. H. S4991, DK, 35th Inf.
MERRITT, Bessie (Becky), W10910, WA, Merritt, John Curtis
MERRITT, J. J. S14533, WL, 34th Inf.
MERRITT, J. K. P. S9882, MT, 11th Inf.
MERRITT, John C. S3180, WA, 48th Va. Vols.
MERRITT, Joseph W. S3056, HD, 34th Inf.
MERRITT, L. W. S14538, WL, 45th Inf.
MERRITT, Larkin, S885, PU, 25th Inf.
MERRITT, Leonard B. S4944, CT, 8th Cav.
MERRITT, Mary Ann, W152, WL, Merritt, Lewis W.
MERRITT, W. M. S7549, CA, 18th Inf.
MERRITT, Wiley, S12132, WI, 44th Inf.
MERRITT, William H. S9461, MU, 8th Inf.

MESSAMORE, Drucilla E. W6300, K, Messamore, George D.
MESSENGER, Samuel M. S5565, PU, 4th (Murray's) Cav.
MESSER, Ann, W9388, CH, Messer, W. T.
MESSER, Elizabeth Jane, W9477, RO, Messer, John
MESSER, George S. S3164, CO, 25th N.C. Inf.
MESSER, John, S3693, CO, 62nd N.C. Inf.
MESSER, William T. S3126, MN, 27th Inf.
MESSICK, Catherine, W5913, CF, Messick, Richard C.
MESSICK, Mattie Jane, W2470, HW, Messick, Wm. F.
MESSICK, R. C. S11927, CF, 17th Inf.
MESSICK, W. F. S1220, HW, 43rd Inf.
METCALF, Absalom, S9452, GE, 29th N.C. Inf.
METCALF, Felicia Zolicoffer, W7668, LI, Metcalf, James Martin
METCALF, Francis M. S1906, H, 19th Ala. Inf.
METCALF, William, S2982, S4548, U, 29th N.C. Inf.
METCALFE, James M. S6670, LI, Huggin's Co. Lt. Art.
METTS, Elzira F. W4867, K, Metts, Ransom D.
MEWBORN, J. L. S14494, SH, 13th Inf.
MEWBORN, J. W. S14495, SH, 13th Inf.
MICHAEL, T. J. S8915, G, 12th Ky. Cav.
MICHIE, Mary, W10429, MN, Michie, R. W.
MICKLES, Stephey, C174, SH, 9th Miss. Inf.
MIDDLETON, A. A. S4783, CH, 9th Cav.
MIDDLETON, Atholinda Viola, W6608, CH, Middleton, James Elbert
MIDDLETON, Jack, S8977, DE, 9th Cav.
MIDDLETON, James Wesley, S7482, K, 16th N.C. Inf.
MIDDLETON, John N. S4723, HR, 23rd Miss. Inf.
MIDDLETON, Mary A. W3598, H, Middleton, Hugh Montgomery
MIDDLETON, Mollie Ann, W5057, HR, Middleton, John Nathaniel
MIDDLETON, Mollie F. W10422, G, Middleton, John Thomas
MIDGET, Samuel, S8117, WL, 4th (McLemore's) Cav.
MIKLES, J. E. sr. S16028, WL, 4th (McLemore's) Cav.
MILAM, Annie B. W1994, D, Milam, Wm. W.
MILAM, H. B. S14022, 21st (Wilson's) Cav.
MILAM, L. L. S2760, O, 5th Inf.
MILBURN, J. H. S12398, O, 7th Ky. Inf.

Index to Tennessee Confederate Pension Applications

MILBURN, Nannie J. W5373, O, Milburn, John H.
MILES, F. R. ("Sam"), S14080, RB, 2nd Ky. Cav.
MILES, G. D. S16004, LI, 4th Ala. Cav.
MILES, G. W. S3435, ST, 50th Inf.
MILES, J. F. S8843, GE, 50th Inf.
MILES, J. R. S14810, WE, 20th Inf.
MILES, John, S862, SN, Undetermined
MILES, John, S16172, LO, 37th Inf.
MILES, Mary Ann, W8255, RB, Miles, Francis Ross
MILES, Nancy Ann, W9181, LO, Miles, John
MILES, R. H. S4197, K, 16th Cav.
MILES, William, S13861, D, 18th Inf.
MILLARD, Bryan J. S12312, CC, 20th N.C. Inf.
MILLARD, Cora D. W5817, CC, Millard, Bryan Jessee
MILLARD, Dr. John, S10123, SU, 1st Co. Home Guards, Sullivan County
MILLARD, E. C. S9974, WA, 63rd Inf.
MILLARD, Elender Eva. W5468, LI, Millard, Thomas
MILLARD, Rebecca Jane, W5636, R, Millard, Anderson Alexander
MILLARD, S. L. S7232, SU, 63rd Inf.
MILLARD, W. A. S10745, LI, 1st (Turney's) Inf.
MILLARD, a. A. S9260, R, 16th Bn. Cav.
MILLER, A. K. S15330, WL, 7th Inf.
MILLER, Amanda J. W115, GR, Miller, Stephen
MILLER, Andrew J. S5547, SE, 61st Inf.
MILLER, Angeline, W2739, MC, Miller, David M.
MILLER, Arminda C. W9765, OV, Miller, Thomas Boin
MILLER, Benjamin F. S3028, 27th Inf.
MILLER, Clara Jane, W3131, T, Miller, Henry Augustus
MILLER, Cyntha Emeline, W7312, WH, Miller, George Washington
MILLER, D. C. S9497, HI, 10th Cav.
MILLER, D. M. S8473, MC, 16th Bn. Cav.
MILLER, David, S4214, HW, 1st N.C. Inf.
MILLER, David, S4540, W, 16th Inf.
MILLER, David, S11842, K, 64th Va. Inf.
MILLER, E. D. S10204, UN, 2nd (Ashby's) Cav.
MILLER, E. Kate, W8784, WA, Miller, Azor
MILLER, E. L. S7667, LE, 11th Inf.
MILLER, Easter Catherine, W3992, SU, Miller, Samuel R.
MILLER, Eliza Jane, W5464, SU, Miller, Solomon S.
MILLER, Elizabeth B. W1173, SU, Miller, Alvin
MILLER, Elizabeth Jane, W9093, SM, Miller, Edwin R.
MILLER, Elizabeth M. W1705, SU, Miller, Jesse B.
MILLER, Elizabeth P. W3180, SU, Miller, Jesse
MILLER, Ella, W10085, SH, Miller, Abraham
MILLER, Emily A. W2590, D, Miller, Wm. Green
MILLER, Emily Ada, W5107, MU, Miller, John Asberry
MILLER, Esther, W7508, BO, Miller, Ely Dixie
MILLER, F. B. S5162, B, 2nd Ark. Inf.
MILLER, F. G. S14937, SU, 29th Va. Inf.
MILLER, Francis Worley, S3171, WA, Conscripts, Guard
MILLER, Frankie, W3412, WE, Miller, John H.
MILLER, G. W. S1643, HM, 45th N.C. Inf.
MILLER, G. W. S7237, WH, 1st (Carter's) Cav.
MILLER, George W. S11209, SH, 1st Art.
MILLER, Georgiana, W6290, W9612, Miller, James F.
MILLER, Harriet Parks, W9353, RB, Miller, Jesse F.
MILLER, Henry, S7136, BO, 60th N.C. Inf.
MILLER, Ida, W10253, MS, Miller, J. L.
MILLER, Ida Weatherly, W10640, MU, Miller, Walter Weslyn
MILLER, Isabella Levina, W5825, H, Miller, Thomas Anderson
MILLER, J. J. S788, D, 45th Inf.
MILLER, J. K. S5960, SN, 30th Inf.
MILLER, J. M. S5793, O, Stewart's Hvy. Art.
MILLER, J. M. S15772, D, 25th Inf.
MILLER, J. M. S15953, GI, 9th Bn. Cav.
MILLER, J. N. S9438, HI, 9th Bn. (Gantt's) Cav.
MILLER, James A. S15758, MC, 4th Ga. Cav.
MILLER, James F. S11328, WE, 154th Sr. Regt. Inf.
MILLER, James Henry, S15991, JE, 3rd (Lillard's) Mtd. Inf.
MILLER, James L. S11344, R, 43rd Inf.
MILLER, James M. S10143, HM, 3rd Confederate Engineer Troops
MILLER, Jesse, S4979, SU, 53rd N.C. Inf.
MILLER, Jesse F. S12307, MT, 2nd (Robison's) Inf.
MILLER, John, S400, SU, 63rd Inf.

Index to Tennessee Confederate Pension Applications

MILLER, John, S10794, HM, 60th Inf.
MILLER, John, S16202, UN, 37th Inf.
MILLER, John A. S722, RU, 2nd Inf.
MILLER, John A. S6285, MU, 6th (Wheeler's) Cav.
MILLER, John A. S15325, WI, 4th (McLemore's) Cav.
MILLER, John Franklin, S12182, T, 42nd N.C. Inf.
MILLER, John Franklin, S15397, D, 42nd N.C. Inf.
MILLER, John H. S10281, WE, 5th Inf.
MILLER, John N. S4957, GE, 8th Ky. Cav.
MILLER, John Q. S8942, O, 1st Hvy. Art.
MILLER, John S. S1713, MS, 19th Inf.
MILLER, Josie, W8210, HI, Miller, Daniel C.
MILLER, Laura E. W10974, H, Miller, Burrus R.
MILLER, M. D. L. S10000, WA, 3rd (Lillard's) Mtd. Inf.
MILLER, M. V. B. S8857, CL, 64th Va. Inf.
MILLER, Margaret A. W1448, HM, Miller, James Deadrick
MILLER, Martha Ann, W3015, T, Miller, Wm. Franklin
MILLER, Martha Caroline, W7351, HE, Miller, Wm. Carett
MILLER, Martha J. W4338, D, Miller, Jerry Wills
MILLER, Martha Jane, W276, SU, Miller, Edward Cox
MILLER, Martha Jane, W7572, CL, Miller, Martin Van Buren
MILLER, Martha Nesbet, W1694, W, Miller, David
MILLER, Martin, S3887, RB, 8th Inf.
MILLER, Mary A. W10918, HW, Miller, Frederick Dewolfe
MILLER, Mary Ann, W1180, WA, Miller, Solomon
MILLER, Mary Elliott, W3029, WA, Miller, James Sevier
MILLER, Mary Hunter, W6700, SH, Miller, Charles Preston
MILLER, Mary L. W8059, HM, Miller, James M.
MILLER, Mary Narcissa, W1412, WE, Miller, Edward Busey
MILLER, Matilda D. W10191, OV, Miller, Moses
MILLER, Moses, S1040, R, 1st Cav.

MILLER, Nancy Elizabeth, W2721, HM, Miller, David Rankin
MILLER, Nora, W2706, SH, Miller, George Washington
MILLER, Obediah, S2447, W, 23rd N.C. Inf.
MILLER, Octava, W5156, L, Miller, Wm.
MILLER, P. C. F. S188, RU, 45th Inf., Follows #190 on film
MILLER, Permelia C. W4096, HI, Miller, James N.
MILLER, Peter A. S4862, DI, 49th Inf.
MILLER, Polly, W6396, SU, Miller, Thomas
MILLER, R. W. S16152, D, 1st Hvy. Art.
MILLER, Rebecca Ann, W2975, R, Miller, Samuel Houston
MILLER, Richard, S10224, SU, 61st Inf.
MILLER, Ruth E. W2575, CF, Miller, Robert J.
MILLER, S. A. S11088, SH, 18th Miss. Cav.
MILLER, S. D. S10235, RU, 45th Inf.
MILLER, S. H. S6109, R, 43rd Inf.
MILLER, S. R. S16674, D, 46th Va. Inf.
MILLER, Salina K. W7467, BO, Miller, Henry
MILLER, Sam, S16272, O, 17th Inf.
MILLER, Sam A. S15591, HN, 5th Inf.
MILLER, Sarah Ann, W1080, MU, Miller, Wm. Rufus
MILLER, Sarah Milinda, W10371, GI, Miller, John
MILLER, Ssamuel R. S9649, SU, 63rd Inf.
MILLER, Stephen, S824, GR, 60th Inf.
MILLER, Susan, W1502, SU, Miller, Adam T.
MILLER, Susan, W2307, L, Miller, Wm. A.
MILLER, T. A. S5731, H, 43rd Inf.
MILLER, T. J. S4094, RU, 2nd Inf.
MILLER, Tennie C. W1565, RU, Miller, Ike Marion
MILLER, Thomas, S2795, SU, 59th Inf.
MILLER, Tracy Sanders, W436, MU, Miller, John Smith
MILLER, W. C. S3210, HE, 9th Cav.
MILLER, W. C. S13342, DI, 6th Ky. Cav.
MILLER, W. L. S13559, SH, 44th Miss. Inf.
MILLER, W. R. S1236, WI, 1st Inf.
MILLER, W. W. S761, HI, 8th Miss. Inf.
MILLER, Wiley Robert, S7416, WE, 51st Inf.
MILLER, William, C162, RU, 11th Cav.
MILLER, William, S1020, M, 58th Inf.
MILLER, William, S5201, FR, 41st Inf.
MILLER, William, S5285, L, 6th Inf.
MILLER, William Henderson, S7712, SN, 28th Inf.

MILLHORN, Elizabeth, W444, SU, Millhorn, James
MILLHORN, Elizabeth Edelin, W7027, SU, Millhorn, Wm.
MILLHORN, G. W. S6720, SU, 1st (Carter's) Cav.
MILLHORN, J. A. S10410, SU, 60th Inf.
MILLHORN, William, S7519, SU, 29th Inf.
MILLIGAN, A. C. S4767, CA, 14th Cav.
MILLIGAN, Eveline D. W3558, JE, Milligan, Lemuel Day
MILLIGAN, Rebecca Beesheba, W4597, CA, Milligan, Alexander Campbell
MILLIGAN, S. Love, W8052, CA, Milligan, Wm. Henry
MILLIGAN, W. H. S4241, CA, 62nd Inf.
MILLIKEN, Ann Melissa, W10858, D, Milliken, George Robards
MILLIKEN, George R. S15916, S15150, D, Huggin's Co. Lt. Art.
MILLIKEN, J. A. S11895, LI, 1st (Turney's) Inf.
MILLIKEN, J. K. S2380, CE, Lt. Art.
MILLIRON, Jacob, S10178, D, 6th (Wheeler's) Cav.
MILLIRON, Nancy Caroline, W9198, D, Milliron, Samuel James
MILLRANY, Lucy Ann, W6813, CF, Millrany, Thomas
MILLRANY, Thomas, S13772, CF, 16th Inf.
MILLS, Alexander, S3779, BR, 62nd Inf.
MILLS, Alvin, S3606, CH, 21st Cav.
MILLS, B. D. S16337, S16534, G, 19th & 20th Cons. Cav., 1st app has Ellis for surname by mistake
MILLS, Dero F. S10140, D, 2nd Cav.
MILLS, E. F. S5821, SU, 63rd Inf.
MILLS, Eletha, W1066, SU, Mills, Frank
MILLS, Emma Catherine, W4493, HR, Mills, Wm. R.
MILLS, F. S925, HR, 9th Inf.
MILLS, F. S12931, HR, 14th Cav.
MILLS, Fred, S2331, HR, 9th Inf.
MILLS, G. A. S12653, DE, Phillips' Co. Lt. Art.
MILLS, J. W. S3253, H, 26th Inf.
MILLS, J. W. S6796, 15th Cav.
MILLS, John, S2518, LI, 84th Inf.
MILLS, John F. S4660, HA, 29th Inf.
MILLS, Laura Lane, W5827, HR, Mills, Augustus
MILLS, Maggie J. W5661, SU, Mills, Edward A.
MILLS, Margaret J. W1255, LI, Mills, John

MILLS, Mary E. W141, O, Mills, Samuel J.
MILLS, W. B. S5142, K, Kain's Battery, Lt. Art.
MILLS, Washington S. S5227, MA, 6th Inf.
MILLS, William Robert, S6679, HR, 14th (Neely's) Cav.
MILLSAP, Mary Elizabeth, W8555, MOO, Millsap, Mike
MILLSAP, Mike, S4938, MOO, 3rd Cav.
MILLSAPS, Julia Anne Katherine, W247, MO, Millsaps, Ransom
MILLSAPS, Mary Ann, W1672, MOO, Millsaps, Luther Wiley
MILNER, R. H. S15259, WE, 33rd Inf.
MILSAPS, W. M. S15030, JO, 1st N.C. Cav.
MILSAPS, andy, S12595, MO, 59th Inf.
MILSTEAD, Casanda, W3192, CH, Milstead, Charles Thomas
MILSTEAD, Charles Thomas, S8554, HR, 16th Cav.
MILUM, George W. S13071, HI, 24th Inf.
MIMS, D. J. S9336, WL, 7th Inf.
MIMS, M. J. S10468, JE, 62nd Inf.
MINATREE, Mary J. W4077, LI, Minatree, David G.
MINCHEY, Richard L. S737, M, 28th Inf.
MINCY, Tinnie D.   See Tinnie D. Barnett
MINICK, James K. P. S4847, SU, Kain's Co. Lt. Art.
MINK, Rachel, W5763, JE, Mink, Wiley B.
MINK, W. B. S10164, JE, 48th Va. Inf.
MINNICK, Mary Bell, W2206, SU, Minnick, James K. P.
MINNIS, Martha, W7119, MO, Minnis, Samuel Y.
MINOR, Charles, S10539, ST, 14th Inf.
MINOR, Margaret P. W8169, ST, Minor, Charles
MINOR, Ned, C110, ST, 10th Cav.
MINOR, William L. S16592, 2nd Ga. Cav.
MINSON, John, S14786, CF, 32nd Va. Inf.
MINSON, Margaret Lamb, W7058, CF, Minson, John
MINTER, Eliza, W6202, MR, Minter, John L.
MINTON, John E. S2694, WY, 45th Inf.
MINTON, Martha Jane, W6206, WY, Minton, J. E.
MINTON, Mary Frances, W7627, PU, Minton, Wm. Carroll
MINTON, T. J. S9669, SQ, 8th (Smith's) Cav.
MINTON, W. C. S13132, PU, 22nd (Barteau's) Cav.
MIRES, Charity A. W8957, WL, Mires, Morgan

MISENHEIMER, M. A. S1207, T, 3rd Inf.
MITCHELL, A. S. S10929, D, 15th Inf.
MITCHELL, Alexander, S12672, 33rd Inf.
MITCHELL, Andrew J. S11465, HE, 35th Inf.
MITCHELL, C. C. S3893, BE, 49th Inf.
MITCHELL, Callie E. W7778, Mitchell, N. A.
MITCHELL, Canseda, W9876, W6828, H, Mitchell, W. Steve
MITCHELL, Carline Elizabeth, W3400, W944, WE, Mitchell, James Daniel
MITCHELL, Chase, S14374, WA, 60th Inf.
MITCHELL, Dulcena, W694, HW, Mitchell, Robert
MITCHELL, Eliza, W470, SM, Mitchell, Henry A.
MITCHELL, Eliza Davis, W7652, MU, Mitchell, Josiah Dabbs
MITCHELL, Elizabeth, W5319, BE, Mitchell, C. C.
MITCHELL, Elizabeth Atlantic, W200, CA, Mitchell, John E.
MITCHELL, Ellen May, W7607, MU, Mitchell, Wm. Terry
MITCHELL, Emma, W8337, CC, Mitchell, Zack A.
MITCHELL, Emma J. W6190, CE, Mitchell, Philip Henry
MITCHELL, G. R. S16407, G, 51st Inf.
MITCHELL, Green Willis, S6443, SH, 28th Miss. Cav.
MITCHELL, H. B. S11991, D, 9th (Ward's) Cav.
MITCHELL, H. L. S12285, WI, 44th Inf.
MITCHELL, H. T. S5570, GI, 32nd Inf.
MITCHELL, Harriett Ann, W814, HE, Mitchell, James Augusta
MITCHELL, Henritta, W10423, W7285, HR, Mitchell, George Washington
MITCHELL, I. R. S3447, LI, 1st (Turney's) Inf.
MITCHELL, Isaac A. S15691, D, Unassigned
MITCHELL, J. A. S3358, W, 35th Inf.
MITCHELL, J. A. S3607, L, 38th Inf.
MITCHELL, J. A. S14386, FR, 23rd Bn. Inf.
MITCHELL, J. C. S10776, LO, Ramsey's Battery, Lt Art
MITCHELL, J. F. S5071, CF, 4th Inf.
MITCHELL, J. N. S8409, HN, 5th Inf.
MITCHELL, J. V. S15945, S16130, HD, 50th Inf.
MITCHELL, J. W. C. S15800, B, 37th Inf.
MITCHELL, James, S8022, PU, 38th Inf.
MITCHELL, James A. S4488, HE, 13th Inf.

MITCHELL, James M. S12907, MN, Undetermined
MITCHELL, James W. S2284, ST, 50th Inf.
MITCHELL, Jennie Wells, W11108, RU, Mitchell, Samuel Hodge
MITCHELL, John M. S2230, WA, 8th Va. Cav.
MITCHELL, John M. S12818, WH, 8th (Dibrell's) Cav.
MITCHELL, John Robert, S8937, WE, 5th Inf.
MITCHELL, Joy, S1484, MR, 35th Inf.
MITCHELL, Judith, W2569, DI, Mitchell, Ballard
MITCHELL, L. C. S14690, LI, 32nd Inf.
MITCHELL, Laura A. W9437, D, Mitchell, A. S.
MITCHELL, Lou H. W8121, SH, Mitchell, H. H.
MITCHELL, Lucy Ellen, W9841, GI, Mitchell, Henry Turner
MITCHELL, Manervia, W3628, WE, Mitchell, Francis Marion
MITCHELL, Margaret O. W6493, Mitchell, Robert Henry
MITCHELL, Mark, S8185, MR, 5th Inf.
MITCHELL, Martha Jane, W9210, L, Mitchell, DeWitt Clinton
MITCHELL, Martin, S4424, PU, 16th Inf.
MITCHELL, Mary E. [McCain], W11002, WE, Mitchell, John Robert, [Later married McCain]
MITCHELL, Moses W. S11196, BR, 39th Ga. Inf.
MITCHELL, N. A. S8502, WE, 55th Inf.
MITCHELL, N. A. S12328, CA, 8th (Smith's) Cav.
MITCHELL, Nancy J. W4939, MO, Mitchell, T. W.
MITCHELL, Olive Jame, W3470, RB, Mitchell, Charles
MITCHELL, P. H. S9857, CE, 9th Bn. Ky. Cav.
MITCHELL, P. T. S7056, SU, 60th Inf.
MITCHELL, Phoeba Ann, W5809, D, Mitchell, J. L.
MITCHELL, Rebecca L. W3610, BE, Mitchell, Allen H.
MITCHELL, Robert L. S12781, OV, 1st Cav.
MITCHELL, S. H. S16539, RU, 45th Inf.
MITCHELL, Sallie Elizabeth, W2930, W8229, HR, Mitchell, Albert Harrison
MITCHELL, Sally J. W8996, LI, Mitchell, L. C.
MITCHELL, Samuel, S3667, S2648, HW, 60th Inf.

MITCHELL, Sarah, W8538, WA, Mitchell, Charles
MITCHELL, Sarah A. W1385, R, Mitchell, Wm. G.
MITCHELL, Sarah Ann, W8402, SU, Mitchell, P. T.
MITCHELL, Sarah Frances, W6609, HE, Mitchell, Andrew Jackson
MITCHELL, Sarah Rebecca, W7382, MU, Mitchell, Wm. H.
MITCHELL, Shem, C8436, MA, 27th Inf., App. numbered on regular Soldiers film
MITCHELL, Soloman, S10635, LI, 1st (Turney's) Inf.
MITCHELL, Spencer, S3025, MR, 5th Cav.
MITCHELL, Sue A. W4385, OV, Mitchell, Robert Lafayette
MITCHELL, T. J. S14794, 22nd Inf.
MITCHELL, Thomas E. S16532, WY, 50th Ala. Inf.
MITCHELL, Thomas J. S10733, 22nd Inf.
MITCHELL, W. S. S7979, 18th Cav.
MITCHELL, W. T. S12643, MU, 3rd (Clack's) Inf.
MITCHELL, William H. S15058, S14183, MU, 6th (Wheeler's) Cav.
MITCHENER, Frank, S7115, MU, 9th Cav.
MITCHIE, R. W. S6230, MN, 19th Inf.
MITCHUM, Mattie, W3710, WE, Mitchum, W. E.
MITCHUM, W. E. S9633, WE, 22nd Inf.
MIZE, Sallie A. W1246, W8274, D, Mize, Wm. Franklin
MIZE, Sarah Annie, W8274, W1246, D, Mize, Wm. Franklin
MOBLEY, Mary Maney, W11118, RU, Mobley, James Gomilion
MOBLEY, Sallie Theresa, W9795, HI, Mobley, Benjamin Bullinger
MOBLY, B. B. S9228, HI, 11th Inf.
MOCK, Florence Wills, W10337, CT, Mock, E. H.
MODENA, Margaret Ann Lyons, W10318, FR, Modena, T. H.
MODINA, Ann, W8749, FR, Modina, D. F.
MODLIN, Z. N. S14336, HO, 43rd N.C. Inf.
MODRALL, John Nelson, S7927, CF, 18th Inf.
MODRALL, Robert Nelson, S6384, RU, 18th Inf.
MODRALL, Sarah E. W3099, RU, Modrall, Robert N.
MOFFETT, Henry, S13700, O, 10th Miss. Cav.

MOFFITT, J. C. S12921, DY, 27th Inf.
MOFFITT, Margaret, W9208, SU, Moffitt, Thomas
MOFFITT, Mary Ann, W9061, W, Moffitt, Hugh Lawson
MOFFITT, Thomas, S1868, SU, 62nd N.C. Inf.
MOFIELD, C. M. S12186, SM, 4th (McLemore's) Cav.
MOFIELD, Cynthia, W3576, SM, Mofield, Thomas
MOFIELD, Margarette, W1287, SM, Mofield, John
MOFIELD, Thomas, S11083, SM, 8th (Dibrell's) Cav.
MOFIELD, William B. S7610, SM, 4th (McLemore's) Cav.
MOIZE, Elizabeth, W3816, MA, Moize, Alford Johnson
MOLES, Elijah, S3987, OV, 8th Ky. Cav.
MOLES, Polly, W6496, OV, Moles, Elijah
MOLLOY, John Gillentine, S9717, MU, 25th Inf.
MOLLOY, M. C. S12726, MU, 48th (Voorhies') Inf.
MOLLOY, Mary Frasier, W6357, D, Molloy, John Gillentine
MONCRIEF, T. J. S2815, SN, 24th Inf.
MONDAY, J. S. S6492, CO, Kain's Co. Lt. Art.
MONEY, D. S. S5954, K, 12th Ga. Inf.
MONEY, J. J. S13402, FR, 34th Inf.
MONEY, N. A. S15773, FR, 34th Inf.
MONFEE, J. M. S14357, SH, 59th Ala. Inf.
MONGER, Sarah R. W4144, LO, Monger, Wiley H.
MONKS, Fannie Amanda, W4685, D, Monks, Thomas B.
MONROE, Alex L. S2937, UN, 1st (Carter's) Cav.
MONROE, Frank, S14719, MA, 6th Inf.
MONROE, J. T. S899, R, 1st Cav.
MONROE, M. S. S5548, JE, 2nd (Ashby's) Cav.
MONROE, Mary Elizabeth, W1206, JE, Monroe, Mordicia S.
MONROE, R. S. S5819, HN, 4th Miss. Inf.
MONSTON, Julia P. W4591, GI, Monston, Richard Victor
MONTAGUE, Adolphus W. S8196, L, 7th (Duckworth's) Cav.
MONTAGUE, Elizabeth A. W3079, SH, Montague, Abraham Young
MONTAGUE, Hettie Hearring, W6824, L, Montague, Adolphus Wiley

Index to Tennessee Confederate Pension Applications

MONTAGUE, James A. S8424, CH, 9th Cav.
MONTAGUE, Marietta, W4015, WY, Montague, Wm. Young
MONTAGUE, W. Y. S11396, WY, 6th (Wheeler's) Cav.
MONTGOMERY, Albert F. S12091, WE, 37th N.C. Inf.
MONTGOMERY, Andrew J. S8252, CC, 13th Ark. Inf.
MONTGOMERY, Bailey, S9794, RU, 20th Inf., Also see James B. Montgomery #16477
MONTGOMERY, Elias, S2785, MOO, 7th (Duckworth's) Cav.
MONTGOMERY, Elizabeth Caroline, W4432, RO, Montgomery, Elbert C.
MONTGOMERY, Frances Minro, W5048, MR, Montgomery, Edward
MONTGOMERY, G. W. S10311, WE, 21st (Wilson's) Cav.
MONTGOMERY, J. C. S12179, MS, 4th (McLemore's) Cav.
MONTGOMERY, J. J. S13192, LO, 63rd Inf.
MONTGOMERY, J. T. S6208, SM, 30th Inf.
MONTGOMERY, James B. S16477, RU, 20th Inf. See also Bailey Montgomery
MONTGOMERY, James R. S10082, D, 154th Sr. Regt. Inf.
MONTGOMERY, John D. S16153, L, 5th Tex. Cav., Application is missing.
MONTGOMERY, John H. S4969, SU, 63rd Inf.
MONTGOMERY, John W. S8083, WE, 31st Inf.
MONTGOMERY, Louisa Jane, W1025, LI, Montgomery, Wm. Moore
MONTGOMERY, Mandy Facilian, W9313, RU, Montgomery, James Bailey
MONTGOMERY, Margaret, W8296, G, Montgomery, D. B. C.
MONTGOMERY, Margaret A. W3984, MU, Montgomery, Henry W.
MONTGOMERY, Mary Jane, W3629, K, Montgomery, John Marshall
MONTGOMERY, Mathew H. S6200, H, 1st (Carter's) Cav.
MONTGOMERY, Mollie, W5491, SH, Montgomery, James E.
MONTGOMERY, Nancy Jane, W1003, WH, Montgomery, Zachariah
MONTGOMERY, S. S. S4198, FR, 32nd Inf.
MONTGOMERY, Sallie Willie, W4035, WE, Montgomery, George W.
MONTGOMERY, Sarah Elizabeth, W10865, WH, Montgomery, Wm. M.
MONTGOMERY, Susan Elizabeth, W10530, H, Montgomery, M. H.
MONTGOMERY, Unity E. W5729, WE, Montgomery, John W.
MONTGOMERY, Uriah, S11419, D, 20th Inf.
MONTGOMERY, W. F. S3676, H, 39th Ga. Inf.
MONTGOMERY, W. F. S5982, SH, 39th Ga. Inf.
MONTGOMERY, W. J. S13548, WE, 47th Inf.
MONTGOMERY, W. M. S1990, LI, 8th Inf.
MONTGOMERY, W. M. S9684, WH, 8th (Dibrell's) Cav.
MONTGOMERY, Zacariah, S1065, WH, 28th Inf.
MONTIETH, Julina, W1908, SU, Montieth, George Washington
MOODY, Amanda R. W8793, SN, Moody, James A.
MOODY, E. W. S2193, WL, 154th Sr. Regt. Inf.
MOODY, G. B. S10061, RB, 14th Inf.
MOODY, H. S2240, ST, 11th Inf.
MOODY, Isaac N. S1107, HN, 20th Cav.
MOODY, J. G. S12277, D, 1st Inf.
MOODY, J. M. S13488, HU, 10th Cav.
MOODY, J. W. S903, SH, 33rd Inf.
MOODY, James A. S563, SN, 2nd Inf.
MOODY, John A. S4958, SU, Unassigned
MOODY, John W. S6493, G, 12th Ky. Cav.
MOODY, Lewis, S14678, LK, Tillman's Div. State Gds.
MOODY, Lizzie, W9829, D, Moody, Wm. Hogan
MOODY, Lucy, W1095, WL, Moody, Samuel Thomas
MOODY, Margaret Susan, W5743, D, Moody, George Boyd
MOODY, Mattie C. W6259, HU, Moody, James Martin
MOODY, R. F. S707, PU, 25th Inf.
MOODY, Samuel M. S9436, HN, 46th Inf.
MOODY, Susan Elizabeth, W10021, HN, Moody, Isaac N.
MOODY, Tilman, S15754, SH, 7th (Duckworth's) Cav.
MOODY, W. H. S8257, D, 1st Inf.
MOODY, W. W. S13514, O, 9th Inf.
MOODY, William W. S12515, JE, 4th Bn. (Branner's) Cav.

MOON, Mary Thomas, W6792, O, Moon, John Alexander
MOONEY, J. H. S7867, G, 16th Inf.
MOONEY, Mattie Elizabeth, W7383, G, Mooney, J. H.
MOONEY, Susan Frances, W2604, WE, Mooney, Wellborn
MOONEYHAM, C. W. S2279, DK, 16th Inf.
MOONEYHAM, Isaac C. S1704, CO, 60th N.C. Inf.
MOONEYHAM, John C. S5861, V, 35th Inf.
MOONEYHAM, Thomas J. S9858, WH, 35th Inf.
MOOR, Mary E. W1743, D, Moor, J. B.
MOORE, A. H. S3940, SU, Burrough's Co. Lt. Art.
MOORE, A. M. S10599, SH, 6th Inf.
MOORE, A. Z. S7000, DK, 50th Inf.
MOORE, Adeline Woolfolk, W7466, Moore, James Dennis
MOORE, Alford, S5749, G, 55th Inf.
MOORE, Ann, W8792, LI, Moore, Joe
MOORE, Ann Hunt, W8924, FR, Moore, Horatio R.
MOORE, Annie E. W3471, D, Moore, Green P.
MOORE, B. H. S7637, CF, 34th Miss. Inf.
MOORE, B. H. S10490, SM, 22nd (Barteau's) Cav.
MOORE, B. P. S5202, MN, 19th Cav.
MOORE, Barbara Frances, W2076, D, Moore, Virgil Burke
MOORE, Bayless, S6579, K, 19th Inf.
MOORE, Benjamin, C250, BR, Regiment not given
MOORE, Benjamin F. S6531, WY, 2nd Ark. Inf.
MOORE, Benjamin F. S6810, MN, 23rd Miss. Inf.
MOORE, C. S. S1579, WE, 20th Inf.
MOORE, Catherine, W8147, MOO, Moore, J. G.
MOORE, Claiborne A. S16466, S15798, WE, 2nd (Woodward's) Ky. Cav.
MOORE, Cleon R. S12542, HW, 63rd Inf.
MOORE, Cordelia Margaret, W3898, D, Moore, John Henley
MOORE, Darthula, W8364, WH, Moore, George W.
MOORE, David N. S16052, 12th Ky. Cav.
MOORE, Dudley, S937, SM, 2nd Cav.
MOORE, E. M. P. S11537, SU, 5th (McKenzie's) Cav.
MOORE, Eliza, W879, MS, Moore, Stephen J.

MOORE, Eliza Davis, W5054, GE, Moore, John
MOORE, Elizabeth, W1649, SQ, Moore, Thomas Jefferson
MOORE, Elizabeth H. W5032, HI, Moore, Wm. H.
MOORE, Elizabeth H. W6925, B, Moore, F. H.
MOORE, Elizabeth Hightower, W8886, W7810, MR, Moore, Alexander Fitzgerald
MOORE, Elizabeth Hollaway, W11012, CO, Moore, Thomas
MOORE, Elizabeth J. W6881, L, Moore, Wm. Anthony
MOORE, Ellen Sarah, W6257, W9920, MA, Moore, Mathias Jones
MOORE, Emma L. W8073, WL, Moore, James E.
MOORE, Eva J. W10899, HY, Moore, Wm. Duncan
MOORE, Eva [Nelson], W10829, MU, Moore, Frank J. [Later married Nelson]
MOORE, F. D. S13127, G, 154th Sr. Regt. Inf.
MOORE, F. H. S5897, B, 3rd (Forrest's) Cav.
MOORE, F. M. S2677, WL, 35th Inf.
MOORE, Frank, S14421, SH, 3rd Miss. Cav.
MOORE, G. M. S8695, PU, 13th Cav.
MOORE, G. W. S1528, GE, 37th Inf.
MOORE, G. W. S5862, F, 13th Inf.
MOORE, George Washington, S8978, F, 15th Cav.
MOORE, George Washington, S11514, CA, 21st (Wilson's) Cav.
MOORE, Green B. S10145, RU, 55th Inf.
MOORE, H. C. W5677, DK, Moore, A. Z.
MOORE, H. L. C. S15811, WH, 16th Inf.
MOORE, H. N. S7409, 12th Tex. Cav.
MOORE, Harriett Lane, W6211, Moore, Wm. C.
MOORE, Hugh A. S13519, HW, 2nd (Ashby's) Cav.
MOORE, J. B. S6054, 12th Inf.
MOORE, J. H. S15383, MT, 14th Ky. Cav.
MOORE, J. M. S4425, SH, 9th Miss. Inf.
MOORE, J. M> J. S9764, 22nd Inf.
MOORE, J. S. S7307, CF, 19th Miss. Inf.
MOORE, J. T. S11888, OV, 8th (Dibrell's) Cav.
MOORE, J. W. S1478, HY, Undetermined
MOORE, J. W. S5111, ST, 50th Inf.
MOORE, J. W. S15245, F, 34th Ala. Inf.
MOORE, James, S5497, SU, 31st Inf.
MOORE, James, S14456, HI, 9th Bn. Cav.
MOORE, James A. S16210, T, 51st Inf.
MOORE, James E. S10530, SH, 8th Miss. Cav.

Index to Tennessee Confederate Pension Applications

MOORE, James Knox, S16063, B, 6th Miss. Cav.
MOORE, James Lewis, S9639, O, 7th Cav.
MOORE, James M. S1163, S14526, WH, 8th (Dibrell's) Cav.
MOORE, James M. S4379, B, 23rd Inf.
MOORE, James W. S413, WA, 37th Inf.
MOORE, Jennie Ella, W5216, MU, Moore, Wm. James
MOORE, Jessee G. S12663, MOO, 4th (McLemore's) Cav.
MOORE, John, C263, HI, 10th Cav.
MOORE, John, S12315, GE, 64th N.C. Inf.
MOORE, John A. S8129, DY, 1st Cav.
MOORE, John A. S15031, D, 7th Inf.
MOORE, John B. S7045, D, 45th Inf.
MOORE, John T. S11123, WH, 8th (Dibrell's) Cav.
MOORE, John T. S16075, D, 6th Ky. Cav.
MOORE, John W. S3833, WL, 8th (Smith's) Cav.
MOORE, John W. S12321, HM, 12th Bn. (Day's) Cav.
MOORE, Joseph, S9058, D, 9th (Bennett's) Cav.
MOORE, Joseph A. S9594, LI, 8th Inf.
MOORE, Julia Ann, W3103, H, Moore, Robert
MOORE, Julia Anna, W4257, HN, Moore, Joseph Thomas
MOORE, Julia Williams, W3517, SH, Moore, Alexander Morgan
MOORE, L. C. S3498, HR, Forrest's Old Regt. Cav.
MOORE, L. D. S2393, DK, 16th Inf.
MOORE, L. J. S4110, DY, 15th Cav.
MOORE, L. J. S9019, H, Thomas' Legion, N.C.
MOORE, Levinia Lemon, W8081, MU, Moore, Robert H.
MOORE, Lucretia, W3572, GI, Moore, Davis
MOORE, M. J. M. S8657, SH, 26th Miss. Inf.
MOORE, Margaret Cornelia, W9912, SH, Moore, Cornelius
MOORE, Martha Eugenia, W4078, GI, Moore, James C.
MOORE, Mary Ann, W902, L, Moore, Wm. J.
MOORE, Mary Ann, W6543, MN, Moore, Benjamin Franklin
MOORE, Mary Artiemissie, W9562, B, Moore, Wyly Tilman
MOORE, Mary E. W356, G, Moore, Wm. S.
MOORE, Mary E. W3153, L, Moore, John A.
MOORE, Mary Frances, W2301, B, Moore, Tillman Tennessee

MOORE, Mary Frances, W5472, O, Moore, Alexander Newell
MOORE, Mary J. W6642, WA, Moore, Richard Carr
MOORE, Mary Jane, W903, L, Moore, Sidney
MOORE, Mary Rhoda, W9133, SH, Moore, John Daniel
MOORE, Mary malinda, W3893, HI, Moore, Robert Totty
MOORE, Matilda, W2127, SU, Moore, James
MOORE, Mattie E. W7748, D, Moore, N. W.
MOORE, Minervia Burgess, W9869, GI, Moore, Alexander DeWitt
MOORE, Mollie, W5004, Moore, Joseph M.
MOORE, Mourning Ella, W5857, HN, Moore, John Warner
MOORE, N. G. S3015, R, 19th Inf.
MOORE, Nancy Ann, W1227, LI, Moore, Joseph T.
MOORE, Nancy Catherine, W3033, HM, Moore, Ephraim Murray
MOORE, Nancy E. W5378, SU, Moore, Alfred H.
MOORE, Nancy Jane, W3817, B, Moore, James Meridith
MOORE, Nancy Jane, W3993, MR, Moore, Richard Jackson
MOORE, Nannie V. W6946, O, Moore, Newton Kelley
MOORE, Nettie Grace, W3502, RU, Moore, T. J.
MOORE, Pattie R. W5154, SH, Moore, Andrew
MOORE, Peter W. S4048, DY, 12th Inf.
MOORE, Peyton, S6100, HR, 14th Cav.
MOORE, Phebe Jones, W3525, MC, Moore, Allen
MOORE, R. C. S4021, WA, 19th Inf.
MOORE, R. M. (Dick), S15858, WY, 48th (Nixon's) Inf.
MOORE, R. P. W1397, WE, Moore, Calvin Simpson
MOORE, R. S. S2462, U, 19th Inf.
MOORE, R. T. S14742, D, 20th Inf.
MOORE, Rachel Jane, W9314, WE, Moore, Claybourn A.
MOORE, Rhoda Ann, W551, BE, Moore, John G.
MOORE, Richard G. S6083, WI, 1st Cav.
MOORE, Richard Jackson, S9213, MR, 4th Cav.
MOORE, Robert I. S15695, MU, 1st (Feild's) Inf.

-245

MOORE, Robert Moore, S14237, GI, 6th (Wheeler's) Cav.
MOORE, Robert T. S265, HI, 9th Cav.
MOORE, Rosa B. W11158, H, Moore, Wm. Antipass, Papers found mixed with 11157 on film
MOORE, S. A. W. S9488, HY, 9th Inf.
MOORE, S. D. S1936, C, 19th Inf.
MOORE, Samuel, S1481, MS, 9th Ala. Inf.
MOORE, Sarah, W9715, G, Moore, Jessie H.
MOORE, Sarah A. W6676, HW, Moore, Cleam R.
MOORE, Sarah Adeline, W3818, K, Moore, Samuel D.
MOORE, Sarah E. W3858, CF, Moore, John Samuel
MOORE, Sarah E. W5053, G, Moore, Robert Yancey
MOORE, Sarah Elizabeth, W4595, G, Moore, Wm.
MOORE, Sarah Elizabeth, W9953, DI, Moore, Frank B.
MOORE, Sarah Ellen, W9920, W6257, MA, Moore, M. J.
MOORE, Sarah Jane, W153, WI, Moore, James Andrew
MOORE, Stephen Petty, S15999, GI, 4th S.C. Inf.
MOORE, Syntha Adeline, W2745, DK, Moore, Levi Douglas
MOORE, T. F. S4285, SH, 41st Inf.
MOORE, T. P. S3964, HE, 5th Ala. Cav.
MOORE, Thomas, S12596, CO, 62nd Inf.
MOORE, Thomas Craven, S5745, HE, 14th Cav.
MOORE, Thomas J. S2963, GE, 61st Inf.
MOORE, W. D. S16519, HY, 3rd (Forrest's) Cav.
MOORE, W. F. S14409, SH, 18th Miss. Cav.
MOORE, W. P. S5464, CO, 60th Inf.
MOORE, W. T. S6352, GI, 5th Ala. Bn. Inf.
MOORE, W. T. S15776, SH, 11th (Holman's) Cav.
MOORE, William, S52, G, 4th Inf.
MOORE, William Anthony, S6759, L, 50th Inf.
MOORE, William G. S68, RU, 18th Inf.
MOORE, William H. H, S1157, HW, 2nd Cav.
MOORE, William J. S5571, RO, 7th N.C. Inf.
MOORE, William James, S14064, MU, 48th (Voorhies') Inf.
MOOREFIELD, John W. S13039, SH, 14th Va. Inf.

MOORELAND, John A. S9314, H, Lookout Art.
MOORING, Mary E. W4984, LK, Mooring, James Dixon
MOORMAN, Cyrus, S11373, B, 41st Inf.
MOORMAN, H. C. S16564, F, 13th Inf.
MOOSE, Susan, W3106, T, Moose, Wm.
MOOSER, Alex Z. S13613, See Alexander Z. Moser
MORAN, Mike, S98, O, 10th Inf.
MORE, Giles, C22, GI, 9th Cav.
MOREFIELD, Joe, S5350, SU, 53rd N.C. Inf.
MOREHEAD, Nannie L. W9315, SH, Morehead, Joseph M.
MOREL, Mary Thompson, W10346, D, Morel, Julius S.
MORELAND, Beverly G. S2463, SM, 28th Inf.
MORELAND, Emily B. W8424, H, Moreland, John Henry
MORELAND, S. J. S11040, S7199, WE, 17th Miss. Inf.
MORELOCK, Hannah, W1204, HW, Morelock, Jacob
MORELOCK, Jonathan B. R. S12896, HM, 12th Bn. (Day's) Cav.
MORELOCK, Nancy, W7262, HM, Morelock, Nathan B.
MORELOCK, Nancy, W8430, HW, Morelock, Samuel
MORELOCK, Nathan B. S9975, HM, 43rd Inf.
MORELOCK, Prissey, W448, SU, Morelock, Baker
MORELOCK, Samuel, S644, HW, 29th Inf.
MORELOCK, Samuel jr. S10038, HW, 31st Inf.
MORELON, B. G. S687, J, 28th Inf.
MORFORD, Henry C. S14387, W, 11th (Holman's) Cav.
MORFORD, Mollie C. W9302, W, Morford, Charles R.
MORGAN, A. W. S6450, CH, 31st Inf.
MORGAN, Andy J. S7066, MO, 59th Inf.
MORGAN, Annie, W6832, HU, Morgan, James
MORGAN, Annie Stephenson, W10881, SH, Morgan, Ephraim Weston
MORGAN, Artilda, W7884, OV, Morgan, Thomas Louis
MORGAN, Benjamin Ledford, S12065, CO, 79th N.C. Inf.
MORGAN, Charles Hynam, S7575, MT, 14th Inf.
MORGAN, Cleopatria, W6557, T, Morgan, John
MORGAN, E. W. S16546, SH, 3rd Miss. Inf.

MORGAN, Edwin James, S6417, SH, 7th (Duckworth's) Cav.
MORGAN, Elizabeth White, W9448, LK, Morgan, James Henry
MORGAN, George H. S8660, HE, 51st Inf.
MORGAN, H. R. S12777, RB, 11th Inf.
MORGAN, HEnry A. S6333, G, 19th Cav.
MORGAN, Henry B. S1949, MOO, 41st Inf.
MORGAN, I. C. S11220, V, 35th Inf.
MORGAN, J. H. S12845, R, 22nd Ala. Inf.
MORGAN, J. J. S8891, OV, 25th Inf.
MORGAN, J. L. S4709, PO, 29th Inf.
MORGAN, J. M. L. S8427, MO, 37th Inf.
MORGAN, J. S. S2031, OV, 8th Cav.
MORGAN, James L. S13017, K, 2nd Ga. Bn.
MORGAN, Jane P. W7008, CH, Morgan, Willis Allen
MORGAN, Jennie B. W7550, V, Morgan, I. C.
MORGAN, Job M. S14770, S14576, J, 8th Inf.
MORGAN, John, S5022, T, 8th (Smith's) Cav.
MORGAN, John, S5940, O, 27th Inf.
MORGAN, John E. S8053, CH, 31st Inf.
MORGAN, John W. S591, J, 4th Inf.
MORGAN, John W. S13382, SN, 20th Inf.
MORGAN, L. B. S12558, CF, 4th (McLemore's) Cav.
MORGAN, Lucinda R. W5493, K, Morgan, James LaFayette
MORGAN, M. L. S14048, O, 27th Inf.
MORGAN, Mahala, W1881, H, Morgan, Silas Marion
MORGAN, Malissa Ellen, W5673, PO, Morgan, John Layfayette
MORGAN, Marena, W8428, PU, Morgan, W. C.
MORGAN, Margaret Elizabeth, W2702, CC, Morgan, Robert Wilson
MORGAN, Mary, W4124, D, Morgan, J. B.
MORGAN, Mary Amanda, W5304, HE, Morgan, G. H.
MORGAN, Mary Eliza, W5702, RB, Morgan, Wm. Albert
MORGAN, Mary Elizabeth, W6146, W, Morgan, George Hampton
MORGAN, Nannie Mai, W4411, RB, Morgan, Hiram Riburn
MORGAN, Nannie Williams, W9994, MU, Morgan, Wm. Porter
MORGAN, Paulina M. W7771, J, Morgan, Jobe M.
MORGAN, Rebecca Jane, W10655, ST, Morgan, James M.
MORGAN, Robert L. S2746, SU, 63rd Inf.
MORGAN, S. G. S8388, DE, 12th Ky. Cav.
MORGAN, S. M. S2444, H, 3rd Inf.
MORGAN, Sarah Tennie, W9203, D, Morgan, John Henry
MORGAN, T. D. S9353, D, Unassigned (Captain of Wagon Train)
MORGAN, Tennie, W7918, D, Morgan, John H.
MORGAN, Thomas L. B. S457, S1342, OV, 8th Cav.
MORGAN, Vina, W2501, WH, Morgan, Algernon Sidney
MORGAN, W. S. S7148, T, 3rd Inf.
MORGAN, W. W. S10303, R, 6th Ga. Cav.
MORGAN, William C. S8701, PU, Shaw's Bn. Cav.
MORGAN, William J. P. S13590, SE, 3rd (Lillard's) Mtd. Inf.
MORGAN, Willie Austin, W10266, SH, Morgan, John Adrian
MORGAN, Zachariah, S4426, W, 35th Inf.
MORIARTY, Thomas, S2754, BE, 55th Inf.
MORISON, J. L. S12263, CL, 1st Va. Cav.
MORITZ, Amelia, W1425, CL, Moritz, John D.
MORRELL, C. R. S2519, SU, 26th Inf.
MORRELL, E. A. S2104, SU, 26th Inf.
MORRELL, Elizzie Jane, W3778, SU, Morrell, Wm. R.
MORRELL, J. C. S15059, CO, 59th Inf.
MORRELL, J. F. S850, SU, 4th Cav.
MORRELL, J. F. E. S14903, WA, 61st Inf.
MORRELL, J. M. S2833, GR, 26th Inf.
MORRELL, James B. S12027, GR, Unassigned (Nitre Bureau)
MORRELL, John R. S3995, SU, 26th Inf.
MORRELL, Joseph O. S637, CT, 60th Inf.
MORRELL, Margaret Edney, W1449, SU, Morrell, Caleb R.
MORRELL, Martha Ellen, W6243, SU, Morrell, Rufus White
MORRELL, Mary, W3566, GR, Morrell, James B.
MORRELL, N. O. S3727, SU, 61st Inf.
MORRELL, Rosannah, W1814, SU, Morrell, Nathan O.
MORRELL, Rufus W. S4004, SU, 63rd Inf.
MORRELL, Ruth, W6615, CT, Morrell, Joseph O.
MORRELL, Susan Catherine, W981, SU, Morrell, Jonathan Franklin
MORRELL, William R. S8540, SU, Undetermined
MORRIS, A. W. S1408, WA, 29th Inf.

MORRIS, Aaron, S16402, S16594, HI, 48th Inf.
MORRIS, Agness T. W2326, WE, Morris, Tandy G.
MORRIS, Allen P. S337, F, 154th Sr. Regt. Inf.
MORRIS, Andrew I. S12894, MT, 26th Va. Inf.
MORRIS, B. F. S6593, DE, 43rd Miss. Inf.
MORRIS, B. R. S3179, S11674, WY, 2nd Miss. Inf.
MORRIS, Bettie Walker, W10239, FR, Morris, Ed
MORRIS, C. L. S15083, WY, 9th Cav.
MORRIS, C. M. S5908, WE, 21st (Wilson's) Cav.
MORRIS, C. T. S7358, FR, 41st Inf.
MORRIS, Catherine Foy, W8825, WI, Morris, Robert Thompson
MORRIS, Chloe Ann, W8663, MS, Morris, Elisha Green
MORRIS, Daniel E. S9113, M, 24th Inf.
MORRIS, E. S12133, FR, 4th (McLemore's) Cav.
MORRIS, Elizabeth E. W5527, FR, Morris, Calvin T.
MORRIS, Elizabeth P. W4948, G, Morris, I. H.
MORRIS, Ellen, W2430, RB, Morris, Wilson Taylor
MORRIS, G. B. C. S5065, HN, 15th Inf.
MORRIS, Gemima, W2153, SN, Morris, Wm. G.
MORRIS, George W. S214, S8420, RB, 49th Inf.
MORRIS, Harriet Serena, W10649, WE, Morris, Joseph C.
MORRIS, Henry T. S2037, HN, 7th Cav.
MORRIS, Ishom H. S12667, G, 8th (Smith's) Cav.
MORRIS, J. B. S5286, DY, 6th Miss. Inf.
MORRIS, J. H. S15629, SH, 23rd Inf.
MORRIS, J. M. S10969, HN, 51st N.C. Inf.
MORRIS, J. P. S14152, O, 3rd Inf.
MORRIS, J. W. S1942, SN, 30th Inf.
MORRIS, James C. S12490, MC, 59th Inf.
MORRIS, James P. S3626, CH, 21st Cav.
MORRIS, Joe, S12484, CE, 18th Inf.
MORRIS, John, S13961, SU, 59th Inf.
MORRIS, John, S15271, CT, 59th Inf.
MORRIS, John H. S14040, HN, 7th Ky. Cav.
MORRIS, John S. S2203, CH, 21st Cav.
MORRIS, John W. S6056, T, 30th N.C. State Troops
MORRIS, Jonathan jr. S15098, WY, 9th Bn. Cav.

MORRIS, Joseph H. S3084, T, 4th Miss. Inf.
MORRIS, Josh K. S15114, F, 9th Inf.
MORRIS, L. W. S10412, GE, 60th Inf.
MORRIS, Leona, W9274, WL, Morris, Richard Garner
MORRIS, Letitia R. W5221, D, Morris, John L.
MORRIS, Luther A. S10737, H, 35th Miss. Inf.
MORRIS, Martha Washington, W6244, CE, Morris, Joseph
MORRIS, Mary, W4932, CH, Morris, John S.
MORRIS, Mary A. W5469, SH, Morris, Thomas
MORRIS, Minnie E. W9938, DE, Morris, B. F.
MORRIS, Missouri, W10924, ST, Morris, Martin Luther
MORRIS, N. E. S15188, WI, 20th Inf.
MORRIS, Nora B. W2052, BL, Morris, Zebulon Montgomery
MORRIS, Paden, C256, HY, Regiment not given
MORRIS, Priscilla, W9788, WY, Morris, Charlie Lee
MORRIS, R. C. S5093, WL, 45th Inf.
MORRIS, Rachel Lucinda, W371, HE, Morris, Wm. Jefferson
MORRIS, Robert, S13031, MC, 59th Inf.
MORRIS, Robert L. S15519, RB, 21st (Carter's) Cav.
MORRIS, Sallie Sharp, W5906, MA, Morris, Edward C.
MORRIS, Samuel W. S9074, SN, 20th Inf.
MORRIS, Sarah Catherine, W716, SN, Morris, John E.
MORRIS, Susan M. W159, MS, Morris, Joel A.
MORRIS, T. P. S11594, S5913, WE, 52nd Inf.
MORRIS, Tandy G. S8330, WE, 5th Inf.
MORRIS, W. C. S439, SN, 20th Inf.
MORRIS, W. R. S8230, WH, 25th Inf.
MORRIS, W. T. S15448, HY, 18th (Newsom's) Cav.
MORRIS, William J. S14088, S14922, O, 27th Inf.
MORRIS, Willie A. W7247, O, Morris, Robert Pink
MORRIS, Z. M. S7647, BL, 20th (Russell's) Cav.
MORRISETT, J. R. S14292, T, 10th Cav.
MORRISETT, James P. S1221, HW, 60th Inf.
MORRISON, Catherine Brown, W8973, RO, Morrison, Marquis Lafayette
MORRISON, E. J. S8541, H, 35th Inf.
MORRISON, E. W. S9479, BO, 37th Inf.
MORRISON, Fannie, W1486, MR, Morrison, James C.

MORRISON, Francis, S4438, R, 5th (McKenzie's) Cav.
MORRISON, G. E. S14435, SH, 3rd (Forrest's) Cav.
MORRISON, Jacob, S3632, GE, 31st Inf.
MORRISON, James Calvin, S5602, MR, 1st (Carter's) Cav.
MORRISON, James E. S4997, LA, 32nd Inf.
MORRISON, Jesse J. S13693, GE, 31st Inf.
MORRISON, M. L. S12387, RO, 5th (McKenzie's) Cav.
MORRISON, Nora E. W7842, CL, Morrison, John L.
MORRISON, Robert, S6201, MT, 13th Ky. Cav.
MORRISON, Thomas B. S8104, RO, 5th Cav.
MORRISON, W. H. S7337, MU, 15th Ark. Inf.
MORRISON, Wyatt, C247, RU, Regiment not given, Application is missing.
MORRISS, Wilburn, S6781, H, 7th Inf.
MORROW, Flora Lucinda, W2765, GE, Morrow, W. J.
MORROW, Hugh J. S433, W, 5th Inf.
MORROW, J. W. S11649, K, Burrough's Co. Art.
MORROW, John M. S15760, RU, 19th Inf.
MORROW, Margaret E. W7758, D, Morrow, A. Green
MORROW, Martin A. sr. S7700, D, 5th Inf.
MORROW, N. F. S13227, LA, 19th (Biffle's) Cav.
MORROW, Phoebe Ann, W257, D, Morrow, John
MORROW, R. J. S10872, WI, 44th Inf.
MORROW, Rebecca Jane, W4506, WI, Morrow, Robert Jackson
MORROW, Robert L. S8246, W, 35th Inf.
MORROW, W. J. S6760, GE, 14th Bn. N.C. Inf.
MORSE, C. M. S13154, WL, 18th Inf.
MORSE, James, S41111, HE, 8th N.C. Inf.
MORSE, Laura Lee, W9284, W8867, WL, Morse, Wm. Harrison
MORTON, Atlas J. S3225, HN, 46th Inf.
MORTON, Dora, W4094, D, Morton, George Hardy
MORTON, Elizabeth, W1626, GU, Morton, Isiah W.
MORTON, George W. S14107, SU, 63rd Inf.
MORTON, Isaac, S4242, S6878, LI, 41st Inf.
MORTON, J. M. S6541, SH, 38th Inf.
MORTON, J. S. S11610, WI, 44th (Consolidated) Inf.
MORTON, Jacob E. S3151, GI, 11th Cav.

MORTON, James Hardison, S14217, MU, 17th Inf.
MORTON, Jennie, W11091, SU, Morton, Nathan D.
MORTON, John H. S14562, D, 10th Ky. Cav.
MORTON, Jonathan M. S5770, SU, 63rd Inf.
MORTON, Martha Ann, W10489, SU, Morton, George W.
MORTON, Mary Byars, W8939, W, Morton, W. C.
MORTON, Mary C. W4117, SU, Morton, Wm. Newland
MORTON, Mary E. W1823, W, Morton, Wm. C.
MORTON, N. D. S10938, SU, 12th Bn. (Day's) Cav.
MORTON, S. F. S13076, SU, 36th Inf.
MORTON, Sarah A. W3444, SU, Morton, Jonathan M.
MORTON, W. T. S11253, D, 6th (Wheeler's) Cav.
MORTON, William P. S3859, GU, 1st (Turney's) Inf.
MOSBY, Charles Winston, S13988, SH, 1st Cav.
MOSBY, Mary Brooks, W9842, D, Mosby, Samuel Gwin
MOSBY, Mary L. [Partee], W10954, RU, Mosby, James Crockett, [Later married Partee]
MOSBY, S. G. S12388, D, 8th (Dibrell's) Cav.
MOSELEY, H. W. S16535, G, 12th Inf.
MOSELEY, Ida Figures, W8548, MU, Moseley, Samuel Starnes
MOSELEY, J. E. S8542, MT, 49th Inf.
MOSELEY, James A. S16182, MS, 23rd Inf.
MOSELEY, Lydia Jane, W1253, WI, Moseley, Wm. Crawford
MOSELEY, Mary H. W6722, RU, Moseley, Edward Archer
MOSELEY, R. H. S15414, WI, 4th (McLemore's) Cav.
MOSELY, Edward Archer, S8342, B, 17th Inf.
MOSELY, Hillery Wood, S3197, L, 31st Inf.
MOSELY, W. H. S5506, HU, Sparkman's Co. Lt. Art.
MOSER, See also Mooser
MOSER, Alexander Z. S12716, S13613, S15159, MU, 21st N.C. Inf.
MOSER, Ben, S14857, WL, 4th (McLemore's) Cav.
MOSER, Joseph E. S12717, MU, 21st N.C. Inf.

MOSER, Luvena, W10222, WL, Moser, Benjamin
MOSER, Martha Jane, W8377, MU, Moser, Alexander
MOSES, Anderson, S8898, MO, 31st Inf.
MOSES, Bettie O. W4090, K, Moses, Samuel D.
MOSES, John, C69, MA, 7th Cav.
MOSES, Lizzie Mitchell, W7012, K, Moses, Frank Armstrong
MOSES, Martin Vincent, S16087, D, 2nd (Robison's) Inf.
MOSES, R. A. S12026, SU, 23rd N.C. Inf.
MOSES, Rachel, W9450, MO, Moses, Anderson
MOSES, Sue Ware, W8938, HY, Moses, James Philip
MOSES, T. L. S5520, SH, 34th Inf.
MOSLEY, Allice, W8412, WA, Mosley, John Nelson
MOSLEY, F. B. S13084, T, 32nd Inf.
MOSLEY, J. R. S14789, MA, 3rd (Forrest's) Cav.
MOSLEY, John, S14629, SU, 60th Inf.
MOSLEY, Louisa Alice, W9679, MS, Mosley, J. A.
MOSS, A. H. S2737, WH, 5th (McKenzie's) Cav.
MOSS, Abraham B. S1409, SU, 63rd Inf.
MOSS, Amanda Lucinda, W9613, SH, Moss, George Washington
MOSS, George W. S11830, CC, 7th Cav.
MOSS, H. R. S8047, MT, 12th N.C. Inf.
MOSS, Henry K. S7825, MS, 20th Inf.
MOSS, I. J. S8084, MT, 12th N.C. Inf.
MOSS, J. H. S8618, C, 48th Va. Inf.
MOSS, Jemima Eviline, W5983, HI, Moss, Thomas Fletcher
MOSS, Jermie, W1937, MS, Moss, Henry K.
MOSS, Louisa A. W1872, MT, Moss, J. H.
MOSS, Margaret A. W3630, WI, Moss, Wm. Giddins
MOSS, Martha Alice, W8494, O, Moss, George W.
MOSS, Mary Peyton, W9722, MA, Moss, W. M.
MOSS, Miriam Amelia, W2453, K, Moss, James Columbus
MOSS, N. F. S12372, HI, 24th Inf.
MOSS, Robert E. S12616, D, 6th (Wheeler's) Cav.
MOSS, Tennessee Caroline, W241, WI, Moss, Newton J.
MOSS, Thomas F. S774, HI, 24th Inf.
MOSS, W. M. S15260, MA, 1st Inf.
MOSS, Whitetta, W10209, WI, Moss, Will Summerfield
MOSS, William, S1689, WL, 18th Inf.
MOSS, William L. S1426, S679, SM, Undetermined
MOSTELLER, W. D. S3980, H, 4th Inf.
MOTLEY, James, S3020, FR, 37th Inf.
MOTLEY, James, S6434, MR, 37th Inf.
MOTLEY, James Joseph, S5691, HY, 12th Inf.
MOTLEY, James Marshal, S10083, HR, 9th Inf.
MOTLEY, William Daniel, S3608, HR, Forrest's Old Regt. Cav.
MOTLOW, Felix, S8176, MOO, 1st (Turney's) Inf.
MOTLOW, Sallie E. [Floyd], W10643, MO, Motlow, Felix Walker, [Later married Floyd]
MOTON, William H. S528, J, 28th Inf.
MOTTERN, Elizabeth, W679, SU, Mottern, Henry
MOTTERN, Henry, S2019, SU, 4th Cav.
MOTTERN, P. H. S5106, GE, Unassigned
MOUNGER, J. E. S14780, A, 16th Bn. (Neal's) Cav.
MOUNGER, James, S13193, LO, 16th Bn. (Neal's) Cav.
MOUNGER, Mattie Elizabeth, W917, H, Mounger, John M.
MOUNGER, Rebecca R. Harris, W5577, K, Mounger, James
MOUTON, J. N. S9023, ME, 3rd (Lillard's) Mtd. Inf.
MOWERY, Sarah Jane, W3343, BR, Mowery, Louis Alexander
MOYE, Henry Williamson, S13061, SN, 12th Ky. Cav.
MOYERS, Rena, W8465, LI, Moyers, Samuel Henry
MOYERS, Samuel H. S7101, LI, 41st Inf.
MULKERON, Helen Marr, W6301, HY, Mulkeron, Joe Haywood
MULLEN, Mary Adeline, W8826, HR, Mullen, Edward Alexander
MULLENDORE, A. L. S6791, SE, 5th (McKenzie's) Cav.
MULLENDORE, Laura B. W5528, SE, Mullendore, Abraham L.
MULLENIX, Mary Pairlee, W472, CA, Mullenix, B. J.
MULLENOX, B. J. S1667, D, 2nd Cav.
MULLENS, Henry Buchanan, W3754, G, Mullens, Robert Wm.

Index to Tennessee Confederate Pension Applications

MULLENS, J. R. S4761, LI, 1st (Turney's) Inf.
MULLENS, Nettie, W108, B, Mullens, David
MULLENS, R. W. S10809, D, 4th Inf.
MULLER, C. P. S144, D, 6th Fla. Inf.
MULLICAN, N. E. W2927, W, Mullican, W. W.
MULLICAN, P. G. S552, W, "Home Guards"
MULLICAN, William W. S1623, W, 16th Inf.
MULLIKEN, Mittie Mildred, W10632, L, Mulliken, Wm. Harvey
MULLINAX, James, S16323, WL, 8th (Smith's) Cav.
MULLINIX, James P. S16278, CA, 22nd (Barteau's) Cav.
MULLINOX, James M. S5287, JE, 1st S.C. Hvy. Art.
MULLINS, Alley, W3994, HA, Mullins, Jerry
MULLINS, Ephraim, S13838, JO, 10th (Dismond's) Ky. Cav.
MULLINS, Florida Ann, W7944, LI, Mullins, John Richardson
MULLINS, G. W. S8820, G, 12th Inf.
MULLINS, H. B. S5771, SU, 19th Inf.
MULLINS, J. T. S5457, LI, 1st (Turney's) Inf.
MULLINS, J. W. S8407, LI, 44th Inf.
MULLINS, James, S5732, B, 23rd Inf.
MULLINS, M. M. S3162, HE, 55th Inf.
MULLINS, Maggie E. W5976, SU, Mullins, Henderson B.
MULLINS, Marilda, W1128, MOO, Mullins, Coleman
MULLINS, Mary A. W11177, HR, Mullins, E. A.
MULLINS, O. H. P. S9077, MU, 34th Inf.
MULLINS, Peter A. S7238, RU, 19th Ala. Inf.
MULLINS, Rebecca Jane, W6260, RU, Mullins, Peter Anderson
MULLINS, Rittia, W1072, CL, Mullins, Riley
MULLINS, Sarah Margret Eliz. W4617, MU, Mullins, Oliver Hazard Perry
MULLINS, W. U. S4363, MOO, 23rd Inf.
MULLINS, William, S2362, B, 41st Inf.
MUMFORD, Thomas J. S12787, S12988, MT, 4th Inf.
MUMPOWER, James C. S16059, WA, Smith's Bn. Reserves
MUNCY, E. H. S8903, W, 8th (Smith's) Cav.
MUNDAY, Sally, W1193, SM, Munday, Wm.
MUNDAY, Susan McGaughey, W475, SM, Munday, Bailey Peyton
MUNFORD, Emma, W372, HI, Munford, Henry H.
MUNROE, Mary E. W7047, D, Munroe, Wm. T.
MUNROE, W. T. S7648, D, 1st Ark. Mtd. Rifles
MUNSAM, Thomas J. S1187, 55th Inf.
MUNSON, Sylvester A. S12394, SH, 13th Inf.
MURCHISON, E. F. S13820, CH, 18th (Newsom's) Cav.
MURDAUGH, L. B. S12271, S16681, HR, Forrest's Old Regt. Cav.
MURDOCK, E. K. S15282, OV, 25th Inf.
MURDOCK, J. M. P. S5639, HM, 48th Va. Inf.
MURDOCK, William J. R. S771, GE, 56th Inf.
MURFF, Martha Missouri, W6455, SH, Murff, Nathan
MURKIN, Herman Luther, S16521, D, 4th Inf.
MURKIN, John A. S3822, D, 1st (Turney's) Inf.
MURKIN, Mary Elizabeth, W1816, D, Murkin, John A.
MURLEY, John Clark, S6122, HR, 154th Sr. Regt. Inf.
MURLEY, Nancy, W2247, HR, Murley, Wm. Hamilton
MURPHEY, James, S16683, HW, 31st Inf.
MURPHEY, John Wesley, S732, HO, 14th Inf.
MURPHEY, Mary, W10324, RB, Murphey, John Coleman
MURPHREE, James D. S305, HI, 42nd Inf.
MURPHY, D. F. S2275, W, 4th Cav.
MURPHY, Fannie, W5112, RU, Murphy, J. K. P.
MURPHY, H. C. S13964, RB, 18th Inf.
MURPHY, J. K. P. S10860, RU, 2nd Ala. Inf.
MURPHY, J. W. S1123, HO, 14th Inf.
MURPHY, Jeremiah, S120, JE, 2nd Inf.
MURPHY, Jerry, S762, JE, 2nd (Walker's) Inf.
MURPHY, John S. S7239, SM, 4th (McLemore's) Cav.
MURPHY, Malissa, W3472, SM, Murphy, John S.
MURPHY, Martha Ann, W849, HO, Murphy, John Wesley
MURPHY, Martha Frances, W614, RB, Murphy, Wm. G.
MURPHY, Mary, W1308, WH, Murphy, Moses
MURPHY, Miles, S10389, RU, 21st (Carter's) Cav.
MURPHY, Molly Grace, W10828, SH, Murphy, John Milton
MURPHY, Moses, S284, MA, 6th Inf.
MURPHY, Robert S. S1561, O, 12th Ky. Inf.
MURPHY, Sarah Lucinda, W841, MS, Murphy, Isah Franklin

MURR, Wesley, S3624, CO, 26th Inf.
MURRAH, Morgan H. S10688, HD, 60th Ga. Inf.
MURRAY, A. P. S9718, MS, Undetermined
MURRAY, Branch, C128, F, 17th Miss. Inf.
MURRAY, Charles, C226, SH, 4th (Murray's) Cav.
MURRAY, D. B. S10365, RU, 8th (Smith's) Cav.
MURRAY, Delia A. W8047, WL, Murray, George W.
MURRAY, G. W. S5584, WL, 7th Inf.
MURRAY, Gilbert, S2905, MC, 43rd Inf.
MURRAY, H. L. W. S932, GI, 3rd Inf.
MURRAY, Ione Saxon, W3247, SH, Murray, Andrew J.
MURRAY, Isabelle, W6002, JO, Murray, James
MURRAY, J. B. S14821, GR, 2nd (Ashby's) Cav.
MURRAY, J. L. w. S1189, GI, 3rd Inf.
MURRAY, James, S781, JO, 38th Va. Inf.
MURRAY, Joseph C. sr. S12335, GR, 2nd (Ashby's) Cav.
MURRAY, Lavanda Jane, W10925, GI, Murray, Oliver Hazard Perry
MURRAY, Matilda Catherine, W7663, MC, Murray, Gilbert
MURRAY, Mollie Anne, W8746, MS, Murray, James Johnstone
MURRAY, Nancy E. W3678, RU, Murray, Hiram
MURRAY, Oliver H. P. S16502, GI, 11th Cav.
MURRAY, R. P. S9583, SU, 60th Inf.
MURRAY, Rachel Elizabeth, W6796, W8096, GR, Murray, Joseph Cobb
MURRAY, Rebecca, W1142, BR, Murray, John Harvey
MURRAY, Sarah E. W9922, DI, Murray, Henry Allen
MURRAY, Susan, W8649, SH, Murray, Wm. Hayden
MURRAY, Thomas B. S174, B, 8th Inf.
MURRAY, Uretha, W201, WA, Murray, Roland P.
MURRAY, William H. S15809, SH, 2nd Miss. Cav.
MURRELL, A. H. D. S1937, FR, 6th Inf.
MURRELL, Benjamin, S407, HU, 10th Cav.
MURRELL, Eliza G. W1840, FR, Murrell, Wm. Estes
MURRELL, Fannie, See Fannie Tyrone
MURRELL, R. C. S10865, HI, 11th Inf.
MURRELL, Worthe, S15721, HY, 18th Miss. Cav.
MURREY, M. N. S15600, 8th (Smith's) Cav.
MURRY, H. C. S4586, MN, 1st Ala. Miss. & Tenn. Inf.
MURRY, Tennessee, W11016, SM, Murry, Wm. C.
MURSER, Michael J. S4117, SU, 63rd Va. Inf.
MURTAUGH, Thomas, S13427, MA, Tobin's Co. Art.
MUSE, George P. S8586, B, 2nd Inf.
MUSE, Harriet, W1496, CF, Muse, Timothy Newton
MUSE, Nannie Anne, W2615, RU, Muse, Wm. Rice
MUSE, Nannie C. W5202, B, Muse, Wm. J.
MUSE, W. J. S10998, B, 1st (Turney's) Inf.
MUSE, William R. S7868, B, 17th Inf.
MUSGROVE, Billie Webster, C215, SH, 8th Miss. Cav.
MUSGROVE, James R. S16574, B, 32nd Inf.
MUSICK, Archibald Gaines, S9634, SU, 48th Va. Inf.
MUSICK, Sarah E. W5971, SU, Musick, Archibald Gaines
MUSSER, Mary A. W2749, JE, Musser, Wm. S.
MUSSER, W. E. S9469, HM, 29th Inf.
MUSSER, William S. S474, JE, 29th Va. Inf.
MUZZALL, Lewis, C65, HN, 20th Cav.
MUZZELL, Stephen W. S13687, 46th Inf.
MYATT, Elizabeth, W1346, CU, Myatt, John C.
MYATT, J. C. S1099, CU, 28th Inf.
MYATT, J. F. S10039, DI, 24th Bn. Sharpshooters
MYATT, Missouri Arkansas, W9913, DI, Myatt, James Franklin
MYATT, Sarah Petty, W9868, DI, Myatt, Wm. Jackson
MYATT, W. J. S15623, DI, 49th Inf.
MYATT, William J. S4065, DI, 49th Inf.
MYERS, Abe, S13390, J, 8th Cav.
MYERS, Alfred A. S1780, T, 1st Hvy. Art.
MYERS, Annie Little, W2909, SH, Myers, George Bogan
MYERS, Calvin E. S16098, S16317, OV, 8th Cav.
MYERS, G. W. S3326, D, 18th Inf.
MYERS, J. B. S1144, HW, 12th Cav.
MYERS, J. K. P. S6879, MN, 11th Miss. Inf.
MYERS, John, S11491, D, 1st Ark. Art.
MYERS, John, S14881, MR, 35th Inf.
MYERS, John N. S6986, GR, 59th Inf.

Index to Tennessee Confederate Pension Applications

MYERS, John P. S14169, HW, 64th Va. Inf.
MYERS, Lavina, W1148, GR, Myers, Wm. A.
MYERS, Lorenzo S. S7571, B, Byrne's Co. Horse Art. Morgan's Cav.
MYERS, Malinda, W1634, JE, Myers, James
MYERS, Margaret Emily, W6530, CT, Myers, Wm. Houston
MYERS, Mary Jane, W5999, D, Myers, John
MYERS, Moses, S14552, 20th (Russell's) Cav.
MYERS, Nancy Jane, W8810, PU, Myers, Abe
MYERS, Susan A. W7606, MN, Myers, J. K. P.
MYERS, T. P. S8727, SN, 28th Inf.
MYERS, W. H. S12278, JO, 1st Cav.
MYERS, William A. S15698, MA, 26th N.C. Inf.
MYLIUS, H. S610, BR, Unassigned (Worked in Button Factory)
MYNATT, Ganum, S5220, RO, 1st Cav.
MYNATT, George W. S1797, GR, Ramsey's Battery, Art.
MYNATT, Matt H. S11351, K, Kain's Battery, Lt. Art.
MYRES, Susannah, W1947, HW, Myres, Isaac B.
MYRICK, John C. S2649, HN, 154th Sr. Regt. Inf.
MYRICK, Laura, W10818, HN, Myrick, John Cornelius
MYRICK, R. L. S3564, HD, 4th Inf.
NABORS, Eliza Jane, W6050, SH, Nabors, John Robert
NABORS, Martha, W589, FR, Nabors, Fleet Benson
NABORS, T. P. S13857, SH, 17th Miss. Inf.
NAFF, Adam F. S7639, GE, 61st Inf.
NAFF, J. M. S5610, WA, 29th Inf.
NAFF, John Wesley, S15959, D, 6th N.C. Cav.
NAFF, Lou F. W7535, SU, Naff, James M.
NAFF, Margaret Logan, W8581, D, Naff, John Wesley
NAFF, Sarah Virginia, W5873, GE, Naff, Adam Ferdinand
NAGLE, Thomas, S1796, MA, 19th Miss. Inf.
NAIL, George Anna, W415, H, Nail, Nicholas Pope
NAIL, James B. S1553, K, Kain's Co. Lt. Art.
NAIL, James B. S16016, BL, 2nd (Ashby's) Cav.
NAIL, N. P. S194, H, 19th Inf.
NAIL, William Stanford, S16176, H, 5th Ga. Inf.
NAILL, Sarah Taylor, W6694, K, Naill, James Bartley

NAILLING, J. W. S13611, O, 4th Inf.
NAILLING, Mary Etta, W8212, O, Nailling, Joseph Willis
NALL, Elisha J. D. S9129, DI, 1st (Feild's) Inf.
NALL, Rosa, W5915, DI, Nall, Elisha J. D.
NANCE, C. P. S15822, D, 5th Tex. Inf.
NANCE, Clena, S12574, B, 41st Inf.
NANCE, James B. S8824, D, 8th (Smith's) Cav.
NANCE, John B. S4599, B, 41st Inf.
NANCE, John M. S9732, HN, 12th Ky. Inf.
NANCE, Mary Catherine, W4682, B, Nance, James W.
NANCE, Matilda Katherine, W3834, B, Nance, John Bradley
NANCE, Payton S. S8272, HN, 5th Inf.
NANCE, William Gallagher, S7508, D, 11th Ala. Cav.
NANNCY, Virginia Green, W1528, WE, Nanncy, Joseph Ledbetter
NANNY, George Robert, S5291, MA, 16th Cav.
NAPIER, R. L. S3230, HR, 29th Inf.
NAPIER, Robert Henry, S6921, D, 11th Inf.
NARRAMORE, R. M. S1772, BL, 35th Inf.
NASH, A. D. S8059, DI, 16th Inf.
NASH, Barbara C. W3016, HI, Nash, Charles A.
NASH, Charles A. S8962, HI, 48th Inf.
NASH, George R. S5721, D, 12th Inf.
NASH, J. A. S13951, ST, 50th Inf.
NASH, James P. S15607, H, 4th Ga. Cav.
NASH, Susan E. W3009, W4933, SH, Nash, Michael V.
NASH, W. J. S12342, SH, 5th Inf.
NASH, william P. S5803, D, 45th Inf.
NASSAUER, Lee, S6231, H, 1st (Feild's) Inf.
NATION, W. W. S12120, H, 16th Bn. Ga. Cav.
NAVE, Eliza Ann Rebecca, W4193, CE, Nave, Josephus
NAVE, Henry V. S5752, SU, 26th Inf.
NAVE, James W. S14477, SU, 63rd Inf.
NAYLOR, A. J. S8153, CH, 18th (Newsom's) Cav.
NAYLOR, H. C. S15638, RU, 18th Inf.
NAYLOR, J. B. S2162, HR, 52nd Inf.
NAYLOR, Mattie C. S. W9545, RU, Naylor, Henry Clay
NEAD, John S. S8811, WA, Undetermined
NEAL, A. H. S4875, GE, 21st Miss. Inf.
NEAL, David C. S16281, GI, 11th (Gordon's) Bn. Cav.
NEAL, G. C. S9603, R, 1st Cav.
NEAL, George A. S1091, 20th Inf.
NEAL, Hannah, W8384, G, Neal, John W.

-253

NEAL, Henderson, S6782, FR, 41st Inf.
NEAL, Henry, C130, MA, Miss. Regt.
NEAL, J. F. S5607, K, 2nd (Ashby's) Cav.
NEAL, J. W. S7649, G, 17th S.C. Inf.
NEAL, James K. P. S4959, GI, 53rd Inf.
NEAL, Jennie M. W4058, WL, Neal, James A.
NEAL, John S. W. S14887, WA, 45th Va. Inf.
NEAL, Joseph, S6904, WL, 45th Inf.
NEAL, Lou Emma, W11139, LA, Neal, David C.
NEAL, Mamie Elizabeth, W8740, W5627, GI, Neal, James Knox Polk
NEAL, Marniva Fine, W6521, R, Neal, Green Calvin
NEAL, Mary Cornelia, W10474, MC, Neal, James Richard
NEAL, Mary I. W4148, GE, Neal, Albert H.
NEAL, Nancy, W3909, FR, Neal, Henderson T.
NEAL, Phoebe Jane, W2125, K, Neal, Wm. Everett Mahoney
NEAL, R. D. S8392, F, 154th Sr. Regt. Inf.
NEAL, Rachel Ellen, W8065, WA, Neal, John S. W.
NEAL, Sarah Jane, W1404, K, Neal, James Franklin
NEBLETT, Catherine Rebecca, W5046, DI, Neblett, Robert Peter
NEBLETT, Clara, W2143, MT, Neblett, Jones Daly
NEBLETT, J. B. S3464, D, 20th Inf.
NEBLETT, Josiah R. S10328, MT, 1st (Feild's) Inf.
NEBLETT, R. P. S6518, DI, 11th Inf.
NEECE, Harrison H. S6, MOO, 41st Inf.
NEECE, Laura M. W7735, PU, Neece, H. H.
NEEDHAM, Elmira, W9743, G, Needham, Jones Wright
NEEDHAM, James W. S15666, G, 12th Cav.
NEEDHAM, Lucy Elizabeth, W7085, MN, Needham, Miles W.
NEEDHAM, Miles M. S2133, UN, 2nd (Ashby's) Cav.
NEEDHAM, Miles W. S6189, MN, 18th Cav.
NEEDHAM, S. G. S8259, MA, 3rd Cav.
NEEDHAM, Thomas M. S8920, BO, 10th N.C. Bn. Cav.
NEEL, Margaret Angaline, W3578, O, Neel, James Wilson
NEEL, Mattie Joe, W9965, SH, Neel, Thomas VanCourt
NEELD, Fannie A. W10813, D, Neeld, Robert A.

NEELD, R. A. S9994, D, Huggin's Co. Lt. Art.
NEELD, Sarah Elizabeth, W1892, LI, Neeld, Thomas J.
NEELEY, A. H. S14910, HA, 64th Va. Inf.
NEELEY, Harriet, W4240, CO, Neeley, R. B.
NEELEY, Katherine Nicholson, W9399, MU, Neeley, Wm. Jasper
NEELEY, Lou B. W1756, MU, Neeley, W. S. L.
NEELEY, Mary Thomas, W8974, HD, Neeley, Wesley Whitfield
NEELEY, Susan Addie, W9345, HR, Neeley, James Calvin
NEELEY, Tennie, W9988, DY, Neeley, Charles Judson
NEELEY, W. A. S11587, HI, 24th Inf.
NEELEY, W. W. S16225, HD, 6th (Wheeler's) Cav.
NEELLEY, Elizabeth Ann, W4854, MU, Neelley, John Wesley
NEELLEY, Samuel, S3842, LA, 48th Inf.
NEELLEY, William M. S14944, LA, 6th (Wheeler's) Cav.
NEELY, Alice Collier, W11017, SH, Neely, James Jackson
NEELY, Alma Sue, W4082, WI, Neely, James Robert
NEELY, C. F. S225, HY, 154th Sr. Regt. Inf.
NEELY, C. M. S1986, SH, 3rd (Forrest's) Cav.
NEELY, Fanny Stephens, W385, HR, Neely, James Jackson
NEELY, G. L. S13727, WI, 32nd Inf.
NEELY, J. C. S8385, HR, 14th Cav.
NEELY, J. S. S11523, HR, 9th Inf.
NEELY, James, S12772, OV, 28th Inf.
NEELY, Joel H. S10806, JO, 37th Va. Inf.
NEELY, Leonora, W1313, SH, Neely, Wm. Thomas
NEELY, Martha Elizabeth, W3107, HY, Neely, Charles F.
NEELY, Mary E. W6478, HR, Neely, Richard James
NEELY, Mary Graham, W3448, OV, Neely, Isaac Berry
NEELY, Mary Jane, W10443, TR, Neely, Wm. J.
NEELY, R. B. S9481, CO, 65th Inf.
NEELY, Roena Chandler, W9248, W4405, DI, Neely, Wm. Albert
NEELY, Sarah Columbus, W6622, MS, Neely, James Thomas
NEELY, W. J. S15935, TR, 20th Inf.

Index to Tennessee Confederate Pension Applications

NEELY, William, S4396, OV, 4th (Murray's) Cav.
NEESE, Daniel J. S16648, HN, 3rd (Forrest's) Cav.
NEESE, Martha Porter, W10596, HN, Neese, John W.
NEFF, Mary A. W4988, MA, Neff, Wm. David
NEFF, Sarah C. W3218, MA, Neff, Samuel H.
NEIGHBORS, Ella Frances, W3769, SH, Neighbors, W. R.
NEIGHBOURS, W. R. S258, L, 4th Inf.
NEIL, E. J. S7703, FR, 1st (Carter's) Cav.
NEIL, Hugh G. S10070, JE, 29th Inf.
NEIL, Joseph, S9836, MC, 62nd Inf.
NEIL, Susan Robeson, W8609, W8437, ME, Neil, Thomas B.
NEIL, T. B. S13945, ME, 26th Inf.
NEILL, Alexander H. S6388, HD, 1st Cav.
NEILL, John H. S8548, PU, 1st Cav.
NEILL, John M. S689, J, Undetermined
NEILL, Rosannah Matilda, W1517, HD, Neill, Alexander Hugh
NEILL, Sarah J. W7540, HD, Neill, Alfred Alexander
NEILL, William M. S5507, J, 3rd East Tenn. Cav.
NEILSON, D. W. S12582, G, 1st Miss. Cav.
NEILSON, J. D. S13405, RU, 4th (McLemore's) Cav.
NEILSON, Pattie Hunt, W6272, RU, Neilson, Joseph Douglas
NELLUMS, Daniel A. S4511, D, 3rd Inf.
NELLUMS, Renie Alvina, W222, MU, Nellums, Daniel Andrew
NELMS, D. W. S12215, SU, 61st Inf.
NELMS, Elizabeth M. W6288, CL, Nelms, James D.
NELMS, J. D. S3499, CL, 29th Inf.
NELMS, John H. S9897, SU, 61st Inf.
NELMS, S. J. S8315, F, 16th Va. Inf.
NELSON, Amanda Jane, W3616, SU, Nelson, Rison Alexander
NELSON, Charles W. S11511, GI, 3rd (Clack's) Inf.
NELSON, D. H. S14405, ST, 8th (Dibrell's) Cav.
NELSON, Daniel Thomas, S10013, DY, 21st (Wilson's) Cav.
NELSON, David H. S16115, CY, 5th Ky. Cav.
NELSON, Eva, See Eva Moore
NELSON, Frederick Moseley, S14232, SH, 7th (Duckworth's) Cav.

NELSON, Henry, C23, G, 19th & 20th Cav.
NELSON, James J. S3372, GI, 53rd Inf.
NELSON, John F. S2964, WA, 60th Inf.
NELSON, John T. S14570, B, 8th Tex. Cav.
NELSON, John Valentine, S1964, MA, 6th Inf.
NELSON, Julia A. W6000, WA, Nelson, John F.
NELSON, Kate Ross, W5067, SH, Nelson, Moses Henderson
NELSON, L. H. S2272, OV, 13th (Gore's) Cav.
NELSON, Laura Miriam, W4912, MU, Nelson, Willoughby Howard
NELSON, Linzy, S3111, MR, 28th Ala. Inf.
NELSON, Louis, C32, L, 7th Cav.
NELSON, M. A. S4729, FR, 2nd Inf.
NELSON, Martha E. W701, WL, Nelson, John W.
NELSON, Mary Catherine, W6337, D, Nelson, Oscar Fitzallen
NELSON, Mildred Gazelle, W6525, SH, Nelson, Frederick Mosely
NELSON, P. H. S1601, MR, 9th Ky. Inf.
NELSON, R. A. S7707, SU, 8th (Smith's) Cav.
NELSON, Rebecca E. W600, MA, Nelson, John V.
NELSON, S. C. S10383, HU, 10th Cav.
NELSON, Sarah A. W5795, WL, Nelson, James A.
NELSON, William, S13800, R, 19th Ala. Inf.
NELUMS, Pink, S123, ST, 14th Inf.
NESBITT, James L. S10788, MT, 14th Inf.
NESBITT, Maria P. W6168, HO, Nesbitt, James M.
NESBITT, N. B. S7826, 55th Inf.
NESBITT, William J. S11060, HD, 1st Cav.
NEVILLS, Lissie June, W4844, MU, Nevills, Clement Harison
NEVILS, Ella Gabrella, W2290, WI, Nevils, Josiah Watkins
NEVINS, Martha A. W922, CY, Nevins, Melton P.
NEVINS, William R. S67, WI, 20th Inf.
NEW, John C. S16080, RU, 23rd Inf.
NEW, Nannie, W10940, L, New, Wm. D.
NEWBERRY, Betty F. W895, WE, Newberry, Wm. D.
NEWBERRY, Elizabethy, W1239, HA, Newberry, Wm. C.
NEWBERRY, Kate, W4538, G, Newberry, Joel M.
NEWBILL, Abraham P. S9965, 1st Va. Reserves

Index to Tennessee Confederate Pension Applications

NEWBILL, Eleonora B. W947, Newbill, Wm. D.
NEWBILL, Grace Meredith, W2423, GI, Newbill, George H.
NEWBILL, R. A. S9268, 20th (Russell's) Cav.
NEWBILL, Thomas, S11662, G, 1st Va. Reserves
NEWBILL, William D. S2991, 55th Inf.
NEWBORN, Mary Anne, W7014, SH, Newborn, Joseph Lemuel
NEWBY, Mattie Paralee, W9397, W, Newby, Wm. Harding
NEWBY, Nancy F. W3925, W, Newby, Wm.
NEWBY, William H. S11054, W, 11th (Holman's) Cav.
NEWCOMB, J. C. S15502, WI, 48th (Voorhies') Inf.
NEWCOMB, William E. S8598, SU, 2nd Ky. Cav.
NEWCOME, Martha, W9999, WI, Newcome, John C.
NEWELL, John M. S11292, D, 1st (Feild's) Inf.
NEWLAND, Ella H. W4375, SU, Newland, Wm. M.
NEWLIN, J. M. S792, RB, 30th Inf.
NEWLON, B. J. S13436, C, 43rd Bn. Va. Partisan Rangers
NEWLON, Elizabeth Worsham, W7859, K, Newlon, Bushrod Jackson
NEWMAN, B. S. S1313, DE, 52nd Inf.
NEWMAN, C. S. S12710, K, 60th Inf.
NEWMAN, Elizabeth, W2274, BR, Newman, P. B.
NEWMAN, Ella, W9633, RU, Newman, J. F.
NEWMAN, G. W. S9950, CF, 28th Cav.
NEWMAN, H. A. S14814, JE, 43rd Inf.
NEWMAN, J. K. S11665, RU, 4th Cav.
NEWMAN, John H. S13883, SH, 4th Inf.
NEWMAN, John R. S16326, D, 9th Cav.
NEWMAN, Julia A. W3012, K, Newman, John A.
NEWMAN, Kate H. W4351, K, Newman, C. S.
NEWMAN, Margaret Donaldson, W1742, K, Newman, Howard Walker
NEWMAN, Mary Elizabeth, W7589, RU, Newman, James K.
NEWMAN, Nannie J. W8396, CF, Newman, George W.
NEWMAN, Olivia Warfield, W6744, SH, Newman, John Baker
NEWMAN, P. B. S9692, BR, 43rd Inf.

NEWMAN, Sarah Horne, W5129, LI, Newman, James Williams
NEWMAN, Thomas W. S10275, K, 35th Inf.
NEWMAN, W. F. S553, WL, 20th Inf.
NEWMAN, William E. S14, F, Wright's Lt. Art.
NEWSOM, Alfred K. S2415, G, 3rd N.C. Inf.
NEWSOM, Amelia, W6534, TR, Newsom, E. M.
NEWSOM, E. M. S10645, SN, 4th (McLemore's) Cav.
NEWSOM, Elizabeth, W1098, CF, Newsom, George W.
NEWSOM, Elizabeth H. W1764, MN, Newsom, Herbert E.
NEWSOM, George W. S1738, CF, 17th Inf.
NEWSOM, James P. S11596, CF, 17th Inf.
NEWSOM, Jane Boyd, W11054, CH, Newsom, John Buxton
NEWSOM, John B. S249, CH, 10th Cav.
NEWSOM, John R. S15673, SH, Wood's Regt. Conf. Cav.
NEWSOM, Margaret E. W779, CH, Newsom, John F.
NEWSOM, Mary Jane, W1775, CH, Newsom, Isaac Jordan
NEWSOM, Rufus, S10286, MA, 20th (Nixon's) Cav.
NEWSOM, Sam, C270, D, Regiment not given
NEWSOM, Silas, C80, D, 20th Inf.
NEWSOM, Susan A. W6361, HY, Newsom, Thomas J.
NEWSOM, Susan P. W6232, B, Newsom, Roland
NEWSOM, William M. S13855, DE, 15th (Stewart's) Cav.
NEWSOM, William S. S11951, D, Browne & Baker's Art.
NEWTON, Alice, W7757, RB, Newton, E. M.
NEWTON, E. M. S15116, RB, 12th Ky. Cav.
NEWTON, Ellen, W3263, SU, Newton, Wm. B.
NEWTON, Lizzie E. W10841, SU, Newton, Worley Embree
NEWTON, Mary Talbot, W7224, LK, Newton, Isham Smith
NEWTON, Nancy Mildred, W3384, HN, Newton, Robert Luke
NEWTON, Peter, S11308, CO, 1st S.C. Inf.
NEWTON, Sallie B. W1429, SU, Newton, James
NEWTON, Sarah, W3158, K, Newton, Peter
NEWTON, Sarah Elizabeth, W1228, GI, Newton, Jefferson Alexander

NEWTON, Smith, S14329, LK, 15th Inf.
NEWTON, W. B. S4060, SU, 63rd Inf.
NEWTON, William H. S8216, MA, 51st Inf.
NIBLETT, Sallie Vance, W2793, DI, Niblett, James Collins
NICELY, Calaway, S6819, GR, 2nd Cav.
NICELY, James P. E. S10831, GR, 2nd (Ashby's) Cav.
NICELY, Mary, W668, GR, Nicely, John S.
NICHALAS, H. M. S11457, PU, 8th Cav.
NICHALSON, Henry H. S2904, SE, 62nd N.C. Inf.
NICHOL, Benjamin Franklin, S12797, RU, Fisher's Co. Art.
NICHOL, Florence G. W5264, D, Nichol, Bradford
NICHOL, Jonathan W. S6275, RU, 8th (Smith's) Cav.
NICHOL, Maggie Angeline, W5088, D, Nichol, Benjamin Franklin
NICHOL, Mary Ready, W6098, RU, Nichol, John W.
NICHOL, Sarah Elizabeth, W2639, D, Nichol, Tilman Harrison
NICHOLAS, M. A. S10807, SH, 2nd (Robison's) Inf.
NICHOLES, J. H. S11397, BE, 5th Inf.
NICHOLS, Alex. B. S16047, SH, Benavide's Tex. Cav.
NICHOLS, Aley, W1047, LI, Nichols, Briggs
NICHOLS, Aley, W1047, LI, Nichols, Briggs
NICHOLS, Alice McPhail, W7079, WI, Nichols, George S.
NICHOLS, Annie Elmo, W5657, MU, Nichols, John Harmon
NICHOLS, Elizabeth Matilda, W695, HU, Nichols, Alfred Tenn. Grayson
NICHOLS, F. M. S2048, D, 1st (Turney's) Inf.
NICHOLS, G. W. S5567, SM, 2nd Cav.
NICHOLS, George S. S152, WI, 19th Cav.
NICHOLS, J. N. S8060, H, 4th Ga. Cav.
NICHOLS, J. W. S2492, B, 35th Inf.
NICHOLS, Jessie, S3752, ST, 84th Va. Militia
NICHOLS, John Harmon, S1488, WL, 11th Inf.
NICHOLS, Katharine, W2388, MT, Nichols, Jesse
NICHOLS, Kittie Ross, W1062, D, Nichols, Jasper
NICHOLS, Mary A. W6875, MU, Nichols, Charles Sydney
NICHOLS, N. m. S16484, D, 3rd Inf.

NICHOLS, Sarah Ann, W6158, PU, Nichols, Henry M.
NICHOLS, William R. S6309, K, 1st S.C. Hvy. Art.
NICHOLSON, Ann Tennessee, W8097, CE, Nicholson, D. B.
NICHOLSON, D. B. S13213, S14244, CE, 49th Inf.
NICHOLSON, Fannie, W5278, HR, Nicholson, George R.
NICHOLSON, G. R. S11545, HY, 12th Cav.
NICHOLSON, Isaac A. C60, D, Comm. Dept. Polk's Corps
NICHOLSON, J. D. S6848, CE, 42nd Inf.
NICHOLSON, J. S. T. S6588, LE, 55th Inf.
NICHOLSON, Mandy A. W7747, SH, Nicholson, M. A.
NICHOLSON, Martha A. W6618, T, Nicholson, Waric David
NICHOLSON, Mary Victoria, W8699, MU, Nicholson, John McLemore
NICHOLSON, Nancy Malinda, W2363, K, Nicholson, H. H.
NICHOLSON, Warwick D. S5708, T, 7th Cav.
NICKEL, J. R. S14660, HN, 46th Inf.
NICKENS, H. C. S5838, MS, 8th (Smith's) Cav.
NICKLES, Elizabeth, W2160, SU, Nickles, David
NICKLES, J. M. S7650, PU, 8th (Dibrell's) Cav.
NICKLES, John W. S10853, MN, 18th (Newsom's) Cav.
NICKLES, Sarah E. W5331, MN, Nickles, John Wesley
NICKS, Henrietta A. W2275, D, Nicks, Richard Augustus
NICKS, Isaac H. S1736, MT, 2nd Ky. Inf.
NICKS, Margaret Ann, W4143, D, Nicks, Wm. Asbury
NICKS, Susannah, W5735, FR, Nicks, John
NIMMO, J. I. S5549, 19th & 20th (Consolidated) Cav.
NIMMO, Vesta, W3521, K, Nimmo, David St. John
NISBET, J. C. S13194, H, 21st Ga. Inf.
NISBET, Louise Bailey, W6797, H, Nisbet, James Cooper
NISBETT, Mattie J. W6419, B, Nisbett, Nathaniel C.
NISBETT, N. C. S4118, B, 45th Inf.
NIX, E. C. S6494, P, 1st Hvy. Art.
NIX, Emily, W793, WI, Nix, Hiram
NIX, George H. S468, MU, 1st Inf.

Index to Tennessee Confederate Pension Applications

NIX, James, S9696, G, 10th Cav.
NIX, John L. S14811, T, 56th Ga. Inf.
NIX, John W. S97, HD, 5th Ky. Inf.
NIX, Matilda, W6392, MA, Nix, George H.
NIX, Robert J. S10, MS, 17th Inf.
NIX, Sarah Josephine, W1582, O, Nix, Rasmus Lucullus
NIX, William, S5002, CF, 1st Ga. State Troops
NIXON, Allan, S5938, MT, 14th Inf.
NIXON, Ann Judson, W640, L, Nixon, John R.
NIXON, Dellie Frances, W8900, SM, Nixon, Jamess
NIXON, Hattie, W4953, SH, Nixon, Wm. Christopher
NIXON, J. C. S16334, SM, 23rd Inf.
NIXON, Polly Ann, W11068, SM, Nixon, James Campbell
NIXON, S. O. S14829, SM, 23rd Inf.
NIXON, W. C. S8876, SH, 4th Inf.
NIXON, W. J. S3849, MU, 7th La. Inf.
NOAH, P. D. S15136, O, 22nd (Barteau's) Cav.
NOAH, T. J. S2395, LI, 32nd Inf.
NOBLES, James, S2255, BE, 14th Inf.
NOBLES, Mary Jane, W2009, BE, Nobles, James
NOBLETT, D. T. S12629, B, 41st Inf.
NOBLETT, Sarah E. W142, MOO, Noblett, James D.
NOBLIN, Jane, W724, CL, Noblin, Charles F.
NOE, J. R. S10910, HM, 61st Inf.
NOE, Jacob, S8239, HM, 61st Inf.
NOE, Jacob L. S5186, HM, 60th Inf.
NOE, John, S12060, HM, 2nd (Ashby's) Cav.
NOE, John M. S1697, HW, 2nd Ky. Mtd. Riflemen
NOE, Martha, W6042, HM, Noe, John
NOE, Nancy C. W3140, HM, Noe, James T.
NOE, Sarah C. W5506, HM, Noe, Joseph R.
NOLAND, J. F. S7308, H, 5th S.C. Cav.
NOLAND, Jane Sadler, W2543, H, Noland, James T.
NOLAND, Margaret, W7830, SE, Noland, P. L.
NOLAND, Peter Lafayett, S12302, SE, 14th N.C. Inf.
NOLAND, Robert C. S8760, D, 1st Confederate Cav.
NOLD, Jane, W1513, MN, Nold, John
NOLD, John, S139, MN, 27th Inf.
NOLEN, Alex, C66, MT, 14th Inf.
NOLEN, J. T. S3318, GI, 13th Inf.
NOLEN, Josie A. W1099, RU, Nolen, John Lewis
NOLEN, Lucy Ann, W1236, GI, Nolen, James Tyre
NOLEN, Michal Margaret, W10546, WI, Nolen, Wm. Stephen
NOLEN, P. Y. S2849, OV, 28th Inf.
NOLES, William, S2118, GI, 44th Inf.
NOLLEY, Mollie B. W2216, SH, Nolley, Thomas Smith
NOLLY, Thomas S. S6067, SH, 4th Inf.
NOONER, Leacy Jane, W4281, G, Nooner, Lafayett
NOREL, Malinda, W6745, H, Norel, John
NORFLEET, J. S. S12889, MT, 49th Inf.
NORFLEETE, George A. S11233, ST, 14th Inf.
NORMAN, Elizabeth Mildred, W2309, D, Norman, Henry Haywood
NORMAN, I. B. S10040, PO, 3rd Inf.
NORMAN, J. T. S5292, L, 1st Confederate Cav.
NORMAN, John, S2517, H, 19th Inf.
NORMAN, John W. S3172, LI, 44th Inf.
NORMAN, Margaret, W2340, HU, Norman, Jonathan
NORMAN, Martha Ann, W1124, M, Norman, John
NORMAN, Rhoda J. W842, H, Norman, John
NORMAN, Robert L. S2335, RU, 18th Inf.
NORMAN, Sallie McLean, W4270, SH, Norman, Henry Hudson
NORMAN, T. J. S8442, HU, 24th Bn. Sharpshooters
NORMAN, W. M. S3837, WY, 54th Inf.
NORMAN, William, S2363, LI, 44th Inf.
NORRED, Aaron L. S2231, HN, 19th Cav.
NORRIS, A. S7246, WH, 19th Inf.
NORRIS, Andrew, S14927, HI, 4th (McLemore's) Cav.
NORRIS, Bill, C276, F, Regiment not given
NORRIS, David M. S14831, PU, 8th (Dibrell's) Cav.
NORRIS, Ephraim, S3119, PO, 62nd N.C. Inf.
NORRIS, Ike, S14691, RU, 39th N.C. Inf.
NORRIS, John R. S12258, HR, 18th Miss. Cav.
NORRIS, Levi J. S13197, FE, 3rd Ark. Inf.
NORRIS, Margaret Elln, W9879, SH, Norris, Wm. Hilliard
NORRIS, William Henderson, S396, WH, 38th Inf.
NORRISS, Martha M. W3189, WH, Norriss, Avery
NORRISS, Mary C. W217, WH, Norriss, Wm. Henderson

NORTH, Eliza Baker, W8099, WI, North, James Abraham
NORTH, J. A. S15283, WI, 22nd (Barteau's) Cav.
NORTH, J. S. S9824, SM, 4th (McLemore's) Cav.
NORTH, Mary K. W10379, B, North, Jonathan Mansfield
NORTH, Mary Virginia, W4095, WL, North, Wm. Patterson
NORTH, P. M. S8952, WL, 4th (McLemore's) Cav.
NORTHCUT, Jasper N. S13412, T, 31st Ala. Inf.
NORTHCUT, Lawson Hill, S6628, GU, 1st (Turney's) Inf.
NORTHCUTT, John B. S1961, CA, 18th Inf.
NORTHERN, Alphia E. W9543, WL, Northern, Sam
NORTHERN, Davis, S11992, GR, 2nd (Ashby's) Cav.
NORTHERN, Nancy Holston, W10230, GR, Northern, Davis
NORTHERN, Solomon, S810, HW, 63rd Inf.
NORTON, Annie Sarah, W7264, H, Norton, John Columbus
NORTON, John W. S7951, G, 12th Inf.
NORTON, R. J. S6820, CF, 44th Inf.
NORTON, Richard, S55, HD, 12th Inf.
NORTON, Settie, W8656, J, Norton, Samuel
NORTON, W. C. S9092, HR, 2nd Miss. Inf.
NORTON, W. L. S4970, CF, 1st (Turney's) Inf.
NORTON, William B. S820, J, 44th Inf.
NORVELL, D. B. S946, L, 35th Inf.
NORVELL, Lucy Douthat, W9209, SU, Norvell, James Wm.
NORVELL, Mary A. W4470, RU, Norvell, Charles B.
NORVELL, Mary Louise, W10772, HY, Norvell, Wm. Henry
NORVELL, W. H. S15843, CC, 12th Ky. Cav.
NORWOOD, Dora Vaughn, W6852, D, Norwood, Robert Wilson
NORWOOD, E. T. S15947, GI, 32nd Inf.
NORWOOD, Eveline Victoria, W7469, SH, Norwood, John Houston
NORWOOD, John H. S10390, SH, 6th Ky. Inf.
NORWOOD, Robert W. S15153, D, 19th & 20th (Consol.) Cav.
NOTT, F. C. S12564, BO, 63rd Inf.
NOWELL, Rhoda Ann, W4641, G, Nowell, Robert Franklin

NOWELL, Smith, C156, L, 7th Cav.
NOWLAND, Edward W. B. S14479, SH, Fagan's Unattached Bn. Ark. Cav.
NOWLIN, George N. S11924, WE, 31st Inf.
NOWLIN, J. T. S10840, B, 23rd Inf.
NOWLIN, Maggie Erin, W4004, Nowlin, Wade Hampton
NOWLIN, Margaret Elizabeth, W4324, B, Nowlin, John Tillman
NOWLIN, Mary, W6954, WE, Nowlin, George W.
NUCHOLS, Elizabeth Hubbell, W1044, BO, Nuchols, James Wesley
NUCKOLLS, Mary Frances, W10344, HR, Nuckolls, Wm. W.
NUCKOLLS, Richard, S3791, SU, 63rd Va. Inf.
NUCKOLLS, Sue Douglass, W10685, SN, Nuckolls, Richard
NUCKOLS, H. F. S11559, PU, 4th Ky. Inf.
NULL, A. J. S6798, D, 31st Ark. Inf.
NULL, James M. S9433, 27th Inf.
NUNLEY, G. W. S14377, DY, 3rd Inf.
NUNLEY, George, S14174, WE, 5th Inf.
NUNLEY, James, S14297, RB, 35th Inf.
NUNLEY, Susan Eveline, W6679, RB, Nunley, James
NUNLEY, W. R. S2916, WE, 44th Inf.
NUNN, John, S3894, CL, 2nd Mo. Inf.
NUNN, Sarah J. W7491, CL, Nunn, John
NUNNELLY, Victoria, W1989, W, Nunnelly, Edwin
NUNNELY, Edwin, S5733, W, Undetermined
NUNNELY, W. R. S5474, W, 16th Inf.
NUNNERLY, James, S10577, BE, 47th Inf.
NUNNERY, Mary Cordelia, W4671, BE, Nunnery, James
NUTT, J. A. S1865, WY, 48th Inf.
NUTT, Sallie, W4922, WY, Nutt, James Alexander
NUTZELL, Conrad, S16688, SH, 15thh Inf.
NUTZELL, Rosina, W4449, SH, Nutzell, Conrad
OAKES, L. S. S12264, CF, 2nd Cav.
OAKLEY, A. D. S10585, CF, 44th Inf.
OAKLEY, C. A. S14086, RU, 11th Inf.
OAKLEY, Elizabeth Frances, W827, DI, Oakley, James Washington
OAKLEY, Frances Ella, W5692, DI, Oakley, Curtis Alexander
OAKLEY, Henry C. S1258, WE, Undetermined
OAKLEY, J. P. S13655, MA, 51st Inf.
OAKLEY, James C. S11932, DI, 4th Inf.

OAKLEY, Mary Barron, W10662, HE, Oakley, James K. Polk
OAKLEY, R. F. S5804, FR, 41st Inf.
OAKLEY, S. W. S6110, DY, 51st Inf.
OAKMAN, Emily Hagood, W5919, H, Oakman, Robert Harper
OAKS, George W. S1494, S, 16th Inf.
OAKS, I. C. S16297, LA, 5th Ala. Inf.
OATES, Celina Jane, W1893, F, Oates, Starnes Kidley
OATES, V. L. S1823, SH, 16th (Logwood's) Cav.
OBAUGH, George T. S5596, GE, 2nd Va. Inf.
OBRIEN, Carrie, W6965, D, O'Brien, Hezekiah
OBRIEN, Mary Ann Elizabeth, W8875, RU, O'Brien, John
OBRIEN, S. M. S1370, WA, 18th Tex. Inf.
OBRIEN, Thomas, S4843, GI, 1st (Turney's) Inf.
OCALLAGHAN, Fannie Ann, W4271, SH, O'Callaghan, John
OCONNER, Patrick, S16570, LA, 1st La. Inf.
ODANIEL, Bryant M. S1029, O, 55th Inf.
ODANIEL, Frances Evelyn, W8515, G, O'Daniel, Robert
ODANIEL, W. H. S3517, MC, 59th Inf.
ODEAR, A. J. S3027, FR, 33rd Ala. Inf.
ODEAR, Katharine, W1235, FR, O'Dear, Andrew Jackson
ODELL, Henry, S9719, CO, 60th Inf.
ODELL, J. P. S5657, A, 63rd Inf.
ODELL, T. F. S10668, SU, Sullivan Co. Reserves
ODELL, Thomas M. S9114, SU, 8th (Smith's) Cav.
ODELL, W. A. S3177, SU, 63rd Inf.
ODELL, William, S2004, SU, 26th Inf.
ODENEAL, L. B. S15651, GI, 32nd Inf.
ODLE, Dave, S7439, WY, 4th (McLemore's) Cav.
ODLE, James A. S3071, OV, 8th Cav.
ODOM, Andrew J. S4496, HD, 38th Inf.
ODOM, Collie, W597, D, Odom, B. F.
ODOM, H. C. S475, CA, 2nd Cav.
ODOM, Isaac H. S15095, ME, 26th Inf.
ODOM, J. A. S14775, SH, 12th Ky. Cav.
ODOM, J. T. E. S6464, SN, 9th (Bennett's) Cav.
ODOM, James W. S6899, RU, 3rd (Forrest's) Cav.
ODOM, John, S2082, ST, 50t Inf.
ODOM, Josephine Bogle, W8960, CA, Odom, Samuel Crisp
ODOM, P. J. S579, CH, 21st Cav.
ODOM, Rachel Agnes, W723, ST, Odom, J. E.
ODOM, Sallie Jane, W9260, CF, Odom, James Henry
ODOM, Samuel C. S16232, S15224, CA, 22nd (Barteau's) Cav.
ODOM, Sarah E. W1909, ME, Odom, Francis Marion
ODOM, Sarah E. W7704, ME, Odom, Isaac H.
ODOM, Susan Caroline, W10823, HU, Odom, Wm. Henry Harrison
ODOM, William F. S3335, RU, 22nd (Barteau's) Cav.
ODONNELL, Rose Kelley, W11031, D, O'Donnell, John
ODUM, Daniel, S3820, W, 4th Inf.
ODUM, James E. S572, MT, 49th Inf.
ODUM, Kate, W2171, WL, Odum, Willie
OEHMING, Isdor Randolph, W2312, FR, Oehming, Benjamin Anderson
OFFICER, Ida Chowning, W10882, OV, Officer, John Holford
OFFICER, Mary Jane, W5397, WH, Officer, David Snodgrass
OFFICER, W. P. S8209, WH, 8th Cav.
OFFIELD, George, S11708, SU, 36th Inf.
OFFIELD, Mary I. W8016, SU, Offield, George
OFFIELD, William, S3554, SU, 26th Inf.
OGARA, Elizabeth, W2740, G, O'Gara, Martin
OGARA, Martin, S4868, G, 9th Inf.
OGDEN, Lydia, W10396, WH, Ogden, Henry
OGILVIE, Annie Lou, W8958, WI, Ogilvie, Wm. Harris
OGILVIE, Bettie Roberts, W9333, WI, Ogilvie, Wm. Franklin
OGILVIE, Charles Henry, S6991, T, Forrest's Old Regt. Cav.
OGILVIE, Mary A. W2454, D, Ogilvie, O. S.
OGILVIE, R. C. S15643, MS, 18th Inf.
OGILVIE, Romelus, S15763, MS, 9th Bn. Cav.
OGILVIE, Theresa Rebecca, W3053, T, Ogilvie, Charles Henry
OGLE, Andrew Thomas, S4282, CE, 42nd Inf.
OGLE, L. H. S9331, U, 29th Inf.
OGLE, Levy, S12498, WI, 20th Inf.
OGLES, H. S14116, CF, 34th Inf.
OGLES, Rebecca C. [Rowland], W11126, MS, Ogles, John C. [Later married Rowland]
OGLESBY, Calvin, S12673, K, 31st Inf.
OGLESBY, Clara M. W4460, TR, Oglesby, D. F.

Index to Tennessee Confederate Pension Applications

OGLESBY, D. F. S12412, TR, 2nd Cav.
OGLESBY, Mary E. [Wiseman], W10467, TR, Oglesby, Thomas E. [Later married Wiseman]
OGLESTREE, Sarah, W10180, OV, Oglestree, Thomas B.
OGLETREE, T. B. S12623, OV, 8th (Dibrell's) Cav.
OGUIN, Annie Rittie, W5553, HI, O'Guin, Patrick G.
OGUIN, Patrick, S6783, HI, 48th (Voorhies') Inf.
OGUIN, R. N. S6025, HU, 11th Inf.
OGWIN, Cornelia, W3370, RB, O'Gwin, Wm. Henry
OHERN, Jerry, S1675, JE, 23rd Inf.
OKELLEY, Elizabeth, W7715, CF, O'Kelley, B. F.
OKELLEY, Elizabeth Ann, W5990, B, O'Kelley, Benjamin Franklin
OLDFIELD, James C. S2885, CF, 4th (McLemore's) Cav.
OLDFIELD, John, S3802, CF, 4th Cav.
OLDHAM, Daisy, W11103, L, Oldham, Gen. Edward Ransdale
OLDHAM, David, S8728, H, 3rd Bn. Cav.
OLDHAM, Edward R. S16638, L, 7th Cav.
OLDHAM, Eliza Jane, W7142, LI, Oldham, Samuel Lewis
OLDHAM, J. M>, S1034, MT, 49th Inf.
OLDHAM, Judah Frances, W9712, W2723, WE, Oldham, Martin VanBuren
OLDHAM, Mariah Lou, W5243, MT, Oldham, I. M.
OLDHAM, Robert, S4208, WL, 8th (Smith's) Cav.
OLDHAM, Samuel L. S8505, LI, 1st Inf.
OLDHAM, W. J. S3274, K, 3rd Cav.
OLDHAM, W. R. S5187, LI, 1st (Turney's) Inf.
OLIPHENT, Rufolphus B. S4090, GE, 64th N.C. Inf.
OLIVE, Joseph Ann, W1213, D, Olive, Jefferson Turner
OLIVE, Louisa, W9897, MN, Olive, Wm. J.
OLIVE, R. B. S13765, HN, 5th Inf.
OLIVE, W. H. S15752, HN, 21st (Wilson's) Cav.
OLIVE, W. J. S12736, MN, 19th (Biffle's) Cav.
OLIVER, A. R. S4199, FR, 32nd Inf.
OLIVER, C. C. S7297, CT, 19th Inf.
OLIVER, Daniel M. S7651, LA, 23rd Inf.

OLIVER, Elizabeth, W3995, HI, Oliver, Wm. Eli
OLIVER, G. W. S1120, O, 47th Inf.
OLIVER, Imogene, W9016, HN, Oliver, Joe
OLIVER, J. L. S14578, O, 47th Inf.
OLIVER, J. P. S15232, D, 6th Ky. Cav.
OLIVER, John, S11868, WH, 50th Inf.
OLIVER, Louisa, W11181, O, Oliver, Allen H.
OLIVER, Luvana Virginia, W3035, O, Oliver, George Washington
OLIVER, Martha, W2607, SU, Oliver, John W.
OLIVER, Martha Elvira, W1933, BO, Oliver, Wm.
OLIVER, Mary E. W10260, CA, Oliver, John H.
OLIVER, Nannie J. W1120, D, Oliver, Felix S.
OLIVER, Narcissa J. W3392, LA, Oliver, Dan M.
OLIVER, Rebecca A. W3429, HN, Oliver, Moses C.
OLIVER, U. C. S10842, SU, 60th Inf.
OLIVER, W. L. S15433, D, 7th Inf.
OLLIS, Louisa Matilda, W5722, CO, Ollis, James Nelson
OMOHUNDRO, J. W. S11202, FR, 44th Va. Inf.
OMOHUNDRO, Maggie Logan, W9979, WL, Omohundro, Orville C.
ONEAL, A. Q. S12283, K, 2nd Ky. Cav.
ONEAL, Ann Warren, W8418, D, O'Neal, Alford M.
ONEAL, Annie Elizabeth, W7494, H, O'Neal, Phillip Sherald
ONEAL, F. M. S8797, MA, 51st Inf.
ONEAL, J. B. S6905, FR, 3rd S.C. Inf.
ONEAL, J. H. S14975, PO, 29th Inf.
ONEAL, Joel A. S8775, CC, 34th Ga. Inf.
ONEAL, Julia, W10599, SN, O'Neal, Wm.
ONEAL, M. V. S14860, PO, 29th Inf.
ONEAL, Mollie Abernathy, W9637, GI, O'Neal, Wm.
ONEAL, P. S. S7849, H, 3rd Inf.
ONEAL, Walter, S7116, DY, 1st Hvy. Art.
ONEAL, William, C157, MA, 12th Miss. Cav.
ONEIL, Harvey D. S7372, MA, 6th Inf.
ONEILL, Cornelius, S3628, 22nd Inf.
ONEILL, E. E. S14994, MU, 2nd (Robison's) Inf.
ONEILL, Peter, S10952, SH, 12th Inf.
ONLY, Anna Elizabeth, W4433, MC, Only, Return John Meigs
ONLY, Malissa D. W641, MC, Only, Edward W.

ONLY, R. J. M. S5701, MC, 3rd Inf.
OPPENHEIMER, Ben, S10544, G, 2nd Ala. Cav.
ORAND, Margaret Ann, W1473, RB, Orand, Wm.
ORE, James A. M. S825, JE, 22nd Tex. Inf.
ORENDUFF, Joseph, S3668, SU, 13th Va. Reserves
ORGAIN, Sallie C. W2956, DI, Orgain, Wm. H.
ORICK, Ibby J. W80, HW, Orick, Benjamin
ORLANDI, Josephine, W4846, SH, Orlandi, Itala Antonio
ORLEANS, Joseph, S9374, O, 10th Miss. Inf.
ORLEANS, Sallie Fine, W6800, O, Orleans, Joseph
ORMAN, Mattie J. W4046, MU, Orman, Robert Lorenzo
ORMAN, Rebecca C. W2327, HI, Orman, John Thomas
ORR, A. Q. S9024, H, 3rd (Lillard's) Mtd. Inf.
ORR, C. J. S10213, MS, 3rd Inf.
ORR, Carson T. S11375, MU, 11th (Holman's) Cav.
ORR, Clay Jones, W9114, MU, Orr, Jacob Kittrell
ORR, Eldora B. W5615, HN, Orr, John S.
ORR, Harriet C. W10281, HN, Orr, Joe P.
ORR, J. K. S15917, MU, 19th (Biffle's) Cav.
ORR, J. P. S13656, HN, 12th Ky. Cav.
ORR, John Hamilton, S13340, B, 18th Inf.
ORR, John S. S9795, HN, 5th Inf.
ORR, Joseph H. S7298, MS, 17th Inf.
ORR, Margaret Catherine, W3289, MS, Orr, Samuel
ORR, Mary Ann, W8680, G, Orr, Wm. Elkana
ORR, Sallie M. W6552, MU, Orr, Carson Thomas
ORR, Susan M. W10036, B, Orr, John Rufus
ORR, W. E. S14662, G, 12th Inf.
ORR, W. H. S12718, MS, 23rd Inf.
ORR, W. M. S16212, MS, 17th Inf.
ORRANT, J. A. S7802, WA, 37th N.C. Inf.
ORRANT, L. W. S7803, WA, 37th N.C. Inf.
ORRICK, Mary L. W1821, MO, Orrick, Felix
ORRICK, Robert B. S6565, HW, 63rd Inf.
ORTNER, Lidia, W1856, LI, Ortner, Wm. Wesley
ORTON, James L. S756, WA, Undetermined
OSBORN, George W. S13931, GE, 1st N.C. Cav.
OSBORN, Lucy, W2842, D, Osborn, James Reed

OSBORN, Mary Ida, W10734, SH, Osborn, R. M.
OSBORNE, Andrew J. S6017, GI, 40th Ga. Inf.
OSBORNE, Frances C. W9032, SU, Osborne, G. W.
OSBORNE, J. B. S2529, CE, 11th Inf.
OSBORNE, J. N. S5046, FR, 4th Inf.
OSBORNE, James Fishback, S14271, G, 33rd Inf.
OSBORNE, Jesse, S12536, WA, 58th N.C. Inf.
OSBORNE, Permelia, W8639, WH, Osborne, Henry
OSBORNE, Prudy G. W7764, GI, Osborne, A. J.
OSBORNE, Sallie Fiteland, W5630, T, Osborne, John Richard
OSBURN, Frank G. S8090, O, 33rd Inf.
OSBURN, J. W. S5411, LI, 53rd Inf.
OSGATHARP, E. G. S13797, CY, 13th Cav.
OSGATHARP, G. B. S759, CY, 8th Cav.
OSGATHORPE, Tilman J. S10226, J, 8th Cav.
OSTEEN, W. H. S16031, B, 21st (Carter's) Cav.
OTEY, Ephriam, C20, WI, Quartermaster Dept.
OTEY, J. H. S14508, WI, 1st (Feild's) Inf.
OTT, John F. S6900, RU, 18th Inf.
OTT, W. A. S14192, H, 23rd Inf.
OUSLEY, Della, W10794, SH, Ousley, Rufus N.
OUTLAW, W. P. S13822, DI, 49th Inf.
OUTTEN, Hallie F. W9648, SH, Outten, Wm. Thomas
OVENDUFF, Susannah Eveline, W3185, SU, Ovenduff, Joseph
OVERALL, Albert H. S3721, RU, 18th Inf.
OVERALL, Harriet Frances, W1598, RU, Overall, Albert Henry
OVERALL, J. P. S15812, T, 7th (Duckworth's) Cav.
OVERALL, Rosanna C. W2428, RU, Overall, Wm. Thomas
OVERALL, William F. S10683, RU, 4th Cav.
OVERBY, Mary J. W4011, HI, Overby, Alexander
OVERBY, Nancy Martin, W2799, FR, Overby, Robert Macks
OVERCAST, John A. S13290, HN, 2nd Miss. Inf.
OVERCAST, T. D. S6001, HN, 18th Cav.
OVERMAN, Margaret, W4219, D, Overman, Jarome Alexander
OVERSTREET, Amanda, W3953, SM, Overstreet, R. H.

OVERSTREET, Emaline, W510, WA, Overstreet, James
OVERSTREET, R. H. S1299, SM, 55th Inf.
OVERTON, J. H. S12664, T, 154th Sr. Regt. Inf.
OVERTON, Jesse, S14250, WE, 27th Inf.
OVERTON, John W. S5494, SN, 24th Inf.
OVERTON, Lizzie, W8228, SN, Overton, John Waller
OWEN, Andrew J. S12208, HE, 9th Cav.
OWEN, C. C. S6296, SH, 1st Ala. Miss. & Tenn. Inf.
OWEN, Charles, S14761, MA, 1st (Carter's) Cav.
OWEN, Charles H. S14229, WE, 20th (Russell's) Cav.
OWEN, D. S. S8284, CH, 9th Ala. Cav.
OWEN, Dansada, W3631, W, Owen, Samuel B.
OWEN, Dora, W8335, MA, Owen, Charles
OWEN, Frusanna M. W526, RU, Owen, David R.
OWEN, George W. S4499, HW, 59th Inf.
OWEN, H. A. S1374, HE, 7th Inf.
OWEN, J. D. S4710, CA, 1st Bn. (McNairy's) Cav.
OWEN, J. L, S11568, D, 11th Inf.
OWEN, J. R. S14875, LA, 27th Ala. Inf.
OWEN, James H. S8386, RU, 24th Inf.
OWEN, James H. S11071, O, 3rd Va. Cav.
OWEN, Jennie Lee, W9245, SH, Owen, Thomas Henderson
OWEN, John A. S11956, O, Richardson's Bn. Va. Art.
OWEN, M. H. S16411, HY, 31st Inf.
OWEN, M. M. S10090, PU, 16th Inf.
OWEN, Martha May, W1980, D, Owen, Joseph Clark
OWEN, Mary Elizabeth, W2812, SH, Owen, Christopher Columbus
OWEN, Mary F. W2006, D, Owen, Obediah F.
OWEN, Mary Jane, W8828, Owen, Abram Ivy
OWEN, Nannie E. W10404, WI, Owen, John Green
OWEN, Nathan, S10857, WI, 1st (Feild's) Inf.
OWEN, S. Caroline, W3753, CA, Owen, James D.
OWEN, S. H. S4652, CA, 23rd Inf.
OWEN, Stephen, S12123, BR, 4th Ga. Cav.
OWEN, Susanna Elizabeth, W9639, GI, Owen, Wm. Pleasant
OWEN, T. A. S7874, CE, 49th Inf.
OWEN, T. G. S9211, MC, 5th Cav.
OWEN, Thomas H. S6714, F, 13th Inf.
OWEN, Thomas P. S8358, L, 7th Cav.
OWEN, Virginia Ann, W6955, WE, Owen, Charles H.
OWEN, W. A. S10709, SH, 12th (Green's) Cav.
OWEN, W. J. S8394, RU, 11th Cav.
OWEN, W. P. S15630, BR, 69th N.C. Inf.
OWEN, W. R. S692, D, 44th Inf.
OWEN, W. R. S4816, MN, 10th Miss. Inf.
OWEN, William, S9033, WI, 6th (Wheeler's) Cav.
OWENS, B. F. S956, HU, 11th Inf.
OWENS, Cynthia Ann, W3003, CE, Owens, Thomas Rufus
OWENS, Cynthia Jane, W2546, HU, Owens, Blythia Fuquay
OWENS, Dennis, S7785, G, 20th Inf.
OWENS, Dudley, S6212, D, 6th (Wheeler's) Cav.
OWENS, Elijah, S6081, G, 47th Inf.
OWENS, Eliza Jane, W4053, HE, Owens, Joseph L.
OWENS, Ellen Crenshaw, W1497, SH, Owens, James Robert
OWENS, Frances M. W340, SM, Owens, Samuel A.
OWENS, James R. S208, SH, 38th Inf.
OWENS, Jesse, S6232, H, 1st Ga. Inf.
OWENS, John B. S1742, HN, 46th Inf.
OWENS, John Henry, S6583, SU, 29th Inf.
OWENS, Lucinda R. W6969, MN, Owens, Daniel S.
OWENS, M. A. W1289, HN, Owens, (Col.) R. A.
OWENS, Margaret J. W72, GR, Owens, John F.
OWENS, Mary E. W3436, SU, Owens, John H.
OWENS, Nannie A. W7972, Owens, Samuel H.
OWENS, Nathan M. S10500, K, 2nd (Ashby's) Cav.
OWENS, R. A. S4248, HN, 46th Inf.
OWENS, Sarah E. W7400, G, Owens, Dennis
OWENS, T. R. S4719, CE, 9th Inf.
OWENS, W. J. S9222, D, 3rd Inf.
OWENS, William, S864, LO, 43rd Inf.
OWENS, William H. S1079, CO, 16th N.C. Inf.
OWENS, William J. S1037, J, 26th Inf.
OWINGS, J. G. S8236, RO, 1st Cav.
OWINGS, William A. S8827, K, 64th Ga. Inf.
OWINGS, William M. S1999, RO, 1st (Carter's) Cav.
OWNBEY, J. W. S5035, H, 1st Ga. State Troops
OWNBY, Cahal Polk, S12686, 5th Inf.

Index to Tennessee Confederate Pension Applications

OWNBY, E. P. S9917, 10th Cav.
OWNBY, S. m. S12085, CA, 20th (Nixon's) Cav.
OWSLEY, T. A. H. S2761, CL, 2nd (Ashby's) Cav.
OXENDINE, Larkin, S5854, CT, 37th N.C. Inf.
OXFORD, Margaret Ann, W4348, C, Oxford, Isaac
OYLER, G. W. S7912, H, 21st Ga. Inf.
OYLER, Sarah Christine, W2241, H, Oyler, George Washington
OYSBORN, Henry, S7428, PU, 8th Inf.
OZANNE, Frank, S14826, SH, Washington's La. Art.
OZMENT, John, S9246, D, 1st Cav.
OZMENT, Nancy Jane, W1670, WL, Ozment, Robert Burton
OZMENT, Robert B. S554, WL, 7th Inf.
PACE, John Carroll, S5076, T, 7th Cav.
PACE, Martha E. J. W997, DY, Pace, James Carroll
PACE, Miley Ann, W10457, G, Pace, Wm. Thomas
PACE, Sarah Margarett, W2840, HI, Pace, Wilson Reavis
PACE, Stacy S. W1360, DY, Pace, Wm. Thomas
PACK, Jeremiah, S14282, H, 1st Ga. Inf.
PACK, John, S1226, CO, 54th N.C. Inf.
PACK, Julia, W7829, CO, Pack, John
PACK, Narcissa, W2642, DK, Pack, John
PACK, Sarah, W3511, DK, Pack, Wm. Madison
PACK, William, S236, CO, 54th N.C. Inf.
PACK, William M. S5143, DK, 35th Inf.
PADEN, John M. S1866, D, 16th Ga. Inf.
PADGETT, Caroline, W3000, H, Padgett, Hicks
PADGETT, Ellen, W7082, D, Padgett, Fletcher Lavender
PADGETT, Emma, W5893, WL, Padgett, John O.
PADGETT, Fletcher L. S9427, D, 11th (Holman's) Cav.
PADGETT, H. B. S1908, DI, 1st (Feild's) Inf.
PADGETT, James Albert, S11574, CO, 22nd N.C. Inf.
PADGETT, William Sidney, S11037, MU, 11th Cav.
PAFFORD, Frances, W5294, BE, Pafford, James Hilliard
PAFFORD, J. H. S4762, BE, 5th Inf.
PAFFORD, R. C. S280, BE, 55th Inf.
PAGE, A. B. S3892, CE, 50th Inf.
PAGE, Beverly, S13009, MT, 8th Ky. Cav.
PAGE, G. H. S4720, RB, 8th Ky. Inf.
PAGE, G. W. S7263, GI, 3rd (Clack's) Inf.
PAGE, George W. S13177, GI, 3rd (Clack's) Inf.
PAGE, J. J. S1820, DI, 51st Inf.
PAGE, J. P. S13909, ST, 2nd Ky. Cav.
PAGE, Lucetta, W4475, MU, Page, David F.
PAGE, Minerva Jane, W6508, WE, Page, Jeremiah Jackson
PAGE, S. J. S16214, WH, 8th Tex. Cav.
PAGE, Sallie Hight, W7080, WL, Page, Albert W.
PAGE, Susan, W5489, DY, Page, Oscar Fitzallen
PAGE, Tabetha Angiline, W7013, MT, Page, Beverly
PAGE, W. H. S14463, D, 10th Cav.
PAINE, Benjamin W. S1817, V, 22nd Inf.
PAINE, Bettie, W2687, D, Paine, Sterling G.
PAINE, Etta E. W, Some papers with #11183 on film
PAINE, Lizzie Rowlett, W6185, SH, Paine, John James
PAINE, S. C. S9976, D, 7th Cav.
PAINE, Smith F. S10953, SE, 64th N.C. Inf.
PAINE, W. R. S5294, V, 16th Inf.
PAINTER, Aaron, S7460, WA, 61st Inf.
PAINTER, Emma L. W10009, SU, Painter, James Watson
PAINTER, Helen Sims, W4176, SH, Painter, Wm. Pinkney
PAINTER, J. W. S7440, SU, 45th Va. Inf.
PAINTER, James C. S143, MOO, 5th Ky. Inf.
PAINTER, Louisa Jane, W622, WA, Painter, Thomas
PAINTER, William Pinckney, S12038, SH, 15th Miss. Inf.
PAIR, Lucinda, W985, O, Pair, J. L.
PAISLEY, Mary Elizabeth, W6762, W520, GI, Paisley, John Milton
PALMER, A. W. S15096, H, 31st Ga. Inf.
PALMER, Angeline, W3603, PU, Palmer, George M.
PALMER, Annie M. W4578, H, Palmer, W. W.
PALMER, Catherine Laws, W11124, D, Palmer, Wm. Asbury
PALMER, J. B. S3710, WI, Allison's Squadron, Cav.
PALMER, Jesse W. S10669, 20th Cav.
PALMER, Martha J. W4402, G, Palmer, Joseph Martin
PALMER, Martha J. W8015, Palmer, Jesse W.

PALMER, Mary Ella, W9733, O, Palmer, John Dabney
PALMER, Nancy Jane, W7441, WL, Palmer, Richard H.
PALMER, R. H. S13880, WL, 7th Inf.
PALMER, Robert D. S9859, B, 17th Inf.
PALMER, Tilman M. S1732, 20th Miss. Inf.
PALMER, W. A. S16162, D, 38th Ala. Inf.
PALMERTREE, J. M. S14486, SH, 1st Miss. Lt Art.
PALMORE, B. B. S9776, CC, 33rd Inf.
PALMORE, Martha, W6010, CC, Palmore, B. B.
PALVADO, Mary, W8352, SH, Palvado, Simon J.
PALVADO, Mary A. W7463, SH, Palvado, Joseph S.
PAMPLIN, John A. S7381, LI, 44th Inf.
PAMPLIN, Joseph, S10722, LI, 41st Inf.
PANGLE, Deliah, W357, OV, Pangle, David
PANGLE, Hugh L. S13498, HM, 4th Tex. Inf.
PANKEY, Florence, W2665, G, Pankey, James L.
PANKEY, James L. S3247, G, 3rd (Forrest's) Cav.
PANKEY, William Huston, S6761, O, 27th Inf.
PANKY, L. N. S12636, DE, 7th (Duckworth's) Cav.
PANTER, Mary, W2248, BL, Panter, Sampson Benjamin
PANTER, W. F. S7652, FR, 8th Inf.
PARADISE, Lemisar, W10631, D, Paradise, David Love
PARAGIN, Lee, C9462, PU, 9th (Cons.) Cav., App. numbered on regular Soldiers film
PARCHMAN, Jesse M. S15994, ST, 50th Inf.
PARCHMAN, N. R. S16060, MT, 2nd Ky. Cav.
PARCHMAN, W. A. S12413, ST, 50th Inf.
PARDUE, G. M. S13155, RB, 42nd Inf.
PARDUE, Martha Washington, W6623, CE, Pardue, David Crockett
PARDUE, Mary, W3366, CE, Pardue, James Lafayette
PARE, Helen Lee, W9147, CH, Pare, Marcus Dean
PARE, M. D. S12958, CH, 31st Inf.
PARHAM, Emma, W8865, WE, Parham, Wm. Weasley
PARHAM, Frances Emiline, W1975, W8829, WI, Parham, Wm. Thomas
PARHAM, Lucy A. W9223, SH, Parham, John Thomas

PARHAM, Mary A. W7349, D, Parham, James Reed
PARHAM, Nancy Catharine, W2044, MU, Parham, Francis Washington
PARHAM, Willia T. S4306, MA, 6th Inf.
PARIS, Bettie, W3724, SN, Paris, John R.
PARIS, John Clark, S16605, G, Unassigned (Emergency Reserve)
PARIS, John R. S3901, SN, 2nd Inf.
PARIS, William Barlow, S9180, GE, 27th S.C. Inf.
PARISH, F. W. S15092, S13499, MA, 21st (Wilson's) Cav.
PARISH, J. J. S10127, G, 31st Inf.
PARISH, Mary Elizabeth, W3883, G, Parish, Thomas Thorne
PARK, Annie E. W1953, O, Park, John S.
PARK, Annie Tennessee, W1048, O, Park, James M.
PARK, Elizabeth McCleod, W1936, MS, Park, Francis Marion
PARK, Emma Denton, W8617, MU, Park, George Wm.
PARK, Francis M. S7183, MS, 41st Inf.
PARK, J. M. S4383, O, 33rd Inf.
PARK, J. R. S14837, RU, 32nd Tex. Inf.
PARK, T. H. S7302, O, 33rd Inf.
PARKER, A. J. S2855, CF, 32nd Inf.
PARKER, A. W. S8866, CA, 4th (McLemore's) Cav.
PARKER, Amanda Jane, W4118, WL, Parker, DeWit Clinton
PARKER, B. F. S10386, HI, 9th Bn. (Gantt's) Cav.
PARKER, Bettie, W5199, F, Parker, Washington Monroe
PARKER, C. S. S4140, HU, 1st (Feild's) Inf.
PARKER, Calista, W1757, MU, Parker, Willard
PARKER, D. C. S2089, WI, 20th Inf.
PARKER, Dora, W9453, GR, Parker, Wm. Haynie
PARKER, Eliza Jane, W5427, MR, Parker, Isaac A.
PARKER, Elizabeth, W8022, F, Parker, W. M.
PARKER, Ella Maude, W8164, W, Parker, George W.
PARKER, Esta Lee, W6734, W9049, W, Parker, Wm. Thomas
PARKER, G. W. S16067, CH, 18th (Newsom's) Cav.
PARKER, Henry Harrison, S6859, L, 16th Ala. Inf.

-265

PARKER, Hiram, S5384, H, 7th Inf.
PARKER, Isaac A. S10621, MR, 18th Bn. Ala. Cav.
PARKER, Isabella Frances, W5145, LK, Parker, Benjamin Franklin
PARKER, J. A. S13580, M, 2nd Ky. Cav.
PARKER, J. A. S15907, HI, 8th (Dibrell's) Cav.
PARKER, J. H. S6334, WA, 60th Inf.
PARKER, J. H. S13214, S12296, FR, 22nd Miss. Inf.
PARKER, J. R. S13337, GU, 35th Inf.
PARKER, James P. S13442, SH, 18th Miss. Inf.
PARKER, Joseph P. S8559, H, 1st Ga. Inf.
PARKER, Laura Ann, W3410, B, Parker, Pinkney D.
PARKER, Lou A. W6366, CF, Parker, Madison
PARKER, M. S. S4926, BE, 5th Inf.
PARKER, Madison, S12912, RU, 1st (Turney's) Inf.
PARKER, Martha A. W6882, GI, Parker, John Wesley
PARKER, Mary Emma, W2424, WH, Parker, C. A.
PARKER, Matt, S2592, FR, 31st Inf.
PARKER, Matt Ayres, W11053, M, Parker, John Arch.
PARKER, Mollie Mason, W10132, SH, Parker, Peyton F.
PARKER, Nancy Mildred, W10578, HI, Parker, Joseph Allen
PARKER, Nat, S13465, CA, 12th La. Inf.
PARKER, Patrick, S3240, H, 49th Ala. Inf.
PARKER, Peyton F. S6730, SH, 12th Cav.
PARKER, Polley Ann, W2821, BE, Parker, Moses Simon
PARKER, Press, S8192, H, Lookout Art.
PARKER, Rebecca, W8811, FR, Parker, Matt
PARKER, Rebecca A. W2441, GI, Parker, Alfred Forest
PARKER, Rosanah Margaret, W4036, B, Parker, John Benjamin
PARKER, Sarah Ann, W1127, ST, Parker, Isaac
PARKER, Sarah J. W3496, HW, Parker, Wm.
PARKER, Sarah L. W1194, G, Parker, George W.
PARKER, Simuel, S3912, HI, 24th Inf.
PARKER, T. J. S3457, DI, Baxter's Co. Lt. Art.
PARKER, Thomas, S14482, CE, 2nd Ky. Cav.
PARKER, Virginia Wiley, W4972, WA, Parker, Francis Asbury
PARKER, W. H. sr. S14323, HD, 26th Ga. Inf.
PARKER, William, S3654, M, 2nd Cav.
PARKER, William H. S10605, HM, 60th Inf.
PARKER, William J. S9694, D, 44th Inf.
PARKES, George W. S1057, JE, 5th Inf.
PARKES, J. M. S6269, WH, 3rd (Lillard's) Mtd. Inf.
PARKESON, Frank M. S10801, DK, 1st Bn. (Colm's) Inf.
PARKEY, Isaac, S10139, HA, 63rd Inf.
PARKISON, R. F. S8555, PU, 13th Cav.
PARKISON, Sarah C. W4639, PU, Parkison, R. F.
PARKMAN, D. A. S327, O, 1st Ky. Inf.
PARKS, Bettie, W10076, MOO, Parks, Rufus Burton
PARKS, D. P. S11176, D, 2nd Regt. Ga. State Line
PARKS, E. T. S9607, LI, 8th Inf. See also Elisha Thomison Parks
PARKS, Elisha Thomison, S14102, LI, 8th Inf. See also E. T. Parks
PARKS, G. W. S15470, MU, 6th (Wheeler's) Cav.
PARKS, George W. S321, W, 16th Inf.
PARKS, Hiram, S9730, CO, 70th N.C. Inf.
PARKS, J. R. S7391, SN, 25th Inf.
PARKS, Joe, S16663, MO, 3rd (Lillard's) Mtd. Inf.
PARKS, John, S2678, WH, 8th Cav.
PARKS, John M. S10025, H, 3rd (Lillard's) Mtd. Inf.
PARKS, Mary Ann, W7372, LI, Parks, Elisha Thomison
PARKS, Thomas Jefferson, S888, L, S.C. State Troops
PARMAN, Samuel Washington, S16644, D, 12th Bn. (Day's) Cav.
PARMAN, Sarah Elizabeth, W1813, D, Parman, Emanuel
PARMLEY, Silas R. S10414, GU, 35th Inf.
PARNELL, R. E. S16516, O, 12th Inf.
PARNELL, William G. S8255, PO, 5th Bn. Ala. Vols.
PARR, Columbus Row, S16290, DY, 4th Inf.
PARR, Isaac C. S1895, GI, 6th Tex. Cav.
PARR, Jennie, W3482, GI, Parr, Isaac Cole
PARRETT, Mahala A. W258, PU, Parrett, James
PARRIGAN, W. H. S8273, OV, 8th Cav.
PARRIS, Nancy A. W9419, WA, Parris, Wm. E.
PARRIS, Susan Surrenia, W4667, GE, Parris, Wm. Borlow
PARRIS, William G. S1132, CO, 54th N.C. Inf.
PARRISH, Abram, S12989, GR, 6th N.C. Inf.

PARRISH, Ann E. W3358, WI, Parrish, J. F.
PARRISH, D. B. S14772, D, Monsarratt's Bn.
PARRISH, John, C166, WI, 2nd Cav.
PARRISH, Julia Moore, W7815, HU, Parrish, Samuel Bryan
PARRISH, Margaret, W73, D, Parrish, Wm. Henry
PARRISH, Margaret A. W1659, MU, Parrish, Levan
PARRISH, Nancy, W8199, HN, Parrish, Thomas B.
PARRISH, Nancy Jane, W4258, W8978, LK, Parrish, Thomas Bedford, Also applied from Henry County
PARRISH, Samuel B. S13195, MU, Unassigned (Gunman)
PARRISH, T. S. S6140, D, Baxter's Co. Lt. Art.
PARRISH, T. T. S9930, G, 2nd Miss. Inf.
PARRISH, Virginia, W1550, DY, Parrish, W. N.
PARROTT, Esmaralda Catherine, W8979, SU, Parrott, Henry Alfred
PARROTT, Henry A. S9381, SU, 19th Inf.
PARROTT, Hiram, S4374, RU, 44th Inf.
PARROTT, John V. S7461, H, 60th Inf.
PARROTT, Nancy, W881, GE, Parrott, James
PARRY, A. C. S9483, JO, 61st Inf.
PARSELEY, James A. S2398, RU, 4th (McLemore's) Cav.
PARSLEY, Ervin, S16324, S16011, DK, Allison's Squadron, Cav.
PARSLEY, M. H. S7011, WE, 20th (Russell's) Cav.
PARSON, W. F. S15218, CU, 37th N.C. Inf.
PARSONS, Lydia Ann, W7620, K, Parsons, Wm. Jackson
PARSONS, W. J. S14624, K, 64th Va. Inf.
PARTAIN, Fannie, W7211, FR, Partain, W. S.
PARTAIN, John B. S2938, SE, Lookout Art.
PARTAIN, Margaret Jane, W4233, SE, Partain, John Benjamin
PARTAIN, Martha C. W6913, DY, Partain, Lewis B.
PARTAIN, Sarah Ann, W2578, MC, Partain, Jesse Franklin
PARTAIN, W. S. S4848, FR, 28th Cav.
PARTEE, J. D. S14801, SH, 18th Miss. Cav.
PARTEE, Mary Emma, W6291, SH, Partee, Jessee Dickens
PARTEE, Mary L.   See Mary L. Mosby
PARTIN, C. H. S6915, GI, 32nd Inf.
PARTIN, L. B. S14124, DY, 3rd Ga. Cav.
PARTON, Robert, S7981, H, 59th Inf.

PARTON, William A. J. S4112, FR, 17th Inf.
PASCHAL, James, S1255, GR, Undetermined
PASCHALL, F. D. S13603, HN, 7th Cav.
PASCHALL, H. W. S5144, WE, 31st Inf.
PASCHALL, Malinda J. W3529, HN, Paschall, John D.
PASCHALL, Mary Catharine, W1006, WE, Paschall, Hiram Washington
PASCHALL, Mary Love, W10820, HN, Paschall, John Wesley Daniel
PASS, E. H. S5530, MO, 63rd Inf.
PASSONS, W. J. T. S12938, WH, 16th Inf.
PATE, B. G. S11734, DY, 12th Inf.
PATE, D. A. S15409, U, 29th N.C. Inf.
PATE, I. J. S3896, CL, 22nd Va. Cav.
PATE, John D. S10643, 10th Cav.
PATE, L. W. S805, WI, 4th Cav.
PATE, Margret Sarah, W3154, SM, Pate, Don Dixon
PATE, Martha Jane, W2784, Pate, Stephen S.
PATE, Martha Jane, W3702, D, Pate, Thomas W.
PATE, Mary S. W948, D, Pate, Wm. N.
PATE, S. H. S16194, WL, 28th Inf.
PATE, William Franklin, S9970, WE, 154th Sr. Regt. Inf.
PATE, William T. S8474, SH, 16th Ala. Inf.
PATE, Winaford L. W4903, CL, Pate, Ira John
PATEN, Daniel, S14410, UN, 50th Va. Inf.
PATRICK, Elizabeth, W143, PU, Patrick, Jenkins
PATRICK, J. M. S1688, BE, 55th Inf.
PATRICK, J. R. S12177, RU, 8th (Smith's) Cav.
PATRICK, Jesse, S546, RU, 23rd Inf.
PATRICK, John, S4922, W, 35th Inf.
PATRICK, W. C. S14986, MT, 42nd Inf.
PATTEN, Sallie Catherine, W7353, GI, Patten, John Allen
PATTENGILL, Samuel, S5023, HO, 50th Inf.
PATTERSON, A. J. S14760, RU, 18th Inf.
PATTERSON, Annie L. W8432, SH, Patterson, M. D.
PATTERSON, B. T. S11693, CC, 47th Inf.
PATTERSON, C. J. S2473, G, 47th Inf.
PATTERSON, Claudis Virginia, W1258, WE, Patterson, Gilbert B.
PATTERSON, Dora B. W9803, SH, Patterson, Samuel Gideon
PATTERSON, E. E. S22, D, 20th Inf.
PATTERSON, Eliza McCormack, W10104, GI, Patterson, Joel Mason

Index to Tennessee Confederate Pension Applications

PATTERSON, Elizabeth J. W358, MS, Patterson, Thomas Marion
PATTERSON, Elizabeth Jane, W6230, BR, Patterson, John Wilson
PATTERSON, Emma B. W2481, CL, Patterson, Houston
PATTERSON, Everitt M. S7818, D, 20th Inf.
PATTERSON, Fannie Grant, W9973, F, Patterson, Henry Johnson
PATTERSON, H. I. S12076, HR, 11th Ala. Cav.
PATTERSON, Henrietta Vannie, W1929, G, Patterson, C. J.
PATTERSON, J. A. S4580, MC, 62nd Inf.
PATTERSON, J. A. S8855, SH, 13th Inf.
PATTERSON, J. B. S2144, MO, 23rd Ga. Inf.
PATTERSON, J. J. S11325, HO, 11th Inf.
PATTERSON, J. M. S7138, MO, 2nd Cav.
PATTERSON, J. M. S16177, GI, 5th Cav.
PATTERSON, J. N. S5051, HO, 10th Cav.
PATTERSON, J. W. S14118, MU, 36th Ga. Inf.
PATTERSON, J. W. S16377, WE, McDonald's Bn.
PATTERSON, James, S10335, MA, 4th Tex. Inf.
PATTERSON, Jesse, S6036, HW, 31st Inf.
PATTERSON, John, S4551, MN, 15th Inf.
PATTERSON, John W. S11437, BR, 1st (Carter's) Cav.
PATTERSON, Louise Ellender, W7187, W10352, MA, Patterson, Jasper Newton
PATTERSON, M. D. S15746, SH, 11th Ala. Cav.
PATTERSON, M. H. S1241, LA, 23rd Inf.
PATTERSON, Margaret L. W9822, CH, Patterson, James B.
PATTERSON, Margaret Louisa, W2703, WL, Patterson, James Thompson
PATTERSON, Martha, W102, MG, Patterson, Robert E.
PATTERSON, Mary, W127, LA, Patterson, Archibald Neal
PATTERSON, Mary, W9384, R, Patterson, James A.
PATTERSON, Mary (Polly), W359, WL, Patterson, Lee
PATTERSON, Mary Boddie, W11115, SN, Patterson, Wm. C.
PATTERSON, Mary Jane, W67, WE, Patterson, W. M. C.
PATTERSON, Mary Virginia, W5631, HR, Patterson, Hobart Ives
PATTERSON, N. S9767, W, 35th Inf.
PATTERSON, Olivia Jane, W9042, RU, Patterson, Archie J.
PATTERSON, Pauline Horner, W10181, G, Patterson, Robert B.
PATTERSON, R. F. S11097, CL, 29th Inf.
PATTERSON, Rachel W. W5944, K, Patterson, Robert F.
PATTERSON, Robert Anderson, S12125, G, 12th (Green's) Cav.
PATTERSON, S. G. S3590, SH, 21st Inf.
PATTERSON, Sanford W. S12575, CE, 49th Inf.
PATTERSON, Sarah, W3439, HW, Patterson, Wm.
PATTERSON, Sarah R. D. I. W909, LA, Patterson, Malcom H.
PATTERSON, Susan Parlee, W5361, MN, Patterson, James Smith
PATTERSON, Thomas, S4561, MT, 50th Inf.
PATTERSON, Thomas M. S11551, HY, 7th Ark. Inf.
PATTERSON, W. A. S12583, HW, 37th Inf.
PATTERSON, W. N. S15730, WL, 18th Inf.
PATTERSON, W. R. S12008, WE, 12th Ky. Cav.
PATTERSON, William, S3327, RO, 59th Inf.
PATTERSON, William, S5521, HW, 31st Inf.
PATTERSON, William Henry, S6316, BR, 19th Inf.
PATTIE, W. B. S3722, GU, 1st (Turney's) Inf.
PATTISON, Anna Holmes, W5382, T, Pattison, Thomas Foster
PATTON, Benjamin F. S11021, K, 60th N.C. Inf.
PATTON, D. L. S10542, LE, 19th (Biffle's) Cav.
PATTON, Frederick M. S5699, WA, 29th N.C. Inf.
PATTON, Helen Amanda, W10103, SH, Patton, Thomas Newton
PATTON, Henry T. S10556, RO, 61st Inf.
PATTON, Horace F. S13494, K, 59th Inf.
PATTON, J. C. S3736, LI, 41st Inf.
PATTON, J. L. S9130, WL, 35th Inf.
PATTON, J. M. S5629, W, 16th Inf.
PATTON, J. N. S11268, HO, 2nd (Robison's) Inf.
PATTON, James P. S5557, MC, 16th N.C. Inf.
PATTON, Jennie Odom, W10038, WL, Patton, John Higgins
PATTON, Jonathan B. S9172, DK, 35th Inf.

Index to Tennessee Confederate Pension Applications

PATTON, L. E. S16503, SH, 2nd Cav.
PATTON, Lou [Flippin], W10686, WL, Patton, John Forbes, [Later married Flippin]
PATTON, Louisa Elizabeth, W10551, MU, Patton, Reloford Melvin
PATTON, Martha Bunch, W10102, SH, Patton, L. E.
PATTON, Martha J. W4286, BL, Patton, John A.
PATTON, Mary E. W10544, WL, Patton, Joseph L.
PATTON, Nancy Amanda, W7410, K, Patton, Horace F.
PATTON, Nelson Gray, S9360, WL, 35th Inf.
PATTON, R. M. S15309, MU, 6th (Wheeler's) Cav.
PATTON, R. M. S16237, MU, 19th (Biffle's) Cav.
PATTON, Robert Bruce, C24, D, 4th Cav.
PATTON, Sallie B. W9435, RO, Patton, Henry Thomas
PATTON, Sallie Rayburn, W10458, CF, Patton, Samuel Sloan
PATTON, Susan Clementine, W9233, GU, Patton, Thomas Benton
PATTON, Susan Mariah, W4098, G, Patton, George Washington
PATTON, T. B. S12062, GU, 44th Inf.
PATTON, W. C. S5047, RB, 14th Inf.
PATTON, W. W. S14827, L, 12th S.C. Inf.
PATTON, William M. S5412, D, 8th Ky. Inf.
PATTY, J. W. S4673, K, 31st Inf.
PATTY, Timothy S. S10631, K, 2nd Cav.
PAUL, M. M. S1835, R, 31st Inf.
PAUL, Tennessee C. W5099, LO, Paul, Meredith M.
PAUL, Uriah, S10990, MS, 3rd (Clack's) Inf.
PAUL, W. B. S5295, H, 31st Inf.
PAYNE, A. W. S9059, MT, 14th Inf.
PAYNE, Ada Bryan, W8504, SH, Payne, Thomas James
PAYNE, C. C. W5345, CC, Payne, Jackson Calhune
PAYNE, Cora Ann, W1686, T, Payne, Daniel Wylie
PAYNE, Daniel Wylie, S8031, T, 51st Inf.
PAYNE, Darthula C. W8275, SU, Payne, Joseph L.
PAYNE, Eliza, W9718, FR, Payne, David
PAYNE, Eliza Jane, W702, MR, Payne, James D.
PAYNE, Elizabeth, W11028, SN, Payne, Edwin Sanders
PAYNE, Elizabeth Cooper, W8422, FR, Payne, McCager
PAYNE, Elizabeth Jane, W3879, H, Payne, Lemuel S.
PAYNE, Emaline, W6773, H, Payne, J. W.
PAYNE, Fanney, W6563, W144, O, Payne, James A.
PAYNE, Florrie Brownlow, W4652, H, Payne, Wm. Henry
PAYNE, G. V. S10812, GE, 5th Cav.
PAYNE, G. W. S12338, SH, 35th Ala. Inf.
PAYNE, Gracie, W4444, MC, Payne, U.
PAYNE, J. W. S8678, MR, 5th Cav.
PAYNE, James D. S1618, MR, 1st Inf.
PAYNE, James M. S10707, ST, 2nd Bn. Ky. Mtd. Rifles
PAYNE, John Booker, S107, T, 4th Inf.
PAYNE, Joseph L. S15826, SU, 60th Inf.
PAYNE, L. S. S11937, H, 1st Ga. Inf.
PAYNE, Lindsey, S11114, H, 40th Miss. Inf.
PAYNE, Lisette Walker, W2709, H, Payne, John Newton
PAYNE, M. C. S8815, FR, 3rd Confederate Cav.
PAYNE, M. V. S9819, SU, 45th Va. Inf.
PAYNE, Martin David, S7364, B, 23rd Inf.
PAYNE, Mary E. W7879, GE, Payne, George Valentine
PAYNE, O. F. S1602, O, 22nd Ga. Inf.
PAYNE, R. C. S7775, RB, Malone's Regt. Ky. Cav.
PAYNE, Sarah Luvinda, W710, T, Payne, John Booker
PAYNE, Susan Mary, W10131, T, Payne, Virgil Lee
PAYNE, Susan Prudence, W3943, DY, Payne, Wylie Flail
PAYNE, T. J. S12414, SH, 12th Cav.
PAYNE, Tillman Price, C81, TR, 4th Cav.
PAYNE, Tink, C284, O, Regiment not given
PAYNE, U. M. S7025, MC, 1st (Carter's) Cav.
PAYNE, William, S2260, T, 34th Miss. Inf.
PAYNE, William H. S4431, SU, 5th (McClellan's) Cav.
PAYTON, J. J. S10152, MU, 9th Bn. Cav.
PEACH, J. A. S10415, WI, 44th Inf.
PEACH, Lewis G. S8321, LI, 8th Inf.
PEACH, Sarah, W6535, WI, Peach, J. A.
PEACH, Susie Sheffield, W8709, B, Peach, Lewis
PEACOCK, George F. S3123, A, 6th Ky. Cav.

Index to Tennessee Confederate Pension Applications

PEACOCK, John W. S13672, B, 4th (McLemore's) Cav.
PEAK, G. A. S13463, CF, 2nd Ga. Inf.
PEAK, James, S12755, WH, 8th (Dibrell's) Cav.
PEAK, Louisa Adeline, W6353, CF, Peak, George Asbury
PEAK, Martha, W9940, ME, Peak, James Knox Polk
PEAK, Molino Delroy, W3108, ME, Peak, Thomas Jefferson
PEAK, Virginia Lee, W9337, H, Peak, C. Standifer
PEAK, William T. S11155, S16332, S4450, MC, 43rd Inf.
PEAL, Nancy Ann, W230, D, Peal, S. D.
PEARCE, George, C135, G, 8th Cav.
PEARCE, H. C. S9258, O, 4th Inf.
PEARCE, John Adams, S15588, S16155, F, 38th Inf.
PEARCE, Malissa Ann, W7841, CH, Pearce, James Starks
PEARCE, Margaret, W2766, SU, Pearce, J. H. C.
PEARCE, Sallie Agnes, W6760, G, Pearce, Henry Clay
PEARCH, James S. S13437, CH, 21st (Wilson's) Cav.
PEARCY, Elizabeth, W2870, D, Pearcy, J. L.
PEARCY, J. W. S564, RU, 45th Inf.
PEARRE, Elvira, W4016, WI, Pearre, Robert H.
PEARSALL, Catherine, W2443, SH, Pearsall, Andrew
PEARSON, C. M. S6528, LI, 4th Inf.
PEARSON, Calvin N. S11612, HR, 17th Inf.
PEARSON, Elizabeth, W5926, HR, Pearson, Stanford
PEARSON, H. L. C. S1312, J, 12th Inf.
PEARSON, Helen Augusta, W7471, R, Pearson, James Henry
PEARSON, James B. S6563, MS, Forrest's Escort, Cav.
PEARSON, James H. S696, R, 1st Cav.
PEARSON, John Enoch, S6558, MOO, 17th Inf.
PEARSON, Josephine, W4514, MA, Pearson, Jonathan Dudley
PEARSON, Nancy M. W9814, FR, Pearson, James Knox Polk
PEARSON, Nannie V. W4295, G, Pearson, Thomas J.
PEARSON, Richard Carroll, S8376, LI, 28th Cav.
PEARSON, T. J. S7125, G, 7th Cav.
PEARSON, Thomas, S270, K, 1st & 11th N.C. Inf.
PEARSON, W. F. S7429, RU, 2nd (Robison's) Inf.
PEARSON, William H. S4256, LI, 8th Inf.
PEAY, J. B. S11412, WI, 25th Cav.
PECK, Elizabeth P. W5836, JE, Peck, Gilbert H.
PECK, James M. S5351, JE, 14th Va. Cav.
PECK, Lizzie I. W7248, JE, Peck, James Montgomery
PECKTOL, Sally T. W1439, SU, Pecktol, Samuel Patton
PEDDICORD, Pattie, W517, J, Peddicord, Carlines
PEEBLES, H. C. S5331, SU, 20th Inf.
PEEBLES, James, S12309, D, 20th Inf.
PEEBLES, Joseph W. S8410, F, 12th Va. Inf.
PEEBLES, Mary Lyon, W9423, WA, Peebles, Wm. Jacob
PEEBLES, Thomas, S10918, D, 15th (Stewart's) Cav.
PEEK, Adaline, W10364, PU, Peek, Robert
PEEK, L. P. S5440, OV, 8th (Dibrell's) Cav.
PEEK, L. T. S2054, OV, 8th Cav.
PEEK, Martha A. W9108, WL, Peek, Uriah
PEEK, Robert, S15011, S16680, PU, 9th (Ward's) Cav., 2nd app# info can be found under #15011
PEEK, Uriah, S16242, WL, 45th Inf.
PEEKS, Jere B. S6544, CT, 59th Inf.
PEEL, Julia, W6554, G, Peel, Wm.
PEEL, William, S4508, G, 40th N.C. Inf.
PEELER, J. N. S13939, LE, 10th (DeMoss') Cav.
PEELER, John, S6215, SU, 59th Inf.
PEELER, Martha A. W1706, SU, Peeler, John
PEELER, W. L. S5991, T, 14th (Neely's) Cav.
PEEPLES, Bettie Clay, W7293, HY, Peeples, B. F.
PEEPLES, Celestia Cincinnati, W2515, O, Peeples, Alford H.
PEEPLES, G. T. S10838, SH, 46th Inf.
PEEPLES, James P. S16536, HN, 5th Inf.
PEEPLES, Rachel Ellen, W7678, H, Peeples, Wm. Oscar
PEERY, Peter, S14938, DY, 22nd Inf.
PELHAM, W. M. S8487, S14263, FR, 17th Inf.
PELL, Sarah Adaline, W5731, HI, Pell, Henry Clark
PELTIER, James W. T. S2318, SU, 14th Inf.
PEMBERTON, A. J. S10944, HU, 10th Cav.
PEMBERTON, Alfred, S6547, BL, 39th Ga. Inf.

PEMBERTON, D. W. S2501, WL, 25th Inf.
PEMBERTON, Margaret F. W360, WL, Pemberton, Robert S.
PEMBERTON, Rachel Manerva, W5228, GR, Pemberton, Caloway
PEMBERTON, Sue C. W8944, SU, Pemberton, T. D.
PENDERGRASS, John T. S11976, PU, 8th (Dibrell's) Cav.
PENDERGRASS, Sarah Elizabeth, W11086, PU, Pendergrass, John T.
PENDERGRASS, William, S4614, SU, 20th Inf.
PENDLETON, C. H. S13338, O, 1st Ky. Cav.
PENDLETON, J. B. S16457, DK, Allison's Squadron, Cav.
PENDLETON, Mary Leona, W7408, O, Pendleton, Charles Henry
PENDLETON, Missouri Freelove, W3739, K, Pendleton, Albert Gallatin
PENDLEY, John M. S3559, B, 35th Inf.
PENDLEY, Posey, S3615, G, 63rd Ga. Inf.
PENGLETON, Mary Ann, W3352, LA, Pengleton, Jefferson K.
PENICK, Louisiana Harriett, W1759, Penick, Joseph Jerome
PENIX, S. M. S3827, SU, 59th Inf.
PENLAND, Florence Osborne, W9777, LO, Penland, Thomas
PENLAND, L. D. S15385, K, 7th Ark. Inf.
PENLAND, Thomas, S16540, LO, Jones' Ga. Inf.
PENN, H. Lee, S9184, MA, 7th (Duckworth's) Cav.
PENN, William, S2181, WE, 39th Ga. Inf.
PENNELL, Mary Elizabeth, W5257, D, Pennell, James Newsom
PENNINGTON, C. S3189, W, 35th Inf.
PENNINGTON, Delila Caroline, W2672, W, Pennington, C.
PENNINGTON, Harriet Eliza, W11033, CE, Pennington, John Robert
PENNINGTON, James, S5024, H, 19th Inf.
PENNINGTON, Mary Wynn, W9512, GE, Pennington, Craig
PENNINGTON, N. A. S13323, DY, 27th Inf.
PENNINGTON, T. J. S6088, MU, 23rd Inf.
PENTECOST, A. J. S6833, WE, 20th (Russell's) Cav.
PENTECOST, John T. S15032, RB, 2nd Ky. Cav.
PENTECOST, Laura A. W11040, WE, Pentecost, Andrew Jackson

PENUEL, Newsom, S6534, D, 9th (Bennett's) Cav.
PEOPLES, B. F. S9060, G, 5th Inf.
PEOPLES, M. L. S15215, WA, East Tenn. Home Guards
PEOPLES, Rutledge, S15392, SU, 1st (Carter's) Cav.
PEPPER, Anna Polk, W10487, SH, Pepper, Samuel Alexander
PEPPER, R. G. S8955, HR, 14th Cav.
PEPPER, S. A. S16315, SH, 29th Miss. Inf.
PERCY, Vidora Ann, W8777, LI, Percy, Josiah Walker
PERDUE, D. C. S10940, CE, 18th Inf.
PERDUE, F. M. S6832, SN, 30th Inf.
PERDUE, T. B. S13090, CE, 4th Inf.
PERIGAN, John R. S3765, SU, 63rd Va. Inf.
PERKINS, Alfred H. Daskiell, S16022, SH, 7th (Duckworth's) Cav.
PERKINS, Daniel Price, S16109, RU, 55th Inf.
PERKINS, Elizabeth James, W8999, SH, Perkins, Alfred H. Dashielle
PERKINS, Frankie Oglesby, W9921, M, Perkins, Thomas F.
PERKINS, J. C. S11506, HY, 48th Ga. Inf.
PERKINS, Lucinda, W2103, MN, Perkins, Warner Perry
PERKINS, Mary, W8004, G, Perkins, Samuel Marion
PERKINS, Mary M. W4965, H, Perkins, Robert
PERKINS, Mattie Currin, W10172, RU, Perkins, D. P.
PERKINS, Mattie T. W10898, MR, Perkins, Andrew J. C.
PERKINS, R. C. S11973, JE, 4th Va. Inf.
PERKINS, Robert, S7046, H, 2nd Ga. Inf.
PERKINS, Thomas F. S14833, S16125, M, 11th Va. Inf.
PERKINS, William R. S16045, SM, 28th Inf.
PERKINSON, J. R. S9034, LA, 15th N.C. Inf.
PERKINSON, Mary Emma, W7112, LA, Perkinson, James Robert
PERKINSON, Sarah E. W3186, LA, Perkinson, Benjamin Eli
PERKY, Patrick, S5923, BO, 37th Inf.
PERMENTER, Mary Jane, W4382, CC, Permenter, R. G.
PERMON, William D. S11324, CL, 25th Va. Cav.
PERRIN, A. J. S11424, LO, 12th Bn. Cav.
PERRIN, Eliza Catherine Hull, W8209, LO, Perrin, Andrew J.

PERRIN, J. A. S5993, GR, 59th Inf.
PERROW, C. H. S12454, GR, 8th Va. Cav.
PERROW, Sue Virginia, W8217, HM, Perrow, Charles Henry
PERRY, See also Pery
PERRY, Alvis, S15518, MA, 21st Cav.
PERRY, B. C. S4843.5, CF, 4th Cav.
PERRY, B. E. S1718, RB, 55th Inf.
PERRY, B. F. S7536, D, 55th Inf.
PERRY, Bell, W9932, HN, Perry, Johns
PERRY, Benjamin, S4019, CF, 4th (McLemore's) Cav.
PERRY, Candes, W2364, M, Perry, Wm.
PERRY, Elizabeth Arbell, W8550, W5071, HN, Perry, John Henry C.
PERRY, Hannah, W10552, SN, Perry, Wilson
PERRY, Henry, S1627, MA, 20th Inf.
PERRY, Henry C. S3181, LI, 40th N.C. Inf.
PERRY, Henry J. S14617, H, 6th (Thompson's) Ga. State Troops
PERRY, Hester Jane, W10610, CE, Perry, Sampson
PERRY, Holdman, S15670, H, 4th Ala. Cav.
PERRY, J. Adaline, W439, SN, Perry, Buck Eaton
PERRY, J. C. S7160, K, 19th Inf.
PERRY, James T. S8346, MA, 14th Inf.
PERRY, Johnetta, W5069, CC, Perry, H. C.
PERRY, Joshua M. S1260, S1629, LA, 53rd Inf.
PERRY, Julina, W5801, D, Perry, Wm. Henry
PERRY, Kate, W6887, HR, Perry, Marcus Nicholas
PERRY, Mallie Elizabeth, W8909, K, Perry, W. R.
PERRY, Mark Nicholas, S8565, HR, Forrest's Old Regt. Cav.
PERRY, Martha Ann, W1758, CC, Perry, Noah Thomas
PERRY, Mattie, W5955, G, Perry, Henry
PERRY, Minerva, W2000, LA, Perry, Joshua
PERRY, Nellie, W7146, CT, Perry, Wm. M.
PERRY, R. M. S12543, WE, 21st (Wilson's) Cav.
PERRY, R. Turner, S7207, D, 11th (Holman's) Cav.
PERRY, Rowena L. W5874, CC, Perry, Barham
PERRY, Sarah, W6385, FR, Perry, Thomas
PERRY, Susan, W408, W, Perry, Joel
PERRY, Thomas, S4858, FR, 32nd Inf.
PERRY, W. M. S4554, CT, 59th Inf.
PERRY, W. T. S7285, CE, Huggin's Co. Lt. Art.

PERRY, W. T. S13521, K, 11th (Holman's) Cav.
PERRY, William, S2002, M, 20th Inf.
PERRY, William M. S12888, D, 22nd Cav.
PERSISE, Jennie, W5333, RB, Persise, John W.
PERSON, B. Alex. S16496, MA, Forrest's Escort, Cav.
PERSON, Fredonia Elizabeth, W3503, MA, Person, James Presley
PERSON, J. P. S10954, MA, 6th Inf.
PERSON, S. B. S10764, MA, 6th Inf.
PERSON, Thomas J. S4716, MA, 6th Inf.
PERY, James M. S1862, SM, Undetermined
PETERMAN, W. B. S5753, SU, 63rd Va. Inf.
PETERS, C. H. S2170, DY, 6th Inf.
PETERS, Daily, S12214, SU, 26th Inf.
PETERS, George W. S2641, WA, 63rd Inf.
PETERS, J. A. S10648, SU, Home Guards
PETERS, Jane, W7154, SU, Peters, George W.
PETERS, Maria, W3145, SU, Peters, John
PETERS, Mary, W4713, SU, Peters, Daily
PETERS, Mary Ann, W33, HR, Peters, Edward J. W.
PETERS, Sarah Jane, W4378, MA, Peters, Charles Henry
PETERS, Sarah M. W5812, SU, Peters, Samuel E.
PETERS, William, S4668, HA, 9th Inf.
PETERSON, J. A. S15036, SE, 10th Ga. Inf.
PETREE, George W. S4833, A, 2nd (Ashby's) Cav.
PETREE, Harriett Newell, W878, A, Petree, George Washington
PETTEY, N. J. S5672, SM, Allison's Squadron, Cav.
PETTIE, Thomas C. S5673, SM, 24th Inf.
PETTIE, W. B. S2353, SM, 8th Inf.
PETTIGNEW, James L. S4763, SH, 2nd Miss. Inf.
PETTIGNEW, Thomas Jackson, S355, DE, 1st & 27th Consol. Inf.
PETTIGNEW, W. R. S3514, G, 1st Miss. Inf.
PETTIJOHN, Jane, W2313, H, Pettijohn, Enoch
PETTUS, Amanda F. [Knight], W4775, SH, Pettus, Wm. T. [Later married Knight]
PETTUS, William F. S1301, GI, 23rd Inf.
PETTWAY, J. M. S5163, TR, 9th (Bennett's) Cav.
PETTY, Columbus, S10452, D, 2nd Bn. Ala. Art.
PETTY, Elizabeth, W8237, PU, Petty, Thomas W.

Index to Tennessee Confederate Pension Applications

PETTY, Emeline, W8898, SM, Petty, Wm.
PETTY, F. T. S13010, GI, 12th Bn. Miss. Cav.
PETTY, G. H. S11080, DI, 42nd Inf.
PETTY, George C. S4200, HI, 42nd Inf.
PETTY, Jesse B. S2638, MU, Maury Art.
PETTY, John, S1216, J, 28th Inf.
PETTY, John A. S985, HI, 48th Inf.
PETTY, M. M. S1339, S6587, O, 10th Cav.
PETTY, Mary E. W3445, MU, Petty, Jessie Branch
PETTY, Mildred T. W176, MN, Petty, John O.
PETTY, Pauline, W3682, D, Petty, Sanford
PETTY, S. S7089, DK, 8th (Smith's) Cav.
PETTY, Sally J. W9080, CF, Petty, Wm. Erwin
PETTY, Sanford Edwards, S7117, D, 1st Inf.
PETTY, Susan Ann, W733, HI, Petty, George C.
PETTY, Susan Ann, W4048, HI, Petty, George Cowen
PETTY, T. H. W. S5441, PU, 8th (Smith's) Cav.
PETTY, Thomas E. S15478, SM, 1st Bn. (Colm's) Inf.
PETTY, W. E. S15303, H, 3rd Va. Reserves
PETWAY, B. F. S11624, CE, 2nd Ky. Cav.
PETWAY, Hinch, S1985, D, 2nd Inf.
PETWAY, Nellie Davis, W6504, D, Petway, Robert Gordon
PETWAY, T. W. S15336, CE, 22nd (Barteau's) Cav.
PETWAY, William Thomas, S963, WL, 2nd Cav.
PEVY, John H. S8130, SH, 30th Miss. Inf.
PEW, James Webster, S4602, LA, 9th Bn. (Gantt's) Cav.
PEWETT, W. P. S5442, HU, 32nd Inf.
PEYTON, J. C. S8976, T, 19th Ala. Inf
PEYTON, J. H. S15131, RU, 45th Inf.
PEYTON, Mary A. W8041, RU, Peyton, James H.
PEYTON, Rufus H. S13892, MU, 9th Bn. (Gantt's) Cav.
PFEIFFER, John G. S15051, D, 1st (Feild's) Inf.
PFLENGER, Parlee, W8457, HN, Pflenger, Wm. Alexander
PFLUEGUER, W. A. S11400, HN, 20th (Russell's) Cav.
PHARRIS, William N. S8702, PU, 8th Cav.
PHELPS, See also Felps
PHELPS, Elizabeth, W9729, H, Phelps, Robert
PHELPS, Ellen, W6544, WE, Phelps, James T.
PHELPS, George W. S11053, WE, 51st Inf.
PHELPS, James T. S4608, WE, 31st Inf.

PHELPS, N. S. S14795, GI, 6th (Wheeler's) Cav.
PHELPS, R. F. S6202, WL, Huggin's Co. Lt. Art.
PHELPS, Rachel Overton, W8694, MU, Phelps, Robert Randolph
PHELPS, Robert, S7980, BR, 4th Inf.
PHELPS, Robert R. S13077, MU, 3rd Inf.
PHELPS, Sarah, W6138, WL, Phelps, Robert Franklin
PHELPS, Sarah Elizabeth, W8443, GI, Phelps, Neal S.
PHELPS, Silas M. S1825, SM, 7th Inf.
PHELPS, Virginia, W5025, HD, Phelps, Wm. H.
PHELPS, W. A. S9671, SQ, 4th Inf.
PHELPS, W. H. S3152, MN, Undetermined
PHIFER, Joseph, S2391, PU, 25th Inf.
PHIFER, Martha Elizabeth, W5761, PU, Phifer, Joseph
PHIFER, Susan, W8012, PU, Phifer, W. H.
PHIFER, W. H. S6792, PU, 25th Inf.
PHILIPS, Elizabeth U. W4791, FR, Philips, Wm. Landers
PHILIPS, G. P. S4010, HD, Moreland's Regt. Ala. Cav.
PHILIPS, M. J. S1237, G, 12th Cav.
PHILLIP, James D. S6864, SN, 20th Inf.
PHILLIPS, A. J. S11246, SH, 51st Inf.
PHILLIPS, Addie Holt, W8911, D, Phillips, Hugh Lawson White
PHILLIPS, Alida Kate, W7186, G, Phillips, Marion Jackson
PHILLIPS, Asa, C220, FR, 1st Inf.
PHILLIPS, B. F. S11815, MS, 41st Inf.
PHILLIPS, Belle, W4358, MO, Phillips, Lemuel Albert
PHILLIPS, Cynthia R. W8340, H, Phillips, Wm.
PHILLIPS, David T. S1509, CC, 6th Inf.
PHILLIPS, Dynishia O. W4031, FR, Phillips, Ezekiel
PHILLIPS, E. S4412, FR, 1st Ark. Cav.
PHILLIPS, Eli, S652, JO, 1st N.C. Cav.
PHILLIPS, Eli, S2820, SU, 63rd Inf.
PHILLIPS, Eliza A. W6589, H, Phillips, Wm. Alfred
PHILLIPS, Elizabeth Ann, W5357, CF, Phillips, Robert L.
PHILLIPS, Fannie J. W9021, MS, Phillips, R. L.
PHILLIPS, George W. S12997, CF, 44th Inf.
PHILLIPS, Harrison, S8278, L, 15th N.C. Inf.
PHILLIPS, Henry M. S13006, WE, 26th Ala. Inf.

-273

PHILLIPS, Henry W. S651, GI, 32nd Inf.
PHILLIPS, Henry W. S964, GI, 32nd Tenn. Regt.
PHILLIPS, J. G. S8412, CF, 44th Inf.
PHILLIPS, J. H. S2971, CL, Undetermined
PHILLIPS, J. J>, S7186, OV, Hamilton's Bn. Cav.
PHILLIPS, J. L. S1445, WL, 55th Inf.
PHILLIPS, James Earvin, S5618, CC, 18th (Newsom's) Cav.
PHILLIPS, James J. S427, GI, 32nd Inf.
PHILLIPS, John, S7092, WA, 60th Inf.
PHILLIPS, John W. S24, WE, 11th Inf.
PHILLIPS, Joseph C. S9516, FE, 8th Cav.
PHILLIPS, Julia, W5335, BO, Phillips, Eli
PHILLIPS, Kate Holden, W2075, SH, Phillips, Joseph Webster
PHILLIPS, L. A. S8178, MO, 2nd S.C. Inf.
PHILLIPS, Mary, W3468, OV, Phillips, Joseph J.
PHILLIPS, Mary, W4365, JO, Phillips, Eli
PHILLIPS, Mary Leanah, W4882, HW, Phillips, Newton Franklin
PHILLIPS, Nancy, W2724, FE, Phillips, Joseph C.
PHILLIPS, Nannie T. W6464, WE, Phillips, John W.
PHILLIPS, Peter, S4971, MOO, 17th Inf.
PHILLIPS, R. G. S7749, 12th Inf.
PHILLIPS, R. L. S8645, CF, 1st Inf.
PHILLIPS, Rachel Annie, W5130, SH, Phillips, Andrew Jefferson
PHILLIPS, Rachel M. W725, G, Phillips, Benjamin
PHILLIPS, Regina, W2953, T, Phillips, James Preston
PHILLIPS, Robert, S7067, O, 22nd (Barteau's) Cav.
PHILLIPS, Sallie, W3523, WY, Phillips, James Irvin
PHILLIPS, Sam B. S13958, CE, 41st Inf.
PHILLIPS, Spencer, S6041, PU, 16th Inf.
PHILLIPS, T. B. S3957, FR, 41st Inf.
PHILLIPS, T. W. S10903, K, 10th Va. Inf.
PHILLIPS, Thomas B. S458, SM, 4th Cav.
PHILLIPS, Virginia W. W4483, K, Phillips, Thaddaeus Warfield
PHILLIPS, W. A. S7353, H, 6th Ga. Cav.
PHILLIPS, W. H. S1, D, 4th Cav.
PHILLIPS, W. S. S10064, RB, 7th Bn. Cav.
PHILLIPS, William, S858, CA, 23rd Inf.
PHILLIPS, William R. S9840, MS, 17th Inf.

PHILLIPS, Wilmoth, See Wilmoth Harrison
PHILLIPS, Z. S. S395, O, 25th Inf.
PHILLIS, Gabrel P. S5352, HD, 7th Ala. Cav.
PHILLPOT, Emma, W4807, SH, Phillpot, Samuel
PHILPOT, W. A. S7047, B, 23rd Inf.
PHIPPS, Isaac, S2525, CL, 12th Bn. Cav.
PHIPPS, J. M. S408, OV, 25th Inf.
PHIPPS, James, S4980, SU, 21st Va. Cav.
PHIPPS, James, S6134, K, 61st Inf.
PHIPPS, James, S13431, GU, 7th Inf.
PHIPPS, Minnie Centennial, W11036, HW, Phipps, Wm. Fletcher
PHIPPS, W. F. S13067, HW, 19th Inf.
PHIPPS, William H. S13549, SU, Sullivan Co. Reserves
PHRASIER, John A. S785, PU, 25th Inf.
PICKARD, John A. S12511, H, 34th Inf.
PICKARD, John L. S7708, HI, 24th Inf.
PICKARD, Julia Ann, W9414, CE, Pickard, Peter Phaney
PICKARD, L. P. S14240, G, 22nd (Barteau's) Cav.
PICKARD, P. P. S13418, CE, 24th Bn. Sharpshooters
PICKEL, Sarah, W1549, ME, Pickel, John
PICKEL, Sarah J. W4957, K, Pickel, George H.
PICKENS, Lou, W3873, BR, Pickens, W. B. (Rev.)
PICKENS, Mary A. W6993, MS, Pickens, Wm. David
PICKENS, R. T. S10637, F, 13th Inf.
PICKENS, Sarah Rachel, W10831, WA, Pickens, Abraham Gregg
PICKENS, William D. S9290, MS, 11th Cav.
PICKET, George W. S12584, LI, 1st (Turney's) Inf.
PICKETT, Sallie E. W1183, D, Pickett, Benjamin Franklin
PICKETT, William H. S13645, MR, 4th (McLemore's) Cav.
PICKLE, John, S8551, ME, 19th Inf.
PIERCE, Addie J. W2725, RU, Pierce, Wm. F.
PIERCE, C. C. S10547, GI, 45th Inf.
PIERCE, Charlotte M. W3457, K, Pierce, H. C.
PIERCE, Elbert D. S5974, R, 16th Bn. (Neal's) Cav.
PIERCE, Eliza, W9944, MA, Pierce, Martin VanBuron
PIERCE, Emma Jane, W3895, F, Pierce, John Cullins
PIERCE, Flora, W1371, BE, Pierce, Iry R.

PIERCE, H. C. S1049, CO, 2nd N.C. Bn.
PIERCE, J. C. S9661, F, 12th (Green's) Cav.
PIERCE, J. H. S6465, SU, 52nd N.C. Troops
PIERCE, James, S1250, WE, 16th Cav.
PIERCE, James E. S1877, GE, 29th Inf.
PIERCE, Joel, S13702, HE, 21st (Wilson's) Cav.
PIERCE, M. V. S4034, G, 52nd Inf.
PIERCE, Millie F. W3553, BE, Pierce, Edward A.
PIERCE, Rice A. S16661, O, 3rd (Forrest's) Cav.
PIERCE, Richard, S12962, HR, 6th Ga. Cav.
PIERCE, Robert, S8000, HM, 31st Inf.
PIERCE, Sallie J. W5231, SU, Pierce, James F.
PIERCE, Sarah E. W4664, PI, Pierce, Robert
PIERCE, W. A. S11379, LA, 23rd Inf.
PIERCE, William, S3306, GI, 41st Inf.
PIERSON, James W. S9841, SN, 30th Inf.
PIGG, George W. S16356, J, 25th Inf.
PIGG, J. C. S11987, GI, 32nd Inf.
PIGG, Martha Elizabeth, W9145, LI, Pigg, Joel Thomas
PIGG, Mary Elizabeth, W4164, W8677, GI, Pigg, John Canian
PIGG, Sarah Fannie, W822, MU, Pigg, Wm. Maury
PIGG, William H. S16247, MU, 9th Bn. (Gantt's) Cav.
PIKE, Frances M. W8321, SN, Pike, John Franklin
PIKE, Hugh P. S10768, W, 63rd Inf.
PIKE, J. M. S11380, D, 55th Inf.
PIKE, John F. S10296, SN, 2nd Inf.
PIKE, Sarah Josephine, W5922, D, Pike, James Madison
PILE, Eliza A. W9928, SU, Pile, George C.
PILE, George C. S12136, SU, 37th Va. Inf.
PILE, John L. S2901, SU, 61st Inf.
PILE, Monroe A. S1547, S192, SU, 61st Inf.
PILKERTON, L. B. S7034, RU, 18th Inf.
PILLOW, Elizabeth, W3483, HN, Pillow, Willis Alexander
PILLOW, J. H. S8579, DY, 4th Inf.
PILLOW, J. W. S5145, WE, 6th (Wheeler's) Cav.
PILLOW, John A. S11340, SN, 13th Ark. Inf.
PILLOW, Mollie, W10661, G, Pillow, Richard Allen
PILLOW, Richard A. S8295, HE, 3rd Inf.
PILLOW, Willis A. S5955, HN, 46th Inf.
PINCKLE, Green Berry, S11789, DY, 25th Ark. Inf.

PINCKLEY, M. C. S121, Unassigned
PINEGAR, John, S2467, DK, 1st Bn. (Colm's) Inf.
PINEGAR, Mary Jane, W1060, DK, Pinegar, John
PINGER, William M. S13665, W, 1st Bn. (Colm's) Inf.
PINION, Lorenzie, S11821, MS, 53rd Inf.
PINKELTON, George W. S13753, GI, 24th Inf.
PINKERTON, D. T. S6621, HI, 42nd Inf.
PINKERTON, Mary Elizabeth, W8505, G, Pinkerton, John Cooper
PINKERTON, William, S9054, HI, 24th Inf.
PINKLETON, J. R. S8729, MU, 53rd Inf.
PINKLETON, Mary, W10256, GI, Pinkleton, John Robert
PINKSTON, J. N. S11658, MU, 53rd Inf.
PIPER, Alexander N. S7832, D, 7th Inf.
PIPER, Eliza Agnes, W6548, SN, Piper, James Henry
PIPER, Joseph H. S5951, SN, 7th Inf.
PIPER, Margaret Ann, W6843, D, Piper, Alexander N.
PIPER, William W. S2617, SM, 23rd Inf.
PIPKIN, D. B. S6495, MA, 7th Cav.
PIPKIN, H. S9995, MA, 14th (Neely's) Cav.
PIPKIN, Maria Jane, W2767, HR, Pipkin, Stephen L.
PIPKIN, Mary Elizabeth, W5580, MA, Pipkin, Hugh
PIPKIN, N. E. S6454, MU, 7th Cav.
PIPKIN, Sibbie (Lillie) W. W9341, G, Pipkin, Francis Marion
PIPKINS, F. M. S15459, G, Hart's Battery, Ark. Art.
PIPPIN, Andrew, S10320, J, 28th Inf.
PIPPIN, John I. S9636, J, 28th Inf.
PIPPIN, Lucinda V. W8533, J, Pippin, Andrew
PIPPIN, Richard F. S7653, PU, 28th Inf.
PIPPIN, Sarah M. W5022, PU, Pippin, Richard F.
PIRTLE, A. J. S3637, D, 3rd N.C. Inf.
PIRTLE, G. W. S5025, HR, 7th Cav.
PIRTLE, Mary Ellen, W3113, HR, Pirtle, Wm. Coleman
PITMAN, Florence A. W11020, W, Pitman, David
PITMAN, Granville, S1771, HY, Thomas' Legion, N.C.
PITMAN, S. A. S5566, MO, 1st (Carter's) Cav.
PITT, Bridger, S13360, DY, 2nd Cav.
PITT, L. H. S5452, DY, 2nd (Robison's) Inf.

PITT, Rosana Temperance, W3617, RB, Pitt, Wm. E.
PITTARD, Andrew Jackson, S13450, HU, 51st Ala. Inf.
PITTARD, Rachel Emiline, W4079, GI, Pittard, John W.
PITTARD, Thomas S. S15747, GI, 3rd (Clack's) Inf.
PITTMAN, Emmalissa, W1327, MO, Pittman, E. M.
PITTMAN, Fannie Clara, W10425, SH, Pittman, Zachary Taylor
PITTMAN, Helen Samantha, W9204, CC, Pittman, John Henry
PITTMAN, Narcissa, W86, MO, Pittman, S. A.
PITTS, Charley, S14390, LK, 1st Bn. Confederate Inf.
PITTS, Ellie Keith, W9322, LI, Pitts, Joel Anderson
PITTS, J. M. S4141, B, 35th Ala. Inf.
PITTS, James J. S12199, LI, 44th Inf.
PITTS, James M. S9355, SH, 5th Ark. Inf.
PITTS, Lilliam White, W11087, RU, Pitts, Frank
PITTS, Ruben, S3913, CA, 18th Inf.
PITTS, Solomon, S3114, DE, 48th Inf.
PITTS, William N. S782, DE, 26th Inf. Ala.
PLANT, John H. S5470, HU, 11th Inf.
PLANT, Mary Eliza, W7671, HU, Plant, John H.
PLANT, Mary Elizabeth, W10668, HU, Plant, Thomas Gideon
PLANT, Mary Gredig, W10192, K, Plant, Robert Vestal
PLATT, Robert B. S16056, H, 1st Miss. Cav. Reserves
PLEASANTS, Mollie L. W3537, F, Pleasants, Charles Polton
PLEMMONS, Adolphus, S4900, MO, 39th N.C. Inf.
PLEMMONS, Robert L. S14523, MC, 39th N.C. Inf.
PLEMMONS, Sarah E. W6052, H, Plemmons, John L.
PLEMMONS, W. J. S2659, SE, 2nd N.C. Inf.
PLEMONS, Clementine, W3417, FR, Plemons, Peter H.
PLEMONS, Peter H. S10329, FR, 23rd Bn. Inf.
PLESS, Martha Harriet, W2410, K, Pless, James Allison
PLESS, Nwton, S7672, B, 17th Inf.
PLUMADORE, Eva, W3452, K, Plumadore, Joseph Edward

PLUMLEE, Amelia Elizabeth, W119, K, Plumlee, Joseph
PLUMLEE, Caroline C. W82, K, Plumlee, Wm. Henry
PLUMLEE, J. Perry, S8445, K, Kain's Co. Lt. Art.
PLUMLEE, James N. S5760, K, Kain's Co. Lt. Art.
PLUMLEE, Samuel R. S2508, CY, Hamilton's Bn. Cav.
PLUMLEE, Sarah A. W6933, K, Plumlee, J. Perry
PLUMLEE, W. H. S1752, K, Kain's Co. Lt. Art.
PLUMMER, C. B. sr. S5188, MT, 3rd Inf.
PLUMMER, Frank E. S4629, FR, 8th N.C. Cav.
PLUMMER, Maria Ann, W5824, MT, Plummer, Carvorn Bruce
PLUMMER, Mary N. W910, P, Plummer, Hugh Kirk
PLUNK, Sydney, S362, MN, 21st Cav.
PLUNKET, Martha Ann, W6949, HI, Plunket, Stephen Alex
PLUNKETT, S. A. S10260, HI, 9th Bn. Cav.
POAG, Joseph S. S13865, GI, 17th S.C. Inf.
POARCH, Lewis I. S2776, MS, 32nd Inf.
POARCH, Susan C. W4342, MS, Poarch, Lewis I.
POATS, Annis A. W1309, HW, Poats, Lims Leander
PODESTA, Permelia Panesi, W3577, SH, Podesta, Louis Edward
POE, Atilda, W3356, L, Poe, Stephen Alexander
POE, Henry, S5465, GE, 3rd Inf.
POE, Ida, W10043, WA, Poe, Wm. Wilburn
POE, J. B. S6111, WE, 46th Inf.
POE, Jhn, S5152, H, 4th Ga. Cav.
POE, L. H. S15627, H, 4th Ga. Cav.
POE, S. A. S5652, L, 28th N.C. Inf.
POE, Sarah jane, W2987, FR, Poe, James Lafayette
POE, William M. S8944, SU, 1st Cav.
POGUE, Addie Conner, W7983, MU, Pogue, Eli Alexander
POGUE, P. H. S16305, SH, 24th Inf.
POGUE, Sally, W2627, MU, Pogue, George W.
POINDEXTER, Christopher C. S11443, T, 7th Cav.
POINDEXTER, J. J. S13301, CY, 1st Cav.
POINDEXTER, Lewis H. S11686, T, 7th Cav.
POINDEXTER, Lula Eliza, W10513, T, Poindexter, Christopher Columbus

POINDEXTER, Thomas William, S4485, HD, 21st (Wilson's) Cav.
POINDEXTER, Virginia Pittman, W3433, T, Poindexter, Christopher Columbus
POINTER, Jennie Brown, W9412, MU, Pointer, Henry C.
POINTER, Sib E. W10692, WE, Pointer, Sam W.
POLANDS, Charles William, S1427, G, 12th Inf.
POLK, Adam L. S987, PU, 28th Inf.
POLK, J. W. S12109, WI, Huggin's Co. Lt. Art.
POLK, Jesse J. S13907, LA, 6th Miss. Cav.
POLK, Sarah Frances, W9501, J, Polk, Adam Little
POLK, William, S13332, F, Forrest's Escort, Cav.
POLLAK, John, S971, LI, 32nd Inf.
POLLARD, Barzillia Betts, S1801, CC, 14th N.C. Inf.
POLLARD, Bettie J. W243, WI, Pollard, Robert L.
POLLARD, Clarissa J. W5201, LA, Pollard, John J.
POLLARD, J. H. S8997, O, 2nd Inf., This # has some of S. M. Horner's Papers
POLLARD, John W. S2394, H, 43rd Inf.
POLLEY, Jeff, S6849, LI, 32nd Inf.
POLLOCK, J. E. S1948, D, 1st Cav.
POLLOCK, Martha, W190, LI, Pollock, Boyers Stevens
POLLOCK, Massie, W1772, LI, Pollock, John
POLLOCK, Priscilla P. W426, MOO, Pollock, Joseph H.
POLLOCK, Robert, S5522, GI, 9th Cav.
POLLOCK, Susan Jane, W8410, GI, Pollock, Robert
POLLY, Bud, S6062, LI, 32nd Inf.
POND, A. J. S4523, SN, 30th Inf.
POND, Amanda West, W4985, SN, Pond, Smith
POND, James T. S7523, RB, 30th Inf.
POND, Smith, S5906, SN, 2nd (Robison's) Inf.
PONDER, James F. S5486, HN, 16th Ala. Inf.
PONDER, James W. S1614, CO, 64th N.C. Inf.
PONDER, Jeremiah, S2700, SM, 45th Inf.
POOL, Andrew J. S793, RB, 25th Inf.
POOL, Corille, W3819, SN, Pool, Andrew Jackson
POOL, I. P. S4489, WL, 45th Inf.
POOL, J. F. S51, CC, 9th Inf.
POOL, James, S9860, F, 14th (Neely's) Cav.
POOL, Jeralline, W6410, CE, Pool, Wm. Henry

POOL, John G. S4747, SH, 12th (Green's) Cav.
POOL, John W. S3788, SN, 25th Inf.
POOL, M. W. S8202, SU, 4th Va. Reserves
POOL, Nathaniel, S1195, HD, 27th Inf.
POOL, Vinie, W1664, SM, Pool, John W.
POOL, W. H. S11493, CE, 49th Inf.
POOL, William R. S5780, RB, 18th Inf.
POOLE, H. R. S14736, RB, 18th Inf.
POOLE, L. D. S3158, R, 26th Inf.
POORE, Almira Samantha, W5991, F, Poore, Edward Hobson
POORE, Catherine Elizabeth, W7148, WA, Poore, LaFayette
POORE, E. H. S12998, F, 13th Inf.
POORE, Lafayette, S11165, WA, 3rd (Lillard's) Mtd. Inf.
POORE, S. C. S2098, V, 8th Cav.
POORE, S. K. S11205, SE, 42nd Inf.
POPE, Alice A. W6512, MA, Pope, David T.
POPE, Amanda M. W1139, DY, Pope, Barnabas J.
POPE, Anna Thornton, W5558, H, Pope, Alepis D.
POPE, B. F. S15560, RU, 45th Inf.
POPE, Cordelia Frances, W10492, H, Pope, John Townson
POPE, Edwin, S13680, WY, 1st (Feild's) Inf.
POPE, Frances Ann, W3538, SM, Pope, Nathan Campbell
POPE, G. A. S12681, GI, 9th Bn. (Gantt's) Cav.
POPE, Harriet, W8413, DY, Pope, W. H.
POPE, John R. S7365, K, 59th Inf.
POPE, John T. S13737, BL, 8th (Dibrell's) Cav.
POPE, John Wiley, S14712, O, Greer's Cav.
POPE, Josie, W8208, DY, Pope, John Wesley
POPE, M. C. S7444, SM, 9th (Bennett's) Cav.
POPE, M. W. S14945, R, Barry's Co. Art.
POPE, Mary A. W9763, SH, Pope, Andrew Rembert
POPE, Mary Jane, W8179, RU, Pope, B. F.
POPE, Myra Belle Carter, W7916, GI, Pope, Gustavus Adolphus
POPE, Rebecca, W9050, R, Pope, Mourel
POPE, Rosa Ann, W9571, WY, Pope, Edwin
POPE, Sue Armine, W6231, MA, Pope, John Lowery
POPE, W. A. S9285, MA, 33rd Inf.
POPE, W. H. S10945, SH, Forrest's Old Regt. Cav.
POPE, W. H. S14805, DY, 20th Cav.
POPE, W. R. S16652, BL, 8th Cav.

POPLIN, Amna M. W5177, B, Poplin, Wm. Richard
POPLIN, John, S690, ME, 26th Inf.
PORCH, Alley Jane, W6553, DI, Porch, Wm. Silons
PORCH, James H. S14609, HU, 10th (DeMoss') Cav.
PORCH, William S. S7376, DI, 11th Inf.
PORTER, Alex. C38, HN, 20th Cav.
PORTER, Alexander, S670, SM, 7th Inf.
PORTER, Augusta A. W7811, GI, Porter, Wm. Anderson
PORTER, B. W. S8834, RB, 2nd Ky. Cav.
PORTER, Belle, W5841, HN, Porter, Nathaniel Bascomb
PORTER, Edward S. S2015, SM, Independent Vols.
PORTER, Eliza A. W3126, LI, Porter, G. W.
PORTER, Ellen, W3301, JE, Porter, James Edward
PORTER, Emaline, W5473, D, Porter, John
PORTER, G. W. D. S4015, LI, 44th Inf.
PORTER, George C. S12063, D, 6th Inf.
PORTER, George W. S14499, RB, 49th Inf.
PORTER, J. K. S9152, HU, 44th Inf.
PORTER, James Polk, S3974, LO, 29th Inf.
PORTER, John A. S14948, FR, 20th Va. Bn. Inf.
PORTER, John W. S15189, R, 16th Bn. Cav.
PORTER, Lizzie McLean, W10310, H, Porter, T. M.
PORTER, Lucy Ann, W4833, H, Porter, James Sterling
PORTER, Marcus L. S4461, S3099, GI, 64th N.C. Inf.
PORTER, Mattie, W9476, G, Porter, John Gideon
PORTER, Mattie R. W7766, LI, Porter, George W. D.
PORTER, Maza, W111, SM, Porter, Alexander
PORTER, Nannie, W3946, MU, Porter, John L.
PORTER, Penelope, W7137, RB, Porter, George W.
PORTER, Priscilla, W154, HI, Porter, Henry Thompson
PORTER, Richard, S2006, RB, 14th Inf.
PORTER, Samuel Shaw, S6190, MU, 48th (Voorhies') Inf.
PORTER, Solomon, S4524, WL, 16th Inf.
PORTER, T. L. S14767, MU, 9th Bn. (Gantt's) Cav.
PORTER, T. M. S10603, 4th Cav.
PORTER, W. A. S10020, MS, 64th N.C. Inf.

PORTER, Willie, W10359, HN, Porter, Felix F.
PORTERFIELD, J. I. S14465, WL, Allison's Squadron, Cav.
PORTERFIELD, Sue Houston, W9593, D, Porterfield, Frank
POSEY, H. K. S338, FR, 2nd Inf.
POSEY, Sarah Ann, W1196, FR, Posey, Hiram K.
POSEY, William M. S2875, LI, 41st Inf.
POSS, Madison, S8470, DK, 12th Ga. Bn. Cav.
POSTLETHWAITE, Rebecca Willis, W1698, HN, Postlethwaite, John Thomas
POSTON, Artelia, W5736, OV, Poston, John Franklin
POSTON, D. C. S9697, J, 8th (Dibrell's) Cav.
POSTON, Elizabeth O. W8021, OV, Poston, Richard T.
POSTON, J. Frank, S4972, OV, 25th Inf.
POSTON, Julina L. W5865, J, Poston, David Crockett
POSTON, L. S. S10050, OV, 25th Inf.
POSTON, Mary J. W6329, OV, Poston, Zadock
POSTON, R. T. S9404, OV, 25th Inf.
POSTON, Sallie, W6559, OV, Poston, Louis Stinson
POSTON, Zadock, S9595, OV, 8th (Dibrell's) Cav.
POTEET, B. A. S4231, BR, 36th Ga. Inf.
POTER, J. P. S10300, M, 24th Inf.
POTTER, Evaline, W2594, MC, Potter, Richard A.
POTTER, Martha Ann, W4686, W, Potter, Andrew Jackson
POTTER, Martha Williams, W6116, HO, Potter, Milton B.
POTTER, Melvina, W734, W3409, HI, Potter, David S.
POTTER, R. A. S2777, MC, 43rd Inf.
POTTER, Susan, W11, DK, Potter, Ozier Denton
POTTER, T. C. S7345, H, 63rd Inf.
POTTER, Thomas J. S15190, JO, 6th N.C. Cav.
POTTER, William J. S7222, D, 11th Bn. (Gordon's) Cav.
POTTS, B. F. S224, MN, 19th & 20th (Consolidated) Cav.
POTTS, C. F. S5072, HN, 5th Inf.
POTTS, Jinsey, W1557, MU, Potts, James Robert
POTTS, John R. S13467, WL, 4th Ala. Cav.
POTTS, Martha Anne, W5607, HN, Potts, Columbus Fernoda

Index to Tennessee Confederate Pension Applications

POTTS, Miles, S13996, MU, 10th Cav.
POTTS, Virginia G. W4384, SH, Potts, Thomas J.
POTTS, W. S. S6594, BE, 7th Cav.
POU, Mary Jane, W10108, SH, Pou, Wm. Henry
POUNDS, F. M. S3064, MN, 10th Miss. Inf.
POUNDS, Martha Jane, W6628, MN, Pounds, Francis Marion
POWEL, Frieda Winter, W6277, SH, Powel, Benjamin
POWELL, Allen H. S7264, MU, 9th Bn. (Gantt's) Cav.
POWELL, Armina, W7294, W, Powell, John William
POWELL, B. T. S12862, H, 60th Ga. Inf.
POWELL, David H. S10084, CC, 15th (Stewart's) Cav.
POWELL, G. W. S8390, G, 22nd Inf.
POWELL, Henry, S640, W, 16th Inf.
POWELL, J. D. sr. S13279, SH, 4th Inf.
POWELL, Jane, W4361, CC, Powell, John P.
POWELL, John, S8708, FR, 17th Inf.
POWELL, John M. S12339, D, 7th Inf.
POWELL, John W. S10427, W, 35th Inf.
POWELL, Johnie, W10496, MN, Powell, Samuel B.
POWELL, Josephine E. W3604, D, Powell, Weldon A.
POWELL, Martha Elizabeth, W7584, WE, Powell, Joshua Wyat
POWELL, Martha Matilda, W5842, W, Powell, Henry
POWELL, Mary B. Wooten, W3476, SH, Powell, Wm.
POWELL, Mary E. W5219, HW, Powell, Edmund Dillahunty
POWELL, Mary E. W10156, ME, Powell, Thomas B.
POWELL, Mary Elizabeth, W6397, SH, Powell, Wm.
POWELL, Mary Jane, W3117, DY, Powell, Benjamin Alfred
POWELL, Mildred Olivia, W9158, ME, Powell, Jacob
POWELL, Moses, S7463, CT, 11th N.C. Inf.
POWELL, P. R. S9796, LI, 38th Ga. Inf.
POWELL, R. W. S9520, O, 2nd Cav.
POWELL, Rutha S. W4717, CO, Powell, Moses
POWELL, S. J. S5221, HW, 9th Ga. Art.
POWELL, Sallie, W4634, SH, Powell, Joseph Deauveaux
POWELL, Sallie F. W2848, HW, Powell, Richard Fain
POWELL, Sarah A. E. W4456, MA, Powell, Wm. Marton
POWELL, T. B. S16465, ME, 3rd Inf.
POWELL, T. B. S16579, ME, 5th (McKenzie's) Cav.
POWELL, Virginia Walker, W3712, HW, Powell, Samuel Perry
POWELL, William H. S5585, ST, 49th Inf.
POWELL, William T. S5674, SM, Allison's Squadron, Cav.
POWERS, Almeda C. W8236, HM, Powers, John T.
POWERS, Arthur B. S3867, MT, 50th Inf.
POWERS, F. B. S12782, ST, 49th Inf.
POWERS, Homer A. S8599, PU, 16th Inf.
POWERS, J. M. S10361, SU, 37th Va. Inf.
POWERS, John S. S5822, GI, 32nd Inf.
POWERS, John T. S4749, HW, 45th Va. Inf.
POWERS, John T. S10565, K, 34th Bn. Va. Cav.
POWERS, John T. S13184, MO, 16th Bn. (Neal's) Cav.
POWERS, John W. S15734, SU, 3rd Regt. N.C. Jr. Reserves
POWERS, Loucilla, W5059, PU, Powers, Homer A.
POWERS, Mary Evannah, W9146, MT, Powers, Samuel Barney
POWERS, R. M. S573, MT, 49th Inf.
POWERS, Rebecca, W7872, SU, Powers, John W.
POWERS, Samuel Barney, S12819, MT, 14th Inf.
POWERS, Sarah Brady, W10211, MO, Powers, John Tolliver
POWERS, Thomas J. S7338, MT, 49th Inf.
POWERS, W. G. S5754, HO, 49th Inf.
POWERS, W. M. S10697, HU, Forrest's Cav.
POWERS, William A. S8431, D, 16th Inf.
POYNER, G. T. S592, WE, 5th Inf.
POYNER, Myra A. W1014, WE, Poyner, George Turner
POYNER, Susan Ellen, W2823, D, Poyner, Isom David
POYNER, Thomas W. S6473, WE, 5th Inf.
POYNER, Tonie, W10603, RB, Poyner, J. D.
POYNER, W. D. S13221, HN, 10th Cav.
PRATER, A. J. S12644, D, 61st Inf.
PRATER, Ann, W7729, WH, Prater, Carington
PRATER, Richard M. S4129, SH, 8th Inf.

Index to Tennessee Confederate Pension Applications

PRATHER, Columbus, S11827, D, Morton's Co. Lt. Art.
PRATHER, George Washington, S4960, D, 60th N.C. Inf.
PRATHER, J. S. S10461, MN, 19th Cav.
PRATHER, Jane, W13, D, Prather, George Washington
PRATHER, Malissa Tennessee, W9092, MN, Prather, John Stanton
PRATHER, T. H. S14007, MN, 20th (Russell's) Cav.
PRATT, F. M. S6414, FR, 13th Inf.
PRATT, George T. S13846, SU, 4th Va. Inf.
PRATT, George Washington, S14604, LK, 5th Inf.
PRATT, Joe H. S7041, S2980, CF, 61st Inf.
PRATT, John H. S549, DE, 27th Inf.
PRATT, Rachel, W856, JE, Pratt, Isaac
PRENTIC, Amanda Brassell, W7289, PU, Prentic, James
PRENTICE, william B. S11793, SM, 24th Inf.
PRESCOTT, Hannah Willis, W10267, SH, Prescott, James A.
PRESLEY, Margaret, W2113, HW, Presley, Temptelan
PRESLEY, Sallie Elizabeth, W2988, K, Presley, Tally B.
PRESLEY, Thomas Jefferson, S5400, HW, 60th Inf.
PRESLEY, William, S1047, BO, 31st Inf.
PRESLEY, William, S5748, H, 3rd Ga. Bn.
PRESNELL, Isaac, S14363, K, 3rd Regt. Confederate Engineers
PRESNELL, Shadrack, S3965, CL, 3rd Conf. Engineer Troops
PRESNELL, Squire, S12959, JO, 58th N.C. Inf.
PRESSLEY, Deborah, W1168, RO, Pressley, G. W.
PRESSLEY, Emeline, See Emeline Harris
PRESSNELL, Martha, W9641, W8157, CL, Pressnell, Shad
PRESSWOOD, James Harvey, S602, BR, 5th Cav.
PRESSWOOD, Joseph, S8088, PO, 5th (McKenzie's) Cav.
PRESTON, Annastasia M. W4355, G, Preston, Stephen Smith
PRESTON, Elizabeth Catherine, W9376, CA, Preston, Hugh
PRESTON, Hugh L. S11663, CA, 4th Cav.
PRESTON, Jesse, S14859, RO, 62nd Inf.
PRESTON, Laura, W10608, SH, Preston, Wade

PRESTON, Lodemia Jane, W5289, SU, Preston, John Tedford
PRESTON, Lucy Emily, W6537, D, Preston, Moses Perry
PRESTON, N. B. S3454, CA, 8th (Smith's) Cav.
PRESTON, Wade, S10582, SH, 2nd Ark. Cav.
PREUETT, Caladona, W291, HI, Preuett, James P.
PREWETT, J. W. S9169, DY, 46th Inf.
PREWITT, George Washington, S11921, HR, 4th Inf.
PREWITT, J. M. S12141, HR, 4th Inf.
PREWITT, M. W. S12206, HR, 18th Miss. Inf.
PREWITT, Mary Spinks, W11143, HR, Prewitt, George Washington
PREWITT, Thomas E. S11818, HR, 4th Inf.
PRICE, A. M. S5904, PO, 19th N.C. Cav.
PRICE, Alice, W6838, MR, Price, James H.
PRICE, Bell Brothers, W4588, DY, Price, Preston Gano
PRICE, C. B. S89, RU, 2nd Inf.
PRICE, Elizabeth J. W561, OV, Price, Wm. O.
PRICE, Ella, W10705, LI, Price, John W.
PRICE, Emma Caroline, W8244, WL, Price, Joseph James
PRICE, Euphilia, W8219, MA, Price, John F.
PRICE, George W. S7732, MA, 18th (Newsom's) Cav.
PRICE, Hezekiah, S15061, JO, Winston's Co. N.C.
PRICE, J. B. S1337, T, 23rd Va. Inf.
PRICE, J. H. S9460, MR, 6th Ala. Inf.
PRICE, J. J. S15567, WL, 45th Inf.
PRICE, J. Y. S14175, MOO, 4th Inf.
PRICE, James T. S8221, SH, Confederate Guards Miss. Art.
PRICE, Jennie Miller, W10284, SU, Price, Wm. Humberson
PRICE, John, S6522, R, 5th (McKenzie's) Cav.
PRICE, John F. S9530, MA, 51st Inf.
PRICE, John M. S9238, SU, 48th Inf.
PRICE, John T. S6811, D, 8th (Smith's) Cav.
PRICE, John W. S14667, LI, 41st Inf.
PRICE, John Williams, S16398, H, McCaskell's Regt. Cav.
PRICE, Leila, W8108, SH, Price, W. R.
PRICE, Linville, S14489, C, 34th N.C. Inf.
PRICE, Lucy Margrett, W1924, MA, Price, George W.
PRICE, Lydda Caroline, W3204, JO, Price, Samuel C.

Index to Tennessee Confederate Pension Applications

PRICE, Martha Mur. Goddard, W4547, D, Price, Elijah Webb
PRICE, Mary Virginia, W5723, SH, Price, Bernard Francis
PRICE, Melissa Alexander, W3372, D, Price, John Thomas
PRICE, Melissa M. W7122, PU, Price, Thomas D.
PRICE, Nancy D. W8116, CF, Price, T. K.
PRICE, Preston Gano, S6376, DY, 11th Inf.
PRICE, R. A. S6210, WL, 45th Inf.
PRICE, R. H. S6645, MN, 154th Sr. Regt. Inf.
PRICE, R. H. S9274, MR, 3rd Confederate Cav.
PRICE, Samuel P. S3944, JO, 16th N.C. Inf.
PRICE, Sarah Frances, W10465, F, Price, James
PRICE, Sarah L. W4961, MC, Price, A. M.
PRICE, Sue E. W6179, D, Price, George Tyre
PRICE, Susan, W177, MN, Price, Thomas T.
PRICE, Susan A. W2670, SH, Price, Thomas
PRICE, Thomas, S9323, L, Hampton's Legion, S.C. Inf.
PRICE, Thomas, S9943, CT, 37th N.C. Troops
PRICE, Thomas D. S14749, PU, 8th (Smith's) Cav.
PRICE, Thomas K. S93, CF, 44th Inf.
PRICE, Tildie Jane, W7621, C, Price, Linville
PRICE, W. O. S1343, OV, 26th Inf.
PRICHARD, C. B. S10777, DY, 28th Ga. Inf.
PRICHARD, Isom, S4201, SU, 48th Va. Inf.
PRICHARD, J. H. S13840, CY, 2nd Ky. Cav.
PRICHARD, J. W. S9098, HI, 48th (Voorhies') Inf.
PRICHARD, James Carroll, S16058, SM, 24th Inf.
PRICHARD, Mary, W4950, DY, Prichard, C. B.
PRICHARD, Rosa Ann, W1605, W1430, DY, Prichard, James Washington
PRIDDY, W. C. S6762, CH, 18th Va. Inf.
PRIDE, Jesse P. S13202, O, 47th Inf.
PRIDE, Susanna A. W5888, O, Pride, J. P.
PRIEST, J. J. S15439, HI, 10th Cav.
PRIEST, John A. S339, MA, 33rd Inf.
PRIEST, Mary K. W840, MA, Priest, John A.
PRIEST, Thomas J. S16156, WE, 48th Inf.
PRIEST, Thomas R. S14074, WI, Forrest's Escort, Cav.
PRIEST, W. C. S5966, SH, 13th Inf.
PRIGMORE, John S. S5643, MR, 5th Inf.
PRILHART, Lemuel, S6415, HM, 1st N.C. Inf.
PRIMM, Jeremiah W. S9370, CE, 6th (Wheeler's) Cav.

PRIMM, Narcissa Elizabeth, W2417, DI, Primm, Horatio Claggett
PRIMM, Paralee, W10466, D, Primm, Newell M.
PRIMM, Rebecca, W1737, RU, Primm, James
PRINCE, E. G. S8885, GI, 32nd Inf.
PRINCE, H. M. S6821, CF, 37th Inf.
PRINCE, J. B. S5146, FR, 3rd Ala. Inf.
PRINCE, J. C. S6262, CF, 37th Inf.
PRINCE, J. R. S4691, B, 37th Inf.
PRINCE, James P. S7897, B, 45th Inf.
PRINCE, Mary, W9125, FR, Prince, Benjamin Paten
PRINCE, Mary Clamenza, W8522, B, Prince, James Pinkney
PRINCE, Nancy Caroline, W1007, B, Prince, Wm.
PRINCE, Newton, S6085, CF, 23rd Inf.
PRINTZ, Lydia R. W7216, D, Printz, Wm. Delancy
PRIOR, James, S6956, OV, 25th Inf.
PRITCHARD, John W. S665, DY, 12th Inf.
PRITCHARD, Maggie, W4242, DY, Pritchard, J. W.
PRITCHARD, Sarah Jane, W4386, SU, Pritchard, Isom
PRITCHETT, J. W. S7795, HN, 5th Inf.
PRITCHETT, Polly, W10270, HN, Pritchett, James Wesley
PRITCHETT, William, S14623, R, 1st (Carter's) Cav.
PRIVETT, Malinda, W6932, MR, Privett, Sam
PRIVETT, Samuel, S5089, MR, 4th (McLemore's) Cav.
PROCTOR, James H. S3696, RU, 45th Inf.
PROFFITT, Benjamin, S5675, JO, 29th Inf.
PROFFITT, G. C. S3080, SM, 84th Inf.
PROFFITT, George E. S8106, RO, 5th Cav.
PROFFITT, J. M. S3022, GR, 61st Inf.
PROFFITT, John W. S10947, CO, 16th N.C. Inf.
PROFFITT, Martha Jane, W3187, PU, Proffitt, George C.
PROFFITT, Sallie, W7478, CO, Proffitt, John M.
PROFIT, Dianna, W8128, JO, Profit, James
PROPES, Mary Ann, W7949, K, Propes, Wm.
PROSER, W. D. S2868, MS, 8th Inf.
PROWELL, John H. S10664, M, 24th Inf.
PROWELL, Sallie E. W3401, WI, Prowell, Andrew M.

PROWELL, Sarah J. W8140, M, Prowell, John H.
PRUETT, Adaline, W4374, SU, Pruett, James Madison
PRUETT, Eliza Ashton, W7876, RU, Pruett, John Madison
PRUETT, Frances A. W3268, G, Pruett, Wm. D.
PRUETT, G. W. S4041, O, 2nd Inf.
PRUETT, J. M. S8821, SU, 2nd N.C. Bn. Inf.
PRUETT, Louisa L. W1725, SN, Pruett, Paul
PRUETT, Lucinda C. W2270, O, Pruett, G. W.
PRUETT, Mary Angeline, W103, SN, Pruett, Silas Barnabas
PRUETT, Roena Catherine, W5302, HI, Pruett, James Samuel
PRUIT, J. W. S6975, DY, 46th Inf.
PRUIT, Nancy, W1864, O, Pruit, James W.
PRUITT, Joseph, S8193, P, 48th (Voorhies') Inf.
PRYOR, J. L. S5293, W, 18th Inf.
PRYOR, John, S5228, K, 61st Inf.
PRYOR, Margaret, W4387, OV, Pryor, James
PRYOR, Mary Ellen, W2182, CA, Pryor, James L.
PRYOR, Nancey Margret, W4427, SH, Pryor, James Brock
PRYOR, P. G. S9453, MR, 4th (McLemore's) Cav.
PRYOR, Temperance S. W2603, MR, Pryor, P. G.
PUCKETT, Andrew P. S3562, B, 4th La. Inf.
PUCKETT, Annie, W4586, DY, Puckett, Calvin Thompson
PUCKETT, Calvin Thompson, S6411, DY, 7th Miss. Cav.
PUCKETT, J. M. S12847, CC, 7th Miss. Cav.
PUCKETT, Jerusha, W9824, RU, Puckett, R. D.
PUCKETT, Lafayette A. S38, 23rd Miss Inf.
PUCKETT, Lucinda A. W4273, Puckett, Lafayette Allen
PUCKETT, Mattie E. W6859, B, Puckett, Arthur P.
PUCKETT, T. J. S9369, D, 2nd (Robison's) Inf.
PUGH, Dawson, C197, HY, 7th Cav.
PUGH, J. A. S9450, ST, 14th Inf.
PUGH, James F. S3385, D, 30th Inf.
PUGH, James M. S5869, U, 25th Va. Cav.
PUGH, Sallie A. W1952, ST, Pugh, Joshua A.
PUGH, frank, S11962, HY, 7th (Duckworth's) Cav.
PULLEN, Aditha L. W10723, HN, Pullen, P. P.
PULLEN, B. P. S11442, LA, 48th Inf.
PULLEN, Ellen, W2794, LA, Pullen, Wm.
PULLEN, Frances Elizabeth, W661, Pullen, James Leonidas
PULLEN, George W. S8812, MU, 3rd Inf.
PULLEN, John Bernard, S11360, T, 7th Cav.
PULLEN, P. P. S12920, HN, 2nd Ky. Cav.
PULLEN, Pearl, W10178, MU, Pullen, George W.
PULLEN, Samuel B. S11681, T, 51st Inf.
PULLEN, Sue, W7387, T, Pullen, Wm. A.
PULLEN, William Allen, S12103, T, 51st Inf.
PULLEN, William C. S14766, HU, 11th Inf.
PULLEY, Rufus, S7991, ST, 50th Inf.
PULLIAM, Mary Eliza, W3299, F, Pulliam, David K.
PULLIAM, Robert, S16555, BR, Undetermined
PULLIN, Elisha, S13601, D, 3rd (Clack's) Inf.
PULLUM, John, S8408, GI, 16th Ala. Inf.
PULLUM, Joshua, S8608, D, 16th Ala. Inf.
PURDOM, Elizabeth Paralee, W1465, MS, Purdom, Mathew Freeman
PURDOM, Sarah R. W2886, MS, Purdom, D. Erwin
PURKEY, Martha, See Martha Holman
PURKYPILE, Christopher, S1447, GR, 59th Inf.
PURPER, William B. S4824, R, 26th Inf.
PURSELL, Sirena Mahon, W9978, DY, Pursell, Joel H.
PURSELY, William Arnett, S9890, O, 12th Ky. Cav.
PURSER, John, S11124, CA, 16th Inf.
PURSER, Joshua, S292, W, 5th Inf.
PURSER, Luke, S11698, W, 16 Inf.
PURSLEY, D. W. S16113, S15469, O, 33rd Inf.
PURSLEY, Eliza Ann, W3156, D, Pursley, Griffith Addison
PURTLE, Susan Jane, W772, DK, Purtle, John L.
PURYEAR, Ella Dorothy, W9926, D, Puryear, David Crockett
PURYEAR, Josephine, W3683, GI, Puryear, John Edward
PURYEAR, Louisa Wardie, W3378, TR, Puryear, Thomas A.
PURYEAR, Mary Maury, W8636, SH, Puryear, Andrew Jackson
PURYEAR, R. H. S14531, HN, 21st (Wilson's) Cav.
PUTMAN, D. T. S15819, B, 26th Ala. Inf.
PUTNAM, D. V. S8665, DI, 11th Cav.
PYBAS, Elizabeth Adelaide, W10834, G, Pybas, Parks Jefferson

Index to Tennessee Confederate Pension Applications

PYBASS, Parke Jefferson, S16291, G, 12th Ky. Cav.
PYLES, J. A. S6665, MA, 13th Inf.
PYLES, Willis C. S13468, MA, 6th Inf.
PYOTT, Alice, W7978, RO, Pyott, Henry Clay
PYOTT, H. C. S14608, H, 43rd Inf.
PYROM, Sterling B. S6513, D, 9th (Bennett's) Cav.
PYRON, Missouri A. W1417, D, Pyron, Sterling B.
PYRON, William R. S11140, HD, 34th Miss. Inf.
QUAILS, B. S. S5401, SU, 63rd Inf.
QUAILS, David E. S8801, SU, 28th Va. Inf.
QUAILS, Eliza E. W1247, SU, Quails, Wm. R.
QUAILS, Elizabeth Jane, W6076, SU, Quails, Benjamin S.
QUAILS, Emory, S3510, SU, 25th Va. Cav.
QUAILS, G. M. S2992, K, 37th Inf.
QUAILS, George M. S3655, GR, 37th Inf.
QUAILS, James A. S2021, SU, 63rd Inf.
QUAILS, William, S4271, CF, 48th (Nixon's) Inf.
QUALLS, Parthena J. W690, PU, Qualls, Francis Rowland
QUALLS, Sarah M. W4851, K, Qualls, George Monrow
QUARLES, Benjamin, S4113, RO, 16th Bn. Cav.
QUARLES, Guy S. S6525, RU, 8th (Smith's) Cav.
QUARLES, Harvey, C214, D, 8th Inf.
QUARLES, Isham, S15262, P, 10th Cav.
QUARLES, J. T. S13660, DK, 8th (Smith's) Cav.
QUARLES, John S. S15428, PU, 8th Inf.
QUARLES, Malissie, W11101, WL, Quarles, James Turner
QUARLES, Mary Ann, W8737, W8045, PU, Quarles, Stephen Decatur
QUARLES, Nannie E. W5207, O, Quarles, George Harrison
QUARLES, R. A. S2256, FR, 8th Inf.
QUARLES, S. D. S6834, PU, 8th (Dibrell's) Cav.
QUARLES, Selia Ann, W8750, PU, Quarles, Wm. Braxton
QUARLES, Virginia Frances, W341, WL, Quarles, Little Berry Jackson
QUARLES, William A. S1411, MT, 42nd Inf.
QUARLES, William Braxton, S8696, PU, 8th Cav.

QUARMBY, Susana Catherine, W6489, SH, Quarmby, Joseph
QUEENER, Jacob M. S5831, MC, 2nd (Ashby's) Cav.
QUEENER, Margaret, W1348, K, Queener, Thomas W.
QUEENER, Martha Caroline, W5007, MC, Queener, Jacob Madison
QUESENBURY, Mary Ann, W1298, WL, Quesenbury, Hugh E.
QUICK, Columbia Elizabeth, W8940, W, Quick, Joseph P.
QUICK, Columbia Elizabeth, W8940, W7649, W, Quick, Joseph P.
QUICK, Jennie, W1575, W, Quick, Wm. C.
QUILLEN, Delila, W135, LE, Quillen, James
QUILLEN, Henry, S10674, HW, 64th Va. Inf.
QUILLEN, Mollie, W8375, W8480, HW, Quillen, Henry
QUILLEN, Nancy J. W10582, LE, Quillen, Lafayette
QUILLEN, W. R. S9555, LA, 17th Miss. Inf.
QUILLIN, Elijah, S10387, WH, 16th Inf.
QUILLIN, Willis, S2477, LE, 3rd (Clack's) Inf.
QUINK, William, S8248, MU, 10th Inf.
QUINLEY, John A. S4810, T, 51st Inf.
QUINN, A. S. S4202, Undetermined
QUINN, P. P. S10885, DE, 5th Inf.
QUINN, Sarah Elizabeth, W9654, MN, Quinn, Thomas Brady
QUINN, Thomas B. S4731, MN, 3rd Tex. Inf.
QUINTEL, Agnes, W8113, SH, Quintel, Charles
QUINTON, J. P. S14732, MT, 29th Inf.
QUINTON, James D. S16333, O, 5th S.C. Inf.
QUSENBY, Hugh E. S1798, WL, 7th Inf.
RABY, John R. S15646, B, 8th Inf.
RABY, P. A. S2293, B, 8th Inf.
RADER, Daniel, S8383, GE, 31st Inf.
RADER, J. A. S108, GE, 61st Inf.
RADER, James P. S1787, SU, 37th Va. Inf.
RADER, Laura L. W2001, GE, Rader, John Asberry (Dr.)
RADER, Lodemia C. W3917, SU, Rader, Calvin M.
RADER, Mary Elizabeth, W9393, SU, Rader, James Polk
RADER, Susan, W6657, GE, Rader, Daniel
RADFORD, Malisa, W2554, WL, Radford, Wm. H
RAGAN, James R. S2204, CF, 22nd Inf.
RAGAN, Mary Louise, W10441, D, Ragan, Wm. Henry

RAGAN, W. H. S16097, MA, 1st (Feild's) Inf.
RAGLAND, Harriet J. W1552, Ragland, John T.
RAGLAND, W. A. S10429, J, 8th (Dibrell's) Cav.
RAGLAND, William H. S16001, PU, 4th (McLemore's) Cav.
RAGSDALE, C. F. S9832, O, 47th Inf.
RAGSDALE, Martha Z. W10739, D, Ragsdale, John L.
RAGSDALE, Octavia Catherine, W8246, O, Ragsdale, Cicero Franklin
RAGSDALE, P. G. S7984, SH, 56th Ga. Inf.
RAGSDALE, Sarah Delilah, W8748, MU, Ragsdale, Francis Marion
RAGSDALE, Tennessee Rebecca, W8962, MU, Ragsdale, John K.
RAIMEY, J. K. S11845, MT, 2nd Ky. Cav.
RAINES, Alsey, S12172, CC, 14th (Neely's) Cav.
RAINES, Annie, W1290, Raines, Henry Harkwell
RAINES, Ella, W9389, CF, Raines, Andrew Jackson
RAINES, J. L. S4092, LK, 12th Ky. Cav.
RAINES, Mary Elizabeth, W3018, HN, Raines, Robert Larkin
RAINES, Mary Jane, W2751, GI, Raines, H. W.
RAINES, R. P. S8899, G, 7th Cav.
RAINES, Robert Larkin, S8892, HN, 46th Inf.
RAINES, Salena L. W8571, MU, Raines, George Luthur
RAINES, William H. S6286, CH, 22nd Inf.
RAINEY, Effie, W10878, SH, Rainey, Wm. Joseph
RAINEY, I.N. S14238, SH, 7th (Duckworth's) Cav.
RAINEY, Isaac H. S10339, GI, 6th (Wheeler's) Cav.
RAINEY, James W. S367, S1442, L, 6th Inf.
RAINEY, John C. S3215, MOO, 8th Inf.
RAINEY, John F. S4364, HI, 48th (Voorhies') Inf.
RAINEY, Martha L. W871, MS, Rainey, G. W.
RAINEY, Nell, W11104, MA, Rainey, Thos. Cicero
RAINEY, Paul, S4915, G, 27th Inf.
RAINEY, S. G. S11024, L, 15th (Stewart's) Cav.
RAINEY, Sallie, W5076, L, Rainey, James W.
RAINEY, T. C. S15142, MA, 7th (Duckworth's) Cav.

RAINEY, Viola, W4323, GI, Rainey, Isaac H.
RAINEY, W. I. S14784, GI, 7th Cav.
RAINEY, W. J. S13717, DY, 4th (McLemore's) Cav.
RAINEY, W. P. S3367, LI, 17th Inf.
RAINS, A. J. S9524, CF, 1st Inf.
RAINS, Elizabeth, W6560, D, Rains, John Bondurant
RAINS, G. L. S9861, L, 33rd Inf.
RAINS, H. W. S1124, GI, 48th Inf.
RAINS, Henlett, S708, GI, 48th Inf.
RAINS, John, S3799, CY, 8th Inf.
RAINS, John W. S10416, G, 20th (Russell's) Cav.
RAINS, Laura M. W3278, MA, Rains, Wm. H.
RAINS, Martha Ann, W3327, CO, Rains, Hiram
RAINS, Mary Ann, W8112, CU, Rains, James M.
RAINS, W. R. S10348, D, 20th Inf.
RAINS, William P. S3414, W, 4th (Murray's) Cav.
RALLS, Francis M. S7102, HN, 5th Inf.
RALSTON, A. S4215, GI, 23rd Inf.
RALSTON, Cornelia A. W1543, GI, Ralston, James Alexander
RAMBA, I. W. S7473, WE, 31st Inf.
RAMBA, Louisa E. W7836, WE, Ramba, J. W.
RAMBO, Eliza E. W799, WE, Rambo, Harvey W.
RAMBO, Elizabeth, W986, MS, Rambo, David
RAMBO, O. H. S11675, SH, 1st Miss. Cav.
RAMBO, William C. S8454, LI, 4th (McLemore's) Cav.
RAMER, Eliza A. W4887, MN, Ramer, Wm. Roark
RAMER, J. S. S13979, MN, 18th (Newsom's) Cav.
RAMER, John, S1934, SN, 55th Inf.
RAMER, L. A. W1349, MN, Ramer, W. M.
RAMEY, Elizabeth S. W6856, MT, Ramey, Samuel E.
RAMEY, Samuel E. S7898, MT, 2nd Ky. Cav.
RAMOR, Lydia Ann, W5436, MN, Ramor, James Samuel
RAMSAY, Jane E. W2273, LA, Ramsay, Robert Manuel
RAMSEY, Abbigail, W1352, PO, Ramsey, Reuben
RAMSEY, Ada Frances, See Ada Frances Cooper
RAMSEY, Austin, S3776, PU, 25th Inf.

RAMSEY, Cornelia, W9525, SN, Ramsey, Zearl Booker
RAMSEY, Elizabeth Colliers, W8922, OV, Ramsey, Wm. Jason
RAMSEY, Emma, W7687, WE, Ramsey, John Jefferson
RAMSEY, Ida Clark, W3938, F, Ramsey, Thomas Polk
RAMSEY, J. A. S8939, D, 11th Cav.
RAMSEY, J. J. S175, LI, 40th Inf.
RAMSEY, James, S14211, HA, 63rd Inf.
RAMSEY, John, S6052, MU, 25th Inf.
RAMSEY, John J. S15048, WE, 4th Ala. Cav.
RAMSEY, John L. S8971, WE, 11th Cav.
RAMSEY, Kate W. W4156, G, Ramsey, G. J.
RAMSEY, Mary, W3725, MS, Ramsey, Daniel B.
RAMSEY, Nancy Ann, W7623, G, Ramsey, Wm. James
RAMSEY, R. N. S15636, G, 55th Inf.
RAMSEY, Robert, S2894, LA, 48th Inf.
RAMSEY, Robert N. S6496, G, 12th Inf.
RAMSEY, S. B. S6323, S16393, GI, 48th Inf.
RAMSEY, Sarah Rixney, W4487, G, Ramsey, Wm. Davis
RAMSEY, Susan R. W4523, D, Ramsey, Edward Tryon
RAMSEY, Thomas P. S10728, F, 41st Inf.
RAMSEY, W. J. S1950, WH, 25th Inf.
RAMSEY, W. J. S15091, G, 4th Tex. Cav.
RAMSEY, Z. B. S14233, WL, 22nd (Barteau's) Cav.
RAN, Margaret Ocoa, W10944, H, Ran, Vincent Lockhart
RANDALL, Martha, W3172, H, Randall, Wm.
RANDALL, William Henry, S9291, GI, 11th Inf.
RANDLE, Emma Chester, W5628, D, Randle, Frederick Douglas
RANDLE, Henry S. S15684, CC, 46th Inf.
RANDLE, Zilphia, W9854, CC, Randle, Henry Smith
RANDOLPH, A. J. S3275, GI, 53rd Inf.
RANDOLPH, A. S. S11684, GI, 32nd Inf.
RANDOLPH, Calvin, S886, PU, 28th Inf.
RANDOLPH, D. W. C. S8807, RB, 14th Inf.
RANDOLPH, E. S4304, WH, 25th Inf.
RANDOLPH, Elizabeth Fountain, W5724, MA, Randolph, J. P.
RANDOLPH, G. W. S12147, MA, Undetermined
RANDOLPH, Harrison, S14391, RB, 30th Inf.

RANDOLPH, Holda, W642, MC, Randolph, Wm. Cantrell
RANDOLPH, J. P. S13449, MA, 31st Inf.
RANDOLPH, Jesse V. S13567, PU, 25th Inf.
RANDOLPH, Lelia Virginia, W5649, SH, Randolph, George Washington
RANDOLPH, Margaret, W10390, LA, Randolph, Adam Stinson
RANDOLPH, Mary Jane, W3734, RB, Randolph, Dewitt Clinton
RANDOLPH, Nancy Jane, W514, PU, Randolph, Calvin
RANDOLPH, S. G. S2862, MN, 27th Ala. Inf.
RANDOLPH, Thomas M. S12314, U, 58th N.C. Inf.
RANDOLPH, W. W. S8048, D, 9th Inf.
RANEY, H. K. S3635, MOO, 41st Inf.
RANEY, Mary Elizabeth, W1873, MOO, Raney, Henry King
RANEY, S. B. S3258, WY, 37th Inf.
RANKHORN, C. M. S6353, DK, 28th Inf.
RANKIN, B. F. S16178, RU, 9th Cav.
RANKIN, C. G. S5371, GE, 61st Inf.
RANKIN, Franklin, S8566, CF, 1st Inf.
RANKIN, Lettie Bennett, W741, H, Rankin, David Byron
RANKIN, Mary Elizabeth, W2471, MS, Rankin, R. S.
RANKIN, Mary Emely, W8298, MS, Rankin, Robert Samuel
RANKIN, Mary Jane, W2037, MR, Rankin, Wm.
RANKIN, Nancy Adeline, W6107, GE, Rankin, Richard A.
RANKIN, R. A. S13142, GE, 61st Inf.
RANKIN, Ruth J. W40, TR, Rankin, James
RANKINS, D. B. S4472, H, 6th (Wheeler's) Cav.
RANSOM, Alexander, C202, B, 24th Inf.
RANSOM, Emma B. W3239, MA, Ransom, Albert W.
RANSOM, Granville M. S12149, MR, 8th (Smith's) Cav.
RANSOM, W. H. S8492, SN, 8th Inf.
RAPER, Monroe, S3808, MO, 62nd Inf.
RAPER, Thomas B. S5983, MO, 62nd Inf.
RASBERRY, John C. S14890, WY, 19th (Biffle's) Cav.
RASBERRY, W. M. S14265, 13th Ark. Inf.
RASBURY, Sarah A. W10101, LE, Rasbury, John C.

RASH, Martha Elizabeth, W1302, PU, Rash, Wm. A.
RASH, Nancy, W6035, J, Rash, Thomas Jefferson
RASH, Thomas J. S10765, J, 28th Inf.
RATCLIFF, Eudora, W9650, D, Ratcliff, Wm. Pope
RATLEDGE, Margaret Arbelia, W10791, G, Ratledge, Manlief Dickerson
RATLEY, William M. S6166, LI, 31st Ala. Inf.
RATLIFF, A. E. S11130, O, 33rd Inf.
RATLIFF, Evan, S6836, LA, 23rd Inf.
RATLIFF, Martha E. W6874, HA, Ratliff, G. J.
RATLIFF, Mary, W7359, O, Ratliff, Alfred Eli
RATLIFF, W. C. S13614, MU, 23rd Inf.
RAULSTON, Michael, S12220, RO, 62nd Inf.
RAWLES, DeKalb, S4061, LI, 8th Inf.
RAWLES, Wesley G. S2642, CE, 1st (Feild's) Inf.
RAWLEY, James W. S2494, D, 12th Inf.
RAWLINGS, Dora Crutchfield, W10163, H, Rawlings, John G.
RAWLINGS, Fannie Frances, W9013, W9174, SH, Rawlings, Richard Jackson
RAWLINGS, John P. S10757, D, 2nd (Robison's) Inf.
RAWLINGS, Thomas K. S10054, MR, 35th Inf.
RAWLS, F. M. S13936, G, 33rd Inf.
RAWLS, Martha Ann, W6649, LI, Rawls, DeKalb
RAWLS, Martha Jane, W6580, G, Rawls, Francis Marion
RAWORTH, Mollie, W8989, HY, Raworth, Dickson Brewer
RAY, A. G. S3570, MOO, 23rd Bn. Inf.
RAY, Aaron, S14173, R, Welker's Bn. Cav.
RAY, Alexander E. S1826, SM, 28th Inf.
RAY, B. H. S6687, OV, 8th (Dibrell's) Cav.
RAY, Bettie E. W5645, WE, Ray, Wm. J.
RAY, Celia Margaret, W8309, PU, Ray, Wm. Larkin
RAY, E. S. S5702, MA, 31st Inf.
RAY, Elizabeth Frances, W5460, WE, Ray, Newton Jasper
RAY, G. W. jr. S2576, PU, 8th Cav.
RAY, George, S6835, PU, 25th Inf.
RAY, George L. S10756, J, 28th Inf.
RAY, H. B. S3212, HD, 53rd Ala. Cav.
RAY, H. M. S1981, OV, 25th Inf.
RAY, Henry, S1286, SM, 44th Inf.
RAY, Henry, S4821, R, 16th Bn. Cav.
RAY, Hugh, S7035, RO, 16th Bn. (Neal's) Cav.

RAY, J. Francis, S8992, MS, 1st Cav.
RAY, J. M. S10264, U, 29th N.C. Inf.
RAY, James H. S7949, CF, 17th Inf.
RAY, James H. S14534, K, Unassigned (Camp of Instruction)
RAY, James R. S2130, K, Burrough's Co. Lt. Art.
RAY, Jennie Wright, W2935, FR, Ray, General Marion
RAY, John, S4273, T, 15th N.C. Inf.
RAY, Joseph, S3981, DK, 50th Inf.
RAY, Kitty, W773, DK, Ray, Joseph
RAY, Louis, S5431, CL, 29th Inf.
RAY, Louisa M. W1010, SM, Ray, Alexander
RAY, Magness L. S7580, OV, 28th Inf.
RAY, Martha, W6581, HD, Ray, H. B.
RAY, Mary Ann, W10759, GI, Ray, Thomas Jefferson
RAY, Mary Ann Elizabeth, W8670, HN, Ray, Robert Carroll
RAY, Mary Elizabeth, W11039, MS, Ray, Wm. Bird
RAY, Mary Polly, W3779, WI, Ray, Jacob
RAY, Nancy Ann, W5852, WE, Ray, John Henry
RAY, Nancy Jane, W3684, OV, Ray, Wm. Houston
RAY, Nayoma, W3890, DK, Ray, Joseph
RAY, Newton J. S2235, WE, 24th Inf.
RAY, R. B. S2993, HR, 19th & 20th (Consol.) Cav.
RAY, Sallie E. W2495, B, Ray, Amos Gore
RAY, Susan, W4992, LO, Ray, Wm.
RAY, T. J. (Pete), S16282, GI, 6th Cav.
RAY, W. H. S2838, MN, 19th Inf.
RAY, W. J. S10065, WE, 12th (Green's) Cav.
RAY, W. M. S4961, MOO, 37th Inf.
RAY, William, S12792, RO, 62nd Inf.
RAY, William B. S3500, MS, 6th Ala. Inf.
RAY, William Houston, S2042, OV, 8th Inf.
RAY, William L. S9061, PU, 8th (Dibrell's) Cav.
RAYBORN, A. J. S10363, D, 16th Inf.
RAYBURN, Almedia W. W3685, CF, Rayburn, Robert Donnel
RAYBURN, Fannie Hager Bush, W8580, D, Rayburn, Andrew Jackson
RAYBURN, John M. S132, PU, 25th Inf.
RAYMER, A. J. W. S11524, D, 2nd (Morgan's) Ky. Cav.
RAYNER, Lawrence, S16157, S9712, T, 1st Hvy. Art.

REA, Sarah V. W9485, MU, Rea, W. M.
REA, W. M. S15751, MU, 53rd Inf.
READ, Henry, C272, L, 7th Cav.
READ, William B. S6090, SN, 9th (Ward's) Cav.
READY, Albert, C97, RU, 23rd Inf.
REAGAN, A. A. S10008, PU, 25th Inf.
REAGAN, Benjamin P. S7076, MO, 3rd (Lillard's) Mtd. Inf.
REAGAN, Duke Riah, S918, WH, 26th Inf.
REAGAN, Emma P. W1590, GI, Reagan, Thomas Caleb
REAGAN, Hopkins T. S1859, FR, 1st Inf.
REAGAN, J. H. S7486, PU, 8th (Dibrell's) Cav.
REAGAN, James Avery, S16070, MC, 16th Bn. (Neal's) Cav.
REAGAN, James H. S1425, BO, 25th Inf.
REAGAN, Joseph, S2869, BO, 69th N.C. Inf.
REAGAN, Kittie, W2333, MO, Reagan, Benjamin P.
REAGAN, Lizzie Buchanan, W10926, MC, Reagan, James Avery
REAGAN, Nettie, W6929, PU, Reagan, A. A.
REAGAN, Susan, W10454, OV, Reagan, Wm.
REAGIN, Fannie H. W9387, D, Reagin, John R.
REAGIN, John R. S9750, D, 1st (Feild's) Inf.
REAMES, Irvin, S2577, CO, 25th N.C. Inf.
REAMS, Mary Elizabeth, W6536, WI, Reams, George Washington
REASON, Kathrine Lucretia, W10297, CC, Reason, George Francis
REASONOVER, John Bover, S6370, SM, 44th Inf.
REASONOVER, T. J. S14777, SH, 29th Miss. Inf.
REASONS, Sarah Clarimont, W2785, GI, Reasons, Grandison Brady
REAVES, F. J. S11474, HI, 11th Inf.
REAVES, John M. S7751, HD, 38th Ala. Inf.
REAVES, L. E. S15869, MU, 24th Inf.
REAVES, L. P. S7918, T, 51st Inf.
REAVES, Virginia, W4962, CC, Reaves, Henry Green
REAVIS, Daniel, S8516, B, 11th Cav.
REAVIS, Fannie Elizabeth, W7363, MA, Reavis, Robert A.
REAVIS, J. J. S9025, FR, 17th Inf.
REAVIS, James, S2264, SU, 2nd N.C. Cav.
REAVIS, R. A. S13118, MA, 20th (Russell's) Cav.
RECTOR, C. M. W529, GE, Rector, Thomas Wilburn
RECTOR, I. E. S10302, PU, 8th (Dibrell's) Cav.
RECTOR, James Madison, S16675, DI, 10th Cav.
RECTOR, Mary Lou, W9526, WH, Rector, Jackson Burnett
RECTOR, McCoger, S5604, SE, 5th N.C. Cav.
REDD, William James, S8762, HR, Forrest's Old Regt. Cav.
REDDELL, James A. S2731, MN, 3rd Inf.
REDDEN, John Wiley, S3010, DI, 11th Inf.
REDDEN, Samuel W. S4380, B, 4th Cav.
REDDICK, George A. S7528, D, 1st (Feild's) Inf.
REDDICK, J. H. S7085, BE, 5th Inf.
REDDICK, Sarah J. W3645, SN, Reddick, James P.
REDDICK, W. S. S14320, SH, 5th (McKenzie's) Cav.
REDFEARN, Harrison, S8749, HR, 22nd Inf.
REDFORD, Belle S. W5667, SH, Redford, Wm. Allison
REDICK, Louise M. W9375, BE, Redick, James H.
REDICK, T. J. S1251, HO, 55th Inf.
REDMAN, A. D. S20, D, 44th Inf.
REDMAN, Martha Jane, W8650, DK, Redman, James Monroe
REDMON, J. C. S11753.5, CL, 64th Va. Mtd. Inf.
REDMON, Job C. S4663, CL, 37th Inf.
REDMOND, Jesse, S4152, DK, 16th Inf.
REDMOND, Lemira, W5794, D, Redmond, Árch.
REDWINE, Sarah Abigal, W3959, BR, Redwine, Wm. Jasper
REECE, Calip, S4443, M, 44th Inf.
REECE, Ellen Frances, W5316, CC, Reece, Jasper Marion
REECE, Joseph M. S8859, CC, 22nd Inf.
REECE, Preston Haywood, S11274, CC, 9th Inf.
REECE, Rhoda C. W991, P, Reece, George W.
REECE, Roana Webb, W9000, PU, Reece, John Aron
REECE, Samuel, S832, SM, 28th Inf.
REED, Amanda Virginia, W5805, RU, Reed, James Burton
REED, Ann Ellen, W3316, T, Reed, Frederick Thomas
REED, Brownlow, S3572, K, 17th Inf.
REED, Celia Jane, W7512, SM, Reed, Jesse
REED, Cynthia Elvira, W10219, G, Reed, Wm. Franklin

REED, E. A. S907, HE, 21st Cav.
REED, E. A. S14638, SH, 5th Miss. Cav.
REED, Elizabeth, W10363, OV, Reed, Andrew Jackson
REED, Ezekiel, S9120, CA, 18th Inf.
REED, Frances Eveline, W3939, MU, Reed, Maxwell Hendrick
REED, G. M. D. S15156, WI, 44th Inf.
REED, J. B. S7149, RU, 18th Inf.
REED, J. W. S9807, WE, 9th Inf.
REED, James, S2716, K, Thomas' Legion, N.C.
REED, Jesse, S5952, SM, 15th Cav.
REED, John R. S6167, HD, 21st (Wilson's) Cav.
REED, John S. S6321, BO, 31st Inf.
REED, John T. S6519, B, 31st Inf.
REED, Louisa Jane, W253, HD, Reed, David M.
REED, Margaret Catherine, W6034, SN, Reed, Thomas Peyton
REED, Nancy M. W4910, B, Reed, John Turner
REED, Nim R. S15955, J, 8th (Dibrell's) Cav.
REED, Patience H. W192, RU, Reed, John Davis
REED, Robert E. S4768, B, 17th Inf.
REED, S. P. S16085, G, 5th Ark. Inf.
REED, Samuel Amos, S14185, MA, 22nd Inf.
REED, T. W. S10716, D, 53rd Inf.
REED, Tennie, W9604.5, RU, Reed, Ezekiel
REED, W. A. S11597, OV, Shaw's Bn. Cav.
REEDER, Almiria A. W3797, DI, Reeder, J. H. L.
REEDER, E. P. S13178, DK, 23rd Inf.
REEDER, J. H. L. S1262, DI, 11th Inf.
REEDER, Lizzie, W8048, MN, Reeder, Wm. A.
REEDER, Telilha Cantrell, W7457, W, Reeder, Edwin Parker
REEDER, W. A. S14425, MN, 19th & 20th (Consol.) Cav.
REEDY, Caroline M. W5428, WA, Reedy, Elisha
REEDY, Elijah E. S2643, WA, 37th Va. Inf.
REEKS, Margaret Frazier, W9659, CE, Reeks, Samuel Harris
REELS, George Washington, S7623, CY, 8th (Dibrell's) Cav.
REEMS, J. M. S7258, CH, 31st Inf.
REEN, Nathan Henry, S16229, SU, Burrough's Co. Lt. Art.
REES, C. C. S14696, SH, 7th Miss. Cav.
REES, D. N. S10808, CT, 1st Ky. Inf.
REES, James R. S2913, MOO, 41st Inf.
REES, Joel, S12292, GI, Forrest's Escort, Cav.
REES, N. B. S8658, B, 41st Inf.

REESE, B. P. S14521, TR, 22nd (Barteau's) Cav.
REESE, Bettie Armstrong, W8741, TR, Reese, Bailey Peyton
REESE, Bettie Wase, W10014, TR, Reese, Wade
REESE, C. C. S15118, SH, 7th Miss. Cav.
REESE, Callihill Minis, S6354, LI, 8th Inf.
REESE, Elizabeth, W1090, B, Reese, James R.
REESE, Emma, W5813, G, Reese, John
REESE, Frances M. W2444, TR, Reese, W. J.
REESE, J. H. S1053, SN, 20th Inf.
REESE, John, S11038, G, 44th Va. Inf.
REESE, Mary, W2928, JE, Reese, Alexander
REESE, Mary Emeline, W7511, GI, Reese, Joel
REESE, NarcisusAnn, W432, Reese, James Solomon
REESE, R. H. S12759, LI, 8th Inf.
REESE, Wade, S15910, TR, 24th Inf.
REEVE, Jennie, W10712, SU, Reeve, Nathan Henry
REEVES, Bettie Ann, W1624, DI, Reeves, John Andrew
REEVES, Charles W. S514, G, 16th Cav.
REEVES, David, S4080, WY, 48th Inf.
REEVES, F. M. S8377, SM, 7th Inf.
REEVES, George W. S14595, WI, 1st (Feild's) Inf.
REEVES, James, C33, WL, 7th Inf.
REEVES, John F. S6636, JO, 26th N.C. Inf.
REEVES, Lucy Ann, W1392, SM, Reeves, Frank M.
REEVES, M. P. S15365, B, 45th Inf.
REEVES, Mary C. W2544, RU, Reeves, Richard Chapman
REEVES, Mary D. W3427, WA, Reeves, Isaac Edward
REEVES, Mary E. W511, MA, Reeves, Charles Washington
REEVES, Mary Elizabeth, W10607, RU, Reeves, Mathew Peyton
REEVES, Narcissa, W5744, HE, Reeves, John Quincey
REEVES, Rebecca F. W10184, RU, Reeves, Ira O.
REEVES, Rosley Malindey, W4982, GU, Reeves, Wm.
REEVES, Sarah S. W8155, LK, Reeves, Hudson
REEVES, W. W. S184, MN, 26th Miss. Inf.
REGEN, Nancy Ellen, W4560, D, Regen, Joseph Struklin
REGG, Josephine, W2049, D, Regg, Charles

REGIN, I. S. S9316, D, 4th (McLemore's) Cav.
REGION, Mary jane, W2200, MU, Region, Joel
REID, D. W. S3540, MN, 27th Inf.
REID, Fred, S14773, SH, 7th La. Inf.
REID, John, S538, 55th Inf.
REID, John A. S9551, HY, 14th Cav.
REID, Laura Josephine, W1053, CH, Reid, James Riley
REID, Maggie Elizabeth, W7945, CH, Reid, Richard Henry
REID, Martha L. W9937, MA, Reid, James G.
REID, Mary Jane, W52, HE, Reid, Eli Arthur
REID, Mattie, W8003, SH, Reid, Will Andrew
REID, Minnie Polk, W10984, SH, Reid, Eugene A.
REID, Nancy Elizabeth, W1921, MN, Reid, Danniel Wm.
REID, Nathan, C94, O, 6th Inf.
REID, R. H. S9351, CH, 27th Inf.
REID, R. H. S12740, D, Shoemaker's Va. Battery
REID, Sarah Brennen, W10877, D, Reid, Richard Henry
REID, Sarah J. W7433, M, Reid, Thomas R.
REID, Susi Boyd, W8587, R, Reid, Martin Van Buren
REID, T. A. S11709, MA, 6th Inf.
REID, T. R. S2196, M, 24th Inf.
REIGER, W. I. S3609, L, Wood's Regt. Miss. Cav.
REINACH, Sarah Stewart, W10282, SH, Reinach, David
REMBERT, Kate C. W9653, SH, Rembert, T. J.
RENEGAN, Elizabeth, W5418, FR, Renegan, Calvin
RENEGAR, Calvin, S9587, FR, 8th Inf.
RENEGAR, Nancy Evaline, W213, G, Renegar, Joseph Hickman
RENEGAR, Thursday, W10216, LI, Renegar, Sanford
RENFRO, Amanda T. W4383, F, Renfro, Marshall S.
RENFRO, B. W. S9261, MU, 3rd Inf.
RENFRO, Henry A. S14974, MG, 32nd Ga. Inf.
RENFRO, James C. S15246, H, 12th Bn. (Day's) Cav.
RENFRO, Laura Swaggerty, W9693, K, Renfro, James Cox
RENFRO, Margaret N. W4494, JO, Renfro, Wm. B.
RENFRO, Rilla, W6126, MU, Renfro, Bryant Ward

RENFRO, Rilla M. W10229, MU, Renfro, Bryant Ward
RENFRO, Susan C. W923, MU, Renfro, John T.
RENFRO, W. H. S9181, MA, 51st Inf.
RENFROE, W. B. S3627, CT, 37th Va. Inf.
RENICK, A. J. S15008, MN, 2nd Miss. Cav.
RENSHAW, Samantha C. W4855, RU, Renshaw, John A.
REYNOLD, Cassie, W292, MS, Reynold, Ezekiel E.
REYNOLD, Charles Richard, S11749, HR, 2nd Ark. Inf.
REYNOLD, G. W. S6721, HO, 10th Cav.
REYNOLD, G. W. S16443, HO, Napier's Bn. Cav.
REYNOLD, George S. S5619, K, 28th Va. Inf.
REYNOLD, George W. S16419, DI, 10th Cav.
REYNOLD, H. A. S14622, WL, 45th Inf.
REYNOLD, J. H. S10698, LI, 7th Ala. Cav.
REYNOLD, J. M. S13271, WE, 22nd Cav.
REYNOLD, James H. S11562, GI, 3rd (Clack's) Inf.
REYNOLD, Jasper, S7729, RB, 6th (Wheeler's) Cav.
REYNOLD, John, S14740, GE, Parmer's N.C. Home Guards
REYNOLD, Z. T. S15964, DY, 22nd (Barteau's) Cav.
REYNOLDS, B. F. S11028, GI, 3rd (Clack's) Inf.
REYNOLDS, Callie, W9761, WL, Reynolds, H. A.
REYNOLDS, Charles Louis, S12012, D, 2nd (Robison's) Inf.
REYNOLDS, Elizabeth Ann V. W7444, WE, Reynolds, James M.
REYNOLDS, Georgia Ann, W7855, HR, Reynolds, Charles Richard
REYNOLDS, J. T. S913, FE, 8th Inf.
REYNOLDS, Lucy Vance, W10676, HW, Reynolds, Wm. H.
REYNOLDS, Nancy Elizabeth, W1480, HD, Reynolds, Redden Washington
REYNOLDS, Nat, S10600, SN, 30th Inf.
REYNOLDS, R. R. S10469, LA, 19th (Biffle's) Cav.
REYNOLDS, Roxie A. W8523, LA, Reynolds, Richard Randolph
REYNOLDS, S. D. S15186, MO, 31st Inf.
REYNOLDS, S. H. S7361, DI, 10th Cav.
REYNOLDS, Sallie Ann, W9617, MO, Reynolds, S. D.

REYNOLDS, Sarah E. W1492, RB, Reynolds, Jasper
REYNOLDS, Sarah J. W3328, MT, Reynolds, Wm. Washington
REYNOLDS, Sarah Jane, W9316, G, Reynolds, Z. T.
REYNOLDS, Susan, W681, FE, Reynolds, T. J.
REYNOLDS, W. A. S13040, HO, 50th Inf.
REYNOLDS, W. J. S10153, WI, Forrest's Escort, Cav.
RHEA, Anna Adelaide, W10414, SH, Rhea, Mathew
RHEA, Emma Louise, W8773, W5008, HR, Rhea, Abram
RHEA, J. B. S7624, F, 4th (McLemore's) Cav.
RHEA, Lewis, S13533, MC, 3rd (Lillard's) Mtd. Inf.
RHEA, Lora Isabella, W6594, HM, Rhea, John Adolphus
RHEA, Margaret Caroline, W9134, JO, Rhea, Robert Campbell
RHEA, Mary E. W8869, CF, Rhea, J. B.
RHEA, Mary Jane, W8633, MC, Rhea, Lewis
RHEA, Matilda A. W3726, SU, Rhea, John Preston
RHEA, Robert, S4373, HM, Unassigned
RHEA, S. W. S9847, SU, 63rd Inf.
RHEA, W. A. S3501, SH, 17th Bn. Cav.
RHEA, William R. S515, WA, 19th Inf.
RHEA, a. S13346, HR, 13th Inf.
RHEAY, Bettie, W9398, W, Rheay, Isaac Fayett
RHOADES, C. S363, SH, 38th Inf.
RHOADES, James Henry, S9382, WE, 20th (Russell's) Cav.
RHOADES, Mary Ann Elizabeth, W6177, WE, Rhoades, James Henry
RHODES, Amelia E. W7769, H, Rhodes, R. L.
RHODES, B. J. S8010, CH, 21st (Wilson's) Cav.
RHODES, Bunivesta, W9122, SH, Rhodes, James Richard
RHODES, D. C. S15027, D, 1st Bn. McNairy's Cav.
RHODES, Harriett, W4609, T, Rhodes, Wm. Thomas
RHODES, J. C. S9013, HE, 27th Inf.
RHODES, J. R. S1650, SH, 1st Ark. Mtd. Rifles'
RHODES, James, S4099, P, 11th Inf.
RHODES, John Allen, S9454, MS, 3rd (Clack's) Inf.
RHODES, Martha Thomas, W8688, HR, Rhodes, Robert James

RHODES, Moses Pinkney, S7773, 22nd Inf.
RHODES, Octava Chopple, W5072, CH, Rhodes, Benjamin Jacob
RHODES, W. C. S1534, SH, 5th Ala. Cav.
RHODES, William Thomas, S1476, SH, 5th Ala. Cav.
RHOTEN, Bettie, W4731, FR, Rhoten, Ben W.
RHOTON, Benjamin W. S2695, FR, 44th Inf.
RHOTON, Mollie, W2207, JE, Rhoton, Jacob Peck
RHYMER, David, S4703, HM, 29th Va. Inf.
RIAL, John Thomas, S757, HI, 48th Inf.
RICE, Alma Phillips, W10989, HO, Rice, Wm. Henry
RICE, Blancha Ann, W2945, DI, Rice, Dan
RICE, Cary G. S3093, L, 9th Inf.
RICE, Eliza Ellen, W5750, L, Rice, Carey Green
RICE, G. A. S6089, DY, 19th (Biffle's) Cav.
RICE, J. M. S10291, K, 29th Inf.
RICE, James Alexander, S12395, S3423, WH, 25th Inf.
RICE, James N. S11903, T, 7th Inf.
RICE, Jesse C. S5123, H, 3rd Cav.
RICE, Jesse C. S7875, ME, 3rd Cav.
RICE, Mariah J. W4072, FR, Rice, David C.
RICE, Mary Eliza, W3045, JE, Rice, Joseph Clay
RICE, Napoleon B. S10276, D, 25th Va. Bn.
RICE, O. A. S8600, WA, 7th Ky. Cav.
RICE, Oliver Thompson, S290, DE, 1st Inf.
RICE, Prudence Tennessee, W2755, MC, Rice, Allen Haley
RICE, Rachel Janette, W1827, CC, Rice, James Yancey
RICE, Rebecca Catherin, W2779, O, Rice, John Walter
RICE, Richard, C138, K, 29th Inf.
RICE, Robert A. S13476, SH, 51st Inf.
RICE, Sarah Elizabeth, W8562, D, Rice, Napoleon Bonapart
RICE, Susan May, W6735, MC, Rice, John Cloud
RICE, T. J. S16277, DY, 12th Inf.
RICE, Thomas, S13393, HY, 9th Inf.
RICE, W. B. S11260, HU, 11th Inf.
RICE, W. H. S11654, HO, 2nd Ky. Cav.
RICE, William H. S16136, S14954, HU, 10th Cav.
RICH, J. M. S3773, FR, 44th Inf.
RICH, J. N. S4473, HW, 60th Inf.
RICH, Joe, S15546, CY, 7th Ky. Cav.
RICH, Jular, W10484, FR, Rich, Joseph M.

Index to Tennessee Confederate Pension Applications

RICH, Laura Bell, W10774, CY, Rich, Joe
RICH, Maggie L. W10202, OV, Rich, Harvy Butler
RICH, Mary Elizabeth, W10261, WL, Rich, Wm. Erastus
RICH, W. E. S11354, WL, 22nd (Barteau's) Cav.
RICHARDS, A. C. S13804, ST, 50th Inf.
RICHARDS, Alexander, S4406, SU, 1st Bn. Inf.
RICHARDS, B. H. S6507, SU, 5th (McClellan's) Cav.
RICHARDS, Benjamin, S4884, CT, 26th Inf.
RICHARDS, Elizabeth E. W128, GR, Richards, Jasper
RICHARDS, G. W. S6128, SU, 26th Inf.
RICHARDS, George C. S7929, RB, 1st Inf.
RICHARDS, George W. S2994, HR, 7th Cav.
RICHARDS, J. A. S3610, W, 8th (Smith's) Cav.
RICHARDS, J. F. S3159, MR, 3rd Cav.
RICHARDS, J. I. S9458, HI, 9th Bn. (Gantt's) Cav.
RICHARDS, J. N. S13025, CC, 31st Ark. Inf.
RICHARDS, J. S. S5805, MC, 31st Inf.
RICHARDS, James, S5153, SU, 26th Inf.
RICHARDS, James, S7474, O, 19th (Biffle's) Cav.
RICHARDS, James S. S9099, MC, 3rd (Forrest's) Cav.
RICHARDS, John S. S6451, CT, Undetermined
RICHARDS, Margaret Ann, W5846, MR, Richards, James Franklin
RICHARDS, Mary Adline, W7269, CC, Richards, James Newton
RICHARDS, Mary J. W949, GR, Richards, Columbus
RICHARDS, Mary Josephine, W1852, HI, Richards, James Ira
RICHARDS, Polly Ane, W6238, DY, Richards, Wm.
RICHARDS, Rutha Ann, W3037, WA, Richards, B. H.
RICHARDS, Sarah Frances, W487, HI, Richards, James H.
RICHARDS, T. M. S694, DY, Undetermined
RICHARDS, W. D. S15019, MR, 4th (McLemore's) Cav.
RICHARDS, W. H. S16647, K, 8th Va. Inf.
RICHARDS, W. W. S4323, MN, 19th & 20th (Consolidated) Cav.
RICHARDS, William, S14198, DY, 9th Bn. Cav.
RICHARDSON, A. J. S9501, HU, 11th Inf.

RICHARDSON, Alpheus W. S6885, OV, 8th Inf.
RICHARDSON, Andrew Jackson, S2668, MOO, 41st Inf.
RICHARDSON, Daniel, S12585, CC, 47th Inf.
RICHARDSON, David, S577, CY, 8th (Dibrell's) Cav.
RICHARDSON, David, S1217, PI, 8th Inf.
RICHARDSON, Emily Catherine, W1558, DI, Richardson, Wm. Turner
RICHARDSON, Eva, W9368, BO, Richardson, Jesse Forrest
RICHARDSON, J. C. S2339, OV, 25th Inf.
RICHARDSON, J. d. S9658, G, 1st Ark. Cav.
RICHARDSON, James, S4973, MS, 41st Inf.
RICHARDSON, James A. S2710, WI, Baxter's Battery, Lt. Art.
RICHARDSON, James A. S9135, MU, 3rd (Clack's) Inf.
RICHARDSON, James J. S10754, G, 10th Cav.
RICHARDSON, Jane T. W5771, OV, Richardson, Joseph C.
RICHARDSON, Jesse F. S6763, BO, 44th N.C. Inf.
RICHARDSON, Lucy Jane, W9972, MU, Richardson, Wm. M.
RICHARDSON, Marienne Hightower, W6172, WI, Richardson, Robert Newton
RICHARDSON, Martha, W5205, FR, Richardson, Wm. Ralie
RICHARDSON, Martin V. S3383, OV, 8th Inf.
RICHARDSON, Mary, W4073, DY, Richardson, Thomas Jefferson
RICHARDSON, Mary Ellen, W3763, OV, Richardson, Martin Van Buren
RICHARDSON, Mary James, W7093, MS, Richardson, James
RICHARDSON, Mary Weller, W10968, W10934, D, Richardson, John Thomas
RICHARDSON, Mattie W. W3686, RU, Richardson, James Henry
RICHARDSON, Philah, W9975, HU, Richardson, A. J.
RICHARDSON, R. N. S13244, WI, 1st (Feild's) Inf.
RICHARDSON, S. R. S8437, MA, 31st Inf.
RICHARDSON, Sarah Augusta, W4329, K, Richardson, John Summerfield
RICHARDSON, Sarah Catherine, W4467, HY, Richardson, Wm. Asberry
RICHARDSON, Sarah T. W1455, MS, Richardson, Charles S.

-291

RICHARDSON, Sue F. W56, GI, Richardson, Wm. Currin
RICHARDSON, T. J. S2567, CC, 12th Inf.
RICHARDSON, Virginia Ann, W4274, MU, Richardson, James Allen
RICHARDSON, W. L. S14750, HY, 38th Inf.
RICHARDSON, W. R. S6158, FR, 32nd Inf.
RICHERT, James, S16653, SH, 9th Miss. Inf.
RICHESON, Laura, W8925, MC, Richeson, Ira R.
RICHEY, H. S. S12111, HI, 10th (DeMoss') Cav.
RICHEY, Joseph, S2995, JE, 2nd Cav.
RICHIE, Melvina Childress, W11070, WE, Richie, Starling C.
RICHIE, R. W. S8816, G, 7th (Faulkner's) Miss. Cav.
RICHMOND, L. A. S10078, G, 7th Inf.
RICHMOND, Maggie Magram, W5898, D, Richmond, Benjamin
RICHMOND, Mary Eliz. [Starr], W3896, G, Richmond, Love Alexander, [Later married Starr]
RICKETS, Charles W. S6002, MU, 9th Bn. (Gantt's) Cav.
RICKETS, Elizabeth, W501, CH, Rickets, Reuben Russel
RICKETTS, Charles W. S872, MU, 9th Bn. Cav.
RICKETTS, David N. S11281, WY, 9th Inf.
RICKETTS, Isabella, W2828, WY, Ricketts, Tennessee Roper
RICKETTS, J. W. S6688, WL, 7th Inf.
RICKETTS, Mary, W1316, HE, Ricketts, John
RICKETTS, Mary F. W10251, WY, Ricketts, David
RICKMAN, Cleopatra Albertine, W2679, MS, Rickman, James Franklin
RICKMAN, E. M. S10134, WE, 17th Inf.
RICKMAN, J. M. S15645, DE, 6th (Wheeler's) Cav.
RICKMAN, Martha A. W10907, DE, Rickman, J. M.
RICKMAN, S. A. S2863, MN, 32nd Miss. Inf.
RICKMAN, W. T. S10108, O, 22nd (Barteau's) Cav.
RICKS, Edison M. S226, HY, 7th Cav.
RICKS, G. T. S15693, SH, 13th Bn. Va. Lt. Art.
RIDDLE, Amanda J. W130, WE, Riddle, Thomas G.
RIDDLE, Elizabeth J. W215, FR, Riddle, Randolph
RIDDLE, John, S8945, BO, 37th Inf.

RIDDLE, Martha Jane, W9415, GR, Riddle, Ephram Perkins
RIDDLE, Sarah Jane, W1037, B, Riddle, Alex
RIDEOUT, W. T. S1720, MA, 26th Ala. Inf.
RIDER, Mary Jane, W6070, MO, Rider, Robert R.
RIDER, Robert R. S9050, MO, 2nd (Ashby's) Cav.
RIDER, Samuel R. S8994, MO, Walker's Bn. Thomas' Legion, N.C.
RIDGE, Godfrey, S3747, HD, 31st Miss. Inf.
RIDGE, Hiram, S13186, D, 2nd (Robison's) Inf.
RIDGE, I. S. S2918, D, 23rd Inf.
RIDGE, R. D. S8517, D, 18th Inf.
RIDGWAY, S. T. S13798, HN, 5th Inf.
RIDINGER, L. B. S5026, CF, 8th (Dibrell's) Cav.
RIDINGS, E. T. S447, HO, 11th Inf.
RIDINGS, Sarah Serena, W8903, HU, Ridings, George Dillard
RIDINGS, Susie, W10028, HU, Ridings, Joel Perry
RIDLEY, George C. S8916, D, McNairy's Bn. Cav.
RIDLEY, J. K. P. S8718, WI, 20th Inf.
RIDLEY, John William, S3237, WH, Thomas' Legion, N.C.
RIDLEY, Mary Jane, W3884, WI, Ridley, Wm. Thomas
RIDLEY, Mildred, W9668, RU, Ridley, Granville S.
RIDLEY, S. J. S14854, D, 6th (Wheeler's) Cav.
RIDLEY, Sallie J. W5705, Ridley, Charles Hampton
RIDLEY, Sinthia Elizabeth, W7792, W8482, HE, Ridley, Wesley Taylor
RIDLEY, Tabitha H. W2864, Ridley, James L.
RIDLEY, W. T. S11938, HE, 55th Inf.
RIDLEY, William T. S27, WI, 20th Inf.
RIETHMEIR, John, S8297, DI, 5th Inf.
RIEVES, E. N. B. S16273, MU, 48th (Nixon's) Inf.
RIEVES, I. O, S8838, RU, 4th (McLemore's) Cav.
RIEVES, Nathaniel Green, S7537, MU, 1st (Feild's) Inf.
RIEVES, Susie Alice, W1991, MU, Rieves, Nathaniel Green
RIEVLEY, Elizabeth J. W11169, H, Rievley, John L.
RIFFEY, David, S6401, K, 25th Va. Inf.
RIGBY, Sam J. S2281, O, 7th Cav.

Index to Tennessee Confederate Pension Applications

RIGGINS, Charles A. S10379, SH, 14th Va. Inf.
RIGGINS, Rosanna Elizabeth, W4453, SH, Riggins, Charles Alexander
RIGGINS, Silas W. S365, MC, 19th Inf.
RIGGINS, THomas, S10680, MC, 3rd Inf.
RIGGS, E. W. S9254, D, 4th (McLemore's) Cav.
RIGGS, Jack, S2311, GI, 1st (Feild's) Inf.
RIGGS, John R. S9768, W, 11th (Holman's) Cav.
RIGGS, Martin, S11846, MC, 59th Inf.
RIGGS, Nannie A. W3446, MS, Riggs, Gideon W.
RIGGS, Sarah Amanda, W4740, GE, Riggs, Jasper N.
RIGGSBEE, Eliza, W6082, SN, Riggsbee, Sydney Bourbon
RIGGSBEE, S. B. S5164, SN, 9th (Bennett's) Cav.
RIGNEY, Charles, S10424, CF, 34th Inf.
RIGNEY, John H. S6332, C, 24th Va. Inf.
RIGNEY, Simon R. S7328, CF, 34th Inf.
RIGSBY, Myra Ann, W3618, SN, Rigsby, David Shadrie
RIGSBY, Richard, S2752, WA, 63rd Inf.
RIGSBY, Richard, S6355, SU, 63rd Inf.
RILEY, Catherine, W331, V, Riley, John
RILEY, Cornelous, S9250, RB, 8th Ky. Inf.
RILEY, Henrietta Josephine, W5376, DY, Riley, James Anderson
RILEY, Isaac, S3970, PI, 4th (Murray's) Cav.
RILEY, J. A. S11413, P, 9th Bn. (Gantt's) Cav.
RILEY, James C. S12951, CH, Crew's Bn. Inf.
RILEY, James T. S14522, SU, 60th Inf.
RILEY, Malinda, W267, MS, Riley, John A.
RILEY, Mary E. W6071, HR, Riley, A. W.
RILEY, Penny, W7824, MS, Riley, Wm. Henry
RILEY, S. M. S7108, LI, 28th Cav.
RILEY, Sanders L. S1855, HD, 2nd N.C. Cav.
RILEY, Thomas J. S8362, HR, 23rd Miss. Inf.
RILEY, W. H. S14635, MS, 4th (McLemore's) Cav.
RINEHART, Elizabeth, W1358, ME, Rinehart, Wm.
RINEHEART, W. M. S2294, ME, 26th Inf.
RING, Victoria B. W9744, MU, Ring, John Martin
RINGO, Martha Eliza, W1845, LI, Ringo, Joseph Henry
RION, John R. S77, RU, Wheeler's Scouts, Cav.
RIPLEY, F. J. S4939, GE, Kain's Co. Lt. Art.
RIPPEY, S. L. S7392, SN, 9th Cav.

RIPPY, Emily Elizabeth, W2711, SN, Rippy, Wm. W.
RIPPY, Isaac, S7561, SN, 6th (Wheeler's) Cav.
RIPPY, J. M. S11919, SN, 9th (Ward's) Cav.
RIPPY, James W. S10297, SN, 9th (Ward's) Cav.
RIPPY, Jesse, S14670, RB, 20th Inf.
RIPPY, Joseph, S660, SN, 20th Inf.
RIPPY, Josephine, W9582, SN, Rippy, Jerry M.
RIPPY, Mary L. W8705, SN, Rippy, James Wesley
RIPPY, Sydney, S9332, SN, 20th Inf.
RIPPY, T. W. S11916, SN, 9th (Ward's) Cav.
RIPPY, Wm. W. S4329, S6003, SN, 20th Cav.
RISER, H. G. S15210, SH, Power's Miss. Cav.
RISER, Stella Coretta, W7605, SH, Riser, Harvey Griffin
RISTINE, Charles E. S16040, K, Ramsey's Battery, Lt. Art.
RITCHEY, Hattie, W7727, H, Ritchey, John T.
RITCHEY, J. T. S14365, H, 1st (Carter's) Cav.
RITTENBERRY, Elvira, W6818, D, Rittenberry, John William
RITTENHOUSE, David G. S10858, SH, 2nd Mo. Cav.
RIVERS, Mary A. W4914, R, Rivers, Robert
RIVERS, Matt, C153, GI, 11th Cav.
RIVERS, Robert, S1297, MC, 59th Inf.
RIVERS, W. B. S8020, G, 51st Inf.
RIVERS, W. H. S3785, D, 17th Inf.
RIVES, Alice, W7207, MS, Rives, Thomas Jefferson
RIVES, B. W. S9365, LI, 1st Trans-Miss. Inf.
RIVES, C. B. S13510, SH, 44th Miss. Inf.
RIVES, Elizabeth Jennings, W6374, D, Rives, Nathaniel Granville
RIVES, N. F. S1227, SH, 154th Sr. Regt. Inf.
RIVES, R. C. S5027, LI, 8th Inf.
RIVES, Rebecca Jane, W6046, W8689, LI, Rives, Robert Clay
RIVES, Sallie, W1178, WH, Rives, Thomas M.
RIVES, Thomas J. S8549, MS, 8th Inf.
ROACH, A. A. S2351, DE, 31st Inf.
ROACH, Cora P. [Linton], W10994, O, Roach, Wm. Henry, [Later married Linton]
ROACH, Nancy Jane, W6235, O, Roach, James Madison
ROACH, Nina, W4626, DE, Roach, Adison Alsbery
ROACH, Philip Emanuel, S1887, HD, 35th Va. Cav.
ROACH, S. H. S14861, D, 20th Inf.

ROACH, Thomas B. S4154, D, 20th Inf.
ROACH, W. C. S4525, MOO, 41st Inf.
ROACH, W. H. S8723, 22nd Inf.
ROAN, Evan Shelby, S10939, MU, 48th (Voorhies') Inf.
ROARK, Dorothy M. W4250, MA, Roark, Elijah
ROARK, Elvira, W7625, HN, Roark, John Lawson
ROARK, J. L. S13522, HN, 3rd Ky. Mtd. Inf.
ROARK, Joseph, S3291, MR, Lookout Art.
ROARK, Katherine, W8272, HW, Roark, Solomon
ROARK, Martha L. W3359, CT, Roark, Nathan W.
ROARK, Mary Elizabeth, W9843, SN, Roark, Iredell Linville
ROARK, N. W. S6812, U, 21st Va. Cav.
ROARK, Rhoda, W10605, SN, Roark, Wm. B.
ROARK, Virginia Anne, W10358, H, Roark, Wm. Marion
ROBASON, Laura Ragan, W10832, MU, Robason, Mark Anderson
ROBBINS, A. M. S14968, HD, 51st Inf.
ROBBINS, James, S7393, OV, Hamilton's Bn. Cav.
ROBBINS, John R. S13515, WL, 45th Inf.
ROBBINS, John S. S15120, K, 20th N.C. Inf.
ROBBINS, Jordan, S13754, WH, 25th Inf.
ROBBINS, Lansden, S2531, PU, 8th (Dibrell's) Cav.
ROBBINS, Louisa M. W2824, MS, Robbins, John Lee
ROBBINS, M. M. S9624, CH, 31st Inf.
ROBBINS, Mary Ann, W7417, R, Robbins, Newton
ROBBINS, Minerva, W743, PI, Robbins, George W.
ROBBINS, Newton, S1746, R, 39th N.C. Inf.
ROBBINS, S. C. S14714, HN, 5th Inf.
ROBBINS, Sarah Elizabeth, W2220, OV, Robbins, James
ROBBINS, Tempie Ann, W6788, WL, Robbins, John Rea
ROBBS, William T. S16682, MA, Lyon's Brigade
ROBENSON, W. T. S6601, D, Undetermined
ROBERSON, I. R. S8131, CH, 21st Inf.
ROBERSON, James, S12210, MR, 4th (McLemore's) Cav.
ROBERSON, L. B. S5973, H, 43rd Inf.
ROBERSON, Martha L. W2062, ME, Roberson, Calvin C.
ROBERSON, Mary, W9772, WI, Roberson, James L.
ROBERSON, Mattie, W904, L, Roberson, Wm. E.
ROBERSON, Penelope Pocahontas, W7061, MR, Roberson, James
ROBERT, Mary Augusta, W7035, D, Robert, U. M.
ROBERT, U. M. S12213, D, 4th Ga. Inf.
ROBERTS, Addie, W2825, SH, Roberts, James Madison
ROBERTS, Amanda Pettis, W7991, GI, Roberts, Noah
ROBERTS, Arsenath, W1495, GU, Roberts, Philip H.
ROBERTS, B. J. S1467, WE, 31st Inf.
ROBERTS, Benjamin F. S3897, WI, 24th Inf.
ROBERTS, D. G. S11682, HD, 6th Miss. Cav.
ROBERTS, Deering J. S15417, D, 20th Inf.
ROBERTS, E. G. S15335, H, 16th S.C. Inf.
ROBERTS, Eli A. S1782, JO, 37th S.C. Inf.
ROBERTS, Eliza Eda, W3787, CF, Roberts, Zephaniah Cunningham
ROBERTS, Elizabeth, W1126, K, Roberts, Lizard F.
ROBERTS, Elizabeth Ann, W3335, HN, Roberts, Richard Francis
ROBERTS, Elizabeth B. W6362, H, Roberts, Wm. B.
ROBERTS, Eugenia Irvine, W3173, HD, Roberts, Louis Coleman
ROBERTS, F. M. S9676, W, 16th Inf.
ROBERTS, Hugh L. S1788, MR, 1st (Carter's) Cav.
ROBERTS, J. J. S12369, WE, 31st Inf.
ROBERTS, J. P. S11974, SH, 10th Miss. Inf.
ROBERTS, James M. S4148, SU, 19th Inf.
ROBERTS, James M. S12268, CO, 50th Inf.
ROBERTS, James S. S4671, DK, 16th Inf.
ROBERTS, Jane, W2547, H, Roberts, T. J.
ROBERTS, Jefferson, S193, J, Unassinged (Recruiting Service)
ROBERTS, Jerusha L. A. W2217, RU, Roberts, Drury Matthew
ROBERTS, John, S2728, GI, 53rd Inf.
ROBERTS, John, S3286, CO, 29th Inf.
ROBERTS, John, S8336, CY, 48th Inf.
ROBERTS, John C. S3146, LI, 35th Inf.
ROBERTS, John K. S8085, WH, 35th Inf.
ROBERTS, John L. S952, WI, Undetermined

Index to Tennessee Confederate Pension Applications

ROBERTS, Josephine, W5589, RU, Roberts, Luceford Madison
ROBERTS, Julia Ann, W5806, CT, Roberts, Wm. White
ROBERTS, L. F. S3011, K, 25th Inf.
ROBERTS, L. T. S6837, WE, 33rd Inf.
ROBERTS, Latitia Warren, W6626, HN, Roberts, P. D. T.
ROBERTS, Leroy, S10180, T, 23rd S.C. Inf.
ROBERTS, Lewis C. S3748, HD, 19th Cav.
ROBERTS, Louisa America, W8575, D, Roberts, John Kelly
ROBERTS, M. L. S10091, B, 23rd Inf.
ROBERTS, Mack C. S4357, WI, 10th Inf.
ROBERTS, Margaret Ann, W810, SU, Roberts, James
ROBERTS, Margaret Isabella, W494, H, Roberts, Joseph Phillip
ROBERTS, Margaret J. W7446, PU, Roberts, Nathan A.
ROBERTS, Martha Caroline, W5271, HU, Roberts, Wm. Anderson
ROBERTS, Martha Gray, W9474, O, Roberts, Oscar St. Clair
ROBERTS, Mary Ann, W3607, WI, Roberts, Mack C.
ROBERTS, Mary Catherine, W2713, MU, Roberts, Eugene
ROBERTS, Mary Corletta, W9030, W2582, OV, Roberts, John S.
ROBERTS, Nancy Adline, W5644, O, Roberts, Robert Alexander
ROBERTS, Nathan A. S4932, J, 17th Inf.
ROBERTS, Noah, S2169, GI, 3rd Tenn. Vols.
ROBERTS, O. S. S7935, O, 22nd Inf.
ROBERTS, O. W. S7240, SM, Allison's Squadron, Cav. See also Oliver W. Roberts
ROBERTS, Oliver W. S9429, SM, Allison's Squadron, Cav. See also O. W. Roberts
ROBERTS, R. A. S6582, L, 31st Inf.
ROBERTS, Rebecca, W160, MO, Roberts, General J.
ROBERTS, S. F. S5475, B, 4th Inf.
ROBERTS, Sarah Ann, W7744, B, Roberts, S. F.
ROBERTS, Sarah E. W10325, D, Roberts, George D.
ROBERTS, Sarah Emaline, W1328, HD, Roberts, James Thomas
ROBERTS, Sarah Harkem, W9022, SU, Roberts, Wm.
ROBERTS, Sarah Turner, W3687, J, Roberts, Jefferson
ROBERTS, Simon P. S5189, J, 17th Inf.
ROBERTS, T. J. S6891, H, Provost Guard (Miss)
ROBERTS, T. M. S12396, H, 3rd Cav.
ROBERTS, W. S. P. S7346, MO, 2nd N.C. Cav.
ROBERTS, W. T. S6096, SH, McDonald's Co. Mo. Art.
ROBERTS, W. W. S6419, CT, 48th Va. Inf.
ROBERTS, William, S240, HW, 31st Inf.
ROBERTS, William, S5296, DI, 11th Inf.
ROBERTS, William, S5698, SU, 63rd Va. Inf.
ROBERTS, William, S15727, RU, Coleman's Scouts
ROBERTS, William A. S16283, P, 20th Inf.
ROBERTS, William J. S12370, WE, 31st Inf.
ROBERTSON, A. A. S11795, SM, 9th (Bennett's) Cav.
ROBERTSON, A. E. S3611, WL, 8th (Smith's) Cav.
ROBERTSON, Ada, W10176, WL, Robertson, Luke Sanders
ROBERTSON, B. A. S4777, CL, 22nd Va. Inf.
ROBERTSON, Christen. Philips, S4646, H, 24th Ga. Inf.
ROBERTSON, Dialthia Olivia, W4539, D, Robertson, James Franklin
ROBERTSON, Eliza Jane, W1787, CL, Robertson, Richard Tolliver
ROBERTSON, Elizabeth I. W5152, BR, Robertson, Felix Grundy
ROBERTSON, Ella, W7475, SN, Robertson, John Ogden
ROBERTSON, H. J. S6575, MU, Maury's Art.
ROBERTSON, H. J. S9014, LA, 5th Ky. Inf.
ROBERTSON, Holcomb, S10360, CH, 21st (Wilson's) Cav.
ROBERTSON, J. F. S11293, D, 30th Inf.
ROBERTSON, J. M. S15447, HO, 10th (DeMoss') Cav.
ROBERTSON, Jackson Van Buren, S7434, HN, 46th Inf.
ROBERTSON, James W. S4725, SN, 2nd (Robison's) Inf.
ROBERTSON, L. S6399, CL, 2nd Bn. Ala. Art.
ROBERTSON, Luke S. S9439, WL, 7th Inf.
ROBERTSON, Lycurgus, S8793, SH, 17th Bn. Cav.
ROBERTSON, M. L. S14567, H, 30th Inf.
ROBERTSON, Mary, W738, ST, Robertson, G. C.

ROBERTSON, Mary Evaline, W1018, SN, Robertson, James Wesley
ROBERTSON, Mary Jane, W1108, WL, Robertson, Zach
ROBERTSON, Mary Jane, W1654, DI, Robertson, David Gay
ROBERTSON, Nancy Caroline, W767, WE, Robertson, Wm. H. A.
ROBERTSON, Nancy Oscar, W380, WL, Robertson, Alexander Edward
ROBERTSON, Rachel M. W5259, HM, Robertson, Daniel J.
ROBERTSON, Rebecca Jane, W8463, RB, Robertson, Wm. Allen
ROBERTSON, Sallie E. W2346, SH, Robertson, Willis Eli
ROBERTSON, Sarah, W4644, SM, Robertson, David
ROBERTSON, Sarah H. W2258, SH, Robertson, Wm.
ROBERTSON, Thomas Harvey, S7764, R, 1st (Carter's) Cav.
ROBERTSON, Vienna, W1902, LI, Robertson, Loderick
ROBERTSON, W. A. S8979, RB, 49th Inf.
ROBERTSON, W. A. S11098, MA, 14th Inf.
ROBERTSON, W. E. S3462, SH, 9th Miss. Cav.
ROBERTSON, William, C142, MU, Undetermined
ROBERTSON, Z. F. S7559, MU, 9th Cav.
ROBESON, J. L. S15767, MU, 11th (Holman's) Cav.
ROBESON, William, S1324, MC, 5th Cav.
ROBEY, W. H. S4526, O, 38th Va. Inf.
ROBINETTE, E. C. S16427, S16410, HM, 7th Cav.
ROBINETTE, Icy, W10971, HM, Robinette, Elbert Chapman
ROBINETTE, William, S12810, HW, 27th Va. Inf.
ROBINS, W. C. S5165, CH, 52nd Inf.
ROBINS, William H. S16560, BE, 21st (Wilson's) Cav.
ROBINSON, A. L. S4460, SU, 48th Va. Inf.
ROBINSON, Addie R. W6713, R, Robinson, Samuel Patton
ROBINSON, Adeline Losh, W9149, R, Robinson, Thomas J.
ROBINSON, Alexander, S11964, PU, 25th Inf.
ROBINSON, Alice Laden, W3731, HD, Robinson, Wm. D.
ROBINSON, Annie, W6269, G, Robinson, George Washington
ROBINSON, B. P. S13085, D, 20th Inf.
ROBINSON, C. M. S9229, WI, 44th Inf.
ROBINSON, D. G. S4338, MN, 32nd Miss. Inf.
ROBINSON, Eliza Ann, W9885, SH, Robinson, Matthew McClung
ROBINSON, Elizabeth, W9137, B, Robinson, Thomas D.
ROBINSON, Ellen E. W8247, CF, Robinson, J. K. P.
ROBINSON, Frances, W5160, SM, Robinson, Wm. H.
ROBINSON, G. H. S15205, JO, 65th N.C. Cav.
ROBINSON, G. W. S16431, WI, 11th Cav.
ROBINSON, Gerald Taylor, S8910, HN, 2nd (Ashby's) Cav.
ROBINSON, Henry H. S16335, S15107, WI, 41st Miss. Inf.
ROBINSON, Israel, S6764, MT, 49th Inf.
ROBINSON, Ittie, W4464, LA, Robinson, Jessie S.
ROBINSON, J. J. S15785, WH, 25th Inf.
ROBINSON, J. S. S4072, DY, Undetermined
ROBINSON, J. W. S11131, O, 33rd Inf.
ROBINSON, J. Y. S1179, T, 3rd S.C. Inf.
ROBINSON, James, C35, D, Undetermined
ROBINSON, James, S13530, JO, 65th N.C. Inf.
ROBINSON, James K. P. S7259, CF, 17th Inf.
ROBINSON, Jesse S. S8017, LA, 6th N.C. Cav.
ROBINSON, John, S2270, WH, 8th (Dibrell's) Cav.
ROBINSON, John M. S7913, MA, 6th Inf.
ROBINSON, John R. S1524, FR, 30th Ala. Inf.
ROBINSON, Josephine, W1462, T, Robinson, John Wesley
ROBINSON, L. S10861, PO, Thomas' Legion, N.C.
ROBINSON, Laura A. W9753, CO, Robinson, James H.
ROBINSON, Lorinda Elizabeth, W4714, Robinson, Samuel A.
ROBINSON, Lucy, W1849, PU, Robinson, Pryor
ROBINSON, Lucy, W9037, B, Robinson, Robert Jamison
ROBINSON, Lucy A. W5829, WI, Robinson, Richard A.
ROBINSON, Margaret Malindy, W5879, RU, Robinson, Alfred Whitfield
ROBINSON, Martha Alice, W4860, WE, Robinson, Phillip R.

ROBINSON, Martha L. W8696, RO, Robinson, Elbert E.
ROBINSON, Mary Alice, W585, G, Robinson, James Henderson
ROBINSON, Mary Ann, W8707, CF, Robinson, Richard
ROBINSON, Mary Ann, W9150, WI, Robinson, H. H.
ROBINSON, Mary Decatur, W6961, G, Robinson, J. L.
ROBINSON, Mead, W10690, MN, Robinson, Francis C.
ROBINSON, Nancy J. W2178, SN, Robinson, Wm. H.
ROBINSON, R. T. S3530, CL, 2nd Cav.
ROBINSON, Richard Andy, S9221, WI, 12th Inf.
ROBINSON, Robert, S469, 15th Cav.
ROBINSON, S. A. S9317, 55th Inf.
ROBINSON, S. N. C. S9617, SM, 28th Inf.
ROBINSON, S. P. C. S14014, R, 16th Bn. (Neal's) Cav.
ROBINSON, Sallie Caruthers, W1750, D, Robinson, Lemuel A.
ROBINSON, Sarah Elizabeth, W2221, MU, Robinson, Charles Washington
ROBINSON, Thomas Costrell, S12793, S9640, MA, Undetermined
ROBINSON, W. H. S1148, M, 2nd Cav.
ROBINSON, William J. S14591, 55th Inf.
ROBINSON, William O. S1180, T, 3rd S.C. Inf.
ROBINSON, William T. S6078, D, 15th Inf.
ROBISON, J. L. S1804, MN, 13th Inf.
ROBISON, James Babb, S8823, SH, 14th Cav.
ROBISON, John Oscar, C199, Undetermined
ROBISON, Josephine, W9731, SH, Robison, John Wesley
ROBISON, M. A. S4386, GE, 60th N.C. Inf.
ROBISON, M. F. S11875, MA, 18th (Newsom's) Cav.
ROBISON, Maggie McGill, W9645, RU, Robison, James Richard
ROBISON, Rebecca Elizabeth, W1122, LA, Robison, Thomas Theodore
ROBLEY, C. B. S9704, MA, 51st Inf.
ROBLEY, Catherine, W1149, HR, Robley, John B.
ROBLEY, John B. S6241, HR, 14th (Neely's) Cav.
ROBSON, Virginia Clara, W1164, SH, Robson, Benidiel P.

ROCHELL, Amanda Jane, W2589, Rochell, James Jasper
ROCHELL, Cynthia Elizabeth, W9430, LE, Rochell, Marcellus Rex
ROCHELL, Elizabeth H. W10112, SH, Rochell, Rufus Smith
ROCHELL, J. J. S3555, 154th Sr. Regt. Inf.
ROCHELL, John, S9643, D, 3rd Ky. Inf.
ROCHELL, Mollie E. W4064, HI, Rochell, T. W.
RODDY, Albert D. S11197, GU, 24th Inf.
RODDY, B. F. S452, GU, 24th Inf.
RODDY, Holston, S12272, MU, Thomas' Legion, N.C.
RODDY, J. G. S7914, CF, 24th Inf.
RODDY, John T. S4864, R, 19th Inf.
RODDY, M. L. S3213, GU, 44th Inf.
RODDY, Martha Elizabeth, W6147, CF, Roddy, Joe G.
RODELSPERGER, Louise, W4751, D, Rodelsperger, Peter
RODEN, Mary Caroline, W10289, MS, Roden, Thomas J.
RODERICK, Andrew, S12356, MC, 71st N.C. Inf.
RODERICK, Lizzie, W, Some papers with #11183 on film
RODES, Tyree, S15253, D, 6th (Wheeler's) Cav.
RODGERS, Betsey Jane, W5101, MC, Rodgers, Houston
RODGERS, Georgia A. W5929, SH, Rodgers, Patrick
RODGERS, J. N. S1103, HR, 34th Inf.
RODGERS, James, S4056, WH, 84th Inf.
RODGERS, James M. S10228, H, 43rd Inf.
RODGERS, Lydia Ann, W437, Rodgers, George Wesley
RODGERS, Mary Margarette, W2841, F, Rodgers, Wm. J.
RODGERS, Matilda Frances, W911, WE, Rodgers, Robert Curin
RODGERS, Samuel L. S3012, HR, 11th Cav.
RODGERS, William, C175, LK, 31st Inf.
RODGERS, William J. S9862, F, 13th Inf.
ROE, Amanda T. W4937, SH, Roe, Benjamin Franklin
ROE, Emma, W5590, MA, Roe, Robert Allen
ROE, Frances Jane, W9254, W10765, T, Roe, Wm. Joseph
ROE, Gale, S5586, HW, 6th Ala. Inf.
ROE, Mary Lou, W7961, H, Roe, Gale

-297

ROFFE, Mary Ann, W1894, WE, Roffe, Willis Francis
ROGAN, John W. S10501, SU, 12th Bn. (Day's) Cav.
ROGERS, A. F. S13919, MC, 3rd (Lillard's) Mtd. Inf.
ROGERS, Alice, W4533, WL, Rogers, Joseph Anderson
ROGERS, Andrew J. S7441, HU, 24th Bn. Sharpshooters
ROGERS, Artela E. W178, GI, Rogers, Leroy W.
ROGERS, Artimesa E. W3708, HU, Rogers, Andrew Jackson
ROGERS, B. D. S12820, WL, 4th (McLemore's) Cav.
ROGERS, Bettie Ann, W8408, K, Rogers, Elbert Sevier
ROGERS, Church, S1108, PU, 28th Inf.
ROGERS, Clarisa M. W5503, GI, Rogers, John Wiley Jefferson
ROGERS, Dona, W10170, DE, Rogers, James Tate
ROGERS, E. S. S12381, K, 25th Inf.
ROGERS, Eleanora Willis, W4478, D, Rogers, Henry Jordan
ROGERS, Eugenia Leon, W5482, SH, Rogers, Wm. Simeon
ROGERS, G. C. S14049, 20th (Russell's) Cav.
ROGERS, G. F. S6356, FR, 45th Inf.
ROGERS, George H. S7457, 12th Ky. Cav.
ROGERS, George W. S2899, 55th Inf.
ROGERS, H. J. S10071, D, 4th (McLemore's) Cav.
ROGERS, H. N. S13712, H, 31st Inf.
ROGERS, I. C. S11982, SH, 48th (Nixon's) Inf.
ROGERS, J. B. S15742, MS, 45th Inf.
ROGERS, J. C. S3377, GI, 32nd Inf.
ROGERS, J. C. S11843, LA, 28th Miss. Cav.
ROGERS, J. M. S5914, MR, 35th Inf.
ROGERS, J. M. S9131, H, 1st Ga. Inf.
ROGERS, J. M. S12682, S16187, SQ, 4th (McLemore's) Cav.
ROGERS, J. R. S4295, SU, 60th Inf.
ROGERS, J. S. S8711, FR, 4th Inf.
ROGERS, J. W. S5372, T, 9th Bn. Cav.
ROGERS, J. W. S6880, HR, 9th Inf.
ROGERS, J. W. J. S9155, GI, 9th Ala. Cav.
ROGERS, James, S8091, HR, 42nd Inf.
ROGERS, James W. S16666, HN, 2nd Ky. Cav.
ROGERS, James Walter, S8980, L, 15th Cav.
ROGERS, Jennie, W1292, SH, Rogers, James Harvey
ROGERS, John, S10672, MR, 36th Ga. Inf.
ROGERS, John Alexander, S2005, WL, 38th Inf.
ROGERS, John G. S15002, MT, 11th Cav.
ROGERS, John T. S10847, MT, 14th Inf.
ROGERS, Jonathan K. S4945, BR, 29th N.C. Inf.
ROGERS, Josiah, S11414, CF, 35th Inf.
ROGERS, L. A. S7538, RU, 37th Inf.
ROGERS, Larkin A. S3829, FR, 1st (Turney's) Inf.
ROGERS, Lucinda, W3920, W1529, HR, Rogers, Samuel Benton
ROGERS, Lucy Reeney, W10151, CL, Rogers, Wm. Franklin
ROGERS, Maggie M. W9901, MS, Rogers, Charles A.
ROGERS, Margaret Owen, W2210, FR, Rogers, J. F.
ROGERS, Martha E. W6135, SH, Rogers, Wm. H.
ROGERS, Martha Lucindy, W7392, H, Rogers, J. M.
ROGERS, Mary Hill, W9888, CF, Rogers, Larkin Alexander
ROGERS, Mary Kirby, W8723, WL, Rogers, Benjamin Duggan
ROGERS, Mary L. W1529, W3920, HR, Rogers, Samuel Benton
ROGERS, Mary Martha, W9883, SH, Rogers, Benjamin Barton
ROGERS, Mary Patterson, W28, B, Rogers, Van Burin
ROGERS, Mattie A. W3163, RU, Rogers, Love Alexander
ROGERS, Nancy, W3489, MR, Rogers, Wm.
ROGERS, Nancy Arminda, W4366, MN, Rogers, Levi Brackstone
ROGERS, Pamelia F. W5298, FR, Rogers, George F.
ROGERS, R. E. S13207, F, 7th (Duckworth's) Cav.
ROGERS, Rachel Fannie, W3021, H, Rogers, James Madison
ROGERS, Rosina D. W381, WL, Rogers, John Alexander
ROGERS, S. B. M. S5052, MR, 4th Inf.
ROGERS, Sarah Elizabeth, W6037, HR, Rogers, John Nichol
ROGERS, Sarah Elizabeth, W11136, SN, Rogers, Thomas Jefferson

ROGERS, Sarah Louise, W4605, Rogers, George H.
ROGERS, Susan, W1930, SU, Rogers, James H.
ROGERS, Thursa, W9863, SQ, Rogers, James M.
ROGERS, W. A. S16571, T, 48th Inf.
ROGERS, W. H. H. S5297, H, 9th Ga. Inf.
ROGERS, W. S. sr. S12373, SH, 6th (Wheeler's) Cav.
ROGERS, William, S2870, MR, 8th (Dibrell's) Cav.
ROGERS, William, S16422, S6243, FR, 1st (Turney's) Inf.
ROGERS, William F. S14913, CL, 37th Inf.
ROGERS, William J. S6303, MC, 16th N.C. Inf.
ROGERS, William S. S14471, MR, 3rd Confederate Cav.
ROLAND, John D. S4717, LI, 2nd (Ashby's) Cav.
ROLAND, Margaret, W3930, CH, Roland, Jacob Henry
ROLAND, Martha Jane, W8941, W, Roland, John F.
ROLLER, Elizabeth C. W547, SU, Roller, Noah
ROLLER, G. W. S7654, SU, 19th Inf.
ROLLER, Jacob, S16617, SU, 59th Inf.
ROLLER, Noah, S6510, SU, 19th Inf.
ROLLINGS, Robert S. S1882, B, 17th Inf.
ROLLINS, Aggie, W4655, SM, Rollins, Ammon
ROLLINS, Arrah, W6193, MA, Rollins, T.
ROLLINS, Daniel, S2265, BL, 14th (Neely's) Cav.
ROLLINS, J. F. S5709, CO, 25th N.C. Inf.
ROLLINS, Jo Ann, W7158, B, Rollins, Robert S.
ROLLINS, Lucinda Minerva, W5648, CO, Rollins, John Franklin
ROLLINS, T. S5695, MA, 18th (Newsom's) Cav.
ROLLS, Lucy Edith, W5386, ST, Rolls, Robert
ROLLS, Martha, W9411, HN, Rolls, Frank Mann
ROLLS, Mary Eliza, W1307, GI, Rolls, Joseph Henry
ROMANS, Soloman, S5685, W, 35th Inf.
ROMINES, Isaac, S5124, OV, 8th (Dibrell's) Cav.
ROMINES, Noah, S16378, WA, 39th Regt. Mtd. Inf.
RONE, Malissa H. W643, O, Rone, John
ROOK, Maggie Elizabeth, W5782, D, Rook, Thomas Campbell

ROOKER, Edward T. S5703, MA, 14th (Neely's) Cav.
ROOKER, James, S8893, OV, 25th Inf.
ROOKER, John W. S250, RB, 11th Inf.
ROOKER, Lizzie Collier, W10114, SN, Rooker, John W.
ROPER, Harvey Albert, S3728, SU, 1st N.C. Inf.
ROPER, Sarah, W4845, SU, Roper, Harvy A.
ROPER, Sarah Caroline, W10510, O, Roper, Albert
ROPP, Ann Catherine, W8461, W10711, K, Ropp, Wm. H.
ROSCOE, Annie Margaret, W10116, D, Roscoe, James Williamson
ROSE, A. B. S14147, SH, 21st (Wilson's) Cav.
ROSE, Darcus C. W3095, T, Rose, Wm. Amos
ROSE, J. M. S6141, BO, 1st N.C. Cav.
ROSE, J. M. A. S14697, H, 35th Inf.
ROSE, James, S11322, MT, 7th Ark. Inf.
ROSE, John Perry, S3076, O, Napier's Bn. Cav.
ROSE, John Wesley, S10601, R, 1st Cav.
ROSE, Mariah, W1665, GR, Rose, Thomas W.
ROSE, Martha Jane, W10431, HR, Rose, W. E.
ROSE, Mary Elizabeth, W8036, SH, Rose, Wm. Washington
ROSE, Nancy Charlotte, W10471, SH, Rose, Robert David
ROSE, Samuel B. S8614, 50th Inf.
ROSE, Samuel S. S4160, CL, 5th Va. Militia
ROSE, Susan Laura, W3741, D, Rose, Pierce H.
ROSE, William A. S3017, T, 12th S.C. Inf.
ROSENBALM, A. J. S8682, FE, Kain's Co. Art.
ROSENBALM, D. H. S9035, U, 37th Inf.
ROSENBAUM, Nancy, W1842, FE, Rosenbaum, Andrew Jackson
ROSINBALM, Martha, W746, CL, Rosinbalm, Wm. Houston
ROSS, Addie Cornelia, W6951, RU, Ross, Oscar
ROSS, Alexander, S3378, SC, 44th Va. Inf.
ROSS, America Louiza, W5992, HO, Ross, Robert Loyed
ROSS, Annie Edwards, W11141, RU, Ross, Frank Emanuel
ROSS, Charles M. S5682, 22nd Inf.
ROSS, D. R. S5098, WA, 12th Bn. Cav.
ROSS, Eliza E. W8119, GI, Ross, J. M.
ROSS, F. M. S5550, F, 7th (Duckworth's) Cav.
ROSS, F. M. S14332, CE, Davis' Legion, Ala. Cav.
ROSS, Frank E. S8867, RU, 32nd Ala. Inf.
ROSS, G. M. D. S7668, WE, 19th & 20th (Consol.) Cav.

ROSS, J. M. S8740, GI, 1st Cav.
ROSS, John A. S5373, GE, 12th Bn. Cav.
ROSS, John Miles, S1982, T, 19th Miss. Inf.
ROSS, Lucy Ann, W8528, Ross, Charles M.
ROSS, Lucy Anna, W7196, CE, Ross, Francis Marion
ROSS, Madison, S3415, DK, 12th Bn. Ga. Lt. Art.
ROSS, Martha Jane, W4512, WA, Ross, David Rankin
ROSS, Oma, W8554, WE, Ross, G. M. D.
ROSS, Oscar, S14517, RU, 45th Inf.
ROSS, R. L. S6266, HO, 50th Inf.
ROSS, Sarah, W2873, MN, Ross, Jesse
ROSS, W. H. S5190, D, 15th Cav.
ROSS, Wiliam T. S5413, SU, 34th Va. Cav.
ROSSOM, Louise Frances, W3688, MT, Rossom, George Thomas
ROSSON, Ann Elizabeth, W5714, MT, Rosson, Wm. Richard
ROSSON, C. T. S14415, F, 3rd Va. Inf.
ROSSON, Michael, S3124, G, 55th Inf.
ROSWELL, Eliza Ann, W6975, BE, Roswell, Thomas Lewis
ROTHERACK, George M. S15602, SH, 11th (Holman's) Cav.
ROTHROCK, Garnet Matilda, W2717, D, Rothrock, Robert Gordon
ROTHROCK, Tennie G. W11050, SH, Rothrock, John Thomas
ROULHAC, J. H. S10431, O, 1st Ky. Inf.
ROUNDTREE, John A. S16678, D, 3rd (Clack's) Inf.
ROUNTREE, Alabama L. W3838, D, Rountree, John A.
ROUSE, William, S5501, WA, 48th Va. Inf.
ROUTIN, James W. S16027, WL, 4th (McLemore's) Cav.
ROUTT, Mary Lou, W8511, LI, Routt, James R.
ROWAN, E. S. S6652, W, 16th Inf.
ROWAN, J. H. S9342, MA, 25th Va. Inf.
ROWAN, Lucy, W2579, W, Rowan, Eldridge Standwick
ROWAN, Lucy Elma, W5754, MA, Rowan, James Harvey
ROWAN, Sarah E. W4157, MO, Rowan, Frank M.
ROWAN, William, S1015, HW, Ramsey's Battery, Lt. Art.
ROWE, A. W. S3359, WL, Sterling's Co. Hvy. Art.

ROWE, Mollie A. W7834, FR, Rowe, Stephen D.
ROWE, S. D. S12144, FR, 3rd Tex. Cav.
ROWE, Will, C249, HN, 2nd Ky. Cav.
ROWE, Wm. Henry Harrison, S8226, U, Winston's Battery, Art.
ROWELL, M. N. S13203, LI, 41st Inf.
ROWELL, S. B. S9225, SH, 42nd Inf.
ROWELL, Thurza Ward, W5699, SH, Rowell, Wm. Augustus
ROWLAND, Amanda H. W2149, W2244, WL, Rowland, David
ROWLAND, George McMain, S13156, CC, 31st Inf.
ROWLAND, H. G. S8071, G, 7th Ky. Inf.
ROWLAND, James L. S12741, MT, 50th Inf.
ROWLAND, Marina Olivia, W10453, DK, Rowland, David
ROWLAND, Martha, W214, W, Rowland, Wm. Carroll
ROWLAND, Nathan S. S7423, MT, 49th Inf.
ROWLAND, Rebecca C. See Rebecca C. Ogles
ROWLAND, William L. S14554, CH, 6th N.C. Cav.
ROWLETT, J. W. S2442, RU, 45th Inf.
ROWLETT, Marthy E. W4993, SH, Rowlett, John W.
ROWSEY, George Washington, S13673, MN, 18th Miss. Cav.
ROWSEY, Martha E. W9623, MN, Rowsey, George Washington
ROY, Carrie, W5197, MC, Roy, Wm.
ROY, Frances Elizabeth, W4398, L, Roy, Thomas Alexander
ROY, John T. S14369, HY, 15th N.C. Inf.
ROY, Margaret Ellen, W10672, L, Roy, Samuel Martin
ROY, S. M. S16662, L, 20th (Nixon's) Cav.
ROY, William, S5045, MC, 3rd (Clack's) Inf.
ROYAL, W. D. S6511, CT, 28th N.C. Inf.
ROYLE, Sarah Jane, W2562, HM, Royle, James
ROYSTER, Charles, S2582, MS, 17th Inf.
ROYSTER, T. E. S14672, SM, 7th Inf.
ROYSTON, James, S6287, SU, 61st Mtd. Inf.
ROZELL, Ashley B. S2503, LI, 49th Ala. Inf.
ROZELL, R. B. S7524, RB, 1st (Feild's) Inf.
RUCKER, Alice Wilson, W1101, WI, Rucker, Elonre D. A.
RUCKER, Angie L. W3825, RU, Rucker, John E.

Index to Tennessee Confederate Pension Applications

RUCKER, Barbara Alvira, W9035, O, Rucker, J. M.
RUCKER, Elizabeth Smith, W9224, LI, Rucker, Wm. Read
RUCKER, H. P. S3864, O, 12th Ky. Cav.
RUCKER, J. E. S14858, D, 11th (Holman's) Cav.
RUCKER, John C. S8210, K, 28th Va. Inf.
RUCKER, Loucinda Angie, W10436, CA, Rucker, John E.
RUCKER, Missouri Ann, W361, WL, Rucker, Sterling Brown
RUCKER, Rachal A. W794, WI, Rucker, Wm. P.
RUCKER, S. B. S555, WL, 7th Inf.
RUCKER, W. T. S13146, RU, 2nd (Robison's) Inf.
RUCKER, William, C111, RU, 2nd Inf.
RUDD, E. L. S3160, R, 1st (Carter's) Cav.
RUDD, Florence, W7201, D, Rudd, Wm. H.
RUDD, Hattie, W4544, H, Rudd, Alexander Montgomery
RUDDER, D. J. S12854, DY, 4th Inf.
RUDOLPH, Vida W. W6569, SH, Rudolph, John Wesley
RUFF, Eliza, W3530, CO, Ruff, Silas J.
RUFFIN, Joel Etheldred, S3328, RB, 50th Inf.
RUFFIN, Thomas D. S8986, DY, 15th Ky. Inf.
RUMAGE, Mollie, W9628, O, Rumage, James
RUMFELT, W. H. S14979, ST, 50th Inf.
RUNDLE, Jonathan, S12624, D, 36th Va. Inf.
RUNDLE, Margaret J. W5764, D, Rundle, Jonathan Theodore
RUNION, J. D. S9977, G, 48th (Voorhies') Inf.
RUNION, J. S. S5028, PO, 62nd Inf.
RUNIONS, Joseph, S6310, BR, 3rd Inf.
RUNIONS, Rachel, W2192, BR, Runions, Joseph
RUNNELLS, A. P. S5029, CF, 45th Inf.
RUNYAN, John Claiborne, S9618, ME, 5th Cav.
RUSH, A. E. S9165, HE, 14th N.C. Inf.
RUSH, Rose, W7310, SU, Rush, Thomas Campbell
RUSH, Sarah E. W6108, G, Rush, Abner
RUSH, Thomas Campbell, S4313, S5443, SU, 60th Ala. Inf.
RUSHING, A. J. S6958, HO, 50th Inf.
RUSHING, Abel, S8632, MA, 6th Inf.
RUSHING, G. B. D. S1917, DE, 28th Tex. Cav.
RUSHING, J. P. S15108, ST, 50th Inf.
RUSHING, J. P. H. S11313, ST, 1st Art.

RUSHING, Mary Eliza, W6128, MA, Rushing, Abel
RUSHING, Sarah Frances, W2218, HN, Rushing, George Hussa
RUSHING, Sue M. W9968, HN, Rushing, John M.
RUSHING, Tennessee B. W4615, D, Rushing, John R.
RUSHING, W. A. S15769, WL, 4th (McLemore's) Cav.
RUSHING, W. H. S2040, HO, 11th Inf.
RUSHTON, Harriett Lucindia, W2523, MU, Rushton, George Washington
RUSSAN, Minnie M. W, Some papers with #11183 on film
RUSSE, L. H. S14838, D, Forrest's Escort, Cav.
RUSSEL, D. L. S3329, GE, Lynch's Battery, Lt. Art.
RUSSELL, Annie, W, Some papers with #11183 on film
RUSSELL, Berry Allen, S5572, G, 20th Inf.
RUSSELL, Ed R. S3780, K, McClung's Co. Lt. Art.
RUSSELL, Elizabeth, W2173, BR, Russell, Wm. H.
RUSSELL, Elizabeth Catherine, W3780, ME, Russell, Felix Grundy
RUSSELL, Frances, W6130, SN, Russell, W. S.
RUSSELL, Frank, C17, WI, Forrest's Escort, Cav.
RUSSELL, George W. S7228, RU, 4th (McLemore's) Cav.
RUSSELL, Hardin T. S1376, RU, 20th Inf.
RUSSELL, Isaac, S13333, S15880, MC, 59th Inf.
RUSSELL, J. C. S13506, HM, 61st Inf.
RUSSELL, J. M. S12683, MU, 9th Bn. (Gantt's) Cav.
RUSSELL, J. T. S306, BR, 5th Cav.
RUSSELL, J. W. S5385, GI, 53rd Inf.
RUSSELL, John, S14065, FR, 19th Inf.
RUSSELL, John H. S6784, LI, 8th Inf.
RUSSELL, John Richard, S16545, CT, 19th Inf.
RUSSELL, John W. S14136, RO, 64th Va. Cav.
RUSSELL, Landers, S13327, CL, 29th Inf.
RUSSELL, Larkin W. S12350, D, 28th Inf.
RUSSELL, Louisa Adeline, W1617, WE, Russell, Wm. Howard
RUSSELL, Maggie Beck, W7213, RO, Russell, J. W.
RUSSELL, Margaret E. W68, B, Russell, James Calloway

-301

RUSSELL, Martha Jane, W4710, B, Russell, Wm. F.
RUSSELL, Martha Rebecca, W6849, PU, Russell, Wm. Newton
RUSSELL, Martha Welburn, W2291, MU, Russell, George Whitfield
RUSSELL, Mary Ann, W6976, B, Russell, Elijah Allen
RUSSELL, Mary Caroline, W3321, W, Russell, Wm. Harry
RUSSELL, Mary Jane, W9808, K, Russell, Samuel Columbus
RUSSELL, Mary Kellow, W1426, G, Russell, Berry Allen
RUSSELL, Mary Sophronia, W8800, ST, Russell, Wm. Gabriel
RUSSELL, Mattie, W10206, HU, Russell, Joab A.
RUSSELL, Miranda M. W3118, HR, Russell, Stephen H.
RUSSELL, Nancy Y. W3826, WH, Russell, Wm. Mansfield
RUSSELL, Peter, C265, LE, Undetermined
RUSSELL, S. C. S800, M, 28th Inf.
RUSSELL, S. C. S3439, GE, 31st Inf.
RUSSELL, S. F. S10324, G, 7th Ky. Cav.
RUSSELL, S. H. S8072, HR, 19th & 20th (Consol.) Cav.
RUSSELL, Susie, W11175, D?, Russell, L. W.
RUSSELL, Tabitah, W488, D, Russell, Hardin Thompson
RUSSELL, Virginia Diehl, W10972, CT, Russell, John Richard
RUSSELL, W. F. S3743, B, 17th Inf.
RUSSELL, W. H. S2480, BR, 62nd Inf.
RUSSELL, W. H. S3843, W, 16th Inf.
RUSSELL, W. N. S2286, W, 16th Inf.
RUSSELL, W. N. S13901, MC, 43rd Inf.
RUSSELL, W. R. S9933, LO, 19th Inf.
RUSSELL, William, S1624, RU, 24th Inf.
RUSSELL, William Gabriel, S12821, MT, 14th Inf.
RUSSELL, William S. S5891, M, 24th Inf.
RUSSWORN, Florence Wetmore, W1812, D, Russworn, Thos. Edwd. Sumner
RUST, Amanda Ellen, W6462, G, Rust, John Wesley
RUST, George E. S1090, O, 12th Inf.
RUST, John W. S10079, G, 19th (Biffle's) Cav.
RUST, L. F. W931, G, Rust, George M.
RUST, Maria Josephine, W1895, W3052, RB, Rust, Wm. Henry

RUST, S. A. S10366, O, 8th (Smith's) Cav.
RUSTON, Joseph, S200, GE, 61st Inf.
RUTH, A. D. S8744, FR, 3rd Bn. Miss. Cav.
RUTH, Rebecca, W5902, H, Ruth, Robert
RUTH, Robert, S13701, MR, 16th Ga. Inf.
RUTHERFORD, Bettie Moore, W9609, SN, Rutherford, Benjamin O.
RUTHERFORD, Felix, S10729, MA, 19th (Biffle's) Cav.
RUTHERFORD, J. F. S11364, MO, 5th Cav.
RUTHERFORD, J. J. S7771, K, 63rd Inf.
RUTHERFORD, J. J. S15438, HA, 50th Va. Inf.
RUTHERFORD, Joseph R. S13556, SU, 59th Inf.
RUTHERFORD, Martha Jane, W5802, SH, Rutherford, Wm. Mumford
RUTHERFORD, Mary Ann, W6249, SU, Rutherford, Ryburn
RUTHERFORD, Melinda Jane, W7024, MO, Rutherford, John Freeland
RUTHERFORD, Phemy, W3689, BE, Rutherford, Robert M.
RUTHERFORD, W. G. S2871, GI, 3rd Ala. Cav.
RUTLAND, James A. S10232, WL, 20th Inf.
RUTLEDGE, Claudia Catherine, W10473, H, Rutledge, Wm. Watkins
RUTLEDGE, E. B. S12211, SN, 9th Cav.
RUTLEDGE, Francis Wager, W1143, GI, Rutledge, Wm. Wallace
RUTLEDGE, James, S5978, V, 25th Inf.
RUTLEDGE, Lee, S9531, MS, 21st Cav.
RUTLEDGE, Louisa, W4872, SN, Rutledge, Elijah Bird
RUTLEDGE, Lucy, W3038, SU, Rutledge, Wade P.
RUTLEDGE, Lucy, W3094, RU, Rutledge, Pleasant R.
RUTLEDGE, Mary Jane, W1874, HM, Rutledge, Richard Keene
RUTLEDGE, Mary Matilda, W6768, K, Rutledge, Samuel Crawford
RUTLEDGE, Mathew, S11299, S13507, SH, 1st Ala. Miss. & Tenn. Inf.
RUTLEDGE, Pleasant R. S2555, RU, 1st Inf.
RUTLEDGE, R. J. S11136, M, 7th Inf.
RUTLEDGE, Richard H. S1298, RU, 18th Inf.
RUTLEDGE, Robert J. S5030, HW, 12th Bn. Cav.
RUTLEDGE, Sallie, W1145, SN, Rutledge, James W.

RUTLEDGE, Samuel C. S10772, K, 12th Bn. (Day's) Cav.
RUTLEDGE, W. D. S1795, CT, 26th Inf.
RUTLEDGE, William G. S2478, HM, Burrough's Co. Lt. Art.
RYALL, Elvira Lozena, W10372, B, Ryall, Albert Princis
RYALS, Catherine Susanna, W530, HE, Ryals, Wm. Noah
RYALS, Joseph Hubbard, S7286, HE, 1st (Feild's) Inf.
RYAN, Giles H. S6298, R, 26th Inf.
RYAN, H. W. S10594, K, 1st Lt. Art.
RYAN, J. M. S11300, U, 61st Inf.
RYBURN, J. P. S. S1231, U, 4th Inf.
RYBURN, S. W. S16425, SU, Washington Co. Reserves
RYE, Alexander B. S1897, MT, 14th Inf.
RYE, Mary Ann, W7185, MT, Rye, A. B.
RYE, Thomas, S8438, HO, 11th Inf.
RYMER, David, S911, PO, 3rd Inf.
RYMER, David W. S4350, BR, 3rd Inf.
RYMER, J. H. S8967, BR, 3rd Inf.
RYMER, Lodaska, W6449, PO, Rymer, John Alexander
RYMER, Rose Ann, W1896, BR, Rymer, James Henry
RYNES, W. M. S10137, MO, 62nd Inf.
RYON, G. H. S743, R, 26th Inf.
SACRA, H. S. S12440, O, 22nd (Barteau's) Cav.
SADLER, Absolum, S12802, SH, McDonald's Bn. Cav.
SADLER, Alice Cath. Patton, W4553, SH, Sadler, Samuel Orlando
SADLER, Augustus, S13703, SH, 2nd Miss. Cav.
SADLER, E. B. S13157, HN, 9th (Ward's) Cav.
SADLER, Edna Hayden, W4687, SH, Sadler, Abraham
SADLER, Ella, W11123, D, Sadler, James Robert
SADLER, Ellen, W5329, SN, Sadler, Henry T.
SADLER, H. T. S434, RB, 30th Inf.
SADLER, J. B. S12908, F, 7th Cav.
SADLER, J. R. S16050, D, 22nd (Barteau's) Cav.
SADLER, Mabel Murtaugh, W10800, SH, Sadler, Wm. Rose
SADLER, Mary A. W5234, HN, Sadler, E. B.
SADLER, Mary Lizzie, W7994, RB, Sadler, W. I.

SADLER, Mary T. W3546, SH, Sadler, Drury
SADLER, W. I. S13923, RB, 8th Ky. Cav.
SADLER, W. R. S15302, SH, 9th Miss. Cav.
SADLER, William, S3795, D, 1st Cav.
SAFLEY, Ramolina, W5465, W, Safley, Robert M.
SAFLEY, Robert M. S1800, W, 16th Inf.
SAGELY, B. L. S12834, CF, 8th (Smith's) Cav.
SAGELY, B. L. S16350, CF, 4th (Baxter's) Cav.
SAILOR, J. J. S11386, SH, 28th Ga. Inf.
SAIN, Andrew, S8987, HR, 14th Cav.
SAIN, Calvin, S12932, HR, 14th Cav.
SAIN, James C. S7247, CF, 6th (Wheeler's) Cav.
SAINE, J. A. S11429, G, 12th Inf.
SAINE, Rebecca Ann, W5220, CF, Saine, Andrew Jackson
SALE, G. B. S16230, T, 7th Cav.
SALTS, William, S2664, WA, 16th Ga. Cav.
SALYER, Peter, S9588, ST, 3rd Ky. Mtd. Inf.
SAMPLES, James, S3593, BR, 29th Inf.
SAMPLES, Nancy E. W3451, MO, Samples, Samuel H.
SAMPLES, Samuel Henry, S3984, MO, 37th Inf.
SAMPLES, Sarah H. W1650, MO, Samples, Wm. H.
SAMPLEY, George W. S3452, MR, 6th Ga. Inf.
SAMPSON, Malissa, W6062, WA, Sampson, Wm. Ward
SAMPSON, Mary Elizabeth, W6767, CL, Sampson, Wm. Henry
SAMPSON, Orville P. S11417, SM, Allison's Squadron, Cav.
SAMPSON, Rebecca, W8066, SM, Sampson, Titus
SAMPSON, Titus, S15251, SM, 44th Inf.
SAMPSON, W. H. S9854, CL, 64th Va. Inf.
SAMS, E. B. S13245, HM, 5th N.C. Cav.
SAMS, Elzira, W8023, SU, Sams, O. E.
SAMS, G. W. S6008, SU, 63rd Inf.
SAMS, J. R. S9300, HM, 29th Inf.
SAMS, Martha, W6178, SU, Sams, G. W.
SAMS, Obediah, S3363, WA, 59th Inf.
SAMS, Owen E. S4555, CT, 4th Cav.
SAMS, Polina, W6551, HM, Sams, J. R.
SAMS, Susan, W350, SU, Sams, Wilson VanBuren
SAMSEL, Joseph, S13173, GR, Lynch's Battery, Lt. Art.
SAMSEL, Sarah Alice, W8013, GR, Samsel, Joseph W.

SAMUEL, George W. S15082, D, 3rd Ky. Cav.
SAMUEL, Sarah Ann Green, W5896, GI, Samuel, Wm. James
SAMUEL, W. J. S2213, GI, 1st (Feild's) Inf.
SAMUELS, Charles G. S15702, MC, 30th Ala. Inf.
SAMUELS, Elizabeth C. W3430, SH, Samuels, John P.
SANDEFER, Malissa Jane, W2968, WE, Sandefer, Wm. Monroe
SANDEFER, W. M. S6822, WE, 61st N.C. Inf.
SANDEFUR, Alice E. W4509, CL, Sandefur, Samuel
SANDEFUR, S. M. S8261, CL, Saltville Va. Art.
SANDERLIN, Thomas Ezekiel, S13946, SH, 16th (Logwood's) Cav.
SANDERS, A. H. S3972, FR, 1st (Turney's) Inf.
SANDERS, A. H. S16071, SU, Home Guards
SANDERS, Amanda, W8018, L, Sanders, Isham Russell
SANDERS, Andrew F. S6655, RU, 18th Inf.
SANDERS, Annie, W10949, D, Sanders, Thomas Crutchfield
SANDERS, Benjamin F. S60, TR, 2nd Inf.
SANDERS, Cattie M. W7480, MN, Sanders, John Wesley
SANDERS, Cordelia, W4302, F, Sanders, John W.
SANDERS, D. J. S14239, RU, 45th Inf.
SANDERS, D. M. S10880, SH, 10th Miss. Inf.
SANDERS, D. S. S13238, HU, 10th Cav.
SANDERS, Ebbie, W6918, O, Sanders, Wm. Harrison
SANDERS, Elizabeth, W3132, FR, Sanders, Jacob Bradley
SANDERS, Fannie J. W7124, RU, Sanders, Drury J.
SANDERS, Fannie Martin, W8516, FR, Sanders, John Turner
SANDERS, Febie H. W2081, HI, Sanders, Francis M.
SANDERS, G. M. S1041, CE, 16th Cav.
SANDERS, George Henry, S16627, L, 3rd (Forrest's) Cav.
SANDERS, George W. S2171, MOO, 1st Inf.
SANDERS, H. A. S5298, MN, 16th Cav.
SANDERS, Harmon Dee, S11920, MU, 19th (Biffle's) Cav.
SANDERS, Henry L. S6440, GI, 1st (Feild's) Inf.
SANDERS, I. N. S11041, WL, 18th Inf.

SANDERS, Isom Russell, S10248, DY, 7th Ala. Cav.
SANDERS, J. B. S5332, FR, 4th Inf.
SANDERS, J. G. S16399, B, 1st Inf.
SANDERS, J. H. S10905, SU, 60th Inf.
SANDERS, J. L. S13086, G, 31st Inf.
SANDERS, J. M. S14128, HU, 10th (DeMoss') Cav.
SANDERS, J. P. S6233, D, 20th Inf.
SANDERS, J. S. S10307, D, 7th Inf.
SANDERS, J. W. S8524, MN, 45th Inf.
SANDERS, Jackson, S11752, GU, 9th Bn. (Gantt's) Cav.
SANDERS, James A. S6012, B, 1st (Turney's) Inf.
SANDERS, James Andrew, S12161, MU, 1st (Feild's) Inf.
SANDERS, James E. S1778, WE, 5th Inf.
SANDERS, James L. S8720, LI, 45th Inf.
SANDERS, James Munroe, S16138, LI, 3rd Cav.
SANDERS, James P. S14125, K, 12th Bn. (Day's) Cav.
SANDERS, James S. S13615, GU, 44th Inf.
SANDERS, John J. S3806, DI, 49th Inf.
SANDERS, John R. S10175, GU, 44th Inf.
SANDERS, John S. S1710, SH, 34th Miss. Inf.
SANDERS, John T. S11203, FR, 17th Inf.
SANDERS, John W. S10346, F, 9th Inf.
SANDERS, L. J. S11995, RB, 30th Inf.
SANDERS, Lillie Ford, W10866, WL, Sanders, Daniel
SANDERS, Lucinder C. W8350, RB, Sanders, L. J.
SANDERS, M. L. W874, WI, Sanders, Robert Harrison
SANDERS, Margaret Ann, W204, HN, Sanders, Thomas Wheeler
SANDERS, Margaret Ann, W978, D, Sanders, Absalom Black
SANDERS, Martha Ann, W9908, RU, Sanders, Thomas Marion
SANDERS, Martha Elizabeth, W9325, O, Sanders, W. T.
SANDERS, Martha Jane, W7053, RU, Sanders, Leonard Newton
SANDERS, Mary, W7277, GU, Sanders, Jackson
SANDERS, Mary Ann, W3388, MN, Sanders, Henry Allen
SANDERS, Mary E. W7231, FR, Sanders, Alexander H.

Index to Tennessee Confederate Pension Applications

SANDERS, Mary Frances, W7327, MU, Sanders, James Andrew
SANDERS, Milton P. S8583, GU, 27th Bn. Cav.
SANDERS, Mollie E. W6532, WA, Sanders, Richard
SANDERS, Nancy Adline, W10107, G, Sanders, J. L.
SANDERS, Nannie E. W5927, D, Sanders, Andrew Jackson
SANDERS, Newton J. S11939, HE, 47th Inf.
SANDERS, Norvell D. S3129, SN, 18th Miss. Inf.
SANDERS, Parham L. S8366, D, Baxter's Co. Lt. Art.
SANDERS, R. A. S1244, D, 45th Inf.
SANDERS, Rachel, W1622, W, Sanders, Wm.
SANDERS, Rhoda Ellen, W8026, K, Sanders, James Preston
SANDERS, Richard, S14360, WA, 21st Va. Cav.
SANDERS, S. H. S11358, SH, 9th Inf.
SANDERS, Sarah Elizabeth, W9152, W9068, B, Sanders, James Anderson
SANDERS, Sarah Margarette, W8604, SU, Sanders, Abraham Henry
SANDERS, Sarah T. W1491, GI, Sanders, Henry Littleton
SANDERS, Sue Elizabeth, W5858, MU, Sanders, Harmon D.
SANDERS, T. D. S13565, G, 47th Inf.
SANDERS, T. F. S15337, MA, 21st (Wilson's) Cav.
SANDERS, T. J. S16558, SH, 27th Miss. Inf.
SANDERS, Thomas Crutchfield, S8194, D, 8th (Smith's) Cav.
SANDERS, Tillie Scott, W10195, LI, Sanders, David Monroe
SANDERS, Tynsa, W6348, Sanders, John M.
SANDERS, Virginia F. W4554, TR, Sanders, Pleasant
SANDERS, W. H. S13970, O, 14th N.C. Inf.
SANDERS, W. M. S6402, S10080, HI, 24th Inf.
SANDERS, William, S8649, W, 11th Cav.
SANDERS, William T. S9610, G, 12th Inf.
SANDIDGE, Henry C. S584, HW, 2nd Ky. Bn.
SANDIDGE, M. P. S6258, SH, 22nd Inf.
SANDIDGE, Perry R. S7581, HW, 2nd Ky. Cav.
SANDIDGE, Sarah Rebecca, W5791, HW, Sandidge, Henry Clay
SANDLIN, I. M. S3259, DK, 7th Inf.
SANDLIN, John F. S10818, LI, 8th Inf.
SANDLIN, Mary J. W3905, DK, Sandlin, Isaac M.
SANDLING, Annie G. W8331, G, Sandling, John H.
SANDLING, John H. S14851, G, 22nd (Barteau's) Cav.
SANDRIDGE, F. M. S709, LI, 17th Inf.
SANFORD, G. W. S15425, S14226, TR, 22nd (Barteau's) Cav.
SANFORD, J. R. S14303, T, 51st Inf.
SANFORD, Joseph L. S1101, CO, 11th N.C. Inf.
SANFORD, Marshall A. S1036, HN, 5th Inf.
SANFORD, Peter, C144, T, Undetermined
SANSOM, Frances Emmily, W1411, DY, Sansom, Sam D.
SAPP, David C. S1588, WH, 28th Inf.
SAPP, Nancy, W1106, WH, Sapp, David Crockett
SAPPINGTON, John M. S15568, G, 3rd (Forrest's) Cav.
SARGEANT, J. W. S15491, MU, 6th (Wheeler's) Cav.
SARGENT, Sallie Rhines, W7938, MU, Sargent, James Wm.
SARTAIN, Angaline Stovall, W10403, SH, Sartain, Linus Whitman
SARTAIN, Bettie Denis, W6917, MR, Sartain, James Robert
SARTAIN, H. H. S8956, GU, 28th Cav.
SARTAIN, James R. S5918, MR, 7th Ala. Inf.
SARTIN, Elizabeth, W798, CF, Sartin, Aaron
SARTIN, J. T. S8298, BR, 1st Confederate Cav.
SASSER, Susan Frances, W3921, HR, Sasser, Joel Stevens
SATTERFIELD, C. C. S14625, ST, 50th Inf.
SATTERFIELD, Cynthia Elya, W5981, LE, Satterfield, John Smith
SATTERFIELD, James, S5466, U, 1st (Carter's) Cav.
SATTERFIELD, Kate, W7385, ST, Satterfield, Charles Columbus
SATTERFIELD, L. J. S15401, MO, 61st Mtd. Inf.
SATTERFIELD, Maggie Elizabeth, W4224, JE, Satterfield, Salastual
SATTERFIELD, W. R. S14264, WL, 4th (McLemore's) Cav.
SATTERFIELD, Wiley, S1077, CO, 26th Inf.
SATTERWHITE, W. H. B. S16215, SN, 55th N.C. Inf.
SAULS, David Crockett sr. S11855, HR, Forrest's Old Regt. Cav.

Index to Tennessee Confederate Pension Applications

SAULS, Elizabeth Ann, W5050, HR, Sauls, David Crockett
SAUNDERS, Ella Lee, W11109, SU, Saunders, James Julian
SAUNDERS, Eugenia C. W193, WA, Saunders, John W.
SAUNDERS, J. W. S16339, S16223, BE, 20th Cav.
SAUNDERS, Mary C. W8060, CL, Saunders, Reuben R.
SAUNDERS, Mary Jane, W2795, MA, Saunders, John Turner
SAUNDERS, Susan Elenora, W2973, D, Saunders, Wm. Daniel
SAVAGE, B. M. S16062, G, 11th Miss. Cav.
SAVAGE, Eli, S13115, RB, 9th (Ward's) Cav.
SAVAGE, Henry, S16672, G, 27th Inf.
SAVAGE, J. R. S13984, D, 11th Inf.
SAVAGE, James, S15234, DE, 51st (Consol.) Inf.
SAVAGE, John H. S3368, HR, 13th Inf.
SAVAGE, M. S. S7819, MS, 51st Ala. Inf.
SAVAGE, Mary E. W6390, D, Savage, J. R.
SAVAGE, Susan Jane, W5965, HR, Savage, John Washington
SAVELY, Almeda Frances, W1761, SN, Savely, John Summers
SAVELY, J. W. S3369, D, 18th Inf.
SAVELY, William H. S10322, SN, 9th (Ward's) Cav.
SAVILLE, John F. S3502, JE, 63rd Inf.
SAWRIE, John W. S943, CC, 6th Inf.
SAWYER, Isaac, S2232, MOO, 23rd Inf.
SAWYER, Nancy Elizabeth, W5408, WE, Sawyer, Samuel Smith
SAWYER, S. S. S8014, WE, 7th Ark. Inf.
SAWYERS, A. J. S8279, JE, 31st Inf.
SAWYERS, G. M. S6234, WE, 53rd Inf.
SAWYERS, George Marion, S401, MS, 53rd Inf.
SAWYERS, George T. S4114, WE, 4th Inf.
SAWYERS, Mary Ann, W1959, WE, Sawyers, George Thomas
SAYLES, James I. S2544, L, 5th Inf.
SAYLES, Zulinda Lynch, W7635, L, Sayles, James I.
SCALES, N. F. S10904, D, Forrest's Escort, Cav.
SCALES, Susan Winchester, W8238, SH, Scales, Dabney Minor
SCALF, Jesse R. S5531, WA, 60th Inf.
SCALF, M. J. W5554, WA, Scalf, Jesse R.

SCALLORN, Charlotte Laura, W3004, Scallorn, Wm. Henry
SCARBOROUGH, Lemuel A. sr. S14111, SH, 13th Inf.
SCARBOROUGH, Louisa Jane, W1765, MA, Scarborough, Joseph Henry
SCARBOROUGH, Martha J. W6099, ST, Scarborough, Samuel Deberry
SCARBOROUGH, Matilda, W5828, ST, Scarborough, Edward A.
SCARBROUGH, Bell Carson, W7160, SH, Scarbrough, Lemuel Alexander
SCARBROUGH, Martha Jeanette, W9216, ST, Scarbrough, Samuel Deberry
SCARBROUGH, Mary Jane, W8509, RO, Scarbrough, Johnathan Mose
SCARBROUGH, William C. S16051, 26th Bn. Cav.
SCARLETT, Mahala, W2053, PU, Scarlett, Thomas Nelson
SCARLETT, Mary Frances, W10145, PU, Scarlett, Silas Nelson
SCATES, William F. S13827, 21st (Wilson's) Cav.
SCHACLETT, H. R. S7613, D, 11th Inf.
SCHELL, Bettie Martin, W2156, SN, Schell, Henry Augustus
SCHLUTER, G. W. S11910, SN, Lane's Tex. Rangers
SCHOLES, M. R. S13108, HU, 11th Inf.
SCHOOLFIELD, H. M. C112, RO, Undetermined
SCHOOLFIELD, Perry A. S5823, MR, 4th (Murray's) Cav.
SCHULTZ, Benjamin F. S2786, CL, 3rd Mo. Cav.
SCIVALLY, Avo, W9172, MOO, Scivally, W. H.
SCIVALLY, J. N. S8963, LI, 41st Inf.
SCIVALLY, John J. S2205, FR, 17th Inf.
SCIVALLY, Millie Ann, W4247, FR, Scivally, John J.
SCIVALLY, Susan Venettie, W2563, FR, Scivally, J. M.
SCIVALLY, William H. S16118, MOO, 12th (Armstead's) Miss. Cav.
SCOBEY, Joseph B. S12645, WL, 7th Inf.
SCOBY, Fanny Penelope, W8592, D, Scoby, James Edward
SCOBY, J. E. S14876, D, 55th Inf.
SCOBY, Mary Ella, W4724, D, Scoby, John Thomas

Index to Tennessee Confederate Pension Applications

SCOGGIN, Thomas H. S5921, GI, 7th Ala. Cav.
SCOGGINS, Jesse, S11774, HR, 18th (Newsom's) Cav.
SCOTT, Anderson D. S7572, SH, 9th Tex. Cav.
SCOTT, Andrew B. S11569, LI, 8th Inf.
SCOTT, Andrew J. S919, WI, 48th Inf.
SCOTT, Asenath Wilder, W3711, K, Scott, Wm. Poston Monroe
SCOTT, Belle H. W5175, D, Scott, J. L.
SCOTT, Drewcilla, W3608, ST, Scott, George W.
SCOTT, Eli P. S3834, G, 45th Inf.
SCOTT, Elizabeth Dillard, W2720, SH, Scott, John Lawson
SCOTT, Elizabeth [Casey], W10695, G, Scott, Eli P. [Later married Casey]
SCOTT, Eugenia Caldwell, W9631, W7000, W8225, MU, Scott, Andrew Jackson
SCOTT, Fannie V. W4688, MU, Scott, Harvey E.
SCOTT, George Y. S15675, SH, 2nd Miss. Reserve Cav.
SCOTT, Howland P. S7070, HR, 4th Ala. Cav.
SCOTT, J. D. S7975, G, 52nd Inf.
SCOTT, J. F. S11683, MA, 6th Inf.
SCOTT, J. M. S1918, 55th Inf.
SCOTT, James B. S8781, MU, 1st Cav.
SCOTT, James C. S5839, LI, 50th Ala. Inf.
SCOTT, James Lewis, S13802, D, Unassigned: Commissary Dept. Trans-Miss.
SCOTT, James N. S15399, SN, 30th Inf.
SCOTT, James Robert, S16442, 7th Ga. Inf.
SCOTT, James S. S7435, HN, 46th Inf.
SCOTT, Laura A. W2905, LI, Scott, James D.
SCOTT, Laura C. W8933, B, Scott, Robert Thomas
SCOTT, Lou W. W9089, SH, Scott, George Young
SCOTT, Louisa, W4703, K, Scott, Shadrack Franklin
SCOTT, Margaret Malinda, W1588, MU, Scott, Wm. McBurton
SCOTT, Mariah A. W9171, LA, Scott, Martin F.
SCOTT, Mark H. S5062, WA, 45th Va. Inf.
SCOTT, Martha Ann, W3047, LI, Scott, Andrew B.
SCOTT, Mary A. (Molly), W10262, W7932, JO, Scott, Wm. M.
SCOTT, Mary Susan, W1130, Scott, James Marshall
SCOTT, N. E. S15942, MA, 4th Ala. Cav.
SCOTT, Robert F. S15488, SH, 12th Cav.

SCOTT, Ruthie, W8778, WH, Scott, James Monroe
SCOTT, S. J. S15390, H, 1st Ga. Inf.
SCOTT, S. P. S15779, WE, 20th (Russell's) Cav.
SCOTT, Sallie Rebecca, W9619, DY, Scott, Allen
SCOTT, Samuel Joseph, S6526, H, 1st Ga. Inf.
SCOTT, Sarah Elizabeth, W1974, GI, Scott, David Columbus
SCOTT, Sarah Elizabeth, W8706, SH, Scott, Thomas Anderson
SCOTT, Scharles, S2720, CF, 4th Inf.
SCOTT, Synthana, W383, CF, Scott, Wm. Marshall
SCOTT, T. J. S12516, SH, 34th Miss. Inf.
SCOTT, Tabitha, W1372, FR, Scott, James
SCOTT, Virginia Elizabeth, W8419, H, Scott, Samuel Joseph
SCOTT, W. W. S11374, BE, 48th Va. Inf.
SCOTT, William M. S7888, GR, 63rd Inf.
SCOTT, William P. M. S10886, K, Wise's Legion, Va. Art.
SCOTT, William W. S8308, V, 22nd Bn. Inf.
SCRIBNER, Amanda D. W6652, MU, Scribner, Lewis Smith
SCRIBNER, Joseph H. S14815, H, Thomas' Legion, N.C.
SCRIBNER, Lewis F. S11737, MU, 6th (Wheeler's) Cav.
SCRIBNER, Mary, W10164, H, Scribner, James Henry
SCRIVENER, John A. S7547, D, 11th Inf.
SCROGGINS, Hiram H. S4410, P, 10th Cav.
SCROGGINS, James McDonald, S10173, H, 36th Inf.
SCROGGINS, Mary A. W1612, R, Scroggins, J. A.
SCRUGGS, B. C. S3503, MN, 5th Cav.
SCRUGGS, Bertha, W10120, GU, Scruggs, John
SCRUGGS, Drury D. S16007, S15990, H, 4th S.C. Inf.
SCRUGGS, Edward, S10607, D, 1st Inf.
SCRUGGS, Henry, S8587, M, 44th Va. Inf.
SCRUGGS, John, S15764, GU, 35th Inf.
SCRUGGS, L. Josephine Watkins, W1718, B, Scruggs, Wm. Finch
SCRUGGS, Mary Elizabeth, W2477, MO, Scruggs, James
SCRUGGS, Sterling, S9062, LI, 50th Ala. Inf.
SCRUGGS, Tennie, W3260, D, Scruggs, Albert Gallatin

SCRUGGS, Virginia Caroline, W1504, GI, Scruggs, John N.
SCRUGGS, W. J. S1134, D, 2nd Inf.
SCRUGGS, W. M. S14335, D, 2nd (Robison's) Inf.
SCURBROUGH, James, S5031, PU, 25th Inf.
SCURLOCK, James K. S2557, CY, 5th Inf.
SEABORN, Jane, W42, BR, Seaborn, J. B.
SEABORNE, Benjamin C. S10866, D, 20th Inf.
SEAGLE, W. L. S12976, HM, 17th Bn. N.C. Troops
SEAGRAVES, Jessee, S5374, BL, 13th Cav.
SEAHORNE, Mary Caroline, W8501, FR, Seahorne, Jasper A.
SEAL, B. B. S7154, CL, 2nd Cav.
SEAL, James M. S4203, U, 1st Cav.
SEAL, Jane, W2083, HA, Seal, Drury
SEAL, R. N. S3541, H, 11th S.C. Inf.
SEAL, Sarah Catherin, W5995, CL, Seal, Bayer Bullard
SEALE, Eliza McCathey, W3220, H, Seale, Reuben Harrison
SEALEY, Susan Ann Malisa, W2184, MU, Sealey, Amis Curtice
SEALS, Mary Frances, W3542, DI, Seals, Abson
SEARCY, R. T. S5956, S6909, SN, 7th Inf.
SEARCY, Shadrick, C235, H, 46th Inf.
SEARS, E. G. S15441, CE, 50th Inf.
SEARS, Isabella, W8317, CE, Sears, Edward Green
SEARS, Richard, S12106, DI, 8th La. Inf.
SEAT, Eli, S1652, WL, 38th Inf.
SEAT, Ellen, W2436, D, Seat, Algemon Sidney
SEAT, J. B. S13475, D, 30th Inf.
SEAT, J. M. S11549, WI, 4th (McLemore's) Cav.
SEAT, Martha Jane, W1322, D, Seat, Sterling Brown
SEATON, A. F. S2660, LI, 44th Inf.
SEATON, E. G. S3443, HN, 5th Inf.
SEATON, J. W. S7449, CH, 52nd Inf.
SEATON, Jacob M. S8839, GE, 61st Inf.
SEATON, Mark L. S9547, GE, 61st Inf.
SEATON, Rachel Mary Ann, W7260, LI, Seaton, Andrew Ferrell
SEATON, Sarah Elizabeth, W1226, CH, Seaton, Wilbon Marion
SEATON, W. M. S6129, CH, 21st (Wilson's) Cav.
SEAVER, W. W. S11267, HW, 12th Bn. (Day's) Cav.
SEAY, A. B. S3346, CO, 5th S.C. Sharpshooters

SEAY, Benjamin, S4497, TR, 57th Va. Inf.
SEAY, Ella M. W6935, SN, Seay, Benjamin
SEAY, Frank M. C145, WI, 24th Inf.
SEAY, Richard H. S11381, DI, 23rd Va. Inf.
SEAY, Susan, W2887, GE, Seay, Presley
SECREST, Mary J. W5588, MS, Secrest, T. J.
SECRIST, T. L. S6827, MS, 19th (Biffle's) Cav.
SEGLE, Louis M. S8455, LE, 1st N.C. Cav.
SEGLE, Martha J. W8154, SE, Segle, L. M.
SEGO, John James, S2644, HE, 27th Inf.
SEHORN, John Franklin, S11613, PU, 5th (McKenzie's) Cav.
SEHORN, L. J. S16008, CF, 34th Ala. Inf.
SEHORN, Lena Gwynn, W8454, B, Sehorn, Wm. Marion
SEHORNE, Alpha P. W2473, FR, Sehorne, Isham J.
SEHORNE, J. N. S4002, FR, 34th Ala. Inf.
SEHORNE, W. M. S4051, B, 34th Ala. Inf.
SEIBER, Jane, W9916, LE, Seiber, Frederick
SELBY, J. S. S11659, PU, 8th Cav.
SELDON, Mary Josphehine, W8050, FR, Seldon, James Montgomery
SELF, Joseph R. S7233, JE, 29th Inf.
SELF, Margaret J. W2197, CO, Self, Jesie S.
SELF, Ophelia T. W533, HU, Self, Abe
SELL, Benjamin L. S6341, SU, 1st (Carter's) Cav.
SELL, John, S3100, SU, 60th Inf.
SELL, Leah, W3484, SU, Sell, Benjamin L.
SELLANS, Catherine Judson, W5635, WL, Sellans, Wm. C.
SELLARS, Artemisia Preston, W9267, WE, Sellars, John Marshall
SELLARS, G. M. S15077, WE, 1st Cav.
SELLARS, J. P. S14431, CT, 6th N.C. State Troops
SELLARS, M. L. S12711, W, 35th Inf.
SELLARS, Mary E. W268, WI, Sellars, Thomas J.
SELLARS, W. C. S3874, WL, 18th Inf.
SELLERS, D. C. S7001, L, 14th Cav.
SELLERS, Harriet Paralee, W3375, D, Sellers, John J.
SELLERS, Mary Emeline, W7070, HE, Sellers, Thomas E.
SELLERS, Phillip, S6881, CH, 51st Inf.
SELLERS, Thomas E. S6075, HE, 19th (Biffle's) Cav.
SELLS, Joseph, S12269, WA, 60th Inf.
SELLS, Mary Vester, W3073, CY, Sells, J. W.
SELLS, Peter G. S1708, FR, 33rd Ala. Inf.

Index to Tennessee Confederate Pension Applications

SELVAGE, John, S3231, RO, 16th Cav.
SELVEY, Bettie Jane, W5137, C, Selvey, Thomas
SEMONES, Mattie J. W8126, K, Semones, Wilson F.
SEMONES, Wilson F. S3781, K, 24th Va. Inf.
SENSABAUGH, Richard Mitchell, S9176, HW, Unassigned (Sappers & Miners Corps)
SENSABAUGH, Susan D. W3454, WA, Sensabaugh, Leonidas F.
SENSABOUGH, Sarah Elizabeth, W7069, HW, Sensabough, Richard Mitchell
SENSING, A. R. S12512, G, 13th Inf.
SENSING, George W. S4797, DI, 49th Inf.
SENSING, J. P. S12513, SH, 13th Inf.
SENSING, Margaret T. W4344, SH, Sensing, John P.
SENSING, Sallie, W1021, DI, Sensing, Archie Benton
SENT, Rebecca E. W9997, D, Sent, Charles Henry
SENTER, Laura Tennessee, W1900, G, Senter, Moses Green
SENTER, M. F. S13383, SN, 20th Inf.
SENTER, Mary J. W5957, HM, Senter, James Orr
SENTER, Neill Alexander, S15839, G, 14th (Neely's) Cav.
SENTER, Zachariah, S12117, K, Burrough's Co. Lt. Art.
SERRETT, Mary, W1891, BE, Serrett, Alvin
SESSUMS, Anna Bryan, W8830, F, Sessums, John H.
SETTERS, J. J. S2154, U, 7th Cav.
SETTLE, George W. S9544, ST, 50th Inf.
SETTLEMIRE, Catherine, W4128, BO, Settlemire, David
SETTLEMURE, David, S1482, BO, 11th N.C. Inf.
SEVIER, C. F. S16426, HD, Confed. States Navy
SEVIER, John V. S14261, HY, 9th Inf.
SEVIER, Mary McClure, W8239, K, Sevier, George Jones
SEVIER, William, S4204, JO, 2nd Inf.
SEWARD, A. N. S9063, SH, 13th Inf.
SEWARD, B. R. S1031, RU, 24th Inf.
SEWELL, A. D. S5870, MC, 36th Ga. Inf.
SEWELL, A. G. S11619, CH, 27th Inf.
SEWELL, Altha Jane, W4012, CH, Sewell, Augustus
SEWELL, George W. C129, H, 14th Miss. Inf.

SEWELL, Isaac S. S2032, OV, 8th Cav.
SEWELL, J. F. S2033, OV, 25th Inf.
SEWELL, Marianna, W3194, MA, Sewell, Joseph Humphrey
SEWELL, Rhena, W210, MN, Sewell, Allen King
SEWELL, S. H. S3809, W, 8th Cav.
SEWELL, Tabitha Jane, W2800, OV, Sewell, Jesse Franklin
SEWELL, Thomas, S2922, DK, 3rd Tex. Cav.
SEXTON, Ada B. W1267, D, Sexton, James M.
SEXTON, E. G. S14800, ST, 50th Inf.
SEXTON, Green A. S8441, HR, 14th Cav.
SEXTON, John, S10979, MR, 4th Ga. Cav.
SEXTON, John T. S9677, ST, 50th Inf.
SEXTON, Kisiah L. W3486, MN, Sexton, R. T.
SEXTON, Mary, W3456, JO, Sexton, Robert
SEXTON, Mary Eliza, W8785, GI, Sexton, Wm. Robert
SEXTON, Mary Jane, W3632, GE, Sexton, Hiram
SEXTON, Mary M. W7025, ST, Sexton, E. G.
SEXTON, Mattie, W5788, Sexton, Wesley Warren
SEXTON, N. O. S13541, MC, 3rd (Lillard's) Mtd. Inf.
SEXTON, Reuben T. S1621, S702, HD, 36th Ga. Inf.
SEXTON, Rosa Lily, W10351, F, Sexton, Green Allen
SEXTON, S. J. S1737, CO, 2nd N.C. Inf.
SEXTON, Sarah A. W2710, CO, Sexton, Pinkney Elijah
SEXTON, Thomas C. S5191, HR, 7th Cav.
SEXTON, Virginia Susan, W9298, GR, Sexton, Wm. D.
SEXTON, W. D. S13917, GR, 51st Va. Inf.
SEXTON, W. F. S4711, LI, 44th Inf.
SEXTON, Wesley Warren, S11182, Capt. William's Co. Cav.
SEYMORE, E. M. S9759, MA, 6th Inf.
SEYMORE, George B. S10832, GR, 2nd (Ashby's) Cav.
SEYMOUR, G. W. S2747, CL, 1st (Carter's) Cav.
SEYMOUR, Mary Jane, W6564, UN, Seymour, James L.
SHACKELFORD, Elijah, C55, MU, 10th Ga. Inf.
SHACKELFORD, Joseph, S13357, LA, 41st Ga. Inf.

Index to Tennessee Confederate Pension Applications

SHACKLEFORD, Sallie, W7756, LA, Shackleford, Joseph
SHACKLETT, Emma A. W4999, D, Shacklett, H. R.
SHAD, Stephen, C82, G, 10th Cav.
SHADDEN, Martha, W1898, R, Shadden, John Alexander
SHAFER, James W. S3057, GE, 60th Inf.
SHAFER, Martha R. W7128, WA, Shafer, James Wm.
SHAMBLIN, W. M. S3424, MC, 43rd Inf.
SHAMLIN, J. M. S14473, MC, 43rd Inf.
SHANE, J. A. S10391, G, 12th Inf.
SHANE, Julia, W4771, G, Shane, James A.
SHANE, Sam, S10980, G, 52nd Inf.
SHANE, Sarah H. W4259, SH, Shane, James Alexander
SHANKLE, A. A. W473, T, Shankle, Jacob T.
SHANKLE, John Wesley, S11977, WE, 21st (Wilson's) Cav.
SHANKLE, Mary Ida, W8754, WE, Shankle, J. W.
SHANKLE, Rachel N. W4787, RO, Shankle, P. H.
SHANKLIN, J. F. S5321, T, 12th Inf.
SHANNON, E. K. S13508, WL, 44th Inf.
SHANNON, I. N. S3504, DI, 9th Inf.
SHANNON, J. A. S2109, HM, 3rd Inf.
SHANNON, James P. S3526, HM, 1st Regt. Engineer Troops
SHANNON, Joice, W3522, WL, Shannon, N. P.
SHANNON, Norman P. S1063, WL, 38th Inf.
SHAPARD, E. S12474, B, 41st Inf.
SHAPARD, Emma F. W7626, B, Shapard, Evander
SHAPARD, J. B. S15380, SH, 3rd (Clack's) Inf.
SHARP, A. A. S14103, K, 12th Bn. (Day's) Cav.
SHARP, Amelia Ann, W4973, H, Sharp, James W.
SHARP, Catherine, W10623, H, Sharp, Gabriel M.
SHARP, Elizabeth, W4868, P, Sharp, Samuel Miles
SHARP, Emma Ella, W6706, K, Sharp, Alfred Alexander
SHARP, Feilding J. S3958, MS, 17th Inf.
SHARP, G. G. S10491, HI, 48th (Voorhies') Inf.
SHARP, G. W. S12822, HI, 48th (Voorhies') Inf.
SHARP, Iowa Clementine, W10822, HI, Sharp, George Washington
SHARP, J. T. S4804, SH, 12th Inf.
SHARP, James, S13160, H, 19th Inf.
SHARP, John J. S12022, D, 3rd (Clack's) Inf.
SHARP, Martha E. W2302, MS, Sharp, J. F.
SHARP, Mary A. W4529, ME, Sharp, James
SHARP, Mary Jane, W823, P, Sharp, John
SHARP, Melissa Wilmuth, W9531, MU, Sharp, Wm. Anderson
SHARP, Peter C. S12430, GR, 2nd Cav.
SHARP, Samuel M. S3330, P, 9th Cav.
SHARP, Susan E. W2963, MS, Sharp, H. M.
SHARP, Virginia Catherine, W9445, HI, Sharp, Green G.
SHARP, W. G. P. S4365, B, 23rd Inf.
SHARP, W. M. S9183, RU, 44th Inf.
SHARPE, Cal, C248, HI, Regiment not given
SHARRETT, Abram G. S4679, GE, 63rd Inf.
SHARROCK, Thomas W. S8378, B, 34th Ga. Inf.
SHASTEEN, William, S2404, FR, 34th Inf.
SHAUB, C. J. S5299, SN, 7th Inf.
SHAUB, Lou Clay, W8379, SN, Shaub, Charles J.
SHAVER, Elmira, W313, R, Shaver, John Q.
SHAVER, Sarah F. W1926, SM, Shaver, John Thomas
SHAVERS, George W. S704, FR, 32nd Inf.
SHAW, A. C. S14199, HY, 31st Inf.
SHAW, Alfred, S12257, CT, 2nd N.C. Inf.
SHAW, Annie Elizabeth, W5853, SH, Shaw, Malcom Mads
SHAW, Arbell F. W2614, MS, Shaw, James Warren
SHAW, C. A. S. S8756, HR, 14th Cav.
SHAW, Craig N. S5842, DY, 15th (Stewart's) Cav.
SHAW, D. N. S10881, JO, 58th N.C. Inf.
SHAW, E. O. S11579, DY, 41st Ala. Inf.
SHAW, F. M. S7204, CC, 14th (Neely's) Cav.
SHAW, Franky, W3781, CT, Shaw, Alfred
SHAW, Harriet Emery, W2463, HD, Shaw, Robert Anderson
SHAW, J. K. P. S8379, SH, Wood's Co. Miss. State Cav.
SHAW, J. O. S11399, WI, 11th (Holman's) Cav.
SHAW, James P. S9275, MU, Maury's Art.
SHAW, John W. S12346, S15407, F, 14th (Neely's) Cav.
SHAW, Julia V. W2438, D, Shaw, James S.
SHAW, M. M. S8380, SH, Bradford's Battery of Miss. Art.

Index to Tennessee Confederate Pension Applications

SHAW, Martha, W7585, MS, Shaw, Richard Franklin
SHAW, Mary, W1912, LI, Shaw, John M.
SHAW, Mary E. W5908, MS, Shaw, John Green
SHAW, Mary Isabel, W7180, JO, Shaw, D. Newton
SHAW, P. J. S14442, DY, Thrawl's Co. Ark. Lt. Art.
SHAW, Parthena, W5535, DY, Shaw, Craig N.
SHAW, R. F. S7002, LI, 53rd Inf.
SHAW, Robert L. S3097, MS, 8th Inf.
SHAW, Sarah E. W5340, SN, Shaw, James L.
SHAW, Sarah Elizabeth, W8082, T, Shaw, Elijah Octavius
SHAW, Sarah Emma, W10137, T, Shaw, Archie Wilson
SHAW, William Augustus, S13370, WI, 11th Cav.
SHEA, Thomas, S1529, S4624, WI, 48th Inf.
SHEA, Thomas, S9397, HR, 9th Inf.
SHEA, Tim, S6424, MN, 19th Miss. Inf.
SHEARIN, Jesse Blanchett, S14096, HR, 13th Inf.
SHEARIN, Lavinia E. W10628, HR, Shearin, Jessie B.
SHEARIN, Martha Isabella, W5272, SH, Shearin, Wm. Braxton
SHEARIN, Nannie, W7178, RU, Shearin, Isaac Wright
SHEARIN, Sterling Brewer, S10897, D, 1st (Feild's) Inf.
SHEARIN, W. T. S9477, MS, 8th (Smith's) Cav.
SHEARIN, William B. S8763, SH, 9th Inf.
SHEARMAN, Anne, W3419, MC, Shearman, John Frank
SHEARON, Mary E. W5637, D, Shearon, Sterling Durham
SHEARON, William T. S5658, HR, 22nd Inf.
SHEARON, Zachary Franklin, S9604, MT, 42nd Inf.
SHEARRON, Z. T. S6543, RB, 42nd Inf.
SHEARWIN, I. W. S8493, D, 1st Inf.
SHEETS, George Wilson, S9158, HR, 1st La. Art.
SHEETS, Isom, S15020, ME, 43rd Inf.
SHEETS, Rachel L. W2378, K, Sheets, David C.
SHEFFEY, Organ T. W3024, GE, Sheffey, Alfred M.
SHEFFIELD, E. V. S15294, MS, 4th (McLemore's) Cav.
SHEFFIELD, James W. S9867, B, 45th Inf.

SHEFFIELD, Laura A. W8926, MS, Sheffield, Columbus Jackson
SHEFFIELD, Mary E. W8758, MS, Sheffield, E. V.
SHELBY, J. M. S11614, SH, 4th Inf.
SHELBY, Margaret, W10224, HI, Shelby, Daniel
SHELBY, Samuel, S1938, R, 16th Bn. Cav.
SHELBY, Wallace, C219, D, Hospital Service
SHELL, Howard, S5489, PO, 29th Inf.
SHELL, Mary, W3827, W9707, MC, Shell, James H.
SHELTON, Amanda B. W3690, H, Shelton, W. T.
SHELTON, Amanda Elizabeth, W4752, CO, Shelton, Martin M.
SHELTON, Anderson, S4750, GR, 29th Inf.
SHELTON, Ann Cornelia, W3770, MA, Shelton, Stephen Lynch
SHELTON, B. F. S11958, GR, 2nd (Ashby's) Cav.
SHELTON, B. M. S4272, CF, 23rd Inf.
SHELTON, Bettie, W7472, CF, Shelton, J. M.
SHELTON, Celia Ann, W3641, HR, Shelton, Daniel Houston
SHELTON, E. A. S11463, R, 3rd N.C. Reserves
SHELTON, E. C. S8601, SU, 4th Va. Reserves
SHELTON, E. E. S9100, LI, 16th Ala. Inf.
SHELTON, Fleming Anderson, S3141, HW, 51st Va. Inf.
SHELTON, Francis M. S1558, GI, 32nd Inf.
SHELTON, Henry F. S1644, LI, 1st Inf.
SHELTON, Iza, S1038, WH, 28th Inf.
SHELTON, J. A. S328, HR, 23rd Miss. Inf.
SHELTON, J. J. S6799, OV, 25th Inf.
SHELTON, J. L. S16307, CC, 12th Ky. Cav.
SHELTON, J. M. S4819, OV, 37th Va. Inf.
SHELTON, J. P. S4741, CF, 4th (McLemore's) Cav.
SHELTON, J. R. S16195, RU, 4th (McLemore's) Cav.
SHELTON, Jacob, S9909, SU, 37th Va. Inf.
SHELTON, James L. S2729, GI, 53rd Inf.
SHELTON, John, S772, D, 11th Inf.
SHELTON, John Elliott, S1793, T, 3rd Ga. Bn. Sharpshooters
SHELTON, John M. S12325, CF, 4th (McLemore's) Cav.
SHELTON, John T. S7972, D, 4th (McLemore's) Cav.
SHELTON, John T. S13695, HW, 22nd Va. Cav.

-311

SHELTON, Leroy, S5459, GI, 53rd Inf.
SHELTON, Lucius, S3276, T, 24th Miss. Inf., Application is missing.
SHELTON, Lydia Jane, W6779, R, Shelton, Erasmus Archer
SHELTON, M. E. S11497, MN, 4th Confederate Inf.
SHELTON, Maria, W7633, MA, Shelton, Abner Clapton
SHELTON, Martha Caroline, W7398, HR, Shelton, James Anderson
SHELTON, Martha J. W373, GI, Shelton, Francis Marion
SHELTON, Martin, S978, CO, 62nd N.C. Inf.
SHELTON, Mary Alice, W8713, MU, Shelton, Thomas Adams
SHELTON, Mary Anne, W9796, MA, Shelton, John Lewis
SHELTON, Mollie, W7315, GR, Shelton, Anderson
SHELTON, Polly, W644, MC, Shelton, Alexander
SHELTON, Polly A. W7699, T, Shelton, J. E.
SHELTON, Rebecca Lee, W6715, WI, Shelton, Wm. Dennis
SHELTON, Robert, S5598, PO, 59th Inf.
SHELTON, Rosaline, W3633, RB, Shelton, T. G.
SHELTON, Sarah J. W7483, HW, Shelton, F. A.
SHELTON, Sophia, W2144, CF, Shelton, James K. P.
SHELTON, W. L. S2206, LI, 41st Inf.
SHELTON, W. R. S11074, T, 18th Inf.
SHELTON, W. T. S3521, BR, 4th (McLemore's) Cav.
SHEMWELL, W. H. S5824, ST, Forrest's Old Regt. Cav.
SHEPARD, Alexander C. S14743, WA, 46th N.C. Inf.
SHEPARD, William N. S5880, D, Undetermined
SHEPHARD, Amanda, W7183, K, Shephard, Andrew Jackson
SHEPHARD, Fannie Millhorn, W7492, SU, Shephard, Patrick Henry
SHEPHARD, J. T. S14392, RB, 18th Inf.
SHEPHARD, R. L. S6906, FR, 4th (McLemore's) Cav.
SHEPHARD, S. G. S14493, WL, 7th Inf.
SHEPHERD, Addie Leana, W9951, RB, Shepherd, James Thomas
SHEPHERD, Andrew J. S9625, K, 51st Va. Inf.
SHEPHERD, James M. S12528, HW, 51st Va. Inf.
SHEPHERD, John C. S2267, D, 9th (Bennett's) Cav.
SHEPHERD, Joseph H. S8475, WA, 11th Va. Inf.
SHEPHERD, Laura, W3691, D, Shepherd, Thomas H.
SHEPHERD, Laura C. W4230, MT, Shepherd, Wm.
SHEPHERD, Martha Jane, W6299, MS, Shepherd, Richard Alonzo
SHEPHERD, T. R. S1384, D, 44th Inf.
SHEPHERD, W. W. S15770, D, Marshall's Co. Art.
SHEPHERD, William, S4576, MT, 14th Inf.
SHEPPARD, Dora Fitts, W2292, TR, Sheppard, Benjamin Franklin
SHEPPARD, Endora, W1456, TR, Sheppard, Frank
SHEPPARD, Margaret Melvina, W2489, K, Sheppard, Wm. Bird
SHERIDAN, J. M. S7947, HN, 20th (Russell's) Cav.
SHERIDAN, John, S2621, HO, 7th La. Inf.
SHERIDAN, Sarah, W2429, D, Sheridan, John
SHERIDAN, Thomas H. S6610, HN, 46th Inf.
SHERLEY, Margaret E. W862, W, Sherley, John W.
SHERMAN, E. G. S9495, WI, Baxter's Co. Lt. Art.
SHERMAN, Sue Jones, W6531, WI, Sherman, Eli Gould
SHERRELL, Adam, S2102, CU, 2nd Cav.
SHERRELL, Andrew, S2103, CU, 2nd Cav.
SHERRELL, Joshua, S8363, PU, 25th Inf.
SHERRELL, Nancy, W3272, CU, Sherrell, Andrew
SHERRILL, Ann Virginia, W9806, HY, Sherrill, Richard Enos Adam
SHERRILL, Elizabeth, W5703, GU, Sherrill, George Alpha
SHERRILL, Hattie, W7362, MC, Sherrill, Lycurgus Lafayette
SHERRILL, L. W. S1587, CH, 6th (Wheeler's) Cav.
SHERRILL, Lycurgus L. S11762, MC, 2nd N.C. Cav.
SHERRILL, Mary Jane, W5966, RU, Sherrill, Wm. T.
SHERRILL, Richard E. S15145, HY, 12th Cav.
SHERRILL, S. S. S941, O, 2nd Cav.

SHERRILL, Sarah E. W10389, LA, Sherrill, Joel
SHERROD, Charlotte Henry, W4861, F, Sherrod, George Taylor
SHERROD, Felix Grundy, S14285, G, 11th Ala. Cav.
SHETLEY, John, S3112, CO, 60th N.C. Inf.
SHETLEY, Mary Ann, W8866, CO, Shetley, John
SHETTER, M. A. S6765, GU, 43rd Inf.
SHIELD, Angeline Gilbert, W495, SE, Shield, Henderson
SHIELDS, B. S. S128, LA, 2nd Miss. Inf.
SHIELDS, Elizabeth Frances, W1073, GI, Shields, Lee Andrew
SHIELDS, George P. S603, GI, 53rd Inf.
SHIELDS, Jacob, S11984, MO, 59th Inf.
SHIELDS, John H. S3390, WY, 48th Inf.
SHIELDS, L. A. S3767, GI, 53rd Inf.
SHIELDS, L. V. W3847, W, Shields, Robert B.
SHIELDS, Mary, W5997, D, Shields, Robert
SHIELDS, Robert, S11357, D, Ramsey's Battery, Lt. Art.
SHIELDS, William Madison, S12226, SH, 8th Bn. Ga. Inf.
SHINAULT, Mary Ophelia, W10039, T, Shinault, Joseph H.
SHIPLEY, Adam, S4391, SU, 63rd Inf.
SHIPLEY, Alice A. W717, K, Shipley, John
SHIPLEY, Amanda, W2564, SU, Shipley, S. P.
SHIPLEY, Ambrose, S10638, SU, "Home Guards"
SHIPLEY, George R. S7132, SU, 3rd Battery, Md. Art.
SHIPLEY, J. M. S1404, WA, 29th Inf.
SHIPLEY, James, S2540, LO, 59th Inf.
SHIPLEY, James H. S2878, WA, 5th Cav.
SHIPLEY, John K. S7133, SU, 29th Inf.
SHIPLEY, Margaret E. W2355, SU, Shipley, Adam
SHIPLEY, Mollie E. W5894, SU, Shipley, John K.
SHIPLEY, Nancy A. W7125, WA, Shipley, Jesse M.
SHIPLEY, S. P. S4885, SU, 60th Inf.
SHIPLEY, Sarah Emaline, W8376, WA, Shipley, Wm.
SHIPLEY, William, S2895, WA, 59th Mtd. Inf.
SHIPMAN, John A. S8904, K, 1st Cav.
SHIPP, Alaminta Frances, W6144, SU, Shipp, John Sterling
SHIPP, J. H. S12952, HI, 48th (Voorhies') Inf.

SHIPP, J. S. S5214, SU, 60th Inf.
SHIPP, James B. S6731, SH, 18th Bn. Miss. Cav.
SHIPP, John T. S310, H, 4th Cav.
SHIPP, Tate, W8495, WL, Shipp, Dave J.
SHIPPER, Frank, S9272, WL, 7th Inf.
SHIRES, C. N. S15276, O, 24th Inf.
SHIRES, J. B. S10614, MU, 24th Inf.
SHIRES, W. M. S10615, MU, 24th Inf.
SHIRLEY, Eliza J. W294, CA, Shirley, Charles
SHIRLEY, F. M. S11226, MR, 3rd Inf.
SHIRLEY, J. W. S3214, W, 35th Inf.
SHIRLEY, Malinda M. W489, HD, Shirley, Franklin
SHIRLEY, W. C. S6216, MR, 6th (Wheeler's) Cav.
SHIRREL, J. A. S2532, CY, 28th & 84th (Consol.) Inf.
SHIVE, Mary Caroline, W6850, O, Shive, W. N.
SHIVE, W. N. S12785, O, 19th Miss. Inf.
SHIVERS, C. T. S2081, FR, Scott's 1st La. Cav.
SHIVERS, Caroline B. W342, MS, Shivers, Ira
SHIVERS, James N. S13824, SH, 4th Inf.
SHIVERS, Va. Albany Bennett, W8967, SH, Shivers, James Norborn
SHOAF, John A. S15799, T, 42nd N.C. Inf.
SHOCKLEY, Lewis, S3018, V, 5th Inf.
SHOCKLEY, Martha G. W8988, MU, Shockley, Wm. Thomas
SHOCKLEY, Rachel, W7303, V, Shockley, Lewis D.
SHOCKLEY, Riley, S29, CF, 5th Inf.
SHOEMAKE, John, S723, SM, Undetermined
SHOEMAKER, Cynthia Jane, W4368, K, Shoemaker, Evin
SHOEMAKER, Evin, S9064, K, 31st Inf.
SHOEMAKER, Thomas R. S12788, K, 29th Inf.
SHOEMAKER, Trophena Ann, W8884, SU, Shoemaker, Wm. Fleenor
SHOFFNER, Nancy Caroline, W2722, B, Shoffner, Robert Wm.
SHOFNER, Ada McMath, W10853, LI, Shofner, James C.
SHOFNER, Harriet M. W3040, MO, Shofner, Peter Lee
SHOFNER, J. C. S16248, LI, Forrest's Escort, Cav.
SHOFNER, Peter L. S2322, CF, 17th Inf.
SHOFNER, William L. S3155, LI, Forrest's Escort, Cav.
SHOOK, Jonathan W. S6106, RO, 65th Ga. Inf.
SHOOK, Mary Laura, W10198, D, Shook, Wm.

SHOOPMAN, Caroline, W2058, SC, Shoopman, Joseph
SHOOPMAN, Joseph, S1536, SC, 3rd Inf.
SHORE, Lucy Catherine, W10501, O, Shore, Thomas Benjamin
SHORES, John M. S3058, GE, 4th Va. Inf.
SHORT, Abraham M. S3059, T, 2nd Miss. Inf.
SHORT, Agnes D. W1730, SH, Short, James M.
SHORT, Elizabeth, W4349, M, Short, Jasper Drury
SHORT, Florence, W7520, GI, Short, James B.
SHORT, Frances Tennessee, W10444, WI, Short, Benjamin Franklin
SHORT, J. D. S2743, M, 24th Inf.
SHORT, James B. S14834, GI, 3rd (Clack's) Inf.
SHORT, Julie Ann, W2169, FR, Short, Ruben Columbus
SHORT, Louminor N. W6482, WI, Short, Thomas Jefferson
SHORT, Mary Elizabeth, W2892, MA, Short, Wm. John
SHORT, Susan Eliza, W4610, T, Short, Isaac Harlin
SHORT, W. F. S12357, HR, Forrest's Old Regt. Cav.
SHOTWELL, Lucy K. W9669, HW, Shotwell, F. A.
SHOULDERS, Celia Jane, W1081, SM, Shoulders, David Timberlake
SHOULDERS, D. T. S8049, SM, 24th Inf.
SHOULTS, Michael, S12475, SH, 18th Miss. Cav.
SHOUN, Martha E. W5664, SU, Shoun, John H.
SHOWN, J. H. S13200, JE, 6th N.C. Cav.
SHRIVER, B. B. S6930, B, 41st Inf.
SHRIVER, Catherine French, W3127, B, Shriver, James G.
SHROAT, Lizzie M. W3447, HO, Shroat, John T.
SHROATE, J. T. S3711, HO, 46th Inf.
SHRUM, John, S6291, MR, 5th Inf.
SHUFF, Isabella Powers, W9085, ST, Shuff, George W.
SHUFORD, JEssie A. W10528, H, Shuford, John E.
SHUGART, E. J. S1129, D, 1st N.C. Inf.
SHUGART, Laura Ellen, W6691, BR, Shugart, Livingston
SHUGART, Livingston, S12009, BR, 2nd (Ashby's) Cav.

SHUGART, W. O. S12806, S15485, BR, 2nd (Ashby's) Cav.
SHULAR, John A. S12184, SE, Thomas' Legion, N.C.
SHULAR, Mary, W4975, SE, Shular, John Alexander
SHULL, F. T. S10367, H, 2nd (Ashby's) Cav.
SHULTS, Frances M. W5346, WE, Shults, Wisdom
SHUMAKER, W. F. S10364, SU, 64th Va. Inf.
SHUMATE, Annie E. W5907, D, Shumate, James C.
SHUMATE, J. C. S7587, D, 20th Inf.
SHUMATE, Lemuel, S2342, GR, 1st (Carter's) Cav.
SHUMATE, T. W. S13674, D, 20th Inf.
SHUTE, Mattie M. W8202, D, Shute, Will Watkins
SHUTE, W. W. S8462, D, 20th Inf.
SHUTTES, E. C. S14340, FR, 8th (Dibrell's) Cav.
SHUTTLE, John, S6174, SU, 63rd Inf.
SHY, George Washington, S5795, SN, 30th Inf.
SHYTLES, W. R. S3556, MN, 9th Ark. Inf.
SIBLEY, Sarah Elizabeth, W11112, GI, Sibley, Felix Woodson
SIFFORD, John, S2787, WA, 58th N.C. Inf.
SIGRAVES, Eliza Harriett, W6239, DY, Sigraves, George Washington
SILER, Anna H. W9589, MA, Siler, Harris W.
SILER, James Lewis, S8023, HR, 26th N.C. Inf.
SILER, Josiah, S15072, HR, 1st N.C. Jr. Reserves
SILER, Mary Ann, W2946, CH, Siler, Edwin H.
SILER, Mary Jane, W9684, HR, Siler, Josiah
SILER, Ruth J. W7777, MA, Siler, James L.
SILLS, Emma Elizabeth, W10642, GI, Sills, Wm. Clinton
SILVER, John, S16295, JE, 29th N.C. Inf.
SILVERS, Narcissa, W2232, K, Silvers, Rice Daniel
SILVERS, R. D. S10093, K, 54th Va. Inf.
SILVERTOOTH, Callie H. W7686, SH, Silvertooth, Jacob
SIMCOCK, J. S. S604, OV, 63rd Va. Inf.
SIMMAMON, Elizabeth, W7409, GR, Simmamon, Wm. Brownlow
SIMMAMON, James P. S6708, HW, 1st (Carter's) Cav.
SIMMERMAN, John A. S8402, WA, 51st Va. Inf.

Index to Tennessee Confederate Pension Applications

SIMMONS, Abigail Caroline, W4904, W1628, WE, Simmons, Andrew Edward
SIMMONS, Annie Lou, W8794, SH, Simmons, Julian A.
SIMMONS, B. C. S10789, MA, 9th Inf.
SIMMONS, Bryant, S6480, V, Unassigned
SIMMONS, C. N. S15060, SN, 6th (Wheeler's) Cav.
SIMMONS, Caroline, W512, WE, Simmons, Andrew
SIMMONS, Caroline, W3215, HN, Simmons, Abram
SIMMONS, David S. S5986, GI, 6th (Wheeler's) Cav.
SIMMONS, David S. S10495, GI, 11th (Gordon's) Cav.
SIMMONS, E. W. S4664, M, 6th (Wheeler's) Cav.
SIMMONS, Elizabeth, W5113, G, Simmons, Samuel Franklin
SIMMONS, F. T. S5402, DY, 14th (Neely's) Cav.
SIMMONS, Frances Caroline, W2104, WE, Simmons, Britton Long
SIMMONS, Gilla H. W1931, M, Simmons, Calvin Green
SIMMONS, J. J. S10652, FR, 17th Inf.
SIMMONS, J. S. S3821, 7th Mo. Cav.
SIMMONS, James F. S12850, LI, 1st (Turney's) Inf.
SIMMONS, James M. S11856, MU, 6th (Wheeler's) Cav.
SIMMONS, Joel, S11838, JO, 37th Va. Inf.
SIMMONS, John W. S10374, F, 7th Cav.
SIMMONS, Julia Emma, W8273, MA, Simmons, Benjamin Coffield
SIMMONS, Lucy Ann, W4476, SH, Simmons, Wm. Eli
SIMMONS, Martha O. W332, HR, Simmons, Benjamin A.
SIMMONS, Nora J. W8588, FR, Simmons, James J.
SIMMONS, Olivia F. W333, HR, Simmons, John H.
SIMMONS, S. F. S13589, G, 8th Ala. Cav.
SIMMONS, Soloman J. S12935, GI, 6th (Wheeler's) Cav.
SIMMONS, T. D. S8725, MU, 32nd Inf.
SIMMONS, Ulla J. W10770, WE, Simmons, Wm. Lemuel
SIMMONS, William, S5987, W, 35th Inf.
SIMMONS, William E. S7808, SH, 42nd Miss. Inf.
SIMMONS, William Thadeus, S13686, SH, 14th Inf.
SIMMS, Sallie M. W9173, LA, Simms, James A.
SIMONS, George W. S7889, V, 35th Inf.
SIMONS, Levi, S3916, HI, 48th Inf.
SIMONS, Mary Ellen, W9247, FR, Simons, Henry F.
SIMPSON, Allis, W9160, SN, Simpson, Wm.
SIMPSON, C. W. S8042, WE, 51st Inf.
SIMPSON, Cora Blount, W9629, HU, Simpson, Thomas Monroe
SIMPSON, Frank M. S10711, ST, 1st Ky. Inf.
SIMPSON, G. C. S7915, MC, 59th Inf.
SIMPSON, G. C. S11966, BR, 59th Inf.
SIMPSON, G. M. S13704, WL, 4th (McLemore's) Cav.
SIMPSON, George F. S11213, LO, 59th Inf.
SIMPSON, J. F. S3844, W, 13th Cav.
SIMPSON, J. T. S4236, WL, Allison's Squadron, Cav.
SIMPSON, James, S7172, HW, 31st Inf.
SIMPSON, James A. S3835, HN, 46th Inf.
SIMPSON, Jesse, S7673, HW, 29th Inf.
SIMPSON, John, S16526, GU, Secret Service
SIMPSON, Joseph W. S8654, MOO, 17th Inf.
SIMPSON, L. A. W1897, FR, Simpson, Rice
SIMPSON, L. E. S16446, DK, 21st Inf.
SIMPSON, Lackey Elizabeth, W7577, ST, Simpson, Francis Marion
SIMPSON, Mary Eliza, W1703, D, Simpson, Wm. Rowan
SIMPSON, Retter, W3023, WE, Simpson, Charles Wesley
SIMPSON, Rice sr. S2347, MOO, 4th Inf.
SIMPSON, Sarah Jane [Heard], W10890, SH, Simpson, George Washington, [Later married Heard]
SIMPSON, T. M. S7109, HU, 1st (Feild's) Inf.
SIMPSON, Thomas, S462, L, 24th S.C. Inf.
SIMPSON, W. A. S15540, O, 19th (Biffle's) Cav.
SIMPSON, W. D. S5403, D, 20th Inf.
SIMS, B. E. S7265, RU, 1st (Feild's) Inf.
SIMS, Caldena, W2942, ME, Sims, George W.
SIMS, Elizabeth C. W7773, LE, Sims, Jesse M.
SIMS, Emma, W4488, WH, Sims, Wm. Glenn
SIMS, Fannie Ann Elizabeth, W5945, MA, Sims, Robert Campbell
SIMS, Georgeia, W9867, K, Sims, Ryan J.
SIMS, Gertrude R. W3692, RU, Sims, Bart E.

-315

SIMS, H. W. S12360, WH, 8th (Dibrell's) Cav.
SIMS, Isabelle, W3619, WH, Sims, Lawson C.
SIMS, J. G. S16602, WH, 8th Cav.
SIMS, J. M. S14078, LE, 19th (Biffle's) Cav.
SIMS, James, S1198, LE, 3rd Inf.
SIMS, Jere, S15382, H, 39th Ga. Inf.
SIMS, L. C. S5386, WH, 8th Cav.
SIMS, Lucy Burt, W277, B, Sims, Wm. Edward
SIMS, Lucy Cummings, W9038, B, Sims, Matthew Benton
SIMS, Lucy Jane, W3453, G, Sims, M. T.
SIMS, Mary Ellen, W10681, CF, Sims, Wm. Polk
SIMS, Mathew Tyler, S11107, G, 45th Inf.
SIMS, R. J. S14980, K, 29th Bn. Ga. Cav.
SIMS, Sarah Isabell, W9962, H, Sims, Jerry Myers
SIMS, Thomas J. S4126, CY, Shaw's Bn. Cav.
SIMS, Thomas J. S8132, C, 16th Cav.
SIMS, W. G. S12180, WH, 16th Inf.
SIMS, W. P. S11350, CF, 11th (Holman's) Cav.
SIMS, William E. S14426, WH, 8th (Dibrell's) Cav.
SIMS, William R. S14950, SH, 18th Miss. Cav.
SINARD, J. H. S5229, GR, 6th Ga. Cav.
SINCLAIR, Frances Virginia, W4083, D, Sinclair, Archibald
SINCLAIR, Missouri Bell, W8258, HN, Sinclair, G. A.
SINDLE, Grace G. W4725, SN, Sindle, Robert Henry
SINDLE, Robert H. S1067, SN, 2nd Inf.
SINGLETON, Celia Ann, W7166, CT, Singleton, H. M.
SINGLETON, Harrison D. S3976, BO, 3rd (Lillard's) Mtd. Inf.
SINGLETON, Henry W. S12158, CT, 6th N.C. Inf.
SINGLETON, Hugh L. S1174, BO, 3rd Inf.
SINGLETON, James C. S14087, CT, 58th N.C. Inf.
SINGLETON, Laura E. W9413, CT, Singleton, James Calvin
SINGLETON, Robert, S1762, BO, 25th Inf.
SINGLETON, Robert L. S10629, B, 17th Inf.
SINGLETON, Sallie E. W7270, B, Singleton, Robert Tipecourt
SINGLETON, Sam, S3121, MN, 19th Cav.
SINK, Ellen B. W3030, SH, Sink, George Franklin
SINK, John H. S12990, SH, 9th Inf.

SINK, Sarah (Sallie) Virg. W9190, W8233, SH, Sink, John Henry
SINKLER, C. F. S2523, O, 27th Inf.
SINKLER, Mary A. W735, O, Sinkler, Charles F.
SINNAMON, W. B. S4661, GR, 1st (Carter's) Cav.
SINNOTT, Della Morgan, W7063, D, Sinnott, H. T.
SIRCY, K. T. S10602, J, 45th Inf.
SIRCY, Martha F. W1458, SM, Sircy, James
SIRLS, Charles, S3033, D, 1st (McNairy's) Bn. Cav.
SISCO, John E. S15898, HI, 49th Inf.
SISCO, Saunders, S5353, J, 28th Inf.
SISK, John, S2323, GI, 53rd Inf.
SISK, Salome Qn. Victoria, W1985, SE, Sisk, Wm. Henry
SISK, W. H. S7816, SE, 37th Inf.
SITZ, James W. S2121, FR, 48th Ala. Inf.
SIZEMORE, E. D. S9987, HA, 43rd Inf.
SIZEMORE, G. M. S7012, HU, 4th Inf.
SIZEMORE, Louisannah, W3261, K, Sizemore, Wm. O.
SIZEMORE, McG. Milley, W3820, BO, Sizemore, Thomas
SIZEMORE, Sallie Ann, W1291, DI, Sizemore, Rufus Hix
SIZEMORE, Thomas, S8975, BO, 62nd N.C. Inf.
SKEFFINGTON, Mary Amelia, W4788, DY, Skeffington, John
SKELLEY, J. B. S14888, MU, Sparkman's Co. Lt. Art.
SKELLEY, Sarah Louise, W4719, WI, Skelley, James Crawford
SKELTON, Eliza A. W4305, HW, Skelton, James
SKELTON, J. M. S16251, HO, 11th Cav.
SKELTON, John, S12374, BR, 19th Inf.
SKELTON, Joseph, S2148, S4339, HW, 12th Cav.
SKELTON, Martha Jane, W4320, H, Skelton, T. B.
SKELTON, S. S6137, G, 5th Miss. Inf.
SKELTON, Sarah Elizabeth, W5508, G, Skelton, Solomon
SKELTON, Thomas N. S16143, CC, 27th Inf.
SKELTON, W. J. S8027, W, 35th Inf.
SKIDMORE, A. J. S14546, FR, 1st (Turney's) Inf.

Index to Tennessee Confederate Pension Applications

SKIFFER, S. H. S7424, MU, 9th Bn. (Gantt's) Cav.
SKILLERN, J. A. P. S9873, GI, 6th (Wheeler's) Cav.
SKILLERN, Sallie Jim, W2796, MA, Skillern, John Henry
SKILLMAN, Millie K. W912, LA, Skillman, Wm. H.
SKIMEHORN, David, S4562, J, 28th Inf.
SKIMERHORN, Malinda, W6692, SN, Skimerhorn, David
SKINNER, G. W. S4907, DY, 43rd Inf.
SLACK, A. E. S6976, MC, 43rd Inf.
SLACK, Alice, W3828, MC, Slack, Abraham
SLACK, Nancy J. W4260, MC, Slack, Abner E.
SLAGEL, Mary Elizabeth, W2768, LA, Slagel, John
SLAGLE, Henry, S11512, C, 4th Ky. Cav.
SLAGLE, J. H. S5236, RO, 43rd Inf.
SLAGLE, John, S9556, LA, 20th Cav.
SLAGLE, William R. S10369, HR, 23rd Inf.
SLAINBECK, William E. S14432, SH, 9th Inf.
SLASS, Mary Louise, W3611, SH, Slass, Joseph Humphreys
SLATER, O. L. S14997, SH, 1st Conf. Army, Art.
SLATTEN, A. C. S6532, V, Unassigned
SLATTEN, John, S6425, W, 16th Inf.
SLATTEN, Mary P. W2492, WH, Slatten, Martin Van Buren
SLATTER, William J. S6554, FR, 1st (Turney's) Inf.
SLAUGHTER, Andrew J. S7248, ME, 43rd Inf.
SLAUGHTER, Benjamin G. S259, FR, Morgan's Ky. Cav.
SLAUGHTER, Cornelia D. W4702, RU, Slaughter, W. B.
SLAUGHTER, David, S1900, SU, 59th Inf.
SLAUGHTER, E. H. S8620, HU, 18th Inf.
SLAUGHTER, George W. S53, MS, 4th Cav.
SLAUGHTER, Hugh, S11826, MU, 8th (Smith's) Cav.
SLAUGHTER, Isaac, S1371, SU, 60th Inf.
SLAUGHTER, Jacob, S161, SU, 59th Inf.
SLAUGHTER, L. G. S11332, SH, 2nd Miss. Cav.
SLAUGHTER, Mariah, W423, SU, Slaughter, David
SLAUGHTER, Martha Caroline, W6217, HU, Slaughter, Edward Hugh
SLAUGHTER, William B. S56, RU, 18th Inf.
SLAYDEN, A. J. S1016, HI, 24th Inf.

SLAYDEN, Augustine Maria, W11146, MT, Slayden, John Dan
SLAYDEN, Florence, W9601, O, Slayden, Wm. Daniel Everett
SLAYDEN, James B. S10225, D, 45th Va. Inf.
SLAYDEN, John D. S15601, MT, 11th Inf.
SLAYDEN, W. D. E. S14908, O, 12th Ky. Cav.
SLEDGE, John W. S8118, WI, 45th Inf.
SLIGAR, Asa, S10522, LO, 43rd Inf.
SLIGAR, C. (Kit), S8478, WH, Daly's Co. Tex. Cav.
SLIGAR, F. M. S15293, WA, 19th Inf.
SLIGAR, F. Marion, S8794, MC, 3rd Inf.
SLIGAR, Henry Martin, S5538, WA, 19th Inf.
SLIGAR, J. L. S9769, ME, 43rd Inf.
SLIGAR, J. W. S16435, 63rd Inf., Applied from Craighead Co. AR
SLIGAR, Jacob E. S3782, MC, 43rd Inf.
SLIGAR, John, S15928, DY, 63rd Inf.
SLIGAR, John W. S7525, PU, 25th Inf.
SLIGAR, Sarah, W8197, H, Sligar, J. L.
SLIGER, Mary Catherine, W10620, MC, Sliger, Jacob Elias
SLIGER, Mary Jane, W691, WA, Sliger, Samuel
SLIGER, T. J. S2348, WA, 60th Inf.
SLIGER, W. L. S7210, PU, 25th Inf.
SLINGER, Phoebe E. W1045, ME, Slinger, Joseph
SLINKARD, John H. S928, S721, D, 20th Inf.
SLINKARD, Susie Canaday, W10928, D, Slinkard, John H.
SLOAN, Anna Dorcas, W8297, D, Sloan, James Theodore
SLOAN, Elizabeth, W7176, D, Sloan, James T.
SLOAN, F. B. S15254, FR, 5th Cav.
SLOAN, J. K. S9801, D, Rock City Guards
SLOAN, J. T. S15317, D, 8th N.C. Inf.
SLOAN, James Theadore, S14127, D, 1st (Feild's) Inf.
SLOAN, Martin, S612, J, 4th Cav.
SLOAN, Mary Elizabeth, W343, WL, Sloan, John Calvin
SLOAN, R. B. S6793, G, 4th Miss. Cav.
SLOAN, Sallie E. W5847, G, Sloan, Ryley B.
SLOAN, Sallie Wilson, W5337, SH, Sloan, John Thomas
SLOAN, Sarah Frances, W2357, D, Sloan, James Alexander
SLOAN, W. H. S7518, D, 1st Inf.
SLOAN, William Henry, S14319, D, 12th Bn. (Day's) Cav.
SLONAKER, Mary,   See Mary White

-317

SMALL, Alice Rebecca, W8776, LI, Small, Robert Jarman
SMALLEN, James K. S5930, LO, 3rd (Lillard's) Mtd. Inf.
SMALLEN, S. M. S3544, LO, 62nd Inf.
SMALLING, Sarah Clay, W10128, B, Smalling, Towning Fugitt
SMALLMAN, M. D. S16069, W, 13th (Gore's) Cav.
SMART, G. S4500, RU, 20th Inf.
SMART, Henry, S7890, K, 51st Va. Inf.
SMART, J. S. S9678, CO, 2nd N.C. Bn.
SMART, Mollie V. W5557, HR, Smart, N. Z.
SMART, Newton Zachariah, S11650, HR, 13th Inf.
SMART, Rufina Angeline, W6060, CO, Smart, Joseph S.
SMARTT, Ezekiel, S9217, GU, 16th Inf.
SMATHERMAN, Martha J. W1030, B, Smatherman, Daniel Dotson
SMEDLEY, W. H. S16368, MR, 34th Inf.
SMITH, A. B. S7266, HA, 2nd (Ashby's) Cav.
SMITH, A. C. S13828, SU, 3rd Ga. Inf.
SMITH, A. G. S8870, DY, 12th Inf.
SMITH, A. J. S2172, ST, 50th Inf.
SMITH, A. P. S14451, RB, 2nd Va. State Troops
SMITH, A. T. S629, D, 49th Inf.
SMITH, Abner C. S3026, PU, 1st La. Cav.
SMITH, Adaline, W2746, SU, Smith, Joseph
SMITH, Addie Florence, W2525, CY, Smith, Joseph
SMITH, Albert J. S3249, WA, 61st Inf.
SMITH, Alexander, S6057, SU, 63rd Va. Inf.
SMITH, Alexander, S13844, CU, 16th Bn. (Neal's) Cav.
SMITH, Alexander C. S8679, LI, 1st Inf.
SMITH, Alice, W10933, RB, Smith, Albert P.
SMITH, Allen, S2075, MO, 2nd (Ashby's) Cav.
SMITH, Allen, S9938, W, 16th Inf.
SMITH, Alta Cora, W6120, J, Smith, Thomas Grisson
SMITH, Amanda, W5830, WH, Smith, John
SMITH, Amanda G. W9574, ST, Smith, Nelson jr.
SMITH, Amanda J. W10244, B, Smith, Samuel Green
SMITH, Angie, W7464, MT, Smith, Benjamin Robert
SMITH, Ann E. W6752, Smith, John T.
SMITH, Ann Eliza, W4159, H, Smith, Wm. Rutledge

SMITH, Anna Duffee, W10660, RU, Smith, Sampson B.
SMITH, Annie, W3693, HW, Smith, David R.
SMITH, Annie, W5650, MN, Smith, James
SMITH, Annie Duval, W5462, D, Smith, Wm. Henry Harrison
SMITH, Annie N. W7519, H, Smith, Frank M.
SMITH, B. B. S2816, S8835, HR, 59th Ala. Inf.
SMITH, B. F. S811, OV, 1st Inf.
SMITH, B. F. S16345, S15674, LI, 18th Ala. Inf.
SMITH, Barbara Jane, W10915, RO, Smith, Wm.
SMITH, Benjamin Franklin, S4149, PU, 52nd Inf.
SMITH, Benjamin R. S7157, MT, 14th Inf.
SMITH, Benjamin W. S1252, LI, 41st Inf.
SMITH, Benjamin W. S2801, J, 18th (Gore's) Cav.
SMITH, Bettie, W6716, H, Smith, John H.
SMITH, Bettie G. W7730, H, Smith, Baxter
SMITH, Bettie J. W7458, WI, Smith, Daniel
SMITH, Blanche, W6501, MT, Smith, McTerrin
SMITH, Burton L. S14949, T, 51st Inf.
SMITH, C. C. S9521, MC, 31st Inf.
SMITH, C. H. S8921, WE, 12th Inf.
SMITH, C. S. S15222, L, 7th Miss. Cav.
SMITH, Caleb B. S11764, LI, 15th S.C. Inf.
SMITH, Caroline, W6899, PO, Smith, Green Berry
SMITH, Cassie, W2957, UN, Smith, James Calvin
SMITH, Catherine, W3885, MN, Smith, Edward
SMITH, Catlett Allensmith, W5440, MT, Smith, Burnley Duke
SMITH, Cattie, W1576, W, Smith, Audley
SMITH, Charles H. S2416, G, 53rd Va. Inf.
SMITH, Chas. T. S13048, SH, Withers' Regt. Lt. Art.
SMITH, Clementine, W6985, W6643, Smith, Littleberry
SMITH, Coleman, S8948, R, 43rd Inf.
SMITH, Coleman Davis, C, SH, Body steward of Sam Davis, Application is missing.
SMITH, Cynthia Elizabeth, W7405, D, Smith, Felix Randolph R.
SMITH, D. B. S11998, W, 16th Inf.
SMITH, D. H. S13925, SN, 9th (Ward's) Cav.
SMITH, D. M. S930, GI, 11th Cav.
SMITH, D. T. S8032, WH, 8th (Dibrell's) Cav.
SMITH, Daniel, S11398, SM, 22nd Inf.
SMITH, David, S3597, GE, 31st Inf.

Index to Tennessee Confederate Pension Applications

SMITH, David, S5125, PO, 3rd Inf.
SMITH, David L. S3140, LI, 41st Inf.
SMITH, David S. S2521, FR, 17th Inf.
SMITH, Delila Mildred, W535, HI, Smith, Theodore Bell
SMITH, Dollie, W9509, WA, Smith, Jacob
SMITH, E. D. S8169, MS, 48th Inf.
SMITH, E. H. Chapman, W4395, GE, Smith, Wm. Hunley
SMITH, E. J. S8530, MR, 4th Inf.
SMITH, Ed. S15486, FR, 22nd (Barteau's) Cav.
SMITH, Edward, S2379, HD, 21st Ga. Inf.
SMITH, Elbert S. S6101, H, 3rd Ala. Inf.
SMITH, Eli, S1723, WL, 7th Inf.
SMITH, Eli, S12262, HU, 50th Inf.
SMITH, Eliza, W10092, A, Smith, Wm.
SMITH, Eliza Jane, W3794, MS, Smith, Wiley Eli
SMITH, Eliza Jane, W4303, HR, Smith, John P.
SMITH, Elizabeth, W1602, H, Smith, Nathaniel H.
SMITH, Elizabeth, W1616, MO, Smith, Wm. R.
SMITH, Elizabeth, W3213, HR, Smith, John W.
SMITH, Elizabeth, W4716, WL, Smith, John
SMITH, Elizabeth, W5074, RO, Smith, Thomas A.
SMITH, Elizabeth Ann, W1282, MO, Smith, Thomas Haywood
SMITH, Elizabeth E. W2574, MA, Smith, Thomas H.
SMITH, Ella C. W1777, WL, Smith, Wm.
SMITH, Ellender R. W4917, HW, Smith, John R.
SMITH, Elmira, W10154, FE, Smith, Thomas Branford
SMITH, Emma, W8056, SH, Smith, Chas. Thos.
SMITH, Emmerson, S844, HW, 63rd Inf.
SMITH, Eunice O. W10214, D, Smith, I. E.
SMITH, F. M. S1760, SU, 6th Inf.
SMITH, F. M. S2110, OV, 25th Inf.
SMITH, F. M. S6365, JO, 63rd Va. Inf.
SMITH, F. P. S4657, PI, 8th (Dibrell's) Cav.
SMITH, Fannie Baugh, W9597, D, Smith, Booker Byrd
SMITH, Fannie Ellha, W1715, MOO, Smith, Wm. B.
SMITH, Fannie Jane, W6994, HY, Smith, Hugh Reden
SMITH, Felix R. R. S15239, D, "Corps of Engineers"
SMITH, Frances, W9073, FR, Smith, Samuel Houston

SMITH, Frank, S11712, BE, 52nd Inf.
SMITH, Frank M. S15192, H, 3rd Inf.
SMITH, G. B. S13749, BR, 11th Ga. Inf.
SMITH, G. H. S7625, HD, 1st Cav.
SMITH, G. T. S291, ME, 43rd Inf.
SMITH, G. W. S1858, HM, 61st Inf.
SMITH, G. W. S2926, BR, 32nd Inf.
SMITH, G. W. S9831, T, 9th Inf.
SMITH, G. W. S10128, SU, 5th Cav.
SMITH, George, S6497, HW, 31st Inf.
SMITH, George Madison, S11679, DY, 20th Cav.
SMITH, George Marten, S6589, MT, 14th Inf.
SMITH, George W. S2258, J, 28th Inf.
SMITH, George W. S2864, MN, 8th Inf.
SMITH, George W. S8730, CH, 21st Cav.
SMITH, Georgia, W1171, B, Smith, Benjamin Franklin
SMITH, H. R. S14992, HY, 2nd Miss. Inf.
SMITH, Harrison, S2733, SM, 24th Inf.
SMITH, Harvey M. S1731, GI, 20th Cav.
SMITH, Henrietta Farah, W5962, DY, Smith, Albert Galiton
SMITH, Henry C. S11722, TR, 4th Cav.
SMITH, Henry Clay, S16468, WL, 4th Cav.
SMITH, Hensley, S1068, SM, 28th Inf.
SMITH, Horace I. S12105, PO, 2nd Ga. Cav.
SMITH, Hugh, S6037, HW, 31st Inf.
SMITH, I. E. S10823, D, 4th (McLemore's) Cav.
SMITH, Imogene, W6044, MT, Smith, Alphonzo Frederick
SMITH, Irene A. W3283, D, Smith, John Morgan
SMITH, Isaac D. S830, PI, 8th Cav.
SMITH, J. A. S3636, H, 4th Cav.
SMITH, J. A. S7724, B, 32nd Inf.
SMITH, J. A. S14159, H, 36th Inf.
SMITH, J. B. S509, FR, 41st Inf.
SMITH, J. C. S5905, H, 1st (Carter's) Cav.
SMITH, J. D. S12118, D, 43rd Inf.
SMITH, J. F. S15794, SH, 15th Cav.
SMITH, J. H. S7382, H, 5th (McKenzie's) Cav.
SMITH, J. H. S9329, S1088, CF, 17th Miss. Inf.
SMITH, J. H. S9348, SH, 26th Miss. Inf.
SMITH, J. H. S11859, H, 1st Ga. Inf.
SMITH, J. J. S7909, WI, 20th Inf.
SMITH, J. K. S4773, RO, 2nd (Ashby's) Cav.
SMITH, J. K. P. S15611, RU, 2nd (Robison's) Inf.
SMITH, J. L. S3586, SU, 63rd Inf.
SMITH, J. L. S5722, LA, 19th (Biffle's) Cav.

Index to Tennessee Confederate Pension Applications

SMITH, J. L. S15720, SH, 18th Miss. Cav.
SMITH, J. M. S8888, O, 3rd Inf.
SMITH, J. N. S9178, SQ, 5th Inf.
SMITH, J. P. S6457, GI, 9th Ala. Inf.
SMITH, J. R. S638, OV, 28th Inf.
SMITH, J. S. S11339, CL, 2nd (Ashby's) Cav.
SMITH, J. S. S15739, G, 14th (Neely's) Cav.
SMITH, J. T. S4219, GI, 3rd Inf.
SMITH, J. T. S7090, H, 5th Cav.
SMITH, J. T. S8463, 1st Ky. Cav.
SMITH, J. T. S11930, MA, 18th (Newsom's) Cav.
SMITH, J. W. S565, GU, Undetermined
SMITH, J. W. S6217, SU, 59th Mtd. Inf.
SMITH, J. Wess, C47, MOO, 17th Inf.
SMITH, Jacob, S6363, WA, White's Co. Sullivan County Reserves
SMITH, Jacob F. S11695, DY, 10th S.C. Inf.
SMITH, James, S3397, MR, 1st Cav.
SMITH, James, S5878, MT, 14th Inf.
SMITH, James, S6498, HW, 3rd Engineer Corps
SMITH, James, S13558, K, 27th Bn. Va. Inf.
SMITH, James B. S10523, D, 1st (Feild's) Inf.
SMITH, James C. S2207, U, 5th Cav.
SMITH, James Grundy, S12219, CA, 45th Inf.
SMITH, James H. S15461, WY, 19th (Biffle's) Cav.
SMITH, James K. S6922, MOO, 44th Inf.
SMITH, James M. S7595, D, 25th Inf.
SMITH, James M. S12899, HI, 8th (Dibrell's) Cav.
SMITH, James M. S13087, D, 8th (Smith's) Cav.
SMITH, Jane, W6469, MN, Smith, Richard A.
SMITH, Jane Andrsn. Cmpbll. W3554, SM, Smith, Fountain Perry
SMITH, Jim, S16405, CC, 11th Inf.
SMITH, Joe, S9541, MA, 9th Cav.
SMITH, Joe P. S13771, RU, 18th Inf.
SMITH, Joel A. S9863, SU, 1st Bn. Va. Inf.
SMITH, John, S678, PU, 28th Inf.
SMITH, John, S4427, U, 1st (Carter's) Cav.
SMITH, John, S5099, JE, 12th Bn. Cav.
SMITH, John, S5568, T, 22nd Inf.
SMITH, John, S6290, GU, 44th Inf.
SMITH, John B. S178, O, 47th Inf.
SMITH, John B. S3633, HW, 31st Inf.
SMITH, John C. S1766, CF, 38th Inf.
SMITH, John C. S13741, WI, 4th (McLemore's) Cav.
SMITH, John Calvin, S3960, LI, 41st Inf.

SMITH, John D. S6300, S16348, SH, 4th (McLemore's) Cav.
SMITH, John E. S3935, DY, 18th Inf.
SMITH, John F. S11311, C, 3rd (Lillard's) Inf.
SMITH, John H. S7426, T, 22nd Inf.
SMITH, John H. S8189, RO, 28th Inf.
SMITH, John J. S3697, SU, 61st Inf.
SMITH, John M. S3975, A, 1st (Carter's) Cav.
SMITH, John M. S13632, K, 2nd (Ashby's) Cav.
SMITH, John M. S14322, D, 1st Confederate Cav.
SMITH, John Morgan, S9685, D, 4th Ky. Inf.
SMITH, John P. S13078, SH, 14th (Neely's) Cav.
SMITH, John T. S15398, H, Undetermined
SMITH, John W. S4933, SN, 2nd Ky. Inf.
SMITH, John W. S6164, LA, Ark. Inf.
SMITH, John W. S11651, HR, 18th Miss. Cav.
SMITH, John W. S14446, LI, 44th Inf.
SMITH, Jonathan, S8626, HA, 64th Va. Cav.
SMITH, Joseph, S1913, SU, 59th inf.
SMITH, Joseph, S5444, WA, 29th Inf.
SMITH, Joseph A. S1687, BO, 1st (Carter's) Cav.
SMITH, Julia J. W1343, RO, Smith, Wm. G.
SMITH, L. B. S6327, 48th (Nixon's) Inf.
SMITH, L. C. S15718, MC, 16th S.C. Cav.
SMITH, L. H. S8421, D, 44th Inf.
SMITH, Leonidas, S13011, S2156, GI, 32nd Inf.
SMITH, Lewis, C108, D, 16th Cav.
SMITH, Lizzie, W4436, RU, Smith, Sherwood
SMITH, Lou R. W2266, BR, Smith, David Francis
SMITH, Louisa, W131, SU, Smith, Francis M.
SMITH, Lowery, S4713, PI, 16th Bn. Cav.
SMITH, Lucinda, W1854, BR, Smith, Hezekiah
SMITH, Lucinda R. W2901, WA, Smith, James R.
SMITH, Lucy, W10863, SM, Smith, Wm. H.
SMITH, Lucy Ann, W6498, O, Smith, George Cephus
SMITH, Lucy D. W6053, D, Smith, Allen Hill
SMITH, Lucy Jane, W9346, H, Smith, David Walter
SMITH, Lutetia, W3320, WH, Smith, Robert
SMITH, Lyda H. W8629, D, Smith, John M.
SMITH, M. F. S11314, MT, 14th Inf.
SMITH, M. K. S13280, MN, 26th Miss. Inf.
SMITH, M. M. S8625, CY, 8th Inf.
SMITH, M. M. S14939, CY, 8th Cav.
SMITH, Mada F. W6358, MU, Smith, John Ellette

SMITH, Mag, W543, WL, Smith, W. C.
SMITH, Maggie A. W5583, MA, Smith, Henry Franklin
SMITH, Maggie F. W6123, DY, Smith, James Josh
SMITH, Margaret, W43, J, Smith, John Dillard
SMITH, Margaret, W162, HM, Smith, Samuel B.
SMITH, Margaret Adline, W6668, M, Smith, Wm. Henry Harrison
SMITH, Margaret E. W1660, SU, Smith, Thomas H.
SMITH, Margaret L. W10713, CL, Smith, James Sterling
SMITH, Marion S. S11652, HR, 18th Miss. Cav.
SMITH, Martha, W7869, CY, Smith, Mordica Milton
SMITH, Martha A. W3232, H, Smith, John C.
SMITH, Martha Ann, W9825, HU, Smith, Thomas Bartlett
SMITH, Martha E. W1804, MR, Smith, Marquett DeLafayette
SMITH, Martha J. W6188, SU, Smith, George Rutledge
SMITH, Martha Jane, W2808, LA, Smith, John W.
SMITH, Martha Jane, W5320, D, Smith, Thomas P.
SMITH, Martha Marietta, W10939, K, Smith, Charles Harry
SMITH, Martha Susan, W1134, Smith, Wm. Milton
SMITH, Martha Virginia, W9634, WI, Smith, Samuel Aaron
SMITH, Mary, W569, LI, Smith, R. F.
SMITH, Mary, W6309, MT, Smith, George W.
SMITH, Mary A. W209, SU, Smith, George W.
SMITH, Mary A. W5674, HW, Smith, Hugh
SMITH, Mary Almeda, W8975, MU, Smith, James
SMITH, Mary Ann, W1158, DI, Smith, James Montgomery
SMITH, Mary Ann, W6711, LI, Smith, Ben J.
SMITH, Mary Ann [Franklin], W10354, LA, Smith, Green B. [Later married Franklin]
SMITH, Mary Burr, W10126, B, Smith, Jasper Newton
SMITH, Mary Cornelia, W6659, SH, Smith, Newton Casper
SMITH, Mary Davis, W3465, Smith, Wm. S.

SMITH, Mary Dougherty, W8848, RU, Smith, Joseph Paten
SMITH, Mary E. W2431, SN, Smith, John W.
SMITH, Mary E. W5885, G, Smith, W. M.
SMITH, Mary E. W8743, DI, Smith, Martin Van Buren
SMITH, Mary Elizabeth, W2251, SU, Smith, Alexander
SMITH, Mary Frances, W8858, RU, Smith, Andrew Harvey
SMITH, Mary I. W10997, ME, Smith, Thomas P.
SMITH, Mary J. W4915, FR, Smith, J. B.
SMITH, Mary J. W10401, GE, Smith, Wm. B.
SMITH, Mary Jane, W4237, F, Smith, Samuel Monroe
SMITH, Mary Jane, W5038, ME, Smith, Gideon Thompson
SMITH, Mary L. W2989, O, Smith, Wm. Jackson
SMITH, Mary S. W374, HI, Smith, Thomas Frazier
SMITH, Mary Sue, W4966, WI, Smith, W. C.
SMITH, Mary Susan, W7331, BL, Smith, Sam M.
SMITH, Matilda, W3190, GE, Smith, David M.
SMITH, Matthew Sims, S717, PU, 16th Inf.
SMITH, Mattie Lou, W11048, D, Smith, Henry Clay
SMITH, Mattie Meadows, W9466, CY, Smith, Mathew Mordicea
SMITH, Mattie P. W3285, HR, Smith, Monroe S.
SMITH, Milla, W1768, SC, Smith, Sterling C.
SMITH, Minnie G. W6354, SU, Smith, John Wright
SMITH, Missouri C. W10688, P, Smith, James Noah
SMITH, Myra Anne, W9488, FR, Smith, Robert George
SMITH, Myra Elizabeth, W9651, K, Smith, John Martin
SMITH, Nancy, W3104, OV, Smith, R. B.
SMITH, Nancy, W6330, MR, Smith, James N.
SMITH, Nancy Ann, W3248, OV, Smith, Franklin M.
SMITH, Nancy C. W269, HN, Smith, Joseph H.
SMITH, Nancy J. W669, R, Smith, Wm. Henry
SMITH, Nannie, W5514, MT, Smith, Richard Hugh
SMITH, Nannie Elizabeth, W6400, D, Smith, Thomas Walace

Index to Tennessee Confederate Pension Applications

SMITH, Nannie L. See Nannie L. Jones
SMITH, Nattie, W4862, MT, Smith, James
SMITH, Nelson, S7491, HO, 7th Inf.
SMITH, Nelson, S15342, GI, 44th Inf.
SMITH, Newton C. S13625, SH, 9th Inf.
SMITH, Orlena Tennessee, W270, R, Smith, James
SMITH, P. H. S12013, LI, 44th Inf.
SMITH, P. S. S11571, MN, 18th (Newsom's) Cav.
SMITH, P. W. S3167, BE, 27th Inf.
SMITH, Patience, W518, BL, Smith, Benjamin Franklin
SMITH, Permelia Adlaide, W4403, D, Smith, James B.
SMITH, Presley (Press), C70, MA, 6th Inf.
SMITH, Priscilla, W4729, HR, Smith, George W.
SMITH, Prissie Elizabeth, W5725, JE, Smith, Wm. Montgomery
SMITH, Purlina Frances, W3944, G, Smith, C. H.
SMITH, R. S5755, MT, 14th Inf.
SMITH, R. H. S2538, HE, 27th Inf.
SMITH, Rachel Elizabeth, W5932, K, Smith, Wm. Harrison
SMITH, Rachel Jane, W8610, D, Smith, Wm. Crawford
SMITH, Rebecca, W10595, D, Knight, Wm. Leonard, See Also Rebecca Knight
SMITH, Rebecca Ann, W9889, DY, Smith, Joe Fletcher
SMITH, Richard G. S10340, WH, 25th Inf.
SMITH, Robert Clinton, S13863, T, 4th Inf.
SMITH, Robert Etcherson, S14008, T, 12th (Green's) Cav.
SMITH, Robert G. S3941, FR, 23rd Inf.
SMITH, Robert Palmer, S16676, SH, 1st Miss. Cav.
SMITH, Rosa, W10166, LI, Smith, Benjamin Franklin
SMITH, Rufus K. S1465, D, 10th Inf.
SMITH, Ruth Ann, W9542, RU, Smith, John Mathew
SMITH, S. A. S14317, S15360, WI, 11th (Holman's) Cav.
SMITH, S. B. S11132, MT, 49th Inf.
SMITH, Sallie, W8654, J, Smith, Joseph Lemiah
SMITH, Sallie Ann, W744, HN, Smith, Thomas Jefferson
SMITH, Sallie Ann, W6456, T, Smith, John Henry
SMITH, Sallie Frances, W7611, D, Smith, Rufus K.
SMITH, Sam M. S14822, BL, 44th Ga. Inf.
SMITH, Samuel, S2744, BO, 3rd Inf.
SMITH, Samuel, S4822, HN, 46th Inf.
SMITH, Samuel, S13364, HU, 20th Inf.
SMITH, Sarah A. W5049, MO, Smith, Allen
SMITH, Sarah Elizabeth, W4969, MA, Smith, Jesse Richard
SMITH, Sarah Frances, W6836, T, Smith, Berton Liton
SMITH, Sarah J. W2747, SU, Smith, Charles W.
SMITH, Sarah Lula, W7856, BR, Smith, George Washington
SMITH, Sarah M. W3212, SU, Smith, John J.
SMITH, Seignei Ora, W3960, HY, Smith, Harvey Mordrell
SMITH, Shirwood W. S9414, RU, Mead's Co. N. Ala. Troops
SMITH, Sidney Helen, W5111, SH, Smith, Alfred Spencer
SMITH, Simeon, S4049, G, 9th Cav.
SMITH, Sinia Amerella, W2797, LI, Smith, Alexander Coleman
SMITH, Soloman, S3766, CL, 3rd Inf.
SMITH, Stephen, S1362, HW, 3rd Inf.
SMITH, Susan Anne, W8923, L, Smith, Granville Dickson
SMITH, Susan Frances, W6294, WL, Smith, John Christopher
SMITH, Susannah, W6636, GU, Smith, John
SMITH, T. C. S10138, 16th Cav.
SMITH, T. H. S3087, MO, 31st Inf.
SMITH, T. H. S4630, CH, 6th Inf.
SMITH, T. P. S13956, CY, 25th Inf.
SMITH, T. P. S15827, ME, 5th (McKenzie's) Cav.
SMITH, T. W. S14853, D, 20th (Nixon's) Cav.
SMITH, Telitha, W3241, J, Smith, John T.
SMITH, Thomas A. S11166, RO, Thomas' Legion, N.C.
SMITH, Thomas F. S1316, HI, 11th Inf.
SMITH, Thomas G. S2539, J, 8th (Dibrell's) Cav.
SMITH, Thomas H. S7517, SU, 61st Inf.
SMITH, Thomas M. S15045, D, 45th Inf.
SMITH, Thomas P. S3431, DE, 49th Inf.
SMITH, Tobitah, W179, D, Smith, Wm. Washington
SMITH, Victoria Brooks, W9199, SH, Smith, Joel Henry

SMITH, W. B. S13650, GE, Thomas' Legion, N.C.
SMITH, W. E. S14785, RU, 18th Inf.
SMITH, W. F. S10400, WI, 24th Inf.
SMITH, W. F. S12238, MR, 55th Ala. Inf.
SMITH, W. G. S2661, RO, 28th Inf.
SMITH, W. H. S11486, M, 24th Inf.
SMITH, W. H. S15040, MA, 11th Miss. Inf.
SMITH, W. Jasper, S9637, F, 6th Inf.
SMITH, W. M. S2802, FE, 16th Cav.
SMITH, W. M. S13790, MU, 48th Inf.
SMITH, W. R. S2295, MO, 154th Sr. Regt. Inf.
SMITH, W. S. S1563, MA, 12th Cav.
SMITH, W. T. S13272, MT, 49th Inf.
SMITH, W. W. S10559, DI, 18th Inf.
SMITH, Wade H. S16298, MT, 2nd Inf.
SMITH, Walter, S6058, S2721, HI, 24th Inf.
SMITH, Wash J. S7287, SH, Wither's Regt. Miss. Vols.
SMITH, William, S4263, S9714, WL, 45th Inf.
SMITH, William, S6114, FE, 16th Bn. Cav.
SMITH, William, S8543, K, 1st Cav.
SMITH, William, S12052, W, 35th Inf.
SMITH, William A. S5620, SH, 4th Inf.
SMITH, William Dickson, S12576, T, 4th Inf.
SMITH, William E. S15958.5, J, 8th (Dibrell's) Cav.)
SMITH, William F. S6288, CY, 13th (Gore's) Cav.
SMITH, William H. S419, HA, 29th Inf.
SMITH, William H. S906, SN, 45th Inf.
SMITH, William H. S12386, SM, 25th Inf.
SMITH, William M. S6278, 12th Inf.
SMITHEAL, Susy Jackson, W4417, T, Smitheal, Green Williamson
SMITHERS, Jacob, S1315, CT, 8th Va. Cav.
SMITHSON, B. F. S10047, WI, 20th Inf.
SMITHSON, Harriet A. W10084, CA, Smithson, James K. P.
SMITHSON, Hezekiah Powers, S16025, LA, 9th Cav.
SMITHSON, J. H. S11143, SN, 20th Inf.
SMITHSON, J. K. P. S2622, CA, 11th Cav.
SMITHSON, James B. S9931, MS, 45th Inf.
SMITHSON, Luvenia, W9401, W8299, WI, Smithson, Sam Henderson
SMITHSON, Margaret, W10407, SU, Smithson, Samuel Dallas
SMITHSON, Martha Jane, W3788, W, Smithson, Isaac Fletcher
SMITHSON, Martha Susan, W2656, WI, Smithson, Benjamin Franklin

SMITHSON, Mary T. W1559, WI, Smithson, James P.
SMITHSON, Robert A. S10417, WI, 2nd Mo. Cav.
SMITHSON, Samuel D. S5523, SU, 26th Inf.
SMITHSON, Samuel H. S1279, WI, 32nd Inf.
SMITHSON, Susan Elizabeth, W8836, MU, Smithson, James R.
SMITHWICK, F. R. W2198, DY, Smithwick, John Quincy
SMOKE, Rachel A. W4668, GE, Smoke, David Little
SMOOT, Thomas R. S10783, O, 22nd Inf.
SMOTHERMAN, D. d. S5094, B, 24th Inf.
SMOTHERMAN, Flora, W10590, HN, Smotherman, James Granville
SMOTHERMAN, J. T. S5166, RU, 24th Inf.
SMOTHERMAN, James H. S12188, PU, 44th Inf.
SMOTHERMAN, L. H. S16613, HE, 4th (McLemore's) Cav.
SMOTHERMAN, Mary Elizabeth, W2033, RU, Smotherman, James Madison
SMOTHERMAN, R. N. S7662, RU, 11th (Holman's) Cav.
SMOTHERMAN, Rhody Ann, W10411, LA, Smotherman, Calvin Keerlee
SMOTHERS, L. S. S3419, O, 44th Inf.
SMOTHERS, Levi, S5300, O, 44th Inf.
SMOTHERS, Marie Etta, W2323, P, Smothers, Pinkney Loton
SMOTHERS, Pinkney L. S3116, P, 22nd N.C. Inf.
SMYTH, A. D. S9765, WE, 52nd Inf.
SMYTH, A. H. S10848, WE, 9th Inf.
SMYTH, John M. S12124, 7th (Duckworth's) Cav.
SMYTHERS, Evaline, W4122, SU, Smythers, Jacob
SNAPP, Andrew J. S3505, SU, 61st Inf.
SNAPP, Darthula J. W6355, SU, Snapp, Robert L.
SNAPP, J. W. S11388, MR, 2nd Va. Cav.
SNAPP, M. J. W5068, MR, Snapp, Jasper Warrick
SNAPP, Mary, W1970, SU, Snapp, Wm. B.
SNAPP, Ritta, W3013, HW, Snapp, Samuel George
SNAPP, Rowena R. W3209, SU, Snapp, Landen K.
SNAPP, T. S. S11588, GE, 5th (McKenzie's) Cav.

SNEAD, I. D. S2266, WA, 27th Va. Cav.
SNEED, Bettie, W8628, W10545, Sneed, Oscar
SNEED, C. F. S7250, JE, 8th Va. Cav.
SNEED, Harriet R. W4446, CE, Sneed, Nicholas Purkins
SNEED, J. H. S13738, GI, 48th (Voorhies') Inf.
SNEED, John H. S9121, WL, 22nd (Barteau's) Cav.
SNEED, Jumous G. S3370, SH, 38th Inf.
SNEED, N. P. S13439, D, 44th Inf.
SNEED, T. H. S15862, D, 20th Inf.
SNEEK, Maria L. W2332, MO, Sneek, Joseph L.
SNELL, James T. S13026, D, 1st (Feild's) Inf.
SNELL, L. V. W15, RU, Snell, Francis M.
SNELL, Sallie P. W6821, D, Snell, James T.
SNELL, Spencer M. S7299, MS, 17th Inf.
SNIDER, Anna Bond, W10165, MA, Snider, John Finlay
SNIDER, Daniel, S9889, WA, 60th Inf.
SNIDER, George W. S7118, MC, 16th Cav.
SNIDER, John F. S16065, MA, Henderson's Co. Miss. Scouts
SNIDER, Rachel J. W4248, WA, Snider, Daniel
SNIDER, Susan, W2122, MC, Snider, George W.
SNIDER, W. R. S1505, WL, 18th Inf.
SNODDY, Delia F. W6204, LI, Snoddy, Pleasant
SNODDY, Eliza E. W10990, B, Snoddy, James Wm. M.
SNODDY, J. W. M. S11369, B, 61st Inf.
SNODDY, T. E. S14516, K, 61st Inf.
SNODGRASS, Eliza J. W7525, WH, Snodgrass, Lafayette Duff
SNODGRASS, Elizabeth, W5820, SU, Snodgrass, Samuel P.
SNODGRASS, L. D. S12861, WH, 8th (Dibrell's) Cav.
SNODGRASS, Louisa Jane Ellen, W7402, SU, Snodgrass, Morgan
SNODGRASS, Mary Jane, W1418, WH, Snodgrass, Joseph
SNODGRASS, Morgan, S4886, SU, 4th Inf.
SNODGRASS, Samuel P. S7776, SU, 59th Inf.
SNODGRASS, W. G. S14874, JE, 2nd (Ashby's) Cav.
SNOW, A. D. S15080, SM, 5th (McKenzie's) Cav.
SNOW, Eli, S13416, MN, 20th Ala. Inf.
SNOW, James M. S865, SM, 26th Inf.
SNOW, Margaret Victorie, W5248, HD, Snow, Richard Daniel
SNOW, R. D. S3656, HD, 13th Inf.
SNOW, W. E. S13786, HN, 16th Cav.
SNYDER, J. H. S3148, MC, 3rd Cav.
SNYDER, Lucinda Angeline, W5290, MC, Snyder, Reuben George
SNYDER, Mahalia Elizabeth, W1489, R, Snyder, Andrew Roddy
SNYDER, R. G. S1096, MC, 30th Inf.
SNYDER, W. M. S16660, R, 3rd Confederate Cav.
SOLMON, J. E. S3260, MT, 14th Inf.
SOLOMON, Martha A. W2347, HY, Solomon, Henry
SOLOMON, Mary Ann, W6389, LI, Solomon, Eldredge Parker
SOLOMON, Phebe Martha, W2958, MT, Solomon, J. E.
SOMERVILLE, W. M. S3729, PU, 20th Ala. Inf.
SOMMERS, James A. S12127, S14453, F, 46th N.C. Inf.
SONS, John, S5915, B, 17th Inf.
SOPER, Susan J. W1726, WL, Soper, John W.
SORRELL, Sidney, S15368, CC, 15th Cav.
SORRELLS, D. S. S3347, CO, 39th N.C. Inf.
SORRELLS, Nancy Elizabeth, W10868, B, Sorrells, Wm. Harvey
SORRELLS, W. H. S8097, LI, 8th Inf.
SOUTH, Annie McClain, W3821, FR, South, George M.
SOUTH, George M. S3034, FR, 32nd Inf.
SOUTH, John C. S15033, SH, 34th Miss. Inf.
SOUTH, John M. S11878, WA, 48th Va. Inf.
SOUTH, M. V. S10841, FR, 32nd Inf.
SOUTH, Sterling L. S2233, GI, 37th Ala. Inf.
SOUTHALL, Julia Ann, W6127, HR, Southall, Augustus Lafayette
SOUTHERLAND, Imogene Latham, W4421, SH, Southerland, James
SOUTHERLAND, Jane Catherine, W6056, SH, Southerland, J. C.
SOUTHERLAND, John C. S12399, SH, Forrest's Old Regt. Cav.
SOUTHERLAND, Nancy Dona, W10580, DI, Southerland, Robert A.
SOUTHERLAND, R. A. S11004, DI, 49th Inf.
SOUTHERLAND, W. L. S7175, GE, 64th N.C. Inf.
SOUTHERLIN, M. H. S14823, B, 1st Ala. Cav.
SOWARD, Henry W. S10820, RO, 63rd Inf.
SOWELL, A. F. S15162, MU, 9th Bn. Cav.

Index to Tennessee Confederate Pension Applications

SOWELL, Fannie E. W6407, W8426, MA, Sowell, Henry Franklin
SOWELL, H. F. S7405, MA, 10th Ark. Inf.
SPADLING, Mollie Elizabeth, W4526, CL, Spadling, Wesley Anderson
SPAIN, Martha Jane, W3735, D, Spain, Wm. Mortimer
SPAIN, William M. S126, RU, 4th Cav.
SPAN, P. A. S7161, DI, 14th Inf.
SPANGLER, A. J. S12890, MO, 51st Va. Inf.
SPANGLER, Barney M. S2078, SU, 60th Inf.
SPANGLER, Columbia V. W3342, HW, Spangler, J. C.
SPANGLER, David, S9589, HW, 63rd Inf.
SPANGLER, Elizabeth B. W10226, SU, Spangler, David
SPANN, Hannah Malinda, W1508, B, Spann, Martin Umphry
SPANN, R. K. S12246, RU, 4th (McLemore's) Cav.
SPARKMAN, Allen S. S954, WI, 44th Inf.
SPARKMAN, Cynthia Jane, W2048, V, Sparkman, John Randolph
SPARKMAN, J. W. S7205, HE, 48th (Nixon's) Inf.
SPARKMAN, Mary Catherine, W2852, HE, Sparkman, John Williams
SPARKMAN, Mary Ellen, W11035, W, Sparkman, Solomon Clay
SPARKMAN, Miranda Evaline, W4570, WH, Sparkman, W. R.
SPARKMAN, Nannie Camp, W10525, MU, Sparkman, Jacob Green
SPARKMAN, Permelia, W9109, W, Sparkman, Elvin
SPARKMAN, Sol, S15332, S10604, V, 8th Cav.
SPARKMAN, T. B. S11221, V, 35th Inf.
SPARKMAN, Temple, S11137, WH, 8th (Dibrell's) Cav.
SPARKS, James W. S177, K, 37th Va. Inf.
SPARKS, Leonia F. W8768, W7553, HU, Sparks, Daniel George
SPARKS, Louisa, W202, RU, Sparks, Mathew S.
SPARKS, M. S. S179, D, 23rd Inf., Follows #180 on film
SPARKS, Nannie Russan, W1195, B, Sparks, Wm. Henry
SPARKS, Nicholas, S3853, CU, 25th Inf.
SPARKS, S. J. S5387, LO, 2nd Cav.
SPARKS, Samuel G.a, S13265, SH, 38th Inf.
SPARKS, Sarah L. W9602, K, Sparks, James W.
SPARKS, Solomon, S6595, PU, 28th Inf.
SPARKS, W. E. S7950, DY, 55th Ala. Inf.
SPARKS, William, S6596, WH, 28th Inf.
SPARKS, William A. S13920, WA, 34th N.C. Inf.
SPARKS, William J. S1705, S1970, K, 1st Cav.
SPAULDING, Laura F. W3533, FR, Spaulding, R. E.
SPAULDING, R. E. S6867, FR, 22nd Va. Inf.
SPEARS, Amanda, W5269, WL, Spears, Lewis E.
SPEARS, J. N. S7152, G, 22nd Inf.
SPEARS, J. T. S8119, WL, 4th (McLemore's) Cav.
SPEARS, Nancy Ezzell, W5229, G, Spears, Joseph Newton
SPEARS, Sideria Mann (Dee), W2756, K, Spears, Christopher Columbus
SPEARS, W. S. S9115, WL, 4th (McLemore's) Cav.
SPECK, G. D. S11864, HR, 45th Miss. Inf.
SPECK, J. J. S7394, OV, 8th Cav.
SPECK, M. E. C. S9309, OV, 8th Inf.
SPECK, Martah F. W3206, WL, Speck, Thomas J.
SPECK, Martha J. W2496, OV, Speck, Michael A.
SPECK, T. J. S11640, HM, Ramsey's Battery, Art.
SPEED, Theodore S. S5060, S6279, MU, 1st (Feild's) Inf.
SPEEGLE, E. M. S6637, HW, 2nd (Ashby's) Cav.
SPEER, A. C. S15160, BO, 59th Inf.
SPEER, America, W4298, RU, Speer, Ephraim A.
SPEER, John R. S13622, GE, Unassigned (Nitre Bureau)
SPEIER, Alexander, S10622, D, 7th La. Inf.
SPEIER, Susan C. W2759, D, Speier, Alex
SPEIGHT, Alice O. W6950, DI, Speight, Westley
SPEIGHT, F. M. S953, O, 5th Inf.
SPEIGHT, J. M. S8318, HN, 33rd Inf.
SPEIGHT, Wesley, S11869, DI, 15th Inf.
SPENCE, Alice Carothers, W7697, HI, Spence, W. Jerome D.
SPENCE, Carlin, W7278, BE, Spence, John Gaston
SPENCE, Eliza Ann, W8841, BE, Spence, Gaston Devro

SPENCE, Lucinda Catherine, W4359, CC, Spence, Joseph Speed
SPENCE, Mary A. W10913, DY, Spence, John
SPENCE, Sarah Emaline, W10533, WE, Spence, Thornton Jefferson
SPENCER, A. S7614, WI, Baxter's Co. Lt. Art.
SPENCER, B. E. S714, MOO, Undetermined
SPENCER, Carter D. S9230, CL, 5th Cav.
SPENCER, D. C. S8418, G, 18th Cav.
SPENCER, George, S4237, D, 1st (Feild's) Inf.
SPENCER, Hiram A. S9075, DI, Baxter's Co. Lt. Art.
SPENCER, J. L. S4428, DY, 15th Inf.
SPENCER, J. R. S843, DK, 28th Inf.
SPENCER, J. T. S12140, BE, 19th (Biffle's) Cav.
SPENCER, John, S7103, DY, 12th Miss. Cav.
SPENCER, Judian, W2580, WI, Spencer, Abraham
SPENCER, Mary E. W2585, RU, Spencer, Lucian B.
SPENCER, Mary Louisa, W9364, MA, Spencer, Wm. C.
SPENCER, Nancy Louisa, W8948, FR, Spencer, Thomas Childs
SPENCER, Philip B. S10616, D, 12th Miss. Cav.
SPENCER, T. F. S13038, MA, 11th Miss. Cav.
SPENCER, T. J. S7697, WE, 12th Ky. Cav.
SPENCER, Thomas C. S3149, FR, 1st Inf.
SPENCER, Thomas J. S2472, MOO, 44th Inf.
SPENCER, Virginia A. W6386, SH, Spencer, Valencote
SPENCER, W. C. S11844, LA, 32nd Inf.
SPENCER, W. J. D. S14806, HI, 11th Inf.
SPENCER, William Henry, S15806, BE, 5th Inf.
SPENCER, Z. S14256, SH, 1st Cav.
SPICER, Elyada, W10053, WE, Spicer, Joe A.
SPICER, Josephine M. W483, WE, Spicer, Solomon
SPICER, Martha O. W2911, SH, Spicer, Robert Augustus
SPICER, Samuel S. S14428, SH, 154th Sr. Regt. Inf.
SPICER, Soloman, S1914, 18th Inf.
SPIDELL, Celia Bush, W9066, D, Spidell, John Benjamin
SPIGGLE, Madison, S3147, MC, 36th Va. Inf.
SPIGHT, Emma Hill, W8976, G, Spight, Lindsey D.
SPIGHT, L. D. S16081, G, 7th Miss. Cav.

SPIKES, Nannie, W4627, WE, Spikes, Henderson Collumbus
SPILLINGS, W. H. S14856, 12th Ky. Cav.
SPINDLE, Sciotha L. W1494, CF, Spindle, Wm. R.
SPINDLE, W. R. S7562, CF, 4th Inf.
SPIVEY, Martha Johnson, W375, GI, Spivey, James
SPIVY, H. J. S7251, GI, 11th (Holman's) Cav.
SPOON, George W. S3634, HM, 61st Inf.
SPRADLING, Elsie, W662, ME, Spradling, John Lilburn
SPRADLING, R. J. S9318, MC, 43rd Inf.
SPRADLING, Wesley Anderson, S9132, CL, 16th Inf.
SPRAKER, Sarah, W4315, UN, Spraker, Stephen
SPRANGLER, Henry F. S15998, HW, 64th Va. Inf.
SPRATT, A. J. S1890, WI, 3rd (Clack's) Inf.
SPRATT, Martha Jane, W6183, WI, Spratt, Wm. Henry
SPRAY, Lewis, S2261, LI, 8th Inf.
SPRIGGS, E. S12963, BR, 2nd (Ashby's) Cav.
SPRIGGS, Mary Elizabeth, W5350, BR, Spriggs, Ezekiel
SPRIGGS, Tempie, W1389, HW, Spriggs, Henry
SPRINGER, Arom T. S10734, MN, 18th (Newsom's) Cav.
SPRINGER, william F. S12983, H, 45th Ala. Inf.
SPRINGFIELD, E. C. S9065, H, Undetermined
SPRINGFIELD, George W. S4209, WL, Shaw's Bn. Cav.
SPRINGFIELD, Serreptha Gartain, W9553, SM, Springfield, George Washington
SPRINKLE, Nancy Caroline, W10998, K, Sprinkle, John Crabtree
SPROLES, Lydia G. W7316, SU, Sproles, David C.
SPROTT, Andrew J. S9051, WI, 3rd (Clack's) Inf.
SPROTT, C. B. S10907, WI, 3rd (Clack's) Inf.
SPROTT, Elizabeth Ellen, W5365, MU, Sprott, Columbus B.
SPROUL, David Crocket, S9590, SU, 25th Va. Cav.
SPROUL, H. G. S5100, CT, 61st Inf.
SPROULS, Lewis, S9434, JE, Jeffress' Battery, Va.

SPROUSE, Gustavus H. S13079, RB, 9th (Ward's) Cav.
SPROUSE, James P. S12326, LA, 16th S.C. Inf.
SPRUGIN, M. E. S11167, SU, 14th Inf.
SPRUNGER, Lizzie, W7740, MN, Sprunger, Giles
SPURGEON, Joe, S14698, LA, 45th Va. Inf.
SPURLIN, George W. S4853, HR, 1st Tenn. Ala. and Miss. Inf.
SPURLOCK, F. M. S5757, DK, 1st Bn. (Colm's) Inf.
SPURLOCK, G. J. S6766, WH, 35th Inf.
SPURLOCK, Johnson Riley, S15065, S13523, J, 4th (Murray's) Cav.
SPURLOCK, Sally Ann, W757, PU, Spurlock, Joseph C.
ST CLAIR, Joshua, S5508, CO, 54th Va. Inf.
ST CLAIR, Sarah Ann, W3251, D, St. Clair, Wm. Richard
ST CLAIR, William R. S9786, D, 22nd Miss. Inf.
ST JOHN, Buenavista, W6222, CA, St. John, Henry Jefferson
ST JOHN, F. G. S3830, PU, 18th Inf.
ST JOHN, H. J. S13871, CA, 18th Inf.
STACEY, A. H. S7048, DI, 8th (Smith's) Cav.
STACEY, Bettie, W7055, MS, Stacey, Joe H.
STACEY, Elizabeth, W8618, MU, Stacey, Joseph Henderson
STACEY, Mary, W427, WH, Stacey, Green
STACEY, R. M. S9502, HU, 10th Cav.
STACEY, Sarah Jane, W344, B, Stacey, John Calvin
STACKER, Blanche, W10395, ST, Stacker, George
STACKER, Grace, W8171, MT, Stacker, Clay
STACY, D. B. S7071, WE, 22nd (Barteau's) Cav.
STACY, James, S4865, HA, 5th (McKenzie's) Cav.
STACY, Sarah Ann, W278, B, Stacy, Robert Jonithan
STAFFORD, A. A. S7944, DY, 9th (Bennett's) Cav.
STAFFORD, A. M. S5676, J, 28th Inf.
STAFFORD, Archibald M. S1228, J, Undetermined
STAFFORD, J. F. S7916, FR, 28th Cav.
STAFFORD, J. T. S9239, F, 13th Inf.
STAFFORD, J. W. S12674, LA, 48th (Nixon's) Inf.
STAFFORD, John B. S5154, F, 14th (Neely's) Cav.
STAFFORD, John W. S3348, MOO, 10th Ky. Cav.
STAFFORD, Martha Ellen, W8429, WA, Stafford, Wm. Henry
STAFFORD, Mary Ann, W2304, F, Stafford, John B.
STAFFORD, Mattie Roane, W11059, SH, Stafford, Joseph Henderson
STAFFORD, Noah, S4012, F, 13th Inf.
STAFFORD, P. M. S4626, T, 13th Inf.
STAFFORD, Sarah, W2872, H, Stafford, James Brennan
STAFFORD, W. H. S2755, WA, 26th N.C. Inf.
STAFFORD, W. H. S8451, O, 7th Bn. Cav.
STAGGS, William E. S3652, LE, 54th Inf.
STAGNER, Theodosiah, W10917, ST, Stagner, Joseph
STAIN, Thalia [Davidson], W10859, SH, Stain, Wm. Fletcher, [Later married Davidson]
STAINBACK, George J. S15505, F, 14th (Neely's) Cav.
STAINBACK, Mary Jane, W9554, W, Stainback, George Tucker
STAINBACK, Rosa Bell, W10737, F, Stainback, George James
STALCUP, Charles T. S10746, K, Thomas' Legion, N.C.
STALCUP, L. F. S16146, S15856, WE, 20th Cav.
STALCUP, Sallie Louisa, W7974, TR, Stalcup, Wm.
STALCUP, Samuel, S12418, O, 20th Inf.
STALEY, Elizabeth J. W203, DI, Staley, James
STALEY, J. D. S7992, K, 62nd Inf.
STALEY, James, S6029, DI, 49th Inf.
STALEY, Mattie A. B. W6809, BO, Staley, David Reese
STALEY, William Spiller, S15790, K, King's Battery, Va. Lt. Art.
STALLING, John R. S4625, WI, 19th (Biffle's) Cav.
STALLINGS, Callie B. W8421, MU, Stallings, John R.
STALLINGS, Daniel S. S6431, MS, 23rd Inf.
STALLINGS, Georgia Ann, W7628, MS, Stallings, Daniel Stanley
STALLINGS, Lucinda, W3822, R, Stallings, James H.
STALLINGS, Thomas, S6253, SE, 16th Inf.

STALLIOUS, Martha S. W8180, SE, Stallious, M. A.
STALLS, Carrie, W7006, SH, Stalls, George Washington
STALLS, George W. S11005, SH, 14th Inf.
STALLS, William M. S14112, HN, 20th (Russell's) Cav.
STAMEY, William R. S8068, MO, 39th N.C. Inf.
STAMM, Sarah Ann, W3415, SH, Stamm, Henry
STAMPER, I. J. S8339, BR, 43rd Inf.
STAMPER, Jane, W894, MT, Stamper, James Madison
STAMPER, Joseph H. S8340, BR, 62nd Inf.
STAMPER, Martha Ann, W4232, BR, Stamper, Isaac Jones
STAMPER, Richard, S6173, ST, 50th Inf.
STAMPER, Sophia Alford, W4690, FR, Stamper, DeWitt Clinton
STAMPS, J. J. S6892, PU, 28th Inf.
STAMPS, Nancy, W1040, PU, Stamps, James Jordon
STAMPS, Sarah Matilda, W9285, D, Stamps, James C.
STANDFIELD, Gabe B. W4863, D, Standfield, Napoleon B.
STANDIFER, A. J. S4974, BL, 62nd Mtd. Inf.
STANDIFER, Benjamin F. S6562, CL, 1st (Carter's) Cav.
STANDIFER, Isiah, S3234, CL, 1st (Carter's) Cav.
STANDIFER, L. L. S9675, BL, 2nd (Ashby's) Cav.
STANDIFER, Sarah, W3420, CL, Standifer, Benjamin F.
STANDIFER, Steven, S2996, CL, 63rd Inf.
STANDRIDGE, E. W. S4264, SH, 18th Ark. Inf.
STANFIELD, A. L. S2507, CH, 52nd Inf.
STANFIELD, A. L. S8643, CH, 51st Inf.
STANFIELD, Benjamin P. S4244, LI, 17th Inf.
STANFIELD, David, S12095, CH, 21st (Wilson's) Cav.
STANFIELD, E. M. S6444, HD, 2nd Bn. Miss. Cav.
STANFIELD, J. D. S9781, HE, 16th Cav.
STANFIELD, J. W. S12349, K, 60th Mtd. Inf.
STANFIELD, Lou Ella Jane, W3954, W6458, WI, Stanfield, Thomas Edwin
STANFIELD, Lucy, W5706, K, Stanfield, Jesse W.
STANFIELD, M. S. S7223, WI, 20th Inf.
STANFIELD, Mahala, W4084, MN, Stanfield, Peyton S.
STANFIELD, Roxana, W7839, L, Stanfield, Wm. Henry
STANFIELD, Sarah A. W3782, HN, Stanfield, Robert Pleasant
STANFIELD, Sarah Jeffres, W4419, HD, Stanfield, Elijah Martin
STANFIELD, Susan, W984, MS, Stanfield, Thomas C.
STANFIELD, Thomas E. S2022, WI, 20th Inf.
STANFIELD, William, S4016, SU, 60th Inf.
STANFIELD, William Henry, S12655, L, 14th (Neely's) Cav.
STANFIELD, William M. S5659, D, 6th (Wheeler's) Cav.
STANFIELD, Zilpha F. W552, T, Stanfield, John Archibald
STANFORD, C. A. S11018, WI, 34th Ala. Inf.
STANFORD, Virginia Tennessee, W4391, WI, Stanford, Cisero Aradius
STANHILL, William C. S1735, WE, 52nd Inf.
STANIFER, Samuel, S894, HA, 63rd Inf.
STANLEY, A. J. S14991, L, 38th Inf.
STANLEY, A. R. S6925, H, 59th Ala. Inf.
STANLEY, Anna E. W3599, SH, Stanley, John D.
STANLEY, B. F. S4142, O, 33rd Inf.
STANLEY, Christina Cox, W718, W, Stanley, Robert M.
STANLEY, D. D. S12100, D, 8th (Smith's) Cav.
STANLEY, J. F. S11455, O, 33rd Inf.
STANLEY, John T. S5683, H, 13th Ga. Cav.
STANLEY, Mahulda Hinston, W7121, LK, Stanley, Richard Nelson
STANLEY, Oliver, S3653, A, 28th N.C. Inf.
STANLEY, R. M. S2880, CA, 8th (Smith's) Cav.
STANLEY, R. N. S566, LK, 9th Inf.
STANLEY, Robert, S13809, D, 30th Inf.
STANLEY, Rosa, W10827, CL, Stanley, Scott
STANLEY, Scot, S15749, CL, 21st Va. Cav.
STANSBURY, David M. S12476, SH, 4th Ky. Cav.
STANTON, Elizabeth E. W136, WA, Stanton, David
STANTON, F. M. S4115, CY, 28th Inf.
STANTON, Mary Ann, W1676, WA, Stanton, John
STANTON, William R. S12331, LI, 25th Inf.

STAPLETON, George, S8923, S15149, SU, 22nd Va. Cav.
STARBUCK, Elizabeth, W2776, SU, Starbuck, Isaiah
STARBUCK, Isaiah, S6013, SU, 57th N.C. Inf.
STARK, Narcissa, W6545, RB, Stark, James Atlas
STARK, W. M. S8253, SH, 10th Miss. Inf.
STARKE, Lula Burns, W6502, SH, Starke, Edwin Temple
STARKEY, Nancy M. W843, MA, Starkey, Wm. Clark
STARKEY, Sarah J. W3159, MA, Starkey, John Rose
STARNES, Hardin, C238, D, 4th Cav.
STARNES, J. B. S4390, FR, 28th Cav.
STARNES, J. M. S2289, SM, 23rd Inf.
STARNES, J. M. S16270, D, 1st Cav.
STARNES, Louisa, W2098, ME, Starnes, Benjamin Franklin
STARNES, Nancy A. W6465, FR, Starnes, Joseph B.
STARNES, Oliver P. S14612, MS, 29th Inf.
STARNES, W. P. S4869, FR, 17th Inf.
STARR, Mary Elizabeth, See Mary Elizabeth Richmond
STARRETT, G. M. S14716, SH, 6th N.C. Inf.
STARRETT, Lodkia Virginia, W6695, SH, Starrett, George Maroni
STATEN, Lucinda Jane, W6377, GE, Staten, Robert
STATEN, Robert, S3714, GE, 63rd Inf.
STATLER, Austin M. S14135, SH, 7th (Duckworth's) Cav.
STATLER, Lavinia P. W7587, SH, Statler, Austin Miller
STATOM, Dean, S1586, FR, 41st Inf.
STATTON, Mary, W4792, SH, Statton, Martin Van Buren
STATZER, James A. S5761, SU, 63rd Inf.
STEADMAN, Anna Eliza, W6982, MA, Steadman, John H.
STEADMAN, Catharine, W3305, K, Steadman, Joshua
STEADMAN, Joshua, S2563, K, 16th N.C. Inf.
STEAKLEY, Wiley, S16505, WH, 1st Confederate Cav.
STEALCUP, Susan M. W7151, HM, Stealcup, C. T.
STEDMAN, Anna E. W7603, MA, Stedman, John Anthony
STEDMAN, M. L. S14776, LI, 1st Ark. Inf.

STEED, James sr. S14156, MC, 5th Cav.
STEEL, Elijah, S13739, S15604, WY, 19th (Biffle's) Cav.
STEELE, Anna Eliza, W9116, W9090, FR, Steele, Newton Alwain
STEELE, Balie Peyton, S1767, CF, 1st (Feild's) Inf.
STEELE, C. C. S3989, MN, 20th Ala. Inf.
STEELE, George W. S1750, RU, 53rd Inf.
STEELE, Harvey, S7322, HW, 64th Va. Inf.
STEELE, J. H. S12999, O, 13th Miss. Cav.
STEELE, Laura W. W10781, L, Steele, Thomas sr.
STEELE, Mary E. W5859, HW, Steele, George Alexander
STEELE, Mary M. W4834, MN, Steele, C. C.
STEELE, Parmelia, W1609, DI, Steele, James
STEELE, Robert D. S10344, HI, 48th (Voorhies') Inf.
STEELE, Sallie A. W4225, RU, Steele, George W.
STEELE, Sarah Evaline, W7899, DI, Steele, Robert D.
STEELE, Sarah Frances, W2754, MS, Steele, John Walters
STEELE, Sarah Jane, W5235, MU, Steele, Silvanus Wood
STEELE, Thomas sr. S16655, L, 7th Cav.
STEELE, William A. jr. S13848, BE, 20th (Nixon's) Cav.
STEELMAN, J. M. S15377, CU, 2nd N.C. Home Guards
STEEN, Samuel, S8886, H, Major Hilliard's Railroad Bn. Ga.
STEGALL, Florence Magnolia, W4581, D, Stegall, Wm. James
STEGALL, Robert, C76, LI, Unassigned, Quartermaster
STEGALL, S. G. S8731, HE, 21st Cav.
STEGER, John J. S13678, F, 7th (Duckworth's) Cav.
STELLER, Missouri O. W6966, G, Steller, Benjamin Franklin
STEPHENS, Bettie, W5695, WE, Stephens, Joseph King
STEPHENS, Daniel, S15023, RU, 2nd Ga. State Troops
STEPHENS, Dora Doyle, W9025, F, Stephens, W. R. D.
STEPHENS, Edward, S11945, GR, 1st East Tenn. Cav.

STEPHENS, Ella, W9416, CY, Stephens, John Hanceford
STEPHENS, Fannie Newell, W3550, SH, Stephens, Robert Keen
STEPHENS, G. S. S13057, HI, 6th (Wheeler's) Cav.
STEPHENS, Henry, S11329, H, 2nd S.C. Rifles
STEPHENS, Isabell, W4326, GR, Stephens, Edward
STEPHENS, J. A. S9166, CY, 8th Inf.
STEPHENS, J. K. S2748, WE, Forrest's Escort, Cav.
STEPHENS, J. M. S4552, FR, 42nd Inf.
STEPHENS, J. M. S5203, CF, 4th Cav.
STEPHENS, Jack, S15420, H, 39th Ga. Inf.
STEPHENS, Jerre B. S5301, CY, 13th Cav.
STEPHENS, John H. S938, GR, 12th Cav.
STEPHENS, Martha Ann, W9357, WE, Stephens, T. J.
STEPHENS, Martha Caruthers, W8626, W8387, CC, Stephens, Wm. M.
STEPHENS, Mattie R. W8831, CA, Stephens, James H.
STEPHENS, Nancy E. W3096, CY, Stephens, J. A.
STEPHENS, Nancy Ellen, W2177, HI, Stephens, James Polk
STEPHENS, R. K. S6149, SH, 3rd Miss. Cav.
STEPHENS, R. S. S6950, HI, 10th Cav.
STEPHENS, Roxie Ann, W2446, HN, Stephens, Wm. Franklin
STEPHENS, Sarah, W562, FE, Stephens, Dode
STEPHENS, Sarah A. W1778, HN, Stephens, W. C.
STEPHENS, Sarah J. W4099, DY, Stephens, Wm. F.
STEPHENS, Susanah, W1323, WA, Stephens, Wm. Catron
STEPHENS, Thomas J. S12547, WE, 20th (Russell's) Cav.
STEPHENS, Thula Jane, W9732, K, Stephens, Wm. Henry
STEPHENS, W. F. S6468, HN, 46th Inf.
STEPHENS, W. H. S12329, D, 20th Inf.
STEPHENS, William R. D. S15476, F, 15th Cav.
STEPHENS, Winnie Richardson, W10558, RU, Stephens, Daniel
STEPHENSON, A. W. S6395, WI, Forrest's Escort, Cav.
STEPHENSON, C. C. S8133, D, 1st (Feild's) Inf.
STEPHENSON, George W. S12279, WI, Forrest's Escort, Cav.
STEPHENSON, J. T. S13894, B, 32nd Inf.
STEPHENSON, James K. S580, K, 19th Inf.
STEPHENSON, John C. S10101, LI, 44th Inf.
STEPHENSON, Margaret Elizabeth, W1117, MU, Stephenson, James White
STEPHENSON, Mary Ann, W3426, DY, Stephenson, Wm. A.
STEPHENSON, Mildred Ann, W3562, LI, Stephenson, Wm. Harison
STEPHENSON, Monroe, C11, MU, 9th Bn. Cav.
STEPHENSON, N. E. W59, B, Stephenson, Wm. Harrison
STEPHENSON, S. N. S7669, CF, 41st Inf.
STEPHENSON, Sarah Jane, W4557, MC, Stephenson, W. A.
STEPHENSON, W. A. S7906, DY, 4th Ala. Cav.
STEPHENSON, W. E. S1495, LA, 23rd Inf.
STEPHENSON, W. H. S9693, CL, 3rd Ala. Inf.
STEPHENSON, W. a. S1338, MC, 29th Inf.
STEPHENSON, W. a. S9833, SH, 13th Inf.
STEPHENSON, Zilphia, W4287, MA, Stephenson, Thomas Nelson
STEPP, Nathan, S4637, GR, 44th Va. Inf.
STEPPE, Mary Ann, W5327, CO, Steppe, Robert
STERCHI, Francis P. S4934, K, 1st (Carter's) Cav.
STERLING, Isaac F. S11490, SH, 1st Miss. Cav.
STERNBERGER, Rose Semon, W6674, SH, Sternberger, Moses
STEVEN, Milton H. S995, WI, 24th Inf.
STEVENS, Eva, W9268, H, Stevens, Jackson
STEVENS, Frances Tennessee, W7324, W, Stevens, Hoggett Goodloe
STEVENS, G. R. S8154, CC, 7th (Duckworth's) Cav.
STEVENS, George W. S3360, K, 31st Inf.
STEVENS, H. B. S4324, WL, 44th Inf.
STEVENS, H. G. S12115, W, 22nd (Barteau's) Cav.
STEVENS, Harriet M. W1332, MA, Stevens, Wm. Allen
STEVENS, Martha, W2798, WI, Stevens, Milton Harvey
STEVENS, Mary E. W9484, SH, Stevens, Leroy
STEVENS, Mary Elizabeth, W1781, F, Stevens, John Henry

STEVENS, Sallie, See Sallie McWhirter
STEVENS, Sarah Ann, W2838, W1644, HR, Stevens, James Edward
STEVENS, W. F. S11089, DY, 11th Tex. Cav.
STEVENS, W. H. S64, CH, 26th Miss. Inf.
STEVENSON, Benjamin F. S13451, H, 4th Ga. Cav.
STEVENSON, Henry C. S8111, RO, 5th S.C. Inf.
STEVENSON, Thomas S. S12224, B, 3rd Inf.
STEVENSON, W. E. F. S10962, GI, 3rd (Clack's) Inf.
STEWART, A. D. S4269, FR, 17th Inf.
STEWART, A. L. S14848, SH, 24th Inf.
STEWART, Alexander H. S3232, H, 6th Ga. Inf.
STEWART, Andrew J. S815, DK, 24th Inf.
STEWART, Annie F. W9816, RB, Stewart, W. C.
STEWART, B. C. S10154, HY, 9th Inf.
STEWART, C. M. S13209, SH, 12th (Green's) Cav.
STEWART, C. W. S776, CH, 62nd Ala. Inf.
STEWART, Charlotte Garner, W5079, SH, Stewart, Wm. Richard
STEWART, Eliza J. W10245, G, Stewart, John Huston
STEWART, George H. S15765, H, 23rd Bn. Ga. Inf. Homes Guards
STEWART, H. A. S15272, HR, 14th Cav.
STEWART, H. P. S10882, FR, 1st (Turney's) Inf.
STEWART, I. G. S6767, FR, 1st (Turney's) Inf.
STEWART, Irena, W1074, WH, Stewart, J. M.
STEWART, Isaac D. S8699, K, 17th Inf.
STEWART, J. C. S3866, HW, 51st Va. Inf.
STEWART, J. M. S16126, LI, 41st Inf.
STEWART, J. S. S5661, WY, 48th (Nixon's) Inf.
STEWART, J. T. S10761, FR, 62nd Ala. Inf.
STEWART, J. W. S15146, MN, 3rd (Clack's) Inf.
STEWART, James, S2722, U, 58th N.C. Inf.
STEWART, Jeremiah M. S14540, FE, 55th Ala. Inf.
STEWART, Jessee, S7563, WI, 22nd (Nixon's) Cav.
STEWART, John A. S3614, CA, 8th (Smith's) Cav.
STEWART, John C. S12823, SH, 51st Inf.
STEWART, John F. S16595, OV, 4th (Murray's) Cav.
STEWART, Judy White, W9144, SH, Stewart, Atablaipa Columbus
STEWART, Littleton, S10833, MU, 48th (Nixon's) Inf.
STEWART, Margaret Jane, W5081, FR, Stewart, Henry Jones
STEWART, Martha Jane, W2279, D, Stewart, Wm. D.
STEWART, Mary, W7291, OV, Stewart, W. J.
STEWART, Mary A. W334, B, Stewart, Wm. Martin
STEWART, Mary A. W1260, LI, Stewart, Wm. C.
STEWART, Mary Eliza, W7384, D, Stewart, Richard Edward
STEWART, Mary Emma, W9584, LI, Stewart, Jessie Milton
STEWART, Mary F. W6426, DK, Stewart, A. J.
STEWART, Mary L. W7177, HW, Stewart, J. C.
STEWART, Mattie Ella, W6822, SH, Stewart, Alexander Lonzo
STEWART, N. H. S12611, MS, 14th (Neely's) Cav.
STEWART, N. J. S4037, HY, 7th Cav.
STEWART, N. T. S9770, W, 5th Inf.
STEWART, Nancy Holmes, W7094, K, Stewart, Isaac Daniel
STEWART, R. A. S11227, SN, 45th Inf.
STEWART, R. E. S11513, D, 9th Bn. (Gantt's) Cav.
STEWART, R. M. S1463, T, 34th Miss. Inf.
STEWART, R. M. S3931, MS, 4th (McLemore's) Cav.
STEWART, R. W. S15173, LI, 41st Inf.
STEWART, Rachel E. W3222, CH, Stewart, Cornelius Wilson
STEWART, Richard W. S12431, S15346, HR, 27th Inf., Also applied from Henderson County
STEWART, Robert Matthew, S5597, MS, 8th (Dibrell's) Cav.
STEWART, Sarah Ann Toff, W2669, ME, Stewart, M. B.
STEWART, Sarah R. W2059, ME, Stewart, Richard
STEWART, Sarah Virginia, W4059, D, Stewart, George Washington
STEWART, Susan S. W7526, MN, Stewart, John Wm.
STEWART, Theresa, W7300, H, Stewart, Alexander Harvey

STEWART, Thomas G. S7822, B, 3rd Ala. Cav.
STEWART, Thomas J. S1646, SM, 8th Cav.
STEWART, Thomas J. S14584, MU, 2nd (Robison's) Inf.
STEWART, W. B. S4722, SH, 12th (Green's) Cav.
STEWART, W. C. S13000, RB, 35th Ala. Inf.
STEWART, W. J. S7013, OV, 8th (Dibrell's) Cav.
STEWART, William C. S6308, WH, 25th (Consol.) Inf.
STEWART, William Carroll, S5946, LI, 1st (Turney's) Inf.
STEWART, William H. S8674, 27th Inf.
STEWART, William Richard, S13564, SH, 3rd (Forrest's) Cav.
STEWART, Zilla, W400, FR, Stewart, Wm. S.
STEWMAN, John H. S5611, W, Harding's Art.
STIDMAN, Nancy, W2570, WA, Stidman, John
STIDMON, John, S7483, WA, 12th Bn. Cav.
STIKES, Joseph W. S14418, HM, 58th N.C. Inf.
STILES, Martha M. W10929, K, Stiles, James C.
STILES, Nancy Caroline, W382, DK, Stiles, Wm.
STILL, Mary Averrilla, W1333, D, Still, Wm. P.
STILLER, Benjamin F. S6499, G, 33rd Inf.
STILLWELL, Jane E. W4459, K, Stillwell, Edward Lee
STILLWELL, Lucinda Emiline, W6208, DY, Stillwell, John Milton
STILLWELL, Sarah J. W5666, SE, Stillwell, Jessee C.
STILT, Mary Williamson, W7502, T, Stilt, John Newton
STILWELL, James M. S1530, DY, 8th Inf.
STINE, Abraham, S3737, SU, Undetermined
STINETT, James L. S9771, GR, 18th Miss. Inf.
STINETT, Johu, S5467, CO, Lynch's Co. Lt. Art.
STINNETT, John S. S2094, BL, 62nd Inf.
STINSON, John K. S4130, M, Undetermined
STINSON, Mary A. W496, WI, Stinson, John
STINSON, Robert, S8570, CL, 22nd Va. Inf.
STIPE, A. B. S7029, MU, 48th (Voorhies') Inf.
STIPE, A. J. S1177, V, 16th Inf.
STIPE, Nancy Cordelia, W5261, MU, Stipe, Abija B.
STIPE, Richard, S176, K, 29th Inf.
STIPE, Susan Parlee, W10708, K, Stipe, Richard
STOBAUGH, Julia Rebecca, W466, MA, Stobaugh, Anselum

STOCKARD, David Franklin, S13161, MU, 3rd (Clack's) Inf.
STOCKARD, J. R. S15944, LE, 9th Cav.
STOCKARD, Mary Jane, W1728, WE, Stockard, George T.
STOCKARD, Mattie Rebecca, W5471, MU, Stockard, David Frank
STOCKDALE, Alabama Flavia, W7328, SH, Stockdale, George Washington
STOCKER, Alexander Y. S7464, TR, 2nd (Robison's) Inf.
STOCKSTILL, Nancy, W116, MOO, Stockstill, Wm. F.
STOCKSTON, Ellen, W3906, OV, Stockston, James Elzy
STOCKSTON, Martha, W7103, PU, Stockston, Bluford Harvey
STOCKSTON, Nannie B. W2455, SU, Stockston, Thomas K.
STOCKTON, B. H. S6768, PU, 25th Inf.
STOCKTON, T. K. S10155, SU, 57th Va. Inf.
STOFFEL, Jordan, S8787, K, 19th Inf.
STOFFELL, Sarah, W9886, K, Stoffell, Zachariah J.
STOKELY, Charles jr. S237, CO, 60th N.C. Inf.
STOKELY, Joseph, S10991, CO, 6th N.C. Inf.
STOKELY, Margaret, W5481, CO, Stokely, Joseph
STOKES, Absolem, S6572, HI, 24th Inf.
STOKES, Frances Elizabeth, W10037, B, Stokes, H. K.
STOKES, H. K. S16367, B, 44th Inf.
STOKES, Martha Maudy, W3899, ME, Stokes, James C. C.
STOKES, T. A. S15047, WI, 3rd Ark. Cav.
STOLSWORTH, Hannah, W3587, K, Stolsworth, Thomas
STONE, Ann Elizabeth, W6118, CC, Stone, Thomas Jefferson
STONE, B. R. S9187, CH, 22nd Inf.
STONE, E. N. S11012, G, 7th (Duckworth's) Cav.
STONE, Edward Franklin, S32, MU, 14th Inf.
STONE, Egenardus Banister, S12383, HR, 22nd Ga. Bn. Hvy. Art.
STONE, Ellen J. W1118, TR, Stone, Wm. N.
STONE, F. M. S4407, CF, 37th Inf.
STONE, Fee, C158, G, Worked on Island No. 10
STONE, G. B. S14038, G, 12th Ky. Cav.
STONE, J. A. S307, CH, 13th Inf.
STONE, J. R. S15690, CY, 10th Ky. Cav.
STONE, James D. S15649, D, 44th Inf.

Index to Tennessee Confederate Pension Applications

STONE, Lizzie P. W4516, G, Stone, E. N.
STONE, Margaret Jane, W987, CH, Stone, Isaac Anderson
STONE, Margett, W1531, CY, Stone, Wm. R.
STONE, Mary Ann, W2704, A, Stone, Silas Murray
STONE, Mary Ann, W9790, MS, Stone, Francis Marion
STONE, Minnie McDowell, W10725, G, Stone, George Banister
STONE, S. M. S6618, A, 55th N.C. Inf.
STONE, Samuel S. S11248, D, 2nd (Robison's) Inf.
STONE, W. C. S11291, SN, 20th Inf.
STONE, W. H. S14283, O, 1st Miss. Lt. Art.
STONE, W. T. S5302, L, 9th Inf.
STONE, William Allen, S8256, DY, 55th Inf.
STONE, William R. S2111, CY, 4th Cav.
STONEBREAKER, George J. S3321, LI, 1st Inf.
STONECIPHER, J. V. S4844, SM, 24th Ga. Inf.
STONECYPHER, Martha Ann, W6603, SM, Stonecypher, John V.
STONER, James P. S4566, DK, 23rd Inf.
STONES, Mary S. W5891, D, Stones, Joseph McEwen
STOOTS, George W. S10323, HY, 57th Va. Inf.
STOPHEL, Owen, S8234, SU, Unassigned
STORMENT, W. D. S7042, G, 32nd Miss. Inf.
STORY, A. T. S6175, GI, 3rd Inf.
STORY, E. F. S13188, LI, 44th Inf.
STORY, James H. S10941, D, 52nd Inf.
STORY, Katherine Cross, W2647, K, Story, Josiah Eugene
STORY, Mary L. W11182, LA, Story, Anderson T.
STORY, Mary Susan, W9002, TR, Story, Jim Will
STOUT, Delilah Minerva, W3114, WA, Stout, Wm. Jackson
STOUT, Leonard, S428, OV, 28th Inf.
STOUT, R. J. S12544, HD, 4th Ala. Cav.
STOUT, Thomas E. S15373, H, Confederate Navy
STOVALL, A. D. S5653, GI, 44th Inf.
STOVALL, Alfred M. S16490, WE, 2nd Cav.
STOVALL, B. M. S5734, B, 2nd Inf.
STOVALL, David H. S7870, B, 23rd Inf.
STOVALL, Fannie E. W9784, WE, Stovall, Alford Madison
STOVALL, Ida, W10094, MA, Stovall, John Wesley

STOVALL, J. R. S16189, MN, 19th & 20th (Consol.) Cav.
STOVALL, James B. S4131, 19th (Biffle's) Cav. County not given
STOVALL, John W. S16092, MA, 12th Ky. Cav.
STOVALL, L. Elizabeth, W3800, G, Stovall, Gustavus Henry
STOVALL, Lula, W10257, GI, Stovall, Wm. David
STOVALL, S. T. S13718, SH, 60 Day Miss. State Troops
STOVALL, Sallie J. W9502, MN, Stovall, John Rudolph
STOVALL, Tennessee, W1369, WI, Stovall, George M.
STOVALL, W. B. S11237, O, 22nd (Barteau's) Cav.
STOVALL, W. D. S8089, GI, 32nd Inf.
STOVER, A. K. S14738, D, 52nd Ga. Inf.
STOVER, J. P. S12025, D, 11th Cav.
STOVER, Robert, C91, CT, Regiment not given
STOWERS, J. T. S4, D, 11th Inf.
STRAIN, John W. S70, BR, 36th Ga. Inf.
STRAIN, Mary Virginia, W1993, L, Strain, Abijah B.
STRALEY, George P. S11742, MU, 3d (Clack's) Inf.
STRANGE, James W. S3137, MC, 19th Inf.
STRANGE, T. J. S1671, HI, 7th Ala. Cav.
STRATTON, Emma Blythe, W9723, SH, Stratton, Beumont Macon
STRATTON, G. B. S11627, SN, 44th Inf.
STRATTON, John H. S5453, SH, 11th Inf.
STRATTON, Lizzie H. W5509, D, Stratton, Wm. O.
STRATTON, Margaret, W4294, GR, Stratton, G. W.
STRATTON, Matt jr. S13444, D, 3rd (Forrest's) Cav.
STRAWN, C. C. S6977, HD, 16th Cav.
STRAWN, J. M. S13908, DY, 20th (Nixon's) Cav.
STRAWN, J. P. S1443, WE, 1st Inf.
STRAWN, John R. S2288, MOO, 1st (Turney's) Inf.
STRAWN, Liza, W4276, DY, Strawn, John Taton
STRAWN, M. J. S448, HD, 3rd & 4th (Consol.) Inf.
STRAWN, Nancy Jane, W8722, DE, Strawn, Maness Jordan

-333

STRAYHORN, J. T. S13318, SH, 1st N.C. Inf.
STRAYHORN, Sarah Margaret, W1690, CC, Strayhorn, Samuel Henry
STREET, A. J. S14959, CE, 11th Inf.
STREET, A. P. S15101, LI, 41st Inf.
STREET, H. W. S11057, DI, 11th (Holman's) Cav.
STREET, Josephine, W8842, LI, Street, Aaron Parker
STREET, Malissie, W10507, DI, Street, David G.
STREET, R. F. S8584, ST, 10th & 11th Cav.
STREET, Sarah Elizabeth, W9812, SH, Street, Luther Calvin
STREET, Wade H. S12416, GI, 20th Cav.
STREETMAN, Mary Amanda, W7641, DI, Streetman, Thomas Jefferson
STREETMAN, T. J. S12330, MT, 56th Ga. Inf.
STRIBLING, John P. S9430, MA, 33rd Inf.
STRICKLAND, G. W. S5066, WA, 29th Inf.
STRICKLAND, G. W. S9218, H, 19th Ala. Inf.
STRICKLAND, Moore, S2788, WA, 58th N.C. Inf.
STRICKLAND, R. Tena, W7976, G, Strickland, Wiley B.
STRICKLAND, William V. S14163, SH, 19th Miss. Inf.
STRICKLER, A. B. S10780, SU, 19th Inf.
STRICKLER, Barbara Gwin, W10024, SU, Strickler, Reuben
STRICKLER, D. S. S15669, K, 2nd Va. Reserves
STRICKLER, John, S9459, SU, 29th Inf.
STRICKLER, Virtie, W10001, SU, Strickler, John
STRINGER, T. H. S14628, GE, 37th Va. Inf.
STRINGFELLOW, W. J. S12577, D, 50th Inf.
STRODE, Lyda, W10029, G, Strode, George W.
STRODE, William T. S5677, J, 28th Inf.
STROMATT, W. K. S9304, CE, 1st Ky. Vols.
STRONG, Cornelia Eloise, W7141, MA, Strong, Jabey Nevil
STRONG, Elizabeth, W2994, SH, Strong, James T.
STRONG, J. L. S11361, SH, 15th (Stewart's) Cav.
STROTHER, William T. S10670, A, 1st Va. Cav.
STROTHERS, William, S3060, WL, 2nd (Robison's) Inf.
STROUD, B. J. S7539, G, 22nd (Nixon's) Cav.

STROUD, Elizabeth Jane, W8403, CA, Stroud, George Stubblefield
STROUD, L. D. S2041, WL, 7th Inf.
STROUD, M. L. S6838, W, 8th Ark. Inf.
STROUD, Mary Jamima, W8467, W, Stroud, Walter Ran
STROUD, W. R. S15804, W, 28th Cav.
STROUP, Daniel S. S10981, HN, 11th N.C. Inf.
STROUP, Samuel P. S4879, SU, 37th Va. Inf.
STUART, A. C. S6527, SH, 37th Miss. Inf.
STUART, Amand N. W1825, HR, Stuart, Wm. Franklin
STUART, Clarise, W6958, DI, Stuart, John Minor
STUART, Henrietta Catharine, W1530, HR, Stuart, Thomas Collier
STUART, J. M. S8316, DI, 11th Inf.
STUART, James H. S11589, CO, 25th Inf.
STUART, James M. S1158, HW, 63rd Inf.
STUART, Minnie Inglesby, W10254, SU, Stuart, James Nelson
STUART, William A. S12704, CY, 19th Inf.
STUBBLEFIELD, Elizabeth Jane, W2625, HW, Stubblefield, Wm. Richard
STUBBLEFIELD, Francis M. S12441, PO, 1st S.C. Art.
STUBBLEFIELD, J. W. S4577, WE, 12th Ky. Inf.
STUBBLEFIELD, James, S4398, GR, 37th Inf.
STUBBLEFIELD, Joe C. S8518, LI, 1st Inf.
STUBBLEFIELD, Maggie, See Maggie Knight
STUBBLEFIELD, Margaret, W5023, WE, Stubblefield, Jarnett Wm.
STUBBLEFIELD, Margaret Elizabeth, W958, HE, Stubblefield, Charles Harrison
STUBBLEFIELD, Mary E. W5203, GR, Stubblefield, Wm.
STUBBLEFIELD, Mary Elizabeth, W8961, DY, Stubblefield, Wm. Washington
STUBBLEFIELD, N. B. S8537, W, 35th Inf.
STUBBLEFIELD, Nancy Jane, W6310, W, Stubblefield, Napoleon Bonaparte
STUBBLEFIELD, W. T. S13528, WE, 21st (Wilson's) Cav.
STUBBLEFIELD, William H. S3761, W, 2nd S.C. Rifles
STUBBS, Corrie Josephine, W10824, H, Stubbs, John Benton
STUBBS, Elrata, W5759, W7236, Stubbs, James Nichols
STUBBS, Jane, W7914, Stubbs, Thomas J.

STUBBS, Thomas J. S13763, 3rd (Forrest's) Cav.
STUCKEY, L. H. S7061, CC, 1st Ala. Inf.
STUDEVANT, Mary jane, W2181, GI, Studevant, Jasper B.
STUDIVANT, Jasper Zurbabel, S5621, LA, 53rd Inf.
STUMP, J. T. S2965, CL, 42nd Va. Inf.
STURDYVANT, James, S2650, MU, 17th Inf.
STURGIL, Robert, S10375, H, 21st Va. Cav.
STURGIS, William Harvey, S12119, O, 47th Inf.
STUTTS, J. H. S3870, MN, 17th Miss. Inf.
STUTTS, James H. S11216, LA, 16th Inf.
STUTTS, Lucy J. W4906, LA, Stutts, James H.
STUTTS, Rebecca Beavers, W10140, MA, Stutts, Wm. J.
STUTTS, W. J. S6959, DY, 21st Cav.
STYLES, Albert C. S1261, PO, 19th Inf.
SUBLETT, B. V. S14129, U, 21st Va. Inf.
SUBLETT, H. A. S8929, G, 18th Inf.
SUBLETT, Willie Anne, W6234, U, Sublett, Benjamin V.
SUDBERRY, A. J. S14384, WE, 4th (McLemore's) Cav.
SUGG, John H. S5644, MT, 49th Inf.
SUGG, Mary E. W1424, D, Sugg, N. T.
SUGG, Sarah Jane, W6481, HO, Sugg, John H.
SUGG, W. T. S7678, D, Unassigned (Commissary Dept.)
SUIT, James M. S15, D, 23rd N.C. Inf.
SULIVAN, Thomas, S4451, G, 22nd Inf.
SULLENGER, Eliza S. W11057, LI, Sullenger, Wm. Alexander
SULLINGER, William A. S10623, LI, 8th Inf.
SULLINS, Pelina, W2027, CA, Sullins, M. Lavander
SULLINS, W. L. S2454, CA, 35th Inf.
SULLIVAN, A. S5178, OV, 25th Inf.
SULLIVAN, Addie Ladelle, W7561, T, Sullivan, Nathan Harris
SULLIVAN, Berry, S6191, LI, 41st Inf.
SULLIVAN, Calloway, S2376, CL, 2nd Cav.
SULLIVAN, Caroline, W2036, HI, Sullivan, Marion
SULLIVAN, Charlotte, W279, WH, Sullivan, Pleasant L.
SULLIVAN, Damaries Elizabeth, W401, CA, Sullivan, Wm. Lee
SULLIVAN, Daniel A. S6671, BR, 65th Inf.
SULLIVAN, G. W. S16049, WL, 8th (Smith's) Cav.

SULLIVAN, Georgean, W4479, MT, Sullivan, James Henry
SULLIVAN, H. R. S7260, RU, 45th Inf.
SULLIVAN, J. A. S2556, WL, 7th Inf.
SULLIVAN, James E. S10004, 12th Inf.
SULLIVAN, Jefferson L. S3522, RU, 7th Inf.
SULLIVAN, Joe, S11147, SM, 44th Inf.
SULLIVAN, John B. S3422, L, 31st Inf.
SULLIVAN, John N. S15642, B, 8th Inf.
SULLIVAN, L. O. S11502, SH, 12th (Green's) Cav.
SULLIVAN, Lee Ann, W1834, OV, Sullivan, Ambros
SULLIVAN, M. E. W3985, RU, Sullivan, H. R.
SULLIVAN, Margaret, W6369, W5598, SH, Sullivan, Wm. Granville
SULLIVAN, Martha Jane, W1082, WE, Sullivan, James B.
SULLIVAN, Mary Ann, W6549, BR, Sullivan, Daniel Asbury
SULLIVAN, Mary Patten, W6840, WL, Sullivan, Wm. M.
SULLIVAN, Melidie Jane, W1866, WE, Sullivan, Wm. Elijah
SULLIVAN, N. H. S5967, T, Forrest's Old Regt. Cav.
SULLIVAN, P. A. S9701, HN, 46th Inf.
SULLIVAN, Squire, S2137, CL, 2nd Cav.
SULLIVAN, Suritha J. W3642, WL, Sullivan, James A.
SULLIVAN, Susan Elizabeth, W7133, Sullivan, James E.
SULLIVAN, Virginia Alice, W7864, SU, Sullivan, Wm. Thomas
SULLIVAN, W. B. S13321, WL, 7th Inf.
SULLIVAN, W. E. S1173, WE, 12th Inf.
SULLIVAN, W. H. S10183, HI, 48th Inf.
SULLIVAN, W. T. S6014, SU, 57th N.C. Inf.
SULLIVAN, William H. S10098, D, 7th Inf.
SULLIVAN, William Mack, S10492, WL, 1st Bn. (Colm's) Inf.
SULLIVAN, Willis J. S16224, D, 3rd (Forrest's) Cav.
SULLIVAN, william, S2189, WI, Baxter's Co. Lt. Art.
SUMERLIN, John W. S12559, CC, 66th N.C. Inf.
SUMERS, R. H. S786, SM, 5th Inf.
SUMMAN, W. C. S3914, HI, 35th Inf.
SUMMAR, J. D. S12939, RU, 22nd (Barteau's) Cav.
SUMMAR, William H. S3130, DK, 23rd Inf.

Index to Tennessee Confederate Pension Applications

SUMMER, A. B. S15130, PU, 35th Inf.
SUMMERS, America Elizabeth, W8268, L, Summers, Wm. Abner
SUMMERS, Bettie, W10207, WE, Summers, Francis S.
SUMMERS, E. J. S3845, BE, 49th Inf.
SUMMERS, F. S. S7450, WE, 5th Inf.
SUMMERS, G. W. S13014, W, 16th Inf.
SUMMERS, J. A. S4042, CA, 4th Cav.
SUMMERS, J. H. S8580, WL, 7th Inf.
SUMMERS, J. M. S13331, F, 26th Bn. N.C. Inf.
SUMMERS, Joel, S16464, JO, 37th Va. Inf.
SUMMERS, Martha E. W1890, GU, Summers, J. W.
SUMMERS, Mary Elizabeth, W393, CH, Summers, John McB.
SUMMERS, Mary Frances, W4406, SH, Summers, Charles Edward
SUMMERS, Rebecca Emily, W10243, DI, Summers, M. C.
SUMMERS, Samantha Ann, W1407, WE, Summers, James M.
SUMMERS, Sarah Emeline, W4721, CA, Summers, John Allen
SUMMERS, Virginia Polk, W4171, SH, Summers, Wm. Eldridge
SUMMERS, William Eldridge, S12389, SH, 37th Miss. Inf.
SUMMERS, William N. S9167, K, 13th N.C. Inf.
SUMMERVILLE, W. H. S7347, RB, 30th Inf.
SUMMITT, Virginia Elizabeth, W2974, D, Summitt, Daniel
SUMNER, Richard Riley, S9760, CO, 1st N.C. Cav.
SUMNER, Tazwell, S7962, SU, Shank's Battery, Va. Art.
SUMNER, W. D. S1909, CH, 1st (Feild's) Inf.
SUMNER, William A. S539, L, 32nd Inf.
SUMROW, W. F. S16508, L, 15th Cav.
SURLES, Addie, W5671, HR, Surles, Ed
SURRATT, Jacob Alva, S1501, BE, 5th Inf.
SUSONG, Mahlan, S12023, WA, 61st Inf.
SUTTLE, Leroy, S12506, D, 3rd (Clack's) Inf.
SUTTON, Ann, W410, B, Sutton, James Porter
SUTTON, C. M>, S5692, SN, 2nd (Robison's) Inf.
SUTTON, Caroline, W1903, G, Sutton, Joseph M.
SUTTON, Flora, See Flora Winn
SUTTON, G. W. S13432, S6203, MN, 2nd Miss. Inf.
SUTTON, Hannah, W2716, SM, Sutton, John Wesley
SUTTON, James, S476, WA, 154th Sr. Regt. Inf.
SUTTON, John, S3029, SM, 16th Inf.
SUTTON, John, S5587, CL, 29th Inf.
SUTTON, John, S10278, D, 11th Cav.
SUTTON, Mary Elizabeth, W5206, H, Sutton, James Montraville
SUTTON, Perlina E. W721, MO, Sutton, Abraham
SUTTON, Robert W. S10271, L, 15th Cav.
SUTTON, W. T. S11726, L, 7th (Duckworth's) Cav.
SWACK, Andrew Jackson, S2241, S7288, WH, 1st Bn. (Colm's) Inf.
SWACK, Sarah Angaline, W1992, WH, Swack, Andrew Jackson
SWAFFER, Ben L. S10068, WL, 1st (Carter's) Cav.
SWAFFORD, A. J. S14227, WH, 35th Ga. Inf.
SWAFFORD, Elizabeth, W3874, MC, Swafford, Ezekiel
SWAFFORD, Eva Jane, W7034, BL, Swafford, John L.
SWAFFORD, John Riley, S2593, MA, 6th N.C. Inf.
SWAFFORD, Margarett, W5279, WH, Swafford, Andrew Jackson
SWAFFORD, Mary Evaline, W1100, BL, Swafford, John P.
SWAGERTY, W. R. S13164, SE, 26th Inf.
SWAIN, Alice E. W3969, RU, Swain, Frank D.
SWAIN, B. B. S10243, RU, 45th Inf.
SWAIN, Byron M. S3922, S2997, G, 31st Inf.
SWAIN, D. F. S6769, RU, 45th Inf.
SWAIN, J. M. S7252, D, 38th Inf.
SWAIN, James M. S8766, D, 45th Inf.
SWALLOWS, A. D. S6659, OV, 25th Inf.
SWAN, J. A. S12247, J, 17th Inf.
SWAN, Mary Ellen, W5215, K, Swan, Samuel Epaminondas
SWAN, S. A. R. S14023, GI, 3rd (Lillard's) Mtd. Inf.
SWAN, W. J. S12872, B, 35th Inf.
SWAN, Winnie, W5366, J, Swan, George W.
SWANER, O. B. R. S2359, LI, 44th Inf.
SWANEY, M. R. S3936, GE, 7th S.C. Art.
SWANGER, David F. S3723, CF, 45th Inf.
SWANGER, David F. S5375, S4434, CA, 45th Inf.
SWANGER, John, S4444, S3724, CF, 18th Inf.

Index to Tennessee Confederate Pension Applications

SWANNER, J. D. S11142, WA, 60th Inf.
SWARINGER, Mary Mesilla, W1805, Swaringer, George Basly
SWATTS, Sarah E. W2807, K, Swatts, Jacob
SWEARINGER, Eli, S16385, WA, 52nd N.C. Inf.
SWEARINGER, G. B. S6702, 19th & 20th (Consol.) Cav.
SWEAT, Rachel, W5102, SH, Sweat, Turney Holley
SWEAT, T. H. S12916, SH, 23rd S.C. Inf.
SWECKER, James F. S5953, GE, 51st Va. Inf.
SWECKER, Mary E. W6979, GE, Swecker, James F.
SWEENEY, Dora Owen, W9513, WL, Sweeney, James Jones
SWEENEY, G. W. S14715, D, 30th Inf.
SWEENEY, H. H. S13756, HR, 3rd Mo. Cav.
SWEENEY, Harvey A. S3686, C, 1st S.C. Art.
SWEENEY, J. L. S13562, WI, Baxter's Co. Lt. Art.
SWEENEY, James C. S12464, D, 10th Cav.
SWEENEY, Lucretia, W7020, C, Sweeney, Harvey Alexander
SWEENEY, Minerva Jane, W7498, WI, Sweeney, Joseph L.
SWEENEY, Moses, S15884, PO, 3rd Ark. Inf.
SWEENEY, Sallie A. W7439, MC, Sweeney, Stephen C.
SWEENEY, Stephen C. S11198, MC, 23rd Inf.
SWEENEY, William G. S9142, WL, 30th Inf.
SWIFT, Aaron, C57, CC, 12th Inf.
SWIFT, Elizabeth Ann, W1505, WH, Swift, James
SWIFT, Fannie, W8381, MT, Swift, Mark Wilson
SWIFT, George W. S13773, CC, 12th Ky. Cav.
SWIFT, H. L. S8981, PU, 13th Cav.
SWIFT, J. W. S4638, HE, 27th Inf.
SWIFT, James M. S8007, CC, 12th Inf.
SWIFT, M. W. S11105, MT, 14th Inf.
SWIFT, Mattie, W478, MT, Swift, Mathew
SWIFT, Olivia, W9514, WL, Swift, George Barney
SWIFT, Thomas B. S7397, S10384, WE, 46th Inf.
SWINDLE, A. E. S13366, BE, 49th Inf.
SWINDLE, Eliza Ann, W129, WH, Swindle, George Washington
SWINDLE, Elizabeth Susan, W2643, BE, Swindle, James Eli
SWINDLE, J. E. S3903, B, 49th Inf.

SWINDLE, William A. S12353, BE, 55th Inf.
SWINEY, A. F. S1435, MS, 4th Inf.
SWINNER, W. F. S3719, SH, 3rd (Clack's) Inf.
SWINNEY, James W. S4232, WE, 55th Inf.
SWISHER, James H. S6435, H, 43rd Inf.
SWOPE, Sophronia C. W8601, SH, Swope, Grandison
SWOR, G. W. L. S12299, HN, 5th Inf.
SWORD, Charles, S13841, SH, 22nd Miss. Inf.
SYKES, Amanda V. W1828, SM, Sykes, Wm. E.
SYKES, Callie, W5547, SH, Sykes, J. P.
SYKES, Cyrus, S1589, MA, 21st (Wilson's) Cav.
SYKES, J. P. S13692, SH, Ross' Brigade, Miss. Cav.
SYKES, L. S. S3917, R, 16th Bn. (Neal's) Cav.
SYKES, Mattie, W8527, ST, Sykes, Thomas Sampson
SYKES, Rebecca Ann, W692, HN, Sykes, James Miller
SYKES, T. S. S15918, ST, 14th Inf.
SYKES, William E. S9641, SM, 55th Inf.
SYKES, William T. S5354, SU, 3rd Battery, Md. Art. C.S.A.
SYLAR, H. H. S493, JA, 1st E. Tenn. Cav.
SYLER, Samantha, W10566, LI, Syler, George Washington
SYLVESTER, David W. S5909, S7150, MO, 3rd (Lillard's) Mtd. Inf.
SYLVESTER, J. M. S14141, SH, 10th Ala. Cav.
TABOR, A. J. S6785, MT, 7th Ky. Cav.
TADLOCK, Lewis M. S5322, GE, Unassigned
TAFTS, M. H. S12742, LI, 44th Inf.
TALBERT, Lyda Elizabeth, W5191, CA, Talbert, Carrol
TALBOT, L. E. S14918, MA, 3rd (Forrest's) Cav.
TALENT, Drucilla J. W8009, PU, Talent, Ike
TALENT, Isel, S1051, PU, 8th Ky. Inf.
TALIAFERRO, L. V. S11839, HY, 7th Inf.
TALIAFERRO, Martha, W2503, K, Taliaferro, Wm. H.
TALIAFERRO, Mary Ellen, W6336, HY, Taliaferro, Charles Simon
TALIAFERRO, Mattie, W9517, HY, Taliaferro, Louis Vernon
TALIAFERRO, W. F. S12254, H, 34th Ga. Inf.
TALLENT, Elizabeth, W10798, MC, Tallent, Leroy Jackson
TALLENT, John, S12274, CF, 1st Cav.
TALLENT, L. J. S15750, GI, 59th Inf.

TALLENT, Mary C. W2066, MO, Tallent, Wm. R.
TALLEY, A. S. S15608, SH, 5th (McKenzie's) Cav.
TALLEY, B. T. S6590, OV, 8th (Dibrell's) Cav.
TALLEY, David Basil, S8195, DY, Baxter's Co. Lt. Art.
TALLEY, James T. S9627, MS, 8th Inf.
TALLEY, John W. S199, LO, 43rd Inf.
TALLEY, Lizzie, W6517, MS, Talley, J. T.
TALLEY, Mary E. W3910, MT, Talley, George F.
TALLEY, Nancy Elizabeth, W5517, DY, Talley, David Basil
TALLEY, S. T. S7104, BR, 62nd Inf.
TALLEY, Spencer B. S14730, WL, 28th Inf.
TALLEY, Thomas R. S10474, D, 9th (Ward's) Cav.
TALLY, Ella, W8506, MT, Tally, Simmons Sullivan
TALLY, H. B. S12514, FR, 4th (McLemore's) Cav.
TALLY, J. M. S11210, DI, 49th Inf.
TALLY, Louisa Leone, W10744, HR, Tally, Robert Franklin
TALLY, R. F. S16099, HR, 14th Cav.
TANKERSLEY, John A. S1151, K, 62nd Inf.
TANKERSLEY, Martha Susan, W1240, MOO, Tankersley, Wm. M.
TANKERSLEY, Melvina, W11034, MOO, Tankersley, Carroll Mandon
TANKERSLEY, William J, S9093, HD, 4th (McLemore's) Cav.
TANKERSLY, Richard, S7582, GI, 53rd Inf.
TANKERSLY, W. M. S6325, MOO, 34th Inf.
TANKESLEY, C. M. S7414, MOO, 34th Inf.
TANNER, E. E. S8307, P, 10th Cav.
TANNER, Frank, S2809, MN, 154th Sr. Regt. Inf.
TANNER, J. G. S13821, D, 11th Cav.
TANNER, John Q. S9356, H, 18th Ga. Inf.
TANNER, Martha, W6602, MN, Tanner, Frank
TANNER, R. W. S15265, MN, 18th (Newsom's) Cav.
TANNER, Rhoe, W4847, O, Tanner, Jonathan Elias
TANSIE, Ed, C7, WE, 31st Inf.
TANT, Frances J. W2818, D, Tant, Frederick
TANT, Frederick, S3988, D, 30th Inf.
TANT, Henry Clay, S4220, D, Unassigned
TANT, Mary Jane, W4373, SH, Tant, Wm. T.
TANT, P. G. S12661, D, 30th Inf.

TAPPS, Catharine Evaline, W4471, WA, Tapps, W. H.
TAPPS, William H. S3909, WA, 64th Inf.
TARKINGTON, Amanda, W2079, D, Tarkington, Joseph
TARKINGTON, J. H. S11555, D, 11th Inf.
TARKINGTON, Mary Jane, W4677, D, Tarkington, John Henry Clay
TARPLEY, A. N. S2883, FR, Huggin's Battery, Lt. Art.
TARPLEY, J. B. S13668, WL, Allison's Squadron, Cav.
TARPLEY, Margaret Elizabeth, W6921, WL, Tarpley, J. B.
TARPLEY, Mary Louisa, W3322, MT, Tarpley, Robert Branch
TARPLEY, Sarah Frances, W1562, FR, Tarpley, Ausbery Nelson
TARRANT, J. H. S13609, DY, 4th Inf.
TARTER, Henry, S15699, HW, 16th Bn. (Neal's) Cav.
TARVER, B. M. S16371, H, Phillip's Legion, Ga. Cav.
TATE, A. H. S12719, WA, 51st Va. Inf.
TATE, Aaron, S3810, P, 10th Cav.
TATE, Adelaide, W7999, SQ, Tate, Dock Mayburn
TATE, Annie E. W4715, SH, Tate, Jesse M.
TATE, C. G. S3236, GU, 35th Inf.
TATE, D. M. S10345, SQ, 3rd Cav.
TATE, F. T. S15017, RB, 2nd Inf.
TATE, G. S. S14926, GI, 6th (Wheeler's) Cav.
TATE, Ida, W11003, G, Tate, Wm. Henry
TATE, J. B. S16265, WL, 7th Inf.
TATE, J. W. S15185, SH, 7th Cav.
TATE, Jane Elizabeth, W2341, D, Tate, Andrew Jackson
TATE, Joseph D. S3587, SU, 29th Inf.
TATE, Joseph Wilson, S10231, HR, 4th Inf.
TATE, Mandy, W9003, SH, Tate, Thomas Cleman
TATE, Mary E. W4243, MO, Tate, W. M.
TATE, Matilda, W362, D, Tate, Zack
TATE, Mattie Duke, W7852, HR, Tate, Robert Alexander
TATE, Nancy A. W5077, O, Tate, John Kelley
TATE, Nancy C. W4894, SU, Tate, Joseph D.
TATE, Phelissa Vanhooser, W9051, D, Tate, Robert P. H.
TATE, R. A. S4849, FR, 17th Inf.
TATE, Robert Alexander, S12343, HR, 16th N.C. Inf.

TATE, Robert Patrick Henry, S12221, D, 4th Cav.
TATE, Thomas C. S14574, SH, 16th N.C. Inf.
TATE, W. M. S1150, MO, 3rd Inf.
TATOM, Alice Madora, W11009, MA, Tatom, Marion Columbus
TATOM, James A. S14270, GI, 10th Ala. Cav.
TATOM, Lucinda Melissa, W7698, HO, Tatom, L. B.
TATOM, M. C. S8550, MA, 15th Cav.
TATUM, Amanda, W97, WL, Tatum, Joseph
TATUM, Ardella, W10217, GI, Tatum, James Abner
TATUM, Ed L. S6500, DI, 6th (Wheeler's) Cav.
TATUM, Elmira S. W7901, SH, Tatum, H. A.
TATUM, H. A. S14130, SH, 1st Cav.
TATUM, ISaac, S5735, WY, 9th Cav.
TATUM, Margaret A. W956, G, Tatum, Joseph J.
TATUM, Mary Jane, W9585, LE, Tatum, Sub Allen
TATUM, Nancy Ellen, W8470, HI, Tatum, Richard Preston
TATUM, R. I. S15857, G, 47th Ga. Inf.
TATUM, S. A. S1903, WY, 24th Inf.
TATUM, S. F. S11238, HD, 12th Cav.
TAYLOE, Sally Love, W5608, BE, Tayloe, Thomas Himan
TAYLOE, T. H. S13311, BE, 7th Cav.
TAYLOR, A. C. S5495, G, 9th (Bennett's) Cav.
TAYLOR, A. M. S10422, GR, 59th Mtd. Inf.
TAYLOR, Alfred, S10589, SU, 63rd Inf.
TAYLOR, Allen Hugh, S9787, 10th (DeMoss') Cav.
TAYLOR, Aneliza E. W8083, G, Taylor, George W.
TAYLOR, Ann, W886, ME, Taylor, John Blevins
TAYLOR, C. M. S16500, DY, Kizer's? Servants
TAYLOR, Carrie B. W9748, B, Taylor, J. N.
TAYLOR, Catherine, W8942, W, Taylor, Jackson
TAYLOR, Catherine Elizabeth, W6424, HR, Taylor, Wm. Alexander
TAYLOR, Catherine Virginia, W5920, SU, Taylor, Robert R.
TAYLOR, Clara S. W5887, MA, Taylor, James Monroe
TAYLOR, Creed, S9772, W, 11th (Holman's) Cav.
TAYLOR, David G. S6931, CF, 28th Cav.

TAYLOR, Delia Adiline, W6454, LI, Taylor, John David
TAYLOR, Drussilla A. W10468, MO, Taylor, Leeroy
TAYLOR, E. H. S5947, CO, 1st (Carter's) Cav.
TAYLOR, E. W. S162, DK, 28th Inf.
TAYLOR, Elias L. S3183, J, 16th Inf.
TAYLOR, Elizabeth, W598, HN, Taylor, H. D.
TAYLOR, Elizabeth, W774, DK, Taylor, John C.
TAYLOR, Elizabeth Miller, W8536, H, Taylor, Wm. Marion
TAYLOR, Elmira H. W7430, D, Taylor, Jesse W.
TAYLOR, Ezekine W. S1535, DK, 28th Inf.
TAYLOR, F. M. S13904, CF, 1st (Turney's) Inf.
TAYLOR, F. M. S14381, MU, 48th Inf.
TAYLOR, Fannie V. W4836, SH, Taylor, Thomas Courtney
TAYLOR, Frank B. S10085, O, 9th Inf.
TAYLOR, G. R. S10784, WE, 12th Ky. Cav.
TAYLOR, H. C. S2308, GI, 3rd Inf.
TAYLOR, H. C. S4274, MN, 26th Miss. Inf.
TAYLOR, Harriet Louiza, W4054, WH, Taylor, Thomas Ed
TAYLOR, Haywood, S574, MU, 1st Inf.
TAYLOR, Henry C. S7695, PU, 25th Inf.
TAYLOR, Henry T. S6501, WI, 45th Inf.
TAYLOR, I. J. S4778, SH, Forrest's Old Regt. Cav.
TAYLOR, Immanuel, S5781, SU, Home Guards
TAYLOR, J. A. S14475, MS, 11th (Holman's) Cav.
TAYLOR, J. C. S14400, G, 19th & 20th Cav.
TAYLOR, J. D. S13094, HW, Jefferies' Battery, Va. Art.
TAYLOR, J. G. S9223, WA, 5th Cav.
TAYLOR, J. G. (Buck), S8668, G, 7th Cav.
TAYLOR, J. H. S11504, WL, 23rd Inf.
TAYLOR, J. M. S227, ST, 50th Inf.
TAYLOR, J. Monroe, S9988, MA, 51st Inf.
TAYLOR, J. S. S6502, HN, 46th Inf.
TAYLOR, J. S. S15421, S11199, WL, 45th Inf.
TAYLOR, James, S1893, SU, 63rd Inf.
TAYLOR, James A. S5660, HY, 7th Cav.
TAYLOR, James F. S7425, DY, Phillip's Battery, Lt. Art.
TAYLOR, James J. S14433, MT, 6th Bn. Ky. Cav.
TAYLOR, James M. S516, WI, 44th Inf.
TAYLOR, James Madison, S12289, HR, 22nd Inf.

TAYLOR, James T. S4600, RU, 8th (Smith's) Cav.
TAYLOR, James W. S2217, T, 7th Cav.
TAYLOR, Jane, W2548, WH, Taylor, Hosea
TAYLOR, Jesse W. S14896, D, 5th Fla. Cav.
TAYLOR, John, S4975, WA, 60th Inf.
TAYLOR, John, S4986, J, 25th Inf.
TAYLOR, John, S5468, ST, 50th Inf.
TAYLOR, John D. S2669, FR, 1st Inf.
TAYLOR, John R. S1790, H, 35th Inf.
TAYLOR, Joseph A. S4621, B, 24th Inf.
TAYLOR, Julia Amanda, W10060, R, Taylor, James O.
TAYLOR, Julia Anna, W7832, H, Taylor, Thomas Daniel
TAYLOR, L. S377, WL, 5th Inf.
TAYLOR, Leroy, S4340, B, 1st (Feild's) Inf.
TAYLOR, Levi R. S5215, DK, 25th Inf.
TAYLOR, Lilla, W9663, L, Taylor, Licurgus Willington
TAYLOR, M. A. W4389, G, Taylor, M. C.
TAYLOR, M. D. L. S9286, LI, 63rd Inf.
TAYLOR, M. K. S3755, WH, 1st (Carter's) Cav.
TAYLOR, Malisa, W4888, DK, Taylor, Lafate
TAYLOR, Malissa Malvinnie, W8285, B, Taylor, John Atkins
TAYLOR, Margaret Ann, W5886, SU, Taylor, Alfred
TAYLOR, Margaret Morton, W3344, SH, Taylor, Samuel Alexander
TAYLOR, Mary, W10368, WE, Taylor, George Robertson
TAYLOR, Mary Beasley, W9289, B, Taylor, Thomas Jefferson
TAYLOR, Mary Dabney, W6162, HY, Taylor, F. M.
TAYLOR, Mary Elizabeth, W1087, DI, Taylor, Wm. Henry
TAYLOR, Mary Ellen, W3588, W6331, MA, Taylor, Robert Wooding
TAYLOR, Mary Jane, W5970, D, Taylor, Wm. Joseph
TAYLOR, Matilda Catherine, W2622, G, Taylor, John Goodwin
TAYLOR, Mattie Dean, W10063, RB, Taylor, Henry Sanford
TAYLOR, Mattie J. W10961, MT, Taylor, James Jay
TAYLOR, Miranda, W857, G, Taylor, Wm. Washington
TAYLOR, Moses, S7395, HR, 7th Cav.

TAYLOR, Nancy, W238, DK, Taylor, Peter Emory
TAYLOR, Nancy, W1635, W, Taylor, Arthur
TAYLOR, Nancy Catherine, W8759, DI, Taylor, Manoah
TAYLOR, Nancy Jane, W5498, CT, Taylor, Thomas E.
TAYLOR, Nancy Pee, W5784, Taylor, A. H.
TAYLOR, P. A. S5555, SH, Forrest's Old Regt. Cav.
TAYLOR, Porter, S15366, WL, 45th Inf.
TAYLOR, R. C. S890, 12th Inf.
TAYLOR, R. R. S14709, SU, 59th Inf.
TAYLOR, R. W. S9214, MA, 33rd Inf.
TAYLOR, Rebecca, W1153, DK, Taylor, Levi R.
TAYLOR, Robert C. S6932, G, 12th Inf.
TAYLOR, Rosa B. W3276, HR, Taylor, Moses
TAYLOR, S. V. S2187, SU, 32nd Mo. Bn.
TAYLOR, Sallie, W8137, RU, Taylor, W. F.
TAYLOR, Sallie Ann, W10534, W5238, WE, Taylor, Rufus Randolph
TAYLOR, Sarah, W1801, SU, Taylor, Immanuel
TAYLOR, Sarah, W8449, MC, Taylor, Herbert
TAYLOR, Sarah Ann, W1121, FR, Taylor, Wm. J.
TAYLOR, Sarah Elizabeth, W5572, CF, Taylor, Robert Benjamin
TAYLOR, Skelton, S11625, WA, 1st Cav.
TAYLOR, Stephen P. S7862, 31st Inf.
TAYLOR, Susan Ann, W1516, SH, Taylor, Peter Abshaw
TAYLOR, Susan L. W832, RU, Taylor, James T.
TAYLOR, T. W. S2526, LI, 44th Inf.
TAYLOR, Tennie Pauline, W6853, R, Taylor, W. H.
TAYLOR, Theo. S12432, GI, 2nd Inf.
TAYLOR, Thomas D. S8320, H, Thomas' Legion, N.C.
TAYLOR, Thomas E. S4502, WH, 16th Inf.
TAYLOR, Thomas J. S8930, B, 45th Inf.
TAYLOR, W. B. S10595, G, 20th (Russell's) Cav.
TAYLOR, W. C. S789, RU, 2nd Inf.
TAYLOR, W. H. S4066, SN, 2nd Cav.
TAYLOR, W. H. S8998, R, 18th Inf.
TAYLOR, W. J. S6357, CF, 11th (Holman's) Cav.
TAYLOR, W. L. S14686, WA, 5th Cav.
TAYLOR, W. L. S15102, H, 1st (Carter's) Cav.

TAYLOR, W. N. S15284, FR, 41st Inf.
TAYLOR, W. W. S11168, RB, 30th Inf.
TAYLOR, William, S6698, DI, Fisher's Co. Art.
TAYLOR, William Alexander, S9039, HR, 7th (Duckworth's) Cav.
TAYLOR, William E. S3307, SU, 20th Inf.
TEAGUE, B. F. S10102, F, 13th Inf.
TEAGUE, Dorcas, W4109, MN, Teague, Josh
TEAGUE, J. R. S12565, MA, 38th Inf.
TEAGUE, James, S10502, F, 2nd Partisan Rangers, Miss. Cav.
TEAGUE, Jeff, S10480, F, 20th (Nixon's) Cav.
TEAGUE, Joshua, S4533, MN, Undetermined
TEAGUE, Joshua Monroe, S2364, MA, 19th Cav.
TEAGUE, Logan, S1062, SU, 26th N.C. Inf.
TEAGUE, Martha Elizabeth, W5075, F, Teague, Benjamin Franklin
TEAGUE, Mary Ann, W4799, PO, Teague, Elisha
TEAGUE, Susan, W4611, HR, Teague, Joseph B.
TEAGUE, Susan A. W7801, MA, Teague, James Riley
TEASLEY, Alexander, S15412, D, 13th Ky. Cav.
TEASLEY, G. W. S3888, CE, 1st (Feild's) Inf.
TEASLEY, L. F. S13171, CE, 49th Inf.
TEASLEY, Mary A. W7490, CE, Teasley, Leonard F.
TEASLEY, Rebecca Jane, W5662, CE, Teasley, George Washington
TEASTER, James H. S6120, CT, 37th N.C. Inf.
TEASTER, Mary Ann, W9493, CH, Teaster, James Harrison
TEEFOTELLER, J. H. S8092, BO, Thomas' Legion, N.C.
TEETERS, G. W. S4594, FR, 44th Inf.
TEFERTALLER, E. L. S3193, MC, 29th Inf.
TEFERTALLER, Mary Catherine, W6261, MC, Tefertaller, Errock Lafayette
TEFFETELLER, Mike, S8001, BO, 37th Inf.
TEFFT, G. T. S11732, HO, 36th Va. Inf.
TEFFT, Latitia Fannie, W9849, SH, Tefft, Julius Lafayette
TEFFT, Louisa S. W5280, HO, Tefft, George Talurage
TEFFT, W. A. S13657, SH, 36th Bn. Va. Cav.
TEFT, E. A. S14791, HO, 16th Va. Cav.
TELL, John, S9698, CA, 18th Inf.
TEMPLE, Annis, W9697, BR, Temple, James D.

TEMPLE, Asenith Henrietta, W10142, D, Temple, Charles Robert
TEMPLE, C. R. S8832, D, Morton's Battery, Lt. Art.
TEMPLE, L. F. S5376, W, 35th Inf.
TEMPLE, W. J. S. S15842, MU, 6th (Wheeler's) Cav.
TEMPLETON, B. B. S7973, B, 23rd Bn. Inf.
TEMPLETON, Burrell, S1620, S1110, MR, 35th Inf.
TEMPLETON, Clarender Anna, W8450, T, Templeton, Richard Springs
TEMPLETON, E. J. S1021, GE, 18th Va. Inf.
TEMPLETON, E. J. S15356, SN, 24th Inf.
TEMPLETON, J. P. S3074, SH, 3rd S.C. Inf.
TEMPLETON, Joe, S5460, MR, 36th Inf.
TEMPLETON, John D. S10868, W, 35th Inf.
TEMPLETON, Lucy F. W3060, GE, Templeton, Edmund J.
TEMPLETON, Maggie, W2372, WH, Templeton, Greenville H.
TEMPLETON, Marender Eveline, W8216, WH, Templeton, Thomas Jefferson
TEMPLETON, Mattie Ann, W9726, LI, Templeton, Robert Henry
TEMPLETON, Robert H. S7187, LI, 44th Inf.
TEMPLETON, Susie, W9976, FR, Templeton, John W.
TEMPLETON, Thomas J. S10081, WH, 16th Inf.
TEMPLIN, David T. S6715, CO, 62nd Inf.
TENNERY, E. K. P. S13394, G, 3rd Inf.
TENNERY, Mary Isabel, W7440, G, Tennery, E. K. P.
TENNISON, Evline, W10078, MN, Tennison, Hiram F.
TENNISON, Hiram F. S5979, HR, 26th Miss. Inf.
TENNISON, Mattie Virginia, W9519, MS, Tennison, Hiram
TERRELL, Ben A. W. S14296, DK, 35th Inf.
TERRELL, Cicero W. S12851, H, 42nd Ga. Inf.
TERRELL, James B. S12956, WI, 3rd (Clack's) Inf.
TERRELL, Nancy Tennessee, W5977, SH, Terrell, Joseph Calvin
TERRELL, W. A. S15316, H, 3rd Va. Cav.
TERRELL, William T. S442, RB, 30th Inf.
TERRENCE, Adella A. W4245, SH, Terrence, James Thomas
TERRY, Almedia Paralee, W10026, CH, Terry, James Carroll

TERRY, Angelina A. C. W1350, PU, Terry, Elijah W.
TERRY, Benjamin, S4341, MC, 16th N.C. Inf.
TERRY, E. C. S9066, G, 1st Ark. Inf.
TERRY, E. J. S1702, CH, 7th Cav.
TERRY, F. B. S10124, H, 17th Inf.
TERRY, H. R. S8732, PU, 25th Inf.
TERRY, Hattie Smith, W7174, SN, Terry, John H.
TERRY, J. C. S6142, CH, 21st (Wilson's) Cav.
TERRY, J. C. S16614, MO, 46th N.C. Inf.
TERRY, John, C255, H, Undetermined
TERRY, John C. S12200, WH, 23rd Inf.
TERRY, John H. S9338, 55th Inf.
TERRY, John H. S13550, SN, 2nd (Robison's) Inf.
TERRY, M. S5922, HN, 5th Inf.
TERRY, Martha Jane, W5325, G, Terry, E. C.
TERRY, Martha Lou, W9323, WH, Terry, J. C.
TERRY, Mary, W6701, HN, Terry, Mike
TERRY, Mary P. W1294, MN, Terry, Walker Jones
TERRY, Mattie J. (P?), W8700, W9661, G, Terry, E. C.
TERRY, Nat G. S3753, B, 17th Inf.
TERRY, Sarah B. W686, CY, Terry, James P.
TERRY, Sarah Jennie, W1711, Terry, John Hill
TERRY, Virginia, W2772, MO, Terry, Benjamin
TERRY, W. C. S9470, CY, 25th Inf.
TERRY, Z. T. S14298, J, 28th Inf.
TERRY, william J. S4178, J, 25th Inf.
TETTLETON, Elizabeth, W5244, MA, Tettleton, Joe
TETTLETON, Joseph, S5167, MA, 6th Inf.
THACKER, J. C. S5901, ST, 49th Inf.
THACKER, Mary Carney, W9898, D, Thacker, James M.
THACKSTON, Eva Drucilla, W3727, D, Thackston, Benjamin Franklin
THARP, Ballard Simpson, S3432, G, 48th Inf.
THARP, C. F. S15357, LI, 32nd Inf.
THARP, Mary Jane, W2964, WY, Tharp, Cary Morris
THARPE, See also Thorpe
THARPE, Nancy M. W8512, LE, Tharpe, Andrew J.
THAXTON, Elizabeth, W4998, SQ, Thaxton, F. K.
THAXTON, F. K. S8304, SQ, 35th Inf.
THAXTON, Mary Ann, W2583, W, Thaxton, Houston Joiner

THIGPEN, R. F. M. S7960, MN, 27th Ala. Inf.
THOMAS, A. D. S15201, ST, 2nd Ky. Cav.
THOMAS, A. E. S9945, WI, 1st (Feild's) Inf.
THOMAS, Add, C267, MU, Undetermined
THOMAS, Adeline, W4780, H, Thomas, Lafayette
THOMAS, Alley Lucinda, W9649, RU, Thomas, George Washington
THOMAS, Ann W. W2545, D, Thomas, H. T.
THOMAS, Atha, S6192, G, 6th Inf.
THOMAS, B. F. S9538, H, 3rd Inf.
THOMAS, Belle McMillan, W5080, K, Thomas, Thomas Jefferson
THOMAS, Ben, C49, MT, 31st Ala. Inf.
THOMAS, Bettie, W2233, BE, Thomas, John Bauden
THOMAS, C. S. S13367, MO, 2nd Inf.
THOMAS, Callaway, S1014, MO, 43rd Inf.
THOMAS, Catherine, W938, MO, Thomas, Reuben
THOMAS, Celia, W4119, W3961, MC, Thomas, George Washington
THOMAS, D. J. S15814, PO, 3rd (Lillard's) Mtd. Inf.
THOMAS, E. D. S7289, WL, 22nd (Barteau's) Cav.
THOMAS, Elizabeth S. W9990, WE, Thomas, M. B.
THOMAS, Elnora, W758, RB, Thomas, George Henry
THOMAS, Evaline, W4785, H, Thomas, Benjamin F.
THOMAS, F. M. S7290, MN, 16th Inf.
THOMAS, Fannie, W4628, MN, Thomas, Wm. N.
THOMAS, Florendie Parilee, W237, BE, Thomas, Wm. Washington
THOMAS, G. C. S14610, FR, 4th (McLemore's) Cav.
THOMAS, G. H. S2, RB, 14th Confederate Regt.
THOMAS, G. S. S7543, RO, 64th Va. Cav.
THOMAS, G. W. S2541, K, 3rd (Lillard's) Mtd. Inf.
THOMAS, G. W. S15492, RU, 1st Bn. (McNairy's) Cav.
THOMAS, H. C. S9489, DI, 49th Inf.
THOMAS, H. W. S3267, MN, 5th Ala. Cav.
THOMAS, Hattie, W10482, JO, Thomas, Hezekia
THOMAS, Henry J. S11783, G, 7th Cav.

THOMAS, Hezekiah, S11531, JO, 58th N.C. Inf.
THOMAS, Hugh, S3591, SE, 37th Inf.
THOMAS, Isaac A. S7196, MS, 4th Cav.
THOMAS, J. A. S10112, HY, 7th Cav.
THOMAS, J. A. S15745, DI, 24th Bn. Sharpshooters
THOMAS, J. E. S2850, MR, 19th Ala. Inf.
THOMAS, J. E. S4764, MR, 14th Ala. Inf.
THOMAS, J. L. S5855, WL, 22nd (Barteau's) Cav.
THOMAS, J. R. S3812, HE, 17th S.C. Inf.
THOMAS, James D. S16671, WI, 4th S.C. Inf.
THOMAS, James F. S15386, O, 32nd Ark. Inf.
THOMAS, James Franklin, S10844, G, 47th Inf.
THOMAS, James K. S10177, MA, 19th (Biffle's) Cav.
THOMAS, James M. S3579, B, 18th Inf.
THOMAS, John, S598, H, 1st Cav.
THOMAS, John C. S2309, WA, 37th Va. Inf.
THOMAS, John H. S15661, MU, 9th Bn. (Gantt's) Cav.
THOMAS, John N. S13618, G, 12th Inf.
THOMAS, John R. S773, HE, 17th Inf.
THOMAS, Joseph C. S13699, CL, 25th Va. Cav.
THOMAS, Julia Anna, W3940, HY, Thomas, Lemual Alston
THOMAS, Kitty, W8565, DI, Thomas, J. A.
THOMAS, L. T. S2074, SM, 55th Inf.
THOMAS, Laura T. W824, SM, Thomas, Leonidus T.
THOMAS, Leander, S2934, K, 1st S.C. Rifles
THOMAS, Lee C. S11306, FR, 23rd Inf.
THOMAS, Liddie Ellen, W3075, MR, Thomas, Jonathan Alexander
THOMAS, Louise Amanda, W1189, MA, Thomas, Wm. James
THOMAS, Lowery, S1224, CO, 62nd Inf.
THOMAS, Lucinda Elizabeth, W5550, G, Thomas, Atha
THOMAS, Lucy M. W5086, MT, Thomas, Benjamin Hardin
THOMAS, Maacha Elizabeth, W3306, G, Thomas, John Smith
THOMAS, Malinda J. W3207, HW, Thomas, Wm. B.
THOMAS, Martha G. W10393, ST, Thomas, Wm. T.
THOMAS, Mary, W4049, RB, Thomas, Archie
THOMAS, Mary E. W9673, WE, Thomas, Wm. Ellis
THOMAS, Mary Emma, W2666, D, Thomas, James Washington
THOMAS, Mary I. W8031, G, Thomas, James Franklin
THOMAS, Mary Virginia, W10241, SU, Thomas, George Washington
THOMAS, Matt, S8655, FR, 59th Ala. Inf.
THOMAS, Mildred Amelia, W6884, MT, Thomas, Nicolis G.
THOMAS, Mollie Bell, W9379, ST, Thomas, Robert Edward
THOMAS, Mollie D. W7951, MU, Thomas, John Howell
THOMAS, N. C. S13150, H, Phillip's Legion, Ga. Inf.
THOMAS, Nancy M. W1172, HE, Thomas, John
THOMAS, Nannie J. W6684, WI, Thomas, Wm. Jackson
THOMAS, Phebe Caroline, W2055, K, Thomas, Caloway
THOMAS, R. J. S9189, SH, 34th Miss. Inf.
THOMAS, Richard F. S3756, G, 2nd Ky. Inf.
THOMAS, S. A. S3945, CE, 18th Inf.
THOMAS, Sallie Redford, W10042, WI, Thomas, Archibald E.
THOMAS, Samuel H. S3425, SH, 20th Cav.
THOMAS, Sarah Lavina, W7691, CL, Thomas, Joseph C.
THOMAS, Selia, W3961, W4119, MC, Thomas, George Washington
THOMAS, Sophronia A. W9299, MA, Thomas, James K.
THOMAS, Susan, W6518, MN, Thomas, Franklin M.
THOMAS, T. J. S10992, HY, 7th (Duckworth's) Cav.
THOMAS, Virginia Bell, W5332, SH, Thomas, Edward Branch
THOMAS, Virginia Randolph, W8383, MU, Thomas, James D.
THOMAS, W. B. S3580, HW, 2nd (Ashby's) Cav.
THOMAS, W. D. S13543, CL, 25th Va. Cav.
THOMAS, W. D. S13869, HN, 29th (Nixon's) Cav.
THOMAS, W. J. S14278, WI, Carter's Scouts, Cav.
THOMAS, W. L. S10543, MS, 14th (Neely's) Cav.
THOMAS, W. N. S13417, MN, 59th Ala. Inf.
THOMAS, W. W. S350, BE, 27th Inf.

THOMAS, Wiley, S8352, CH, 27th Inf.
THOMAS, William Graham, S10751, SU, 48th Va. Inf.
THOMAS, William J. S575, S1548, CC, 51st Inf.
THOMAS, Wm. E. S16380, WE, McDonald's Bn.
THOMASON, Catherine, W8619, BE, Thomason, James
THOMASON, G. J. G. S7789, 21st (Wilson's) Cav.
THOMASON, H. M. S3013, MR, 39th Ga. Inf.
THOMASON, James, S13446, G, 55th Inf.
THOMASON, James S. S12604, B, 55th Inf.
THOMASON, M. M. S4387, O, 21st Cav.
THOMASON, Malinda Frances, W590, MU, Thomason, Riley (James)
THOMASON, Matthew N. S15929, D, 55th Ala. Inf.
THOMASON, Nancy Francies, W10758, D, Thomason, John Given
THOMASON, Rita, W5591, ST, Thomason, J. G.
THOMASON, Rosie L. W7837, CC, Thomason, T. D.
THOMASON, Sarah Catherin, W4145, HU, Thomason, James Henderson
THOMASON, Sarah Rebecca, W4517, HM, Thomason, James
THOMASON, Winnie Jane, W1841, RU, Thomason, Adam T.
THOMASSON, Rhoda V. W7109, D, Thomasson, Edwin Watson
THOMASSON, T. D. S10401, CC, 35th Inf.
THOMASSON, W. L. S215, PU, 16th Cav.
THOMBERG, A. L. S14911, D, 30th Inf.
THOMISON, Cornelia Ann, W8641, R, Thomison, Wm. Patton
THOMISON, Siddie, W9927, LI, Thomison, Thomas
THOMISON, W. P. S16055, R, 19th & 20th (Consol.) Cav.
THOMPKINS, Socrates, S12300, L, 15th S.C. Inf.
THOMPSON, A. S2914, CC, 7th Miss. Inf.
THOMPSON, A. A. S4439, MS, 8th Inf.
THOMPSON, A. F. W450, HU, Thompson, Wm. Henry
THOMPSON, A. J. S3163, GI, 1st Inf.
THOMPSON, A. J. S5126, 12th Inf.
THOMPSON, A. J. S10009, SU, 63rd Inf.
THOMPSON, A. N. S6537, D, 49th Inf.

THOMPSON, Absalom, S10055, WA, 16th Cav.
THOMPSON, Adaline Miller, W8637, SH, Thompson, John D.
THOMPSON, Alex. S13985, G, 38th Inf.
THOMPSON, Alexander, S16101, MA, 38th Inf.
THOMPSON, Alice, W10893, DI, Thompson, James Balden
THOMPSON, Annette Connor, W7482, F, Thompson, Wm. Damarcus
THOMPSON, Arena A. W579, HN, Thompson, Reuben V.
THOMPSON, B. B. S2780, LI, 24th Inf.
THOMPSON, B. T. S1590, MT, Undetermined
THOMPSON, Bartley, S12094, WA, 16th Cav.
THOMPSON, Beedy, W3837, WI, Thompson, Eppes J.
THOMPSON, Bolinda Taylor, W10269, L, Thompson, L. O.
THOMPSON, Bryant, S7513, MC, 16th Bn. (Neal's) Cav.
THOMPSON, C. W. S10739, D, 6th (Wheeler's) Cav.
THOMPSON, Catherine, W4206, CL, Thompson, Wm. G.
THOMPSON, Catherine Quintina, W2064, HI, Thompson, Wm. Carothers
THOMPSON, Charles A. S7498, D, 1st (Feild's) Inf.
THOMPSON, Charlotte E. W882, HU, Thompson, Wm. H.
THOMPSON, Della, W10296, DI, Thompson, Thomas D.
THOMPSON, E. A. S2872, WL, 4th (McLemore's) Cav.
THOMPSON, E. G. S10209, HI, 19th (Biffle's) Cav.
THOMPSON, E. L. S6966, PU, 8th (Dibrell's) Cav.
THOMPSON, Eliza, W6957, BR, Thompson, Wm.
THOMPSON, Elizabeth, W2199, WA, Thompson, Isaac Newton
THOMPSON, Elizabeth Fain, W3109, D, Thompson, Robert Adolphus
THOMPSON, Ellen, W3380, MA, Thompson, W. H. H.
THOMPSON, Fannie Jane, W9063, CF, Thompson, Larry
THOMPSON, Francis R. S14215, LI, 5th Ky. Inf.

THOMPSON, G. W. S2455, FR, 41st Inf.
THOMPSON, G. W. S4062, H, 8th Inf.
THOMPSON, George R. H. S57, WL, 18th Inf.
THOMPSON, George W. S3448, FR, 4th Cav.
THOMPSON, H. W. S2405, GI, 44th Inf.
THOMPSON, Hardy, S7208, SN, 9th (Bennett's) Cav.
THOMPSON, Henry B. S10769, H, 3rd Ala. Inf.
THOMPSON, Henry M. S16646, HA, Rhett Art.
THOMPSON, Huldah B. W6079, B, Thompson, Wm. Thomas
THOMPSON, Isaac, S1876, S6591, C, 64th Va. Inf.
THOMPSON, J. B. S5173, PO, 59th Inf.
THOMPSON, J. B. S8334, DI, Baxter's Co. Lt. Art.
THOMPSON, J. E. S10094, MT, 9th Inf.
THOMPSON, J. F. S5048, PU, 25th Inf.
THOMPSON, J. H. S7930, W, 4th (McLemore's) Cav.
THOMPSON, J. H. S12173, G, 38th Inf.
THOMPSON, J. K. P. S7737, MS, 41st Inf.
THOMPSON, J. L. S627, G, 9th Cav.
THOMPSON, J. M. S7726, H, 39th N.C. Inf.
THOMPSON, J. M. S15830, CC, 55th Inf.
THOMPSON, J. O. S420, G, 14th Cav.
THOMPSON, J. R. S12425, WH, 16th Inf.
THOMPSON, J. W. S9982, WI, 24th Inf.
THOMPSON, Jacob C. S6150, GE, 61st Inf.
THOMPSON, James H. S15628, FR, 1st (Turney's) Inf.
THOMPSON, James T. S13829, MA, 18th Ala. Inf.
THOMPSON, James W. S16621, SN, 24th Inf.
THOMPSON, Joe A. S12477, B, 41st Inf.
THOMPSON, John, S7804, MS, 41st Inf.
THOMPSON, John, S12384, HR, 22nd Inf.
THOMPSON, John B. S3520, UN, Allison's Squadron, Cav.
THOMPSON, John DeKalb, S13529, T, 12th (Green's) Cav.
THOMPSON, John J. S251, HN, 5th Inf.
THOMPSON, John W. S6770, WA, 60th Inf.
THOMPSON, Joseph, S11851, ME, 5th (McKenzie's) Cav.
THOMPSON, Joseph F. S14512, K, 19th Inf.
THOMPSON, Joseph Newton, S16445, SH, 44th Miss. Inf.
THOMPSON, Kitty Logan, W10446, D, Thompson, James C.
THOMPSON, L. L. S7766, MS, 41st Inf.

THOMPSON, Lettie Cannon, W9837, B, Thompson, Zach
THOMPSON, Maggie A. W10456, HI, Thompson, Tommie C.
THOMPSON, Margaret, W1382, MC, Thompson, Bryant
THOMPSON, Margaret Elizabeth, W6302, SU, Thompson, Andrew Jackson
THOMPSON, Margaret L. W8693, W7984, MU, Thompson, Robert Hoker
THOMPSON, Marshall, C229, D, 4th Cav.
THOMPSON, Martha, W3463, ME, Thompson, Joseph
THOMPSON, Martha Elizabeth, W2017, MS, Thompson, John
THOMPSON, Mary A. W7867, MS, Thompson, Lindsey L.
THOMPSON, Mary Ann, W3338, D, Thompson, Milten Lafayette
THOMPSON, Mary C. W7039, WH, Thompson, James Robertson
THOMPSON, Mary E. W497, LI, Thompson, Hugh W.
THOMPSON, Mary Frances, W6029, W, Thompson, J. H.
THOMPSON, Mary J. W1295, D, Thompson, James A.
THOMPSON, Mary J. W4231, MC, Thompson, Silvester Rice
THOMPSON, Mary J. W8341, HU, Thompson, Wm. Tazewell
THOMPSON, Mary Jane, W820, G, Thompson, Jesse Leander
THOMPSON, Matilda Elizabeth, W10854, HA, Thompson, Henry M.
THOMPSON, Nancy, W7418, MN, Thompson, John
THOMPSON, Nancy Jane, W1151, OV, Thompson, Raleigh J.
THOMPSON, Ola Belle, W7455, WA, Thompson, A. B.
THOMPSON, Otis Dunlap, S11716, MT, 14th Va. Inf.
THOMPSON, P. C. S16123, CE, 2nd Ark. Inf.
THOMPSON, Parmelia, W2787, WL, Thompson, Wm. Dillard
THOMPSON, Patsy M. W4616, BR, Thompson, Terrel
THOMPSON, Permelia Emerline, W5622, D, Thompson, Swan W.
THOMPSON, R. A. S3444, SN, 7th Inf.

THOMPSON, R. J. S2113, OV, 8th (Dibrell's) Cav.
THOMPSON, R. M. S2803, CL, 29th Inf.
THOMPSON, R. R. S1496, D, 48th Inf.
THOMPSON, R. V. S3506, HN, 5th Inf.
THOMPSON, Robert H. S1973, K, 48th Va. Inf.
THOMPSON, Rowena E. W3488, D, Thompson, John Claiborne
THOMPSON, S. R. S8065, MO, 31st Inf.
THOMPSON, Sallie, W10236, Thompson, Andrew J.
THOMPSON, Sallie A. W6737, SH, Thompson, A. W.
THOMPSON, Sallie E. W11088, WA, Thompson, James Franklin
THOMPSON, Sallie Jewell, W9378.5, WL, Thompson, Johnie B.
THOMPSON, Sarah Elizabeth, W6756, MT, Thompson, James Edward
THOMPSON, Sarah H. W6624, LI, Thompson, B. B.
THOMPSON, Sarah Irene, W3046, DI, Thompson, James J.
THOMPSON, Sarah Jane, W2382, D, Thompson, Wm. Riley
THOMPSON, Sarah Jane, W3853, CL, Thompson, Wm. Alexander
THOMPSON, Scipio, S11276, D, 19th (Biffle's) Cav.
THOMPSON, Susan, W11029, CO, Thompson, W. C.
THOMPSON, Susan Ann, W7367, CE, Thompson, Wm. W.
THOMPSON, T. D. S13103, D, 11th Inf.
THOMPSON, T. J. S5573, T, 46th Miss. Inf.
THOMPSON, Temperance W. W5399, WL, Thompson, T. W.
THOMPSON, Terrel, S3031, PO, 5th (McKenzie's) Cav.
THOMPSON, Thomas, S15654, G, 47th Inf.
THOMPSON, V. D. S12948, SM, 22nd (Barteau's) Cav.
THOMPSON, W. A. S3270, WE, 5th Inf.
THOMPSON, W. D. S10738, F, 14th (Neely's) Cav.
THOMPSON, W. H. H. S7526, MA, 19th (Biffle's) Cav.
THOMPSON, W. J. S6481, MS, 17th Inf.
THOMPSON, W. N. S7891, PU, 8th (Dibrell's) Cav.
THOMPSON, W. T. S3598, HU, 11th Inf.
THOMPSON, W. W. S15119, CE, 50th Inf.

THOMPSON, William, S340, GE, 29th Inf.
THOMPSON, William, S12824, BR, 65th Ga. Inf.
THOMPSON, William A. S12848, K, 39th N.C. Inf.
THOMPSON, William Columbus, S13054, CO, 60th N.C. Inf.
THOMPSON, William G. S2966, CL, 29th Inf.
THOMPSON, William H. S10850, H, 51st Va. Inf.
THOMPSON, William T. S12015, B, 23rd Inf.
THOMPSON, William W. S10357, G, 4th (McLemore's) Cav.
THOMSON, J. B. S14605, SH, 42nd Inf.
THOMSON, W. P. S5230, LO, 65th Ga. Inf.
THORN, William, S13885, WA, 1st Va. Cav.
THORNBURG, Cynthia, W4005, JE, Thornburg, James R.
THORNBURG, Daniel E. S8719, WA, 29th Inf.
THORNBURG, Elizabeth, W3957, WA, Thornburg, Daniel E.
THORNBURG, J. N. S4908, JE, 61st Inf.
THORNBURG, Nora, W10553, SN, Thornburg, Andrew L.
THORNE, Emma O. W5123, G, Thorne, Wm. T.
THORNLEY, Donie, W5441, L, Thornley, Thomas W.
THORNLEY, James, S10238, D, Unassigned (Medical Dept.)
THORNLEY, T. W. S8988, L, Unassigned
THORNTON, A. J. S6633, HI, 10th Cav.
THORNTON, Arite, W1482, BE, Thornton, George Washington
THORNTON, Edward, C177, T, Unassigned, Teamster
THORNTON, Elizabeth Lina. W4480, BE, Thornton, George M.
THORNTON, George M. S3927, BE, 5th Inf.
THORNTON, J. R. S12849, HR, 6th Inf.
THORNTON, James R. S6933, MA, 6th Inf.
THORNTON, John F. S14106, HU, 8th (Dibrell's) Cav.
THORNTON, Josephine Elizabeth, W6625, HD, Thornton, Milds Van Buren
THORNTON, Lucinda Mary, W223, DE, Thornton, Wm. Benjamin
THORNTON, M. V. S14305, HD, Nichol's Ark. Regt.
THORNTON, R. N. S15216, D, 9th (Ward's) Cav.
THORNTON, Reubin N. S16530, D, 15th Cav.

THORNTON, W. J. S91, HU, 5th Inf., Follows #93 on film
THORP, Andrew Jackson, S4784, LE, 6th (Wheeler's) Cav.
THORP, C. M. S4081, WY, 9th Cav.
THORPE, See also Tharpe
THORPE, Margaret Viranns, W4170, HN, Thorpe, Wm. Logan
THRASHER, J. S. S9817, H, 7th Ga. Inf.
THRASHER, Lilly James, W10598, H, Thrasher, Jessie Scaife
THROCKMORTON, Anne N. W8010, SH, Throckmorton, Craig Francis
THROCKMORTON, C. F. S12560, HN, 11th Ala. Cav.
THROGMORTON, James Douglass, S9168, HN, 49th Inf.
THRONEBERRY, J. P. S4156, CF, 44th Inf.
THUM, Mattie A. W8665, L, Thum, John G.
THURMAN, E. S. S3518, MU, 3rd (Clack's) Inf.
THURMAN, J. M. S3173, GI, 53rd Inf.
THURMAN, John, S13032, H, 4th Ga. Cav.
THURMAN, Margaret Jane, W10709, H, Thurman, John
THURMAN, Mary Catherine, W7877, MU, Thurman, Ervin S.
THURMAN, Van, S2367, R, 43rd Inf.
THURMOND, E. S. S7330, DY, 15th & 16th (Consol.) Cav.
THURMOND, Mary Frances, W10851, L, Thurmond, James A.
THURSTON, Edward, S13914, LO, 26th Inf.
THURSTON, Sarah, W8027, LO, Thurston, Edward
THWEAT, Alice K. W6682, MS, Thweat, Pleasant S.
THWEATT, Martha James, W2005, B, Thweatt, John Henry Harrison
TIBBS, E. C. S3658, HY, 4th Ala. Cav.
TIBBS, Maggie Gaddy, W9372, D, Tibbs, John James
TICER, G. W. S6509, T, 51st Inf.
TIDWELL, Aquilla, S6235, HI, Baxter's Co. Lt. Art.
TIDWELL, F. F. S12310, DI, 11th Inf.
TIDWELL, Georgia Anne, W3477, H, Tidwell, W. M.
TIDWELL, Harriet Wiley, W9071, GI, Tidwell, Charles Wesley
TIDWELL, L. S12773, WE, 21st (Wilson's) Cav.

TIDWELL, Lou, W10362, MN, Tidwell, John W.
TIDWELL, Magdaline K. W5055, DI, Tidwell, Franklin Fulton
TIDWELL, Marshall, C268, HI, 24th Inf.
TIDWELL, Mary Ann, W7036, WE, Tidwell, Levy
TIDWELL, Moses H. S11422, D, 49th Inf.
TIDWELL, Robert S. S13015, GR, 69th N.C. Inf.
TIDWELL, S. M. S9735, HU, Baxter's Co. Lt. Art.
TIDWELL, William B. S9020, MU, 35th Ala. Inf.
TIGNOR, John M. S15878, D, 24th Inf.
TILFORD, J. W. S14792, D, 7th Inf.
TILFORD, Samuel sr. S4765, CF, Undetermined
TILFORD, Virginia Frances, W1829, CF, Tilford, Samuel
TILLER, A. P. S7339, MA, 6th Inf.
TILLER, William B. S8391, LI, 26th Ala. Inf.
TILLEY, Alice, W9438, D, Tilley, Henry Henderson
TILLEY, Jeremiah C. S12165, RO, Welker's Bn. Cav.
TILLEY, John G. S974, GR, 1st Ky. Cav.
TILLEY, Joseph, S9349, JO, 37th N.C. Inf.
TILLEY, Sarah C. W3694, GR, Tilley, John G.
TILLISON, James K. S10355, SU, 1st Va. Inf.
TILLISON, Nancy Ellen, W6175, SU, Tillison, James K. Polk
TILLMAN, A. M. S8847, CF, Lynn's Co. Partisan Rangers
TILLMAN, Bryant, S9713, T, 1st Hvy. Art.
TILLMAN, Calvin, S5828, HR, 17th Cav.
TILLMAN, Caroline, W363, MS, Tillman, Timothy Terrell
TILLMAN, Dicey Ann, W3164, WE, Tillman, Bennett
TILLMAN, J. A. S7876, HR, 9th Inf.
TILLMAN, J. W. S15256, WE, 12th Ky. Cav.
TILLMAN, Jane Hannah, W2413, L, Tillman, James H.
TILLMAN, Lizzie, W6180, HR, Tillman, Joshua A.
TILLMAN, Sophia C. W10696, WE, Tillman, Joe Wm.
TILLY, Belle, W2950, SU, Tilly, Edward
TILLY, Mary L. W9, RO, Tilly, Wm. M.
TILMAN, Bettie, W1904, WE, Tilman, James Calvin

TILSON, Elizabeth, W3064, U, Tilson, James W.
TILSON, H. C. S8457, SH, 29th Inf.
TIMBERLAKE, Eveline, W1241, SM, Timberlake, Fountain Pitts
TIMBS, Silas Green, S16565, G, Undetermined
TIMBS, Susan Matilda, W10914, G, Timbs, Silas Green
TIMERLAKE, Fountain P. S5678, SM, 7th Inf.
TIMERLAKE, S. R. S9959, F, 15th Miss. Inf.
TIMMER, Margaret Ann, W1477, SH, Timmer, Henry Clay
TIMMONS, George A. S14234, G, Huggin's Co. Lt. Art.
TIMMONS, Nancy Evans, W10793, MU, Timmons, Thomas Jefferson
TIMMONS, T. J. S16433, WI, 9th Bn. Cav.
TIMMONS, William, S10470, H, 4th Ga. Cav.
TIMMS, V. T. S632, CH, 18th Inf.
TIMS, Ann, W3804, HR, Tims, V. T.
TIMS, J. H. S10016, CH, Moreland's Regt. Ala. Cav.
TIMS, John H. S8924, HR, Newman's Cav.
TINDALL, Annie Judson, W1751, D, Tindall, John A.
TINDALL, John A. S2188, D, 9th (Bennett's) Cav.
TINDALL, Mary Lou, W9052, MU, Tindall, Wm. Henry H.
TINDER, Frances Ellen, W3323, CC, Tinder, Richard
TINKER, Jesse, S3174, MO, 3rd Inf.
TINKER, Phillip P. S3846, WA, 64th Inf.
TINKLE, Meda, W5930, G, Tinkle, Robert Franklin
TINKLE, R. F. S13675, G, 47th Inf.
TINNEN, William M. S5562, T, 12th (Green's) Cav.
TINNIN, Hessie Ann, W10671, D, Tinnin, Wm. E.
TINNON, Fannie Evans, W6131, GI, Tinnon, Wm. Armine
TINSLEY, Lucy Sherman, W10938, HY, Tinsley, Henry B.
TIPPS, Dudley, S2651, LI, 17th Inf.
TIPPS, J. C. sr. S2208, MOO, 41st Inf.
TIPPS, Jacob, S2066, MOO, 17th Inf.
TIPPS, Jane Rebecca, W6343, LI, Tipps, Dudley
TIPPS, John, S2789, FR, 41st Inf.
TIPPS, Mattie Ross, W7943, D, Tipps, Wm. Pinkney
TIPPS, W. P. S7509, D, 5th Inf.

TIPTON, Andrew H. S13882, H, 3rd Ga. Cav.
TIPTON, G. W. S15039, H, 60th Ga. Inf.
TIPTON, Pleas, S6771, DY, 4th Inf.
TIPTON, Rufus M. S1412, HA, 37th Va. Inf.
TISDALE, Laura T. W7975, D, Tisdale, David Merincather
TISDEL, Francis M. S6097, MU, 24th Inf.
TITSWORTH, Electa, W5939, DK, Titsworth, John P.
TITSWORTH, John P. S2469, DK, 1st Bn. (Colm's) Inf.
TITTLE, G. W. S2773, HU, 60th Inf.
TITTLE, George W. S16168, SN, Kain's Co. Lt. Art.
TITTLE, Mary Elizabeth, W5094, H, Tittle, George Washington
TODD, A. F. S861, DY, 12th Inf.
TODD, C. M. S4205, R, 1st Ala. Cav.
TODD, Caleb Washington, S1802, RU, 23rd Inf.
TODD, Elizabeth Prater, W9211, RU, Todd, Aaron Wilson
TODD, J. H. S16630, GI, 8th (Smith's) Cav.
TODD, James G. S2056, OV, 12th Bn. Ga. Lt. Art.
TODD, Jane, W1687, WE, Todd, Wm. Harvey Lawson
TODD, John M. S6555, ME, 5th Cav.
TODD, John S. S9782, 21st (Wilson's) Cav.
TODD, Juliet H. Pitts, W1083, D, Todd, Wm. F.
TODD, Mary Ellen, W2348, MA, Todd, James Madison
TODD, Mary Old, W2060, LI, Todd, Wm. Melvin
TODD, Nancy Angeline, W10498, G, Todd, Wm. Cas.
TODD, Sallie, W7108, DY, Todd, Alexander Franklin
TODD, Samuel N. S4157, GI, 16th Ala. Inf.
TODD, Susan Elizabeth, W2822, Todd, J. M.
TODD, Susan Elizabeth, W6669, CF, Todd, Wm. Jefferson
TODD, W. H. L. S4962, WE, 27th Inf.
TODD, W. J. S8640, RU, 2nd Inf.
TODD, Wilson, S10420, W, 23rd Inf.
TOLBERT, Carrel, S7768, CA, 17th Inf.
TOLBERT, Davis, S10162, CL, 4th Bn. Va. Cav.
TOLER, Catherine M. W7042, H, Toler, Joseph Marion
TOLER, Joe M. S15128, H, 25th Va. Bn. Inf.
TOLIVER, Henry T. S9052, RU, Allison's Squadron, Cav.

Index to Tennessee Confederate Pension Applications

TOLLESON, Annie Elise, W5609, SH, Tolleson, E. B.
TOLLEY, John D. S1967, LI, 8th Ky. Inf.
TOLLEY, William P. S10349, FR, 1st (Turney's) Inf.
TOLLISON, Soloman, S1929, WH, 1st Inf.
TOLLIVER, Elizabeth, W5432, RU, Tolliver, Wm. Martin
TOMERLIN, Ann Chanty, W1038, GI, Tomerlin, James Washington
TOMERLIN, James W. S5339, S4543, GI, 32nd Inf.
TOMISON, Logan, S641, HW, 16th Inf.
TOMLINSON, Adelia Mildred, W3165, SU, Tomlinson, Richard
TOMLINSON, Dona, W11125, F, Tomlinson, Junius
TOMLINSON, J. B. S16226, MU, 6th (Wheeler's) Cav.
TOMLINSON, J. H. S11727, WE, 20th (Russell's) Cav.
TOMLINSON, John, S13971, L, 31st Inf.
TOMLINSON, Martha Isabel, W1031, WA, Tomlinson, Elijah Allen
TOMLINSON, Martha Lucy, W4528, MU, Tomlinson, Wm.
TOMLINSON, Mary Catherine, W994, WL, Tomlinson, James Browning
TOMLINSON, Merrit B. S16203, MU, 3rd (Clack's) Inf.
TOMLINSON, Nancy Emily, W9919, L, Tomlinson, John
TOMLINSON, W. S. S9177, MC, 36th Ga. Inf.
TOMPKINS, J. E. S9591, RU, 45th Inf.
TOMPKINS, Sallie, W9794, RU, Tompkins, Albert G.
TONEY, Nancy J. W8668, HM, Toney, Robert J.
TONEY, R. J. S3277, HM, Undetermined
TOOMBE, James W. S90, RU, 47th Inf.
TOOMBS, Nancy America, W7509, MU, Toombs, James L.
TOOMBS, Sarah J. W2281, RU, Toombs, Joel
TOOMEY, Richard A. S15168, HI, 6th (Wheeler's) Cav.
TORBETT, Darthula A. W7352, SU, Torbett, Wm. F.
TORBETT, Isaac, S3977, K, Humald's Battery, Art.
TORBETT, John A. S10624, SU, 60th Inf. & 1st Special Bn. La. Inf.

TORBETT, P. S. S13940, MR, 4th (McLemore's) Cav.
TORBETT, S. M. S9503, MR, 4th Cav.
TORBETT, William P. S9864, SU, 60th Inf.
TORIAN, Antionette Elizabeth, W5131, SH, Torian, Christopher Columbus
TORRENCE, Elizabeth Click, W7878, GI, Torrence, Thomas Newton
TORRENCE, T. N. S15204, GI, 4th N.C. Inf.
TOSH, James M. S11898, WE, Unassigned (Work Shop)
TOSH, Naomi Duncan, W5270, WE, Tosh, James M.
TOTTY, B. A. S9971, BE, 5th Inf.
TOTTY, James, S3621, HI, 9th Bn. Cav.
TOTTY, Mary Jebane, W5875, BE, Totty, B. A.
TOTTY, Rebecca, W2406, HI, Totty, Willeferel Davis
TOTTY, Thomas S. S2438, DI, 11th Inf.
TOUMBS, James L. S3982, MU, 48th (Voorhies') Inf.
TOWERY, P. C. S10845, R, 3rd (Lillard's) Mtd. Inf.
TOWLES, Elizabeth, W3579, W, Towles, John Wm.
TOWLES, J. T. S10596, F, 14th (Neely's) Cav.
TOWNES, James M. S2756, 12th Inf.
TOWNES, Tabitah Ann, W4337, Townes, James M.
TOWNLEY, Eveline, W3620, HN, Townley, John L.
TOWNLY, George C. S12153, HN, 10th Mo. Inf.
TOWNS, Alice, W10213, WL, Towns, Wm. T.
TOWNS, Alice Crockett, W9191, Towns, Henry Clay
TOWNS, John Wesley, S588.5, D, 20th Inf.
TOWNS, Sarah, W1468, D, Towns, John Wesley
TOWNS, William, S10099, WL, 30th Inf.
TOWNSEND, A. W. S16642, MG, 10th (Johnson's) Ky. Cav.
TOWNSEND, Albert M. S16372, S7541, HN, 42nd Inf.
TOWNSLEY, Rosaline Etta, W9783, O, Townsley, Wm. Washington
TOWNSLEY, W. W. S9337, G, 19th (Biffle's) Cav.
TOWREY, P. C. S3223, R, 26th Inf.
TOWRY, Mary Jane, W1055, LI, Towry, George W.
TOWRY, William, S11156, K, 37th Inf.

Index to Tennessee Confederate Pension Applications

TOZER, Samuel, S3067, HR, 22nd Inf.
TRACEY, A. P. S4787, DK, 7th Inf.
TRACY, C. T. S8688, D, 7th Ky. Cav.
TRAFFENTELL, Syney F. S15740, WA, N.C. State Reserves
TRAINER, J. H. S10010, F, 14th Bn. Miss. Lt. Art.
TRAINHAM, C. C. S10516, SU, 56th Va. Inf.
TRAMMEL, Isaac, S1515, S1055, W, 16th Inf.
TRANTHAM, Newton J. S8507, T, 7th Cav.
TRANUM, D. C. S1405, WA, 56th Inf.
TRASH, Mattie Allen, W9212, SH, Trash, W. T.
TRATTER, Sylvanus, S4549, DI, 14th Inf.
TRAVIS, D. M. S9226, MT, Forrest's Cav.
TRAVIS, D. T. S8041, HM, 31st Inf.
TRAVIS, Eudorah Caroline, W4037, WE, Travis, Joseph H.
TRAVIS, J. H. S4805, FR, 28th Cav.
TRAVIS, JAmes M. S7323, CF, 34th Provisional Army
TRAVIS, Jack, C42, 27th Inf.
TRAVIS, James E. S12953, WE, 7th (Duckworth's) Cav.
TRAVIS, Kate, W10942, MOO, Travis, J. H.
TRAVIS, Liddia, W1514, JE, Travis, Wm. Henry
TRAVIS, Littleton W. S12783, WE, 7th Cav.
TRAVIS, Mary Frances, W2634, CF, Travis, Wm. J.
TRAVIS, Nancy A. W4216, HM, Travis, D. T.
TRAVIS, Nancy Prior, W293, FR, Travis, James Parks
TRAVIS, Narcissa E. W1250, HN, Travis, Wm. E.
TRAVIS, William, S1235, HM, 31st Inf.
TRAVIS, William H. S4429, K, 31st Inf.
TRAWICK, Ruth Ann, W6816, SM, Trawick, Charles Milton
TRAXLER, Anderson, S6772, B, 17th Inf.
TRAYLOR, Addie, W504, HU, Traylor, Thomas Benton
TRAYLOR, Hulda, W9442, U, Traylor, Allen
TRAYLOR, Lou C. W5549, HU, Traylor, W. S.
TRAYLOR, Stephen, S4233, HO, 10th (DeMoss') Cav.
TRAYWICK, Harrison N. S13652, SH, 62nd Ala. Inf.
TREADWAY, James, S7077, HR, 5th Miss. Inf.
TREADWAY, Mary Ann, W11021, RU, Treadway, Henry Harding
TREADWAY, Mary Jane, W2995, RO, Treadway, Levi Jackson

TREADWELL, Daniel, S3794, P, 9th Cav.
TREADWELL, R. A. S11394, MA, 7th Inf.
TREANOR, John Duke, S3336, D, 1st Bn. (McNairy's) Cav.
TREDWAY, Julia C. W1918, WA, Tredway, Daniel Bayless
TREDWAY, Levi J. S4277, R, 43rd Inf.
TREECE, W. S. S5424, HM, Unassigned
TRENT, Mary J. W6003, K, Trent, Joseph D.
TRENT, Nellie T. W4120, MO, Trent, Thomas D.
TRENTHAM, A. J. S12348, R, 16th Bn. (Neal's) Cav.
TREVATHAN, Charity E. W4604, O, Trevathan, Francis Marion
TREVATHAN, Martha Frances, W2902, HN, Trevathan, Albert Green
TREVATHAN, Mary E. W8715, R, Trevathan, A. J.
TRIBBLE, Louisa Clardy, W180, B, Tribble, Patrick Henry
TRIBBLE, W. H. S5049, SH, 17th Miss. Inf.
TRICE, John E. S14879, MT, 14th Inf.
TRICE, Laura V. W10265, D, Trice, James E.
TRIDDLE, Alfred, S4993, B, 41st Inf.
TRIGG, A. J. S16472, GI, 11th (Holman's) Cav.
TRIGG, Fannie E. W3397, WL, Trigg, Stephen Chenault
TRIGG, Guy S. S14762, H, 22nd Va. Cav.
TRIGG, Stephen C. S11552, WL, 3rd Mo. Inf.
TRIM, Martha E. W7905, HR, Trim, Samuel H.
TRIM, Samuel Henderson, S191, T, 41st Ala. Inf.
TRIPLET, John, S4606, HO, 12th Inf.
TRIPLETT, C. B. S4234, HU, 1st (Feild's) Inf.
TRIPLETT, Frank, S2534, BR, 36th Inf.
TRIPLETT, John, S12798, HO, 24th Bn. Inf.
TRIPLETTE, Mary, W9792, JO, Triplette, Thomas Toliver
TRIPP, Aaron W. S7291, MOO, 44th Inf.
TRIPP, Francis M. S1834, LI, 44th Inf.
TRIPP, Jonathan Houston, S9319, CF, 44th Inf.
TRIPP, Sallie A. W7717, CF, Tripp, J. H.
TRIPP, Thomas H. S3477, LI, 44th Inf.
TRIVETT, Joel, S14401, CT, 58th N.C. Inf.
TROBAUGH, William A. S11666, T, 51st Inf.
TROBAUGH, William T. S2967, GE, 29th Inf.
TROGDEN, A. W. S2635, HU, 11th Inf.
TROGDEN, Andrew P. S12403, WH, 4th Inf.
TROOP, Ellen, W9464, LI, Troop, John G.
TROOP, J. G. S3176, MS, 8th Inf.
TROTT, M. C. W5, B, Trott, Wm. Joseph

Index to Tennessee Confederate Pension Applications

TROTTER, Amanda, W7868, MT, Trotter, John Wm.
TROTTER, B. F. S9790, HU, 10th Cav.
TROTTER, Bettie, W4407, HU, Trotter, Benjamin F.
TROTTER, J. W. S4859, MT, 50th Inf.
TROUSDALE, A. C. S5782, HN, 5th Inf.
TROUSDALE, Alice Eugenia, W11110, H, Trousdale, James H.
TROUSDALE, Eunice N. W854, HN, Trousdale, Felix Grundy
TROUSDALE, Martha jane, W2884, D, Trousdale, Wm. Felix
TROUSDALE, Virginia A. W4074, HN, Trousdale, James M.
TROUSDALE, Wilson, S8416, MU, 48th Inf.
TROUT, Archibald W. S7180, K, 54th Va. Inf.
TROUT, James Marcus, S15886, MA, 3rd Ky. Cav.
TROUT, Nancy Katherine, W6704, O, Trout, Samuel Barton
TROUT, Nannie L. W6413, DY, Trout, Jacob Uriah
TROUT, Sam B. S9352, O, 5th Inf.
TROUT, W. H. S14710, T, 22nd Bn. Va. Inf.
TROUT, Wiley S. S8245, DY, 47th Inf.
TROUTT, JEremiah, S7325, M, 20th Inf.
TROUTT, Katherine, W2550, SN, Troutt, Jeremiah
TROUTT, Lydia, W458, SN, Troutt, Elijah
TROXLER, Martha, W6956, B, Troxler, Anderson
TROXLER, Mary Ann, W8887, CF, Troxler, Micajah
TROXLER, Sarah Jane, W1467, B, Troxler, Andrew Jackson
TROXWELL, Emma Cordilia, W5540, SU, Troxwell, Samuel
TROXWELL, Samuel, S5127, CT, Marshall's Battery, Art.
TRUCE, John R. S15007, HM, 37th Inf.
TRUE, Martha Ann, W2948, LA, True, David Hamilton
TRUEHEART, S. D. S896, SH, 38th Inf.
TRULL, John E. S16024, CC, Forrest's Provost Guard
TRULL, Leona E. W8551, CC, Trull, J. E.
TRULL, Mary Catherine, W8405, G, Trull, James Nathaniel
TRULL, Mollie Padgett, W11171, D, Padgett, Robert

TRUSS, George Nash, S12891, MA, 10th Ala. Inf.
TRUSS, Mary Weaks, W10013, MA, Truss, George Nash
TRUSTA, Eliza Fitzallen, W2833, SH, Trusta, Robert Burton
TRUSTY, J. W. S8567, SH, 15th Miss. Inf.
TRUSTY, Margaret Armeedy, W9834, SH, Trusty, James Wm.
TUBBS, Layer C. S10191, DE, 52nd Inf.
TUCK, Charles P. S4570, CF, 32nd Inf.
TUCKER, A. S4213, DE, 27th Inf.
TUCKER, Annie, W7802, H, Tucker, John Samuel
TUCKER, Annie O'Haver, W5777, SH, Tucker, John O.
TUCKER, C. L. S15894, SH, 8th Confederate Unit
TUCKER, Clara L. W4994, SH, Tucker, Adolphus Fenton
TUCKER, Cynthia Anna, W5056, D, Tucker, John Wesley
TUCKER, D. W. S9401, B, 44th Inf.
TUCKER, Dessie, W7822, LI, Tucker, M.
TUCKER, E. F. S15163, LI, Forrest's Escort, Cav.
TUCKER, Elizabeth, W8534, GI, Tucker, Samuel Houston
TUCKER, Emily J. W10277, GI, Tucker, Callaway Garner
TUCKER, G. H. S9886, WL, 4th (McLemore's) Cav.
TUCKER, G. W. S12825, O, 17th Inf.
TUCKER, George W. S14840, 55th Inf.
TUCKER, Grattan, S13443, L, 4th Va. Cav.
TUCKER, H. H. S2377, DY, 32nd Inf.
TUCKER, J. B. S14031, GU, 20th Ala. Cav.
TUCKER, J. O. S14429, SH, 6th Miss. Cav.
TUCKER, J. R. C. S369, GI, 53rd Inf.
TUCKER, J. W. S6523, DE, 10th Cav.
TUCKER, J. W. S15711, HI, 49th Inf.
TUCKER, James M. S2611, GI, 3rd Inf.
TUCKER, Jarratt, S1166, WL, 4th Cav.
TUCKER, John, S13080, GE, 31st Inf.
TUCKER, John T. S6703, MU, 1st (Feild's) Inf.
TUCKER, John T. S7797, G, 19th & 20th (Consol.) Cav.
TUCKER, John W. S5, WI, Maney's Lt. Art.
TUCKER, Joseph, S6043, HW, 29th Inf.
TUCKER, Joseph, S9900, U, 2nd N.C. Cav.
TUCKER, M. S14967, LI, 6th (Wheeler's) Cav.
TUCKER, M. V. S2192, LI, 44th Inf.

TUCKER, Malinda J. W563, WA, Tucker, Thomas Henry
TUCKER, Mary E. W34, GI, Tucker, Wm. M.
TUCKER, Mary Frances, W4465, LI, Tucker, Martin V.
TUCKER, Mary Jane, W3695, MU, Tucker, John T.
TUCKER, Mary V. W2939, CC, Tucker, J. R. C.
TUCKER, Mary Virginia, W9102, MU, Tucker, Wm. Franklin
TUCKER, Matthew Wilson, S3670, SH, 7th Mo. Inf.
TUCKER, Melissa, W4925, GI, Tucker, James Madison
TUCKER, Melissa J. W4408, CF, Tucker, T. H.
TUCKER, Minerva Adeline, W1551, DY, Tucker, Howell Harris
TUCKER, Nannie, W8620, MU, Tucker, Wm. Franklin
TUCKER, Nettie Wells, W10048, D, Tucker, Wilson Monroe
TUCKER, Olivia, W9491, O, Tucker, Wm. J.
TUCKER, Phebe, W1509, GE, Tucker, Branch
TUCKER, R. G. S2371, F, 13th Inf.
TUCKER, R. Gideon, S6015, FR, 44th Inf.
TUCKER, R. H. S6102, DE, 18th (Newsom's) Cav.
TUCKER, R. W. S4150, FR, 16th Inf.
TUCKER, Robert B. S7253, K, McClung's Co. Lt. Art.
TUCKER, S. H. S4474, MG, 44th Inf.
TUCKER, Sarah Bathesheba, W6418, DE, Tucker, Reuben Houston
TUCKER, Sarah Clemintine, W1469, WE, Tucker, Wm. Irvine
TUCKER, Sarah Jane, W9520, GE, Tucker, John
TUCKER, Solomon, S775, DE, 23rd Inf.
TUCKER, T. H. S2242, WA, 60th Inf.
TUCKER, T. H. S2652, CF, 16th Inf.
TUCKER, W. G. S1325, CF, 4th Inf.
TUCKER, W. I. S6813, WE, 33rd Inf.
TUCKER, W. J. S14153, O, 15th Inf.
TUCKER, W. M. S13799, MU, 1st (Feild's) Inf.
TUCKER, William Allen, S10441, LI, 23rd Inf.
TUCKER, William F. S5034, GE, 31st Inf.
TUCKER, William H. S13852, H, 60th Ga. Inf.
TUCKER, William M. S10630, MS, 34th Inf.
TUGGLE, Richard, C176, SH, 13th Inf.
TULEY, C. M. M. S9264, LI, 1st (Turney's) Inf.

TULLASS, T. R. S13893, WI, 4th (McLemore's) Cav.
TULLOCH, Sophia J. W1487, GE, Tulloch, Elijah Matison
TULLY, L. B. S9967, DY, 12th Inf.
TUNE, John W. S10086, O, Phillip's Co. Lt. Art.
TUNNELL, A. D. S14600, CF, 29th Miss. Inf.
TUNSTILL, Alice, W9771, WL, Tunstill, W. M.
TURBYFILL, J. B. S14613, CT, 58th N.C. Inf.
TURBYVILLE, James A. S4288, K, 1st Bn. (Colm's) Inf.
TURLEY, Irene Ragner, W10687, SH, Turley, Thomas Battle
TURLEY, Mary Ann, W1503, W3842, H, Turley, John Atlas
TURNAGE, C. B. S1468, O, 18th Inf.
TURNAGE, John L. S10985, T, 51st Inf.
TURNAGE, Narcissa Belle, W6323, O, Turnage, Charles Bransford
TURNBO, Evaline J. W345, MU, Turnbo, John L.
TURNER, A. J. S2900, HI, 24th Inf.
TURNER, Alexander R. S5303, MA, 14th Cav.
TURNER, Armilda, W3032, CU, Turner, D. C.
TURNER, B. S. S2629, CA, 35th Inf.
TURNER, Bettie A. W9380, WL, Turner, Thomas M.
TURNER, Bickey, W6100, DK, Turner, Wm.
TURNER, Chesley, S1517, DK, 28th Inf.
TURNER, Chesley sr. S5107, DK, Undetermined
TURNER, D. C. S7166, CU, 28th Inf.
TURNER, D. T. S14536, MA, 33rd Inf.
TURNER, E. L. sr. S46, RU, 1st Inf.
TURNER, Eliza Abigail, W5793, CY, Turner, Marcus Aurelias
TURNER, Elizabeth J. W971, SU, Turner, George W.
TURNER, Ella Deleslin, W6487, MA, Turner, David Travis
TURNER, Emma Jerene, W10433, MA, Turner, David Wm.
TURNER, F. A. S10011, D, 11th (Holman's) Cav.
TURNER, Feling, S1416, DK, 16th Inf.
TURNER, George, S4686, SU, 61st Inf.
TURNER, Gilbert H. S9122, MS, 17th Inf.
TURNER, Granville B. S13792, CY, 7th Cav.
TURNER, Isaac, S5101, HO, 50th Inf.
TURNER, J. F. S9234, O, 16th N.C. Inf.
TURNER, J. J. S15394, FR, 1st (Turney's) Inf.
TURNER, J. L. S14161, D, 1st Inf.

Index to Tennessee Confederate Pension Applications

TURNER, J. Net, S14274, SN, 2nd (Robison's) Inf.
TURNER, James, S10425, HM, 4th Inf.
TURNER, James T. S6802, G, 47th Inf.
TURNER, James W. S3127, LI, 25th Ala. Inf.
TURNER, Jennie Lee, W9317, WI, Turner, Gilbert Hunn
TURNER, Jeremiah, S4737, RB, 7th Inf.
TURNER, John, S5992, BL, 43rd Inf.
TURNER, John B. S6095, D, 1st (Turney's) Inf.
TURNER, John William, S1480, MU, 1st Inf.
TURNER, Jonathan, S5090, MR, 4th (McLemore's) Cav.
TURNER, Kate Hobson, W2297, D, Turner, James Frank
TURNER, Laura Portis, W9864, T, Turner, Yancey Burton
TURNER, Lilly Witt, W10714, Turner, Alexander Randolph
TURNER, Louis E. S10144, SH, 3rd Miss. Cav.
TURNER, Louisey Jane, W693, HD, Turner, Thomas Martin
TURNER, Marietta L. W795, WI, Turner, John Wm.
TURNER, Martha H. W6499, SH, Turner, Cyrus Augustus
TURNER, Martha Jane, W9078, SM, Turner, Wm. Addison
TURNER, Mary, W6825, HM, Turner, James
TURNER, Mary, W6978, WH, Turner, Chesley
TURNER, Mary E. (Peebles), W10875, D, Turner, Uriah
TURNER, Mary Jane, W5796, LI, Turner, R. T.
TURNER, Nannie Emily, W5769, SH, Turner, Louis Edgar
TURNER, Peter, C103, RB, 30th Inf.
TURNER, R. C. S1203, CO, 60th N.C. Inf.
TURNER, Robert J. S14138, D, 1st (Feild's) Inf.
TURNER, Robert T. S10411, LI, 12th Ala. Inf.
TURNER, Sarah Elizabeth, W2271, SN, Turner, Jeremiah
TURNER, Sarah Elizabeth, W3264, G, Turner, J. M.
TURNER, Tennessee, W22, MU, Turner, Thomas H.
TURNER, Udora C. W9638, HI, Turner, Andrew Jackson
TURNER, Virginia McLemore, W10699, SH, Turner, John B.
TURNER, W. C. S8433, D, 9th Cav.
TURNER, W. E. S6455, T, 7th Miss. Cav.
TURNER, W. N. S13789, O, 13th Cav.
TURNER, William, S329, SU, 26th Inf.
TURNER, William, S3738, DK, 28th & 84th (Consol.) Inf.
TURNER, William, S8141, WY, 1st Cav.
TURNER, William B. S9280, GU, 39th Ga. Inf.
TURNER, William P. S3246, K, 1st (Carter's) Cav.
TURNER, William P. S4909, A, 1st (Carter's) Cav.
TURNER, Willis, S7821, HI, 24th Inf.
TURNER, Yancey B. S10959, T, 7th (Duckworth's) Cav.
TURNIPSEED, Mary Elizabeth, W4360, SH, Turnipseed, John Adam Fletcher
TURNLEY, William Henry, S15261, MT, 2nd Ky. Cav.
TURPIN, JEsse, S2257, B, 45th Inf.
TURPIN, Jesse, S8036, B, 17th Inf.
TUTT, H. D. S14942, WI, 6th Tex. Cav.
TUTTLE, William H. S11309, OV, 37th Va. Bn. Cav.
TWITTY, L. S11090, MS, 17th Inf.
TWITTY, Mary Tison, W11111, LI, Twitty, Leonard Henley
TWOMEY, Richard A. See Toomey
TYLER, F. J. (Rev.), S13913, GI, 9th Bn. (Gantt's) Cav.
TYLER, Hugh C. S5128, HN, 5th Inf.
TYLER, Mary Elizabeth, W10113, H, Tyler, Wm. Thaddeus
TYLER, Sarah Almarinda, W1793, HI, Tyler, James Washington
TYLER, Tennessee Adline, W4401, HN, Tyler, Hue C.
TYLER, Winnie, W, Some papers with #11183 on film
TYLOR, Martha E. W112, MU, Tylor, Wm. Carroll
TYNE, J. A. S9026, H, 3rd (Lillard's) Mtd. Inf.
TYNER, Georgia Hunter, W10876, D, Tyner, James Sevier
TYNER, J. S. S13750, D, 19th Inf.
TYNS, Fannie M. W6492, HY, Tyns, John E.
TYREE, David W. S5129, MU, 55th (Brown's) Inf.
TYREE, J. H. S11563, SM, 9th (Bennett's) Cav.
TYREE, Mary Ann, W6876, MS, Tyree, David Walter
TYREE, Mary Dance, W9647, G, Tyree, Cyrus Hardy
TYREE, Mary Emerline, W3829, PU, Tyree, Robert J.

TYREE, Reuben, S6666, WA, 51st Va. Inf.
TYREE, Robert J. S2578, PU, 4th Inf.
TYREE, T. J. S5131, WY, 19th (Biffle's) Cav.
TYRONE, Fannie [Murrell], W10697, SH,
    Tyrone, James Henry, [Later married
    Murrell]
TYRONE, J. H. S6566, SH, 14th Miss. Inf.
TYSON, Alfred, C119, MA, 12th Ky. Cav.
TYSON, G. M. S14104, MA, 12th Ky. Cav.
TYSON, W. F. S8525, MN, 4th N.C. Cav.
UMBLES, A. J. S4212, MS, 37th Inf.
UNDERHILL, A. I. S8755, WL, 18th Inf.
UNDERHILL, Mollie L. W7820, D, Underhill,
    Alex Irvin
UNDERWOOD, Bettie, W7150, WE,
    Underwood, H. H.
UNDERWOOD, Carroll A. S957, WL, 45th Inf.
UNDERWOOD, Eleanor Dalton, W6937, O,
    Underwood, Thomas Benton
UNDERWOOD, Elisha P. S6508, WL, 45th Inf.
UNDERWOOD, G. W. S2645, CL, 18th N.C.
    Inf.
UNDERWOOD, Henry H. S4480, WE, 10th
    Cav.
UNDERWOOD, James, S1135, HW, 29th Inf.
UNDERWOOD, Jane, W5116, D, Underwood,
    James Richardson
UNDERWOOD, John W. S16106, MU, 22nd
    (Barteau's) Cav.
UNDERWOOD, Martha M. W4693, WL,
    Underwood, Elisha P.
UNDERWOOD, Mary J. W2832, HW,
    Underwood, Joseph
UNDERWOOD, S. G. S3184, WL, 9th Cav.
UNDERWOOD, Thomas, S1923, HW, City Bn.
    Va.
UNDERWOOD, Thomas Benton, S11365, O,
    22nd (Barteau's) Cav.
UNDERWOOD, Thomas J. S2817, WH, 16th
    Inf.
UNDERWOOD, W. A. S14972, RU, 24th Inf.
UNDERWOOD, W. E. S216, RB, 30th Inf.
UNDERWOOD, W. G. S9876, FR, 1st (Feild's)
    Inf.
UNDERWOOD, William B. S6941, MT, 15th
    Inf.
UPCHURCH, Ausel M. S414, GE, 58th Inf.
UPCHURCH, Carter H. S5147, J, 25th Inf.
UPCHURCH, John Franklin, S16463, SU, 9th
    Bn. N.C. Reserves
UPCHURCH, Lucy, W2636, RU, Upchurch, W.
    W.

UPCHURCH, Martha Ann, W9658, HN,
    Upchurch, John Frank
UPCHURCH, Mary E. W8104, RU, Upchurch,
    R. L.
UPCHURCH, Richardson, S3904, MO, 26th
    N.C. Inf.
UPCHURCH, Robert L. S11, RU, 45th Inf.
UPCHURCH, Ross, S13319, J, 16th Inf.
UPCHURCH, Thomas, S14897, PU, 4th
    (Murray's) Cav.
UPCHURCH, W. H. S7550, GE, 26th N.C. Inf.
UPCHURCH, W. W. S1431, RU, 45th Inf.
UPTON, D. M. S6918, O, 15th Inf.
UPTON, Nannie Bell, W6184, O, Upton, Daniel
    M.
URSERY, Dusty, W9383, GI, Ursery, J. M.
URSERY, W. C. S9398, CC, 31st Inf.
USELTON, Alfred, S6699, CF, 17th Inf.
USELTON, Ellen Jane, W7646, GI, Uselton, J.
    B.
USELTON, J. B. S5988, GI, 18th Inf.
USERY, J. M. S9605, GI, 31st Inf.
USREY, T. J. S10762, FR, 17th Inf.
USSELTON, J. W. S3803, CF, 44th Inf.
USSERY, A. S4850, FR, 17th Inf.
USSERY, Angeline, W1553, HR, Ussery, Wm.
    C.
USSERY, Emily, W1621, CH, Ussery, Dempsey
USSERY, W. C. S5304, HR, 13th Inf.
UTLEY, M. V. S1977, BE, 16th Ark. Inf.
UTLEY, Mattie, W5986, L, Utley, F. M.
UTLEY, Mattie O. W9846, MA, Utley, Wm.
    Leonidas
UTLEY, Sarah P. W2256, BE, Utley, Martin
    VanBuren
UTLEY, Thomas B. S13803, MA, Napier's Bn.
    Cav.
VACCARO, Abraham B. S11272, SH, 3rd
    (Forrest's) Cav.
VACCARO, Bart, S12734, SH, 154th Sr. Regt.
    Inf.
VACCARO, Celestine, W7339, SH, Vaccaro,
    Bartholomew
VACCARO, Ida Bradford, W7279, SH,
    Vaccaro, Abraham Baptista
VADEN, Althea, W9371, PU, Vaden, Wm.
    Winston
VADEN, M. W. S11282, WI, 27th Ala. Inf.
VADEN, N. B. S12720, WI, 45th Inf.
VALENTINE, John R. S12864, MA, 12th Ky.
    Cav.
VALENTINE, M. V. B. S10229, HN, 46th Inf.

Index to Tennessee Confederate Pension Applications

VALENTINE, Mary Katherine, W4330, HN, Valentine, Martin VanBuren
VALENTINE, T. R. S9190, O, 46th Inf.
VALENTINE, Thomas, S9525, WE, 52nd Inf.
VALENTINO, J. Louis, S15208, S13887, D, 7th Ga. Inf.
VALLENTINE, Missouri E. W7223, HN, Vallentine, Thomas S.
VANBIBER, Jacob, S6482, HD, 1st Tex. Legion (Cav.)
VANCE, Bettie, W8832, B, Vance, Daniel B.
VANCE, David, S3952, SU, 63rd Inf.
VANCE, E. B. S14337, WA, 63rd Va. Inf.
VANCE, Isabella, W1744, RU, Vance, Wm. Henry
VANCE, J. N. S9925, OV, 8th (Dibrell's) Cav.
VANCE, James, S12940, K, 3rd (Lillard's) Mtd. Inf.
VANCE, Mahala, W4601, CA, Vance, Thomas
VANCE, Martha, W7940, K, Vance, James
VANCE, Mary Boyce, W5490, SU, Vance, David
VANCE, Mary Jane, W3071, MO, Vance, John
VANCE, Melia, W5967, OV, Vance, John Newton
VANCE, Susan, W3584, SU, Vance, Isaac
VANCE, Thomas D. S13204, WA, 58th N.C. Inf.
VANCE, W. H. S1847, CA, 18th Inf.
VANCLEAVE, Jasper N. S12826, 46th Inf.
VANDERFORD, James A. S488, MA, 5th Ark. Inf.
VANDERGRIFF, J. B. S12977, RU, 8th (Smith's) Cav.
VANDERGRIFF, Linsey, S5976, GR, 1st (Carter's) Cav.
VANDERGRIFF, Rachel Malinda, W1979, UN, Vandergriff, Linzy
VANDERGRIFF, W. J. S47, RU, 18th Inf.
VANDERGRIFT, Margaret A. C. M. W4442, K, Vandergrift, James Robert
VANDERPOOL, C. C. S5231, SM, Allison's Squadron, Cav.
VANDIVER, W. C. S9557, LA, 48th (Nixon's) Inf.
VANDYCK, Sarah M. W. W7559, HN, VanDyck, John S.
VANDYKE, A. M. S5648, HE, 13th Inf.
VANDYKE, Calistie Alline, W1688, HE, VanDyke, Joseph Daniel
VANDYKE, Elizabeth M. W5933, HE, VanDyke, Angus Marshal

VANDYKE, John S. S5179, HN, 7th Cav.
VANHOOSER, John, S11254, DK, 16th Inf.
VANHOOSER, Melvina, W9780, W, Vanhooser, John
VANHOY, A. N. S7515, CT, 4th Bn. N.C. Reserves
VANHOY, N. H. S14200, CT, 1st N.C. Cav.
VANHUSS, Nancy E. W2461, BE, VanHuss, Dan H.
VANN, John W. S5116, WL, 7th Inf.
VANPELT, J. K. S4221, SH, 6th Inf.
VANPELT, J. W. S16679, D, 4th Inf.
VANTREASE, Abbie, W9954, WL, Vantrease, J. W.
VANTREASE, Clarissa, W9572, WL, Vantrease, Richard
VANTREASE, Polk, S7679, WI, 1st Ala. Cav.
VANTREESE, J. L. S1075, WL, Undetermined
VANTREESE, Jane Isabell, W570, MA, Vantreese, Thomas
VANTREESE, Josie, W7391, WL, Vantreese, Polk
VANTREESE, R. T. S11946, SM, 4th (McLemore's) Cav.
VANVLEEK, Emma, W632, FR, VanVleek, Abram
VANZANT, Isaac, S10920, FR, 41st Inf.
VANZANT, Jacob H. S8317, FR, 41st Inf.
VANZANT, Sarah, W7113, FR, Vanzant, Isaac
VARDELL, W. A. S12612, RB, 20th Inf.
VARNELL, Josiah, S494, JA, 5th Inf.
VARNELL, W. E. S10781, H, Phillip's Legion, Ga. Inf.
VARNEX, Watson, S3287, CO, 29th Inf.
VAUGHAN, D. J. S6371, D, 7th Tenn. Inf.
VAUGHAN, Leila Riker, W10740, D, Vaughan, Charles H.
VAUGHAN, Mary Ruth Loving, W3364, D, Vaughan, John D.
VAUGHAN, R. D. S7684, WL, 7th Tenn. Inf.
VAUGHN, A. M. S7850, RU, 21st (Carter's) Cav.
VAUGHN, Arthur, S15788, OV, 25th Inf.
VAUGHN, B. F. S13714, D, 44th Inf.
VAUGHN, Benjamin, S15992, WI, 10th Cav.
VAUGHN, C. C. S15774, MU, 6th (Wheeler's) Cav.
VAUGHN, C. H. S16320, D, 4th (McLemore's) Cav.
VAUGHN, Catherine, W6367, HW, Vaughn, John
VAUGHN, E. P. S8571, WE, 46th Inf.

VAUGHN, Ella D. W1731, WL, Vaughn, E. D.
VAUGHN, Ephraim, S2439, PU, 25th Inf.
VAUGHN, Fannie Ann, W1405, W1463, RU, Vaughn, John Lytle
VAUGHN, G. W. S6987, CA, 8th (Smith's) Cav.
VAUGHN, H. C. S6362, DK, 8th (Smith's) Cav.
VAUGHN, H. W. S3563, DY, 13th Inf.
VAUGHN, Huie J. W4195, G, Vaughn, Elizka Randolph
VAUGHN, I. L. S10292, K, 60th Inf.
VAUGHN, Isabella Caroline, W5347, WE, Vaughn, James Thomas
VAUGHN, J. J. S11891, WE, 31st Inf.
VAUGHN, J. L. S7683, RU, 23rd Inf.
VAUGHN, James T. S10156, WE, 5th Inf.
VAUGHN, Jane, W586, DK, Vaughn, James Madison
VAUGHN, Jemima, W3559, GU, Vaughn, Robert
VAUGHN, John, S5636, HA, 62nd Inf.
VAUGHN, John Franklin, S5445, RU, 1st (Feild's) Inf.
VAUGHN, John T. S15475, D, 22nd (Barteau's) Cav.
VAUGHN, Kittie Sheffield, W5336, MC, Vaughn, James S.
VAUGHN, L. M. S14055, SH, 12th Inf.
VAUGHN, Louisa Jane, W8697, WI, Vaughn, Wm. Anderson
VAUGHN, Malinda Elizabeth, W5476, D, Vaughn, Howard
VAUGHN, Margaret C. W2595, RU, Vaughn, John Franklin
VAUGHN, Mary Ann, W9040, RU, Vaughn, M. R.
VAUGHN, Mary Jane, W6074, SH, Vaughn, T. R.
VAUGHN, Micha Temperance, W9241, RU, Vaughn, R. H.
VAUGHN, Mose, S12037, T, 51st Inf.
VAUGHN, Richard J. S1444, CH, 31st Miss. Inf.
VAUGHN, S. C. S12750, MN, 43rd Miss. Inf.
VAUGHN, Sarah Catherine, W6540, RU, Vaughn, Richard Daniel
VAUGHN, Sarah Frances, W775, DY, Vaughn, Hayes Wood
VAUGHN, Sarah Frances, W9142, D, Vaughn, Benjamin Franklin
VAUGHN, Susan C. W708, WL, Vaughn, Henry Blanton
VAUGHN, T. J. S9402, MS, 53rd Inf.
VAUGHN, T. W. S6143, SH, 37th Miss. Inf.
VAUGHN, Thomas M. S10514, HN, 20th (Russell's) Cav.
VAUGHN, Thomas Smith, S8776, O, 20th Inf.
VAUGHN, William, S5832, HR, 22nd Inf.
VAUGHT, Catharine J. W2314, WI, Vaught, James Zachariah
VAUGHT, Ophelia Wolfe, W8846, D, Vaught, Stephen
VAUGHTER, Sarah J. W4200, RU, Vaughter, John B.
VAWTER, A. J. S7505, 12th Inf.
VAWTER, Frances, W6861, G, Vawter, Andrew Jackson
VAWTER, Margie, W1678, G, Vawter, Wm. H.
VEAL, Jane, W6988, DY, Veal, Thomas George
VEAL, Thomas G. S11803, DY, Burrough's Co. Lt. Art.
VEATCH, Mary A. W5749, D, Veatch, Wm. T.
VEATCH, William T. S3507, J, 8th Inf.
VENABLE, J. R. S11031, DI, 6th Ky. Inf.
VENABLE, James, S1828, HN, 20th Cav.
VENABLE, James W. S11906, RO, 8th Va. Cav.
VENABLE, Jane, W770, HN, Venable, John Brown
VENABLE, Joe, S9067, HN, 9th Ala. Inf.
VENABLE, Mary Elizabeth, W4211, WI, Venable, Wm. G.
VENABLE, Mary Wooding, W10783, R, Venable, Charles Woodson
VENABLE, Sarah Elizabeth, W7843, MG, Venable, James W.
VENABLE, T. W. S11458, H, 1st Ga. Cav.
VERHINE, Elizabeth E. W8787, O, Verhine, John Prince
VERHINE, John P. S16286, O, 20th Cav.
VERNELL, C. V. S2153, LI, 17th Ala. Inf.
VERNON, A. J. S13719, HR, 4th Inf.
VERNON, Elizabeth D. W1493, HI, Vernon, Wm. A.
VERNON, Izora, W1373, HE, Vernon, James B.
VERNON, J. A. S13959, WI, 24th Inf.
VERNON, Martha Susie, W10123, WI, Vernon, James Adam
VERNON, Samantha A. W4340, B, Vernon, Wm. Tinsley
VERNON, Susan McMahon, W9311, WI, Vernon, J. A.
VERNON, T. C. S15989, WI, 20th Cav.
VERNON, W. T. S5168, B, 24th Inf.

Index to Tennessee Confederate Pension Applications

VERTREES, Peter, C36, SN, 6th Ky. Cav.
VESEY, Katherine Lillian, W10873, SH, Vesey, Marcellus Lauderdale
VESEY, Marcellus Lauderdale, S16649, SH, 14th Miss. Inf.
VEST, Alexander, S10463, JE, 29th N.C. Inf.
VESTAL, A. J. S8798, CH, 51st Inf.
VESTAL, Charlotte Kinnard, W9402, MU, Vestal, Aaron Thomas
VICE, M. S. S12448, D, 4th S.C. Militia
VICK, E. J. S4351, GE, 4th (Consol.) Inf.
VICK, Elizabeth P. W4809, SH, Vick, Howell Ransom
VICK, Tennie C. W1466, D, Vick, Wm. Allen
VICK, W. J. S1070, GI, 53rd Inf.
VICKERS, J. W. S2781, LI, 44th Inf.
VICKERS, T. M. S15198, MT, 12th Ky. Cav.
VICKERS, W. M. S2569, LI, 44th Inf.
VICTORY, Isaac, S7615, RU, 4th (McLemore's) Cav.
VILLENES, T. J. S15877, RB, 30th Inf.
VILLINES, Alice Wilder, W5227, W8243, D, Villines, Dallas Madison
VINCENT, C. D. S10236, O, 4th Mo. Cav.
VINCENT, Eliel, S4916, ME, 43rd Inf.
VINCENT, Evaline, W281, ME, Vincent, Wm. Jasper
VINCENT, Eveline, W53, ME, Vincent, Elill
VINCENT, Hugh T. S2923, ME, 3rd Inf.
VINCENT, J. A. S13557, MS, 3rd (Clack's) Inf.
VINCENT, J. O. S10181, WE, 12th Ky. Cav.
VINCENT, Martha S. W6919, D, Vincent, Solomon Yarbrough
VINCENT, Mary Jane, W9680, WE, Vincent, John O.
VINCENT, Narcissa, W3310, ME, Vincent, H. T.
VINCENT, O. B. S1087, WE, 31st Inf.
VINCENT, Sallie Doak, W6977, O, Vincent, Christopher Domer
VINCENT, T. E. S3804, CF, 44th Inf.
VINCENT, William J. S818, R, 3rd Inf.
VINEYARD, Hiram M. S3460, GR, 1st (Carter's) Cav.
VINEYARD, Martha E. W5232, GR, Vineyard, Hiram M.
VINEYARD, W. I. S5833, HW, 48th Va. Inf.
VINEYARD, William, S13074, GR, 12th Bn. (Day's) Cav.
VINSON, B. P. S12069, ST, 50th Inf.
VINSON, Caroline O. W7701, WE, Vinson, J. J.
VINSON, Drusilla, W4390, WE, Vinson, Josephus L.
VINSON, Frances, W4598, CA, Vinson, James
VINSON, Henry, S1685, J, 8th Cav.
VINSON, Isabell, W3225, WH, Vinson, Henry
VINSON, J. H. S15974, WL, 12th Ky. Cav.
VINSON, J. W. S13392, WE, 26th Miss. Inf.
VINSON, James, S821, J, Shaw's Bn. Cav.
VINSON, James, S13062, CA, 8th (Smith's) Cav.
VINSON, James Calvin, S4595, ST, 50th Inf.
VINSON, Lissie, W1807, J, Vinson, James
VINSON, Lucy, W6675, D, Vinson, Daniel
VINSON, Thomas J. S13740, CA, 8th (Smith's) Cav.
VINSON, Thomas S. S15726, SN, 1st (Field's) Battery, La. Art.
VINSON, William, S2818, W, 18th Inf.
VISER, Sallie A. W4332, SH, Viser, James Harvey
VIVRETT, Rebecca Jane, W5383, WL, Vivrett, Wm. Bond
VONKANNON, James F. S15514, SH, 3rd Bn. Mo. Cav.
VOORHIES, Milda, W1960, GI, Voorhies, Wm. Milton
VOSS, James Ransom, S9978, MU, 54th Inf.
VOSS, Mary Ann, W5138, L, Voss, John
VOSS, Nancy C. W2414, L, Voss, Z. S.
VOSS, William Allen, S12128, MU, 19th (Biffle's) Cav.
VOWELL, Elizabeth Hayes, W1154, WI, Vowell, James Robert
VOYLES, Newton A. S16673, SH, Undetermined
WACASTER, Belle, W10340, SH, Wacaster, John Thomas
WACASTER, W. W. S4680, CT, 49th N.C. Inf.
WADDELL, Albert A. S10960, T, 41st Ala. Inf.
WADDELL, J. W. S14527, HY, 3rd (Forrest's) Cav.
WADDELL, W. S. S15911, WI, 44th Inf.
WADDILL, J. E. S13965, G, 60th N.C. Inf.
WADDLE, John B. S4127, CY, 25th Inf.
WADDLEY, Mary F. W1354, G, Waddley, Henry A.
WADDY, J. T. S11570, WI, 4th (McLemore's) Cav.
WADE, C. A. S3416, W, 4th Inf.
WADE, C. N. S14347, G, 12th Inf.
WADE, Charles H. S2355, CA, 5th Inf.

WADE, Cora Moore, W5499, SH, Wade, Wm. Allen
WADE, Electra Pickens, W8543, G, Wade, George Washington
WADE, G. H. S12266, R, 43rd Inf.
WADE, James W. S13592, T, 51st Inf.
WADE, Jarret, S6907, MC, 5th (McKenzie's) Cav.
WADE, John B. S7026, D, Huggin's Co. Lt. Art.
WADE, John W. S13496, RU, 18th Inf.
WADE, Lou M. W8586, W4931, G, Wade, Isham Phelan
WADE, Margaret, W8833, J, Wade, James Webster
WADE, Nancy Catherine, W10630, GR, Wade, General Jackson
WADE, Nancy Davis, W6582, R, Wade, Granville H.
WADE, O. H. S2778, CC, 12th Cav.
WADE, R. Thomas, S8795, F, 14th Cav.
WADE, Ruth Jane, W7396, W, Wade, C. A.
WADE, Salome J. W4123, WE, Wade, Wm. H.
WADE, Sarah Ann, W7808, LA, Wade, Wm. Alford
WADE, Sarah Ann Watkins, W10203, GI, Wade, Ephrem
WADE, Sarah Jane, W4133, F, Wade, Richard Thomas
WADE, William, S15544, DK, 35th Inf.
WADE, William Alfred, S5117, GI, 44th Inf.
WADE, Wilson Watkins, S16086, S16544, G, 12th (Green's) Cav.
WADKINS, William M. S715, LI, 48th Inf.
WADLEY, Emma S. W7939, W7885, MA, Wadley, Felix Washington
WADLEY, F. W. S9147, MA, 27th Inf.
WADLEY, Martha Perlina, W1666, HE, Wadley, Wm. Burnor
WAGENER, J. L. S5840, SH, 13th Inf.
WAGGONER, Ann Eliza, W8969, B, Waggoner, Wm. Jeferson
WAGGONER, Betty, W4032, MOO, Waggoner, Charley L.
WAGGONER, Felix M. S30, LI, 8th Inf.
WAGGONER, Margaret Elizabeth, W8552, D, Waggoner, Wiley B.
WAGGONER, Martha F. W3757, LI, Waggoner, Riley
WAGGONER, Mary Ann, W221, MOO, Waggoner, James Marion
WAGGONER, Wyley B. S13480, D, 2nd (Robison's) Inf.
WAGNER, Annie, W2464, SU, Wagner, Michael
WAGNER, J. W. S10570, CF, 32nd Inf.
WAGNER, John W. S1471, MS, 44th Inf.
WAGNER, Michael, S2713, SU, 19th Inf.
WAGONER, Frederick, S4697, MN, 18th Cav.
WAGONER, Louisa Frances, W4100, SN, Wagoner, Amos Hall
WAGONER, Minerva Summerfield, W2961, CC, Wagoner, David
WAGONER, W. R. S13902, FR, Forrest's Escort, Cav.
WAGSTER, John, S11729, G, 12th Inf.
WAGSTER, Robert A. S11884, G, 4th Inf.
WAID, John C. S15925, LI, 8th Inf.
WAID, Margaret, W10105, LI, Waid, John C.
WAIDE, W. A. S2209, MOO, 44th Inf.
WAIR, James P. S8656, D, 20th Inf.
WAIT, Rachel Annie, W5087, SH, Wait, Rochambean Lafayette
WAITES, Fannie Elizabeth, W10212, PU, Waites, John Rhodes
WAITS, John R. S5305, OV, 84th Inf.
WAKEFIELD, J. F. S2594, GI, 18th (Newsom's) Cav.
WAKEFIELD, J. F. S10609, GI, 41st Inf.
WAKEFIELD, Jennie, W4841, H, Wakefield, Wm. Payton
WAKEFIELD, Mary, W9264, FR, Wakefield, James H.
WAKEFIELD, O. S6378, D, Undetermined
WAKEFIELD, W. L. S13422, MU, 11th (Holman's) Cav.
WALACE, Lettie Ann, W1851, CA, Walace, Wm. Henry
WALDEN, Arselina, W9551, RU, Walden, Samuel
WALDEN, Jesse, S3402, MR, 4th Ga. Cav.
WALDEN, Nancy, W1200, MR, Walden, Jesse
WALDEN, Newton, S3338, CC, 10th Ala. Inf.
WALDEN, P. A. S14981, SH, 41st Inf.
WALDEN, S. A. S13397, RU, 20th Inf.
WALDING, Jane, W3233, L, Walding, James A.
WALDRIDGE, John H. S35, GI, 1st Inf.
WALDRON, Estelle Golibart, W4815, SH, Waldron, Cook Mitchell
WALDRON, Isaac, S11978, K, 42nd Va. Inf.
WALDROP, A. J. S12130, GI, 3rd (Clack's) Inf.
WALDROP, David H. S2510, MU, 3rd Inf.
WALDROP, Eugenia C. W8142, GI, Waldrop, Andrew J.
WALDROP, J. A. S5524, PO, 59th Inf.

Index to Tennessee Confederate Pension Applications

WALDROP, Mary Jane, W443, MU, Waldrop, D. H.
WALDROPE, Eli, S6156, HM, 5th Bn. N.C. State Troops
WALDROPE, Joseph, S10586, U, 58th N.C. Inf.
WALKER, A. S1121, DK, 1st Bn. Inf.
WALKER, A. B. S5102, GE, 12th Cav.
WALKER, A. H. S4052, DY, 12th Inf.
WALKER, A. P. H. S11116, R, 1st Bn. S.C. Reserves
WALKER, A. S. S9094, ME, 26th Inf.
WALKER, A. W. S7436, PU, 28th Inf.
WALKER, Alexander W. S6505, DK, 16th Inf.
WALKER, Ann D. W6503, WI, Walker, G. W.
WALKER, Archie L. S2968, K, 63rd Inf.
WALKER, Bailey, C118, DY, 13th Inf.
WALKER, Bettie, W7898, BE, Walker, Alexander Newton
WALKER, C. T. S16341, SH, 1st Ark. Inf.
WALKER, Cassandra, W4445, GI, Walker, Thomas J.
WALKER, Cyrena Elizabeth, W3166, R, Walker, Sam
WALKER, Dovie Ann, W10947, MOO, Walker, Moses
WALKER, E. S. S16376, MC, 59th Mtd. Inf.
WALKER, Elgin T. S11667, T, 51st Inf.
WALKER, Elizabeth Clarasy, W2899, MN, Walker, James R.
WALKER, Elizabeth Smith, W9309, GI, Walker, Francis Marion
WALKER, Ellen, W8966, MO, Walker, Gustavis A.
WALKER, Ellen, W10588, T, Walker, James
WALKER, Emma J. W9685, MA, Walker, Joseph N.
WALKER, Eudora Paty, W2383, DI, Walker, Samuel Thomas
WALKER, F. M. S7241, GI, 19th (Biffle's) Cav.
WALKER, Flora Nicholson, W8591, SH, Walker, John Valent. Freeman
WALKER, G. W. S2714, WI, 48th Inf.
WALKER, G. W. S4437, R, 8th (Dibrell's) Cav.
WALKER, George W. S16204, FR, 2nd (Ashby's) Cav.
WALKER, Helen Gordon, W3249, GI, Walker, Calvin Harvey
WALKER, Isaac L. C258, HI, Regiment not given
WALKER, J. M. S14962, MA, 27th Ala. Inf., Alias R. J. Freeman #15709
WALKER, J. P. S281, CH, 16th Cav.

WALKER, J. P. S13027, CF, 44th Inf.
WALKER, J. Vance, S11204, MC, Conscripts Camp of Instruction
WALKER, J. W. S8894, CE, 14th Inf.
WALKER, J. W. S10210, O, 33rd Inf.
WALKER, Jacob A. S7781, FR, 16th Inf.
WALKER, James, S11330, FR, 17th Inf.
WALKER, James H. S3433, HN, 7th Cav.
WALKER, James V. S5806, MC, 3rd Inf.
WALKER, Joe H. S14783, V, 16th Inf.
WALKER, John, S7348, 55th Inf.
WALKER, John H. S1919, RO, 26th Inf.
WALKER, John J. S2491, GI, 11th Cav.
WALKER, John K. S14034, HY, 6th N.C. Inf.
WALKER, John W. S6385, WH, 10th Ky. Inf.
WALKER, Jonathan, S15696, UN, 63rd Inf.
WALKER, Josephine B. W2874, T, Walker, John Lafayette
WALKER, Joshua, S8011, S4179, MT, 14th Inf.
WALKER, Kiziah, W7896, MC, Walker, James Vance
WALKER, Luvisa B. W3986, G, Walker, Wm. H.
WALKER, Martha, W1702, MOO, Walker, Sidney
WALKER, Martha A. W145, CF, Walker, Wm. M.
WALKER, Martha Jane, W4220, PU, Walker, Abram Washington
WALKER, Mary, W1570, ST, Walker, James H.
WALKER, Mary A. W181, MOO, Walker, Zachariah A.
WALKER, Mary Agnes, W8489, HY, Walker, Benjamin Simmens
WALKER, Mary Alice, W7358, MU, Walker, Wm. Overton
WALKER, Mary Aurelia, W8885, SH, Walker, John Parks
WALKER, Mary Christenia, W8892, MN, Walker, Robert Mormon
WALKER, Mary F. W2092, LI, Walker, Elijah W.
WALKER, Mary Jane, W7345, GI, Walker, Robert S.
WALKER, Minnie Elizabeth, W5586, SH, Walker, John Wm.
WALKER, Molly, W6471, GI, Walker, Thomas Monroe
WALKER, Moses (Buck), S16116, MOO, 12th (Forrest's) Cav.
WALKER, Nancy A. W256, RO, Walker, Charles

WALKER, Nancy A. W6067, FR, Walker, John W.
WALKER, O. D. S6773, DK, 16th Inf.
WALKER, P. A. S6951, DY, 20th (Russell's) Cav.
WALKER, Pleasant H. S12112, HI, 42nd Inf.
WALKER, R. G. S15901, MU, 6th (Wheeler's) Cav.
WALKER, R. S. S4917, GI, 53rd Inf.
WALKER, Robert A. S10447, T, 16th Bn. N.C. Cav.
WALKER, Robert D. S2072, HO, 50th Inf.
WALKER, Sallie, W5541, PU, Walker, Wm. H.
WALKER, Samuel, S5558, R, 1st (Carter's) Cav.
WALKER, Sarah Ann, W7163, MU, Walker, Wm. Thomas
WALKER, Sarah E. W4371, RO, Walker, John H.
WALKER, Susan Margaret, W3621, MC, Walker, Joseph Henry
WALKER, T. A. S15831, L, 7th (Duckworth's) Cav.
WALKER, T. J. S8526, MN, 21st Cav.
WALKER, T. J. S8782, HI, 24th Inf.
WALKER, Talitha, W170, HA, Walker, Peter
WALKER, Thomas A. S3403, JE, 1st Tex. Cav.
WALKER, Thomas J. S8364, GI, 1st Cav.
WALKER, W. A. S3622, WY, 1st Cav.
WALKER, W. H. S504, MC, 3rd (Vaughn's) Inf.
WALKER, W. H. S9934, G, 24th Inf.
WALKER, W. H. S11459, PU, 8th Cav.
WALKER, W. J. S2234, MOO, 22nd N.C. Inf.
WALKER, W. L. S13286, T, 12th Inf.
WALKER, W. O. S13162, MU, 6th (Wheeler's) Cav.
WALKER, W. T. S13766, MU, 9th Bn. (Gantt's) Cav.
WALKER, W. W. S6138, W, 23rd Inf.
WALKER, William, S1943, RU, 2nd Inf.
WALKER, William, S11183, MT, 42nd Inf.
WALKER, William A. S6366, WY, 6th (Wheeler's) Cav.
WALKUP, J. A. S3308, CA, 32nd Inf.
WALKUP, James, S11420, CE, 53rd Inf.
WALKUP, James D. S7851, D, 11th Va. Inf.
WALKUP, Sarah Elizabeth, W3749, RU, Walkup, J. A.
WALKUP, William J. S10578, CA, 8th (Smith's) Cav.
WALL, Ada, W6215, MN, Wall, Newton

WALL, Adelle Coleman, W8651, SH, Wall, Wm. Henry
WALL, Ardenia Catherine, W8338, F, Wall, James Brown
WALL, B. P. S13808, HN, 46th Inf.
WALL, Cincinnatus, S5414, MT, 14th Inf.
WALL, Elizabeth Bowen, W8492, GI, Wall, G. W.
WALL, Ezekiel P. S13316, MU, 1st Cav.
WALL, Fannie, W4959, SH, Wall, Oney C.
WALL, Frank G. S15046, MN, 1st (Feild's) Inf.
WALL, J. F. S15041, HN, 5th Inf.
WALL, J. M. See J.M. Walls
WALL, J. P. S14556, ST, 50th Inf.
WALL, James B. S7095, F, Forrest's Old Regt. Cav.
WALL, John T. S7616, GI, 53rd Inf.
WALL, Joseph D. S8911, O, 33rd Inf.
WALL, L. H. S10454, F, 2nd Ky. Cav.
WALL, Letitia Luis, W4521, MT, Wall, John Samuel
WALL, Louisa, W6439, SH, Wall, Micajah
WALL, Louisa, W8725, ST, Wall, James P.
WALL, Martha Axie, W9963, SH, Wall, James K. Polk
WALL, Mary Ann, W1470, MT, Wall, Cincinnatus
WALL, Mary Elizabeth, W3593, GI, Wall, John T.
WALL, Mary M. W5367, WL, Wall, John M.
WALL, N. T. S12966, DK, 2nd Ga. Cav.
WALL, NEwton, S4325, MN, 45th Inf.
WALL, Perry A. S14083, H, 5th S.C. Inf.
WALL, Rebecca J. W10520, O, Wall, J. D.
WALL, Sallie, W8301, H, Wall, Perry A.
WALL, Sarah Ellen, W6007, SH, Wall, Wm. Neal
WALLACE, A. T. S9215, MS, 8th Cav.
WALLACE, Benjamin F. S1525, K, 31st Inf.
WALLACE, E. D. S4588, SN, 2nd (Robison's) Inf.
WALLACE, Elizabeth [Jones], W10963, HU, Wallace, James Tyler, [Later married Jones]
WALLACE, Fannie B. W2584, H, Wallace, James A.
WALLACE, G. E. S10283, ST, 50th Inf.
WALLACE, George B. S13643, HE, 27th Inf.
WALLACE, Isaac A. S10227, H, 36th Inf.
WALLACE, J. C. S14735, WH, 8th (Dibrell's) Cav.
WALLACE, J. K. P. S5306, LI, 8th Inf.

WALLACE, J. M. S12984, ST, 50th Inf.
WALLACE, J. W. S3725, MA, 23rd Bn. Inf.
WALLACE, James, S914, CA, 18th Inf.
WALLACE, James F. S14012, D, 4th (McLemore's) Cav.
WALLACE, Jane, W1519, RO, Wallace, Wm.
WALLACE, Jesse B. S5807, MC, 59th Inf.
WALLACE, Laura Virginia, W5301, CU, Wallace, Simon Doyle
WALLACE, M. M. S14602, ST, 50th Inf.
WALLACE, Margaret I. W3634, BO, Wallace, Abram L.
WALLACE, Mary Elizabeth, W3056, LI, Wallace, James K. P.
WALLACE, Mary M. W10437, CA, Wallace, Wm. H.
WALLACE, Melissa Duncan, W11038, MS, Wallace, A. T.
WALLACE, Nancy K. W4313, H, Wallace, Isaac A.
WALLACE, Phebe A. W3709, SN, Wallace, Elmore Douglass
WALLACE, Robert D. S6070, SH, Forrest's Old Regt.
WALLACE, Robert M. S13856, M, 24th Inf.
WALLACE, Sallie, W7622, D, Wallace, James Franklin
WALLACE, Sallie Burden, W7894, WH, Wallace, John Calvin
WALLACE, Sarah A. W6944, SH, Wallace, Robert Delafield
WALLACE, Sarah Jane, W8568, ST, Wallace, M. M.
WALLACE, Thomas, S3783, HW, 29th Inf.
WALLACE, Willie Alma, W5461, ST, Wallace, George Evans
WALLEN, Janie, W9005, HW, Wallen, John G.
WALLEN, John G. S3645, HA, 2nd Cav.
WALLER, Andrew J. S939, PU, 43rd Inf.
WALLER, Andrew J. S5432, DK, 43rd Inf.
WALLER, E. S7303, RU, Carter's Scouts, Cav.
WALLER, E. M. W1766, GR, Waller, L. F.
WALLER, Eliza, W3622, LO, Waller, Hardin
WALLER, Fannie, W7071, RU, Waller, Ephraim
WALLER, George R. S10887, D, Wheeler's Scouts, Cav.
WALLER, J. L. S12442, RO, 19th Inf.
WALLER, James R. S9068, D, Carter's Scouts, Cav.
WALLER, John P. S3331, RO, 63rd Inf.

WALLER, Kate Garner, W8558, D, Waller, George Ralston
WALLER, Lou R. W3080, D, Waller, Wm.
WALLER, Lucinda Matilda, W9306, RO, Waller, George Pickell
WALLER, Manerva T. W10317, HY, Waller, Thomas Washington
WALLER, Martha Ann, W3976, ST, Waller, Benjamin Lenard
WALLER, Mary Eliza, W1471, D, Waller, John
WALLER, Mary Jane, W10147, G, Waller, Jonas Memory
WALLER, McNairy C. S14033, S14664, D, 1st (Feild's) Inf.
WALLER, Rebecca E. W1954, F, Waller, Henry Benjamine
WALLER, Sallie, W3019, WI, Waller, B. R.
WALLER, Sarah A. W2293, A, Waller, George
WALLER, Sarah Killingsworth, W7862, K, Waller, John Polk
WALLER, Sophronia Edeline, W3563, K, Waller, Henry Allen
WALLER, Susie Sneed, W9188, D, Waller, John Rains
WALLER, Thomas J. S10973, WI, 4th (McLemore's) Cav.
WALLER, W. N. S4817, CL, 4th (Consolidated) Inf.
WALLER, William, S9324, D, Carter's Scouts, Cav.
WALLING, Martha, W8270, W, Walling, Shelby
WALLING, Martha Jane, W2497, SU, Walling, Leander Jackson
WALLING, Shelby, S1147, V, 16th Inf.
WALLINGSFORD, Thomas W. S4298, DY, 52nd Inf.
WALLIS, J. T. S13489, HU, 10th Cav.
WALLIS, Lou Crecy, W5457, WE, Wallis, Stephen
WALLIS, Mary A. W10421, D, Wallis, Charles G.
WALLIS, Nannie, W7664, ST, Wallis, Taylor
WALLIS, Sarah Jane, W1938, H, Wallis, Henry
WALLIS, Stephen, S5865, WE, 55th Inf.
WALLIS, Taylor, S13185, ST, 4th Ky. Inf.
WALLIS, W. C. S5834, MC, 43rd Inf.
WALLIS, W. N. S5863, MC, 43rd Inf.
WALLS, Frances Ann, W10736, RU, Walls, George Washington
WALLS, G. N. S3382, GI, 32nd Inf.
WALLS, George W. S13063, RU, 12th Inf.

WALLS, H. M. S7626, MS, 41st Inf.
WALLS, J. D. S5622, B, 17th Inf.
WALLS, J. M. S1930, LI, 5th Inf.
WALLS, Mary Jane, W7360, MS, Walls, James David
WALSH, Annie Eveline, W3236, Walsh, Thomas
WALSH, Eliza Cassie, W6085, MR, Walsh, George Washington
WALSH, Fannie, W11067, HU, Walsh, Patrick
WALSH, G. W. S7899, MR, 45th Inf.
WALSH, Genetta, W8392, JO, Walsh, Wm. H.
WALSH, John, S11255, JO, 65th Inf.
WALSH, Mary, W2337, MT, Walsh, James
WALSH, Pat, S14195, HU, Thos. Porter's Art.
WALSH, Thomas, S5446, 6th Inf.
WALSH, William H. S11234, JO, Unassigned
WALT, Mary Trask, W9902, SH, Walt, Martin Vanburen
WALTER, Mary J. W519, WA, Walter, George
WALTER, Mary L. W7742, WA, Walter, Wm.
WALTERS, A. J. S11468, WE, 20th Cav.
WALTERS, A. V. S12284, MA, 23rd Miss. Inf.
WALTERS, C. A. S10921, MU, Sparkman's Co. Lt. Art.
WALTERS, D. H. S185, HW, 12th Cav.
WALTERS, Elijah, S1777, HW, 16th Bn. Cav.
WALTERS, Elijah, S8494, HW, 12th Cav.
WALTERS, Henry Harrison, S11634, MU, 9th Cav.
WALTERS, James W. S109, 19th & 20th (Consol.) Inf.
WALTERS, Sarah Ann, W4662, Walters, James W.
WALTERS, Sarah Jane, W8226, WE, Walters, Andrew Jackson
WALTERS, Soloman, S7057, HW, 16th Bn. Cav.
WALTERS, William, S6638, WA, 63rd Inf.
WALTHAL, Sallie Whitfield, W8496, MT, Walthal, Thomas Washington
WALTHALL, J. H. S2352, OV, 8th Inf.
WALTON, Bettie, W3137, DY, Walton, Tyree Harris
WALTON, H. A. S1489, HE, 2nd Inf.
WALTON, J. W. S10699, SH, 1st Miss. Inf.
WALTON, John L. S8495, HW, 12th Bn. Cav.
WALTON, John L. S11261, WI, 20th Inf.
WALTON, Mary Frances, W1331, D, Walton, Josiah
WALTON, Peter, S7663, MS, 4th (McLemore's) Cav.

WALTON, Sallie Salina, W6983, SH, Walton, Thomas Hobson
WALTON, Samuel W. S10261, D, 20th Inf.
WALTON, Thomas H. S8281, SH, 3rd Miss. Cav.
WALTON, Urildia Carson, W10790, SN, Walton, J. L.
WALTON, William T. S11407, SH, 50th Ala. Inf.
WALWORK, Elizabeth M. W3282, D, Walwork, Wm. B.
WAMPLER, David, S4490, SU, 29th Va. Inf.
WAMPLER, Ellen Cecil, W9064, H, Wampler, J. B.
WANMAKER, Lydia Naomi, W1663, GU, Wanmaker, James
WARBRITTON, Agnes, W3623, Warbritton, Henry Newton
WARBRITTON, Ella Augusta, W4820, Warbritton, Benjamin Franklin
WARD, Albert G. S8015, SE, 31st Inf.
WARD, America, W5391, W, Ward, Rufus
WARD, Ann W. W9839, RU, Ward, Robert M.
WARD, Bettie, W10334, CH, Ward, Thomas D.
WARD, Clara P. W4920, SH, Ward, John W.
WARD, Elvira J. W2114, WE, Ward, Pinkney M.
WARD, F. F. S13586, HN, 1st Ky. Cav.
WARD, Harriet S. W7009, SE, Ward, Albert G.
WARD, Hattie Brown, W10003, HN, Ward, Rufus K.
WARD, Isaac, S11847, SE, 31st Inf.
WARD, J. R. S15148, D, 12th Ala. Inf.
WARD, J. W. S7705, G, 12th Ky. Cav.
WARD, J. W. S15378, DK, 35th Inf.
WARD, Jesse B. S12760, MA, 18th (Newsom's) Cav.
WARD, John, S6967, ME, 5th (McKenzie's) Cav.
WARD, John A. S13224, F, 1st N.C. Cav.
WARD, John B. S11741, SM, 8th (Smith's) Cav.
WARD, John F. S15570, S15737, LK, 5th Inf.
WARD, John K. S3322, S16394, LI, 1st (Turney's) Inf.
WARD, John S. S701, ME, 5th Cav.
WARD, Lucy Amanda, W2970, GU, Ward, Wm. Hudson
WARD, Mary, W10797, RU, Ward, James
WARD, Mary A. W137, WE, Ward, Hayden E.
WARD, Mary Frances, W845, Ward, Wm. Thomas

WARD, Melissa E. W4821, RB, Ward, Wm. Henry
WARD, Mose, C262, HI, 24th Inf.
WARD, Nancy Malissa, W4006, O, Ward, Robert D.
WARD, Nannie S. W6834, H, Ward, James Ralston
WARD, P. M. S8877, WE, 52nd Inf.
WARD, Patrick I. S4206, O, 34th Inf.
WARD, R. D. S1580, O, 47th Inf.
WARD, R. M. S7892, RU, 45th Inf.
WARD, Rachel Agness, W8354, DY, Ward, Robert Madison
WARD, Rufus, S453, V, 16th Inf.
WARD, Sallie, W1324, WH, Ward, Wm.
WARD, Sarah, W1063, WL, Ward, C. W.
WARD, Susan H. W1846, D, Ward, James Best
WARD, Susan Margaret, W8061, G, Ward, J. W.
WARD, T. D. S10770, MA, 21st (Wilson's) Cav.
WARD, Tabitha, W1932, D, Ward, John Henry
WARD, William H. S1161, GU, 4th N.C. Inf.
WARDEN, James L. S1694, S1617, OV, 8th (Dibrell's) Cav.
WARDEN, James M. S10771, LI, 44th Inf.
WARDEN, Robert, S9642, CL, 2nd Cav.
WARDEN, S. C. S4293, DE, 27th Inf.
WARDLOW, Betsy Ann, W5709, MN, Wardlow, Charlie Wesley
WARDLOW, Elizabeth Jane, W7821, MN, Wardlow, James Wm.
WARDLOW, J. W. S10462, MN, 32nd Miss. Inf.
WARE, A. D. S3905, W, 16th Inf.
WARE, Charles, C205, W, 16th Inf.
WARE, Elizabeth B. W4140, Ware, John Calvin
WARE, Mary Boyd, W8602, T, Ware, Joseph Henry
WARE, Mollie A. W8812, MU, Ware, Wm. A.
WARE, Samuel, S8709, H, 1st Ga. Bn. Inf.
WAREN, Martha A. W1592, HI, Waren, John Thomas
WARF, Sarah A. E. W5166, WL, Warf, Wm. G.
WARF, W. G. S13158, WL, 38th Va. Inf.
WARFIELD, Doras Pollard, W7693, MT, Warfield, George Waters
WARFIELD, Florence Nelson, W10182, SH, Warfield, Wm. Pollock
WARFIELD, H. C. S10109, RB, 11th Inf.
WARFORD, B. M. S695, SM, 7th Inf.
WARLICK, James P. S1032, MA, 6th Inf.

WARLICK, Lafayette, S13246, HM, 32nd N.C. Inf.
WARMACK, A. J. S2698, W, 35th Inf.
WARMACK, Dallas, S7590, WE, 2nd (Robison's) Inf.
WARMACK, F. G. S2699, W, 16th Inf.
WARMACK, John P. S993, SN, 44th Inf.
WARMACK, Sarah, W3933, BE, Warmack, T. J.
WARMACK, William, S9682, BE, 5th Inf.
WARNER, Ella Mary, W6889, WL, Warner, Richard
WARNER, James Polk, S16073, MS, 8th (Smith's) Cav.
WARNER, Richard, S10014, MS, 23rd Inf.
WARNER, S. J. S8721, MS, 11th Cav.
WARR, James M. S3872, F, 13th Inf.
WARREN, Edward A. S10524, WI, 32nd Inf.
WARREN, Elizabeth C. W8334, HI, Warren, Wm. C.
WARREN, George W. S3297, GI, 32nd Inf.
WARREN, Hulda Reynolds, W7076, WE, Warren, James Jefferson
WARREN, Isaac R. S8073, G, 44th Inf.
WARREN, J. A. S13781, LA, 48th Inf.
WARREN, J. A. sr. S9442, P, 42nd Inf.
WARREN, J. N. S14679, RB, 4th (McLemore's) Cav.
WARREN, J. R. S13033, H, 12th Ga. Inf.
WARREN, John, S8604, HR, 4th Inf.
WARREN, Julia, W10908, SH, Warren, Wm. Mandred
WARREN, Letitia Thompson, W4689, B, Warren, Charles A.
WARREN, Louisa Virginia, W6614, H, Warren, John Randolph
WARREN, Luzaney, W5753, HI, Warren, Cornelius
WARREN, Maria L. W5097, WL, Warren, Elisha E.
WARREN, Marmon D. S6926, MOO, 41st Inf.
WARREN, Mary Catherine, W9082, WY, Warren, Sam Burns
WARREN, Mary E. W5834, WL, Warren, Wm. Farmer
WARREN, Mary E. W10755, WL, Warren, Thomas E.
WARREN, Mary Frances, W4422, G, Warren, Archie Prior
WARREN, Milton B. S12227, S16467, S16489, WY, 1st Cav.

WARREN, Mittie J. W5542, G, Warren, Isaac Richard
WARREN, P. A. W682, SU, Warren, Wm. E.
WARREN, Perilla, W5715, OV, Warren, Wm. Henry
WARREN, S. B. S14782, WY, 19th (Biffle's) Cav.
WARREN, Sallie C. W8757, MU, Warren, Thomas Armstrong
WARREN, Sarah, W1450, LE, Warren, W. C.
WARREN, Susan, W2018, HU, Warren, Emzie
WARREN, Tabitha A. W1451, WL, Warren, Berryman G. T.
WARREN, Thomas E. S13275, RB, Allison's Squadron, Cav.
WARREN, Thomas V. S6896, H, 4th Ala. Inf.
WARREN, W. C. S12390, HI, 24th Inf.
WARREN, W. H. S8646, RB, 8th (Smith's) Cav.
WARREN, W. N. S14015, SN, 9th (Bennett's) Cav.
WARREN, William, S1056, CO, 22nd N.C. Inf.
WARREN, William T. S9405, R, 8th (Smith's) Cav.
WARRICK, Margaret F. W2741, CF, Warrick, James H.
WARRICK, Nancy Ellen, W10275, K, Warrick, Wm. Henry Harrison
WARWICK, John W. S13867, K, 26th S.C. Inf.
WARWICK, Margaret Elizabeth, W7165, K, Warwick, John Wesley
WASHBURN, Lucetta Butler, W6216, J, Washburn, Lafayette
WASHBURN, Mark C. S1386, MN, 17th Inf.
WASHER, Eliza, W2599, ST, Washer, James
WASHER, James, S4793, S2173, ST, 14th Inf.
WASHINGTON, Guy, S7119, DI, 3rd Ark. Inf.
WASSOM, John W. S10184, R, 1st (Carter's) Cav.
WASSOM, Lucinda, W2586, SU, Wassom, James L.
WASSOM, P. M. S110, J, 16th Inf.
WASSON, F. P. S6082, HN, 4th Ala. Cav.
WASSON, J. F. S13296, HU, 19th (Biffle's) Cav.
WASSON, J. L. S9069, HN, 4th Ala. Cav.
WASSON, Mary Frances, W2813, HN, Wasson, Finis Pinkney
WASSON, Sarah Margaret, W5698, J, Wasson, Pleasant Marion
WATERHOUSE, Cyrus, S5333, H, Barry's Co. Lt. Art.

WATERS, C. N. S2630, H, 40th Ga. Inf.
WATERS, J. W. S4448, SE, 2nd N.C. Cav.
WATERS, Mary Eliza, W3900, HI, Waters, Zachariah John
WATERS, Mary Eugenia, W1339, WI, Waters, Benjamin Frank
WATERS, Pauline, W10397, GI, Waters, Mark Smith
WATERS, Sarah ann, W2373, SE, Waters, John Wesly
WATERS, Thomas J. S16658, WY, 4th Ala. Cav.
WATKINS, D. F. S15926, MU, 6th (Wheeler's) Cav.
WATKINS, Eliza, W6048, RU, Watkins, John W.
WATKINS, Isaac G. S1665, JE, 3rd Inf.
WATKINS, J. W. S1322, WE, 10th N.C. Station Art.
WATKINS, Jennie Mays, W5150, MU, Watkins, Sam R.
WATKINS, John T. S6226, 46th Inf.
WATKINS, John W. S14017, D, McClung's Battery, Art.
WATKINS, K. C. S1885, HO, 5th Cav.
WATKINS, Lucinda Spain, W7105, D, Watkins, John Wm.
WATKINS, Lula Elizabeth, W8485, SH, Watkins, Marcet Ruffin
WATKINS, Mary P. W3001, SU, Watkins, Richard Henry
WATKINS, Mary Turner, W9594, SH, Watkins, Benjamin F.
WATKINS, Nancy Eveline, W6038, JE, Watkins, Isaac George
WATKINS, Robert B. S4981, SU, 63rd Inf.
WATKINS, Sallie T. W3128, HY, Watkins, James B.
WATKINS, Samuel Aaron, S16383, K, 17th Va. Inf.
WATKINS, Sarah, W9422, WL, Watkins, Robert Ruse
WATKINS, Sarah G. W10188, HY, Watkins, J. B.
WATKINS, Sue Cannon, W10064, SH, Watkins, Thomas R.
WATKINS, Thomas D. S8466, D, 11th Bn. Cav.
WATKINS, Thomas J. S15640, T, 14th (Neely's) Cav.
WATKINS, WAde, C269, L, 48th Inf.
WATSON, A. P. H. S6794, WI, 32nd Inf.

WATSON, Alice Louise, W1638, D, Watson, Wm. F.
WATSON, Annie, W3996, MS, Watson, W. F.
WATSON, Coleman, S15722, MU, 65th Ga. Inf.
WATSON, Coleman, S15795, PO, 60th Ga. Inf.
WATSON, E. E. S5307, SU, 63rd Inf.
WATSON, E. H. S16284, MU, 9th Cav.
WATSON, Elison, S6559, SE, 25th N.C. Inf.
WATSON, George A. S13895, GI, 6th (Wheeler's) Cav.
WATSON, George W. S3036, MO, 59th Inf.
WATSON, J. A. S15009, CY, 8th Cav.
WATSON, J. H. S5334, BE, 1st Mo. Inf.
WATSON, J. R. S12087, PU, 25th Inf.
WATSON, J. T. S16470, MA, 6th Inf.
WATSON, J. W. S4013, LA, 19th (Biffle's) Cav.
WATSON, J. W. S5892, LI, 28th Inf.
WATSON, James H. S926, BR, 5th Cav.
WATSON, James M. S13553, SH, 1st Ala. Inf.
WATSON, John, S13180, MU, 48th (Voorhies') Inf.
WATSON, John G. S958, T, 42nd Miss. Inf.
WATSON, John J. S2430, CL, 26th N.C. Inf.
WATSON, Julia, W4848, MO, Watson, Robert D.
WATSON, L. E. S16110, WL, 27th N.C. Inf.
WATSON, L. H. S7596, BR, 65th Inf.
WATSON, Lois, W6705, CY, Watson, James Francis Monroe
WATSON, Lucy Caroline, W8834, BE, Watson, Allen Washington
WATSON, M. L. S8422, D, 49th Inf.
WATSON, Mack G. S10059, D, Forrest's Escort, Cav.
WATSON, Margaret Frances, W5236, GI, Watson, George Allen
WATSON, Mary, W3063, DY, Watson, Wm. Henry
WATSON, Mary, W3924, MO, Watson, Jasper
WATSON, Mary Corda [Blevins], W10763, JO, Watson, Thos. Jackson, [Later married Blevins]
WATSON, Mary E. W4154, MO, Watson, James C.
WATSON, Mary Emily, W7798, GI, Watson, W. E.
WATSON, Mat J. S11476, MA, 6th Inf.
WATSON, Nancy Ann, W4919, WL, Watson, R. T.
WATSON, Nancy Jane, W8420, SU, Watson, E. E.

WATSON, Nathan D. S3560, B, 17th Inf.
WATSON, Rev. J. W. S10660, SU, Jackson's Home Guards
WATSON, Robert, S3226, MO, 62nd Inf.
WATSON, Sallie Abagile, W3081, MU, Watson, Simeon
WATSON, Samuel A. S9805, WE, 50th N.C. Inf.
WATSON, Sarah A. W8161, BR, Watson, L. H.
WATSON, Sarah F. W7776, DK, Watson, John C.
WATSON, Simeon, S9136, WI, 3rd (Clack's) Inf.
WATSON, W. E. S2915, GI, 11th Bn. (Holman's) Cav.
WATSON, W. F. S3440, LI, 8th Inf.
WATSON, W. P. S11294, D, Harding Art.
WATSON, William W. S1983, WA, 60th Inf.
WATT, Mattie, W5752, MA, Watt, Wm.
WATT, T. J. S11056, G, 52nd Inf.
WATT, T. J. S12420, MA, 52nd Inf.
WATT, William, S9944, MA, 6th Inf.
WATTENBERGER, Martha Ann, W3382, ME, Wattenberger, John
WATTERSON, Minerva B. W3728, HW, Watterson, Wm. H.
WATTERSON, William H. S3879, HW, 19th Inf.
WATTS, Alexander B. S8868, MA, 37th N.C. Inf.
WATTS, Anderson, S3705, BE, 7th S.C. Inf.
WATTS, Anna Harty, W7378, H, Watts, Wm. Julius
WATTS, B. S4825, WE, 7th Cav.
WATTS, C. H. S9133, G, 3rd (Forrest's) Cav.
WATTS, Dollie, W, Some papers with #11183 on film
WATTS, F. M. S11356, RB, 30th Inf.
WATTS, J. H>, S61, RU, 1st Cav.
WATTS, Sarah Ann, W2445, RU, Watts, J. H.
WATTS, Sarah Virginia, W5901, G, Watts, Charles Henry
WATTS, Steven D. S12827, F, 14th Cav.
WATTS, Thomas, S13266, CE, 30th Inf.
WATTS, Wealthy Jane, W5026, RB, Watts, Francis Marion
WAYNES, Jacob, S7134, UN, 1st Cav.
WEAKLEY, Cornelia Virginia, W10199, MT, Weakley, George Washington
WEAKLEY, G. W. S13072, CE, 42nd Inf.
WEAKLEY, Josephine Jones, W9221, RU, Weakley, Samuel Murford

WELCH, Emily Jane, W9200, MS, Welch, John Robert
WELCH, Frances, W2063, PU, Welch, John
WELCH, Frances E. W2213, DE, Welch, Jeremiah Benton
WELCH, G. R. S16357, RU, 45th Inf.
WELCH, Isaiah, S4794, DE, 18th (Newsom's) Cav.
WELCH, J. H. S794, CO, 2nd N.C. Inf.
WELCH, J. H. S9143, MS, 17th Inf.
WELCH, J. H. S13376, MU, 23rd Inf.
WELCH, J. W. S12613, MS, 17th Inf.
WELCH, James A. S6193, PU, 25th Inf.
WELCH, James H. S5525, WA, 26th Inf.
WELCH, John, S4084, DI, 11th Inf.
WELCH, John L. S5308, WE, 31st Inf.
WELCH, Margaret C. W2133, MS, Welch, Charles S.
WELCH, Martha J. W5323, MS, Welch, Stephen J.
WELCH, Mary Frances, W4414, DY, Welch, Wm. Green
WELCH, Nancy Garrett, W11052, MU, Welch, James Washington
WELCH, Patrick, S1311, MA, 15th Inf.
WELCH, Preston J. S7744, RO, 2nd Cav.
WELCH, R. H. S13500, SH, 3rd (Forrest's) Cav.
WELCH, Sallie J. W8813, W5305, MS, Welch, Wm. Harvey
WELCH, Sarah Catharine, W6629, SU, Welch, George Washington
WELCH, Wesley, S8483, DI, Baxter's Battery, Art.
WELCH, Winnie, W1767, DE, Welch, Isaiah
WELCKER, Hester A. W2608, K, Welcker, Benjamin Franklin
WELLBANKS, H. H. S11892, WE, 15th Inf.
WELLKER, Francis Marion, S12687, DY, 2nd Ky. Inf.
WELLONS, Charles Marmaduke, S10031, HR, 22nd Inf.
WELLONS, Maria Louise, W6296, HR, Wellons, C. M.
WELLS, Alice, W1498, MT, Wells, James Henry
WELLS, Elizabeth, W1972, D, Wells, James M.
WELLS, Elizabeth E. W6685, GR, Wells, Ellington
WELLS, Fannie, W7038, MU, Wells, Wm. T.
WELLS, Isabella, W6604, LI, Wells, James Marion
WELLS, J. C. S13019, LI, 32nd Inf.
WELLS, J. M. S15043, LI, 41st Inf.
WELLS, J. T. S14537, SH, 4th Inf.
WELLS, J. W. S7752, SH, 15th Miss. Inf.
WELLS, James Grayar, S15606, MA, 21st (Wilson's) Cav.
WELLS, James Henry, S7430, MT, 49th Inf.
WELLS, John F. S13942, MU, 3rd (Clack's) Inf.
WELLS, Joseph A. S16645, RU, Unassigned
WELLS, Lucy Collier, W10435, MS, Wells, Mark L.
WELLS, M. H. S13635, GE, 31st Inf.
WELLS, Martha A. W4110, GI, Wells, Wm. H.
WELLS, Martha Emeline, W6936, MS, Wells, John Cole
WELLS, Mary W. W4658, GE, Wells, Samuel H.
WELLS, Mattie Ann, W8532, GI, Wells, Wm. Henry
WELLS, Rhoda Clamanda, W6928, GE, Wells, Marson Hanson
WELLS, Sarah Jane, W4898, WY, Wells, Elias
WELLS, W. H. sr. S14060, LI, 32nd Inf.
WELLS, W. T. S10895, MU, 3rd (Clack's) Inf.
WELSH, Mary, W259, D, Welsh, Thomas
WENDEL, Hallie B. W10330, W6101, DY, Wendel, James Brown
WENDEL, James B. S2931, DY, 4th Inf.
WESCOAT, Octavia, W905, HN, Wescoat, Sam E.
WESSON, Emma, W4438, SH, Wesson, Joseph Nathaniel
WEST, Adlade, W10891, WH, West, Alex
WEST, Alexander, S4753, PU, 3rd Confederate Engineer Troops
WEST, Annie Conners, W11001, D, West, John
WEST, C. A. W9192, SN, West, Isaac Moody
WEST, Caroline, W513, GI, West, John Hensley
WEST, Carrie Lockridge, W9183, MU, West, James Isaac
WEST, Dorthula Ann, W7912, J, West, James H.
WEST, E. M. S1965, CO, 3rd S.C. Inf.
WEST, Eliza Ellen, W4708, D, West, George Washington
WEST, Elizabeth, W687, PU, West, Granville Finley
WEST, Elizabeth, W4558, MO, West, Joseph V.
WEST, Elizabeth, W9468, GI, West, Wilborn Chesley
WEST, Elizabeth Evans, W9734, GI, West, Wm. Harrison

Index to Tennessee Confederate Pension Applications

WEST, Elizabeth Green, W6753, MC, West, Samuel T.
WEST, Elmyra Taylor, W9076, HO, West, James Sturdivant
WEST, Fredonia, W6345, D, West, Johnson Bascom
WEST, George T. S891, M, Undetermined
WEST, George Washington, S529, CF, 1st Fla. Inf.
WEST, H. W. S3508, OV, 25th Inf.
WEST, Harrison, S7451, SM, 28th Inf.
WEST, I. P. S14143, L, 1st Bn. (Cox's) Inf.
WEST, Isabella L. W4019, FR, West, Levi
WEST, J. F. S2757, BE, 3rd Ky. Inf.
WEST, J. H. S623, M, 28th Inf.
WEST, J. H. S4369, DY, 33rd Inf.
WEST, J. S. S13149, HO, 2nd Ky. Cav.
WEST, J. V. S1506, MO, 59th Inf.
WEST, J. W. S16452, SN, 9th Cav.
WEST, James B. S622, J, 28th Inf.
WEST, James H. S5323, D, Huggin's Co. Lt. Art.
WEST, Jesse, S6774, MO, Thomas' Legion, N.C.
WEST, John, S11425, FR, 41st Inf.
WEST, Johnson Bascom, S13997, D, 1st Ky. Cav.
WEST, L. M. S2796, T, 21st Inf.
WEST, Laura Louise, W9896, MO, West, Thomas Monley
WEST, Levi, S3646, FR, 35th Ala. Inf.
WEST, Lou Ersie (Raper), W11121, WH, West, Jasper L.
WEST, Lucinda, W6278, H, West, W. R.
WEST, Malvina M. W7886, SM, West, John Ridly
WEST, Margaret, W9568, R, West, Wm. Thomas
WEST, Martha, W657, CF, West, Wm. M.
WEST, Mary Ann, W7504, L, West, Isaac Peter
WEST, Mary J. W6627, B, West, George W.
WEST, Mercer W. S7014, MT, 1st Ky. Cav.
WEST, Milley, W2193, SM, West, Harrison
WEST, Nancy, W4901, CO, West, Elihu Moore
WEST, Sam T. S9650, MC, 5th Cav.
WEST, Sarah A. W1520, MA, West, John Wm.
WEST, Sarah F. W1084, SM, West, Jesse
WEST, Sarah Frances, W5659, T, West, Lafayette Melvin
WEST, Stephen, S2250, OV, 8th Cav.
WEST, Thomas M. S16684, MC, Thomas' Legion, N.C. Inf.
WEST, Thomas W. S13247, SN, 20th Inf.
WEST, W. C. S11796, SM, 22nd (Barteau's) Cav.
WEST, W. H. S11912, GI, 6th (Wheeler's) Cav.
WEST, W. L. C. S13001, S15633, GI, 20th (Nixon's) Cav.
WEST, William J. S15810, GI, 53rd Inf.
WEST, William M. S10072, S11115, SH, Forrest's Old Regt. Cav.
WEST, Willis Riley, S13016, H, 1st Ga. Inf.
WEST, Wilson, S4001, PU, 25th Inf.
WESTBROOKS, Martha Jane, W2257, P, Westbrooks, J. N.
WESTCOAT, S. E. S1739, WE, 9th Inf.
WESTERN, A. M. S12917, HN, 46th Inf.
WESTERN, Sophia Arrilie Davis, W9425, DE, Western, Robert Davis
WESTMORELAND, J. M. S4918, HR, 34th Miss. Inf.
WESTMORELAND, Pennie E. W2616, MU, Westmoreland, Robert W.
WETZEL, William H. S6622, HW, 29th Va. Inf.
WHALEN, G. J. S6886, RO, 1st (Carter's) Cav.
WHALEN, J. K. P. S5388, H, 1st Cav.
WHALEY, H. S7664, WE, 31st Inf.
WHAN, John, S6934, WE, 20th Cav.
WHARTON, Alex (Big Alex), C71, MA, 154th Sr. Regt. Inf.
WHARTON, Alex (Little Alex), C72, MA, 21st Cav.
WHARTON, Frank, C167, HY, 14th Cav.
WHARTON, Martha Hanie Wheeler, W8679, CA, Wharton, John Henry
WHARTON, Mary Driskel, W6757, SH, Wharton, George H.
WHARTON, Mary Jane, W1383, GI, Wharton, Wm. Thomas Harris
WHARTON, W. T. H. S3194, LA, Forrest's Escort, Cav.
WHEAT, J. S. S10948, HI, 9th Bn. (Gantt's) Cav.
WHEAT, Mary B. W3934, HI, Wheat, Joseph S.
WHEATLEY, Addie J. S4876, HE, 22nd Inf.
WHEATLEY, G. P. S189, HE, 27th Inf.
WHEATLEY, H. L. S2000, BE, 55th (Brown's) Inf.
WHEATLEY, J. C. S2251, BE, 55th Inf.
WHEATLEY, Martha, W7700, BE, Wheatley, James Con.
WHEELER, Alpha Corsilia, W11047, MC, Wheeler, John W.

-367

WHEELER, Catharine A. W1342, K, Wheeler, W. C.
WHEELER, Charles Newton, S11086, D, 1st (Carter's) Cav.
WHEELER, Emma J. W8358, F, Wheeler, Richard R.
WHEELER, G. S. S15279, F, Eldridge's Co. Lt. Art.
WHEELER, George W. S8057, BR, 34th Ga. Inf. & 4th Ga. Cav.
WHEELER, Hopkins, S1023, S716, J, 25th Inf., 716 follows 639; out of order on film
WHEELER, J. H. S14346, BL, 36th Ga. Inf.
WHEELER, James W. S12898, SH, Phillip's Co. Lt. Art.
WHEELER, Lenna, W11049, BL, Wheeler, James H.
WHEELER, Mary M, W1724, W, Wheeler, Alfred D.
WHEELER, Matilda Catherine, W7479, H, Wheeler, Wm. Henry
WHEELER, N. M. S4043, B, 1st Cav.
WHEELER, Samantha, W8194, B, Wheeler, Mike
WHEELER, Thomas, S2527, WH, 8th (Dibrell's) Cav.
WHEELER, W. W. S8802, L, 4th Inf.
WHEELER, William A. S7685, B, 41st Inf.
WHEELING, Lucinda Smith, W9259, D, Wheeling, Christn. Ed. Charles
WHEELIS, Amos, S8373, WE, 12th Ky. Cav.
WHEELIS, Susan E. W10124, WE, Wheelis, Amos
WHEELOCK, Mary Caroline, W2105, LO, Wheelock, Noah Wilburn
WHELESS, Sarah B. W536, D, Wheless, James
WHERRY, W. C. S7576, HU, 10th (DeMoss') Cav.
WHIATHEY, Henrietta, W6086, HE, Whiathey, George Pierce
WHILLOCK, A. S1433, U, 62nd Inf.
WHIPPLE, Susan, W6164, CO, Whipple, John
WHISENHUNT, Cindia, W5073, CT, Whisenhunt, Noah
WHISENHUNT, Noah, S5684, CT, 6th N.C. Inf.
WHISMAN, James A. S14402, WA, 63rd Inf.
WHISMAN, Mary Elizabeth, W7819, WA, Whisman, James Alexander
WHITAKER, F. Clementine, W645, MC, Whitaker, George Edward

WHITAKER, J. C. S14498, P, 48th (Voorhies') Inf.
WHITAKER, J. M. S15434, PU, 25th Inf.
WHITAKER, L. J. S16514, PU, 25th Inf.
WHITAKER, Mary A. H. W4364, D, Whitaker, John G.
WHITAKER, Mary Ann, W4126, MS, Whitaker, Francis Marion
WHITAKER, Mary Elizabeth, W8508, PU, Whitaker, John Harrison
WHITAKER, Mary Jane, W3696, D, Whitaker, James Monroe
WHITAKER, Rachel Caroline, W587, MN, Whitaker, James Martin
WHITAKER, Robbin, S624, J, Hamilton's Bn. Cav.
WHITE, A. A. S4647, DY, 20th (Russell's) Cav.
WHITE, A. T. S8783, SH, 9th Inf.
WHITE, Alex L. S5309, LI, 3rd Inf.
WHITE, Alice [Jennings], W10936, T, White, Rederick Thomas, [Later married Jennings]
WHITE, Amanda, W9577, DY, White, Bert Rufus
WHITE, B. F. S14205, WI, 44th Inf.
WHITE, B. F. sr. S4475, SU, 4th Va. Inf.
WHITE, C. B. R. S10356, DY, 15th (Stewart's) Cav.
WHITE, C. I. S10167, MU, 48th Inf.
WHITE, Daniel, S5462, DI, Baxter's Co. Lt. Art.
WHITE, Daniel F. S691, RU, 24th Inf.
WHITE, David F. S1832, RU, 24th Inf.
WHITE, Dick, C134, HY, 6th Inf.
WHITE, E. E. S5355, OV, 13th Cav.
WHITE, E. W. S4681, DI, 26th Inf.
WHITE, Elias E. S9078, D, 8th (Dibrell's) Cav.
WHITE, Ellen, W8433, SU, White, Thomas Wm.
WHITE, F. Marion, S15648, WI, 50th Inf.
WHITE, Fannie, W9439, M, White, James Braxton
WHITE, Francis Marion, S11415, HD, 1st Confederate Cav.
WHITE, Geneva, W9616, O, White, John
WHITE, George, S6007, D, 1st Art.
WHITE, H. L. S429, S1622, BE, 5th Inf.
WHITE, H. L. S1074, RB, 14th Bn. Cav.
WHITE, Harriet Baker, W3585, D, White, James Park
WHITE, Henrietta H. W1606, HU, White, W. C.
WHITE, Henry A. S8878, HD, 9th Cav.

Index to Tennessee Confederate Pension Applications

WHITE, I. H. S6091, DE, 27th Inf.
WHITE, Ira Dotson, S3337, GI, 48th Inf.
WHITE, Isaiah, S13929, D, Hamilton's Bn. Cav.
WHITE, J. A. S3854, H, 8th Cav.
WHITE, J. B. S14098, M, 6th (Wheeler's) Cav.
WHITE, J. C. S9596, BE, 52nd Inf.
WHITE, J. D. S6222, DY, 19th (Biffle's) Cav.
WHITE, J. E. S11222, WE, 22nd Inf.
WHITE, J. H. S2034, OV, 8th Cav.
WHITE, J. J. S11326, RB, 49th Inf.
WHITE, J. J. S14798, WE, 20th (Russell's) Cav.
WHITE, J. M. S7546, H, 5th (McKenzie's) Cav.
WHITE, J. M. S12400, 41st Inf.
WHITE, J. M. T. S9870, MS, 4th (McLemore's) Cav.
WHITE, J. P. S10208, R, 1st (Carter's) Cav.
WHITE, J. P. S16227, S6722, DI, Baxter's Battery, Lt. Art.
WHITE, J. W. S. S7551, ST, 24th Inf.
WHITE, James, S1894, SU, 63rd Inf.
WHITE, James L. S12507, MU, 6th (Wheeler's) Cav.
WHITE, James M. S12202, WE, 32nd Inf.
WHITE, Jasper, S15457, HD, Phillip's Co. Lt. Art.
WHITE, Jessee, S3218, HI, Baxter's Co. Lt. Art.
WHITE, John, S15138, O, 9th (Elliott's) Mo. Cav.
WHITE, John E. S6204, R, 1st (Carter's) Cav.
WHITE, Josie O. W1064, DE, White, Hugh L.
WHITE, Juda Catherine, W9949, CY, White, Eli E.
WHITE, L. H. S13294, D, Undetermined
WHITE, Laura E. W7307, WE, White, James E.
WHITE, Lillian Campbell, W8835, L, White, George H.
WHITE, Lizzie Fisher, W9826, MA, White, Hugh Lawson
WHITE, Lucy A. W6399, D, White, Isaiah
WHITE, M. D. S9825, SM, 4th (McLemore's) Cav.
WHITE, M. L. S4704, WY, 51st Inf.
WHITE, Malinda Jane, W625, G, White, Dancy
WHITE, Margaret E. W6417, WI, White, Benjamin Franklin
WHITE, Mary, W2903, HM, White, Jacob
WHITE, Mary Josephine, W1510, MS, White, Benjamin Franklin
WHITE, Mary Josephine, W2480, RU, White, Wm. Jasper
WHITE, Mary L. W736, D, White, Coleman
WHITE, Mary [Slonaker], W10738, WA, White, James Bishop, [Later married Slonaker]
WHITE, Matthias, S16026, S16316, MU, 9th Cav.
WHITE, Millie Ann, W8211, DI, White, Wm. Marshall
WHITE, Minnie, W10472, RU, White, Richard Henry
WHITE, Nancy Alabama, W606, MU, White, Daniel
WHITE, Nancy Ann, W467, CF, White, Robert Gilbert
WHITE, Ophelia, W7220, MU, White, James Lewis
WHITE, Parthena, W2773, LA, White, George Washington
WHITE, Parthena, W8279, DI, White, Daniel
WHITE, R. A. S2790, HE, 27th Inf.
WHITE, R. H. S1874, 15th Cav.
WHITE, Richard A. S613, HE, 31st Inf.
WHITE, Robert L. S1190, HY, 9th Inf.
WHITE, Robert T. S12735, SH, 2nd Inf.
WHITE, Ruth, W10279, BL, White, Isaac Easterly
WHITE, Sarah Annie, W7016, MU, White, Henry Reuben
WHITE, Sarah Elizabeth, W10746, LE, White, Mathias
WHITE, Sarah Elizabeth, W10993, RB, White, John James
WHITE, St. Leger, S8054, MU, 2nd (Robison's) Inf.
WHITE, T. B. S10690, SH, 1st Miss. Inf.
WHITE, T. H. S15012, RB, 14th Inf.
WHITE, T. J. S9232, G, 17th Inf.
WHITE, Thomas H. S16609, FR, 4th (McLemore's) Cav.
WHITE, Thomas William, S9101, SU, 63rd Inf.
WHITE, Virginia A. W10278, WE, White, James J.
WHITE, Virginia Annie, W5733, G, White, Wm. Hamilton
WHITE, W. C. S5077, HU, 24th Inf.
WHITE, W. C. S8113, G, 23rd Inf.
WHITE, W. I. S12320, HU, 11th Inf.
WHITE, W. J. S2842, RU, 24th Inf.
WHITE, W. M. S1381, DI, 11th Inf.
WHITE, W. M. T. S7120, D, 45th Inf.
WHITE, William David, S7665, GI, 53rd Inf.
WHITE, William H. S4249, HE, 53rd Inf.
WHITE, William H. S6026, W, 16th Inf.

Index to Tennessee Confederate Pension Applications

WHITE, William M. S14951, MR, 4th Ga. Cav.
WHITE, William T. S5216, WL, 24th Inf.
WHITE, William W. S9979, HE, 27th Inf.
WHITED, Matilda W. W98, WL, Whited, George
WHITEHEAD, Bettie T. W5533, RB, Whitehead, Robert Hardwood
WHITEHEAD, Caroline Isabella, W1169, D, Whitehead, Andrew Jackson
WHITEHEAD, Ella May, W7438, HY, Whitehead, Wm. Jasper
WHITEHEAD, Ellen Elizabeth, W4561, SH, Whitehead, Richard Cornelious
WHITEHEAD, Henry B. S14188, SH, 1st Hvy. Art.
WHITEHEAD, Hugh, S5155, DK, 16th Inf.
WHITEHEAD, James M. S5526, PU, 8th (Dibrell's) Cav.
WHITEHEAD, Joseph L. S3323, SH, 13th Inf.
WHITEHEAD, Louisa Jane, W2516, PU, Whitehead, James Madison
WHITEHEAD, Mary E. W2315, H, Whitehead, Isaac Thomas
WHITEHEAD, Mary T. W335, SM, Whitehead, John
WHITEHEAD, Rhoda Almira, W6632, MA, Whitehead, John Thomas
WHITEHEAD, Robert, S2568, MU, 9th Cav.
WHITEHEAD, W. J. S15143, HY, 38th Inf.
WHITEHEAD, William L. S6301, HD, 5th Miss. State Troops
WHITELAW, Bettie, W10419, HY, Whitelaw, J. P.
WHITELOW, Wright, C206, C236, HY, 7th & 3rd (Forrest) Cav.
WHITESCARVER, Maddaline, W1837, WL, Whitescarver, Reuben M.
WHITESCARVER, R. M. S6144, WL, 8th (Smith's) Cav.
WHITESHEAD, James M. S435, PU, 8th Cav.
WHITESIDE, Agnes Lipscomb, W5670, B, Whiteside, Henry Clay
WHITESIDE, Charlie, C113, HI, 48th Inf.
WHITESIDE, G. H. S11580, MU, 9th Bn. (Gantt's) Cav.
WHITESIDE, G. R. S6850, MU, 6th (Wheeler's) Cav.
WHITESIDE, J. T. S15537, MA, 6th Inf.
WHITESIDE, Nannie Lou, See Nannie Lou Lawrence
WHITESIDES, W. R. S12637, T, 17th S.C. Inf.
WHITFIELD, G. W. S4880, H, 1st Ala. Cav.
WHITFIELD, Henry, S16395, MT, 15th Ky. Cav.
WHITFIELD, J. W. S14011, GI, 3rd (Clack's) Inf.
WHITFIELD, Jennie Vaughn, W10900, MT, Whitfield, Harvey
WHITFIELD, Margaret A. W2526, BE, Whitfield, F. C.
WHITFIELD, S. C. S16287, WI, 24th Inf.
WHITFIELD, Sarah, W6550, H, Whitfield, Gordon W.
WHITFIELD, T. H. S15121, WI, 20th Inf.
WHITFORD, C. C. S14787, ST, 1st Hvy. Art.
WHITFORD, Jennie, W8441, ST, Whitford, Christopher Columbus
WHITLEY, Annie, W9165, W7537, CC, Whitley, Wiley Washington
WHITLEY, Drury A. S1844, WI, 1st Ark. Inf.
WHITLEY, J. W. S2423, GI, 53rd Inf.
WHITLEY, James, S6292, MU, 48th (Voorhies') Inf.
WHITLEY, Lillian, W9903, SH, Whitley, Rufus Daniel
WHITLEY, Mariah, W6173, D, Whitley, D. A.
WHITLEY, R. D. S15353, HR, 3rd N.C. Cav.
WHITLEY, W. W. S9720, CC, 1st Miss. Inf.
WHITLEY, William, S14925, O, 11th (Holman's) Cav.
WHITLOCK, Nat F. S6466, SU, 26th Inf.
WHITLOCK, S. M. S3387, CO, 62nd N.C. Inf.
WHITMAN, Virginia P. W10522, GI, Whitman, James Wm.
WHITNEY, Dan C. S10625, HM, 1st (White's) Special Bn. La. Inf.
WHITSETT, Sarah E. W6747, MS, Whitsett, John
WHITSITT, John C. S8043, WE, 16th Cav.
WHITSITT, Samuel Porter, S13745, D, 6th (Wheeler's) Cav.
WHITSON, Alzira, W5328, U, Whitson, John W.
WHITSON, Buena S. W6970, CY, Whitson, Andrew J.
WHITSON, Carrie Lee, W10017, W, Whitson, Wm. V.
WHITSON, John W. S12614, U, 29th N.C. Inf.
WHITSON, Louisa, W8186, LO, Whitson, Wm.
WHITSON, Stephen, S2807, FR, 5th Cav.
WHITSON, William, S5796, CO, 5th Cav.
WHITSON, William V. sr. S15479, W, 14th Cav.

WHITTAKER, James M. S3364, D, Lewis' Bn. Ala. Cav.
WHITTAKER, John Golithan, S2218, D, 23rd Inf.
WHITTAKER, John Harrison, S13921, PU, 25th Inf.
WHITTAKER, Mary A. W459, WY, Whittaker, Wm. Lion
WHITTAKER, Sue A. W9262, P, Whittaker, John Cary
WHITTEN, G. W. S4082, WY, 9th Cav.
WHITTEN, H. B. S5765, GE, 28th Va. Inf.
WHITTENBERG, Mary A. W768, H, Whittenberg, Wm. Wesley
WHITTHORNE, Rebecca Watson, W5341, MU, Whitthorne, Wm. J.
WHITTINGTON, Sallie E. W5369, JO, Whittington, W. W.
WHITTLE, Archimedes, S15825, R, 26th Inf.
WHITUS, Nancy L. W1174, B, Whitus, George W.
WHITUS, R. L. S14658, RU, 24th Inf.
WHITWELL, Mary M. W9742, MU, Whitwell, Thomas
WHITWORTH, Catherine, W844, MA, Whitworth, Ezekiel Travis
WHITWORTH, R. D. S8788, MA, 6th Inf.
WICKER, D. W. S252, O, 9th Inf.
WIDDERS, John A. S2343, S5756, UN, 31st Inf.
WIDENER, Fannie, W10424, WA, Widener, Elijah
WIDENER, J. M. S16487, UN, 13th Bn. Va. Reserves
WIDENER, M. T. S4635, LI, 12th Bn. Ala. Cav.
WIDENER, Nancy Ann Pickle, W9358, WA, Widener, L. M.
WIDICK, C. W. S6901, RB, 30th Inf.
WIDNER, L. M. S15093, WA, 63rd Va. Inf.
WIDNER, Rebecca J. W2571, CT, Widner, Cavin
WIERICK, James Larkin, S1378, R, 5th Cav.
WIERICK, Katie, W3697, R, Wierick, J. L.
WIERICK, Sarah, W2115, RO, Wierick, George W.
WIGGINS, James P. S3565, G, 17th Inf.
WIGGINS, Matilda Jane, W4477, HR, Wiggins, Wm. Henry
WIGGINS, Othella Swann, W7677, SH, Wiggins, Thomas J.
WIGGINS, William H. S6469, HR, 4th Inf.
WIGGS, Jennie L. W9029, MS, Wiggs, Irwin T.

WIGGS, Martha Emaline, W5291, D, Wiggs, T. W.
WIGGS, Mary Jane, W1721, RU, Wiggs, Daniel Patton
WIGGS, T. W. S8531, RU, 45th Inf.
WILBON, Mattie J. W3750, MA, Wilbon, John R.
WILBOURN, Mary S. W7068, F, Wilbourn, Jasper Gibbs
WILBOURNE, J. G. S11687, F, 1st Miss. Inf.
WILCOX, Dora, S11469, GU, 32nd Inf.
WILCOX, John B. S9259, CT, 23rd N.C. Inf.
WILCOX, Mary Eliza, W5479, SH, Wilcox, Thomas Wm.
WILCOX, William I. A. S15710, MS, 53rd Inf.
WILCOX, William Lewis, S10708, DY, 12th Cav.
WILDER, Charles, S4631, HA, 5th (McKenzie's) Cav.
WILDER, David, S4353, HA, 5th Cav.
WILDER, Jane, W1065, HA, Wilder, Thomas
WILDER, Mary, W769, HA, Wilder, Sterling
WILDER, Sarah Frances, W1376, BO, Wilder, Clark C.
WILDER, Thomas, S4718, GR, 5th (McKenzie's) Cav.
WILDS, George B. S16626, H, 7th Ky. Inf.
WILES, James P. S8676, SH, 15th Cav.
WILES, Martha Ann, W4033, LI, Wiles, Stephen P.
WILES, S. P. S3349, LI, 8th Inf.
WILES, William H. S1526, D, Undetermined
WILEY, James A. S9868, L, 2nd Miss. Cav.
WILEY, Martha C. W3274, Wiley, Samuel Houston
WILEY, Samuel H. S9597, 46th Inf.
WILEY, William H. S10032, MU, 9th Bn. (Gantt's) Cav.
WILHITE, E. M. S7084, PU, 13th Cav.
WILHITE, Halliad, S5192, WH, 8th Cav.
WILHITE, Rebecca Narcissa, W6886, PU, Wilhite, Elijah McCamal
WILHOIT, Elizabeth, W5996, GE, Wilhoit, Emanuel
WILHOIT, J. W. S15908, MOO, 41st Inf.
WILHOIT, P. R. S15797, H, 8th Ga. Inf.
WILHOIT, Virginia Moore, W9143, W9235, B, Wilhoit, Thomas Phillipp
WILIFORD, T. J. S5866, OV, 2nd (Ashby's) Cav.
WILKENS, Mary H. W10504, DK, Wilkens, James

WILKERSON, A. V. S881, WL, 7th Inf.
WILKERSON, Charles, C59, HY, 1st Cav.
WILKERSON, Dock W. S12166, HY, 45th Inf.
WILKERSON, G. W. S1864, RB, 4th Cav.
WILKERSON, John W. S8872, D, 18th Va. Inf.
WILKERSON, Letitia C. W2509, HR,
    Wilkerson, Thomas Owen
WILKERSON, Lucinda, W6001, RB,
    Wilkerson, Albert VanBuren
WILKERSON, Mary Ann, W805, DK,
    Wilkerson, Marion Francis
WILKERSON, W. A. S13585, F, 14th (Neely's) Cav.
WILKERSON, W. W. S614, DY, 5th Inf.
WILKERSON, William, S11538, H, 21st Ga. Inf.
WILKERSON, William H. S14364, LO, 63rd Inf.
WILKERSON, William W. S1567, G, 5th Inf.
WILKERSON, Zariak J. S14350, S15973, MS, 42nd Ga. Inf.
WILKES, Annie Heiskell, W10837, D, Wilkes, James Horace
WILKES, Dora Davis, W5519, MU, Wilkes, James Howell
WILKES, Effie, W9460, MS, Wilkes, Miceor E.
WILKES, Elvira O. W4177, MU, Wilkes, Richard Sparks
WILKES, Florence A. W5803, W, Wilkes, John I.
WILKES, J. W. S9799, SH, 18th Va. Inf.
WILKES, James H. S12615, MU, 3rd Ark. Cav.
WILKES, John I. S12705, WE, 24th Miss. Bn. Cav.
WILKES, John L. S8840, MU, 11th Cav.
WILKES, M. E. S8796, MS, 11th Cav.
WILKES, Nim, C1, MU, Forrest's Headquarters
WILKES, Sophia Emeline, W4235, HR, Wilkes, Benjamin
WILKES, Ulyses L. S12586, SN, 9th (Bennett's) Cav.
WILKINS, Isaac, S3873, K, 1st Northern Va. Engineer Corps
WILKINS, James (Bill), S16561, DK, Undetermined
WILKINS, James M. S6270, MU, 6th (Wheeler's) Cav.
WILKINS, Minnie Swayne, W10343, SH, Wilkins, Wm. Goodwin
WILKINS, Robert W. S9609, S15501, F, 51st Inf.

WILKINSON, Ann Eliza, W8840, GI, Wilkinson, Tyree Rhode
WILKINSON, Charles W. S4667, SN, 9th (Bennett's) Cav.
WILKINSON, Clara L. W8714, D, Wilkinson, Wm. Henry
WILKINSON, Emma Sue, W6264, FR, Wilkinson, John A.
WILKINSON, George H. S14068, RU, 1st (Feild's) Inf.
WILKINSON, John A. S8568, CF, 44th Inf.
WILKINSON, John R. S11421, MA, 4th (McLemore's) Cav.
WILKINSON, Louisa Catharine, W5778, HR, Wilkinson, Nathaniiel Lawrence
WILKINSON, N. L. S13381, HR, 14th Cav.
WILKINSON, Octavine, W7335, RU, Wilkinson, George H.
WILKINSON, Pleasant Fletcher, S12465, HR, 154th Sr. Regt. Inf.
WILKINSON, Sallie Elizabeth, W6240, MA, Wilkinson, John Robert
WILKINSON, Sallie Independence, W8473, HR, Wilkinson, Pleasant Fletcher
WILKINSON, Thomas J. S16525, SN, 22nd Cav.
WILKINSON, Thomas V. S14793, S10334, SH, 51st Inf.
WILKINSON, W. A. S13715, B, 1st (Feild's) Inf.
WILKINSON, William Henry, S1223, CO, 11th N.C. Inf.
WILKS, Elizabeth, W8943, L, Wilks, W. S.
WILKS, John T. S7745, SN, 2nd (Robison's) Inf.
WILKS, Josephine, W3729, SN, Wilks, Edward I.
WILKS, Sallie Gibson, W8664, SN, Wilks, John Talbas
WILKS, Sarah J. W3580, RB, Wilks, Thomas A.
WILLARD, D. B. S6690, WL, Allison's Squadron, Cav.
WILLARD, Lissie, W7239, WL, Willard, Daniel Burt
WILLBANKS, Ruth Minerva, W4838, LK, Willbanks, D. W.
WILLBANKS, W. D. S11676, LK, 7th Miss. Cav.
WILLCOX, Isaiah, S15463, JO, 65th N.C. Inf.
WILLEFORD, Robert P. S133, RU, 2nd Inf.
WILLEFORD, W. Y. S2392, GI, 32nd Inf.

Index to Tennessee Confederate Pension Applications

WILLETT, George W. S14790, WA, 3rd Conf. Engineers
WILLETTE, Ambrose, S1111, CO, 62nd Inf.
WILLHANKS, Margaret M. W8145, WE, Willhanks, John D.
WILLHOIT, Emanuel, S5169, GE, 64th N.C. Inf.
WILLIAMS, A. A. S6680, R, 43rd Inf.
WILLIAMS, A. F. S7893, SH, 1st (Turney's) Inf.
WILLIAMS, A. H. S9070, RU, Carter's Scouts
WILLIAMS, A. J. S341, WH, 28th Inf., Follows 342 on film
WILLIAMS, A. J. S7300, O, 7th Inf.
WILLIAMS, A. J. S10312, G, 9th (Bennett's) Cav.
WILLIAMS, A. M. S11077, CC, 51st Inf.
WILLIAMS, Adeline, W6872, WL, Williams, David Travis
WILLIAMS, Alexander L. P. S10723, RB, 56th Va. Inf.
WILLIAMS, Allen W. S5715, D, 24th Inf.
WILLIAMS, Alonia, W10434, DI, Williams, George Coleman
WILLIAMS, Anderson, S801, WL, 1st Cav.
WILLIAMS, Anderson, S4607, HA, 5th (McKenzie's) Cav.
WILLIAMS, Andrew F. S15559, HI, 20th Inf.
WILLIAMS, Ann, W2374, RU, Williams, Charlie Hay
WILLIAMS, Ann, W5918, SH, Williams, Absolum Flint
WILLIAMS, Annie Walker, W5611, G, Williams, W. Boyd
WILLIAMS, Artie Artelia, W7966, MA, Williams, James Lee
WILLIAMS, B. B. S1633, D, 2nd Ky. Cav.
WILLIAMS, B. M. S4119, CA, 8th (Smith's) Cav.
WILLIAMS, Barbara Ann, W2644, HN, Williams, John M. L.
WILLIAMS, Ben, S1462, MU, 53rd Inf.
WILLIAMS, Benjamin, S9471, GR, 1st (Carter's) Cav.
WILLIAMS, Benjamin Franklin, S2061, HI, Sparkman's Co. Lt. Art.
WILLIAMS, Bettie, W3795, G, Williams, John J.
WILLIAMS, Bettie, W10541, WL, Williams, Julius H.
WILLIAMS, C. M. S8703, GI, 32nd Inf.

WILLIAMS, Cassie C. W4008, D, Williams, Adolphus N.
WILLIAMS, Catherine A. W5223, WE, Williams, Jasper A.
WILLIAMS, Charity Bourne, W3507, MT, Williams, Henry A.
WILLIAMS, Charles P. S13823, GI, 53rd Inf.
WILLIAMS, Cordelia E. W7197, D, Williams, Wm. H. H.
WILLIAMS, Crofford, S13597, HN, 46th Inf.
WILLIAMS, D. A. S1670, CH, 6th Inf.
WILLIAMS, D. H. S10503, 27th Inf.
WILLIAMS, D. S. S5490, W, 4th (McLemore's) Cav.
WILLIAMS, D. T. S2282, WL, 7th Inf.
WILLIAMS, Delilah Norman, W6474, D, Williams, Anderson Franklin
WILLIAMS, Dilla, W6054, G, Williams, John Kirkpatrick
WILLIAMS, Eliza, W539, RU, Williams, John C.
WILLIAMS, Eliza A. W829, W750, TR, Williams, Allen Wade
WILLIAMS, Elizabeth, W5114, H, Williams, Andrew Alexander
WILLIAMS, Elizabeth, W11066, CF, Williams, U. B.
WILLIAMS, Elizabeth C. W2769, SU, Williams, Jeremiah
WILLIAMS, Elizabeth Melor, W2596, GI, Williams, Cuthbert Miles
WILLIAMS, Emma, W4356, MA, Williams, Hiram
WILLIAMS, F. G. S6038, DI, 11th Inf.
WILLIAMS, F. M. S744, 12th Inf.
WILLIAMS, F. M. S12071, SH, 18th Miss. Cav.
WILLIAMS, F. S. S12706, ST, 50th Inf.
WILLIAMS, Fannie, W889, CE, Williams, Thomas W.
WILLIAMS, Fannie, W9275, WL, Williams, Samuel C.
WILLIAMS, Freddie Maude, W10560, HY, Williams, John Thomas
WILLIAMS, Frederick, S6386, GR, 37th Inf.
WILLIAMS, G. H. C98, C225, RU, 18th Inf., 225 is missing.
WILLIAMS, G. L. S13608, MT, 2nd Ky. Cav.
WILLIAMS, G. P. S7566, L, 20th Inf.
WILLIAMS, G. W. S378, G, 12th Inf.
WILLIAMS, G. W. S8285, P, 48th Inf.
WILLIAMS, George ann, W5923, D, Williams, Adam

-373

Index to Tennessee Confederate Pension Applications

WILLIAMS, H. C. S12449, HN, 46th Inf.
WILLIAMS, H. K. S10056, DI, 49th Inf.
WILLIAMS, H. T. S4299, SN, 7th Inf.
WILLIAMS, H. T. S13433, WL, 7th Inf.
WILLIAMS, Harriet, W3863, WI, Williams, Henry
WILLIAMS, Henry, S9191, WI, 8th (Dibrell's) Cav.
WILLIAMS, Henry, S15231, H, 12th Ga. Cav.
WILLIAMS, Henry R. S14348, L, 19th & 20th (Consol.) Cav.
WILLIAMS, J. A. S3749, W, 24th Inf.
WILLIAMS, J. A. S4769, T, 12th Cav.
WILLIAMS, J. A. S9707, WE, 20th Ala. Inf.
WILLIAMS, J. B. S15778, MT, 14th Inf.
WILLIAMS, J. C. S8822, G, 12th Inf.
WILLIAMS, J. G. S8476, DY, 154th Sr. Regt. Inf.
WILLIAMS, J. H. S14883, WL, 8th (Smith's) Cav.
WILLIAMS, J. J. S2210, LI, 44th Inf.
WILLIAMS, J. M. S2824, OV, 28th Inf.
WILLIAMS, J. M. S3573, K, 29th Inf.
WILLIAMS, J. P. S14634, HR, 14th (Neely's) Cav.
WILLIAMS, J. R. S5447, WE, 7th Ky. Inf.
WILLIAMS, J. S. S9705, D, 30th Inf.
WILLIAMS, J. T. S8187, WH, 8th (Dibrell's) Cav.
WILLIAMS, J. T. S12656, GE, 19th Inf.
WILLIAMS, J. W. S1153, 4th Cav.
WILLIAMS, J. W. S4180, J, 4th Cav.
WILLIAMS, J. W. S8970, FR, 17th Inf.
WILLIAMS, James, S556, MR, 11th Inf.
WILLIAMS, James, S11296, H, 31st Inf.
WILLIAMS, James H. S360, SM, 24th Inf.
WILLIAMS, James H. S4941, T, 51st Inf.
WILLIAMS, James L. S6676, D, 6th (Wheeler's) Cav.
WILLIAMS, James L. S10289, MA, 27th Inf.
WILLIAMS, James N. S7466, CH, 6th Inf.
WILLIAMS, James P. S16362, D, 2nd (Robison's) Inf.
WILLIAMS, James R. S21, WE, 3rd Ky. Inf.
WILLIAMS, James W. S10795, 12th Inf.
WILLIAMS, James W. S16340, WI, 4th (McLemore's) Cav.
WILLIAMS, Jerry, S3019, S4071, SU, 59th Inf.
WILLIAMS, Jesse Wesley, S9036, RU, 8th (Smith's) Cav.
WILLIAMS, John, S2465, CY, 1st Cav.
WILLIAMS, John C. S783, RU, 18th Inf.

WILLIAMS, John D. S3687, WA, 60th Inf.
WILLIAMS, John F. S6409, CF, 55th Ala. Inf.
WILLIAMS, John F. S15468, HW, 31st Inf.
WILLIAMS, John H. S3862, DK, 1st Ark. Mtd. Riflemen
WILLIAMS, John H. S12829, H, 46th Va. Inf.
WILLIAMS, John J. S3089, G, 12th Inf.
WILLIAMS, John L. S9653, ME, 5th (McKenzie's) Cav.
WILLIAMS, John M. S16549, CH, 6th Inf.
WILLIAMS, John R. D. S16158, GI, 9th Bn. (Gantt's) Cav.
WILLIAMS, John S. S16005, DY, 22nd Inf.
WILLIAMS, John T. S5310, G, 12th Inf.
WILLIAMS, John W. S2436, MN, 19th Cav.
WILLIAMS, John W. S6475, 8th Ark. Inf.
WILLIAMS, Jones, S6978, G, 14th Tex. Cav.
WILLIAMS, Joseph F. S4103, SN, 7th Inf.
WILLIAMS, Joseph P. S6716, HM, 61st Inf.
WILLIAMS, Joseph P. S12756, MT, 14th Inf.
WILLIAMS, Josephus W. S1615, 4th Cav.
WILLIAMS, Kibbie, W9918, WL, Williams, James A.
WILLIAMS, Kitty, W9893, RU, Williams, Charlie Richard
WILLIAMS, L. F. S7689, SM, 44th Inf.
WILLIAMS, L. S. S13421, CF, 41st Inf.
WILLIAMS, Laura, W5250, D, Williams, J. L.
WILLIAMS, Laura E. W2504, GE, Williams, John H.
WILLIAMS, Laura Gillikin, W10307, K, Williams, W. S.
WILLIAMS, Lemuel, S4811, T, 51st Inf.
WILLIAMS, Linnie, W5170, DY, Williams, Samuel Anderson
WILLIAMS, Lou Anne, W6868, MT, Williams, Thomas M.
WILLIAMS, Lucinda, W2168, HU, Williams, Wm. M.
WILLIAMS, Lucy Adams, W6159, T, Williams, Felix Grundy
WILLIAMS, Luke Lee, S7162, HR, 154th Sr. Regt. Inf.
WILLIAMS, M. C. S12646, HM, 37th N.C. Inf.
WILLIAMS, M. L. S16670, SH, 12th Inf.
WILLIAMS, M. P. S4639, MS, 35th Inf.
WILLIAMS, Maggie, W10847, GI, Williams, John R. D.
WILLIAMS, Malvina, W739, D, Williams, Wm. Alexander
WILLIAMS, Margaret Jane, W10895, MU, Williams, Joel Hubble

WILLIAMS, Martha Ann, W2645, HN, Williams, William Cleavelan
WILLIAMS, Martha Elizabeth, W2626, HW, Williams, Wm. Louis
WILLIAMS, Martha J. W7354, SE, Williams, Wm. O.
WILLIAMS, Martha Jane, W6761, D, Williams, Phillip W.
WILLIAMS, Martha Lucretia, W2389, J, Williams, James Whitson
WILLIAMS, Martha Matilda, W2021, Williams, Joe Washington
WILLIAMS, Mary, W5619, PU, Williams, Wm.
WILLIAMS, Mary Catherine, W1942, T, Williams, James Harvey
WILLIAMS, Mary Emeline, W1423, WE, Williams, Wm. Henry
WILLIAMS, Mary Jane, W5400, MA, Williams, D. A. Follows 5265 on Soldiers film
WILLIAMS, Mary M. W5483, MU, Williams, Robert Nichols
WILLIAMS, Mary S. W4636, GE, Williams, Thomas L.
WILLIAMS, Mary Sarah, W3290, SU, Williams, Gustavus A.
WILLIAMS, Matilda Agnes, W8546, D, Williams, James Madison
WILLIAMS, Mattie J. W5993, G, Williams, Zackaria Nowell
WILLIAMS, Milliyan M. E. W9377, MC, Williams, H. P.
WILLIAMS, N. B. S6689, CF, 24th Inf.
WILLIAMS, N. C. S5589, B, 2nd Cav.
WILLIAMS, N. J. S13459, ST, 33rd Inf.
WILLIAMS, Nackie, W8256, WL, Williams, Howell W.
WILLIAMS, Nancy, W6728, PU, Williams, James M.
WILLIAMS, Nancy J. W6006, FR, Williams, L. Shaw
WILLIAMS, Nancy Manuriah, W3011, RU, Williams, Wm. Burton
WILLIAMS, Nash, S12913, RU, Huggin's Co. Lt. Art.
WILLIAMS, P. T. S8403, O, 33rd Inf.
WILLIAMS, Paralee, W10440, Williams, James W.
WILLIAMS, Pollie, W2154, J, Williams, Isac
WILLIAMS, Polly Ann, W1753, SM, Williams, Anderson
WILLIAMS, R. C. S3038, CF, 2nd Ala. Inf.
WILLIAMS, R. J. S14308, CH, 6th Inf.
WILLIAMS, Rachel A. W3223, WL, Williams, Newton J.
WILLIAMS, Rebecca, W999, HN, Williams, Harrison
WILLIAMS, Rebecca F. W883, GI, Williams, Thomas Benton
WILLIAMS, Rebecca Jane, W5530, G, Williams, John Thomas
WILLIAMS, S. B. S7827, G, 19th (Biffle's) Cav.
WILLIAMS, S. G. S3566, HN, 46th Inf.
WILLIAMS, S. H. S11451, G, 5th (McKenzie's) Cav.
WILLIAMS, Sallie, W8481, O, Williams, Andrew Jackson
WILLIAMS, Samuel F. S727, MC, 2nd Ark. Inf.
WILLIAMS, Sarah E. W1388, HM, Williams, Joseph P.
WILLIAMS, Sarah E. W3490, RU, Williams, Jesse W.
WILLIAMS, Sarah J. W3181, K, Williams, Samuel Jackson
WILLIAMS, Sarah J. W6633, DI, Williams, Henry K.
WILLIAMS, Sarah Katherine, W9065, MU, Williams, Edward Thomas
WILLIAMS, Stanfield F. S1359, WI, 32nd Inf.
WILLIAMS, Susan, W1689, HI, Williams, George W.
WILLIAMS, Susan, W10889, SU, Croom, John Wilson, See Also Susan Croom
WILLIAMS, Susan Angline, W3160, WE, Williams, Samuel
WILLIAMS, Susan Mildred, W3034, K, Williams, James W.
WILLIAMS, Sylvester J. S10825, D, 20th Inf.
WILLIAMS, T. F. S9242, HN, 46th Inf.
WILLIAMS, Thomas J. S8050, J, 4th Cav.
WILLIAMS, Thomas M. S8813, MT, 8th Ky. Mtd. Inf.
WILLIAMS, Thomas Samuel, S13947, S10752, MU, 11th (Holman's) Cav.
WILLIAMS, Thomas W. S3673, DI, Harding's Lt. Art.
WILLIAMS, Tillie W. W8057, H, Williams, John Henry
WILLIAMS, U. A. S14460, HU, 37th Ala. Inf.
WILLIAMS, Virginia E. W2375, CC, Williams, R. G.
WILLIAMS, W. A. S3220, D, 14th Inf.
WILLIAMS, W. B. S9626, G, 12th Inf.
WILLIAMS, W. H. H. S6456, D, 38th Inf.

Index to Tennessee Confederate Pension Applications

WILLIAMS, W. H. H. S7753, SH, Forrest's Old Regt. Cav.
WILLIAMS, W. J. S4326, WL, 45th Inf.
WILLIAMS, W. M. S5311, WH, 6th Ala. Inf.
WILLIAMS, W. P. S13413, G, Unassigned (Got up cattle beef)
WILLIAMS, W. R. S2440, MO, 31st Inf.
WILLIAMS, W. T. S15748, D, 9th (Ward's) Cav.
WILLIAMS, W. W. S3098, FR, 1st (Turney's) Inf.
WILLIAMS, William, S3574, G, Undetermined
WILLIAMS, William B. S7791, RU, 2nd (Robison's) Inf.
WILLIAMS, William Duncan, S16664, D, Morgan's Scouts
WILLIAMS, William O. S7998, SE, 29th Va. Inf.
WILLIAMS, Wm. P. S2271, WH, 28th Inf.
WILLIAMS, Z. M. S14596, G, Carter's Scouts, Cav.
WILLIAMSON, A. K. S9416, PU, 17th Inf.
WILLIAMSON, Bettie Carter, W9167, MA, Williamson, John George
WILLIAMSON, C. A. S9431, J, Cleburn's Escort, Cav.
WILLIAMSON, Charles C. S8619, CF, 29th Inf.
WILLIAMSON, Elizabeth F. W8175, MR, Williamson, John A.
WILLIAMSON, Elizabeth Jane, W906, Williamson, George W.
WILLIAMSON, Fannie, W7161, G, Williamson, W. Y.
WILLIAMSON, G. S5032, DY, 12th Inf.
WILLIAMSON, Isaac W. S5204, LI, 41st Inf.
WILLIAMSON, J. F. S11660, MA, 14th Cav.
WILLIAMSON, J. G. S16416, MA, 16th Ga. Inf.
WILLIAMSON, J. H. S2310, GI, 3rd Inf.
WILLIAMSON, John A. S11840, MR, 44th Inf.
WILLIAMSON, Joseph Mitchell, S16009, J, 17th Inf.
WILLIAMSON, Katherine, W7380, Williamson, Sylvanus Walker
WILLIAMSON, Martha Ann, W9705, J, Williamson, Joseph Mitchel
WILLIAMSON, Mary, W10627, LI, Williamson, Isaac Wesley
WILLIAMSON, Mary Ellen, W271, SH, Williamson, Francis Henry
WILLIAMSON, Nancy Rebecca, W7280, DY, Williamson, George Washington
WILLIAMSON, S. W. S7510, 12th Inf.
WILLIAMSON, Sammie L. W4009, D, Williamson, James Polk
WILLIAMSON, Sarah Jane, W228, GI, Williamson, Robert Rush
WILLIAMSON, Susan Jane, W3901, PO, Williamson, John Coffee
WILLIAMSON, T. T. S3088, K, 6th S.C. Inf.
WILLIAMSON, Tinsley R. S2035, WA, 28th Va. Inf.
WILLIAMSON, W. R. S2174, MOO, 41st Inf.
WILLIAMSON, W. W. S16121, S15443, FR, 6th Ala. Cav.
WILLIAMSON, W. Y. S15209, G, 47th Inf.
WILLIAMSON, Wesley H. S2112, 11th Cav.
WILLIAMSON, William R. S5312, MA, 6th Inf.
WILLIFORD, David J. S16615, SH, 7th N.C. Inf.
WILLIFORD, Eula D. W10806, SH, Williford, David Judson
WILLIFORD, W. D. S14403, SH, 44th Miss. Inf.
WILLIN, John, S3101, SU, Undetermined
WILLING, David, S10103, HM, 1st (Carter's) Cav.
WILLINGHAM, Alice Ann, W7516, H, Willingham, John Wesley
WILLINGS, George W. S6549, JE, 31st Inf.
WILLIS, A. H. S5532, HM, 37th Inf.
WILLIS, C. M. S9004, L, 15th Cav.
WILLIS, Catherine Anderson, W8569, FR, Willis, Wilson
WILLIS, John M. S9383, ME, 5th (McKenzie's) Cav.
WILLIS, M. E. C. S12985, S10380, HW, 2nd (Ashby's) Cav.
WILLIS, Mary, W7718, HM, Willis, A. H.
WILLIS, Sallie N. W3002, MT, Willis, L. R.
WILLIS, Texana, W7229, RO, Willis, John M.
WILLIS, Thomas W. S16137, RB, 30th Inf.
WILLIS, William M. S12104, MU, Sparkman's Co. Lt. Art.
WILLKIE, Ellen Brennan, W3945, D, Willkie, Pinkney Octavius
WILLOUGHBY, E. R. S12941, CC, 19th & 20th Consol. Cav.
WILLOUGHBY, Frances C. Marshall, W8603, MT, Willoughby, John Henry
WILLOUGHBY, William H. S7342, HN, 46th Inf.
WILLS, H. J. S15132, WL, Shaw's Bn. Cav.
WILLS, Mary C. W3841, HW, Wills, Henry

WILLS, W. S6823, D, 1st (Feild's) Inf.
WILLS, W. H. S1073, S547, SU, 29th Inf.
WILLSHIRE, Maggie, W4213, SH, Willshire, James Dillard
WILLSHIRE, W. T. S10117, SH, Ballentine's Miss. Cav.
WILLSON, E. W. S3250, RB, 14th Inf.
WILLSON, Jeptha, S8498, MC, 62nd N.C. Inf.
WILLSON, William, S3906, SE, 8th (Smith's) Cav.
WILMETH, B. W. S3594, HM, 3rd Va. Cav.
WILMOT, Carrie V. W5151, B, Wilmot, Daniel Hix
WILMOTH, John C. S11061, HW, 42nd Va. Inf.
WILSON, A. R. S6775, MT, 42nd Inf.
WILSON, A. S. S2927, SU, 4th Va. Inf.
WILSON, Alice B. W9324, MU, Wilson, John J.
WILSON, Amanda M. W9713, H, Wilson, Wm. Moore
WILSON, Amanda Melvina, W966, MR, Wilson, Nathaniel
WILSON, Annie Elizer, W4041, CF, Wilson, Francis Marion
WILSON, B. F. S13073, CE, 49th Inf.
WILSON, Benjamin T. S8179, WI, 45th Inf.
WILSON, C. J. S10639, RB, 2nd Ky. Cav.
WILSON, C. P. S6039, HW, 31st Inf.
WILSON, C. P. S7965, G, 16th Cav.
WILSON, Caroline, W10235, CF, Wilson, C. B.
WILSON, Carrie E. W2760, HN, Wilson, Robert A.
WILSON, Catherine Josephine, W6546, SH, Wilson, John McCamy
WILSON, Celey Ann, W5697, ST, Wilson, John Decalb
WILSON, Charles Calhoun, S13210, SH, Hardie's Bn. Ala. Cav.
WILSON, Crocket, S12900, WL, 25th Inf.
WILSON, Daniel W. S11516, SH, 11th Inf.
WILSON, David H. S13743, RU, 11th (Holman's) Cav.
WILSON, E. W. See E. W. Willson
WILSON, Ed, S1632, WL, 24th Inf.
WILSON, Edward, S13335, U, 58th N.C. Inf.
WILSON, Elisha, S196, RB, 14th Inf.
WILSON, Eliza Ann, W6903, D, Wilson, Thomas Henry
WILSON, Eliza Melvin, W555, WI, Wilson, Reuben
WILSON, Ellen Ward, W10700, H, Wilson, Leroy Halsey

WILSON, Emma Fox, W10991, MS, Wilson, Isaac William
WILSON, Florence, W9714, GI, Wilson, Frank F.
WILSON, Franklin F. S8465, GI, 53rd Inf.
WILSON, Frederic N. S8713, HN, 46th Inf.
WILSON, G. W. S14242, L, 12th Inf.
WILSON, George W. S4343, H, 1st Inf.
WILSON, H. S5961, HN, 20th Inf.
WILSON, H. R. S4501, RU, 24th Inf.
WILSON, Henry, S14560, WY, 3rd Ala. Cav.
WILSON, Isaac W. S8301, MS, 17th Inf.
WILSON, J. B. S13912, G, 12th Inf.
WILSON, J. C. S6053, S8164, RB, 1st (Feild's) Inf.
WILSON, J. D. S11753, MO, 59th Inf.
WILSON, J. E. S12992, F, 13th Inf.
WILSON, J. F. S3768, SH, 38th Inf.
WILSON, J. F. S11525, GI, 20th (Nixon's) Cav.
WILSON, J. H. S15523, R, 26th Inf.
WILSON, J. P. S11099, MN, 21st (Wilson's) Cav.
WILSON, J. W. S4870, SH, 25th Inf.
WILSON, J. W. S16294, RB, 1st Cav.
WILSON, Jack, S5313, MOO, Hudson's Battery, Miss.
WILSON, James C. S2851, GU, 14th Inf.
WILSON, James M. D. S195, CF, 8th Inf.
WILSON, Jeptha, See Jeptha Willson
WILSON, Jesse, S8069, T, 8th (Dibrell's) Cav.
WILSON, Joel E. S8659, HE, 51st Inf.
WILSON, John, S8879, LO, 1st Cav.
WILSON, John A. S13251, SH, 12th (Green's) Cav.
WILSON, John B. S4342, B, 22nd Ala. Inf.
WILSON, John Hamilton, S5356, MC, 16th Cav.
WILSON, John M. S8296, HE, 15th Miss. Vols.
WILSON, John M. S15257, WE, 33rd Inf.
WILSON, John M. S15547, G, 1st (Carter's) Cav.
WILSON, John Milton, S8761, WI, 44th Inf.
WILSON, John O. S9339, SH, 19th (Biffle's) Cav.
WILSON, John T. S3108, LI, 1st Inf.
WILSON, John W. S567, RU, 2nd Inf.
WILSON, John W. S5448, SH, Undetermined
WILSON, Joseph P. S13495, P, 42nd Inf.
WILSON, Josephine Salina, W8411, SH, Wilson, C. C.
WILSON, Josephus C. S16183, RB, 1st (Feild's) Inf.

WILSON, Kate, W3997, WL, Wilson, H. B.
WILSON, Leroy H. S16103, H, 4th Ala. Cav.
WILSON, Louisa Ann, W7132, H, Wilson, John Holmes
WILSON, Louiza, W5240, H, Wilson, John H.
WILSON, Lucendia Coldonia, W9603, LO, Wilson, John H.
WILSON, M. H. S3480, W, 35th Inf.
WILSON, M. L. S221, O, 24th Inf.
WILSON, Manda M. W1674, CF, Wilson, Wm. P.
WILSON, Manervia, W416, OV, Wilson, Wm. H.
WILSON, Margarette, W1808, RB, Wilson, Elisha
WILSON, Marina V. W5028, MT, Wilson, Amos Ross
WILSON, Martha Ann, W5194, HE, Wilson, John M.
WILSON, Martha Cunningham, W9094, D, Wilson, Wm. Thomas
WILSON, Martha Elizabeth, W5575, HE, Wilson, Joel E.
WILSON, Martha S. W7557, WI, Wilson, John M.
WILSON, Mary, W1819, MOO, Wilson, A. J.
WILSON, Mary E. W324, WI, Wilson, Samuel B.
WILSON, Mary E. W1922, RB, Wilson, John Wesley
WILSON, Mary Elizabeth, W3771, RB, Wilson, John
WILSON, Mary Elizabeth, W10883, SH, Wilson, Wm. Blackstock
WILSON, Mary Ella, W3736, G, Wilson, Wm. Hugh
WILSON, Mary Emma, W10019, SH, Wilson, Joseph C.
WILSON, Mary M. W3182, CA, Wilson, Martin V.
WILSON, Mary Rebecca, W3455, SH, Wilson, George Washington
WILSON, Matthew G. S15404, LO, 1st Regt. Hvy. Art.
WILSON, Minerva, W10975, CF, Wilson, Wm. Franklin
WILSON, Mollie Ladora, W7967, HR, Wilson, Charles Milton
WILSON, Nancy Julie, W6167, P, Wilson, Joseph P.
WILSON, O. T. S10893, BE, 5th Inf.
WILSON, Overton, S10347, OV, 25th Inf.
WILSON, P. G. S9592, SH, 34th Miss. Vols.
WILSON, Patrick, S790, CA, 4th Cav.
WILSON, R. A. S2151, HN, 46th Inf.
WILSON, R. J. S8218, BR, 29th Inf.
WILSON, Rachel Joan, W2334, DI, Wilson, Wm. Wesley
WILSON, Reubin, S3417, WI, 11th Cav.
WILSON, Ruth Berrien, W3752, K, Wilson, Christopher Jenkins
WILSON, Sallie, W7538, CF, Wilson, John Wesley
WILSON, Sallie B. W9503, SH, Wilson, John Alexander
WILSON, Samuel Franklin, S12865, SN, 2nd (Robison's) Inf.
WILSON, Samuel M. S5222, LO, 43rd Inf.
WILSON, Samuel O. S13125, O, 15th Cav.
WILSON, Sarah, W3835, SH, Wilson, John Oscar
WILSON, Sarah Elizabeth, W5098, MT, Wilson, Cave Johnson
WILSON, Sarah Jane, W5675, Wilson, George W.
WILSON, Saretha G. W6751, F, Wilson, J. E.
WILSON, Temple C. S4045, T, 3rd Ark. Inf.
WILSON, Tennessee Irene, W703, HN, Wilson, Hardin
WILSON, Thomas H. S8912, RU, 1st Inf.
WILSON, Thomas J. S9962, RU, 20th Inf.
WILSON, Thomas Wesley, S1042, W, 35th Inf.
WILSON, W. J. S5389, WH, 8th Cav.
WILSON, W. J. S14568, H, 26th Ga. Inf.
WILSON, W. M. S1653, G, 11th Cav.
WILSON, W. M. S5723, MC, 43rd Inf.
WILSON, W. M. S15634, D, 8th (Smith's) Cav.
WILSON, W. P. S3463, CF, 18th Inf.
WILSON, W. S. S11590, HN, 7th Cav.
WILSON, William, See also William Willson
WILSON, William D. S311, HN, 46th Inf.
WILSON, William D. S3332, HW, 45th Inf.
WILSON, William Morgan, S4257, D, 6th (Wheeler's) Cav.
WILSON, William N. S10654, JO, 33rd Inf.
WILSON, William Newton, S2887, DK, 4th Cav.
WILSON, William T. S12311, SN, 17th Inf.
WILSON, William W. S111, WI, 10th Cav.
WILSON, Winnie C. W6470, JO, Wilson, Wm. N.
WILY, John, S7340, MU, 9th Bn. Cav.
WIMBERLEY, A. J. S11988, HN, 21st (Wilson's) Cav.

Index to Tennessee Confederate Pension Applications

WIMBERLEY, F. N. S1679, G, 5th Inf.
WIMBERLEY, Ida May, W9028, ST, Wimberley, John S. P.
WIMBERLEY, Mary Louise, W2316, GU, Wimberley, James Claiborn
WIMBERLY, B. F. S7956, G, 46th Inf.
WIMBERLY, G. W. S12419, DI, 23rd Inf.
WIMBERLY, Jane, W6065, CA, Wimberly, John Carroll
WIMBERLY, John S. P. S14688, ST, 14th Inf.
WIMBERLY, Sarah Louisa, W4883, CA, Wimberly, Wm. Alfred
WIMBERLY, W. A. S2283, CA, 23rd Inf.
WIMBERLY, W. D. S6430, HN, 46th Inf.
WINBURN, Hepsey Elizabeth, W5429, CC, Winburn, Henry Clay
WINCHESTER, Coleman, S13999, HN, 2nd Ky. Cav.
WINCHESTER, Elizabeth, W10285, HN, Winchester, Coleman
WINDLE, Mary Clementine, W2155, OV, Windle, Alfred Lafayette
WINDLE, W. W. S9243, OV, 8th Inf.
WINDROW, Wyatt, C251, RU, Regiment not given
WINFIELD, Henry, C282, SH, Bodyguard to Jeff Davis
WINFIELD, Minerva M. W3381, RB, Winfield, Wm. Seal
WINFORD, Benjamin F. S11719, LI, 32nd Inf.
WINFORD, Nicey Pinkney, W3070, LI, Winford, George Riley
WINFORD, W. W. S9082, B, 32nd Inf.
WINFREE, B. C. S4266, SM, 24th Inf.
WINFREE, H. q. S7842, DK, 5th Inf.
WINFREE, Mary S. W8318, SM, Winfree, Thomas L.
WINFREE, Nancy S. W3119, DK, Winfree, Henry L.
WINFREY, A. J. S12354, D, 22nd (Barteau's) Cav.
WINFREY, James H. S5846, HW, 29th Inf.
WINFREY, Reubin G. S12019, RU, 23rd Inf.
WINFREY, W. B. S10125, SM, 44th Inf.
WINGO, Margaret Carolyn, W6989, HO, Wingo, Robert Anderson
WINGO, Mary C. W6209, Wingo, T. R.
WINGO, Robert A. S13551, HO, 2nd Ky. Cav.
WINHAM, James, S7003, SN, 7th Inf.
WINKLE, Mary M. W4060, GE, Winkle, Jacob
WINKLER, Carrie Alice, W6906, D, Winkler, Peyton Herbert
WINKLER, Peyton H. S7224, D, 30th Inf.
WINKLER, Sarah, W1835, D, Winkler, W. B.
WINN, Flora [Sutton], W11010, MO, Winn, Robert R. [Later married Sutton]
WINN, John W. S12548, B, 55th Inf.
WINN, L. Z. S15970, B, 11th (Holman's) Cav.
WINN, Peter T. S5091, T, 1st Hvy. Art.
WINN, R. R. S3269, MO, 37th Ga. Inf.
WINN, William Riley, S11217, MS, 8th (Smith's) Cav.
WINN, Wilson, S9985, MT, 14th Inf.
WINNETT, Martha Ann, W5515, B, Winnett, Elkanah
WINNETT, P. C. W146, CF, Winnett, Thomas M.
WINSET, Delaney Helen, W10602, O, Winset, Wm. Robert
WINSETT, William R. S477, BL, 1st Cav.
WINSTEAD, Alice, W527, HU, Winstead, Thomas Hartford
WINSTEAD, Bridget A. W3796, K, Winstead, W. D.
WINSTEAD, William D. S180, K, 16th N.C. Inf.
WINSTON, Maniel, C155, SH, 9th Inf.
WINSTON, Thirza, W3082, WE, Winston, James M.
WINTER, Nora Ann, W7657, JE, Winter, Edward White
WINTERS, A. B. S8946, HO, 46th Inf.
WINTERS, John A. S5623, RB, 11th Inf.
WINTERS, Mary F. W4504, HO, Winters, A. B.
WINTERTON, Katherine, W2633, SH, Winterton, Thomas
WINTON, John, S8613, CF, 28th Cav.
WINTON, Matilda Elizabeth, W4734, CF, Winton, Wm. Blanton
WIRT, J. D. S6717, F, Forrest's Old Regt. Cav.
WIRYCK, James A. S2038, RO, 62nd Inf.
WISDOM, J. M. S15180, O, 20th Cav.
WISE, Anderson, S1122, CO, 50th Inf.
WISE, Mary Ann, W74, MOO, Wise, James W.
WISE, Tracy Byrum, W4178, MA, Wise, Wm. Pleasant
WISE, W. P. S10220, MA, Carne's Battery, Art.
WISEHART, Benjamin L. S142, HN, 5th Inf.
WISEHART, Sallie E. W10462, HN, Wisehart, George W.
WISEMAN, A. N. S8710, S8003, 20th (Nixon's) Cav.
WISEMAN, Audley, S6697, W, 35th Inf.
WISEMAN, Elijah, S3967, B, 7th Inf.

WISEMAN, Howell, S13435, TR, 30th Inf.
WISEMAN, John W. S229, TR, 9th Cav.
WISEMAN, Liza Ann, W5866, Wiseman, Alfred Newton
WISEMAN, Mary E. See Mary E. Oglesby
WISEMAN, Mary M. W8289, O, Wiseman, James P.
WISEMAN, Nancy C. W87, FR, Wiseman, Wiley M.
WISEMAN, Robert C. S2839, MOO, 41st Inf.
WISEMAN, Sallie E. W2, B, Wiseman, Wm. Robert
WISEMAN, Sarah F. W6457, W9403, W, Wiseman, Andley
WISEMAN, W. J. S13664, HN, 20th (Nixon's) Cav.
WISEMAN, W. Y. S10165, SN, 9th Cav.
WISENER, F. H. S2340, OV, 28th Inf.
WISENER, Susan Joanna, W1571, OV, Wisener, Felix Harbert
WISER, Docie, W2140, RU, Wiser, Wm. Harrison
WISER, J. M. S8058, PU, 8th (Dibrell's) Cav.
WISER, John M. S8538, CF, 4th Cav.
WISER, John W. S7640, CF, 24th Inf.
WISER, Mary E. W5437, CF, Wiser, John W.
WISER, Oregon T. W5195, CF, Wiser, John M.
WISER, William H. S8028, RU, 44th Inf.
WITCHER, James, S3792, SU, 8th (Smith's) Cav.
WITHAM, A. E. S16036, SH, 1st Conf. Cav.
WITHAM, Mollie J. W9725, SH, Witham, A. E.
WITHERINGTON, Melvina A. W10721, G, Witherington, Stephen
WITHERS, George W. S1939, D, 30th Inf.
WITHERS, James, C133, SH, 3rd Miss. Cav.
WITHERSPOON,   See also Weatherspoon
WITHERSPOON, E. F. S11228, MA, 12th Ky. Cav.
WITHERSPOON, Gaines Cicero, S13941, WL, 8th (Smith's) Cav.
WITHERSPOON, H. H. S11861, MA, 7th (Duckworth's) Cav.
WITHERSPOON, J. M. S593, G, 31st Inf.
WITHERSPOON, T. J. S16566, WE, 31st Inf.
WITHERSPOON, William, S11572, MA, 7th (Duckworth's) Cav.
WITT, Hughes Taylor, S7274, HM, 60th Inf.
WITT, John H. S4701, PO, 29th Inf.
WITT, Mollie, W2883, G, Witt, Caleb Jasper
WITT, N. B. S5342, PO, 36th Inf.

WITT, Sallie Ann, W8276, SU, Witt, Wm. Henry
WITT, William H. S10057, SU, 61st Inf.
WITTINGTON, Susan E. W7443, MU, Wittington, Aurelius K.
WITTY, Sallie Ann (Jewell), W10886, WL, Witty, Hiram Carpenter
WIX, W. A. S13134, R, 18th S.C. Inf.
WOFFORD, Mark. J. S3959, H, Lookout Art.
WOHLFORD, R. L. S14855, HM, 50th Va. Inf.
WOLAVER, G. W. S2073, LI, 12th Inf.
WOLF, Alfred, S1133, S733, MR, 29th Inf.
WOLF, C. F. S8368, SU, 59th Inf.
WOLF, E. H. S10917, GR, 26th Inf.
WOLF, Ella M. W3031, HW, Wolf, James K.
WOLFE, E. S. S11310, WA, 59th Inf.
WOLFE, F. M. S11192, SU, White's Co. Sullivan County Reserves
WOLFE, Jane, W2947, HA, Wolfe, Elijah
WOLFE, John, S4354, HA, 5th Cav.
WOLFE, Malissa C. W4720, SU, Wolfe, Creed F.
WOLFE, Mary P. W8451, WA, Wolfe, Elbert S.
WOLFE, Nicholas, S4527, HA, 5th (McKenzie's) Cav.
WOLFE, Robert E. S10258, SU, 51st Va. Inf.
WOLFE, Virginia A. W2536, SU, Wolfe, Virginia A.
WOLFENBARGER, Martha, W1330, HA, Wolfenbarger, George F.
WOLFORD, Elkand D. S10531, SU, 60th Inf.
WOLFORD, Frances V. W4782, SU, Wolford, Elkanah D.
WOLFORD, Sallie Mauk, W9478, WA, Wolford, Jacob Droke
WOLFORD, William G. S11169, SU, 19th Inf.
WOLFORD, William M. S8264, SU, 60th Inf.
WOMACK, A. E. S322, W, 23rd Inf.
WOMACK, A. J. S5808, FR, 17th Inf.
WOMACK, Catherine S. W433, FR, Womack, Wm. R.
WOMACK, Daniel, S8841, MC, 5th Cav.
WOMACK, F. G. S6960, W, 16th Inf.
WOMACK, F. M. S10999, CF, 24th Inf.
WOMACK, J. M. S4987, M, 35th Inf.
WOMACK, J. P. S15122, D, 18th Inf.
WOMACK, James J. S3639, W, 16th Inf.
WOMACK, Jordan Hale, S7019, LA, Forrest's Escort, Cav.
WOMACK, Mary O. W9463, CF, Womack, F. M.

Index to Tennessee Confederate Pension Applications

WOMACK, Milanda, W2019, W, Womack, Amos Edward
WOMACK, Nannie, W3624, M, Womack, John Mulican
WOMACK, Nola [Lawson], W10663, SH, Womack, John, [Later married Lawson]
WOMACK, Sarepta E. W2472, MC, Womack, Daniel
WOMACK, T. N. S4581, GI, 8th Inf.
WOMACK, W. R. S1765, FR, 5th Ky. Inf.
WOMACK, Wiley G. S3205, CF, 17th Bn. (Newman's) Cav.
WOMACK, William D. S1320, SN, 5th Inf.
WOMACK, William H. S8459, SM, 28th Inf.
WOOD, Adelia C. W6102, PU, Wood, John P.
WOOD, Arlene V. W7394, HM, Wood, Joseph Robert
WOOD, C. C. S9435, SH, 6th Inf.
WOOD, David Thompson, S12842, RU, 11th (Holman's) Cav.
WOOD, Elizabeth, W6324, A, Wood, Alfred Jefferson
WOOD, Emma Smothers, W9338, CC, Wood, Francis John
WOOD, F. J. S8715, CC, 27th Inf.
WOOD, F. M. S1354, DE, 10th Cav.
WOOD, G. K. S4563, HU, 1st (Feild's) Inf.
WOOD, Georgia Ann, W4267, HD, Wood, James J.
WOOD, Henry Milton, S3091, G, 12th Inf.
WOOD, J. A. S12883, SU, 48th Va. Inf.
WOOD, J. J. S3471, HD, 12th Miss. Cav.
WOOD, James, S4706, MS, 32nd Inf.
WOOD, John P. S10282, OV, 3rd Engineer Troops
WOOD, John W. S9877, SU, 48th Inf.
WOOD, Joseph R. S2046, S2939, HM, 3rd Regt. Engineer Corps
WOOD, Levy Bennett, S12799, HM, 9th Inf.
WOOD, Linnie J. W2294, CA, Wood, Wm. Jackson
WOOD, Lodica D. W1123, RU, Wood, Andrew J.
WOOD, Luke, S12727, H, 21st Ga. Inf.
WOOD, Lydia A. W4428, D, Wood, R. F.
WOOD, M. E. C222, H, Undetermined
WOOD, Margaret Lucy, W7906, HR, Wood, Nathaniel E.
WOOD, Martha Caroline, W4310, MA, Wood, Wm. Phillip
WOOD, Mary E. W8952, H, Wood, Luke
WOOD, Mary Jane, W6597, HM, Wood, Levi Bennett
WOOD, Mary P. W3499, SH, Wood, Wm. Harvey
WOOD, Mary T. W7106, RU, Wood, David Thompson
WOOD, Nancy Mahalia, W8563, WE, Wood, Wm. K.
WOOD, Nathaniel Ellis, S11117, HR, Forrest's Old Regt. Cav.
WOOD, R. F. S12918, D, Carter's Scouts, Cav.
WOOD, Sarah Ruth, W4563, SU, Wood, John W.
WOOD, Sophronia E. W3431, D, Wood, W. H.
WOOD, T. W. S8922, B, 18th Inf.
WOOD, Thomas R. S12191, MA, 19th (Biffle's) Cav.
WOOD, W. B. S869, MU, 48th Inf.
WOOD, W. H. S1327, GR, 62nd Ga. Inf.
WOOD, W. H. S7996, D, 9th Bn. Cav.
WOOD, W. P. S6776, HD, 18th (Newsom's) Cav.
WOOD, William D. S7004, W, 16th Inf.
WOOD, William Morrison, S12290, SU, Va. Military Institute
WOODALL, Ada, W2328, RB, Woodall, Thomas Christopher
WOODALL, Lemina, W9162, MS, Woodall, Wm. Preston
WOODALL, Mary Allen, W6940, MT, Woodall, Wiley W.
WOODALL, Thomas C. S6788, RB, 7th Inf.
WOODALL, W. P. S15199, MS, 11th (Holman's) Cav.
WOODALL, Wesley C. S1360, RU, 44th Inf.
WOODALL, Wiley W. S9095, MT, 42nd Inf.
WOODARD, Emma, W10957, LI, Woodard, John W.
WOODARD, Emma Bradshaw, W5139, LI, Woodard, J. L.
WOODARD, H. T. S9532, LI, 32nd Inf.
WOODARD, J. J. S10566, GI, 48th (Voorhies') Inf.
WOODARD, J. W. S14134, LI, 44th Inf.
WOODARD, James R. S3261, LI, 1st (Turney's) Inf.
WOODARD, Lucinda, W3783, U, Woodard, B. W.
WOODARD, Margaret Catharine, W5265, B, Woodard, Wm. Robert

-381

Index to Tennessee Confederate Pension Applications

WOODARD, Richard J. S2222, S5156, GI, 11th Cav., 5156 immediately precedes 2222 on film
WOODARD, Tabitha Almeda, W4663, GI, Woodard, Thomas Newton
WOODARD, W. R. S6289, MOO, 19th Inf.
WOODFIN, Elizabeth Frances, W6645, MR, Woodfin, Samuel Chose
WOODFIN, Mary E. W9106, RU, Woodfin, Hugh Lawson White
WOODFIN, S. C. S6732, MR, 18th Inf.
WOODLEE, Jane, W6698, GU, Woodlee, James Jefferson
WOODMORE, John F. S904, MT, 50th Inf.
WOODROOF, Lucretia, W2118, RU, Woodroof, James Thomas
WOODROOF, Rebecca A. W2914, D, Woodroof, Richard
WOODRUFF, John W. S11581, D, Unassigned (Gunsmith)
WOODRUFF, Mattie White, W7155, D, Woodruff, John White
WOODRUFF, W. F. S8635, MOO, 8th Inf.
WOODRUFF, W. H. S5509, CH, 21st (Wilson's) Cav.
WOODRUM, William S. S12675, WL, 45th Inf.
WOODS, D. W. S6910, LI, 35th Ala. Inf.
WOODS, F. T. S8263, T, 2nd Tex. Inf.
WOODS, G. W. S1783, MOO, 17th Inf.
WOODS, H. C. S14050, O, 2nd Va. Cav.
WOODS, J. B. S4283, W, 8th (Dibrell's) Cav.
WOODS, J. F. S10113, K, 52nd Ga. Inf.
WOODS, J. H. C. S3584, LI, 41st Inf.
WOODS, James, S15610, D, 1st Art.
WOODS, John, C264, LE, Undetermined
WOODS, John W. S6467, HI, 9th Bn. (Gantt's) Cav.
WOODS, Joseph, S8155, A, 4th Cav.
WOODS, Kate Duffy, W9852, CE, Woods, James Campbell
WOODS, Leah Clementine, W3740, HR, Woods, James Allen
WOODS, Louisa Jane, W9263, H, Woods, William I.
WOODS, Mary Ann, W6591, DE, Woods, Franklin Marion
WOODS, Mattie, W7199, W7485, SH, Woods, F. T. 7485 is missing
WOODS, Nancy E. W811, HI, Woods, John W.
WOODS, Nannie, W2969, LI, Woods, J. H. C.
WOODS, Nannie M. W3087, D, Woods, Garland
WOODS, Rachel, W1820, SU, Woods, Isaac
WOODS, Sallie Hayes, W9026, O, Woods, Henry Clay
WOODS, Smith, C77, DY, 20th Cav.
WOODS, Susan, W1707, SU, Woods, Wm. Jackson
WOODS, Thomas H. S14894, B, 17th Inf.
WOODS, W. H. S8628, 55th Inf.
WOODS, William Robinson, S14258, HR, 12th Cav.
WOODSON, Armindia A. W6248, SH, Woodson, Thomas Stanley
WOODSON, J. N. S13639, MT, 14th Inf.
WOODSON, Susan Frances, W3318, MA, Woodson, Peter S.
WOODSON, Thomas S. S12676, MT, 1st Ky. Inf.
WOODWARD, Charles B. S10336, K, 52nd Ga. Inf.
WOODWARD, Mary A. W8928, MS, Woodward, E. W.
WOODWARD, Nannie D. W5133, DE, Woodward, Wm. W.
WOODWARD, Sarah Jain, W2407, CL, Woodward, Alexander Fletcher
WOODWARD, W. J. S7398, SN, 2nd Cav.
WOODWARD, W. Ward, S4289, DE, Norfolk's Lt. Art. Va.
WOODY, Alexander, S2312, CU, 16th Bn. Cav.
WOODY, David, S3532, R, 16th Bn. (Neal's) Cav.
WOODY, Elizabeth, W5762, CO, Woody, James
WOODY, Harrison, S16285, CU, 28th Inf.
WOODY, James, S1898, CO, 60th N.C. Inf.
WOODY, James, S12800, RO, 62nd Inf.
WOODY, Nancy Jane, W7208, K, Woody, Wm. Marion
WOODY, Polly Ann, W2134, CU, Woody, Preston Alexander
WOODY, S. S. S11713, O, Sparkman's Co. Lt. Art.
WOODY, Sarah, W8582, CO, Woody, W. J.
WOODY, Susan, W4913, R, Woody, David
WOODY, W. J. S10451, JE, 5th (McKenzie's) Cav.
WOODY, W. M. S7772, K, 60th N.C. Inf.
WOOLARD, Fannie, W9276, WL, Woolard, James A.
WOOLAVER, J. W. S1455, A, 29th Inf.
WOOLAVER, Mary E. W1387, MS, Woolaver, Robert G.

Index to Tennessee Confederate Pension Applications

WOOLBRIGHT, Harriet, W3058, D, Woolbright, Asa Chandler
WOOLBRIGHT, Randle, S13281, MT, 25th Inf.
WOOLDRIDGE, D. H. S3739, WE, 14th Cav.
WOOLDRIDGE, Mollie C. W1141, SH, Wooldridge, J. Alex
WOOLLARD, M. B. S13474, WL, 28th Inf.
WOOLVERTON, B. S. S8439, HR, 21st Cav.
WOOSLEY, Ann Elizabeth, W4111, B, Woosley, John Crawford
WOOSLEY, Arabella Josephine, W8499, B, Woosley, Thomas Alexander
WOOSLEY, G. P. S4692, B, Jackson's Co. Forrest's Escort, Cav.
WOOSLEY, Rebecca Jane, W10722, B, Woosley, Giles Polk
WOOSLEY, Thomas A. S4347, B, 17th Inf.
WOOSLEY, William C. S4464, B, 41st Inf.
WOOTEN, A. J. S8506, H, 6th Ga. Cav.
WOOTEN, A. W. S16504, LA, 3rd Inf.
WOOTEN, Arrie Elizabeth, W6962, H, Wooten, Wm. Dow
WOOTEN, B. H. S10230, GU, 50th Inf.
WOOTEN, Bailey P. S7527, RU, 4th Inf.
WOOTEN, Cornelia J. W10842, LA, Wooten, Albert Washington
WOOTEN, J. B. S16058.5, CF, 4th N.C. Inf.
WOOTEN, J. C. S5463, B, 41st Inf.
WOOTEN, J. D. S7068, CA, 35th Inf.
WOOTEN, Mary Ann, W615, PU, Wooten, Benjamin Harrison
WOOTEN, Mary Matilda, W2003, CF, Wooten, W. J.
WOOTEN, Parlee, W2123, SM, Wooten, Robert W.
WOOTEN, W. B. S3065, SM, 9th Cav.
WOOTON, Fanny H. W5292, CF, Wooton, Jonathan D.
WOOTON, Martha Elizabeth, W1191, CA, Wooton, Jesse David
WOOTTEN, William B. S6824, SM, 9th (Ward's) Cav.
WORD, George, C28, G, 20th Cav.
WORD, R. Q. S14201, RU, 7th Inf.
WORK, Malissa Tennessee, W7456, DI, Work, Robert J.
WORK, R. J. S7999, DI, 11th Inf.
WORK, Susan Ann, W6865, D, Work, Wm. Lovill
WORKMAN, I. E. S8240, MU, 15th Cav.
WORKMAN, James E. S13744, SU, 14th N.C. Inf.
WORKMAN, Martha Adeline, W6729, SU, Workman, James Ellis
WORKMAN, Mathias G. S7717, WE, 61st Ky. Capitol Guards
WORKMAN, Samuel, S14580, MC, 8th Mo. Inf.
WORLEY, Arrie Malinda, W2283, WH, Worley, James
WORLEY, D. B. S1193, CY, 5th Inf.
WORLEY, David, S961, OV, 5th Inf.
WORLEY, David B. S4683, DK, 16th Inf.
WORLEY, J. M. S9731, HI, 48th (Voorhies') Inf.
WORLEY, James, S7324, WH, 52nd Ga. Inf.
WORLEY, Lucy Elender, W646, SN, Worley, John Wm.
WORLEY, Martha Ella, W3170, SU, Worley, Elbert Sevier
WORLEY, Mary Elizabeth, W2020, DK, Worley, David Benjamin
WORLEY, T. C. S15062, D, 11th (Holman's) Cav.
WORLEY, William, S4408, LI, 28th Inf.
WORRELL, Amanda J. W6574, CC, Worrell, James Ransom
WORRICK, James H. S3558, CF, 4th Cav.
WORSHAM, George W. S1724, GI, 1st Cav.
WORSHAM, Nettie Garrett, W9510, W6031, MR, Worsham, Wm. Johnson
WORTHAM, W. E. S6148, ST, 15th Inf.
WORTHINGTON, C. C. S16309, BL, 13th (Gore's) Cav.
WORTHINGTON, Margaret, W2478, H, Worthington, Wm.
WORTHINGTON, Mary, W7200, R, Worthington, S. P.
WORTHINGTON, Mary A. W468, GR, Worthington, Shubal G.
WORTHINGTON, Mary Addie, W9595, G, Worthington, Daniel
WORTHINGTON, S. P. S11857, BL, 2nd (Ashby's) Cav.
WORTHINGTON, Samuel M. S4063, A, 19th Inf.
WORTHINGTON, Samuel sr. S14895, V, 16th Inf.
WORTHINGTON, Sarah Catherine, W1535, A, Worthington, Jesse Brown
WRAGG, J. L. S9761, SH, 1st Ga. Cav.
WRAGG, Sarah Elizabeth, W3911, SH, Wragg, James Langdon
WRAY, A. E. S3851, WL, 45th Inf.

WRAY, Emily F. W9529, SN, Wray, George F.
WRAY, George F. S11133, SN, 20th Inf.
WRAY, J. B. S11206, SH, 28th Miss. Cav.
WRAY, Martha T. W6372, SH, Wray, James Bennett
WRAY, Mary Elizabeth, W1899, WL, Wray, A. E.
WRAY, Porcia Hayes, W3998, MA, Wray, Granville Webster
WRAY, R. G. S4064, HI, 9th Cav.
WRAY, Tula Coleman, W3889, D, Wray, Wm. Anderson
WRAY, W. E. S8767, CC, 35th Ga. Inf.
WREN, J. H. S2732, MN, 31st Inf.
WREN, John M. S7877, G, Caruther's Battery, Hvy. Art.
WREN, Nancy J. W7738, G, Wren, John M.
WRENCH, Elizabeth Jane, W8847, SH, Wrench, T. W.
WRIGHT, A. S3474, RO, Thomas' Legion, N.C.
WRIGHT, Aaron Hampton, S7086, D, 20th Inf.
WRIGHT, Aaron S. S1159, HW, 31st Inf.
WRIGHT, Albert A. S8165, LI, Huggin's Co. Lt. Art.
WRIGHT, Alfred, S12066, GE, 25th N.C. Inf.
WRIGHT, Amos Lafayette, S12014, 21st (Wilson's) Cav.
WRIGHT, Andrew J. S3418, WI, 20th Inf.
WRIGHT, Anna, W10778, RO, Wright, W. J.
WRIGHT, Austin, C280, T, 7th Cav.
WRIGHT, Bettie C. W8484, SH, Wright, James
WRIGHT, C. B. S11214, M, 24th Inf.
WRIGHT, Charles Erin, W6895, Wright, Wm. M.
WRIGHT, Christiana Snider, W6383, W7347, MA, Wright, Noell Zachariah
WRIGHT, Clementine, W7130, RO, Wright, A.
WRIGHT, Clinton, S6063, G, 1st Md. Cav.
WRIGHT, D. L. S7734, SN, 30th Inf.
WRIGHT, Delia E. W5146, G, Wright, Benjamin P.
WRIGHT, Eldridge, S10846, WE, 31st Inf.
WRIGHT, Elender Bethena, W2730, W, Wright, James Walker
WRIGHT, Eli J. S4067, DK, 5th Inf.
WRIGHT, Elizabeth, W4632, RU, Wright, James W.
WRIGHT, Elizabeth Jane, W2952, D, Wright, John Edward
WRIGHT, Enoch P. S1274, CL, 37th Inf.
WRIGHT, Evalina C. W7539, W9394, G, Wright, John C.

WRIGHT, Evelyn Clay, W9394, W7539, G, Wright, John Calvin
WRIGHT, F. B. S7556, HI, 24th Inf.
WRIGHT, Fannie Cursey, W3120, G, Wright, Clinton
WRIGHT, Fredrica Oliver, W10505, SH, Wright, Jesse Clay
WRIGHT, George G. S13255, MN, 2nd Ky. Cav.
WRIGHT, Harvey J. S13297, SH, 38th Inf.
WRIGHT, Henry J. S728, DE, 1st Cav.
WRIGHT, Isaac, S6248, MS, 24th Inf.
WRIGHT, J. G. S3679, WI, 20th Inf.
WRIGHT, J. J. S7467, SH, 15th Cav.
WRIGHT, J. W. S7740, CH, 32nd Inf.
WRIGHT, James, S2324, MC, 16th Cav.
WRIGHT, James M. S3855, H, 19th Inf.
WRIGHT, James S. S11896, WL, 45th Inf.
WRIGHT, James W. S1641, W, 16th Inf.
WRIGHT, James W. S10504, D, 20th Inf.
WRIGHT, John, S9498, GE, 29th N.C. Inf.
WRIGHT, John Bell, S13287, DY, 15th Cav.
WRIGHT, John C. S15139, G, 22nd Inf.
WRIGHT, John H. S3715, MC, 7th Inf.
WRIGHT, John T. S15364, D, 8th (Smith's) Cav.
WRIGHT, John Thomas, S13112, MU, 19th (Biffle's) Cav.
WRIGHT, John W. S10066, SH, 13th Inf.
WRIGHT, Joseph B. S6851, MU, 9th Bn. Cav.
WRIGHT, Joseph M. S10982, HM, 12th Bn. (Day's) Cav.
WRIGHT, Joseph Thomas, S10247, D, 11th Cav.
WRIGHT, L. B. S7714, K, 6th Inf.
WRIGHT, L. D. S15374, DI, 11th (Holman's) Cav.
WRIGHT, Lecy Elizabeth, W5737, DI, Wright, Wm.
WRIGHT, Lillie Mai, W11025, WI, Wright, Andrew Jackson
WRIGHT, Louisa Jane, W3195, HM, Wright, Jacob
WRIGHT, Malinda, W7616, K, Wright, James
WRIGHT, Martha Jane, W3022, MU, Wright, J. B.
WRIGHT, Martha S. W1248, WL, Wright, Josiah H.
WRIGHT, Mary J. W4837, SN, Wright, Scroggins
WRIGHT, Mary Jane, W6463, W8319, D, Wright, Wm. Alexander

Index to Tennessee Confederate Pension Applications

WRIGHT, Mattie Jane, W9072, GI, Wright, J. M.
WRIGHT, Moses W. S11692, WL, 20th Inf.
WRIGHT, Nancy, W5463, MC, Wright, John Henry
WRIGHT, Nancy Caroline, W2141, WH, Wright, Wesley Deskin
WRIGHT, Penelope E. W6914, SN, Wright, Robert Barr
WRIGHT, Polly Ann, W88, MC, Wright, Thomas
WRIGHT, R. B. S6683, SN, 2nd (Robison's) Inf.
WRIGHT, R. H. S5977, CH, 14th Cav.
WRIGHT, R. Jane, W3201, WL, Wright, James L.
WRIGHT, Rachel Ann, W8744, WL, Wright, Moses Washington
WRIGHT, Richard H. S7060, MA, 38th Inf.
WRIGHT, S. Columbus, S10930, HN, 7th (Duckworth's) Cav.
WRIGHT, S. F. S12843, W, 16th Inf.
WRIGHT, Sallie H. W2456, O, Wright, Robert M.
WRIGHT, Sallie J. W8608, W8801, MU, Wright, Wm. Newton
WRIGHT, Sallie Jane, W5118, MU, Wright, John Thomas
WRIGHT, Sarah A. W8345, MU, Wright, Perrin
WRIGHT, Sarah Tennessee, W6992, D, Wright, Wade Hampton
WRIGHT, Scoggins, S7835, SN, 30th Inf.
WRIGHT, Sparrell B. S6377, K, 11th Va. Inf.
WRIGHT, Susan Adeline, W2335, MU, Wright, George Franklin
WRIGHT, Susan Frances, W10879, MA, Wright, Sterling Columbus
WRIGHT, T. C. S4732, RO, Thomas' Legion, N.C.
WRIGHT, Thomas, S1106, MO, 63rd Inf.
WRIGHT, Thomas P. S7809, RU, 24th Inf.
WRIGHT, Thomas Porter, S12517, HN, 7th Ark. Inf.
WRIGHT, Thomas W. S13113, RU, 45th Inf.
WRIGHT, W. M. S1549, DE, 1st Cav.
WRIGHT, W. M. S7810, DI, 10th (DeMoss') Cav.
WRIGHT, W. T. S11062, D, 20th Inf.
WRIGHT, W. a. S10135, D, 16th Bn. Cav.
WRIGHT, Wade H. S3990, D, 20th Inf.
WRIGHT, William, S14585, GI, 1st (Carter's) Cav.
WRIGHT, William H. S15069, BR, 62nd Inf.
WRIGHT, William J. S13293, RO, Kain's Battery, Lt. Art.
WRIGHT, William M. S1199, DE, 1st Cav.
WRIGHT, William N. S13806, MU, 32nd Inf.
WRINKLE, Parilee B. W7913, Wrinkle, Amos Lafayette
WRYE, James M. S5476, D, 38th Inf.
WRYE, Nancy Tennessee, W3801, D, Wrye, Wm. Henry
WRYE, William H. S8627, WL, 45th Inf.
WYATT, Billie, C165, LK, 3rd Mo. Cav.
WYATT, Frances, W5035, MN, Wyatt, James Wm.
WYATT, G. H. S8556, HR, 18th Cav.
WYATT, I. W. S11101, ST, 50th Inf.
WYATT, J. F. S7627, DI, 24th Bn. Sharpshooters
WYATT, J. W. S4116, MN, 28th Inf.
WYATT, J. W. S5736, DE, 52nd Inf.
WYATT, James A. S10487, GR, 37th Inf.
WYATT, James S. S9153, SH, 38th Inf.
WYATT, James W. S3085, MN, 8th Inf.
WYATT, L. L. S2928, MN, 28th Ala. Inf.
WYATT, Marion, S7721, CH, 22nd Inf.
WYATT, Martha Jane, W5027, W4781, GR, Wyatt, James Alexander
WYATT, Mary Adaline, W7037, ST, Wyatt, Irvin
WYATT, Mary E. W5710, SH, Wyatt, James Summerfield
WYATT, Nancy A. W3361, DI, Wyatt, Wm. A.
WYATT, Nancy E. W2065, DE, Wyatt, Jessee
WYATT, Richard F. S9292, GR, 37th Inf.
WYATT, Sarah Elizabeth, W9959, W4776, MA, Wyatt, Warren A.
WYATT, Stephen, S6358, SU, 63rd Va. Inf.
WYATT, William, S784, DE, 27th Inf.
WYCUFF, Caroline, W2253, R, Wycuff, James K. P.
WYCUFF, James K. P. S1275, S1432, S1475, R, 62nd Inf., 1275 is ripped and missing contents
WYLIE, Charles P. S8142, D, 22nd (Barteau's) Cav.
WYLIE, Cynthia Indiana, W8356, SH, Wylie, James Lewis
WYLIE, Emma L. W3084, D, Wylie, Charles P.
WYLIE, James Lewis, S6238, SH, 12th Cav.
WYLIE, Mollie F. W4275, SH, Wylie, Cyrus
WYLLIE, Allen L. S13501, SN, 2nd (Robison's) Inf.

-385

Index to Tennessee Confederate Pension Applications

WYLY, J. Harris, S14647, BE, 3rd Mtd. Inf.
WYNIGER, Rebecca Ann, W10621, HN, Wyniger, James J.
WYNN, Belle, W4828, RB, Wynn, John Henderson
WYNNE, Jemima Powell, W260, D, Wynne, John J.
WYNNE, John G. S2412, DY, Bell's Brigade
WYNNE, John H. S10644, WL, 4th (McLemore's) Cav.
WYNNE, L. A. S15889, D, 3rd (Consol.) Inf.
WYNNE, Ora, W9736, DY, Wynne, John Goodman
WYNNE, Sallie A. W6176, WL, Wynne, John Henry
WYNNS, George H. S15969, HN, 5th Inf.
WYNNS, J. Whit, S14142, D, 22nd (Barteau's) Cav.
WYNNS, Rhoda Elizabeth, W9004, D, Wynns, Joel Whitten
WYONT, Nannie Duke, W11157, G, Wyont, David Hosea, 11157 also has papers from other app's.
WYRICK, Eliza Jane, W9866, JE, Wyrick, Philip
WYRICK, JAmes A. S14586, GR, 2nd (Ashby's) Cav.
WYRICK, John, S7701, C, 36th Va. Inf.
WYRICK, Nannie Emiline, W8799, K, Wyrick, James Harvey
WYRICK, Phillip, S8134, S14928, K, 1st (Carter's) Cav.
WYRICK, Soloman, S8274, DY, 1st Cav.
YACHRA, Larkran, S3534, O, 3rd Miss. Cav.
YADEN, T. H. S3000, GR, 37th Inf.
YADON, Joseph, S14989, UN, 1st (Carter's) Cav.
YANCEY, Callie F. W4978, SH, Yancey, James Edwin
YANCEY, L. F. S7072, F, 7th (Duckworth's) Cav.
YANCEY, Thomas, S421, G, 12th Inf.
YANCEY, William F. S10026, MA, 19th & 20th (Consol.) Cav.
YANSEY, George W. C207, O, 4th Ga.
YARBER, Nancy, W4325, MC, Yarber, Newton
YARBER, Newton, S7427, MO, 63rd Inf.
YARBOROUGH, Mickie J. W7493, SH, Yarborough, John J.
YARBOROUGH, William R. A. S4940, D, 22nd Ala. Inf.
YARBRO, John T. S13181, DE, 10th Cav.

YARBROUGH, F. A. S5314, FR, 4th Cav.
YARBROUGH, G. W. S14067, MS, 32nd Inf.
YARBROUGH, George W. S14246, 20th Cav.
YARBROUGH, J. M. S5810, MS, 8th (Smith's) Cav.
YARBROUGH, J. S. S6084, MS, 4th Cav.
YARBROUGH, J. W. S4779, SH, 7th Cav.
YARBROUGH, John E. S2604, RB, 2nd Inf.
YARBROUGH, Linsey, S1523, MR, 19th Ala. Inf.
YARBROUGH, Lucretia, W5013, HR, Yarbrough, Wm. Ira
YARBROUGH, Lucy, W8735, MS, Yarbrough, George Whitfield
YARBROUGH, Lydia C. W2276, D, Yarbrough, W. R. A.
YARBROUGH, Miles, S6271, ST, 50th Inf.
YARBROUGH, N. E. S6556, ST, 14th Inf.
YARBROUGH, R. A. S2735, GI, 11th Cav.
YARBROUGH, Sallie Frances, W3014, DI, Yarbrough, Thomas Luis
YARBROUGH, Sarah Elizabeth, W8549, HR, Yarbrough, John Crocket
YARBROUGH, W. C. S6139, MN, 21st (Wilson's) Cav.
YARBROUGH, W. J. S6263, HR, 14th Cav.
YARNELL, Mary, W4021, A, Yarnell, Joseph
YARNELL, Rachell, W3977, A, Yarnell, Richard H.
YARNELL, Sofrona A. W10271, A, Yarnell, Milton Tate
YATES, Calvin, S243, D, 5th Inf.
YATES, Columbus, S11065, LO, 6th Ga. Cav.
YATES, D. A. S16455, CT, 1st N.C. Inf.
YATES, Elizabeth, W4579, LO, Yates, Columbus
YATES, Elizabeth A. W1366, F, Yates, Ed A.
YATES, Emma L. W3303, MT, Yates, H. A.
YATES, J. H. S5825, RB, 9th Miss. Inf.
YATES, J. K. P. S4309, RO, 16th Cav.
YATES, J. M. S16147, G, 5th Ky. Cav.
YATES, James M. S15801, G, 5th Inf.
YATES, James P. S122, CF, 44th Inf.
YATES, Larkin, S3769, V, 5th Cav.
YATES, Louiza Jane, W6611, CO, Yates, Nathaniel
YATES, Lydia Jane, W4630, RB, Yates, James Henry
YATES, M. S15104, G, 12th Ky. Cav.
YATES, Martha, W5592, MO, Yates, James
YATES, Mary Ann, W2086, GI, Yates, Charles E.

386-

YATES, Mathew, S8076, G, 7th Ky. Cav.
YATES, Nellie L. W4986, D, Yates, Thomas James
YATES, P. C. S271, SH, 13th Inf.
YATES, Robert H. S657, LO, 21st Va. Inf.
YATES, Sarah C. W3091, D, Yates, Alvin
YATES, Virginia Ann, W2566, HN, Yates, Thomas Jefferson
YATES, W. H. S15182, SH, 13th Inf.
YEAMAN, Minerva, W1699, SM, Yeaman, Nathaniel T.
YEARGAN, C. H. S7225, DK, Allison's Squadron, Cav.
YEARMAN, R. H. S9806, SM, 9th (Ward's) Cav.
YEARWOOD, James H. S1625, GE, 5th S.C. Inf.
YEARWOOD, Nancy Adalaid, W5410, GE, Yearwood, J. H.
YEARY, W. W. S8593, CL, 50th Va. Inf.
YEATMAN, Mollie Hill, W6673, K, Yeatman, Wm. Eugene
YEATMAN, William Eugene, S12942, K, 2nd (Robison's) Inf.
YERBER, Newton, S4559, MO, 63rd Inf.
YEWS, William Thomas, S4481, CH, 6th (Wheeler's) Cav.
YOAKLEY, Elizabeth E. W7591, SU, Yoakley, Wm. F.
YOE, Ann Eliza, W2073, K, Yoe, John Wm.
YOKELEY, A. D. S8488, GI, 53rd Inf.
YOKELEY, P. H. S15895, GI, Farris' Bn. Mo. Lt. Art.
YOKLEY, Ann Rebecca, W6941, GI, Yokley, Andrew Dean
YOKLEY, E. H. S12830, JO, 54th N.C. Inf.
YOKLEY, E. M. S16308, W, 2nd Cav.
YOKLEY, N. A. S7573, MR, 4th Ky. Cav.
YORK, Elizabeth Frances, W6678, CC, York, Wm. Blackburn
YORK, Jennie, W8684, SH, York, Moses Alexander
YORK, Lizzie, W9836, W, York, Eli Milton
YORK, Margaret Rachel, W4075, WI, York, John W.
YORK, Mary D. W1655, SU, York, Uriah L.
YORK, Moses Alexander, S10435, T, 19th (Biffle's) Cav.
YORK, William B. S12078, CC, 6th Inf.
YOST, George Anna, W7241, GE, Yost, Henry Clay

YOST, H. C. S14923, GE, 63rd Inf.
YOST, J. M. S8602, SU, Unassigned (Nitre & Mining Bureau)
YOST, Rebecca Ellen, W4333, SU, Yost, James McCoy
YOUNG, A. A. H. S14681, L, 9th Inf.
YOUNG, Alfred, S8757, GI, 3rd Inf.
YOUNG, Amelia A. W8054, L, Young, A. H. H.
YOUNG, Belle V. W9598, LI, Young, John Wm.
YOUNG, Catherine Annette, W5245, WH, Young, Charles Coller
YOUNG, Charles C. S13767, WH, 41st Inf.
YOUNG, Clementine Steel, W8206, SU, Young, Thomas Patterson
YOUNG, D. C. S3138, S9037, O, 26th Inf.
YOUNG, D. E. S10455, HN, 5th Inf.
YOUNG, D. N. S14579, 55th Inf.
YOUNG, E. J. S3604, W, 3rd Hvy. Art.
YOUNG, Eliz. Rebecca Carol. W7688, D, Young, Wm. Henry
YOUNG, Emma C. W10272, D, Young, Jacob
YOUNG, Emma M. W6363, L, Young, G. Whit
YOUNG, Eugenia Judson, W3479, MA, Young, Benjamin Franklin
YOUNG, Fanny, W3478, GI, Young, Alfred
YOUNG, Frances, W3253, RU, Young, W. C.
YOUNG, Frances Elizabeth, W8791, SM, Young, Lewis H.
YOUNG, G. W. S3744, FR, 1st (Turney's) Inf.
YOUNG, G. W. S13972, L, 7th (Duckworth's) Cav.
YOUNG, Gabriel, S8135, LI, 41st Inf.
YOUNG, Isaiah F. S697, H, 6th Ala. Inf.
YOUNG, J. A. S12882, RU, 6th (Wheeler's) Cav.
YOUNG, J. B. S7828, WL, 4th (McLemore's) Cav.
YOUNG, J. H. S11629, HY, 35th Miss. Inf.
YOUNG, J. M. S14071, MA, 6th Cav.
YOUNG, J. P. S3998, GU, 1st (Turney's) Inf.
YOUNG, J. W. S9134, PU, 4th Cav.
YOUNG, Jacob, S14916, D, 4th (McLemore's) Cav.
YOUNG, James C. S3760, SH, Undetermined
YOUNG, James E. S664, OV, 8th Cav.
YOUNG, James E. S8074, MN, 17th Miss. Inf.
YOUNG, John T. S3961, CH, 21st Cav.
YOUNG, Joshua, S6777, J, Unassigned
YOUNG, Julia Ann, W5178, J, Young, Thomas
YOUNG, Julia Jane, W9881, K, Young, John Lamertine

YOUNG, Lillie Margarett, W2733, RU, Young, Joseph
YOUNG, Mallissa, W2365, J, Young, Duke
YOUNG, Martha A. W2940, O, Young, Dewit C.
YOUNG, Mary, W5779, WH, Young, Daniel W.
YOUNG, Mary Catharine, W1610, HD, Young, Richard Washington
YOUNG, Mary Elizabeth, W1216, WL, Young, James
YOUNG, Mary Jane, W1815, WE, Young, Wm. J.
YOUNG, Mary L. W8200, WL, Young, J. W.
YOUNG, Mary Susan, W737, FR, Young, Isaac
YOUNG, Mattie Jane, W7807, GI, Young, Napoleon Bonapart
YOUNG, Medora J. W7301, GI, Young, Nathaniel A.
YOUNG, N. S2145, HI, 24th Inf.
YOUNG, Nancy Jane, W5466, GU, Young, James Polk
YOUNG, Napoleon B. S82, J, 8th Inf.
YOUNG, Napoleon B. S2598, GI, 32nd Inf.
YOUNG, Narcissa, W6717, SN, Young, Wright
YOUNG, Nathaniel A. S2481, GI, 32nd Inf.
YOUNG, Ophelia Elizabeth, W1943, WL, Young, Casmire Fleetwood
YOUNG, P. R. S3199, JE, 25th N.C. Inf.
YOUNG, Rhoda Ann, W9170, MU, Young, Wm. L.
YOUNG, S. n. S8323, CA, 11th Cav.
YOUNG, STephen M. S5811, MC, 3rd Engineer Corps
YOUNG, Sallie, W6181, J, Young, Napoleon Bonapart
YOUNG, Sarah, W6055, DK, Young, John Lawson
YOUNG, Sarah Jane, W719, O, Young, Andrew J.
YOUNG, Sarah Jane, W7562, HN, Young, David E.
YOUNG, Sarah Louise, W10625, D, Young, Tom
YOUNG, Sarah Pickett, W7551, H, Young, Franklin Isaac
YOUNG, Susan, W6253, D, Young, Wm. Robert
YOUNG, Susan Mildred, W5431, MA, Young, James Madison
YOUNG, Tabitha E. W6541, G, Young, James Franklin
YOUNG, Tabitha P. W6640, FR, Young, George W.
YOUNG, Tennessee, W5538, D, Young, David Winson
YOUNG, Thomas, S1335, J, 28th Inf.
YOUNG, Thomas, S7619, DK, 1st Bn. (Colm's) Inf.
YOUNG, Thomas C. S14284, GI, 32nd Inf.
YOUNG, Virginia Frances, W4331, T, Young, Wiley Tinsley
YOUNG, W. A. S12657, BR, 36th Ga. Inf.
YOUNG, W. C. S10974, RU, 45th Inf.
YOUNG, W. H. S5315, D, 7th Inf.
YOUNG, W. J. S3875, MN, 21st (Wilson's) Cav.
YOUNG, W. R. S7275, D, 20th Inf.
YOUNG, Wiley T. S7747, T, 14th (Neely's) Cav.
YOUNG, William A. S2315, GI, 32nd Inf.
YOUNG, William Henderson, S12322, J, 28th Inf.
YOUNG, William Henry, S14513, D, 18th Inf.
YOUNG, William L. S8200, MU, 48th (Voorhies') Inf.
YOUNG, Willie Cornelia, W3548, HR, Young, Joseph Herbert
YOUNG, Wright, S10591, SN, 4th (McLemore's) Cav.
YOUNGBLOOD, B. F. S8574, W, 1st Cav.
YOUNGBLOOD, Charles F. S1974, K, Humald's Battery, Art.
YOUNGBLOOD, G. W. S6045, MN, 24th Ga. Inf.
YOUNGBLOOD, J. A. S6908, RO, 23rd Ga. Inf.
YOUNGBLOOD, Mary A. W7749, RO, Youngblood, J. A.
YOUNGBLOOD, Sarah Ann, W1335, K, Youngblood, Charles F.
YOUNGBLOOD, W. E. S4356, W, 11th Inf.
YOUNGBLOOD, W. H. S14206, H, 35th Miss. Inf.
YOUNGBLOOD, William J. S7952, K, 1st Ga. Regulars
YOUNGER, Bettie, W4902, MN, Younger, Josiah
YOUNGER, J. G. S14917, L, 53rd Va. Inf.
YOUNGER, Josiah, S13101, MN, 18th (Newsom's) Cav.
YOUREE, Anthony P. W825, SN, Youree, Patrick S.

Index to Tennessee Confederate Pension Applications

YOUREE, David L. S7267, RU, 8th (Smith's) Cav.
YOUREE, George C. S7268, RU, 8th (Smith's) Cav.
YOUREE, Henry, C12, SN, 2nd Cav.
YOUREE, Patrick S. S967, SN, 2nd Inf.
YOUREE, Sallie Watkins, W7336, RU, Youree, Wm. Hall
YOUREE, W. H. S8260, RU, 14th Cav.
ZACHARY, Black, S11990, LK, 3rd Miss. Cav.
ZACHARY, R. A. S13587, F, 16th Bn. (Neal's) Cav.
ZELLNER, Jennie A. W3434, SH, Zellner, John Wm.
ZELLNER, John W. S6326, SH, 13th Inf.
ZELLNER, Martha Adline, W1791, SH, Zellner, Marion
ZELLNER, Sarah R. W3513, D, Zellner, Wm. James
ZIMMERMAN, Angeline, W745, SN, Zimmerman, Verdinan
ZIMMERMAN, Hugh Lawson, S4384, GI, 1st (Turney's) Inf.
ZIMMERMAN, Jacob C. S8423, WA, 60th Inf.
ZIMMERMAN, Sarah E. W5646, SU, Zimmerman, J. C.
ZORN, W. G. S10174, H, 5th Ga. Inf.
ZWINGLE, C. C. S12964, W, 35th Inf.

APPENDIX

MISSING SOLDIERS APPLICATIONS

83	1232	4467	8581	14862
130	1234	4693	9486	15073
151	1254	5205	9565	15140
166	1284	5280	9645	15187
173	1290	5535	9674	15389
254	1307	5580	9752	15396
294	1329	5646	9865	15543
330	1345	5814	10001	15714
432	1348	5890	10148	16078
498	1453	6311	10325	16153
545	1469	6340	10399	16211
611	1474	6392	10554	16213
642	1594	6564	10604	16244
648	1609	6586	10673	16423
654	1749	6632	11201	16432
656	1791	6648	11212	16598
875	1921	6840	11269	
887	2071	6841	11312	
915	2468	6842	11565	
962	2983	6843	11635	
979	3188	6871	11820	
988	3191	6957	12380	
996	3204	6990	12641	
1064	3276	7039	12844	
1078	3394	7126	13088	
1094	3413	7229	13222	
1126	3429	7360	13235	
1139	3486	7661	13518	
1145	3550	7902	13669	
1149	3620	8353	13839	
1156	3838	8354	14183	
1169	3918	8429	14404	

MISSING WIDOWS APPLICATIONS

25	4537	7988	8824	10308
63	4549	8096	8868	11011
81	4995	8182	8881	11056
505	5279	8192	8890	11113
880	5501	8248	9107	11137
1913	6743	8573	9169	11149
1978	6958	8577	9225	11150
2623	6959	8690	9243	11151
3416	7088	8718	9370	11152
4022	7343	8821	9630	11153
4468	7485	8822	9670	11154
4473	7596	8823	10082	11155

MISSING COLORED MEN'S PENSIONS

43	195	230	243	266
84	196	231	245	
193	223	232	246	
194	225	242	247	

www.ingramcontent.com/pod-product-compliance
Lightning Source LLC
Chambersburg PA
CBHW031702230426
43668CB00006B/80